Handbook of Intelligence

Spurred by the new developments in a rapidly expanding field, Robert J. Sternberg has brought together a stellar list of contributors to provide a comprehensive, broad, and deeply thematic review of intelligence that will be accessible to both scholar and student. The field of intelligence is lively on many fronts, and this volume provides full coverage on topics such as behavior–genetic models, evolutionary models, cognitive models, emotional intelligence, practical intelligence, and group differences. The 28 chapters in the handbook are divided into 9 parts: I. The Nature of Intelligence and Its Measurement, II. Development of Intelligence, III. Group Analyses of Intelligence, IV. Biology of Intelligence, V. Intelligence and Information Processing, VI. Kinds of Intelligence, VII. Testing and Teaching Intelligence, VIII. Intelligence, Society, and Culture, and IX. Intelligence in Relation to Allied Constructs.

The handbook will serve as an authoritative resource on all aspects of theory, research, and measurement in the field of intelligence.

Robert J. Sternberg is IBM Professor of Psychology and Education in the Department of Psychology at Yale University. He is author of *Thinking Styles, Metaphors of Mind*, and *The Psychologist's Companion*, and editor of the *Handbook of Creativity*.

HANDBOOK OF
Intelligence

Edited by

Robert J. Sternberg

Yale University

CAMBRIDGE
UNIVERSITY PRESS

PUBLISHED BY THE PRESS SYNDICATE OF THE UNIVERSITY OF CAMBRIDGE
The Pitt Building, Trumpington Street, Cambridge, United Kingdom

CAMBRIDGE UNIVERSITY PRESS
The Edinburgh Building, Cambridge CB2 2RU, UK   http://www.cup.cam.ac.uk
40 West 20th Street, New York, NY 10011-4211, USA   http://www.cup.org
10 Stamford Road, Oakleigh, Melbourne 3166, Australia
Ruiz de Alarcón 13, 28014 Madrid, Spain

First published 2000

Printed in the United States of America

Typeface Stone Serif 9/12 pt. and Antique Olive   *System* LaTeX 2_ε [TB]

A catalog record for this book is available from the British Library.

Library of Congress Cataloging in Publication Data
Handbook of intelligence / edited by Robert J. Sternberg.
      p.   cm.
    Includes indexes.
        ISBN 0-521-59371-9 (hardcover), – ISBN 0-521-59648-3 (pbk.)
        1. Intellect.   2. Intelligence levels.   3. Intelligence tests.
    4. Psychology, Comparative.   I. Sternberg, Robert J.
    BF431.H31865   2000
    153.9 – dc21   99-24437
                                                                      CIP

ISBN 0 521 59371 9 hardback
ISBN 0 521 59648 3 paperback

This book is dedicated to the memory of Samuel Messick, a scholar who, in the tradition of the early pioneers in the study of human intelligence, valiantly sought to merge issues of theory and measurement, and of research and application, in the study of human intelligence.

Contents

Preface

We make judgments about people's intelligence everyday – in conversations with people, in reading about people, in listening to news stories about people. Societies also have designed special occasions in which intelligence can be assessed – intelligence tests, aptitude tests, job interviews, university application essays, and the like. But what is this *intelligence* about which so many judgments are being made?

The *Handbook of Intelligence* provides what is perhaps the most comprehensive account available of what intelligence is, how it is assessed, how it is developed, and how it affects society and its institutions. There are few questions about intelligence that are not addressed somewhere in the scope of this handbook. The handbook is written not only for psychologists but for any educated individual with an interest in the study of intelligence. Educators, anthropologists, sociologists, philosophers, cognitive scientists, neuroscientists, and laypeople alike will find the chapters of this book written in a manner that is both easily readable and quickly understandable. Because the coverage of the book is so broad, it can be read as a reference on an as-needed basis for those who would like information about a particular topic, or from cover to cover either as a sourcebook or as a textbook in a course dealing with human intelligence.

The *Handbook of Intelligence* complements the *Encyclopedia of Human Intelligence* that I edited (Sternberg, 1994) in that it provides a topical rather than an alphabetical account of topics in human intelligence. Of course, the handbook is also more up-to-date. The handbook also follows upon and supersedes the *Handbook of Human Intelligence* (Sternberg, 1982), published about 20 years ago. The present handbook, in addition to being more up-to-date, is considerably more comprehensive. Its 28 chapters (compared with 15 in the 1982 handbook) cover additional topics that, since the 1980s, have blossomed into important areas of study, such as social intelligence, practical intelligence, emotional intelligence, and the teaching of intelligence. Other topics that might have been included in the earlier handbook but were not are also included, such as giftedness, group differences in intelligence, animal intelligence, the neuropsychology and psychophysiology of intelligence, tests of intelligence, the interpretation of intelligence test scores, and the relation of intelligence to creativity and wisdom. In addition, the development of intelligence is now divided into two chapters, one on development in childhood and one on development in adulthood.

The book is divided into nine main parts. Each part deals with a somewhat different aspects of intelligence.

Part I, The Nature of Intelligence and Its Measurement (Chapters 1–3), deals with general issues in what intelligence is and how it is measured. In this part, Robert J. Sternberg discusses the concept of intelligence, Nathan Brody reviews the history of theories and measurements of intelligence, and Janet E. Davidson and C. L. Downing present contemporary models of intelligence.

Part II, Development of Intelligence (Chapters 4–6), deals with how intelligence develops from conception to old age. In this part, Elena L. Grigorenko discusses heritability and intelligence,

Zhe Chen and Robert S. Siegler review the topic of intellectual development in childhood, and Cynthia A. Berg covers the topics of intellectual development in adulthood.

Part III, Group Analyses of Intelligence (Chapters 7–9), deals with how particular groups differ from one another in intelligence. In this part, Douglas Detterman, Lynne Gabriel, and Joanne Ruthsatz discuss intelligence and mental retardation; Carolyn Callahan analyzes intelligence and giftedness; and John Loehlin provides an overall review of group differences in intelligence.

Part IV, Biology of Intelligence (Chapters 10–12), covers intelligence in nonhuman organisms as well as biological issues in human intelligence and its evolution. In this part, Thomas Zentall reviews the literature on animal intelligence; Harry Jerison discusses the evolution of intelligence; and Philip Vernon, John Wickett, P. Gordon Bazana, and Robert Stelmack elucidate the neuropsychology and psychophysiology of human intelligence.

Part V, Intelligence and Information Processing (Chapters 13–15), covers the relation of intelligence to information processing at all levels in both humans and computers. In this part, Ian Deary discusses simple information processing and intelligence, David Lohman provides an overview of complex information processing and intelligence, and Roger Schank and Brendon Towle deal with artificial intelligence.

Part VI, Kinds of Intelligence (Chapters 16–18), covers some of the major kinds of intelligence that researchers are investigating today. In this part, John Kihlstrom and Nancy Cantor discuss social intelligence; Richard K. Wagner reviews work on practical intelligence; and John Mayer, Peter Salovey, and David Caruso discuss emotional intelligence.

Part VII, Testing and Teaching Intelligence (Chapters 19–22), covers issues of how intelligence is tested and taught. In this part, Susan Embretson and Karen McCollam discuss psychometric approaches to the understanding and measurement of intelligence, Alan Kaufman reviews tests of intelligence, Mark Daniel elucidates interpretation of intelligence test scores, and Tina Grotzer and David Perkins discuss teaching of intelligence.

Part VIII, Intelligence, Society, and Culture (Chapters 23–25), covers how intelligence relates to the broader context in which it is found. In this part, Richard Mayer reviews work on intelligence and education, Craig Ramey discusses issues of intelligence and public policy, and Robert Serpell elucidates the relation of intelligence and culture.

Part IX, Intelligence in Relation to Allied Constructs (Chapters 26–28), covers how intelligence relates to other constructs sometimes associated with intelligence. In this part, Moshe Zeidner and Gerald Matthews discuss intelligence and personality, Robert J. Sternberg and Linda O'Hara cover intelligence and creativity, and Robert J. Sternberg covers intelligence and wisdom.

The *Handbook of Intelligence* will meet the needs of anyone curious about the nature of intelligence and how intelligence affects society and culture. It should serve as a comprehensive source of information for many years to come.

RJS
New Haven, CT

Contributors

P. Gordon Bazana, School of Psychology, University of Ottawa, Montpetit Hall, Ottawa, Ontario K1N 6N5, Canada

Cynthia A. Berg, Department of Psychology, 502 Behavioral Science Building, Salt Lake City, UT 84112

Nathan Brody, Wesleyan University, Department of Psychology, Middletown, CT 06459–0408

Carolyn M. Callahan, University of Virginia, 140, Ruffner Hall, 405 Emmet Street, Charlottesville, VA 22903

Nancy Cantor, The University of Michigan, Room 3068, Fleming Building, Ann Arbor, MI 48109

David Caruso, Work-Life Strategies, 2701 Summer Street, Stamford, CT 06905

Zhe Chen, Psychology Department, Baker Hall 342 C, Carnegie Mellon University, Pittsburgh, PA 15213–3890

Mark H. Daniel, Test Publishing, American Guidance Service, 4201 Woodland Road, Publishers' Building, Circle Pines, MN 55014–1796

Janet E. Davidson, Department of Psychology, Box 16, 0615 SW Palatine Hill Road, Lewis & Clark University, Portland, OR 97219–7899

Ian J. Deary, Department of Psychology, The University of Edinburgh, 7 George Square, Edinburgh EH 8 9JZ, Scotland, UK

Douglas K. Detterman, Department of Psychology, Mather Memorial Building 109, Case Western Reserve University, Cleveland, OH 44106

C. L. Downing, Department of Psychology, Box 16, 0615 SW Palatine Hill Road, Lewis & Clark University, Portland, OR 97219–7899

Susan E. Embretson, Department of Psychology, University of Kansas, Lawrence, KS 66045–0501

Lynne T. Gabriel, Department of Psychology, Mather Memorial Building 109, Case Western Reserve University, Cleveland, OH 44106

Elena L. Grigorenko, Department of Psychology, Yale University, P.O. Box 208205, New Haven, CT 06520–8205

Tina A. Grotzer, Graduate School of Education, Harvard University, 315 Longfellow Hall, Appian Way, Cambridge, MA 02138–3752

Harry J. Jerison, 503 West Rustic Road, Santa Monica, CA 90402–1115

Alan S. Kaufman, 42 Quarry Road, Stamford, CT 06903

John F. Kihlstrom, Department of Psychology, University of California – Berkeley, 3210 Tolman Hall, MC 1650, Berkeley, CA 94720–1650

John C. Loehlin, Department of Psychology, University of Texas, Austin, TX 78712

David F. Lohman, College of Education, University of Iowa, 366, Lindquist Center, Iowa City, IA 52242

Gerald Matthews, Department of Psychology, University of Dundee, Dundee, Scotland

John D. Mayer, Department of Psychology, University of New Hampshire, Conant Hall, Durham, NH 03824

Richard E. Mayer, Department of Psychology, University of California at Santa Barbara, Santa Barbara, CA 93106

Karen M. Schmidt McCollam, Department of Psychology, Gilmer Hall, University of Virginia, Charlottesville, VA 22903

Linda A. O'Hara, Department of Psychology, Yale University, P.O. Box 208205, 2 Hillhouse Avenue, New Haven, CT 06520–8205

David N. Perkins, Graduate School of Education, Harvard University, 315 Longfellow Hall, Appian Way, Cambridge, MA 02138–3752

Sharon Landesman Ramey, Civitan International Research Institute, P.O. Box 313, University of Alabama–Birmingham, Birmingham, AL 35294–0001

Craig T. Ramey, Civitan International Research Institute, P.O. Box 313, University of Alabama–Birmingham, Birmingham, AL 35294–0001

Joanne M. Ruthsatz, Department of Psychology, Mather Memorial Building 109, Case Western Reserve University, Cleveland, OH 44106

Peter Salovey, Department of Psychology, Yale University, P.O. Box 208205, New Haven, CT 06520–8205

Roger C. Schank, Institute for the Learning Sciences, 1890 Maple Avenue, Suite 300, Evanston, IL 60201

Robert Serpell, Department of Psychology, University of Maryland – Baltimore County, 1000 Hilltop Circle, Baltimore, MD 21250

Robert S. Siegler, Psychology Department, Baker Hall 342 C, Carnegie Mellon University, Pittsburgh, PA 15213–3890

Robert M. Stelmack, School of Psychology, University of Ottawa, Montpetit Hall, Ottawa, Ontario K1N 6N5, Canada

Robert J. Sternberg, Department of Psychology, Yale University, P.O. Box 208205, 2 Hillhouse Avenue, New Haven, CT 06520–8205

Brendon Towle, Department of Computer Science, Northwestern University, Evanston, IL 60208

Philip A. Vernon, Department of Psychology, University of Western Ontario, London, Ontario N6A 5C2, Canada

Richard K. Wagner, Department of Psychology, Florida State University, Copeland at College, Tallahassee, FL 32306

John C. Wickett, School of Psychology, University of Ottawa, Montpetit Hall, Ottawa, Ontario K1N 6N5, Canada

Moshe Zeidner, School of Education, University of Haifa, Mt. Carmel, Haifa 31905, Israel

Thomas R. Zentall, Department of Psychology, University of Kentucky, Lexington, KY 40506

PART I

THE NATURE OF INTELLIGENCE AND ITS MEASUREMENT

CHAPTER ONE

The Concept of Intelligence

ROBERT J. STERNBERG

Looked at in one way, everyone knows what intelligence is; looked at in another way, no one does. Put another way, people all have conceptions – which also are called folk theories or implicit theories – of intelligence, but no one knows for certain what it actually is. This chapter addresses how people conceptualize intelligence, whatever it may actually be.

WHY CONCEPTIONS OF INTELLIGENCE MATTER

Why should we even care what people think intelligence is as opposed only to valuing whatever it actually is? There are at least four reasons people's conceptions of intelligence matter.

First, implicit theories of intelligence drive the way in which people perceive and evaluate their own intelligence and that of others. To better understand the judgments people make about their own and others' abilities, it is useful to learn about people's implicit theories. For example, parents' implicit theories of their children's language development will determine at what ages they will be willing to make various corrections in their children's speech. More generally, parents' implicit theories of intelligence will determine at what ages they believe their children are ready to perform various cognitive tasks. Job interviewers will make hiring decisions on the basis of their implicit theories of intelligence. People will decide who to date on the basis of such theories. In sum, knowledge about implicit theories of intelligence is important because this knowledge is so often used by people to make judgments in the course of their everyday lives.

Second, implicit theories of scientific investigators ultimately give rise to their explicit theories. It thus is useful to find out what these implicit theories are. Implicit theories provide a framework, or lay of the land, that is useful in defining the general scope of a phenomenon – especially a not-well-understood phenomenon. These implicit theories can suggest what aspects of the phenomenon have been more or less attended to in previous investigations.

Third, implicit theories can be useful when an investigator suspects that existing explicit theories are wrong or misleading. If an investigation of implicit theories reveals little correspondence between the extant implicit and explicit theories, the implicit theories may be wrong. But the possibility also needs to be taken into account that the explicit theories are wrong and in need of correction or supplementation. For example, some implicit theories of intelligence suggest the need for expansion of some of our explicit theories of the construct.

Finally, understanding implicit theories of intelligence can help elucidate developmental and cross-cultural differences. As mentioned earlier, people have expectations for intellectual performances that differ for children of different ages. How these expectations differ is in part a function of culture. For example, expectations for children who participate in Western-style schooling are almost certain to be different from those for children who do not participate in such schooling – or at least they should be (Greenfield, 1997).

This chapter is divided into four parts. First, I discuss lay conceptions of intelligence. This discussion is divided into two sections. The first section deals with Western conceptions, and the second with conceptions from other parts of the world. The second part of the chapter deals with what might be called expert conceptions of intelligence. This discussion is divided into three sections. First, I discuss definitions of intelligence that have been proposed by experts. I then describe some conceptions of experts inferred by means other than direct definitions. Last I delineate some of the usually implicit metaphors that have driven explicit theories of intelligence proposed by experts. The third part of the chapter deals with implicit theories of how intelligence relates to society at large, and the fourth part consists of a brief summary and some conclusions.

LAY CONCEPTIONS OF INTELLIGENCE
Western Conceptions of Intelligence

Some of the studies of implicit theories of intelligence among mainland U.S. adults have been conducted by my collaborators and myself. We have been involved in three major sets of studies. The first was on implicit theories of intelligence, academic intelligence, and everyday intelligence in laypersons and experts (Sternberg, Conway, Ketron, & Bernstein, 1981). The second set was on implicit theories of intelligence as well as wisdom and creativity in laypersons and experts in various fields of endeavor (Sternberg, 1985c). A third set of studies was on implicit theories of intelligence across the adult life span (Berg & Sternberg, 1985).

In the first set of studies (Sternberg et al., 1981), three factors emerged from analyzing ratings of the ideally intelligent person as supplied by laypersons. The factors were labeled Practical Problem Solving, Verbal Ability, and Social Competence. The first factor included behaviors such as reasoning logically and well, identifying connections among ideas, and seeing all aspects of a problem. The second factor included behaviors such as speaking clearly and articulately, having verbal fluency, and conversing well. The third factor included behaviors such as accepting others for what they are, admitting mistakes, and displaying interest in the world at large. Sternberg (1985c) obtained fairly similar results in the second set of studies.

In the third set of studies, Berg and Sternberg (1985) investigated the development of implicit theories of intelligence over the life span. Their participants ranged in age from 20 to 83 years and were divided into three groups averaging 30, 50, and 70 years of age. The main finding of interest was that older individuals tend to view everyday competence as more important in characterizing the difference between individuals of average and exceptional intelligence than do younger individuals. Moreover, middle-aged and older individuals tend to combine crystallized intelligence with problem-solving abilities for most age-specific prototypes. Thus, the distinction between fluid (abstract-reasoning) and crystallized (knowledge-based) abilities seems less important to the older individuals than to the younger ones.

Some of the most interesting work on implicit theories of intelligence has been done by investigators seeking an understanding of the nature of intelligence in children. Siegler and Richards (1982) asked college students what they thought intelligence is at different ages. In particular, participants were asked to describe the nature of intelligence in 6-month-olds, 2-year-olds, 10-year-olds, and adults. The authors reported the five traits (in order of the frequency of mention) that most often were mentioned as characterizing intelligence at different ages. At 6 months old, these traits were recognition of people and objects, motor coordination, alertness, awareness of the environment, and verbalization. At 2 years of age, they were verbal ability, learning ability, awareness of people and environment, motor coordination, and curiosity. At 10 years old, they were verbal ability, followed by learning ability, problem-solving ability, reasoning ability – all tied for second place in frequency of mention – and creativity. At the adult level, the traits were reasoning ability, verbal ability, problem-solving ability, learning ability, and creativity. Clearly, there is a trend toward conceiving of intelligence as less perceptual–motor and as more cognitive with increasing age.

One of the more interesting studies of implicit theories regarding children's intelligence was done with teachers rather than with college students. Fry (1984) asked teachers at the primary, secondary, and tertiary levels about their conceptions of intelligence. Elementary school teachers tended to emphasize social variables such as popularity, friendliness, respect for law and order, and interest in the environment in their conceptions of intelligence. Secondary teachers, in contrast, were inclined to stress verbal variables, such as verbal fluency and energy, in their conceptions. The tertiary teachers tended to regard cognitive variables such as reasoning ability, broad knowledge, logical thinking, and the ability to deal maturely with problems as most important to intelligence. Thus, the teachers at the three levels in effect recapitulated the three factors obtained by Sternberg et al. (1981) in their study of implicit theories, but the emphasis was on the applicability of different factors at different ages. Problem-solving ability applied most to teachers' conceptions of college students' intelligence, verbal ability to their conceptions of secondary school students' intelligence, and social competence to their conceptions of elementary students' intelligence.

Yussen and Kane (1985) studied conceptions of intelligence, but they used as their participants children rather than adults. They interviewed students in the first, third, and sixth grades. Children were asked questions concerning such issues as visible signs of intelligence, qualities associated with intelligence, the constancy or malleability of intelligence, and the definition of intelligence. The authors found that older children's conceptions were more differentiated than were those of younger children and that with advancing age children increasingly characterized intelligence as an internalized quality. But older children were less likely than younger children to think that overt signs indicate intelligence. Older children also are less global in the qualities they associate with intelligence than are younger children. There is a tendency as well for younger children to think of intelligence largely in terms of social skills but for older children to think of intelligence largely in relation to academic skills.

Dweck (1999; Dweck & Elliott, 1983) has also investigated concepts of intelligence among children and has found that children generally have one of two kinds of concepts regarding the plasticity of intelligence. "Entity theorists" believe that intelligence is something you are born with and that its level remains constant across the life span. Because these children believe that there is not much they can do to increase their intelligence, they tend to be oriented toward showing intelligence through their performance. They are often afraid to make mistakes, particularly if they will be observed by others, and attempt to "look good" to others in their work. "Incremental theorists," on the other hand, believe that intelligence is something that increases throughout the life span and that the method of increase is through learning. They are inclined, therefore, to be learning rather than performance oriented and to seek new challenges that will help them improve their intelligence.

Nicholls (1990) has also studied children's conceptions of abilities. Like Dweck, he found that children differ in their conceptions of intelligence and its relationship to effort. Some children view effort and ability as largely differentiated, whereas others do not. Nicholls also found that children differ in their overall conceptions of intelligence. Some children view the development of intelligence as involving effortful learning or acquisition of information, whereas others do not. Also, as children become more sophisticated, they begin to differentiate the acquisition of information from problem solving with information.

Conceptions of Intelligence around the World

In some cases, Western notions about intelligence are not shared by other cultures (Berry, 1984; Sternberg & Kaufman, 1998). For example, the Western emphasis on speed of mental processing is not shared by many cultures (Sternberg et al., 1981). People in other cultures may even be suspicious of the quality of work done very quickly and may emphasize depth rather than speed of processing. They are not alone. Some prominent Western theorists have pointed out the importance of depth of processing for full learning and understanding of what one learns (e.g., Craik & Lockhart, 1972).

Yang and Sternberg (1997a) have reviewed Chinese philosophical conceptions of intelligence. The Confucian perspective emphasizes the characteristic of benevolence and of doing what is right. As in the Western notion, the intelligent person spends much effort in learning, enjoys learning, and persists in lifelong learning with enthusiasm. The Taoist tradition, in contrast, emphasizes the importance of humility, freedom from conventional standards of judgment, and full knowledge of oneself and of external conditions.

The difference between Eastern and Western conceptions of intelligence may persist even today.

Yang and Sternberg (1997b) studied contemporary Taiwanese conceptions of intelligence and found five factors underlying these conceptions: (a) a general cognitive factor, much like the general factor in conventional Western tests of intelligence; (b) interpersonal intelligence; (c) intrapersonal intelligence; (d) intellectual self-assertion; and (e) intellectual self-effacement. In a related study but with different results, Chen (1994) found three factors underlying Chinese conceptions of intelligence: nonverbal reasoning ability, verbal reasoning ability, and rote memory. The difference may be due to different subpopulations of Chinese, to differences in methodology, or to differences in when the studies were done.

Chen and Chen (1988) explicitly compared the concepts of intelligence of Chinese graduates from Chinese-language versus English-language schools in Hong Kong. They found that both groups considered nonverbal reasoning skills as the most relevant skills for measuring intelligence. Verbal reasoning skills and social skills were next and then numerical skills. Memory was seen as least important. The Chinese-language-schooled group, however, tended to rate verbal skills as less important than did the English-language-schooled group. Moreover, in an earlier study, Chen, Braithwaite, and Huang (1982) found that Chinese students viewed memory for facts as important for intelligence, whereas Australian students viewed such memory skill as of only trivial importance.

Das (1994), also reviewing Eastern notions of intelligence, has suggested that in Buddhist and Hindu philosophies, intelligence involves waking up, noticing, recognizing, understanding, and comprehending but also includes such things as determination, mental effort, and even feelings and opinions in addition to more intellectual elements.

Differences between cultures in conceptions of intelligence have been recognized for some time. Gill and Keats (1980) noted that Australian university students value academic skills, whereas Malay students value practical skills as well as speech and creativity. Dasen (1984) found that Malay students emphasize social and cognitive attributes in their conceptions of intelligence.

Western schooling also emphasizes other things (Srivastava & Misra, 1996) such as generalization or going beyond the information given (Connolly & Bruner, 1974; Goodnow, 1976), speed (Sternberg,

1985a), minimal moves to a solution (Newell & Simon, 1972), and creative thinking (Goodnow, 1976). Moreover, silence is interpreted as a lack of knowledge (Irvine, 1978). In contrast, the Wolof tribe in Africa views people of higher social class and distinction as speaking less (Irvine, 1978). This difference between the Wolof and Western notions suggests the usefulness of looking at African notions of intelligence and its manifestations in behavior as possible contrasts to Western notions.

Ruzgis and Grigorenko (1994) have argued that, in Africa, conceptions of intelligence revolve largely around skills that help to facilitate and maintain harmonious and stable intergroup relations; intragroup relations are probably equally important and at times more important. Serpell (1974, 1977, 1982) found that Chewa adults in Zambia emphasize social responsibilities, cooperativeness, and obedience as important to intelligence; intelligent children also are expected to be respectful toward adults. Kenyan parents also emphasize reasonable participation in family and social life as important aspects of intelligence (Super & Harkness, 1986). In Zimbabwe, the word for intelligence, *ngware*, actually means to be prudent and cautious, particularly in social relationships. Among the Baoule, service to the family and community and politeness toward, and respect for, elders are seen as key to intelligence (Dasen, 1984).

Wober (1974) investigated concepts of intelligence among members of different tribes in Uganda as well as within different subgroups of the tribes. Wober found differences in concepts of intelligence within and between tribes. The Bagandans, for example, tended to associate intelligence with mental order, whereas the Batoro tribespeople were inclined to associate it with some degree of mental turmoil. On semantic–differential scales, Bagandan tribespeople thought of intelligence as persistent, hard, and obdurate, whereas the Batoro thought of it as soft, obedient, and yielding.

Harkness and Super (1983) analyzed concepts of intelligence among the Kokwet of western Kenya. He found that intelligence in children seemed to be conceived differently from intelligence in adults. The word *ngom* was applied to children and seemed to note responsibility, highly verbal cognitive quickness, the ability to comprehend complex matters quickly, and good management of interpersonal relations. The word *utat* was applied to adults and suggested inventiveness, cleverness, and sometimes wisdom and unselfishness. A separate word, *keelat*, was used to signify smartness or sharpness.

Similar emphasis on social aspects of intelligence has been found as well among two other African groups – the Songhay of Mali and the Samia of Kenya (Putnam & Kilbride, 1980). The Yoruba, another African tribe, emphasize the importance of depth of listening rather than just referring to intelligence and of being able to see all aspects of an issue and to place the issue in its proper overall context (Durojaiye, 1993).

The emphasis on the social aspects of intelligence is not limited to African cultures. Notions of intelligence in many Asian cultures also emphasize the importance of the social aspects of intelligence more than do the conventional Western or IQ-based notions (Azuma & Kashiwagi, 1987; Lutz, 1985; Poole, 1985; White, 1985).

It should be noted that neither African nor Asian notions emphasize exclusively social notions of intelligence. In a collaborative study with several investigators, Sternberg and Grigorenko (1997; Sternberg et al., in press) have studied conceptions of intelligence in rural Kenya. In one such rural village, well over 90% of the children are infected with parasitic infections. Consequently, they experience stomachaches quite frequently. Traditional medicine suggests the usefulness of a large variety of natural herbal medicines that can be used to treat such infections. It appears that at least some of these – although perhaps a small percentage – actually work. More important for our purposes, however, is that children who learn how to self-medicate with these natural herbal medicines are viewed as being at an adaptive advantage over those children who do not have this kind of informal knowledge. Clearly, the kind of adaptive advantage that is relevant in this culture would be viewed as irrelevant in the West, and vice versa.

Although these conceptions of intelligence emphasize social skills much more than do conventional Western conceptions of intelligence, they simultaneously recognize the importance of cognitive aspects of intelligence. Note, however, that there is no one overall Western or even U.S. conception of intelligence. Okagaki and Sternberg (1993) found that different ethnic groups in San Jose, California, had rather different conceptions of what it means

to be intelligent. For example, Latino parents of schoolchildren tended to emphasize the importance of social competence skills in their conceptions of intelligence, whereas Asian parents tended rather heavily to emphasize the importance of cognitive skills. Anglo parents also placed greater emphasis on cognitive skills. Teachers, representing the dominant culture, emphasized cognitive rather than social competence skills more. The rank order of children of various groups' performance (including subgroups within the Latino and Asian groups) could be predicted perfectly by the extent to which their parents shared the teachers' conceptions of intelligence. That is, teachers tended to reward those children who were socialized into a view of intelligence that happened to correspond to the teachers' own. Yet, social aspects of intelligence, broadly defined, may be as important as, or even more important than, cognitive aspects of intelligence in later life. For example, a team that needs to complete a cognitive task may not be able to do so if members are unable to work together. Heath (1983) also found differences in conceptions of intelligence between White and Black groups characterized by the Black groups' emphasizing nonverbal communication skills more and the White groups' placing more emphasis on verbal communication skills.

EXPERT CONCEPTIONS OF INTELLIGENCE
Expert Definitions of Intelligence

Perhaps the most famous or infamous definition of intelligence, depending upon one's point of view, was proposed by Boring (1923) in an article in *The New Republic*. Boring proposed that intelligence is what tests of intelligence test. Boring was not so foolish as to believe that this operational definition was the end of the line for understanding intelligence. On the contrary, he saw it as a "narrow definition, but a point of departure for a rigorous discussion ... until further scientific discussion allows us to extend [it]" (p. 35).

To the extent that some view the definition as infamous, it is probably because they see this definition as seriously flawed. First, it seems to define away intelligence rather than defining it. To this day, it is not totally clear what intelligence tests measure, and thus it cannot be clear on the basis of this definition what intelligence is. Second, tests of intelligence do not intercorrelate perfectly, and therefore they do not produce a singular entity of the kind the definition implies. Or if they do, it is a subset of what they measure rather than the whole thing (Spearman, 1927). Third, the definition is extremely conservative in that it never will enable us to understand intelligence in a way that goes beyond the traditional tests. Finally, many view the definition as circular.

Probably the most famous study of experts' definitions of intelligence was done by the editors of the *Journal of Educational Psychology* ("Intelligence and its measurement," 1921). Contributors to this issue provided several different definitions as follows:

1. The power of good responses from the point of view of truth or facts (E. L. Thorndike);
2. The ability to carry on abstract thinking (L. M. Terman);
3. Sensory capacity, capacity for perceptual recognition, quickness, range or flexibility of association, facility and imagination, span of attention, quickness or alertness in response (F. N. Freeman);
4. Ability to learn or having learned to adjust oneself to the environment (S. S. Colvin);
5. Ability to adapt oneself adequately to relatively new situations in life (R. Pintner);
6. The capacity for knowledge and knowledge possessed (B. A. C. Henmon);
7. A biological mechanism by which the effects of a complexity of stimuli are brought together and given a somewhat unified effect in behavior (J. Peterson);
8. The capacity to inhibit an instinctive adjustment, the capacity to redefine the inhibited instinctive adjustment in the light of imaginally experienced trial and error, and the capacity to realize the modified instinctive adjustment in overt behavior to the advantage of the individual as a social animal (L. L. Thurstone);
9. The capacity to acquire capacity (H. Woodrow);
10. The capacity to learn or to profit by experience (W. F. Dearborn); and
11. Sensation, perception, association, memory, imagination, discrimination, judgment, and reasoning (N. E. Haggerty).

To the extent that there are common themes in these definitions, they would appear to be with respect to the ability to adapt to the environment and the ability to learn. Other contributors to this symposium did not provide clear definitions of intelligence but concentrated instead on how to test it.

Of course, there have been many definitions of intelligence since those represented in the journal symposium, and an essay has been written on the nature of definitions of intelligence (Miles, 1957). But a subsequent symposium was designed to update the earlier one.

Two dozen experts (including one team of two) in the field of intelligence were asked to define intelligence 65 years later (Sternberg & Detterman, 1986). The panelists were Anne Anastasi, Paul Baltes, Jonathan Baron, John Berry, Ann Brown and Joseph Campione, Earl Butterfield, John B. Carroll, J. P. Das, Douglas Detterman, William Estes, Hans Eysenck, Howard Gardner, Robert Glaser, Jacqueline Goodnow, John Horn, Lloyd Humphreys, Earl Hunt, Arthur Jensen, James Pellegrino, Sandra Scarr, Roger Schank, Richard Snow, Robert Sternberg, and Edward Zigler. Rather than try to review each definition here, I will summarize the main similarities and differences between the two symposia (see Sternberg & Berg, 1986).

First, at least some general agreement exists across the two symposia regarding the nature of intelligence. The correlation between frequencies of listed behaviors was .50, indicating moderate overlap in present and past conceptions. Attributes such as adaptation to the environment, basic mental processes, and higher order thinking (e.g., reasoning, problem solving, decision making) were prominent in both listings.

Second, certain themes were prominent in both symposia. The issue of the one versus the many – Is intelligence one thing or is it manifold? – continued to be of concern, although no consensus existed in either symposium. The issue of breadth of definition also continued to be of concern. As in the earlier symposium, some panelists in the 1986 symposium defined intelligence quite narrowly in terms of biological or cognitive elements, whereas others included a broader array of elements, including motivation and personality. The issue of breadth, like that of the one versus the many, remains unresolved.

Third, despite similarities in views over the 65 years, some salient differences in the two listings could also be found. Metacognition – conceived of as both knowledge about and control of cognition – played a prominent role in the 1986 symposium but virtually no role at all in the 1921 symposium. The salience of metacognition and executive processes can be attributed to the rise of the computational metaphor in the current study of intelligence. In the later symposium, a greater emphasis also was placed on the role of knowledge and the interaction between knowledge and mental processes. The change in emphasis was not entirely with respect to functions that occur within the organism. The later panelists showed considerable emphasis on the role of context, and particularly of culture, in defining intelligence, whereas such emphasis was absent in the earlier symposium.

Definitions of intelligence tend to be based on classical views of concepts (Katz, 1972) whereby an attempt is made to specify the defining attributes of intelligence, that is, what attributes are individually necessary and jointly sufficient for a person to be considered intelligent. Neisser (1979) pointed out that intelligence may instead be prototypically organized, meaning that there are no clear defining attributes but rather only characteristic attributes that tend to be typical of intelligent persons. In this view, an intelligent person would be someone displaying certain attributes, but there would be no particular attributes that could be identified as necessary and sufficient for describing a person as intelligent.

Another possibility is that there is no prototype. On views of intelligence involving not just a single ability but many, one could argue that there are so many different ways to be intelligent that no one prototype or even small number of prototypes would suffice to characterize a person as intelligent. Rather, it may be that we have stored in our minds multiple exemplars of intelligent people, and we assess a person's intelligence in relation to these exemplars. For example, there might be someone we know who is test-smart, someone who is high in common sense, and so on. Such a model would be based on multiple-exemplar theories of concept meanings (see, e.g., Ross & Spalding, 1994).

Inferences about Expert Conceptions of Intelligence

HISTORICAL VIEWS. Historically, some scholars who have explored intelligence would be considered experts, but not in the field of intelligence. These are writers, philosophers, theologians, and others who, in the course of their writings, speculated on but did not attempt precisely to define the nature of intelligence. Some of these speculations are summarized here. (For a more nearly complete analysis, see Sternberg, 1990.)

Homer, in the *Odyssey*, distinguished between good looks and good thinking. He noted that one man may make a poor physical impression but speak in an articulate and persuasive way. Another man may be handsome but lack the ability to communicate well with others.

Plato had much to say regarding the nature of intelligence. Perhaps his most well-known comments are in the dialogue *Theaetetus*. Socrates asks Theaetetus to imagine that there exists in the mind of man a block of wax that is of different sizes in different men. The block of wax also can differ in hardness, moistness, and purity. Socrates, citing Homer, suggests that when the wax is pure and clear and sufficiently deep, the mind easily will learn and retain information and will not be subject to confusion. It only will think things that are true, and because the impressions in the wax are clear, these impressions will be distributed quickly into their proper places on the block of wax. But when the wax is muddy or impure or very soft or very hard, there will be defects of the intellect. People whose wax is soft will be good at learning but be apt to forget. People whose wax is hard will be slow to learn but will retain what they learn. People whose wax is shaggy or rugged or gritty, or whose wax has an admixture of earth or dung, will have only indistinct impressions. Those with hard wax will have the same because there will be no depth to their thoughts. If the wax is too soft, the impressions will be indistinct because they easily can be confused or remolded.

Aristotle also had some well-formed views on the nature of intelligence. In the *Posterior Analytics Book 1* he conceived of intelligence in terms of "quick wit." For example, an intelligent person seeing someone in conversation with a man of wealth might conclude quickly that the person is seeking to borrow money from the man of wealth.

CONTEMPORARY VIEWS. In the studies mentioned earlier, Sternberg (1985c; Sternberg et al., 1981) looked at expert as well as lay views. Experts were all in the field of psychology. In the

Sternberg et al. (1981) study, comparable factor analyses were carried out for experts as for laypersons. Three interpretable factors emerged for the experts. They were verbal intelligence, problem-solving ability, and practical intelligence. These factors were similar to those of laypersons but had a somewhat more academic slant in terms of the behaviors that loaded highly on them.

Sternberg (1985c) looked at expert conceptions, but in this study, the experts were professors in the fields of art, business, philosophy, and physics. The experts had somewhat different conceptions of intelligence that seemed to reflect the requirements of scholarship in their fields. Whereas professors of art emphasized knowledge and the ability to use that knowledge in weighing alternative possibilities and in seeing analogies, business professors emphasized the ability to think logically, to focus on essential aspects of a problem, and to follow others' arguments easily and to see where these arguments lead. The emphasis on assessment of argumentation in business professors' implicit theories is far weaker in art professors' implicit theories. Philosophy professors emphasize critical and logical abilities very heavily – especially the ability to follow complex arguments, to find subtle mistakes in these arguments, and to generate counterexamples to invalid arguments. The philosophers' view very clearly emphasizes those aspects of logic and rationality that are essential in analyzing and creating philosophical arguments. Physicists, in contrast, place more emphasis on precise mathematical thinking, on the ability to relate physical phenomena to the concepts of physics, and on the ability to grasp the laws of nature quickly. Thus, experts tended, sometimes subtly, to emphasize the skills important in their profession when queried as to their implicit theories of intelligence.

Metaphors Underlying Experts' Conceptions of Intelligence

I have argued that several identifiable metaphors underlie experts' conceptions of intelligence (Sternberg, 1985b, 1990).

GEOGRAPHIC METAPHOR. A first metaphor, a geographic metaphor, views intelligence as a map of the mind. Examples of theorists holding this view include Spearman (1927), Thurstone (1938), Guilford (1967), Cattell (1971), Vernon (1971), and Carroll (1993). The basic unit of analysis in this metaphor is the factor that typically is alleged to be a source of individual differences among people. This metaphor has as some of its advantages its (a) clear specification of proposed mental structures; (b) direct operationalization through mental tests; and (c) availability of sophisticated quantitative machinery for implementation. Possible disadvantages are (a) insufficient emphasis on mental processing, (b) difficulties in falsification of theories based on exploratory factor analysis, (c) very strong dependence on individual differences, (d) rotational indeterminacy in exploratory factor analysis, and (e) questionable generalizability to everyday intelligence.

COMPUTATIONAL METAPHOR. A second metaphor is a computational one. Examples of theorists who have adopted this metaphor are Simon (1976), Hunt (1978), and Sternberg (1977). The basic unit of analysis is the elementary information process (or component). Exponents of this metaphor typically use reaction-time analysis, protocol analysis, and computer simulation in their research. Some advantages of this metaphor are (a) its detailed specification of mental processes and strategies, (b) real-time analysis of task performance, and (c) the availability of sophisticated quantitative and computer machinery for implementation. Some possible disadvantages are (a) insufficient emphasis on mental structures as sources of individual differences, (b) our uncertainty as to whether the mind really is well modeled by a computer, and (c) the questionable generalization of these theories to everyday life.

BIOLOGICAL METAPHOR. A third metaphor is a biological one. Some of the main theorists here are Luria (1973, 1980), Hebb (1949), Halstead (1951), and, more recently, Vernon (Vernon & Mori, 1992; Wickett & Vernon, 1994). The main unit of analysis varies across theories. For Hebb, it was the cell assembly; for Vernon, speed of neuronal conduction. Others, like Luria and Halstead, have proposed structural theories linking parts of the brain to various intellectual functions. A number of different methods of analysis have been used, including measurement of evoked potentials, measurement of speed of neuronal conduction, assessment of hemispheric specialization, and use of radioactive tracers to trace via positron emission tomography (PET) or functional magnetic resonance imaging (fMRI) scanning parts of the brain that are involved in different kinds of mental tasks. Some advantages of this metaphor are that it (a) links intelligence to its sources in the brain, (b) often employs fairly precise experimental and measurement techniques, and (c) carries the intriguing possibility, not yet realized, of culture-reduced or even culture-fair measurement. Some disadvantages are that (a) the results of the approach are largely a promissory note not yet usable in any practical application; (b) a tendency exists to ignore the contexts in which intelligence manifests itself; and (c) the claims for the approach, especially with regard to causality, go beyond the data. This last point is worth a bit of elaboration. Suppose, as has been claimed, that some measurement of a resting electroencephalography (EEG) proves to be related to scores on a test of intelligence (Hendrickson, 1982; see chapters in Eysenck, 1982). It is not clear from this correlation that the underlying biological process is somehow causative of intelligence. For example, cognitive processing may be responsible for the correlation: Brighter individuals may use the time to think, whereas less bright individuals do not. Or biological and cognitive processing may both be dependent on something else. For example, electroencephalography is only an index of certain kinds of brain activity, the nature of which is unclear. Other measures, such as evoked potentials, really suffer from the same limitation.

GENETIC–EPISTEMOLOGICAL METAPHOR. A fourth metaphor is a genetic–epistemological one. The main theorist is Piaget (1972). The fundamental unit of analysis is the schema. Typical methodology is close observation via case studies and experimentation. Some advantages of this metaphor are its (a) comprehensiveness as a theory of intelligence and intellectual development, (b) the incredible range of research that has been done under the metaphor on children of all ages all around the world, and (c) the detail with which many structures and processes have been described. Some disadvantages are (a) the concentration of the theory on the logical and scientific aspects of intelligence as opposed to other aspects of intelligence, (b) the placement of the commencement of the last

stage of intellectual development at roughly 11 or 12 years old, almost certainly before individuals have reached intellectual maturity, and (c) the overestimation of ages at which children are capable of showing various intellectual performances.

ANTHROPOLOGICAL METAPHOR. A fifth metaphor is an anthropological one. The question here is that of what forms intelligence takes as a cultural invention. The basic unit of analysis is the individual in interaction with his or her cultural context. Examples of anthropologically oriented theorists are Berry (1984), Cole (1996), and Greenfield (1997). Advantages of this metaphor are its (a) recognition of cultural roles in determining what constitutes intelligent behavior and possibly even the nature of intelligence, (b) greater potential cross-cultural applicability of theorizing, and (c) the recognition of the need to gear testing of intelligence to the cultural context. Some disadvantages are that (a) cognitive functioning is specified imprecisely or not at all, (b) specification of theories tends to lack crucial details, and (c) extreme relativist positions – that intelligence differs in nature in each culture – lack parsimony.

SOCIOLOGICAL METAPHOR. This metaphor emphasizes the importance of socialization in intelligence. Well-known theorists include Vygotsky (1978) and Feuerstein (1980). For Vygotsky, a particularly important construct is internalization, whereby the child watches behavior in social interactions and then internalizes – takes into him or herself – relevant aspects of the situation and makes them his or her own. For Feuerstein, a key construct is mediated learning, which is knowledge acquisition that occurs when a mediator, usually a parent or teacher, explains the environment to the child. Advantages of this metaphor are its (a) recognition of the importance of internalization of experiences initially encountered with others, (b) recognition of the role of the mediator in internalization, and (c) recognition of the difference between latent capacity and manifest developed ability. Some disadvantages are (a) lack of detailed specification as to how internalization takes place, (b) questionable validity of the actual measurement operations for Vygotsky's zone of proximal development – the difference between performance before and after mediation, and (c) ambiguities regarding conclusions that can be drawn from many training studies.

SYSTEMS METAPHOR. The systems metaphor is based on the notion that intelligence is a complex system that integrates many levels of analysis, including geographic, computational, biological, anthropological, sociological, and others. The unit of analysis is the system and its elements in interaction. Examples of theorists are Gardner (1983, 1993) and Sternberg (1985b, 1997). Some advantages of this metaphor are (a) its recognition of the complexity of intelligence, (b) its integration of multiple levels of analysis, and (c) the breadth of abilities included within the theories. Some disadvantages are that (a) it is difficult although not impossible to test the theories; (b) the theories are very complex, making them less parsimonious; and (c) some of the theories tend to be specified more in breadth than in depth.

Metaphors are not right or wrong. They can be useful differentially, however. Most likely, their usefulness depends on purpose. Thus, which metaphor one best adopts depends on the purposes for which one needs a metaphor.

IMPLICIT THEORIES OF INTELLIGENCE AND SOCIETY

I have suggested that there are three major implicit theories of how intelligence relates to society as a whole (Sternberg, 1997). These might be called Hamiltonian, Jeffersonian, and Jacksonian. These views are not based strictly, but rather, loosely, on the philosophies of Alexander Hamilton, Thomas Jefferson, and Andrew Jackson, three great statesmen in the history of the United States.

The Hamiltonian view, which is similar to the Platonic view, is that people are born with different levels of intelligence and that those who are less intelligent need the good offices of the more intelligent to keep them in line, whether they are called government officials or, in Plato's term, philosopher-kings. Herrnstein and Murray (1994) seem to have shared this belief when they wrote about the emergence of a cognitive (high-IQ) elite, which eventually would have to take responsibility for the largely irresponsible masses of nonelite

(low-IQ) people who cannot take care of themselves. Left to themselves, the unintelligent would create, as they always have created, a kind of chaos.

The Jeffersonian view is that people are equal in terms of political and social rights and should have equal opportunities, but they do not necessarily avail themselves equally of these opportunities and are not necessarily equally rewarded for their accomplishments. People are rewarded for what they accomplish, given equal opportunity, rather than for what they might have, or should have, or could have accomplished. Those who fail are not rewarded equally, just because they gave it a chance, with those who succeed. In this view, the goal of education is not to favor or foster an elite, as in the Hamiltonian tradition, but rather to allow children the opportunities to make full use of the skills they have. My own views are similar to these (Sternberg, 1997).

The Jacksonian view is that all people are equal, not only as human beings but in terms of their competencies – that one person would serve as well as another in government or on a jury or in almost any position of responsibility. In this view of democracy, people are essentially intersubstitutable except for specialized skills, all of which can be learned. Related views are proposed by Ericsson (1996). In this view, we do not need or want any institutions that might lead to favoring one group over another.

CONCLUSION

Implicit theories of intelligence and of the relationship of intelligence to society perhaps need to be considered more carefully than they have been because they often serve as underlying presuppositions for explicit theories and even experimental designs that are then taken as scientific contributions. Different theorists and experimentalists start from different sets of presuppositions and may believe that they are arguing over the science of a matter when in fact they are arguing past each other because of the differing presuppositions they bring to their scientific investigations. For example, the same book (Jensen, 1998) that one scholar might view as obsessive and preoccupied with the existence of what is really a somewhat limited general factor (Neisser, 1999) might be viewed by another scholar as a courageous and scientific exploration of truths that the softer-minded or politically correct might wish to explain away (Bouchard, 1999). Until scholars are able to discuss their implicit theories and thus their assumptions, they are likely to talk past rather than to each other in discussing their explicit theories and their data.

ACKNOWLEDGMENT

Preparation of this chapter was supported under the Javits Act Program (Grant R206R950001) as administered by the Office of Educational Research and Improvement, U.S. Department of Education. Grantees undertaking such projects are encouraged to express their professional judgment freely. This chapter, therefore, does not necessarily represent the positions or policies of the Office of Educational Research and Improvement or the U.S. Department of Education, and no official endorsement should be inferred.

REFERENCES

Azuma, H., & Kashiwagi, K. (1987). Descriptions for an intelligent person: A Japanese study. *Japanese Psychological Research, 29*, 17–26.

Berg, C. A., & Sternberg, R. J. (1985). A triarchic theory of intellectual development during adulthood. *Developmental Review, 5*, 334–370.

Berry, J. W. (1984). Towards a universal psychology of cognitive competence. In P. S. Fry (Ed.), *Changing conceptions of intelligence and intellectual functioning* (pp. 35–61). Amsterdam: North-Holland.

Boring, E. G. (1923, June 6). Intelligence as the tests test it. *New Republic, 35*, 35–37.

Bouchard, T. J. (1999). The definitive case of *g*. [Review of the book *The g factor: The science of mental ability*.] *Contemporary Psychology, 44*, 133–135.

Carroll, J. B. (1993). *Human cognitive abilities: A survey of factor-analytic studies*. New York: Cambridge University Press.

Cattell, R. B. (1971). *Abilities: Their structure, growth and action*. Boston: Houghton Mifflin.

Chen, M. J. (1994). Chinese and Australian concepts of intelligence. *Psychology and Developing Societies, 6*, 101–117.

Chen, M. J., Braithwaite, V., & Huang, J. T. (1982). Attributes of intelligent behaviour: Perceived relevance and difficulty by Australian and Chinese students. *Journal of Cross-Cultural Psychology, 13*, 139–156.

Chen, M. J., & Chen, H. C. (1988). Concepts of intelligence: A comparison of Chinese graduates from Chinese and English schools in Hong Kong. *International Journal of Psychology, 223*, 471–487.

Cole, M. (1996). *Cultural psychology: A once and future discipline*. Cambridge, MA: Harvard University Press.

Connolly, H., & Bruner, J. (1974). Competence: Its nature and nurture. In K. Connolly & J. Bruner (Eds.), *The growth of competence*. New York: Academic Press.

Craik, F. I. M., & Lockhart, R. S. (1972). Levels of processing: A framework for memory research. *Journal of Verbal Learning and Verbal Behavior, 11*, 671–684.

Das, J. P. (1994). Eastern views of intelligence. In R. J. Sternberg (Ed.), *Encyclopedia of human intelligence* (Vol. 1, pp. 387–391). New York: Macmillan.

Dasen, P. (1984). The cross-cultural study of intelligence: Piaget and the Baoule. *International Journal of Psychology, 19*, 407–434.

Durojaiye, M. O. A. (1993). Indigenous psychology in Africa. In U. Kim & J. W. Berry (Eds.), *Indigenous psychologies: Research and experience in cultural context*. Newbury Park, CA: Sage.

Dweck, C. S. (1999). *Self-theories: Their role in motivation, personality, and development*. Philadelphia: Psychology Press.

Dweck, C. S., & Elliott, E. S. (1983). Achievement motivation. In P. H. Mussen (General Ed.) & E. M. Heatherington (Vol. Ed.), *Handbook of child psychology: Vol. 4. Socialization, personality, and social development* (4th ed., pp. 644–691). New York: Wiley.

Ericsson, K. A. (Ed.). (1996). *The road to excellence*. Mahwah, NJ: Erlbaum.

Eysenck, H. J. (Ed.). (1982). *A model for intelligence*. Berlin: Springer-Verlag.

Feuerstein, R. (1980). *Instrumental enrichment: An intervention program for cognitive modifiability*. Baltimore, MD: University Park Press.

Fry, P. S. (Ed.). (1984). *Changing conceptions of intelligence and intellectual functioning: Current theory and research*. Amsterdam: North-Holland.

Gardner, H. (1983). *Frames of mind: The theory of multiple intelligences*. New York: Basic.

Gardner, H. (1993). *Multiple intelligences: The theory in practice*. New York: Basic.

Gill, R., & Keats, D. M. (1980). Elements of intellectual competence: Judgments by Australian and Malay university students. *Journal of Cross-Cultural Psychology, 11*, 233–243.

Goodnow, J. J. (1976). The nature of intelligent behavior: Questions raised by cross-cultural studies. In L. Resnick (Ed.), *The nature of intelligence* (pp. 169–188). Hillsdale, NJ: Erlbaum.

Greenfield, P. M. (1997). You can't take it with you: Why abilities assessments don't cross cultures. *American Psychologist, 52*, 1115–1124.

Guilford, J. P. (1967). *The nature of human intelligence*. New York: McGraw-Hill.

Halstead, W. C. (1951). Biological intelligence. *Journal of Personality, 20*, 118–130.

Harkness, S., & Super, C. M. (1983). The cultural construction of child development: A framework for the socialization of affect. *Ethos, 11*, 221–231.

Heath, S. B. (1983). *Ways with words*. New York: Cambridge University Press.

Hebb, D. O. (1949). *The organization of behavior: A neuropsychological theory*. New York: Wiley.

Hendrickson, A. E. (1982). The biological basis of intelligence. Part I: Theory. In H. J. Eysenck (Ed.), *A model for intelligence* (pp. 151–196). Berlin: Springer-Verlag.

Herrnstein, R. J., & Murray, C. (1994). *The bell curve*. New York: Free Press.

Hunt, E. B. (1978). Mechanics of verbal ability. *Psychological Review, 85*, 109–130.

Intelligence and its measurement: A symposium. (1921). *Journal of Educational Psychology, 12*, 123–147, 195–216, 271–275.

Irvine, J. T. (1978). "Wolof magical thinking": Culture and conservation revisited. *Journal of Cross-Cultural Psychology, 9*, 300–310.

Jensen, A. R. (1998). *The g factor: The science of mental ability*. Westport, CT: Praeger/Greenwood.

Katz, J. J. (1972). *Semantic theory*. New York: Harper and Row.

Luria, A. R. (1973). *The working brain*. New York: Basic.

Luria, A. R. (1980). *Higher cortical functions in man* (2nd ed., rev. & expanded). New York: Basic.

Lutz, C. (1985). Ethnopsychology compared to what? Explaining behavior and consciousness among the Ifaluk. In G. M. White & J. Kirkpatrick (Eds.), *Person, self, and experience: Exploring Pacific ethnopsychologies* (pp. 35–79). Berkeley: University of California Press.

Miles, T. R. (1957). On defining intelligence. *British Journal of Educational Psychology, 27*, 153–165.

Neisser, U. (1979). The concept of intelligence. In R. J. Sternberg & D. K. Detterman (Eds.), *Human intelligence: Perspectives on its theory and measurement*. Norwood, NJ: Ablex.

Neisser, U. (1999). The great *g* mystery. [Review of the book *The g factor: The science of mental ability*.] *Contemporary Psychology, 44*, 131–133.

Newell, A., & Simon, H. A. (1972). *Human problem solving*. Englewood Cliffs, NJ: Prentice Hall.

Nicholls, John G. (1990). What is ability and why are we mindful of it? A developmental perspective. In R. J. Sternberg & J. Kolligian, Jr. (Eds.), *Competence considered* (pp. 11–40). New Haven, CT: Yale University Press.

Okagaki, L., & Sternberg, R. J. (1993). Parental beliefs and children's school performance. *Child Development, 64*, 36–56.

Piaget, J. (1972). *The psychology of intelligence*. Totowa, NJ: Littlefield Adams.

Poole, F. J. P. (1985). Coming into social being: Cultural images of infants in Bimin–Kuskusmin folk psychology. In G. M. White & J. Kirkpatrick (Eds.), *Person, self, and experience: Exploring Pacific ethnopsychologies* (pp. 183–244). Berkeley: University of California Press.

Putnam, D. B., & Kilbride, P. L. (1980). *A relativistic understanding of social intelligence among the Songhay of Mali and Samia of Kenya*. Paper presented at the meeting of the Society for Cross-Cultural Research, Philadelphia, PA.

Ross, R. H., & Spalding, T. L. (1994). Concepts and categories. In R. J. Sternberg (Ed.), *Handbook of perception and cognition: Thinking and problem solving* (pp. 119–148). San Diego, CA: Academic Press.

Ruzgis, P. M., & Grigorenko, E. L. (1994). Cultural meaning systems, intelligence and personality. In R. J. Sternberg and P. Ruzgis (Eds.), *Personality and intelligence* (pp. 248–270). New York: Cambridge.

Serpell, R. (1974). Aspects of intelligence in a developing country. *African Social Research*, No. 17, 576–596.

Serpell, R. (1977). Strategies for investigating intelligence in its cultural context. *Quarterly Newsletter of the Institute for Comparative Human Development*, 11–15.

Serpell, R. (1982). Measures of perception, skills, and intelligence. In W. W. Hartup (Ed.), *Review of child development research* (Vol. 6, pp. 392–440). Chicago: University of Chicago Press.

Siegler, R. S., & Richards, D. D. (1982). The development of intelligence. In R. J. Sternberg (Ed.), *Handbook of human intelligence* (pp. 896–971). New York: Cambridge University Press.

Simon, H. A. (1976). Identifying basic abilities underlying intelligent performance of complex tasks. In L. B. Resnick (Ed.), *The nature of intelligence* (pp. 65–98). Hillsdale, NJ: Erlbaum.

Spearman, C. (1927). *The abilities of man*. London: Macmillan.

Srivastava, A. K., & Misra, G. (1996). Changing perspectives on understanding intelligence: An appraisal. *Indian Psychological Abstracts and Review, 3*, 1–34.

Sternberg, R. J. (1977). *Intelligence, information processing, and analogical reasoning: The componential analysis of human abilities*. Hillsdale, NJ: Erlbaum.

Sternberg, R. J. (1985a). *Beyond IQ: A triarchic theory of human intelligence*. New York: Cambridge University Press.

Sternberg, R. J. (1985b). Human intelligence: The model is the message. *Science, 230*, 1111–1118.

Sternberg, R. J. (1985c). Implicit theories of intelligence, creativity, and wisdom. *Journal of Personality and Social Psychology, 49*, 607–627.

Sternberg, R. J. (1990). *Metaphors of mind: Conceptions of the nature of intelligence*. New York: Cambridge University Press.

Sternberg, R. J. (1997). *Successful intelligence*. New York: Plume.

Sternberg, R. J., & Berg, C. A. (1986). Quantitative integration: Definitions of intelligence: A comparison of the 1921 and 1986 symposia. In R. J. Sternberg & D. K. Detterman (Eds.), *What is intelligence? Contemporary viewpoints on its nature and definition* (pp. 155–162). Norwood, NJ: Ablex.

Sternberg, R. J., Conway, B. E., Ketron, J. L., & Bernstein, M. (1981). People's conceptions of intelligence. *Journal of Personality and Social Psychology, 41,* 37–55.

Sternberg, R. J., & Detterman, D. K. (1986). *What is intelligence?* Norwood, N.J.: Ablex.

Sternberg, R. J., & Grigorenko, E. L. (1997). The cognitive costs of physical and mental ill health: Applying the psychology of the developed world to the problems of the developing world. *Eye on Psi Chi, 2,* 20–27.

Sternberg, R. J., & Kaufman, J. C. (1998). Human abilities. *Annual Review of Psychology, 49,* 479–502.

Sternberg, R. J., Nokes, K., Geissler, P. W., Prince, R., Okatcha, F., Bundy, D. A., & Grigorenko, E. L. (in press). The relationship between academic and practical intelligence: A case study in Kenya. *Intelligence.*

Super, C. M., & Harkness, S. (1986). The developmental niche: A conceptualization at the interface of child and culture. *International Journal of Behavioral Development, 9,* 545–569.

Thurstone, L. L. (1938). *Primary mental abilities.* Chicago: University of Chicago Press.

Vernon, P. E. (1971). *The structure of human abilities.* London: Methuen.

Vernon, P. A., & Mori, M. (1992). Intelligence, reaction times, and peripheral nerve conduction velocity. *Intelligence, 8,* 273–288.

Vygotsky, L. S. (1978). *Mind in society: The development of higher psychological processes.* Cambridge, MA: Harvard University Press.

White, G. M. (1985). Premises and purposes in a Solomon Islands ethnopsychology. In G. M. White & J. Kirkpatrick (Eds.), *Person, self, and experience: Exploring Pacific ethnopsychologies* (pp. 328–366). Berkeley: University of California Press.

Wickett, J. C., & Vernon, P. A. (1994). Peripheral nerve conduction velocity, reaction time, and intelligence: An attempt to replicate Vernon and Mori. *Intelligence, 18,* 127–132.

Wober, M. (1974). Towards an understanding of the Kiganda concept of intelligence. In J. W. Berry & P. R. Dasen (Eds.), *Culture and cognition: Readings in cross-cultural psychology* (pp. 261–280). London: Methuen.

Yang, S., & Sternberg, R. J. (1997a). Conceptions of intelligence in ancient Chinese philosophy. *Journal of Theoretical and Philosophical Psychology, 17,* 101–119.

Yang, S., & Sternberg, R. J. (1997b). Taiwanese Chinese people's conceptions of intelligence. *Intelligence, 25,* 21–36.

Yussen, S. R., & Kane, P. (1985). Children's concept of intelligence. In S. R. Yussen (Ed.), *The growth of reflective thinking in children* (pp. 207–241). New York: Academic Press.

CHAPTER TWO

History of Theories and Measurements of Intelligence

NATHAN BRODY

FRANCIS GALTON

Just 6 years after the publication in 1859 of Darwin's *On the Origin of Species*, his cousin Francis Galton published two articles in *Macmillan's Magazine* jointly entitled "Hereditary Talent and Character." These articles were expanded into a book published in 1869 on hereditary genius. Galton's book combined Darwin's ideas about natural selection with the work of the Belgian statistician Quetelet (1849). Galton argued that genius is a normally distributed and heritable characteristic of humans. Galton believed in racial hierarchies. He argued that the ancient Greeks were as superior to his English contemporaries in their capacity for genius as his contemporaries were superior to Africans and their American descendants.

Galton's Measurement of Simple Processes

Galton established a laboratory in the South Kensington Museum of London in 1882 for the measurement of individual differences. For a small fee, visitors to the museum were given a battery of tests designed to measure auditory and visual sensory discrimination abilities as well as reaction times to stimuli and the ability to exert hand-squeeze pressure on a dynamometer. The choice of measures was influenced by the beliefs of the British empiricist philosophers about the importance of knowledge derived from sensations as a foundation for complex cognitive functioning and by a belief held by Galton that the sensory discriminative capacities of idiots are impaired. He assumed that individuals with high intelligence would have keener discriminative capacities than individuals with low intelligence (Galton, 1883).

Galton's interest in the measurement of relatively simple cognitive functions as a basis for understanding genius was the progenitor of an active area of research at the end of the 19th century. James McKeen Cattell was an American student of Wundt's (receiving his degree in 1886) who was interested in individual differences. In 1890 Cattell published a paper entitled "Mental Tests and Measurements" in which he described measures of 10 psychological functions, including measures of tactile discrimination, absolute thresholds for pain, weight discrimination, reaction time for auditory stimuli, and so forth. Cattell was the first to use the term *mental test*. The program of research initiated by Cattell was influenced by Galton. Galton wrote a commentary to Cattell's 1890 paper endorsing the research and indicating that it would be useful to relate scores from the psychological measures to ratings of intellectual eminence.

Several other psychologists assessed large groups of individuals in the 1890s. Jastrow (1891–1892) administered a similar battery of tests to undergraduates at the University of Wisconsin and subsequently developed a large battery of tests for discrimination ability, reaction times, and memory for lines, colors and forms, as well as the ability to judge tachistoscopically presented stimuli that he used to assess visitors to the Columbian exhibition in Chicago in 1893 (see Philippe, 1894). Boas tested a large sample of school children when he was at

Clark University in 1891 using measures of memory, hearing, and vision (see Bolton, 1891–1892).

Binet's Reaction

Binet was opposed to the attempt to measure intelligence by focusing on elementary cognitive processes. He was convinced that intelligence must be studied by focusing on complex mental processes. He was influenced by the findings of studies conducted in Germany. Oehrn (1895) studied individual differences in memory for digits, ability to add numbers, and the abilities to read and to write from dictation. In reviewing this research, Binet and Henri (1896) noted that individual differences seemed to be more varied in complex rather than simple functions. Binet was also influenced by the work of Ebbinghaus (1897), who administered tests of calculation, memory for digits, and a series of tests called cancellation tests involving the completion of missing elements of words and letters in sentences. Ebbinghaus administered these tests several times over the course of a school day to assess the influence of fatigue on children's performance. The cancellation test was assumed to provide insight into individual differences in intelligence because it required an individual to combine disparate elements into a comprehensive analysis. Ebbinghaus noted that individual differences in measures of relatively simple cognitive functions, such as tests of digit-span memory and calculation, did not exhibit a clear relationship to differences in intelligence as assessed by academic performance. By contrast, tests of cancellation – a complex measure involving combination – were related to individual differences in intelligence. Binet and Henri (1896) expressed their doubts about a program of research in intelligence devoted to the study of individual differences in simple functions. They were "astonished by the considerable place reserved to the sensations and simple processes, and by the little attention lent to superior processes" (Binet and Henri, 1896). They believed that an adequate assessment of individual differences would require one to assess inter alia memory for designs, sentences, musical phrases, and so forth; imagery; imagination, as assessed by the ability to discuss the meanings suggested by abstract words or to construct stories; comprehension; suggestibility; and aesthetic judgments.

Binet and Henri provided examples of the measures that they thought could be used to assess these complex functions.

The debate about the relative importance of simple or complex tasks for the measurement of intelligence is manifested in what are arguably the two most important papers in the history of research on intelligence: Spearman's paper of 1904 and Binet and Simon's paper published in 1905. Spearman developed a theory; Binet and Simon developed a test. Both the theory and the test shaped research on intelligence for the remainder of the 20th century.

SPEARMAN'S PAPER
Empirical Foundation

The empirical components of Spearman's research were derivative, that is, they were based on an attempt to measure individual differences in sensory-discrimination capacities and to relate performance on these measures to measures of academic performance and to ratings of intellectual capacity for samples of school children. Spearman criticized many of the earlier studies on this problem noting that, with the exception of Wissler (1901), they did not report the results of correlations, relying instead on subjective impressions about relationships. Wissler's study was the first to use the coefficient of correlation to assess relationships among psychological measures. His study reported relationships for a series of reaction-time and sensory-discrimination measures and measures of academic performance. He obtained correlations for his battery of tests and noted that different measures of psychological functions did not correlate positively nor did they correlate with grades. This study was enormously influential. The study was conducted at Columbia University in James McKeen Cattell's laboratory. It represented a comprehensive analysis of the attempt to measure intelligence using the methods that Cattell had advocated for 15 years beginning with a paper published in 1886. The results of the study were instrumental in ending the attempt to measure intelligence by the techniques initially advocated by Galton. Spearman (1930) noted that he was not aware of Wissler's work at the time he collected his data, and, if he had been, he probably would not have conducted his study.

Spearman's Theory

Spearman (1904a) obtained correlations among several measures of sensory-discrimination ability. He noted that the correlations were positive and that there was an ability to discriminate that could be assessed by an aggregate index. He related sensory-discrimination ability measures to measures of academic achievement. He noted that these latter measures were positively correlated with each other and were positively correlated with his measures of sensory-discrimination ability. All of the correlations in his matrix were positive.

Spearman noted that correlations between measures could be attenuated by the presence of errors of measurement. In a paper published in the same issue of the *American Journal of Psychology* he developed a formula that may be used to correct obtained correlations for errors of measurement (Spearman, 1904b). Spearman obtained aggregate indices of discrimination ability and aggregate indices of intellectual ability as determined by academic performance. The disattenuated correlation between the two led him to the conclusion "that the *common and essential element in the Intelligences coincides with the common and essential element in the Sensory Functions*" (Spearman, 1904a, p. 269, italics in original).

Spearman developed a theory to account for the correlations in the matrix he had obtained. Spearman assumed that there must be a common intellectual ability that accounted for the positive manifold of correlations. He labeled this g for general intelligence. He assumed that the variance on a particular measure could be partitioned into a component attributable to g and to a second specific source of variance s. This "two factor theory" of intelligence has a number of consequences. If the specificities associated with each measure are independent, and if s is uncorrelated with g, then the correlation between any two measures of intelligence is attributable to the extent to which they share g. Measures that have a high g-to-s ratio will tend to correlate with each other more substantially than measures that have low g-to-s ratios. Thus, measures of intelligence may be arrayed in a hierarchy in terms of their g loadings. A matrix of correlations formed by tests ordered in rows defined by descending g loadings will exhibit declining row and column values.

BINET'S TEST

Spearman's theory was based on the attempt to measure intelligence using the techniques advocated by Galton. Binet attempted to measure intelligence using the kinds of complex tasks advocated in his paper with Henri published in 1896. Binet's attempt to develop a test of intelligence floundered on his inability to develop quantitative indices of the several different complex functions that he thought should be measured. In 1904 at a conference in Germany, Henri presented a paper (written jointly with Binet) indicating that the attempts to measure intelligence using the methods recommended in their 1896 paper had been unsuccessful (see Wolf, 1973). It was impossible to obtain a sufficient number of measures in a limited period of time that would provide a full picture of an individual's intellectual functioning. A year later, Binet and Simon (1905) published the first test of intelligence. The test was developed in response to Binet's appointment as scientific advisor to a commission appointed to study the needs of retarded and abnormal children. The need to produce an instrument appears to have galvanized Binet and led him to overlook some of his own beliefs about the inability of any quantitative index to assess fully the idiographic complexity of intellect present in each person.

Binet and Simon wanted to develop an instrument that would allow examiners to ascertain the level of functioning of a child and to decide whether it was appropriate to provide that child with special educational opportunities. The test resembled a modern test in four respects. First, it was a test primarily of complex mental functions, including tests of vocabulary and comprehension (e.g., What is the thing to do when you are sleepy?). Second, the items attempted to assess different kinds of abilities. Third, the test could be administered without special laboratory equipment. Fourth, the items were grouped according to difficulty. Binet and Simon believed that children who were retarded generally performed at a level comparable to that of normal children who were younger.

Binet published two revisions of the test. The 1908 revision involved a shift to an emphasis on normal children and included specific age-graded equivalents for each item. The 1911 revision expanded the test using five items at each age, allowing for the calculation of a fractional mental age (see Peterson, 1926). Binet never converted mental age scores to IQs. Stern (1912) invented the IQ index. In its original version it was the ratio of mental age to chronological age multiplied by 100.

SUMMARY: THE FOUNDATION

Binet and Spearman disagreed substantively and stylistically. Spearman was at home in the realm of mathematical abstractions. He sought to find a coherent and even brutally simplified structure beyond the multiplicity of form and observation presented by the natural world. Binet was endlessly fascinated by nuance and difference – appreciative of the idiographic complexity involved in understanding intelligence as revealed in the life of a particular individual. Spearman was attracted to the methodological simplicities of the German psychophysical tradition. Binet, by contrast, shared William James's distaste for Fechnerian psychophysics and believed that its precision was illusory with respect to understanding anything as complex as intelligence (see James, 1890, p. 549). And, they were equally skeptical of each other's achievement. Spearman (1927) thought that Binet's test was of little importance in elucidating what he took to be the essential problem – understanding g – although he thought that his theory provided a rationale for Binet's attempt to derive a single index to represent the intellectual functioning of a child. Binet (1905) reviewed the two papers published by Spearman in 1904. Binet wrote that he was astonished at the claim that intelligence could be related to sensory-discrimination ability. He also indicated that the notion of g as a singular entity was mistaken because two individuals could obtain the same score using quite different knowledge and skills. Binet's skepticism was shared by the American psychologist who developed an English version of Binet's test, Lewis Terman. Terman (1930) disliked Spearman's dogmatism and excessive faith in mathematical reasoning.

This brief review of early research provides a foundation for the consideration of five thematic issues that will structure this chapter. First, is it appropriate, as Spearman implied, to think of intelligence as singular? Second, what is the relationship between intelligence and simple and complex cognitive processes assessed in the psychology laboratory? How did Binet's and Spearman's views on this issue influence and relate to subsequent research? Third, is intelligence heritable? Was Galton correct? Fourth, what was done and what should be done with Binet's invention, the intelligence test? Fifth, Binet had a test, and Spearman had a theory: neither really had a clear notion of what was being measured by tests of intelligence. What is intelligence?

THE ONE–MANY PROBLEM

g Is not Enough

Is intelligence one thing or many things? Spearman's analytic procedures provide an elegant way of testing a matrix for the presence of a single general ability and of determining the g loading or saturation of a particular measure. Applications of the method indicate that g does not account for all of the covariance in the matrix. In his 1904 paper, Spearman analyzed correlations between measures of knowledge of Latin grammar and Latin translation and French prose and French dictation. He noted that the disattenuated correlations between these pairs were higher than would be expected by an analysis of their g loadings. He believed that g accounted for only 74% of the common variance in these two aggregates. Thus, there must be specific factors in addition to g. Spearman ignored these additional sources of variance in the matrix. For him, g was the critical construct, and "specific communities" (Spearman's term for sources of variance other than g that contributed to covariance in the matrix) were incidental perturbations.

In his first published paper designed to test ideas advanced by Spearman and Binet, Cyril Burt (1909–1910) obtained correlations for a battery of tests. Burt noted that he obtained a positive manifold providing evidence for the presence of a general factor. He also noted that there was evidence for a specific factor related to sensory discrimination ability and that thus g could not account for all of the covariance in the matrix.

Thurstone's Theory

The first systematic attempt to focus on sources of variance in a matrix of correlations of ability measures that were independent of g was undertaken in the work of Louis Thurstone (1931, 1938a; Thurstone and Thurstone, 1941). Thurstone developed the method of multiple factor analysis to ascertain independent factors present in a matrix of correlations. The choice of factors was guided by the criterion of "simple structure" that mandated a factor structure in which tests loaded highly on a single factor and had near-zero loadings on other factors. This method of analyzing the matrix resulted in a decomposition of the variance on a particular test into several independent factors. So, too, an individual could be described by a profile of strengths and weaknesses for each of several abilities. Thurstone's analyses led him to assume the existence of several primary ability factors, including verbal comprehension, number facility, spatial reasoning, memory, deduction, and inductive abilities.

Thurstone's analyses and Spearman's analyses could not initially have been more at odds with each other. Thurstone's methods would work if g was not present in the matrix of correlations. If most of the covariance in a matrix of abilities was attributable to g, it would be impossible to obtain simple structures for factors that were independent of each other. Spearman's methods for determining the g loading of different tests would not be successful if substantial portions of the covariance in the matrix were attributable to group factors that were independent of g.

Rapprochement

Despite their diametrically opposed emphases, Spearman and Thurstone were able to resolve their differences. Thurstone noted that it was not possible to obtain simple structure for analyses of ability matrices derived from individuals who differed widely in intelligence. The factors had to be obliquely related to one another or to be correlated. If factors were correlated, then it was possible to perform a second-order factor analysis leading to the derivation of g. Spearman recognized that g did not account for all of the covariance in the matrix (recall he had already noted this in 1904). It was possible to resolve their differences by using a hierarchical model of intelligence in which specific abilities were related to each other and in which g was a superordinate factor present at the apex of the ability structure.

There were, to be sure, different emphases on the importance of g and different methods of factor analyses that were related to these different emphases. British factor analysts such as Vernon (1950) preferred to begin their analysis by analyzing the g variance in the matrix and then analyzing the residual variance. In Vernon's analyses the two most important specific factors were labeled $k:m$ – a factor that was defined by measures of mechanical and spatial ability and $v:ed$ – a factor defined by verbal abilities and by other abilities that were related to educational exposures such as mathematical reasoning. American factor analysts preferred to start with specific abilities and then derive one or more higher order abilities by an analysis of the relationships that obtained among the specific abilities or factors. But general agreement existed about the presence of a hierarchical structure.

Guilford's Theory

In the 1960s, Guilford developed a model of intelligence that was not hierarchical (Guilford, 1967, 1977, 1981, 1985; Guilford & Hoepfner, 1971). Guilford began with a descriptive analysis of tests that could be used to measure intelligence. He developed a three-dimensional taxonomy that permitted him to classify any test with respect to its position on the dimensions of operation, product, and content. He distinguished five operations: cognition (knowing), memory, divergent production (generation of alternatives), convergent production, and evaluation. Each of these operations could be applied to one of four types of contents: figural, symbolic, semantic, and behavioral. The application of these processes to these contents could result in one of six products: units, classes, relations, systems, transformations, and implications. There are 120 independent abilities in the model defined by all possible combinations of position on each of the three facets of the model. Guilford (1977) subsequently modified the model to distinguish between two types of figural contents, auditory and visual, leading to an expansion of the number of independent factors to 150.

Guilford used "targeted rotations" in which the factors were defined before an examination of the correlation matrix and the loadings of tests on predefined factors were examined. The procedure usually resulted in factors that were not clearly defined by tests with high loadings, and the factors that were obtained were not highly replicable (Brody & Brody, 1976). Horn and Knapp (1973) demonstrated that randomly chosen targeted rotations were equivalent to Guilford's targeted rotations with respect to the fit between test loadings and factors.

Guilford (1981) subsequently modified his theory to allow for the possibility of higher order structures. He assumed that tests that shared a common dimensional position would be related to each other. The 150 first-order factors would combine to form 85 second-order factors, and these 85 second-order factors would combine to form 16 third-order factors. For example, memory for semantic units would form a first-order factor, memory for units would be a second-order factor, and memory would form a third-order factor. This model was never extensively tested and in some preliminary analyses was not well supported by the data (see Brody, 1992; Kelderman, Mellenbergh, & Elshout, 1981).

Cattell's Theory

Raymond Cattell (1963, 1971, 1987; Horn & Cattell, 1966) developed a theory of intelligence based on the distinction between two different *g* components: fluid intelligence or *gf* and crystallized intelligence or *gc*. Fluid ability was viewed as a biologically influenced dimension of *g* that declines over the adult life span, whereas *gc* was believed to be influenced by education and cultural exposures and was not assumed to decline over the adult life span. Cattell's theory was supported by second-order factor analyses that incorporated at the first-order Thurstone ability factors; *gf* and *gc* were higher order factors. Modifications in the theory resulted in the specification of five second-order factors. In addition to *gf* and *gc*, there were memory, visualization, and speed factors. The factors *gf* and *gc* are oblique, often correlating in excess of .5.

The most comprehensive analysis of the structure of ability factors is found in Carroll (1993). Carroll reanalyzed the canon of ability matrices (over 450 matrices) and developed a three-stratum taxonomic structure in which *g* exists as the singular third-order stratum at the apex of a hierarchical structure of abilities. In his conception, arrayed below *g* at the second stratum are eight abilities rank ordered with respect to their loading on *g*. Ranked from highest to lowest *g* loading, these are fluid intelligence, crystallized intelligence, general memory and learning, broad visual perception, broad auditory perception, broad retrieval ability, broad cognitive speediness, and processing speed (reaction-time decision speed). Each of the second-stratum abilities is related to several narrow first-stratum dimensions of ability.

Summary and Conclusion

Viewed from the perspective of the present, the attempt to analyze correlation matrices to uncover the taxonomic structure of abilities was dominated by the presence of a recalcitrant reality that imposed its structure on the efforts of psychologists to represent reality in a distorted manner. However intense the debates, and however ingenious the analysis methods, two fundamental results governed the outcomes of the search for the structure of abilities. First, virtually all measures of cognitive function were positively correlated with each other. Matrices of ability measures usually contain a *g* factor that accounts for about 50% of the covariance in the matrix. Second, *g* does not exhaust all of the covariance in the matrix. There are narrower ability measures that must be postulated to account for relationships in the matrix. The only theorist who wished to avoid these results was Guilford, and he was able to do this only by developing methods of analysis that allowed him to circumvent the discipline provided by the need to obtain congruence between theory and data. This does not imply that the analysis of ability matrices initiated by Spearman in 1904 is the preferred method for ascertaining the taxonomic structure of abilities. One could begin elsewhere, for example, by a search for the biological structures that influence the development of intelligence or perhaps by an analysis of the achievements that are valued in different cultures.

THE EXPERIMENTAL FOUNDATION OF INTELLIGENCE

Why It Died

For much of the 20th century, the attempt to integrate the study of individual differences in intelligence with the experimental psychology of cognitive processes was moribund. There are at least four reasons for the end of what had been a more collaborative relationship between these areas of research in the 19th century. First, the extreme nature of Spearman's conclusion that discrimination abilities and higher order mental processes are one and the same thing struck many of his contemporaries as a mistaken notion. We have already noted that Binet expressed astonishment at this conclusion. Edward Lee Thorndike, a student of James McKeen Cattell's, wrote a letter to Spearman in 1904 in which he interpreted Spearman's results as follows:

In measuring any sensory activity we measured a complex of the mere sensory capacity and the capacity to understand instructions, to be attentive and ambitious, to use all the clues that might be available in making the judgment. These latter factors would be practically identical with the factors involved in what we call intellect.... the sensory activity as measured is not a function of the mere reception of stimuli but involves the so-called higher powers (letter from Thorndike to Spearman reproduced in Joynson, 1989, pp. 328–329).

Spearman realized that his conclusions were badly worded, and in a footnote to Burt's paper published in 1909 he wrote the following:

I did not mean (as others have naturally taken it) that intelligence was based on sensory discrimination; if anything, vice versa. I take both the sensory discrimination and the manifestations leading a teacher to impute a general intelligence to be based on some deeper fundamental cause (Spearman, in Burt, 1909–1910, p. 165).

Spearman and Thorndike were in partial agreement: Whatever the reason for a relationship between sensory-discrimination ability and intelligence, the study of discrimination ability would not lead to an understanding of intelligence. If Spearman's original claims were absurd on their face, and if mature reflection about them led to doubt about the viability of a research program designed to elucidate the ways in which complex intellectual skills might derive from basic cognitive processes, then there was no reason to pursue the study of basic cognitive processes to understand intelligence.

Second, the invention of tests of intelligence provided psychologists with a technology that led to a shift from laboratory-based research to applied issues. Tests could be used to allocate individuals to different educational tracks and to select individuals for various job opportunities. There were many studies of the distribution of test scores and studies

of continuity and change in intelligence. Psychometric investigations focused on the properties of tests, including an analysis of item characteristics, factor structures, and the reliability and predictive validity of test scores. Virtually all of this research was conducted outside of laboratories designed to study cognitive processes.

Third, for much of this century, many experimental psychologists were interested in the study of animal learning as a way of understanding cognitive processes. Such prominent learning theorists as Tolman (1932) and Hull (1943) believed that the fundamental principles of human cognition could be understood by the analysis of the learning abilities of rats.

Fourth, Wissler's results and the results of an earlier study by Sharp (1898–1899) convinced many psychologists that the study of the experimental foundations of intelligence was not viable. Sharp, working in Titchener's laboratory, tested seven graduate students on a subset of measures proposed by Binet and Henri in their compendium of suggested tests of higher mental functions, including tests of memory, imagination, and attention. Sharp relied on subjective impressions of the results; quantitative analyses were not used. She concluded that "a lack of correspondences in the individual differences observed in the various tests was quite as noticeable as their presence" (Sharp, 1898–1899, p. 389). She also concluded that more could be learned about individual differences by using complex rather than simple elementary processes, although she did not include any measures of elementary processes in her investigation. And she concluded that the tests would probably yield little of value for the structural introspective approach to psychology in vogue in Titchener's laboratory. Given the nature of the sample and the lack of quantitative detail in the report of the study results, it is unclear what, if anything, should have been the appropriate conclusion to be drawn from Sharp's study.

Wissler's study was criticized by Spearman (1904a). He noted that 22 tests were administered to groups in 45 minutes. In addition, the tester was required to note a number of physical features of the examinees. The reaction-time measures were derived from three or four observations and could not have been very reliable. Given the restrictions in range of talent of the subjects and the rather casual way in which the tests were administered, it is not unreasonable to conclude that the empirical results had little or no value. Irrespective of their empirical merit, there is no doubt that Wissler's conclusions contributed to the belief that elementary cognitive processes studied in laboratory settings could not provide insights into the nature of intelligence.

Deary (1994) reviewed studies of the relationships between intelligence and elementary sensory processes carried out at the turn of the century. He noted that the results of these studies actually supported Spearman's findings. Spearman (1904a) obtained correlations ranging from .25 to .47 between sensory-discrimination indices and academic performance used as an index of intelligence. Burt (1909–1910) obtained correlations close to .30 between measures of ability to discriminate between line lengths and estimates of intelligence. Thorndike, Lay, and Dean (1909) reported a correlation between estimates of intelligence and discrimination ability of .23. Spearman's results were supported by the empirical studies of his contemporaries, although the conclusions derived from Wissler's less adequate findings were those that defined what many psychologists believed to be true.

Rebirth: Complexity Redux

The 19th-century integration between laboratory research and the study of intelligence was revived in the 1960s, 1970s, and 1980s. Neisser's book *Cognitive Psychology* was published in 1967 and summarized an emerging body of research on cognitive processes. Two journals were founded that published many studies relating individual differences in intelligence to laboratory-based measures. *Intelligence* was founded by Detterman in 1977 and *Personality and Individual Differences* was founded by Eysenck in 1980.

The influence of the information-processing approach to intelligence can be observed in research by Hunt and his colleagues. Hunt, Lunneborg, and Lewis (1975) studied laboratory tasks that were assumed to be related to verbal ability. In one of the first studies of this type, Hunt required subjects to make identity judgements for tachistoscopically presented letter pairs. Identical stimuli consisted of letters that were physically identical (e.g., *AA*) or semantically identical (e.g., *Aa*). Reaction times for semantically identical stimuli were longer than reaction times for physically identical stimuli. The difference in reaction times was assumed to be a measure of the time taken to access semantic codes. Individuals with high verbal ability had more rapid access to semantic codes than individuals with low verbal ability.

Sternberg (1977) developed componential analyses designed to obtain measures of individual differences in performance on several components that were required to solve analogies problems. Sternberg began with a theory of the task that specified the way in which several component processes combined to influence task performance. By varying characteristics of the task, it is possible to obtain measures of individual differences for each of the components that determine task performance. Sternberg's analyses represented a novel approach to the study of individual differences. The idea that an understanding of intelligence could be derived by studying complex cognitive tasks has it origins in the 19th century. But earlier research relied on an examination of the products of performance to infer the processes that led to successful performance. Componential analyses are based on the experimental manipulation of task properties. Sternberg's research and Hunt's research may be viewed as an attempt to integrate the study of individual differences in intelligence with an experimental approach to cognitive processes.

Rebirth: Simplicity Redux

There was also a revival of the experimental study of elementary cognitive processes as a basis for understanding intelligence. Jensen spent a sabbatical in England in Eysenck's Department in 1964 (see Jensen, 1997). Eysenck told Jensen about studies by Roth (1964) in which measures of reaction time were obtained using an apparatus consisting of a series of lights arrayed in a semicircle. Subjects were required to press a button under each light as quickly as possible to indicate when the light was turned on. The time taken to move from the home button to the button under each light increased as the number of possible lights that could be lit increased. Roth found that the slope of increase in reaction times as a function of the size of the set of possible stimuli was inversely related to intelligence. Jensen (1982, 1987) subsequently initiated a program of research relating performance on measures of reaction time based on the use of Roth's apparatus and individual differences in intelligence. Jensen's first substantial summary of this research was published in 1982 in a book edited by Eysenck entitled *A Model for Intelligence*. In the same volume, Brand and Deary reported the results of studies of inspection times. Inspection-time tasks present subjects with pairs of stimuli that are noticeably different. In one version of this task, two lines differing in length are presented to a subject followed by two thick lines that occlude the previously presented stimuli and act as a backward mask. The minimal duration for accurate judgment of line lengths is obtained. The duration threshold is inversely related to intelligence.

Deary (1986) indicated that inspection-time measures are similar to measures used by James McKeen Cattell in 1886. Cattell (1886) obtained measures of the time required to judge the color of a stimulus presented against a gray background accurately, and he obtained thresholds for the time required to judge letters and words using an apparatus that was similar to a tachistoscope. He believed that the time taken to judge stimuli was related to individual differences in intelligence.

Evaluative Comments

The attempt to relate intelligence to such relatively elementary processes as reaction times and inspection times, and the attempt to relate intelligence to the relatively complex processes measured in componential analyses and in Hunt's measure of speed of access to semantic codes bears more than a superficial resemblance to two analogous approaches characteristic of research in the 19th century. One approach based on reaction time and inspection time measures was reductionist and, in terms of a contemporary metaphor, a bottom–up analysis seeking an understanding of complex intellectual processes from an analysis of allegedly elementary information-processing abilities. The other approach assumes that an understanding of complex intellectual processes can only be attained by studying performance of relatively complex tasks. Each approach has its strengths and weaknesses. The great strength of the approach based on an analysis of individual differences in performance of a complex task is that such an analysis is ipso facto an analysis of the cognitive processes that define complex intellectual achievements. Two difficulties are characteristic of the approach relating intelligence to complex cognitive processes. First, it is difficult to obtain cross-situational generality from the analysis of componential parameters of performance of a particular task. Such parameters do not invariably predict performance on related parameters based on analyses of performance in other tasks. Second, it is often the case that the parameters of greatest interest to the cognitive psychologist are not those that relate most substantially to individual differences in intelligence. For example, in the Hunt et al. (1975) study of speed of access to semantic codes, the measure derived from the task that has the highest correlation with verbal ability is the average reaction time for judgments of semantically and physically identical stimuli – not the theoretically meaningful parameter of the excess time taken to access semantic as opposed to physical identity of stimuli.

The bottom–up approach partially circumvents the problem of cross-situational generality of parameters. Reaction- and inspection-time measures are relatively remote in form and character from the tasks used to measure intelligence. There are also difficulties with this approach. The correlations between elementary processing measures and performance on more complex tasks are relatively low. There is no credible theory explaining the processes by means of which, if any, complex intellectual skills derive from simple measures. In addition, the relationships that are derived have been interpreted in a manner analogous to that of Thorndike in his letter to Spearman about the relationship between sensory-discrimination ability and intelligence. The alleged simplicity of the tasks may be illusory. Complex intellectual skills may not derive from more elementary processes, but attempts to measures simple processes may unwittingly be contaminated by the effects of strategies. (See Egan, 1994, for a contrary view with respect to inspection time.)

HEREDITY AND ENVIRONMENT

Virtually all of the pioneers in the study of intelligence believed intelligence to be a heritable trait. All of the pioneers were also aware of the possibility that the development of intelligence could be impeded by inadequate environmental exposures. Spearman (1904a) noted that sensory-discrimination ability, which he wrongly believed was at the core of intelligence, was influenced by environmental exposures associated with social class background. Binet (1911) noted that there were differences in performance on his tests for children with different social backgrounds, which he attributed to the extent to which the environment provided adequate stimulation of the development of intelligence. It was widely recognized that any measure of ability must of necessity reflect the opportunity for individuals to acquire the knowledge or skill assessed by a measure of intelligence, although individuals with comparable exposures might differ in the development of intellectually relevant skills and knowledge for genetic reasons. Thorndike et al. (1926, p. 436) asserted that there were truisms or axioms that the community of researchers in the field of intelligence accepted:

All researchers would accept the following axiom. (1) If two men had been subjected to identical circumstances in life, each and every difference between them would be due to original nature.... Not all researchers would accept the following axiom: Intellectual tasks, success in which requires zero training ... do not exist and cannot exist.

If performance on all measures of intelligence is determined by a mixture of opportunity to acquire knowledge and a genetically influenced ability to benefit from environmental exposures, how is it possible to ascertain the extent to which genetic and environmental influences contribute to performance on measures of intelligence?

Family Studies

Galton (1869) tabulated the incidence of eminence among relatives of individuals who were eminent. He observed that the incidence of eminence was related to the closeness of the family relationship, that is, first-degree relatives (fathers and sons) of eminent individuals were more likely to be eminent than second-degree relatives (grandparents and grandsons). Galton noted that it could be argued that the immediate family of eminent individuals might be eminent because of environmental influences associated with family social advantages rather than for genetic reasons. Although family background influences and genetic influences are thoroughly confounded in studies of natural families, Galton believed that his data supported a genetic rather than an environmental influence on

eminence. He noted that many eminent men had impoverished social backgrounds. If family influence produced eminence, why was it possible to find eminent individuals among individuals being reared by families that were not socially privileged?

Galton's studies of intellectual eminence were followed by several other "pedigree" studies. Among the most famous of these were Goddard's studies of the Kallikaks.

Goddard (1912) attempted to separate the influence of nature and nurture in pedigree studies by studying the descendants of Martin Kallikak, a pseudonymous Revolutionary War soldier who was alleged to have had an affair with a feebleminded woman who gave birth to a son named Martin Kallikak, Jr. One of the descendants of this woman was a resident in the Vineland Training School for the Feebleminded directed by Goddard. Martin Kallikak married a woman from a socially privileged background. The descendants of the feebleminded woman were judged to have much lower intelligence than the descendants of the married family of Martin Kallikak. Goddard assumed that this provided strong evidence of the dominance of nature over nurture. Goddard's methods do not really separate nature and nurture. Kallikak's illegitimate descendants may have been influenced by the disadvantaged circumstances associated with the family in which they were reared as well as by the alleged influence of the genes they received from their mother.

Twin Studies

Galton introduced the study of the twin method as a way of ascertaining genetic and environmental influences on intelligence. Galton (1883) was aware that there are two types of twins – monozygotic (MZ) and dizygotic (DZ). He did not distinguish between same-sex DZ twins and MZ twins, although he argued that twins who were similar at birth continued to be similar, and twins who were dissimilar at birth continued to be dissimilar even though they were exposed to a similar environment. He believed that these data provided evidence in support of the dominance of nature over nurture.

Thorndike (1905) noted that twin pairs might differ on a continuum of similarity. He administered tests of ability to twins of different ages and noted that older twins were not more similar to each other than younger twins, suggesting to him that the effects of common rearing did not produce similar abilities. He believed that his data provided support for the dominance of nature over nurture. Thorndike also argued that the environment might produce differences in achievements. He stated his position as follows:

The relative differences in certain mental traits ... are due almost entirely to ancestry, not in training; but that this does not in the least deny that better methods of training might improve all their achievements fifty per cent (Thorndike, 1905, p. 11).

Perhaps the first twin study to resemble modern studies was that of Newman, Freeman, and Holzinger (1937). These researchers attempted to study same-sex DZ twins and MZ twins. They assumed that it would be possible to use various physical features that were highly heritable as a basis of determining whether a twin pair was monozygotic or dizygotic. They found that the twin pairs they classified as MZ were more similar in intelligence than those they classified as DZ. In addition, Newman et al. obtained a correlation of .67 on intelligence for 19 MZ twin pairs who were reared apart.

Adoption Studies

The first studies attempting to separate nature and nurture by the use of an adoption design were published in the 1920s. Among the most important studies of this period was a study by Burks (1928), who compared correlations between adoptive parents and their adopted children with correlations between natural parents and their biological children on tests of intelligence. The control families and the adopted families were matched on a variety of indices of social background. She noted that the midparent to child correlation for the foster children was .20, and the comparable correlation for midparent to child correlation for natural parents was .52. She analyzed her data using the biometrical procedures developed by Wright (1921) and concluded that the heritability of intelligence was close to .8 and that the home environment accounts for approximately 17% of the variance in IQ.

Conclusion

By the end of the fourth decade of this century, evidence in favor of the view of intelligence as a heritable trait had been obtained. Twin studies indicated that MZ twins were more alike than DZ twins on measures of intelligence. The MZ twins reared apart were similar in intelligence. Adopted children exhibited lower correlations with their adopted parents' intelligence test scores than with the test scores of natural parents.

Controversies and New Developments

A belief in the importance of genetic influences on intelligence was challenged in two books written in 1961 and 1974, respectively. J. McV. Hunt (1961) believed that intelligence is substantially malleable and indicated that appropriate modifications early in life might increase intelligence substantially. Hunt's beliefs about the malleability of intelligence were reminiscent of arguments made at the turn of the century. Binet (1911) argued against the "brutal pessimism" of those who believed intelligence to be unmalleable. He advocated the use of techniques of mental orthopedics designed to increase the intelligence of children. The quotation from Thorndike provides clear evidence that the belief in the malleability of intelligence could be coexistent with the belief in the heritability of intelligence. Hunt did not cite studies demonstrating that IQ could be substantially increased by planned interventions. His argument was based in part on evidence from animal studies that indicated that failures to provide adequate stimulation might have long-term impacts on intellectual development. Hunt also relied on studies of brain damage analyzed by Hebb (1942). Children demonstrated better recovery than adults, suggesting greater malleability in development for interventions early in life than for interventions later in life. Hunt's ideas influenced the development of Headstart programs in the United States.

Kamin (1974) presented a critical reanalysis of adoption data and twin research data, pointing to various flaws in the data and arguing that there was little evidence for the heritability of IQ. Kamin analyzed the results of a study of twins reared apart published by Burt at the end of his career indicating that separated MZ twins correlated .86 in intelligence. Kamin noted that the correlation for separated MZ twins remained remarkably the same in several different reports of Burt's studies even as the sample sizes for the studies changed with the addition of new twin pairs. Whether Burt had forged his data, or collected his data and reported the findings incorrectly, is difficult to ascertain (see Hearnshaw, 1979, and Joynson, 1989, for conflicting views of the ''Burt affair''). Kamin attempted to create a penumbra of uncertainty about evidence for the heritability of intelligence.

Many of the uncertainties surrounding research on the heritability of intelligence have been resolved in the past 2 decades since the publication of Kamin's book. It is now widely recognized that intelligence is a heritable trait. Part of the change in opinion is attributable to better adoption and twin studies and new studies of MZ twins reared apart. In large measure, these new developments may be viewed as providing incremental evidence to results that emerged before the end of the fourth decade of this century. There was, however, one new set of findings that has done much to change views about the importance of genetic influences on intelligence. With the exception of Skodak and Skeels' study published in 1949, none of the studies of adoption had obtained longitudinal data. Most of the studies of the influence of adoption had obtained data for relatively young children; indeed much of the data on genetic influences on intelligence that were available dealt with preadolescent children. Erlenmeyer-Kimling and Jarvik (1963) and Bouchard and McGue (1981) summarized kinship relationships for intelligence. Their summaries were overwhelmingly determined by data on children.

Skodak and Skeels found that the correlations between adopted children and their biological mothers increased as children grew older, attaining a final value of .41 when the children varied in age from 11 to 17 years. In a thorough and sophisticated review of all of the data on the heritability of IQ published in 1972, Jencks noted that the Skodak and Skeels' data are anomalous. The correlations obtained between biological parents and their adopted children appeared to be too high to be accommodated to his model-fitting procedures. The possibility that the heritability of IQ for older children might be larger than the heritability of IQ for young children was not considered.

In the 1980s, three adoption studies were reported that led to a reassessment of genetic and environmental influences on IQ. Scarr and Weinberg (1983) studied the influences of the biological parents' ed-

ucational level on the IQs of adopted children when the children were between 16 and 22 years old and obtained correlations of .28 and .43 for biological mothers and fathers, respectively, which are values comparable to the corresponding correlations for natural parents rearing their own children. Loehlin, Horn, and Willerman (1988) analyzed longitudinal data obtained from the Texas Adoption Study and noted that correlations between the IQs of adopted children and the IQs of their adoptive parents declined in a 10-year longitudinal study, whereas the correlations between the IQs of the biological mothers and their adopted children remained constant. They also noted that correlations between biologically unrelated siblings reared in the same home declined to near-zero values in their 10-year longitudinal follow. Phillips and Fulker (1989) analyzed data from the Colorado Adoption Project and obtained increasing correlations in a longitudinal study for relationships between biological parents' IQs and the IQs of their adopted children and declining values for the relationship between the IQ of adoptive parents and the IQs of their adoptive children (for newer results from this study see Plomin et al., 1997). In 1987, Plomin and Daniels wrote an influential paper dealing with these new findings indicating that relationships in intelligence for biologically unrelated children reared together after early childhood were essentially zero and that relationships between adoptive parents and their adoptive parents were also near zero after childhood. These data may be interpreted as indicating that most of the environmental influences on intelligence for older individuals are those that lead children reared in the same family to differ from one another. These data imply that the heritability of intelligence increases from early childhood to adulthood. Whether declining family influences on IQ obtain across the entire social spectrum is unknown. Contemporary research provides little guidance about the effects of being reared in extreme poverty.

WHAT HAPPENED TO BINET'S INVENTION?
The Development of Tests

Binet's scales were enthusiastically received by American psychologists. Goddard translated the scales into English and believed that they provided accurate indices of the intellectual functioning of the residents of his institution.

Terman, like Goddard, was a student of G. Stanley Hall's at Clark University. In 1916, Terman published an English-language version of Binet's test – the Stanford–Binet. Terman's test was designed to produce approximately equal means and standard deviations for IQ scores for individuals of different ages.

Goddard and Terman joined a committee headed by Yerkes to develop a test of intelligence for military recruits in World War I (Yerkes, 1921). Yerkes and his colleagues developed group tests of intelligence that were eventually administered to 1,750,000 military recruits. There were two versions of the test: the Army Alpha and the Army Beta. The former was used to test literate individuals, and the latter was used to test individuals who were illiterate or who were not fluent in English. The tests were used as a basis for rejection of individuals for the military as well as for the assignment of individuals to different kinds of military training. The tests relied on a deviation IQ in which an individual's performance was scaled by comparisons with the performance of the cohort of individuals taking the exam. Test scores were converted to a scale in which the mean was arbitrarily set at 100 and the standard deviation was 15. Terman and Merrill (1960) eventually adopted deviation IQs in the 1960 revision of the Stanford–Binet scales. Deviation IQs were also used by Wechsler in the various versions of his tests (see Wechsler, 1958).

In the 1930s, group tests of intelligence were developed that were widely administered to students in public schools. The Henmon–Nelson tests were introduced between 1932 and 1935 (Henmon & Nelson, 1932–1935). These tests used a multiple-choice format and were administered to elementary school children in grades 3–8. The California Test of Mental Maturity was designed for use with pupils in grades 7–14. The California tests were designed to provide profiles of abilities reflecting the idea that intelligence may optimally be construed as being multifactorial (Sullivan, Clark, & Tiegs, 1936–1939). Thurstone also published an experimental version of a multifactorial measure designed to be used in the public schools (Thurstone, 1938b).

The development of tests for college admissions derived from the work of Brigham at Princeton in the 1920s (see Downey, 1961). This work eventually led to the development of the Scholastic Aptitude Tests (SAT) in 1937, which were designed to measure verbal and quantitative aptitudes using a multiple-choice format.

To What End?

By the end of the fourth decade of this century the testing of intelligence in America had become common. Controversies were attendant upon the use of the tests. Individuals involved in research on intelligence advocated social policies that many found objectionable. Research on intelligence was used to support eugenic arguments that influenced ideas about who should reproduce – a topic considered by Galton in 1869 and by Herrnstein and Murray in 1994. Results of the Army testing program in World War I were used to promote stereotypical views of Southern European immigrants and led Brigham, one of the psychologists involved in the development of the testing program, to argue for restricted immigration to the United States and for the development of programs designed to restrict the propagation of "defective strains" (Brigham, 1923). And many individuals involved in research on intelligence, beginning with Galton and extending to the contemporary writings of Eysenck (1971), Herrnstein and Murray (1994), and Jensen (1998), believed that Africans and their descendants differed in intelligence from White people for genetic reasons.

Virtually all of the pioneers in the study of intelligence recognized that performance on a measure of intelligence derives from a mixture of opportunities to acquire knowledge and from differences in native endowment, that is, from nature and nurture. If individuals differ in their exposure to knowledge and information, then the use of a test of intelligence for assignment of individuals to various social roles may be viewed as a device for reinforcing social privilege. Walter Lippman, a famous journalist wrote a series of articles criticizing the use of IQ tests. He viewed them as devices for reproducing social privilege (see Block and Dworkin, 1976). McClelland, writing in 1973, expressed a similar view comparing performance on tests of intelligence with knowledge of Latin in the Middle Ages. Latin was taught to a small group of individuals. If a test of knowledge of Latin had been used to assign social privileges to individuals in the Middle Ages, it would have reinforced the privileged position of individuals who had access to the relevant training. So, too, tests of intelligence could be viewed as devices to reward individuals arbitrarily who, by virtue of their social position, had access to the relevant knowledge that was assessed by the test.

There is an alternative position. The extent to which individuals develop intellectual abilities and skills may reflect native endowments that are not tied to family background. The use of the tests as a basis for assigning social privileges to individuals becomes a way of defeating social privilege. This idea derives from Galton's observation that genius could be attained by individuals whose background was not privileged. Herrnstein and Murray (1994) argued that increased reliance on the SAT led to a Harvard student body that was defined by intellectual ability rather than by social privilege.

Controversies about the use of tests for selection were also present in debates in England about the relative merits of comprehensive as opposed to grammar schools (see Carroll, 1985; Hearnshaw, 1979, Chapter 7; and Simon, 1974). Grammar schools required tests as a basis for admission. Grammar schools were viewed as elitist. Defenders of the grammar school, such as Burt, argued that the use of tests would enable intellectually gifted children to obtain an education comparable to that provided at "public" schools, which were expensive boarding schools that educated the children of Britain's socially privileged affluent families. On the basis of this view, the use of tests for admission to grammar schools would broaden the social background of students attending Britain's universities.

Although secondary school education has been overwhelmingly comprehensive rather than selective in America, high schools that use tests as a condition of entry do exist. Such schools as Dunbar in Washington D.C., a segregated school for African-Americans, Hunter in New York, and Boston Latin School, are among a group of American public secondary schools that have used tests of academic and intellectual ability as a condition of entry and have long histories of successful education of students from moderate or underprivileged backgrounds. The graduates of these schools have attained records of academic distinction in many selective colleges and universities in the United States. Of course, it is entirely possible that they would have been academically successful if they had attended a comprehensive non-selective school.

In a presidential address to the American Psychological Association, Lee J. Cronbach noted that psychology needed to develop methods for combining what he called the "two disciplines of scientific psychology" (Cronbach, 1957). An optimal program of applied psychology would be one in which environments are created that are designed to cater to individuals with different abilities. In 1977, Cronbach and Snow comprehensively surveyed the literature dealing with what they called aptitude X instructional interactions to ascertain whether there was a scientific basis for recommending the assignment of individuals dissimilar in intellectual abilities and in other personal characteristics to different educational exposures. They were disappointed to discover that the literature provided little or no basis for individuating educational experiences. They found that most of the replicated findings in the literature indicated g to be invariably related to educational outcomes. It was possible to design curricular experiences that would decrease the slope of the relationship between g and academic achievement, but there were no educational procedures that would eliminate the influence of g. The g factor could provide a basis for assigning individuals to different educational experiences. Assignments of individuals to different tracks based on performance on tests of intelligence generally have little or no effect on performance in the elementary school, although assignment to different learning experiences within the same classroom is marginally beneficial – especially where the structure of the curriculum is appropriately differentiated to reflect different learning abilities (Rogers, 1994). Whether IQ tests provide an optimal basis for such assignments is unclear. Teachers should be aware of their students' educational accomplishments, and such knowledge might well provide an equally sound or even superior basis for assigning different educational experiences to students. It is also possible that newer research, published after Cronbach and Snow's survey of the literature, may provide information about optimal ways of assigning individuals to different educational experiences that take into account abilities other than g (see Sternberg, Ferrari, Clinkenbeard, & Grigorenko, 1996 for one such example).

WHAT IS INTELLIGENCE?

Toward the end of his life, Binet (1911) noted that intelligence is contained in the meaning of four terms: comprehension, inventiveness, direction, and criticism. He noted that intelligence is a process directed toward an understanding of the external world that works toward a reconstruction. The reconstruction must be subject to a critical evaluation. A symposium on the definition of intelligence published in 1921 produced a profusion of definitions and little agreement (Thorndike et al., 1921). In 1986 Sternberg and Detterman published a follow-up to the 1921 symposium noting the presence of some areas of agreement combined with considerable disagreement about the appropriate definition of intelligence. In 1923 Boring defined intelligence as what the tests test. Such a definition may be viewed as a frivolous attempt to beg the question or perhaps as being congruent with Spearman's argument that the tests measure whatever it is that is common to all of the tests that form a positive manifold. This does not provide a definition of the common element in the tests. Thorndike et al. (1926) argued that the common element is derived from associations among many different elements. They asserted that "...the higher forms of intellectual operation are identical with mere association or connection-forming, depending upon the same sort of physiological connections but requiring *many more of them*" (Thorndike et al., 1926, p. 414, italics in original). This hypothesis was analogous to one developed by Thomson (1916), who argued that the appearance of a general factor was a consequence of the overlap existing among discrete elements that are used to solve various intellectual tasks. Thus, the positive manifold is a consequence of relationships among discrete elements combined according to the laws of chance. Spearman (1927) argued that g is related to mental energy and to cognitive processes he defined as involving the eduction of correlates and relations. The eduction of relations involves the ability to note relations between two or more ideas as "instanced when a person becomes aware, say, that beer tastes something like weak quinine...or that the proposition 'All A is B' proves the proposition that 'Some A is B.'" The eduction of correlates involves the ability to derive a correlative idea from an idea and a rela-

tion as evidenced by the ability to "hear a musical note and try to imagine the note a fifth higher" (Spearman, 1927, pp. 165–166). Spearman also indicated that intelligence is related to the "apprehension of one's own experience," noting that individuals differ in the power of introspection. He also asserted that "nothing of the sort appears to have yet been measured" (Spearman, 1927, pp. 164–165). Spearman's theory of g and Thomson's interpretation of g are metaphorical – neither was closely related to an empirical research program. Contemporary theorists have not attained consensus about the definition of intelligence or about a theory of g.

A FINAL COMMENT

Binet, Galton, and Spearman are the progenitors of the contemporary study of intelligence. Their contributions resonate in our contemporary discussions of research on intelligence. Galton's belief in genetic influences on intelligence is widely accepted. His belief in a genetic hierarchy of ability defined by ancient Greeks, British people, and Africans is analogous to contemporary discussions of a racial hierarchy of Asians, Whites, and Africans (see Jensen, 1998; Lynn, 1987; Rushton, 1995). Although belief in a racially defined, genetically influenced hierarchy of intelligence is not accepted by many contemporary students of intelligence, such beliefs continue to be expressed. A majority of psychologists assumed to be knowledgeable about intelligence surveyed by Snyderman and Rothman in 1990 believed that racial differences in scores on intelligence tests were partially determined by genetic differences between individuals with different racial identities. Galton's belief in a relationship between intelligence and elementary cognitive processes is related to an active program of contemporary research. Spearman's belief in the overwhelming importance of g is present in many contemporary discussions (see, e.g., Jensen, 1998), and attempts to measure intelligence similar to those initiated by Binet are common.

We know how to measure something called intelligence, but we do not know what has been measured. We do know that whatever has been measured is predictive of performance in academic settings. And, we know that what we have measured is influenced by a person's genes. We do not know what, if anything, should be done with this knowledge. A study of the history of research on intelligence may inform us about how prescient our forbears were. In large measure we know what they knew, we do not know what they did not know, and what many find controversial and objectionable in their work is equally so today when similar ideas are advanced by our contemporaries.

REFERENCES

Binet, A. (1905). Analyse de C. E. Spearman, the proof and measurement of association between two things and general intelligence objectively determined and measured. *L'Année Psychologique, 11*, 623–624.

Binet A. (1911). *Les idees modernes sur les enfants*. Paris: Flammarion.

Binet, A., & Henri, V. (1896). La psychologie individuelle. *L'Année Psychologique, 2*, 411–465.

Binet, A., & Simon, T. (1905). Methodes nouvelles por le diagnostic du niveau intellectuel des anormaux. *L'Année Psychologique, 11*, 191–244.

Block, N. J., & Dworkin, G. (1976). *The IQ controversy*. New York: Pantheon.

Bolton, T. L. (1891–1892). The growth of memory in children. *American Journal of Psychology, 4*, 362–380.

Bouchard, T. J., Jr., & McGue, M. (1981). Familial studies of intelligence: A review. *Science, 212*, 1055–1059.

Boring, E. G. (1923). Intelligence as the tests test it. *New Republic, 35*, 35–37.

Brand, C. R., & Deary, I. J. (1982). Intelligence and "inspection time." In H. J. Eysenck (Ed.), *A model for intelligence*. Berlin: Springer-Verlag.

Brigham, C. C. (1923). *A study of American intelligence*. Princeton, NJ: Princeton University press.

Brody, E. B., & Brody, N. (1976). *Intelligence: Nature, determinants, and, consequences*. New York: Academic Press.

Brody, N. (1992). *Intelligence* (2nd ed.). San Diego: Academic Press.

Burks, B. S. (1928). The relative influence of nature and nurture upon mental development: A comparative study of foster parent–foster child resemblance and true parent–true child resemblance. *Yearbook of the National Society for the Study of Education, 27*, 219–316.

Burt, C. (1909–1910). Experimental tests of general intelligence. *British Journal of Psychology, 3*, 94–177.

Carroll, J. B. (1985). The measurement of intelligence. In R. J. Sternberg (Ed.), *Handbook of human intelligence* (pp. 29–120). Cambridge, U.K.: Cambridge University Press.

Carroll, J. B. (1993). *Human cognitive abilities: A survey of factor-analytic studies*. New York: Cambridge University Press.

Cattell, J. M. (1886). The time taken up by cerebral operations. *Mind, 11*, 220–242, 377–392, 524–538.

Cattell, J. M. (1890). Mental tests and measurements. *Mind, 15*, 373–381.

Cattell, R. B. (1963). Theory of fluid and crystallized intelligence: A critical experiment. *Journal of Educational Psychology, 54*, 1–22.

Cattell, R. B. (1971). *Abilities: Their structure and function*. Boston: Houghton Mifflin.

Cattell, R. B. (1987). *Intelligence: Its structure growth and action*. Amsterdam: North-Holland.

Cronbach, L. J. (1957). The two disciplines of scientific psychology. *American Psychologist, 12*, 671–684.

Cronbach, L. J., & Snow, R. E. (1977). *Aptitudes and instructional methods*. New York: Irvington.

Darwin, C. (1859). *The origin of species*. London: Murray.

Deary, I. J. (1986). Inspection time: Discovery or rediscovery. *Personality and Individual Differences, 7*, 625–631.

Deary, I. J. (1994). Sensory discrimination and intelligence: Postmortem or resurrection? *American Journal of Psychology, 107*, 95–115.

Downey, M. T. (1961). *Carl Campbell Brigham: Scientist and educator*. Princeton, NJ: Educational Testing Service.

Ebbinghaus, H. (1897). Über eine neue Methode zur Prüfung geistiger Fähigkeiten und ihre Anwendung bei Schulkindern. *Zeitschrift für angewandte Psychologie, 13*, 401–459.

Egan, V. (1994). Intelligence, inspection time, and cognitive strategies. *British Journal of Psychology, 85*, 305–316.

Erlenmeyer-Kimling, L., & Jarvik, L. F. (1963). Genetics and intelligence: A review. *Science, 142*, 1477–1479.

Eysenck, H. J. (1971). *Race, intelligence, and education*. London: Temple Smith.

Eysenck, H. J. (Ed.). (1982). *A model for intelligence*. Berlin: Springer-Verlag.

Galton, F. (1869). *Hereditary genius: An inquiry into its laws and consequences*. London: Macmillan.

Galton, F. (1883). *An inquiry into human faculty*. London: Macmillan.

Goddard, H. H. (1912). *The Kallikak family*. New York: Macmillan.

Guilford, J. P. (1967). *The nature of human intelligence*. New York: McGraw-Hill.

Guilford, J. P. (1977). *Way beyond the IQ: Guide to improving intelligence and creativity*. New York: McGraw-Hill.

Guilford, J. P., & Hoepfner, R. (1971). *The analysis of intelligence*. New York: McGraw-Hill.

Hearnshaw, L. S. (1979). *Cyril Burt: Psychologist*. Ithaca, NY: Cornell University Press.

Hebb, D.O. (1942). The effects of early and late brain injury upon test scores, and the nature of normal adult intelligence. *Proceedings of the American Philosophical Society, 85*, 275–292.

Henmon, V. A. C., & Nelson, M. J. (1932–1935). *Henmon–Nelson test of mental ability*. Boston: Houghton Mifflin.

Herrnstein, R. J., & Murray, C. (1994). *The bell curve: Intelligence and class structure in American life*. New York: Free Press.

Horn, J. L., & Cattell, R. B. (1966). Refinement and test of the theory of fluid and crystallized intelligence. *Journal of Educational Psychology, 57*, 253–270.

Horn, J. L., & Knapp, J. R. (1973). On the subjective character of the empirical base of Guilford's structure-of-intellect model. *Psychological Bulletin, 80*, 33–43.

Hull, C. L. (1943). *Principles of behavior*. New York: Appleton-Century-Crofts.

Hunt, E., Lunneborg, C., & Lewis, J. (1975). What does it mean to be high verbal? *Cognitive Psychology, 7*, 194–227.

Hunt, J. M. (1961). *Intelligence and experience*. New York: Ronald.

James, W. (1890). *Principles of psychology*. New York: Dover.

Jastrow, J. (1891–1892). Some anthropological and psychologic tests on college students – A preliminary survey. *American Journal of Psychology, 4*, 420–427.

Jencks, C. (1972). *Inequality*. New York: Harper and Row.

Jensen, A. R. (1982). Reaction time and psychometric *g*. In H. J. Eysenck (Ed.), *A model for intelligence* (pp. 93–132). Berlin: Springer-Verlag.

Jensen, A. R. (1987). Individual differences in the Hick paradigm. In P. A. Vernon (Ed.), *Speed of information processing and intelligence* (pp. 101–175). Norwood, NJ: Ablex.

Jensen, A. R. (1997). Introduction: Hans Eysenck and the study of intelligence. In H. Nyborg (Ed.), *The scientific study of human nature: Tribute to Hans J. Eysenck at eighty*. Oxford, U.K.: Pergamon.

Jensen, A. R. (1998). *The g factor*. New York: Praeger.

Joynson, R. B. (1989). *The Burt Affair*. London: Routledge.

Kamin, L. J. (1974). *The science and politics of IQ*. Potomac, MD: Erlbaum.

Kelderman, H., Mellenbergh, G. J., & Elshout, J. J. (1981). Guilford's facet theory of intelligence: An empirical comparison of models. *Multivariate Behavioral Research, 16*, 37–61.

Loehlin, J. C., Willerman, L., & Horn, J. M. (1989). Modeling IQ change: Evidence from the Texas Adoption Project. *Child Development, 60*, 993–1004.

Lynn, R. (1987). The intelligence of mongoloids: A psychometric, evolutionary and neurological theory. *Personality and Individual Differences, 8*, 813–844.

McClelland, D. C. (1973). Testing for competence rather than for "intelligence." *American Psychologist, 28*, 1–14.

Neisser, U. (1967). *Cognitive psychology*. New York: Appleton-Century-Crofts.

Newman, H. H., Freeman, F. N., & Holzinger, K. J. (1937). *Twins a study of heredity and environment*. Chicago: University of Chicago Press.

Oehrn, A. (1895). Experimentelle Studien zur Individualpsychologie. *Psychologischen Arbeiten, 1*, 92–152.

Peterson, J. (1926). *Early conceptions and tests of intelligence*. New York: World Book Company.

Philippe, J. (1894). Jastrow. – Exposition d'anthropologie de Chicago. – Tests psychologique. *L'Année Psychologique, 1*, 522–526.

Phillips, K., & Fulker, D. W. (1989). Quantitative genetic analysis of longitudinal trends in adoption designs with application to IQ in the Colorado Adoption Project. *Behavior Genetics, 19*, 621–658.

Plomin, R., & Daniels, D. (1987). Why are children in the same family so different from each other? *Behavioral and Brain Sciences, 10*, 1–16.

Plomin, R., Fulker, D. W., Corley, R., & DeFries, J. C. (1997). Nature, nurture, and cognitive development from 1–16 years: A parent-offspring adoption study. *Psychological Science, 8*, 442–447.

Quetelet, M. (1849). *Letters on probabilities*. London: Layton.

Rogers, K. B. (1994). Ability grouping. In R. J. Sternberg (Ed.), *Encyclopedia of Human Intelligence*. Vol. 1 (pp. 5–10). New York: Macmillan.

Roth, E. (1964). Die Geschwindigkeit der Verarbeitung von Information und ihr Zusammenhang mit Intelligenz. *Zeitschrift für Experimentelle und Angewandte Psychologie, 11*, 616–622.

Rushton, J. P. (1995). *Race, evolution, and behavior*. New Brunswick, NJ: Transaction Publishers.

Scarr, S., & Weinberg, R. A. (1983). The Minnesota Adoption Studies: Genetic differences and malleability. *Child Development, 54*, 260–267.

Sharp, S. E. (1898–1899). Individual psychology: A study in psychological method. *American Journal of Psychology, 10*, 329–391.

Simon, B. (1974). *The politics of educational reform, 1920–1940*. London: Lawrence and Wishart.

Skodak, M., & Skeels, H. M. (1949). A final follow-up study of 100 adopted children. *The Pedagogical Seminary and Journal of Genetic Psychology, 77*, 3–9.

Snyderman, M., & Rothman, S. (1990). *The IQ controversy, the media and public policy*. New Brunswick, NJ: Transaction.

Spearman, C. (1904a). "General Intelligence" objectively determined and measured. *American Journal of Psychology, 15*, 201–293.

Spearman, C. (1904b). The proof and measurement of association between two things. *American Journal of Psychology, 15*, 72–101.

Spearman, C. (1927). *The abilities of man*. London: Macmillan.

Spearman, C. (1930). Charles Spearman in C. Murchison (Ed.), *A history of psychology in autobiography*. Worcester, MA: Clark University Press.

Stern, W. L. (1912). *Psychologischen Methoden der Intelligenz-Prüfung*. Leipzig: Barth.

Sternberg, R. J. (1977). *Intelligence, information processing and analogical reasoning: The componential analysis of human abilities*. Hillsdale, NJ: Erlbaum.

Sternberg, R. J., & Detterman, D. K. (1986). *What is intelligence? Contemporary viewpoints on its nature and definition*. Norwood, NJ: Ablex.

Sternberg, R. J., Ferrari, M., Clinkenbeard, P., & Grigorenko, E. L. (1996). Identification, instruction, and assessment of gifted children: A construct validation of a triarchic model. *Gifted Child Quarterly, 40*, 129–137.

Sullivan, E. T., Clark, W. W., & Tiegs, E. W. (1936–1939). *California Test of Mental Maturity*. Los Angeles: California Test Bureau.

Terman, L. M. (1916). *The measurement of intelligence*. Boston: Houghton Mifflin.

Terman, L. M. (1930). Trails to psychology. In G. Murchison (Ed.), *A history of psychology in autobiography*. Vol. 2. Worcester, MA: Clark University Press.

Terman, L. M., & Merrill, M. A. (1950). *The Stanford–Binet Intelligence Scale*. Boston: Houghton Mifflin.

Thomson, G. H. (1916). A hierarchy without a general factor. *British Journal of Psychology, 8*, 271–281.

Thorndike, E. L. (1904). Letter to Charles Spearman. 17 October 1904. Reproduced in R. B. Joynson (1989). *The Burt affair*. London: Routledge.

Thorndike, E. L. (1905). Measurements of twins. *Columbia University Contributions to Philosophy and Psychology, 13*, 1–64.

Thorndike, E. L., Bergman, M. V., Cobb, & Woodyard, E. (1926). *The measurement of intelligence*. New York: Bureau of Educational Research, Columbia University.

Thorndike, E. L., Lay, W., & Dean, P. R. (1909). The relation of accuracy in sensory discrimination to general intelligence. *American Journal of Psychology, 20*, 364–369.

Thorndike, E. L. (1921). Intelligence and its measurement: A symposium. *Journal of Educational Psychology, 12*, 123–147, 195–216, 271–275.

Thurstone, L. L. (1931). Multiple factor analysis. *Psychological Review, 38*, 406–427.

Thurstone, L. L. (1938a). *Primary mental abilities*. Chicago: University of Chicago Press.

Thurstone, L. L. (1938b). *Tests for primary mental abilities: Experimental edition*. Washington, DC: American Council on Education.

Thurstone, L. L., & Thurstone, T. G. (1941). *Factorial studies of intelligence*. Chicago: University of Chicago Press.

Tolman, E. C. (1932). *Purposive behavior in animals and men*. New York: Appleton-Century-Crofts.

Vernon, P. E. (1950). *The structure of human abilities*. London: Methuen.

Wechsler, D. A. (1958). *The measurement and appraisal of adult intelligence* (4th ed.). Baltimore: Williams and Wilkins.

Wissler, C. (1901). The correlates of mental and physical tests. *Psychological Review*, Monograph No. 3.

Wolf, T. H. (1973). *Alfred Binet*. Chicago: University of Chicago Press.

Wright, S. (1921). Systems of mating. *Genetics, 6*, 111–178.

Yerkes, R. M. (Ed.). (1921). *Psychological examining in the United States Army*. Memoirs, National Academy of Sciences, Vol. 15.

CHAPTER THREE

Contemporary Models of Intelligence

JANET E. DAVIDSON AND C. L. DOWNING

CONTEMPORARY MODELS OF INTELLIGENCE

What does it mean for someone to be intelligent or for one person to be more intelligent than another? Not surprisingly, the answers to these questions depend upon the level at which they are addressed. Because intelligence is assessed by members of a society, its conceptualization often takes several forms that can vary according to when, where, and how the assessment occurs.

Despite the inherent difficulty in defining and measuring human intelligence, the goal is a worthy one. Understanding a society's views of intelligence and making these views explicit means that valuable talents can be identified and fostered. In addition, finding the sources of this elusive construct advances our scientific knowledge about the workings of the human mind.

One method for understanding intelligence is through theory-based models. These models often use metaphors to explain existing research on intelligence and clarify future questions (Sternberg, 1990). However, they must also meet certain criteria to be useful to society and to science. First, the models must be based on relevant assumptions and empirical support, build on previous knowledge, and be falsifiable. Second, the elements and the mechanisms by which the elements interact need to be well specified and internally consistent. Third, the models should describe, explain, and predict intelligent behavior over time and across situations. Finally, the models must be fruitful in generating new research and applications that advance the field of intelligence. These criteria are similar to those cited in the literature on theories (Davidson, 1990; Hempel, 1966; Kaplan, 1964).

This chapter will describe four types of contemporary models of human intelligence: neural efficiency, hierarchical, contextual, and complex systems. Because of space limitations, only a sample of the current views will be presented. After each description, we will return to the question: Is this type of model useful? In other words, we will analyze whether each of the four types fit our criteria for an intelligent model of intelligence.

THE NEURAL EFFICIENCY MODEL

Many theorists believe that the heart of intelligence is actually the brain. According to this view, the neurophysiological bases of mental ability must be discovered for intelligent behavior to be understood and properly measured. The premise behind the neural efficiency model is that highly intelligent people have brains that operate more accurately and more quickly than those of less intelligent individuals. Because of advances in technology, several techniques now provide direct measurement of the brain's efficiency. These techniques include evoked potentials, cerebral glucose metabolic rates (CGMRs), and nerve conduction velocity (NCV).

Evoked Potentials

Imagine a measure of intelligence that requires no overt responses or prior knowledge on the part of the examinees. Individuals simply sit in a comfortable chair and listen to tones presented at random intervals. Attached to each person's scalp are electrodes measuring evoked potentials that reflect the brain's electrical activity in response to the tones. According to A. E. Hendrickson (1982) and D. E. Hendrickson (1982), individuals with low intelligence quotients (IQs) will show a fair amount of variability in their electrical brain activity because they have errors in the transmission of information through the cortex of their brains. In contrast, high-IQ individuals will have relatively error-free transmission and therefore will show little variability in their evoked potentials.

To test the hypothesis that intelligence reflects neural accuracy, the Hendricksons developed a method of data analysis that essentially simulated a string being placed on top of the waveform produced from the averaged evoked potentials (AEPs). Long string lengths reflected consistency of the electrical activity, and short ones reflected variability caused by errors in transmission. The intriguing finding in this research was that the string-length measure had a correlation of approximately .80 with IQ. In other words, the researchers found an extremely strong relationship between the consistency of the electrical activity in people's brains and the responses they gave on the Wechsler Adult Intelligent Scale. More sophisticated analyses have since replaced the string test, and a relation between AEPs and IQ has been found with visual as well as auditory stimuli (Ertl & Schafer, 1969; Reed & Jensen, 1992).

It should be noted that high correlations between AEPs and IQ are not always replicated (Barrett & Eysenck, 1992), although some relation is usually obtained. The correlations have ranged between about .20 and .80. One explanation for the inconsistent results is that studies differ in the attentional demands they place on subjects (Bates & Eysenck, 1993). In a recent study (Bates, Stough, Mangan, & Pellet, 1995), high-IQ subjects showed shorter string lengths in an attention-demanding condition than they did in a condition with no attentional requirements. In contrast, low-IQ subjects showed longer string lengths in the attended than the unattended condition. These researchers concluded that their results support higher neural efficiency and capacity in the high-IQ subjects rather than greater neural accuracy.

Along similar lines, a relationship has been found between IQ and neural adaptability. More specifically, higher IQ subjects, unlike ones with lower IQs, showed higher amplitude AEPs in response to unexpected items and lower amplitude AEPs in response to expected ones (Schafer & Marcus, 1973; Schafer, 1979). According to Schafer (1982), efficient, intelligent brains are flexible in responding to stimuli; they use more neurons to process novel or unexpected stimuli and fewer neurons to process familiar or expected information.

Another promising line of research involves integrating measurement of evoked potentials with performance on an inspection-time task. The inspection-time task is a well-studied information-processing index that reflects the speed of intake of simple information (Deary & Stough, 1996). On a typical inspection time task, individuals are asked to look at two parallel, vertical lines of obviously unequal length and determine which of the two lines is longer. The lines are presented for various durations and are usually followed by a visual mask that interrupts visual processing. Unlike many information-processing tasks, reaction time is not an issue for the inspection-time task; individuals are encouraged to take as long as they want to make a decision. Inspection time is usually determined by the duration of stimulus exposure needed for each individual to achieve a certain level of accuracy. Inspection time accounts for approximately 20% of the variance in performance on intelligence tests (Deary & Stough, 1996). In addition, evoked potentials collected early in the processing of the vertical lines distinguish individuals with high performance on measures of inspection time and IQ (Caryl, 1994). This finding suggests that efficient stimulus–analysis mechanisms underlie intelligent behavior.

Cerebral Glucose Metabolic Rates

Further support for the neural efficiency model comes from studies using positron emission tomography (PET) to measure cerebral glucose metabolic rates (CGMRs) while individuals perform a range of tasks. When the brain performs mental activities, it compensates for its consumption of energy by metabolizing glucose. Individual differences have been found in the amount of energy expended by the brain on any given task. More specifically, individuals who obtain high-IQ scores have brains that expend less energy, and consequently consume less glucose, than the brains of individuals with lower IQ scores (Haier et al., 1988).

In addition, individuals who showed the greatest improvement in performance over time on a complex video game also showed the largest decrease in the metabolism of glucose in some areas of their brains and higher levels of metabolism in brain areas related to the task (Haier, 1992). This result indicates a strong relationship between the brain's efficiency and learning. It also suggests that, at some point, researchers will be able to identify specific areas of the brain that are most active and most efficient during the performance of different mental tasks.

Nerve Conduction Velocity

Some studies of nerve conduction velocity (NCV) and intelligence also support the neural efficiency model. Nerve conduction velocity measures transmission speed as electrical impulses travel from one part of the body to another. Faster conduction velocity in the median nerve of the arm (Vernon & Mori, 1992) and in the hand (Barrett, Daum, & Eysenck, 1990) were found to be related to higher IQ scores. This result is especially intriguing given that the NCV involves no cognitive activity and was measured in the peripheral nervous system. However, it should be noted that research on the relation between NCV and intelligence is still in its early stages, and some results have not been replicated (Reed & Jensen, 1991; Wickett & Vernon, 1994).

Critique of the Neural Efficiency Model

The neural efficiency model is appealing for several reasons. From a scientific standpoint, the model provides an uncomplicated, reductionistic view of intelligence as a biological phenomenon. It makes sense to study the organ associated with intelligence directly rather than resort to making inferences about the brain from behavioral measures. From a practical standpoint, neurophysiological measurements provide a glimmer of hope for "culture-fair" measurement of intelligence. Physiological measures are less likely to penalize anyone for insufficient prior knowledge or poor test-taking skills.

Unfortunately, no contemporary model of intelligence is problem free. As noted earlier, empirical support for the neural efficiency model is inconsistent. It is not clear why some studies show high correlations between IQ and the physiological measures, whereas studies similar in design do not. Stimulus intensity, placement of electrodes, and task demands are some of the variables that influence the size of the correlation. Unfortunately, the effects of these variables are not well understood (Eysenck, 1994).

Another problem for the neural efficiency model is that the empirical support is based on the assumption that IQs are a valid, stable, and sufficient standard of comparison for the physiological measurements. Many of the chapters in this volume and elsewhere (Gardner, 1983; Sternberg, 1985) present persuasive evidence that IQ is an incomplete measure of intelligence. It is not yet known whether AEPs, CGMRs, and NCVs will correlate with more broadly defined measures of intelligence. Although it appears that the neurophysiological measures are related to school-like abilities, their relation to less-speeded intellectual accomplishments of adulthood is unclear. In addition, extensive work still needs to be done cross-culturally to determine if the relation between the neurophysiological measures and intelligence is obtained in different cultures.

Finally, at this time, the neural efficiency model is not fully explanatory. The mechanisms causing neural efficiency in the brain still need to be established. Similarly, the direction of causality is unknown. It is tempting to conclude that brain efficiency is the underlying cause of high intelligence. However, another possibility is that neurophysiological functions and cognitive performance are reflections of some other aspect of physiological or psychological functioning that has not yet been discovered. Unfortunately, correlational studies cannot explain causation. Different types of experiments will need to clarify the relationship between the brain's efficiency and an individual's intelligent behavior.

In short, the neural efficiency model shows a great deal of promise for advancing research and knowledge in the field of intelligence. The relation between physiological measures and intelligent behavior is intriguing. However, the mechanisms by which the brain and behavior interact to produce intelligence need to be specified and more broadly tested. Fortunately, the model has tremendous heuristic value; current empirical support is encouraging and will no doubt continue to generate a great deal of research in this area.

HIERARCHICAL MODELS

The basic assumption underlying psychometric models, including hierarchical ones, is that the structure of intelligence can be discovered by analyzing the interrelationship of scores on mental-ability tests. To develop these models, large numbers of people are given many types of mental problems. The statistical technique of factor analysis is then applied to the test scores to identify the "factors," or latent sources, of individual differences in intelligence. For example, if performance on one type of problem is highly related to performance on another type, the abilities measured by the two types are viewed as being interrelated. A set of interrelated abilities is referred to as a factor.

Current hierarchical models can best be understood in terms of two earlier psychometric theories: Spearman's and Thurstone's. Spearman (1927) found a single important factor to be related to performance on all types of mental abilities tests. He labeled this the general factor (g) and believed it to correspond to a fixed amount of "mental energy" that an individual can assign to different tasks at different times. He also found what he considered to be a less important set of specific factors (s), each of which was related to performance on a single type of mental-ability test, such as arithmetic computations, or vocabulary.

Thurstone (1938), however, found no evidence for a general factor of intelligence when he used a wider range of mental tests and a somewhat different version of factor analysis than Spearman used. Instead, Thurstone's analysis revealed seven independent factors, or primary mental abilities, that could be given psychological interpretations. These primary abilities are verbal comprehension (knowing the definitions of words), word fluency (quickly producing large numbers of words), number facility (computations and mathematical problem solving), space (mentally rotating pictures or objects), perceptual speed (quickly recognizing features of stimuli), induction (solving analogies and finding rules or principles in completion problems), and memory (remembering lists of words, pictures, or numbers).

Because a fair amount of data fit neither Spearman's nor Thurstone's models of intelligence, most current psychometric models propose a hierarchical structure to intelligence. This type of structure places one or more general factors at the top of the hierarchy and delegates specific factors to lower levels. More precisely, when first-order factors are correlated with each other, then a second-order factor is constructed to explain the intercorrelations. The first-order factors appear at the bottom of a hierarchical structure, and the broad, second-order factors are at the stratum above them. Similarly, third-order factors might be needed to account for intercorrelations between second-order factors. Third-order factors are even more general than the second-order factors and appear above them in a hierarchical model. In other words, the higher a factor is on a hierarchical model, the farther removed it is from people's actual performance on psychometric tests.

Two contemporary hierarchical models, in particular, help reconcile Spearman's and Thurstone's views of intelligence. The theory of fluid and crystallized intelligence (gf–gc theory) clarifies Spearman's notion of a general factor and is useful in explaining development from infancy through adulthood (Horn, 1994). Carroll's three-stratum theory (1993) is based on the meta-analysis of a wide-range of psychometric results, including the data that shaped gf–gc theory.

gf–gc Theory

The gf–gc theory received its name because early versions (Cattell, 1943, 1963) of the theory proposed that general intelligence has two major parts: fluid intelligence (gf) and crystallized intelligence (gc). The theory has since been updated to include other second-order factors in its hierarchical structure (Horn, 1986). The addition of these factors was based on five types of evidence: individual differences in performance (structural evidence), developmental changes from infancy through adulthood (developmental evidence), the relationship between psychometric performance and neurophysiological functioning (neurocognitive evidence), predictions of school and occupational performance (evidence of achievement), and relationships between cognitive behavior and biological relatedness (behavioral–genetic evidence).

The gf–gc theory can be thought of as a two-stratum model. The broad, second-order factors constitute the top stratum and are based on over 40 first-order factors that form the lower stratum. These first-order factors include Thurstone's primary mental abilities. In addition, Horn's hierarchical theory organizes the second-order abilities functionally according to their level of information processing (Horn, 1986).

The gf and gc factors represent the highest level of cognitive function, which is *relation education* (or inference). The gf factor includes the abilities to perceive relationships among stimulus patterns, to comprehend implications, and to draw inferences from relationships. It is dependent on the efficient functioning of the central nervous system, rather than on prior experience and cultural context. Standardized tests measure this type of intelligence through analogies, series completions, and other tasks involving abstract reasoning. The gc factor, which is dependent on experience and education within a culture, consists of the set of skills and knowledge that individuals acquire throughout their life spans. It includes the first-order abilities of verbal comprehension, evaluation of semantic relationships, and cognition of semantic relationships. Standardized tests measure gc through vocabulary, general knowledge, and verbal comprehension questions. Quantitative knowledge (gq) is a form of gc that has its own processes of acquisition and retention; therefore, it is often portrayed as a separate construct in the model. There is some disagreement about the sources of gf and gc. Cattell (1941) proposed that gf is derived from genetic and biological influences, whereas gc reflects mainly environmental influences. Horn (1994), however, cites evidence that both factors have distinct heritabilities and cultural influences.

The next level of information processing, *perceptual organization*, provides input to the relation education level. Perceptual organization includes processing speed, the ability to visualize information, and the ability to process auditory information.

The third level is *association processing*. It includes the ability to acquire and retrieve information from short-term memory and the fluency of information retrieval from long-term memory.

The lowest level of function in Horn's hierarchical model is *sensory reception*. It consists of two basic sensory detection capabilities: the ability to detect a large amount of visual information in one's environment and hold it in iconic memory and the ability to detect auditory information in one's environment and hold it in echoic memory.

The gf–gc theory explains and predicts intellectual development across the life span (Horn, 1994; Horn & Donaldson, 1976). Infants' abilities mostly center around the lowest levels of the hierarchy. As children develop, they become better able to perform tasks that are representative of the higher levels of function. However, some abilities are vulnerable to injuries to the central nervous system. If the effects of these irreversible injuries accumulate during adulthood, certain abilities can decrease. The abilities most susceptible to decline are fluid intelligence, short-term memory, and processing speed. Because other abilities, such as crystallized intelligence and retrieval from long-term memory, are less affected by the central nervous system, these abilities either increase or remain stable during adulthood.

The Three-Stratum Theory

The three-stratum theory (Carroll, 1993, 1996) is based on Carroll's comprehensive reanalysis of more than 460 datasets reported in the psychometric literature. This model is similar to other hierarchical models (Gustafsson, 1988) but differs notably from gf–gc theory in the inclusion of a third-order general factor at the apex of its hierarchy.

More specifically, Carroll portrays the structure of intelligence as a pyramid. The top of the pyramid, Stratum III, is the conceptual equivalent of Spearman's g. Although Carroll does not support Spearman's interpretation of g as representing mental energy, he agrees that g underlies all intellectual activity and has a high degree of heritability.

The middle of the pyramid, Stratum II, consists of eight factors that are differentially influenced by g. These broad abilities, which are similar to the second-order factors in the gf–gc theory, represent enduring characteristics of individuals that can influence their performance in a given domain. The eight abilities are fluid intelligence, crystallized intelligence, general memory and learning, broad visual perception, broad auditory perception, broad retrieval ability, broad cognitive speediness, and processing speed. The order in which the abilities are listed here reflects the degree that each one is influenced by (or correlated with) the general factor of intelligence. For example, fluid intelligence is the factor most related to g; processing speed is the least related.

The base of the pyramid, Stratum I, consists of numerous specific abilities such as quantitative reasoning and lexical knowledge. As in the $gf–gc$ model, some of these factors represent Thurstone's primary mental abilities. Each ability at Stratum I is related to one or more of the eight abilities that compose Stratum II.

Carroll emphasized that his three strata are not rigidly defined. Abilities in each stratum merely reflect their degree of generality in governing a wide range of intelligent behavior. Stratum I represents very specialized skills that reflect the acquisition of particular strategies or specific types of knowledge; Stratum II contains somewhat specialized abilities that occur in broad domains of intelligent behavior; and Stratum III has one ability, g, that underlies all aspects of intellectual activity. Because generality is a matter of degree, some abilities may be difficult to assign to a stratum. Therefore, Carroll acknowledged that intermediate strata may exist between the three strata he identified.

Recent research supports the three-stratum model. For example, Bickley, Keith, & Wolfe (1995) performed a hierarchical confirmatory factor analysis on test scores obtained from over 6,000 participants of varying ages. These participants were part of the standardization sample for the Woodcock–Johnson PsychoEducational Battery–Revised (McGrew, Werder, & Woodcock, 1991). This test battery was designed to represent many of the abilities in Horn's $gf–gc$ theory. All abilities were highly correlated with g, and results from a confirmatory factor analysis supported a strict interpretation of the three-stratum model. However, a modified version of the three-stratum model provided an even better fit of the data. This modified version suggests the possible existence of intermediate factors that fall between the second and third strata in Carroll's model; these intermediate factors represent gf, gq, and gc.

Critique of the Hierarchical Models

The two hierarchical theories just described meet many of our criteria for models of intelligence. First, both theories build on previous research and help reconcile many of the earlier psychometric findings. More specifically, they illustrate how Spearman's and Thurstone's positions can fit together to explain the structure of intelligence. Second, the $gf–gc$ and three-stratum theories embody a large amount of empirical evidence in support of a well-specified hierarchical structure to intelligence. The three-stratum theory, in particular, provides a comprehensive depiction of the general and specialized abilities and their interrelationships that underlie performance on mental tests. There is also considerable and reassuring overlap in the broad factors that have been proposed and tested by various researchers. Third, these hierarchical theories describe, explain, and predict performance on mental tests over time and across a wide range of problems. The $gf–gc$ model, in particular, provides useful explanations and predictions about intellectual development across the life span. Finally, these theories and their predecessors have generated a great deal of research on human intelligence. In addition to providing insights about the structure of intelligence, these theories, when used in conjunction with performance on information-processing tasks, help illuminate and classify the nature of cognitive processes (Carroll, 1993). They have also influenced the complex systems models that will be discussed later in this chapter and have resulted in the development of theory-based tests such as the Woodcock–Johnson PsychoEducational Battery.

However, the use of different batteries of tests, different factorial rotations of the data, and different interpretations of the results of the factor analysis can lead to different hierarchical models. For example, Horn's $gf–gc$ theory does not propose g as a latent source of individual differences in intelligence, whereas Carroll's three-stratum theory does. Partly because of differences between the hierarchical models, g has become a controversial and pervasive issue for contemporary theories of intelligence. Even nonpsychometric researchers are expected to justify why they have or have not incorporated the psychometric concept of g into their theories. Unfortunately, it is not clear exactly what g represents. Horn (1989) viewed g as basically a statistical artifact. Another interpretation is that g is a unitary dimension of general mental ability that underlies intellectual performance and is particularly evident on tests of abstract reasoning (Carroll, 1993; Spearman, 1927). Ceci (1996) argues that g could be the result of one or more variables such as environmental, biological, metacognitive, motivational, temperamental, or an interlocked set of independent variables. Obviously, a better understanding of g would provide a better understanding of the structure of intelligence.

To understand g, it seems necessary to understand its relationship with gf (fluid intelligence). Some confirmatory factor analyses have been unable to distinguish g from gf (Gustafsson, 1984, 1988). Horn (1989) interpreted this finding as support for his view that intelligence is more specific than g; a single factor does not account for all individual differences in intellectual performance. Carroll (1993) proposed that the strong relationship between g and gf might be due to the high degree of heritability of both factors. Another hypothesis is that g and gf represent essentially the same abilities (Gustafsson, 1988). Recent research suggests that gf is not identical to g but may belong between Stratum II and Stratum III in Carroll's model (Bickley, Keith, & Wolfe, 1995). It is possible that measures of g require specific skills that are not necessarily needed in measures of gf; however, the exact nature of these skills is not yet known. In general, the mental processes that result in intelligent performance on mental tests and in other situations need more specification.

In short, clarifying what g does and does not tell us about intellectual abilities will further our knowledge about the nature of intelligence. Theories and research in the field can then move forward, either with g as an established foundation or without the need to explain its absence.

CONTEXTUAL MODELS

Many models of intelligence are based on the views and laboratory research of Western societies. An absolutist position on intelligence assumes that intelligence involves species-wide mental processes and responses (Berry, 1994). According to this position, the theories and assessment techniques of Western cultures apply to individuals everywhere. In contrast, contextual models are based on the assumption that

intelligence often has different meanings and instantiations in different contexts, particularly in different cultures. Research supports this assumption by demonstrating that what is considered intelligent behavior in one culture is sometimes thought to be rather idiotic in other cultures (Berry & Bennett, 1992; Das, 1994; Wober, 1974).

In a classic example of cultural variability in definitions of intelligent behavior, Cole, Gay, Glick, and Sharp (1971) asked some Kpelle people in Liberia to sort 20 objects. Even though the objects fit four linguistic categories (food, food containers, clothing, and implements), the participants made functional pairings, such as placing a knife and a potato together. The researchers finally asked how a fool would do the sorting. The Kpelle participants then sorted the items linguistically, which is the style of sorting considered to be intelligent in many cultures.

In general, the context in which intelligence is assessed can lead to differences in the conclusions drawn about intelligence. For example, a study of Brazilian street children (Carraher, Carraher, & Schliemann, 1985) demonstrated that these 9-to-15-year-olds could add, subtract, and multiply information in their heads if the problems were put in the context of items that they sold. The children were less good, however, at manipulating numbers associated with items they did not sell. The lowest performance was found on problems in which numbers were presented in an abstract form. Similarly, Ceci and Bronfenbrenner (1985) studied children's monitoring of time in home and laboratory settings. In particular, they looked at how children deal with time pressure in problem-solving tasks as a function of where they are doing the task. They found that the pattern of results was completely different in the two settings. Ceci and Roazzi (1994) propose that social, mental, and physical contexts can all influence intellectual performance.

Contextual theories of intelligence place different degrees of emphasis on the role of context in intelligence. Relativistic theories base their descriptions and assessments of intelligence on its indigenous meanings (Berry, 1994; Berry, Irvine, & Hunt, 1987). In other words, intelligence is defined in terms of its specific meaning within a cultural context. For example, because intelligence in Africa means slowness and conformity (Wober, 1974), the construct of intelligence is quite different in Africa than it is in cultures that value speed of thought or creativity. The extreme form of relativism implies that intelligence has no universal attributes. Therefore, quantitative comparisons of individuals' levels of intelligence in different contexts are invalid.

Other theories of intelligence fall in between the absolutist and relativistic perspectives (Berry, 1994). These theories assume that abilities internal and external to individuals contribute to their intelligence. Mental processes are internal characteristics common to all human populations. Variations in how the universal mental processes are transformed into intelligent responses and competencies are primarily the result of variations in external cultural factors. According to the law of cultural differentiation (Irvine & Berry, 1988), intellectual development occurs in, and is shaped by, ecological and cultural contexts. Therefore, variations in context need to be understood before variations in intelligence can be understood.

Berry and Irvine (1986) proposed an ecological model that describes four somewhat hierarchical levels of context and the ways each one influences intelligent behavior. Level 1, the highest level, is the ecological context in which the person lives. This is the setting in which humans interact with their physical environment. It consists of resources and other relatively permanent characteristics that provide a context for one's actions within a cultural system. Adaptive responses to one's ecological context lead to achievements and the acquisition of customs. Level 2, the experiential context, provides a foundation for learning and development within the ecological context. It includes deliberate training and recurrent experiences. The psychological outcome of this level is a repertoire of long-term abilities, traits, and attitudes that have been learned through socialization and enculturation. Level 3, the situational context, involves immediate environmental circumstances or experiences, such as daily activities, that lead to specific short-term actions. Level 4 is the assessment context. This level occurs when psychologists or similar individuals manipulate an individual's environmental characteristics to obtain test scores or behavioral responses from the individual. If the testing is not nested within the individual's other three contexts, then the test results will not be representative. In other words, intelligent behavior is determined by the ecological, experiential, and situational contexts within

each culture. Therefore, it can only be understood and fairly assessed within these contexts.

Critique of the Contextual Models

The contextual models emphasize that intelligence is not a universal trait or set of abilities that can accurately be assessed by conventional intelligence tests. Neisser (1976) was among the first to stress the importance of connecting cognitive–psychological research to the real-world realities it is supposed to explain. Unfortunately, his message has only recently started to have an impact on the field of intelligence.

In general, contextual views of intelligence are based on a large amount of empirical support demonstrating the effects of context on performance. These scientific findings have implications for conceptions and assessments of intelligence. By their very nature, contextual models also provide explanations of intelligent behavior within a given time and situation. These models have been influential in moving the field of intelligence beyond a static IQ-based approach.

However, the current contextual models do not provide definitive specifications on when and how to integrate context into research on intelligence. Different types and amounts of integration are likely to produce different results and views on intelligence. Similarly, individual differences in intellectual performance within a context are not fully explained. For example, contextual theories do not specify mechanisms to account for how and why some individuals acquire particular types of knowledge or select certain strategies whereas other individuals within the same context do not.

In short, the contextual approach provides an important reminder to researchers and practitioners to be cautious in interpreting and applying their own culture's theories of intelligence. Even though more specification would be useful to the field, the contextual views emphasize that external factors need to be taken into account before intelligence can be fully understood.

COMPLEX SYSTEMS MODELS

Many models of intelligence focus primarily on the physiological or cognitive components of intelligence, and they often use IQ as their only measure of intelligence. However, three contemporary views are much broader in scope. They combine and extend aspects of the biological, hierarchical, and contextual models in their conceptualization of intelligence as a complex system that includes interactions between mental processes, contextual influences, and multiple abilities. According to the complex systems models, intelligence is dynamic and can change when environmental conditions change.

The Triarchic Theory of Intelligence

According to Robert Sternberg's triarchic theory (1985, 1988, 1997), there are three interacting aspects to intelligence. The first, which is internal to the individual, consists of the information-processing skills that guide intelligent behavior. The second aspect involves the ability to create an optimal match between one's skills and one's external environment. The third involves the ability to capitalize on one's experiences to process both novel and unfamiliar information successfully. Each of these aspects will be described in depth.

THE INTERNAL ASPECT OF INTELLIGENCE. According to the triarchic theory, intelligence can partially be understood in terms of the mental mechanisms that drive intelligent behavior. These information processing skills include the metacomponents, performance components, and knowledge acquisition components that formed the basis of Sternberg's earlier "componential" theory (Sternberg, 1977).

Metacomponents are higher order mental processes that intelligent individuals use effectively to guide their problem-solving efforts. These components, which are common to all tasks, include the following:

1. Identifying that a problem exists and needs to be solved.
2. Defining the givens, goals, and obstacles of the problem.
3. Selecting the lower order processes that will be needed to solve the problem.
4. Choosing an appropriate strategy for solving the problem.
5. Selecting a mental representation or "mental map" of the givens, the relations among the givens, and the goals found in the problem.
6. Allocating one's attention and other mental resources for use in solving the problem.
7. Monitoring how well one is achieving one's goals during problem solving.
8. Evaluating the results once a solution has been reached.

According to Sternberg (1985), individual differences in the use of these metacomponents can explain the persistent appearance of g in factor analytic studies of intelligence.

In contrast, performance components are lower order mental processes that intelligent individuals use to implement the instructions given by the metacomponents. Performance components are often specific to the type of problem being solved. They can include processes such as encoding the elements of a problem, comparing the available answer options with one's mentally generated solution, justifying one's response, and physically making the response.

Like the performance components, the knowledge-acquisition components are lower order mental processes. They allow intelligent individuals to learn how to acquire the knowledge that is necessary for problem solving. Sternberg has found three types of knowledge-acquisition components are especially important for intellectual behavior. These types are selective encoding, selective combination, and selective comparison.

Selective encoding involves determining which elements in a set of information are relevant for one's purposes and which are not. Various situations present an individual with large amounts of information, yet only some of it is relevant to one's goals. For example, teachers generally have the problem of too much material to cover in a short period of time. Intelligent teachers select information that is relevant for their pedagogical purposes and do not focus on less important material.

Selective combination involves putting together relevant elements of information to form an integrated whole. Intelligent teachers often develop a way to put together several facts in a way that provides a coherent picture for their students.

Selective comparison involves finding a relationship between new information and information already stored in one's memory. For example, intelligent teachers often relate new classroom material to information that students have already learned. Relating new information to old information can help the students learn the material more quickly and thoroughly.

Sternberg proposes that the metacomponents, performance components, and knowledge-acquisition components occur and are valued in all cultures. However, what is considered an intelligent instantiation of these components may differ across cultures because problems and values often vary across cultures.

The internal (or componential) part of the triarchic theory has been tested extensively with a range of participants and problems. For example, Sternberg and his colleagues found that intelligent problem solvers were more likely than less intelligent ones to spend more time using the components of encoding, strategy planning, and solution monitoring (Sternberg, 1988).

THE EXTERNAL ASPECT OF INTELLIGENCE. According to the triarchic theory, a second aspect of intelligence involves the practical application of the metacomponents, performance components, and knowledge-acquisition components to real-world contexts. Intelligent individuals often know when and how to adapt to a particular environment. If adaptation does not work, they know when and how to change the environment to fit their needs and abilities. If shaping the environment is not a viable option, they know when and how to select a more suitable environment.

The practical aspect of intelligence allows one to acquire tacit knowledge in environments in which strategies for success are not explicitly taught or always verbalized. For example, Wagner and Sternberg (1985) found that some business executives did not score particularly well on standard tests of intelligence yet did quite well on tests of tacit knowledge about business. These executives learned how to allocate their time and energy in a business situation even though they were not expert at allocating their time and energy in a standardized test situation.

THE EXPERIENTIAL ASPECT OF INTELLIGENCE. The third aspect of intelligence involves capitalizing on one's experiences to solve relatively novel problems and quickly automatize procedures. Many intelligent individuals are quite skillful at insightful processing of new information. They use the knowledge-acquisition components of selective encoding, selective combination, and selective comparison described earlier to extract and apply relevant information that is often nonobvious in new situations. For example, research on these three processes revealed that intellectually gifted children spontaneously applied the processes when solving novel problems. In contrast, students of average intellectual ability needed to be told explicitly what information to encode, how to combine the information, and what information to compare (Davidson & Sternberg, 1984).

In addition to coping with novelty, many intelligent individuals quickly make the transition from conscious and deliberate mental processing of a task to subconscious, automatic processing. This transition allows a person to conduct certain procedures effortlessly and to perform more than one task at a time.

Coping with novelty and automatizing procedures are interrelated skills that are important in all cultures. The efficient processing of new information allows intelligent individuals the mental resources to learn and automatize this information quickly. In turn, automaticity frees attentional resources and working memory so individuals can consciously focus on new information.

PATTERNS OF INTELLIGENCE. The internal, external, and experiential aspects of intelligence work together. However, individuals who are strong in one aspect are not necessarily strong in the other two. According to Sternberg, what intelligent individuals of all cultures have in common is the ability to capitalize on their strengths and improve upon, or compensate for, their areas of weakness.

More specifically, some individuals are particularly adept at using the metacomponents, performance components, and knowledge-acquisition components to analyze and compare information. According to Sternberg, these individuals are demonstrating analytic intelligence. Other individuals show creative intelligence when they use the mental components of intelligence to create new products or make new discoveries. Practical intelligence involves using the mental components to help one adapt to, shape, or select an environment that is appropriate for oneself. Sternberg and his colleagues (Sternberg, Ferrari, Clinkenbeard, & Grigorenko, 1996) found that students who were taught in a way that matched their analytic, creative, or practical abilities achieved at higher levels than students who were given instruction that did not match their abilities.

Multiple Intelligences

Like Sternberg, Howard Gardner rejects the conception of intelligence as a unitary ability. However, Gardner's theory of multiple intelligences (MI) focuses more on domains of intelligence and less on mental processes than does the triarchic theory.

According to MI theory (Gardner, 1983, 1998), there are at least eight fairly independent, equally important types of intelligences that have evolved in the human species and are valued in a wide range of cultures. An intelligence is defined as "the ability to solve problems, or to create products, that are valued within one or more cultural settings" (Gardner, 1993). Individuals develop one or more intelligences through genetic inheritance, training, and socialization of cultural values. In other words, the intelligences evolve through interactions between one's biological predispositions and the opportunities provided by one's environment.

Three of the intelligences – linguistic, logical–mathematical, and spatial – are related to abilities measured by conventional intelligence tests. Linguistic intelligence involves the abilities to use language to explain, convince, and remember information and to clarify meaning. Logical–mathematical intelligence is the ability to operate on relationships in abstract symbol systems and to evaluate ideas and quantities logically. Spatial intelligence involves skill in perceiving and transforming visual–spatial relationships.

The remaining five types – musical, bodily–kinesthetic, intrapersonal, interpersonal, and naturalist – are valued in most cultures even though they are not measured by conventional intelligence tests. Musical intelligence includes sensitivity to various musical properties and the ability to appreciate, produce, and combine pitch, tones, and rhythms. Bodily–kinesthetic intelligence is the skillful use of one's body. Intrapersonal intelligence reflects the understanding of one's own motives, emotions, strengths, and weaknesses. Interpersonal intelligence involves understanding of, and sensitivity to, other people's motives, behaviors, and emotions. Naturalist intelligence is Gardner's latest addition to his theory (Gardner, 1998). It involves

understanding the patterns found in natural environments.

Although Gardner believes that the intelligences are relatively independent from each other, he acknowledges that they can work together within a domain. For example, complex word problems in mathematics require logical–mathematical and linguistic intelligences. Similarly, expert musicians probably need bodily–kinesthetic, interpersonal, intrapersonal, and musical intelligences to perform well in their field.

MI theory, unlike some of the other theories of intelligence, is not based on patterns of paper-and-pencil test scores. Instead, Gardner used several types of evidence to support the existence of the eight relatively independent intelligences. One type of evidence was neuropsychological data showing that damage to certain areas of the brain impairs some abilities but not others. In some ways the mind seems to be organized according to content areas, and each area relies on its own neural structures. Another source of evidence included the uneven performance of autistic children, idiot savants, prodigies, and gifted individuals who excel in some areas but not in others. High competence in one kind of intelligence was not found to be predictive of high competence in the other kinds. A third source of evidence was that each intelligence has its own developmental course and an identifiable set of mental operations. Musical intelligence, for example, develops more or less independently from the other kinds of intelligences and, unlike the other kinds, it requires the ability to discriminate pitches. Another source was that certain competences occur in several cultures and show an evolutionary history that seems to be related to a primordial form of expression in other species. A fifth source of evidence for MI theory was that certain abilities are expressed through culturally determined symbol systems. For example, musical intelligence has one type of notation, mathematical intelligence becomes encoded in another type, and linguistic intelligence has its own symbols and rules. These concrete symbol systems allow the intelligences, which cannot be expressed in pure form, to be applied to specific domains within a culture.

Although Gardner acknowledges that standardized psychometric measures can reveal a general factor, he claims that the narrow scope of these measures severely limits g's explanatory and predictive value.

Because Gardner and his colleagues believe the intelligences are best measured in the contexts in which they naturally occur, they concluded that paper-and-pencil tests are inadequate assessments (Chen & Gardner, 1997; Gardner, 1992). Consequently, MI theory has been tested through observations and tasks conducted in real-world settings. For example, Adams (as cited in Chen & Gardner, 1997) went into the homes of 4-year-old children to test the relationship between the preschooler's logical–mathematical, linguistic, artistic, interpersonal, musical, and mechanical abilities. Performance on a series of diverse gamelike tasks, called the Spectrum Field Inventory, revealed that the six cognitive abilities showed very little relationship to each other. In fact, only 10% of the sample of children displayed the same level of performance on all tasks. However, the results from this study have limited generalizability because the sample size was small ($n = 42$) and consisted mostly of middle- to upper-class children.

The Bioecological Model

In his bioecological theory, Ceci (1996; Ceci, Rosenblum, de Bruyn, & Lee, 1997) proposed that intelligence is a function of the interactions between innate potential abilities, environmental context, and internal motivation. Like Gardner, Ceci believes that there are multiple innate potential abilities that can be fostered by specific contexts; an individual can be strong in some abilities and weak in others. Unlike MI theory, the bioecological model is explicitly developmental and process-oriented in nature.

According to the bioecological theory, each person's innate abilities are derived from a system of biological resource pools. These multiple pools are statistically independent from one another. Each pool is responsible for different aspects of one's information-processing capabilities, such as contrast-detection skill, memory capacity, and visual-rotation ability.

Interaction with environmental resources determines whether an innate cognitive potential will succeed or fail in its development. Domain-specific cognitive processes, domain-specific knowledge, and other aspects of one's context help shape and develop one's biological predispositions. In turn, the predispositions help shape one's context. This ongoing interactive process results in changes that can themselves lead to more changes. In other words,

one set of changes caused by the interplay between biological endowments and critical ecological contexts can begin a cascading effect that shapes each person's development. Even relatively small changes in one process can eventually result in larger changes to other processes. The consequence is that human development is nonadditive and synergistic rather than linear.

The timing of the interchange between innate potential abilities and environmental resources is sometimes critical to intellectual development. Some neural connections disappear if they do not receive specific contextual stimulation during sensitive periods of development. When neural connections are lost, certain potential abilities do not fully develop. Similarly, certain environmental experiences can result in the formation of rich neural connections that promote the development of an individual's cognitive abilities.

According to the bioecological model, an individual's environmental resources are of two related types (Ceci et al., 1997). One type, called proximal processes, involves enduring, reciprocal interactions between the developing child and the objects, people, activities, and symbols in his or her immediate environment. These positive interactions allow the child to develop progressively more complex forms of intelligent behavior. In other words, proximal processes play the important role of transforming genotype into phenotype. The second type of resource, called distal resources, consists of the dimensions of one's environment that influence the form and quality of the proximal processes. Many stable distal resources, such as books and consistently safe neighborhoods, are more likely than less enriched settings to foster high levels of proximal processes. In turn, high levels of proximal processes are related to high levels of intelligent behavior. For example, a parent's background, parenting style, and stress level are distal resources that help shape the parent–child interactions leading to the proximal process of attachment. Later in life, children who had secure attachments during infancy are more likely to show better performance in school than children who were insecurely attached.

Although the interchanges between biological and environmental resources are necessary for intellectual development, they are not sufficient. According to the bioecological model, individuals must be motivated to capitalize on their innate abilities and take advantage of their particular environments. When people are motivated in certain areas, they tend to elaborate on their mental representations of information related to those areas. Because elaborate mental representations lead to more efficient cognitive processing, individuals are often better able to process and retrieve information if it is in the context of some domains than if it is in the context of others. For example, Ceci and Liker (1986) found that men who were quite successful in their betting at race tracks and who generated complicated mental strategies for predicting winners of the races did not demonstrate the same complexity or type of reasoning in other contexts. In fact, these men had an average IQ that was slightly below the population average. According to the bioecological model, motivation contributes to uneven intellectual performance across domains. Similarly, knowledge in a given domain influences one's mental processes and reasoning skills, which results in uneven intellectual performance across domains.

Critique of the Complex Systems Models

In their explanations of why human intellectual performance is often high in some contexts and low in others, these three complex systems models emphasize the range, malleability, and complexity of intelligent behavior. Through this emphasis, they advance the field of intelligence beyond a narrow, static conception of intelligence. In particular, these three models help explain how mental capacities develop and change over time and across situations. In addition, the complex systems models build upon and help integrate subfields of intelligence by incorporating aspects of the biological, psychometric, information-processing, and contextual approaches. Unlike some of the more traditional theories of intelligence, these models are attentive to a wide range of physiological, cognitive, and developmental research.

Even though the three models emphasize different aspects of intelligence, they are not mutually exclusive of each other. As Sternberg notes (1997), his analytic, practical, and creative patterns of intelligence can be applied to Gardner's symbolic domains of intelligences. For example, someone with analytic and linguistic intelligence might excel as a literary critic. An individual with practical and mathematical intelligence might become an accountant.

A talented painter probably has creative and spatial intelligence. In other words, the internal, external, and experiential aspects of the triarchic theory are mostly compatible with MI theory. Similarly, the bioecological theory is compatible with the triarchic and MI theories in that it helps explain how individuals develop their patterns and domains of intelligences.

As implied earlier, one of the strengths of the complex systems theories is that they reflect a scientific and societal desire to view intelligence in a way that is broad enough to reflect its full complexity. Although each of these three models should be commended for its breadth, each one needs more depth before its validity and utility can be established. Without further elaboration of the different elements of each model and specification of how the elements interact, it is not clear how any of the three complex systems models can be fully tested or completely disconfirmed. Similarly, it is not obvious how to establish whether any of the models is missing mental components or intelligences.

Fortunately, parts of each complex systems theory can be subjected to an empirical test. For example, the triarchic theory views the metacomponents of intelligence as being relatively domain general, whereas MI theory and the bioecological theory emphasize domain specificity. A thorough examination of how well individuals apply the metacomponents to a wide range of content areas will help shed light on the issue of domain generality versus domain specificity. Until each model can be tested in its entirety, partial tests will help guide modifications and help ensure that each model is on the right track in its assumptions.

CONCLUSIONS AND IMPLICATIONS

How intelligent are these models of intelligence? If one's definition of intelligence includes the ability to learn from incomplete instruction (Resnick & Glaser, 1976), then the answer is that these models are quite intelligent. The creators of these contemporary models learned from the ambiguities and flaws of previous research. For example, the current hierarchical models resolve some of the problems found in Spearman's and Thurstone's models. The contextual and complex systems models explain previously confusing patterns of uneven performance on mental tasks. In general, the contemporary models seem more extensive and promising than the ones that came before them. To borrow Sternberg's definition of intelligence (1986), the later models capitalized on the strengths of the earlier ones and avoided many of their weaknesses.

Similarly, if one's definition includes the ability to adapt to circumstances (Binet & Simon, 1916), then these models demonstrate a great deal of intelligence. The contemporary models were constructed in response to the changing needs within science and society to view intelligence as something more than what conventional intelligence tests measure. The contextual and complex systems models, in particular, have a broad conception of intelligence. The neural efficiency model is a response to a scientific need to understand the physiological underpinnings of intelligence.

On the surface, these four types of models seem quite different. The neural efficiency model focuses on the physiological aspects of intelligence. The hierarchical models examine the structure of the mind in terms of the latent sources of individual differences in mental abilities. The contextual models emphasize the external sources that influence or create the construct of intelligence. Finally, the complex systems models view intelligence in terms of multiple, interacting dimensions. In other words, each type of model analyzes and explains a different level (or set of levels) of intelligence. Each one provides a different answer to the questions of what it means for someone to be intelligent or for one person to be more intelligent than another.

However, there is at least one commonality in the four types of models reviewed here. They all seem to value adaptability of cognitive processing as an important aspect of intelligence. For example, the neural efficiency model encompasses neural adaptability. The hierarchical models incorporate fluid intelligence, which involves the ability to adapt to novel information. The contextual models view intelligence in terms of adaptability to one's culture or context. The complex systems models explain intelligence, or intelligences, as adapting potential abilities to the values and demands of one's culture.

If these contemporary models have one common weakness, it is that they all need more specification. The neural efficiency model does not fully explain the relationship between the brain and intelligence.

The hierarchical models have not clarified exactly what a general factor of intelligence represents or how psychometric scores relate to, and explain, intelligent behavior in a range of situations. The contextual models do not explain how and why individual differences in intelligence occur within a given context. Finally, the complex systems models are vague in terms of how their different aspects operate and interact.

The diversity of the types of contemporary models is impressive. At one time the field of intelligence was dominated by the psychometric models and then by theories developed through the information-processing methodology. Ten years ago, this chapter would have included a section on information-processing models of intelligence and focused less on the biological, contextual, and complex systems views. Now new types of models are in the field playing a large role in shaping and advancing our conceptions of intelligence. These new models incorporate and extend the information-processing models. At the same time, many of them are attentive to the contexts in which intelligent behavior occurs. Individually, each model focuses on a different aspect of what it means to be intelligent. Taken together, these contemporary models help establish a comprehensive view of intelligence and provide new directions for productive research.

REFERENCES

Barrett, P. T., Daum, I., & Eysenck, H. J. (1990). Sensory nerve conduction and intelligence: A methodological study. *Journal of Psychophysiology, 4*, 1–13.

Barrett, P. T., & Eysenck, H. J. (1992). Brain evoked potentials and intelligence: The Hendrickson paradigm. *Intelligence, 16*, 361–381.

Bates, T., & Eysenck, H. J. (1993). String length, attention, and intelligence: Focused attention reverses the string length–IQ relationship. *Personality and Individual Differences, 15*, 362–371.

Bates, T., Stough, C., Mangan, G., & Pellet, O. (1995). Intelligence and complexity of the averaged evoked potential: An attentional theory. *Intelligence, 20*, 27–39.

Berry, J. W. (1994). Cross-cultural variations in intelligence. In R. J. Sternberg (Ed.), *Encyclopedia of human intelligence* (pp. 316–322). New York: Macmillan.

Berry, J. W., & Bennett, J. A. (1992). Cree conceptions of cognitive competence. *International Journal of Psychology, 27*, 73–88.

Berry, J. W., & Irvine, S. H. (1986). Bricolage: Savages do it daily. In R. J. Sternberg & R. K. Wagner (Eds.), *Practical intelligence: Nature and origins of competence in the everyday world* (pp. 271–306). Cambridge University Press.

Berry, J. W., Irvine, S. H., & Hunt, E. B. (Eds.). (1987). *Indigenous cognition: Functioning in cultural context.* Dordrecht, Netherlands: Nijhoff.

Bickley, P. G., Keith, T. Z., & Wolfe, L. M. (1995). The three-stratum theory of cognitive abilities: Test of the structure of intelligence across the life span. *Intelligence, 20,* 309–328.

Binet, A., & Simon, T. (1916). *The development of intelligence in children* (E. S. Kite, Trans.) Baltimore, MD: Williams & Wilkins.

Carraher, T. N., Carraher, D. W., & Schliemann, A. D. (1985). Mathematics in the streets and in schools. *British Journal of Developmental Psychology, 3,* 21–29.

Carroll, J. B. (1993). *Human cognitive abilities: A survey of factor-analytic studies.* Cambridge: Cambridge University Press.

Carroll, J. B. (1996). A three-stratum theory of intelligence: Spearman's contribution. In I. Dennis & P. Tapsfield (Eds.), *Human abilities: Their nature and measurement.* Mahwah, NJ: Lawrence Erlbaum Associates.

Cattell, R. B. (1941). Some theoretical issues in adult intelligence testing. *Psychological Bulletin, 38,* 592.

Cattell, R. B. (1943). The measurement of adult intelligence. *Psychological Bulletin, 40,* 153–193.

Cattell, R. B. (1963). Theory of fluid and crystallized intelligence: A critical experiment. *Journal of Educational Psychology, 54,* 1–22.

Caryl, P. G. (1994). Early event-related potentials correlate with inspection time and intelligence. *Intelligence, 18,* 15–46.

Ceci, S. J. (1996). *On intelligence: A bioecological treatise on intellectual development.* (Expanded Edition). Cambridge, MA: Harvard University Press.

Ceci, S. J., & Bronfenbrenner, U. (1985). Don't forget to take the cupcakes out of the oven: Strategic time-monitoring, prospective memory and context. *Child Development, 56,* 175–190.

Ceci, S. J., & Liker, J. (1986). Academic and nonacademic intelligence: An experimental separation. In R. J. Sternberg & R. K. Wagner (Eds.), *Practical intelligence* (pp. 119–142). New York: Cambridge University Press.

Ceci, S. J., Rosenblum, T., de Bruyn, E., & Lee, D. L. (1997). A bio-ecological model of intellectual development: Moving beyond h^2. In R. J. Sternberg & E. L. Grigorenko (Eds.), *Intelligence, heredity, and environment* (pp. 303–321). New York: Cambridge University Press.

Ceci, S. J., & Roazzi, A. (1994). The effects of context on cognition: Postcards from Brazil. In R. J. Sternberg & R. K. Wagner (Eds.), *Minds in context: Interactionist perspectives on human intelligence* (pp. 74–101). New York: Cambridge University Press.

Chen, J., & Gardner, H. (1997). Alternative assessment from a multiple intelligences theoretical perspective. In D. P. Flanagan, J. L. Genshaft, & P. L. Harrison (Eds.), *Contemporary intellectual assessment: Theories, tests, and issues* (pp. 105–121). New York: Guilford Press.

Cole, M., Gay, J., Glick, J., & Sharp, D. W. (1971). *The cultural context of learning and thinking.* New York: Basic Books.

Das, J. P. (1994). Eastern views of intelligence. In R. J. Sternberg (Ed.), *Encyclopedia of human intelligence* (pp. 387–391). New York: Macmillan.

Davidson, J. E. (1990). Intelligence recreated. *Educational Psychologist, 25* (3&4), 337–354.

Davidson, J. E., & Sternberg, R. J. (1984). The role of insight in intellectual giftedness. *Gifted Child Quarterly, 28,* 58–64.

Deary, I. J., & Stough, C. (1996). Intelligence and inspection time: Achievements, prospects, and problems. *American Psychologist, 51,* 599–608.

Ertl, J. P., & Schafer, E. W. P. (1969). Brain response correlates of psychometric intelligence. *Nature, 223,* 421–422.

Eysenck, H. J. (1994). EEG evoked potentials. In R. J. Sternberg (Ed.), *Encyclopedia of human intelligence* (pp. 391–394). New York: Macmillan.

Gardner, H. (1983). *Frames of Mind: The theory of multiple intelligences.* New York: Basic Books.

Gardner, H. (1992). Assessment in context: The alternative to standardized testing. In B. Gifford & M. O'Connor (Eds.), *Alternative views of aptitude, achievement, and instruction.* Boston: Kluwer.

Gardner, H. (1993). *Frames of mind: The theory of multiple intelligences* (10th anniversary edition). New York: Basic Books.

Gardner, H. (1998). Are there additional intelligences? The case for naturalist, spiritual, and existential intelligences. In J. Kane (Ed.), *Education, information, and transformation* (pp. 111–132). Englewood Cliffs, NJ: Prentice Hall.

Gustafsson, J. E. (1984). A unifying model for the structure of intellectual abilities. *Intelligence, 8,* 179–203.

Gustafsson, J. E. (1988). Hierarchical models of individual differences in cognitive abilities. In R. J. Sternberg (Ed.), *Advances in the psychology of human intelligence.* (Vol. 4, pp. 35–71). Hillsdale, NJ: Erlbaum.

Haier, R. J. (1992). Cerebral glucose metabolism and intelligence. In P. A. Vernon (Ed.), *Biological approaches to the study of human intelligence.* Norwood, NJ: Ablex.

Haier, R. J., Siegel, B. V., Jr., Nuechterlein, K. H., Hazlet, E., Wu, J. C., Paek, J., Browning, H. L., & Buchsbaum, M. S. (1988). Cortical glucose metabolic rate correlates of abstract reasoning and attention studied with positron emission tomography. *Intelligence, 12,* 199–217.

Hempel, C. G. (1966). *The philosophy of natural science.* Englewood Cliffs, NJ: Prentice Hall.

Hendrickson, A. E. (1982). The biological basis of intelligence. Part I: Theory. In H. J. Eysenck (Ed.), *A model for intelligence* (pp. 151–196). New York: Springer-Verlag.

Hendrickson, D. E. (1982). The biological basis of intelligence. Part II: Measurement. In H. J. Eysenck (Ed.), *A model for intelligence* (pp. 197–228). New York: Springer-Verlag.

Horn, J. L. (1986). Intellectual ability concepts. In R. J. Sternberg (Ed.), *Advances in the psychology of human intelligence* (Vol. 3, pp. 35–77). Hillsdale, NJ: Erlbaum.

Horn, J. L. (1989). Models of intelligence. In R. L. Linn (Ed.), *Intelligence, measurement, theory, and public policy* (pp. 29–33). Urbana: University of Illinois Press.

Horn, J. L. (1994). Theory of fluid and crystallized intelligence. In R. J. Sternberg (Ed.), *Encyclopedia of human intelligence* (pp. 443–451). New York: Macmillan.

Horn, J. L., & Donaldson, G. (1976). On the myth of intellectual decline in adulthood. *American Psychologist, 31*, 701–719.

Irvine, S. H., & Berry, J. W. (1988). The abilities of mankind: A reevaluation. In S. H. Irvine & J. W. Berry (Eds.), *Human abilities in cultural context* (pp. 3–59). New York: Cambridge University Press.

Kaplan, A. (1964). *The conduct of inquiry: Methodology for behavioral science*. San Francisco: Chandler.

McGrew, K. S., Werder, J. K., & Woodcock, R. W. (1991). *WJ-R technical manual: A reference on theory and current research*. Chicago: Riverside.

Neisser, U. (1976). *Cognition and reality: Principles and implications of cognitive psychology*. San Francisco: Freeman.

Reed, T. E., & Jensen, A. R. (1991). Arm nerve conduction velocity (NCV), brain NCV, reaction time, and intelligence. *Intelligence, 15*, 33–47.

Reed, T. E., & Jensen, A. R. (1992). Conduction velocity in a brain nerve pathway of normal adults correlates with intelligence level. *Intelligence, 16*, 259–272.

Resnick, L. B., & Glaser, R. (1976). Problem solving and intelligence. In L. B. Resnick (Ed.), *The nature of intelligence* (pp. 205–230). Hillsdale, NJ: Erlbaum.

Schafer, E. W. P. (1979). Cognitive neural adaptability: A biological basis for individual differences in intelligence. *Psychophysiology, 16*, 199.

Schafer, E. W. P. (1982). Neural adaptability: A biological determinant of behavioral intelligence. *International Journal of Neuroscience, 17*, 183–191.

Schafer, E. W. P., & Marcus, M. M. (1973). Self-stimulation alters human sensory brain responses. *Science, 181*, 175–177.

Spearman, C. (1927). *The abilities of man*. New York: Macmillan.

Sternberg, R. J. (1977). *Intelligence, information processing, and analogical reasoning: The componential analysis of human abilities*. Hillsdale, NJ: Erlbaum.

Sternberg, R. J. (1985). *Beyond IQ: A triarchic theory of human intelligence*. New York: Cambridge University Press.

Sternberg, R. J. (1988). *The triarchic mind: A new theory of human intelligence*. New York: Cambridge University Press.

Sternberg, R. J. (1990). *Metaphors of mind*. New York: Cambridge University Press.

Sternberg, R. J. (1997). The triarchic theory of intelligence. In D. P. Flanagan, J. L. Genshaft, & P. L. Harrison (Eds.), *Contemporary intellectual assessment: Theories, tests, and issues* (pp. 92–104). New York: Guilford Press.

Sternberg, R. J., Ferrari, M., Clinkenbeard, P. R., & Grigorenko, E. L. (1996). Identification, instruction, and assessment of gifted children: A construct validation of a triarchic model. *Gifted Child Quarterly, 40*(3) 129–137.

Thurstone, L. L. (1938). *Primary mental abilities*. Chicago: University of Chicago Press.

Vernon, P. E., & Mori, M. (1992). Intelligence, reaction times, and peripheral nerve conduction velocity. *Intelligence, 16*, 273–288.

Wagner, R. K., & Sternberg, R. J. (1985). Practical intelligence in real-world pursuits: The role of tacit knowledge. *Journal of Personality and Social Psychology, 49*, 436–458.

Wickett, J. C., & Vernon, P. A. (1994). Peripheral nerve conduction velocity, reaction time, and intelligence: An attempt to replicate Vernon and Mori. *Intelligence, 18*, 127–132.

Wober, M. (1974). Towards an understanding of the Kiganda concept of intelligence. In J. W. Berry & P. Dasen (Eds.), *Culture and cognition* (pp. 261–280). London: Methuen.

PART II

DEVELOPMENT OF INTELLIGENCE

CHAPTER FOUR

HERITABILITY AND INTELLIGENCE

ELENA L. GRIGORENKO

HERITABILITY AND INTELLIGENCE

One need only think of one's fellow men and women to realize that individual intellectual make-ups vary in numerous ways. Psychology's most long-standing indicator of individual differences in intellectual functioning is the intelligence quotient (IQ). Although IQ was originally invented to differentiate children into groups of those whose level of intellectual functioning corresponds to that of peers of similar age and those whose level of mental functioning does not,[*] it has since evolved into the most frequently used indicator of individual differences (or variability) in intellectual functioning. The point of this chapter, however, is not to analyze individual differences in IQ per se, but, rather, the *sources* of these differences. In other words, what forces make people similar (or dissimilar) in IQ[†]?

The sources of variability in IQ have been the subject of a field known as the psychology of individual differences. This subfield is one of the oldest in psychology, and, like any mature field, it has witnessed successive theoretical transformations. In this case, different theories have been employed to explain the etiology of the traits in which people differ (e.g., Kimble, 1993). The landmark of research on the etiology of individual differences in IQ is the concept of heritability, a statistic describing the proportion of phenotypic (observed) differences among individuals in a population that can be attributed to genetic differences between them. It has been said that there are very few subfields in psychology as controversial and yet sterile as that of heritability-based studies of IQ (Danzinger, 1997). The debates concerning these studies are remarkable in number and pervasiveness. The controversies begin with the essential question of the interestingness and meaningfulness of the concept of heritability for psychology (e.g., Block, 1995), continue with the methodology underlying individual-differences research in IQ (e.g., Feldman & Otto, 1997), and culminate with a questioning of this research's major findings and interpretations (e.g., Wahlsten & Gottlieb, 1997).

---

[*] In 1905, when they published their test, Binet and Simon (1916) claimed that the goal of the endeavor was to differentiate children into groups of those who would succeed (because they have enough intelligence) and those who would fail (because they lack intelligence) in school. The authors limited their objective to the technical goal of devising an instrument suitable for determining pupil's fitness for different educational programs. Binet and Simon provided a means for calculating a single intelligence score but cautioned that its meaning was blurry and that the score should be used merely as a matter of practical convenience when it was necessary to make a decision regarding the placement of a child.

[†] An important point of clarification must be made here at the outset of the main argument. In many writings on heritability studies of IQ, the authors use the terms IQ, intelligence, and general cognitive ability factor (so-called g-factor) interchangeably. As others have said multiple times, however, heritability studies of intelligence are in reality limited to IQ. Thus, such an extension of the terminology (from IQ to intelligence) is justifiable only if it is assumed that there is nothing more to intelligence than IQ. Correspondingly, the assumption that there is more to intelligence than IQ makes the interchangeability of the terms *IQ* and *intelligence* incorrect. Therefore, the term IQ will be employed throughout the chapter (unless a different term appears in a directly cited original source).

This chapter asserts that the heritability approach to the etiology of individual differences in human traits in general and in IQ in particular (hereafter *heritability paradigm*) has completed its mission in the science of individual differences. The heritability paradigm has been useful for psychology because it has established a tradition of referring not exclusively to environments, but also to genes, as we attempt to understand the etiology of individual differences in intellectual functioning. Having established *who* the players are (i.e., genes and environments), the field needs to account for *how* the game is played (i.e., how genes and environments coact in producing individuality). The heritability paradigm was instrumental in the first inquiry, but is not suited for the second. This chapter alleges that an improved understanding of the etiology of individual differences in intellectual functioning will come from a new paradigm now taking shape, the paradigm of measuring rather than estimating etiological contributions of genes and environments.

THE HERITABILITY APPROACH: THE FLAVOR OF A PARADIGM

Why Call It a Paradigm?

Scientists' interpretations of the heritability paradigm's meaning and significance for psychology vary. Some view the paradigm as a scientific endeavor (e.g., Hunt, 1997), whereas others claim that it is an infertile invention of psychologists – one of the field's dead ends (Danzinger, 1997). The term heritability paradigm refers here to a distinct methodological tradition of studying sources of individual variability in human traits. This tradition is also known as the decomposition of phenotypic variance into so-called genetic and environmental components. It is important to note that the heritability paradigm refers only to studies decomposing observed phenotypic variance in *human traits* into its *estimable* (not measured!) components. Sir Francis Galton established the foundation for the heritability paradigm, which subsequently evolved, through many transformations, into a strong subfield of research, as manifested by numerous pathbreaking works (e.g., Jinks & Fulker, 1970; Neale & Cardon, 1992; Plomin, DeFries, McClearn, & Rutter, 1997). The essence of this paradigm is its assumption of (1) the deterministic role of genes and environments in the emergence of individual differences in a trait, (2) the separability of nature and nurture as distinct forces that contribute independently to individual developmental trajectories, and (3) the estimability of the relative contributions that variabilities in genes and environments make to the variability in human traits.

Why is it important to classify the heritability approach as a paradigm? This label helps us recognize the global role of heritability studies in the broader context of the field of individual differences. The heritability approach's importance and its social–historical role in the promotion of biological factors' significance for the emergence of individuality has been discussed by the approach's proponents (e.g., Plomin, DeFries, McClearn, & Rutter, 1997; Plomin & Petrill, 1997) as well as by doubters (e.g., Danzinger, 1997) and opponents (e.g., Wahlsten, 1998; Wahlsten & Gottlieb, 1997). Whether they accept or reject this approach, scientists do not question its significance for the development of science. Now, however, the field is concerned with where we stand today and what we should do next. In this regard, classifying the heritability approach as a paradigm eases us into a discussion of the inevitability of paradigmatic shifts (Kuhn, 1962, 1977) and so facilitates our demonstration of the heritability approach's explanatory limitations and the need for a new paradigm.

According to Kuhn (1962), a scientific paradigm is characterized by scientific achievements that are (1) sufficiently unprecedented to attract an enduring group of adherents, (2) sufficiently open-ended to leave many challenging and interesting problems for researchers to address and resolve, and (3) sufficiently developed to be characterized by distinct rules and standards for scientific practice. The claim here is that the heritability paradigm meets these requirements. With its formation in the late 1960s and early 1970s, the paradigm (1) promised to provide answers to interesting questions (e.g., the importance of genetic variability for human-trait variability) and attracted a brilliant group of scientists, (2) pointed to a general direction of development but left plenty of space for the formulation of specific questions, and (3) developed a sophisticated methodological apparatus serving its own needs. Moreover, the developmental trajectory of the heritability approach matches that identified by philosophers of science as indicative of paradigmatic development. In particular, the approach is characterized by common theoretical presuppositions and methodology (a set of common practices for advancing the theory) (Smith, 1997). In addition, the establishment of the heritability paradigm was marked by the formation of a specialized journal (*Behavior Genetics*), which publishes most of the relevant research, the foundation of a supportive professional society (The Behavior Genetics Association), and the claim for a special place in the educational curriculum (there are numerous textbooks in the field, some of which have been republished in successive editions).

Paradigms gain their status because they are more successful than their competitors (or predecessors) at solving a few problems. They appear with the promise of answering unresolved questions, but they are initially resisted until, eventually, disputes are resolved and the dominant paradigm begins to rule. Once this battle for establishment is over, scientists working within the dominant paradigm engage primarily in enhancing and extending the paradigm, making it stronger and more powerful. Ironically, by doing all of this, they lay the groundwork for its eventual elimination. The claim of this chapter is that the heritability paradigm has exhausted its explanatory power and slowly is being forced out of the field.

This argument will be articulated in three steps. First, I provide a summary of the paradigm's current state-of-the-art heritability studies of IQ. Second, I point to several observations that are anomalous with respect to the heritability paradigm. Finally, I discuss some possible ways of enhancing our understanding of the etiology of individual differences in IQ and point to some exciting developments that form the basis for a new emerging paradigm in the field.

Heritability Paradigm and IQ: The State of the Art

Every paradigm addresses three main sets of problems (Kuhn, 1962). The first set has to do with the identification of those facts, among the many facts known in the field, that are significant for the paradigm. In the case of the heritability paradigm, which of the facts accumulated in the field of individual differences in IQ should be considered important?

The second set of problems concerns matching significant facts with theory. In other words, once the significant facts have been selected, what kinds of inferences can be made from them? Finally, the third set of problems has to do with the articulation of theory. How does the paradigm interpret the significant facts and link them with the theory? The facts of concern for the heritability paradigm are familial (relative) resemblance in IQ. The method that matches the observed IQ similarity–dissimilarity to theory is the decomposition of phenotypic variance. Measured IQ differences are accounted for by reference to genes and environments. The ultimate interpretation of these findings is aimed at identifying important and unimportant agents of developmental IQ trajectories (e.g., Harris, 1995; Rowe, 1997).

The heritability paradigm of IQ is a concrete scientific achievement supported by multiple thorough studies and a characteristic set of preconceptions and beliefs. This paradigm embraces all kinds of commitments – theoretical (expressed in the use of the index of heritability, h^2), methodological (expressed in the utilization of distinct methodologies), instrumental (expressed in preferences for specific software), and even philosophical (expressed in support for Mendelian ideas of genetic determinism). As a powerful tool shaping scientific consciousness, the heritability paradigm is prerequisite to the perception, processing, and interpretation of many phenomena. In other words, for its followers, the heritability paradigm structures the world, sorting the smorgasbord of the observed reality of individual differences in IQ into neatly packaged boxes labeled "genes" and "environments," as well as the somewhat messier box labeled "genes and environments: interactions and correlations." In the next section I explain how this packaging is done.

Selected Concepts

For the purpose of the following discussion, I must define several crucial concepts.

The value observed when an individual's IQ is measured is referred to as a *phenotypic value* (or *phenotype*). Thus, every individual in a population can be characterized by his or her phenotypic value (IQ score). If enough individuals are measured on the trait, the parameters of the distribution (mean, variance, and higher moments) of the phenotypic values can be characterized for a population. This distribution quantifies individual differences in IQ in a given population.

The question is how to explain this distribution. In other words, how can the phenotypic values be divided into components so that they can be attributed to different causes? The first and most evident division is into components attributable to genotype and environment. The *genotype* refers to the unique constellation of genes possessed by the individual, and the *environment* refers to all the nongenetic influences determining the phenotype.

The importance of the phenotype–genotype distinction is that it depicts the relation between observable and unobservable characteristics: an observable trait (phenotype) is not a perfect indicator of an individual's latent qualities (genotype). These differences between the phenotype and the corresponding genotype can be accounted for by environmental influences (or environmental deviations). For example, monozygotic (identical) twins are often thought of as having identical genotypes,[*] yet one might have a higher IQ than the other because of differences in environment. These relationships between the individual's phenotype (P), the individual's genotype (G), and the environment (E) can be expressed in a simple mathematical scheme as

$$P = G + E.$$

However, researchers often divide both contributions (G and E) into their subcomponents. Then,

$$P = (A + D + I) + (S + N),$$

where A refers to additive effects (the combined effects of alleles[*] both within and between genes), D refers to dominant effects (those resulting from interactions between alleles), I refers to epistatic effects (those resulting from interactions between different genes), S refers to environmental effects shared by all family members, and N refers to nonshared (individualized) environmental effects.

This formula, however, depicts only the general components of a phenotype. To describe the variability (i.e., individual differences) of a phenotype in a population, the concept of variance is used. The total variance is the phenotypic variance, or the variance of phenotypic values, and is the sum of the separate components. In other words,

$$V_P = V_G + V_E = (V_A + V_D + V_I) + (V_S + V_N).$$

This representation, however, requires certain clarifications. First, genotypic and environmental components may be correlated; then V_P will be increased by twice the covariance of G and E (this term is usually referred to as genotype–environment correlation, $2\mathrm{Cov}(G)(E)$). Second, interactions between genes and environments may occur, introducing yet another additional term to the equation (this term is referred to as genotype–environment interaction, V_{GXE}).

On the basis of this decomposition of variance, the heritability coefficient is defined as the indicator of the contribution of genes to the variation in a trait (phenotypic variation). If this coefficient is defined as V_A/V_P, it is called heritability in the narrow sense. If it is defined as V_G/V_P, it is referred to as heritability in the broad sense.

The representation of the phenotypic variance through its components, however, is nothing more than a coherent abstraction. It is handy in allowing us to picture causal influences on the phenotype, but it becomes "alive" only when it is linked to indicators of similarities and dissimilarities between relatives.

---

[*] Apparently, a closer look at this widely held belief provided rather interesting results (for a brief review, see Martin, Boomsma, & Machin, 1997). Hall, for example, reported on the genetic differences that take shape between identical twins during fetal development (1996a,b). Moreover, researchers question the accuracy of the term *identical* when referring to monozygotic (MZ) twins, pointing out that there are monochorionic (MC) and dichorionic (DC) MZ twins, both of which are genotypically and phenotypically rather discordant (Keith & Machin, 1997; Machin, 1996). In particular, it is claimed that MC–MZ twins are more similar in behavioral and less similar in biological phenotypes than DC–MZ twins (Charlemaine & Pons, 1998). Whether the MZ twins' differences are significant enough to jeopardize the dogma of the genetic similarity of identical twins has yet to be determined.

---

[*] An allele is a variant of a gene; in any given gene, an individual has two alleles, one inherited from a mother and the other inherited from a father.

IQ: Years of Research on Thousands of Pairs of Relatives

The literature covering genetic and environmental influence on IQ is immense. Consequently, this review section is selective and focuses primarily on mainstream, widely discussed data and representative findings.* Extensive summaries of the current state of heritability studies of IQ have recently been provided by numerous researchers (e.g., Bouchard, 1998; Plomin & Petrill, 1997; Sternberg & Grigorenko, 1997). The essence of this research can be captured by one statement: "genetic influence on individual differences in intelligence is significant and substantial"(Plomin & Petrill, 1997, p. 56). So, all that is left to do is to understand what "significant and substantial" mean. What evidence underlies this rather vague but hard-won conclusion?

People living together by their own choice, whether blood relatives or not, are more similar in their IQ than a random group of people not living together. For example, the correlation for IQ scores of randomly chosen, genetically unrelated people not living together is .06; the correlation for IQ scores of genetically unrelated students attending a boarding school and living in one dormitory is .37; the correlation for genetically unrelated spouses is .42; the correlation for IQ scores of biological parents and offspring living together is about .33 (Grigorenko, unpublished data†). Whereas the first correlation is obviously very different from the rest, the other three correlations do not appear to differ substantially from each other. However, even though the correlations of individuals living together look similar, the causal reasoning underlying this superficial similarity differs from one instance to the next.

The correlation between students sharing a dormitory may be attributable to studying in the same school and living in the same dormitory. In addition, it may be that certain schools are sought by, or seek, people with similar genotypes. For example, by establishing a certain minimum achievement test score as the key to the school door, schools effectively select not only for IQs but also for certain genotypes. Thus, students share much of their environments and, as a result of the school-selection policy, may carry similar genotypes as well.

The correlation between spouses could be attributed to assortative mating (i.e., nonrandom mating of human couples, where the choice of the partner is driven by similarity in IQ) and spousal convergence (increased similarity of those living together owing to their overlapping environmental experiences). It also could be that correlation between spouses results from their carrying similar genotypes. For example, let us assume that high-IQ levels are seen in individuals carrying the genotypes A, B, and C; middle-range IQ people tend to have genotypes D, E, and F; and lower-level IQ people tend to have genotypes G, H, and J. Then, those who have a high IQ (individuals with genotypes A, B, and C) and select spouses who also have a high IQ (i.e., selecting partners with genotypes A, B, and C) will also be selecting the spouses' genotypes. Therefore, phenotypic IQ correlations between spouses might, in fact, reflect correlations between their genotypes. In other words, one spouse might resemble another not only because the two live together but also because each, in selecting a partner similar to himself or herself intellectually, selected an individual with a similar genotype. Spouses share environments and, most likely, have similar genotypes.

The correlation for IQ scores of biological parents and offspring is, approximately, of the same magnitude as that of spouses and of students living in one dormitory. Unlike the other two correlations, this correlation is not due to "accidental" (phenotype-based) correlation of genotypes – by definition of biological relatedness, parents and their offspring share genes. However, they also share the environments of their families.

---

* The review does not deal with several important issues such as the following: heritability-based studies of IQ in minority populations (e.g., Levin, 1994, 1997; Loehlin, 1992; Waldman, Wainberg, & Scarr, 1994), studies of IQ in populations of developing countries (e.g., Pal, Shyam, & Singh, 1997), estimates and interpretations of environmental effects (e.g., Rowe, 1997), and developmental fluctuations of heritability–environmentality coefficients (e.g., McGue et al., 1993).

† The proximity of these correlations is illustrative even though they are sample-specific and their 95% confidence intervals are rather large.

So, all three IQ correlations between people willingly or unwillingly living together could be explained by reference to both genetic and environmental influences. In other words, speculations regarding the causal nature of all three correlations include genes and environments as explanatory factors. When it comes to quantifying these explanatory factors, the first two correlations (between students in the same dormitory and between spouses) are informative only when both latent causes (genes and environments) are somehow measured. On the other hand, the third correlation (between parents and child) could be informative even when genes and environments are not measured because this correlation could be compared with correlations between other types of relatives.

This peculiarity of parent–offspring correlation prompted a discovery of quasi-experimental designs that have been productively utilized in research on the etiology of individual differences in IQ. Basic ideas for these designs were developed by Sir Francis Galton, who, in searching for a way to distinguish the genetic and environmental sources of IQ variability, suggested using both twins and adoptive families (Galton, 1876, 1883). If we assume that differences in IQ are attributable (significantly and substantially) to genetic differences, and if we know the degree to which individuals are biologically related to each other, as well as whether they share or do not share the same family environment, a pyramid of expectations for correlations between different pairs of relatives' IQ scores can be constructed. Genetically related family members living together are expected to be more similar than genetically unrelated members of families formed by adoption. Biological siblings living together are expected to be more similar than half-siblings living together, because, on average, the former share 50% of their genes, whereas the latter have only 25% of their genes in common. Different corresponding expectations could be mapped out for family members of different degrees of relatedness; the general rule is that the smaller the degree of genetic relatedness, the lower the correlation for IQ scores. Figure 4.1 summarizes the results of hundreds of studies conducted on the IQs of relatives of various degrees living together and apart. And indeed, in general, the correlations fit the expectations nicely – the more genetically distant the relatives are, the less their IQ scores resemble each other.

The major claim of the heritability paradigm is that information about familial resemblance can be used to unravel the sources of interindividual variability in IQ. The crucial piece of information that needs to be obtained is the correlation of IQs in pairs of relatives. Knowledge of the causal structures of these correlations permits – when correlations between different pairs of relatives are combined – the estimation of the contribution of genes and environments. (For example, identical twins reared together share all of their genes, and they live in one home; thus, the factor that should explain the fact that the correlation between their IQs is not 1 is some constellation of environmental influences experienced by the twins differently). This is the essence of the heritability paradigm – within it, the variance attributable to genes and environment can be *estimated*; it does not have to be *measured*.

Even though these sources may be described quantitatively in many ways, the most popular statistic used is that of the heritability coefficient (often referred to as heritability, or h^2). When estimated from different pairs of relatives (e.g., genetic relatives adopted apart versus genetic relatives reared together), the heritability coefficient varies significantly (e.g., Bouchard & McGue, 1981). These differences, however, are attributable to method variation (Plomin et al., 1997). In particular, h^2 appears to be higher when obtained by comparing the resemblance between individuals reared apart than when obtained by comparing the similarity between individuals reared together. When pooled across different studies (that is, across different cohorts, different age groups, and different types of relatives), the heritability coefficient is considered to be estimated reliably. Let me comment briefly on some of these studies.

Family Studies

Since the late 1920s, when the first studies regarding familial resemblance for IQ were conducted, dozens of studies have been published (for review, see Bouchard & McGue, 1981). There is a consensus that the data can be divided into two parts, the so-called old (conducted before 1980) and new (conducted after 1980) studies. The older studies had relatively small samples, were less

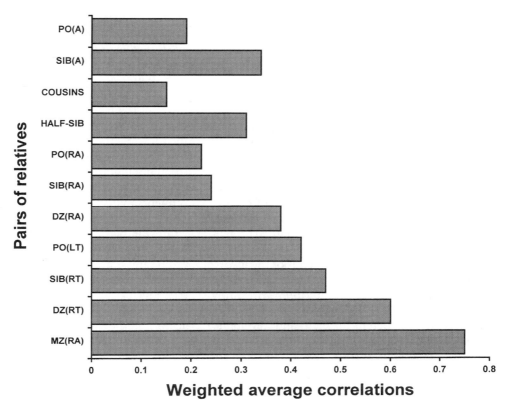

FIGURE 4.1. Family, twin, and adoption data on the correlations between pairs of relatives' IQ. RT – reared together, RA – reared apart, LT – living together, MZ – monozygotic (identical) twins, DZ – dizygotic (fraternal) twins, Sib – siblings, PO – parent-offspring, A – adopted. Adapted from Bouchard and McGue (1981), Loehlin (1989), and Plomin and Petrill (1997).

sophisticated methodologically, and provided rather high estimates of heritability (with a median correlation of about .42). The newer studies (e.g., the Hawaii study, DeFries, Vandenberg, & McClearn, 1976; DeFries et al., 1979) are characterized by larger sample sizes and more sophisticated methodology. The correlations obtained in these studies tend to be lower (e.g., $r = .26$; DeFries, Corey, Johnson, Vandenberg, & Wilson, 1982).

Three explanations of these differences have been suggested. First, the mismatch between the old and the new data may be attributable to environmental and genetic changes in the studied populations that occurred in the time frame between the new and the old studies. This explanation seems plausible for environmental effects (life has changed dramatically since the 1930s), but unlikely for genetic components. Second, there may be restriction of range in the new data (Caruso, 1983). The newer data were collected primarily from middle-class white families, which offer somewhat less variation in IQ than is observed in a normal population and thus limit the current findings to a group with IQ above average.

The third, most plausible, explanation highlights the role of methodological differences between the old and new studies. The methodological procedures in the newer studies are more standardized. Moreover, although the older studies were extended for a longer period of time, the newer studies involved tests administered to many families at the same time in the same testing facilities.

Twin Studies

The first behavioral–genetic twin study focusing on IQ was conducted by Merriman (1924). Since then, many thousands of twins around the world have served as recruits in studies of general and specific cognitive abilities. Meta-analyses of these data (Bouchard & McGue, 1981; Loehlin & Nichols,

1976) suggest a heritability of about .50. These estimates are not corrected for the effects of either assortative mating or nonadditive genetic variance.

A detailed review of the twin studies of IQ is beyond the scope of this chapter. However, several of them have addressed specific issues that are of interest to our broad discussion. For example, researchers summarized monozygotic (MZ) and dizygotic (DZ) twin correlations for general cognitive ability by age (McGue et al., 1993). The difference between MZ and DZ twin correlations increases slightly from early to middle childhood and then increases dramatically in adulthood. Another important finding resulted from a study of 300 pairs of same-sex twins and 100 nontwin siblings evenly distributed by gender and ages (from 7 to 12 years). The pairs were oversampled at the low and high ends of the IQ distribution (Detterman, Thompson, & Plomin, 1990; Thompson, Detterman, & Plomin, 1993). This study indicated, among other findings, that heritability of IQ appears to be different for high- and low-ability subjects, suggesting that different genetic mechanisms may be involved in the manifestation of individual differences in IQ at different ends of the IQ distribution.

Adoption–Separation Studies

Most adoption studies, like family and twin studies, have also investigated the heritability of IQ. The range of obtained estimates of correlations between biological relatives, though broad (from .22 to .72), results in a mean heritability score of about .50, meaning that genetic differences among individuals account for about half of the differences in their performance on IQ tests.

The adoption studies that attracted the most attention are those of MZ twins reared apart. These studies tend to suggest higher heritability estimates than those discussed earlier. The correlation obtained on 45 pairs of MZ twins participating in the Minnesota Study of Twins Reared Apart was .78 (Bouchard, Lykken, McGue, Segal, & Tellegen, 1990). A study of Swedish twins included 48 pairs of MZ twins reared apart and reported the same correlation of .78 (Pedersen, Plomin, Nesselroader, & McClearn, 1992).

Numerous family, twin, and adoption studies have been combined into global analyses using a model-fitting approach (Chipuer, Rovine, & Plomin,

1990; Loehlin, 1989). This approach allows one to analyze simultaneously the data collected in different studies and to obtain more elaborate and precise estimates of genetic and environmental contributions than is possible by comparing simple correlations. The outcome of these analyses places the estimate of the heritability of intelligence at 50–51% (Plomin & Neiderhiser, 1992). Unlike many scientific findings, this one fits with laypeople's interpretation of the impact of genes and environments on variability in IQ – the observed variability is half genetic and half environmental; both genes and environments matter.

This internal consistency of the results obtained within the heritability paradigm is interpreted differently by different scientists. Some say that these results are sufficiently convincing to declare the nature–nurture controversy regarding IQ resolved (e.g., McGue, Bouchard, Iacono, & Lykken, 1993), whereas others bemoan the wasted resources and lack of interpretability they perceive as the end result of this half-and-half finding (e.g., Fischer & Silvern, 1985; Gottlieb, 1992; Lerner, 1991; Oyama, 1985). However, the internal consistency of the data obtained within a paradigm does not make that paradigm "right" (Kuhn, 1962). Paradigms shift, not because of data consistency or lack thereof but rather because the old paradigm is incapable of either offering a new step for the development of the field or explaining new observations.

Voices of Concern

As they grappled with the conclusion that variability in IQ is half attributable to variability in genes and half attributable to variability in environments, scientists expressed a variety of concerns; some of these concerns came from within the paradigm (i.e., from those who believe in the paradigm and want to strengthen it), and some came from outside of the paradigm (i.e., from those who suggest dismissing the paradigm altogether).

It Is Right, But...

The within-paradigm concerns can be summarized in five different points.

First, the summary reports present mostly weighted average (or median) correlations delivered to readers without confidence intervals. An evaluation of the original sources, however, reveals rather large confidence intervals. Bouchard (1998), for example, pointed out that the 95% confidence interval for the SATSA's (Swedish Adoption/Twin Study of Aging) correlations of .32 was .30–.56, and that, for the MISTRA's (Minnesota Study of Twins Reared Apart) correlations, this interval was .13–.71 (for DZ twins reared apart). Similarly, the confidence interval for the correlation of .62 between elderly twins (McClearn et al., 1997) was .29–.73 (Feldman & Otto, 1997). Such nitpicking, however, is important – unfortunately, the confidence intervals are too large to be ignored.

Second, heritability coefficients apply to particular populations at particular times. Lewontin (1974) stressed that the statistic of heritability provides us with a local analysis of a trait under certain environmental conditions in a population characterized by a given distribution of genotypes unique to a given time. As a statistic of a given moment, heritability cannot offer any information about either what has happened, what will happen, or what might happen. It does not reveal any evolutionary history, and it does not forecast the future. To illustrate, consider a specific population characteristic, such as birth rate. Birth rate reflects the state of a population at a given historical moment. For example, in Russia, before the beginning of Perestroika, the birth rate was 16 per 1,000. Since then it has decreased steadily, reflecting the conditions of the society and current complications associated with child rearing. The birth rate was 8.9 per 1,000 in 1996 (*Semia v. Rossii*, 1997). Because of the way it is defined, heritability depends on the two elements of the proportion, G and P. In turn, P depends on E. Therefore, any change in either G or E may be reflected in a change of the heritability coefficient. To be specific, any environmental change may result in a change in h^2. The "stability" of heritability is no higher than that of birth rate or the number of roller-blades in a population.

In particular, the heritability coefficient is expected to go down when (a) the variability of environments is increased (e.g., by offering many types and forms of schooling) or (b) the variability of genes is decreased (e.g., by creating a population of genetic clones). On the contrary, the heritability coefficient is expected to go up when (a) the variability of environments is decreased (e.g., by instituting uniform schooling) or (b) the genetic variability

is increased (e.g., by quantifying this variability in a large sample of pairs of relatives representative of different populations).

The third major concern is that heritability provides a "state" rather than "process" description of the functioning behind IQ. The following example illustrates the distinction between these two types of description: (a) a circle is the locus of all points equidistant from a given point; (b) to construct a circle, rotate a compass with one arm fixed until the other arm has returned to its starting point. According to Euclid, if one carries out the process described in (b), he or she will produce the object defined in (a). Sentence (a) provides a state description of a circle, whereas sentence (b) gives a process description. Much scientific activity follows this tradition: Once they obtain the description of a phenomenon, scientists attempt to find the differential equations for the processes that will result in the phenomenon. What is troublesome about the concept of heritability is that the step from (a) to (b) is unclear. Estimates of h^2 do not bring scientists any closer to understanding underlying processes, regardless of the precision or imprecision of the estimate. Even elaborate longitudinal multivariate models that decompose the phenotypic correlations between relatives obtained at different developmental stages (see, for example, Fulker, Cherny, & Cardon, 1993; Loehlin, Horn, & Willerman, 1989) and state whether the trait is influenced by similar or different sets of genes at different developmental stages, cannot overcome this problem – there is a huge gap between the indices of heritability and any understanding of the biological processes that result in these indices.

Fourth, often the heritability coefficient is inflated as a result of the subsuming of the contributions of higher order interactions between the components of the equation. Specifically, it has been shown that the presence of interaction between genes and shared environments (the detection of which requires very large datasets rarely obtainable in practice) tends to inflate the estimates of V_G and, correspondingly, the estimates of h^2 (Molenaar, Boomsma, & Dolan, 1999). Moreover, the presence of interaction between genes and nonshared environments tends to inflate the estimates of V_N (Molenaar, Boomsma, & Dolan, 1999). Owing to statistical power constraints, there is a lack of empirical research stressing the importance of these higher order effects. As a result, the artificially suppressed contribution of V_S can be erroneously interpreted as a lack of the importance of shared environments (e.g., Harris, 1995).

Finally, the generalizability of findings on IQ heritability is extremely limited because most of the data have come from predominantly White, middle-class, North American and European populations. With the exception of only a few studies (e.g., Moore, 1986; Scarr & Weinberg, 1977; Scarr, Weinberg, & Waldman, 1993), populations outside of these narrow parameters have not been studied. Because heritability estimates are population-specific, extreme caution is necessary when extending current knowledge to different populations. Moreover, the vast majority of the relative correlations were derived from samples of individuals between 9 and 20 years of age (Bouchard & McGue, 1981; McGue, Bouchard, Iacono, & Lykken, 1993). Recent studies (for a review, see Plomin & Petrill, 1997) show some fluctuations in heritability estimates across the life span. Thus, it appears that the obtained heritability estimate of 50–51% is not applicable to individual variation in IQ at all stages of the life span; it is also unclear whether h^2 fluctuations observed in different age groups are reflective of environmental or biological events.

In sum, scientists who accept the heritability paradigm as the leading paradigm in the field have some specific concerns regarding both findings (see the preceding discussion) and their interpretations (Sternberg & Grigorenko, 1999). Yet, the imprecise and confounded nature of the h^2 estimates, their fluctuations in different populations and at different developmental stages, and the overall lack of generalizability of the findings are generally thought of as correctable. According to this contingent of scientists, good studies should bring desirable improvements to the heritability paradigm; the paradigm itself, however, is still considered dominant.

It Is Wrong . . .

Others, however, have challenged both the theory underlying the heritability paradigm and the nature of the data acquired by it. Theoretical challenges to global heritability estimates come from (a) those who question the meaning and the appeal of the concept of heritability for psychology (e.g., Block, 1995), (b) those who question statistical aspects of heritability estimates (e.g., Schönemann, 1994, 1997), and (c) those who reinterpret the dogma of genetic determinism and, consequently, reject the concept of heritability in its classic form (e.g., Gottlieb, 1992).

The Usefulness of the Concept

Quite a few psychologists and historians of the sciences have voiced doubt regarding the usefulness of the concept of heritability for psychology (e.g., Block, 1995; Danzinger, 1997). An interesting characteristic of heritability is that, as with any population statistic, it can be calculated for any trait as long as that trait is distributed; in other words, heritability can be estimated for a trait even if we do not know what the trait is.

In a discussion of the value of heritability for psychology, Block (1995) stresses the importance of the distinction between *genetic determination* and *heritability*. Genetic determination has to do with what is inherited (i.e., received from ancestors by genetic transmission) and therefore responsible for the value of the trait. Heritability concerns what is responsible for observed variation in values of the trait (i.e., what proportion of the total trait variation in the population can be accounted for by genetic variation). Conceptually, genetic determination is applicable to individuals (i.e., the statement *I have green eyes because my mother has green eyes, and my father has blue eyes* makes sense), whereas heritability is applicable only to groups and populations (i.e., the statement *The heritability of my IQ is 50%* does not make sense).

A trait can be highly heritable in the absence of genetic determination. Some time ago, when only men flew planes, the heritability of knowing how to fly a plane was high, because differences in whether a person had this knowledge were "accounted for" by a chromosomal difference, XX versus XY. Now that flying is no longer a privilege only of men, the heritability of knowing how to fly has undoubtedly decreased. What is remarkable is that never – neither at the beginning of the century, nor now – has flying a plane been genetically determined. Moreover, the heritability of a trait can change dramatically, ranging from near 0 to near 1. Consider the example of haircuts. Long ago, when people did not get their hair cut, there were no haircuts, and the variation in length of hair corresponded primarily to the variation in genes (those with "hairy" genes had longer hair than those with "nonhairy" genes). Of course, there was some variation attributable to variability in environment (e.g., the quality of diet), but heritability was high because most of the observed difference in hair length was due to variation in genes. Then, people began cutting their hair, and variation by gender and culture marked the history of haircutting. At certain historical moments, in certain cultural groups, both men and women cut their hair (e.g., Tibetan warriors); at other times and in other places both did not cut their hair (e.g., medieval Scotland), and in other situations the overwhelming majority of men cut their hair (e.g., Soviet society from the 1940s to the 1960s). Along with fashion, heritabilities changed, ranging from almost 0 to almost 1, with all kinds of intermediate stops in between. That is, the heritability coefficient does not imply constancy – both the value and the meaning of h^2 vary across times and places.

What is remarkable is that most of the findings interpreted as evidence for the genetic determination of IQ in particular have come from studies of mental retardation (for review, see Burack, Hodapp, & Zigler, 1998). The accumulated evidence shows overwhelmingly that one wrong turn in the process of human development caused by a single gene mutation or a number of other genetic mechanisms can significantly alter brain development and function, resulting in mental retardation. Wahlström (1990) compiled a list of 503 separate disorders associated with mental retardation. Of these, 69 were mapped to 1 of the 22 chromosomes, and 73 were linked to the X chromosome; clearly, the human genome plays a crucial role in mental retardation. Let us consider a few illustrations.

Down's syndrome, for example, is genetically determined, but not heritable. The rate of Down's syndrome is 0.9 per 1,000 live births in mothers under the age of 33, but it increases to 2.8 in mothers between 35 and 38, and to 3.8 in mothers who are 44 years of age or older (Trimble & Baird, 1978). About 95% of Down's syndrome cases occur as a result of nondisjunction of chromosome 21, primarily in the mother's germ cells (Gardner & Sutherland, 1996; Mikkelsen, Poulsen, Grimsted, & Lange, 1980). Nondisjunction refers to a phenomenon in which, instead of receiving only one copy of a chromosome, a germ cell receives two copies. When this germ cell is fertilized, the resulting cell has three copies of a given chromosome. Nondisjunction is strongly related to maternal age. There are also speculations regarding possible paternal nondisjunctions resulting from the effect of environmental toxins (Olshan, Bard, & Teschke, 1989) on spermatogenesis. The relevant mechanism that is likely to be involved in the development of mental retardation is an imbalance in gene dosage (i.e., the amount of inherited genetic material). In other words, what matters is not what is inherited by the offspring, but rather how much is inherited. It has been shown that, compared with diploid (normal) cells, blood levels of gene products involved in trisomies (cells having three copies of one chromosome) are about 1.5 times the normal values (Epstein, 1986). The general biological mechanism must produce the right gene product in the right amount; dosage effects can have dramatic developmental impacts, specifically or nonspecifically disrupting regulatory mechanisms during development.

Two genetic phenomena, *imprinting* (chromosomal rearrangement arising on a chromosome of specific parental origin) and *deletion–microdeletion* (chromosomal truncation), have been discovered within the last few years and appear to play an important role in the genetics of mental retardation. A variety of genetic syndromes (Jacobsen syndrome, Smith–Magenis syndrome, Prader–Willi syndrome, Angelman syndrome, Williams syndrome, etc.), which differ significantly at the phenotypic level, have one severe phenotypic trait in common (mental retardation) and have been shown to share similar genetic mechanisms.

The point of this brief excursion into the genetics of mental retardation is to demonstrate the wide variety of genetic mechanisms that result in the manifestation of low IQ and underline the current depth of knowledge about these mechanisms. Again, most so-called mental retardation phenotypes present a whole spectrum of various symptoms, of which low IQ is only one. Yet not a single gene involved in the development of mental retardation has been shown to be associated with normal variation in IQ. So, although proponents of the heritability paradigm often cite these findings as evidence of the importance of the genome in IQ-based variation (e.g., Plomin & Petrill, 1997), note that (a) neither of these specific genes or general genetic mechanisms (e.g., chromosomal abnormalities) have been implicated in IQ variation (and there is no a priori reason to believe that they should be) and (b) none of these related discoveries were made within the heritability paradigm (most occurred in the field of molecular genetics). In other words, there have been all sorts of recent discoveries relating genetic phenomena to mental retardation and low IQ, but the heritability paradigm cannot utilize this information or be credited with facilitating these advances that produced it.

Another important facet of the debate over the usefulness of the concept of heritability for psychology concerns the meaning of two concepts of "baseline" and "derivative" environment. The baseline (or as Kitcher, 1996, refers to it, "normal") environment might be defined either as (1) that which is most frequently present in a population or (2) that which allows the trait to develop to the benefit of its carrier. A derivative environment is one that has been modified when compared with a particular baseline environment. A good illustration of the distinction between these two types of environment can be found in the varying developmental pathways of phenylketonuria (PKU), which is the major form of hyperphenylalaninemia (HPA), a condition caused by altered functioning and activity of the enzyme phenylalanine hydroxylase (PAH), which is involved in the metabolic processing of phenylalanine. The prevalance of PKU varies in different racial and ethnic groups (Scott & Cederbaum, 1990); the highest rates (1 in 10,000) are observed among Northern Europeans (DiLella & Woo, 1987). The genetic mechanism of this disorder is best understood when compared with other conditions related to mental retardation. Phenylketonuria is an autosomal recessive condition with the locus for PAH assigned to the short arm of chromosome 12 (Lidsky et al., 1984). Since this discovery, 73 different PAH-gene mutations each of a different nature, different population origins, and different magnitudes of outcome have been described (Kayaalp et al., 1996). Thus, researchers (Okano et al., 1991; Svensson, von-Dobeln, Eisensmith, Hagenfeldt, & Woo, 1993) have established associations between different mutations and the degree of PAH enzyme activity. In turn, the level of the reduction in enzyme activity appears to be related to the level of mental retardation (Ramus, Forrest, Pitt, Saleeba, & Cotton, 1993).

Phenylketonuria usually is referred to as a classic example of an environmentally alterable genetic disorder. The treatment involves dietary restriction of phenylalanine during early life and was initially declared to be almost 100% effective (e.g., Smith & Wolff, 1974). Recent studies, however, have indicated somewhat less impressive results. Although dietary treatment significantly reduces the effects of the mutation in those detected and treated at birth, as compared with untreated sibs, the phenylalanine diet does not lead to a complete remediation of the defect. Specifically, the IQs of children with treated PKU are estimated to be 4 to 7 points below the IQs of their unaffected sibs (Koch, Azen, Freidman, & Williamson, 1984). Furthermore, discontinuing the diet at the age of 10 can lead to a decline in intellectual performance, reading, and spelling (Fishler, Azen, Friedman, & Koch, 1989), and in treated women maternal PKU is associated with high rates of birth defects and subsequent mental retardation in offspring (Lenke & Levy, 1980).

In spite of all these complcations, however, PKU is an excellent example of a condition that was once thought to be genetically determined; now this belief is questioned. Specifically, the concept of genetic determination does not fit here because what is genetically determined is not the condition of mental retardation but rather the disruption of the phenylalanine metabolism mechanism, which might then lead to the development of mental retardation if there is phenylalanine in the diet. So, as Block (1995) argues, what manifests itself as genetically determined depends on what the baseline environment is. In a phenylalanine-diet environment, PKU, the disease phenotype, appears to be genetically determined, whereas in a phenylalanine-free-diet environment, it appears not to be genetically determined. One might say that the baseline environment is the naturally occurring one and, therefore, has to be considered as the primary one. This argument, however, is not directly relevant to my point here, which is that the heritability coefficient is insensitive to the nominal characteristics of the environment (i.e., whether the environment is baseline or derivative). In two qualitatively different environments, the h^2 – the proportion of genetic and environmental variations in the causation of the trait differences in the population – will be different, but the heritability paradigm does not have an apparatus to explain how to account for this difference.

Finally, however neat the heritability paradigm's separation of environmental and genetic factors appears to be at first glance, it is loaded with complications and confounding factors that have become obvious from other nonheritability-based studies. For example, researchers have consistently found that mildly retarded children come from families of low socioeconomic status (SES) at a significantly elevated frequency (Birch, Richardson, Baird, Horobin, & Illsley, 1970; B. Hagberg, G. Hagberg, Lewerth, & Lindberg, 1981; Rao, 1990). Hence, specifically low SES might turn out to be a much more important environmental risk factor than would be evident from the observed variation in social backgrounds within the middle of the normal range (Capron & Duyme, 1989). This phenotype-dependent environmental conditioning is difficult (virtually impossible!) to detect by means of heritability-based studies. Furthermore, it has been observed that obstetric and perinatal complications are seen at a higher frequency among mentally retarded children (Hagberg et al., 1981; Rao, 1990; Rutter, Tizard, & Whitmore, 1970). However, the causality of this phenomenon is difficult to establish owing to the presence of confounding factors – for example, low birth weight is also related to social disadvantage (Read & Stanley, 1993) but does not appear to be of high heritability. There is also the possibility of a recursive influence of parental mental retardation on children's development (Keltner, 1994). Unfortunately, there is not much research on the characteristics of the home environments provided by parents with mental retardation (Dowdney & Skuse, 1993; Tymchuk, 1992). Typically, parents of mildly retarded children are of both low IQ and low SES, and several adversities affecting rearing practices are associated with these factors (Broman, Nichols, Shangnessy, & Kennedy, 1987; Lamont & Dennis, 1988). Thus, overall, the research indicates that the negligible importance of gene–environment interactions in data drawn from the general population (Plomin, DeFries, & Fulker, 1988) might turn out to be important in special subpopulations. It is reasonable to suggest that children who are at risk biologically (genetically) may be more likely to be adversely affected by poor rearing conditions (Sameroff & Chandler, 1975). Clearly, it is difficult to pinpoint any pure

contribution of environmental influences as they are defined in the heritability-based approach. No matter which "environmental" factor is examined, it operates in combination with something else, whether this "something else" is genes or other biological agents.

In sum, the concept of heritability has been perceived by many (e.g., Block, 1995; Gottlieb, 1992) to be a misguided approach to interpreting the significance of genes and environments for the development of IQ. The biological evidence that is presented as supportive of genetic involvement in IQ comes from studies of mental retardation, *all* of which have been performed outside of the heritability paradigm. As a statistic of a given historical moment, heritability cannot offer any information about what would happen if, for example, new environmental agents were to be introduced into the population. The impact of a new environmental agent can be predicted only if the biological mechanism of the studied trait is understood – and heritability does not help us understand this underlying biological mechanism. It is important to note that those who question the value of the "notoriously elusive goal" (Feldman & Otto, 1997) of decomposing the phenotypic variance of IQ – attributing some portion to genes and some to environment – do not question the importance of genetic variation for individual differences in intellectual functioning (e.g., Wahlsten & Gottlieb, 1997). The critics, however, stress the potential hazard of guesswork when models are fitted that do not contain measured indicators of either environment or genes (Block, 1995).

Statistical Aspects of Heritability Estimates

There are several ways to calculate the heritability coefficient, depending on the type of data (i.e., whether they were collected using twins, siblings, parent-offspring pairs or other types of relatives) and software (i.e., generic or specialized) available. Different methods make different assumptions that often result in biased heritability estimates. Thus, for example, the most frequently used method in the twin literature is that utilizing the formula $2(r_{MZT} - r_{DZT})$ (Falconer, 1990). This way of calculating h^2 makes two assumptions: the assumption of the equal environment of MZ and DZ twins and the assumption of the additive nature of all genetic variance, both of which have been questioned in the literature (e.g., Grigorenko & Carter, 1996; Chipuer, Rovine, & Plomin, 1990, respectively).

Similarly, researchers questioned several other assumptions made in the calculation of heritability estimates for human traits (e.g., Capron, A. R. Vetta, & A. Vetta, 1998; Hirsch, 1990; Vetta, 1980) as well as various statistical techniques used in different methods of heritability estimates (Schönemann, 1989, 1993, 1994, 1997). In short, statistical methods of obtaining heritability estimates have been criticized for making unrealistic assumptions regarding the true random nature of genetic and environmental variables (Schönemann, 1993), omitting interaction terms from heritability equations (Schönemann, 1994; Wahlsten, 1990), and ignoring the importance of assortative mating (Capron, A. R. Vetta, & A. Vetta, 1998). Critics also have questioned the adequacy of fit of the selected models when the data are reanalyzed (Feldman & Otto, 1997; Schönemann, 1989, 1994) and doubted the adequacy of the underlying genetic model (Weiss, 1992, 1995).

Developmental Systems Theory

The basis of this line of criticism of the heritability paradigm is in dialectical biology (Levins & Lewontin, 1985) and the developmental systems theory (Ford & Lerner, 1992; Gottlieb, 1992). These approaches question the concept of heritability and even revise the concept of genetic determination itself (Strohman, 1997). According to researchers promoting these approaches, the gene is an integral part of the complex metabolic system of a cell, and the gene's functions are limited to coding for the linear structure of a specific polypeptide. The cellular consequences of this protein, however, depend on the complex environment of the cell in which the protein is synthesized. Moreover, the overall "fate" of this cell, as well as its role in the development of the organism, depends on surrounding cells. In turn, the developmental trajectory of the individual organism depends on the environmental context in which this organism exists and develops. The performance of a given gene (i.e., its functional status and characteristics of action) is governed by events external to the gene (i.e., those involving other genes, those occurring in the gene's cellular environment, and even events external to the organism). Thus, conditionality is the prerequisite of the developmental system.

A mutation (whether inherited or acquired) of a specific gene may dramatically alter the trajectory of individual development, but it does not necessarily code for a specific behavioral outcome. Moreover, it is assumed that mutations occur more often in organisms that are more sensitive to external perturbations and less capable of self-regulation in the presence of a harmful environmental agent. Similarly, a wild (original, not mutated) variant of a gene does not code for any specific trait; even if the gene contributes to phenotypic variability in a trait, its effects are contingent and relative.

According to this approach, the heritability paradigm (1) is based exclusively on a population–genetic tradition and does not concern itself with individual developmental trajectories, (2) views only heritable sources as important for evolution, and (3) promotes a nondevelopmental understanding of developmental outcomes (Wahlsten & Gottlieb, 1997).

In sum, the external criticism of the heritability paradigm is concerned with (1) the importance and interest that the concept of heritability holds for psychology (having shown that genes matter, what else can we accomplish using this paradigm?), (2) the adequacy of its methodological apparatus (like any analytic method, the estimation of h^2 rests on several simplifying assumptions; the concern here is whether, when researchers impose these simplifications, they throw out the baby with the bath water), and (3) heritability's engagement with abstract "population" sources of variance rather than with concrete developmental realizations.

NEW DATA, NEW CONCERNS

The paradigm of heritability, in its various proliferated forms, has traveled around the world. It originated in England, initially thrived in North America, and then was forced out. It then returned to Europe, briefly visited Russia, went back to the United States, and so on. In each country it has visited, the paradigm has left behind followers and opponents. Historians of science claim that the outcome of a visit by the heritability paradigm depends on the nature of the political and ideological system of the given country (Danzinger, 1997). But, leaving aside the various ways that ideology has colored the heritability paradigm during its world voyage, let us look at some of the paradigm's scientific properties.

One of the internal properties of the human heritability paradigm is that it is not falsifiable. Yet, as clearly enunciated by Popper (1968), falsifiability is the very essence of scientific inquiry. By interpreting a few bits of data, scientists come up with a hypothesis that reaches beyond the data. This hypothesis then forms a scientific context (a framework) in which experimental work is designed with the goal of verifying or refuting the core hypothesis. The longer the hypothesis can withstand these examinations, the more influential and lasting it is. As long as the heritability paradigm is referred to as scientific (Bouchard, 1998), there should be experimental ways to verify it. Experiments are conducted in plants and animals, but owing to the specifics of studying human beings (namely, the taboo of conducting experimental genetic research on people), verifying experiments are performed on other nonhuman species. So, for now, the major analytic tool that is used in the evaluation of the heritability paradigm with respect to humans is the classification of observations (both experimental – that is, acquired through experimenting with nonhumans – and nonexperimental – that is, acquired through nonexperimental research on humans) into anomalous and normal with respect to the paradigm. Several sources (e.g., Bouchard, 1998; Plomin & Petrill, 1997) provide evidence of observations that support the paradigm.* The following discussion will serve as a starting point for an inquiry into those observations that are not consistent with the paradigm.

Anomalous Observations

In its rush to complete its "first project" – namely, showing the power of genes to shape human traits – the heritability paradigm did not pause to explain many discrepancies not covered by its current theory. Note that the paradigm makes no attempt to elicit the unexpected; indeed, most phenomena that do not fit into one of the neat boxes supplied by the paradigm are ignored (a practice that is common

---

* Very few paradigms actively seek their disconfirmation. In this regard, the heritability paradigm is not exceptional (e.g., Simonton, 1994). In its attempt to expand and confirm itself, the heritability paradigm has attempted to decompose the variation in variables that has been traditionally thought of as environmental, such as life events (Billig, Hershberger, Iacono, & McGue, 1996).

to many other paradigms as well). Scientists working within a paradigm generally do not attempt to create new theories (Barber, 1961) but rather direct their research at articulating what the paradigm has already established. These scientists struggle to incorporate new observations into the old paradigm. Among such observations are (1) the increasingly apparent dependency of h^2 estimates on population allele frequencies, (2) the effect of pleiotropy, and (3) the ever more apparent lack of differentiation between genetic and environmental forces in the mutual action that shapes individuality (discussed in this section). This section of the chapter is designed to point to such observations and show how current findings simultaneously loosen the stereotypes of the heritability paradigm (so that even its proponents talk about going "beyond" h^2) and provide the incremental data necessary for a fundamental paradigm shift.

Searching for Genes
Heritability and Gene Frequencies

Let us return for a minute to the representation of the phenotype (P) provided at the beginning of this chapter. In the description of all causal contributions to the P, it has been mentioned that its genetic component comprises A (additive), D (dominant), and I (epistatic) genetic influences. Even though there has been some suggestion of the importance of I (Chipuer et al., 1990) for variation in IQ, nobody would dispute that it is mostly A and D that matter. But what are A and D? And, correspondingly, how are V_A, V_D, and V_I determined?* In brief, each component of genetic variance is derived on the basis

---

* Because phenotype is measurable, the corresponding value is called *phenotypic value*. The value associated with the influence of the genotype is referred to as *genotypic value*, and the value associated with the influence of the environment is referred to as *environmental deviation*. The term *deviation* is used here for a particular reason. In a given population, the mean phenotypic value is equated to the mean genotypic value; therefore, the departure of the observed phenotypic value from the genotypic value is attributable to deviating influences of the environment. The term *population mean* is used interchangeably with the terms *mean phenotypic* or *mean genotypic* values.

In principle, genotypic value is measurable, but in practice it is not (with the exception of some very special and very limited cases). For the purposes of deduction, it is common to assign arbitrary values to genotypes of interest. Let us consider a gene with two alleles, B and β, and assume that of

of genotypic values and counts of the alleles constituting this genotype in the population. In other words, all genetic terms contributing to the phenotypic variance are dependent upon the nature and frequencies of the inherited alleles.

Because the value of heritability depends on the magnitude of all the components of variance, a change in any one of those will affect h^2. Therefore, because allele frequencies vary drastically from population to population, and because all the genetic components of heritability are dependent on gene frequencies, heritability estimates also vary from population to population. For example, smaller populations that have been fairly isolated for a significant time often undergo a change in their initial allele frequencies, and thus certain alleles are observed much more often than expected and others are seen much more rarely than expected. Such populations are expected to show lower heritabilities than do larger populations. The most "powerful" alleles in terms of their contribution to the phenotypic variance are those whose frequencies are in the middle

the two alleles, allele B increases the phenotypic value. Then the genotypic value of the homozygote BB is referred as $+b$, that of the homozygote $\beta\beta$ is referred to as $-b$, and that of the heterozygote $B\beta$ (or βB) is referred to as d. These genotypic values can be put on a scale as shown in Figure 4.A.

Now we can show how the allele frequencies (i.e., how often given alleles are seen in a given population) influence the trait population mean. Let the allele frequencies of B and β be p and q, respectively. On the basis of classic laws of population genetics (for detail, see Plomin, DeFries, McClearn, & Rutter, 1997), we can determine the genotype frequencies as p^2 for BB, $2pq$ for $B\beta$, and q^2 for $\beta\beta$. The mean value in the whole population is obtained by multiplying the value of each genotype by its frequency and summing over the three genotypes:

$$\text{Population mean} = p^2b + 2pqd + (-q^2b)$$
$$= b(p - q) + 2dpq.$$

To understand the meaning of this formula, mentally convert frequencies to numbers of individuals. The multiplication of the value of a given genotype by the number of individuals carrying this genotype gives a sum of values of individuals with that genotype. Summing similar values over the three genotypes (BB, $B\beta$, and $\beta\beta$) gives the sum of values of all individuals; dividing this sum by the total number of individuals gives the population mean. Thus, the contribution of any gene to the population mean (if it is assumed

that this gene has only two variants—two alleles B and β) has two terms, b $(p - q)$, reflecting the impact of the homozygotes, and $2dpq$, reflecting the impact of the heterozygotes. Different types of relationships between B and β (no dominance or complete dominance) result in different values whose range is $2b$. The case of overdominance broadens this range of values.

As mentioned previously, this example is the simplest one possible — the analyzed trait is controlled by only one gene, and there are only two alternative variants of this gene, alleles B and β. However, the more scientists learn about the genetics of complex traits, the stronger the belief that most human traits of interest to the field of psychology involve the function of many genes. The contributions of several genes and their joint effect on the mean can also be of different types. For simplicity, let us assume that a combination of effects of different genes on a trait is by addition (note, however, that there are also nonadditive — that is, dominant and epistatic — combinations). For example, if the genotypic value of BB is b and that of CC is c, then the genotypic value of $BBCC$ is $b+c$. Consequently, the population mean resulting from the joint effects of several genes is the sum of the contributions of each of the separate loci:

$$\text{Population mean} = \sum b(p - q) + 2\sum dpq.$$

Now let us go one step farther in our analytical deductions to reach the definition of genetic additive effects (A). The issue here is in relating the concept of genotypic value to that of the genetic transmission from parent to offspring. Parents pass on their genes and not their genotypes; genotypes are assembled anew each generation. Therefore, a different concept is needed to refer to genes and not genotypes; this concept is termed *average effect*. Average effect depends on the genotypic values b and d and on the allele frequencies. To illustrate, let us assume that a number of gametes, all carrying allele B, unite at random with gametes from the population (i.e., the frequencies of the occurrences of gametes drawn from the population are determined by the frequencies of B and β). Then the mean of the genotypes so produced differs from the population mean by the average effect of allele B. Another way to grasp the meaning of average effect is to define it through allele substitution. Let us assume that one could change one allele type (e.g., β) chosen at random into

FIGURE 4.A. Arbitrary assigned genotypic values. The zero point of the scale shows the mid-point between the values of the homozygotes. The value d of the heterozygote depends on the degree of dominance of the allele B over the allele β (or vice versa). The case of no dominance ($d = 0$) puts the genotypic value of $B\beta$ right of the zero point, mid-way between the two homozygotes. If B is dominant over β, then $d > 0$, and if β is dominant over B, then $d < 0$. If dominance is complete, then $d = +b$ (or $-b$, depending on the nature of the dominance). If there is overdominance, $d > +b$ or $d < -b$.

Genotype	$\beta\beta$		βB	BB
Genotypic				
Value	$-b$	0	d	$+b$

range. The effects of varying allele frequencies have been investigated for traits whose variation is accounted for by the variation in many genes (so-called polygenic traits), and it has been found that the impact of varying population-specific allele frequencies is dramatic even for the traits involving many genes (Kendler & Kidd, 1986). Thus, in populations with different allele frequencies, even if environmental conditions in these populations are similar, h^2 for the same phenotypic trait might differ considerably.

The overwhelming majority of textbooks on quantitative and behavioral genetics that present decomposition of phenotypic variance discuss the relationships between allele frequencies and genetic variance components. In short, all the components of genetic variance are dependent on gene frequencies, and thus *any* estimates of these components are *only* for the population from which they were estimated. The complications involved in interpreting heritability estimates across different populations are obvious. In the late 1950s, when the principle of

another allele type (e.g., B) and register the resulting change of the observed phenotypic value. Having repeated this substitution multiple times, one could calculate the change in the population mean produced by this procedure; this change will indicate the average effect of the allele substitution. If the substituted allele is allele β, then two types of substitutions might happen: (1) $B\beta$ will transform into BB (and the frequency of such events will be p, i.e., the population frequency of the allele β), changing the value from d to $+b$, and, correspondingly, the effect will be $(b - d)$ and (2) $\beta\beta$ will transform into BB (and the frequency of such events will be q, i.e., the population frequency of the allele B), changing the value from $-b$ to d, and the effect will be $(d + b)$. The average effect of the allele substitution is $p(b - d) + q(d + b) = b + d(q - p)$. Note that the average effect of the allele substitution is the difference between the average effects of the two alleles B and β.

Finally, the last concept that needs to be introduced is that of *breeding value*. Recall that the usefulness of the concept of average effect arises from the fact that parents pass on their alleles and not their genotypes to their offspring. Consequently, it is the average effects of the parents' alleles that determine the mean genotypic value of their progeny. Therefore, there is a need for a concept that describes a characteristic of a parent through characteristics of his or her offspring. This concept is breeding value, which is the value of an individual, judged by the mean value of his or her progeny. To grasp this concept, think of a polygamist whose spouses were taken at random from the population and who has numerous offspring. Then, the breeding value of this polygamist is twice the mean deviation of his or her progeny from the population mean (the deviation has to be doubled because the polygamist provides only half the genes in the offspring; the other half comes at random from population). The more offspring from different spouses the polygamist has, the higher the precision of the estimate of his or her breeding value. What is very important to understand is that, similar to the concept of average effect, the concept of breeding value is characterized by a double-dependency, that is, the dependency from the individual and the dependency from the population. As much as the average effect is a property of both the quality of the allele (e.g., whether it is allele B or β) and its frequency in the population, the breeding value is a property of the individual (i.e., his or her genotype) and the population from which his or her mates are drawn (i.e., the population mean).

Breeding value can be defined in terms of average effects: it is the sum of the average effects of the alleles carried by the individual (the sum is taken over the pair of alleles at each gene and over all genes). Multiplying the breeding value of each genotype by the frequency of this genotype in the population and obtaining the sum over such products for all genotypes in the population gives the mean breeding value. Often the breeding value is referred to as the *additive genotype*, and variation in breeding value is attributed to additive effects of genes. In terms of variance,

$$V_A = 2pq[b + d(q - p)]^2$$

(for detail, see Falconer & Mackay, 1996).

This concept is the main reason the preceding eight paragraphs were presented. To summarize, the breeding value expresses the value transmitted from parents to offspring and, therefore, (1) the expected breeding value of any individual is the average of the breeding values of the two parents, (2) the expected breeding value is also the individual's expected phenotypic value, and (3) the variance of breeding value (also referred to as additive genetic variance) is determined by the nature of the transmitted alleles and their population frequencies.

The final part of this technical insertion is devoted to the dominant genetic component of phenotypic variance. Dominant effect (dominant deviation) is determined, for a single locus, by the difference between the genotypic value G and the breeding value A. Dominance is a property resulting from the "inequality" of the different alleles of one gene. When all alleles are equal in their rights, there is no dominance, and breeding value coincides with genotypic value. Dominant effect results from pairing two alleles with different rights; these alleles interact within a gene, causing genotypic value to deviate from breeding value. Like the average effects of genes and the breeding values of genotypes, the dominance deviations are also dependent on gene frequency. In terms of variance,

$$V_D = 2pqd^2 \quad \text{(for detail, see Falconer & Mackay, 1996).}$$

Similarly, it can be shown that the V_I component of the phenotypic variance is also dependent on allele frequencies. This is so because, if the genes interact with each other showing epistatic interaction, the derivation of the properties of interaction variances rests on its subdivision into components (e.g., if two genes interact with each other, the decomposing the variance was first developing (e.g., Kempthorne, 1955) and the heritability paradigm had just started to penetrate the field of psychology, it seemed unrealistic that one could actually know the frequencies of different alleles in different populations. At that time, there were no genetic markers, very limited genetic maps, slow computers, and astronomically high prices for genotyping. The argument then was that, in practice, a researcher could not be concerned with allele frequencies and

component of variance will include the interaction of additive components of the two genes plus the interaction of the dominance in one gene with the additive component in the other, and so on). Because each subcomponent of the epistasis variance is dependent on allele frequencies, the term is also dependent on them.

The impact of gene frequency on the genetic components of variance is shown in Figure 4.B. On the basis of this graph, the general conclusion can be drawn that contributions of genes to genetic variance differ, depending on the frequencies of these genes in a population. Specifically, alleles contribute much more variance when at intermediate frequencies than when at high or low frequencies. In particular, recessive alleles contribute very little variance at low frequencies.

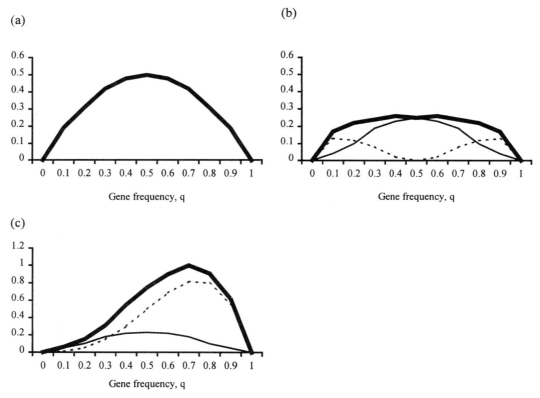

FIGURE 4.B. The relationship between allele frequency and the magnitude of the genetic components of variance arising from a single gene with two alleles (adapted from Falconer & Mackay, 1996). Genotypic variance is shown in thick lines, additive variance — in broken lines, and dominance variance — in thin lines. The gene frequency, q, is that of the recessive allele (correspondingly, $p = 1 - q$). The graphs (a)-(c) show different degrees of dominance. The graph (a) reflects the case when there is no dominance ($d = 0$). Note that in this case the genotypic variance is all additive, and it is at maximum when $p = q = .5$. In the second case, (b), the graph shows the case of pure overdominace ($b = 0$). The dominance variance is greatest when $p = q = .5$. The additive variance, however, is zero at $p = q = .5$, and maximal when $q \sim .1$ ($p \sim .9$) and $q \sim .9$ ($p \sim .1$). It is remarkable that in this case genotypic variance remains practically constant over a wide range of gene frequency. Its composition, however, changes profoundly. In (c), dominance is complete ($d = b$). Note that the genotypic variance is maximal at $q \sim .7$, the dominance variance is greatest when $p = q = .5$ (same as in graph (b)), and the additive variance is greatest when $p \sim .75$.

allele effects because they were unknown. But now allele frequencies are known (or at least can be determined at fairly low costs). About 10 years ago scientists concerned themselves only with the estimation of the components of phenotypic variance because this was their only option at the time. Thirty years ago the main "ideological" task of those who believed that genetic variation plays a role in the variation of human traits was to show that genes matter. The heritability paradigm offered a way to do so. But these scientists have made their point – by the late 1980s most social and behavioral scientists and educators who were surveyed acknowledged the role of genetic factors in individual differences (Snyderman & Rothman, 1987, 1988). The scientific public has been convinced. To move forward, researchers have to overcome the limitations of decomposition and start measuring and counting. In fact, they have started doing so (Daniels et al., 1998; Neale, 1997; Martin, Boomsma, & Machin, 1997).

Consider the following illustration. In 1996, two groups working independently, one in Israel (Ebstein et al., 1996) and another at NIH (Benjamin et al., 1996), reported a link between a so-called Novelty Seeking trait (characterized by excitability, thrill-seeking, and a quick temper) and a gene expressed in limbic areas of the brain and involved in the activity of the neurotransmitter dopamine, which, among other things, transmits sensations of pleasure. The studies focused on one allele of the gene (DRD4) in which a segment of the gene's molecular code is repeated seven times in a row (a so-called 7-repeat allele). The scores on the trait of Novelty Seeking appeared to be higher in people with the sevenfold repetition. Subsequent studies, however, did not confirm the original findings or yielded only marginally significant results (limited to only one of the subscales of the Novelty Seeking scale, namely, Exploratory-Excitability; for a review, see Baron, 1998). These inconsistent results raise a question that keeps coming up in the field of behavior genetics and in the field of psychiatric genetics: Were the original observations a false positive?

The hallmarks of true robust findings in this field are (1) their confirmation by multiple replications, (2) a low prior probability of selecting the "right" candidate genes, and (3) population admixture. The last is primarily due to ethnic variation – as has been discussed earlier, populations differ dramatically from each other in their frequencies of different alleles. For example, a worldwide survey of various alleles in the DRD4 gene showed that the 7-repeat allele with which the trait of Novelty Seeking was associated appeared quite frequently in the Americas (about 48%) but only occasionally in East and South Asia (about 2%), demonstrating significant variation in allele frequencies in different populations (Chang, Kidd, Livak, Pakstis, & Kidd, 1996). The highest frequency of the allele-7 repeat was that of 78% in the Ticuna (an Amerindian tribe), and the lowest was 1% (for the Japanese). If the claim is true, and there is indeed an association between the score on Novelty Seeking and the presence of the allele-7, then should heritability estimates of Novelty Seeking be significantly lower in Japan and significantly higher among the Ticuna Indians (assuming, of course, that breeding value of allele-7 is the same in the two populations)? It could be, of course, that the variation in the trait of Novelty Seeking is associated with different alleles in different populations. However, this would seem to be a rather inefficient way for nature to orchestrate such a variation. If one assumes that ancestors of modern humans who left Africa long ago (Tishkoff et al., 1996) in search of a better life would have been higher on Novelty Seeking than those who stayed behind, why did nature not preserve this variation?

These broader evolutionary questions, however, are beyond the scope of this essay. The point here is to show the inherent dependency of heritability estimates on population allele frequencies. When the heritability paradigm appeared, the state of science did not allow us to ascertain detailed descriptions of the genes involved in a given trait. Now this is possible. The old heritability paradigm of decomposition should be replaced by a paradigm of measurement. If we are interested in understanding the biology underlying the development of human traits and the way this biology is realized in a concrete individual maturing in a given environment, we cannot simply continue to decompose variance.

QTL(s), Pleiotropy, and Other Complications

Quantitative Traits

How does it come about that the intrinsically discontinuous variation resulting from genetic transmission (an individual either inherits an allele from his or her parents or does not, but there is no state in between) manifests itself in the continuous variation of a human trait (in our case, IQ)? There are two reasons for this "paradox." First, by far, most human traits are affected by many genes rather than one.* Second, variation from different, nongenetic sources is superimposed. In other words, if, on top of this pseudo-continuous variation resulting from the involvement of many genes, the truly continuous variation of nongenetic sources were superimposed, the edges of distinct values would become totally blurred – the variation as we see it in a population is continuous no matter how precise our measurement instruments are.

Reconsider, for a moment, the genetics generally taught in school. That genetics was primarily concerned with Mendelian characteristics (qualitative conditions of an either–or type: Mendel's peas were either yellow or green). The difference between genes concerned with qualitative and quantitative traits lies in the magnitude of their effects relative to other sources of variation. A gene with an effect

---

* Consider a simplified example (adapted from Falconer & Mackay, 1996). Let us suppose that there is a trait A that is observed in a population at six values (i.e., there are six phenotypic values of trait A, $x = 0$, $x = 1$, $x = 2$, $x = 3$, $x = 4$, and $x = 5$) and that the variation in trait A is fully determined by genes. Now, let us assume that trait A is affected by five genes, each with two alleles at equal frequency ($p = q = 0.5$). Finally, suppose that there is complete dominance of one allele at each gene: the relationship between dominant alleles and trait A is such that each dominant allele adds one unit of measurement to the values of the trait. Thus, there are six discrete values of trait A, and these values are determined by whether the individual has the dominant allele present at each of the five loci ($x = 0$ if none of the five loci has a dominant allele, $x = 1$ if one of the five loci has a dominant allele, $x = 2$ if two loci have dominant alleles, and so on). Again, there are only six phenotypic values in the population — thus, if the utilized measurement is sufficiently accurate, then every measured individual is unambiguously placed in his or her value group.

What if there were more genes contributing to trait A, but each of them had a smaller effect? This genetic mechanism would result in the existence of more phenotypic values with smaller differences between them. Given that the differences between the values are small, they would be much more difficult to detect (unless there are ideal instruments whose measurement error is negligibly small). Thus, with an increase in the number of genes involved and a decrease in the differences between the values (and, correspondingly, a decrease of the ratio of the true value to its measurement error), the discontinuities between different phenotypic values would become unrecognizable.

large enough to result in observable discontinuity (i.e., it leads to the existence of distinct values of a trait, usually 0 [no] or 1 [yes]) can be studied individually and is referred to as a *major* gene even if there are other genes contributing to the trait as well as other nongenetic sources of variation. A gene with an effect that is not large enough to produce a gap (discontinuity) in phenotypic values cannot be studied individually and is referred to as a *minor* gene. Yet, this classification is simplistic, and there are, in fact, genes that produce intermediate effects and are unclassifiable as either major or minor. The variation in a trait resulting from the simultaneous influences of many genes is referred to as *polygenic* variation; the corresponding mode of inheritance is called *polygenic* inheritance.

In the context of this chapter, the reasonable question to ask is how do we know that so-called continuous traits (e.g., IQ) are controlled by many genes? Researchers point to two lines of evidence (Falconer & Mackay, 1996). The first strand of evidence is analytical – many observations obtained through various sources in general agree well with what is expected from the theory of polygenic inheritance. The second line of evidence is experimental – there are actually methods by which genes affecting quantitative traits can be mapped to particular chromosomal locations (in other words, these methods allow the determination of precise locations of genes of interest). Genes identified with these methods are called Quantitative Trait Loci (QTLs).

Note that a complete description of genes involved in the control of a given trait must take the genes into account individually; that is, it must consider allele frequencies and the magnitude of the effect of each allele on the trait of interest. Again, up to a couple of years ago, it was impossible even to conceive of a detailed characterization of genetic constellations involving more than two or three genes. To compensate for this absence of knowledge about the genes' individual properties, theoretical work had to make some unrealistic assumptions, such as the assumption that the frequencies of all genes involved in a given QTL are more or less the same, and the assumption that there are unidentified (indefinite) numbers of genes acting on a trait.

Psychologists interested in IQ have grown increasingly familiar with the term QTLs. Those who had not come across it before (e.g., in the work of

Plomin, 1997; Plomin & Petrill, 1997) encountered it in the spring of 1998 in newspaper headlines announcing the identification of yet another susceptibility gene for IQ.* The first susceptibility gene, located on chromosome 6, had been reported 3 years earlier (Skuder et al., 1995), but this finding was later refuted by the same group of scientists (Petrill et al., 1998). The first positive finding was obtained in a smaller group of children, and a second finding was obtained in an enlarged group that subsumed the first sample (but dropped the low-IQ group). There have also been two other weak positive signals among over 100 negative or uninformative ones (Ball et al., 1998; Daniels et al., 1998; Plomin, McClearn, & Smith, 1994; Plomin, McClearn, & Smith, 1995). In its current state, the project utilizes DNA material from 51 children whose IQs averaged 103 and 51 children with a mean IQ of 136 in the target group as well as 40 extremely high-IQ individuals and 50 average-IQ individuals in the replication sample. To avoid many possible complications resulting from studying a genetically heterogeneous sample, Plomin and his colleagues confined their study to a group of White Americans of mixed origin. In this current sample, the researchers reported allelic association between IQ and an allele in a region located very close to the gene IGF2R (an insulin-like growth factor receptor gene) (Chorney et al., 1998). Almost all the subjects in the target sample had one or both of the most common versions of the gene, allele 4 and allele 5. But almost half of the high-IQ group had at least one copy of allele 5 – a rate twice as high as that in the average group. The finding was replicated in 102 other children, half of them with a superhigh IQ average of 160.

For this finding to be considered robust, it must be replicated in many other studies and across different populations. What needs to be discussed here, however, is not necessarily the specific finding (which may or may not hold) but the broader meaning of

the QTL project for IQ. This discussion embraces three different issues: (1) whether heritability studies were a prerequisite of any kind for the QTL study, (2) whether the finding of such statistical association is proof of causation, and (3) what it can possibly mean that the variation in such an extremely powerful gene as the IGF2R receptor gene contributes to variation in IQ.

As far as the first issue is concerned, heritability studies cannot be credited with laying especially important groundwork for the QTL study. Heritability studies did not suggest where to start looking for genes or what covariates (whether biological or environmental) should be taken into account. The IQ QTL study that matured within the heritability paradigm did not find anything useful there that would take the inquiry to a "new stage that goes beyond merely demonstrating the importance of genetic influence on behavior" (Plomin, 1997, p. 85). In other words, it is time to move forward, but there is not much to take from the heritability studies beyond the mere demonstration of the importance of genetic influences. Even some proponents of the heritability paradigm have gone mainstream (Plomin, 1997), that is, have started looking for specific genes whose variant forms might contribute to variation in IQ.

The second issue for discussion concerns whether the finding of an allele association is proof of causation. The answer is no; to show biological causation of a certain phenotype, one must understand the biological mechanism resulting in a given phenotype. In fact, there are multiple conditions under which an association can exist, and only two of them ([1] a true etiological significance of the associated allele and [2] linkage between the associated allele and the gene with etiologically relevant variation) may be informative of underlying biological mechanisms. By itself, the fact of association, unfortunately, is not a causal finding – it is an unknown probability of a causal finding. In addition, the methodological paradigm of association studies utilized in this research has been alleged to prompt nonreplicable results and yield little if any insight into disease (Kidd, 1993). Note also that the polygenic model of IQ is not the only model that has been discussed. Weiss (1992, 1995), for example, has presented his data supporting the major gene hypothesis for IQ. Moreover, much of the

---

* A remarkable characteristic of this study is its brevity. Many other studies of complex human traits are preceded by sophisticated analyses of patterns of intragenerational transmission of the trait of interest, subsequent determination of a sample size powerful enough to detect genes for given effects (Risch & Marikangas, 1996), and efforts to control for various environmental covariates (Goldin et al., 1997). The future will show whether this brevity will result in fascinating discoveries or a series of nonreplications.

work contributing to our understanding of the biological mechanisms of complex traits has been conducted with the use of experimental animal models. Thus, to be on the cautious side, identifying a gene in which the variation co-occurs with the variation in a small restricted sample at moderate levels of *p*-values is far removed from understanding the underlying biological mechanism of IQ.

Finally, the third issue raises yet another layer of discussion. Little is known about the IGF2R receptor gene (or insulin-like growth factor 2, a multifaceted hormone). The IGF2R receptor has been reported to play a role in cancer, and thus it is hypothesized that this gene may influence both the development and everyday metabolism of the brain, although neither role has been proven (De Souza et al., 1995). Tens of thousands of genes have been found to be expressed in the adult brain, and many more genes are involved in brain development and maturation (Sutcliff, 1988). All in all, the IGF2R *is not* a specialized IQ gene. It appears that this gene has numerous other functions, but, somehow, it appears to be relevant also to variation in IQ. This multifunctional property of the IGF2R necessitates a consideration of pleiotropy.

Pleiotropy

Pleiotropy is the property of a gene to affect two or more traits such that the segregating gene (i.e., the gene transmitted from generation to generation) causes simultaneous variation in the traits it affects (Falconer & Mackay, 1996). The effect of pleiotropy primarily has been studied as a common property of major genes. For example, genes that increase growth rate increase stature and weight and, therefore, tend to cause correlation at the phenotypic level. The magnitude of correlation resulting from pleiotropy expresses the degree to which two (or more) traits are influenced by the same gene or genes. These correlations may be positive, indicating that transmitted genes increase both phenotypic characteristics, or negative, indicating that some genes increase one trait and decrease the other. Therefore, pleiotropy does not necessarily cause a detectable phenotypic correlation; if genes act in different directions, the phenotypic correlation between the traits might not be detectable.

Pleiotropic genes do not follow the classic interpretation of genetic determinism according to which a gene (or genes) determines a trait. A pleiotropic gene influences processes inside a cell, participating in the development of a wide array of phenotypes. Because of pleiotropy, the same genes can be classified as major with respect to one trait and minor with respect to another. The fields of plant and animal genetics have accumulated many examples of mutations affecting multiple phenotypic characteristics (Barton, 1990; Wagner, 1996). There also has been a substantial amount of analytical work on pleiotropy. In particular, analytical research has shown that, even when one of these mutations becomes a subject of a certain type of selection (even though other single mutation results in a small phenotypic change), phenotypic-correlations will be observed more often than by chance, even though their genetic causes might not correlate (Waxman & Peck, 1998).

To gain an intuitive understanding of the effects of pleiotropic genes, consider the following example. The importance of the dopamine signaling system in the brain is well known, and researchers have discovered several genes involved in the function of this system. Lately, however, many scientists have become interested in other systems in the brain that might influence the functioning of the dopamine system. Kręzel and colleagues (Kręzel et al., 1998) studied the impact of mutations on the system of retinoic acid in mice. They found that mutations in different retinoic acid receptors resulted in locomotor defects related to dysfunction of the mesolimbic signaling pathway. As a result of this research, scientists suggested that altered vitamin A signaling could be implicated in the etiology of pathologies that have been linked to dysfunction of dopaminergic systems (e.g., Parkinson's disease and schizophrenia). In addition, in the process of summarizing research on mutant mice with disrupted functions of the retinoid system and pointing out the highly pleotropic effects caused by these mutations, the researchers suggested that, given the broad distribution of retinoid receptors in the central nervous system, the disruption of the function of the retinoic acid genes might influence not only the dopamine system but also the functioning of other systems modulated by retinoid signaling.

To complicate matters, it might be that certain genes are not only "designed" to be pleiotropic, they can also become pleiotropic if the cell has a need for them to do so. For example, it is a widely accepted belief that individual neurons in the central nervous system release only a single fast transmitter, and therefore they are specialized and controlled by specialized genes. Recent findings, however, show that a single neuron can generate a corelease of a faster glycinergic component and a slower GABAergic (γ-aminobutyric acid) component to activate functionally distinct receptors in the postsynaptic cells targeted by this neuron (Jonas, Bischofberger, & Sandkühler, 1998). The functional meaning of this mechanism is not yet understood, but it points to an enormous plasticity of the brain and, correspondingly, to the enormous plasticity of the genes involved in brain functioning. This latest discovery suggests that a single neuron can respond in one of three ways (releasing only glycine, only GABA, or both). Why would the brain go to such efforts to have two transmitters activating an identical conductance mechanism and available for release from the same synapse (Nicoll & Malenka, 1998)? Two hypotheses have been offered. One suggests that this "double precision" is necessary for motor coordination that often depends on precise timing. The second hypothesis suggests that cotransmission may enable compensatory mechanisms to become activated in the event of genetic defects in one of the transmitting units. It is possible that genes controlling the production of specific neurotransmitters are coacting by monitoring each other's status and being prepared to organize a cell rescue operation by engaging in the control of other phenotypes.

The bottom line of this discussion is that there may be no genes such that their variation directly contributes to the variation in IQ. In fact, because IQ is a complex reflector of many lower level information processes, it may be a collector of various sporadic correlations of some genes with something else. For example, there is no doubt that phenotypic variability in many cognitive processes is linked to variability in the synaptic concentrations of neurotransmitters. Most likely, the variability in these concentrations is largely due to variability in the relevant genes. Is there any evidence to support the hypothesis that, for some reason, this variability in the neurotransmitters' genes would be more relevant to variability in IQ than to variability in other cognitive processes? Quite the contrary. Even within the heritability paradigm, there are voices discussing the

substantial (estimated!) genetic overlap across different cognitive abilities (Petrill, 1997). The rapidly unfolding picture of complexities linking genes to cellular processes, environments, and behaviors suggests that we reconsider the old maps we have used to navigate between genes and behavior – and perhaps design new guides for the future.

The Complexities of Genetic Mechanisms

In this section, two examples of genetic mechanisms involved in different cognitive phenotypes are discussed. These mechanisms are illustrative of the complexities that are, most likely, characteristic of the biological mechanisms of any particular phenotype of interest to psychologists. Note that the work presented here was done outside the heritability paradigm.

The most common cause of inherited mental retardation is the so-called *fragile X syndrome* affecting 1 in 1,500–2,000 males and 1 in 2,000–2,500 females (Webb, Bundley, Thake, & Todd, 1986) with the prevalence estimates varying across populations, ranging from the highest incidence among males in Finland (1 in 1,250) to the lowest among females in Australia (1 in 5,000) (Sherman, 1996). This X-chromosome anomaly accounts for about 50% of X-linked mental retardation. Retardation caused by this syndrome is usually in the mild-to-moderate range (IQ of 35 to 69) with some individuals experiencing severe retardation and others demonstrating normal intelligence. This syndrome, along with several other baffling human diseases (e.g., myotonic dystrophy and Huntington's disease), is caused by an expansion of a repeated sequence of three nucleotides within a gene on the X-chromosome. The peculiar characteristic of these repeated sequences is that, with each generation, these repeats are replicated and the sequence gets longer, eventually compromising the function of the genes. The manifestation of the effect is controlled by a dominant mechanism – as long as at least one of the two alleles is sufficiently expanded, the full pathology occurs. In addition, in most cases, the severity of the disease is a function of the length of the repeat (the longer the repeat, the more severe the condition).

Several simultaneous reports implicating the role of the trinucleotide repeat sequence in the region containing the FMR-1 gene appeared in 1991

(Davies, 1991; Oostra, 1996). Individuals in the general population show 6 to 50 trinucleotide repeats. However, clinically and cytogenetically normal obligate carriers, that is, those phenotypically normal individuals whose children are affected with the disorder (both male and female), show anywhere between 50 and 200 repeats. This expanded sequence (the stretch of DNA including >50 repeats), called premutation, is unstable and is likely to expand up to 200 or more repeats. The fragile X syndrome is characterized by the presence of a full mutation, one that is greater than 200 repeats. Studies designed to investigate the importance of the full mutation showed that individuals with a number of repeats higher than 200 do not express the FMR-1 gene (Pieretti et al., 1991). Even though the complete pathway connecting the FMR-1 gene to the phenotype of the fragile X syndrome has not yet been found, it is known that this gene is expressed in the brain – specifically in the cytoplasm of neurons (Devys, Lutz, Rouyer, Belloeq, & Mandel, 1993). The role of this gene in the manifestation of the syndrome is now established (De Boulle et al., 1993; Gedeon et al., 1992).

In the context of this essay, the genetic mechanism of fragile X is of interest for two reasons. First, what is transmitted in families in this case is not a complete phenotype (e.g., the phenotype of mental retardation) but rather a set of symptoms, which, if the repeat keeps expanding, increasingly grow worse with each generation. What is interesting, however, is that phenotypically such ''intermediate'' individuals can be identified only backwards, that is, only after the full manifestation of the disease in their descendents. In other words, the carriers of the expanding repeat whose length has not crossed the pathological threshold are not phenotypically different from normal individuals.

Second, similar to the biological mechanism of Down's syndrome, fragile X is also genetically determined but not heritable. According to current views (Singer, 1998), the expansion most likely occurs initially in the germ cells or early embryos, where, during the process of DNA replication in the cell cycle, DNA polymerase may ''stutter'' on the repeats and, while stuttering, multiply them.

We can further expand our appreciation of the complexity of genetic mechanisms latent to complex traits by considering, for example, studies of

long-term memory. It long has been known that synaptic plasticity (i.e., the ability of neurons to alter the strength of their synaptic connections with activity and experience) plays a critical role in memory storage. On the basis of this knowledge, molecular studies of gene expression regulating long-lasting synaptic plasticity initially focused on the identification of positive regulators of these processes. Recent work, however, has revealed that long-lasting forms of synaptic plasticity require not only a prolonged activation of the positive regulatory system but also the withdrawal of inhibitory restraints stopping or preventing memory storage. Some researchers (e.g., Abel, Martin, Bartsch, & Kandel, 1998) suggest that there should be so-called ''memory suppressor genes'' whose product inhibits memory storage. According to this hypothesis, at least two clusters of genes are involved in long-term storage – one regulating induction and another regulating inhibition (or its withdrawal). Correspondingly, presumably, differences in gene expression should be driven by learning needs: some memory genes will increase their expression in response to neuronal activity, whereas other genes will have their expression suppressed. Today's molecular instruments allow researchers to use approaches aimed at comparing gene expression in experimental organisms during different types and stages of neuronal activity. These systems can be studied only holistically; in other words, changes in gene expression should be registered in the context of neuronal activity, which is, in fact, an external (environmental, if you wish) event with regard to the genes. Genes change their expression patterns in response to synaptic activity; this system is inherently interactive, and thus any attempt to differentiate the genetic and environmental components of the system is fundamentally flawed. I will consider this interconnectedness more fully in the following discussion of gene functions in environments.

Genes in Environments

One of the harshest criticisms of the heritability paradigm centers on its assumption of the separability of the main effects of genes and environments. In fact, this concern is as old as the paradigm itself. In 1913, Leonard Darwin, the son of Charles Darwin and President of the British Eugenics Society at the time, published a paper in which he wrote, ''It is impossible to compare heredity as a whole with environment as a whole as far as their effects are concerned; for no living being can exist for a moment without either of them" (p. 153). Yet the convenience of splitting the phenotypic variance into its components overrode the concerns of Leonard Darwin and many others. But the observations keep piling up to suggest that development is messy and cannot be divided neatly into causal forces of genes and environments. The following examples illustrate how genes interact with different types of environments. These environments range from cellular to cultural, covering a wide spectrum of influences experienced by a developing and maturing individual (whether animal or human). At this point, relatively little is known about detailed aspects of coactions of genes and environments in regard to human intellectual functioning. This is why some of the illustrations that follow come from studies of cognitive functioning in animals, whereas others are taken from human studies of phenotypes besides IQ. The following few paragraphs illustrate the types of genetic and environmental coactions that form complex behavioral phenotypes. These samples may serve as templates for our thinking about the mechanisms that result in individual differences in intellectual functioning.

Genes and Cellular Environments

To understand the degree of intimacy between genes and the cellular environments in which they exist, consider studies of choline, one of the essential nutrients required for maintenance of normal health (Blusztajn, 1998). Meck, Williams, and their colleagues (Meck, Smith, & Williams, 1989; Meck & Williams, 1997a,b) have studied the links between the availability of choline during fetal development and several cognitive indicators. The researchers controlled the amount of choline in the diets of rats during that period of pregnancy that is characterized by high cell division and programmed cell death in the fetal brain (days 11 through 17). There were three different groups of rats ingesting, respectively, (1) no choline, (2) control amounts of choline, and (3) three times the control amounts of choline. Aside from these critical pregnancy periods, the mothers and the offspring were provided a normal diet. Apparently, these alterations of the amounts of choline during a fairly short time resulted in life-long be-

havioral changes in the offspring. As adults, offspring of the group (3) mothers were comparatively more adept at temporal memory, spatial, and attention tasks. In contrast, the group (1) mothers' offspring were impaired in several attentional and memory tasks. Moreover, the offspring of group (3) mothers maintained their memory performance and did not show the memory decline that is normally observed in old age. Neurophysiological and neurochemical (respectively, Cermak, Holler, Jackson, & Blusztajn, 1998; Pyapali, Turner, Williams, Meck, & Swartzwelder, 1998) data suggest that prenatal choline availability is linked to hippocampal synaptic plasticity by lowering the threshold of long-term potentiation and increasing the release of the neurotransmitter acetylcholine. Both of these mechanisms are important for learning and memory (Bliss & Collingridge, 1993; Fibiger, 1991).

These findings stress yet again the naiveté of the belief that cellular machinery is simply run by magic words read off of DNA. On the contrary, DNA is as sensitive to the state of the cell as the cell is sensitive to the information kept in the genome. Moreover, in some extreme situations, the cellular machinery imposes unequivocal control over the genes. Observations similar to those described above turn around the deterministic notion of the linear DNA-behavioral trait paradigm and the assumption of the separability of genetic and environmental influences.

Genes and Experiences

Nature itself "plans" for – leaves space for – experience. For example, researchers (Crair, Gillespie, & Stryker, 1998) have studied the role of visual experience in the development of cats' visual cortex. In general, patterned visual experience in a cat begins when its eyes open about a week after birth. By the time they are 2 weeks old, cats have developed cortical maps for orientation and ocular dominance. The scientists studied the development of maps for orientation and ocular dominance in normal and binocularly deprived cats (i.e., cats deprived of patterned visual experience by bilateral lid suture before the time of eye opening). The findings showed that early pattern vision appeared unimportant because cortical maps developed identically in normal and binocularly deprived cats up to the age of 3 weeks. These results seem to support the hypothesis of the innate basic structure of cortical maps; the formation of these maps appears to be genetically determined. Later patterned experience, however, was crucial for further visual cortex development, namely, for maintaining the responsiveness and selectivity of cortical neurons. Crair et al. (1998) interpreted their findings as an illustration of the interaction between innate and experiential factors in cortex development. Genes set up basic maps, and then experience refines and enhances them; the development of the visual cortex goes through a sequence of experience-independent and experience-dependent stages.

This interpretation, which assumes that the initial establishment of connections in the developing nervous system is genetically determined, has been questioned further. The common belief until very recently was that connections in the developing nervous system are formed initially by an activity-independent process of axon pathfinding and target selection. This initial establishment was thought to be refined by neural activity at later stages of life. In recent experiments, however, researchers have obtained results that suggest that activity-dependent processes occur even in the initial steps of cortical target selection by thalamic axons (Catalano & Shatz, 1998). By infusing a chemical into cats during the early period of the axons' networking, researchers blocked the spontaneous action-potential activity generated in the retina. As a result, the majority of neurons, rather than projecting themselves into the visual cortex, projected themselves into other brain areas that normally are bypassed by the moving axons; those axons that did make it to the cortex were topographically disorganized. It appears, then, that even the initial steps of the establishment of cortical connections are activity-dependent.

To explore the role of experience in higher mammals' genotypes, let us consider another interesting piece of evidence from recent studies challenging the "no-new-neurons-in-adults" dogma (Barinaga, 1998). Previous work has shown that lower species, including birds and rodents, produce brain neurons throughout their lives. Higher animals also have been studied previously, but no evidence of neurogenesis in adults was revealed (Rakic, 1985). Recently, however, researchers (Gould, Tanapat, McEwen, Flugge, & Fuchs, 1998) reported that adult mar-

moset monkeys make new neurons in the hippocampus. Moreover, studies suggest that stress reduction (Gould & McEwen, 1995) and enriching experiences (Kempermann, Kuhn, & Gage, 1998) may increase the rate of neurogenesis. Together, these results suggest that experiences can regulate the neuronal replacement rate. Scientists have not yet explained why Rakic had negative results in rhesus monkeys, whereas Gould and McEwen had positive results in marmosets. Certainly, both of the findings have to be replicated to settle the issue and investigate possible ramifications for humans. Moreover, another challenge concerns how a newborn neuron is incorporated into existing neuronal nets and what possible advantages and disadvantages this newcomer might bring with it. Though farfetched, the hypothesis that neurogenesis may be important for enhancing learning and memory at later life stages appears to be worth considering.

This set of observations reveals yet another layer of complexity in the structure connecting genes and behaviors. What becomes more and more apparent is that an understanding of how genes act and what happens in the cell when learning and memory occur is possible only when a specific gene is identified and its relations with its surroundings are characterized. The heritability paradigm has yet to uncover even one new gene relevant to human intelligence.

Genes and Living Environments

Let us consider the example of the impact of living environments by reviewing some aspects of cancer research. It is now commonly accepted that most cancer results from an interaction of genetics and the environment (Doll, 1996; Perera, 1996; Perera & Weinstein, 1996), but genetic factors by themselves explain only about 5% of all cancer (Knudson, 1985; Venitt, 1994). The other 95% of cancer can be attributed to environmental factors coacting with genetic and acquired susceptibility (Perera, 1997).

In prevention work, two common approaches have been used. The first focuses on helping individuals modify hazardous lifestyles. The second approach emphasizes limiting involuntary exposure to carcinogens by regulating work and life conditions. The common basis for both approaches is the assumption that all individuals in a population have the same biological response to a specified dose of carcinogen. However, these approaches have been unable to facilitate risk assessment and prevention in specific populations – even though in recent years the need to account for interindividual variation in susceptibility has become a central concern of health policymakers.

This need to describe and classify different interactive environment–susceptibility pathways to cancer has resulted in the emergence of a new approach, molecular epidemiology, which relies on biomarkers and the specification of various environmental exposures to study risk factors in specific populations. In the process of defining risk for cancer, molecular epidemiologists have documented several striking interactions between biological (susceptibility) and environmental factors (Perera, 1997). Among the biological markers of special interest are genes encoding metabolic–detoxification enzymes, and the two most harmful environmental carcinogens are polycyclic aromatic hydrocarbons (PAH), which are a product of the oxidation of fossil fuels, and aromatic amines, which are present in cigarette smoke. Here are some illustrations of the complexity of the interaction of biological susceptibility markers and environmental carcinogens.

In general, variation in a number of so-called metabolic genes strongly influences individual biological responses to environmental carcinogens. As a result of exposure to carcinogens, residues of different metabolic processes attach themselves to DNA, forming structures called adducts and causing procarcinogenic DNA damage. It has been shown that, in general, smokers and those who have high rate of exposure to PAH tend to have more PAH–DNA adducts. This relation, however, is not uniform for everybody. Perera (1996), for example, found considerable interindividual variation in carcinogene-DNA binding under equivalent conditions of exposure.

Specifically, some carcinogenic products may arise during the early catalytic stages of many chemicals (ranging from steroids to pollutants). These stages are carried out by so-called P450 enzymes. The production of P450 enzymes is controlled by several genes, including CYP1A1, which yields a product that metabolizes some PAH. This gene is polymorphic; that is, in the population, it exists in several variants. About 10% of Caucasians have a form of

the enzyme that is associated with an increased risk of lung cancer in smokers. In turn, some research has shown that increased lung cancer risk is associated with some variance of CYP1A1 (Kawajiri, Eguchi, Nakachi, Sekiya, & Yamamoto, 1996; Nakachi, Imai, Hayashi, Watanbe, & Kawajiri, 1991; Xu, Kelsey, Wiencke, Wain, & Christiani, 1996). Most crucially, when researchers compared light smokers with and without these "susceptible" CYP1A1 genotypes, the risk for the former was seven times the risk of the latter. When, however, heavy smokers with and without the genotype were compared, the risk of those with susceptibility genotypes was less than twice the risk of heavy smokers without the genotype (Kawajiri, et al., 1996; Nakachi et al., 1991).

Enzymes operating at the later stages of the catalysis of chemicals generally detoxify carcinogenic metabolites to produce excretable products. One of these enzymes, GSTM1, detoxifies reactive intermediates of PAH. The gene producing this enzyme is entirely deleted in about 50% of Caucasians. There is considerable evidence that GSTM1 deletion is associated with an increased risk of bladder and lung cancer (Bell et al., 1993; McWilliams, Sanderson, Harris, Richert-Boe, & Henner, 1995). The complexity of susceptibility–exposure interactions is illustrated by the observation that individuals with genotypes with GSTM1 deletion had a negligible risk of developing bladder cancer in the absence of exposure to tobacco smoke. It appears, however, that smoke exposure puts these individuals at higher risk because PHA–DNA adducts were higher in persons with GSTM1 deletion (Kato, Bowman, Harrington, Blomeke, & Shields, 1995; Ryberg, Hewer, Phillips, & Haugen, 1994a,b).

In short, it appears that the formation of adducts and the appearance of mutations in response to exposure is strongly modulated by variation in metabolic genes. This genetic variation, which influences the metabolic activation or detoxification of carcinogenic chemicals, is an important determinant of population risk. It is interesting to note that much of the research suggests that specific variation in metabolic genes has a greater impact on procarcinogenic adducts and cancer risk when exposure to carcinogens is low (Perera, 1997). It is possible (even though this might not hold for all types of variation) that at higher exposures environmental insults override genetic variation.

The complexity of individual responses to environmental carcinogens becomes even more apparent when such factors as nutrition and preexisting health conditions are considered. For example, several studies showed that smokers with the genotype with GSTM1 deletion whose diet lacked certain micronutrients, such as α-tocopherol and specific carotenoids, might have reduced protection against carcinogen-caused damage of DNA (Mooney et al., 1997; Mooney & Perera, 1996).

The work on cancer briefly described above underlines the importance of the "dosage" of environmental influences on specific genotypes. Apparently, general population laws do not hold for all subpopulations. If population is stratified by the types of genotypes of its members (note the need to know precisely what these genotypes are), its different strata may demonstrate a whole range of sensitivities to special environmental agents. In the case of intellectual functioning, heritability of IQ is an abstract indicator obtained in ill-defined populations characterized by a heterogeneity of variance reflective of the superimposing of different distributions on each other. Any meaningful interpretation of the links between genes and environments with regard to intellectual functioning can only be based on the identification, quantification, and description of specific genotypes and specific environments.

Genes and Culture

Finally, consider an example showing the impact of social rules on the genome. The strict rules of the Hindu caste system have controlled the marriage choices of its followers for more than 3,000 years. This cultural tradition has left a clear mark on the genes of modern Hindus. When scientists analyzed markers on the Y chromosome (one of the sex chromosomes inherited only through the paternal line) and mitochondrial DNA (inherited only through the maternal line), they discovered an interesting pattern (for a brief report, see Gibbons, 1998). Using genetic material collected from Hindu men of different castes, researchers quantified genetic distances between the castes. On the basis of mitochondrial DNA, they found that such distances are smaller between the upper and middle castes, and between the middle and lower castes, than between the upper and lower castes. On the basis of

an examination of Y-chromosome DNA, scientists found that men in the higher castes did not share any more genetic markers with men in the lower castes than they did with men in the middle castes, suggesting little crossing of caste lines. Taken together, these data suggest that Hindu women sometimes married up, thereby ascending the social ladder into higher castes. Hindu men, however, tended to stay in the castes into which they were born. This clustering means that these men's maternal ancestors had moved up from adjacent castes, mixing the genes between neighboring castes. This finding came as no surprise – the strict social rules enhancing women's movement upward has been documented in cultural–historical records (Kao & Sinha, 1997) and fiction (Roy, 1997). What is worth noting in the context of this chapter is, once again, the blended coaction of genes and environments in certain cultural contexts. Moreover, the mating practices of Hindu society impose a methodological challenge to the statistical models underlying the heritability paradigm (e.g., Capron et al., 1998); unless genetic similarity between spouses within each caste is quantified and embedded in heritability estimates, traditional paradigmatic methods of obtaining h^2 based on correlations between relatives will result in biased parameter estimates. In addition, the results from this study demonstrate the power of genetic research (when it involves detailed quantification of the genes involved) to reveal social history – something that the heritability paradigm is not equipped to do with its decomposition tools.

This section of the chapter has introduced into the discussion of the heritability paradigm several issues that, for a variety of reasons, have not been attended to sufficiently within the heritability paradigm. These issues are (1) the dependence of the h^2 estimates of population-specific allele frequencies, (2) the importance of pleiotropic effects in understanding the biological mechanisms underlying phenotypically correlated traits, (3) the complexity of the genetic mechanisms accountable for the variation in complex phenotypic traits, and, finally, (4) the integrated role of environment in the phenotypic manifestation of underlying genetic variation. One explanation for such inattentiveness is that the paradigm simply does not have the tools to deal with these issues.

In the light of all these concerns, where would I like the field to go? The answer I would like to offer is simple in one sense and complex in another. It is simple because it can be expressed in essentially one brief statement: we have to *identify, measure, and analyze the mechanisms involved*. Yet this solution is also complex because the objects of identification, measurement, and analyses (whether they are specific genes or specific environments) should be included in models, not as other phenotypic correlations for multivariate analyses based on the same ideology (e.g., Plomin & Petrill, 1997), but as the observed components of the carefully designed systems we are modeling. Ever since the appearance of the heritability paradigm, we have had to estimate because we could not afford to measure. Now we can afford to measure and therefore should control our habit of estimating. What developments in the field of psychology and in other fields permit me to assert that we can afford to measure?

WHAT IS COMING DOWN THE PIKE?

All areas of science develop as blends of theory and observation. However, without some theory – even a somewhat simplistic, reductionistic, and vague theory – one has no idea what to observe and what experiments to design. It is difficult to overestimate the role of the heritability-based approach in communicating the importance of the variability in genes for the variability in phenotypic traits. But this has been done. What is coming up next?

In Genetics

The magnitude of what is coming down the pike is breathtaking. In the three decades since biologists cracked the genetic code (that is, found the key to translating DNA into proteins), they have been working continuously on the "personification" of the DNA code. Which interindividual variation in nucleotides C(s), T(s), G(s), and A(s) is important and which is not? Geneticists now are in a better position to answer this question than ever before.

One novel development is the search for SNPs (single nucleotide polymorphisms, pronounced *snips*). The SNPs' endeavor engages academic laboratories and private companies and relies on governmental and private money around the world. The hope here is that researchers can nail down which genes contribute to the development of diseases that involve many genes (e.g., schizophrenia and diabetes). The basic strategy of this initiative is to collect a few hundred thousand single-based variations in human DNA in major population categories with the goals of quantifying genetic variation, studying variable forms of known genes, and providing new mapping points in the human genome. The major investment of private money in this operation is driven by its potential outcome – it could provide a tool for quickly screening genotypes. For example, a collaboration between a drug company named Affymetrix, Inc., and a group of scientists at MIT is expected to result in the creation of a sensor that identifies 2,000 or more SNPs. This sensor is an electronic device coated with a preset DNA sequence that probes a test material and provides an extensive amount of information on the makeup of the probed genotype.

The implication of having these data is very attractive; this information could allow us to personalize a variety of treatment approaches (both biomedical and behavioral). For example, several pharmaceutical companies want specialized SNPs maps to screen out patients who are less likely to respond to drugs in clinical trials because of the variant genes they carry. The SNPs endeavor also sets up new possibilities for drug treatment in the future. Picture this: You come to your physician with a complaint, but instead of giving you a prescription for your symptoms, he or she runs a quick DNA test for you and modifies a general drug formula so that "your" drug conforms to the particular molecular structures associated with your genotype; the effectiveness of your treatment is enhanced. Drug treatment could be personalized to overcome such complications as drug resistance and side effects. Another example is even more extreme. When, through the use of SNPs, the genes involved in the manifestation of complex multigene conditions are identified, clinicians will be able to assess an individual's predisposition to those diseases based on his or her SNP repertoire.

These clinical applications, however, will also provide much information that can be used in the search for the sources of variability in complex behavioral traits. Over the next decade, scientists will identify thousands of genes that directly and indirectly influence behavior (Hamer, 1997). But now, instead of guessing and estimating the additive component of the genetic variance, researchers will be able to measure it. And it looks as if the state of technology and the cost of this measurement will permit the quantification of differences in genotypes in different populations, age groups, and biological relations.

In Psychology

Living things (whether they are one-cell organisms or human beings) use DNA to store the instructions for making the proteins that build cells and direct them to develop into a complete organism. The DNA chain is made up of four different units (A, C, T, and G). These units group into three-letter "words" called codons, and each codon specifies an amino acid, which, in turn, is a building block of a protein (a complex polypeptide consisting of many amino acids). Specialized cellular machinery copies the DNA code onto RNA and delivers this code to cell protein factories, where it is used as a guide to direct the assembly of a polypeptide from amino acids. The synthesized proteins modulate functional systems of inhibitory and excitatory networks in the neocortex (which is considered the physiological basis of complex cortical information processing). The dynamics of these systems are extremely complex (Hasselmo, 1995). Different neurotransmitters interact with a variety of receptors; in turn, activation of different receptors can produce different effects on the excitability of a diverse group of cortical neurons. Thus, what cortex event will happen, and how it will affect the flow of information in cortical circuits, depends on the mode of action of a given neurotransmitter at a given receptor located on a specific subgroup of neurons (which, in turn, depending on which particular cortical network they belong to, have particular post-synaptic actions and connections). Such differential modulation of subgroups of neurons by specific neurotransmitter systems, which are responsive to minuscule fluctuations in environments, provides a substrate for fine control of information flow in the cortical network (Xiang, Huguenard, & Prince, 1998). The widely accepted belief in modern neuroscience is that the function of this cortical network is the substrate of human psychological processes.

The rapid development of the neurosciences and the usage of functional magnetic resonance imaging (fMRI) and positron emission tomography (PET) methodologies to map neurophysiological responses to cognitive, emotional, or sensory stimulation (e.g., Posner & Raichle, 1994; Raichle, 1998) in principle open up new possibilities for genetic studies of complex cognitive phenotypes. The challenge here is to figure out how to quantify these activities – at the level of metabolic and neurotransmitter events unfolding, first, in response to various types of stimulation, and, second, in response to participants' own thoughts and emotions – while also taking into account the variation in the genes of interest (e.g., genes involved in dopaminergic and GABAergic systems). There are some examples of such studies, even though they are still rare (Japan Science & Technology Corporation and Uppsala University PET Centre, 1997). This field embraces two exciting lines of development – one centers on how genes are involved in the biochemical activity of the brain (Sutcliff, 1988), and the other on how biochemical traces in the brain caused by mental activity (e.g., Mlot, 1998; Knudsen, 1998; Schacter, 1998) influence gene expression.

Another line of research focuses on the improved measurement of environments as well as measurement of adaptive reactions in response to changing environments. For example, one of the newly developing research trajectories has to do with the paradigm of challenging adaptive systems. One of the classic lines of research in psychology addresses the adaptation of people's motor behavior in response to environmental perturbations. This direction was pioneered by Helmholtz (1867), who was the first to suggest studying the behavioral shifts that occur in the visual field when prism glasses are worn over the eyes. This work was extended by numerous researchers (for review, see Welch, 1978) and transferred to different modalities (e.g., speech, Houde & Jordan, 1998). What is going to happen with the gene–environment systems when they are studied in changing environments? The heritability paradigm cannot predict the fluctuations in h^2 when new environments are introduced into a system. Those responses need to be measured so that differences between actualized and unactualized genotypes (Ceci, de Bruyn, & Lee, 1997) can be explored.

Such studies of adaptive environments in conjunction with an increased understanding of the genetic mechanisms involved in the realization of a particular phenotype may lead to remarkable remedial outcomes. Consider, for example, the following: The production of color vision is accomplished in normal people with the use of short-, middle-, and long-wavelength pigments. There are different types of color blindness, most of which are genetically determined. Researchers studying the relative preservation of color vision in deuteranomalous individuals (color-blind men who lack the gene for the middle-wavelength cone pigment) suggested that the degree of preservation of trichromatic vision by these color-blind individuals was related to their brains' ability to split long-wavelength pigments that could substitute for the missing middle-wavelength one (J. Neitz, M. Neitz, & Kainz, 1996). To compensate for this genetic defect, computer software could be developed that would take advantage of the brain function of the deuteranomalous individual to give them a fuller range and vividness of color vision (Altschuler & Lades, 1997).

And last, but not least, studies investigating the sources of individual variation in cognition should take advantage of new developments in the fields of cognitive and cultural psychologies. The heritability paradigm has almost exclusively investigated IQ and other conventional indexes of mental ability while consciously ignoring new developments in the field of cognitive psychology (Bouchard, 1998). This choice is inherent to the paradigm because, for phenotypic correlations to be decomposable, they have to meet specific psychometric standards. These standards, as well as traditional indexes of mental abilities, have been shown to have differential relevance in environments outside school (e.g., Sternberg, 1998). In addition, methods of investigating sources of individual variability in non-Westernized developmental systems have to be considered.

Thus, the new technological, methodological, and theoretical developments in psychology and genetics warrant a heavier reliance on the measurement of both genetic and environmental components than ever before. And these developments in the field are acknowledged not only by those working outside of the heritability paradigm (e.g., Greenspan, 1997) but also by those who fall within this traditional framework (e.g., Plomin, 1997). Whether we continue to study the etiology of individual differences in IQ or replace IQ with some other indicator(s) of intellectual functioning, it is clear that our approaches should change. And, as demonstrated earlier much information has been accumulated within the last few years that permits formulating hypotheses regarding possible mechanisms underlying phenotypic variation in intellectual functioning and forms a great starting point for advances in the field.

ON THE CHANGE OF PARADIGMS: "THE KING IS DEAD, LONG LIVE THE KING!"

Some, of course, would argue that what changes with a paradigm shift is only the scientists' interpretation of phenomena. Phenomena themselves are fixed. Thus, Priestley and Lavoisier both saw oxygen, but their interpretations of what they saw differed. Aristotle and Galileo both saw pendulums, but they interpreted what they had seen differently. The relevant point made by Kuhn (1962) is that it is not only interpretations that change. When a paradigm changes, the data that scientists collect on the same phenomenon alter as well. It is as if scientists need to put on Helmholtz's glasses; they need to confront the same phenomena as before – but see them transformed.

Much outstanding effort has been invested in reaching this point of transformation. The contribution of the heritability paradigm is hard to overestimate. It has (1) convinced the majority of scientists of the relevance and importance of variability in genes for variability in intellectual functioning; (2) provided theoretical bases for several studies that are viewed as outstanding examples of psychological research in terms of their methodology, power, and explanatory outcomes; (3) led to remarkable methodological and instrumental developments; and (4) resulted in formulating numerous unresolved questions serving now as new directions of scientific development (e.g., developmental changes and molecular bases of individual differences in intellectual functioning).

Notwithstanding, the heritability paradigm of studying behavioral traits has primarily bypassed the biology and psychology of environments in favor of a top–down decompositional approach. In this approach, cognitive functioning is modeled as consisting of separate functional modules, each performing a discrete mental process (whether reflected in IQ or any other index), each of which is controlled by a separate set of genes and by separate sets of environments.

The simplicity of interpretations of the contribution of genetic variability to complex human behavioral phenotypes can be attributed to researchers' overall oversight regarding the enormous variability and plasticity of existing genetic mechanisms. It is fair to say that every week a new piece of information is revealed that stresses the complex nature of the genome. However, the overly simplistic interpretation of the role of environment in heritability-paradigm studies has a different etiology. On the surface, despite powerful evidence demonstrating the impact of environmental influences on IQ, the position of the environmentalists in the so-called nature–nurture IQ debate has been magnitudes weaker than that of the hereditarians. This inequality resulted in part from some environmentalists' acceptance of IQ as an indicator of some underlying latent trait of unquestionable reality (Danzinger, 1997). The history of the concept of IQ shows that it appeared and developed as an essentially hereditarian construct; by accepting IQ and using a somewhat weak methodology in their research, environmentalists unwittingly facilitated the establishment of the heritability paradigm. Within the paradigm, the complexity of environment gets reduced to so-called nonshared environmental contributions (Samelson, 1985). With regard to IQ, the environmental position appears to be so weak that some researchers, in contrasting it to the hereditarian position, refer to the latter as scientific and the former as humanistic (Hunt, 1997). No subtlety there!

The shifting of paradigms, just like the annual change of the seasons, cannot be avoided and cannot be forced; it is a matter of converging experience. The empirical measurement of what constitutes the causal forces referred to as genes and environments will allow the field to target individual trajectories of development. There is increasing evidence pointing to the importance of variants in many complex human conditions. In Francis Collins' words,* "there are no perfect specimens" (Lin, 1996); researchers have to encounter as many specimens as possible.

* Collins is the director of the National Human Genome Research Institute.

New molecular–genetic and epidemiological data illustrate the complexity of environment–gene interactions – not one gene but multiple genes are involved in the control of complex traits, and the effects of these genes are modulated by such factors as ethnicity, age, gender, nutritional status, and harmful environmental exposure. In this respect, what is important is to pinpoint combinations of genes and environments that matter. The greatest potential outcome of behavior–genetic studies of intellectual functioning (whether of general or specific cognitive abilities) is in knowing enough about the interplay between genes and environment to design interventions that protect the susceptible subgroups. Such a "best" intervention study could be carried out on the basis of knowledge of differential risk resulting from predisposing genotypes, nutrition impairments, ethnicity, age, gender, and health. This intervention would require the development of education, health monitoring, and behavior modification programs – all carefully designed to have maximum impact. In other words, the fallacious default assumption of population homogeneity (on which the decomposition-of-variance is based) needs to be replaced with the awareness of the importance of knowledge about the distribution of exposure and susceptibility within the population (Hattis, 1991).

The complexity of the systems researchers are trying to study is awe-inspiring. And what is important now is precision. This essential level of precision cannot be obtained through the guessing games of decomposition but must be supported by identification, measurement, and the analysis of the mechanisms.

The whole purpose of this chapter is prescriptive. I advocate change in what scientists need to do to deal better with the question of the etiology of individual differences. I argue that, in attracting the attention of the scientific community to the role of genes, heritability studies of IQ have fulfilled their mission. Furthermore, using examples from the field of psychology and other sciences, I envisage understanding the mechanisms of the interactions of specific genes and specific environments for the sake of enhancing our appreciation of the complexities that result in the emergence of individuality. Because I limited my discussion largely to questioning the role of the heritability paradigm for the progress of the science of individual differences, I may have come across as one transmitting the values of a natural scientist. If I did, it is even more important that I state the following.

First, dismissing the usefulness of the heritability paradigm in future studies of individual differences in intellectual functioning does not resolve the question of what needs to be studied. I intentionally limited myself to a review of IQ, but, in debate of the significance of this concept for the field of psychology, I join those who say that this concept is largely a social invention (Danzinger, 1997; Smith, 1997; Stenberg, & Grigorenko, 1997) rather than a transcendent property of nature. Understanding individual differences in intellectual functioning is a very important query, but in doing so scientists should not restrict themselves to socially constructed entities, the life span of which might be limited by the length of the epoch that invented them.

Second, in stressing the importance of understanding the mechanics of the genome involvement in intellectual functioning and in opposing the simplistic strategy of decomposition, I biased this chapter toward genes. No individuality, regardless of how detailed its biochemical portrait is, can be understood without considering the person's intentions, moral values, and cultural and political context. However, scientists often go for the biochemistry – they can make a difference in their laboratories at this level, whereas any progress at the contextual level (even understanding familial environment) involves political will, which is beyond the reach of scientific reasoning.

And yet, although I appreciate the complexity of human activity and human life, I still believe that the road to understanding it requires precision – that is, identification, measurement, and analysis.

ACKNOWLEDGMENTS

I would like to acknowledge invaluable commentaries on the earlier version of this chapter kindly offered to me by Drs. Judith Adkins, Irina Sirotkina, Roger Smith, and Robert Sternberg. Preparation of this chapter was supported by Grant R206R50001 under the Javits Act from the Office of Educational Research and Improvement, U.S. Department of Education. Positions taken here do not necessarily represent those of the Office of Education or the U.S. Government, and no support of my positions should be inferred.

REFERENCES

Abel, T., Martin, K. C., Bartscn, D., & Kandel, E. R. (1998). Memory suppressor genes: Inhibitory constraints on the storage of long-term memory. *Science, 279,* 238–241.

Altschuler, E. L., & Lades, M. (1997). Color vision, genetics, and computers? *Science, 278,* 788.

Ball, D., Hill, L., Eley, T., Chorney, M., Chorney, K., Thompson, L. A., Detterman, D. K., Benbow, C., Lubinsky, D., Owen, M., McGuffin, P., & Plomin, R. (1998). Dopamine markers and general cognitive ability. *Neuroreport, 9,* 347–349.

Barber, B. (1961). Resistance by scientists to scientific discovery. *Science, CXXXIV,* 596–602.

Barinaga, M. (1998). No-new-neurons dogma loses ground. *Science, 279,* 2041–2042.

Baron, M. (1998). Mapping genes for personality: Is the saga sagging? *Molecular Psychiatry, 3,* 106–108.

Barton, N. H. (1990). Pleiotropic models of quantitative variation. *Genetics, 124,* 773–782.

Bell, D. A., Taylor, J. A., Paulson, D. F., Robertson, C. N., Mohler, J. L., & Lucier, G. W. (1993). Genetic risk and carcinogen exposure: A common inherited defect of the carcinogen-metabolism gene glutathione S-transferase M1 (GSTM1) that increases susceptibility to bladder cancer. *Journal of the National Cancer Institute, 85,* 1559–1564.

Benjamin, J., Li, L., Patterson, C., Greenberg, B. D., Murphy, D. L., & Hamer, D. H. (1996). Population and familial association between the D4 dopamine receptor gene and measures of novelty seeking. *Nature Genetics, 12,* 81–84.

Billig, J. P., Hershberger, S. L., Iacono, W. G., & McGue, M. (1996). Life events and personality in late adolescence: Genetic and environmental relations. *Behavior Genetics, 26,* 543–554.

Binet, A., & Simon, T. (1916). *The development of intelligence in children.* Baltimore: Williams & Wilkins. (French original published in 1905).

Birch, H. G., Richardson, S. A., Baird, D., Horobin, G., & Illsley, R. (1970). *Mental subnormality in the community: A critical and epidemiological study.* Baltimore: Williams & Wilkins.

Bliss, T. V. P., & Collingridge, G. L. (1993). A synaptic model of memory: Long-term potentiation in the hippocampus. *Nature, 361,* 31–39.

Block, N. (1995). How heritability misleads about race. *Cognition, 56,* 99–128.

Blusztajn, J. K. (1998). Choline, A vital amine. *Science, 281,* 794–795.

Bouchard, T. J. (1998). Genetic and environmental influences on adult intelligence and special mental abilities. *Human Biology, 70,* 257–279.

Bouchard, T. J., Lykken, D. T., McGue, M., Segal, N. L., & Tellegen, A. (1990). Sources of human psychological differences: The Minnesota Study of Twins Reared Apart. *Science, 250,* 223–228.

Bouchard, T. J., & McGue, M. (1981). Familial studies of intelligence: A review. *Science, 212,* 1055–1059.

Broman, S., Nichols, P. L., Shaughnessy, P., & Kennedy, W. (1987). *Retardation in young children: A developmental study of cognitive deficit* . Hillsdale, NJ: Lawrence Erlbaum Associates.

Burack, J., Hodapp, R. M., & Zigler, E. (Eds.) (1998). *Handbook of mental retardation and development.* New York: Cambridge University Press.

Capron, C., & Duyme, M. (1989). Assessment of the effects of socioeconomic status on IQ in a full cross-fostering study. *Nature, 340,* 552–554.

Capron, C., Vetta, A. R., & Vetta, A. (1998). Genetic model fitting in IQ, assortative mating and components of IQ variance. *Race, Gender, & Class, 5*(3), 51–60.

Caruso, D. R. (1983). Sample differences in genetics and intelligence data: Sibling and parent–offspring studies. *Behavior Genetics, 13,* 453–458.

Catalano, S. M., & Shatz, C. J. (1998). Activity-dependent cortical target selection by thalamic axons. *Science, 281,* 559–562.

Ceci, S. J., Rosenblum, T., de Bruyn, E., & Lee, D. Y. (1997). A bio-ecological model of intellectual development: Moving beyond h^2. In R. J. Sternberg, & E. L. Grigorenko. Intelligence, heredity, and environment (pp. 303–322). New York: Cambridge University Press.

Cermak, J. M., Holler, T., Jackson, D. A., & Blusztajn, J. K. (1998). Prenatal availability of choline modifies development of the hippocampal cholinergic system. *FASEB Journal, 12,* 349–357.

Chang, F.-M., Kidd, J. R., Livak, K. J., Pakstis, A. J., & Kidd, K. K. (1996). The world-wide distribution of alleles frequencies at the human domapine D4 receptor locus. *Human Genetics, 98,* 91–101.

Charlemaine, C., & Pons, J. C. (1998). What monozygotic twins tell us about genetic determinism. *Race, Gender, & Class, 5*(3), 12–40.

Chipuer, H. M., Rovine, M., & Plomin, R. (1990). LISREL modelling: Genetic and environmental influences on IQ revisited. *Intelligence, 14,* 11–29.

Chorney, M. J., Chorney, K., Seese, N., Owen, M. J., Daniels, J., McGuffin, P., Thompson, L. A., Detterman, D. K., Benbow, C., Lubinsku, D., Eley, T., & Plomin, R. (1998). A quantitative trait locus associated with cognitive ability in children. *Psychological Science, 9,* 159–166.

Crair, M., Gillespie, D. C., & Stryker, M. P. (1998). The role of visual experience in the development of columns in cat visual cortex. *Science, 279,* 566–570.

Daniels, J., Holmans, P., Williams, N., Turic, D., McGuffin, P., Plomin, R., & Owen, M. J. (1998). A simple method for analyzing microsatellite allele image patterns generated from DNA pools and its application to allelic association studies. *American Journal of Human Genetics, 62,* 1189–1197.

Danzinger, K. (1997). *Naming the mind.* Thousand Oaks, CA: Sage.

Darwin, L. (1913). Correspondence, Heredity and Environment. *Eugenic Review, 5,* 153–154.

Davies, K. (1991). Breaking the fragile X. *Nature, 351,* 439–440.

De Boulle, K., Verkerk, A. J. M. H., Reyniers, E., Vits, L., Hendrick, J., Van Roy, B., Van Den Bos, F., de Graaff, E., Oostra, B. A., & Willems, P. J. (1993). A point mutation in the FMR-1 gene associated with fragile X mental retardation. *Nature Genetics, 3,* 31–35.

DeFries, J. C., Corey, R. P., Johnson, R. C., Vandenberg, S. C., & Wilson, J. R. (1982). Sex-by-generation and ethnic group-by-generation interactions in the Hawaii, Family Study of Cognition. *Behavior Genetics, 12,* 223–230.

DeFries, J. C., Johnson, R. C., Kuse, A. R., McClearn, G. E., Polovina, J., Vandenberg, S. G., & Wilson, J. R. (1979). Familial resemblance for specific cognitive abilities. *Behavior Genetics, 9,* 23–43.

DeFries, J. C., Vandenberg, S. G., & McClearn, G. E. (1976). Genetics of specific cognitive abilities. *Annual Review of Genetics, 10,* 179–201.

Detterman, D. K., Thompson, L. A., & Plomin, R. (1990). Differences in heritability across groups differing in ability. *Behavior Genetics, 20,* 369–384.

De Souza, A. T., Hankins, G. R., Washington, M. K., Fine, R. L., Orton, T. C., & Jirtle, R. L. (1995). Frequent loss of heterozygosity on 6q at the mannose 6-phosphate/insulin-like growth factor II receptor locus in human hepatocellular tumors. *Oncogene, 10,* 1725–1729.

Devys, S., Lutz, Y., Rouyer, N., Belloeq, J.-P., & Mandel, J.-L. (1993). The FMR-1 protein is cytoplasmic, most abundant in neurons and appears normal in carriers of a fragile X premutation. *Nature Genetics, 4,* 335–340.

DiLella, A., & Woo, S. L. C. (1987). Molecular basis of phenylketonuria and its clinical applications. *Molecular Biology and Medicine, 4,* 183–192.

Doll, R. (1996). Nature and nurture: Possibilities for cancer control. *Carcinogenesis, 17,* 177–184.

Dowdney, L., & Skuse, D. (1993). Parenting provided by adults with mental retardation. *Journal of Child Psychology and Psychiatry, 34,* 25–48.

Ebstein, R. P., Novick, O., Umansky, R., Riel, B., Osher, Y., Blaine, D., Bennett, E. R., Nemanov, L., Katz, M., & Belmaker, R. H. (1996). Dopamine D4 receptor (*DRD4*) exon III polymorphism associated with the human personality trait of novelty seeking. *Nature Genetics, 12,* 78–79.

Epstein, C. J. (1986). *The consequences of chromosomal imbalance: Problems, mechanisms and models.* New York: Cambridge University Press.

Falconer, D. S. (1990). *Introduction to quantitative genetics.* New York: Longman Group.

Falconer, D. S., & Mackay, T. F. C. (1996). *Quantitative genetics.* Essex, England: Addison Wesley Longman, Ltd.

Feldman, M. W., & Otto, S. P. (1997). Twin studies, heritability, and intelligence. *Science, 278,* 1383–1384.

Fibiger, H. C. (1991). Cholinergic mechanisms in learning, memory and dementia: A review of recent evidence. *Trends in Neuroscience, 14,* 220–223.

Fischer, K. W., & Silvern, L. (1985). Stages and individual differences in cognitive development. *Annual Review of Psychology, 36,* 613–648.

Fishler, K., Azen, C. G., Friedman, E. G., & Koch, R. (1989). School achievement in treated PKU children. *Journal of Mental Deficiency Research, 33,* 493–498.

Ford, D. H., & Lerner, R. M. (1992). *Developmental systems theory: An integrative approach.* Newbury Park, NJ: Sage.

Fulker, D. W., Cherny, S. S., & Cardon, L. R. (1993). Continuity and change in cognitive development. In R. Plomin & G. E. McClearn (Eds.), *Nature, nurture and psychology* (pp. 77–97). Washington, DC: American Psychological Association.

Galton, F. (1876). The history of twins as a criterion of the relative powers of nature and nurture. *Royal Anthropological Institute of Great Britain and Ireland Journal, 6,* 391–406.

Galton, F. (1883). *Inquiries into human faculty and its development.* London: Macmillan.

Gardner, R. J. M., & Sutherland, G. R. (1996). *Chromosomal abnormalities and genetic counseling.* New York: Oxford University Press.

Gedeon, A. K., Baker, E., Robinson, H., Parlington, M. W., Gross, B., Korn, B., Poustka, A., Yu, S., Sutherland, G. R., & Mulley, J. C. (1992). Fragile X syndrome without CGG amplification has an FMR-1 deletion. *Nature Genetics, 1,* 341–344.

Gibbons, A. (1998). Anthropologists probe genes, brains at annual meeting. *Science, 280,* 380–381.

Goldin, L. R., Bailey-Wilson, J. E., Borecki, I. B., Falk, C. T., Goldstein, A. M., Suarez, B. K., & MacCluer, J. Q. (Eds.). (1997). Genetic Analysis Workshop 10. *Genetic Epidemiology, 14,* 549–1137.

Gottlieb, G. (1992). *Individual development and evolution. The genesis of novel behavior.* New York: Oxford University Press.

Gould, E., & McEwen, B. S. (1995). Neuronal birth and death. *Current Opinion in Neurobiology, 3,* 676–682.

Gould, E., Tanapat, P., McEwen, B. S., Flugge, G., & Fuchs, E. (1998). Proliferation of granule cell precursors in the dentate gyrus of adult monkeys is diminished by stress. *Proceedings of the National Academy of Sciences of the United States of America, 95,* 3168–3171.

Greenspan, S. I. (1997). Twin studies, heritability, and intelligence. *Science, 278,* 1384–1385.

Grigorenko, E. L., & Carter, A. S. (1996). Co-twin, peer, and mother–child relationships and IQ in a Russian adolescent twin sample. *Journal of Russian and East European Psychology, 34*(6), 59–87.

Hagberg, B., Hagberg, G., Lewerth, A., & Lindberg, U. (1981). Mild mental retardation in Swedish school children: 1. Prevalence. *Acta Paediatrica Scandinavica, 70,* 441–444.

Hall, J. G. (1996a). Twinning: Mechanisms and genetic implications. *Current Opinion in Genetics & Development, 6,* 343–347.

Hall, J. G. (1996b). Twins and twinning [editorial]. *American Journal of Medical Genetics, 61,* 202–204.

Hamer, D. (1997). The search for personality genes: Adventure of a molecular biologist. *Current Directions in Psychological Science, 6,* 111–115.

Harris, J. R. (1995). Where is the child's environment? A group socialization theory of development. *Psychological Review, 102,* 458–489.

Hasselmo, M. E. (1995). Neuromodulation and cortical function: Modeling the physiological basis of behavior. *Behavioural Brain Research, 67,* 1–27.

Hattis, D. (1991). Use of biological markers and pharmacokinetics in human health risk assessment. *Environmental Health Perspectives, 90,* 229–238.

Helmholtz, H. V. (1867). *Treatise on psychological optics* (Vol. 3).

Hirsch, J. (1990). A nemesis for heritability estimation. *Behavior and Brain Sciences, 13,* 137–138.

Houde, J. F., & Jordan, M. I. (1998). Sensimotor adaptation in speech production. *Science, 279,* 1213–1216.

Hunt, E. (1997). Nature vs. nurture: The feeling of *vijà dé.* In R. J. Sternberg & E. L. Grigorenko (Eds.), *Intelligence, heredity, and environment* (pp. 531–551). New York: Cambridge University Press.

Japan Science & Technology Corporation and Uppsala University PET Centre. (1997). Subfemtomole Biorecognition Project report.

Jinks, J. L., & Fulker, D. W. (1970). Comparison of biometrical genetical, MAVA, and classical approaches to the analysis of human behavior. *Psychological Bulletin, 73,* 311–349.

Jonas, P., Bischofberger, J., & Sandkühler, J. (1998). Corelease of two fast neurotransmitters at a central synapse. *Science, 281,* 419–424.

Kao, H. S. R., & Sinha, D. (Eds.) (1997). *Asian perspectives on psychology. Cross-cultural research and methodology series* (Vol. 19). New Delhi, India: Sage Publications, Inc.

Kato, S., Bowman, E. D., Harrington, A. M., Blomeke, B., & Shields, P. G. (1995). Human lung carcinogen-DNA adduct levels mediated by genetic polymorphisms in vivo. *Journal of the National Cancer Institute, 87,* 902–907.

Kawajiri, K., Eguchi, H., Nakachi, K., Sekiya, T., & Yamamoto, M. (1996). Association of CYP1A1 germ line polymorphisms with mutations of the p53 gene in lung cancer. *Cancer Research, 56,* 72–76.

Kayaalp, E., Carter, K., Waters, P. J., Byck, S., Treacy, E., Scriver, C. R., & the PAH Mutation Analysis Consortium (1996). Mutant PAH genotypes and associated metabolic phenotypes: A meta-analysis. *American Journal of Human Genetics, 4,* A201.

Keith, L., & Machin, G. (1997). Zygosity testing; current

status and evolving issues. *The Journal of Reproductive Medicine, 42,* 699–707.

Keltner, B. (1994). Home environments of mothers with mental retardation. *Mental Retardation, 32,* 123–127.

Kempermann, G., Kuhn, H. G., & Gage, F. H. (1998). Experience-induced neurogenesis in the senescent dentate gyrus. *Journal of Neuroscience, 18,* 3206–3212.

Kempthorne, O. (1955). The theoretical values of correlations between relatives in random mating populations. *Genetics, 40,* 153–167.

Kendler, K. S., & Kidd, K. K. (1986). Recurrence risks in an oligogenic threshold model: The effect of alterations in allele frequency. *Human Genetics, 50,* 83–91.

Kidd, K. K. (1993). Associations of disease with genetic markers: *Déjà vu* all over again. *American Journal of Medical Genetics (Neuropsychiatric Genetics), 48,* 71–73.

Kimble, G. A. (1993). Evolution of the nature–nurture issue in the history of psychology. In R. Plomin & G. E. McClearn (Eds.), *Nature, nurture and psychology* (pp. 3–26). Washington, DC: American Psychological Association.

Kitcher, P. (1996). Fascinating genetalk. In *An unequal inheritance,* New York: Simon & Schuster.

Knudsen, E. (1998). Capacity for plasticity in the adult owl auditory system expanded by juvenile experience. *Science, 279,* 1531–1533.

Knudson, A. G. (1985). Hereditary cancer, oncogenes, and antioncogenes. *Cancer Research, 45,* 1437–1443.

Koch, R., Azen, C., Freidman, E. G., & Williamson, M. L. (1984). Paired comparisons between early treated PKU children and their matched sibling controls on intelligence and school achievement test results at eight years of age. *Journal of Inherited Metabolic Disorders, 7,* 86–90.

Kręzel, W., Ghyzelinck, N., Samad, T. A., Dupé, V., Kastner, P., Borrelli, E., & Chambon, P. (1998). Impaired locomotion and dopamine signaling in terinoid receptor mutant mice. *Science, 279,* 863–867.

Kuhn, T. (1962). *The structure of scientific revolutions.* Chicago: The University of Chicago Press.

Kuhn, T. (1977). *The essential tension: Selected studies in scientific tradition and change.* Chicago: The University of Chicago Press.

Lamont, M. A., & Dennis, N. R. (1988). Aetiology of mild mental retardation. *Archives of Diseases in Childhood, 63,* 1032–1038.

Lenke, R. R., & Levy, H. L. (1980). Maternal phenylketonuria and hyperphenylalanemia: An international survey of the outcome of treated and untreated pregnancies. *New England Journal of Medicine, 303,* 1202–1208.

Lerner, R. M. (1991). Changing organism-context relations as the basic process of development: A developmental contextual perspective. *Developmental Psychology, 27,* 27–32.

Levin, M. (1994). Comment on the Minnesota Transracial Adoption Study. *Intelligence, 19,* 13–20.

Levin, M. (1997). *Why race matters: Race differences and what they mean.* Westport, CT: Praeger.

Levins, R., & Lewontin, R. (1985). *The dialectical biologist.* Cambridge, MA: Harvard University Press.

Lewontin, R. (1974). The analysis of variance and the analysis of causes. *American Journal of Human Genetics, 26,* 400–411.

Lidsky, A. S., Robson, K. J. H., Thirumalachary, C., Barker, P. E., Ruddle, F. H., & Wodd, S. L. C. (1984). The PKU locus in man is on chromosome 12. *American Journal of Human Genetics, 36,* 527–535.

Lin, H. J. (1996). Smokers and breast cancer. 'Chemical individuality' and cancer predisposition. *JAMA, 276,* 1511–1512.

Loehlin, J. C. (1989). Partitioning environmental and genetic contributions to behavioral development. *American Psychologist, 44,* 1285–1292.

Loehlin, J. C. (1992). Should we do research on race differences in intelligence? *Intelligence, 16,* 1–4.

Loehlin, J. C., Horn, J. M., & Willerman, L. (1989). Modeling IQ change: Evidence from the Texas Adoption Project. *Child Development, 60,* 993–1004.

Loehlin, J. C., & Nichols, R. C. (1976). *Heredity, environment, and personality.* Austin: University of Texas Press.

Machin, G. A. (1996). Some causes of genotypic and phenotypic discordance in monozygotic twin pairs. *American Journal of Medical Genetics, 61,* 216–228.

Martin, N., Boomsma, D., & Machin, G. (1997). A twin-pronged attack on complex traits. *Nature Genetics, 17,* 387–392.

McGue, M., Bouchard, T. J., Jr., Iacono, W. G., & Lykken, D. T. (1993). Behavioral genetics of cognitive ability: A life-span perspective. In R. Plomin & G. E. McClearn (Eds.), *Nature, nurture and psychology* (pp. 59–76). Washington, DC: American Psychological Association.

McClearn, G. E., Johansson, B., Berg, S., Pedersen, N. L., Ahern, F., Petrill, S. A., & Plomin, R. (1997). Substantial genetic influence on cognitive abilities in twins 80 or more years old. *Science, 278,* 1560–1563.

McWilliams, J. E., Sanderson, B. J. S., Harris, E. L., Richert-Boe, K. E., & Henner, W. D. (1995). Glutathione S-transferase M1 (GSTM1) deficiency and lung cancer risk. *Cancer Epidemiology, Biomarkers & Prevention, 4,* 589–594.

Meck, W. H., Smith, R. A., & Williams, C. L. (1989). Organizational changes in cholinergic activity and enhanced visuospatial memory as a function of choline administered prenatally or postnatally or both. *Behavioral Neuroscience, 103,* 1234–1241.

Meck, W. H., & Williams, C. L. (1997a). Characterization of the facilitative effects of perinatal choline supplementation on timing and temporal memory. *Neuroreport, 8,* 2831–2835.

Meck, W. H., & Williams, C. L. (1997b). Simultaneous temporal processing is sensitive to prenatal choline availability in mature and aged rats. *Neuroreport, 8,* 3045–3051.

Merriman, C. (1924). The intellectual resemblance of twins. *Psychological Monographs, 33,* 1–58.

Mikkelsen, M., Poulsen, H., Grinsted, J., & Lange, A. (1980).

Non-disjunction in trisomy 21: Chromosomal hetero-morphisms in 110 families. *Annals of Human Genetics*, *44*, 17.

Mlot, C. (1998). Probing the biology of emotion. *Science*, *280*, 1005–1007.

Molenaar, P. C., Boomsma, D. I., & Dolan, C. V. (1999). The detection of genotype-environment interaction in longitudinal genetic models. In M. L. LaBuda & E. L. Grigorenko (Eds.), *On the way to individuality: Current methodological issues in behavioral genetics* (pp. 53–70). Commack, New York: Nova Science Publishers, Inc.

Mooney, L. A., Bell, D. A., Santella, R. M., Van Bennekum, A. M., Ottman, R., Paik, M., Blaner, W. S., Lucier, G. W., Covey, L., Young, T. L., Cooper, T. B., Glassman, A. H., & Perera, F. P. (1997). *Carcinogenesis*, *18*, 503–509.

Mooney, L. A., & Perera, F. P. (1996). Application of molecular epidemiology to lung cancer chemoprevention. *Journal of Cellular Biochemistry — Supplement*, *25S*, 63–68.

Moore, E. G. J. (1986). Family socialization and the IQ test performance of traditionally and transracially adopted black children. *Developmental Psychology*, *22*, 317–326.

Nakachi, K., Imai, K., Hayashi, J., Watanbe, J., & Kawajiri, K. (1991). Genetic susceptibility to squamous cell carcinoma of the lung in relation to cigarette smoking dose. *Cancer Research*, *51*, 5177–5180.

Neale, M. C. (1997). *Mx: Statistical Modeling*, 3rd ed. (Box 980126, MCV, Richmond, VA 23298).

Neale, M., & Cardon, L. R. (1992). *Methodology for genetic studies of twins and families, NATO ASI Series*. Dordrecht, The Netherlands: Kluwer Academic Press.

Neitz, J., Neitz, M., & Kainz, P. M. (1996). Visual pigment gene structure and the severity of color vision defects. *Science*, *274*, 801–804.

Nicoll, R. A., & Malenka, R. C. (1998). A tale of two transmitters. *Science*, *281*, 360–361.

Olshan, A. F., Bard, P. A., & Teschke, K. (1989). Parental occupation exposure and the risk of Down's syndrome. *American Journal of Human Genetics*, *44*, 646–651.

Oostra, B. A. (1996). FMR1 protein studies and animal model for FXS. In R. J. Hagerman & A. Cronister (Eds.), *Fragile X syndrome: Diagnostics, treatment, & research* (pp. 193–209). Baltimore, MD: The Johns Hopkins University Press.

Oyama, S. (1985). *The ontogeny of information: Developmental systems and evolution*. Cambridge: Cambridge University Press.

Pal, S., Shyam, R., & Singh, R. (1997). Genetic analysis of general intelligence 'g': A twin study. *Personality and Individual Differences*, *22*, 779–780.

Pedersen, N. L., Plomin, R., Nesselroader, J. R., & McClearn, G. E. (1992). A quantitative genetic analysis of cognitive abilities during the second half of the life span. *Psychological Science*, *3*, 346–353.

Perera, F. P. (1996). Molecular epidemiology: Insights into cancer susceptibility, risk assessment, and prevention. *Journal of the National Cancer Institute*, *88*, 496–509.

Perera, F. P. (1997). Environment and cancer: Who are susceptible? *Science*, *278*, 1068–1073.

Petrill, S. A. (1997). Molarity versus modularity of cognitive functioning? A behavioral genetic perspective. *Current Directions in Psychological Science*, *6*, 96–99.

Petrill, S. A., Ball, D., Eley, T., Hill, L., Plomin, R., McClearn, G. E., Smith, D. L., Chorney, K., Chorney, M., Hershz, M., Detterman, D. K., Thompson, L. A., Benbow, C., & Lubinski, D. (1998). Failure to replicate a QTL association between a DNA marker identified by EST00083 and IQ. *Intelligence*, *25*, 179–184.

Pieretti, M., Zhang, F., Fu, Y.-H., Warren, S. T., Oostra, B. A., Caskey, C. T., & Nelson, D. L. (1991). Absence of the expression of the FMR-1 gene in fragile X syndrome. *Cell*, *86*, 817–822.

Plomin, R. (1997). Current directions in behavioral genetics: Moving into the mainstream. *Current Directions in Psychological Science*, *6*, 85.

Plomin, R., DeFries, J. C., & Fulker, D. W. (1988). *Nature and nurture during infancy and early childhood*. Cambridge, UK: Cambridge University Press.

Plomin, R., DeFries, J. C., McClearn, G. E., & Rutter, M. (1997). *Behavioral Genetics*. New York: W. H. Freeman and Company.

Plomin, R., & Neiderhiser, J. M. (1992). Quantitative genetics, molecular genetics, and intelligence. *Intelligence*, *15*, 369–387.

Plomin, R., McClearn, G. E., & Smith, D. L. (1994). DNA markers associated with high versus low IQ: The IQ QTL Project. *Behavior Genetics*, *24*, 107–118.

Plomin, R., McClearn, G. E., & Smith, D. L. (1995). Allelic associations between 100 DNA markers and high versus low IQ. *Intelligence*, *21*, 31–48.

Plomin, R., & Petrill, S. A. (1997). Genetics and intelligence: What is new? *Intelligence*, *24*, 53–78.

Popper, K. (1968). *The logic of scientific discovery*. New York: Harper & Row.

Posner, M. I., & Raichle, M. E. (1994). *Images of mind*. New York: Scientific American Library/Scientific American Books.

Pyapali, G. K., Turner, D. A., Williams, C. L., Meck, W. H., & Swartzwelder, H. S. (1998). Prenatal dietary choline supplementation decreases the threshold for induction of long-term potentiation in young adult rats. *Journal of Neurophysiology*, *79*, 1790–1796.

Raichle, M. E. (1998). Behind the scenes of functional brain imaging: a historical and physiological perspective. *Proceedings of National Academy of Sciences*, *95*, 765–772.

Rakic, P. (1985). Limits of neurogenesis in primates. *Science*, *227*, 1054–1056.

Ramus, S. J., Forrest, S. M., Pitt, D. B., Saleeba, J. A., & Cotton, R. G. H. (1993). Comparison of genotypes and intellectual phenotype in untreated PKU patients. *Journal of Medical Genetics*, *30*, 401–405.

Rao, J. M. (1990). A population-based study of mild mental handicap in children: Preliminary analysis of bostetric associations. *Journal of Mental Deficiency Research, 34,* 59–65.

Read, A. W., & Stanley, F. J. (1993). Small-for-gestational-age term birth: The contribution of socio-economic, behavioral and biological factors to recurrence. *Paediatric and Perinatal Epidemiology, 7,* 177–194.

Risch, N., & Merikangas, K. (1996). The future of genetic studies of complex human diseases. *Science, 273,* 1516–1517.

Rowe, D. C. (1997). A place at the policy table? Behavior genetics and estimates of family environmental effects on IQ. *Intelligence, 24,* 133–158.

Roy, A. (1997). *The god of small things.* New Delhi, India: Harper Perennial.

Rutter, M., Tizard, J., & Whitmore, K. (Eds.) (1970). *Education, health, and behavior.* London: Longman.

Ryberg, D., Hewer, A., Phillips, D. H., & Haugen, A. (1994a). p53 mutations in lung tumors: Relationship to putative susceptibility markers for cancer. *Cancer Research, 54,* 1551–1555.

Ryberg, D., Hewer, A., Phillips, D. H., & Haugen, A. (1994b). Different susceptibility to smoking-induced DNA damage among male and female lung cancer patients. *Cancer Research, 54,* 5801–5803.

Samelson, F. (1985). Organization for the kingdom of behavior: Academic battles and organizational policies in the twenties. *Journal of the history of the Behavioral Sciences, 21,* 33–47.

Sameroff, A. J., & Chandler, M. J. (1975). Reproductive risk and the continuum of caretaking casualty. In F. D. Horowitz (Ed.), *Review of child development research* (Vol. 4, pp. 187–224). Chicago: University of Chicago Press.

Scarr, S., & Weinberg, R. A. (1977). Intellectual similarities within families of both adopted and biological children. *Intelligence, 1,* 170–191.

Scarr, S., Weinberg, R. A., & Waldman, I. D. (1993). IQ correlations in transracial adoptive families. *Intelligence, 17,* 541–555.

Schacter, D. (1998). Memory and awareness. *Science, 280,* 59–60.

Schönemann, P. H. (1989). New questions about old heritability estimates. *Bulletin of the Psychonomic Society, 27* (2), 175–178.

Schönemann, P. H. (1993). A note on Holzinger's heritability coefficient h^2. *Chinese Journal of Psychology, 35,* 59–65.

Schönemann, P. H. (1994). Heritability. In R. J. Sternberg (Ed.), *Encyclopedia of human intelligence* (pp. 528–536). New York: Macmillan.

Schönemann, P. H. (1997). On models and muddles of heritability. *Genetica, 99,* 97–108.

Scott, C. R., & Cederbaum, S. D. (1990). Disorders of amino acid metabolism. In A. E. H. Emery & D. H. Rimoin (Eds.), *Principles and practice of medical genetics* (pp. 1639–1673). Edinburgh: Churchill Livingstone.

Semia v. Rossii [Family in Russia]. (1997), 4.

Sherman, S. (1996). Epidemiology. In R. J. Hagerman & A. Cronister (Eds.). *Fragile X syndrome: Diagnostics, treatment, and research* (pp. 165–192). Baltimore, MD: The Johns Hopkins University Press.

Simonton, D. (1994). *Greatness.* New York: The Guilford Press.

Singer, R. H. (1998). Triplet-Repeat Transcripts: A role for RNA in disease. *Science, 280,* 696–698.

Skuder, P., Plomin, R., McClearn, G. E., Smith, D. L., Vignetti, S., Chorney, K., Chorney, M., Kasaesa, S., Thompson, L. A., Detterman, D. K., Petrill, S. A., Daniels, J., Owen, M. J., & McGuffin, P. (1995). A polymorphism in mitochondrial DNA associated with IQ? *Intelligence, 21,* 1–12.

Smith, R. (1997). *The Norton history of the human sciences.* Dunmore, PA: W. W. Norton & Company, Inc.

Smith, J., & Wolff, O. H. (1974). Natural history of phenylketonuria and early treatment. *Lancet, 2,* 540–544.

Snyderman, M., & Rothman, S. (1987). Survey of expert opinion on intelligence and aptitude testing. *American Psychology, 42,* 137–144.

Snyderman, M., & Rothman, S. (1988). *The IQ controversy, the media and public policy.* New Brunswick, NJ: Transaction Books.

Sternberg, R. J., & Grigorenko, E. L. (Eds.). (1997). *Intelligence, heredity, and environment.* New York: Cambridge University Press.

Sternberg, R. J., & Grigorenko, E. L. (1999). Myths in psychology and education regarding the gene-environment debate. *Teachers College Record,* 536–553.

Sternberg, R. J. (1998). "How intelligent is intelligence testing?" *Scientific American Presents, 9,* 12–17.

Strohman, R. C. (1997). The coming Kuhnian revolution in biology. *Nature Biotechnology, 15,* 194–200.

Sutcliff, J. G. (1988). mRNA in the mammalian central nervous system. *Annual Review of Neuroscience, 11,* 157–198.

Tishkoff, S. A., Dietzsch, E., Speed, W., Pakstis, A. J., Kidd, J. R., Cheung, K., Bonné-Tamir, B., Santachiara-Benerecetti, A. S., Morla, P., Krings, M., Pääbo, S., Watson, E., Risch, N., Jenkins, T., & Kidd, K. K. (1996). Global patterns of linkage disequilibrium at the CD4 locus and modern human origins. *Science, 271,* 1380–1387.

Thompson, L. A., Detterman, D. K., & Plomin, R. (1993). Differences in heritability across groups differing in ability, revisited. *Behavior Genetics, 23,* 331–336.

Trimble, B. K., & Baird, P. A. (1978). Maternal age and Down syndrome: Age specific incidence rates by single year intervals. *Journal of Medical Genetics, 2,* 1.

Tymchuk, A. K. (1992). Predicting adequacy of parenting by people with mental retardation. *Child Abuse and Neglect, 16,* 1165–1166.

Venitt, S. (1994). Mechanisms of carcinogenesis and individual susceptibility to cancer. *Clinical Chemistry, 40,* 1421–1425.

Vetta, A. (1980). Correlation, regression, and biased science. *The Behavior and Brain Sciences, 3,* 357–358.

Wagner, G. P. (1996). Apparent stabilizing selection and the maintenance of neutral genetic variation. *Genetics, 143,* 617–619.

Waldman, I. D., Wainberg, R. A., & Scarr, S. (1994). Racial-group differences in IQ in the Minnesota Transracial Adoption Study: A reply to Levin and Lynn. *Intelligence, 19,* 29–44.

Wahlsten, D. (1990). Insensitivity of the analysis of variance to heredity–environment interaction. *Behavioral and Brain Sciences, 13,* 109–161.

Wahlsten, D. (1998). Origins of genetic determinism in medieval creationism. *Race, Gender, & Class, 5*(3), 90–107.

Wahlsten, D., & Gottlieb, G. (1997). The invalid separation of effects of nature and nurture: Lessons from animal experimentation. In R. J. Sternberg & E. L. Grigorenko (Eds.), *Intelligence, heredity, and environment* (pp. 163–192). New York: Cambridge University Press.

Wahlström, J. (1990). Gene map of mental retardation. *Journal of Mental Deficiency Research, 34,* 11–27.

Waxman, D., & Peck, J. R. (1998). Pleiotropy and preservation of perfection. *Science, 279,* 1210–1213.

Webb, T. P., Bundley, S., Thake, A., & Todd, J. (1986). The frequency of the fragile X chromosome among schoolchildren in Coventry. *Journal of Medical Genetics, 23,* 396–399.

Weiss, V. (1992). Major genes of general intelligence. *Personality and Individual Differences, 13,* 1115–1134.

Weiss, V. (1995). The advent of a molecular genetics of general intelligence. *Intelligence, 20,* 115–124.

Welch, R. B. (1978). *Perceptual modifications: Adapting to altered sensory environments.* New York: Academic Press.

Xiang, Z., Huguenard, J. R., & Prince, D. A. (1998). Cholinergic switching within neocortical inhibitory networks. *Science, 281,* 985–988.

Xu, X., Kelsey, K. T., Wiencke, J. K., Wain, J. C., & Christiani, D. C. (1996). Cytochrome P450 CYP1A1 MspI polymorphism and lung cancer susceptibility. *Cancer Epidemiology, Biomarkers, and Prevention, 5,* 687–692.

CHAPTER FIVE

Intellectual Development in Childhood

ZHE CHEN AND ROBERT S. SIEGLER

Intellectual development is a vast topic – far too large even to begin to summarize in a single, relatively brief chapter. Therefore, this review is, of necessity, extremely selective. It includes two sections. The first briefly describes six theories of intellectual development, three longstanding ones and three more recent ones. The second focuses on a core area of intellectual development in which progress has been especially notable over the two decades since the previous edition of this handbook: the development of problem solving and learning.

THEORETICAL APPROACHES

Traditional Theories

PSYCHOMETRIC APPROACHES. Psychometric theories are aimed at explaining individual and developmental differences in performance on standardized tests of intellectual performance – especially IQ tests. Underlying such theories is the assumption that intelligence can be assessed in terms of latent sources of individual differences or "factors." Psychometric theories can be divided by the number of factors that they emphasize: one, a few, or many. Consider a prominent example of each. Spearman (1927) emphasized that underlying all intellectual performance is a single common general factor (g). Thurstone (1938) proposed that intelligence involves seven primary mental abilities: verbal comprehension, verbal fluency, number, spatial visualization, memory, reasoning, and perceptual speed. Guilford (1967) hypothesized the existence of 180 ability factors based on the possible combinations of three dimensions that were present in all tasks: content, operation, and product. The one-few-many trichotomy also applies to nonpsychometric theories of intellectual development. For example, Piaget's theory emphasizes a single operational intelligence, privileged-domains theories (e.g., Carey, 1985; Gardner, 1993; Wellman & Gelman, 1998) emphasize a small number of intelligences, and sociocultural theories (Cole, 1996; Rogoff, 1998) view intelligence in terms of performance within a vast number of contexts.

At the time of the writing of Siegler and Richards (1982), psychometric test scores had been shown to be quite useful with individuals age 5 years and older. The evidence included demonstrations that individual differences are quite stable from age 5 or 6 through adulthood, that test scores are closely related to concurrent school performance at each age in that range, and that test scores early in this age range predict later school achievement quite accurately. A different picture, however, emerged at younger ages. Traditional tests of infant intelligence proved not to be accurate predictors of later development. For example, scores on the Bayley Scale, which assesses individual infants' behavior relative to a variety of developmental milestones, are not very predictive of children's performance on later tests (Lipsitt, 1992; McCall, 1979, 1981).

More recent measures of infants' information processing have been found to be more predictive than the infant intelligence tests of later intelligence tests scores. Some of the most commonly used measures of information processing involve performance on habituation tasks. In habituation tasks, a picture or object is shown repeatedly, and infants' looking time is recorded after each presentation. With repeated presentation, infants pay less and less attention to the increasingly familiar picture or object. This is the phenomenon of *habituation*. When a new item replaces the old one or is presented along with the old one, infants typically show increased attention. This is the phenomenon of *dishabituation*.

Rates of habituation and dishabituation during the first 6 months predict IQ scores for a surprisingly long time thereafter. The more rapidly that infants stop looking at a familiar picture, and the more rapidly they resume looking at a novel one, the higher their IQ score tends to be 4 or 6 years later (Fagan & Singer, 1983; McCall & Carriger, 1993; Sigman, Cohen, Beckwith, & Parmelee, 1986). Habituation and dishabituation rates in infancy also have been shown to be related to the likelihood of learning disabilities as much as 5 years later (Fagan & Detterman, 1992; Rose, Feldman, & Wallace, 1992; Rose & Wallace, 1985). It should be noted, though, that the correlation between these measures of information processing in infancy and performance on later standardized tests is typically modest ($rs = .35–.50$).

One process that seems to underlie the correlations is efficiency of encoding (Bornstein, 1985; Bornstein & Sigman, 1986; Ceci, 1990; Colombo, 1995; Sternberg, 1981). Rose and Feldman (1997) found that 7-month-olds' performance on visual recognition memory tasks, which reflects the rapidity and precision with which infants encode information about the target stimulus, is a relatively strong predictor of 11-year-olds' IQ. Other studies also suggest that encoding plays a large role in the efficiency of information processing (Bronson, 1991; Freeseman, Colombo, & Coldren, 1993). For example, Colombo, Freeseman, Coldren, and Frick (1995) found that those infants who rapidly demonstrate a preference for novel stimuli focused on global features first and then moved to local elements. In contrast, infants who were slow to show such a preference attended to local features for prolonged periods. Infants who showed a novelty preference rapidly also engaged in more extensive scanning than those who needed a longer familiarization time. Taken together, these findings suggest that efficiency in encoding essential information underlies some of the continuity between early information processing and later psychometric test scores.

Despite the stability of children's test scores, the use of a single score as a measure of intelligence has several drawbacks. A single number, or even several numbers measuring the status of different dimensions of intelligence, can hardly capture the richness and complexity of intelligence, learning abilities, and creativity. Another limitation of such numerical measures of intelligence results from their failure to take into account the social and cultural contexts that shape all types of intellectual performance (Ceci, 1990; Sternberg, 1985b; 1997).

Several efforts have been made in recent years to address these criticisms and to broaden the psychometric approach. One particularly important type of extension has been to examine the cognitive processes that underlie performance on tasks used to measure intelligence (Ackerman, 1989; Carpenter, Just, & Shell, 1990; Kyllonen & Shute, 1989). One information-processing component that has proved to be a good predictor of general intelligence is efficiency of thinking (Jensen, 1988). For example, the time that children require to discriminate stimuli is moderately correlated with general intelligence (Kranzler & Jensen, 1989). Other studies (e.g., Geary, 1994; Geary & Burlingham-Dubree, 1989) have revealed that effective strategy choices on simple addition problems is related to IQ.

Perhaps the most comprehensive approach to identifying the processing elements that underlie performance on IQ tests is Sternberg's triarchic theory (e.g., Sternberg, 1985a). As the name suggests, the triarchic theory includes three subtheories of intelligence: the cognitive process, contextual, and experiential subtheories (Figure 5.1). The cognitive process subtheory concerns the ways in which intelligent behavior is generated. Three classes of information-processing components are posited in this subtheory: performance components, knowledge-acquisition components, and metacomponents. *Performance components* are the basic processes involved in intellectual activities: encoding, inference, mapping, and application. *Knowledge-acquisition components* focus on processes involved in learning. They include selective encoding of relevant information, selective combination of incoming information, and selective comparison of new information to existing knowledge. *Metacomponents* are higher order executive processes that determine which performance and learning components

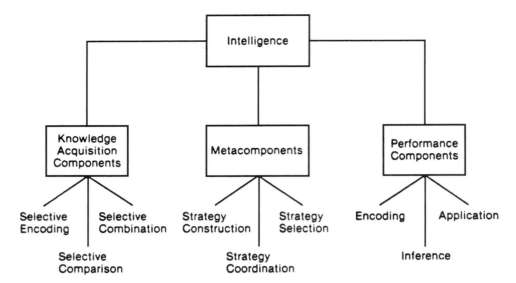

FIGURE 5.1. A schematic diagram of Sternberg's triarchic theory (1985a) of intelligence.

will be used and in what sequence. They include planning, monitoring, and evaluating problem solutions. Children with higher IQs execute all three types of components more efficiently than those with lower IQs (Davidson & Sternberg, 1984; Johnson & Mervis, 1994; Marr & Sternberg, 1986).

The triarchic theory also includes contextual and experiential subtheories. The contextual subtheory proposes that more intelligent individuals are more skillful in adapting to environments in which they find themselves, in selecting environments in which they can function well, and in shaping environments to fit their capabilities. The experiential subtheory focuses on the relation between internal capacities and the external world. The basic hypothesis is that individuals with higher intelligence are superior in dealing with novel situations and in automatizing processing in familiar situations.

The triarchic theory has proved to be valuable in describing and explaining individual and developmental differences in intelligence. However, like all current theories of intellectual development, it has distinct limits. In particular, the theory has not specified how its components interact, and it remains to be demonstrated whether the separate components can be assessed in ways that maintain the reliability and validity of traditional intelligence tests while adding theoretical precision and a broader scope.

PIAGET'S THEORY. Like Spearman, Piaget posited a single, general intelligence. Unlike Spearman, he asserted that this intelligence progresses through a sequence of qualitatively distinct forms or stages: the sensorimotor stage (birth–2 years), the preoperational stage (2–7 years), the concrete-operational stage (7–12 years), and the formal-operational stage (12 years–adulthood).

In the sensorimotor stage, infants' intelligence is realized only in sensorimotor schemes; that is, motor behavior directed toward objects or the infant's own body. The primary source of early development is children's interactions with objects and the environment. As infants progress through this period, their motoric schemes become increasingly interrelated and complex until they culminate in the ability to form internal symbolic representations. One important intellectual achievement toward the end of this stage is the acquisition of object permanence, the understanding that objects continue to exist when they are hidden. Another critical accomplishment is imitation of observed behaviors. The emergence of these capabilities indicates the emergence of mental representations.

In the preoperational stage, the key characteristic of intelligence is the ability to represent thought in language, mental imagery, and other symbolic means. This ability to form symbolic representations leads to more efficient learning and problem solving. One key achievement of children in this stage is the acquisition of what Piaget termed "qualitative identity," the realization that objects' basic qualities do not change even when their appearance changes. The thinking of children in this stage, however, is still portrayed as rigid, lacking in logic, and limited to focusing on one aspect of a situation at a time. A key deficiency of preoperational children's thinking is egocentrism, the inability to distinguish the symbolic viewpoint of others from the child's own. Another limitation is centration: the child's thinking is preoccupied and misled by an object's perceptual features.

During the concrete-operational stage, children's thinking is viewed as more logical, flexible, and organized than in the previous stage. Milestones during this stage include the mastery of different forms of conservation and the ability to classify objects or events according to multiple, simultaneously applied criteria, rather than just one. Children are now capable of solving various conservation problems such as recognizing that the amount of water does not change when it is poured from one container to another of a different shape. These abilities illustrate decentration, which entails the capacity to recognize that a change in one dimension (the height of the water) is compensated for by a change in another dimension (the width), and reversibility, the capacity to imagine the water being returned to the original container as proof of conservation. However, children's thinking in this stage remains relatively unsystematic and tied to tangible situations rather than being extended to abstract and imaginary situations as well.

During the formal-operational stage, children become capable of flexible, logical, scientific reasoning. The distinguishing characteristic of formal operations is the capacity for hypothetical-deductive reasoning. When faced with a problem, adolescents start with a general theory about various possibilities that might effect an outcome, from it deduce specific testable hypotheses, and go on to test them in a systematic, unbiased fashion.

Piaget's theory also included a general characterization of the mechanisms that produce cognitive growth. He started from the assumption that human intelligence is a biological adaptation of a complex organism to a complex environment. He viewed two intellectual functions as paramount: *adaptation* and *organization*. Adaptation involves building mental structures through direct interaction with the environment. It occurs through the simultaneous and complementary processes of assimilation and accommodation. Assimilation refers to the transformation of information from the external environment so that it fits into the individual's existing ways of thinking. Accommodation refers to the transformation of existing ways of thinking in response to new information and experiences.

The second key intellectual function identified by Piaget is organization, which involves the internal rearrangement and linking together of mental structures such that these structures become part of a broad network of structures that can be applied to the external world. The processes of adaptation and organization explain how children's thinking progresses from one stage to another with experience and maturation and how their cognitive systems interact with their external environments.

Piaget's theory remains the most prominent approach to the development of intelligence. It covers the full age range from birth to adolescence, includes a very broad range of types of thinking, and depicts a clear and dramatic sequence of qualitatively different stages. It also has contributed to many other theories of intellectual development – in particular to the group of theories collectively labeled neo-Piagetian theories (e.g., Case, 1985, 1992; Demetriou, Efklides, & Platsidou, 1993; Fischer & Farrar, 1987; Halford, 1993; Pascual-Leone, 1987).

These neo-Piagetian theories are distinguished by an attempt to maintain the strengths of Piaget's approach while shoring up some of the weaknesses. One common direction has been to bring together concepts from Piaget's theory and concepts from information-processing theories such as capacities, goals, and strategies. Like Piaget, neo-Piagetians postulate mental representations or structures that grow in complexity with age and that produce broad unities in children's thinking at a given age. Unlike Piaget, neo-Piagetians propose change mechanisms such as increasing memory capacity or synchronization of processing in different regions of the brain as factors that produce transitions from one level of thinking to another. Although the particulars of the change mechanisms differ, neo-Piagetian theories propose that increasingly powerful information-processing capacities are at the core of the change process.

One prominent neo-Piagetian approach is Case's (1985) theory, which emphasizes working-memory capacity as a determinant of intellectual growth. With brain maturation and experience, working memory capacity increases so that a cognitive operation that previously required all working-memory resources can be accomplished through using only part of the available cognitive resources. Changes in information-processing efficiency also enable children to construct more advanced central conceptual structures, "networks of semantic nodes and relations that represent children's core knowledge in a domain that can be applied to the full range of tasks that domain entails" (Case & Okamoto, 1996, p. v). Case and Okamoto (1996) described central conceptual structures in numerical, spatial, and social domains. Each of these three major central conceptual structures becomes increasingly complex with age, and thus at age 6, all three central conceptual structures focus on a single dimension, whereas at age 8, each conceptual structure can coordinate two dimensions. For example, 6-year-olds' space conceptual structure represents either the shape or the location of objects in an isolated manner, whereas 8-year-olds' conceptual structure represents the shape and location of objects simultaneously.

Piaget and neo-Piagetians depict a linear and orderly picture of how intelligence grows. However, more recent findings suggest that cognitive development is considerably more complex and children's thinking far more variable than depicted in these models (Flavell, 1982, 1992; Siegler & Ellis, 1996). The variability in children's thinking is greater among different tasks that measure understanding of the same concept and within individual children's thinking about a single concept than Piaget realized. Another limitation of Piagetian and neo-Piagetian theories is the underestimation of early conceptual competencies. Recent research indicates that very young children are far more cognitively competent than Piaget believed, especially in such central domains as mechanics, biology, and psychology (e.g., Gopnik & Meltzoff, 1997; Wellman & Gelman, 1998).

INFORMATION-PROCESSING THEORIES. Perhaps the most obvious weakness of the psychometric and Piagetian approaches is that they provide little specific explanation concerning the processes in-

volved in intellectual change. In contrast, the issue of how intellectual change occurs is central within information-processing theories. The fundamental assumptions of information-processing theories are that the human mind is a complex, symbol-manipulating system through which information flows and that changes in mental functioning occur through some combination of improvements in basic capacities, strategies, and content knowledge (Klahr, 1992). In general, instead of a focus on stages of intellectual development, the emphasis of information-processing approaches is on precise-analyses of the mechanisms that produce intellectual development.

Several information-processing theorists have posited that change is produced by the process of self-modification; in other words, the outcomes of children's own intellectual activities lead to changes in the way they think. An example of this self-modification process can be found in Siegler and Shipley's (1995) strategy-choice model. In this model, children's use of a variety of arithmetic strategies to solve problems leads to increased knowledge about the overall effectiveness of the strategies, the difficulty of specific problems, and the relative effectiveness of each strategy on subclasses of problems. The knowledge gained from using the strategies, in turn, influences children's future strategy choices. Similarly, in Klahr's self-modifying production systems (e.g., Klahr & MacWhinney, 1998; Simon & Klahr, 1995), new productions are created, and existing productions are modified as a result of the system's activities.

A recent, important extension of information-processing approaches is the connectionist approach. Connectionist systems are computer simulations that consist of a large number of elementary processing units (*nodes*) that are connected by a set of pathways (*links*). Most such simulations are organized into three layers: input, output, and hidden layers. Each layer has numerous nodes. When a problem is presented, the nodes of the input layer provide an initial representation of it. The nodes of the output layer produce the system's response to the problem. The nodes within the hidden layer combine the information from input and output units in complex, nonlinear computations that determine their own activation. The nodes typically are connected within a given layer and between layers. A given unit fires when the amount of activation it receives exceeds a threshold. Knowledge, concepts, strategies, and rules are represented implicitly as patterns of connections among the units in the system rather than explicitly.

Within connectionist models, learning occurs through associative competition among the elementary processing units. Learning is a process of reducing the discrepancy between the system's output and the correct output. Once the system is shown the correct answer to a problem, it changes the strengths of connections among the processing units in ways that reduce the discrepancy. Connectionist simulations have successfully modeled the processes involved in children's acquisition of knowledge of object permanence; phonology; grammar; balance scales; number conservation; time, speed, and distance concepts; and many other aspects of intellectual development (MacWhinney & Chang, 1995; Marchman, 1992; McClelland, 1995; Munakta, McClelland, Johnson, & Siegler, 1997; Shultz, Schmidt, Buckingham, & Mareschal, 1995).

Recent Approaches

Over the past two decades, several new theories of intellectual development have been proposed. Three of the most influential are *privileged-domains theories, sociocultural theories*, and *cognitive-evolution theories*.

PRIVILEGED-DOMAINS THEORIES. Although Piaget viewed intelligence as a unified whole that governs understanding of concepts in all domains, and information-processing approaches search for domain-general processes that underlie learning in all domains, privileged-domain theories search for specialized abilities and conceptual structures that are unique to evolutionarily important domains (Carey, 1985; Keil, 1994; Gelman & Williams, 1998; Wellman & Gelman, 1992, 1998). Within this view, human cognition does not depend on a single, domain-general system. Rather, the mind is fundamentally domain-specific. That is, cognitive abilities are specialized to process and represent specific types of information.

Infant's and young children's surprisingly advanced understanding of certain important areas has led some researchers to hypothesize that infants are born equipped with special learning mecha-nisms for acquiring information in domains that are important to human functioning (Gallistel, Brown, Gelman, & Keil, 1991; Gelman & Williams, 1998; Keil, 1989). These domains include learning language, perceiving objects, recognizing faces, identifying living and nonliving things, and learning numbers.

Gelman (1990; Gelman & Williams, 1998) has proposed one such account of concept learning. She averred that intellectual development in core domains starts with core skeletal structures that include knowledge of what to attend to and encode in relevant environments. The skeletal structures also set a range of possible interpretations of the stimuli, thus enhancing the efficiency of learning. Experience, in turn, results in elaboration of these structures. From the earliest days of life, children greatly benefit as learners from the innate skeletal structures that organize core domains.

One good example of a domain-specific skeletal structure can be seen in young children's understanding of living things (Keil, 1989, 1994). After hearing a story about a skunk that was surgically altered so that it looked like a raccoon, children reported that the animal was still a skunk, despite its altered appearance. However, children did not reason in the same way when they heard similar stories about artifacts; a key that was melted down and stamped into pennies was no longer a key. Thus, even preschool children possess certain abstract, informal, core structures that enable them to understand animate things as distinct from artifacts. These core structures are hypothesized to be critical to the development and acquisition of more elaborated knowledge.

A related way of thinking about how young children are able to learn evolutionarily important information quite quickly is to posit the existence of constraints that limit the range of hypotheses that they consider. This approach has been used to explain the rapidity of children's vocabulary acquisition (Markman, 1992; Woodward & Markman, 1998). Markman and her coworkers have focused on three constraints on word learning: (1) the *whole object constraint*, by which children assume that a word used to label an object refers to the object as a whole rather than to its parts or properties; (2) the *taxonomic constraint*, by which children assume that a word applies to all other objects of the same class rather than only to the individual object; and (3) the *mutual exclusivity constraint*, by which children assume that each object has a single name. These constraints help young children learn the names of objects without much trial and error; in a sense, they predispose them to guess correctly more often than not. Thus, constraints, like skeletal structures, increase the efficiency of learning by channeling children's efforts in fruitful directions.

A third approach to the issue of how young children learn certain types of information as quickly as they do is to assume that they possess rudimentary theories of especially important domains. Three theories have received the most attention: a theory of physics (e.g., Spelke, 1994), a theory of psychology (e.g., Flavell & Miller, 1998), and a theory of biology (e.g., Hatano & Inagaki, 1994). These theories are not axiomatic, logically-consistent, tightly-organized systems like theories of physics. Rather, they are defined by four less stringent criteria: fundamental categories unique to the domain, causal explanations unique to the domain, unobservable explanatory constructs, and coherent organization (Wellman & Gelman, 1998). Nascent theories appear to be present quite early: from birth for the theory of physics, from 18 months for the theory of psychology, and from 2 or 3 years for the theory of biology (Wellman & Gelman, 1998). The theories help children learn by providing a basis for predicting and interpreting occurrences in novel situations and for organizing a large number of particulars in terms of a small set of causal principles that apply to different types of entities. For example, even 7-month-olds realize that different causal principles apply to people and to inanimate objects as indicated by their showing suprise when an inanimate object appears to start moving on its own but not when a person does.

Privileged-domain theories have helped to motivate research by demonstrating that key concepts and reasoning skills in important domains begin their development far earlier than previously believed. They also have provided intriguing explanations of why young children sometimes learn rapidly. Yet these theories have not described the domain-specific learning mechanisms that are said to produce this rapid learning. They also have not indicated how children's experiences and performance in specific domains contribute to their conceptual understanding; the conceptual understanding is simply said to be present without explication of how it is acquired and elaborated (see Gelman, 1997; Siegler, 1997; Sophian, 1997, for recent discussions of these issues). Active pursuit of these issues should lead to a deeper understanding of why children are able to learn so quickly in certain domains.

SOCIOCULTURAL THEORIES. Traditional approaches to intellectual development have paid relatively little attention to the fact that learning usually occurs in a world of other people. Instead of viewing the child within a social and cultural context, most theories have focused on the mental structures that individual children construct. According to sociocultural theories, however, intellectual development cannot be understood without placing children's thinking in a sociocultural context and considering the social interactions in which children participate.

The sociocultural perspective has its roots in Vygotsky and Leont'ev's sociohistorical theories. They viewed individual development as an aspect of sociohistorical activities and held that children and their social environment collaborate to mold intelligence in culturally adaptive ways. Extending this perspective, contemporary sociocultural theories examine how sociocultural contexts and interactions shape development. They view the child participating in ongoing activity, generally involving other people, as the best unit at which to analyze intellectual development (Miller, 1993; Rogoff, 1998).

Cultures differ in the kinds of thinking that are valued and in the ways that concepts and skills are learned (Ceci, 1990; Rogoff, 1998; Sternberg, 1997). For example, children's mathematical learning is influenced by parents' values, beliefs, and knowledge; other adults' teaching efforts and interaction styles; and the technologies and number systems available in the culture (Miller, Smith, Zhu, & Zhang, 1995; Stevenson, Lee, & Stigler, 1986).

Studies inspired by sociocultural theories have shown that parents help children learn by identifying goals, encouraging children to find ways to achieve the goals, and discussing strategies with them (Azmitia, 1996; Ellis & Rogoff, 1986). Parents also adjust the level of their assistance in response to children's level of success or errors on the tasks. The extent to which parents make these adjustments is positively related to learning (Rogoff,

Radziszewska, & Masliello, 1995; Saxe, Gearhart, & Guberman, 1984). Children also actively shape their own learning through use of available tools, strategies, and skills.

At present, sociocultural theories serve more as a framework for thinking about development and as a motivation to consider the social, cultural, and historical context within which children learn than as a clear set of empirical principles and predictions. Given the growing amount of research within this tradition, such principles and predictions may soon emerge.

COGNITIVE-EVOLUTION THEORIES. Several recent models of intellectual development have drawn analogies between the evolution of species and the evolution of children's thinking (Changeux & Dehaene, 1989; Cziko, 1995; Siegler, 1996; Thelen, 1992). For example, Siegler's (1996) overlapping waves theory holds that, as in the biological domain, variation, selection, and inheritance are the engines that drive cognitive change. In particular, the overlapping waves theory hypothesizes that (1) at any one time, children think in a variety of ways about most phenomena; (2) these varied ways of thinking compete with each other for a prolonged period of time; and (3) the more advanced ways of thinking gradually become increasingly frequent. These assumptions are illustrated in Figure 5.2. Thus, cognitive-evolution theories raise such questions as what is the set of alternative approaches that children use at a given age, what factors influence their choice of which approach

to use in specific circumstances, and what mechanisms lead to discovery of new approaches and changing distributions of choices among existing approaches.

The overlapping waves pattern of data illustrated in Figure 5.2 has been observed across ages ranging from infancy to old age and across such varied tasks as serial recall, arithmetic, time telling, spelling, reading, motor activity, rule learning, tool use, moral reasoning, and scientific reasoning. In all of these areas, children have been found to use multiple strategies at any given age with the variability existing within individual subjects as well as between them. In all of the domains, children also have been found to shift toward the more advanced approaches with age and experience. Siegler and colleagues have proposed computational models to account for children's strategy choices and discoveries on these tasks (Shrager & Siegler, 1998; Siegler & Shipley, 1995). The basic assumption about learning that underlies these models is that the problem-solving process yields information about the effectiveness of each strategy on different types of problems, which shapes the system's future strategy selections (see Figure 5.3). The model of discovery creates new candidate strategies from subroutines within existing strategies; those candidate strategies that are in accord with the principles that underlie legitimate addition strategies are then tried. If they prove effective relative to previously available strategies, their use increases; if not, they are soon abandoned.

Evolutionary theories bring to the foreground the fact that at every level of cognitive development children's thinking is much more varied than

FIGURE 5.2. An overlapping waves depiction of a typical pattern of intellectual development.

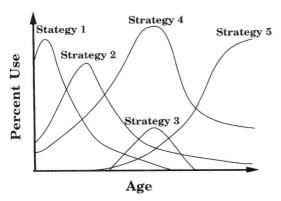

FIGURE 5.3. Overview of the Siegler & Shipley (1995) adaptive strategy choice model.

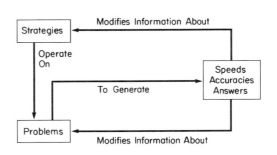

stage theories or privileged-domains theories have assumed. Examining varied ways of thinking not only allows a more accurate depiction of cognitive growth than has been available previously, it also facilitates efforts to understand the process of change. Like the privileged-domains and sociocultural theories, however, it is a theory of an important part of cognitive development rather than a theory of cognitive development as a whole. Integrating its findings about cognitive change with findings on early competence and the role of the sociocultural context is among the major challenges facing evolutionary theories.

Thus far, we have briefly described some major theories of intellectual development. In the remainder of the chapter, we examine recent empirical work in an area that is central to all of the theories: problem solving and learning. Effective problem solving and learning have been considered to be hallmarks of intelligence since early in the history of intelligence research. Illustratively, such skills figured prominently in experts' definitions of intelligence at a 1921 symposium on this topic (e.g., Colvin, 1921; Dearborn, 1921; Woodrow, 1921). In the next section, we discuss recent research on the development of problem solving and learning with the focus on early competencies and on the process of intellectual change.

RECENT RESEARCH ON CHILDREN'S PROBLEM SOLVING AND LEARNING

Early Competencies

Over the last 20 years, a vast amount of evidence has been obtained concerning infants' conceptual understanding. Infants have been shown to have far more understanding than previously hypothesized of such key concepts as object permanence, number, time, space, and mechanics. This research has been well described in several recent reviews (e.g., Baillargeon, 1994; Haith & Benson, 1998; Spelke & Newport, 1998; Wellman & Gelman, 1998) and therefore will not be the focus of our discussion.

Under facilitative conditions, infants also display impressive reasoning and problem-solving skills, including causal inferences, deferred imitation, means-end analysis, transfer of cognitive skills, and analogical problem solving. These discoveries have received less attention in recent reviews; we therefore discuss them below.

CAUSAL INFERENCE. The ability to draw causal inferences is vital for almost all reasoning and problem solving. It is not surprising, therefore, that infants draw causal inferences from early in the first year. In one of the first demonstrations of this ability, Leslie (1984) habituated 6-month-old infants to a "launching" event in an animated film in which a moving red brick made contact with a green brick and "caused" the green brick to move immediately along an appropriate trajectory. Infants dishabituated when shown sequences in which the green brick started moving before the red brick hit it or when a temporal delay occurred between the time of contact and the subsequent movement.

More recent research by Oakes and Cohen (1990, 1994) using more realistic objects pinpointed a developmental change in infants' causal understanding. After habituating to a causal event, 6- and 7-month-olds typically did not respond differentially to movement that occurred immediately after contact, a few seconds after contact, or before contact. They also did not dishabituate to a greater extent if the object that was struck moved at a perpendicular angle to the motion of the object that struck it than if it moved in a more standard path. In contrast, 10-month-olds dishabituated to a greater extent to the nonimmediate, noncontact, and perpendicular movement sequences (Oakes & Cohen, 1990; Oakes, 1994). Thus, during the first year of life, causal understanding increases considerably, which provides a basis for improvements in representing and imitating sequential actions, solving analogy problems, and planning and transferring problem-solving strategies.

DEFERRED IMITATION. Piaget (1952) argued that infants younger than 18 months are incapable of imitating novel actions that happened hours or days earlier because they cannot mentally represent the original event. More recent findings, however, indicate that infants as young as 6 months are capable of imitating novel activities, such as pressing a recessed button on a box to trigger a beeping sound, even after a 24-hour delay (Barr, Dowden, & Hayne, 1996).

Bauer and Mandler (1989) modeled more complex action sequences, such as those involving three sequential actions, and found that 1-year-olds accurately reproduced the event sequences. One such sequence involved making a rattle by putting a block into a barrel, covering it up, and shaking it. Toddlers and infants not only reenacted the modeled actions when later encountering the same props but also generalized the actions to novel materials when some of the original props were replaced by new ones (Bauer & Dow, 1994). Other studies (Barnat, Klein, & Meltzoff, 1996) showed that 14-month-olds generalized the observed action sequences across test contexts. Toddlers also can make use of the causal relations among event sequences to organize their representations (Mandler & McDonough, 1995). Infants reproduced action sequences more systematically when the actions had enabling relations (e.g., in the rattle example, the actions must be performed in a given order for the rattle to function) than when the order of actions was arbitrary (Bauer & Mandler, 1989, 1992).

Although infants as young as 6 months exhibit deferred imitation for two-step events delayed over a week (Barr, Dowden, & Hayne, 1996), deferred imitation improves with age. Older toddlers reproduce observed actions more systematically than younger children (Bauer & Dow, 1994), imitate more complex multiple-action sequences (Bauer & Hertagaard, 1993), generalize the actions more widely (Barr, Dowden, & Hayne, 1996), and remember the actions longer (Meltzoff, 1988a, 1988b). Such deferred imitation demonstrates that infants are capable of constructing enduring internal representations. The imitation provides infants with a powerful learning tool that makes possible the acquisition of problem-solving strategies they see other people use.

MEANS-ENDS ANALYSIS. Means-ends analysis involves comparing a goal with a current situation and reducing the differences between them until the goal is met. Like causal inference and deferred imitation, this ability is present by the end of the first year. Willatts (1984) presented 9-month-olds with a foam rubber barrier behind which was a cloth. Infants in the experimental condition encountered a configuration in which a small, attractive toy rested on the far end of the cloth. Those in the control condition saw a configuration in which the toy was beside, rather than on top of, the cloth. The task in the experimental condition required infants to retrieve the toy by first removing the barrier and then pulling the cloth on which the toy was supported. Willatts found that infants in the experi-

mental group typically removed the barrier and then went on to pull the cloth and retrieve the toy. In contrast, infants in the control group tended to pick up the barrier, play with it, and ignore the cloth. The results suggested that 9-month-olds could plan appropriate solutions.

Willatts and Rosie (1988) showed that slightly older infants also apply means-ends analysis to three-step tasks. In the experimental condition, 10- to 12-month-olds were presented a barrier located in front of a piece of cloth on which a string rested. The other end of the string was attached to a toy. Retrieving the toy required removing the barrier, pulling the cloth, and grasping and pulling the string. In the control condition, infants saw the same arrangement of barrier, cloth, string, and toy, except that the toy could not be retrieved because it was not attached to the string. Children in the experimental condition were more likely to remove the barrier, were quicker to contact and pull the cloth, and more often pulled the string and retrieved the toy. Thus, by the end of their first year, infants can systematically reduce the distance between their current state and goal attainment until the goal is achieved.

TRANSFER OF COGNITIVE SKILLS. Very young children have also been found able to transfer skills (Brown, 1989; Case, 1985). For example, Brown (1990) trained 2- and 3-year-old children to use a rake or hook to bring a toy within reach. The tools were painted with a red and white candy-cane pattern. After successfully using the tool to obtain the goal object, the child was provided with another set of tools. These included a tool that shared surface features but not functional features with the original tool (a candy-cane patterned straight stick) and a tool that shared functional but not surface features with it (a solid-colored hook). Children tended to select the tool that was functionally similar to the training tools and thus successfully transferred the problem solution.

Chen, Sanchez, and Campbell (1997) demonstrated that even younger children can transfer some skills. Ten- and 13-month-olds attempted to solve problems that required combining two subgoals to bring a toy within reach. The procedure involved presenting each infant with three tasks that differed in surface features but that could be solved by pursuing the same sequence of subgoals. Each task possessed a similar structure to those used by Willatts and Rosie (1988) and described two paragraphs ago. The three successively presented problems differed in the surface characteristics of the barriers, strings, cloths, and toys.

Infants initially were given several opportunities to solve the first problem. Regardless of the success of these efforts, actions that would obtain the toy were then modeled by the experimenter, and the child was encouraged to imitate them. Thirteen-month-olds demonstrated effective transfer of the modeled solution strategy across the three isomorphic problems. One-fourth of this older group successfully solved the first problem, and over 50% solved the second and third problems. The 10-month-olds also learned and transferred the solution strategy to a subsequent problem but only after seeing the adult solve two problems. These findings indicate that 1-year-olds can construct relatively abstract and flexible representations by extracting a common solution principle from isomorphic problems even when few superficial features are shared.

ANALOGICAL PROBLEM SOLVING. Piaget (Inhelder & Piaget, 1958; Piaget, 1952) claimed that solving classical analogies requires formal-operational reasoning, which does not emerge until early adolescence. Essentially consistent with this view, subsequent studies indicated that children below 10 years of age experience difficulty in solving clas-

sical analogy problems (Sternberg & Rifkin, 1979). To explain these and other findings, Gentner (1989) proposed that young children focus on surface features and only older children focus on deeper structural relations.

These conclusions, however, have been challenged by recent findings concerning young children's analogical and symbolic reasoning (DeLoache, 1995; Goswami, 1996). Goswami and Brown (1990a,b) proposed that young children experience difficulty in solving classic analogy problems not because they are incapable of detecting and mapping structural relations but because they are not familiar with the particular tasks. To test this interpretation, Goswami and Brown (1990b) presented 4-year-olds with simple analogy tasks whose content was familiar to them, such as bird:nest::dog:?. The children needed to select the picture from among four possibilities that would best complete the analogy. As shown in Figure 5.4, the four pictures included one that was the best completion (a doghouse), one that was an associate (a bone), one that was a member of the same superordinate category as well as being semantically related (a cat), and one that was a member of the same basic level category (another dog). Even 4-year-olds most often selected the correct completion for the analogy, thus demonstrating that they can appreciate analogical relations and override lower order relations.

PROCESS MODELS OF EARLY COMPETENCE. As indicated in this section, research over the past two

FIGURE 5.4. An example of analogical problem-solving tasks used by Goswami and Brown (1990b).

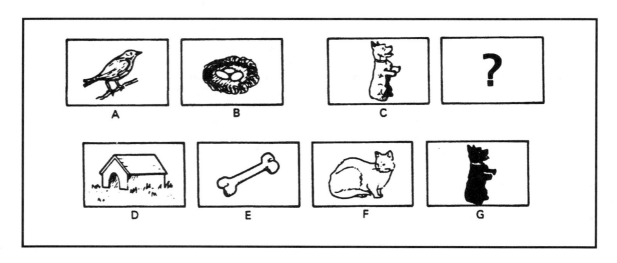

decades has revealed impressive intellectual competencies in infants and young children. These demonstrations, however, have rarely been accompanied by explanations of the developmental process by which children acquire these abilities. The challenge is to explain why very young children display relatively advanced knowledge and skill in some situations, but also why considerably older ones fail to display comparable knowledge and skill in other situations.

One of the few such explanations that has been generated is a recent connectionist model of the development of object permanence (Munakata et al., 1997). In this model, the system repeatedly was presented codes that corresponded to a barrier and an object; the barrier moved back and forth, occluding the object during part of its movement. The system learned from the experience gradually and went from initially maintaining object representations only through short occlusions to maintaining the representations over longer and longer ones. With a small amount of experience, the network's internal representation of an occluded object was sufficient to drive a low threshold output such as looking. With more training, the representation of the occluded object developed sufficiently to allow more complex forms of output such as reaching. The model thus demonstrated a way in which looking measures could reveal representations of occluded objects long before reaching measures indicated object permanence, as defined by Piaget. It also illustrates how seeing objects disappear behind barriers and reappear on the other side of them could lead to competence via looking and reaching measures.

Munakata et al. (1997) is one of the few studies that have modeled how changes occur in infants' thinking. In research with older children, however, the process of change has increasingly become a central topic. It is to this subject that we now turn.

Later Developments

Several recent models of cognitive development in older children have emphasized variability of thinking, transition, and nonlinear change. For example, dynamic systems theories (Fischer & Bidell, 1998; Fischer & Granott, 1995; Molenaar, 1986; Thelen, 1992; Thelen & Smith, 1998; Van Geert, 1994) address the issue of what circumstances lead to the developing system being stable, what circumstances lead it to change, and what occurs during periods of change. Two key assumptions of such dynamic systems approaches are that general dynamic principles determine the degree of stability that is present at any given time and that, during periods of rapid change, diverse ways of thinking and acting coexist and compete. Research in a wide variety of domains supports these basic assumptions, as described in the following paragraphs.

MICROGENETIC METHODS. Studying intellectual growth requires observing the changing ways of thinking while the changes are occurring. Traditional cross-sectional and longitudinal designs do not allow precise analyses of change. The observations of intellectual competence are separated too far in time for much to be learned about the change process. These traditional methods of studying development leave open a large number of possible pathways to change, especially because changes in children's thinking often do not proceed by the most direct route we can imagine. Children discover new approaches, temporarily abandon superior new ways of thinking, and regress to less sophisticated approaches. Different children also follow different paths to learning (e.g., Karmiloff-Smith, 1984; Piaget, 1971).

Microgenetic methods offer a promising way to meet the challenges inherent in trying to understand such complex changes (Kuhn, Garcia-Mila, Zohar, & Anderson, 1995; Siegler & Crowley, 1991). The approach is defined by three characteristics: (1) an observation period spanning the time from the beginning of the period of rapid change to the stable use of target ways of thinking; (2) a high density of observations relative to the rate of change; and (3) intensive, trial-by-trial assessments of ongoing cognitive changes, both qualitative and quantitative.

A study conducted by Karmiloff-Smith (1986) illustrates how microgenetic methods can yield information about change that could not emerge from traditional cross-sectional or longitudinal designs. Children were asked repeatedly to draw maps for an ambulance driver to follow in getting to a hospital. From the first drawing to the final one, children's maps improved substantially; that was not surprising. More surprising was the frequent regressions from more informative, or more efficient maps, to less informative or less efficient forms. For example, children often figured out how to draw efficient maps without redundant information, then drew maps with redundant information, and then returned to the earlier, less efficient forms. Without the trial-by-trial analyses afforded by the microgenetic approach, such regressions would not have been discovered.

Microgenetic methods have been adopted by researchers with a variety of theoretical perspectives: Piagetian, neo-Piagetian, sociocultural, information processing, and dynamic systems. The approach has proved useful for studying infants (Adolph, 1997), preschoolers (e.g., Siegler & Jenkins, 1989), school-age children (e.g., Coyle & Bjorklund, 1997), adolescents and college students (Kuhn et al., 1995), and elderly adults (Siegler & Lemaire, 1997). It has proved useful for studying diverse domains, including development of motor skills (Thelen, 1984), attentional strategies (Miller & Aloise-Young, 1996), memory strategies (Bjorklund, Coyle, & Gaultney, 1992), arithmetic (Alibali & Goldin-Meadow, 1993), conceptual understanding (Church & Goldin-Meadow, 1986), social problem solving (Wertsch & Hickmann, 1987), scientific reasoning (Kuhn et al., 1995; Schauble, 1996), pictorial representation (Karmiloff-Smith, 1986, 1992), and analogical reasoning (Chen & Klahr, in press). Microgenetic methods also have proved revealing for studying such fundamental issues as developmental differences in learning (Kuhn et al., 1995; Schauble, 1996), differences in learning between children with higher and lower IQs, and differences in learning of children with more and less prior knowledge of the content domain (Johnson & Mervis, 1994).

Despite this variation in populations and content domains, microgenetic studies have yielded several consistent findings concerning the way in which intellectual change occurs. Three of the most consistent findings include the high degree of variability in individual children's thinking, the adaptiveness of their strategy choices throughout the learning process, and the halting and uneven ways in which new strategies are discovered and generalized. The large majority of this microgenetic research has been performed with 4-year-olds and older children, but, where available, research with infants and toddlers will also be noted.

VARIABILITY OF THINKING. Studies that have assessed children's thinking on a trial-by-trial basis have consistently found substantial variability. This variability is not limited to different individuals using different strategies, though people certainly do differ in their strategy use. Instead, the variability exists within individual children as well as between them. Infants who crawl down a ramp on one trial will slide down on their bellies on another trial and will slide in a sitting position on a third trial (Adolph, 1997). One- and 2-year-olds who attempt to obtain an out-of-reach toy by turning to their parent for help on one trial will attempt to climb on the table on another trial, reach for an effective tool for reeling in the toy on another trial, and reach for an ineffective tool on another trial (Chen & Siegler, 1998). Four- and 5-year-olds who solve one simple addition problem by counting from 1 will solve another by counting from the larger of the two addends and will solve a third by retrieving the answer from memory (Geary & Burlingham-Dubree, 1989; Siegler & Shrager, 1984). Nine-year-olds who recall categorically related objects by rehearsing the individual names on one trial will recall them by physically sorting the objects on another trial and by naming categories on a third (Coyle & Bjorklund, 1997). Twelve-year-olds and adults who perform systematic scientific experiments in one trial will perform uncontrolled experiments in another (Kuhn et al., 1995; Schauble, 1996).

Part of this variability is attributable to different problems' eliciting different distributions of strategies. That is not the whole story, however. Even when presented the same problem on two occasions close in time, children use different strategies quite often. In studies of single-digit addition, number conservation, and time telling, children have been found to use different strategies on roughly one-third of trials when identical problems are presented earlier and later (Siegler, 1995; Siegler & McGilly, 1989; Siegler & Shrager, 1984). This variability is not attributable to learning. The changes have been from more advanced to less advanced strategies almost as often as they are from less advanced to more advanced ones. It also is notable that the variability is present even in problems such as number conservation, where one strategy, relying on the type of transformation that was performed, is logically superior to others, such as relying on the relative lengths of the rows.

The variability of thinking is even evident within a single trial. Studies that have examined gesture and speech have frequently noted that children's gestures express more advanced understanding than their verbal statements (Alibali & Goldin-Meadow, 1993; Church & Goldin-Meadow, 1986; Perry, Church, & Goldin-Meadow, 1988). Children often use varying combinations of memory strategies in different trials (Coyle & Bjorklund, 1997).

This variability is not limited to brief transition periods. Rather, it is characteristic of long stretches of development, and, in at least some cases, is present from early in development through adulthood. In single-digit addition, for example, multiple strategies are used by the large majority of children between ages 4 and 9 years (Geary & Burlingham-Dubree, 1989; Siegler, 1987). Even among adults, roughly half use strategies such as counting from the larger addend and decomposing problems into two simpler problems to solve single-digit addition problems (LeFevre, Sadesky, & Bisanz, 1996).

This variability is important not just for an accurate description of thinking but also for understanding learning. Microgenetic studies have revealed that the amount of variability in the performance of a task before children receive relevant experience with it is positively correlated with how well children learn from the experience (Alibali & Goldin-Meadow, 1993; Coyle & Bjorklund, 1997; Graham & Perry, 1993; Siegler, 1995). In one such demonstration, Perry, Church, and Goldin-Meadow (1988) found that 9- and 10-year-olds' speech and gestures on mathematical equality problems fairly often showed mismatches on a given trial. Those children who showed such mismatches on a pretest were more likely to benefit from instruction than those who did not. Similarly, 5-year-olds who used a greater number of strategies on a pretest, and more often used multiple strategies on a single pretest trial, learned more from a conservation training procedure (Siegler, 1995). This relation to learning was among the reasons that Miller and Coyle (1998) concluded, "Variability clearly is a theoretically interesting phenomenon rather than an uninteresting nuisance to be eliminated by pretraining or practice trials" (p. 9).

STRATEGY CHOICES. Knowing multiple strategies creates a need to select which one to use on each new problem. From surprisingly young ages, children choose adaptively among the strategies they know. For example, one common choice is whether to state an answer retrieved from memory or to use a backup strategy (a strategy other than retrieval) to generate the answer. This choice is one that children face when solving simple arithmetic problems, when reading and spelling words, when remembering phone numbers, and in many other situations. The complexity of the choice stems from the fact that retrieval is faster than other approaches and also yields very accurate answers on some problems but leads to inaccurate answers on other problems. From very young ages, children choose in a very sensible way; the easier the problem, the more often they rely on retrieval (Geary & Burlingham-Dubree, 1989; Siegler, 1986). Similarly, when choosing among alternative backup strategies, children are especially likely to choose a strategy that works well on that type of problem. When solving an addition problem with a large difference between the addends, such as $2 + 9$, first and second graders are especially likely to count from the larger addend rather than counting from 1 (Siegler, 1987).

Strategy choices are influenced not only by problem difficulty but also by the episodic success of strategies. Children are more likely to switch strategies from one trial to the next when the strategy did not yield success on the previous trial (Coyle & Bjorklund 1997). The combination of being wrong on the immediately preceding trial and also having used a strategy that had a higher rate of success is especially likely to lead to strategy switching on the next trial (McGilly & Siegler, 1989).

Microgenetic studies have revealed that strategy choices tend to be adaptive from early in the learning process but also that they become increasingly adaptive with experience. In a study by Lemaire and Siegler (1995), second graders were presented single-digit multiplication problems three times: the first presentation was about a week after multiplication instruction began, the second was two months later, and the third was four months after that. Even on the first testing occasion, strategy choices were quite adaptive. However, the adaptiveness of the choices (measured by the correlation between problem difficulty and frequency of use of retrieval on that problem) increased substantially from the first to the second testing and somewhat more from the second to the third testing.

Another study of a totally different domain with much younger subjects showed a similar pattern. From early in learning, infants who needed to locomote down ramps tended to adopt more conservative strategies (e.g., sliding on their back) when the ramp was steeper. However, adjustment of strategies to the steepness of the ramp became increasingly precise with age and locomotor experience (Adolph, in press).

THE DISCOVERY PROCESS. Microgenetic methods have yielded particularly interesting information about the circumstances and behaviors that accompany generation of new ways of thinking. They make possible examination of what led up to discoveries, what the experience of discovery is like, and how new discoveries are generalized beyond their initial context.

One consistent finding is that generation of new approaches occurs when existing approaches have been successful as well as when they have led to failure. A number of models of discovery have followed the adage, "Necessity is the mother of invention" (e.g., Newell, 1990; van Lehn, 1990). These models generate new approaches only when existing approaches fail. Microgenetic observations, however, indicate that discoveries occur following successes as well. For example, Miller and Aloise-Young (1996) found that 71% of preschoolers' initial uses of the optimal strategy during a selective attention task followed success with the previous problem. Karmiloff-Smith (1986) made similar observations concerning older children's discoveries on a map-drawing task, as did Siegler and Jenkins (1989) with simple arithmetic and Siegler (1995) with number conservation. Thus, discovery does not require prior failure.

A second consistent finding is that performance during the trial of discovery and often in the immediately preceding trials tends to be halting, fragmented, and weakly organized. One sign is unclear explanations. On the trial of discovery and immediately before it, children tend to give a greater number of vague explanations than at other times (Graham & Perry, 1993). They generate more disfluencies, false starts, repairs, and long pauses than they typically do (Alibali, McNeil, & Perrott, 1996; Perry & Lewis, 1999; Siegler, 1989) and their explanations more often diverge from their gestures (Alibali & Goldin-Meadow, 1993; Perry & Goldin-Meadow 1988). On some tasks, they continue to maintain that they are using longstanding strategies for at least a few trials after nonverbal indices unambiguously indicate that they are using a new, more insightful, approach (Siegler & Stern, 1998).

A third characteristic of strategy discoveries that has been revealed by microgenetic studies is their limited immediate generalization. Adults as well as children who generate precise experiments on scientific reasoning tasks often regress to generating confounded experiments soon after (Kuhn et al., 1995; Kuhn & Phelps, 1982; Schauble, 1990; 1996). Children who discover advanced number conservation and insightful arithmetic strategies often soon regress to previous, less advanced approaches (Siegler, 1995; Siegler & Jenkins, 1989; Siegler & Stern, 1998).

A fourth characteristic is that newly discovered strategies often do not lead to immediate improvements in performance even though they will in the long run. This phenomenon has been labeled a "utilization deficiency" by Miller (1990) and has been found to characterize initial use of several memory and attention strategies (Miller & Seier, 1994). In one microgenetic study that illustrated this phenomenon, Coyle and Bjorklund (1997) showed that for second graders, number of strategies used was consistently unrelated to recall; that for fourth graders, the two were always positively related; and that for third graders, the two were unrelated on earlier trials and positively related on later ones. Apparently, the third graders at first failed to benefit from using more diverse strategies, including newly-generated ones, but with practice became able to do so.

Thus, microgenetic studies have yielded several consistent findings about cognitive variability, strategy choice, and strategy discovery. They also show potential for bringing together insights from traditional developmental and psychometric theories and theories of cognitive evolution. This potential is illustrated in the next section.

INTEGRATING COMPARATIVE AND MICROGE-NETIC STUDIES. The picture of cognitive change yielded by microgenetic studies contrasts with that yielded by comparative studies – studies that contrast children who differ on preexisting status variables such as age, IQ, and expertise. Variability is greater, regressions are more frequent, and immediate benefits of new procedures are less certain in the microgenetic than in the comparative studies. In large part, this is due to the different time grains of microgenetic and comparative studies. The microgenetic studies intensively sample change during the period in which behavior is most variable, in which there are the greatest number of regressions to earlier forms of behavior, and in which benefits in the central task are least certain to accompany strategic changes.

Although the pictures yielded by the two approaches are different, they cannot ultimately be incompatible. After all, it is the same cognitive system that is being described. And careful analyses often show that the differences between groups that differ on status variables are less extreme than they at first appear. For example, although traditional portrayals of many skills depict younger children as consistently using one approach and older children as consistently using a different approach, trial-by-trial examinations often indicate that their strategies overlap and that substantial strategic variability exists at both ages (Siegler, 1996).

Therefore, studies that unite comparative and microgenetic perspectives seem especially promising. Such studies have the potential to indicate exactly how the comparative variables exercise their effects. They can reveal exactly what processes differ between the learning of older and younger children, more and less intelligent children, and children with more and less expertise in the particular area.

A recent study of 4- and 5-year-olds' learning about balance scales (Siegler & Chen, 1998) illustrates the potential of studies that integrate comparative and microgenetic approaches. Previous studies of children's learning about balance scales had established that age and initial encoding are related to learning. Older children and children who encode more of the relevant dimensions learn more from feedback experience than younger children and children whose encoding is less complete (Siegler, 1976, 1978). However, the previous studies had not revealed exactly how the process of learning differs between children who differ in age or previous knowledge. To reveal how age and initial encoding

exercise their effects, Siegler and Chen conducted a microgenetic study of balance-scale learning by children of different ages and different initial knowledge.

The same balance-scale apparatus that had been used in previous studies was again employed. On each side of the fulcrum were four pegs on which metal weights could be placed. The arm of the balance could tip left or right or could remain level, depending on how the weights were arranged. A lever could be set to hold the balance scale's arm motionless, or could be released so that the amount of weight and the location of the weight on each side would determine the arm's movement.

Young children had been found in earlier studies to use one of three approaches on these problems. Most 4-year-olds and some 5-year-olds do not use any task-relevant rule; they guess, alternate between choosing the left and right sides, or proceed in some other way unrelated to either weight or distance from the fulcrum. Other 4-year-olds and most 5-year-olds use an approach that Siegler (1976) labeled Rule I. A child using Rule I predicts which side of the balance scale will go down solely according to the number of weights on each side of the fulcrum. If weight is the same, the child predicts "balance"; otherwise, the child predicts that the side with the greater weight will go down. A small percentage of 5-year-olds, and a larger percentage of older children, use an approach that Siegler (1976) labeled Rule II. Children who use Rule II rely on weight if the two sides have different amounts of weight, but if the weight is equal, they predict that the side with its weight farther from the fulcrum will go down.

Rule use can be assessed through the different predictions yielded by different approaches to particular types of problems. Two types of problems, and the predictions yielded in response to them by each of the three approaches described in the previous paragraph, are shown in Figure 5.5. On weight problems, children who did not use a relevant rule would be accurate far less often than children who used either Rule I or Rule II. On distance problems, children who used no rule would perform at chance, those who used Rule I would be consistently incorrect, and those who used Rule II would be consistently correct.

In Siegler and Chen (1998), 4- and 5-year-olds who used either no rule or Rule I were presented feedback

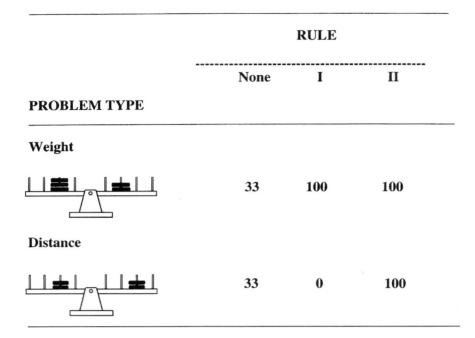

	RULE		
PROBLEM TYPE	**None**	**I**	**II**
Weight	33	100	100
Distance	33	0	100

FIGURE 5.5. Predicted percentage of correct answers on each problem type for children using each balance scale rule.

on a set of distance problems. For each trial during the learning phase, children were asked to predict the scale's behavior. After they observed the outcome, they were asked to explain why that outcome occurred. A rule assessment approach, like that used in the previous studies, was used to assess children's rules before they encountered the feedback problems (the pretest) and after they encountered them (the posttest).

This design allowed us to examine simultaneously the contribution to rule learning of *distal variables* and *proximal variables*. Distal influences on learning are qualities, processes, and knowledge that we can measure before people encounter experiences that promote learning. In this experiment, they included age, pretest rule use, and pretest encoding; in principle, they could include any measure of prior status. Proximal influences on learning are processes that occur within the learning situation. In this situation (and many others), four proximal processes were expected to be present:

Noticing potential explanatory variables that were previously unattended; operationally, children were said to notice the role of distance if they referred to the locations of the disks on at least one of their explanations of why a given side of the balance scale went down.

Formulating a predictive rule; operationally, children were said to have formulated a predictive rule if they at least once stated that a given side went down because its disks were farther from the fulcrum and then on the next trial predicted that the side with its disks farther from the fulcrum would go down.

Generalizing the rule to novel problems; operationally, this meant using the rule on at least 80% of trials after it was formulated.

Maintaining the new rule under less facultative circumstances; operationally, this meant using the new rule on the posttest, where no feedback was given.

The results of this study replicated those of previous studies. All three distal variables that had been shown to influence learning about balance scales once again influenced learning. A regression analysis indicated that pretest rule use accounted for 28% of the variance in whether children used Rule II on the posttest; pretest encoding of distance accounted for an additional 14%, and age accounted for a further 4%. Older children, children whose pretest encoding of distance was more accurate, and children who used Rule I on the pretest were all more likely to learn Rule II.

Analysis of the contribution of the four proximal variables yielded a more detailed portrait of how learning occurred. As shown in Figure 5.6, only 40% of the children ever met the criterion for noticing the locations of the disks. Of those who did, about 75% formulated a rule that included distance as a variable. Of those who formulated such a rule, about 70% generalized the rule to the remaining problems. Finally, of those who generalized the distance rule during the feedback phase, almost 90% used it on the posttest. Thus, in general, failing to notice that distance from the fulcrum varied on the two sides seemed to be the biggest impediment to learning.

Separate analyses of learning of 4-year-olds and of 5-year-olds indicated that noticing the variation in distance was especially problematic for the younger children. As shown in Figure 5.6, only 17% of 4-year-olds noticed variations in distance. Of those who did, about half met the criteria for each subsequent component (bottom panel). In contrast, 64% of 5-year-olds noticed the variation in distance. About 80% of them met each further criterion. Seen from another perspective, almost all of the 4-year-olds who did not learn Rule II failed even to notice distance, whereas almost half of the 5-year-olds who did not learn Rule II noticed distance but failed at a later component. To summarize, failing to notice the variation in distance was the largest impediment to learning, especially for the younger children, but difficulty with each of the subsequent components also led to a considerable number of children not mastering Rule II.

One of the greatest benefits of integrating comparative and microgenetic approaches is that the microgenetic analyses allow us to examine the specific ways in which distal influences exercise their effects. In the Siegler and Chen study, differ-

A

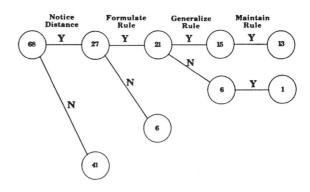

B

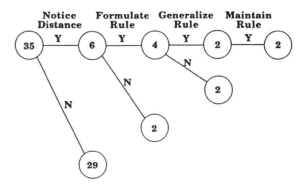

C

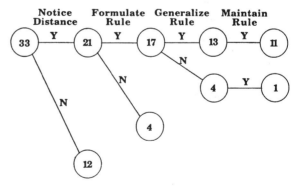

FIGURE 5.6. Number of children in Siegler & Chen (1998) succeeding (top path) and failing (descending branches) in executing each proximal process (Panel A: both ages; Panel B: 4-year-olds; Panel C: 5-year-olds).

ent distal variables predicted whether children succeeded in attaining different learning components. Pretest encoding of distance and age predicted noticing. This made sense; encoding of distance on the pretest indicated that variable was being noticed, and older children, with greater processing resources, presumably can sample the environment more completely and notice more variables. In contrast, within the set of children who noticed variations in distance, whether children used a systematic, task-relevant rule on the pretest (generally Rule I) was the best predictor of whether they formulated a more advanced rule. Again this made sense; children who systematically based predictions on the status of the variable they knew about previously, weight, were more likely to formulate a new rule that included another variable, distance. Finally, within the set of children who formulated a new rule that included distance, pretest rule use predicted generalization of the rule. Once again this made sense because children who used Rule I on the pretest, like those who generalized Rule II during the learning phase, needed to apply the rule consistently once they formulated it.

To summarize, Siegler and Chen's findings indicate that developmental differences in learning arose through two distal variables that were correlated with age – initial rule use and initial encoding – and that helped older children to execute several proximal processes: noticing the potential explanatory role of a key variable, formulating a more advanced rule, and generalizing the rule. Thus, considering the proximal processes at work during the learning phase as well as the distal influences already present at the time of the pretest yielded a richer understanding of cognitive change.

This emphasis on identifying the proximal variables through which distal variables exercise their effects is based on the same logic as Sternberg's (e.g., 1985a) approach to studying intelligence. Sternberg's goal was to identify the sources of high- and low-IQ children's differing performance on a variety of inductive and deductive reasoning tasks. He traced the differing performance to differential execution of both specific proximal processes, such as mapping and application, and families of proximal processes, such as learning components and metacomponents. For example, Sternberg and his colleagues found that high-IQ children especially excel at the execution of learning components (Davidson & Sternberg, 1984; Marr & Sternberg, 1986). The present approach of identifying the proximal variables through which distal variables exercise their effects can be viewed as a generalized version of Sternberg's approach. It is not just IQ and age that

can be examined with this approach; any distal variable, whether it be sex, cultural background, prior knowledge, personality type, or socioeconomic status could all be examined in this way.

SUMMARY AND FUTURE DIRECTIONS

Klahr and Wallace (1976) proposed that there were two central issues in the study of cognitive development: the issue of the innate kernel and the issue of change processes. The first issue corresponded to the question, What capabilities are present from early in life? The second issue corresponded to the question, How do children move beyond these early capabilities to acquire the more advanced capabilities of older children and adults?

We now know a great deal about these questions that we did not know when Klahr and Wallace posed them. Much of this new knowledge concerns infants' and very young children's cognitive capabilities. Simply put, they can think in much more sophisticated ways than anyone realized 15 or 20 years ago. These cognitive capabilities include general problem-solving and learning skills as well as understanding of basic concepts. By their first birthday, infants are able to draw causal inferences, to reason analogically, to perform means–ends analysis, to transfer problem-solving strategies to new contexts, and to form enduring representations that allow them to imitate novel actions that they saw much earlier.

We also have learned a great deal about the process of cognitive growth. We now know that cognition is highly variable throughout development and that the amount of variability is positively correlated with the probability of learning from relevant experiences. We also know that children choose adaptively among strategies from early in the learning process with the choices becoming increasingly adaptive and shaping the future course of development. We also know a fair amount about the discovery of new strategies: that behavior on the trial of discovery, and often just before, tends to be halting, fragmented, and disorganized; that discoveries occur in the context of success, as well as failure; that generalization of most new discoveries is slow; and that immediately after discoveries, children often gain only limited benefit from using the new approach. Finally, we are starting to understand the proximal processes through which broader variables, such as age and IQ, exercise their effects on learning.

What we do not yet know, however, is at least as notable as what we do know. One fundamental area in which our understanding is limited concerns the exact mechanisms that produce cognitive change. The finer grained descriptions of change that have been obtained in the past 15 years considerably constrain the range of possible mechanisms. In particular, the omnipresent variability of cognition and the slow generalization of new ways of thinking indicate that developmental mechanisms do not need to produce sudden, large jumps because that is not the way that children's intellectual development proceeds. Rather, to mirror empirical knowledge of development, change mechanisms must produce cognitive growth in a gradual and incremental fashion. Connectionist and symbolic models represent a start toward the goal of specifying developmental mechanisms, but at present it is only a start. There are simply too few such models to be able to identify and test competing predictions in ways that would lead to empirically based tests and refinements of the proposed mechanisms. As more such models are formulated, exciting progress in testing and refining hypothesized mechanisms should become possible.

A second large gap in our understanding concerns how to integrate current theories of intellectual development. These theories are not so much alternatives to each other as attempts to answer different questions. Privileged-domains theories focus on early competence in a small number of important areas. Sociocultural theories provide a perspective on how participation in social activities influences intellectual development. Cognitive-evolution theories provide detailed accounts of the processes through which children choose among existing strategies and generate new ones. Together with previously formulated psychometric, Piagetian, and information-processing theories, these theories cover a great deal of the vast terrain of intellectual development and contain many insights. However, they remain largely isolated from each other. Integrating the diverse insights and topics addressed by these approaches into a single, coherent theory (or better yet, several alternative coherent theories) remains the largest challenge to understanding intellectual development.

REFERENCES

Ackerman, P. L. (1989). Individual differences and skill acquisition. In P. L. Ackerman, R. J. Sternberg, & R. Glaser (Eds.), *Learning and individual differences: Advances in theory and research*. New York: W.H. Freeman and Company.

Alibali, M. W., & Goldin-Meadow, S. (1993). Gesture-speech mismatch and mechanisms of learning: What the hands reveal about a childs state of mind. *Cognitive Psychology, 25*, 468–523.

Alibali, M. W., McNeil, N. M., & Perrott. (1996). What makes children change their mind: Changes in encoding lead to changes in strategy selection. In M. A. Gernsbacher & S. Derry (Eds.), *Proceedings of the 20th Annual Conference of the Cognitive Science Society* (pp. 36–41). Mahwah, NJ: Erlbaum.

Adolph, K. E. (1997). Learning in the development of infant locomotion. *Monographs of the Society for Research in Child Development, 62*, (3, Serial No. 251).

Azmitia, M. (1996). Peer interactive minds: Developmental, theoretical, and methodological issues. In P. B. Baltes & U. M. Staudinger (Eds.), *Interactive minds: Life-span perspectives on the social foundations of cognition*. New York: Cambridge University Press.

Baillargeon, R. (1994). How do infants learn about the physical world? *Current Directions in Psychological Science, 3*, 133–140.

Barnat, B. B., Klein, P. J., & Meltzoff, A. N. (1996). Deferred imitation across changes in context and object: Memory and generalization in 14-month-old infants. *Infant Behavior and Development, 19*, 241–252.

Barr, R., Dowden, A., & Hayne, H., (1996). Developmental changes in deferred imitation by 6- to 24-month-old infants. *Infant Behavior and Development, 19*, 159–170.

Bauer, P. J., & Dow, G. A. (1994). Episodic memory in 16- and 20-month-old children: Specifics are generalized but not forgotten. *Developmental Psychology, 30*, 403–417.

Bauer, P. J., & Hertsgaard, L. A. (1993). Increasing steps in recall of events: Factors facilitating immediate and long-term memory in 13.5–16.5-month-old children. *Child Development, 64*, 1204–1223.

Bauer, P. J., & Mandler, J. M. (1989). One thing follows another: Effects of temporal structure on 1- to 2-year-olds' recall of events. *Developmental Psychology, 25*, 197–206.

Bauer, P. J., & Mandler, J. M. (1992). Putting the horse before the cart: The use of temporal order in recall of events by one-year-old children. *Developmental Psychology, 28*, 441–452.

Bjorklund, D. F., Coyle, T. R., & Gaultney, J. F. (1992). Developmental differences in the acquisition and maintenance of an organizational strategy: Evidence for utilization deficiency hypothesis. *Journal of Experimental Child Psychology, 54*, 434–438.

Bornstein, M. H. (1985). Infant into adult: Unity to diversity in the development of visual categorization. In

J. Mehler and R. Fox (Eds.), *Neonate cognition: Beyond the blooming buzzing confusion.* Hillsdale, NJ: Erlbaum.

Bornstein, M. H., & Sigman, M. D. (1986). Continuity in mental development from infancy. *Child Development, 57,* 251–274.

Bronson, G. W. (1991). Infant differences in rate of visual encoding. *Child Development, 62,* 44–54.

Brown, A. L. (1989). Analogical learning and transfer: What develops? In S. Vosniadou & A. Ortony (Eds.), *Similarity and analogical reasoning.* New York: Cambridge University Press.

Brown, A. L. (1990). Domain-specific principles affect learning and transfer in children. *Cognitive Science, 14,* 107–133.

Carey, S. (1985). *Conceptual change in childhood.* Cambridge, MA: MIT Press.

Carpenter, P. A., Just, M. A., & Shell, P. (1990). What one intelligence test measures: A theoretical account of the processing in the Raven Progressive Matrices Test. *Psychological Review, 97,* 404–431.

Case, R. (1985). *Intellectual development: A systematic reinterpretation.* New York: Academic Press.

Case, R. (1992). *The mind's staircase: Exploring the conceptual understandings of children's thought and knowledge.* Hillsdale, NJ: Erlbaum.

Case, R., & Okamoto, Y. (1996). The role of central conceptual structures in the development of children's numerial, literacy, and spatial thought. *Monographs of the Society for Research in Child Development 61,* (1–2, Serial No. 246).

Ceci, S. J. (1990). *On intelligence . . . more or less: A bioecological treatise on intellectual development.* Englewood Cliffs, NJ: Prentice Hall.

Changeux, J. P., & Dehaene, S. (1989). Neuronal models of cognitive functions. *Cognition, 33,* 63–109.

Chen, Z., & Klahr, D. (in press). All other things being equal: Children's acquisition of the Control of Variables Strategy. *Child Development.*

Chen, Z., Sanchez, R., & Campbell, T. (1997). From beyond to within their grasp: The rudiments of analogical problem solving in 10- and 13-month-old infants. *Developmental Psychology, 33,* 790–801.

Chen, Z., & Siegler, R. S. (1998, April). *Not beyond their grasp: Microgenetic analyses of infants' strategy discovery and generalization.* Paper presented at the XIth Biennial International Conference on Infant Studies, Atlanta, GA.

Church, R. B., & Goldin-Meadow, S. (1986). The mismatch between gesture and speech as an index of transitional knowledge. *Cognition, 23,* 43–71.

Cole, M. (1996). *Cultural psychology: A once and future discipline.* Cambridge, MA: Harvard University Press.

Colombo, J. (1995). On the neural mechanisms underlying developmental and individual differences in visual fixation in infancy: Two hypotheses. *Developmental Review, 15,* 97–135.

Colombo, J., Freeseman, L. J., Coldren, J. T., & Frick, J. E. (1995). Individual differences in infant fixation duration: Dominance of global versus local stimulus properties. *Cognitive Development, 10,* 271–285.

Colvin, S. (1921). What I conceive intelligence to be. *Journal of Educational Psychology, 12,* 136–139.

Coyle, T. R., & Bjorklund, D. F. (1997). Age differences in, and consequences of, multiple- and variable-strategy use on a multitrial sort-recall task. *Developmental Psychology, 33,* 372–380.

Cziko, G. (1995). *Without miracles: Universal selection theory and the second Darwinian revolution.* Cambridge, MA: MIT Press.

Davidson, J. E., & Sternberg, R. J. (1984). The role of insight in intellectual giftedness. *Gifted Child Quarterly, 28,* 58–64.

Dearborn, W. F. (1921). Intelligence and its measurement: A symposium. *Journal of Educational Psychology, 12,* 210–212.

DeLoache, J. S. (1995). Early symbol understanding and use. *The Psychology of Learning and Motivation.* New York: Academic Press.

Demetriou, A., Efklides, A., & Platsidou, M. (1993). The architecture and dynamics of developing mind. *Monographs of the Society for Research in Child Development* (Serial No. 234).

Ellis, S., & Rogoff, B. (1986). Problem solving in children's management of instruction. In E. Mueller & C. Cooper (Eds.), *Process and outcome in peer relationships.* Orlando, FL: Academic Press.

Fagan, J. F., III, & Detterman, D. H. (1992). The Fagan Test of Infant Intelligence: A technical summary. *Journal of Applied Developmental Psychology, 13,* 173–193.

Fagan, J. F., & Singer, L. T. (1983). Infant recognition memory as a measure of intelligence. In L. P. Lipsitt (Ed.), *Advances in infancy research* (Vol. 2, pp. 31–78). Norwood, NJ: Ablex.

Fischer, K. W., & Bidell, T. R. (1998). Dynamic development of psychological structures in action and thought. In W. Damon (Series Ed.) & R. M. Lerner (Vol. Ed.), *Handbook of child psychology: Vol. 1. Theoretical models of human development* (5th ed.). New York: Wiley.

Fischer, K. W., & Farrar, M. J. (1987). Generalizations about generalization: How a theory of skill development explains both generality and specificity. *International Journal of Psychology, 22,* 643–677.

Fischer, K. W., & Granott, N. (1995). Beyond one-dimensional change: Parallel, concurrent, socially distributed processes in learning and development. *Human Development, 38,* 302–314.

Flavell, J. H. (1982). On cognitive development. *Child Development, 53,* 1–10.

Flavell, J. H. (1992). Cognitive development: Past, present, and future. *Developmental Psychology, 28,* 998–1005.

Flavell, J. H., & Miller, P. H. (1998). Social cognition. In W. Damon (Series Ed.) & D. Kuhn & R. S. Siegler (Vol. Eds.),

Handbook of child psychology: Vol. 2, Cognition, Perception & Language (5th ed.). New York: Wiley.

Freeseman, L. J., Colombo, J., & Coldren, J. T. (1993). Individual differences in infant visual attention: Four-month-olds' discrimination and generalization of global and local stimulus properties. *Child Development, 64,* 1191–1203.

Gallistel, C. R., Brown, A. L., Gelman, R., & Keil, F. C. (1991). Lessons from animal learning for the study of cognitive development. In S. Carey & R. Gelman (Eds.), *The epigenesis of mind: Essays on biology and cognition* (pp. 3–36). Hillsdale, NJ: Erlbaum.

Gardner, H. (1993). *Multiple intelligences: The theory in practice.* New York: Basic Books.

Geary, D. C. (1994). *Children's mathematical development: Research and practical implications.* Washington, DC: American Psychology Association.

Geary, D. C., & Burlingham-Dubree, M. (1989). External validation of the strategy choice model for addition. *Journal of Experimental Child Psychology, 47,* 175–192.

Gelman, R. (1990). First principles organize attention to and learning about relevant data: Number and the animate–inanimate distinction. *Cognitive Science, 14,* 79–106.

Gelman, R. (1997). Constructing and using conceptual competence. *Cognitive Development, 12,* 305–314.

Gelman, R., & Williams, E. (1998). Constraints on thinking and learning. In W. Damon (Series Ed.) & D. Kuhn & R. S. Siegler (Vol. Eds.), *Handbook of child psychology: Vol. 2. Cognition, Perception & Language* (5th ed.). New York: Wiley.

Gentner, D. (1989). The mechanisms of analogical transfer. In S. Vosniadou & A. Ortony (Eds.), *Similarity and analogical reasoning.* London: Cambridge University Press.

Gopnik, A., & Meltzoff, A. (1997). *Words, thoughts and theories.* Cambridge, MA: MIT Press.

Goswami, U. (1996). Analogical reasoning and cognitive development. In H. Reese (Ed.), *Advances in Child Development and Behavior, Vol. 26.* New York: Academic Press.

Goswami, U., & Brown, A. (1990a). Melting chocolate and melting snowmen: Analogical reasoning and causal relations. *Cognition, 35,* 69–95.

Goswami, U., & Brown, A. (1990b). Higher-order structure and relational reasoning: Contrasting analogical and thematic relations. *Cognition, 36,* 207–226.

Graham, T., & Perry, M. (1993). Indexing transitional knowledge. *Developmental Psychology, 29,* 779–788.

Guilford, J. P. (1967). *The nature of human development.* New York: McGraw-Hill.

Haith, M., & Benson, J. (1998). Infant cognition. In W. Damon (Series Ed.) & D. Kuhn & R. S. Siegler (Vol. Eds.), *Handbook of child psychology: Vol. 2. Cognition, Perception & Language* (5th ed.). New York: Wiley.

Halford, G. S. (1993). *Children's understanding: The development of mental models.* Hillsdale, NJ: Erlbaum.

Hatano, G., & Inagaki, K. (1994). Young children's naive theory of biology. *Cognition, 50,* 171–188.

Inhelder, B., & Piaget, J. (1958). *The early growth of logical thinking from childhood to adolescence.* New York: Basic Books.

Jensen, A. R. (1988). Speed of information processing and population differences. In S. H. Irvine & J. W. Berry (Eds.), *Human abilities in cultural contexts* (pp. 105–145). New York: Cambridge University Press.

Johnson, K. E., & Mervis, C. B. (1994). Microgenetic analysis of first steps in children's acquisition of expertise on shorebirds. *Developmental Psychology, 30,* 418–435.

Karmiloff-Smith, A. (1984). Children's problem solving. In M. Lamb, A. L. Brown, & B. Rogoff (Eds.), *Advances in developmental psychology* (Vol. 3, pp. 39–89). Hillsdale, NJ: Erlbaum.

Karmiloff-Smith, A. (1986). Stage/structure versus phase/process in modeling linguistic and cognitive development. In I. Levin (Ed.), *Stage and structure: Reopening the debate.* Norwood, NJ: Ablex.

Keil, F. C. (1989). *Concepts, kinds, and cognitive development.* Cambridge, MA: MIT Press.

Keil, F. C. (1994). The birth and nurturance of concepts by domains: The origins of concepts of living things. In L. A. Hirschfeld & S. A. Gelman (Eds.), *Mapping the mind: Domain specificity in cognition and culture.* New York: Cambridge University Press.

Klahr, D. (1992). Information processing approaches to cognitive development. In M. H. Bornstein & M. E. Lamb (Eds.), *Developmental psychology: An advanced textbook* (3rd ed.). Hillsdale, NJ: Erlbaum.

Klahr, D., & MacWhinney, B. (1998). Information processing. In W. Damon (Series Ed.) & D. Kuhn & R. S. Siegler (Vol. Eds.), *Handbook of child psychology: Vol. 2. Cognition, Perception & Language* (5th ed.). New York: Wiley.

Klahr, D., & Wallace, J. G. (1976). *Cognitive development: An information processing view.* Hillsdale, NJ: Erlbaum.

Kranzler, J. H., & Jensen, A. R. (1989). Inspection time and intelligence: A meta-analysis. *Intelligence, 13,* 329–347.

Kuhn, D., & Phelps, E. (1982). The development of problem solving strategies. In H. Reese (Ed.), *Advances in child development and behavior, Vol. 17.* New York: Academic Press.

Kuhn, D., Garcia-Mila, M., Zohar, A., & Andersen, C., (1995). Strategies of knowledge acquisition. *Monographs of the Society for Research in Child Development, 60* (4, Serial No. 245).

Kyllonen, P. C., & Shute, V. J. (1989). A taxonomy of learning skills. In P. L. Ackerman, R. J. Sternberg, & R. Glaser (Eds.), *Learning and individual differences: Advances in theory and research.* New York: W.H. Freeman and Company.

LeFevre, J. A., Sadesky, G. S., & Bisanz, J. (1996). Selection of procedures in mental addition: Reassessing the problem-size effects in adults. *Journal of Experimental Psychology: Learning, Memory & Cognition, 22,* 216–230.

Lemaire, P., & Siegler, R. S. (1995). Four aspects of strategic change: Contributions to children's learning of multiplication. *Journal of Experimental Psychology: General, 124*, 83–97.

Leslie, A. M. (1984). Spatiotemporal continuity and the perception of causality in infants. *Perception, 13*, 287–305.

Lipsitt, L. P. (1992). Discussion: The Bayley Scales on infant development: Issues of prediction and outcome revisited. In C. Rovee-Collier & L. P. Lipsitt (Eds.), *Advances in infancy research* (Vol. 7). Norwood, NJ: Ablex.

MacWhinney, B., & Chang, F. (1995). Connectionism and language learning. In C. Nelson (Ed.), *The Minnesota Symposium on Child Psychology*. Hillsdale, NJ: Erlbaum.

Mandler, J. M., & McDonough, L. (1995). Long-term recall in infancy. *Journal of Experimental Child Psychology, 59*, 457–474.

Marchman, V. (1992). Constraint on plasticity in a connectionist model of the English past tense. *Journal of Cognitive Neuroscience, 5*, 215–234.

Markman, (1992). Constraints on word learning: Speculations about their nature, origins and domain specificity. In M. R. Gunnar & M. P. Maratsos (Eds.), *The Minnesota Symposium on Child Psychology* (pp. 59–101). Hillsdale, NJ: Erlbaum.

Marr, D. B., & Sternberg, R. J. (1986). Analogical reasoning with novel concepts: Differential attention of intellectually gifted and nongifted children to relevant and irrelevant novel stimuli. *Cognitive Development, 1*, 53–72.

McCall, R. B. (1979). The development of intellectual functioning in infancy and the prediction of later IQ. In J. D. Osofsky (Ed.), *Handbook of infant development*. New York: Wiley.

McCall, R. B. (1981). Early predictors of later IQ: The search continues. *Intelligence, 5*, 141–148.

McCall, R. B., & Carriger, M. S. (1993). A meta-analysis of infant habituation and recognition memory performance as predictors of later IQ. *Child Development, 64*, 57–79.

McClelland, J. L. (1995). A connectionist perspective on knowledge and development. In T. J. Simon & G. S. Halford (Eds.), *Developing cognitive competence: New approaches to process modeling*. Hillsdale, NJ: Erlbaum.

McGilly, K., & Siegler, R. S. (1989). How children choose among serial recall strategies. *Child Development, 60*, 172–182.

Meltzoff, A. N. (1988a). Infant imitation and memory: Nine-month-olds in immediate and deferred tests. *Child Development, 59*, 217–225.

Meltzoff, A. N. (1988b). Infant imitation after a 1-week delay: Long-term memory for novel acts and multiple stimuli. *Developmental Psychology, 24*, 470–476.

Miller, P. H. (1990). The development of strategies of selective attention. In D. F. Bjorklund (Ed.), *Children's strategies: Contemporary views of cognitive development* (pp. 157–184). Hillsdale, NJ: Erlbaum.

Miller, P. H. (1993). *Theories of developmental psychology.* (3rd ed.). New York: W.H. Freeman and Company.

Miller, P., & Aloise-Young, P. (1996). Preschoolers' strategic behaviors and performance on a same–different task. *Journal of Experimental Child Psychology, 60*, 284–303.

Miller, P. H., & Coyle, T. R. (in press). Developmental change: Lessons from Microgenesis. In E. K. Scholnick, K. Nelson, S. A. Gelman, & P. H. Miller (Eds.), *Conceptual Development: Piaget's Legacy*. Hillsdale, NJ: Erlbaum.

Miller, P. H., & Seier, W. S. (1994). Strategy utilization deficiency in children: When, where and why. In H. W. Reese (Ed.), *Advances in Child Development and Behavior, Vol. 25* (pp. 107–156). New York: Academic Press.

Miller, K. F., Smith, C. M., Zhu, J., & Zhang, H. (1995). Preschool origins of cross-national differences in mathematical competence: The role of number-naming systems. *Psychological Science, 6*, 56–60.

Molenaar, P. C. (1986). On the impossibility of acquiring more powerful structures: A neglected alternative. *Human Development, 29*, 245–251.

Munakata, Y., McClelland, J. L., Johnson, M. H., & Siegler, R. S. (1997). Rethinking infant knowledge: Toward an adaptive process account of successes and failures in object permanence tasks. *Psychological Review, 104*, 686–713.

Newell, A. (1990). *Unified theories of cognition.* Cambridge, MA: Harvard University Press.

Oakes, L. M. (1994). The development of infants' use of continuity cues in their perception of causality. *Developmental Psychology, 30*, 869–879.

Oakes, L. M., & Cohen, L. B. (1990). Infant perception of a causal event. *Cognitive Development, 5*, 193–207.

Oakes, L. M., & Cohen, L. B. (1994). Infant causal perception. In C. Rovee-Collier & L. P. Lipsitt (Eds.), *Advances in infancy research, Vol. 9*. Norwood, NJ: Ablex.

Pascual-Leone, J. (1987). Organismic processes for Neo-Piagetian theories: A dialectical causal account of cognitive development. *International Journal of Psychology, 22*, 531–570.

Perry, M., Church, R. B., & Goldin-Meadow, S. (1988). Transitional knowledge in the acquisition of concepts. *Cognitive Development, 3*, 359–400.

Perry, M., & Lewis, J. L. (1999). Verbal imprecision as an index of knowledge in transition. *Developmental Psychology, 35*, 749–759.

Piaget, J. (1952). *The origins of intelligence in children.* New York: International University Press.

Piaget, J. (1971). *The construction of reality in the child.* New York: Ballantine.

Rogoff, B. (1998). Cognition as a collaborative process. In W. Damon (Series Ed.) & D. Kuhn & R. S. Siegler (Vol. Eds.), *Handbook of child psychology: Vol. 2. Cognition, perception & language* (5th ed., pp. 371–420). New York: Wiley.

Rogoff, B., Radziszewska, B., & Masliello, T. (1995). Analysis of developmental processes in sociocultural activities. In L. Martin, K. Nelson, & E. Tobach (Eds.), *Sociocultural psychology: Theory and practice of doing and knowing* (pp. 125–149). Cambridge, UK: Cambridge University Press.

Rose, A. S., & Feldman, J. F. (1997). Memory and speed: Their role in the relation of infant information processing to later IQ. *Child Development, 68*, 630–641.

Rose, A. S., Feldman, J. F., & Wallace, I. F. (1992). Infant information processing in relation to six-year cognitive outcomes. *Child Development, 63*, 1126–1141.

Rose, A. S., & Wallace, I. F. (1985). Visual recognition and memory: A predictor of later cognitive functioning in preterms. *Child Development, 56*, 843–852.

Saxe, G. B., Gearhart, M., & Guberman, S. B. (1984). The social organization of early number development. In B. Rogoff & J. V. Wertsch (Eds.), *Children's learning in the "Zone of proximal development"* (pp. 19–30). San Francisco: Jossey-Bass.

Schauble, L. (1990). Belief revision in children: The role of prior knowledge and strategies for generating evidence. *Journal of Experimental Child Psychology, 49*, 31–57.

Schauble, L. (1996). The development of scientific reasoning in knowledge-rich contexts. *Developmental Psychology, 32*, 102–119.

Shrager, J., & Siegler, R. S. (1998). SCADS: A model of children's strategy choices and strategy discoveries. *Psychological Science, 5*, 405–410.

Shultz, T. R., Schmidt, W. C., Buckingham, D., & Mareschal, D. (1995). Modeling cognitive development with a generative connectionist algorithm. In T. Simon & G. Halford (Eds.), *Developing cognitive competence: New approaches to process modeling*. Hillsdale, NJ: Erlbaum.

Siegler, R. S. (1976). Three aspects of cognitive development. *Cognitive Psychology, 8*, 481–520.

Siegler, R. S. (1978). The origins of scientific reasoning. In R. S. Siegler (Ed.), *Children's thinking: What develops?* Hillsdale, NJ: Erlbaum.

Siegler, R. S. (1986). Unities across domains in children's strategy choice. In M. Perlmutter (Ed.), *Perspectives on intellectual development: The Minnesota symposia on child psychology, Vol. 19*, Hillsdale, NJ: Erlbaum.

Siegler, R. S. (1987). The perils of averaging data over strategies: An example from children's addition. *Journal of Experimental Psychology: General, 116*, 250–264.

Siegler, R. S. (1995). How does change occur: A microgenetic study of number conservation. *Cognitive Psychology, 28*, 225–273.

Siegler, R. S. (1996). *Emerging minds: The process of change in children's thinking*. New York: Oxford University Press.

Siegler, R. S. (1997). Beyond competence – Toward development. *Cognitive Development, 12*, 323–332.

Siegler, R. S., & Chen, Z. (1998). Developmental differences in rule learning: A microgenetic analysis. *Cognitive Psychology, 36*, 273–310.

Siegler, R. S., & Crowley, K. (1991). The microgenetic method: A direct means for studying cognitive development. *American Psychologist, 46*, 606–620.

Siegler, R. S., & Ellis, S. (1996). Piaget on childhood. *Psychological Science, 7*, 211–215.

Siegler, R. S., & Jenkins, E. A. (1989). *How children discover new strategies*. Hillsdale, NJ: Erlbaum.

Siegler, R. S., & Lemaire, P. (1997). Older and younger adults' strategy choice in multiplication: Testing predictions of ASCM using the choice/no-choice method. *Journal of Experimental Psychology: General, 126*, 71–92.

Siegler, R. S., & McGilly, K. (1989). Strategy choice in children's time-telling. In I. Levin & D. Zakay (Eds.), *Time and human cognition: A life span perspective*. The Netherlands: Elsevier.

Siegler, R. S., & Richards, D. D. (1982). The development of intelligence. In R. J. Sternberg (Ed.), *Handbook of human intelligence*. Cambridge University Press.

Siegler, R. S., & Shipley, C. (1995). Variation, selection, and cognitive change. In T. Simon and G. Halford (Eds.), *Developing cognitive competence: New approaches to process modeling*. Hillsdale, NJ: Erlbaum.

Siegler, R. S., & Shrager, J. (1984). Strategy choices in addition and subtraction: How do children know what to do? In C. Sophian (Ed.), *The origins of cognitive skills* (pp. 229–293). Hillsdale, NJ: Erlbaum.

Siegler, R. S., & Stern, E. (1998). Conscious and unconscious strategy discoveries: A microgenetic analysis. *Journal of Experimental Psychology: General, 127*, 377–397.

Sigman, M., Cohen, S. E., Beckwith, L., Asarnow, R., & Parmelee, A. H. (1991). Continuity in cognitive abilities from infancy to 12 years of age. *Cognitive Development, 6*, 47–57.

Simon, T., & Klahr, D. (1995). A theory of children's learning about number conservation. In T. Simon & G. Halford (Eds.), *Developing cognitive competence: New approaches to process modeling*. Hillsdale, NJ: Erlbaum.

Sophian, C. (1997). Beyond competence: The significance of performance for conceptual development. *Cognitive Development, 12*, 281–304.

Spearman, C. (1927). *The abilities of man: Their nature and measurement*. New York: Macmillan.

Spelke, E. S. (1994). Initial knowledge: Six suggestions, *Cognition, 50*, 431–445.

Spelke, E. S., & Newport, E. L. (1998). Nativism, empiricism, and the development of knowledge. In W. Damon (Series Ed.) & R. M. Lerner (Vol. Ed.), *Handbook of child psychology. Vol. 1. Theoretical models of human development.* (5th ed.). New York: Wiley.

Sternberg, R. J. (1981). Novelty-seeking, novelty-finding, and developmental continuity of intelligence. *Intelligence, 5*, 149–155.

Sternberg, R. J. (1985a). *Beyond IQ: A triarchic theory of human intelligence*. New York: Cambridge University Press.

Sternberg, R. J. (1985b). Introduction: What is an information-processing approach to human abilities? In

R. J. Sternberg (Ed.), *Human abilities: An information-processing approach*. New York: W.H. Freeman and Company.

Sternberg, R. J. (1997). The concept of intelligence and its role in lifelong learning and success. *American Psychologist, 52*, 1030–1037.

Sternberg, R. J., & Rifkin, B. (1979). The development of analogical reasoning processes. *Journal of Experimental Child Psychology, 27*, 195–232.

Stevenson, H., Lee, S., & Stigler, J. (1986). Achievement in mathematics. In H. Stevenson, H. Azuma, & K. Hakuta (Eds.), *Child development and education in Japan*. New York: W.H. Freeman.

Thelen, E. (1992). Development as a dynamic system. *Current Directions in Psychological Science, 1*, 189–193.

Thelen, E., & Smith, L. B. (1998). Dynamic systems theories. In W. Damon (Series Ed.) & R. M. Lerner (Vol. Ed.), *Handbook of child psychology: Vol. 1. Theoretical models of human development*. (5th ed.). New York: Wiley.

Thurstone, L. L. (1938). Primary mental abilities. *Psychometric monographs*.

van Geert, P. (1994). *Dynamic systems of development: Change between complexity and chaos*. Hemel Hempstead, Hertfordshe: Harvester Wheatsheaf.

van Lehn, K. (1990). *Mind bugs: The origins of procedural misconceptions*. Cambridge, MA: MIT Press.

Wellman, H. M., & Gelman, S. A. (1992). Cognitive development: Foundational theories in core domains. *Annual Review of Psychology, 43*, 337–375.

Wellman, H. M., & Gelman, S. (1998). Acquisition of knowledge. In W. Damon (Series Ed.) & D. Kuhn & R. S. Siegler (Vol. Eds.), *Handbook of child psychology: Vol. 2. Cognition, Perception & Language* (5th ed.). New York: Wiley.

Wertsch, J. V., & Hickmann, M. (1987). Problem solving in social interaction: A microgenetic analysis. In M. Hickmann (Ed.), *Social and functional approaches to language and thought* (pp. 251–266). San Diego, CA: Academic Press.

Willatts, P. (1984). The stage IV infants' solution of problems requiring the use of supports. *Infant Behavior and Development, 7*, 125–134.

Willatts, P., & Rosie, K. (1989, April). Planning by 12-month-old infants. Paper presented at the biennial meeting of the Society for Research in Child Development, Kansas City, MO.

Woodrow, H. A. (1921). Intelligence and its measurement: A symposium. *Journal of Educational Psychology, 12*, 207–210.

Woodward, A. L., & Markman, E. M. (1998). Early word learning. In W. Damon (Series Ed.) & D. Kuhn & R. S. Siegler (Vol. Eds.), *Handbook of child psychology: Vol. 2, Cognition, Perception & Language* (5th ed.). New York: Wiley.

CHAPTER SIX

Intellectual Development in Adulthood

CYNTHIA A. BERG

As for writing, I still write — at age 72. My experience is that I have to strive harder, tire sooner and come apart at the seams more completely than was the case when I was younger. The aging mind has a bagful of nasty tricks, one of which is to tuck names and words away in crannies where they are not immediately available and where I can't always find them (E. B. White in Taylor, 1984, p. 113).

There is often a mysterious growth of the mind, which we can trace to no particular efforts or studies, which we can hardly define, though we are conscious of it. We understand ourselves and the past, and our friends and the world better (Channing as cited in Taylor, 1984, p. 102).

These two quotations illustrate the tension that exists in the literature regarding age-related differences in intelligence across adulthood. The view that intelligence largely declines in adulthood has perhaps received the longest and most overwhelming support. Intelligence during adulthood is characterized by declines in the speed of mental processes, in abstract reasoning, and in several measures of memory performance (see Salthouse, 1991, for a review). However, much empirical and theoretical work characterizes adult intellectual development as being marked by progressive growth in the ability to integrate cognitive, interpersonal, and emotional thought so that the type of synthetic understanding of self and others that Channing spoke of is possible (see Labouvie-Vief, 1992, for a review). As will be seen throughout the chapter, in a life-span theoretical perspective these two perspectives are not considered to be inconsistent, but rather the development of intelligence is seen as a balance between such losses and gains (Baltes, 1987; Labouvie-Vief, 1992).

The question of what happens to adult intelligence across the life span has sparked tremendous debate and controversy (see Baltes & Schaie, 1976; Horn & Donaldson, 1976; Schaie, 1974). Horn and Donaldson (1976) argued that intellectual decline is inevitable: "if one lives long enough, decrement in at least some of the important abilities of intelligence is likely to occur" (p. 701). Schaie (1974) referred to the view of declining adult intelligence as "at best a methodological artifact and at worst a popular misunderstanding of the relation between individual development and sociocultural change" (p. 802). As highlighted by Horn's focus on "important abilities," at least part of the controversy over adult intelligence as decline versus maintenance and improvement arose over different conceptions about the nature of adult intelligence and about development. Before reviewing the literature on adult intelligence, we must explore what is meant by intelligence and by development.

DEFINITIONS OF INTELLIGENCE AND DEVELOPMENT

Intelligence

Although a great deal of research in the field of adult intelligence has operated under the assumption that adult intelligence is "what an intelligence test measures," numerous theorists have raised concerns about using traditional intelligence tests to measure the intelligence of adults across the life span (Baltes, Dittmann-Kohli, & Dixon, 1984;

117

Berg & Sternberg, 1985; Demming & Pressey, 1957; Labouvie-Vief, 1992). Intelligence tests were originally designed to predict the academic success of children; however, such prediction is not relevant to older adults who are typically outside of the academic environment. Many theoreticians have described a different nature of intelligence across the life span (e.g., Labouvie-Vief, 1992) in which "domains of psychological functioning other than performance on intelligence tests gain in relative significance" (Baltes et al., 1984, p. 50). The focus in adulthood is on domains such as family life, health, personal and professional development, and social intelligence rather than school.

In this chapter, the term intelligence will be used to refer to *the mental abilities and processes involved in providing an optimal fit between oneself and one's environment.* This definition of intelligence has a long-standing history in the field of intellectual development. The view of intelligence as adaptation is the key to Piaget's notion of intelligence (1976) and has been present in many contextually based notions of intelligence (Berg & Sternberg, 1985; Sternberg, 1985). This view of intelligence makes apparent two aspects in the expression of intelligence: *abilities and mental processes that lie within the individual and how these abilities and mental processes transact the constraints and opportunities of the context.* Thus, intelligence does not reside solely within an individual's mind but in how an individual uses abilities and mental processes to transact with, adapt to, and shape his or her environment.

This view of intelligence is apparent in numerous theoretical positions on adult development and aging. For instance, the triarchic theory of intelligence proposed by Sternberg (1985) and extended to adult development and aging by Berg and Sternberg (1985) explicitly defines intelligence as residing in an interaction between the individual's abilities and processes and their expression within different contexts. In the triarchic theory, the context in which individuals must adapt may differ across adult development in terms of the demands and constraints that are present (e.g., shift out of the work context as a result of retirement). As these contexts shift across the life span, the abilities and processes necessary for successful adaptation may vary at different developmental epochs. Berg and Sternberg (1992) found through an examination of adults' concep-

tions of intelligence that adults perceived the abilities needed for successful adaptation as differing in importance across adulthood. Adults perceived intelligence to consist of three distinct subabilities (i.e., interest in, and ability to deal with, novelty; verbal ability; and everyday competencies) whose importance to the assessment of intelligence differed across development. For instance, characteristics associated with the interest in, and ability to deal with, novelty were perceived to be most important for young adults and less important for middle-aged and older adults, whereas characteristics associated with everyday competencies and verbal ability were considered to be more important for middle-aged and older adults than young adults.

P. B. Baltes and M. M. Baltes' (1990; see also Baltes et al., 1998) notion of selective optimization with compensation also focuses on the interplay between the individual and context. Individuals are posited to select across the life span from a variety of domains and goal possibilities those that can be enhanced and correspondingly to compensate for abilities and processes that may be showing elements of decline. Thus, individuals are thought to actively select out of some contexts and into others that can maximize their strengths and minimize their weaknesses in abilities and processes. For instance, older adults seem to leave jobs that require quick sensorimotor performance (Barrett, Mihal, Panek, Sterns, & Alexander, 1977), perhaps because they are selecting into other work environments that may rely less on their declining speed of performance. In addition, older adults report that they attempt to optimize and compensate at work through impression management (Abraham & Hansson, 1995). Many current theories of life-span development include this self-regulatory notion of intellectual development (Backman & Dixon, 1992; Brandtstädter & Greve, 1994; Heckhausen & Schulz, 1995) in which individuals regulate their own fit to changing contexts.

VIEW OF DEVELOPMENT

The view of development adopted in this chapter is a life-span developmental perspective (Baltes, 1987; Baltes, Lindenberger, & Staudinger, 1998). As outlined by Baltes (1987, Baltes et al., 1998), this perspective views development as an expression of both ontogenetic, and cultural and historical changes. The life-span developmental perspective again points to the importance of examining individual intellectual development as situated within, and in comparison across, the contexts in which it is expressed.

An important methodological issue within the field of life-span development, the influence of cohort effects, illustrates how an individual's intellectual development is situated within his or her historical context. Cohort effects were revealed by Schaie (1984) to be an important factor in understanding cross-sectional differences in intellectual development. That is, cross-sectional methods for examining intellectual development in which individuals of different ages are compared at one point in time confound age and cohort (generational membership or normative influences that are held in common with those in one's birth cohort). A comparison of age differences uncovered via a variety of methodological designs (e.g., cross-sectional, longitudinal, cross-sequential) revealed that a substantial proportion of the age-related differences in intellectual functioning could be accounted for by cohort effects. Thus, factors associated with historical time (e.g., years of education held by adults in different generations, generational differences in educational systems) were reflected in many of the differences that were thought to be representative of age differences in intellectual functioning.

Many of the tenets of life-span development are consonant with a view of intelligence as the individual transacting his or her context (Baltes et al., 1998). First, intellectual development is characterized by multidirectionality; that is, intelligence takes pluralistic forms across development (e.g., linear increase, maintenance, some decline, increase followed by maintenance and then decline), depending on the ability in question and the context in which that ability is examined. Second, great interindividual variability is posited to occur in life-span development, in part due to aspects of the contexts that different individuals traverse across development. Third, great plasticity (within-person variability) is found in intellectual performance, depending on the supportive conditions present within the context.

This chapter will review theoretical and empirical work that illustrates the development of adult intelligence (1) in the mental abilities and processes that are thought to be important for adaptation and

(2) in how those mental abilities and processes vary as they are applied across different contexts. Instead of an exhaustive survey of the research oriented toward individual abilities and processes situated in context, the review will provide illustrative research to support general principles of intellectual development. The chapter ends with a call for research that integrates these aspects of adult intelligence and questions and issues for the future of the field of adult intellectual development.

Research drawn from three theoretical perspectives will be used to review the existing literature on the development of adult intelligence: psychometric, information-processing, and contextual. These perspectives were chosen for two reasons: (1) because of their prominence in the field at the current time (see Berg & Klaczynski, 1996; Schaie, 1996a; Sternberg & Berg, 1992) and (2) because of their emphasis on the abilities and processes individuals use to adapt to their life contexts. The psychometric and the information-processing approaches focus on the abilities and processes that reside within the "individual." The contextual approach focuses on how the expression of those individual abilities and processes may vary, depending on the social and historical context in which intelligence is expressed. Although the perspective taken in this chapter is that abilities and processes do not reside within the individual but at the transaction of the individual and his or her context, the research literature has generally assumed that abilities and processes are within the head of the individual. Thus, the reader may initially get the impression that abilities and processes are a property of the individual that he or she applies in different contexts, which is not the perspective of this chapter. As will be seen in the concluding section, intellectual development from the perspective advanced in the paper should be examined as the *process* whereby the individual transacts with his or her context.

INDIVIDUAL MENTAL ABILITIES AND PROCESSES

Abilities

In specifying the number and kinds of categories of mental abilities that characterize intellectual development, the field has drawn heavily from work on the structure or nature of intelligence in psychometrics. The psychometric perspective defines intelligence as those cognitive products that characterize intellectual differences between individuals at various developmental periods (Horn & Hofer, 1992; Schaie, 1996a). The field of adult intelligence had been dominated by the psychometric perspective until the 1980s (see Schaie, 1996a; Schaie & Willis, 1996, for a complete treatment of the psychometric perspective). This approach comes the closest to defining intelligence as "how well one scores on an intelligence test."

In the psychometric perspective, the nature of intelligence is first investigated by measuring the performance of individuals on specific intelligence tests. Statistical procedures are then utilized that summarize and illuminate the structure underlying the organization of individuals' performance on these intelligence tests. Distinct abilities can be characterized as those that do not cluster together and those that show different trajectories across development. Although issues of the number and kinds of mental abilities characterizing intelligence were a matter of great dispute (see Reinert, 1970, for a review), a consensus has emerged that adult intelligence consists of a small number (2–12) of different components that remain largely unchanged in their organization across adult development (Horn & Hofer, 1992).

The following review will be restricted to three different abilities currently considered distinct in terms of their content and developmental trajectory: fluid intelligence, crystallized intelligence, and everyday intelligence (see Schaie & Willis, 1996). The psychometric literature (see Baltes et al., 1998, for a review) has uncovered that different abilities display different developmental functions (multidirectionality), that there is extensive variability in adult intelligence at any particular age (interindividual variability), and that there is great modifiability of adult intelligence (plasticity).

FLUID AND CRYSTALLIZED INTELLIGENCE. One of the most robust and long-standing divisions of intelligence is the fluid and crystallized distinction of Cattell and Horn (e.g., Cattell, 1971; Horn, 1968). Fluid intelligence is said to be measured best by tasks that require adaptation to new situations and for which prior learning provides relatively little advantage. Crystallized intelligence is best measured by tasks in which the problem solving of the task has been learned as a result of education and acculturation, or both. Measures of fluid intelligence include tests of abstract reasoning, spatial orientation, and perceptual speed, whereas measures of crystallized intelligence include tests of verbal ability such as vocabulary and arithmetic abilities (see Figure 6.1 for example items from the Primary Mental Abilities Test (PMA), the measure that has been most extensively investigated by Schaie, 1996b).

1. MULTIDIRECTIONALITY OF INTELLIGENCE. The multidirectionality of adult intelligence refers to the display of different developmental patterns by distinct abilities. Fluid intelligence has been described by Horn and Hofer (1992) as abilities that are vulnerable to aging. As can be seen in Figure 6.2, cross-sectional functions of these two different types of abilities are distinct, and cross-sectional declines are largest for measures of fluid intelligence.

FIGURE 6.1. Examples of test items from the Primary Mental Abilities Test (taken from Schaie & Willis, 1996).

Verbal Meaning

Old　a. Good　b. Ancient　c. Wise　d. Respected

Space

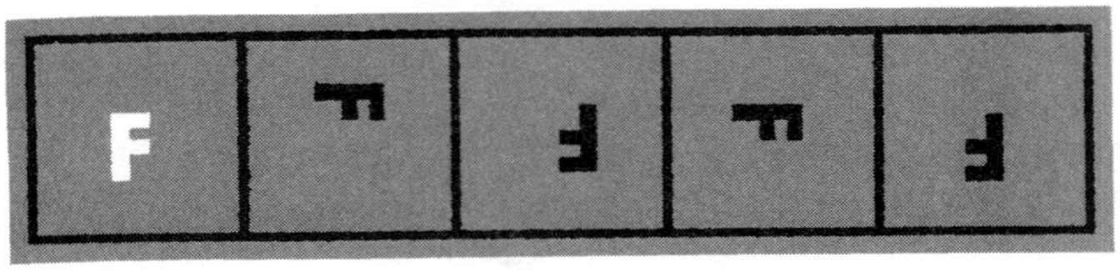

Reasoning

a b w c d x e f　　b y d g

Number

a.	b.			
46	28		a.	R　W
15	39		b.	R　W
27	12			
88	77			

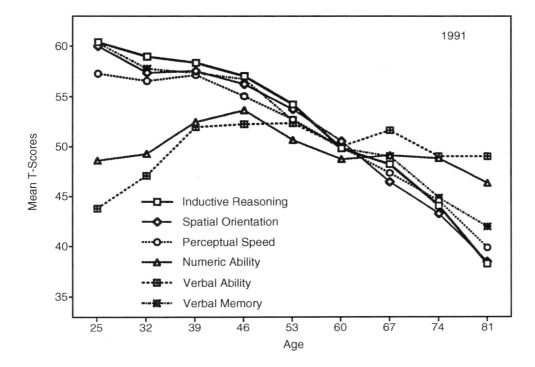

FIGURE 6.2. Cross-sectional age gradients in six primary mental abilities (taken from Schaie, 1996).

The developmental function of crystallized intelligence is largely stable until the sixth decade of life with decline thereafter. The findings reported above are for cross-sectional studies of intellectual development. Longitudinal research (in which the same individuals are followed across time) suggests that even for fluid intelligence, decline does not begin generally until between ages 60 and 70, whereas decline in crystallized intelligence occurs nearly a decade later after age 70 (Schaie, 1996b).

Because of these robust age-related differences in performance, much effort has been expended to try to explain the difference between these vulnerable and maintained abilities. The basic distinction between fluid and crystallized intelligence relies on the difference between abilities that are novel versus familiar and those that do not and do require the application of knowledge. Thus, the distinction has been interpreted as indicating differences in the ability to deal with novelty versus the ability to apply one's knowledge in relatively familiar settings. However, careful work that controls for the degree of task novelty for individuals across the life span has not been conducted. Some theorists (Cattell, 1963; Horn, 1968) have interpreted differences in

the functions of fluid and crystallized intelligence as reflective of a stronger genetic base to fluid intelligence, although heritability estimates for both abilities are about equal (Nichols, 1978).

The differences in developmental function of fluid and crystallized intelligence may be due, in part, to generational gains in intelligence referred to as the *Flynn effect* (Flynn, 1987). Flynn demonstrated generational gains in intelligence (ranging from 5 to 25 IQ points) across countries, and the largest gains occurred for tests of fluid intelligence rather than crystallized intelligence. Thus, cross-sectional decreases in fluid intelligence across age may not be attributable to declines in fluid intelligence in late life but to increases in the level of fluid intelligence expressed by young adults (reflecting later generations). Even longitudinal results can be influenced by these generational gains because longitudinal data may be based on revised norms that reflect these generational gains, thereby producing what appears to be intellectual decline for older adults in fluid intelligence. These findings are consonant with the cohort effect uncovered by Schaie and others (see Schaie, 1996, for a review).

Multidirectionality of abilities is also present in the distinction between the mechanics and pragmatics of intelligence advanced by Baltes (1987; Baltes et al., 1998), which parallels the distinction between fluid and crystallized intelligence. In making the analogy to a computer, Baltes et al. (1998) refer to these two aspects as the hardware (mechanics) versus the software (cognitive pragmatics) of the mind. The mechanics contain the basic information processing of the cognitive system, irrespective of the content of those processes, and are indexed by the speed and coordination of elementary processing operations such as might be assessed on tests of simple discrimination, selective attention, and so forth. The pragmatics of intelligence refer to content-rich, experience-based declarative and procedural knowledge that one acquires during the course of socialization. As is true for the empirical findings on the distinction between fluid and crystallized intelligence, Baltes et al. (1998) found that abilities representative of the mechanics of intelligence declined linearly from young adulthood until old age, whereas abilities representative of the pragmatics were stable throughout the adult years. For instance, no age differences were found on measures of reasoning about life planning (representative of pragmatics); however, linear decline was found in the speed of comparing information in short-term memory (representative of the mechanics of intelligence).

2. INTERINDIVIDUAL VARIABILITY OF MENTAL ABILITIES. Variability in intellectual development not only occurs for individuals across intellectual abilities but for the same intellectual ability across individuals. That is, there is extensive interindividual variability for a single intellectual ability within a specific age group. Although Schaie's (1996b) work consistently revealed mean cross-sectional differences in overall performance, scores varied considerably within age group. Schaie (1988) explicitly studied this variability by examining the proportion of overlap in intellectual abilities with the distribution present for young adults (at age 25). Even in their late 80s, 53% of individuals overlapped with the distribution for young adults, thus scoring well above the mean for their age group on the verbal meaning subtest (a measure of crystallized in-

telligence). Even in late life, therefore, a substantial proportion of individuals perform comparable to a group of young adults in measures of crystallized and fluid intelligence despite general age differences in mean levels of performance.

Variability also exists in the longitudinal patterns of decline, maintenance, and improvement that individuals demonstrate. Schaie and Willis (1986) found that by categorizing older individuals (mean age = 72 years) as having declined versus having remained stable in their performance on the space and reasoning tests of the PMA over a 14-year period, the majority of individuals (46.7%) of the sample remained stable on both measures, whereas only 21% declined in both measures. Schaie (1989) further reports that even for those individuals who were followed into their 80s, virtually no one showed universal declines across all five subtests of the PMA. An extensive body of research has now been compiled to understand what distinguishes individuals who show substantial intellectual decline from those who show maintenance and improvement in intellectual development. Schaie (1996b) found that individual differences in the developmental function of intelligence are due to a host of factors such as genetic endowment, incidence of chronic disease, educational background, occupational pursuits, the stimulating versus passive nature of daily life activities, and personality styles such as rigidity and flexibility.

3. PLASTICITY OF MENTAL ABILITIES. Research on the intraindividual plasticity of intelligence has focused on the modifiability of intelligence through intervention. Over the last two decades substantial research has revealed that intervention can lead to significant gains in abilities such as problem-solving tasks (Denney, 1979), perceptual speed (Hoyer, Labouvie, & Baltes, 1973), and fluid intelligence (Baltes & Lindenberg, 1988; Willis, 1987). In general, intervention efforts have been aimed at those abilities that show the greatest decline: largely abilities of fluid intelligence and processes representative of the mechanics of intelligence.

Results from intervention studies indicate that the plasticity of human intelligence among older adults is substantial (see Willis, 1987 for a review). For instance, results from the Seattle Training Study, a component of Schaie's Seattle Longitudinal Study (Schaie, 1996b) indicate that intervention boosted older adults' performance back to the level present more than a decade before. Schaie and Willis trained individuals in five 1-hour sessions in spatial ability or reasoning ability. For those who had shown decline in performance on either of these tests over the preceding 14-year period, training was effective in returning their performance nearly to the original level. For individuals who had remained stable over the preceding 14-year period, training raised their performance beyond the level they had demonstrated 14 years previously. Not only is training effective in the short run, but gains produced through training are maintained over as many as 7 years (Neely & Backman, 1993; Willis & Nesselroade, 1990). However, training effects are fairly limited to tests in which training occurs and do not extend to intelligence tests that are different in kind (e.g., training in fluid intelligence tests does not extend to performance on crystallized intelligence tests, see Baltes & Willis, 1982).

EVERYDAY INTELLIGENCE. Everyday intelligence is an ability that has only recently been examined within the field of adult intelligence (see Berg & Klaczynski, 1996, for a review). The examination of everyday intelligence arose as researchers were concerned with using traditional tests of intelligence (e.g., measures of fluid and crystallized intelligence) exclusively to measure the intelligence of adults who were largely outside of academic environments. A variety of definitions and distinctions exist regarding the meaning of everyday intelligence. Some define everyday intelligence as the expression of more basic fluid and crystallized abilities that permit adaptive behavior within a specific class of everyday situations (Willis & Schaie, 1986). Many current definitions involve distinctions between abilities critical for everyday intelligence and abilities that are required to perform well on more traditional measures of intelligence (e.g., measures representative of fluid and crystallized intelligence) (Neisser, 1976; Wagner, 1986). Much of the measurement of everyday intelligence has focused on solving problems that are ill-structured as to their goals and their solution (e.g., may not contain one correct answer) and that are frequently encountered in daily life (e.g., Cornelius & Caspi, 1987; Denney, 1989). Everyday intelligence has been thought to be particularly important for measuring the intelligence of middle-aged and older adults, both by laypeople (see

earlier discussion of Berg & Sternberg, 1992) and theorists (Baltes et al., 1984; Berg, 1990; Sinnott, 1989). Everyday intelligence is thought to be used in individuals' work environments (Colonia-Willner, 1998; Wagner & Sternberg, 1985), in making routine decisions (Johnson, 1990), in dealing with complex health decisions (Meyer, Russo, & Talbot, 1995), and in solving tasks that are required to maintain independence (Willis & Schaie, 1993) in many daily life situations. Two issues have dominated work on everyday intelligence: (1) the extent to which everyday intelligence is a manifestation of other more traditional intellectual abilities such as fluid and crystallized intelligence, and (2) whether the pattern of age differences in everyday intelligence mirrors that of fluid or crystallized intelligence (see Berg & Klaczynski, 1996 for a review).

Research by Willis and her colleagues provides the best evidence that everyday intelligence is an expression of fluid and crystallized abilities. She approaches everyday intelligence as an adult's ability to perform activities considered essential for living independently (e.g., meal preparation, managing finances, using the telephone). Willis and colleagues utilized a variant of the ETS Basic Skills Test to measure everyday intelligence. This test is a multiple-choice test that contains items requiring individuals to read and abstract information from maps, medication labels, technical documents (e.g., IRS forms) and newspaper text. Such items have a single correct answer, are scored as either correct or incorrect, and are quite similar in their structure and format to traditional comprehension questions on intelligence tests. Willis and Schaie (1986) reported substantial correlations between performance on the Basic Skills Test and a measure of fluid ($r = .83$) and crystallized ($r = .78$) intelligence. Diehl, Willis, and Schaie (1995) reported that measures of fluid intelligence also predicted observational assessments of older adults that were designed to be variants of the paper and pencil measures.

Other researchers who have used more ill-structured measures of everyday intelligence have not found such strong evidence for the hierarchical nature of intellectual abilities whereby everyday intelligence is simply a manifestation of more traditional intellectual abilities. For instance, many researchers utilize measures that involve presenting adults with hypothetical problem scenarios and asking the examinees to generate multiple strategies for problem solution (Denney & Palmer, 1981; Denney & Pearce, 1989; Denney, Pearce, & Palmer, 1982) or rate the effectiveness of a preset group of strategies (e.g., Blanchard-Fields, Janke, & Camp, 1995; Cornelius & Caspi, 1987). For instance, adults might be presented with a problem involving how to fix one's broken lawnmower or with a decision-making task regarding which insurance plan to purchase. Studies using such measures have found only modest relationships (*r*s range between .2 and .4) between measures of fluid and crystallized intelligence and measures of everyday intelligence (Camp, Doherty, Moody-Thomas, & Denney, 1989; Cornelius & Caspi, 1987).

The developmental function of everyday intelligence has been examined to determine if its direction is more similar to the pattern uncovered for crystallized or fluid intelligence. The pattern of age differences in everyday intelligence varies dramatically, depending on the criterion used for optimal everyday problem-solving performance. For instance, Denney and her colleagues (Denney & Palmer, 1981; Denney & Pearce, 1989) used the number of "safe and effective solutions" generated and found that middle-aged adults generated the most number of solutions, whereas young and older adults produced fewer solutions. Berg et al. (1994) found no age differences when utilizing individuals' own ratings of how effective they were in solving their own everyday problems. Cornelius and Caspi (1987) found that everyday problem solving increased with adult age when the criterion of how closely individuals' ratings of strategy effectiveness matched a "prototype" of the optimal everyday problem solver. Studies have also reported age differences in the strategies individuals report for dealing with everyday problems (more problem-focused or emotion-focused strategies), although inconsistencies exist in the pattern of results (see Berg et al., 1998, for a discussion), and disagreements occur as to whether a particular strategy type reflects more effective everyday problem solving (contrast Berg et al., 1998 with Heckhausen & Schulz, 1995); therefore, conclusions regarding the developmental function of strategy selection in everyday problem solving are equivocal.

Several studies examining everyday problem solving within a neo-Piagetian or postformal operational perspective (extending and reformulating Piaget's theory to the study of adult development) have also found evidence for growth in late adulthood (Labouvie-Vief, 1992). The formal operational reasoning of late adolescents and young adults, with its focus on logic, is replaced with more sophisticated structures in middle and late adulthood that are characterized by more relativistic reasoning that involves a synthesis of logic, the irrational, emotive, and personal. Blanchard-Fields, for instance, (1986, 1994; Blanchard-Fields & Norris, 1994) found evidence of increases in everyday intelligence in some conditions using measures that tap the extent of integrative attributional reasoning (integrating dispositional and situational components) in social dilemmas.

These inconsistencies in the relation between measures of everyday intelligence and fluid and crystallized intelligence and in the developmental function of everyday intelligence are probably due to multiple types of everyday intelligence being represented by these diverse measures. Marsiske and Willis (1995), which is the only work to date on the structure of everyday problem solving, indicated that different measures of everyday intelligence are indeed measuring distinct constructs, which are not highly related. In addition, the inconsistencies may be due to the fact that everyday problem-solving measures range from those that are quite similar in structure and format to traditional measures of intelligence (e.g., ETS Basic Skills Test) to those that diverge greatly from intelligence test items (e.g., ill-structured hypothetical problems characteristic of daily living). Such diverse measures may not be equally reflective of how individuals adapt to their everyday environments.

SUMMARY. This review of the intellectual abilities that individuals use to adapt to their context presents a fairly complex picture of adult intellectual development that emphasizes variability at multiple levels of analysis. First, variability exists in the developmental function of intelligence, depending on the ability in question and the extent to which performance relies on accumulated experience and acculturation. Developmental differences are most prominent when assessed through abilities that require novel application (fluid intelligence) rather than familiar application (crystallized intelligence). Second, variability exists at any age between individuals, and there is some evidence that this variability is most prominent in late adulthood (see Morse,

1993, for a review). Third, variability also exists at the intraindividual level, for intervention studies have shown great modifiability of individual abilities at any age. Work on everyday intelligence reveals that this ability may show less decline across age than is present for fluid intelligence. The relation, however, between everyday intelligence and measures of fluid and crystallized intelligence depends on the specific criterion used to assess everyday intelligence.

Mental Processes

Researchers who have examined the mental abilities individuals use to adapt to their life contexts have focused on end products such as one's performance on an intelligence test. Those who have focused on mental processes, however, address the question of how those mental products are produced through mental processes.

The mental processes that individuals use to adapt to their contexts and how those mental processes change across development have largely been addressed from the information-processing perspective. The information-processing perspective focuses on the processes (e.g., representations, strategies, executive processes, availability of resources) by which an individual performs an intellectual task (Salthouse, 1992b). The focus is on how individuals mentally solve an intellectual task through basic-level processes of encoding, retrieving, and comparing information, as well as higher order executive processes used to plan how to solve a problem and monitor one's solution strategy. A key developmental question within this perspective has been whether the age differences in mental abilities discussed previously can be isolated to particular processing components or whether they are due to a limited number of mental resources that impact many mental processes.

LOCALIZATION OF AGE-DIFFERENCES IN PROCESSING COMPONENTS. The emphasis of much of the work examining age differences in mental processes has been on localizing the specific processes responsible for the age differences seen in measures of fluid intelligence and understanding why those processes are intact with respect to crystallized performance. Because many models of mental processes are represented by flowcharts that map the order of the processes, Salthouse (1992b) refers to these efforts as identifying "which box is broken?" (p. 267).

These localization efforts begin by mapping out and measuring the cognitive processes that individuals go through when performing a specific task. In general, researchers have assumed that the processes and strategies characterizing young adults' performance will also characterize older adults' performance, although such an assumption may not always be valid (see Adams, Labouvie-Vief, Hobart, & Dorosz, 1990; Berg, Klaczynski, Calderone, & Strough, 1994).

In mapping age differences in processes, no age differences have been found in individuals' metacognitive abilities. The term metacognitive abilities refers to individuals' knowledge about memory or cognition (e.g., relative difficulty of remembering different types of information) and individuals' ability to monitor their own cognitive processes (allocating time to study material not yet mastered, accurate judgements concerning cognitive performance). No age differences have been found in either type of metacognitive abilities (Cavanaugh, 1996; Hultsch & Dixon, 1990). Thus, older individuals are aware of their own cognitive functioning and are able to monitor its functioning as well as young adults.

However, age differences have been found in many other processing components to such an extent that some have concluded it may not be fruitful to isolate which of the "boxes" or components is broken or deficient. For example, research examining age differences in spatial visualization (see space subtest of PMA, Figure 6.1), a measure of fluid intelligence, typically shows age-related declines beginning in the 30s (see Figure 6.2). Numerous attempts were made by investigators to localize which process is responsible for these age differences. This work drew on models of mental rotations ability developed by Shephard and Metzler (1971) that specify processes involved in the successful completion of mental rotations items. These processes include a serial order of processing stages beginning with encoding the stimuli followed by an analog mental rotation of the stimuli into congruence, comparisons of the representations, and finally a motor response. Numerous studies (Berg, Hertzog, & Hunt, 1982; Cerella, Poon, & Fozard, 1981; Gaylord & Marsh, 1975; Hertzog, Vernon, & Rypma, 1993) reported that older adults were slower in each of the mental processes (e.g., encoding, rotating, comparing, deciding) than young adults. Thus, age differences could not be localized to any one particular process.

The results from work with the spatial visualization test is consonant with a large body of research that tries to localize age differences in a wide variety of abilities such as reasoning and memory (Salthouse, 1991). These failures to isolate the small number of processing components responsible for age-related differences in fluid intelligence performance led many theorists to speculate that a smaller number of processing resources are responsible for the large number of differences seen in processing components (see Figure 6.3). Thus, the processing resources view has been gaining support as a more parsimonious explanation of intellectual development than the localization approach.

PROCESSING RESOURCES. Two processing resources have been most frequently postulated and investigated as responsible for age-related differences in processing components: speed of processing and working memory capacity (Salthouse,

FIGURE 6.3. Schematic illustration of the difference between the localization approach and the reduced resources approach to cognitive aging (taken from Salthouse, 1991).

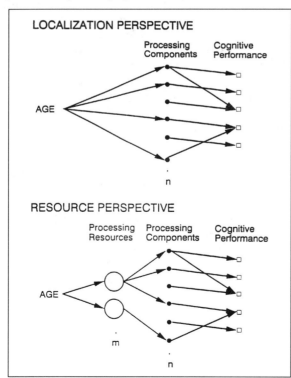

1991). Interestingly, these processing resources have also been theorized to be responsible for age-related changes in processing components during childhood and adolescence (Case et al., 1996; Kail, 1991; Salthouse & Kail, 1983).

1. *Speed of processing.* The idea that speed of processing may be a resource responsible for age-related differences in processing components comes from research showing that older adults' performance across a wide variety of tasks slows at similar rates (Birren, 1974). Several meta-analyses of young and older adults' performance suggest that older adults' performance on a wide variety of tasks with diverse procedures slows at a fairly constant function of young adults' performance (Cerella, 1990; Hale, Myerson, Smith, & Poon, 1988). Several large-scale studies have been conducted to examine the role of speed of processing in age differences in measures of fluid intelligence (Hertzog, 1989; Salthouse, Kausler, & Saults, 1988).

For instance, Salthouse et al. (1988) examined speed of processing (measured by the time needed to make relatively simple comparisons) and its influence on measures of fluid intelligence (e.g., series completion, geometric analogies, and spatial reasoning tasks). Depending on the specific measure used to indicate processing speed, between 13 and 32% of the age differences in measures of cognitive performance were associated with age differences in speed. Much higher estimates of the age-related variance in cognitive performance that is attributable to processing speed come from a study by Hertzog (1989). He found that controlling for measures of speed of processing (operationalized as perceptual speed, tasks such as number comparison, and finding As in a string of letters) in the performance of other cognitive tasks reduced the age-related variance in cognitive performance by an average of 92%. The results from a large number of studies (see Salthouse, 1992a, for a review) now provide moderate support for speed of processing as a resource responsible for some of the age-related differences in cognitive tasks.

2. *Working memory capacity.* Working memory capacity is a processing resource that has often been postulated as responsible for the age differences found in processing components. Working memory capacity refers to the amount of information that can

be stored and processed in a sort of mental scratch pad used when performing nearly every cognitive task. Age differences in working memory capacity have been implicated in age differences in nearly every type of mental ability: language and comprehension (Cohen, 1988; McDowd, Oseas-Kreger, & Filion, 1995; Hasher & Zacks, 1988) and spatial relations and abstract reasoning (Salthouse, Mitchell, Skovronek, & Babcock, 1989).

Numerous studies have explored whether age differences in working memory are associated with age differences in cognitive performance (e.g., Salthouse, 1992a; Salthouse, Mitchell, Skovronek, & Babcock, 1989). Salthouse (1992a) had subjects from 18 to 83 years of age perform the computation span and a variety of fluid intelligence tasks such as the Raven's Advanced Progressive Matrices, the Shipley Abstraction Test, paper folding, integrative reasoning, geometric analogies, and cube assembly. In the computation span task, participants were presented with a series of simple arithmetic problems in which they are asked to indicate the correct answer and to remember the final digit in each of the problems and respond accordingly at the end. The results from these studies indicate that working memory is associated with about 50% of the age-related variance in measures of cognitive functioning. Thus, working memory can be viewed as an important mediator of the age-related differences in many measures of cognitive function (Salthouse, 1991, 1992a, for reviews).

Summary

The review of the mental processes that adults use to perform intelligence tasks indicates that age differences exist in several mental processes. Current thinking within the field indicates that the age differences found in many mental processes may be due to age differences in two processing resources: speed of response and working memory capacity. A substantial body of evidence is now accumulating that indicates that these two processing resources may be responsible for a substantial portion of the age-related variance in mental abilities or products.

CONTEXT OF ADULT INTELLECTUAL DEVELOPMENT

The preceding review has focused on characteristics within the individual (abilities and processes) that researchers believe are utilized as individuals adapt to their contexts across development. Although intelligence is viewed in this chapter as the mental abilities and processes whereby individuals adapt to multiple contexts, the literature thus far has not examined the process of adaptation. Rather, the literature has focused on the fact that abilities and mental components may be differently expressed in multiple contexts. Although the research reviewed portrays a view of the context as setting up specific constraints and opportunities to which the individual passively adapts, the view taken in the chapter is not as unidirectional or passive as it may seem. That is, individuals do not passively apply their abilities and processes to static contexts that contain different opportunities and constraints. Rather the adaptation process is a dynamic one in which the individual's abilities and processes as well as the context are simultaneously shaped and altered.

The theoretical perspective that has most often been used to understand the context of adult intelligence is the contextualist perspective (Berg & Calderone, 1994; Berg & Sternberg, 1985; Dixon, 1992). Such a perspective defines intellectual development as reflecting the specific contexts – sociocultural, biological, and historical – in which development occurs (Laboratory of Comparative Human Cognition, 1982; Rogoff, 1982; Vygotsky, 1978). From this perspective intellectual development is examined as occurring within different contexts. That is, intellectual development is posited to be disparate across groups of individuals who are situated in different contexts. To the extent that contextual demands and opportunities are different across the adult life span, different measurements of intelligence may be needed.

Although extensive studies detailing the context of adult intelligence at different times during development have not been conducted, much speculation has occurred as to how the landscape and context of adults across the life span vary in a way that influences intellectual development. The context of older adults differs from that of young adults in many ways. The proximity of older adults to formal schooling environments is much less than that of young adults who recently completed high school or are currently enrolled in college. Many fewer older adults are in daily contact with the work context, due to retirement, as compared with young adults. Older adults differ from young adults in the complexity versus passivity of their daily life activities, which may be important for sustaining intellectual functioning (Scheidt & Schaie, 1978). Older adults may also differ from young adults in the frequency of social interaction (Antonucci & Akiyama, 1987), which may affect opportunities for collaborative problem solving.

For instance, as individuals move from young adulthood to late adulthood, there is a move away from contact with formal schooling environments. Differences in the number of years of education and the type of educational experiences that these years represent have been examined as an important factor in understanding cohort effects (Schaie, 1996a). In addition, Rogoff's (1982) treatment of the influence of formal schooling on cognitive performance suggests that intellectual performance may be influenced because most adults are not in formal schooling environments. The memorization, categorization, and speed of response required in most Western schools have been found to influence many aspects of cognitive performance, including spontaneous use of strategies to remember information, abstract reasoning, and the ability to draw formal logical conclusions (Laboratory of Comparative Cognition, 1982; Rogoff, 1982). In fact, comparisons of young and older adults who are both in formal schooling environments often show reduced or no age differences in intellectual performance (Jacewicz & Hartley, 1979; Parks, Mitchell, & Perlmutter, 1986), although interpretations of these data are complex.

Research on the context of adult intellectual development is in its relative infancy compared with work on the individual abilities and processes that reside within the individual. Research will next be reviewed illustrating two issues that have been prominent thus far in this work: (1) how intellectual development varies across different contexts and (2) how the social context may facilitate intellectual performance.

Variability in Intellectual Development across Different Contexts

Research that examines how individuals adapt their mental abilities and processes to fit the specific contextual constraints and opportunities of the context and correspondingly shape their con-

texts to provide a better fit with their mental needs has largely been conducted for adults by focusing on only one specific age group (e.g., Lave, 1989; Scribner, 1986). For instance, Scribner (1986) found that adult dairy workers adapted their arithmetic strategies depending on the specific constraints of the size of boxes and number of bottles involved in the delivery order. Much less work has been done, however, comparing adults across the life span in the ways in which abilities and processes are adapted to fit contextual conditions. The research reviewed typically compares individuals of different ages who occupy disparate contexts to understand how contextual demands may reflect different intellectual abilities and processes rather than focusing on the same individuals and how they respond to different contexts.

COMPLEXITY OF WORK ENVIRONMENTS. One environmental variable that has been examined as being influential for shaping the development of adult intelligence is the complexity and stimulation of one's work environment. Kohn and Schooler (1983) examined the relation between the extent to which one's work-related activities involve independent thought and judgment (which they call substantive complexity) and ideational flexibility (a combined measure of fluid intelligence tests and responses to questions representing flexibility in dealing with complex intellectual activities). Results from their longitudinal study of men between the ages of 24 to 64 years of age indicate that the more substantive the complexity of one's job, the greater the incremental gains in intellectual performance over a 10-year period. The same relations between job complexity and intelligence hold for women doing complex housework (Schooler, 1984). Furthermore, Miller and Kohn (1983) found that individuals with greater ideational flexibility were involved in more intellectually engaging leisure activities (e.g., reading books versus watching television). Although these studies suggest that a complex work environment assists in maintaining intellectual functioning, these studies are unable to rule out the possibility that individuals who maintain their intellectual functioning are more apt to pursue and stay in challenging work environments. However, these results are consistent with those of researchers (Gribbin, Schaie, & Parham, 1980; Hulstch, Hammer, & Small,

1993) who found that engaging in more complex and stimulating daily life activities is related to modest facilitation of intellectual performance.

DOMAIN OF EVERYDAY PROBLEM SOLVING. A growing literature now exists that demonstrates that everyday intelligence is different when examined within different domains of functioning (Berg et al., 1998; Blanchard-Fields, Chen, & Norris, 1997; Cornelius & Caspi, 1987). The domain of everyday intelligence is used to refer to the context in which problems occur (e.g., school, work, home) and the types of demands present in problem contexts (e.g., interpersonal versus achievement). Sansone and Berg (1993) reported that the context of everyday intelligence differs across the life span such that domains of work and family are particularly salient during middle adulthood and domains such as family and health are more salient in late adulthood. Contextual differences are thought to be important in understanding developmental differences in everyday problem solving because developmental differences may reflect the reality that individuals occupy different contexts and thereby experience disparate problems across the life span. Berg et al. (1998) and Blanchard-Fields et al. (1997) found that the strategies adults used to deal with everyday problem-solving situations and the attributions they made for the behavior of individuals within the problem varied depending on the context in which everyday problems were couched. For instance, individuals reported utilizing strategies that were more interpersonally focused for more interpersonally relevant domains such as family and friends and strategies that were focused more on behavioral action for more achievement-oriented domains (Berg et al., 1998). Berg et al. (1998) reported that these context effects may have been observed because different contexts elicit different representations of problem situations and goal orientations, which subsequently influence strategy selection.

FAMILIARITY OR EXPERIENCE WITH THE DOMAIN. Individual differences in the familiarity of young and older adults with the materials and context of intellectual assessment have also been examined. Familiarity and experience with the contexts of intellectual assessment are important because in-dividuals may express their abilities and mental processes differently when they are familiar with the constraints and opportunities of the context versus when they are unfamiliar with these features. Cornelius (1984) reported that older adults perceived traditional intelligence tests as less familiar than did young adults. Thus, comparisons of young and older adults on intelligence tests may place older adults at a relative disadvantage because they may be less familiar with how to apply their mental processes and products in specific intellectual assessment contexts.

Results have clearly shown that intellectual performance is superior for both young and older adults when assessed in contexts that are familiar to individuals – either when individuals are given materials with which they are familiar (Smith & Baltes, 1990) or when individuals are given extensive practice with the intellectual task (Berg et al., 1982). The research has been equivocal, however, as to whether differential familiarity is a factor that can help to explain age differences in intellectual performance.

Several studies now have examined the problem-solving performance of young and older adults with problems that were constructed to be more familiar or more normative for one age group or the other. Smith and Baltes (1990) found that adults performed best on measures of wisdom when the problems were more normative for the examinee's age group. Denney and colleagues also found that adults performed best when presented everyday problems more normative for their age group (Denney et al., 1982). However, Denney and Pearce (1989) found that familiar materials were not able to eliminate age differences in that older adults performed less well than young adults even when older adults were performing with materials that had been explicitly designed by older adults to be those with which they would perform better than young adults. Research examining how memory performance is facilitated by familiar materials is consistent (Barrett & Watkins, 1986; Worden & Sherman-Brown, 1983) in showing that older adults tend to perform better with materials with which they are more familiar (e.g., remembering words that were in frequent use during their adulthood years versus contemporary equivalents).

Another strategy for examining the role of familiarity with the abilities and operations under examination has been to assess intellectual functioning in areas of relative expertise versus less expertise (see Bosman & Charness, 1996; Salthouse, & Mitchell 1990). This research has focused on how extensive amounts of practice, as would characterize individuals who practice some ability or process daily in their jobs (e.g., typists and reaction time) may alter the typical declines seen in measures of intellectual performance. Domain-relevant performance in which individuals have had extensive experience (e.g., chess and bridge experts, architects and their spatial ability, typists) tends to show a developmental trajectory of maintenance, whereas what appears to be the same process or ability assessed in a less familiar or contextualized fashion may demonstrate a trajectory of decline (Charness, 1981; Salthouse, 1984). For instance, Salthouse (1984) reported that typists varying in age showed the typical declines in speed of performance when assessed via a reaction-time task but did not show any age-related declines in speed of processing when typing. The maintenance of speed of processing with familiar materials appeared to be due to older adults' adopting a different strategy for typing than young adults. Thus, older adults may have compensated for some declines in intellectual functioning by adapting their cognitive strategies to fit optimally with the typing task. Research that examines familiarity with materials by giving individuals extensive practice with some task, however, does not often fully eliminate age differences and sometimes shows an exacerbation of age differences (see Berg et al., 1982; Denney, 1979). Thus, extensive practice may be required before individuals are able to fit their abilities and processes optimally to the constraints of the intellectual context.

Social Context of Adult Intellectual Development

Recently, several investigators have examined the social context of adult intellectual development (see Baltes & Staudinger, 1996b, for a review). This work emphasized how the process of adapting to one's environment may involve other individuals as collaborators, support providers, and sources of information (see also Berg, Meegan, & Deviney, 1998; Berg et al., 1998). Schaie's (1996b) analyses of adult married couples suggests that one's spouse may serve as an important collaborator. His work indicates that

individuals' intellectual performance benefits from having a spouse who is performing better than oneself intellectually.

Work within the social context of intelligence questions the typical view of intelligence as residing within an individual's mind and instead begins to talk about constructs such as interactive minds (Baltes & Staudinger, 1996a) and the sociocultural mind (Rogoff, 1990) to illustrate the transactive nature of minds. Baltes and Staudinger (1996a) characterized interactive minds as implying

that the acquisition and manifestation of individual cognitions influence and are influenced by cognitions of others and that these reciprocal influences between minds contribute to the activation and modification of already available cognitions as well as to the generation (development) of new ones (p. 7)

Several studies now point to the important role that others play in the process whereby individuals use their mental processes and abilities to adapt to their context. Staudinger and Baltes (1996; Staudinger, 1996) have examined the social context of wisdom. Wisdom is operationalized as expertise in knowledge of the fundamental pragmatics of life. Their measure of wisdom taps the pragmatics of intelligence and involves problems that describe a difficult life-planning scenario (e.g., a middle-aged woman who desires to pursue career and educational opportunities for herself at a time when her adult son needs assistance with rearing his young children). Individuals are asked to solve this problem, and their responses are coded for the amount of procedural and factual knowledge individuals mention, an understanding of the contextual complexities present in the solution, a person's management of uncertainty, and so forth. Staudinger and Baltes examined the ability of individuals to solve life-planning problems under several conditions that varied the extent of social interaction. Anchoring the individual end of assessment was the typical form of assessment in which an individual was asked to perform the task alone. A condition designed to elicit a moderate amount of social facilitation was a condition in which individuals were asked to think about the task when informed by what another person, whose advice he or she typically seeks, would encourage them to consider. The greatest facilitation was expected when an individual was allowed to discuss the task with another person and then respond individually. The results indicated that the best performance occurred when individuals worked in dyads and when working with the implied other (these conditions were not different from each other). Working individually (the typical form of assessment) was particularly ineffective compared with these other conditions. Thus, individuals' performance can benefit from face-to-face interaction with others as well as implied interaction.

Research by Dixon and colleagues further suggests the process whereby social facilitation may occur. For instance, Dixon and Gould (1996) examined the text recall of young and older married couples. Dixon and Gould (1996) and Gould, Kurzman, and Dixon (1994) found that older married couples performed as well as younger married couples on measures of amount of information recalled (in direct opposition to a large body of research, see Hultsch & Dixon, 1990). When the interaction patterns between husbands and wives were examined, older couples appeared to engage in more strategy discussion at a point when text recall was declining to a greater extent than did young adults. Dixon and Gould (1996) interpreted such results to mean that older adults may be compensating for their declines in individual recall through strategies that may elicit more text recall. Older married adults may be more able to engage in such strategies than young couples because of their extensive relational history (Berg et al., 1998).

The research on the social facilitation of intellectual performance has implications for older adults' collaborative problem solving in numerous tasks of everyday intelligence (e.g., calculating taxes, decisions regarding retirement planning, difficult medical decisions). Furthermore, this work is suggestive of a different type of intellectual assessment. For instance, Vygotsky's (1978) work suggests that the difference between individual performance and what an individual accomplishes with the assistance of others could be used as a measure of intellectual competence rather than individual performance alone. This zone is thought to reflect latent potential or soon-to-be developing competence. Although Brown and Ferrara (1985) suggested that such a form of intellectual assessment may be useful across the life span, this form of assessment has not yet been adopted in the field.

Summary

The research reviewed illustrates the powerful role of the context in affecting the expression of intellectual abilities and processes and in potentially altering the course of intellectual development. Although the research in this area is still growing, the research suggests that intellectual development varies according to the complexity of one's daily life context and that the familiarity, content, and social nature of one's context influence the expression of many abilities and processes.

CONCLUSIONS AND FUTURE RESEARCH DIRECTIONS

This chapter has painted a complex and rich view of the potential changes that occur across adult development in intelligence. The three perspectives (psychometric, information-processing, and contextual) utilized to review work oriented toward the view of intelligence as comprising abilities and processes situated in context each add an important, if not essential, dimension of intellectual functioning. The psychometric perspective begins by surveying the landscape of intelligence with a focus on intellectual products throughout the life course. From this perspective we see the variability that exists across different intellectual abilities, within an ability across persons, and within a specific individual across intervention. The information-processing perspective endeavors to understand the processes by which intellectual products are formed by examining the processes, representations, and strategies individuals use to perform specific intellectual tasks. Age differences in processes may well be due to more general processing resources (e.g., speed of processing and working memory capacity) that underlie many intellectual performances. The contextual perspective takes the intellectual products and processes investigated by the first two perspectives and places these in a larger sociocultural context. The complexity, familiarity, domain, and social nature of the context have influences on the form and content, as well as the quality, of the intellectual products and processes.

This chapter illustrates how research within the field of adult intellectual development has largely focused separately on the abilities and processes that reside within the mind of the individual or on the differential expression of abilities and processes within different contexts, within rather different theoretical perspectives. However, as should be clear from the review, any measurement of intellectual performance draws on abilities and processes and is assessed within a context that has particular constraints and opportunities. Thus, we could reframe any of the research reviewed on any particular aspect of intelligence (e.g., abilities) and recast it as involving the other aspects of intelligence. For instance, research that examines age-related differences in measures of fluid intelligence has typically been framed as demonstrating age-related decline in basic-level abilities for which prior education and acculturation are of relatively little advantage. However, within the view of intelligence taken within this chapter, these age differences may be understood as showing age-related differences in processing resources expressed within an environment (the typical testing situation) that is less familiar to older adults than to young adults and that contains certain demands (e.g., highly speeded responses in an environment that is asocial). Too often work that is focused on a specific component of intelligence (e.g., context) neglects how other aspects of intelligent functioning may be involved (abilities or processes). A more complete, albeit complex, view of intelligence would emerge if research were oriented toward understanding all three of these aspects of intelligent performance (i.e., abilities, processes, and contexts) across adult development.

The view of intelligence advanced in this chapter as *the mental abilities and processes that an individual uses to fit optimally with his or her context* suggests, however, another avenue for research that focuses specifically on the process of adaptation. Because the contexts to which adaptation is directed differ across adult development, individuals must adapt their own mental abilities and processes to fit with the changing context and correspondingly to change the context to fit one's own mental abilities and processes better. However, as is illustrated herein, individuals' abilities and processes as well as their context are dynamically changing across adult development.

Research is needed that specifically addresses how individuals adapt to these changing abilities, processes, and contexts. For instance, research could ex-amine how adults' mental abilities and processes are adapted in the face of contextual changes such as changing jobs, retirement, or loss of spouse (as potential collaborative partner) and correspondingly how individuals change their contexts to adapt to these demands (e.g., change job requirements to fit better with one's own needs, use friends as collaborators after the loss of a spouse). Furthermore, research must explore how individuals' awareness of changes in their own abilities and processes (e.g., speed of response, fluid intelligence) may foster cognitive adaptations such as compensations (e.g., Backman & Dixon, 1992) or contextual adaptations such as the use of memory aids or switching contexts (Dixon, 1992). Such research might explore how these adaptations take place during naturally occurring transitions and changes in contexts and abilities and processes as well as more experimentally controlled changes.

Multiple models of life-course change can be useful in guiding these research efforts. For instance, P. B. Baltes and M. Baltes' (1984) model of selective optimization with compensation addresses how individuals may consciously select out of contexts perceived to be inconsistent with current cognitive needs and into others that optimize fit. Backman and Dixon (1992) used the notion of compensation to understand how individuals may alter cognitive abilities and processes when a mismatch is perceived to occur between the individual and environmental demands. Brandtstädter and Greve's (1994) model of the self explores how individuals may change their intellectual goals to provide a more optimal fit between changing abilities, processes, and contexts. These models place the individual in an important role as regulator of his or her own life-span intellectual development. The self-regulatory process suggested by these models is in need of explicit empirical examination.

As research begins to examine this process whereby mental processes and abilities are adapted to provide an optimal fit to specific contexts, research will need to examine how factors that have not traditionally been examined as relevant for intelligence (e.g., personality, attitudes, stress, and coping strategies) may influence this adaptation process. Numerous personality correlates over the years have been identified with intellectual functioning. Modest relationships have been found between intellectual functioning and perceptions of efficacy (Lachman & Leff, 1989), attitudes toward aging (Levy, 1996), and personality styles of rigidity and flexibility (Schaie, 1996b). Such personality characteristics have recently been incorporated into ideas about adult intelligence (Ackerman, 1996; Sternberg & Ruzgis, 1994). The integration of social, emotional, and cognitive factors in understanding intellectual development in adulthood has been underscored in neo-Piagetian models of intellectual development (Labouvie-Vief, 1992).

To conclude, the answer to the question of what happens to intelligence across adulthood is a complex one, which includes many qualifiers. The form of intellectual development depends on what one means by intelligence (i.e., what abilities are under consideration, the processes that are required by the intellectual performance) and on aspects of the context in which the performance occurs. Furthermore, the factors that influence intellectual development may differ for individuals whose contexts present different intellectual demands. Thus, both White and Channing (quoted at the beginning of the chapter) are correct in their characterization of adult intellectual development. It includes both the decline in quickness and memory and the growth of synthetic understanding of self and others that White and Channing described. The challenge for the future of the field of adult intelligence is how to incorporate these views of losses and gains into a vision of adult intelligence as optimally transacting the contexts of life. This future must include an understanding of how individuals incorporate and manage these gains and losses in the regulation of their own intellectual development.

ACKNOWLEDGMENT

The author would like to thank the following people for their comments on an earlier draft of the chapter: Robert Sternberg, Sean P. Meegan, Frances, P. Deviney, Eric Cleaveland, Amy Leishman, and J'Lene George.

REFERENCES

Abraham, J. D., & Hansson, R. O. (1995). Successful aging at work: An applied study of selection, optimization, and compensation through impression management. *Journal of Gerontology, 50B*, pp. 94–103.

Ackerman, P. L. (1996). A theory of adult intellectual development: Process, personality, interests, and knowledge. *Intelligence, 22*, 227–257.

Adams, C., Labouvie-Vief, G., Hobart, C. J., & Dorosz, M. (1990). Adult age group differences in story recall style. *Journal of Gerontology: Psychological Sciences, 45*, pp. 17–25.

Antonucci, T. C., & Akiyama, H. (1987). Social networks in adult life and a preliminary examination of the convoy model. *Journal of Gerontology, 42*, 519–527.

Backman, L., & Dixon, R. A. (1992). Psychological compensation: A theoretical framework. *Psychological Bulletin, 112*, 1–125.

Baltes, P. B. (1987). Theoretical propositions of life-span developmental psychology: On the dynamics between growth and decline. *Developmental Psychology, 23*, 611–626.

Baltes, P. B., & Baltes, M. M. (1990). Psychological perspectives on successful aging: The model of selective optimization with compensation. In P. B. Baltes & M. M. Baltes (Eds.), *Successful aging: Perspectives from the behavioral sciences* (pp. 1–34). New York: Cambridge University Press.

Baltes, P. B., Dittmann-Kohli, F., & Dixon, R. A. (1984). New perspectives on the development of intelligence in adulthood: Toward a dual-process conception and a model of selective optimization with compensation. In P. B. Baltes & O. G. Brim, Jr. (Eds.), *Life-span development and behavior* (Vol. 6, pp. 33–76). New York: Academic Press.

Baltes, P. B., & Lindenberger, U. (1988). On the range of cognitive plasticity in old age as a function of experience: 15 years of intervention research. *Behavior Therapy, 19*, 283–300.

Baltes, P. B., Lindenberger, U., & Staudinger, U. M. (1998). Life-span theory in developmental psychology. In W. Damon (Series Ed.) R. M. Lerner (Vol. Ed.), *Handbook of child psychology*, Theoretical Models of Human Development (Vol. 1, pp. 1029–1143). New York: Wiley.

Baltes, P. B., & Schaie, K. W. (1976). On the plasticity of intelligence in adulthood and old age: Where Horn and Donaldson fail. *American Psychologist, 31*, 720–725.

Baltes, P. B., & Staudinger, U. M. (1996a). Interactive minds in a life-span perspective: prologue. In P. B. Baltes & U. M. Staudinger (Eds.), *Interactive minds: Life-span perspectives on the social foundation of cognition* (pp. 1–34). New York: Cambridge University Press.

Baltes, P. B., & Staudinger, U. M. (Eds.) (1996b). *Interactive minds: Life-span perspectives on the social foundation of cognition*. New York: Cambridge University Press.

Baltes, P. B., & Willis, S. L. (1982). Plasticity and enhancement of intellectual functioning in old age: Penn State's adult development and enrichment project (ADEPT). In F. I. M. Craik & S. E. Trehub (Eds.), *Aging and cognitive processes* (pp. 353–389). New York: Plenum.

Barrett, G. V., Mihal, W. L., Panek, P. E., Sterns, H. L., & Alexander, R. A. (1977). Information processing skills predictive of accident involvement for younger and older commercial drivers. *Industrial Gerontology, 4*, 173–182.

Barrett, G. V., & Watkins, S. K. (1986). Word familiarity and cardiovascular health as determinants of age-related recall differences. *Journal of Gerontology, 41*, 222–224.

Berg, C. (1990). What is intellectual efficacy over the life course?: Using adults' conceptions to address the question. In J. A. Rodin, C. Schooler, & K. W. Schaie (Eds.), *Self-directedness: Causes and effects throughout the life course* (pp. 155–181). Hillsdale, NJ: Erlbaum.

Berg, C. A., & Calderone, K. S. (1994). The role of problem interpretations in understanding the development of everyday problem solving. In R. J. Sternberg & R. K. Wagner (Eds.), *Mind in context: Interactionist perspectives on human intelligence* (pp. 105–132). New York: Cambridge University Press.

Berg, C. A., Hertzog, C., & Hunt, E. (1982). Age differences in the speed of mental rotation. *Developmental Psychology, 18*, 95–107.

Berg, C. A., & Klaczynksi, P. (1996). Practical intelligence and problem solving: Searching for perspectives. In F. Blanchard-Fields & T. M. Hess (Eds.), *Perspectives on cognition in adulthood and aging*. New York: McGraw-Hill.

Berg, C. A., Klaczynski, P., Calderone, K. S., & Strough, J. (1994). Adult age differences in cognitive strategies: Adaptive or deficient. In J. Sinnott (Ed.), *Interdisciplinary handbook of adult lifespan learning* (pp. 371–388). Westport, CT: Greenwood Press.

Berg, C. A., Meegan, S. P., & Deviney, F. P. (1998). A social contextual model of coping with everyday problems across the life span. *International Journal of Behavioral Development, 22*, 239–261.

Berg, C. A., & Sternberg, R. J. (1985). A triarchic theory of intellectual development during adulthood. *Developmental Review, 5*, 334–370.

Berg, C. A., & Sternberg, R. J. (1992). Adults' conceptions of intelligence across the life span. *Psychology and Aging, 7*, 221–231.

Berg, C. A., Strough, J., Calderone, K. S., Sansone, C., & Weir, C. (1998). The role of problem definitions in understanding age and context effects on strategies for solving everyday problems. *Psychology and Aging, 13*, 29–44.

Birren, J. E. (1974). Translations in gerontology – From lab to life: Psychophysiology and speed of response. *American Psychologist, 29*, 808–815.

Blanchard-Fields, F. (1986). Reasoning on social dilemmas varying in emotional saliency: An adult developmental perspective. *Psychology and Aging, 1*, 325–333.

Blanchard-Fields, F. (1994). Age differences in causal attributions from an adult developmental perspective. *Journal of Gerontology: Psychological Sciences, 49*, P43–P51.

Blanchard-Fields, F., Chen, Y., & Norris, L. (1997). Everyday problem solving across the life span: The influence of domain-specificity and cognitive appraisal. *Psychology and Aging, 12*, 684–693.

Blanchard-Fields, F., Jahnke, H. C., & Camp, C. (1995). Age differences in problem-solving style: The role of emotional salience. *Psychology and Aging, 10*, 173–180.

Blanchard-Fields, F., & Norris, L. (1994). Causal attributions from adolescence through adulthood: Age differences, ego level, and generalized response style. *Aging and Cognition, 1*, 67–86.

Bosman, E. A., & Charness, N. (1996). Age-related differences in skilled performance and skill acquisition. In F. Blanchard-Fields & T. M. Hess (Eds.), *Perspectives on cognition in adulthood and aging* (pp. 428–453). New York: McGraw-Hill.

Brandtstädter, J., & Greve, W. (1994). The aging self: Stabilizing and protective processes. *Developmental Review, 14*, 52–80.

Brown, A. L., & Ferrara, R. A. (1985). Diagnosing zones of proximal development. In J. V. Wertsch (Ed.), *Culture, communication, and cognition: Vygotskian perspectives*. Cambridge, Cambridge University Press.

Camp, C. J., Doherty, K., Moody-Thomas, S., & Denney, N. W. (1989). Practical problem solving in adults: A comparison of problem types and scoring methods. In J. D. Sinnott (Ed.), *Everyday problem solving: Theory and applications* (pp. 211–228). New York: Praeger.

Case, R., Okamato, Y., Griffin, S., McKeough, A., Bleiker, C., Henderson, B., & Stephenson, K. (1996). The role of central conceptual structures in the development of children's thought. *Monographs of the Society for Research in Child Development, 61*, No. 1–2, Serial No. 246.

Cattell, R. B. (1963). Theory of fluid and crystallized intelligence: A critical experiment. *Journal of Educational Psychology, 54*, 1–22.

Cattell, R. (1971). *Abilities: Their structure, growth, and action*. New York: Houghton Mifflin.

Cavanaugh, J. (1996). Memory self-efficacy as a moderator of memory change. In F. Blanchard-Fields & T. M. Hess (Eds.), *Perspectives on cognitive change in adulthood and aging* (pp. 488–507). New York: McGraw-Hill.

Cerella, J. (1990). Aging and information processing rate. In J. E. Birren & K. W. Schaie (Eds.), *Handbook of the psychology of aging* (pp. 201–221). San Diego, CA: Academic Press.

Cerella, J., Poon, L. W., & Fozard, J. L. (1981). Mental rotation and age reconsidered. *Journal of Gerontology, 36*, 620–624.

Charness, N. (1981). Age and skilled problem solving. *Journal of Experimental Psychology: General, 110*, 21.

Cohen, G. (1988). Age differences in memory for texts: Production deficiency or processing limitations? In L. L. Light & D. M. Burke (Eds.), *Language, memory and aging* (pp. 171–190). New York: Cambridge University Press.

Colonia-Willner, R. (1998). Practical intelligence at work: Relationship between aging and cognitive efficiency among managers in a bank environment. *Psychology and Aging, 13*, 45–57.

Cornelius, S. W. (1984). Classic pattern of intellectual aging: Test familiarity, difficulty and performance. *Journal of Gerontology, 39*, 201–206.

Cornelius, S. W., & Caspi, A. (1987). Everyday problem solving in adulthood and old age. *Psychology and Aging, 2*, 144–153.

Demming, J. A., & Pressey, S. L. (1957). Tests indigenous to the adult and older years. *Journal of Counseling Psychology, 4*, 144–148.

Denney, N. W. (1979). Problem solving in late life: Intervention research. In P. B. Baltes & O. G. Brim (Eds.), *Lifespan development and behavior* (Vol. 2, pp. 37–66). New York: Academic.

Denney, N. W. (1989). Everyday problem solving: Methodological issues, research findings, and a model. In L. W. Poon, D. C. Rubin, & B. A. Wilson (Eds.), *Everyday cognition in adulthood and late life* (pp. 330–351). New York: Cambridge University Press.

Denney, N. W., & Palmer, A. M. (1981). Adult age differences on traditional and practical problem-solving measures. *Journal of Gerontology, 36*, 323–328.

Denney, N. W., & Pearce, K. A. (1989). A developmental study of practical problem solving in adults. *Psychology and Aging, 4*, 438–442.

Denney, N. W., Pearce, K. A., & Palmer, A. M. (1982). A developmental study of adults' performance on traditional and practical problem-solving tasks. *Experimental Aging Research, 8*, 115–118.

Diehl, M., Willis, S. L., & Schaie, K. W. (1995). Older adult's everyday competence: Observational assessment and cognitive correlates. *Psychology and Aging, 10*, 478–491.

Dixon, R. (1992). Contextual approaches to adult intellectual development. In R. J. Sternberg & C. A. Berg (Eds.), *Intellectual development*. New York: Cambridge University Press.

Dixon, R. A., & Gould, O. N. (1996). Adults telling and retelling stories collaboratively. In P. B. Baltes & U. M. Staudinger (Eds.), *Interactive minds: Life-span perspective on the social foundation of cognition* (pp. 221–241). New York: Cambridge University Press.

Flynn, J. R. (1987). Massive IQ gains in 14 nations: What IQ tests really measure. *Psychological Bulletin, 101*, 171–191.

Gaylord, S. A., & Marsh, G. R. (1975). Age differences in the speed of a spatial cognitive process. *Journal of Gerontology, 30*, 675–678.

Gould, O. N., Kurzman, D., & Dixon, R. A. (1994). Communication during prose recall conversations by young and old dyads. *Discourse Processes, 17*, 149–165.

Gribbin, K., Schaie, K. W., & Parham, I. A. (1980). Complexity of life style and maintenance of intellectual abilities. *Journal of Social Issues, 36*, 47–61.

Hale, S., Myerson, J., Smith, G. A., & Poon, L. W. (1988). Age, variability, and speed: Between-subjects diversity. *Psychology and Aging, 3*, 407–410.

Hasher, L., & Zacks, R. T. (1988). Working memory, comprehension, and aging: A review and a new view. *The Psychology of Learning and Motivation, 22*, 193–225.

Heckhausen, J., & Schulz, R. (1995). A life-span theory of control. *Psychological Review, 102*, 284–304.

Hertzog, C. (1989). Influences of cognitive slowing on age differences in intelligence. *Developmental Psychology, 25*, 636–651.

Hertzog, C., Vernon, M. C., Rypma, B. (1993). Age differences in mental rotation task performance: The influence of speed/accuracy tradeoffs. *Journal of Gerontology: Psychological Sciences, 48*, pp. 150–156.

Horn, J. L. (1968). Organization of abilities and the development of intelligence. *Psychological Review, 75*, 242–259.

Horn, J. L., & Donaldson, G. (1976). On the myth of intellectual decline in adulthood. *American Psychologist, 31*, 701–719.

Horn, J. L., & Hofer, S. M. (1992). Major abilities and development in the adult period. In R. J. Sternberg & C. A. Berg (Eds.), *Intellectual development* (pp. 44–99). New York: Cambridge University Press.

Hoyer, W. J., Labouvie, G. V., & Baltes, P. B. (1973). Modification of response and speed deficits and intellectual performance in the elderly. *Human Development, 16*, 233–242.

Hultsch, D. F., & Dixon, R. A. (1990). Learning and memory in aging. In J. E. Birren & K. W. Schaie (Eds.), *Handbook of the psychology of aging* (3rd ed. pp. 258–274). San Diego: Academic.

Hultsch, D. F., Hammer, M., & Small, B. J. (1993). Age differences in cognitive performance in later life: Relationships to self-reported health and activity life style. *Journal of Gerontology: Psychological Sciences, 48*, pp. 1–11.

Jacewicz, M. M., & Hartley, A. A. (1979). Rotation of mental images by young and old college students: The effects of familiarity. *Journal of Gerontology, 34*, 396–403.

Johnson, M. M. S. (1990). Age differences in decision making: A process methodology for examining strategic information processing. *Journal of Gerontology: Psychological Sciences, 45*, 75–78.

Kail, R. (1991). Developmental change in speed of processing during childhood and adolescence. *Psychological Bulletin, 109*, 490–501.

Kohn, M. L., & Schooler, C. (1983). *Work and personality*. Norwood, NJ: Ablex.

Laboratory of Comparative Human Cognition (1982). Culture and intelligence. In R. J. Sternberg (Ed.), *Handbook of human intelligence* (pp. 642–719). Cambridge UK: Cambridge University Press.

Labouvie-Vief, G. (1992). A Neo-Piagetian perspective on adult cognitive development. In R. J. Sternberg & C. A. Berg (Eds.), *Intellectual development*. New York: Cambridge University Press.

Lachman, M. E., & Leff, R. (1989). Perceived control and

intellectual functioning in the elderly: A 5-year longitudinal study. *Developmental Psychology, 25,* 722–728.

Lave, J. (1989). *Cognition in practice.* New York: Cambridge University Press.

Levy, B. (1996). Improving memory in old age through implicit self-stereotyping. *Journal of Personality and Social Psychology, 71,* 1092–1107.

Marsiske, M., & Willis, S. L. (1995). Dimensionality of everyday problem solving in older adults. *Psychology and Aging, 10,* 269–283.

McDowd, J. M., Oseas-Kreger, D. M., & Filion, D. L. (1995). Inhibitory processes in cognition and aging. In F. N. Dempster & C. J. Brainerd (Eds.), *Interference and inhibition in cognition* (pp. 363–400). San Diego, CA: Academic Press.

Meyer, B. J. F., Russo, C., & Talbot, A. (1995). Discourse comprehension and problem solving: Decisions about the treatment of breast cancer by women across the lifespan. *Psychology in Aging, 10,* 84–103.

Miller, K. A., & Kohn, M. L. (1983). The reciprocal effects on job conditions and the intellectuality of leisure-time activities. In M. L. Kohn & C. Schooler (Eds.), *Work and personality* (pp. 217–241). Norwood, NJ: Ablex.

Morse, C. K. (1993). Does variability increase with age? An archival study of cognitive measures. *Psychology and Aging, 8,* 156–164.

Neely, A. S., & Backman, L. (1993). Long-term maintenance of gains from memory training in older adults: Two $3\frac{1}{2}$-year follow-up studies. *Journal of Gerontology, 48,* 233–237.

Neisser, U. (1976). General, academic, and artificial intelligence. In L. B. Resnick (Ed.), *The nature of intelligence* (pp. 135–144). Hillsdale, NJ: Erlbaum.

Nichols, R. C. (1978). Twin studies of ability, personality and interest. *Homo, 29,* 158–173.

Parks, D. C., Mitchell, D. B., & Perlmutter, M. (1986). Cognitive and social functioning across adulthood: Age or student status differences? *Psychology and Aging, 1,* 248–254.

Piaget, J. (1976). *The psychology of intelligence.* Totowa, NJ: Littlefield, Adams & Co.

Reinert, G. (1970). Comparative factor analytic studies of intelligence throughout the human life-span. In L. R. Goulet & P. B. Baltes (Eds.), *Life-span developmental psychology: Research and theory* (pp. 467–484). New York: Academic Press.

Rogoff, B. (1982). Integrating context and development. In M. E. Lamb & A. L. Brown (Eds.), *Advances in developmental psychology* (Vol. 2, pp. 125–170). Hillsdale, NJ: Erlbaum.

Rogoff, B. (1990). *Apprenticeship in thinking: Cognitive development in social context.* New York: Oxford University Press.

Salthouse, T. A. (1984): Effects of age and skill in typing. *Journal of Experimental Psychology: General, 113,* 345–371.

Salthouse, T. A. (1991). *Theoretical perspectives on cognitive aging.* Hillsdale, NJ: Erlbaum.

Salthouse, T. A. (1992a). *Mechanisms of age–cognition relations in adulthood.* Hillsdale, NJ: Erlbaum.

Salthouse, T. A. (1992b). The information-processing perspective on cognitive aging. In R. J. Sternberg & C. A. Berg (Eds.), *Intellectual development* (pp. 261–277). New York: Cambridge University Press.

Salthouse, T. A., & Kail, R. (1983). Memory development throughout the life span: The role of processing rate. In P. B. Baltes (Ed.), *Life-span development and behavior* (Vol. 5, pp. 89–116). New York: Academic Press.

Salthouse, T. A., Kausler, D. H., & Saults, J. S. (1988). Utilization of path analytic procedures to investigate the role of processing resources in cognitive aging. *Psychology and Aging, 3,* 158–166.

Salthouse, T. A., & Mitchell, D. R. (1990). Effects of age and naturally occurring experience on spatial visualization performance. *Developmental Psychology, 26,* 845–854.

Salthouse, T. A., Mitchell, D. R., Skovronek, E., & Babcock, R. L. (1989). Effects of adult age and working memory on reasoning and spatial abilities. *Journal of Experimental Psychology: Learning, Memory, and Cognition, 15,* 507–516.

Sansone, C., & Berg, C. A. (1993). Adapting to the environment across the life-span: Different process or different inputs? *International Journal of Behavioral Development, 16,* 215–241.

Schaie, K. W. (1974). Translations in gerontology – from lab to life: Intellectual functioning. *American Psychologist, 29,* 802–807.

Schaie, K. W. (1984). Historical time and cohort effects. In K. A. McCloskey & H. W. Reese (Eds.), *Life-span developmental psychology: Historical and generational effects* (pp. 1–15). New York: Academic Press.

Schaie, K. W. (1988). Variability in cognitive functioning in the elderly: Implications for societal participation. In A. D. Woodhead, M. A. Bender, & R. C. Leonard (Eds.), *Phenotypic variation in populations: Relevance to risk assessment* (pp. 191–212). New York: Plenum.

Schaie, K. W. (1989). The hazards of cognitive aging. *Gerontologist, 29,* 484–493.

Schaie, K. W. (1996a). Intellectual development in adulthood. In J. E. Birren & K. W. Schaie (Eds.), *Handbook of the psychology of aging* (pp. 266–286). New York: Academic Press.

Schaie, K. W. (1996b). *Intellectual development in adulthood: The Seattle Longitudinal Study.* New York: Cambridge University Press.

Schaie, K. W., & Willis, S. L. (1986). Can decline in adult intellectual functioning be reversed? *Developmental Psychology, 22,* 223–232.

Schaie, K. W., & Willis, S. L. (1996). Psychometric intelligence and aging. In F. Blanchard-Fields & T. Hess (Eds.), *Perspectives on cognitive change in adulthood and aging.* New York: McGraw-Hill.

Scheidt, R. J., & Schaie, K. W. (1978). A situational

taxonomy for the elderly: Generating situational criteria. *Journal of Gerontology, 33*, 348–357.

Schooler, C. (1984). Psychological effects of complex environments during the life span: A review and theory. *Intelligence, 8*, 259–281.

Scribner, S. (1986). Thinking in action: Some characteristics of practical thought. In R. J. Sternberg & R. Wagner (Eds.), *Practical intelligence: Origins of competence in the everyday world* (pp. 143–162). New York: Cambridge University Press.

Shepard, R. N., & Metzler, J. (1971). Mental rotation of three-dimensional objects. *Science, 171*, 701–703.

Sinnott, J. D. (Ed.). (1989). *Everyday problem solving: Theory and applications.* New York: Praeger.

Smith, J., & Baltes, P. B. (1990). Wisdom–related knowledge: Age/cohort differences in response to life-planning problems. *Developmental Psychology, 26*, 494–505.

Staudinger, U. M. (1996). Wisdom and the social–interactive foundation of the mind. In P. B. Baltes & U. M. Staudinger (Eds.), *Interactive minds: Life-span perspectives on the social foundation of cognition* (pp. 276–318). New York: Cambridge University Press.

Staudinger, U. M., & Baltes, P. B. (1996). Interactive minds: A facilitative setting for wisdom-related performance? *Journal of Personality and Social Psychology, 71*, 746–762.

Sternberg, R. J. (1985). *Beyond IQ: A triarchic theory of human intelligence.* New York: Cambridge University Press.

Sternberg, R. J., & Berg, C. A. (1992). *Intellectual Development.* Cambridge, UK: Cambridge University Press.

Sternberg, R. J., & Ruzgis, P. (1994). *Personality and intelligence.* Cambridge, UK: Cambridge University Press.

Taylor, C. (1984). *Growing on: Ideas about aging.* New York: Van Nostrand Reinhold.

Vygotsky, L. S. (1978). *Mind in society.* Cambridge, MA: Harvard University Press.

Wagner, R. K. (1986). The search for intraterrestrial intelligence. In R. J. Sternberg & R. K. Wagner (Eds.), *Practical intelligence: Origins of competence in the everyday world* (pp. 361–378). New York, Academic Press.

Wagner, R. K., & Sternberg, R. J. (1985). Practical intelligence in real-world pursuits: The role of tacit knowledge. *Journal of Personality and Social Psychology, 48*, 436–458.

Willis, S. L. (1987). Cognitive training and everyday competence. In K. W. Schaie (Ed.), *Annual Review of Gerontology and Geriatrics* (Vol. 7, pp. 159–188). New York: Springer-Verlag.

Willis, S. L., & Nesselroade, C. S. (1990). Long-term effects of fluid ability training in old-old age. *Developmental Psychology, 26*, 905–910.

Willis, S. L., & Schaie, K. W. (1986). Practical intelligence in later adulthood. In R. J. Sternberg & R. K. Wagner (Eds.), *Practical intelligence: Nature and origins of competence in the everyday world* (pp. 236–268). New York: Cambridge University Press.

Willis, S. L., & Schaie, K. W. (1993). Everyday cognition: Taxonomic and methodological considerations. In J. M. Puckett & H. W. Reese (Eds.), *Life-span developmental psychology: Mechanisms of everyday cognition.*

Worden, P. E., & Sherman-Brown, S. (1983). A word-frequency cohort effect in young versus elderly adults' memory for words. *Developmental Psychology, 19*, 521–530.

PART III

GROUP ANALYSES OF INTELLIGENCE

CHAPTER SEVEN

Intelligence and Mental Retardation

DOUGLAS K. DETTERMAN, LYNNE T. GABRIEL, AND JOANNE M. RUTHSATZ

INTELLIGENCE AND MENTAL RETARDATION: PAST, PRESENT, AND FUTURE

As we approach a new millennium, it seems appropriate to take stock. Where have we been and where are we going? This is particularly true of mental retardation and intelligence. Have researchers and specialized workers accomplished anything in their centuries of effort with the mentally retarded? Has the study of mental retardation added anything to our understanding of intelligence? Does research on intelligence provide help in understanding mental retardation?

For those of us who work in the field and look at our day-to-day progress, it often seems as if little is getting accomplished. We still do not have a very complete understanding of mental retardation and its relationship to intelligence. There certainly is no cure for mental retardation. But pessimism may simply be a function of our limited vision. We look at the present but lose sight of the past. Perhaps if the span traveled were viewed from more distant horizons, it might give a more optimistic picture.

In this chapter, we will examine several areas of mental retardation research and theory to try to answer these questions. First, we will consider definitions of mental retardation and how they have changed. Second, we will examine basic research

Author Note: Parts of this work were supported by Grant No. HD07176 from the National Institute of Child Health and Human Development, Office of Mental Retardation. Requests for reprints may be sent to D. K. Detterman, Department of Psychology, Case Western Reserve University, Cleveland, OH 44106. E-mail:dkd2@po.cwru.edu

that has attempted to understand mental retardation in terms of basic cognitive processes. Third, and finally, we will consider a sampling of the applied research that has attempted to devise interventions for the mentally retarded.

Definitions of Mental Retardation

Studying mental retardation is one way to study intelligence. It has only been within the past few decades that researchers have come to appreciate the contribution that mental retardation has made and can make to our understanding of general intellectual ability. Even today, though, some intelligence researchers consider mental retardation as a special case that does not need to be explained by general theories of intelligence. In fact, intelligence is central to the definition of mental retardation. Intelligence tests provide an accurate diagnostic criterion for the definition of mental retardation.

Detterman (1983, 1987) outlined three stages in the history of mental retardation research that are pertinent when discussing the impact of this research on general intelligence theories and the definition of mental retardation. This section will outline those stages and discuss the definitions of mental retardation during each stage, focusing on how the definitions changed as the knowledge of the scientific community changed.

The first stage lasted from the middle of the 19th century to the early years of the 20th century. During this stage, efforts were made to identify people with mental retardation because those who were mentally ill and those who were mentally retarded were often not differentiated (Doll, 1962;

Scheerenberger, 1987). Only when the scientific study of mental retardation began in the late 1800s did a formal definition begin to emerge. In particular, two French researchers, Itard and Esquirol, described deficient mental processes that prevented individuals from coping with everyday demands (Doll, 1962, 1967).

The introduction of the Binet scales to the United States made a significant impact on the field. Beginning in 1910, the concept of intellectual functioning, or IQ, was the dominant criterion for diagnosing mental retardation (Reschly, 1992). In fact, the first official classification scheme of the American Association on Mental Retardation (AAMR), published in 1921, strongly emphasized using (usually) a Binet IQ as the criterion for diagnosis. In this classification scheme, three levels of mental retardation were recognized as defined by the following IQ levels: moron (IQ 50–75), imbecile (IQ 25–50), and idiot (IQ < 25).

It is hard for us to appreciate the positive impact tests of intelligence have made on the diagnosis of mental retardation. Before intelligence tests were available, there was no way to diagnose mental retardation. Persons with mental retardation were often institutionalized for life under horrible conditions. There was seldom any thought of treatment. In a very real sense, the development of IQ tests opened a new world of possibility for the mentally retarded.

The beginning of the 20th century through World War II marks the second stage of mental retardation research. At the beginning of the century, most researchers were convinced that people with mental retardation were incapable of doing much of anything. They were thought incapable of learning or other more complex cognitive skills. Research during this era focused on determining what people with mental retardation could or could not do. Much to their surprise, researchers discovered that people with mental retardation could do numerous things, including learning and remembering information. With training, people with mental retardation could learn to do many tasks necessary for everyday living. Because of these findings the definitions suggested by Doll (1934, 1941) placed greater emphasis on social competence than on intellect. However, measures of social competence were neither as available nor as precise as standardized IQ tests, and thus IQ was still the dominant diagnostic criterion. Doll's definitions were never formally adopted by AAMR, but they were influential throughout the 1940s and 1950s (Reschly, 1992).

The "remarkable" discovery that people with mental retardation could learn and remember led researchers to conclude that the behavior of people with mental retardation and the behavior of people of average intelligence actually form a continuum of ability (Detterman, 1987). For theorists, this continuum represented a challenge: to account for the whole spectrum of general intellectual ability, including the intelligence of those labeled mentally retarded. Unfortunately, most theorists did not accept this challenge, claiming that theories of intelligence should not be required to predict behavior in people with mental retardation (Detterman, 1987).

The last stage of mental retardation research, from the end of World War II to the present, built on the descriptive research of the past era and has been focused on determining the causes of mental retardation. During this era, a division between scientific research and advocacy and rights has emerged. The definitions advanced during this era, especially the most current AAMR definition (Lukkasson, 1992), are often regarded as most useful for advocacy purposes, not research.

The 1961 version of the AAMR definition described mental retardation as "subaverage general intellectual functioning which originates during the developmental period and is associated with impairment in adaptive behavior" (Heber, 1961, p. 3). Although adaptive behavior was considered a criterion for diagnosis, IQ was still considered the primary criterion because tests of adaptive behavior were not well-standardized (Reschly, 1992). The definition also established five levels of mental retardation: borderline, mild, moderate, severe, and profound. The borderline diagnosis extended the upper IQ limit from a previously accepted level of 70–75 to a level of 85.

Macmillan and Reschly (1997) noted two problems with this classification scheme. First, although adaptive behavior and intellectual functioning were needed for diagnosis, only IQ was used to identify the levels mentioned in the preceding paragraph. Second, the borderline diagnosis was considered very controversial. With an upper IQ limit of 85, approximately 16% of the population would be considered to have mental retardation (using only the

IQ criterion) as opposed to 3% when the traditional cutoff level was used. This increased proportion in the borderline category included large numbers of people from some minority groups and people of low socioeconomic status (SES) as mentally retarded (Macmillan & Reschly, 1997).

Researchers in the field criticized this new classification scheme on several grounds. The main criticism was the absence of scales to assess the adaptive behavior domain. Often, clinical judgement was used as opposed to a formal assessment. Zigler, Balla, and Hodapp (1984) argued that the diagnosis of impaired adaptive behavior made through clinical assessment led to low agreement between examiners, resulting in an unreliable classification system.

Another criticism of adaptive behavior was made by Clausen (1967, 1968, 1972), who noted that as IQ decreased, adaptive behavior decreased as well. Because the two dimensions were so highly correlated, mental retardation was still being diagnosed on IQ alone and not with the combination of IQ and adaptive behavior. Adaptive behavior scales often correlate as high as .60 with IQ test scores. This correlation is nearly as high as the correlation of two IQ tests with each other.

The AAMR definitions of the 1970s and 1980s (Grossman, 1973, 1977, 1983) were slightly modified versions of the 1961 definition that incorporated substantial changes in emphasis. The 1973 version referred to mental retardation as "significantly subaverage general intellectual functioning existing concurrently with deficits in adaptive behavior and manifested during the developmental period" (Grossman, 1973, p. 5). The description "significantly subaverage" meant an IQ of two or more standard deviations below the population (i.e., an IQ or 70 or below). This was a return to the traditional scheme, which eliminated the borderline category. Another change was replacing the "associated with" to "existing concurrently" when discussing adaptive behavior. This change elevated adaptive behavior to equal importance with intellectual functioning despite objections from critics (Macmillan & Reschly, 1997).

Although the 1983 version of the definition was the same as the 1973 version, the 1983 manual contained recommendations regarding the use of absolute IQ scores. The upper limit was actually a range of 70–75 (Grossman, 1983). Although this lack of precision would prove helpful for service providers in offering services to a large number of individuals, it would be a dilemma for researchers, who need to define their populations precisely. The imprecision made it difficult to determine levels of mental retardation as well (Reschly, 1992).

The exact cutoffs preferable to researchers were a real problem for service providers. Often laws requiring care would state a specific cutoff for the provision of a particular service. For example, a person might be required to have a 50 IQ or lower to be eligible for services provided by a sheltered workshop. A person with an IQ test score of 51 would be ineligible for the service. Even if there were a consensus among service providers that the person would profit from a sheltered workshop environment, the service provider was left with only a few options. He or she could find a test that gave an IQ below 50, or the test score could be fudged.

The most current AAMR definition, published in 1992, characterizes mental retardation by

significantly subaverage intellectual functioning, existing concurrently with related limitation in two or more of the following applicable adaptive skill areas: communication, self-care, home living, social skills, community use, self-direction, health and safety, functional academics, leisure, and work. Mental retardation manifests before age 18 (Lukkason, 1992, p. 3).

The most obvious change from the previous definitions is the addition of 10 specific adaptive skill areas rather than an overall adaptive skill level. However, the problems with including adaptive behaviors that were identified 30 years ago still exist today, namely, how to assess adaptive behavior accurately. Some researchers argue that "no measures that have suitable psychometric characteristics for assessment of adaptive behavior are available for all these domains" (Jacobson & Mulick, 1992, p. 11). The picture is blurred even further when the upper IQ limit for diagnosis is discussed, which is actually a range of 70–75. This ambiguity makes the issue of classification very difficult for research purposes. The definition has been criticized for its imprecision regarding classification for research purposes and scientific interests (Belmont & Borkowski, 1994; MacMillan, Gresham, & Siperstein, 1993). Clearly, the definition was designed for advocacy purposes (Macmillan & Reschly, 1997). There is more "wiggle room" in this definition. The classification of mental retardation is more heavily left to the judgement of professionals than to the score on a single test.

Although AAMR and other advocacy groups have focused on the abilities of people with mental retardation and what they can accomplish with enough support, scientific researchers interested in the underlying cause of mental retardation have moved in the other direction and have attempted to find what is "missing" in people with mental retardation. In other words, if intelligence, loosely defined, is the ability to perform well on IQ tests, then people who do not do well on IQ tests have low intelligence. Presumably, people with low intelligence have a cognitive deficiency. The interesting question, then, is what exactly is the deficiency? What "works" in intellectually average people that "does not work" in people with mental retardation?

To answer the question, researchers have applied models from other areas of psychology to people with mental retardation in an attempt to discover which process is deficient. This approach is often referred to as the deficit model of mental retardation. It was hoped that once the underlying process causing mental retardation was discovered, an appropriate intervention based on improving the function of that process could be developed. In this way, the incidence of mental retardation could be reduced through interventions or even eliminated. The two major areas on which mental retardation researchers concentrated were memory and attention.

Memory in the Mentally Retarded

One of the most widely used memory models for mental retardation research was an adaptation of the Atkinson and Shiffrin (1968) and Waugh and Norman (1965) models suggested by Ellis (1970). In the Ellis model, information flows through a series of stores: very short-term memory (VSTM), primary memory (PM), secondary memory (SM), and tertiary memory (TM). The stores are defined by their capacity, by how quickly information is lost from them, and by the way forgetting occurs. Information moves between stores by means of two processes: perceptual attention and rehearsal. Perceptual-attentional processes allow information to be transferred from VSTM to PM, whereas rehearsal prevents decay of information in PM and allows it to be moved to SM.

Using this paradigm, researchers tried to determine which memory store or process causes the differences seen between people with mental retardation and people without mental retardation in performing memory tasks. However, instead of finding the one memory store or process producing the deficits, researchers found deficits in every area. Selected studies examining each memory store or process are reviewed below.

Very Short-Term Memory

Very short-term memory is a sensory-specific representation of a stimulus event (Ellis, 1970) and has a relatively limitless capacity and a very brief duration (Sperling, 1960). Researchers have compared the performance of normal mental age- or chronological age-matched individuals with the performance of people with mental retardation on VSTM tasks to define similarities or differences between groups. The two types of tasks generally used are partial report and masking. Partial-report techniques involve cueing subjects at various intervals after the onset of the stimulus to attend to only a part of the stimulus array. This time interval is termed the interstimulus interval, and people with mental retardation perform more slowly than controls at all interstimulus intervals (Friedrich, Likbuman, Craig, & Winn, 1977; Likbuman & Friedrich, 1972; Pennington & Luszcz, 1975). Generally, the slower performance of people with mental retardation is taken as evidence of deficits in VSTM for such people (Headrick & Ellis, 1964; Pennington & Luszcz, 1975). However, partial-report data could be confounded by strategy use or prior learning (Ross & Ward, 1978; Sheingold, 1973).

The other method used to study VSTM is masking. Masking involves presenting a target stimulus for a short duration followed by the masking stimulus, which covers the target stimulus and makes it difficult to perceive the target. Studies using this method have reported that people with mental retardation do not process information efficiently because of a decreased VSTM capacity (Galbraith & Gliddon, 1972; Hornstein & Mosley, 1987; Welsandt & Meyer, 1974). It is possible that people with mental retardation cannot keep information in VSTM long enough to determine what the relevant cues are before the onset of the mask (Hornstein & Mosley,

1987). Overall, the evidence points in the direction of a deficit in VSTM.

Primary Memory

Primary memory (PM) is limited in capacity and has a longer duration than VSTM (Ellis, 1970). Researchers generally define PM by the recency effect. The recency effect is demonstrated by superior recall of the last few items on a list. Interestingly, researchers found that people with mental retardation and normal control subjects performed equally well on the last few positions of a list (Ellis, 1970). It was concluded that the groups had functionally similar PM (Belmont & Butterfield, 1969; Ellis, 1970), and differences in overall performance on memory tasks were attributed to a lack of active strategy use (Ellis, 1970). The view that there is no PM deficit in people with mental retardation has been widely accepted. However, this finding is questionable (Detterman, 1979). There have been a few studies that have at least suggested the possibility that a PM deficit exists (Cohen & Sandberg, 1977; Dugas & Kelas, 1974).

Rehearsal

Rehearsal is the ability to maintain information in PM for as long as possible so it can be moved to SM. Rehearsal includes naming items, repetition of items, chunking, and grouping. Not surprisingly, rehearsal has been extensively studied in people with mental retardation. Most reviews have concluded that people with mental retardation are less likely to use strategies such as rehearsal than chronological age- or mental age-matched controls (Butterfield & Belmont, 1977; Borkowski & Cavanaugh, 1979; Campione, Brown, & Ferrara, 1982).

Ellis (1970) used numerous memory tasks to examine rehearsal and the transfer of information from PM to SM. As mentioned previously, people with mental retardation and normal controls both demonstrated similar recency effects. However, when the two groups were compared for items remembered from the beginning of a list, or the primacy effect, people with mental retardation recalled far fewer items. The differential performance on these tasks was attributed to a rehearsal deficit. That is, people with mental retardation did not use active rehearsal to maintain information. Although they do not adopt strategies spontaneously, people with mental retardation can be trained to employ strate-

gies to increase performance on memory tasks. However, these strategies are short-lived (Borkowski & Cavanaugh, 1979). Therefore, it is widely accepted that a rehearsal deficit exists. In fact, the rehearsal deficit was the major focus of researchers during the 1970s and 1980s. Attempts were made to get mentally retarded subjects to use active strategies as they processed information. When we consider educational interventions, we will see that the most effective approaches seem to encourage active use of strategy.

One issue that was never resolved in all of the research on strategic use in persons with mental retardation was if the absence of strategy use is the primary deficit in mental retardation or simply the reflection of a more primary deficit. It is hopeful to think that a low IQ is simply the reflection of processing information the wrong way. Once a person is taught to process correctly, the problem is solved. On the other hand, a person may use bad strategies in processing information because they are not reinforced sufficiently when he or she uses strategies. For example, a statistics student could memorize the statistics book but the time required would far exceed the benefit. In the same way, a person with mental retardation might not obtain sufficient return from using strategies because of more basic information processing deficits.

To show that the use of strategies is the primary deficit would require a study showing that, when they used strategies, persons with mental retardation perform the same as persons of normal intelligence. We are unaware of any study, free of ceiling effects, that has ever produced equality between mentally retarded and normal subjects, though there have been many attempts.

Secondary and Tertiary Memory

Ellis (1970) divided long-term memory into secondary and tertiary memory. Secondary memory has limited storage but a greater capacity and duration than PM. Tertiary memory is the long-term store for over-learned information. Its capacity and duration are virtually limitless, but information can be lost through interference or be inaccessible owing to difficulties with retrieval.

The majority of studies dealing with TM in people with mental retardation have serious methodological problems (Belmont, 1966; Detterman, 1979). The basic argument is that it is extremely difficult, if not impossible, to assess long-term memory truly because of deficits that exist earlier in the system. If people with mental retardation do not encode information properly, cannot hold enough information in memory, and cannot transfer the information to a longer term store, then measuring long-term memory is confounded by all of these factors. Simply put, there cannot be a measure of long-term memory without considering the processes and stores that contribute to it. However, a few studies have shown long-term memory deficits in people with mental retardation (Prehm & Mayfield, 1970; Sperber, Ragain, & McCauley, 1976). Not enough sound studies exist to make any firm conclusions about TM in people with mental retardation.

Overall, it seems that Ellis (1978) was accurate when he suggested that people with mental retardation have a deficit that begins at stimulus onset and persists throughout the entire system. Similarly, Detterman (1979) concluded every process to be deficient to some degree and labeled it the "everything deficit." Further evidence to support the "everything deficit" hypothesis comes from a study that examined the basic cognitive processes of mentally retarded people and college students (Detterman et al., 1992). This study systematically investigated each memory store, memory process, or both, and found deficits for nearly every store or process for the adults with mental retardation. The basic conclusion regarding memory in people with mental retardation is that no specific deficit could be identified as a single explanation of their poorer performance.

Attention and Mental Retardation

This section will briefly describe some of the theories of attention that have been applied to mental retardation research. These theories include structural components and cognitive processing as they relate to attention as well as some of the research that has been done in this area.

In 1963, Zeaman and House postulated that individual differences in the performance of discrimination tasks seen in people with mental retardation could be attributed to attentional differences rather than differences in learning or extinction. They described discriminative learning as a chain of two responses. The first is attending to the rel-

evant dimension of a stimulus, and the second is approaching the correct cue for that particular dimension. Several parameters defined their model, including initial attention preferences, initial cue preferences, learning and extinction rate, and the number of stimulus dimensions. They found that individual differences in intelligence were related to attention. However, preference for initial cues did not vary with intelligence, nor did learning rate parameters.

Fisher and Zeaman (1973) proposed a model that combined the earlier Zeaman and House (1963) attention theory with the Atkinson and Shiffrin (1968) memory model. The important change to this model was the role assigned to information retention. Retention was described as a change in the focus of attention resulting from a change in the contents of memory. Zeaman and House (1979) reported that some components of their theory were related to intelligence. Initial probability of attending to the relevant dimension of a stimulus distinguished the performance of mentally retarded people with higher and lower levels of intelligence. Thus, direction of attention was included as a fixed component in the model. Learning and extinction rate were not related to intelligence. However, the capacity of short-term memory and the ability to attend to more than one dimension of a stimulus were related to intelligence in this model.

In 1984, Carr proposed that attention is an executive process within a limited capacity system. Attentional processes select a goal, plan sequences designed to reach the goal, and monitor the execution of those plans. Attentional processes also filter irrelevant stimuli and actively process relevant information in STM. Within this framework, Carr proposed that the limited-capacity system in people with mental retardation is drained by each attentional component. This results in speed–accuracy trade-offs and work-storage trade-offs in people with mental retardation.

Conclusions about Past Research

An enormous amount of research was conducted from the 1960s through the 1980s on the cognitive abilities of persons with mental retardation. Very little of this research is being conducted now. Did it serve any useful purpose? The answer to this question is an emphatic yes. Before this research was conducted, persons with mental retardation were seen as incapable of learning even the simplest material. The cognitive research boom of the last 40 years has shown unambiguously that persons with mental retardation are capable of learning and remembering even complex materials. Previously, there was a tendency to think of people with mental retardation as a separate species not subject to the principles of cognitive psychology. Today, any comprehensive theory of intelligence or cognition must account for mental retardation in the same way it must account for genius.

Has this research accomplished anything of a practical nature? Again the answer is yes. For example, the Fagan Test of Infant Intelligence is a direct descendant of the Zeaman and House model of attention. In a later section of this chapter, we shall see that portions of the research have been translated into academic interventions that seem to be effective across the full range of IQs. More generally, the research on persons with mental retardation has led to the development of cognitive tasks that can be used with very low-functioning persons who may have IQs as low as four standard deviations below the mean. This technology may have important uses in the future.

If this research was so successful, why is it almost extinct? We believe the answer to this question lies in the nature of general intelligence, or *g*. Cognitive processes do not exist in isolation but are well-integrated into a complex system (Detterman, 1987a, 1994). Because all of these cognitive process are interdependent, it is very difficult to identify a deficit in a single part of the system. If there is a single deficit, this deficit would almost surely affect the functioning of the entire system – particularly if the deficit were in an important or central process of the system. It may be difficult or impossible to identify specific deficits using only behavioral measures. This may be particularly true of the mentally retarded because cognitive processes are known to correlate more highly in the mentally retarded than in persons of higher levels of intelligence (Detterman & Daniel, 1989). The identification of deficits may require the coordination of underlying biological processes with behavioral measures. And we believe this is the direction cognitive research on mental retardation is headed.

FUTURE DIRECTIONS

Mental retardation research holds an exciting future. Several new directions should prove worthwhile in our attempt to understand the broader concept of intelligence. Two of these directions are phenotypic mapping and savant syndrome.

Phenotypic Mapping

A phenotype is the "observable or measurable expression of a gene or genes" (Berini & Kahn, 1987). Studying behavioral phenotypes simply means studying phenotypes of individuals with specific genetic disorders (O'Brien, 1992). In general, it is believed that individuals with a specific genetic syndrome may exhibit similar physical or behavioral traits as compared with individuals with other causes of mental retardation because they share a common genetic anomaly (Dykens, 1995; Epstein, 1993).

Once behavioral phenotypes are identified, phenotypic mapping can be employed. Phenotypic mapping means using molecular genetic techniques to define the physical region of a chromosome that is likely to contain the gene(s) whose over- or under-expression is at least partly responsible for a phenotypic feature (Korenberg, 1993). Phenotypic mapping is commonly studied using aneuploid syndromes. An aneuploid syndrome is one in which there is an imbalance in the copy number of genes – either too few (as in Turner's syndrome) or too many (as in Down's syndrome). The goal of phenotypic mapping is to discover which genes are responsible for particular features of the phenotype, especially the most devastating ones, so that they can be prevented in the future (Epstein, 1993).

Although some phenotypic features have been mapped successfully, other more complex features still require further investigation. Most of the medical conditions associated with Down's syndrome have been fairly well mapped – perhaps because of the medical backgrounds and training of the researchers who are actively mapping the chromosome. In contrast, the cognitive domains are not as well established. Collaboration between the medical and cognitive researchers is needed to define the regions associated with mental retardation better. Given the extensive research on cognitive processes in the mentally retarded, this is a superb opportunity to apply the cognitive methodologies that have already been developed and to correlate them with underlying biological processes.

The regions containing the genes for the mental retardation associated with Down's syndrome are extremely broad and not well defined. Profound mental retardation is associated with bands 21q21.1 to 21q21.3, whereas mild mental retardation is associated with bands 21q11.2 to 21q21.3 and also bands 21q22.12 to qter (Korenberg, 1995). These regions are extremely large, in molecular terms, and need to be narrowed considerably.

Generally, performance on IQ tests is the characteristic used to define mental retardation. Research has shown that intelligence is a trait that is probably affected by the interaction of many genes as opposed to one or even a small number of genes. It is possible that an IQ score is too complex a measure to be mapped adequately to a small chromosomal region. Perhaps using tasks that measure more basic cognitive abilities would be helpful. The chromosomal region(s) responsible for basic cognitive abilities might be smaller, and thus easier to define, than complex cognitive abilities.

One such test of basic abilities is the Cognitive Abilities Test (CAT; Detterman, 1988). The CAT is an integrated, computer-administered battery of cognitive tasks that test for individual differences in cognitive abilities. The battery consists of tasks such as simple and choice reaction time, recall and recognition tasks, stimulus discrimination, and tasks that assess learning. The CAT has been used with persons at all levels of intelligence. Studies have examined persons with mental retardation (Caruso & Detterman, 1983a; Conners & Detterman, 1987; Detterman, 1987b; Detterman & Daniel, 1989; Detterman et al., 1992), including Down's syndrome (Kim, 1995; Detterman, Gabriel, & Spry, 1997), and intellectually average persons (Caruso & Detterman, 1983b; Detterman, 1987a; Detterman & Andrist, 1990). In sum, using less complex better-defined cognitive abilities may prove fruitful in the phenotypic mapping of mental retardation associated with Down's syndrome and other genetic disorders associated with mental retardation.

Overall, it appears that phenotypic mapping is one approach that will aid in defining the genetic basis for Down's syndrome and other chromosomal abnormalities. Phenotypic mapping has been successful in pointing out chromosomal regions that are (at least partly) responsible for some phenotypic features associated with Down's syndrome. In particular, band 21q22 is involved in the genesis of the characteristic facial appearance, mental retardation, and heart disease (Korenberg et al., 1990). It is also believed that two regions on the long arm of chromosome 21 are involved in producing mental retardation. However, collaboration is needed between medical and psychological researchers to define better the cognitive features that need to be investigated. It is anticipated that the molecular mapping of Down's syndrome will meet with continued success provided that the molecular data from more individuals with partial trisomy becomes available, higher resolution techniques are developed, and phenotypic features continue to be better defined.

Savant Research

The second promising area of research in mental retardation that might prove fruitful in understanding general intelligence is work with savants. A savant is a person with mental retardation who demonstrates one or more skills above the level expected of nonretarded individuals (Hill, 1978). The skills in the savant population seem to fall within a few general categories. Categories include artistic talent (Tredgold, 1914, 1922; Selfe, 1978; Rimland & Hill, 1984), fine sensory discrimination (Tredgold, 1922; Horwitz, Kestenbaum, Person, & Jarvik, 1965), exceptional musical talent (Rimland & Hill, 1984; Rimland & Fein, 1988; Anastasi and Levee, 1960; Owens & Grimm, 1941; Rimland & Fein, 1988; Sloboda, Hermelin, & O'Connor, 1985; Viscott, 1970), exceptional memory (Jones, 1926; Tredgold, 1914; Treffert, 1988; Hill, 1978), and mathematical ability (Critchley, 1979; Rife & Snyder, 1931; Rimland & Hill, 1984). Another category of savant skills is calendar calculating. Calendar calculating is the ability to determine, usually within a few seconds the day of the week on which a particular date fell or will fall without consulting a calendar. Many cases are cited throughout the literature, but most early accounts are simply colorful descriptions of individual calendar calculators (Horwitz, Kestenbaum, Person, & Jarvik, 1965).

It has only been in the last few decades that investigators have tried to do more than provide case reports of savants. Instead, the focus has become finding the mental processes behind the skills and the methods the savants use to determine the various dates. Several theories to explain calendar calculating have been proposed, including concrete thinking, sensory deprivation, compensation and motivation, memory, and concentration (Hill, 1978). Knowledge of calendar rules and regularities has also been suggested (O'Connor & Hermelin, 1984). Several mathematical formulas for calculating dates have been proposed, although most researchers in the area feel they are too complex for savants to use (Spitz, 1994). However, some have suggested that people of average intelligence could learn to use them to calendar calculate if given the time or motivation (Ericsson & Faivre, 1988; Hill, 1978; Hoffman, 1971). In fact, two studies have successfully trained people of average intelligence to calendar calculate (Addis, as cited in Ericsson & Faivre, 1988; Gabriel, 1997). Because there are relatively few savant calendar calculators, training people to perform savant tasks could provide researchers with greater numbers of people to study. Individuals trained to perform a savant task could be compared with actual savants, which could provide insight into the methods that actual savants may be using. Understanding the processes behind a savant skill would help researchers understand what cognitive processes do and do not contribute to general intelligence. The particular advantage of studying savant skills is that the unique skills displayed by savants appear to be a contradiction to g. In a well-integrated system, abilities across people should be highly correlated. Because savants display a single outstanding skill, portions of the cognitive system must somehow be independent of the rest of the system. Understanding which parts of the cognitive system are contributing to these savant skills may give leverage in understanding the whole system and how it is integrated in more typical people.

GENERAL CONCLUSIONS ABOUT BASIC RESEARCH

Research within the field of mental retardation has proven helpful for the broader understanding of intelligence. By applying mainstream psychological paradigms to persons with mental retardation, we come to understand more about their cognitive

functioning and how it relates to our overall notion of intelligence. This is as true today as when research on mental retardation research was in its infancy. As in any area of research, the questions always get more complex and the answers more sophisticated. What seemed an enormous accomplishment at the time it was realized, when viewed from a more distant vantage point, may seem silly. For example, to us, those researchers who asked if the mentally retarded could learn simple material seem extremely naive. However, in an environment where nearly everyone thought that the mentally retarded were incapable of learning anything and should be locked away for life, this research had enormous practical consequences for those affected and for society in general. Given this perspective, it is amazing how much we have accomplished in the last 100 years and particularly in the last 50 years.

THE EDUCATION OF CHILDREN WITH MENTAL RETARDATION

The education of children with mental retardation is a relatively new concept that has blossomed within the last two centuries. Historically, individuals with limited mental capabilities were at best ignored but often mistreated. Inspired by the work being done at the end of the 18th century with deaf children, Jean Marc Itard, a French physician, began to speculate that children with limited mental capabilities could be helped by environmental influences (Kirk & Johnson, 1951).

Itard found an opportunity to confirm his theory. Itard subscribed to the beliefs of sensationalism or what would today be labeled as environmental influences on intelligence. The sensationalists believed intelligence to develop through the exposure of the senses to education. Although Itard had many opponents from the genetic, or what was then known as nativism, position, he began a 5-year educational intervention with a boy, whom he named Victor, found living alone in the forest of Aveyron.

Even though Itard eventually gave up his attempt to educate Victor, declaring it a failure, it is a classic story about the beginnings of educational interventions with the mentally retarded. Victor was without language and appeared to have sensory deprivation. He could not discriminate between hot and cold. Itard worked to enhance Victor's mental capabilities through the use of his senses. Modest improvements in his abilities were obtained. Victor was able to read a few words and to associate them with the correct object. However, Victor remained largely mute until his death.

Although Itard eventually gave up his work with mentally retarded children, he inspired his student Edward Seguin and many others who began the search for educational interventions for the mentally retarded. Edward Seguin is best remembered for his progressive views of education. He emphasized the individualization of education, the need to begin with an area of interest for the child, and to enjoy an open and comfortable relationship between child and teacher. Modern day interventions and remediation for children with mental retardation are founded on many of the same principles of environmental interventions that Itard, Seguin, and other early philosophers subscribed to. The following section will review more recent early childhood programs aimed at preventing and remediating mental retardation.

The Abecedarian Project was one of the more famous attempts targeted at preventing mild mental retardation (Ramey & Campbell, 1992). It was one of several early intervention programs that sprung from the hope that mild mental retardation could be prevented through environmental interventions for children at risk for mild mental retardation. Children selected for the Abecedarian Project were from low-resource families. Children from low-resource families are at higher risk for academic failure, which is predictive of unfavorable life experiences (Herrnstein & Murray, 1994). Children in low-resource situations experience higher rates of grade retention than children in middle-class families (Lazar, Darlington, Murray, Royce, & Snipper, 1982). The Abecedarian Project intended to intervene at infancy and enhance the academic outcome of children at risk for mental retardation by enhancing their cognitive abilities.

The Abecedarian Project began in 1972 at the University of North Carolina. The researchers devised an index to estimate the risk factor for mental retardation each child faced. The children were then matched and randomly assigned to either the experimental or the control group. All children in the program, both the experimental and control groups, were entitled to social services and medical treatments. Children in the control group also received nutritional supplements to counteract any effect that may have resulted from the meals children in the experimental group received during preschool hours. The only difference between the experimental and control groups was that the experimental children received educational intervention from the time they entered the program at an average age of 8.8 weeks until they entered kindergarten.

Children in the experimental group attended a traditional high-quality day-care center. The program began at 7:45 a.m. and ran through 5:30 p.m. for 5 days each week and 50 weeks per year. Special emphasis was placed on language development. Children encountered typical preschool activities such as water play, sandboxes, puzzles, and one-to-one instruction from the staff. Testing was done when children reached 54 months of age. The General Cognitive Index score for the experimental group was 101. The mean General Cognitive Index score for the control group was 91, $t = 4.00$, $p < .001$. Children in the experimental group sustained a 10-point gain over the control group. The project then entered its second phase, the follow-through program.

The follow-through program was initiated to study the effect of grade-school intervention on children at risk of failure. The researchers for the Abecedarian project were aware of the usual fade-out effects for IQ gains made in early intervention programs. The follow-through segment was intended to provide evidence on the following two issues:

1. Could the traditional fade-out effect be prevented with further educational support?
2. Could groups that began an intervention program in the early grades increase their academic achievement?

Children in the experimental and control groups were matched and then randomly assigned to one of two groups. Half of the children in the experimental group continued to receive special services and tutoring during the early grade-school years and half were placed into the control group. The original control group was also divided into two sections: half the children entered the experimental group and half remained in the control group. This structure set up four separate groups for the investigators to study. The first group received the experimental intervention in both the preschool intervention and the follow-through section. The second group received the preschool intervention, but additional intervention was discontinued at school age. The third group received no intervention during the preschool years but special services during the early years of grade school, and the final group remained untreated throughout the entire project.

Children who took part in the follow-through segment of intervention were given a graduate-level home or school teacher who was used as a liaison between the two environments. The resource teacher met with the classroom teacher to review current classroom topics and inquire about the progress of the follow-through student. The resource teacher would then supplement the educational material presented in class with additional review work. The material was presented during weekly meetings with the parents at which not only was academic achievement discussed but also the child's behavioral report from the classroom teacher.

The follow-through project hoped to create an atmosphere of trust and cooperation between the child's home and school environment. Parents were instructed to review the material that the resource teacher provided for their child. The average reported time spent on the review material was 15 minutes each day (Ramey & Campbell, 1992).

Children who had preschool intervention scored significantly higher on the Wechsler test for cognitive ability, though the differences were small. However, there was no significant IQ gain for children who only participated in the follow-through program. The lack of substantial and sustainable IQ differences between groups have led some to conclude the program was ineffective (Spitz, 1984). Because substantial IQ gains were not realized for the follow-through program, academic gains for each group were assessed.

The academic achievement scores for the children who participated in the Abecedarian preschool and follow-through program exhibited a trend for academic achievement to increase as a function of the amount of time spent in an intervention program. The children who served as controls for the entire project had the lowest academic achievement scores as measured on both the school-administered California Achievement test for reading and the Woodcock–Johnson test. The average score for reading in the control group was at the 19th percentile, whereas the preschool plus follow-through group scored at the 41st percentile. The academic outcome for mathematical achievement followed the same pattern. Children who received intervention services for longer periods functioned at higher rates. The control group average for mathematical ability measured at the 33rd percentile, whereas the preschool plus follow-through group had a mean score at the 51st percentile.

The results from the Abecedarian project are typical of results often found in this area: (1) Large gains in IQ can be obtained with intensive early intervention programs. (2) These gains are lost if intervention is discontinued. (3) Even if intervention is continued, IQ gains are usually lost. What seems to be improved are achievement variables, including an increased percentage of students who completed high school, a lower percentage of special education placements, and so forth. To the best of our knowledge, no interventions have shown sustained IQ gains through the use of intervention. However, they also consistently show several less direct effects on outcome. The longer the intervention is maintained, the more likely are these effects to occur. A major issue that is frequently debated is how important the less direct effects are and if they justify the expense of intervention.

Programs like the Abecedarian project use conventional methods of intervention. It might be possible to make bigger gains using more refined intervention methods. Research that identifies strategies that impact on the educational achievement of school-aged children with mild mental retardation is a current topic in the educational literature. These methods were, at least indirectly, inspired by cognitive research on the use of strategies.

Children are often not diagnosed with mild mental retardation until they reach school age. Several investigators have developed programs aimed at increasing the cognitive ability and the behavioral strategies children with mild mental retardation have at their disposal. Instrumental Enrichment is one such intervention proposed by Feuerstein, Randi, and Rynders (1988).

Feuerstein bases his theory of Instrumental Enrichment on the firm belief that intelligence is modifiable. The basis of intervention stems from belief that low-functioning individuals did not have sufficiently modified interactions with the environment as infants or young children. Children who did not have a mediator (parent, teacher, caregiver) to interpret the environment and point out relevant information did not benefit cognitively in the same way children with adequate attention did. Feuerstein believes that mediation with the environment will modify the cognitive structures of children with mild mental retardation and allow them to function at elevated levels.

Feuerstein identified three necessary steps for the modification of human cognitive ability. The first step is the evaluation of the individual through the learning potential assessment device (LPAD). This device is meant to measure the individual's capacity to learn. The LPAD is a dynamic approach to discover a child's readiness or ability to learn and is different from traditional IQ tests, which are considered a static form of assessment. Once the assessment is done the individual enters the second stage of the program, Instrumental Enrichment (IE), which entails learning to learn. The program provides the child with strategies to enhance performance in academic and real-world situations. The final phase of the program is the adjustment of the environment to produce supportive formats for people with mental retardation.

The first step in the modification of cognitive structures for children with mental retardation is the LPAD. The LPAD acts first as an assessment and then as a tool for understanding the cognitive deficits each child displays and finally as a tool to assess gains made through modification. The identification of deficits gives the educator a valid understanding of why the child is low functioning. Rather than being concerned with the child's answers, the modifier is interested in the process by which the child reached his or her answer. By identifying a child's individual cognitive deficits, the moderator can develop specific tasks or strategies to work with for each child. After the child's deficits have been identified, remediation can begin. Following the remediation, the child is retested on similar but novel items to judge how much he or she was able to benefit from the remediation.

The second phase of intervention, IE, has been accepted as a successful intervention strategy for individuals with mental retardation (Feuerstein, Rand,

Hoffman, Hoffman, & Miller, 1979). Unlike traditional educational goals, children are not taught crystallized pieces of information. The goal of IE is to increase the learning capacity of each child through the mediated instruction of relevant strategies that proficient learners spontaneously employ. Typical IE programs for children with mental retardation are implemented for 5 to 7 hours each week for a period of 2 years.

Instrumental enrichment is concerned with three separate stages of processing: input, elaboration, and output. During the input stage, attention is focused on the learner's ability to scan relevant material in a systematic way. The mediator is interested in leading the child to gather information in an effective manner. The mediator may present the child with a paper that has four dots equal distances away from each other. The mediator may ask the child to count the dots. The child may continually lose count because he or she does not scan the material in a systematic manner. The mediator may then introduce a left-to-right, top-to-bottom scanning procedure that will aid in the systematic gathering of information. This exercise may be repeated in novel situations until the child internalizes the strategy and produces it at the appropriate time.

The second stage of processing the IE is elaboration. Mediators are concerned that the information gathered be dealt with in an instructive manner. The mediator encourages the child to integrate the present material with past information and possible future outcomes. Children with mental retardation have difficulty with processing material from more than one source at a time. Their learning potential is greatly decreased from what is referred to as an episodic grasp of reality.

The output phase in many ways is the most difficult for children with mental retardation. Even after the new information has been gathered and elaborated on in a meaningful way, children have difficulty producing an appropriate response or output. Through constant feedback from the mediator, children are encouraged to take their time to formulate an answer that reflects their understanding of the information at hand. The program has developed its slogan from this section of the intervention ("Just a minute . . . let me think").

The final phase of intervention for persons with mental retardation is Shaping Modifying

Environments. Persons who travel through the first two steps of the intervention, LPAD and IE, need an environment that is able to stimulate their modified cognitive structures and then support their individual needs to function in a meaningful way in society. Often adults and children with mental retardation are isolated or tolerated within their environments. This lack of stimulation will only hinder their ability to function at their optimal level.

The IE program has shown promising effects experimentally. Rand, Tannenbaum, and Feuerstein (1988) investigated the effect of IE on 600 culturally deprived children with mental retardation. The 300 IE subjects received 300 hours of IE intervention over the course of 2 years. This intervention took place during portions of the regular school day. The comparison group received 300 hours of additional instruction in reading, mathematics, and writing. After 1 year the IE group significantly outperformed the comparison group on the PMA (Primary Mental Abilities Test). The difference persisted throughout the testing period, which continued until 2 years after the intervention program ended. The gains made by the experimental group increased as a function of time, which is different from the fade-out effect displayed by most intervention with low-functioning children.

Feuerstein's method of intervention for children with mental retardation is one form of remediation. The IE program places its emphases on changing the cognitive structure of the learner. Other research places its emphasis on changing the learning situation in which retarded learners function. Although most programs are not mutually exclusive, they do have a major focus. Recent investigation has highlighted the effectiveness of peer-tutoring. Peer-tutoring differs from IE intervention in that its focus is generally on increasing content-bound material. Instrumental enrichment was developed to instruct mentally retarded individuals in strategies that would enhance their ability to learn new material. The program is intentionally content free. Peer-tutoring is usually targeted at one or two subjects with the hope of increasing performance within that specific domain. Usual targets are reading comprehension and mathematics. What they share in common is an emphasis on strategic performance by the learner.

The term peer-tutoring is used throughout the literature to refer to both same-age and cross-aged tutors. We will use the term peer-tutor exclusively for same-aged tutoring pairs. This will be done to avoid confusion over the relationship that exists within each tutoring pair. Peer tutoring has advantages and disadvantages when compared with reciprocal peer tutoring and cross-age tutoring. Peer-tutoring programs take advantage of students within the same classroom. Usually an academically advanced student is used to tutor an academically delayed student in a specific subject.

Peer tutoring has had encouraging academic results for both the tutor and the tutee in reading, spelling, mathematics, and writing when compared with traditionally taught control groups (Cloward, 1977; Cohen, Kulik, & Kulik, 1982; Topping, 1987). Peer-tutoring actively engages the tutor and the tutee in the target academic activity and gives students an opportunity to respond, which is vital for academic growth (Delquadri, Greenwood, Whorton, Carta, & Hall 1986). Peer-tutoring provides immediate feedback and increases the time students are engaged in academic activity. Increased amounts of time engaged in academic activity has been demonstrated to have a positive correlation with academic achievement (Greenwood, 1991).

Peer-tutoring has innate drawbacks, however, because of the social implications involved with same-aged students' being identified as tutor and tutee. As children age, they become increasingly sensitive to the social implications of their status within this pair (DePaulo, Tang, Webb, Hoover, Marsh, Litowitz, 1989). Reciprocal tutoring, also known as classwide tutoring, offers a solution to the status problems that occur in peer tutoring. Cross-age tutoring is another alternative arrangement that provides an abundance of competent tutors without the social stigma associated with dividing same-aged classmates into tutor and tutee roles.

Cross-age tutoring is the use of an older student to tutor a younger one. In America, cross-age tutoring has its historical roots in the one-room school house. In this setting, one teacher was often employed to instruct several children of different ages. Older children were used to help younger students with their lessons. Cross-age tutoring is rarely used in today's classrooms because age segregation is prevalent within our educational system.

Research that surrounds cross-age tutoring has shown that it is an effective educational intervention for children at risk of failure (Cohen, Kulik, Kulik, 1982; Limbrick, McNaughton, & Glynn, 1985; Maher, 1982; Sharpley, Irvine, & Sharpley, 1983). Cross-age tutoring provides the opportunity for students to respond and increases engaged time, which is vital for academic growth (Delquadri, Greenwood, Whorton, Carta, & Hall, 1986). Cross-age tutoring provides the younger tutee and the older tutor with accelerated, academically relevant gains when compared with control students receiving traditional education. Accelerated academic gains are critical for children who have fallen behind their classmates and are thus at risk of failure.

Cross-age tutoring programs that use low-achieving or troubled adolescents as tutors have produced encouraging outcomes for those individuals and the younger students that they tutor. Although, traditionally, tutoring employs a high achiever to tutor a low achiever, research indicates that struggling adolescents can be effective tutors with younger children (Maher, 1982).

Programs that use struggling adolescents as cross-age tutors have reported positive changes for affective measures along with cognitive gains. Tutors reported increased self-esteem (Pino, 1990; Yogev & Ronen, 1982) and a reduction in truancy (Lazerson, Foster, Brown, & Hummel, 1988). Affective and academic changes made as a result of assuming a tutoring role for low-achieving high school adolescents have had a positive effect on decreasing dropout rates (Sosa, 1986).

Studies done using handicapped children to tutor nonhandicapped students are rare. However, Top and Osguthorpe (1987) did report reading outcomes for 78 handicapped fourth through sixth graders employed as tutors for nonhandicapped first graders. The handicapped tutors were randomly assigned to the tutor or nontutor group.

The tutees were 82 first-grade students who were not in any special classroom setting. However, their teachers had identified them as in need of reading practice. The first-grade students were also randomly assigned to either the tutee or control group.

The tutors were trained in techniques that aided them in their new role. Specific reading instruction was not given. The handicapped tutors were instructed in ways to prompt their students and in appropriate praising behaviors. The students spent 15–20 minutes each day 4 days a week in their tutoring sessions. The program lasted 14 weeks. The control students received similar reading time in their traditional classrooms.

The results indicated that the handicapped students who served as tutors significantly outperformed the handicapped control students in reading achievement as measured on the Woodcock–Johnson reading achievement test. The first-grade students who received the one-on-one attention from the handicapped tutors also outperformed their first-grade counterparts in reading achievement as measured by a standardized Woodcock–Johnson reading test.

Evaluation of Educational Interventions

Although special education has generally not been very special (Detterman & Thompson, 1997), there are a few hopeful signs for future possibilities. It is not surprising that progress in a field that has been under investigation is slow. It is encouraging that the interventions that do show some signs of being useful are direct, or at least indirect, descendents of cognitive research with the mentally retarded. All of these interventions have been frequently criticized for flaws in research methods, subject populations, and methods of assessment (see Spitz, 1986 for examples). But it is not surprising that applied research is a lot less precise than more basic research. The most optimistic part of the story is that there is a line that can be traced from basic research to application. A century ago, no such connection existed. Interventions were based on very basic philosophical ideas unsupported by basic research. That has changed over the course of the last century, and that change has been all for the better.

GENERAL CONCLUSIONS

This chapter has sketched the panorama of research in mental retardation over the last century with particular emphasis on the last 40 years. Our intention was to give the reader a thumbnail sketch of where researchers have been and where they may be going in this field. We believe we have captured the essential features of the landscape, but others may provide a different viewpoint.

The questions remaining are those we posed at the beginning of this chapter: Has research in mental retardation accomplished anything? We believe it has. Although the progress may be glacial in speed, when viewed for a long period of time, movement is apparent. Of particular note is the closer linkage of basic research with applied research. Although this connection is still weak, there is reason to hope that it will grow stronger in the future.

Another accomplishment of research in mental retardation is that it has changed our conceptions of persons with mental retardation. People who, at one time, were viewed as unsalvageable are now regarded as people who can learn and accomplish. This is quite a radical change to occur in less than 100 years.

Has research in mental retardation contributed anything to our understanding of intelligence? We think it undoubtedly has. First, the initial use of intelligence tests was to classify mentally retarded persons. Widespread use of IQ tests for classification of the mentally retarded led to the accumulation of enormous amounts of data about the correlates of IQ. Second, the cognitive approach to understanding human intelligence, which is the dominant approach to the study of intelligence today, can be directly traced to research in mental retardation. These are not small accomplishments.

Finally, has the study of intelligence increased our understanding of mental retardation? To some extent it has. However, there are few theories of intelligence that attempt to explain mental retardation in any systematic way. Some theorists still believe that an explanation of mental retardation is appropriately beyond the scope of a theory of intelligence. We do not agree with this position. Until the explanation of mental retardation is an integral part of theories of intelligence, theories of intelligence will be incomplete.

Over the next century, there is reason to hope that the connection between intelligence and mental retardation will be more fully, and perhaps even completely, explicated. Advances in genetics, brain imaging and recording, and neuroscience may allow the connection of behavioral data collected over the last 50 years with underlying biological processes. Perhaps at the end of the next century, whoever writes this chapter will be giving us more definitive answers to the questions we have not answered, posing new questions, and wondering if they have really accomplished anything over the last 100 years.

REFERENCES

Anastasi, A., & Levee, R. (1960). Intellectual defect and musical talent: A case report. *American Journal of Mental Deficiency, 64,* 695–703.

Atkinson, R. C., & Shiffrin, R. M. (1968). Human memory: A proposed system and its control processes. In K. W. Spence & J. T. Spence (Eds.), *The psychology of learning and motivation: Vol. 2* (pp. 90–195). New York: Academic Press.

Belmont, J. M. (1966). Long-term memory in mental retardation. In N. R. Ellis (Ed.), *International review of research in mental retardation: Vol. 1* (pp. 219–255). New York: Academic Press.

Belmont, J. M., & Borkowski, J. (1994). Prudence, indeed, will dictate...review of *Mental retardation: Definition, classification, and systems of support* (9th ed.). *Contemporary Psychology, 39,* 495–496.

Belmont, J. M., & Butterfield, E. C. (1969). The relations of short-term memory to development and intelligence. In L. P. Lipsitt & H. W. Reese (Eds.), *Advances in child development and behavior: Vol. 4* (pp. 29–82). New York: Academic Press.

Berini, R. Y., & Kahn, E. (1987). *Clinical genetics handbook.* Oradell, NJ: Medical Economics Books.

Borkowski, J. G., & Cavanaugh, J. C. (1979). Maintenance and generalization of skills and strategies by the retarded. In N. R. Ellis (Ed.) *Handbook of mental deficiency, psychological theory, and research* (2nd ed., pp. 569–617). Hillsdale, NJ: Erlbaum.

Butterfield, E. C., & Belmont, J. M. (1977). Assessing and improving the cognitive functions of mentally retarded people. In I. Bialer & M. Sternlicht (Eds.), *The psychology of mental retardation: Issues and approaches.* New York: Psychological Dimensions.

Campione, J. C., Brown, A. L., & Ferrara, R. A. (1982). Mental retardation and intelligence. In R. J. Sternberg (Ed.), *Handbook of human intelligence* (pp. 392–490). London: Cambridge University Press.

Carr, T. H. (1984). Attention, skill, and intelligence: Some speculations on extreme individual differences in human performance. In R. Sperber, C. McCauley, & P. Brooks (Eds.), *Learning and cognition in the mentally retarded* (pp. 189–215). Baltimore: University Park Press.

Caruso, D. R., & Detterman, D. K. (1983a). Stimulus encoding by retarded and nonretarded adults. *American Journal of Mental Deficiency, 96,* 649–655.

Caruso, D. R., & Detterman, D. K. (1983b). Individual differences in short-term memory and their relationship to item identification. *American Journal of Psychology, 96,* 527–537.

Clausen, J. A. (1967). Mental deficiency: Development of

a concept. *American Journal of Mental Deficiency, 71*, 727–745.

Clausen, J. A. (1968). A comment on Halpern's note. *American Journal of Mental Deficiency, 72*, 950.

Clausen, J. A. (1972). Quo vadis, AAMD? *The Journal of Special Education, 6*, 51–60.

Cloward, R. D. (1977). Studies in tutoring. *The Journal of Experimental Education, 36*, 14–25.

Cohen, P. A., Kulik, J. A., and Kulik, C. C. (1982). Educational outcomes of tutoring: A meta-analysis of findings. *American Educational Research Journal, 19*, 237–248.

Cohen, R. L., & Sandberg, T. (1977). Relation between intelligence and short-term memory. *Cognitive Psychology, 9*, 534–554.

Conners, F. A., & Detterman, D. K. (1987). Information processing correlates of computer assisted word learning in mentally retarded students. *American Journal of Mental Deficiency, 91*, 606–612.

Critchley, M. (1979). The divine banquet of the brain. New York: Raven Press.

Delquadri, J. C., Greenwood, C. R., Whorton, D., Carta, J. J., & Hall, R. V. (1986). Classwide peer tutoring. *Exceptional Children, 52*, 535–542.

DePaulo, B. M., Tang, J., Webb, W., Hoover, C., Marsh, K., & Litowitz, C. (1989). Age differences in reactions to help in a peer tutoring context. *Child Development, 60*, 423–439.

Detterman, D. K. (1979). Memory in the mentally retarded. In N. R. Ellis (Ed.), *Handbook of mental deficiency, psychological theory, and research* (2nd ed., pp. 727–760). Hillsdale, NJ: Lawrence Erlbaum Associates.

Detterman, D. K. (1983, March). Assessing cognitive deficits in the mentally retarded. Paper presented at the Gatlinburg Conference on Mental Retardation, Gatlinburg, TN.

Detterman, D. K. (1987a). Theoretical notions of intelligence and mental retardation. *American Journal of Mental Deficiency, 92*, 2–11.

Detterman, D. K. (1987b). What does reaction time tell us about intelligence? In P. A. Vernon (Ed.), *Speed of information processing and intelligence* (pp. 177–199). Norwood, NJ: Ablex.

Detterman, D. K. (1988). *CAT: Cognitive Abilities Tests.* Cleveland, OH: Case Western Reserve University.

Detterman, D. K. (1994). A system theory of intelligence. In D. K. Detterman (Ed.). *Current topics in human intelligence: Vol. 4. Theories of intelligence* (pp. 85–115). Norwood, NJ: Ablex.

Detterman, D. K., & Andrist, C. G. (1990). The effects of instruction on elementary cognitive tasks sensitive to individual differences. *American Journal of Psychology, 103*, 367–390.

Detterman, D. K., & Daniel, M. H. (1989). Correlations of mental tests with each other and with cognitive variables are highest for low IQ groups. *Intelligence, 13*, 349–359.

Detterman, D. K., Gabriel, L. T., Spry, K. (1997). Cogni-

tive skills and aging in persons with Down syndrome. Manuscript submitted for publication.

Detterman, D. K., Mayer, J. D., Caruso, D. R., Legree, P. J., Conners, F., & Taylor, R. (1992). Assessment of basic cognitive abilities in relation to cognitive deficits. *American Journal of Mental Retardation, 97*, 251–286.

Detterman, D. K., & Thompson, L. A. (1997). IQ, schooling, and developmental disabilities: What's so special about special education? *American Psychologist, 52*, 1082–1091.

Doll, E. A. (1934). Social adjustment of the mental subnormal. *Journal of Educational Research, 28*, 36–43.

Doll, E. A. (1941). The essentials of an all-inclusive concept of mental deficiency. *American Journal of Mental Deficiency, 46*, 214–219.

Doll, E. A. (1962). A historical survey of research and management of mental retardation in the United States. In E. P. Trapp & P. Himmelstein (Eds.), *Readings on the exceptional child* (pp. 21–68). New York: Appleton-Century-Crofts.

Doll, E. A. (1967). Historical review of mental retardation, 1800–1965: A symposium. *American Journal of Mental Deficiency, 72*, 165–189.

Dugas, J. L., & Kellas, G. (1974). Encoding and retrieval processes in normal children and retarded adolescents. *Journal of Experimental Child Psychology, 17*, 177–185.

Dykens, E. M. (1995). Measuring behavioral phenotypes; Provocations from the "new genetics." *American Journal of Mental Retardation, 99*, 522–532.

Ellis, N. R. (1970). Memory processes in retardates and normals. In N. R. Ellis (Ed.), *International review of research in mental retardation, Vol. 4* (pp. 1–32). New York: Academic Press.

Ellis, N. R. (1978). Do the mentally retarded have poor memory? *Intelligence, 2*, 41–54.

Epstein, C. J. (1993). The conceptual bases for the phenotypic mapping of conditions resulting from aneuploidy. In C. J. Epstein (Ed.), *The phenotypic mapping of down syndrome and other aneuploid conditions* (pp. 1–18). New York: Wiley-Liss.

Ericsson, K. A., & Faivre, I. A. (1988). What's exceptional about exceptional ability? In L. K. Obler & D. Fein (Eds.), *The exceptional brain: Neuropsychology of talent & special abilities* (pp. 436–473). New York: Guilford Press.

Feuerstein, R., Rand, Y., Hoffman, M., Hoffman, M., & Miller, R. (1979). Cognitive modifiability in retarded adolescents: Effects of instrumental enrichment. *American Journal of Mental Deficiency, 83*, 539–550.

Feuerstein, R., Rand, Y., & Rynders, J. E. (1988). *Don't accept me as I am: Helping retarded people to excel.* New York and London, Plenum Press.

Fisher, M. A., & Zeaman, D. (1973). An attention-retention theory of retardate discrimination learning. In N. R. Ellis (Ed.), *International review of research in mental retardation: Vol. 6* (pp. 159–256). New York: Academic Press.

Friedrich, D., Likbuman, T., Craig, F., & Winn, F. (1977). Readout times from iconic memory in normal and retarded adolescents. *Perceptual and Motor Skills, 34,* 467–473.

Gabriel, L. T. (1997). An investigation of calendar calculation using "manufactured" savants. Unpublished master's thesis.

Galbraith, G. C., & Gliddon, J. B. (1972). Backward visual masking with homogeneous and patterned stimuli: Comparison of retarded and nonretarded subjects. *Perceptual and Motor Skills, 34,* 903–908.

Greenwood, C. R. (1991). Classwide peer tutoring: Longitudinal effects on reading, language, and mathematics achievement of at-risk students. *Journal of Reading, Writing, & Learning Disabilities International, 7,* 105–123.

Grossman, H. J. (Ed.). (1973). *Manual on terminology and classification in mental retardation.* Washington, DC: American Association on Mental Deficiency.

Grossman, H. J. (Ed.). (1977). *Manual on terminology and classification* (Rev. ed.). Washington, DC: American Association on Mental Deficiency.

Grossman, H. J. (Ed.). (1983). *Classification in mental retardation* (3rd ed.). Washington DC: American Association on Mental Deficiency.

Hasher, L., & Zacks, R. T., (1979). Automatic and effortful processes in memory. *Journal of Experimental Psychology: General, 108,* 356–388.

Hasher, L., & Zacks, R. T. (1984). Automatic processing of fundamental information. *American Psychologist, 39,* 1372–1388.

Headrick, M. W., & Ellis, N. R. (1964). Short-term visual memory in normals and retardates. *Journal of Experimental Child Psychology, 1,* 339–347.

Heber, R. (1961). Modifications in the manual on terminology and classification in mental retardation. *American Journal of Mental Deficiency, 65,* 499–500.

Herrnstein, R. J., & Murray, C. A. (1994). *The bell curve: Inelligence and class structure in Americans life.* New York: Free Press.

Hill, A. L. (1978). Savants: Mentally retarded individuals with special skills. In N. R. Ellis (Ed.), *International review of research in mental retardation, Vol. 9* (pp. 277–298). New York: Academic Press.

Hoffman, E. (1971). The idiot savant: A case report and a review of explanations. *Mental Retardation, 9,* 18–21.

Hornstein, H. A., & Mosley, J. L. (1987). Iconic memory deficit of mildly mentally retarded individuals. *American Journal of Mental Deficiency , 91,* 415–421.

Horwitz, W. A., Kestenbaum, C., Person, E., & Jarvik, L. (1965). Identical twins – "idiot savants" calendar calculators. *American Journal of Psychiatry, 121,* 1075–1079.

Jacobson, J. W., & Mulick, J. A. (1992). A new definition of mentally retarded or a new definiton of practice? *Psychlogy in Mental Retardation and Developmental Disabilities, 18,* 9–14.

Jones, H. E. (1926). Phenomenal memorizing as a "special ability." *Journal of Applied Psychology, 10,* 367–377.

Kim, L. Y. (1995). *Contrast sensitivity in adults with Down syndrome and its effect on cognitive abilities and age.* Unpublished doctoral dissertation.

Kirk, S. A., & Johnson, G. O. (1951). *Educating the retarded child.* Boston, MA: Houghton Mifflin Company.

Korenberg, J. R. (1993). Toward a molecular understanding of Down syndrome. In C. J. Epstein (Ed.), *The phenotypic mapping of Down syndrome and other aneuploid conditions* (pp. 87–115). New York: Wiley-Liss.

Korenberg, J. R. (1995). Mental modeling. *Nature Genetics, 11,* 109–111.

Korenberg, J. R., Bradley, C., & Disteche, C. M. (1992). Down syndrome: Molecular mapping of the congenital heart disease and duodenal stenosis. *American Journal of Human Genetics, 50,* 294–302.

Korenberg, J. R., Kawashima, H., Pulst, S. M., Ikeuchi, T., Ogasawara, N., Yamamoto, K., Schonberg, S. A., West, R., Allen, L., Magenis, E., Ikawa, K., Taniguchi, N., & Epstein, C. J. (1990). Molecular definition of a region of chromosome 21 that causes features of the Down syndrome phenotype. *American Journal of Human Genetics, 47,* 236–246.

Lazar, I., Darlinton, R., Murray, H., Royce, J., & Snipper, A. (1982). Lasting effects of early education: A report from the Consortium for Longitudinal Studies. *Monographs of the Society for Research in Child Development, 47* (2–3, Serial No. 195).

Likbuman, T., & Friedrich, D. (1972). Threshold measures of sensory register storage (perceptual memory) on normals and retardates. *Psychonomic Science, 27,* 357–358.

Limbrick, E., McNaughton, S., & Glynn, T. (1985). Reading gains for underachieving tutors and tutees in a cross-age tutoring programme. *Journal of Child Psychology and Psychiatry, 26,* 939–953.

Luckasson, R. (Ed.). (1992). *Mental retardation: Definition, classification and systems of support.* Washington, DC: American Association on Mental Retardation.

Macmillan, D. L., Gresham, F. M., & Siperstein, G. N. (1995). Heightened concerns over the 1992 AAMR definition: Advocacy versus precision. *American Journal on Mental Retardation, 98,* 325–335.

Macmillan, D. L., & Reschly, D. J. (1997). Issues of definition and classification. In W. E. MacLean (Ed.), *Ellis' handbook of mental deficiency, psychological theory and research* (3rd ed. pp. 47–74). New Jersey: LEA Publishers.

Maher, C. A. (1982). Behavioral effects of using conduct problem adolescents as cross-age tutors. *Psychology in the Schools, 19,* 360–364.

O'Brien, J. (1992). Behavioral phenotypes and their measurement. *Developmental Medicine and Child Neurology, 34,* 365–367.

O'Connor, N., & Hermelin, B. (1984). Idiot savant calendar calculators: Maths or memory? *Psychological Medicine, 14,* 801–806.

Owens, W. A., & Grimm, W. (1941). A note regarding exceptional musical ability in a low grade imbecile. *Journal of Educational Psychology, 32,* 636–637.

Pennington, F. M., & Luszcz, M. A. (1975). Some functional properties of iconic storage in retarded and nonretarded subjects. *Memory and Cognition, 3,* 295–301.

Pino, C. (1990). Turned on by tutoring. *American Educator, 14,* 35–36.

Prehm, M. J., & Mayfield, S. (1970). Paired-associate learning and retention in retarded and nonretarded children. *American Journal of Mental Deficiency, 74,* 622–625.

Ramey, C. T., & Campbell, F. A. (1992). Poverty, early childhood education, and academic competence: The Abecedarian experiment. In A. Huston (Ed.), *Children in poverty* (pp. 190–221). New York: Cambridge University Press.

Rand, Y., Tannenbaum, & Feuerstein, R. (1988) *Don't accept me as I am; Helping retarded people to excel* (Appendix D). New York and London: Plenum Press.

Reschly, D. J. (1992). Mental retardation: Conceptual foundation, definitional criteria, and diagnostic operations. In S. R. Hynd & R. E. Mattison (Eds.), *Assessment and diagnosis of child and adolescent psychiatric disorders: Vol. II. Developmental disorders* (pp. 23–67). Hillsdale, NJ: Lawrence Erlbaum Associates.

Rife, D. C., & Snyder, L. H. (1931). Studies in human inheritance VI: A genetic refutation of the principles of "behavioristic" psychology. *Human Biology, 3,* 547–559.

Rimland, B., & Hill, A. L. (1984). Idiot Savants. In J. Wortis (Ed.), *Mental retardation and developmental disabilities* (Vol. 13, pp. 155–169). New York: Plenum Press.

Rimland, B., & Fein, D. A. (1988). Special talents of autistic savants. In L. K. Obler & D. A. Fein (Eds.), *The exceptional brain: Neuropsychology of talent & special abilities* (pp. 474–493). New York: Guilford Press.

Ross, L. E., & Ward, (1978). The processing of information from short-term visual store: Developmental and intellectual level. In N. R. Ellis (Ed.), *International review of research in mental retardation.* Vol. 9 (pp. 1–28). New York: Academic Press.

Scheerenberger, R. C. (1987). A history of mental retardation. Baltimore: Brookes.

Schweinhart, L. J., & Weikart, D. P. (1989). The High/Scope Perry Preschool Study: Implications for early childhood care and education. *Prevention in Human Services, 7,* 109–132.

Selfe, L. (1978). *Nadia: A case of extraordinary drawing ability in an autistic child.* New York: Academic Press.

Sharpley, A. M., Irvine, J. W., & Sharpley, C. F. (1983). An examination of the effectiveness of a cross-age tutoring program in mathematics for elementary school children. *American Educational Research Journal, 20* (1), 103–111.

Sheingold, K. (1973). Developmental differences in intake and storage of visual information. *Journal of Experimental Child Psychology, 16,* 1–11.

Sloboda, J. A., Hermelin, B., & O'Connor, N. (1985). An exceptional musical memory. *Music Perception, 3,* 155–170.

Sosa, A. S. (1986). Valued youth partnership program: Dropout prevention through cross-age tutoring. *Newsletter, Intercultural Development Research Association* (ERIC Document Reproduction Service Nos. ED 279 764 and ED 279 765).

Sperber, R. D., Ragain, F. D., & McCauley, C. (1976). Reassessment of category knowledge in retarded individuals. *American Journal of Mental Deficiency, 81,* 227–234.

Sperling, G. (1960). The information available in brief visual presentations. *Psychological Monographs, 74* (11, Whole No. 498).

Spitz, H. H. (1986). The raising of intelligence: A selected history of attempts to raise retarded intelligence. Hillsdale, NJ: Lawrence Erlbaum Associates.

Spitz, H. H. (1994). Lewis Carroll's formula for calendar calculation. *American Journal of Mental Retardation, 98,* 601–606.

Top, B. L., & Osguthorpe, R. T. (1987). Reverse-role tutoring: The effects of handicapped students tutoring regular class students. *The Elementary School Journal, 87,* 413–423.

Topping, K. (1987). Peer tutored paired reading: Outcome data from ten projects. *Educational Psychology, 7,* 133–145.

Tredgold, A. F. (1914). *Mental deficiency.* New York: William Wood.

Tredgold, A. F. (1922). *Mental deficiency* (pp. 334–345). New York: William Wood.

Treffert, D. A. (1988). The idiot savant: A review of the syndrome. *American Journal of Psychiatry, 145,* 563–572.

Viscott, D. S. (1970). A musical idiot savant. *Psychiatry, 33,* 494–515.

Waugh, N. C., & Norman, D. A. (1965). Primary memory. *Psychological Review, 72,* 89–104.

Welsandt, R. F., & Meyer, P. A. (1974). Visual masking, mental age, and retardation. *Journal of Experimental Child Psychology, 18,* 512–519.

Yogev, A., & Ronen, R. (1982). Cross-age tutoring: Effects on tutors' attributes. *Journal of Educational Research, 75,* 261–268.

Zeaman, D., & House, B. (1963). The role of attention in retardate discrimination learning. In N. R. Ellis (Ed.), *Handbook of mental deficiency* (pp. 159–223). New York: McGraw-Hill.

Zeaman, D., & House, B. (1979). A review of attention theory. In N. R. Ellis (Ed.), *Handbook of mental deficiency, psychological theory and research* (2nd ed., pp. 63–120). Hillsdale, NJ: Erlbaum.

Zigler, E., Balla, D., & Hodapp, R. (1984). On the definition and classification of mental retardation. *American Journal of Mental Deficiency, 89,* 215–230.

CHAPTER EIGHT

Intelligence and Giftedness

CAROLYN M. CALLAHAN

What do we mean when we call a child or adult gifted? How do we assess giftedness? Is giftedness synonymous with high intelligence? High IQ? What other constructs are considered to be part of the giftedness construct? To what degree is adult giftedness related to childhood aptitude and to what degree are factors such as motivation, effort, or learning style predictive of eminence? Is giftedness unidimensional or multidimensional? Is genius the same as being gifted? What is the relationship of creativity to giftedness? Does giftedness exist, or is it an invention of society to represent what we value in children and adults, or is it simply an artifact of educators' desires to sort students? The debate surrounding these questions and the presumed answers have affected the ways that schools have done business for most of this century.

Outstanding performance and expertise are recognized and praised in all societies, but not all societies value and reward the same talent. The label gifted (or talented, highly able, bright, smart, capable, wise, or intelligent) is not assigned to the same exceptional performance across all societies or to persons with the same particular constellation of traits. Some societies extend their recognition beyond the domain of cognitive accomplishments to include physical or athletic prowess or artistic, performing, and productive talents. For example, basketball prowess is much more highly valued in our society than in any other. Even when a society limits its conception of superior ability to the domain of intellectual functioning or intelligence, it is difficult to find consensus regarding the meaning of giftedness.

Certainly, the diversity among definitions of intelligence given by eminent theorists represents an underlying source of disparity among definitions of giftedness (Sternberg & Detterman, 1986). Arguments surrounding the dimensionality of intelligence, the assessment of intelligence, the heritability of intelligence, and the stability of intelligence are paralleled in educators' debates regarding giftedness. In addition, debates regarding the meaning, application, and implications of the term *gifted* are rooted in the ways various definitions of intelligence are integrated into a conception or definition of giftedness, in the relevance and importance of nonintellective factors, in the relative emphasis placed on performance versus potential, and in the degree to which constructs like creativity are equivalent, superordinate, or component factors of giftedness.

In Western cultures, particularly in schools, the dominant operational definitions of giftedness are based on the use of standardized individual and group measures of IQ that have evolved from the Standford–Binet test. Hence, this chapter will begin with an overview of the historical relationships between the intelligence testing movement and the corresponding dominance of the IQ definition of giftedness that has evolved. Then a sample of representative definitions of giftedness reflecting changing conceptions of intelligence during the last three decades will be used to illustrate the range of variability in current thinking. Finally, the chapter includes a review of the issues underlying discussions of the value or relevance of the various definitions and a summary of promising developments in the research on gifted children and adults that may inform practice in identifying and providing appropriate educational interventions.

BACKGROUND AND INFLUENCES

Interest in the gifted individual as a phenomenon to be studied in conjunction with the study of intelligence can be traced to the work of Sir Francis Galton (1869). His study of intelligence and giftedness, *Hereditary Genius*, focused on a retrospective examination of distinguished persons and their families. On the basis of Galton's observations that the distinguished persons he studied seemed to come from families with many other eminent figures, he concluded exceptional achievement to be a result of inherited sensory ability (i.e., what he believed to be intelligence). Galton's beliefs about the high heritability of intelligence and giftedness have had profound influence on societal attitudes and associated educational beliefs and practice surrounding the identification of gifted children and the services provided by schools. The line of influence from Galton to the study of giftedness in the United States is most directly traceable through his influence on the work of Lewis Terman.

The Influence of Terman

The concept of intelligence as measured by an IQ test and the study of giftedness in the United States have been intertwined since Terman modernized and Americanized the Binet–Simon test to create the Stanford–Binet Intelligence Scale (Terman, 1916). Given that Terman had included the study of "genius" as a component of his master's thesis and studied "seven bright and seven dull boys" (Terman, 1925, p. 1) for his doctoral thesis, it is not surprising that shortly after the completion of his work on the Stanford–Binet test he began his classic longitudinal work on gifted individuals. Applying the Stanford–Binet test to select his sample of more than 1500 gifted children (defined as those nominated by their teachers and scoring above 140 on that instrument*), Terman undertook to assess this

---

* All children under 11 scored at least 140. Lower cutoff scores were used for older students, and 132 was the lowest score of those included in the sample who were tested with the Stanford–Binet.

sample along mental, physical, social, personality, and character–moral dimensions. The legacy of that work has been a lasting and seemingly immutable tie between the concept of general intellectual ability as measured by intelligence tests and the concept of giftedness, at least in research and practice, during most of the 20th century. Tannenbaum (1996) reported, for example, that 13 of 22 empirical studies published in *Gifted Child Quarterly* in the years 1991 and 1992 list IQ test score results as the sole measure or the prominent measure in defining their samples. Abeel, Callahan, and Hunsaker (1994) found that intelligence tests were the most frequently used assessment tools in local school divisions to identify gifted students. The emphasis given to the use of traditional, individually administered IQ tests for the assessment of cognitive abilities in the training of school and clinical psychologists provides continual reinforcement to acceptance of the IQ score as the penultimate assessment of giftedness.

Terman's work in intelligence testing reflected Galton's beliefs in the heritability and permanence of the traits of intelligence. The relative stability of scores of his group on the IQ tests he developed affirmed this belief. (Terman and his associates explained individual variation as artifacts of testing procedures; Cravens, 1992.) The manifestation of a belief in the inherent nature and stability (and even heritability) of intelligence in educational practice has been the assumption that "giftedness" is a trait within the individual and it is the task of schools to "find it."

Terman's longitudinal study also provided an array of descriptive characteristics of children and adults who score more than two standard deviations above the mean on intelligence tests (Terman et al., 1925; Terman & Oden, 1947; Terman & Oden, 1959). The children in his sample were found to be normal or superior in all aspects of intellectual, as well as physical, behavioral, and moral dimensions studied, which countered the prevalent view held at that time that highly intelligent persons are abnormal or deviant. These characteristics are still the most commonly cited defining traits of giftedness in textbooks and articles on the subject of gifted children and their education (see, for example, Davis & Rimm, 1998, and Gallagher & Gallagher, 1994). Not surprisingly, these lists often reflect characteristics measured by the Stanford–Binet test (locating, remembering, or recognizing factual details; possessing a large vocabulary; having exceptional ability to perceive relationships among details, etc.). Subsequent lists derived from later studies parallel the findings of Terman in the intellectual domain – perhaps because of a heavy reliance on the same test or highly correlated tests for defining the samples of those studies.

In the early 1940s the Standford–Binet test was used to select students for the Hunter College Elementary School from the top 1% of the population. The school was established by Leta Hollingworth based on her conclusion that early recognition of extraordinary intelligence and provisions of appropriate educational opportunities contributed to greater accomplishment and an improved quality of social and emotional adjustment (Morelock & Feldman, 1997). The median score of these children on the Stanford–Binet test during the first 10 years of the school's existence was 151. Her studies of the ''highly gifted'' did not yield the same results as those of Terman. Although both samples were successful in school, Hollingworth concluded that the highly gifted (defined as those with IQ scores above 150) tended to have several adjustment problems, including (1) failure to develop desirable work habits in school, (2) difficulty in finding a suitable peer group (often becoming social isolates), and (3) vulnerability because of an intellectual capacity to understand major ethical or moral issues that developed in advance of their emotional capacity to deal with them (Morelock & Feldman, 1997).

CONCEPTIONS OF GIFTEDNESS

One of the other ramifications of the strong bond between the use of IQ scores to define and assess intelligence and the education of the gifted has been to limit discussion, debate, and research focusing on the relationships of conceptions of intelligence to conceptions of giftedness. With the notable exception of the publication of *Conceptions of Giftedness* (Stenberg & Davidson, 1986), the literature on this topic has been sparse. Even among those who propose alternative definitions of giftedness, the degree to which these theorists make specific connections between the construct of intellectual abilities and the construct of giftedness varies considerably. The construct of giftedness is sometimes directly con-

nected with a specific theory of intelligence (e.g., Sternberg, 1986a), sometimes intentionally ignored or dismissed by the authors (e.g., Stanley & Benbow, 1986), sometimes vague, and sometimes presumed to be understood.

The existing definitions of giftedness and conceptions of giftedness have also varied based on (1) the degree to which intellectual ability is the core of the definition or one of many ways that giftedness is defined, (2) the way intelligence is conceptualized (independent of, or combined with, other cognitive constructs such as creativity, and (3) the ways that cognitive domains of performance (including creativity and intelligence) are combined with other nonintellective factors (such as personality).

The IQ Definition of Giftedness

As I have mentioned, the IQ test has dominated the assessment of giftedness, and in much of the research literature and the practice of identifying and serving gifted children the IQ definition prevails. Terman aimed at assessing intelligence as abstract, symbolic thought (Morelock & Feldman, 1997) with the Simon–Binet test. That concept and the consequent measure of aptitude reflected by a single score on an intelligence test is often accepted as a sufficient definition of giftedness in state policy and by local school division practice (Abeel, Callahan, & Hunskaker 1994). The IQ definition does not rely on any theory; rather, the success of the IQ test in predicting school success suffices.

The Federal Definition of Giftedness

The most widely accepted definition of giftedness (based on citations and the number of state policy documents such as regulations for gifted programs) was first offered by the U.S. Office of Education (also known as the USOE or Marland definition). According to this definition gifted and talented children were those who demonstrated achievement and/or potential ability in any of the following areas:

1. General intellectual ability
2. Specific academic aptitude
3. Creative or productive thinking
4. Leadership ability
5. Visual and performing arts
6. Psychomotor ability. (Marland, 1972, p. 10)

When this definition was revised in 1993, the categories remained essentially the same with gifted and talented students now defined as follows:

Children and youth with outstanding talent perform or show the potential for performing at remarkably high levels of accomplishment when compared with others of their age, experience, or environment.

These children and youth exhibit high performance capability in intellectual, creative, and/or artistic areas, possess an unusual leadership capacity, or excel in specific academic fields. They require services or activities not normally provided by the schools (U.S. Department of Education, 1993, p. 3).

The categories within this definition are interpreted to be independent of one another. Further, the category of general intellectual ability has most often been interpreted to mean "highly intelligent" and is operationalized as the top 3–5% of students as measured by intelligence tests (Abeel, Callahan, & Hunsaker, 1994). In essence, when school divisions translate this definition into practice, they most often accept the IQ definition of giftedness.

Renzulli's Three-Ring Definition

Renzulli (1978) criticized the USOE definition as having three particular shortcomings. First, he asserted that the categories were not parallel because both *fields of human endeavor* such as specific academic aptitude and visual and performing arts and *processes* such creativity, general intellectual ability and leadership that can be brought to bear on performance areas were included. Second, he maintained that the categories were not mutually exclusive, but rather, overlapping. And finally, he was critical of the omission of nonintellective factors, including task commitment, from the conception of giftedness offered. He also criticized *any* definition based on simply IQ or analytic intelligence as insufficient in defining the construct of giftedness. As an alternative he offered a definition based on his interpretation of the literature on giftedness as manifested in children and adults.

Renzulli (1986) asserted that there are two kinds of giftedness. The first, he calls "schoolhouse giftedness." According to Renzulli, schoolhouse giftedness is the type of giftedness assessed by IQ and other cognitive ability tests. He also calls giftedness of this sort "test-taking or lesson-learning gifted-

ness" (p. 57). Although he conceded that students identified as the top 3–5% of the population using such a conception are likely to earn high grades and do need modifications in the pace and content of their instruction, he noted that these assessments and the factors measured with such instruments only account for a limited amount of school success and fail to identify many students who will become "creative-producers," (i.e., those who he claims will come to be recognized as gifted). His three-ring definition asserts that the creative–productive gifted individuals possess three clusters of traits: well above average ability, creativity, and task commitment.

Renzulli contended that above average ability can be defined as either general ability (including such constructs as abstract thinking, information processing, verbal and numerical reasoning, and spatial relations) *or* it can be defined as specific ability to acquire knowledge. He lists chemistry, ballet, mathematics, sculpture, photography, and musical composition as examples of specific abilities. General ability in Renzulli's model is assessed by tests of general aptitude or intelligence. Specific abilities are assessed by tests of specific aptitude or achievement (or, if highly correlated with general aptitude, by measures of general ability – such as might be the case with mathematics and chemistry). Renzulli contended that "persons who are capable of performance or have the potential for performance that is representative of the top 15–20% of any given area of human endeavor" (p. 67) should be considered to have this cluster identified as above average ability. Renzulli considered ability to be a relatively stable trait. Task commitment represents a directed form of motivation brought to bear on a particular problem or task. Task commitment differs from general motivation in its more limited focus and in being a state characteristic rather than a trait characteristic. Creativity is a combination of characteristics such as fluency, flexibility, and originality; openness to experience; curiosity; sensitivity to detail; and aesthetics.

The manifestation of giftedness in Renzulli's model is an interaction among the three clusters and is not a stable trait. He also chose to define gifted behavior rather than gifted persons. "Gifted behavior consists of behaviors that reflect an interaction among [these] three basic clusters.... Gifted and talented children are those possessing or capable of developing this composite set of traits and applying them to any potentially valuable area of human performance" (p. 73). As this definition suggests, Renzulli's conception of giftedness also leads to the position that giftedness is a trait (or even more appropriately, a set of behaviors) to be developed with much of the responsibility for providing talent development opportunities resting in the school.

Tannenbaum's Psychosocial Definition

Tannebaum was also highly critical of the use of intelligence tests as the standard for identifying the gifted. "At best, IQ tests are designed to identify those who have in them to qualify some day as professors in the sciences, philosophy, mathematics, artist history, or literature, not as creative scientists, philosophers, mathematicians, artists, poets, playwrights, or novelists" (1996, p. 55). He contends that "giftedness in children . . . denotes their potential for becoming critically acclaimed performers or exemplary producers of ideas in spheres of activity that enhance the moral, physical, emotional, social, intellectual, or aesthetic life of humanity" (Tannenbaum, 1986, p. 33). Tannenbaum, like Renzulli, asserted that *producing* knowledge, rather than consuming it, is the indicator of giftedness, and he also considered giftedness to be a constellation of factors beyond intellectual ability. However, the elements that Tannenbaum associated with the development of giftedness extend beyond the individual. He included superior general intelligence (the *g* factor), exceptional special aptitude in some arena, nonintellective factors (e.g., motivation and self-concept), environmental influences, and chance or luck to be necessary for fulfillment of the promise of becoming gifted.

Sternberg's Triarchic Model of Giftedness

The triarchic model of giftedness flows from the triarchic theory of intelligence. The three elements of intelligence (componential, experiential, and contextual) are translated into analytic, creative and practical giftedness. The componential subtheory focuses on information processing, including metacomponents, performance components, and knowledge-acquisition components. An individual with strengths in this area would be likely to score well on traditional IQ tests and could be identified as gifted using traditional assessment procedures that rely heavily on intelligence tests. Persons with

strengths in the experimental subtheory (the ability to respond appropriately and uniquely to novel tasks and situational demands and to automatize information processing) are more creative. Finally, the contextual subtheory is defined as "purposive adaptation to, shaping of, and selection of real-world environments relevant to one's life" (Sternberg, 1986a, p. 235). Within this model of intelligence and conception of giftedness, exceptional abilities may manifest themselves in any one of the three domains. Sternberg did not specify a formula or relative balance necessary for giftedness; however, in his theory the most gifted (those with the most "successful intelligence") are seen to be those who are both strong in all three domains *and* able to balance these three dimensions, knowing when and how to use each (Sternberg, 1997). Further, Sternberg's theory acknowledges that the particular processes involved in each component may differ from discipline to discipline and does not claim independence of components. Rather, the components are viewed as interactive in creating exceptionally able performance (1986).

Gardner's Model of Multiple Intelligences

Gardner's model of intellectual ability (1983, 1993a), the Multiple Intelligence (MI) model has been translated by educators of the gifted into identification procedures that generate groups of students classified as gifted in one or more of the intelligences he has suggested: linguistic, logical-mathematical, spatial, musical, bodily-kinesthetic, interpersonal, and intrapersonal (Plucker, Callahan, & Tomchin, 1996; Maker, Neilson, & Rogers, 1994; Starnes, n.d.). Within this model, an intelligence is defined as "an ability or set of abilities that permit an individual to solve problems or fashion products that are of consequence in a particular cultural setting" (Ramos-Ford & Gardner, 1977, p. 55). Further, Ramos-Ford and Gardner asserted that the seven are not intended to be restrictive, but rather, to extend the concept of intelligences beyond the linguistic domain traditionally assessed in schools. They also noted that the model proposes these intelligences as "potentials or proclivities that are realized or not depending on the cultural context in which individuals are reared and the opportunities presented for the identification, expression and development of the several intelligences" (p. 55).

Within the schemes for identifying giftedness according to the particular intelligence domains specified by Gardner, the domains are considered independent, and the processes for identification rely on performance assessments and teacher judgments of the presence or absence of traits as listed by Gardner in describing a domain.

Feldman's Developmentalist Position

Developmentalists have not paid particular attention to the phenomenon of giftedness with the exception of Feldman (1986). Feldman, like most contemporary theorists, has viewed the IQ as a narrow and limiting way to define giftedness (or human abilities in general). Through his study of prodigies he has concluded that giftedness is domain-specific rather than generalizable and manifests itself in the process of development, "not only in the mastery of a challenging domain," but in the "reorganization of the structure of that domain" (p. 287), which he calls creativity. He reserves the term *genius* for those "extremely rare occasions when an entire domain is fundamentally reorganized" (p. 287).

Like Tannenbaum and Gardner, Feldman posits that prodigious behavior in children and giftedness in adults reflect a "co-incidence" of forces within and outside the individual. Feldman aligns these forces with the individual's life span, the developmental history of the field or domain, historical or cultural trends bearing on individuals, and evolutionary time. One category of force within the life span is intraindividual factors (biological and psychological) that predispose an individual toward giftedness in a particular field. This category includes biological propensities such as "brain-based" intelligences (defined as potential for development within particular fields) as well physical or acoustical facilities. Feldman also considers the point in the life span at which a child is introduced to a field and the social and emotional environment to be critical factors in the development of giftedness. These are considered environmental factors (familial, societal, or cultural). The historical time frame reflects the opportunity to learn (such as the math–science emphasis following the launch of Sputnik) and the developmental stage of the discipline. Finally, cultural and biological evolutionary factors interact to support or suppress the development of particular talents.

Julian Stanley and Precocity

Julian Stanley disavowed interest in conceptualizing giftedness (Stanley & Benbow, 1986) but rather focused on mathematical precocity. He avoided psychological constructs. "It is as if trying to be psychological throws us off course and into a mire of abstract dispositions" (p. 361). In reality, however, his definitions of precocity or potential talent seem to rest on narrowly conceptualizing individual talents according to specific aptitude and achievement indicators such as the SAT–M. Mathematical precocity is defined as the ability to reason well within the discipline and symbol system of mathematics. Although Stanley focused on mathematics initially, later work included identifying verbal abilities and suggesting that the work be expanded to include specific talent in "music, art, and any other competencies that can be specified in product or performance terms" (p. 361).

Although not exhaustive of the definitions that have been offered, these definitions represent the psychometric, information processing, and developmental conceptions offered to researchers and practitioners who struggle with the conceptualization of giftedness in studying the phenomenon and providing appropriate educational services.

INFLUENCE OF INTELLIGENCE TESTING ON SELECTING A CONCEPTION OF GIFTEDNESS AND CARRYING OUT THE PROCESS OF IDENTIFYING GIFTED CHILDREN

The early association of giftedness with IQ scores derived from atheoretical instruments led to atheoretical practices in identifying gifted students and providing educational interventions. Initially, many systems of identifying gifted children relied exclusively on a single intelligence test score (for example, schools like the Hunter Elementary School discussed earlier). Later developments in creating identification schemes and strategies continued to rely on either the scores on the Stanford–Binet (or other individualized or group tests highly correlated with the Stanford–Binet or Wechsler scales), achievement tests, and often checklists and rating scales (based on characteristics of the sample of gifted students who were identified using IQ tests). Current school practice and public policy continue to be greatly influenced by the dominance of intelligence tests in defining human abilities. Gifted students were (and still are in many school districts) simply those who scored in the top 5% or top 1% on IQ tests. Even though Terman (1959) later questioned the equating of intelligence test scores with giftedness, several states still prescribe a minimum score on an intelligence test as a determinant of eligibility for funding (U.S. Department of Education, 1993). As an illustration of the way that the construct of giftedness has been inextricably linked with intelligence test scores, consider the choice of language in the following statements from a recent textbook in the field of gifted education (Davis & Rimm, 1998): "It is difficult to be gifted when tested with the Stanford–Binet, Fourth Edition" (p. 73). "As with the Stanford–Binet Fourth Edition, it is more difficult to be gifted when tested with the WISC III"(p. 74). These statements reflect the belief that one is only gifted when the intelligence test score authenticates the characteristic.

Not surprisingly, the magnitude of the intelligence test score has been used to categorize individuals further within the general group of identified gifted persons. Such labels as "exceptionally gifted," (IQ 150 and over), "severely and/or profoundly gifted" (IQ 180 and over) (Webb, Meckstroth, & Tolan, 1982), and "moderately gifted" are assigned based on achieving an arbitrarily specified cutoff score on an intelligence test (Morelock & Feldman, 1997; Newland, 1976). This has led to criticisms of current revisions of intelligence tests such as those offered by Davis and Rimm (1998) of the various forms of the WISC because "the highest possible score on the Wechsler tests is 155.... [T]he renorming of the WISC-III in 1991 generally shifted IQ scores down about five points. However, at the high end of the distribution, where gifted children score, WISC-III scores run about 8 or 9 points lower than WISC-R scores" (p. 74). The Stanford–Binet, Fourth Edition, is similarly criticized by the same authors for not "differentiating among highly gifted children" (p. 74).

The continued atheoretical nature of the practice of identifying gifted children is illustrated by the recommendation that practitioners substitute Raven's Progressive Matrices (RPM) (Ford, 1996) for traditional intelligence tests when evaluating children from minority or low socioeconomic groups for placement in gifted programs. Substituting an untimed, nonverbal assessment of inductive reasoning using visual patterns as stimuli for the more verbally oriented IQ assessments that assess a very differently configured set of cognitive skills is recommend as means of finding higher test scores for students in the target groups. Mills, Ablard, and Brody (1993) have concluded "there isn't enough information at present to fully understand what the RPM is measuring and what it [a score from the RPM] means in terms of programming" (p. 186), which raises questions about the constructs being assessed when the RPM and more traditional IQ tests are used interchangeably.

A similar lack of commitment to a theoretical construct underlying giftedness is reflected in the practice of using a system called matrix identification for screening and placement of gifted students in special services. The most popular model used is the Baldwin Identification Matrix (Baldwin, 1985). The application of matrices begins with assigning points for specified, but arbitrary, levels of performance on tests and other assessment tools (e.g., IQ tests, achievement tests, teacher checklists or rating scales, portfolios). For example, an IQ score of 130 or greater may earn 5 points, an IQ score between 120 and 130 may earn 4 points, and so forth. A reading achievement score at the 97th percentile may be assigned 5 points; scoring between the 90th and 96th percentile may earn 4 points, and so on. A teacher rating scale with a total of 30 points may earn 5 points, and one between 25 and 29 may earn 4 points. Then, a single score is created by adding these matrix scores together with the presumption that the sum represents an assessment of "giftedness."

Is Giftedness Unitary or Multidimensional?

The first issue in considering the multidimensionality of giftedness is reflected in definitions in which intellectual ability is one of many factors or dimensions of giftedness. The U.S. Office of Education (Marland definition) is a case in point. It lists the domains of general intellectual ability, specific academic aptitude, creative or productive thinking, leadership ability, and the visual and performing arts (Marland, 1972). The implication of the definition was that general intellectual ability is a category independent of the other categories and that abilities in each category should be evaluated independently. Similarly, Renzulli, Gardner, and Feldman view giftedness as multidimensional in considering multiple specific areas or disciplines in which talents may be manifest.

THE DIMENSIONALITY OF GIFTEDNESS AND THE DIMENSIONALITY OF INTELLIGENCE. The debate over the unitary, multidimensional, hierarchical nature of intelligence among theorists and researchers will certainly receive ample attention in other chapters. The degree to which diversity of opinion in the field of psychology regarding the dimensionality of intelligence has influenced the literature and practice in education of the gifted is evidenced through theorists such as Guilford, Gardner, and Sternberg.

Although unitary conceptions of intelligence and giftedness (when defined as intellectual ability) have dominated the fields of the psychology and education of the gifted, there have been notable exceptions in literature and practice. The first was the work of Guilford (1967) in the development of the Structure of the Intellect (SI) model. After the publication of the 120-factor multidimensional model of intellectual functioning across the domains of content, process, and product and the development of instructional materials based on that model by one of Guilford's students, several programs for the gifted used the model as a means of identifying gifted students and identifying student strengths and weaknesses according to dimensions of the "cube." Educators implemented instructional activities aimed at the development of specific intellectual abilities (Meeker & Meeker, 1986). Guilford did not suggest using the SI model or the related instruments for identifying gifted students, and the existing literature does not offer any substantive evidence that either the instruments used or the instructional models based on this conception of intelligence of giftedness are effective for either. The more wide ranging impact of Guilford's work was to suggest that there are important dimensions of human capability not measured by intelligence tests. In calling attention to the divergent production "slab" of his model (1967) and the general construct of creativity (1950), Guilford opened the discussion of the possibilities of seeing intelligence, and subsequently giftedness, as a combination of factors extending beyond convergent thinking.

The multidimensionality of giftedness across components or factors of intelligence is also part of the triarchic theory of Sternberg (1985, 1986a) and the multiple intelligences model of Gardner. Gardner proposed that intelligence is itself multidimensional, but rather than categorizing the dimensions as levels of content, process, and product as Guilford did, Gardner addressed multidimensionality across areas of human performance. Like the Marland definition of giftedness, the Multiple Intelligence model has been criticized for presuming independence of categories (e.g., Scarr, 1989), and the models of Guilford and Gardner are criticized for presuming a fixed set of abilities (Sternberg, 1994). Even though Gardner has acknowledged the interrelationships among the intelligences, the interpretations of the model for defining giftedness and identifying gifted children have presumed independent categories. Analyses of assessment tools designed to assess the MI model have not validated their use for identification of independent categories of giftedness (Plucker, Callahan, & Tomchin, 1994).

Sternberg's notions of intelligence and giftedness, as discussed earlier, clearly are multidimensional but are so along the dimensions of information processing domains rather than along discipline dimensions. In addition, Sternberg posits that it is not simply the abilities that are critical for achieving eminence but also the ability to ascertain what we are good at, to find ways to compensate for the things we are not good at, and to match the strengths we have with the task we elect to do.

Renzulli (1986) included general ability and specific abilities in constituting the "well above average ability" component of his definition of giftedness. The descriptions he provided of these concepts suggest that he sees the ability component as multidimensional. The general ability component includes many of those traits suggested in the three areas of Sternberg's theory of intelligence (high levels of abstract reasoning, verbal and spatial reasoning, spatial relations, memory, adaptation to and the shaping of novel situations, automatization of information processing, etc.), although the specific ability domain is described as the "application of the various combinations of the above general abilities to one or more specialized areas of knowledge or areas of human performance [and the] capacity for acquiring and making appropriate use of advanced amounts of tacit knowledge, technique logistics, and strategy in the pursuit of particular problems, etc." (p. 75).

Through his study of prodigies, Feldman has concluded that there are specific sets of cognitive functions and processes that distinguish the expert or gifted individual in a given domain. Like others to be discussed later, he posits that it is not simply the cognitive abilities that distinguish the gifted but a combination of qualities, including "propensities such as talent and personality differences; characteristics of the context within which an individual pursues mastery; characteristics of those who are critical influences on the process such as parents, teachers, and peers; and the state of development of all the various fields that might be mastered at a given moment" (p. 291).

INTELLIGENCE, CREATIVITY AND GIFTEDNESS

As the dicussion of the unitary or multifaceted nature of giftedness suggests, much of the debate over the unitary nature of giftedness has often included discussions of the relationship of creativity to intelligence. Most significant in bringing attention to, and stimulating discussion of, the relationship of these constructs was Guilford's Presidential Address to the American Psychological Association in 1950. That address, combined with his work on the structure of intellect, although largely dismissed as an artifact of the methodology of factor analysis by some cognitive psychologists (e.g., Horn & Knapp, 1973), was very influential in stimulating debate about the dimensions of intelligence and in loosening the grip, at least slightly, that intelligence tests had on the definition of giftedness. Further, the degree to which components of Guilford's model of intellectual functioning were those of creative thinking as well (e.g., divergent production and transformation), the model became part of an expanding debate about the independence of creativity and intelligence, the overlap in functions, and the relative roles of the two constructs in defining giftedness. In Guilford's SI model, the structure of intelligence is presumed to include dimensions that are creative. The presentation of creativity as an integral component of intellectual ability was inherent in Guilford's model; however, later theoreticians and practitioners such as Torrance (1966) chose to split the divergent production slab of the cube away from the rest of the structure and treat that dimension of thinking independently for assessment and instruction.

Certainly the field of education for the gifted has embraced the concept of creativity in its definitions. The construct of creativity in relation to giftedness has been at times integrated with the notion of intelligence and giftedness (as in the models of Guilford and Sternberg). At times creativity is considered a construct independent of the intelligence construct but critical to forming the construct of giftedness. For example, the Marland definition cited previously lists creativity as a category of giftedness separate from those of intellectual ability or specific academic abilities and the visual and performing arts.

The more dominant views in the field of education for the gifted reflect creativity as an independent dimension of giftedness, as described in the Marland definition, or as a fundamental concept within the gifted construct. Piirto (1992), for example, calls creativity "the underpinning, the basement, the foundation, which permits giftedness to be realized" (p. 24). This view is also represented by Renzulli's (1978) definition of giftedness in which creativity's interaction with above-average ability and task commitment is the foundation for gifted behaviors. Renzulli (Renzulli, Reis, & Smith, 1981) initially included many of the cognitive processes others associate with creativity (e.g., ideational fluency and originality) with general intellectual ability; and, he recommended the use of creativity tests in the same publication (generally based on those concepts) as an indicator for spotting generalability. In later works he described the creativity component (1986) in his definition of giftedness as

Fluency, flexibility and originality of thought.
Openness to experience; receptive to what is new and different (even irrational) in the thoughts, actions, and products of oneself and others.
Curious, speculative, adventurous, and "mentally playful;" willing to take risks in thought and action, even to the point of being uninhibited.
Sensitive to detail, aesthetic characteristics of ideas and things; willing to act on and react to external stimulation and one's own ideas and feelings (p. 75).

Although some considered giftedness and creativity to be synonymous (Tannenbaum, 1986), other researchers and theoreticians such as Amabile (1989) and Runco and Albert (1986) carefully distinguished giftedness from creativity. Tannenbaum considered giftedness and creativity to be the "potential for becoming an outstanding producer or performer, not just a consumer, spectator, or amateur appreciator of ideas" (p. 49). Albert and Runco (1986) recognized giftedness as a separate construct but believed that the differences are unimportant at the highest levels of ability (presumably an intellectual ability separate from creativity).

Sternberg's definition of intelligence describes a component of creative or synthetic intelligence. In other writings, he described intelligence, wisdom, and creativity as three distinct, although interrelated, constructs (Sternberg, 1986b, 1989). With Lubart (Sternberg & Lubart, 1993), Sternberg singled out creativity as a distinct type of giftedness stemming from "a confluence of six resources – intellectual processes, thinking styles, personality, motivation and environment" (p. 7).

The research, which shows no relationship between IQ scores and measures of creativity beyond an IQ of 120, is often used as evidence in support of arguments of the independence of the construct (Tannenbaum, 1996). However, the assessments used are clearly designed to be independent; the IQ tests are traditional, convergent instruments, and creativity is assessed with measures of divergent thinking. Although creativity has been embraced by the field, the use of tests in the assessment of creativity remains as widely criticized (if not more so) as the use of the IQ test to test the domain of intelligence (Tannenbaum, 1996). "Such tests capture, at best, only the most trivial aspects of creativity" (Sternberg, 1986b).

OTHER PSYCHOLOGICAL CONSTRUCTS AND GIFTEDNESS

The many proposals for structures of intelligence influence the debate regarding the multidimensionality of giftedness, but there are also other psychological constructs that have been variously combined with intelligence as factors in describing giftedness. Although the original USOE definition and subse-

quent versions of that definition have made no case for nonintellective dimensions of giftedness, several theorists in the field have made much of personality factors, social factors, and even luck as part of their definitions (e.g., Feldhusen, 1986; Feldman, 1986; Renzulli, 1986; Tannenbaum, 1986).

Feldhusen (1986) adds positive self-concept and achievement motivation to general intellectual ability to create his conception of giftedness. The definition of giftedness proposed by Tannenbaum also included self-concept and motivation, but the complete manifestation of giftedness includes a "right blending" (1986, p. 49) of a set of "nonintellective" traits factors combined with superior general intellectual ability, distinctive special abilities, a challenging environment, and the "smile of good fortune" (p. 49). He includes motivation to achieve, self-concept, and interest in academic and artistic activities among other personality traits in his set of "nonintellective traits" that predict giftedness. He contends that "the five factors interact in different ways for separate talent domains, but they are *all* represented in some way in *every* form of giftedness" (p. 49).

As mentioned, Renzulli (1986) includes task commitment as one of the three critical components of giftedness. Renzulli distinguishes task commitment from general motivation, maintaining that task commitment is a state rather than a trait. It applies to particular tasks of high interest at particular times, leading Renzulli to contend that giftedness is a set of behaviors occurring in certain students under particular circumstances at particular times. In describing task commitment he includes the indicators of

The capacity for high levels of interest, enthusiasm, fascination, and involvement in a particular problem, area of study, or form of general expression.

The capacity for perseverance, endurance, determination, hard work, and dedicated practice.

Self-confidence, a strong ego and a belief in one's ability to carry out important work; freedom from inferiority feelings, drive to achieve.

The ability to identify significant problems within specialized areas; the ability to tune in to major channels of communication and new developments within given fields (p. 75).

POTENTIAL VERSUS PERFORMANCE

In defining the gifted, the early USOE definitions (Marland, 1972) considered "those with demonstrated achievement and/or potential" (p. 2). The current U.S. Department of Education definition (1993) includes those having "high performance capability" (p. 3). The translation of potential and demonstrated capabilities into theory and practice has taken many forms. The most traditional of these has been the use of intelligence tests as an indicator of potential for high achievement and the use of achievement tests, grades, portfolios and products, and performance as evidence of demonstrated giftedness.

Tannenbaum (1986) contended that it is not appropriate to identify giftedness in the child. Rather, he contends, in children we may *only* recognize potential giftedness. He uses the term "potentially gifted" to distinguish those who have the promise to become an outstanding performer or producer.

Renzulli (1986) recommended the creation of "talent pools" that represent the potentially gifted. Viewing the general and specific abilities as measured by standardized tests as more consistent traits, he recommended that these serve as the basis for establishing a group of children who are then presented activities and opportunities through which gifted behaviors may emerge. These activities and opportunities are designed to allow for further assessment of creativity and task commitment of potentially gifted students.

The distinction between potential giftedness and demonstrated giftedness is often not reflected in identification or in theory. The arguments about the degree to which intelligence tests simply measure current learning aside, most identification schemes use a combination of measures of cognitive ability and achievement (through standardized tests, grades, or both).

CONTINUED USE OF THE INTELLIGENCE TEST AS THE CRITERION FOR GIFTEDNESS AND BARRIERS TO CHANGE

Despite the widespread discussions of alternative conceptions of intelligence and giftedness, concerns relating to cultural bias, widespread agreement about the limited scope of assessment of cognitive processes, and the presentation of alternative means of assessing a broad spectrum of intellectual abilities, the intelligence test remains the dominant tool used in the assessment of giftedness and in the screening and placement of students in school programs for the gifted (Abeel, Callahan, & Hunsaker, 1994). It also remains the dominant indicator of giftedness used in publications in the field of gifted education.

Alternatives to traditional tests for identifying giftedness that are offered face many barriers to acceptance. First, the most dominant individual intelligence tests (the WISC-R and WISC III and the Stanford–Binet IV) are most familiar and are most recommended to those who make most assessment recommendations and decisions in schools. For example, in a recent publication on giftedness "for school personnel," Genshaft, Bireley, and Hollinger (1995) included a full chapter by Sternberg on the triarchic theory of intelligence (Sternberg, 1995). Then, in the very next chapter on the identification of giftedness they provided an extensive discussion of the relative merits of various individualized and group intelligence tests (Bireley, 1995) with only a passing reference to the unavailability of published assessments relating to the models offered by Gardner and Sternberg.

The lack of published, standardized alternatives and the lack of reliability and validity evidence for innovative assessment procedures inhibits the assessment of broader and more theory-based definitions of giftedness (Plucker, Callahan, & Tomchin, 1996). In some cases, the theory itself, the proponents of the theory, or both mitigate against the development of standardized, published assessments. Gardner, for instance, resists the assessment of the components of his model in a limited time frame, arguing that full assessment of the potentials he posits rests on observations over time in tasks that represent performance in the seven (now eight) domains he has specified. Schools intent on identifying a pool of potentially gifted students must invest considerable time and resources for such a model – resources that are not readily available.

In other cases, test publishers have been reluctant to invest in the development and publishing of instruments that do not follow the same form and format of the "standards" of intelligence testing or do not correlate highly with existing assessments of intellectual ability (Sternberg, 1992). Just as the producers of vehicles with internal combustion engines have resisted the development and marketing of vehicles using alternative fuel sources, the publishers of the traditional assessment tools have much to lose without a guarantee of gain by offering alternatives.

GIFTEDNESS AND GENIUS

Terman's early, multivolume works reporting on his study of gifted children carried the title *Genetic Studies of Genius*. Unfortunately, this title has created the long-lasting impression that advocates of gifted children are elitist in their beliefs that giftedness is an inherited (and racially influenced) trait and that the only individuals who should be labeled gifted are those who exhibit extremely advanced thought and productivity ("one in a million"). Terman acknowledged in 1954 that the use of the term genius for his high-IQ subjects (who did turn out to be, for the most part, accomplished in their professions) was inappropriately applied to his sample. Feldman contends that the word has come to incorporate "the combined meanings of high intelligence and achieved eminence" (1979, p. 38). In his research he has defined genius relative to development in a domain of knowledge. "A creative contribution meriting the designation genius is one that transforms an entire domain of human knowledge" (Morelock & Feldman, 1991, p. 362).

In describing genius, Jensen provides the following statement delineating between genius and "magician" that may provide us with a useful distinction between the gifted individual and the extraordinary:

An ordinary genius is a fellow that you and I would be just as good as, if we were only many times better. There is no mystery to how his mind works. Once we understand what he has done, we feel certain that we, too, could have done it. It is different with magicians. They are, to use mathematical jargon, in the orthogonal complement of where we are and the working of their minds is for all intents and purposes incomprehensible. Even after we understand what they have done, the process by which they have done it is completely dark. (Quoted in Jensen, 1996, p. 396 and reported there as quoted in Kanigel, 1991, p. 281.)

GIFTEDNESS AS A SOCIAL CONSTRUCT

Within the educational field, there is a faction who contend that giftedness is not a cognitive construct but rather a social construct (Pendarvis & Howley, 1996; Sapon-Shevin, 1987, 1994). Their arguments reflect the concerns that educators of the gifted have constructed groupings based on intelligence that result in *"reify[ing]"* the concept of giftedness (Borland, 1996, p. 134). Borland (1997) agreed that "giftedness is not a fact of nature or something educators have discovered. Instead, it is a socially constructed concept" (p. 6). He believes that the social circumstances arising from compulsory education and "rampant use of mental tests" led to this construction in our society. The debate around the constructs of intelligence and giftedness is tied very closely in these authors' writings to the introduction of the particular terms to the psychological–scientific literature. The constructs are criticized most seriously for the creation of a "qualitative existential dichotomy in which there are two distinct groups of humans: the gifted and the rest of humanity" (Borland, 1997, p. 9). Sapon-Shevin suggests that we should acknowledge "that without school rules and policies, legal and educational practices designed to provide services to gifted students, this category would cease to exist" (Sapon-Shevin, 1994, p. 17). Although she concedes individual differences in the ways and rates at which students learn, she asserts that the category exists at the behest of "a system that, for a variety of reasons, wishes to measure, select, and sort students in this manner" (p. 18). In the case of Borland and Sapon-Shevin, the creation of a category of giftedness is not only a misuse of intelligence tests but also an unnecessary dichotomy that fails to reflect the continuum of abilities, the many ways in which ability is manifested and documented, and the empirical instructional needs of the group created by the label.

CONTINUING QUESTIONS AND ISSUES IN THE RESEARCH

Understanding the Development of Giftedness

The understanding of characteristics of gifted students still rests largely on the work of Terman and other researchers who have used intelligence tests as the basis for identifying samples. In addition, what we know about giftedness is also largely derived from group data. As Cravens (1992) has pointed out, in Terman's time

the individual could not be understood as existing apart from the group that nature or society had assigned him or her. . . . To Terman and his associates it made no sense to discuss individuals qua individuals, for insofar as they were concerned, individuals could not exist apart from the group to which they belonged, in this case the group being that of geniuses apart from their group (pp. 187–188).

Research conducted between Terman's time and the early 1970s continued in this vein. The work of Roe and Torrance on characteristics of creative individuals similarly looked at traits across groups. To this end, much of what has been written about the gifted focuses on what the child or adult *is* rather than how that person *came to be*. Gruber's study of Darwin (1981) and Feldman's (1991) study of prodigies broke the mold and began the case-study, qualitative examination of exceptional individuals, which allows for the generation of hypotheses relating to the relationships between the circumstance of the environment to the gifted individual's development. Recent works by Gardner (1993b) and Feldman, Csikszentmihalyi, and Gardner (1994) have extended this work to a systems model, which includes the person and his or her characteristics, the developmental status of a particular domain (defined as "a formally organized body of knowledge associated with a given field" [p. 22]), and the field of the domain (all those who influence the structure of the domain – the teachers, the critics, and peers in the discipline). Further qualitative investigations of their model, in combination with carefully designed quantitative research, have the potential for illuminating our understandings of the complex interactions among factors that influence the development of giftedness. Walberg and his colleagues (e.g., Wallace & Walberg, 1987; Filippelli & Walberg, 1997) have also contributed to the identification of the ways the use of qualitative study of the gifted individual illuminates an understanding of the dynamic interactions between the individual's cognitive and personality traits with

environmental conditions. Although most of the research has been done retrospectively (and using historical data) to identify eminent individuals whose accomplishments clearly are agreed upon as representing gifted behavior, the models generated provide the hypotheses for further research in understanding the dynamics of the development of eminence.

Developing Appropriate Educational Interventions

Certainly, the use of intelligence testing to create an elite group of students with special privilege and tracking practices associated with the grouping of students is questionable, as Borland (1997), Sapon-Shevin (1987, 1994) and many others who believe giftedness is only a social construct have argued. However, the arguments fail to address the questions that underlie the reasons such constructs were invented. First, although the label may appear to be fairly recent, have not societies nurtured and recognized talent? Further, there is no reason to believe that Binet or Terman, or the many hundreds of psychologists who have studied intelligence or cognitive processes, were interested in creating an elite society or in giving parents ammunition for creating special privileges for their children. Binet undertook the study of individual differences in performance and ability to help determine appropriate instructional interventions for at-risk students, and Terman's intention was to gain an understanding of the development of students with high levels of cognitive functioning. If schools did not exist we would label fewer students learning disabled and fewer students gifted (Sapon-Shevin, 1994), but we do have schools and we do recognize that some students struggle and some are not challenged. If schools consistently recognized a continuum of differences and adjusted school learning to meet individual needs, and if schools recognized a broader concept of abilities, we would see less need to label our children. Might it be that the labels emerge when the children are not appropriately challenged? The need for labeling appears to be decreasing among those who advocate for highly able children (Borland, 1994). An emerging challenge to educators and psychologists is to forge a path of theory and research that broadens the conceptions and understandings of intelligence and giftedness so that instructional programs and curricula are geared to assessing educational needs and the appropriate level of challenge of all students, including those with abilities that distinguish them from their peers. We can no longer be content with assuming an intelligence test score tells us who is gifted or likely to exhibit gifted behaviors. Our object must be to understand differences across the span of cognitive abilities and disciplines and the relationships of those differences to learning so that the development of full potential is available to all children.

Unfortunately, much of the research defining giftedness and its relationship to intellectual ability has been divorced from the research on educational programs and practice with several notable exceptions. Stanley and his colleagues, although rejecting the notion of general intelligence and focusing on the specific domain of mathematical reasoning, have provided considerable evidence that acceleration of the mathematics curriculum for middle-school-age students who score exceptionally well on the College Board Scholastic Aptitude Test (SAT-M, now called the Scholastic Achievement Test) can be a highly effective strategy for encouraging early completion of high school and college (Stanley & Benbow, 1986). Two specific types of accleration have been studied by Stanley and his colleagues as part of the Study of Mathematically and Precocious Youth (SMPY). The subjects in the early studies of fast-paced mathematics classes followed in many cases by early admission to college were tracked for several years to document academic success and social adjustment (Benbow, Lubinski, & Suchy, 1996; Stanley, 1996). The second type of acceleration program developed and studied by the staff at the Center for the Advancement of Academically Talented Youth at Johns Hopkins University is known as DT–PI (Diagnostic Testing followed by Prescriptive Instruction). Benbow (1986) describes the DT–PI model as a fast-paced instructional program with the following specific series of steps:

1. Determining the student's current level of knowledge using appropriate standardized tests;
2. Pinpointing areas of weakness by analyzing items missed on a given test;
3. Devising an instructional program that targets those

areas of weakness and allows the student to achieve mastery on a second form of the test; and
4. Proceeding to the next higher level in mathematics and repeating steps 1–3 (p. 12).

Benbow (1986) provided case study data to document the success of the strategy among students with exceptionally high scores on the SAT-M.

Reis et al. (1993) have also provided evidence that the instructional strategy of compacting the curriculum does not negatively impact a child's performance on standardized achievement measures. In curriculum compacting, the teacher assesses the current level of performance of a student in disciplines where he or she is achieving above grade level, and then, through diagnostic assessment of the teacher's choosing determines which knowledge, skills, or understanding from the upcoming unit of instruction have already been mastered. Next, the teacher develops group and individual programs for ensuring command of the areas in which the student was found to have deficiencies. Finally, the students engage in alternative accelerated or enriched curriculum during the time that would have been spent rehearsing already known material. Reis and her colleagues found that even when the teachers in their study eliminated significant portions of instruction (40–50%) based on a child's achievement level, these children achieved as well as or higher than students whose curriculum had not been compacted.

Reis and Renzulli (1982) have also provided evidence for the assertions that students who are identified using the three-ring definition of giftedness produce products that are similar to those produced by students identified according to definitions requiring extraordinary aptitude and achievement scores. The products of students who scored between the 6th and 15th percentile on intelligence assessments (the three-ring sample) and products of students scoring in the top 5% on intelligence tests were judged to be of equal quality.

Current research on the triarchic model of human intelligence provides the closest tie between a theory of intelligence, a theory of giftedness, and the effects of educational programming practice (Sternberg, Ferrari, Clinkenbeard, & Grigorenko, 1996). This research examined the degree to which compatibility in the processes of identifying, instructing, and assessing high-school-age gifted students in an introductory psychology course using the triarchic model enhances achievement in that domain. As part of the research paradigm, tests of the relative independence of three triarchic abilities (analytic, creative, and analytic) were verified. More important, from an instructional perspective, "students who were placed in a course that matched their pattern of abilities performed better than students who were mismatched" (p. 136) across assessments of analytic, creative, and practical achievements and on multiple-choice and essay assessments. Further, students who scored high across domains were able to perform as well as their counterparts with strengths in only one area across all conditions. Continued research examining the usefulness of the model in other discipline areas and across age levels is warranted as is research that looks at the effectiveness of using models of intelligence to guide our practice in development of talent.

COMMON GROUND

Despite the many interpretations of the term giftedness and an uneven history of appropriate use of intelligence to define and assess giftedness, there seems to be an emerging consensus in the literature of general principles.

Intellectual ability, particularly as measured by a single IQ score, is one of the best predictors of what Renzulli has called "schoolhouse giftedness," but is insufficient to explain or predict creative productivity in children or adults and is certainly not a perfect predictor of scholastic success either. "High IQ offers a hint of how well an individual *may* fare in a variety of tasks, without guaranteeing how well he or she *will* fare, and in what specific domain of excellence" (Tannenbaum, 1996, p. 47).

Giftedness (or nongiftedness), like intelligence, is not immutable or fixed in stone for the lifetime of the individual. Further, there is increasing discomfort with the notion that a child is gifted or not gifted, particularly when the categorization is based on a single assessment such as an intelligence test score. Increasingly, we see broadened theoretical definitions of giftedness offered either through "disjunctive" conceptualizations such as those of the U.S. Department of Education or "conjunctive" definitions such as those of Renzulli or Sternberg (Borland, 1997). The tendency to label behaviors

rather than the child (Renzulli et al., 1981) also reflects an uneasiness with a permanent, immutable labeling process and recognition of the malleability of cognitive abilities and the interactions with so many other intellectual, personality, and environmental factors in the manifestation of giftedness. Further, much more specification of the interactions of general cognitive processes with specific domain abilities and knowledge as well as noncognitive factors has become the focus of understanding high-level performance.

Multiple criteria for the identification of giftedness are not seen as effective in broadening the conception of giftedness nor for offering more guidance on appropriate educational interventions if they simply provide further testimony to the same attributes identified by the IQ score.

It is most significant that the categorization of children has taken a back seat to attempts to understand the instructional and psychological needs of the individuals who are highly able or who have the potential for displaying gifted behaviors in specific and general domains of performance. Increasingly, researchers have shifted concerns from the process of finding the "right test" to finding ways to match the capabilities of children to the instructional program and support systems necessary to translate intellectual potential into adult accomplishment.

ACKNOWLEDGMENT

This research was supported under the Javits Act Program (Grant R206R50001) administered by the U.S. Department of Education's Office of Educational Research and Improvement. The findings and opinions expressed here do not reflect the Office's positions or policies.

REFERENCES

Abeel, L. B., Callahan, C. M., & Hunsaker, S. L. (1994). *The use of published instruments in the identification of gifted students.* Washington, DC: National Association for Gifted Children.

Amabile, T. M. (1989). *Growing up creative: Nurturing a lifetime of creativity.* New York: Crown.

Baldwin, A. Y. (1985). *The Baldwin identification matrix 2.* New York: Trillium.

Benbow, C. P. (1986). SMPY's model for teaching mathematically precocious students, In J. S. Renzulli (Ed.), *Systems and models for developing programs for the gifted and talented.* Mansfield center, CT: Creative Learning Press.

Benbow, C. P., Lubinski, D., & Suchy, B. (1996). The impact of SMPY's educational programs from the perspective of the participant. In C. P. Benbow & D. Lubinski (Eds.), *Intellectual talent* (pp. 266–300). Baltimore: The Johns Hopkins University Press.

Bireley, M. (1995). Identifying high ability/high achievement giftedness. In J. Genshaft, M. Bireley, & C. L. Hollinger (Eds.), *Serving gifted and talented students: A resource for school personnel* (pp. 49–66). Austin, TX: Pro-ed.

Borland, J. H. (1994). Gifted education and the threat of irrelevance. *Journal for the Education of the Gifted, 19,* 129–147.

Borland, J. H. (1997). The construct of giftedness. *Peabody Journal of Education, 72,* 6–20.

Cravens, H. (1992). A scientific project locked in time: The Terman genetic studies of genius, 1920s–1950s. *American Psychologist, 47,* 183–189.

Davis, G. A., & Rimm, S. B. (1998). *Education of the gifted and talented* (4th ed.). Boston: Allyn & Bacon.

Feldhusen, J. F. (1986). A conception of giftedness. In. R. J. Sternberg & J. E. Davidson (Eds.), *Conceptions of giftedness* (pp. 112–127). New York: Cambridge University Press.

Feldman, D. H. (1979). Extreme giftedness. In A. H. Passow (Ed.), *The gifted and talented: Their education and development. The 78th yearbook of the National Society for the Study of Education* (pp. 335–351). Chicago: University of Chicago Press.

Feldman, D. H. (1986). Giftedness as a developmentalist sees it. In. R. J. Sternberg & J. E. Davidson (Eds.), *Conceptions of giftedness* (pp. 285–305). New York: Cambridge University Press.

Feldman, D. H. (1991). *Nature's gambit: Child prodigies and the development of human potential.* New York: Teachers College Press.

Feldman, D. H., Csikszentmihalyi, M., & Gardner, H. (1994). *Changing the world: A framework for the study of creativity.* Westport, CT: Praeger.

Filippelli, L. A., & Walberg, H. J. (1997). Childhood traits and environmental conditions of women scientists. *Gifted Child Quarterly, 41,* 95–104.

Ford, D. Y. (1996). *Reversing underachievement among gifted black children.* New York: Teachers College Press.

Gallagher, J. J., & Gallagher, S. A. (1994). *Teaching the gifted child* (4th ed.). Boston: Allyn & Bacon.

Galton, F. (1869). *Hereditary genius.* London: Macmillan.

Gardner, H. (1983). *Frames of mind: The theory of multiple intelligences.* New York: Basic Books.

Gardner, H. (1993a). *Multiple intelligences.* New York: Basic Books.

Gardner, J. (1993b). *Creating minds: An anatomy of creativity seen through the lives of Freud, Einstein, Picasso, Stravinski, Eliot, Graham, and Ghandi.* New York: Basic Books.

Genshaft, J. L., Bireley, M., & Hollinger, C. L. (Eds.). (1995). *Serving gifted and talented students: A resource for school personnel.* Austin, TX: Pro-ed.

Guilford, J. P. (1950). Creativity. *American Psychologist, 5,* 444–454.

Guilford, J. P. (1967). *The nature of human intelligence.* New York: McGraw-Hill.

Gruber, H. (1981). *Darwin on man.* Chicago: University of Chicago Press.

Horn, J. L., & Knapp, J. R. (1973). On the subjective character of the empirical base of Guilford's structure-of-intellect model. *Psychological Bulletin, 80,* 33–43.

Jensen, A. R. (1996). Giftedness and genius: Crucial differences. In C. P. Benbow & D. Lubinski (Eds.), *Intellectual talent* (pp. 393–409). Baltimore: The Johns Hopkins University Press.

Maker, C. J., Neilson, A. B., & Rogers, J. A. (1994). Intelligence and creativity in multiple intelligences. *Teaching Exceptional Children, 27*(1), 4–18.

Marland, S. P. (1972). *Education of the gifted and talented: Vol. 1. Report to the Congress of the United States by the U.S. Commissioner of Education.* Washington, DC: Department of Health, Education and Welfare.

Meeker, M., & Meeker, R. (1986). The SOI system for gifted education. In J. S. Renzulli (Ed.), *Systems and models for developing programs for the gifted and talented* (pp. 194–215). Mansfield Center, CT: Creative Learning Press.

Mills, C. J., Ablard, K. E., & Brody, L. E. (1993). The Raven's Progressive Matrices: Its usefulness for identifying gifted/talented students. *Roeper Review, 14,* 183–186.

Morelock, M. J., & Feldman, D. H. (1991). Extreme precocity. In N. Colangelo & G. A. Davis (Eds.), *Handbook of gifted education* (pp. 347–364). Boston: Allyn & Bacon.

Morelock, M. J., & Feldman, D. H. (1997). High-IQ, extreme precocity, and savant syndrome. In N. Colangelo & G. A. Davis (Eds.), *Handbook of gifted education 2nd ed.,* (pp. 439–459). Boston: Allyn & Bacon.

Pendarvis, E., & Howley, A. (1996). Playing fair: The possibilities of gifted education. *Journal for the Education of the Gifted, 60,* 215–233.

Piirto, J. (1982). *Understanding those who create.* Dayton, OH: Ohio Psychology Press.

Plucker, J. A., Callahan, C. M., & Tomchin, E. M. (1996). Wherefore art thou, multiple intelligences? Alternative assessments for identifying talent in ethnically diverse and low income families. *Gifted Child Quarterly, 40,* 81–92.

Ramos-Ford, V., & Gardner, H. (1997). Giftedness from a multiple intelligences perspective. In N. Colangelo & G. A. Davis (Eds.), *Handbook of gifted education* (2nd ed., pp. 439–459). Boston: Allyn & Bacon.

Reis, S. M., & Renzulli, J. S. (1982). A research report on the revolving door identification model: A case for the broadened conception of giftedness. *Phi Delta Kappan, 63,* 619–620.

Reis, S. M., Westberg, K. L., Kulikowich, J., Caillard, F., Hebert, T., Plucker, J., Percell, J. H., Rogers, J. B., & Smist, J. M. (1993). *Why not let high ability students start school in January? The curriculum compacting study.* Storrs, CT:

University of Virginia, National Research Center on the Gifted and Talented.

Renzulli, J. S. (1978). What makes giftedness? Reexamining a definition. *Phi Delta Kappan, 60*, 180–184, 261.

Renzulli, J. S. (1986). The three-ring conception of giftedness: A developmental model of creative productivity. In R. J. Sternberg & J. E. Davidson (Eds.), *Conceptions of giftedness* (pp. 53–92). New York: Cambridge University Press.

Renzulli, J. S., Reis, S. M., & Smith, L. H. (1981). *The revolving door identification model*. Mansfield Center, CT: Creative Learning Press.

Runco, M. A., & Albert, R. S. (1986). The threshold theory regarding creativity and intelligence: An empirical test with gifted and non-giftedchildren. *Creative Child and Adult Quarterly, 11*, 212–18.

Sapon-Shevin, M. (1987). Giftedness as a social construct. *Teachers College Record, 41*, 39–48.

Sapon-Shevin, M. (1994). *Playing favorites: Gifted education and the disruption of community*. Albany, NY: State University of New York.

Scarr, S. (1989). Protecting general intelligence: Constructs and consequences for interventions. In R. Linn (Ed.), *Intelligence: Measurement, theory and public policy* (pp. 74–118). Chicago: University of Illinois.

Stanley, J. C. (1996). In the beginning: The study of mathematically precocious youth. In C. P. Benbow & D. Lubinski (Eds.), *Intellectual talent* (pp. 225–245). Baltimore: The Johns Hopkins University Press.

Stanley, J. C., & Benbow, C. P. (1986). Youths who reason exceptionally well mathematically. In R. J. Sternberg & J. E. Davidson (Eds.), *Conceptions of giftedness* (pp. 361–387). New York: Cambridge University Press.

Starnes, W. T. (n.d.). A model program for identifying young underserved gifted students. In C. M. Callahan, C. A. Tomlinson, & P. M. Pizzat, (Eds.), *Contexts for promise: Noteworthy practices and innovations in the identification of gifted students* (pp. 43–60). Charlottesville, VA: National Research Center on the Gifted and Talented, University of Virginia.

Sternberg, R. J. (1985). *Beyond IQ: A triarchic theory of human intelligence*. New York: Cambridge University Press.

Sternberg, R. J. (1986a). A triarchic theory of intellectual giftedness. In R. J. Sternberg & J. E. Davidson (Eds.), *Conceptions of giftedness* (pp. 223–243). New York: Cambridge University Press.

Sternberg, R. J. (1986b). Intelligence, wisdom, and creativity. *Educational Psychologist, 21*, 175–190.

Sternberg, R. J. (1989). Intelligence, wisdom, and creativity: Their matures and interrelationships. In R. Linn (Ed.), *Intelligence: Measurement, theory, and public policy* (pp. 117–146). Chicago: University of Illinois.

Sternberg, R. J. (1992). Ability tests, measurements and markets. *Journal of Educational Psychology, 84*, 134–140.

Sternberg, R. J. (1994). Commentary: Reforming school reform: Comments on *Multiple intelligences: The theory in practice. Teachers College Record, 95*, 561–569.

Sternberg, R. J. (1995). Changing conceptions of intelligence and their impact upon the concept of giftedness: The triarchic theory of intelligence. In J. Genshaft, M. Bireley, & C. L. Hollinger (Eds.), *Serving gifted and talented students: A resource for school personnel* (pp. 33–48). Austin, TX: Pro-ed.

Sternberg, R. J. (1997). Still smarting. *Teacher Magazine, 8*, 40–41.

Sternberg, R. J., & Davidson, J. E. (Eds.). (1986). *Conceptions of giftedness*. New York: Cambridge University Press.

Sternberg, R. J., & Detterman, D. K. (Eds.). (1986). *What is intelligence? Contemporary viewpoints on its nature and definition*. Norwood, NJ: Ablex.

Sternberg, R. J., Ferrari, M., Clinkenbeard, P., & Grigorenko, E. L. (1996). Identification, instruction, and assessment of gifted children: A construct validation of a triarchic model. *Gifted Child Quarterly, 40*, 129–137.

Sternberg, R. J., & Lubart, T. I. (1993). Creative giftedness: A multivariate investment approach. *Gifted Child Quarterly, 37*, 7–15.

Tannenbaum, A. J. (1986). Giftedness: A psychosocial approach. In R. J. Sternberg & J. E. Davidson (Eds.), *Conceptions of giftedness* (pp. 21–252). New York: Cambridge University Press.

Tannenbaum, A. J. (1996). The IQ controversy and the gifted. In C. P. Benbow & D. Lubinski (Eds.), *Intellectual talent* (pp. 44–77). Baltimore: The Johns Hopkins University Press.

Terman, L. (1916). *The measurement of intelligence*. Boston: Houghton Mifflin.

Terman, L. et al., (1925). *Genetic studies of genius: Vol. I. Mental and physical traits of a thousand gifted children*. Stanford, CA: Stanford University Press.

Terman, L. (1959). *The discovery and encouragement of exceptional talent*. Stanford, CA: Stanford University Press.

Terman, L., & Oden, M. H. (1947). *Genetic studies of genius: Vol. IV. The gifted child grows up*. Stanford, CA: Stanford University Press.

Terman, L., & Oden, M. H. (1959). *Genetic studies of genius: Vol. V. The gifted group at mid-life: Thirty-five years' follow-up of a superior group*. Stanford, CA: Stanford University Press.

Torrance, E. P. (1966), *Tests of creative thinking*. Lexington, MA: Personnel Press.

U.S. Department of Education. (1993). *National excellence: A case for developing America's talent*. Washington, DC: Author.

Wallace, T., & Walberg, H. J. (1987). Personality traits and childhood environments of eminent essayists. *Gifted Child Quarterly, 31*, 65–69.

Webb, J. T., Meckstroth, E. A., & Tolan, S. S. (1982). *Guiding gifted children: A practical source for parents and children*. Columbus: Ohio Psychology Press.

CHAPTER NINE

Group Differences in Intelligence

JOHN C. LOEHLIN

INDIVIDUAL AND GROUP DIFFERENCES

Individual differences are primary; group differences are secondary. The individual is the biological and societal unit that develops, that learns, that thinks, that wants, that feels, that acts. The group is a collection of individuals – sometimes just that, sometimes with a structure of its own.

The individual members of any species, such as humans, have a great many characteristics in common; indeed, judged against the varied forms of life on this earth one might deem them virtually indistinguishable. Yet from a viewpoint within the human species, we see them as differing in an array of biological and psychological characteristics, and these differences are often of intense social, personal, and economic interest to us.

On the basis of such individual variation, individuals may be classified in numerous ways and for various purposes into subgroups. A particular human may be placed simultaneously into groups according to age, sex, occupation, ancestry, religious preference, marital status, home ownership, political party affiliation, sexual orientation, television viewing habits, taste in soft drinks, and any number of other criteria. These classifications can be said to be secondary in the sense that they derive from already-existing characteristics of the individual; that someone may choose to classify an individual into one or another category does not in itself change that individual in any way whatsoever – although, of course, the individual's or others' reactions to this act of classification may have such an effect.

When we classify individuals into different categories according to any of the preceding attributes, we can observe or measure the individuals on some other trait of interest and see whether there is any average difference in this trait between the individuals in different categories. If there is, we may well want to ask further questions: Why is this so? Is it equally true for different subdivisions within the category? Does it hold over variations in age, place, and time?

A trait that has often been considered in this way is intelligence, as measured by typical IQ or similar tests. For example, members of the U.S. standardization sample for the 1981 revision of the Wechsler Adult Intelligence Scale, classified in various ways, had the IQ means and standard deviations given in Table 9.1.

Several points may be noted. First, each of the 1,880 individuals in the sample is multiply classified according to sex, race, residence, and occupation. Each individual contributes to the averages of whatever categories he or she is classified in; the act of classifying does not affect the IQ score of the classified individual. A given person who has (say) an IQ score of 107 has that score whether he or she happens to be a black urban male skilled worker or a white female professional who lives in the country.

Second, there are differences between the mean IQs of people in different groups. Sometimes these are small such as a couple of IQ points (sex, residence), and sometimes the differences are larger (15 IQ points for race, 22 points between professionals and unskilled workers).

TABLE 9.1. Some Subgroup Means and Standard Deviations for Full-Scale IQ for the WAIS–R Standardization Sample

Category	N	M	SD
Sex			
Male	940	100.9	15.3
Female	940	98.7	14.9
Race			
White	1664	101.4	14.7
Black	192	86.9	13.0
Residence			
Urban	1421	100.3	15.2
Rural	459	98.4	14.8
Occupation			
Professional			
and technical	206	111.0	13.4
White-collar	409	104.1	12.6
Skilled worker	213	99.5	12.6
Semiskilled	404	93.1	14.2
Unskilled	68	89.1	15.2

Note: Subgroups omitted — race "Other;" occupation "Not in labor force."
Source: Data from Reynolds, Chastain, Kaufman, & McLean (1987).

Third, an important fact often overlooked is that the variation within groups remains very nearly as large as the variation in the population as a whole. The observed standard deviations within subgroups range from 12.6 to 15.3 IQ points as against a standard deviation of about 15.1 in the total sample. A pair of unskilled laborers picked at random from among the 68 in the sample would be, on average, as different from each other in IQ as any pair of individuals randomly picked from the sample as a whole. Furthermore, this will be pretty much the case for individuals within any of the other categories in the table – the within-group standard deviations (SDs) run from 83 to 101% of that for the total sample. Even though the group means differ for IQ, the vast majority of the population variation lies within the subgroups, not between them. Personal attitudes or social policies based on the assumption that groups that differ on average in IQ are essentially homogeneous for this trait are egregiously in error and do much mischief. This error has a name. It is called *stereotyping*.

Nevertheless, even if group differences properly play second fiddle to individual differences, and even though they are often badly misinterpreted, average differences between groups remain an object of legitimate scientific and popular interest. A better understanding of group differences, what they do and do not mean, can contribute to a saner attitude toward members of groups other than one's own. A study of group differences can also offer clues to important questions in human evolutionary and social history or shed light on mechanisms of individual development. Finally, anyone who aspires to *change* group differences (e.g., in academic or occupational achievement) is surely well advised to understand their causes.

This chapter will look at some of the evidence and issues relevant to group differences in intelligence, considering in turn the four categories listed in Table 9.1: sex or gender, race or ancestry, rural–urban residence, and occupation. As we shall see, not all group differences are alike.

Male–Female Differences in Intelligence

The quick summary is that there are no consistent and dependable male–female differences in general intelligence as measured by standard IQ tests. One reason for this is that a lack of sex bias is often a criterion in the construction of such tests. Items that tend on average to favor males are balanced by items that tend on average to favor females. The important point, however, is that this is relatively easy to do. Many items of both sorts can be found among tasks generally agreed upon as tapping some aspect of intellectual abilities. Even in an age before such item balancing was customary, overall sex differences on intelligence tests tended to be trivial (Terman, 1916).

Certain specific varieties of cognitive performance do, however, consistently show sex differences. Males, for example, on average obtain higher scores for mental rotation items, which require the testee to judge how an object would look if it were rotated in space. One meta-analysis of studies with such tests estimated the average male–female difference to be .9 SD, the equivalent of $13\frac{1}{2}$ points on an IQ-type scale (Masters & Sanders, 1993). On the other hand, females tend to have an advantage on verbal tests involving the fluent production of words belonging to a category, such as synonyms. Skill in mathematics goes both ways. Girls tend to be superior during the early school years, when the computational aspects of the subject predominate; boys later, when the inferential aspects do (Hyde, Fennema, & Lamon, 1990).

Mathematical ability also supplies a good illustration of one important aspect of group differences: the effect that a modest difference between two groups in means and standard deviations can have on proportions at the extremes. Hedges and Nowell (1995) analyzed sex differences in mental abilities in six large nationally representative samples of U.S. high school students and young adults tested between 1960 and 1992. One of the areas measured in all six studies was mathematical abilities. Males, at these ages, averaged slightly higher in mathematical skills, but the differences in means were small: .03 to .26 standard deviations across the different studies. Males were also slightly more variable: the male standard deviations were 2 to 12% larger. The combination of these apparently modest differences resulted, however, in nearly twice as many males as females among the top 5% of scorers. At higher levels of mathematical talent there can be an even greater disproportion. One study found 13 boys for every girl in a sample estimated to include roughly the top .01% of the ability distribution (Benbow & Stanley, 1983).

Hedges and Nowell's analysis included several different abilities and found mean differences in both directions (girls averaged higher for reading, perceptual speed, and memory; boys for science, spatial ability, and mechanical reasoning). However, the difference in variability was in the same direction across all the areas: variability tended to be greater for boys. This meant that in areas where boys had higher means, boys substantially outnumbered girls at the top, and for areas where boys had lower means, boys substantially outnumbered girls at the bottom. For the other alternatives, the effects of means and variabilities tended to cancel, and the proportions of boys and girls were not very different.

The reasons why average sex differences in special abilities exist are still controversial. Some authors have suggested that biological differences, such as the effect of sex hormones on brain differentiation, may be responsible. Others have emphasized differences in the socialization experiences of

boys and girls. An instructive glimpse of the range of such viewpoints can be found in the various commentaries to an article by Benbow (1988) on sex differences in mathematical talent.

In assessing such divergencies of viewpoint, one should keep in mind that we are not necessarily in an either–or situation here: nature and nurture can work in parallel. Socialization practices may track biological realities, and behavior can lead to biological changes. A great deal of careful empirical research will be required before the causes of sex differences in cognitive skills are well understood. Paradoxically, one reason the problem is difficult is that there are only two sexes. This means that there are a great many variables, biological and social, all correlated with the observed sex difference and with each other, making it all too easy to conclude erroneously that a given variable is a cause of an observed sex difference when it is only a correlate.

IQ Differences in Groups Defined by Ancestry

An even more contentious difference in average IQ test scores emerges when individuals are sorted into groups according to their ancestry – so-called racial or ethnic differences. In most of the studies to be discussed, racial classification is based on self-identification, and thus the sorting by ancestry is approximate at best.

Table 9.2 provides an illustration of observed differences in average test performance for U.S. subgroups of differing racial–ethnic ancestry. The table is based on a nationwide survey conducted in the

TABLE 9.2. Average Scores for U.S. 12th-graders of Differing Ancestry Expressed in an IQ Metric

Group	Verbal Test	Nonverbal Test
European Americans	102	102
African Americans	85.5	85.9
Asian Americans	98.2	101.5
Native Americans	88.9	95.0

Note: European-American mean set to 102 (see Flynn, 1984). The SD used (set to 15) was the unweighted mean for the three minority groups because the European-American SD was restricted by test ceiling.
Source: Data rescaled from means in Coleman et al. (1996, Supplemental Appendix).

mid-1960s under the auspices of the U.S. Office of Education and popularly known as the "Coleman Report" (Coleman et al., 1966). It includes a wider range of ethnic groups than most such studies. Although the report is careful to avoid describing the tests as "intelligence tests," their content was much like that of typical group-administered IQ tests; in Table 9.2 the report's scores have been converted to an IQ scale for comparability to Table 9.1 and other values given in this chapter.

As is typically found in such data, the differences between Americans of predominantly European ancestry and predominantly African ancestry are substantial – here, the equivalent of 16 or 17 IQ points, a little over a standard deviation. Americans of Asian ancestry, although a group subjected historically to much discrimination and prejudice in the United States, scored nearly as high as Americans of European ancestry – particularly on the nonverbal test. The scores of the Native Americans were intermediate and were again higher on the nonverbal test.

In the following sections, we consider the three minority groups in turn using as a point of reference the European American majority.

AFRICAN AMERICANS. An average difference on the order of one standard deviation between U.S. individuals of predominantly European ancestry (Whites) and predominantly African ancestry (Blacks) has been evident ever since the advent of mass intelligence testing (Shuey, 1966; Osborne & McGurk, 1982). The scores of military draftees in three wars – World War I, World War II, and Vietnam – showed average differences between Blacks and Whites of one to one-and-a-half standard deviations (summarized in Loehlin, Lindzey, & Spuhler, 1975). Furthermore, the Black–White differences show up at an early age – well before the time of school entry. Three samples tested with the Stanford–Binet test showed IQ differences of the order of one standard deviation between Black and White 3-year-olds (Montie & Fagan, 1988; Peoples, Fagan, & Drotar, 1995). Of course, it should be remembered that these are differences in averages and that individual Blacks and Whites at all ages vary almost as widely as do individuals in the population at large (and that describing them as Blacks and Whites is a decided oversimplification).

Although a substantial average difference between U.S. Blacks and Whites in cognitive test performance has persisted for many years, there is evidence to suggest that in recent decades it may have shrunk somewhat. Hedges and Nowell (1998) carried out a meta-analysis based on six national studies. The trend for 12th graders in these 6 studies over the 27 years from 1965 to 1992 was for the average Black–White difference to decrease from about 1.2 to about .8 standard deviations.

Hedges and Nowell also found the variability in the African-American samples to be somewhat smaller. The standard deviations for Blacks averaged about 89% of those for Whites with no obvious increasing or decreasing trend over time. The combination of a lower mean and reduced standard deviation for African Americans had major consequences at the upper extreme: Among Blacks a much smaller fraction scored at a level that would place them in the top 5% overall. Across the different studies, scorers at this level were relatively 8 to 20 times more frequent among Whites than Blacks, and, given that the population contains fewer Blacks to begin with, the absolute numerical discrepancies are much greater than this. Of course, so far this is simply descriptive, not explanatory.

Finally, the differences between Americans of predominantly African and predominantly European ancestry are not uniform across all the subtests of IQ tests but appear to follow what has been referred to as the *Spearman hypothesis*, namely, that the difference is greater the more highly the subtests are correlated with g – the general factor representing what the various cognitive skills involved in IQ tests have in common (Jensen, 1985). Tests of verbal comprehension or spatial ability, for example, tend to show larger Black–White differences than do tests of memory or perceptual speed and accuracy and also tend to correlate more highly with overall IQ and load more highly on the general factor. The *Spearman effect* appears to show up early. It has been reported in the data of 3-year-olds (Peoples et al., 1995). It should be emphasized that observation of the Spearman effect at the level of empirical measurement does not necessarily imply any particular cause (such as a genetic origin). A variety of views on this point may be found among the commentators on Jensen's article (see Jensen, 1985). The controversial issue of possible genetic and environmental contribution to U.S. group differences will be discussed later.

ASIAN AMERICANS. There is some dispute as to whether Asian Americans obtain higher average scores on IQ tests than European Americans or score at about the same level. Richard Lynn has estimated that the IQs of Asians in their native countries average around 106 but that those of Asian Americans might be a little lower (Lynn, 1991). In contrast, James Flynn has argued that many studies that have compared the test scores of various Asian-American samples with U.S. norms have involved an artifact, namely, they have failed to allow for the prevailing upward creep of IQ test performance over time (the so-called ''Flynn effect''; Flynn 1984, 1996). When the results from studies using just Asian-American samples were adjusted for this effect and combined with those from studies in which both groups were simultaneously measured on the same tests, Flynn found little overall IQ difference between European and Asian Americans – perhaps a couple of IQ points in favor of European Americans (Flynn, 1991).

There is, however, a difference between IQ subtests primarily measuring visuo-spatial skills and those primarily measuring verbal skills. Asian Americans (and Asians in Asia) tend to do relatively better on visuo-spatial tests than on verbal tests. Such differences have, for example, been obtained between Americans of Japanese ancestry and of European ancestry in Hawaii, where they have been found to be stable across two generations despite major changes in the degree of acculturation to American ways (Nagoshi & Johnson, 1987).

There is also a large difference in how effectively Asian Americans and European Americans convert their cognitive skills into professional and occupational achievement (Weyl, 1969). Flynn estimated that Asian Americans tend to achieve at a level characteristic of European Americans with IQs 10 to 20 points higher. This is partly because a greater proportion of Asian Americans who are qualified for higher education in fact undertake it and partly due to their being able to succeed at lower ability levels by working harder (Flynn, 1991).

NATIVE AMERICANS. This term refers to groups such as the Inuit (Eskimos) and peoples of various American Indian tribal origins (Hopi, Cheyenne, Iroquois, etc.). They are Native Americans in the sense of having been in the Western Hemisphere much longer than European or African Americans, although they themselves are believed to have come to North America from Asia some tens of thousands of years ago.

Numerous studies measuring cognitive abilities among Native Americans peoples have been reported over the last three-quarters of a century; a review may be found in McShane and Berry (1988). Many of these studies were flawed by the problems involved in giving standardized tests to groups with differing cultural and linguistic backgrounds and varying degrees of acculturation to Western ways.

Nevertheless, a few general conclusions seem warranted. On the whole, Native Americans tend to perform comparably to European Americans on nonverbal tests – particularly those with a visuo-spatial emphasis. Lynn (1991) listed 14 studies conducted with Native Americans between 1952 and 1984, mostly using Wechsler IQ tests, from which he computed an average IQ score for visuo-spatial performance. These IQs ranged from 91 to 105 across the different studies – 7 of the 14 studies yielded average visuo-spatial IQs of 100 or better.

Typically, Native American groups obtain lower verbal IQs. In many of the earlier studies, this was confounded with the fact that the tests were given in English, and English was a second language for the group concerned. However, Lynn restricted his tabulation to groups for which English was the first language, and it still showed verbal IQs averaging some 20 points below visuo-spatial ones.

One factor depressing verbal relative to nonverbal performance may be hearing loss resulting from middle-ear infections in infancy and early childhood for which Native American populations appear to be at a high risk. Several studies have shown an association between a history of middle-ear infections and lower verbal IQs in individuals from Native American populations (summarized in McShane & Berry, 1998). But the same advantage of nonverbal over verbal skills is characteristic of Asian Americans, with whom Native Americans share common ancestry. Thus, one might also consider genetic factors resulting from shared evolution in the distant past. For the present, any such explanation remains speculative. However, direct genetic research could support or refute this hypothesis in the future as genes related to a verbal–spatial difference are identified in both groups and shown to be the same or different in frequency in the two groups.

RURAL–URBAN DIFFERENCES IN IQ

A generation or two ago, average U.S. rural–urban IQ differences were substantial, averaging about $6\frac{1}{2}$ IQ points (Terman & Merrill, 1937). In more recent years, the difference declined to about 2 IQ points (e.g., Table 9.1). The urban–rural difference is now so small that recent IQ test standardizations have not even bothered to stratify their samples by this variable. The most obvious explanations for this trend are the changes that have taken place in the environment. Rural and urban populations are much less different in their experiences than once was the case. Rural children nowadays are bused to consolidated schools rather than having to walk to a one-room schoolhouse, both urban and rural populations can watch the same television programs and read the same books and magazines, and improved roads and transportation have greatly decreased rural isolation. Farming itself is much more a high-technology enterprise than it once was. But at the same time there has also been much rural–urban migration, which is a process that can change IQ differences without changing IQs and which would need to be considered in a complete account. For example, the proportion of the U.S. male work force involved in farming decreased from 42% in 1900 to 25% in 1930 to 4% in 1970 (Featherman & Hauser, 1978).

OCCUPATIONAL DIFFERENCES IN IQ

As noted in Table 9.1, different categories of occupations have different average levels of IQ, although, again, there is a wide range of IQs within occupational groups, and thus occupation is not a good predictor of the IQs of individuals. Occupational level is often combined with other related measures such as education and income in a broad variable of socioeconomic status (SES). Considered as a continuous variable, SES falls outside the scope of this chapter, although in categorical form, as in comparisons among defined social classes, it could qualify.

Nowhere is the distinction between *cause*, *effect*, and mere *correlation* more important than when considering the relationship of occupation (or other SES-related categories) and IQ. Among adults, a person's IQ may be an important reason why he or she is in a given occupation. Occupations vary widely in the extent of abstract reasoning and problem solving they demand. Furthermore, some occupations, such as the professions, may require lengthy educational programs for entry into them, and success in these programs may require substantial cognitive skills. Even to be admitted to the educational programs may depend on performance on IQ-related tests. Thus, an individual's IQ may be a cause of his or her occupation (although rarely the sole cause – aspirations and interests do matter!). On the other side, it has been suggested that the IQ test score of an adult may also be to some extent an *effect* of his or her occupation. Authors such as Kohn and Schooler (1983) have emphasized the role of complex jobs in sustaining or enhancing the intellectual competence of those who occupy them.

It is when we come to the children whose parents occupy different positions in the social structure that the ground becomes most treacherous. It is obvious that a parent's occupation, income, and education have substantial effects on the environment in which a child grows up. It has seemed obvious to some that the reason that children with parents of higher social status tend to have higher IQs than do children of parents of lower social status is because of the differences in the environments that the parents provide for their children. But in fact favorable environments may be correlated with, not causal to, childrens' IQs. Children could tend to resemble their parents in IQ because of the genes parents transmit to their children, not because of the environments the parents supply. An intermediate view is that, although in childhood there is a causal effect of family environment on childrens' IQs, this effect is fairly modest in size. Furthermore, it is transitory and tends to dissipate as children grow older; thus, by the time the children reach adulthood, the effect of family environment has dropped virtually to zero, and family resemblance depends almost entirely on the genes that parents and their children share (see, e.g., McGue, Bouchard, Iacono, & Lykken, 1993).

GENES AND ENVIRONMENTS IN INDIVIDUAL AND GROUP DIFFERENCES

It is a truism that both genes and environmental factors influence the development of cognitive skills in individuals and that they are so deeply intertwind in their effects that, for any given individual, it would be virtually hopeless to try to untangle them. But all is not lost. The methods of behavior genetics permit the estimation of the extent to which genetic and environmental variation contribute to the observed differences among individuals in a population for a given trait. Moreover, these methods permit the environmental contribution to be broken down into two parts: the environment that is shared by family members, and the environment that is idiosyncratic to individuals. This latter breakdown is of particular interest in the present context because among those things that family members usually have in common are their ethnic identity, their rural or urban status, and the occupation of the parents.

Behavior genetic methods rely on the comparison of groups sharing varying degrees of genetic and environmental resemblance. The most widely used procedures are the comparison of identical and fraternal twins and the study of adoptive families. Other designs, such as the comparison of full-, half-, and step-siblings in step-families, the study of identical twins reared apart, and the studies of the families of identical twins, are also sometimes used. These methods have been extensively applied to IQ (and to a lesser extent to specialized cognitive abilities). The conclusions for populations in the United States and Western Europe may be quite briefly summarized; for the detailed evidence see textbooks and reviews such as those of Plomin, DeFries, McClearn, and Rutter (1997); McGue et al. (1993); McCartney, Harris, and Bernieri (1990); Neisser et al. (1996), and the sources they cite. Note that the conclusions depend on age.

1. Among young children, say aged 3 or 4 years, all three factors – genes, shared environment, and individual environment – contribute in roughly equal degrees to individual IQ differences.
2. As children grow older, the genes increase in importance in explaining individual differences in IQ, and the role of shared family environment decreases.
3. By adulthood, the genes are responsible for something like one half to three quarters of IQ differ-

ences among individuals, and the effects of the person's childhood family environment have dwindled to near zero.
4. Measures of specific cognitive skills such as verbal and spatial ability, which are correlated with each other and with IQ, show a similar but quantitatively weaker pattern. Their distinctive aspects (after partialing out general ability) may show separate genetic or shared environmental influences, or both.

These statements are about individual differences. To what extent are the genes and environment responsible for *group* differences in IQ?

First, it should be emphasized that because genes are important contributors to individual differences does not automatically mean that genes will be important contributors to group differences. It is logically possible for environmental factors to be wholly responsible for group differences on a trait for which individual variation is mostly genetic. Height is highly heritable, but if one were to take two groups of children randomly and give members of one group hormone treatments enhancing growth and members of the other group hormone treatments retarding growth, one would produce an average height difference between the two groups that would be entirely environmental in origin.

One should, of course, not leap to the conclusion that because a group difference *could be* entirely environmental, it therefore *is* entirely environmental. That remains an empirical question. Moreover, the answer need not always be the same across groups or characteristics. For example, rural–urban IQ differences may turn out to be largely environmental, whereas occupational differences may prove to have a substantial genetic component, or differences between Americans of Asian and European ancestry may not have the same basis as differences between Americans of African and European ancestry.

Given that no flat answer will do for every case, what evidence is available for the relative roles of genes and environments in the various kinds of group differences that have been described in this chapter?

This question will be discussed quite briefly for differences associated with sex, urban–rural, and socioeconomic groupings, and then differences due to ancestry will be considered at somewhat greater length.

Sex Differences: Genetic or Environmental?

There is a simple, correct answer here, and that answer is "mostly genetic." Except for the occasional developmental mess-up, mammalian maleness or femaleness results from the presence or absence of a genetic region on the Y chromosome – a difference that leads to a series of hormonal events shaping biological and behavioral development in the male or female direction (for a review, see Collaer and Hines, 1995). However, the interesting question for most people is not the original source of the difference but how the process works out. Are the observed male–female differences in the patterning of abilities a fairly immediate consequence of brain differentiation under the influence of hormones or an indirect consequence of hormone-influenced primary and secondary sex characteristics (genitalia, body size and shape, etc.) whose effects on cognitive development are via the assignment of individuals to the gender statuses Male and Female and the environmental consequences to which this leads?

In any event, the genes involved in this process appear *not* to be those that account for individual variation in general intelligence. As noted previously, the sexes do not differ much, if at all, on average levels of IQ, although individuals within each sex vary widely, in part for genetic reasons. The reasons for the observed gender differences in specific cognitive skills remain controversial.

Rural–Urban Differences: Genetic or Environmental?

As noted earlier, because the U.S. rural–urban IQ gap has changed substantially over the course of a few decades, it seems likely that changes in the environment are chiefly responsible. Unfortunately, this does not pin down which environmental changes these are because rural–urban environmental differences in the United States have decreased in many ways during the period in question. If the genes have played any role in urban–rural IQ differences, possible mechanisms to be considered would be (a) selective migration, if the individuals moving to the cities were on average higher in IQ than those who remained behind, and (b) a greater degree of inbreeding in isolated rural communities, because inbreeding tends to lower IQs (e.g., Agrawal, Sinha, &

Jensen, 1984). Both of these processes could change rapidly over time and thus be consistent with effects that occur within a generation or two.

Occupational Differences: Genetic or Environmental?

Here there is good reason to believe that the observed average IQ differences in the United States are at least partly genetic. The underlying mechanism is occupational mobility based on cognitive skill. Individuals with higher IQs, other things being equal, are more likely to be able to satisfy the educational requirements for entering higher status occupations and (to the extent that these occupations do in fact require high levels of cognitive skill) more likely to perform well in them. If IQ differences lead (to some extent) to different jobs, and reflect (to some extent) different genes, one expects occupational mobility to lead to average genetic differences between the individuals in different occupations. This argument has been particularly emphasized by Herrnstein (1973; Herrnstein & Murray, 1994). Clearly, this is not a matter of direct genetic inheritance of occupation; it is a matter of the inheritance of genes that influence the development of cognitive skills – skills that in turn affect an individual's occupational outcomes. In a differently organized society – for example, one stratified along caste lines – the story could be different. Whether a group difference is genetic may depend on environmental conditions as well as on genes.

To what extent are the genes involved in occupational IQ differences? Many factors affect occupational success, and cognitive skill is only one of them. A Norwegian study based on some 1,000 twin pairs tested in connection with compulsory military service estimated that about 43% of the differences in occupational level among males born in the era since World War II reflected the genes (Tambs, Sundet, Magnus, & Berg, 1989). The genes accounted for somewhat larger proportions of differences in education (about 51%) and IQ (about 66%). A recent U.S. study based on full and half siblings yielded roughly comparable figures: 42% for income, 68% for education, and 64% for IQ (Rowe, Vesterdal, & Rodgers, 1999). The authors concluded that genes and shared family environment both contribute significantly to the association between IQ and SES-related variables among individuals in the United States with the genes carrying somewhat more weight.

Thus it is likely that IQ differences between U.S. occupations are partially genetic, although far from completely so. Individual differences in IQ within occupations remain large, and much of that variation is genetic. Occupation remains a weak predictor, at best, of an individual's IQ or of an individual's genes.

Racial and Ethnic Differences: Genetic or Environmental?

It is fairly safe to conclude that at least some of the average IQ differences among U.S. groups whose ancestry differs are environmental in origin. At least among children, family environments are known to affect IQ, and different U.S. racial–ethnic groups tend to differ in many family environmental variables (e.g., Brooks-Gunn, Klebanov, & Duncan, 1996). But different U.S. racial–ethnic groups also differ in the frequencies of various genes. Do these genetic differences contribute to the observed differences in level or patterning of cognitive skills among these groups? And if they do, is this a substantial or a trivial contribution?

These questions have vexed Americans – academics and laymen alike – for many years. Perhaps the two main foci of this debate in recent decades were Jensen's long article in the *Harvard Educational Review* (Jensen, 1969), "How Much Can We Boost IQ and Scholastic Achievement?" and Herrnstein and Murray's (1994) book *The Bell Curve*. Interestingly, neither of these works focused primarily on group differences, and neither made a strong claim that there is a genetic component to U.S. racial–ethnic differences. However, both brought down the wrath of their critics by saying that there might be such a component and that this possibility deserved scientific investigation.

GROUP DIFFERENCES IN WHAT INTELLIGENCE IS? One way of rendering any simple approach moot is the claim that various U.S. subgroups differ in fundamental ways in their approach to intellectual tasks and that these differences make it inappropriate to compare their performance in schools or on standard IQ tests. Boykin (1986) suggested, for example, that the African-American subculture differs from the U.S. majority culture along such dimensions as spirituality, harmony, verve, expressive individualism, communalism, and so on, and that these differences are the reasons U.S. Blacks tend to do badly in schools and on tests. One might argue that with friends like this, who needs enemies? What racist is going to object to the notion that U.S. Blacks may be better suited for life in a tribal community than for success in a modern Western technological society? Nevertheless, it is a possibility to be considered, and there have been some studies addressed to this point. Of course, the issue is not whether such subcultural differences exist but whether they have substantial effects on IQ.

An obvious first question is to ask whether intelligence is the same thing in different U.S. racial–ethnic groups. One kind of evidence concerns the factor structure of cognitive skill measures: Is it the same across groups? That is, though means may differ, do the test interrelationships remain the same? DeFries et al. (1974) compared the factor structure of a battery of 15 cognitive tests for samples of individuals in Hawaii with predominantly Japanese or predominantly European ancestry. They found the same four factors in both groups with nearly identical factor loadings. A recent study of nearly 270,000 young U.S. adults who took the Air Force Officer Qualifying Test between 1981 and 1993 compared the factor structure of its 16 subtests for subgroups self-identified as White, Black, Hispanic, Asian American, and Native American (Carretta & Ree, 1995). The subgroup sizes varied from 212,238 for Whites to 2,551 for Native Americans. The factor structure and the factor loadings proved to be nearly identical across the groups.

Another approach looks at differences in performance on IQ tests at the level of individual items. Are the patterns of item difficulty – which items are easy, which are hard – the same in different racial–ethnic groups? Jensen (1980, Chapter 11) reviewed a considerable amount of evidence suggesting that at least for U.S. Blacks and Whites the rank order of item difficulties on standard tests is highly correlated across groups and that item x race interactions are nonexistent or small. Where such differences do appear, they can typically be reduced or eliminated by taking overall level of performance into account. That is, item difficulties for Black and White children performing at the same level – for example, a comparison of Black schoolchildren with

White children a year or two younger – are even more similar than for Black and White children of the same chronological age.

A related approach is to see whether the interrelationships among variables related to developmental outcomes such as ability or achievement are different in different racial or ethnic groups. One such study (Rowe, Vazsonyi, & Flannery, 1994) compared covariance matrices for several different U.S. racial–ethnic subgroups in seven samples. Each sample permitted the comparison of two to four of the following groups: African Americans, Hispanic Americans, Asian Americans, European Americans. Comparisons were based on covariance matrices among 6 to 11 variables per study, including measures of family, home, and peer environments, and child outcome variables such as test scores, delinquency, and school grades. The result was that the covariance matrices did not differ significantly across racial–ethnic groups. The authors suggested that this is evidence that the developmental processes are basically similar for individuals in all of the groups and that differences in outcome depend on differences in input. They drew no conclusion as to whether these differences in input might be genetic, environmental, or both.

If we conclude, then, that (approximately) the same thing is being measured by intelligence tests in different U.S. racial–ethnic subgroups and that what is measured relates in (approximately) the same way to other measures of childhood environments and outcomes, we still must ask whether the observed group differences on this trait are due to differences in the distributions of genes in the different groups, or to differences in the distributions of one or more environmental factors (possibly prenatal, or if postnatal, relatively early, prior to 3 years of age for United States Blacks and Whites, anyway).

Several different kinds of evidence bear on this issue. Studies of interracial adoptions and of race mixture provide perhaps the most direct evidence.

ADOPTION STUDIES OF RACIAL–ETHNIC GROUP DIFFERENCES. When infants of one racial group are reared by parents of another, if the children tend to display the characteristics of the adopting group, it is prima facie evidence for postnatal environmental effects, and if they tend to display the characteristics of the group from which they came, it is prima facie evidence for the genes or prenatal effects.

There have been several interracial adoption studies. One study involved children of differing ancestries adopted into White homes in Minnesota (Scarr & Weinberg, 1976; Weinberg, Scarr, & Waldman, 1992; Waldman, Weinberg, & Scarr, 1996). A smaller study compared Black and interracial children adopted into White and Black homes (Moore, 1986). Two studies examined Korean and Southeast Asian infants adopted into U.S. homes, and a small study examined Korean infants adopted into homes in Belgium.

The Minnesota study by Scarr and her colleagues included several groups of children of differing ancestries adopted into White middle-class homes plus biological children of the adoptive parents. The children were given IQ tests in childhood at an average age of 7 years and tested again 10 years later in late adolescence. The average IQs, corrected for norm shifts ("Flynn effect") are given in Table 9.3 for several relevant groups: adoptees with one African-American and one European-American parent, adoptees with two African-American parents, adoptees with two European-American parents, adoptees of Asian or Native American parentage, and biological offspring of the adoptive parents. Some of these groups were quite small, but the results appear consistent with the following generalization: Rearing in an advantaged home has a positive effect during childhood, but this largely fades away by late adolescence. The means at the time

---

TABLE 9.3. Mean IQs for Children of Different Ancestries Growing Up in White Middle-Class Homes in Minnesota

Adoptees' Parentage	Number of Children	Original Study	10 Years Later
Black–Black	21	91.4	83.7
Black–White	55	105.4	93.2
White–White	16	111.5	101.5
Asian or Indian	12	96.1	91.2
Birth children	101	110.5	105.5

Note: All means adjusted for norm shifts over time ("Flynn-corrected"). Black–White refers to adoptee with one Black and one White biological parent, etc.
Source: Data from Waldman, Weinberg, & Scarr (1996).

of follow-up are about what one would expect to see for children in these groups growing up in their own homes in the United States (Lynn, 1994). (The Asian–Indian group is perhaps a bit on the low side, but the numbers are small.) This result is consistent with the typical finding from behavior genetics that shared family environmental effects on IQ are appreciable in childhood but decline to low levels by adulthood.

That this result occurs despite all the children's being socioeconomically advantaged – reared in good homes with caring parents, attending good schools, and so on – makes variables of the latter sort less plausible for explaining the average IQ differences among corresponding groups in the U.S. population. This leaves genetic, prenatal environmental, and preadoptive environmental explanations.

Unfortunately, these are to some degree confounded in these data: the White adoptees had fewer and more favorable preadoptive placements than the Black groups, and the Asian–Indian adoptees had more and worse ones. The last were placed in the adoptive homes quite late (average age of 5 years); the other groups were placed at earlier and more comparable ages (average age of $1\frac{1}{2}$ years). The children with one Black and one White biological parent (designated Black–White in the table) had somewhat more favorable conditions in a number of preadoptive variables than did the group with both biological parents black (Black–Black). Thus, the Minnesota data, although consistent with a genetic or prenatal explanation of the group differences, fall short of decisively demonstrating this to be the case.

A second adoption study, which obtained rather different results, compared 26 Black–Black and 20 Black–White children adopted into Black or White adoptive homes (Moore, 1986). All children were placed in their adoptive home by the age of 2 years and were given a standard IQ test (WISC) at ages 7 to 10. The Black–Black and Black–White children adopted into White homes can be compared with the corresponding groups in the Minnesota transracial study. After mean IQs are adjusted for age of norms, the mean was 108.7 for 9 Black–Black children adopted into White homes and 107.2 for 14 Black–White children similarly adopted compared with the corresponding 91.4 and 105.4 obtained at the original testing in Minnesota. The samples in the Moore study are quite small, of course, but as the data stand, the Black–Black group is substantially higher in average IQ than the corresponding Minnesota group, and there is no evidence of a difference in IQ between the Black–Black and the Black–White children.

The Moore study also allowed comparison between Black and Black–White children growing up in White and Black adoptive homes. Here there was a substantial difference in favor of the White adoptive homes. The Black children adopted into Black homes averaged 15 IQ points below the Black children adopted into White homes, and the biracial children adopted into Black homes averaged 11 points below the biracial children adopted into White homes.

The absence of a difference between Black and biracial children and the presence of a difference between Black and White adoptive homes suggest postnatal environmental causes rather than differences in the genes or prenatal environments. However, these causes do not appear to be a difference of a gross socioeconomic sort. All three sets of adoptive parents were predominantly middle class. The adoptive mothers' education averaged 15.1 years in Minnesota and 16.0 years in each of the groups in the Moore study. The fathers' education averaged 16.9, 17.3, and 15.6 years, respectively. Moore found differences in mother–child interaction styles in the Black and White adoptive homes that she believed might have been responsible for the IQ differences. However, given the smallness of the samples and the inconsistencies with the Minnesota findings, one would want to see a replication of the basic results before making too many inferences about them.

The three studies of Asian adoptees found that, despite often adverse preadoption experiences, these groups did relatively well on IQ tests in childhood. The largest study (Winick, Meyer, & Harris, 1975) was based on 141 Korean girls who had been adopted as infants or toddlers into U.S. homes and were currently of elementary school age (grades 1 to 8). For 111 of these children, IQ tests were available from school records. The average IQ was 107 – presumably somewhat inflated by norm shifts. Given the varying and unspecified IQ tests involved, a precise adjustment cannot be made, but if we assume that the typical test norms were 10-to-15 years old, this figure should be adjusted downward about 4 IQ points. Even with that, these children appeared to be showing quite satisfactory cognitive development.

A smaller study investigated 25 preschool-age children born in Southeast Asia and adopted into U.S. homes (Clark & Hanisee, 1982). All children were placed in their adoptive homes before the age of 3 years (average age 11 months) and were tested with the Peabody Picture Vocabulary Test at ages averaging somewhat under 4 years. The mean obtained IQ was 120, which would adjust to about 116 if one allows for norm changes. At these ages, we would expect family environment to have a considerable effect on children's IQs. These adoptive families, like those in the Minnesota and Moore studies, were middle to upper-middle class. Parents' years of education are not given, but it is stated that both parents typically had college degrees. Characteristic occupations for fathers are given as engineers, ministers and teachers – the same three occupations named as typical for adoptive fathers in the Minnesota study.

A third adoption study of Asians involved a small group of 19 Korean children adopted by families in Belgium (Frydman & Lynn, 1989). The average age of adoption was about $1\frac{1}{2}$ years. The children were tested with a French version of the WISC at an average age of 10 years. They obtained a mean IQ of 119 norm-corrected to about 110. An interesting feature of this study was that these Belgian-reared Asian children showed the same superiority of visuo-spatial over verbal skills discussed earlier in connection with Asian and Asian-American children reared by their own parents (in this study, mean performance IQ exceeded mean verbal IQ by about 13 points). Because of the small size of the sample and the fact that one cannot absolutely rule out some French language handicap owing to early exposure to Korean, one cannot put too much weight on these particular results. Nevertheless, this is the sort of outcome one would expect to find if there is a genetic component to the different patterning of verbal and visuo-spatial abilities in Asians and Europeans.

RACIAL MIXTURE STUDIES OF RACIAL–ETHNIC GROUP DIFFERENCES. These have been largely confined to African and European mixtures, although they could obviously be extended to Asian and European mixtures, for example, in Hawaii or Southeast Asia.

The basic idea is simple: Individuals, all considered African Americans, vary widely in the proportion of their genes that came from European ancestors. If (a) there is an appreciable difference between Europeans and Africans in the frequencies of genes influencing intelligence, favoring Europeans, and if (b) the genes affecting intelligence act in a straightforward additive fashion, and if (c) the genes derived from African and European ancestors are reasonably representative of their ancestral gene pools, then African Americans who have more genes derived from European ancestors should score higher on measures of intelligence than African Americans who have fewer genes derived from European ancestors.

It will be recalled that this is just what happened in the Minnesota transracial adoption study: African-American adoptees with one Black biological parent outscored African-American adoptees with two Black biological parents. But this was not the case in the Moore study. And several other studies involving race mixture have also reported a different outcome.

One of these is an early study by Witty and Jenkins (1936), who obtained information about the ancestry of African-American children of very high IQ. If there is a difference in the ancestral gene pools that is related to IQ, one would expect high-IQ African-American children to have a disproportionate share of European ancestry. However, they did not and were very similar to unselected African-American samples in this regard. Information about ancestry was obtained by interview in both cases.

Two studies have looked at blood-group genes in African-American samples – in both studies, these were twins who had been blood tested to determine their zygosity and for whom cognitive test scores were also available. One study (Loehlin, Vandenberg, & Osborne, 1973) asked whether genes that are more common among European Americans than among African Americans tended to be associated with high test performance in the African-American subsample. They were not in samples of 20 and 22 African-American twin pairs from Georgia and Kentucky (a total of 84 individuals). The second study (Scarr, Pakstis, Katz, & Barker, 1977), done in Philadelphia, estimated the odds of European versus African ancestry for each African American in the sample and correlated these odds ratios with cognitive test scores. There were 72 African-American twin pairs (144 individuals). Whether there were low correlations or no correlations between ancestry and test scores depends on what measure you look at: There was a correlation of about +.10 between estimated European ancestry and performance on Ravens' Progressive Matrices, a correlation of about −.12 for a memory measure, and approximately zero correlations for a couple of other tests and for the first principal component among the set of cognitive measures. The simplest conclusion is that no relationship at all has been demonstrated, and this was the conclusion of the authors. However, I mention the actual numbers for two reasons. First, the positive correlation is with a measure on which Blacks tend to do relatively poorly, and the negative correlation is for an ability on which they tend to do relatively well. It is plausible that European genes might be more helpful for the former than the latter. Second, the estimate of European ancestry, judging from the data the authors provided, has a reliability of about .19. This means that correlations of around .40 would be as high as one could expect even if the proportion of genes deriving from European ancestors was in fact perfectly correlated with cognitive skills in this population. Against this background, correlations like .10 and .12 – if real – are not so trivial. (In the Loehlin et al. data, the situation was even less appealing psychometrically; the estimated reliability of a measure of European ancestry for African-American individuals would have been zero. The authors did not take this approach but acknowledge that the power of the different one they chose might be quite limited.) Research using larger samples and better techniques for estimating ancestry is called for and quite feasible.

Finally, a study in Germany gave IQ tests to illegitimate children whose mothers were German but whose fathers were either Black or White soldiers from the Allied Occupation Forces stationed in Germany after World War II (Eyferth, 1961). The children were tested with a German version of the WISC at ages between 5 and 13 years. No average IQ difference was found between children with White and Black fathers. On the face of it, the presence of genes of African origin had no adverse effect on the IQs of the group of children who had Black fathers. Flynn (1980) concluded, on the basis of extensive analysis, that differential selection of various kinds could not plausibly explain this – that there

most likely were substantial differences in the average IQs of the Black and White fathers involved but that these differences failed to make the average IQs of the two groups of children different, as one would expect them to do if there were a genetic contribution to the racial–ethnic group difference.

Interpretation of this study is complicated by the presence of a race x sex interaction. Among the boys, those with Black fathers averaged below those with White fathers; but among the girls it was the other way around – those with White fathers did worse. Looked at differently, the boys and girls with Black fathers were approximately equal in mean IQ (96 and 97, respectively). The boys and girls with White fathers were markedly unequal (101 and 93, respectively). These last two samples were fairly small (37 boys, 33 girls), and thus perhaps this 8-point difference is a statistical fluke. In some sense, it must be at least partly such. After all, the standardization population of this test consisted of children of German women whose mates had genes of European origin! The test does show a difference in IQ that tends to favor boys, but less – about 4 IQ points, judging from Eyferth's graphs. The samples of children with Black fathers are larger, 81 boys and 90 girls, and so should be somewhat more stable. But that leaves us with the question of why the offspring of the black fathers do not show the sex difference that the population seems to. Back to "more research is necessary."

The mothers of the biracial children in this study were all of predominantly European ancestry (German women). So, as it happens, were nearly all the mothers of the Black–White children in the Minnesota study (66 White mothers, 2 Black mothers). What happens if one compares Black–White children whose mothers are Black with Black–White children whose mothers are White? Willerman and his colleagues did just this, using the children of Black–White couples from a large collaborative study done under the auspices of the National Institues of Mental Health (Willerman, Naylor, & Myrianthopoulos, 1970). At age 4, the average IQ of the children of 61 interracial couples whose mothers were White was 100.9. The average IQ of the children of 27 interracial couples whose mothers were Black was 93.7. Both values are presumably inflated owing to changing norms, but the difference between them is of chief interest, and adjusting both will not affect it. That difference is about 7 IQ points, half a standard deviation, in favor of the children with White mothers. The two kinds of couples did not differ notably as to either mothers' or fathers' average level of education, nor had the children differed at birth in average birthweight, length at birth, or estimated duration of gestation. The children in both groups would have had, on average, about 40% genes of African origin and 60% genes of European origin (given typical estimates of about 20% European admixture among African Americans). Yet the ones whose mothers were White averaged about 7 IQ points higher than the ones whose mothers were Black. The two groups should be genetically equivalent (barring exotic effects from cytoplasmic inheritance or genetic imprinting), and thus the difference between them is presumably environmental in some form. It seems not to be due to any gross socioeconomic difference between the two kinds of couples, given their equivalence in educational level, nor is it due to the sort of prenatal factors that would affect birthweight or length of gestation. However, subtler prenatal or postnatal environmental effects are not excluded.

RACIAL–ETHNIC EFFECTS: CONCLUSIONS. Tentatively, the difference in patterning of abilities between Americans of Asian ancestry and Americans of European ancestry looks as though it may be at least partly genetic, based on its stability over acculturation, its presence in the one small adoption study in which it was assessed, and because Native Americans, who share common ancestry, show a similar pattern. But clearly, more and better evidence would be welcome, and some could easily be obtained (e.g., verbal-performance differences among U.S. Asian adoptees).

African-American and European-American differences appear to be something else. The results of the Moore study, the Eyferth study, and Witty and Jenkins do not appear to be genetic, nor do the two bloodgroup studies, although they may not have much power. The Scarr study suggests a genetic difference, on its face, although there is some confounding of variables. Is there an alternative explanation for the difference between the Black–Black and Black–White groups in this study? Well, one possibility lies in the prenatal environment

provided by Black and White biological mothers. The Black–Black group, of course, all had Black mothers. In the Black–White group, virtually all of the birth mothers were White (66 of 68). Willerman and his colleagues found that in interracial couples it made a difference whether the mother was Black or White: The children obtained higher IQs if she was White. They suspected that this difference was due to the postnatal environment, but it could, of course, have been in the prenatal one.

U.S. Black children in general have Black birth mothers, and U.S. White children have White ones. Could this be part of the reason that there is a difference in their average IQs? It would certainly be premature to give a simple yes answer to this question. The results of the Moore study are on their face opposed, but are somewhat equivocal, because race was correlated with treatment in that study – 70% of the biracial children were placed in the White adoptive homes. As in Minnesota, the birth mothers of the biracial children were mostly White (Moore, 1980/81). Overall, there is about a five-point average IQ difference in favor of the biracial children, which is consistent with (some) genetic or prenatal effect. However, within the two adoptive categories the difference between Black and biracial children vanishes, which is consistent with an entirely postnatal effect. Because of the confounding, neither inference can confidently be drawn. And of course the 6 and 14 biracial children in this study are precariously small groups from which to draw any sweeping inferences.

So we are left with the usual conclusion: More research is needed. First, this research needs to pin down the extent to which the environmental contribution to the Black–White IQ difference is prenatal or postnatal. Then it needs to isolate the particular mechanisms involved. In this process, genetic differences should not be completely ignored. It is quite conceivable, for example, that they might be involved in interaction with environmental factors in creating a particular group difference even when they do not seem to have main effects. In one possible scenario, genetic differences in mothers may lead to prenatal environmental differences for their children.

Note that our tentative conclusion assigns different bases to different U.S. racial–ethnic IQ differences. For a contrasting view that places

Asian-American, European–American, and African-American IQs along a single dimension, along with many other differences among these groups, see Rushton (1995).

Molecular Genetics and Group Differences

Attempts are currently being made to identify individual genes contributing to variation in behavioral characteristics, including intelligence (Petrill, et al. 1996). Such efforts are still at an early stage, but if they are successful, as they may well be at some point, this could have important implications for the study of group differences. If one had an array of genes known to be related to general intelligence within the groups in question, one could simply ask: Do these genes differ in frequency between the groups? If the answer is yes, one would conclude that the group difference had at least some genetic component.

Whether such a finding would be of any importance in a practical sense would depend on the usual sorts of considerations: How much of a difference are we talking about? What do we know about the operation of the particular genes involved? Do we know how to intervene in their functioning? Would we want to? At present, of course, these are purely hypothetical questions. For a complex trait such as intelligence they are likely to remain in this status for some time. If and when they change from hypothetical to real, the relations between individual and group differences outlined in this chapter will continue to apply.

Group Differences, Individual Differences, and Ethical Dilemmas

It should be clear from the discussion so far that knowledge of an individual's membership in sex, racial, or occupational categories is not generally a good basis for drawing conclusions concerning his or her intellectual skills. If you need to know about these, give the person an appropriate test. Yet weak associations can be the basis of considerable economic advantage if one is selecting a few candidates from among many applicants (e.g., Lubinski & Humphreys, 1996).

To sharpen the issues, consider the case of sex differences in mathematical ability discussed earlier. Recall that small differences between boys and girls in means and variances, at a level that would make gender virtually useless in estimating the mathe-

matical ability of a typical individual, can lead to marked disproportion at the extremes – the ratio of 13 boys to 1 girl in the top .01% of talent was mentioned. Suppose that one were searching for individuals at this level of mathematical talent. One could cut one's search costs roughly in half by a simple expedient: Only consider boys. From the standpoint of economy and efficiency, this strategy would have much to commend it. But is it fair to the girls (few though they may be) who would automatically be excluded under such a strategy although they in fact are qualified? Efficiency and fairness are both virtues, but here they are in conflict. People differ in the extent to which they value one over the other, and such differences provide dilemmas for social policy. These are real, not spurious, dilemmas. Scientists cannot solve them; they lie in the domain of ethics, law, and politics. (If this example does not persuade you, try substituting Whites and Blacks for boys and girls).

The relationship between individual and group differences can produce several such dilemmas. One is that if a test used for selection is fair at the individual level, it will be unfair at the group level (Schmidt & Hunter, 1974). It is assumed that the groups in question differ in their average scores on the test and that the measurement is less than perfect and better than random. "Fair at the individual level" means that the decision for every individual has as small an error as possible – averaging over all individuals – and is not biased by his or her group membership. "Unfair at the group level" means that the proportion of individuals selected from the two groups will not be the same as the proportion of individuals actually qualified in the two groups – more will be selected from the higher-scoring group. Most people value both individual and group fairness, but they differ in the relative importance they assign to the two. Hence, such matters produce policy dilemmas.

These are not dilemmas that this chapter can resolve, for they involve issues of ethics and politics rather than the facts science can yield. But such facts can often be relevant to the feasibility of proposed solutions, and thus research on individual and group differences remains vital in a responsible and responsive society. Readers who wish to pursue such issues further might find of interest a special issue of the journal *Intelligence* (Gottfredson, 1997) on intelligence and social policy and an issue of the journal *Psychology, Public Policy, and Law* (Lubinski, 1996) dealing with the applications of research on individual differences.

GENERAL CONCLUSIONS

Group differences, though accounting for less human variation than individual differences, still deserve attention. Different kinds of group differences may have different explanations in terms of their genetic and environmental origins: The four kinds discussed in this chapter – sex differences, rural–urban differences, occupational differences, racial–ethnic differences – all look quite distinctive at the level of mechanism.

Average group differences, on the scale of those observed for IQ and specialized cognitive skills, have little predictive power for individuals. Knowledge of whether a person is male or female, is African-, Asian-, or European-American, lives in the city or the country, or has a particular occupation, only very slightly reduces our uncertainty concerning his or her IQ. Stereotyping, the assumption that the members of such categories are much more homogeneous than they are, is simply a mark of ignorance regarding the facts. If one needs to make a decision about a person that involves his or her intellectual abilities, one will obtain *vastly* more accurate results by assessing these directly than by relying on group averages – even though no assessment can reduce errors to zero.

But it is also the case that moderate differences between two groups in average level on a trait can lead to considerable disproportion at the extremes; differences in variance may offset or exacerbate such disproportions. Genuine ethical dilemmas can arise in such cases. No amount of knowledge of the facts can remove such dilemmas, which involve conflicts in values. Nevertheless, a grasp of the facts can clarify the problem and focus attention on the critical issues to be resolved.

REFERENCES

Agrawal, N., Sinha, S. N., & Jensen, A. R. (1984). Effects of inbreeding on Raven matrices. *Behavior Genetics, 14,* 579–585.

Benbow, C. P. (1988). Sex differences in mathematical reasoning ability in intellectually talented preadolescents: Their nature, effects, and possible causes. *The Behavioral and Brain Sciences, 11,* 169–232.

Benbow, C. P., & Stanley, J. C. (1983). Sex differences in mathematical reasoning ability: More facts. *Science, 222,* 1029–1031.

Boykin, A. W. (1986). The triple quandary and the schooling of Afro-American children. In U. Neisser (Ed.), *The school achievement of minority children* (pp. 57–92). Hillsdale, NJ: Erlbaum.

Brooks-Gunn, J., Klebanov, P. K., & Duncan, G. J. (1996). Ethnic differences in children's intelligence test scores: Role of economic deprivation, home environment, and maternal characteristics. *Child Development, 67,* 396–408.

Carretta, T. R., & Ree, M. J. (1995). Near identity of cognitive structure in sex and ethnic groups. *Personality and Individual Differences, 19,* 149–155.

Clark, E. A., & Hanisee, J. (1982). Intellectual and adaptive performance of Asian children in adoptive American settings. *Developmental Psychology, 18,* 595–599.

Coleman, J. S., Campbell, E. Q., Hobson, C. J., McPartland, J., Mood, A. M., Weinfeld, F. D., & York, R. L. (1966). *Equality of Educational Opportunity.* Washington, DC: U.S. Department of Health, Education, and Welfare.

Collaer, M. L., & Hines, M. (1995). Human behavioral sex differences: A role for gonadal hormones during early development? *Psychological Bulletin, 118,* 55–107.

DeFries, J. C., Vandenberg, S. G., McClearn, G. E., Kuse, A. R., Wilson, J. R., Ashton, G. C., & Johnson, R. C. (1974). Near identity of cognitive structure in two ethnic groups. *Science, 183,* 338–339.

Eyferth, K. (1961). Leistungen verschiedener Gruppen von Besatzungskindern im Hamburg–Wechsler Intelligenztest für Kinder (HAWIK). *Archiv für die gesamte Psychologie, 113,* 222–241.

Featherman, D. L., & Hauser, R. M. (1978). *Opportunity and change.* New York: Academic Press.

Flynn, J. R. (1980). *Race, IQ and Jensen.* London: Routledge & Kegan Paul.

Flynn, J. R. (1984). The mean IQ of Americans: Massive gains 1932 to 1978. *Psychological Bulletin, 95,* 29–51.

Flynn, J. R. (1991). *Asian Americans: Achievement beyond IQ.* Hillsdale, NJ: Erlbaum.

Flynn, J. R. (1996). What environmental factors influence intelligence: The relevance of IQ gains over time. In D. K. Detterman (Ed.), *Current topics in human intelligence. Vol. 5: The environment* (pp. 17–29). Norwood, NJ: Ablex.

Frydman, M., & Lynn, R. (1989). The intelligence of Korean children adopted in Belgium. *Personality and Individual Differences, 10,* 1323–1325.

Gottfredson, L. S. (Ed.). (1997). Intelligence and social policy [Special issue]. *Intelligence, 24*(1), 1–320.

Hedges, L. V., & Nowell, A. (1995). Sex differences in mental test scores, variability, and numbers of high-scoring individuals. *Science, 269,* 41–45.

Hedges, L. V., & Nowell, A. (1998). Black-white test score convergence since 1965. In C. Jencks & M. Phillips (Eds.), *The black–white test score gap.* Washington, DC: Brookings Institution.

Herrnstein, R. J. (1973). *I.Q. in the meritocracy*. Boston: Little, Brown.

Herrnstein, R. J., & Murray, C. (1994). *The bell curve: Intelligence and class structure in American life*. New York: The Free Press.

Hyde, J. S., Fennema, E., & Lamon, S. J. (1990). Gender differences in mathematics performance: A meta-analysis. *Psychological Bulletin, 107*, 139–155.

Jensen, A. R. (1969). How much can we boost IQ and scholastic achievement? *Harvard Educational Review, 39*, 1–123.

Jensen, A. R. (1980). *Bias in mental testing*. New York: The Free Press.

Jensen, A. R. (1985). The nature of the black–white difference on various psychometric tests: Spearman's hypothesis. *The Behavioral and Brain Sciences, 8*, 193–263.

Kohn, M. L., & Schooler, C. (1983). *Work and personality: An inquiry into the impact of social stratification*. Norwood, NJ: Ablex.

Loehlin, J. C., Lindzey, G., & Spuhler, J. N. (1975). *Race differences in intelligence*. San Francisco: Freeman.

Loehlin, J. C., Vandenberg, S. G., & Osborne, R. T. (1973). Blood group genes and Negro–White ability differences. *Behavior Genetics, 3*, 263–270.

Lubinski, D. (Ed.). (1996). Applied individual differences research [Special issue]. *Psychology, Public Policy, and Law, 2* (2), 187–392.

Lubinski, D., & Humphreys, L. G. (1996). Seeing the forest from the trees. *Psychology, Public Policy, and Law, 2*, 363–376.

Lynn, R. (1991). Race differences in intelligence: A global perspective. *Mankind Quarterly, 31*, 255–296.

Lynn, R. (1994). Some reinterpretations of the Minnesota Transracial Adoption Study. *Intelligence, 19*, 21–27.

Masters, M. S., & Sanders, B. (1993). Is the gender difference in mental rotation disappearing? *Behavior Genetics, 23*, 337–341.

McCartney, K., Harris, M. J., & Bernieri, F. (1990). Growing up and growing apart: A developmental meta-analysis of twin studies. *Psychological Bulletin, 107*, 226–237.

McGue, M., Bouchard, T. J., Jr., Iacono, W. G., & Lykken, D. T. (1993). Behavioral genetics of cognitive ability: A life-span perspective. In R. Plomin & G. E. McClearn (Eds.), *Nature, nurture, & psychology* (pp. 59–76). Washington, DC: American Psychological Association.

McShane, D., & Berry, J. W. (1988). Native North Americans: Indian and Inuit abilities. In S. H. Irvine & J. W. Berry (Eds.), *Human abilities in cultural context* (pp. 385–426). Cambridge, U.K.: Cambridge University Press.

Montie, J. E., & Fagan, J. F., III (1988). Racial differences in IQ: Item analysis of the Stanford-Binet at 3 years. *Intelligence, 12*, 315–332.

Moore, E. G. J. (1980/81). The effects of cultural style on black children's intelligence test achievement (doctoral dissertation, University of Chicago, 1980). *Dissertation Abstracts International, 41*, 3014A.

Moore, E. G. J. (1986). Family socialization and the IQ test performance of traditionally and transracially adopted black children. *Developmental Psychology, 22*, 317–326.

Nagoshi, C. T., & Johnson, R. C. (1987). Cognitive ability profiles of Caucasian vs Japanese subjects in the Hawaii Family Study of Cognition. *Personality and Individual Differences, 8*, 581–583.

Neisser, U., Boodoo, G., Bouchard, T. J., Jr., Boykin, A. W., Brody, N., Ceci, S. J., Halpern, D. F., Loehlin, J. C., Perloff, R., Sternberg, R. J., Urbina, S. (1996). Intelligence: Knowns and unknowns. *American Psychologist, 51*, 77–101.

Osborne, R. T., & McGurk, F. C. J. (Eds.). (1982). *The testing of Negro intelligence* (Vol. 2). Athens, GA: Foundation for Human Understanding.

Peoples, C. E., Fagan, J. F., III, & Drotar, D. (1995). The influence of race on 3-year-old children's performance on the Stanford–Binet: Fourth Edition. *Intelligence, 21*, 69–82.

Petrill, S. A., Plomin, R., McClearn, G. E., Smith, D. L., Vignetti, S., Chorney, M. J., Chorney, K., Thompson, L. E., Detterman, D. K., Benbow, C., Lubinski, D., Daniels, J., Owen, M. J., & McGuffin, P. (1996). DNA markers associated with general and specific cognitive abilities. *Intelligence, 23*, 191–203.

Plomin, R., DeFries, J. C., McClearn, G. E., & Rutter, M. (1997). *Behavioral Genetics* (3rd ed.). New York: W. H. Freeman.

Reynolds, C. R., Chastain, R. L., Kaufman, A. S., & McLean, J. E. (1987). Demographic characteristics and IQ among adults: Analysis of the WAIS–R standardization sample as a function of the stratification variables. *Journal of School Psychology, 25*, 323–342.

Rowe, D. C., Vazsonyi, A. T., & Flannery, D. J. (1994). No more than skin deep: Ethnic and racial similarity in developmental process. *Psychological Review, 101*, 396–413.

Rowe, D. C., Vesterdal, W. J., & Rodgers, J. L. (1999). Herrnstein's syllogism: Genetic and shared environmental influences on IQ, education, and income. *Intelligence*, (in press).

Rushton, J. P. (1995). *Race, evolution, and behavior*. New Brunswick NJ: Transaction.

Scarr, S., Pakstis, A. J., Katz, S. H., & Barker, W. B. (1977). Absence of a relationship between degree of white ancestry and intellectual skills within a black population. *Human Genetics, 39*, 69–86.

Scarr, S., & Weinberg, R. A. (1976). IQ test performance of black children adopted by white families. *American Psychologist, 31*, 726–739.

Schmidt, F. L., & Hunter, J. E. (1974). Racial and ethnic bias in psychological tests: Divergent implications of two definitions of test bias. *American Psychologist, 29*, 1–8.

Shuey, A. M. (1966). *The testing of Negro intelligence* (2nd ed.). New York: Social Science Press.

Tambs, K., Sundet, J. M., Magnus, P., & Berg, K. (1989). Genetic and environmental contributions to the covariance between occupational status, educational attainment, and IQ: A study of twins. *Behavior Genetics, 19,* 209–222.

Terman, L. M. (1916). *The measurement of intelligence.* Boston: Houghton Mifflin.

Terman, L. M., & Merrill, M. A. (1937). *Measuring intelligence: A guide to the administration of the new revised Stanford–Binet tests of intelligence.* Boston: Houghton Mifflin.

Waldman, I. D., Weinberg, R. A., & Scarr, S. (1996, August). *Genetic and environmental influences on IQ change in the Minnesota Transracial Adoption Study.* Paper presented at meeting of the International Society for the Study of Behavioral Development, Quebec City, Canada.

Weinberg, R. A., Scarr, S., & Waldman, I. D. (1992). The Minnesota Transracial Adoption Study: A follow-up of IQ test performance at adolescence. *Intelligence, 16,* 117–135.

Weyl, N. (1969). Some comparative performance indexes of American ethnic minorities. *Mankind Quarterly, 9,* 106–119.

Willerman, L., Naylor, A. F., & Myrianthopoulos, N. C. (1970). Intellectual development of children from interracial matings. *Science, 170,* 1329–1331.

Winick, M., Meyer, K. K., & Harris, R. C. (1975). Malnutrition and environmental enrichment by early adoption. *Science, 190,* 1173–1175.

Witty, P. A., & Jenkins, M. D. (1936). Intra-race testing and Negro intelligence. *Journal of Psychology, 1,* 179–192.

PART IV

BIOLOGY OF INTELLIGENCE

CHAPTER TEN

Animal Intelligence

THOMAS R. ZENTALL

ANIMAL INTELLIGENCE

With some justification, humans place themselves at the top of the evolutionary scale. If we rule out the exceptional sensory and response skills of certain nonhuman animals, clearly the sum of our intellectual capacity, measured in almost any way, exceeds that of other animals. The role of our intelligence in the domination of our species over others is clear, but in the broader perspective of evolution, intelligence per se can be viewed quite differently. Our species-centric view of intelligence may be self-serving, but as a general characteristic it correlates only superficially (and perhaps even negatively) with most measures of evolutionary success.

Survival, or more specifically, survival of the genes (Dawkins, 1976) is the measure of evolutionary success. From a purely biological perspective, the ideal survival "machine" is a simple, perhaps one-celled, organism (e.g., bacteria). By some estimates, bacteria, in spite of their small size, account for as much biomass as all other life forms combined, including plants (Gould, 1996). The survival strategy of bacteria is to reproduce quickly and often with sufficient genetic variability to accommodate changes in the environment. This has proven to be a very effective strategy also for more complex organisms like insects and many fishes. An alternative strategy is to invest more in the genetic carrier (the individual organism) and to build within the organism the flexibility required for survival.

Intelligence, in its simplest form, can be thought of as the built-in flexibility that allows individual organisms to adjust their behavior to relatively rapidly changing environments (Stenhouse, 1974, p. 61). An example of the need for flexibility comes from the varied foraging behavior of animals. For some animals, a stable supply of a highly specific food may be quite predictable (e.g., eucalyptus leaves in the environment of the koala or bamboo leaves in the environment of the panda) – at least until recently. For most animals, however, environments are much less predictable, and their predisposed eating preferences must be much more flexible (e.g., most seed-eating birds will eat a variety of seeds). For still other animals, the environment is sufficiently unpredictable that it is impossible to specify directly (by genetic means) what food will be available to an individual. For these animals to survive, more general (abstract) "rules" must be available. For such animals, rules about what to eat may not be based on the sight or taste of what is ingested but on the *consequences* of ingestion to the individual. Instead of instructing the animal to eat eucalyptus leaves or to eat a certain class of seeds, these genes tell the animal that if it feels bad after eating a certain new food, it should avoid eating more of that food. Such general rules allow for the behavioral flexibility that we call learning.

But there is a price to pay for this added flexibility. The animal must sometimes suffer the consequences of eating something bad, and if the novel taste is associated with a substance containing poison, the animal may not survive to use its new-found knowledge. The creation and maintenance of a nervous system capable of such learning represents a cost as well. For many animals, the benefits of the capacity for simple associative learning outweigh the cost. For some animals, however, the negative consequences are sufficiently costly that the simple learning rules are not enough.

Some animals have found ways to reduce this cost. Rats, which live in highly unpredictable environments, have acquired (genetically) the ability to learn the consequences of eating a novel food in a single experience, even when those consequences are experienced hours after the food was ingested (Garcia & Koelling, 1966). Rats have also developed the ability to transmit food preferences socially. If a rat has experienced the smell of a novel food on the breath of another rat, it will prefer a food with that smell over another equally novel food (Galef, 1988), and it may also be able to assess the consequences for the other rat of having eaten a novel food (Kuan & Colwill, 1997).

But what if this degree of flexibility is still not enough to allow for survival? In the case of humans, for example, our poorly developed sense of smell, our relatively poorly developed gross motor response (e.g., slow running speed), and our relative physical weakness may not have allowed us to hunt competitively with other predators (e.g., large cats). This competition must have come about slowly enough for us to have developed weapons and tools, complex forms of communication (language), and complex social structure (allowing for cooperation, teamwork, and reciprocation). According to this view, although our intellect appears to have given us a clear advantage over other animals, its evolution is likely to have emerged as the result of relative weakness (Morris, 1967). Furthermore, it is not obvious that intelligence per se is particularly advantageous for survival. Many of our closest physical and intellectual animal relatives (e.g., the chimpanzee, the orangutan, and the gorilla) are endangered species, whereas many "less intelligent" species (e.g., mice) are quite prolific.

Discussions of animal intelligence often presume that there is inherent value in intelligence. For humans, a strong case can be made for such an argument (although one could also argue that with our propensity to produce nuclear weapons, to overuse our resources, and to pollute our environment, our intelligence is actually threatening our survival). In our case, intelligence has had a runaway effect on our ability to adapt to change (an effect that Dawkins, 1976, calls hypergamy), which has allowed us to acquire and pass on knowledge and to change our environment radically (through culture rather than by genetic program). But intelligence has not had such an obviously beneficial effect on any other animal species. In general, the correlation between intelligence and numeric success is negative. One could even say that, in general, intelligence can be viewed as making the best out of a bad situation or as arriving at a complex solution to problems that other species either avoid or manage to solve in simpler ways. As we evaluate the various intellectual capacities of other animals, we should try to keep in mind that there is no inherent advantage to complexity, nor does it represent progress in any sense other than the relative recency of its appearance (Gould, 1996).

The Comparative Approach: Two Warnings

First, most people have a vague idea of the relative intelligence of animals. As a general rule, those species that are more like us physically are judged to be more intelligent. But we must be careful in making such judgements because we humans are the ones deciding what is intelligent behavior. We make up the rules and the testing procedures, and those tests may be biased in favor of our particular sensory, motor, and motivational systems (Macphail, 1985). We should avoid letting such nonintellectual differences affect our assessment of intellectual capacity.

Unfortunately, it is often not possible to control for all of these factors (i.e., it may be impossible to devise species-fair tests). Bitterman (1965, 1975) has suggested that a relational view of animal learning be used to correct for peripheral differences in sensory capacity and motor coordination. He suggested that rather than looking for differences in the rate at which different species can learn to discriminate between two stimuli, for example, we might look at differences in an animal's ability to *learn from that experience*. In other words, to what extent can learning a discrimination facilitate the learning of new discriminations. Then, using original learning as a baseline, one can ask if the *pattern* of learning successive discriminations (i.e., learning set, Harlow, 1949) differs between species.

Although logically sound, this approach assumes that peripheral and motivational factors do not interact with measures of intelligence, but they probably do. For example, Bitterman (1978) argued that goldfish show no benefit from prior experience with discriminations (i.e., they show no improvement in learning repeated discrimination reversals) and thus, they show no evidence of *learning to learn*, but Mackintosh (1978) noted that minor procedural changes can result in clear evidence for improvement in learning with experience by goldfish. Thus, attempts to make direct comparisons of intelligence among species have not been very useful, unless those species are closely related (see Kamil, 1988).

Second, we must guard against the opposite bias: the tendency to interpret behavior as intelligent because of its similarity to intelligent human behavior. In evaluating research addressing the cognitive capacity of animals I will adopt Morgan's (1894) position that it is not necessary to interpret behavior as complex (more cognitive) if a simpler (less cognitive) account will suffice. Thus, cognitive interpretations will always be contrasted with simpler, associative-learning accounts. Although the experimental study of animal cognition is relatively new (e.g., Hulse, Fowler, & Honig, 1978; Honig & Fetterman, 1992; Ristau, 1991a; Weiskrantz, 1985; Zentall, 1993a) its roots can be traced back to Tolman (1932). I will start with several classical issues concerned with the nature of learning and intelligence in animals.

RELATIONAL AND DIMENSIONAL LEARNING
Absolute versus Relational Learning

One of the most basic cognitive capacities is not being bound to the absolute properties of a stimulus. At an intuitive level, it must be the case that animals are capable of making relative judgments. The light reflected from an object will differ greatly, depending on ambient illumination, and yet animals show little loss of stimulus control when tested under lighter or darker conditions of illumination. Such simple evidence of relational learning can readily be accommodated by an absolute theory of learning (Hull, 1943; Spence, 1937) by considering gradients of stimulus generalization established during training. Thus, an animal may respond appropriately to new test stimuli if those stimuli are similar to the original training stimuli.

Spence's (1937) elaboration of the absolute theory of learning has considerable explanatory power. Its assumption that discrimination learning establishes gradients of excitation and inhibition that summate algebraically can account for several phenomena that otherwise would appear to suggest relational learning (see Riley, 1968, for an excellent discussion of absolute and relational theories). The best known of these phenomena are transposition and the easy-to-hard effect.

Transposition

If rats are trained to select a particular value of dark gray (S+) rather than a particular value of lighter gray (S−) when given a choice between the S− and a still lighter value of gray, they will choose the S− rather than the novel brightness (Kendler, 1950). This finding suggests that the animals learn the *relationship* between the training stimuli (i.e., they learn to choose the darker stimulus) and that they use that relationship, rather than the absolute values of the stimuli, when presented with the test stimuli. This result appears to be difficult to explain in terms of learning about the absolute properties of the training stimuli. However, if one assumes that excitation that accrues to the S+ will generalize to the S− (and beyond), and that inhibition accruing to the S− is somewhat weaker than the excitation at that point, then the resulting net excitatory gradient can predict transposition without the need to posit relational learning (Spence, 1937).

Easy-to-Hard

If rats are trained on an easy black–white discrimination, it appears to facilitate their acquisition of a difficult dark-gray–light-gray discrimination relative to controls only exposed to the difficult discrimination (Lawrence, 1952). Lawrence (1955) argued that training with two widely separated points along a dimension establishes the dominance of (or draws attention to) the dimension defined by those points over other dimensions. Logan (1966) has shown, however, that Spence's gradient-summation account can explain Lawrence's findings in the absence of relation learning.

Overtraining Reversal Effect

Another phenomenon that has suggested dimensional learning is the overtraining reversal effect (Reid, 1953). If rats, for example, are trained to criterion on a simple simultaneous discrimination, it will take them more trials to reverse that discrimination than if they had been overtrained on the original discrimination before the reversal. According to Mackintosh's (1965) attentional account, there are dimensional analyzers that get strengthened gradually when stimuli along that dimension are differentially associated with reinforcement. Once the discrimination has been acquired, the dimensional analyzer continues to gain salience with added experience. When reversal training begins, overtrained animals continue to respond to stimuli based on the training dimension, whereas criterion-trained animals do not.

Although other accounts have been proposed for the overtraining reversal effect, Mackintosh's analyzer theory provides the best explanation of the many findings that have been reported using the overtraining reversal procedure. The overtraining reversal effect has important implications for a general theory of animal intelligence because the animals appear to learn not only that black, rather than white, is the stimulus to which responses are reinforced but also that brightness is the relevant dimension. The notion of a dimensional analyzer implies that the animal has the ability to abstract a dimension from the *relation* between two stimuli, the $S+$ and the $S-$.

LEARNING TO LEARN

Can an animal use prior learning to facilitate new learning (i.e., can animals learn to learn)? There are two ways in which this question has been asked.

Serial Reversal Learning

First, if an animal learns a simple simultaneous discrimination between two stimuli (an $S+$, to which responses are reinforced and an $S-$ to which responses are extinguished) and then, following acquisition, the discrimination is reversed (the $S+$ becomes $S-$ and the $S-$ becomes $S+$), and then reversed again, repeatedly, are successive reversals learned faster than earlier reversals? Animals trained on this serial-reversal task generally show improvement within a few reversals, although it appears that rats show more improvement than pigeons, and pigeons show more improvement than goldfish (Bitterman & Mackintosh, 1969). Although Bitterman (1965) has attributed these differences to phyletic differences in learning, Mackintosh (1969)

attributes them to the differential ability of these species to maintain *attention* to the relevant dimension (see earlier discussion of the overtraining reversal effect).

Learning Set

The second approach to learning to learn is to look for improvement in the rate at which discriminations involving new stimuli are learned. This phenomenon, known as learning set (Harlow, 1949), has been studied primarily using visual discriminations with monkeys, but good evidence for such effects has also been found with olfactory discriminations in rats (Slotnick & Katz, 1974). In the limit, learning of a new discrimination or of a reversal, can occur in a single trial. When it does, it is referred to as a win-stay-lose-shift strategy because stimulus choice is completely controlled by the consequences of choice on the preceding trial alone. One means of developing such a strategy is to *learn to forget* the consequences of trials before the immediately preceding trial. Research has shown, in fact, that memory for the specific characteristics of the stimuli from prior discriminations actually declines as the number of discriminations learned increases (Meyer, 1971). Similarly, in serial reversal research, as experience with reversals increases, at the start of each session, animals appear to treat the stimuli independently of their value on the day before (Bitterman, 1975). Thus, animals approach optimal learning by learning to ignore the effects of all but the most recent experience.

SERIAL LEARNING

When rats learn to navigate a multiple unit maze, their learning can be described in terms of a chain of stimulus–response associations (Hull, 1943). But it is also possible that they are able to represent the maze in the form of a cognitive map (Tolman, 1932). Although a chained-association account appears to be more parsimonious than a cognitive map, when conditions are such that reliable external cues (e.g., stimuli at the choice points of the maze) are not available, the notion of a cognitive map (or of an internal representation of a series of responses) becomes more plausible. For example, Straub and Terrace (1981) have shown that pigeons can learn to respond in a particular order to the randomly displayed, simultaneous presentation of a set of stimuli. More important, when one or more stimuli are removed from the display the pigeons remain quite accurate (the remaining stimuli are selected in the appropriate order). If each stimulus served as a cue for the following response, as suggested by a chained-association account, such performance on test trials should not be possible.

It also appears that these representations can be used more effectively if they can be organized into categories, hierarchies, or chunks (Terrace, 1991; see also Fountain, Henne, & Hulse, 1984), or if their organization can be facilitated by the presence of an underlying relational rule (e.g., a monotonically decreasing reward pattern; Hulse & Dorsky, 1977). Thus, stimulus-response chains provide an incomplete account either of the complexity of associations that can develop among serial stimuli or of the higher order relations that can influence learning about them.

STIMULUS CLASS FORMATION

Perceptual Classes

Pigeons are remarkably adept at responding selectively to photographs of natural scenes, depending on whether there is a human form present (Herrnstein & Loveland, 1964) or a more abstract object present (e.g., trees or water, Herrnstein, Loveland & Cable, 1976). Those objects need not be anything that the pigeons might actually have encountered in their past (e.g., underwater pictures of fish, Herrnstein & deVilliers, 1980). To demonstrate that the pigeons do not simply memorize a list of pictures and their appropriate responses, Herrnstein et al. showed that the pigeons would respond appropriately to new examples of the positive and negative stimulus sets. Furthermore, Edwards and Honig (1987) found that a set of pictures representing a person–no-person class could be learned significantly faster than when those same pictures were assigned randomly to the positive and negative sets.

A different approach to the formation of stimulus classes has been reported by Pepperberg (1983; see also Premack, 1976). Pepperberg's African gray parrot has demonstrated the ability to respond with an appropriate vocalization (e.g., "blue" or "four-corner") to verbal questions involving the identification of stimulus properties (e.g., What color? or

What shape?) of particular objects; these learned labels could then be applied to novel stimuli.

In the case of perceptual classes, all the stimuli in the positive set have certain characteristics. For the kind of natural classes used by Herrnstein and his colleagues, those characteristics may be quite difficult to specify, but there is certainly some physical similarity among the stimuli within such classes. There are cases, however, in which the stimuli within a class are no more perceptually similar than the stimuli outside of that class.

Stimulus Equivalence

The term *stimulus equivalence* may be used when, following training, *arbitrary* (i.e., initially unrelated) stimuli come to have *emergent* relational properties that arise by means of common representations (Zentall & Smeets, 1996). Specifically, when two unrelated stimuli are associated with the same response or outcome, the two stimuli may come to "mean the same thing." Other terms that have been used to describe similar stimulus relations include stimulus class formation, functional equivalence, common coding, and stimulus substitutability. When used formally, however, stimulus equivalence has been defined by the demonstration of three specific emergent stimulus relations: reflexivity, symmetry, and transitivity (Sidman, 1990).

REFLEXIVITY OR IDENTITY. Reflexivity is the relation between a stimulus and itself or generalized identity. Identity (or sameness) is one of most fundamental human concepts. The simplest way to test for the ability to use an identity relation is to train animals on a task in which an identity relation is present (the "instructional" portion of the task) and then ask if that experience will generalize to novel stimuli (that are not differentially more similar to one of the training stimuli). Zentall and Hogan (1976, 1978; see also 1974, 1975) showed that when pigeons are trained on a matching or oddity task with shapes, the birds transferred to the same task (matching to matching, or oddity to oddity) involving novel colors performed significantly better than those transferred to the other task involving those same colors (matching to oddity, or oddity to matching).

Wilson, Mackintosh, and Boaks (1985) have argued, however, that transfer data of this kind may result entirely from a natural predisposition by pigeons to prefer stimuli that are relatively novel (see also Herrnstein, 1985). Although there is little evidence for such a predisposition (see Zentall, Hogan, Edwards, & Hearst, 1980; in fact pigeons appear to be somewhat neophobic and are afraid of novelty), pigeons could learn to use relative novelty (i.e., the degree to which a comparison stimulus has very recently been seen as a sample) as a cue. For example, in the case of generalized matching the pigeon could learn to choose the comparison that is relatively familiar, and in the case of oddity, the comparison that is relatively unfamiliar (Wilson et al.). However, although it may seem more parsimonious to attribute the transfer of matching and oddity to relative familiarity and novelty, such an account is conceptually indistinguishable from generalized identity.

Because pigeons are somewhat neophobic, the use of novel stimuli in assessing the use of identity by pigeons (and perhaps other animals as well) may result in novelty avoidance, which in turn may lead to the underestimation of identity transfer. Convergent evidence for the role of identity in the acquisition of matching tasks can be obtained, however, using all familiar stimuli (Zentall, Edwards, Moore, & Hogan, 1981). Pigeons trained in either matching or oddity were then presented with test trials in which the matching or the nonmatching comparison was systematically replaced with stimuli familiar to the pigeons from training (both as correct and incorrect comparisons) but not in the context of the test sample (see Zentall et al., 1981, for details).

The results suggest that pigeons use the identity relation to learn both matching and oddity. For the matching task, replacing the correct or matching comparison resulted in correct comparison choices. For the oddity task, however, replacing the incorrect comparison (which also removes the matching comparison) resulted in poor performance. Furthermore, in neither case did replacement of the nonmatching comparison affect performance. Taken together, the results of transfer tests involving novel stimuli and those involving replacement of correct and incorrect comparisons with familiar stimuli indicate that identity can play an important role in learning by animals.

A higher (relational) form of identity or same–different learning has been demonstrated by Pepperberg (1987b) in a parrot. After having learned the appropriate color and shape labels for objects in response to the question What color? or What shape? the parrot was then trained with a subset of objects to respond with the appropriate category label to the question What's same? or What's different? The parrot not only acquired this task (i.e., it could respond appropriately with "color" or "shape"), but it transferred at a high level to new combinations of training objects and to novel objects.

A different version of relational same–different learning has been demonstrated in chimpanzees (Thompson, Oden, & Boysen, 1997). In this modified version of matching-to-sample, the sample consisted of a pair of objects that either were the same (e.g., AA) or were different (e.g., BC). Two pairs of comparison objects also were presented, one for which the relation to the sample matched (e.g., DD in the case of an AA sample) and the other for which the relation to the sample did not match (e.g., EF in the case of an AA sample). High levels of relational same–different matching were found for all of the adult chimpanzees tested. Apparently, the chimpanzees had learned to match relations, not just stimuli.

SYMMETRY OR BIDIRECTIONAL ASSOCIATIONS. The second defining property of stimulus equivalence is symmetry. When a relation is symmetrical it indicates that if A = B, then it is also true that B = A. Although there is some evidence for the development of bidirectional associations in Pavlovian conditioning experiments, especially early in training (Spetch, Wilkie, & Pinel, 1981), animals have a strong tendency to learn that X *leads* to Y, rather than X and Y *go together*.

Bidirectional learning between arbitrary events has also been examined in the context of two-alternative conditional-discrimination tasks (similar to matching but in which the relation between samples and comparisons is completely arbitrary, i.e., none of the stimuli match). When samples and comparisons are interchanged, however, little evidence for bidirectional learning has been found (Gray, 1966; Hogan & Zentall, 1977; Lipkens, Kop, & Matthijs, 1988; Richards, 1988; Rodewald, 1974; Sidman, Rauzin, Lazar, Cunningham, Tailby, & Carrigan, 1982). In some of these cases, transfer may not have been found because the tests involved the exchange not only of the temporal order of the stimuli but also of their spatial location. Better evidence for bidirectional learning has been found when one of the discriminations involves stimuli that are biologically important (i.e., food; Hearst, 1989; Sherburne & Zentall, 1995; Zentall, Sherburne, & Steirn, 1992).

TRANSITIVITY OR MEDIATION. The third defining property of stimulus equivalence is transitivity. When a relation is transitive it means that if A = B, and B = C, then A = C. The best evidence for transitivity in animals comes from two lines of Pavlovian conditioning research: sensory preconditioning and second-order conditioning. In sensory preconditioning, one stimulus is paired with another in Phase 1. Then in Phase 2, the second stimulus is paired with a biologically important event (e.g., food). Evidence for transitivity is found if a conditioned response is elicited when the first stimulus is reintroduced (see Seidel, 1959). In second-order conditioning, the first two phases are reversed. Thus, training starts with the pairing of a stimulus with a biologically important event. Then, in Phase 2, the first stimulus is paired with a second. Finally, the second stimulus is presented alone, and evidence for transitivity is found when a conditioned response is elicited (see Rescorla, 1980).

Recently, evidence has been reported for emergent transitive relations in an instrumental context (Steirn, Jackson-Smith, & Zentall, 1991; see also Kuno, Kitadate, & Iwamoto, 1994). Pigeons were initially trained using an associative learning task in which two stimuli, A1 and A2, were each associated with a unique outcome, B1 or B2 (food or no-food), respectively. The food and no-food outcomes were then presented as conditional stimuli associated with correctly responding to comparison stimuli C1 and C2, respectively. Finally, when the pigeons were presented with A1 and A2 samples, they showed significant choice of the C1 and C2 comparisons, respectively.

Functional Equivalence

The term functional equivalence has sometimes been used to describe the two classes of stimuli that are formed by stimuli involved in serial reversal training for which reinforcement contingencies are similar. For example, Vaughan (1988) trained

pigeons to respond to 20 randomly selected pictures of trees (S + s) and not to respond to 20 other randomly selected pictures of trees (S − s). Following acquisition, the discrimination was reversed, and then reversed again, repeatedly. Following a large number of reversals, at the start of a reversal, the pigeons began responding appropriately after the first three or four exemplars from each set (i.e., as soon as they had determined to which set of stimuli responses were being reinforced).

Classes of this type have an interesting property. There is no simple verbal label (e.g., trees) to identify them. They are generally described by humans as stimuli that, because of their common reinforcement histories, "go together."

Common Coding

The term common coding has been used to describe the results of a form of matching-to-sample procedure in which two or more samples are each associated with the same comparison stimulus. Following training on this task (often referred to as many-to-one matching), evidence has been found for the development of emergent relations between samples associated with the same comparison.

The most direct evidence for the common representation of arbitrary samples associated with the same comparison comes from transfer of training designs (Lea, 1984) in which, following many-to-one training, one member of each of the presumed stimulus classes is associated with a new pair of comparisons. It can then often be shown that the remaining members of each class are also associated with the new comparisons (Urcuioli, Zentall, & DeMarse, 1995; Urcuioli, Zentall, Jackson-Smith, & Sterin, 1989; Wasserman, DeVolder, & Coppage, 1992; see also Zentall, Sherburne, & Urcuioli, 1993). This robust transfer-of-training effect has also been demonstrated in simpler Pavlovian contexts (Honey & Hall, 1989; see also Hall, 1996).

Additional support for emergent stimulus relations following many-to-one matching training comes from the difficulty of reversing sample-comparison associations involving one member of each presumed stimulus class but not the other (Nakagawa, 1986; Zentall, Sterin, Sherburne, & Urcuioli, 1991). Furthermore, Kaiser, Sherburne, Steirn, and Zentall (1997) have found that samples associated with the same comparison are more difficult to discriminate from each other than samples associated with different comparisons.

Finally, convergent support for emergent relations between samples associated with the same comparison comes from the relative slopes of retention functions following training with many-to-one matching. Typically, when variable-duration delays are inserted between samples and comparisons of a delayed matching task, the resulting retention functions are considerably flatter when the samples are hues than when they are line orientations (i.e., the orientation of a line is not remembered as well as a hue; Farthing, Wagner, Gilmour, & Waxman, 1977; Urcuioli & Zentall, 1986; Zentall, Urcuioli, Jagielo, & Jackson-Smith, 1989). When many-to-one training involves a hue and a line orientation mapped onto the same comparison, however, the slopes of the hue-sample-trial and line-orientation-sample-trial retention functions are remarkably similar (Urcuioli et al., 1989; Zentall et al., 1989). The implication of retention-function similarity is that the underlying memories are also similar.

The importance of stimulus class formation as a critical component of intelligence cannot be overstated. For example, the formation of stimulus classes plays an integral role in the acquisition of human language (e.g., vocabulary). The ability of small-brained organisms like pigeons to develop *arbitrary* stimulus classes suggests that this capacity is much more pervasive than once thought.

MEMORY STRATEGIES

Prospective Processes

Traditionally, animal memory has been viewed as a rather passive process. According to this view, sensory events can leave a trace that may control responses even when the event is no longer present (Roberts & Grant, 1976). More recently, however, it has been suggested that animals can actively translate or code the representation of a presented stimulus into an expectation of a yet-to-be-presented event (Honig & Thompson, 1982). The use of expectations, or prospective coding processes, has important implications for the cognitive capacities of animals. If the expectation of a stimulus, response, or outcome can serve as an effective cue for responding, this suggests that animals may be capable of exerting active control over memory and, in particular,

may suggest they have the capacity for active planning.

The notion of expectancy as an active purposive process can be attributed to Tolman (1932; see also Dickinson, 1985). Although one can say that a dog salivates when it hears a bell because it *expects* food to be placed in its mouth, the demonstration that an expectation can serve as a discriminative stimulus (i.e., as the basis for making a choice), makes clear the cognitive nature of expectancy.

THE DIFFERENTIAL OUTCOMES EFFECT. If a conditional discrimination is designed such that a correct response following one sample results in one kind of outcome (e.g., food) and following the other sample results in a different kind of outcome (e.g., water), one can show that acquisition of the conditional discrimination is faster (Trapold, 1970) and retention is better (Peterson, Wheeler, & Trapold, 1980). But more direct evidence that outcome expectancy can serve as a *cue* for comparison choice comes from transfer-of-training research with pigeons. If other stimuli that have been directly associated with the same differential outcomes replace the original samples, positive transfer typically results (e.g., Peterson, 1984; Edwards, Jagielo, Zentall, & Hogan, 1982). This line of research indicates that presentation of a sample creates an expectation by the pigeon of a particular kind of outcome and that expectation can then serve as the basis for comparison choice (Sherburne & Zentall, 1998).

Once one has accepted the notion that outcome expectancies can control comparison choice, it may not be surprising to learn that they can bridge delays better than the sample memories themselves (Sherburne & Zentall, 1998). After all, hedonic outcomes are of great importance to animals. But there is also evidence that *nonhedonic* events such as the anticipation of a stimulus (or a response) can affect response accuracy (e.g., Honig & Thompson, 1982).

PROSPECTIVE CODING STRATEGIES. Perhaps the most impressive demonstration of memory strategies in animals comes from rats' performance on the radial arm maze (Cook, Brown, & Riley, 1985). This apparatus consists of a central platform with perhaps 12 baited arms radiating from the center. The rat enters each arm in any order, and the trial ends when all the arms have been entered at least once. An error is defined by more than one entry into a particular arm.

Rats acquire this task, to a high level of accuracy, very rapidly. Memory can then be assessed by interrupting the trial with a retention interval (perhaps 15 min) spent off the maze and then allowing the rat to complete the trial. To assess the rat's memory strategy, the point in the trial at which the rat is removed is varied from trial to trial. If, while off the maze, the rat remembers the places it has been, retrospectively, then the probability of making an error (corrected for opportunity and possible selection bias) should increase as the point of delay interpolation comes later in the trial. This should occur because the rat has more to remember later in the trial. If, however, the rat remembers the places yet to be visited, prospectively, then the probability of making an error should decrease as the point of delay interpolation comes later in the trial. This should occur because the rat has fewer yet-to-be-visited places to remember later in the trial. Cook et al. (1985) found that early in the trial (when the delay was interpolated after 2, 4, or 6 arm entries) the probability of an error increased. Thus, early in the trial the rat appeared to remember where it had been earlier during that trial. Later in the trial (when the delay was interpolated after 8 or 10 arm entries), however, the probability of an error decreased. Thus, later in the trial the rat appeared to remember where it still had to go in that trial. What is especially remarkable about this finding, according to this account, is that prior to the delay each animal must remember both the arms that it has visited and those not yet visited. Then, at the time of removal from the maze (or during the retention interval), the rat must "decide" which set of arms it will remember. Similar findings have been reported for pigeons with an operant-chamber analog of the radial arm maze (Steirn, Zentall, & Sherburne, 1992; Zentall, Steirn, & Jackson-Smith, 1990).

Directed Forgetting

The notion of directed forgetting is borrowed from human memory research. It implies that memory is an active, rather than an automatic process. Presumably, following presentation, items that participants are instructed to forget will not be well stored or maintained in memory, and thus they should not be well retained. The simplest form of directed for-

getting in animals involves the omission procedure. Pigeons are trained, for example, on a matching task and then a fixed duration delay is introduced between the sample and the comparisons. On "forget" trials, during the delay, the pigeons are cued that there will be no test of sample memory (i.e., the trial is over). On probe trials, however, the "forget" cue is presented, but there is also a test of sample memory. Matching accuracy in these probe trials is generally below that of uncued "remember" trials (see Roper & Zentall, 1993).

Unfortunately, when the omission procedure is used, the "forget" cue not only signals that memory will not be tested but it also signals that the animal will not get fed and that no response to a comparison stimulus will be required. If one controls for these artifacts by using a substitution procedure (e.g., a simple simultaneous discrimination is substituted for the comparisons on "forget" trials in training), typically, no evidence of directed forgetting has been found. But, as has been noted by Roper and Zentall, (1993) this procedure may not sufficiently encourage the pigeon to stop maintaining the sample in memory. In the human version of the task, forgetting is encouraged because prior "remember" items can be rehearsed between identification of the "forget" cue and presentation of the next item. Better evidence for directed forgetting in pigeons can be demonstrated, however, if on "forget" trials in training, one approximates the human directed-forgetting procedure by allowing the animal to *reallocate* its memory from the sample to an alternative memory (Kaiser, Sherburne, & Zentall, 1997; Roper, Kaiser, & Zentall, 1995).

TOOL USE

It has been argued that the use of tools by humans has greatly enhanced human fitness and thus has played an important role in the evolution of human intelligence (Barash, 1979, p. 221). This position is not well supported by the widespread but unsystematic use of tools by various unrelated species.

For example hamadryas baboons have been seen to use the ends of their tails as a "sponge" to obtain otherwise inaccessible water (Schonholzer, 1958, as cited by Kummer & Goodall, 1985). More obvious examples that involve objects not part of the animal's body include the sea otter's use of a rock placed on its chest against which to strike shellfish (Drickamer, Vessey, & Meikle, 1996, p. 285). Similarly, Egyptian vultures have been seen dropping rocks on ostrich eggs (Goodall & van Lawick, 1966), and the selection and use of appropriate rocks for cracking open nuts and the stripping of leaves from straight twigs and use for termite "fishing" by chimpanzees is well documented (Kummer & Goodall, 1985). Finally, I found particularly innovative the use of bait (sometimes edible sometimes inedible) by certain green-backed heron to attract fish within striking range (Higuchi, 1986).

Although one's definition of what constitutes a tool may exclude some examples of what others might include (e.g., When a gull repeatedly flies over rocks and drops a mussel it is carrying, do the rocks constitute a tool?), it is not obvious where one should draw the line to distinguish tool use from other less intelligent behavior.

REASONING

Reasoning can be thought of as a class of cognitive behavior for which correct responses during test trials require an *inference* based on initial experience. For obvious reasons, although most research on reasoning in animals has been done with higher primates (e.g., chimpanzees), there is evidence that some reasoning-like behavior can be demonstrated in a variety of animal species.

Transitive Inference

In its simplest form, the transitive inference task can be described as follows: if A is greater than B (A > B), and B > C, then it can be inferred that A > C (where the letters A, B, and C represent arbitrary stimuli). A correct response in this relational learning task requires that an inference be made about the relation between A and C that can only be derived from the two original propositions. To avoid potential problems with end-point effects (i.e., C is never greater than anything, and A is always greater in all comparisons in which it appears), the task usually involves four propositions: A > B, B > C, C > D, and D > E, and the test involves the choice between the non-end-points B and D.

When humans are tested for transitive inference, the use of language allows for the propositions to be completely relational. Often relative heights are assigned to individuals identified only by name (e.g., given that Arnold is taller than Bob, and that Bob is taller than Charles, who is taller, Arnold or Charles). With animals, however, there is no way to present such relational propositions without also presenting the actual values of the stimuli. And if the actual values differ, then a correct response can be made without an inference being made (i.e., based on the absolute values).

McGonigle and Chalmers (1977) argued that a nonverbal relational form of the task could be represented by simple simultaneous discriminations (S+ S−). Thus, A > B can be represented as A+ B−, B > C as B+ C−, and so on. With four proportions an animal would be exposed to A + B−, B + C−, C + D−, and D + E−. Stimulus A is always positive and E is always negative, but B and D, stimuli that were never paired during training, share similar reinforcement histories. Thus, if animals order the stimuli from A is best to E is worst, then B should be preferred over D. Findings consistent with transitive inference have been reported in research with species as diverse as chimpanzees (Gillan, 1981), rats (Davis, 1992), and pigeons (Fersen, Wynne, Delius, & Staddon, 1991). Although some have argued that these results can be accounted for without postulating that an inference has been made (Couvillon & Bitterman, 1992; Fersen et al., 1991; Steirn, Weaver, & Zentall, 1995; Wynne, Fersen, & Staddon, 1992), transitive inference effects have been found when these presumably simpler mechanisms have been controlled (Weaver, Steirn, & Zentall, 1997).

CONSERVATION AND ANALOGICAL REASONING. The conservation of liquid volume task, made popular as a test of cognitive development by Piaget (1952), was developed to test for the inference that if two liquid volumes are initially the same and one of the volumes is transformed by pouring it into a container of a different shape (the heights of the liquids in the two containers are quite different following the transformation), the volumes must be still the same. Woodruff, Premack, and Kennel (1978) developed a nonverbal version of this task that they used to test for conservation in Sarah, a chimpanzee. Not only did Sarah indicate (by means of previously acquired use of "same" and "different" tokens) that transformation of shape did not cause two like volumes to be different, but she also indicated that two initially dissimilar volumes continued to be different following a transformation that resulted in liquid levels of similar height. Furthermore, Sarah was unable to judge the relative volume of the liquids correctly if the transformation was made out of sight (i.e., when no inference could be made). Thus, correct responding required observation of the original state of the containers and the transformation. This series of experiments is particularly noteworthy for its careful control of possible extraneous variables.

Another example of reasoning by a chimpanzee, analogical reasoning, has been reported by Gillan, Premack, and Woodruff (1981). Sarah was shown pictures of previously encountered objects in the relation A is to B as A′ is to X with a choice of B′ and C′ as a replacement for X. Sarah's reliance on the analogical relationship was tested by varying only the initial stimulus pair. Thus, in one trial she was presented with, for example, "lock" is to "key" as "paint can" is to "?" with a choice of "can opener" and "paint brush," and in another trial with "paper" is to "pencil" as "paint can" is to "?" with a choice of the same "can opener" and "paint brush." In the first case Sarah selected the "can opener;" in the second, the "paint brush."

COUNTING

The term numerical competence is often used in animal research because the more common term, counting, carries with it the surplus meaning that accompanies the human verbal labels given to numbers. That this distinction is an arbitrary one based on limitations of response (output) capacity rather than conceptual ability is suggested by Pepperberg's (1987a) work with generalized number use (in verbal English) in an African gray parrot.

An excellent review of the animal counting literature is provided by Davis and Memmott (1982; see also Boysen & Capaldi, 1993; Davis & Pérusse, 1988), who concluded that counting does not come easily. "Although counting is obtainable in infra humans, its occurrence requires considerable environmental support" (Davis & Memmott, 1982, p. 566). In contrast, Capaldi (1993) concluded that, under the right conditions, animals count routinely. In simple but elegant experiments, Capaldi demonstrated that, following training, rats can anticipate whether they will get fed or not for running down an alley, depending solely on the number of successive times that they have run down that alley without having gotten fed (e.g., Capaldi & Verry, 1981). Capaldi has also shown that rats can count independently the number of one kind of food versus another and, furthermore, that they can transfer that learning to new foods (Capaldi & Miller, 1988).

The difference in conclusion reached by Davis and Memmott and by Capaldi has general implications for the study of intelligence in animals (including humans). The context in which one looks for a particular capacity may determine whether one will find evidence for it or not. Because we, as human experimenters, devise the tasks that serve as the basis for the assessment of intelligence, we must be sensitive to the possibility that these tasks may not be optimal for eliciting the behavior we are assessing. Much of our view of the evolutionary scale of intelligence may be biased in this way by species differences in sensory, response, and motivational factors.

Perhaps the most impressive demonstration of numerical competence in an animal was reported by Boysen and Berntson (1993). A chimpanzee, Sheeba, was first trained in the correspondence between Arabic numerals and number of objects. When she was then shown a number of objects seen at two or three different locations (e.g., three objects at one site and one object at another), she pointed to the numeral 4, the sum of the objects. Finally, she was shown Arabic numerals at two different sites, and she spontaneously pointed to the numeral that represented the sum of the two numerals she had seen.

LANGUAGE

It has been argued that the use of language alone may distinguish human intelligence from that of other vertebrate animals (Macphail, 1985). Furthermore, Macphail has proposed that if other animals could acquire language, they might be capable of humanlike intelligence (i.e., language is merely the vehicle by which intelligence expresses itself).

We are the only species to develop, on our own, the flexible form of communication based on arbitrary symbols that we call language. With training, however, other species may be able to acquire such forms of communication. One of the most widely reported and least understood lines of research in animal intelligence involves projects concerned with the acquisition of language in chimpanzees (see also Pepperberg, 1997, on the acquisition of human-based codes by a parrot and Herman, Kuczaj, & Holder, 1993; Herman, Pack, & Morrel-Samuels, 1993, on receptive language acquisition by dolphins).

The three best known of the chimpanzee projects are Gardner and Gardner's (1969) sign learning project (see also Patterson's, 1978, work with a gorilla), Premack's (1976) token learning project, and the Rumbaughs' (Rumbaugh, 1977) keyboard learning project.

Although these projects are identified by the nature of the responses required of their animals, they are better distinguished by differences in their conceptual approaches. The Gardners chose sign language because it is an accepted form of human language, and acquisition and mastery skills by a chimpanzee could be compared directly with those of humans by sign-trained observers unfamiliar with the animals. The use of tokens in Premack's research allowed for more careful control over the set of possible responses. Premack's research focused more on the *conceptual* nature of language, including such characteristics as same–different learning, negation, property of, and causality. The Rumbaughs' work with Austin and Sherman focused on the functional use of language in communication (Savage-Rumbaugh, 1984). For example, they established conditions in which solution of a problem by one chimpanzee required the production and reception by another chimpanzee of a complex list of symbols representing a request for a tool.

Whether the communication skills acquired by these chimpanzees qualify as language depends in part on how language is defined. Unfortunately, there is little agreement on the necessary and sufficient characteristics of language. For such a definition to be useful, it must be sufficiently liberal to include within its scope, not only hearing-impaired humans who use sign language but also young children and many developmentally delayed adults who have restricted but functionally adequate language skills.

THEORY OF MIND

An organism has a theory of mind when it demonstrates an understanding of what another organism may know. When Susan sees a hidden object moved to second hidden location after Billy has left the room and Susan understands that Billy will probably look for the object in the first location rather than in the second, we say that Susan has a theory of mind because she understands what Billy can and cannot know (see Frye, 1993). To demonstrate theory of mind in an animal is a bit more complex because, in the absence of language, theory of mind must be inferred from other behavior.

Self-Recognition

Recognition of the similarity between ourselves and others would seem to be prerequisite for theory of mind. If we can recognize ourselves in a mirror, we can see that we are similar to others of our species. Gallup (1970) has shown that not only will chimpanzees exposed to a mirror use it for grooming, but, if their face is marked while they are anesthetized, they will use the mirror to explore the mark tactually. Furthermore, both prior experience with the mirror and the presence of the mirror following marking appear to be necessary for mark touching to occur. Although mirror-directed mark touching appears to occur in other higher apes (orangutans and perhaps also in gorillas), no evidence of self-recognition has been found in monkeys, even with extensive mirror experience (Gallup & Suarez, 1991).

Imitation

Certainly, if an organism understands what another knows, it should be able to benefit from that understanding by taking the perspective of another. One form of perspective taking involves the capacity to imitate another (Piaget, 1951). But evidence for true imitative learning requires that one rule out (or control for) other sources of facilitated learning following observation (see Whiten & Ham, 1992; Zentall, 1996). One procedure that appears to control for all artifactual sources of facilitated learning following observation is the two-action method (Dawson & Foss, 1965). Specifically, imitation is said to occur if observers exposed to a demonstrator performing a response in one of two topographically different ways perform the response with the same topography as their demonstrator (Heyes & Dawson, 1990). For example, Akins and Zentall (1996) trained some Japanese quail demonstrators to step on a treadle and others to peck at the same treadle for food. When observer quail were exposed to one or the other demonstrator, they matched the behavior of their demonstrator with a high probability (see also Zentall, Sutton, & Sherburne, 1996).

Perhaps the most impressive example of animal imitation comes from a test of generalized imitative learning reported by Hayes and Hayes (1952) with a home-raised chimpanzee named Viki. Using a set of 70 gestures, Viki was trained to replicate each gesture when the experimenter said, "Do this." More important, when she was directed to, Viki also accurately repeated 10 novel arbitrary gestures (see also Custance, Whiten, & Bard, 1995).

Deception

If an animal can deceive, one could argue that it must know what another knows. Certainly, functional deception can be trained. Woodruff and Premack (1979) trained chimpanzees to point to the container that held food in order to receive food. The chimpanzees then learned that one trainer would give them the food for pointing to the container that held the food, whereas the other would give them the food only if they pointed to a container that did not hold food. Although the chimpanzees learned to respond appropriately, there was no indication that they *intended* to deceive the trainer (Dennett, 1983).

Whiten and Byrne (1988) described three levels of deception, each involving a presumably greater degree of intentionality. The first, concealment, involves hiding an object that might be taken away by another animal or concealing one's interest in an object obtained by another for the apparent purpose of having a better chance to take it away.

The second level of deception, distraction, involves behavior that is more active than concealment. It may involve a vocalization that draws another animal's attention away from a desired object. It may also involve what has been called lying (Jolly, 1991), as in the case of predator false alarm calls that appear to have distraction as their motive.

The third level of deception, creating an image, involves concealment of the nature of a social interaction. An example of this kind of concealment was suggested by de Waal (1982). It involved a male chimpanzee that limped, presumably because of an injury, but it did so selectively, only when it could

be seen by dominant males. The assumption is that by limping the likelihood of an aggressive response from a dominant male would be reduced.

Jolly (1991) suggested that there is a fourth level of intentionality, one that involves *social tools*. At this level, one animal may use another to interact with a third. An example of this kind of behavior is when a mother chimpanzee distracts her offspring because he is annoying others (Fouts & Fouts, 1989).

The problem with interpreting experiments on deception is that in each of these cases intentionality must be *inferred* from behavior. Intentionality is difficult to assess in any organism. Consider, for example, the difficulty we humans have in assessing the intentionality of an individual who has committed a crime (e.g., battery). Was it self-defense, an impulsive act, or premeditated behavior? Intentionality is particularly difficult to assess in a nonverbal organism, and the more different an organism is from us, the more difficult it is for us to conclude that the behavior is intentional. Consider the difference between the context-dependent limping chimpanzee described by de Waal (1982) and the broken-wing display of the piping plover, a behavior that has the effect of leading predators away from its nest (Ristau, 1991b).

Perspective Taking

One account of imitation is that the observer can take the perspective of (or put itself in the role of) the demonstrator. But children do not develop the ability to take the perspective of another until they are 5–7 years old. If Japanese quail can imitate, it is unlikely that they do so by taking the perspective of the demonstrator.

Povinelli, Nelson, and Boysen (1990) attempted a version of the child's theory of mind task described earlier (Frye, 1993). Chimpanzees first were trained to select a box towards which a trainer was pointing to receive a reward. When they were tested with two trainers (who were pointing at different boxes), one that had been present when the box was baited and the other that had been absent, the chimpanzees chose the box indicated by the "knower" over the one indicated by the "guesser." But as Heyes (1998) has noted, in this and other similar procedures (involving, for example, a "guesser" with a bag over his head), the preference for the "knower" did not show up on the very first trials, and the number of test trials was sufficient that the chimpanzees could have *learned* to use the "knower's" behavior as a cue rather than to infer the "knower's" knowledge.

Cooperation and Altruism

Cooperation and altruism are special cases of intelligent behavior because they represent a form of social behavior for which the actions of the organism have implications for the well-being of another organism. Although true cooperation and altruism are closely related to theory of mind, many forms of these behaviors (e.g., the cooperation among dogs hunting in a pack, and maternal behavior) are strongly biologically predisposed, and thus cognitive accounts are unnecessary. Other cases of cooperation can more parsimoniously be interpreted as the use of another animal as a discriminative stimulus. Skinner (1962), for example, trained pigeons to "hunt" on each trial for the response key to which a response would be reinforced. He then placed two pigeons side by side and added the contingency that the two "correct" response keys (which were always at the same vertical level) should be pecked simultaneously. The pigeons readily adjusted to the new contingency and often got fed, but their functional cooperation can be explained as the use of movement of one pigeon toward a response key as a discriminative stimulus for the other pigeon to peck the same key at the same time.

Examples of altruistic behavior based on variants of parental behavior (e.g., adoption of others' offspring) can be explained more parsimoniously in terms of "errors" in biologically predisposed behavior. Furthermore, although a certain level of intelligence may be required for true, cognitively-based cooperation and altruism to take place, it is also clear that intelligence is not sufficient. Thus, neither phenomenon should be generally viewed as a measure of human intelligence.

Although theory of mind in animals is a relatively new area of research, it promises to be an exciting point of contact between the human and animal cognitive literature.

CONCLUSIONS

The broad range of positive research findings that has come from investigating the cognitive abilities of animals suggests that many of the "special capacities" attributed to humans may differ from those of other animals more on quantitative than on qualitative grounds. In the case of many cognitive learning tasks, once we learn how to ask the question appropriately (i.e., in a way that is accommodating to the animal's natural propensities), animals often surprise us with their capacity to use complex relations.

In evaluating the animal intelligence literature (and for that matter, the human intelligence literature as well), we must be sensitive to errors of overestimation and of underestimation. Errors of overestimation can come from results that on the surface appear to be cognitive functioning in animals but that can be accounted for more parsimoneously in noncognitive terms (Zentall, 1993b). Spence's (1937) gradient-summation account of transposition is a good example. Errors of underestimation can come from our bias to present animals with tasks that involve procedures convenient to us (i.e., that are compatible with our sensory, response, and motivational systems). Learning set can be demonstrated quite readily in primates using three-dimensional objects (Harlow, 1949). In rats, however, learning set can best be demonstrated using olfactory discriminations (Slotnick & Katz, 1974).

Errors of underestimation can also come from our ability to instruct verbally competent humans but not other animals concerning the "rules" of the task as distinct from the capacity being assessed. In a test of memory, humans can be told, "Remember when you we here yesterday, you learned two lists of words. Please write down all the words that you can remember from the first list." With animals, "understanding" of the task instructions is generally confounded with the capacity being assessed, and creative means may be needed to isolate one from the other (Zentall, 1997). The absence of verbal capacity can also determine the response obtainable from the animal. Consider how different it would be to conduct the children's version of the theory of mind task with animals. How would one ask an animal where another animal would indicate that an object can be found? The accurate assessment of animal intelligence will require the vigilance, on the one hand, to evaluate cognitive functioning against simpler accounts and, on the other hand, to determine the conditions that will maximally elicit the animal's cognitive capacity.

There are some animal researchers (e.g., many radical behaviorists) who would argue that the concept of cognition is unnecessary – in all animals, including humans. It is perhaps even an epiphenomenon. But as Griffin (1991) has noted, such an anticognitive position "is often taken by scientists as evidence of considerable rigor when, in fact, it may be little more than an excuse for neglecting or ignoring an important scientific problem" (p. 7).

ACKNOWLEDGMENTS

Preparation of this chapter was made possible by Grant MH 55118 from the National Institute of Mental Health and by Grant IBN 9414589 from the National Science Foundation.

REFERENCES

Akins, C., & Zentall, T. R. (1996). Evidence for true imitative learning in Japanese quail. *Journal of Comparative Psychology, 110*, 316–320.

Barash, D. (1979). *The whisperings within: Evolution and the origin of human nature*. New York: Penguin.

Bitterman, M. E. (1965). Phyletic differences in learning. *American Psychologist, 20*, 396–410.

Bitterman, M. E. (1975). The comparative analysis of learning. *Science, 188*, 699–709.

Bitterman, M. E., & Mackintosh, N. J. (1969). Habit reversal and probability learning: Rats, birds, and fish. In R. M. Gilbert & N. S. Sutherland (Eds.), *Animal discrimination learning* (pp. 163–185). New York: Academic Press.

Boysen, S. T., & Berntson, G. G. (1989). Numerical competence in a chimpanzee (*Pan troglodytes*). *Journal of Comparative Psychology, 103*, 23–31.

Boysen, S. T., & Capaldi, E. J. (Eds.). (1993). *The development of numerical competence: Animal and human models*. Hillsdale, NJ: Erlbaum.

Capaldi, E. J. (1993). Animal number abilities: Implications for a hierarchical approach to instrumental learning. In S. T. Boysen & E. J. Capaldi (Eds.). *The development of numerical competence: Animal and human models* (pp. 191–209). Hillsdale, NJ: Erlbaum.

Capaldi, E. J., & Miller, D. J. (1988). Counting in rats: Its functional significance and the independent cognitive processes that constitute it. *Journal of Experimental Psychology: Animal Behavior Processes, 14*, 3–17.

Capaldi, E. J., & Verry, D. R. (1981). Serial order anticipation learning in rats: Memory for multiple hedonic events and their order. *Animal Learning & Behavior, 9*, 441–453.

Cook, R. G., Brown, M. F., & Riley, D. A. (1985). Flexible memory processing by rats: Use of prospective and retrospective information in the radial maze. *Journal of Experimental Psychology: Animal Behavior Processes, 11*, 453–469.

Couvillon, P. A., & Bitterman, M. E. (1992). A conventional conditioning analysis of "transitive inference" in pigeons. *Journal of Experimental Psychology: Animal Behavior Processes, 18*, 308–310.

Custance, D. M., Whiten, A., & Bard, K. A. (1995). Can young chimpanzees imitate arbitrary actions? Hayes and Hayes (1952) revisited. *Behaviour, 132*, 837–859.

Davis, H. (1992). Transitive inference in rats (*Rattus norvegicus*). *Journal of Comparative Psychology, 106*, 342–349.

Davis, H., & Memmott, J. (1982). Counting behavior in animals: A critical evaluation. *Psychological Bulletin, 92*, 547–571.

Davis, H., & Pérusse, R. (1988). Numerical competence in animals: Definitional issues, current evidence, and a new research agenda. *Behavioral and Brain Sciences, 11*, 561–615.

Dawkins, R. (1976). *The selfish gene*. New York: Oxford University Press.

Dawson, B. V., & Foss, B. M. (1965). Observational learning in budgerigars. *Animal Behaviour, 13*, 470–474.

Dennett, D. C. (1983). Intentional systems in cognitive ecology: The "panglossian paradigm" defended. *Behavioral and Brain Sciences, 6*, 343–355.

de Waal, F. B. M. (1982). *Chimpanzee politics*. New York: Harper & Row.

Dickinson, A. (1985). Actions and habits: The development of behavoural autonomy. In L. Weiskrantz (Ed.), *Animal intelligence* (pp. 67–78). Oxford: Clarendon.

Drickamer, L. C., Vessey, S. H., & Meikle, D. (1996). *Animal behavior* (4th ed.). Dubuque, IA: W. C. Brown.

Edwards, C. A., & Honig, W. K. (1987). Memorization and "feature selection" in the acquisition of natural concepts in pigeons. *Learning and Motivation, 18*, 235–260.

Edwards, C. A., Jagielo, J. A., Zentall, T. R., & Hogan, D. E. (1982). Acquired equivalence and distinctiveness in matching-to-sample by pigeons: Mediation by reinforcer-specific expectancies. *Journal of Experimental Psychology: Animal Behavior Processes, 8*, 244–259.

Farthing, G. W., Wagner, J. W., Gilmour, S., & Waxman, H. M. (1977). Short-term memory and information processing in pigeons. *Learning and Motivation, 8*, 520–532.

Fersen, L. V., Wynne, C. D. L., Delius, J. D., & Staddon, J. E. R. (1991). Transitive inference formation in pigeons. *Journal of Experimental Psychology: Animal Behavior Processes, 17*, 334–341.

Fountain, S. B., Henne, D. R., & Hulse, S. H. (1984). Phrasing cues and hierarchical organization in serial pattern learning by rats. *Journal of Experimental Psychology: Animal Behavior Processes, 10*, 30–45.

Fouts, R. S., & Fouts, D. H. (1989). Loulis in conversation with the cross-fostered chimpanzees. In R. A. Gardner, B. T. Gardner, & T. E. Van Cantfort (Eds.), *Teaching sign language to chimpanzees* (pp. 293–307). Albany, NY: SUNY Press.

Frye, D. (1993). Causes and precursors of children's theory of mind. In D. F. Hay & A. Angold (Eds.), *Precursors and causes of development and psychopathology*. Chichester, England: Wiley.

Galef, B. J., Jr. (1988). Imitation in animals: History, definition, and interpretation of data from the psychological laboratory. In T. R. Zentall & B. G. Galef, Jr. (Eds.), *Social learning: Psychological and biological perspectives* (pp. 3–28). Hillsdale, NJ: Erlbaum.

Gallup, G. G. (1970). Chimpanzees self-recognition. *Science, 167*, 86–87.

Gallup, G. G., & Suarez, S. D. (1991). Social responding to mirrors in rhesus monkeys: Effects of temporary mirror removal. *Journal of Comparative Psychology, 105*, 376–379.

Garcia, J., & Koelling, R. A. (1966). Relation of cue to consequence in avoidance learning. *Psychonomic Science, 4*, 123–124.

Gardner, R. A., & Gardner, B. T. (1969). Teaching sign language to a chimpanzee. *Science, 165*, 664–672.

Gillan, D. J. (1981). Reasoning in the chimpanzee: II. Transitive inference. *Journal of Experimental Psychology: Animal Behavior Processes, 7*, 150–164.

Gillan, D. J., Premack, D., & Woodruff, G. (1981). Reasoning in the chimpanzee: I. Analogical reasoning. *Journal of Experimental Psychology: Animal Behavior Processes, 7*, 1–17.

Goodall, J., & Lawick, H., van (1966). Use of tools by Egyptian vultures. *Nature, 212*, 1468–1469.

Gould, S. J. (1996). *Full house*. New York: Harmony.

Gray, L. (1966). Backward association in pigeons. *Psychonomic Science, 4*, 333–334.

Griffin, D. R. (1991). Progress toward a cognitive ethology. In C. A. Ristau (Ed.), *Cognitive ethology: The minds of other animals* (pp. 3–17). Hillsdale, NJ: Erlbaum.

Hall, G. (1996). Learning about associatively activated stimulus representations: Implications for acquired equivalence and perceptual learning. *Animal Learning & Behavior, 24*, 233–255.

Harlow, H. F. (1949). The formation of learning sets. *Psychological Review, 56*, 51–65.

Hayes, K. J., & Hayes, C. (1952). Imitation in a home-raised chimpanzee. *Journal of Comparative and Physiological Psychology, 45*, 450–459.

Hearst, E. (1989). Backward associations: Differential learning about stimuli that follow the presence versus the absence of food in pigeons. *Animal Learning & Behavior, 19*, 280–290.

Herman, L. M., Kuczaj, S. A., II, & Holder, M. D. (1993). Responses to anomalous gestural sequences by a language-trained dolphin: Evidence for processing of semantic relations and syntactic information. *Journal of Experimental Psychology: General, 122*, 184–194.

Herman, L. M., Pack, A. A., & Morrel-Samuels, P. (1993). Representational and conceptual skills of dolphins. In H. L. Roitblat, L. M. Herman, & P. E. Nachtigall (Eds.), *Language and communication: Comparative perspectives* (pp. 403–442). Hillsdale, NJ: Erlbaum.

Herrnstein, R. J. (1985). Riddles of natural categorization. In L. Weiskrantz (Ed.), *Animal intelligence* (pp. 129–143). Oxford: Clarendon.

Herrnstein, R. J., & DeVilliers, P. A. (1980). Fish as a natural category for people and pigeons. In G. H. Bower (Ed.), *The psychology of learning and motivation* (Vol. 14, pp. 59–95). New York: Academic Press.

Herrnstein, R. J., & Loveland, D. H. (1964). Complex visual concept in the pigeon. *Science, 146*, 549–551.

Herrnstein, R. J., Loveland, D. H., & Cable, C. (1976). Natural concepts in pigeons. *Journal of Experimental Psychology: Animal Behavior Processes, 2*, 285–301.

Heyes, C. M. (1998). Theory of mind in nonhuman primates. *Behavioral and Brain Sciences, 21*, 101–134.

Heyes, C. M., & Dawson, G. R. (1990). A demonstration of observational learning in rats using a bidirectional control. *Quarterly Journal of Experimental Psychology, 42B*, 59–71.

Higuchi, H. (1986). Bait-fishing by the green-backed heron *Ardeola striata* in Japan. *Ibis, 128*, 285–290.

Hogan, D. E., & Zentall, T. R. (1977). Backward associative learning in the pigeon. *American Journal of Psychology, 90*, 3–15.

Honey, R. C., & Hall, G. (1989). The acquired equivalence and distinctiveness of cues. *Journal of Experimental Psychology: Animal Behavior Processes, 15*, 338–346.

Honig, W. K., & Fetterman, J. G. (Eds.). (1992). *Cognitive aspects of stimulus control*. Hillsdale, NJ: Erlbaum.

Honig, W. K., & Thompson, R. K. R. (1982). Retrospective and prospective processing in animal working memory. In G. Bower (Ed.), *The psychology of learning and motivation* (Vol. 16, pp. 239–283). Orlando, FL: Academic Press.

Hull, C. L. (1943). *Principles of behavior*. New York: Appleton-Century-Crofts.

Hulse, S. H., & Dorsky, N. P. (1977). Structural complexity as a determinant of serial pattern learning. *Learning and Motivation, 8*, 488–506.

Hulse, S. H., Fowler, H., & Honig, W. K. (Eds.). (1978). *Cognitive processes in animal behavior*. Hillsdale, NJ: Erlbaum.

Jolly, A. (1991). Conscious chimpanzees? A review of recent literature. In C. A. Ristau (Ed.), *Cognitive ethology: The minds of other animals* (pp. 231–252). Hillsdale, NJ: Erlbaum.

Kaiser, D. H., Sherburne, L. M., Steirn, J. N., & Zentall, T. R. (1997). Common coding in many-to-one matching by pigeons as evidenced by reduced discriminability of commonly coded stimuli. *Psychonomic Bulletin & Review, 4*, 378–381.

Kaiser, D. H., Sherburne, L. M., & Zentall, T. R. (1997). Directed forgetting in pigeons resulting from the reallocation of memory-maintaining processes on forget-cue trials. *Psychonomic Bulletin & Review, 4*, 559–565.

Kamil, A. C. (1988). A synthetic approach to the study of animal intelligence. In D. W. Leger (Ed.), *Nebraska symposium on motivation: Vol 35. Comparative perspectives in modern psychology* (pp. 257–308). Lincoln, NE: University of Nebraska Press.

Kendler, T. S. (1950). An experimental investigation of transposition as a function of the difference between training and test stimuli. *Journal of Experimental Psychology, 40*, 552–562.

Kuan, L.-A., & Colwill, R. (1997). Demonstration of a socially transmitted taste aversion in the rat. *Psychonomic Bulletin & Review, 4*, 374–377.

Kummer, H., & Goodall, J. (1985). Conditions of innovative behaviour in primates. In L. Weiskrantz (Ed.), *Animal intelligence* (pp. 203–213). Oxford: Clarendon.

Kuno, H., Kitadate, T., & Iwamoto, T. (1994). Formation of transitivity in conditional matching to sample by pigeons. *Journal of the Experimental Analysis of Behavior, 62*, 399–408.

Lawrence, D. H. (1952). The transfer of a discrimination along a continuum. *Journal of Comparative and Physiological Psychology, 45*, 511–516.

Lawrence, D. H. (1955). The applicability of generalization gradients to the transfer of a discrimination. *Journal of Genetic Psychology, 52*, 37–48.

Lea, S. E. G. (1984). In what sense do pigeons learn concepts? In H. L. Roitblat, T. G. Bever, & H. S. Terrace (Eds.), *Animal cognition* (pp. 263–276). Hillsdale, NJ: Erlbaum.

Lipkens, R., Kop, P. F., & Matthijs, W. (1986). A test of symmetry and transitivity in the conditional discrimination performance of pigeons. *Journal of the Experimental Analysis of Behavior, 49*, 395–410.

Logan, F. A. (1966). Transfer of discrimination. *Journal of Experimental Psychology, 71*, 616–618.

Mackintosh, N. J. (1965). Selective attention in animal discrimination learning. *Psychological Bulletin, 64*, 124–150.

Mackintosh, N. J. (1969). Comparative studies of reversal and probability learning: Rats, birds, and fish. In R. M. Gilbert & N. S. Sutherland (Eds.), *Animal discrimination learning* (pp. 137–162). New York: Academic Press.

Mackintosh, N. J. (1978). Cognitive or associative theories of conditioning: Implications of an analysis of blocking. In S. H. Hulse, H. Fowler, & W. K. Honig (Eds.), *Cognitive processes in animal behavior* (pp. 155–175). Hillsdale, NJ: Erlbaum.

Macphail, E. M. (1985). Vertebrate intelligence: The null hypothesis. In L. Weiskrantz (Ed.), *Animal intelligence* (pp. 37–50). Oxford: Clarendon.

McGonigle, B. O., & Chalmers, M. (1977). Are monkeys logical? *Nature, 267*, 694–696.

Meyer, D. R. (1971). Habits and concepts of monkeys. In L. E. Jarrard (Ed.), *Cognitive processes of nonhuman primates* (pp. 83–102). New York: Academic Press.

Morgan, C. L. (1894). *Introduction to comparative psychology*. New York: Scribner.

Morris, D. (1967). *The naked ape: A zoologist's study of the human animal*. New York: McGraw-Hill.

Nakagawa, E. (1986). Overtraining, extinction, and shift learning in a concurrent discrimination in rats. *Quarterly Journal of Experimental Psychology, 38B*, 313–326.

Patterson, F. G. (1978). The gestures of a gorilla: Language acquisition in another pongid. *Brain and Language, 5*, 72–97.

Pepperberg, I. M. (1983). Cognition in the African grey parrot: Preliminary evidence for auditory/vocal comprehension of the class concept. *Animal Learning & Behavior, 11*, 179–185.

Pepperberg, I. M. (1987a). Interspecies communication: A tool for assessing conceptual abilities in an African grey parrot. In G. Greenberg & E. Tobach, (Eds.), *Language, cognition, and consciousness: Integrative levels* (pp. 31–56). Hillsdale, NJ: Erlbaum.

Pepperberg, I. M. (1987b). Acquisition of the same–different concept by an African grey parrot (*Psittacus erithacus*): Learning with respect to categories of color, shape, and material. *Animal Learning & Behavior, 15*, 423–432.

Pepperberg, I. M. (1997). Social influences on the acquisition of human-based codes in parrots and nonhuman primates. In C. T. Snowdon & M. Hausberger (Eds.), *Social influences on vocal development* (pp. 157–177). Cambridge, UK: Cambridge University Press.

Peterson, G. B. (1984). How expectancies guide behavior. In H. L. Roitblat, T. G. Bever, & H. S. Terrace (Eds.), *Animal Cognition* (pp. 135–148). Hillsdale, NJ: Erlbaum.

Peterson, G. B., Wheeler, R. L., & Trapold, M. A. (1980). Enhancement of pigeons' conditional discrimination performance by expectancies of reinforcement and nonreinforcement. *Animal Learning & Behavior, 8*, 22–30.

Piaget, J. (1951). *Play, dreams, and imitation in childhood*. New York: Norton.

Piaget, J. (1952). *The child's concept of number*. New York: Norton.

Povinelli, D. J., Nelson, K. E., & Boysen, S. T. (1990). Inferences about guessing and knowing by chimpanzees. *Journal of Comparative Psychology, 104*, 203–210.

Premack, D. (1976). *Intelligence in ape and man*. Hillsdale, NJ: Erlbaum.

Reid, L. S. (1953). Development of noncontinuity behavior through continuity learning. *Journal of Experimental Psychology, 46*, 107–112.

Rescorla, R. A. (1980). *Pavlovian second-order conditioning: Studies in associative learning*. Hillsdale, NJ: Lawrence Erlbaum Associates.

Richards, R. W. (1988). The question of bidirectional associations in pigeons' learning of conditional discrimination tasks. *Bulletin of the Psychonomic Society, 26*, 577–579.

Riley, D. A. (1968). *Discrimination learning*. Boston: Allyn and Bacon.

Ristau, C. A. (Ed.). (1991a). *Cognitive ethology: The minds of other animals*. Hillsdale, NJ: Erlbaum.

Ristau, C. A. (1991b). Aspects of the cognitive ethology of an injury-feigning bird, the piping plover. In C. A. Ristau (Ed.), *Cognitive ethology: The minds of other animals* (pp. 91–126). Hillsdale, NJ: Erlbaum.

Roberts, W. A., & Grant, D. S. (1976). Studies of short-term memory in the pigeon using the delayed matching-to-sample procedure. In D. L. Medin, W. A. Roberts, & R. T. Davis (Eds.), *Processes of animal memory* (pp. 79–112). Hillsdale, NJ: Erlbaum.

Rodewald, H. K. (1974). Symbolic matching-to-sample by pigeons. *Psychological Reports, 34*, 987–990.

Roper, K. L., Kaiser, D. H., & Zentall, T. R. (1995). Directed forgetting in pigeons: The role of alternative memories in the effectiveness of forget cues. *Animal Learning & Behavior, 23*, 280–285.

Roper, K. L., & Zentall, T. R. (1993). Directed forgetting in animals. *Psychological Bulletin, 113*, 513–532.

Rumbaugh, D. M. (Ed.). (1977). *Language learning by a chimpanzee: The Lana project.* New York: Academic Press.

Savage-Rumbaugh, E. S. (1984). Acquisition of functional symbol use in apes and children. In H. L. Roitblat, T. G. Bever, & H. S. Terrace (Eds.), *Animal Cognition* (pp. 291–310). Hillsdale, NJ: Erlbaum.

Seidel, R. J. (1959). A review of sensory preconditioning. *Psychological Bulletin, 56*, 58–73.

Sherburne, L. M., & Zentall, T. R. (1995). Delayed matching in pigeons with food and no-food samples: Further examination of backward associations. *Animal Learning and Behavior, 23*, 177–181.

Sherburne, L. M., & Zentall, T. R. (1998). The differential outcomes effect in pigeons is not reduced by eliminating differential response-outcome associations: Support for a two-process account. *Animal Learning & Behavior, 26*, 378–387.

Sidman, M. (1990). Equivalence relations: Where do they come from? In H. Lejeune & D. Blackman (Eds.), *Behavior analysis in theory and practice: Contributions and controversies* (pp. 93–114). Hillsdale, NJ: Erlbaum.

Sidman, M., Rauzin, R., Lazar, R., Cunningham, S., Tailby, W., & Carrigan, P. (1982). A search for symmetry in the conditional discrimination of rhesus monkeys, baboons, and children. *Journal of the Experimental Analysis of Behavior, 37*, 23–44.

Skinner, B. F. (1962). Two "synthetic social relations." *Journal of the Experimental Analysis of Behavior, 5*, 531–533.

Slotnick, B. M., & Katz, H. M. (1974). Olfactory learning-set formation in rats. *Science, 185*, 796–798.

Spence, K. W. (1937). The differential response in animals to stimuli varying within a single dimension. *Psychological Review, 44*, 430–444.

Spetch, M. L., Wilkie, D. M., & Pinel, J. P. J. (1981). Backward conditioning: A reevaluation of the empirical evidence. *Psychological Bulletin, 89*, 163–175.

Steirn, J. N., Jackson-Smith, P., & Zentall, T. R. (1991). Mediational use of internal representations of food and no-food events by pigeons. *Learning and Motivation, 22*, 353–365.

Steirn, J. N., Weaver, J. E., & Zentall, T. R. (1995). Transitive inference in pigeons: Simplified procedures and a test of value transfer theory. *Animal Learning & Behavior, 23*, 76–82.

Steirn, J. N., Zentall, T. R., & Sherburne, L. M. (1992). Pigeons' performances of a radial-arm-maze analog task: Effect of spatial distinctiveness. *Psychological Record, 42*, 255–272.

Stenhouse, D. (1974). *The evolution of intelligence.* London: George Allen & Unwin.

Straub, R. O., & Terrace, H. S. (1981). Generalization of serial learning in the pigeon. *Animal Learning & Behavior, 9*, 454–468.

Terrace, H. S. (1991). Chunking during serial learning by a pigeon: I. Basic evidence. *Journal of Experimental Psychology: Animal Behavior Processes, 17*, 81–93.

Thompson, R. K. R., Oden, D. L., & Boysen, S. T. (1997). Language-naive chimpanzees (*Pan troglodytes*) judge relations between relations in a conceptual matching-to-sample task. *Journal of Experimental Psychology: Animal Behavior Processes, 23*, 31–43.

Tolman, E. C. (1932). *Purposive behavior in animals and men.* New York: Century.

Trapold, M. A. (1970). Are expectancies based on different reinforcing events discriminably different? *Learning and Motivation, 1*, 129–140.

Urcuioli, P. J., & Zentall, T. R. (1986). Retrospective memory in pigeons' delayed matching-to-sample. *Journal of Experimental Psychology: Animal Behavior Processes, 12*, 69–77.

Urcuioli, P. J., Zentall, T. R., & DeMarse, T. (1995). Transfer to derived sample-comparison relations by pigeons following many-to-one versus one-to-many matching with identical training relations. *Quarterly Journal of Experimental Psychology, 48B*, 158–178.

Urcuioli, P. J., Zentall, T. R., Jackson-Smith, P., & Steirn, J. N. (1989). Evidence for common coding in many-to-one matching: Retention, intertrial interference, and transfer. *Journal of Experimental Psychology: Animal Behavior Processes, 15*, 264–273.

Vaughan, W., Jr. (1988). Formation of equivalence sets in pigeons. *Journal of Experimental Psychology: Animal Behavior Processes, 14*, 36–42.

Wasserman, E. A., DeVolder, C. L., & Coppage, D. J. (1992). Non-similarity based conceptualization in pigeons via secondary or mediated generalization. *Psychological Science, 6*, 374–379.

Weaver, J. E., Steirn J. N., & Zentall, T. R. (1997). Transitive inference in pigeons: Control for differential value transfer. *Psychonomic Bulletin & Review, 4*, 113–117.

Weiskrantz, L. (Ed.). (1985). *Animal intelligence.* Oxford: Clarendon.

Whiten, A., & Byrne, R. W. (1988). Tactical deception in primates. *Behavioral and Brain Sciences, 11*, 233–244.

Whiten, A., & Ham, R. (1992). On the nature and evolution of imitation in the animal kingdom: Reappraisal of a century of research. *Advances in the Study of Behavior, 21*, 239–283.

Wilson, B., Mackintosh, N. J., & Boaks, R. A. (1985). Matching and oddity learning in the pigeon: Transfer effects and the absence of relational learning. *Quarterly Journal of Experimental Psychology, 37B*, 295–311.

Woodruff, G., & Premack, D. (1979). Intentional communication in the chimpanzee: The development of deception. *Cognition, 7*, 333–362.

Woodruff, G., Premack, D., & Kennel, K. (1978). Conservation of liquid and solid quantity by the chimpanzee. *Science, 202*, 991–994.

Wynne, C. D. L., Fersen, L., von, & Staddon, J. E. R. (1992). Pigeons' inferences are transitive and the outcome of elementary conditioning principles: A response. *Journal of Experimental Psychology: Animal Behavior Processes, 18*, 313–315.

Zentall, T. R. (Ed.). (1993a). *Animal cognition: A tribute to Donald A. Riley*. Hillsdale, NJ: Erlbaum.

Zentall, T. R. (1993b). Animal cognition: An approach to the study of animal behavior. In T. R. Zentall (Ed.), *Animal cognition: A tribute to Donald A. Riley* (pp. 3–15). Hillsdale, NJ: Erlbaum.

Zentall, T. R. (1996). An analysis of imitative learning in animals. In C. M. Heyes & B. G. Galef, Jr. (Eds.), *Social learning and tradition in animals* (pp. 221–243). New York: Academic Press.

Zentall, T. R. (1997). Animal memory: The role of instructions. *Learning and Motivation, 28*, 248–267.

Zentall, T. R., Edwards, C. A., Moore, B. S., & Hogan, D. E. (1981). Identity: The basis for both matching and oddity learning in pigeons. *Journal of Experimental Psychology: Animal Behavior Processes, 7*, 70–86.

Zentall, T. R., & Hogan, D. E. (1974). Abstract concept learning in the pigeon. *Journal of Experimental Psychology, 102*, 393–398.

Zentall, T. R., & Hogan, D. E. (1975). Concept learning in the pigeon: Transfer of matching and nonmatching to new stimuli. *American Journal of Psychology, 88*, 233–244.

Zentall, T. R., & Hogan, D. E. (1976). Pigeons can learn identity, difference, or both. *Science, 191*, 408–409.

Zentall, T. R., & Hogan, D. E. (1978). Same/different concept learning in the pigeon: The effect of negative instances and prior adaptation to the transfer stimuli. *Journal of the Experimental Analysis of Behavior, 30*, 177–186.

Zentall, T. R., Hogan, D. E., Edwards, C. A., & Hearst, E. (1980). Oddity learning in the pigeon as a function of the number of incorrect alternatives. *Journal of Experimental Psychology: Animal Behavior Processes, 6*, 278–299.

Zentall, T. R., Sherburne, L. M., & Steirn, J. N. (1992). Development of excitatory backward associations during the establishment of forward associations in a delayed conditional discrimination by pigeons. *Animal Learning & Behavior, 20*, 199–206.

Zentall, T. R., Sherburne, L. M., & Urcuioli, P. J. (1993). Common coding in a many-to-one delayed matching task as evidenced by facilitation and interference effects. *Animal Learning & Behavior, 21*, 233–237.

Zentall, T. R., & Smeets, P. M. (Eds.). (1996). *Stimulus class formation in humans and animals*. Amsterdam: North-Holland.

Zentall, T. R., Steirn, J. N., & Jackson-Smith, P. (1990). Memory strategies in pigeons' performance of a radial-arm-maze analog task. *Journal of Experimental Psychology: Animal Behavior Processes, 16*, 358–371.

Zentall, T. R., Steirn, J. N., Sherburne, L. M., & Urcuioli, P. J. (1991). Common coding in pigeons assessed through partial versus total reversals of many-to-one conditional discriminations. *Journal of Experimental Psychology: Animal Behavior Processes, 17*, 194–201.

Zentall, T. R., Sutton, J. E., & Sherburne, L. M. (1996). True imitative learning in pigeons. *Psychological Science, 7*, 343–346.

Zentall, T. R., Urcuioli, P. J., Jagielo, J. A., & Jackson-Smith, P. (1989). Interaction of sample dimension and sample-comparison mapping on pigeons' performance of delayed conditional discriminations. *Animal Learning & Behavior, 17*, 172–178.

CHAPTER ELEVEN

The Evolution of Intelligence

HARRY J. JERISON

THE EVOLUTION OF INTELLIGENCE

Definition: *Intelligence is the behavioral consequence of the total neural-information processing capacity in representative adults of a species, adjusted for the capacity to control routine bodily functions.*

In the first edition of this chapter I suggested the broad definition of intelligence above, which remains my working definition. The adjustment is estimated from the regression of brain size on body size in appropriate samples of species. Intelligence is thus defined as equivalent to encephalization. If one can accept it, this definition enables us to present an evolutionary history of intelligence that can be tied directly to the fossil record of the brain. There is a fine fossil record, which can be analyzed as the evolution of the brain's information processing capacity. Relating information processing to brain size involves simple, straightforward, and unusually reliable bivariate regressions. (For many critical relationships one finds correlation coefficients $r > .99$.) That, in a nutshell, is the way I have always approached the problem (Jerison, 1973, 1982, 1985, 1991). Although inspired by the great psychologist Karl Lashley (1949), my definition is obviously broader than those of most psychologists, but I believe that the definition is fundamentally correct and that it provides useful and sometimes surprising insights for an intuitive understanding of the nature of human intelligence.

At present, the contribution of an evolutionary analysis is primarily on the nature of the fundamental dimensions of human intelligence. Although variation is the stuff of evolution, the clearest insights are with respect to mean values of traits rather than their variability. The relevant conclusion about individual differences, the topic that is perhaps of most concern to students of human intelligence, is that their magnitude for behavioral measurements is appropriate for their expected values for brain traits. There is not much to be said about the source of this variability. The fundamental dimensions that are appropriate for my analysis are somewhat different from the abilities often associated with intelligence. My dimensions are the more classical ones: perception and cognition as opposed to communication, learning, and social behavior, and I will emphasize the place of perceptual–cognitive activity. The route to this conclusion is less obvious than it may seem to be from our intuitions, and much of this chapter is a development of the evidence, mainly from morphological data on the evolution of the brain.

EVOLUTION AND THE PROBLEM OF DEFINITION

That it is important to resolve the problem of definition is evident from Hunt's (1983) critical review and in his comment that I had undertaken "an impossible task" in writing about the evolution of intelligence. He was evidently concerned with the more conventional meanings of intelligence, which are usually analyzable only in trivial ways in an evolutionary framework. Such definitions typically reduce our topic to a catalog of abilities in different species and the bare statement that they are either present or absent in a given species. Without detailing the abilities that might define intelligence, I will outline their place in my approach. Here, first, is a good list, as presented by Hodos (1988, pp. 100–101):

The following is a list of behavioral abilities that usually are considered as fundamental dimensions of human intelligence (Sternberg, 1985; Humphreys, 1985; and Horn, 1985) and that seem appropriate as dimensions of animal intelligence. I have added "tool use" because it frequently is cited as an indicator of animal intelligence.

- speed of learning
- retrieval of information from long-term memory
- decision making
- problem solving
- communication in symbolic form
- counting
- spatial-relations ability
- concept formation
- rule learning
- tool use

According to Macphail's (1982) review of the distribution of abilities such as these among vertebrates, one might conclude that all nonlinguistic abilities are shared by all vertebrate species. In evolutionary terms, they would be plesiomorphies, suggesting that they evolved as very early adaptations at the root of the vertebrate phylogenetic tree. The only apomorphic (derived, and perhaps advanced) aspect of intelligence would be represented by language, which Macphail saw as a uniquely human ability. Later in this chapter I will support a weaker version of these surprising inferences from Macphail's conclusions, but in view of the variety of behavioral adaptations in living animals, they cannot be taken seriously as they stand. Yet these inferences would be inescapable were we to define intelligence by the dimensions listed by Hodos. We would be stymied by an essentially semantic problem of definition, which would obscure the scientifically valuable evolutionary contribution to our understanding of intelligence.

Evolutionary facts are about the genetic systems (genotypes) that determine organismic (phe-notypic) structure and function and about the change in these genotypes and phenotypes over time. Theories try to explain the reasons for the change: Darwinian natural selection for phenotypes, and random non-Darwinian genetic drift applied primarily to genotypes. It should be emphasized that there is no debate about the facts. The debates are about the theories and are primarily about the rate of evolution and the relative importance of selection versus drift. (See Dawkins, 1987, for an excellent readable introduction to current evolutionary theory. See Bickerton, 1990; Deacon, 1997; Donald, 1991; Greenfield, 1991; and Pinker, 1994, for views on language evolution, especially on its relation to the evolution of brain; and see Dennett, 1995, for a philosopher's discussion of current controversies in evolutionary theory. Popular "evolutionary psychology" as represented, for example, by Buss, 1994, which is primarily an application of sociobiology [Wilson, 1975, 1978] to social psychological issues, does not yet appear to contribute to the material that I will cover in this chapter.)

Regardless of how it is defined, the consensus is that intelligence is a complex phenotypic trait, the evolution of which must be traced to changing genetic systems. Like most phenotypic traits, intelligence is determined by the interaction of genes and environment. It is commonplace to recognize this for behavioral analysis, but it may not be appreciated that it is equally true for the brain. The structure and function of mammalian brains are determined by an intricate interaction between a genetic blueprint and pre- and postnatal environments in which neurons and supporting brain tissue develop. We now know that even the elegant maps drawn to depict sensory and motor systems as if specified by a blueprint are, in fact, subject to environmental modification (Merzenich & Kaas, 1980).

In recommending a strategy for studying animal intelligence, Hodos argued against a "general-intelligence model and general brain indices such as total weight or total volume." He recommended instead "that we concentrate our efforts on determining the relationships between specific morphological components of the brain and specific intellectual abilities. By accepting the multidimensional natures of both the brain and intelligence we will have better opportunities to uncover the relationships between the two" (Hodos, 1988, p. 104.) To the extent that there is a consensus on the issue, it is well represented by Hodos.

My approach is almost the opposite. I hold that view despite my agreement with Hodos about the multidimensional nature of brain and intelligence. From broad perspectives such as Sternberg's (1988) triarchic theory of intelligence, and even from the more restricted definitions implicit in psychometric tests (Carroll, 1997), human intelligence is multidimensional. It is safe to assume that animal intelligence is also multidimensional. In addition, I recognize a fundamental truth in Macphail's conclusion about the extent to which abilities that might normally be thought of as differentiated in the course of evolution are in fact shared. Finally, although there have been many advances in the study of animal behavior, Lashley's (1949) view of a half-century ago remains substantially correct: The only biological correlate of animal intelligence that has been discovered thus far is one based on general brain indices (cf. Weiskrantz, 1985). For the present, an evolutionary analysis remains possible only for a kind of general intelligence.

The evolutionary analysis begins with the brain's operations, which, in the control of complex behavior, involve neural systems distributed through much of the brain (Goldman-Rakic, 1988). Although the behavior that is controlled may be dissected by a multivariate analysis, the interconnections and interplay among the underlying neural systems that control the behavior are so extensive that their evolution probably occurred by changes in some generalized genetic instructions that regulate the development of the central nervous system. This is consistent, also, with behavior genetic analysis of human cognitive functioning (Petrill, 1997).

It may be helpful to consider the way the genetic information can be encoded. A possible genetic blueprint of a species may include code for the following instruction to regulate growth in a primordial nerve cell: Perform 32 cell divisions and then stop. If that instruction were followed and no cells died, 4,294,967,296 nerve cells would be produced. Imagine now a major (but small) mutation, that changed the number of cell divisions from 32 to 34. This small change would yield 17,179,869,184 nerve cells. Were these fated to be neocortical neurons, the mutation would be about right to distinguish the

number of neurons in the brain of a chimpanzee from that in a human (Pakkenberg & Gundersen, 1997). In this example, the code may seem overly simple, but it is that kind of code that can be written, and it is a code that would have a very great morphometric effect. Instructions that are significantly more complex may be beyond the capacity of genes to encode information.

Once a feature of the genetic blueprint is carried out and generates a particular neural phenotype, there remains the issue of how the phenotype actually works for an animal. How would the "dimensions" listed by Hodos work as functions of the brain? A model neurobehavioral phenotype for decision making is suggested by Ewert's (1974) experiments on the control of tongue-flicking predation by toads. From microelectrodes implanted in a particular brain structure (the superior colliculus), one records electrical activity of single nerve cells that are part of a network. The toad is stimulated by having a small dark spot pass in front of one eye at a specified rate. When the rate of action potentials is within certain limits, reflex motor control systems are activated to release the tongue to fly out in a quick movement directed toward the stimulus. The limits can be described as a window of activity for the decision as to whether or not a certain moving stimulus was present. In nature, the adequate stimulus is typically a small insect flying within range, and the effect is to enable a toad to catch a fly. Although later research (Roth, 1987) indicates that the situation is more complex, Ewert's results suggest how connections could be made between neural activity and overt behavior.

Decision making is among the abilities listed by Hodos, and a mechanism for decision making by neural networks in living animals is suggested by Ewert's report. Although it is natural enough, there are many limitations to this approach to a component of intelligence. Is the neural mechanism identified in the toad similar to mechanisms in other decision making, such as the behavior of a rat at a choice point? The neural decision making by the toad, involving a "window" that is a criterion for whether or not an event is a signal, can be treated as a problem in signal detectability (Swets, 1964). A rat's decision about which way to turn in a maze, on the other hand, seems to be determined by a map in its head (Olton, 1985), and one assumes that its neural basis is related to a representation of that map. The neural basis may thus be in some kind of pattern recognition involving computations that may not be the same as those for a signal detection problem. By analogy with information processing in computers, it is clear that much more computational power is required for pattern recognition than for signal detection (Minsky, 1985). Ewerts's experiments are elegant, but the correct inference from them may be that decision making is not a unitary trait, and it may have to be subdivided at least into decisions about signals versus nonsignals as opposed to decisions about patterns or representations.

Perhaps the most important limitation is our ignorance of the genetic basis for the neural substrate of the toad's behavior. We do not understand the connection between genetic instructions and the actual assembly of a neural network that controls the fly-catching behavior. The analysis of the toad's fly-catching, even if it remains somewhat controversial (Roth, 1987), has been an unusual achievement in experimental analysis. But consider the problem we set for the genetic code if it were required to describe in detail how to assemble the network and then how to make it work. If one were to design a machine to do this kind of job, it would require pages of blueprints and specifications before it could be built as well as instruction manuals on how to work it. A genetic code that would contain comparably detailed instructions could not fit on the chromosomes that are available to carry the information. The code can only be of a kind that can be written by the genetic material – perhaps of the kind in my example of how to produce the neurons in chimpanzee and human neocortex.

To imagine phenotypic neural instruction programs for Hodos's list, the best we can do now is to work from analogies to computer programs for artificial neural networks. If that is our model, species may differ in the number of lines of program that their brains can write, but following the analogy to computer programs, it is difficult to imagine genetic programs capable of specifying all of the details of the different abilities in Hodos's list. Like a computer program, the genetic programs could have the same vocabulary, which could be equivalent to a programming language, or the corresponding machine language. The genetic code could probably handle such a vocabulary (as in the ASCII code for letters of an alphabet). But how would it handle the amount of information that specifies the different sentences and graphics that we need when we describe the different activities that take place when each of the abilities is exercised? Although we know from a behavioral analysis that the information exists, we do not know how it is stored and retrieved as neural information.

Our present understanding of the neural substrate of intelligence is thus limited to a sense of the processing capacity that is encumbered. One trusts that we will develop a greater understanding of the details of that capacity and the way it is distributed among the behavioral dimensions of intelligence. But even when we do, we will continue to be interested in total capacity as well as in the partitioning. Aside from the practical limits of what is presently analyzable, I believe it wrong to reject a notion of "general intelligence" as reflected in total neural capacity. The idea that we should restrict ourselves to the functioning of the parts without concern for the whole is as absurd as a concern for the whole without considering the functioning of the parts. It happens that at present we can do much better at analyzing the whole rather than its parts.

My working definition, though concerned primarily with overall processing capacity, also directs our attention to neural control systems and their evolution. It is, thus, a bottom–up view that begins with the origins of intelligence in its neural substrate. Extended to behavior, the approach seeks an understanding of human intelligence as having evolved from roots in perhaps distantly related adaptations in other species.

From fundamental aspects of neural structure and function in different species (Butler & Hodos, 1996; Johnson, 1990; Welker, 1990), the evolution of between-species variation in the specializations of brains makes it clear that processing capacity is partitioned in different ways in different species. Simians (anthropoid primates, i.e., monkeys, apes and humans) are almost unique among mammals in their visual specialization, and this is reflected in the expansion of visual neocortex. They are unique among land mammals in the reduction of their olfactory system at the level of the olfactory bulbs, a fact that I find significant for the early evolution of human language (Jerison, 1991). Bats are specialized in their use of echolocation for a three-dimensional picture of their external world, and most of their neocortex is auditory (Grinnell, 1995). The evolution of perceptual capacities has been a story of specialization, and if we recognize the close relationship between perception and cognition, we will appreciate that it is necessary to think of the evolution of intelligences in the plural.

Before reviewing the evidence, let me foreshadow my conclusions that are most relevant for human intelligence. Most of my conclusions are about between-species relationships, but I will report that there is, indeed, a small correlation between brain size and intelligence for psychometric definitions of human intelligence (Willerman, Schultz, Rutledge, & Bigler, 1991). The puzzling decoupling of within- from between-species variation that I discussed in the first edition of this chapter is no longer a puzzle. It does not exist. The correlation, though low, is appropriate for our views of the heritability of human intelligence, and its discovery solves a scientific problem. I will also present a scenario for the evolution of human language and conclude that it is primarily cognitive and perceptual and only secondarily has it evolved into an adaptation for communication.

VERTEBRATE HISTORY

The evolution of the brain and of intelligence is part of the history of the evolution of life on earth and should be seen in the context of that history (Doolittle, Feng, Tsang, & Cho, 1996; Schopf, 1992). The earth and solar system are about 4.5 billion years old, and the earliest evidence of life is from about 3.5 billion years ago. The first vertebrates were jawless fish, "agnathans," and their fossils are from the early Paleozoic era, about a half billion (0.5×10^9) years ago. Figure 11.1 is a phylogenetic tree (cf. Carroll, 1988) showing the subsequent evolution of the major vertebrate groups. One can read evolutionary distance and relatedness among these groups from the tree.

The earliest metazoans (multicellular animals) appeared about 600 million years ago (ma), before the beginning of the Paleozoic era. The greatest extinction of metazoan species, which divides the Paleozoic from the Mesozoic era, occurred about 250 ma. The most famous of extinctions is the later one that separates the Mesozoic from the Cenozoic era, which occurred 65 ma when an object about 5 miles

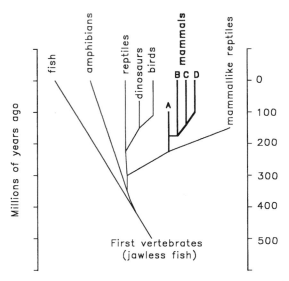

FIGURE 11.1. The phylogeny of the vertebrates. Mammalian phylogeny indicated in boldface. Group A indicates major groups now extinct such as the triconodonts and multituberculates but also the parent groups of living species. Groups B, C, and D are the monotremes, marsupials, and placentals, respectively, with approximate ages at splitting from the main line indicated on the ordinate.

in diameter gouged out a hole in what is now the Caribbean Sea, near the Yucatan peninsula. The extinction of dinosaurs is often referred to the K–T event (Cretaceous–Tertiary Mass Extinction Event), the K–T boundary separating the Cretaceous period of the Mesozoic era from the Tertiary period of the Cenozoic era.

The first tetrapods were amphibians, appearing almost 400 ma, and the reptiles appeared "shortly" thereafter, about 350 ma. The first birds probably evolved as small specialized dinosaurs with feathers, an event that occurred during the early to middle Mesozoic era, at least 150 ma. Mammals evolved even earlier, at least 225 ma from therapsid (mammallike) reptiles, and the separation of the dinosaur (archosaurian, or "ruling reptile") lineage from the therapsid lineage occurred at least 300 ma. This and later dating are important for identifying minimum age for some of the plesiomorphies of intelligence.

Within the mammals, the placentals appeared 100 ma. Primates may have diverged from other species of placental mammals during the late Cretaceous period, about 70 ma. There are morphologically "good" primates known as fossils that are early Cenozoic and are about 55 million years old; other primatelike mammal fossils are about 60 million years old. And there are a few Cretaceous primatelike mammal teeth that are at least 70 million years old. One can pick one's date for the divergence of primates from other mammals, but it happened a long time ago. An authoritative detailed discussion of primate evolution, including the quantitative analysis of the evolution of the primate brain, is available in Martin (1990), and a popular illustrated review of all of the history of the mammals is in Savage & Long (1986).

Our dates must be evaluated with respect to the common and the unique traits that we can recognize in various living animals, including the human animal. We know that many morphological traits, such as whether one has five fingers or a hoof, or a wing or an arm, diverged relatively rapidly from a basal condition. According to recently developed evidence (Tobias & Clarke, 1996), it was only about 3 ma that the primate foot with an opposable digit suitable for grasping and climbing evolved into the human foot specialized for walking and running. This, by the way, is evidence of the persistence of arboreal locomotion in some australopithecine hominids. Fully terrestrial habits evolved within the australopithecines and after hominids had separated from the Great Apes. The conclusion to emphasize is that evolution can be relatively rapid when environmental requirements drive it appropriately.

In the face of such evidence of rapid evolution and diversification of morphological traits, can we assume that behavioral traits (and their neural substrates) could remain stable over very long periods of time? Oddly, the assumption turns out to be not unreasonable, because the nervous system is one of the more conservative biological systems with respect to evolutionary change. This may be due, in part, to the plasticity of neural tissue, because the genetic program can be rather general and rely on environmental effects during early growth and development to mold the complete adaptations of neural networks. The genetic program may thus retain common elements in very distantly related species. Behavioral evidence points to the same conclusion. For many years the literature of operant conditioning was a litany of reports of behaviors in pigeons and rats that were operationally indistinguishable (Skinner, 1957), suggesting similar mechanisms in these two very distantly related species. Although it may

be incorrect to assume common mechanisms for behavior in these mammals and birds, the simplest assumption is that they are homologies, despite the 300-million-year interval available for their divergent evolution. Ethologists, zoologists, and comparative psychologists have been amused at the naiveté of the Skinnerians about behavioral functions, but the behavioral data are consistent with the assumption of a plesiomorphy: that the behaviors are based on homologous neural traits shared by rats and pigeons (and mammals and birds).

UNIFORMITIES IN BRAINS

Vertebrate brains are organs consisting of networks of neurons and their supporting tissue. The principles of nerve action in the transmission of information are substantially the same in all multicellular animals, which is a metazoan plesiomorphy that makes it possible to use almost any neuron from any species as a model for neuronal action. (Much of what we know about single neurons has been learned in experiments on invertebrates – horseshoe crabs and squids.) If we consider the neuron as the morphological unit for processing capacity, then the number of neurons is a measure of that capacity in any vertebrate.

The plesiomorphic status of at least some of the abilities mentioned by Hodos as defining intelligence is evident from current research on the neural basis of conditioning. These neural mechanisms appear to be similar enough in mammals, fruit flies, and sea slugs to have inspired recent analyses of the fundamentals of conditioning and learning from the physiology of neural networks in these species (Byrne, 1987; Tully, Preat, Boynton, & Del Vecchio, 1994). Neural capacity may thus define intelligence in any species with a neural network, whether or not one normally thinks of the species as intelligent. Intelligence is not an all-or-none trait, and its evolutionary roots may appear in distant and "primitive" animals. These roots may represent a shared trait or suite of traits that evolved more than half a billion years ago in the earliest metazoans.

There are additional uniformities in the structure of neurons and networks that evolved later in mammalian brains, when the neocortex appeared as an evolutionary novelty. Although mammalian neurons differ considerably in the amount of arborization, their cell bodies are fairly constant in size. Cortical cell bodies are typically about 10 or 20 μm in diameter. The number of synapses per unit volume of cortical tissue appears to be constant, regardless of species (Schüz & Demnianenko, 1995). There is another remarkable neocortical uniformity: excepting only primary visual cortex in primates, where the number is about twice as large, in land mammals there appears to be a constant number of neurons beneath a given amount of surface area, regardless of species and regardless of the part of the cortex that is examined (Rockel, Hiorns, & Powell, 1980), which is a particularly useful result for the analysis of the meaning of brain size.

In the mammalian species in which Powell and his colleagues have done the counting, the number is about 15,000,000 neurons per cm^2 of cortical surface. Because cortical surface area will obviously be different in brains of different size, we should be able to relate the processing capacity of a brain between-species to its gross size. Figure 11.2 shows how well we can do just that. It is a graph of cortical surface area as a function of brain size in 50 different species of mammals, and it is the basic justification

for considering brain size as a reliable estimator of total information-processing capacity.

How old is the adaptation represented by the surface–volume relationship in the mammalian brain? The answer is in Figure 11.1. The mammalian stocks B, C, and D (monotremes, marsupials, and placentals) had their most recent common ancestor 175 ma. The evolutionary logic is that the surface–volume function, as a brain trait presently shared by species from all three groups, evolved either as having descended from the common ancestor or by convergent evolution. Given the likely complexity of the genetic instructions required for the blueprint that produces the trait in living species, the probability of its having evolved independently in all of the species represented on the graph is low, and one can safely conclude that the mechanism of folding in the mammalian cortex evolved early in mammalian evolution (Van Essen, 1997; Welker, 1990). It was then conserved in succeeding generations.

Among the additional conclusions from Figure 11.2, note, first, the regression line and the associated correlation coefficient. To two significant figures, the correlation is perfect ($r = 1.00$), suggesting an almost deterministic rather than probabilistic association. The numerical value of the slope of the regression line, which is .91, is equally important. One expects a 2/3 slope in logarithmic coordinates to relate surface to volume in similar solids. This means that as brains evolved to different sizes, they changed their shape, affecting the amount of surface area per unit volume. Their change in shape is generated, of course, by folding the outer cortical surface into convolutions. The high correlation means that the folding follows a very orderly rule, which is given by the equation of the regression line.

Myths of popular psychology of mind–brain relations include the notion that convolutedness is related to intelligence. Figure 11.2 shows, to the contrary, that it is related primarily to brain size. We can do more to destroy the myth. There are the two small polygons on the graph labeled "dolphin" and "human." These are minimum convex polygons drawn about all of the presently available data on bottlenose dolphins (*Tursiops truncatus*, $N = 13$) and on humans ($N = 23$). The dolphin polygon lies entirely above the regression line, and the human polygon lies almost entirely below the regression

FIGURE 11.2. The relationship between cortical surface and gross brain size in 50 species of mammals. Each point represents a species. In addition, two labeled minimum convex polygons indicate within-species variability in humans ($N = 23$) and dolphins (*Tursiops truncatus*, $N = 13$). Several species are labeled by name to indicate the diversity of the sample. (From Jerison, 1991, by permission.)

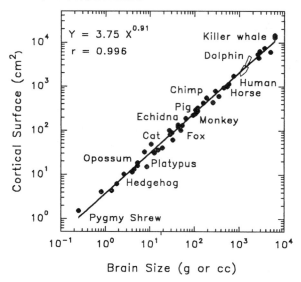

line. The differences between the polygons and the regression are both statistically significant ($p < .02$). In other words, dolphin brains are *more* convoluted than average for mammals and, more shocking, human brains are *less* convoluted. Rather than give up our self-image as the smartest of the mammals, we probably would prefer to give up the idea that intelligence is related to convolutedness.

There are methodological lessons on scales of measurement and on the significance of residuals. The scales in Figure 11.2 are logarithmic. This is more than a convenience for graphing an extensive range of data. The size of living things is determined by cell division, and increments in size are normally doublings of the number of cells in the organ. It is, therefore, appropriate to scale biological size to show equal steps of doubling as equal distances on the scale. Logarithmic scales have that characteristic. This is not to say that logarithmic scales are not convenient. I was led to this kind of analysis by Stevens's (1946, 1951) classic report on psychophysical scaling in which he pointed out the didactic utility of graphing data on logarithmic coordinates. When one's data graph as a straight line, the slope of the line is the exponent of the independent variable in a linear power function. As shown in the equation on the graph, cortical surface is a function of the .91 power of brain size.

The statistical lesson is on the meaning of residuals. With a correlation of .996 between cortical surface area and brain size, essentially all of the variance is "explained" by the regression, and less than 1% remains to be accounted for by other factors. So small a residual would normally be thought of as representing an error-of-measurement factor — random noise, as it were. The data on human and dolphin, however, show that even so small a residual can represent a significant effect.

ALLOMETRY AND ENCEPHALIZATION

The main lesson from Figure 11.2 is that brain size estimates information-processing capacity in mammals, and we can, therefore, go on to consider how and why species differ in that capacity. One obvious difference is due to body size. From the way the body is mapped on the brain, small species should be expected to have smaller brains than large species. The relationship is now well known, and it is the basis

for further analysis of the evolution of processing capacity.

The between-species correlation between brain weight and body weight within a class of vertebrates is about $r = .90$; that is, about 80% of the between-species variance in brain size is explained by differences in body size. The regression line that can be fitted to the data gives the expected brain size for a body size and describes what biometricians refer to as an "allometric" relationship (Harvey & Pagel, 1991). The residual for each species is the distance of the species from the regression line. Because the scaling is logarithmic, that distance is a quotient and has been called an encephalization quotient (*EQ*).* In words, an encephalization quotient is the ratio of the measured brain weight to the expected brain weight when the expected weight is determined by an allometric equation. (Compare my working definition of intelligence at the beginning of this chapter.) It is a between-species measure of the degree to which the brain became enlarged beyond the requirement of body size.

Historically, the analysis into allometric and encephalization components was described as dividing the brain's size into a somatic factor and a psychic factor (Manouvrier, 1883; see Jerison, 1973). We can now appreciate it from an information-processing perspective as distinguishing between processing capacity required to run the body and remaining capacity that is, in some sense, related to intelligence.

Although I have calculated my share of encephalization quotients (*EQs*), I prefer to avoid the technicalities by describing the data nonparametrically, constructing minimum convex polygons that contain all of the data of each group. The analysis for living vertebrates is presented in Figure 11.3, and the method of constructing a polygon is illustrated for living reptiles in Figure 11.4.

---

* A computational reminder: The logarithm of a quotient is the difference between the logarithms of the numerator and denominator. Consider the human encephalization quotient *EQ*, for example. Human average brain weight is about 1,400 g for a 65-kg body, and expected brain weight in mammals for that body size (which can be read from a regression line) is about 200 g. The human *EQ* is thus the ratio $1,400/200 = 7$. After working with logarithms we have $\log 1400 - \log 200 = \log 7$, or $3.15 - 2.30 = 0.85$; 7 is the antilog of 0.85. Our brains are about seven times as large as average for 65 kg mammals.

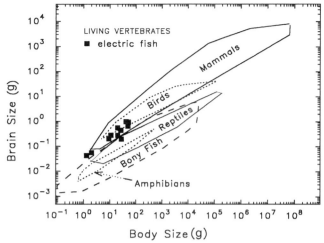

FIGURE 11.3. Brain-body relations in 1,954 living vertebrate species enclosed in minimum convex polygons. The samples are 647 mammals, 180 birds, 1,027 bony fish, 41 amphibians, and 59 reptiles. (Unpublished data on fish, courtesy of Professors Andy Bass for electric fish, and Roland Bauchot for other bony fish.)

I have drawn polygons around five data sets representing the usual living vertebrate classes. These are the mammals (Worthy & Hickie, 1986), birds (Mlikovsky, 1977), reptiles (Platel, 1979), amphibians (Thireau, 1975), and bony fish (Class Osteichthyes, Ridet & Bauchot, 1990). The allometric exponents (least-squares slopes of the regressions) are about 3/4 for mammals and about 1/2 for the other classes (Martin, 1981, 1983). It should be evident from the graph, however, that the polygons are similar for all of the groups and differ mainly in the range of body sizes and, of course, their vertical displacement from one another. For the problem of the evolution of intelligence, the most important differences are between mammals and birds versus their ancestors among the reptiles. I discuss this in detail later (Figure 11.4) in conjunction with the fossil evidence.

Mammals and birds are approximately equally encephalized and are "higher vertebrates"; reptiles, amphibians, and bony fish are "lower vertebrates" in the positions of their polygons in brain-body space. A closer look complicates the picture, which is approximately correct for most of the 50,000 living vertebrate species. However, about 2% of the species are exceptions. These are the classes Agnatha (70 species) and Chondrichthyes (800 species), and

a few dozen species of electric fish, which would normally be graphed with other bony fish (about 25,000 species in the class Osteichthyes). In the interest of clarity I have omitted the exceptional polygons from the graph (see Butler & Hodos, 1996, Fig. 5-10, p. 81), but to suggest the complexity, I show the available data on electric fish in relation to the polygon for other bony fish.

The jawless fish (class Agnatha: lampreys and hagfish) are somewhat less encephalized than any other living vertebrates. Because living agnathans are sometimes considered degenerate in an evolutionary sense, often living parasitically by attaching themselves to other fish, their low encephalization may be a secondary specialization rather than their original vertebrate status. Although we have data on their fossil ancestors, it is impossible to estimate the size of their brains (Stensiö, 1963; Jerison, 1973). Data on cartilaginous fish (class Chondrichthyes, i.e., sharks, rays, and skates) overlap those of mammals and bony fish. This appears to have been true also in an ancestral shark of 300 ma (Zangerl & Case, 1976), which would identify the sharks as having been the first vertebrates to "experiment" with encephalization. Too little is known about the lives of sharks and rays to suggest a behavioral interpretation of their encephalization. For the present it remains a scientific enigma.

The anomalous data on mormyrid electric fish are certainly related to their reliance on unusual senses for information about their environments (Bullock, 1993; Butler & Hodos, 1996). The enlarged mormyrid brain is due to a unique enlargement of the cerebellum, rather than forebrain, presumably in connection with processing information from their electric organs. The neural circuitry involves the lateral line system and the eighth cranial nerve (Butler & Hodos, 1996; pp. 181–183). The data on these electric fish, which I show on the graph, are appropriately aligned with respect to allometry; they differ from other bony fish in encephalization.

One should interpret the data on electric fish within the same framework that works for mammals and birds, although their cerebellar specialization may be different enough from forebrain specialization to note it if one elaborated the definition. We may choose to distinguish cerebellar from forebrain sources of neural information-processing capacity that defines intelligence, but even that may not be necessary in the light of recent reports of cognitive functions associated with mammalian cerebellar activity (Squire, 1987). It makes sense to me to keep the definition as simple as possible and to treat the behavioral capacity of electric fish as, perhaps, an unusual example of a different kind of intelligence. It is clearly an exotic intelligence when compared with the processing capacity that evolved in mammals, which was essentially a forebrain enlargement associated with the evolution of the cerebral cortex (Jerison, 1990). Electric fish are a diversion for the present concern with antecedents for human intelligence, but the unusual excess of processing capacity in electric fish is a challenge to animal behaviorists to find out why it is there.

The evidence on the relationship between brain size and processing capacity is from mammalian data. We can assume, however, that because nerve cells are packed efficiently in brains, at least a similar relationship exists in other vertebrates. In that case, we may equate processing capacity with brain size on the ordinate of Figure 11.3. We then conclude, first, that within each vertebrate group most of the variation of processing capacity is an allometric effect of the evolution of smaller or larger bodies and not a result of selection for additional capacity related to intelligence. Allometry accounts for about 80% of the variance in brain size, leaving no more than 20% or so to be accounted for by encephalization. (I summarize some factor analytic data in the next paragraph.) We can conclude, second, that mammals and birds are similar in processing capacity and that both are "higher vertebrates" relative to the other groups. The cartilaginous fish and electric fish remain exceptions to be explained by future research.

For a more precise view of the present diversity in processing capacity, I performed a principal components factor analysis on mammalian data (Stephan, Frahm & Baron, 1981), a 12×76 data matrix with 12 variates determined for each of 76 species of mammal. The species, by taxonomic order, were 28 insectivores, 3 tree shrews, 18 prosimians, and 27 simian primates (including apes and humans). The variates were 10 parts of the brain (four cortical components, basal ganglia, diencephalon, mesencephalon, cerebellum, medulla, and olfactory bulbs), total brain weight, and total body weight. Reported elsewhere in more detail (Jerison, 1991), the analysis demonstrated that two factors accounted for 98% of the variance. The first factor, which accounted for 86% of the variance, was a general size factor heavily loaded in all of the variates except the olfactory bulbs. The second factor was a special factor loaded mainly on olfactory bulb size, which accounted for 13% of the variance. The special olfactory bulb factor is undoubtedly an artifact of the large number of primate species in the sample. Simian primates all have atypically small olfactory bulbs, whereas the other species were normal mammals in this respect. The variance in olfactory bulbs across this sample of species is artificially inflated because the distribution is bimodal. The appearance of this factor in the analysis emphasizes how unusual the reduction of olfactory bulbs is as an adaptation of simian primates.

I repeated the factor analysis, adding a measure of encephalization (EQ) as a thirteenth variate, and, as expected, an additional factor had to be extracted to account for the variance. A general size factor was still strongest, accounting for 73% of the variance, and the olfactory bulb factor was still evident as a special factor with its effect reduced slightly to 11% of the variance. The third factor was an encephalization factor represented on the same variates as the general size factor as well as the new encephalization variate and accounting for 14% of the variance. The interpretation is fairly obvious. Encephalization is correlated with developments in many different structures in the brain. Excepting the olfactory bulbs, the parts of the brain that were analyzed were about equally heavily loaded on the encephalization factor.

There are two important conclusions. First, the brain hangs together. If one knows the size of one part or of the whole brain in a species, one can estimate with surprising accuracy the size of most other parts. If one were to draw bivariate graphs, as in Figure 11.2, with a part of the brain shown as a dependent variable and total brain size as the independent variable, each graph would be similar in appearance to Figure 11.2 and would also indicate correlations close to $r = .99$ (Jerison, 1991). Second, the different parts of the brain contribute in very similar ways to variation in overall brain size and in an encephalization component of brain size. I relate this to the distribution of processing through much of the brain. For example, although vision is in a sense localized as a function of visual cortex, it is now recognized that many other parts of the brain, including regions in the temporal and frontal lobes, are activated by visual stimulation. The mammalian brain controls major behavioral domains by systems widely distributed throughout the brain (Goldman-Rakic, 1988).

All of these results encourage us to analyze the evolution of processing capacity and encephalization from the analysis of brain–body relationships. The evolutionary analysis is supported by an excellent fossil record, which enables us to learn the actual history of encephalization (and, by inference, of intelligence) in all vertebrates. The record is clearest for the evolution of mammals and birds relative to their ancestors among the reptiles.

FOSSIL BRAINS AND BODIES

A fossil brain is actually a cast, an endocast, molded by the cranial cavity of the skull of the fossil. Because all mammalian brains are packed tightly in the cranial cavity, an endocast is shaped like the brain that it replaces. During its growth, the brain actually shapes the inner walls of the skull to mirror a brain's external surface, and an endocast can be analyzed as if it were an undissected brain.

In most living species of mammals, an endocast is quite brainlike in appearance, showing details of the fissural pattern in the neocortex and the vermis of the cerebellum as well as the superficial veins and arteries. Endocasts are equally good in birds. They are not quite as good in some very large-brained species, such as humans, elephants, and cetaceans, in which the pattern of gyri and sulci is sometimes obscured, but these endocasts look as brainlike as a freshly removed brain when the dura is still in place. In "lower vertebrates," however, the brain does not usually fill the cranial cavity, and endocasts are useful mainly to estimate brain size (Jerison, 1973).

Fossils provide other information for understanding brain evolution and for extrapolations to behavior. Body size can be estimated from the postcranial skeleton to analyze encephalization in fossil vertebrates in the same way as in living species. Details of structure, such as the shape of teeth, forelimbs, and hindlimbs, can enable one to analyze feeding habits,

gait, and other behavior (Alexander, 1989; Feduccia, 1993). There is even fossil evidence on social behavior in dinosaurs, which has been reconstructed from the aggregation of fossilized eggs, bones, and foot and tail prints (Horner & Gorman, 1988). There is also a fossil record of sensory structures, which is useful for reconstructing the information about the external world that was available to fossil animals. Olfactory bulbs and nasal turbinals are visible on the endocast and the skull and are related to the evolution of the sense of smell (Jerison, 1991). There are fossil middle-ear bones and cochlea, which are important for the analysis of the evolution of hearing (Allin, 1975, 1986). The orientation of the orbits of the eye provides evidence on the evolution of binocular vision (Martin, 1990, pp. 318–323), and the placement of the hyoid bones on fossil humans has been the basis for speculations on the evolution of the voice box and of articulated speech (Lieberman, 1984).

The analysis of the evolution of intelligence, defined in terms of processing capacity, is based on adding data on fossils to Figure 11.3 to reveal the history of encephalization. An important clue about the origin of intelligence is in a qualitative analysis of the positions of early mammals and their ancestors among the reptiles, compared with living species of mammals and reptiles in this graph. One can then speculate knowledgeably about the selection pressures on mammallike reptiles of the beginning of the Mesozoic era, about 250 ma, because these were the reptiles that were eventually to be transformed into the earliest mammals.

As mentioned earlier, mammallike reptiles (therapsids) had been the dominant reptiles of the Permian period at the end of the Paleozoic, and some of their species had survived the greatest of all mass extinctions in the history of life, which occurred at the Permo–Triassic border. Another group of reptiles, the archosaurians, including the dinosaurs, appeared at about that time, and it is not unreasonable to think of therapsids and archosaurians as competing for major ecological niches during the Triassic period at the beginning of the Mesozoic. From the remains of their brains and their bodies, species in both groups were "good" reptiles, quite comparable in the adequacy of all adaptations that can be read from skeletons. Nevertheless, by the middle of the Mesozoic era, the therapsids had lost the competition and gone extinct. Not quite extinct. One group survived as slightly modified "reptiles," much reduced in body size and with several other detectable modifications. We have renamed them "mammals."

Among the modifications in the mammals was an enlarged brain, which was probably a solution for a packaging problem. The adaptational problem was where to put some additional neural machinery required by a mammal as an only slightly modified reptile but adapted for life in twilight and at night rather than the usual diurnal niche of Mesozoic reptiles. I develop the scenario in the next section in detail to describe the adaptation and the packaging problem. First, let me review what actually happened to the brain.

The fossil evidence of the brain in the earliest mammals, which lived about 225 ma, can presently be inferred only from external features of the skull. (The fossils exist, but endocasts have not yet been prepared.) These features are consistent with those in skulls of somewhat later Mesozoic species in which encephalization has been measured. The oldest endocast is from a species that appeared about 150 ma, *Triconodon mordax*, and it was several times larger than expected in a reptile of its size. *Triconodon* was a tiny animal, about the size of living moles and shrews, and probably similar in behavioral adaptations. It is significant for the view that nocturnicity was a mammalian characteristic of the time that all Mesozoic mammals were small, none larger than living house cats. Their size was a defense against predation during the day, for they could hide in burrows out of sight of large diurnal predatory reptiles. Although advanced in encephalization compared with reptiles, all Mesozoic mammals were encephalized to about the same degree. Although there were other evolutionary changes, the stasis in encephalization in mammals evidently lasted for at least 150 million years.

Following the great extinctions at the K–T boundary that ends the Mesozoic era, mammals became diversified in body size, and some species weighed several hundred kilograms. Presumably these early Cenozoic species had "discovered" terrestrial niches left empty by the disappearance of dinosaurs. But

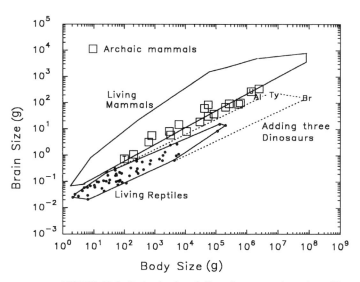

FIGURE 11.4. Brain–body relations in mammals and reptiles with each class enclosed in a minimum convex polygon. Labeled archaic mammals are the Mesozoic *Triconodon mordax* (T) and the early Cenozoic *Uintatherium anceps* (U). Labeled dinosaurs are *Allosaurus* (Al), *Tyrannosaurus* (Ty), and *Brachiosaurus* (Br).

their brains continued to be relatively small for the first 10 million years of the Cenozoic era, 55 to 65 ma, becoming enlarged only to the extent required by allometry. The record is quantified in Figure 11.4.

Data on encephalization in Figure 11.4 are presented against the background of the minimum convex polygons for living mammals and for living and fossil reptiles. The reptilian polygon, extended to include some dinosaurs, pictures the status of the group from which mammals evolved. Fossil data on therapsids, which were the immediate ancestors of true mammals, all fall within the polygon of living reptiles (Jerison, 1973; Hopson, 1979).

Archaic species are defined as members of orders that are now entirely extinct. Their data in Figure 11.4 are the small square symbols. *Triconodon* is identified with a "T," and the largest of the archaic species, *Uintatherium*, a large ungulate that lived about 50 ma in what is now Utah, is identified with a "U." It is clear that as a group the archaic mammals were not encephalized beyond the level achieved by the earliest mammals. The data on archaic species lie close to the lower margin of living mammals, although all are above a reptilian grade of encephalization.

These are the data that support the conclusion that the earliest mammals had "discovered" an available adaptive zone early in their evolution, which required some enlargement of the brain relative to their reptilian ancestors. The zone was evidently fairly stable throughout the Mesozoic era, and from Figure 11.4 we can also recognize that some living species require no higher level of encephalization. Those living species include the insectivores as well as opossums among the marsupials.

I have entered the individual living reptilian data points to indicate how a minimum convex polygon is constructed. If one imagines the living reptile points as a set of pegs, a minimum convex polygon is made by the smallest possible string that can be pulled tightly to enclose all of the pegs. The outer pegs support the string.

Data on dinosaurs in Figure 11.4 are for your entertainment, but they also demonstrate the power of the analysis of gross brain size and the adequacy of the polygons for a scientific analysis. If we pose the frequently asked question, Did dinosaurs become extinct because of their walnut-size (i.e., terribly small) brains?, we can answer with Figure 11.4. With respect to their brains, the three dinosaurs added to Figure 11.4 were normal reptiles. These dinosaur species, *Allosaurus* (Al), *Tyrannosaurus* (Ty), and *Brachiosaurus* (Br) were not unusually small-brained. Dinosaurs did not go extinct for lack of brains.

THE LOCALIZATION AND INTEGRATION OF INFORMATION PROCESSING

Having reviewed the facts, we can now turn to the explanations for the expansion of information-processing capacity when the mammals first evolved. Brain tissue is metabolically among the most expensive of bodily tissues (Aiello & Wheeler, 1995). Evolution is often thought of as an optimizing process in which costs are balanced by benefits, and the question is, What benefits were associated with the enlargement of the brain in these mammals to make its energetic cost worthwhile? The answer has to be speculative, of course, because we were not on the scene when the critical events occurred. The issue is to present a reasonable scenario. With a few calculations on living brains, I develop such a scenario on the basis of how reptiles

and mammals presently use information about the environment to guide their movements. I follow the uniformitarian hypothesis, a version of parsimony that states that the laws of nature in the past were the same as in the present (Simpson, 1970).

The scenario begins by recognizing that most Paleozoic reptiles were diurnal and relied primarily on visual information to guide their movements. I suggest that the therapsids became extinct when the ruling reptiles displaced them in diurnal niches and that aberrant nocturnal therapsids that we know retrospectively as mammals survived. They had evolved adaptations for nocturnal niches in which they did not face competition or predation from archosaurians.

Life in nocturnal niches depends on sensory modalities other than vision. For my scenario I calculate the amount of neural machinery required to use nonvisual senses to be computationally equivalent to the visual system. For convenience, I work with auditory information, as if the earliest mammals were batlike in relying on echolocation. We know that living bats construct a three-dimensional world from such auditory information and that their world is comparable to our visual world (Grinnell, 1995). Visual and auditory senses for distance information may both be spatial senses, but the neural machinery for vision and audition is packaged in different ways.

The neural control of visual information in amphibians and reptiles involves significant amounts of information processing that occurs in the neural retina of the eye (Lettvin, Maturana, McCulloch, & Pitts, 1959). Additional processing is performed at subcortical neural centers such as the superior colliculi ("optic lobes"), and although some analysis may take place in their forebrains, these species have no cerebral cortex. Ewert's analysis described earlier was primarily of activity in the colliculi.

From data on living species, one can estimate that there were several hundred thousand retinal ganglion cells in each eye of the reptilian forbears of the mammals. There should have been about several million nerve cells in other layers of the neural retina (cf. Polyak, 1957; Roth, 1987) and comparably large numbers of photoreceptors. The computational problem is to determine the effect on the organization of the brain if one were to replace the reptilian diurnal neural retinal system with other neural sensory systems. This had to be accomplished by early mammals if their movements after dark were to be coordinated with information about the environment.

If in the earliest mammals the auditory system were to evolve as a primary system for distance information, the sensory information and the location of the neural control networks would be quite different from that in the visual system. In living reptiles there are only between 50 and 1,000 sense cells (hair cells) in each cochlea, indicating that hearing has a relatively minor role in their lives (Wever, 1978). However, even in mammals such as bats, where we know that the auditory system is critically important, there are only about 35,000 sense cells (hair cells) in each cochlea. This number, so much smaller than the number of photoreceptors, is typical for all living mammals.

The neural analysis by any sensory system converts sensory data into information about the external environment, and the initial information received by the sense cells has to be analyzed by neural networks elsewhere in the system. This analysis itself could be similar in auditory and visual systems. We saw something of how that analysis can take place in the example of neural control in Ewert's toads, which enables them to "know" how to catch a fly. The amount of analysis may be similar for an equivalent analysis with the auditory system, for example, in the way echolocating bats catch moths (Grinnell, 1995). This is more detail than we need to know about how the system may function, however. Our problems are only how large must the system be and where it would be.

These are packaging problems. It may take as many as 5,000,000 neurons in each retina of a reptile, or 10,000,000 neurons in all, to process information about the environment useful for the control of movement. We can assume (as a first approximation, of course) that this is the number of neurons that would be required to do the same job with auditory and other nonvisual modalities. In no nonvisual system is there a peripheral structure comparable to the neural retina as a place to pack the neurons of the network. For example, in the peripheral auditory apparatus there is space beneath the basilar membrane of the cochlea for the auditory bipolar cells, but no more than the same number of bipolars as hair cells can be stored there.

The argument also follows, with somewhat more detail, from the hierarchical structure of the networks. Retinal photoreceptors in reptiles communicate directly with as many as 1,000,000 first-order retinal bipolar neurons, which then communicate with even more "association neurons" in the retina, and it is these that communicate with the ganglion cells, which are the cell bodies of the optic nerve. The retinal neurons for processing visual information are, thus, second-, third-, or fourth-order neurons in a synaptic chain. The comparable hierarchy in the auditory system in all living vertebrates has a maximum of 70,000 first-order bipolar neurons peripheral to the brain in the spiral ganglion. The second-, third-, and fourth-order auditory neurons are all in the brain proper. They are in the medulla, midbrain and thalamus in lower vertebrates, and in mammals there is an additional level of neural processing in the neocortex. If the early mammals were to do with hearing (and other modalities) what their reptilian ancestors did with vision, they had to evolve networks to do the equivalent processing, presumably with a similar hierarchical structure. As we have seen, something of the order of 10,000,000 neurons are in the retinal neural networks, and for the other modalities to do the job, this is the number that would have to be packed in the brain.

This is the same as the total number of cortical neurons in the half-gram mouse brain (Braitenberg & Schüz, 1991). If we were to add the amount of processing capacity performed in the neural retina to the brain proper, we would have to add the equivalent of a mouse brain to the premammalian reptile brain. We have to add about 0.5 g of brain.

With these numbers we can return to our data on fossils. To model the reptilian ancestors of mammals I take the unusually small early Mesozoic therapsid, Thrinaxodon, which weighed about 500 g and had a 0.4 g brain. As the early mammal, we have already met Triconodon, which weighed about 100 g and had a 0.7 g brain. Evolving from a Thrinaxodon-sized therapsid to a Triconodon-sized mammal required a half order of magnitude reduction in body size and an appropriately adjusted brain size. From a regression analysis of the data of Figure 11.4, I can estimate the expected brain size in a 100-g therapsid reptile as 0.15 g. To transform the therapsid into Triconodon we would add the difference between 0.7 g and 0.15 g, or 0.55 g of brain, which is a four- or five-fold increase in brain size. The transformation added a mouse-sized brain, as it were, which is the right amount of encephalization according to our calculations.

We now have a complete answer. The amount of encephalization that occurred when the earliest mammals evolved can be explained as a solution of a packaging problem of where to put the extra processing machinery for the sensory systems (10,000,000 neurons) that had to replace or supplement vision. From comparative neuroanatomy we infer that the extra machinery was packed into a new neural forebrain structure that evolved in mammals, the cerebral cortex. However, sometimes even a simple solution has complications, and one effect of this kind of packaging may be the major clue to the relationship of encephalization to intelligence.

Several different nonvisual systems would have contributed information for this scenario – in particular the auditory, olfactory, and tactile systems. In addition, the visual system could continue to provide information about the external environment for a nocturnal species, provided that it evolved to be sensitive to weak visual stimuli that are available in the evening or at night. The rod system of the retina, basically a mammalian specialization, is appropriate for these responses. There are, thus, four different neural systems to provide information about the external environment, and in living mammals they are packed into different regions in the cortex.

The complication for the operation of these systems occurs because the information from the different component systems would refer to a common set of events in the external environment. The neural response to the information from each modality would presumably be similar to that recorded from the superior colliculi of Ewert's toads, bursts of firing of nerve cells in a network, and there would be no way to identify the bursts as having originated in a common environmental event. The analysis of the information from several sensory systems would have to be integrated in some way, and more neural machinery would be required to effect the integration.

The integration presumably took the form of identifying common features in the information from each modality, such as a description of the source as an object in an external world. There would also have to be codes with regard to where the object was and when the object was sensed. In short, the integration would be in terms of events in the real world as we know it with objects placed in space and time. From a computational perspective, the brain's problem is a pattern recognition problem rather than a simple signal detection problem. In more classical terms, one might consider the problem as the creation of perceptual worlds or *Umwelten* (von Uexküll, 1934), and this seems to me a good characterization of the work of a mammalian brain – in particular of the cerebral cortex. In effect the brain's work is to create a real world, or in less dramatic terms, to provide knowledge about the real world. This is very different from a brain as a reflex machine implied by Ewert's toads.

If I were to go beyond the working definition with which I introduced this chapter, it would be to restrict "intelligent" processing to pattern recognition. I would attempt to distinguish this kind of integrative activity from the brain's work as a reflex machine, although one assumes that both integrative and reflex activities occur in all mammalian brains. The critical added processing is the creation of a real world by the brain, as it were, or, in less dramatic terms, the added processing supports the integrative activity that enables an animal to know the real world. This seems to me a fundamental feature of intelligence in any animal. One reason to resist going beyond the working definition, however, is the difficulty one would face in attempting an operational bottom–up approach within such a definition. At a fundamental level, one would have to specify purely neural distinctions between pattern recognition and signal detection. In direct analysis of neural activity it is impossible to make such a distinction. The computational analogy is to attempt to distinguish, in a blind test, between small samples of machine code for a pattern recognition program from samples of code during a signal detection program and to identify the programs. It is presumably possible, but it would be a formidable problem in cryptanalysis.

BRAIN AND PERCEPTION

Because I have tied the evolution of intelligence to the evolution of encephalization and analyze the major advance in encephalization that occurred when the mammals evolved as having involved a shift in perceptual modalities, I must digress briefly to comment on the brain's role in perception. It is conventional in neuropsychology to draw maps of the brain indicating localized sensory and motor areas, and in older maps one drew "silent areas" representing association cortex. Much of that view has been recognized for several decades as unsustainable (Diamond, 1977). Association functions that relate the activities of sensory and motor systems to one another are intercalated among the sensory and motor areas, and those areas extend over almost the entire neocortex (Jones & Powell, 1970). There are no silent areas. Furthermore, we recognize that sensory analysis at the level of the neocortex usually involves multiple projections of superficially similar information. There are many duplicate maps of the body on the brain, including at least a dozen separate projections in the primate brain from different parts of the visual field (Zeki, 1993).

"Images of mind" (Posner, 1994), determined by metabolic activity in the brain and recorded as positron emission tomography (PET) and functional magnetic resonance imaging (fMRI) scans of the living brain, show that foci of activity correlated with behavior and experience are spread through many parts of the brain. Although such images demonstrate localized activation by specialized human mental activities, the "local" regions are very extensive. Because there are about 15,000,000 neurons under a square centimeter of cortex, and a typical human brain scan localizes activity in at least several square centimeters of cortex, a "localization" actually involves a very wide area and very large amounts of processing capacity. One should note, too, the extent to which there are multiple activation patterns, which suggests interaction among parts of the brain. There are usually several regions of maximum activity rather than a single focal region responsive to a mental activity. The extent to which functions are localized is partly a function of the way the measurements are performed. Localized functions are measurable as activity in single nerve cells, but these cells are presumably parts of extensive networks of neurons. All or almost all of these networks process information from the external environment. It is most significant that these networks, which can be characterized as supporting perceptual and cognitive processing, can account for essentially all of the cortical surface.

In the quantitative example of mammalian encephalization as the solution to a packaging problem, I "explained" the increase in brain size as related entirely to perceptual and cognitive processing. The additional tissue was assumed to be doing sensory analysis of the kind done in the neural retina of frogs (Lettvin et al., 1959), and it was also thought to be integrating that analysis as knowledge of a real world. It is interesting that when one analyzes the work of the brain in living monkeys and humans, one also correlates neural activation with handling information from the external world. We describe the behavioral aspects of the work as attending and responding to images, sounds, words, and ideas (Posner, 1994). Returning to the computer analogy, one can make the point that good pattern recognition is the most demanding work that computers can do and requires the most processing capacity. One can reach a similar conclusion about brains. To generate knowledge of the external world, to perceive that world and understand its structure and function, is the brain's most demanding work and is the basic reason for the brain's enlargement. I have tried to show how this was true early in mammalian evolution, and I believe that it remains true in living mammals, including humans.

BIRDS

I can review the entire fossil record of the encephalization of birds in a few paragraphs, but it is worth additional space to emphasize the different kinds of intelligences that have evolved. Although few fossil avian endocasts have been retrieved, they cover enough of the time period during which birds have lived to enable one to outline the history. The earliest bird, *Archaeopteryx*, lived about 150 ma, and, as in Mesozoic mammals, its brain was at the lower edge of the avian polygon of Figure 11.3. It was very small-brained as a bird, but it was more encephalized than any of its close relatives among reptiles.

Birds as a group are now generally considered to be a surviving group of dinosaurs (but see Feduccia, 1996). For paleoneurologists, however, *Archaeopteryx* is better viewed as a transitional form between birds and reptiles. Its brain was about twice as large as expected in dinosaurs and other reptiles, and it was birdlike in completely filling the cranial cavity (Jerison, 1973). It lacked a Wulst, however, the characteristic telencephalic gyrus in living birds that is the major forebrain visual center. Birds and mammals had a most recent common ancestor about 300 ma (see Figure 11.1), and the long period of their divergent evolution is reflected in their brains. Birds do not have neocortex, but the telencephalon of their forebrain appears to be homologous to neocortex according to its thalamic connections (Karten, 1991; cf Butler & Hodos, 1996).

No more than a dozen fossil endocasts are known for birds, but from these it appears that their encephalization paralleled that of mammals. A Wulst became evident in late Mesozoic and early Cenozoic birds, which still were less encephalized than average, specifically in the size of their forebrain. But bird endocasts have been indistinguishable from those of their living relatives since at least 20 ma.

Among living birds, pigeons are relatively small brained, although we know that their behavioral capacities are impressive. They almost replaced rats as the standard subject in much of the operant conditioning literature, and all of the effects of schedules of reinforcement demonstrable in mammals (including humans) have been demonstrated in pigeons (Skinner, 1957). Among their more unusual abilities, pigeons are evidently as good as or better than humans in perceiving patterns such as faces (Herrnstein, 1985).

The most encephalized of living birds are crows and parrots. Perhaps the most impressive of all recent reports on the intellectual capacities of nonhuman animals has been on the accomplishments of one gray parrot (Pepperberg, 1994). There are, of course, many anecdotes attesting to the intelligence of crows and other corvids. One normally finds positive correlations between laboratory measures of animal intelligence and encephalization, although they are difficult to evaluate, in part because it is difficult to arrange comparable behavioral tests in different species. Macphail (1982) reviewed the literature on the performance of crows and other corvids with numbers, learning sets, and so forth, noting that they perform comparably to primates.

Although birds and mammals are comparable in performance in laboratory tests involving the abilities cited by Hodos as related to intelligence, I believe it is true that birds have specialized in the evolution of fixed action patterns (FAPs), whereas mammals have specialized in behaviors requiring greater plasticity. These are different specialized intelligences, but it is inappropriate to treat either as more advanced than the other. The biological criterion for evolutionary success is often the number of different species present or the total number of individuals. There are about twice as many bird species as mammals species (9,750 versus 4,629 according to standard sources), and if we exclude the rogue mammalian species, *Homo sapiens*, the biomass of birds is probably comparable to that of mammals (cf. Young, 1962). In these nonjudgmental times, perhaps one can leave it at that, vowing to stop considering "bird-brained" as a pejorative in view of the present success of these feathered dinosaurs.

CENOZOIC ENCEPHALIZATION IN NONHUMAN MAMMALS

The Cenozoic era began 65 ma and continues to the present. I outline the record of encephalization during that time now; full reviews are in Falk (1987), Jerison (1973, 1985) and Martin (1990). During the Paleocene geological epoch, covering the first 10 million years of the Cenozoic, encephalization remained at the same grade as during the Mesozoic for almost all groups. A possible exception is one primatelike species (*Plesiadapis*) that may have been somewhat more encephalized than its contemporaries. Primates are among the more ancient of living orders of mammals, and possible primate teeth have been found in Cretaceous geological strata of about 70 ma.

There was a clear increase in encephalization in the progressive orders of mammals during the following epoch, the Eocene (55–35 ma; "progressive" refers only to the fact that the order includes living species). For example, the early Eocene equid, *Hyracotherium*, may have been somewhat encephalized beyond the Mesozoic grade although clearly less encephalized than later equids.

A major advance in encephalization occurred in most mammalian species after the great extinction event known as the Grand Coupure, which signaled a transition from the Eocene to the Oligocene epoch (35–22 ma). Equids, as represented by *Mesohippus*, for example, reached the grade of encephalization of average living mammals during the Oligocene;

that is, their encephalization quotient was $EQ = 1.0$. Among the Oligocene primates of that epoch, the North American fossil tarsioid, *Rooneyia*, was more encephalized than any of its mammalian contemporaries and had reached the grade typical for living tarsioid species. However, the North African primates of 30 ma, in particular *Aegyptopithecus*, a possible ancestor for living simians, were relatively small-brained, comparable to Eocene lemuroid species and only slightly more encephalized than average Oligocene mammals, but somewhat less encephalized than average living mammals. The Eocene tarsioids and all Oligocene and later primates had brains with characteristic primate external configuration, lemurlike in shape, and an appropriately positioned sylvian fissure. By the early Miocene epoch (22–5 ma) simian primates had advanced to their present level as about twice as encephalized as average mammals, and the one prosimian endocast of the epoch was comparable to that of living species in size.

Although the pattern was complex (Figure 11.5), there was a trend toward encephalization detectable in most orders of mammals during the Cenozoic, although a Mesozoic grade persists in some living groups. The evidence from ungulate and carni-

vore fossil brains is that the encephalization was driven by the enlargement of the cerebral neocortex (Jerison, 1990, 1994). Among the more "primitive" of living mammals, opossums and insectivores are indistinguishable in encephalization from their Cretaceous relatives. At some time between the Oligocene and the Miocene, rodents reached their present grade, about twice that of the smallest-brained living mammals but half as encephalized as average. Primates have, in general, been advanced compared with other mammals with respect to the beginning of the increase in relative brain size, but all of the groups with the exception of *Homo sapiens* among the primates had reached their present typical grade of encephalization early in the Miocene epoch (22–5 ma).

The hominid lineage is first known from australopithecines, and the record of their brain is known from mid-Pliocene times, about 3.5 ma. Their brains were at first comparable in size to living

FIGURE 11.5. The time course of encephalization in vertebrates. Encephalization quotients are approximate relative to average living mammals in which the quotient is defined as 1.0.

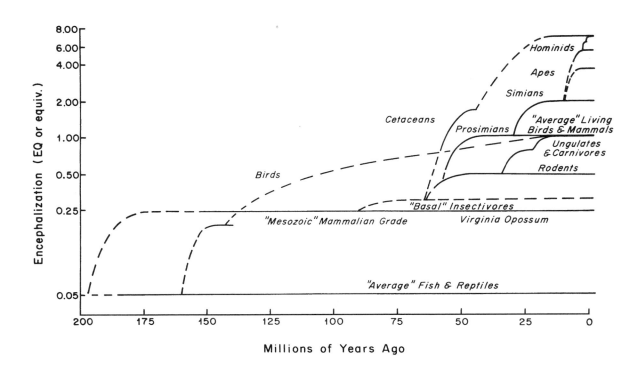

chimpanzees, about 400 ml in volume. The early gracile species were typically somewhat smaller bodied than living apes, however, with body sizes estimated as about 30 kg, and later australopithecine brains were probably about 500 ml in volume; these ancestors were somewhat more encephalized than living great apes. Fossil apes from that time are not known, but Miocene apes were also small-bodied, and they had much smaller brains, about 200 ml.

The dramatic advance in hominid encephalization occurred near the end of the Pliocene and beginning of the Pleistocene (1.8 ma–10,000 years ago) with the advent of the genus *Homo* in the habiline species of about 2 ma and the erectus species, first known 1.6 ma. The largest, but also best, habiline endocast displaces 775 ml. Early erectus endocasts are only slightly larger, 800 ml or so, but the last of the erectus fossils, which lived about 500,000 years ago, included individuals with endocasts well within the range of living human brains, displacing perhaps 1200 ml.

Paleoanthropologists continue to debate the status of the Neandertals, whether they were members of the same species as ours, *Homo sapiens*, or whether they were a different species (Trinkaus & Shipman, 1993). The Neandertal brain cannot be distinguished in any neurologically significant way from living human brains. There are perhaps a dozen endocasts that have been examined, and they overlap the living human range, averaging somewhat larger.

For a sense of the measurements, here are data on cranial capacity in 12 Neandertal endocasts described by Coon (1962) compared with a modern sample from 44 male and 30 female cadavers (Davis & Wright, 1977). The Neandertals' cranial capacity ranged from 1,271 ml to 1,641 ml, with a mean of 1,485 ml, standard deviation (SD) = 112 ml. The entire recent sample ranged from 1,119 ml to 1,655 ml, mean = 1,391 ml, SD = 120 ml. The statistics: $t = 2.669$, $df = 84$, $p < .01$. However, if we assume sexism among the Neandertals in that only male skulls were preserved (which happened to be likely for most of this sample), the picture changes. In the male recent sample, mean capacity was 1,428 ml, SD = 117. The statistics are then $t = 1.548$, $df = 54$, $.20 > p > .10$. In my view the difference is a myth. At best it is too small to be interesting. Although the endocasts of Neandertals are somewhat elongated compared with those from re-

cent cadavers, I would draw no inferences from the difference in shape.

The human brain, whether known from Neandertals or from "true" humans, reached its present grade of processing capacity within the past half million years, and it has been at the level throughout that period. Modern *Homo sapiens* are known in Europe from about 250,000 years ago as contemporaries of the Neandertals. Evidence of human culture is much more recent. The oldest verified artifacts (paintings, carvings, etc.), other than tools, are known from less than 50,000 years ago. It is something of a puzzle for those concerned with brain–behavior relations to find so long a period when the human brain had reached its present grade of processing capacity and was not using that capacity for artistic cultural activities.

Before one interprets this history in terms of the evolution of intelligence, there are two aspects of encephalization as an evolutionary trait in mammals that should be kept in mind. First, encephalization is not a unitary trait. Although the brain "hangs together," that is, the size of one part can typically be estimated rather well from the size of other parts (e.g., Figure 11.2), the differences described under the rubric of "proper mass" demonstrate that the actual measure of encephalization results from convergent evolution. Bats and mice may be equally encephalized, but most of the increase in brain size in insect-eating (microchiropteran) bats can be attributed to expansion of auditory cortex (Grinnell, 1995), whereas mice are more normal mammals in the allocation of brain mass to various sensorimotor systems (Johnson, 1990).

Closer to home, humans and dolphins are another example. As species, we are comparable to one another in brain size and in encephalization. The human's is a normal primate brain, much enlarged because of the evolution of the language areas, but the allocation of processing capacity to the major lobes of the neocortex is the same as in other primates relative to gross brain size. Even the vaunted expansion of the prefrontal neocortex in humans turns out to be exactly as expected for a primate brain that evolved to human brain size. (Deacon, 1997, claims the opposite, but there are flaws in his analysis. The acceptable data are in Uylings & Van Eden, 1990; and in Semendeferi, Damasio, Frank & Van Hoesen, 1997. See also Jerison, 1997.) The dolphin brain is more unusual, having increased in the size of the auditory system, but with a rather different histological structure – a structure different enough that it has been characterized as primitive (Morgane, Jacobs, & Galaburda, 1986). Primitive or not, brains reach their mature size in different species by different adaptations, contributing differently to the mass of tissue that evolved, even when the total mass indicates equal encephalization in different species.

Similarities in encephalization are almost always results of convergent evolution, and for this reason it is fundamentally impossible to use them taxonomically for cladistic analysis to judge evolutionary distance among groups (cf. Johnson, 1990). This fact is the reason for emphasizing that if we define intelligence, as I have, in terms of encephalization, embedded in this definition is the idea that it was not a unitary intelligence that evolved. Rather, a variety of intelligences, in the plural, evolved in mammals and birds. This reflects an evolutionary truism. Species are adapted to different ecological niches, each unique in some respects. Uniqueness defines a species, and uniqueness is with respect to behavior as well as morphology. The brain control for unique behavior is obviously unique in some respect for each species, and the "excess" processing capacity involved in that control will constitute a unique aspect of the intelligence of the species.

There is an unusual feature in the history of primate encephalization that is also worth special mention. It is evident in the history of prosimians when comparing late Eocene species with Miocene and later species, in the history of simians when comparing Oligocene species with later ones, and in human history when comparing Pliocene australopithecines with the genus *Homo*. In each group, classification based on reliable nonneural skeletal features of the earliest members indicates that encephalization was not one of the features to characterize the group. The brain's enlargement occurred later than other adaptations to the ecological niche that each group found. This is not true for other mammalian groups (e.g., the equids mentioned earlier), where the evidence indicates that encephalization to a particular grade was part of the suite of traits that could define the group. This suggests that in attempting to explain encephalization in primates, one should seek to discover critical features of their niches that would have made it advantageous to have an enlarged brain. The evolution of primate encephalization would then be understood to be a response to a feature of the niche that had already been successfully occupied before the enlargement of the brain occurred. Evolutionists today might describe it as anagenetic evolution within the clade.

Asynchrony between brain evolution and the evolution of other traits has been too little appreciated. Evolutionists of a century ago assumed that human evolution had been driven by the enlargement of the brain. The expected "missing link" between apes and men was an apelike creature that had somehow mutated into a large-brained apelike man and as a result of its newfound wisdom could somehow evolve to new heights of excellence to become less like the beasts and more like the angels. Great expectations can lead to great errors, and in this instance they provided the setting for the notorious Piltdown fraud. An unknown party, religiously committed to the evolutionary dogma of his time (evidence points to a man's doing it), fiddled with an orangutan lower jaw and ground its teeth to make them look human, found an old human cranium and upper jaw, and fiddled with those teeth to match those of the orangutan. He then dyed the pieces to look appropriately ancient and fossil-like and salted a diggable area in Piltdown in England with these two "fossils." (The culprit probably also wanted to prove that all good things began in England – at that time, 1913, the good European fossil hominids were from France and Germany.) Some honest evolutionists were alerted to the discovery of a primate fossil, and they found the two pieces following an appropriate search of the area. The bones entered the literature of human evolution as "*Eoanthropus dawsoni*" (Dawson may have been the culprit; as discoverer, he was honored by the species name). It is to the credit of paleoanthropologists that the fraud was exposed by a dramatic piece of scientific detective work (Wiener, 1955).

MAMMALIAN AND AVIAN "INTELLIGENCE"

According to our working definition we can trace a history of intelligence as increasing levels of information-processing capacity, which evolved in mammals and birds during the past 200 million years. It is graphed in Figure 11.5. The processing capacity in birds was fundamentally to control fixed action patterns, whereas in mammals it involved plasticity of some kind. Within the mammals many "intelligences" evolved.

I have mentioned the bat's world as a three-dimensional space created from information encoded as echolocation. One can find examples in more closely related groups. Outstanding among these is the discovery by Welker and his colleagues (Welker, 1990) of the differences in the organization of the brain in raccoonlike mammals (procyonids) that are correlated with their behavior patterns. Raccoons explore their environment with their forepaws, and the somatosensory areas of their brains are expanded so that each pad and digit of the forepaw has a distinct representation. Their close relatives, the coatis, which explore analogously with their snouts, have comparable expanded representation for the snout. The principle, which I have called "proper mass," is that the amount of brain tissue devoted to the control of a process is related to the importance of the process in an animal's life. That the bat's neocortex is primarily auditory (Grinnell, 1995) is another example. Closer to home, the enormous size of the human language areas alerts us to examine the importance of this adaptation, which is the subject of the next section.

The steplike progression in mammalian encephalization suggests a reason for some of the adaptations. Dawkins & Krebs (1979) describe them as arms races in which competitive adaptations develop in different species to enable them to maintain their viability relative to one another. The concept was developed in part to explain the relationship between carnivores and herbivores suggested by the data on their encephalization, which is comparable in these two groups of mammals; distributions of EQ have similar means and variance. But in the fossil record, there appeared to be a kind of leapfrogging with samples of carnivorous species always somewhat more encephalized than samples of herbivorous species from the same general geological period (Jerison, 1973). Very few species could be sampled for this conclusion, and these were from very broad ranges of time, of the order of 20 million years per group. Until better and larger samples from shorter periods can be developed, the conclusion remains tentative. The analysis of brain evolution in dinosaurs, however, also based on a small number of species, supports the view that predators are likely to be more encephalized than prey (Hopson, 1979).

Without going through all of the reasons, we can probably agree that carnivory requires more processing capacity than herbivory, that hunters require more information about the external world than is required by the hunted. One would normally expect the kind of relationship between the distributions of EQ that existed in the past. That it is absent in populations of living species, where the sample is large and truly of contemporaries, weakens the hypothesis. However, true or false, the hypothesis makes the point about the variety of intelligences that evolved. It is clear that different kinds of processing are required for the life of the successful predator compared with the life of the (equally) successful prey. Whether more is required for the one as compared with the other is unsettled, but there should be no question about their having to be different.

There is a special problem with laboratory studies of animal intelligence. Animals from all species that are studied in laboratory settings are usually successful in solving whatever problems are put to them. One conclusion from Macphail's (1982) review of the results of such studies is that we should not underestimate the ingenuity of human experimenters in training their animals to do their tasks. A second conclusion is that the laboratory procedures, which focus on a functional (input–output) analysis of behaviors, tended to minimize a role for species and individual differences. The laboratory, in effect, removes the context within which behavior mechanisms evolved, and, in a sense, it tests the extent to which processing capacity that may have evolved in connection with specific environmental requirements can be applied to problem solving in the novel environment of the laboratory. The conclusion must be that it has not been possible to discover laboratory tasks that are beyond the processing capacity that evolved in any of the animals that have been tested.

Bitterman (1988), in an elegant series of experiments, has been able to show that honeybees perform like rats and other mammals in many complex learning tasks often thought of as involving higher mental processes. Herrnstein's pigeons (1985) evidently see the world much as we do and can learn perceptual categorizing that follows the same rules as those used by humans. Pepperberg's (1994) gray parrot seems almost human in submitting to a variety of animal intelligence tests, and it has the additional advantage of a parrot's tongue.

When the learning sets procedure was first developed (Klüver, 1933; Harlow, 1949), it seemed to be a kind of intelligence test for animals with a "scale of nature" effect that ranked the species studied in the laboratory. People were best, followed by great apes, then monkeys, then prosimians, then cats. Rats seemed incapable of solving the problems. The picture was elegant (Passingham, 1982) and evidently makes sense for primates. Rumbaugh (1997) has been able to show that related tasks, measured with his "transfer index," do discriminate well among living primates and that their performance correlates highly with measures of encephalization. The elegant learning-sets picture was nevertheless complicated by the discovery that rats, supposedly incapable of succeeding in these tasks, could succeed if the task were modified appropriately. All that was needed was a sensory modality that was natural for rats to promote them to the class of species capable of learning set formation, and Slotnick and Katz (1974) found the modality: olfaction. It is not easy to arrange olfactory learning sets, but these experimenters succeeded.

One can extend the catalog of abilities that have been examined in the laboratory. But in a sense they miss the point. The evolutionary view is that whatever intelligence evolved in a species evolved in an environmental context, and it is inappropriate to assess it independently of that context.

When the assessment removes the context, something other than what evolved is being examined. A kind of uncertainty principle is at work. When we test intelligent behavior out of context, we have removed a major part of what there is to test. To use an evolutionary metaphor, if one thinks of intelligence as an adaptation, any laboratory test of intelligence is actually testing the extent to which the intelligence that evolved was preadaptive for the new environment encountered in the laboratory. This is one reason for my preference for the analysis of the evolution of processing capacity without specifying the way it is used. In my working definition my only specification is that it should be independent of the fraction of processing capacity that is correlated with bodily functions.

HUMAN INTELLIGENCE AND THE PROBLEM OF LANGUAGE

We are one species among, perhaps, 5,000 mammalian species and almost 50,000 vertebrate species. According to my working definition, intelligence evolved in at least 14,000 of those, the birds and mammals, and although we may be especially interested in our own status, the evolutionary issue is broad and the rules that I have been discussing are applicable to all species. There is an advantage, however, in illustrating the way the rules apply in at least one example, and it is appropriate to choose the human species as the example. Among other things, if perceptual–cognitive aspects of information processing are to be emphasized, it helps to work with a species in which we have so intimate a knowledge of the processing. We know ourselves.

There are two rules I wish to emphasize. First, evolution is adaptive, that is, it is a solution of a kind of engineering problem set by a changing environment. The adaptations track the environmental change. They do not anticipate environmental change. Although it could turn out to be preadaptive for a future environment at some future time, intelligence could only be adaptive to the conditions of its time as it evolved. Second, the special rule for neural evolution is that nervous tissue is energetically expensive, and neural adaptations should be expected to solve the environmental problem with as little neural tissue as possible. These rules indicate that to understand the evolution of human intelligence we must reconstruct the environment in which hominid species evolved as the hominid and ape lines split apart about 5 ma, and we must think carefully about the utility of the enlargement of the hominid brain in the face of the increased energetic cost. We no longer need measure encephalization quotients because hominid body size has remained reasonably constant during this period. It will be enough to look at changes in absolute brain size for clues.

The change in processing capacity is recorded in the evolution of brain size (Falk, 1987). Australopithecine brains of 2 ma to 4 ma were about 400 to 500 ml in volume. The first *Homo* species, *H. habilis*, appeared between 2 and 2.5 ma, and its brain size ranged between about 600 and 775 ml; the largest of these sizes (in the specimen identified as ER 1470) is also the best determined. The next of our ancestors was *H. erectus*, first known from Africa of about 1.6 ma. The species was first discovered in Java and was called "Pithecanthropus erectus" of about 1 ma, and the latest are from Peking, first called "Sinanthropus" and dated to about 0.5 ma. Its brain's volume ranged from about 800 ml to about 1250 ml, thus overlapping living human brains. I have already mentioned the Neandertals. They and individuals that are more definitely in the *H. sapiens* lineage are first known from about 0.25 ma, and their brain sizes are in the living human range. In round numbers the range of endocranial volumes is about 1,100 to 1700 ml with a mean of about 1400 ml. This record is not of a lineage but of specimens that have been recovered. The consensus at present is that humans evolved from an australopithecine species but that most of the fossil australopiths are from side branches. The habilines are thought of as close to the main line as are the erectus specimens. But in every instance one should think of a branching tree, and specimens are always at least partly branched off from the main line of descent. However, the evolution of processing capacity, as represented by the individuals on which we have data, presumably occurred on the main line to exactly the same extent.

The first problem about human intelligence is why it evolved in the first place. As we learn more about the behavioral capacities of great apes we become increasingly impressed by how adaptable they are. "Language" competence in great apes, especially as revealed by the Atlanta group (Savage-Rumbaugh et al., 1993) is impressive – in particular when it turns out that human linguistic categories are required to describe that competence adequately. The australopithecines of 3.5 ma had brains no larger than some of these linguistically trained chimpanzees.

To digress slightly about brain size in australopithecines and chimpanzees, reported australopithecine brain volumes (Falk, 1987) are usually contrasted with mean chimpanzee brain weight of about 350 grams and body weight of about 50 kg. It has been natural to assume a slight advantage for the hominids, suggesting that the evolutionary enlargement of the brain had already begun. I believe that this was the case, especially in the light of the absence of data on brain size in the ape lineage of that period. But there are problems. One of the chimpanzees (Austin) in the Atlanta project died recently, and although the data have not yet been published, I understand that its brain weighed about 500 g, near the top of the australopithecine range. The animal weighed more than 100 kg compared with the 20 to 40 kg estimated for the gracile australopithecines, and perhaps body size has to be considered for this comparison. The data on Austin, which are several

standard deviations above the range of brain and body sizes as reported in the literature, indicate how difficult it can be to reason from the available quantitative data. It is hard enough to get good estimates on the fossils, and the report on Austin's necropsy shows why one prefers to reason from order-of-magnitude differences rather than mere doublings of size. But we work with what we have, and the encephalization of the hominids is as well documented as any evidence in the fossil record.

Although I have occasionally indicated some skepticism about reasoning from the fissural patterns of hominid endocasts, it is possible to identify some of the fissural patterns in these (see Jerison, 1990, for more discussion). It seems to be true that the australopithecine brain was different in pattern from living ape brains and that the difference may be related to the beginnings of language. Furthermore, in the living human brain, the enlargement is related primarily to the evolution of language and related activity (Deacon, 1997). Following my second rule, the Ockham's razor that tells us that the amount of brain should be minimized for any adaptation, the implication is that something happened when the hominids evolved that made it more economical to enlarge the brain than to do anything else, and that something probably had to do with the beginnings of language. The situation is analogous to the events that differentiated mammals from therapsids, the entry into a nocturnal niche that required expansion of nonvisual neural systems. Our thought problem is, therefore, to identify the niches open to the first hominids and differentiate them from niches occupied by their cousins that remained proper apes.

The events are from about 5 ma, the beginning of the Pliocene, according to the current consensus about the final branching of the hominoids into hominids and pongids. There is a good environmental event that could have required unusual adaptations, a major climatic change related to the drying of the Mediterranean Sea and the expansion of desert and savannah at the expense of rain forest in northern Africa (Pilbeam, 1984). Although morphological evidence indicates that the earliest hominids remained competent tree dwellers (Tobias & Clarke, 1996), my scenario sees their adaptation as discovering a niche for increased predation to supplement the omnivorous diet that still characterizes at least some great apes. (Gorillas remain pure herbivores, but chimpanzees are known to feast on an occasional monkey. In the laboratory one feeds one's simian subjects an occasional bit of liver, and they do enjoy it.) That niche, coupled with the strange simian reduction in the olfactory bulbs, is the basis for my scenario. I see the first hominids as discovering the niche for social predators and model the niche after that of living wolves.

To reconstruct that environment, imagine the range of the hominoids (hominids and apes) of 5 ma as similar to that of living chimpanzees and gorillas, living in the rain forest and near grassy plains. With the drought that reduced the rain forest, some populations living at the edge of the forested region, and like most of their conspecifics feeding on an occasional rodent or monkey, could improve their diets by preying more extensively on other animals. The present daily range of chimpanzees and gorillas is only a few hundred square meters, although they wander through much wider areas. Wolves, which are the model social predators for my analysis, have daily ranges of many square kilometers (Peters & Mech, 1975), and this extended range is one requirement for a successful predator. Potential prey are not as concentrated as leaves, fruits, and grasses, and the predator must hunt them down and know where to hunt. Like Olton's rats, a proper predator must have a map of its range in its head and be able to work with that map.

The adaptational problem faced by the hero or heroine of this scenario was to navigate a much more extensive range than that normal for a simian primate. The problem is more severe than one might guess. The map in the head is mediated by a neural system, often identified as hippocampal (O'Keefe & Nadel, 1978) but clearly also involving important olfactory inputs. Wolves manage their range by an elaborate scent-marking system, and sensory analysis involving olfactory codes about which we, as proper primates, have no intuitive understanding. Laboratory studies (Eisenberg, 1981) indicate that olfactory cues in effect name names for an animal, and from the way dogs (as domesticated wolves) mark their territories and sniff out information on other animals, we sense that these cues are more meaningful to them than to us. Our sense is poor because our olfactory bulbs, which, were we normal mammals, would be comparable in size to those of wolves (about 5 ml in volume), are a fraction of that size (about 0.1 ml in volume). To adapt to the environment of a social predator, hominids had to discover other sense modalities to do for their mapmaking system what olfaction does for wolves.

For my scenario, the earliest hominids used primarily the auditory channel to "mark" their range, in a sense talking to themselves to remember objects that they had already identified with the excellent diurnal primate visual system with which they were endowed. The naming could not be with a fixed-action-pattern adaptation because the objects in their external world would differ from hunt to hunt. Yet the requirement would not be for unusually large amounts of additional processing capacity. All that would be required is a single vocal pattern to encode a bit of the external world. I would imagine a small increase in processing capacity in auditory "association" cortex, where the signals would arrive, as well as circuitry to connect that to the brain's various visual systems to ensure that encoding was working, and finally circuits to the mapping system of the brain, which would include the "old cortex" hippocampal system. There would be almost no measurable encephalization that could be identified with this kind of adaptation.

Note that I do not relate this adaptation to the development of a communications system, to social organization, or to learning ability. All mammals communicate with conspecifics about many matters, and the communication is controlled by brain systems that need not be very extensive. The codes are limited and close to fixed-action patterns. Warning signals by deer, in which the tail is flapped to reveal a white flag as it were, are typical examples, and these seem to be inherited behavior patterns. Even the famous examples of signals among vervet monkeys (Cheney & Seyfarth, 1990), which are developed as the animals mature, appear to have a major FAP base in that the same code is available early in development to all normal monkeys, although it is shaped by experience. Communication is not a dimension of animal behavior that normally requires a large brain. The same is true for social behavior and interactions, and the same is true for the fundamentals of learning. What does require an enlarged brain is the integrative knowledge about the environment, and this is the kind of information that goes into a map.

That communication or social behavior does not require enlarged brains does not mean that they might not benefit from an enlarged brain. The initial enlargement of the brain in hominids, according to my scenario, had to do only with supporting a new habit, predation, but it could have secondary effects on other adaptations. If I am correct in assigning a role to vocalization and audition for marking a territory, this role would have an immediate effect on other behavior. The model for the effect is in behavior of echolocating bats. When these animals hunt for insects, they emit sound signals that echo from their prey, and they use the echoes to locate the prey and eventually eat them. Bats hunt in very large numbers, and the evidence now is that echoes from a signal emitted by one bat can be used by another bat to locate prey. It is a kind of communication. If our first hominids marked their territory vocally and one of their fellows was within hearing distance, the mark would also stimulate the fellow. They could communicate. The communication would have a feature that most animal communication lacks. Instead of merely commanding an action or directing attention to an event in the external environment, the sound that marked the territory would be recorded as an event in the listener's environment, much like that in the vocalizer's. Communication would occur by sharing mental images.

This pretty much completes my scenario. I see language as having begun as a vocal marking system related to the construction of a map of an extended range analogous to the scent-marking system of wolves that enables them to navigate their range. That the system could be used for direct communication of mental images made it a potential communications system for hominids. The effect might have been immediate, but to incorporate it into genetic systems takes time. From the fossil data the time was a few million years with progress toward improving the system as a communications system but always with the feature that what was communicated was mental imagery, one's knowledge of the external world.

Although it is obviously speculative, this evolutionary insight identifies language as fundamentally a cognitive–perceptual adaptation, which was preadaptive for the human style of communication. It may clarify our understanding of studies of "language" in chimpanzees, which I enclose with quotation marks to suggest a fundamental difference from human language. Like other laboratory studies of animal abilities, those on ape language are tests of the extent to which the processing capacity that has evolved in apes can be used to do what language does for people. And like laboratory studies of all animal abilities, we are properly impressed with the extent to which the animals succeed at the job we give them. But there is no reason to assume that when an ape communicates about a "water bird" (using sign language for "water" in conjunction with other signs for "bird" to identify a duck; see Fouts & Mills, 1997) that the neural mechanisms are the same as when a child uses words in the same way. On the other hand, we should recognize that the roots of language may be shared by humans and apes, and that, in fact, the neural mechanisms may be similar.

The scenario is easy to develop further, but I can conclude by suggesting a simple experiment and a final remark on language and intelligence. One can perform brain scans with chimpanzees much as in humans. The human language areas are localized grossly by such scans, and brain activation can be explored in language-trained apes, much as it is in humans. One can compare the patterns of activity and then decide whether the neural systems are likely to be homologous in apes and humans. One vexing problem for analysis is the evolution of lateralization of the language areas. As identified by gross anatomy, the brain structures are similar in extent in the two halves of the brain, but one typically identifies only one half with language as conventionally understood. If scans show ape "language" as lateralized, it would be evidence for a homology with human language.

I have no scenario to explain the lateralization of language functions, which is reflected structurally in some brain asymmetry but not in a significant difference between of the two hemispheres of the brain in overall size. It is easier to treat the hemispheres as having become enlarged in humans in a balanced way, involving a perceptual–cognitive capacity that includes verbal language as typically localized primarily in the left hemisphere and a Gestalt-like "other" representational (language) system in the right hemisphere. The unique adaptation that we call human intelligence may then be the broadly defined language as a perceptual–cognitive adaptation.

Although variation is the basis of Darwinian natural selection, evolutionary analysis contributes little to understanding variations in human intelligence. The fossil record has nothing to contribute to that topic, nor can we learn much from the literature on variation in human brain size. The politically charged debates on the topic make it difficult to discuss as a scientific issue (cf. Gould, 1981; Herrnstein & Murray, 1994; Kamin, 1974; Rushton, 1995; Wilson, 1978). There are real race differences in brain size (Rushton, 1995), if one defines race sociologically rather than genetically to be politically correct, but it is difficult to know what to make of them. There are larger and more interesting, but also more perplexing, sex differences in brain size. Men's brains are about 130 g heavier (about 1 SD) than women's. Pakkenberg & Gundersen (1997) report the number of neocortical neurons in men and women: about 22.8 billion in men and 19.3 billion in women. Brain size is not related to body size in humans, and the sex difference in brain size cannot be explained on the basis of body size or composition. There is a significant effect of age, which indicates that about 10% of the brain's neurons are lost during a normal lifetime. Within a race, within a sex, and within an age group there is a correlation of about .4 between brain size and IQ (Willerman et al., 1990). These are the facts. Sex differences in intelligence are so difficult to evaluate that psychometricians in effect assume no difference and adjust test items to produce parity. Race differences, which, from the brain size data should be much smaller, are simply not discussable in any scientific forum. At best such differences would be relevant for judgments about populations rather than individuals, and as a society we are not capable of distinguishing between such judgments. (Perhaps a school curriculum forcing all of us to learn statistics might help, but one foresees objections.) My personal view is that, until the scientific problems are better understood, the issue is political and that this works reasonably well in democracies if each affected group is prepared to protect itself from negative discrimination by appropriate political pressure.

REFERENCES

Aiello, L. C., & Wheeler, P. (1995). The expensive-tissue hypothesis: The brain and the digestive system in human and primate evolution. *Current Anthropology, 36,* 199–221.

Alexander, R. M. (1989). *Dynamics of dinosaurs and other extinct giants.* New York: Columbia University Press.

Allin, E. F. (1975). Evolution of the mammalian middle ear. *Journal of Morphology, 147,* 403–438.

Allin, E. F. (1986). The auditory apparatus of advanced mammal-like reptiles and early mammals. In N. Hotton III, P. D. MacLean, J. J. Roth, and E. C. Roth (Eds.), *The evolution and ecology of mammal-like reptiles* (pp. 283–294). Washington, DC: Smithsonian Institution Press.

Bickerton, D. (1990). *Language and species.* Chicago: University of Chicago Press.

Bitterman, M. E. (1988). Vertebrate-invertebrate comparisons. In H. J. Jerison and I. L. Jerison (Eds.), *Intelligence and evolutionary biology* (pp. 251–276). Berlin: Springer-Verlag.

Braitenberg, V., & Schüz, A. (1991). *Anatomy of the cortex: Statistics and geometry.* Berlin: Springer-Verlag.

Bullock, T. H. (1993). *How do brains work?* Boston: Birkhauser.

Buss, D. M. (1994). The strategies of human mating. *American Scientist, 82,* 238–249.

Butler, A. B., & Hodos, W. (1996). *Comparative vertebrate neuroanatomy.* New York: Wiley-Liss.

Byrne, J. H. (1987). Aplysia, associative modification of individual neurons. In G. Adelman (Ed.), *Encyclopedia of neuroscience* (Vol. 1, pp. 65–67).

Carroll, J. B. (1997). Psychometrics, intelligence, and public perception. *Intelligence, 24,* 25–52.

Carroll, R. L. (1988). *Vertebrate paleontology and evolution.* New York: Freeman.

Cheney, D. L., & Seyfarth, R. M. (1990). *How monkeys see the world: Inside the mind of another species.* Chicago: University of Chicago Press.

Coon, C. S. (1962). *The origin of races.* New York: Alfred A. Knopf.

Davis, P. J. M., & Wright, E. A. (1977). A new method for measuring cranial cavity volume and its application to the assessment of cerebral atrophy at autopsy. *Neuropathology and Applied Neurobiology, 3,* 341–358.

Dawkins, R. (1987). *The blind watchmaker.* New York: Norton.

Dawkins, R., & Krebs, J. R. (1979). Arms races between and within species. *Proceedings of the Royal Society (London), 205B,* 489–511.

Deacon, T. W. (1997). *The symbolic species: The co-evolution of language and the brain.* New York: W. W. Norton.

Dennett, D. C. (1995). *Darwin's dangerous idea.* New York: Simon & Schuster.

Diamond, I. T. (1979). The subdivisions of the neocortex: A proposal to revise the traditional view of sensory, motor, and association areas. *Progress in Psychobiology and Physiological Psychology, 8,* 1–43.

Donald, M. (1991). *Origins of the modern mind.* New York: Basic Books.

Doolittle, R. F., Feng, D.-F., Tsang, G., & Cho, E. Little. (1996). Determining divergence times of the major kingdoms of living organisms with a protein clock. *Science, 271*, 470–480.

Eisenberg, J. F. (1981). *The mammalian radiations.* Chicago: University of Chicago Press.

Ewert, J. P. (1974). The neural basis of visually guided behavior. *Scientific American, 230*, 34–42.

Falk, D. (1987). Hominid paleoneurology. *Annual Review of Anthropology, 16*, 13–30.

Feduccia, A. (1993). Evidence from claw geometry indicating arboreal habits of *Archaeopteryx. Science, 259*, 790–793.

Feduccia, A. (1996). *The origin and evolution of birds.* New Haven: Yale University Press.

Fouts, R., & Mills, S. T. (1997). *Next of kin: What chimpanzees have taught me about who we are.* New York: Morrow.

Goldman-Rakic, P. S. (1988). Topography of cognition: Parallel distributed networks in primate association cortex. *Annual Review of Neurosciences, 11*, 137–166.

Gould, S. J. (1981). *The mismeasure of man.* New York: Norton.

Greenfield, P. M. (1991). Language, tools and brain: The ontogeny and phylogeny of hierarchically organized sequential behavior. *Behavioral and Brain Sciences, 14*, 531–595.

Grinnell, A. D. (1995). Hearing in bats: an overview. In R. R. Fay & A. M. Popper (Eds.), *Hearing by bats.* (pp. 1–36). Heidelberg: Springer-Verlag.

Harlow, H. F. (1949). The formation of learning sets. *Psychological Review, 56*, 51–65.

Harvey, P. H., & Pagel, M. D. (1991). *The comparative method in evolutionary biology.* Oxford: Oxford University Press.

Herrnstein, R. J. (1985). Riddles of natural categorization. *Philosophical Transactions of the Royal Society (London), B 308*, 129–144.

Herrnstein, R. J., & Murray, C. (1994). *The bell curve: Intelligence and class structure in American life.* New York: Free Press.

Hodos, W. (1988). Comparative neuroanatomy and the evolution of intelligence. In H. J. Jerison & I. Jerison (Eds.), *Intelligence and evolutionary biology.* New York: Springer-Verlag.

Hopson, J. A. (1979). Paleoneurology. In C. Gans, R. G. Northcutt, & P. Ulinski (Eds.), *Biology of the reptilia* (Vol. 9. pp. 39–146). New York: Academic Press.

Horn, G. (1985). *Memory, imprinting, and the brain.* Oxford: Clarendon Press.

Horner, J. R., & Gorman, J. (1988). *Digging dinosaurs.* New York: Harper & Row.

Humphreys, L. G. (1985). General intelligence. In B. Wolman (Ed.), *Handbook of intelligence.* New York: Wiley.

Hunt, E. (1983). Intelligence on intelligence [Review of the book *Handbook of human intelligence* (1st ed.)] *Contemporary Psychology, 28*, 901–903.

Jerison, H. J. (1973). *Evolution of the brain and intelligence.* New York: Academic Press.

Jerison, H. J. (1982). The evolution of biological intelli-gence. In R. J. Sternberg (Ed.), *Handbook of human intelligence* (pp. 723–791). New York: Cambridge University Press.

Jerison, H. J. (1985). Issues in brain evolution. *Oxford Surveys in Evolutionary Biology, 2*, 102–134.

Jerison, H. J. (1990). Fossil evidence on the evolution of the neocortex. In E. G. Jones & A. Peters (Eds.), *Cerebral cortex* (Vol. 8A, pp. 285–309). New York: Plenum.

Jerison, H. J. (1991). *Brain size and the evolution of mind: 59th James Arthur lecture on the evolution of the human brain.* New York: American Museum of Natural History.

Jerison, H. J. (1994). Evolution of the brain. In D. Zaidel (Ed.), *Neuropsychology (handbook of perception and cognition)* (2nd ed., pp. 53–82). New York: Academic Press.

Jerison, H. J. (1997). Evolution of prefrontal cortex. In N. Krasnegor, R. Lyon, & P. Goldman-Rakic (Eds.), *Development of the prefrontal cortex: Evolution, neurobiology, and behavior* (pp. 9–26). Baltimore: Paul H. Brookes Company, Inc.

Johnson, J. I. (1990). Comparative development of somatic sensory cortex. In E. G. Jones & A. Peters (Eds.), *Cerebral cortex.* (Vol. 8B, pp. 335–449). New York: Plenum.

Jones, E. G., & Powell, T. P. S. (1970). An anatomical study of converging sensory pathways within the cerebral cortex of the monkey. *Brain, 93*, 793–820.

Kamin, L. J. (1974). *The science and politics of IQ.* Hillsdale, NJ: Erlbaum.

Karten, H. J. (1991). Homology and evolutionary origins of the 'neocortex.' *Brain, Behavior and Evolution, 38*, 264–272.

Klüver, H. (1933). *Behavior mechanisms in monkeys.* Chicago: University of Chicago Press.

Lashley, K. S. (1949). Persistent problems in the evolution of mind. *Quarterly Review of Biology, 24*, 28–42.

Lettvin, J. Y., Maturana, H. R., McCulloch, W. S., & Pitts, W. H. (1959). What the frog's eye tells the frog's brain. *Proc. Institute of Radio Engineers, 47*, 1940–1951. (Also in McCulloch, W. S. (1965). *Embodiment of mind.* pp. 230–255. Cambridge, MA, MIT Press.)

Lieberman, P. (1984). *The biology and evolution of language.* Cambridge: Harvard University Press.

Macphail, E. M. (1982). *Brain and intelligence in vertebrates.* Oxford: Clarendon.

Manouvrier, L.-P. (1883). Sur l'interpretation de la quantité dans l'encéphale et dans le cerveau en particulier. *Bulletin de la Société d'Anthropologie, Paris, 3*, 137–323.

Martin, R. D. (1981). Relative brain size and basal metabolic rate in terrestrial vertebrates. *Nature, 293*, 57–60.

Martin, R. D. (1983). *Human brain evolution in ecological context. James Arthur lecture on the evolution of the human brain.* New York: American Museum of Natural History.

Martin, R. D. (1990). *Primate origins and evolution: A phylogenetic reconstruction.* London: Chapman & Hall.

Merzenich, M. M., & Kaas, J. H. (1980). Principles of organization of sensory-perceptual systems in mammals.

Progress in Psychobiology and Physiological Psychology, 9, 1–42.

Minsky, M. (1985). *The society of mind.* New York: Simon & Schuster.

Mlikovsky, J. (1977). *Beitrage zur Evolution des Vogelgehirnes* (Doctoral dissertation, Martin Luther Universitaet, Halle, 1977). (Copy on deposit, Biomedical Library, UCLA, Los Angeles.)

Morgane, P. J., Jacobs, M. S., & Galaburda, A. (1986). Evolutionary morphology of the dolphin brain. In R. J. Schusterman, J. A. Thomas, & F. G. Wood (Eds.), *Dolphin cognition and behavior: A comparative approach.* Hillsdale, NJ: Erlbaum.

O'Keefe, J., and Nadel, L. (1978). *The hippocampus as a cognitive map.* Oxford: Oxford University Press.

Olton, D. S. (1985). The temporal context of spatial memory. *Philosophical Transactions of the Royal Society (London), B308*, 79–86.

Pakkenberg, B., & Gundersen, H. J. G. (1997). Neocortical neuron number in humans: Effect of sex and age. *Journal of Comparative Neurology, 385*, 312–320.

Passingham, R. E. (1982). *The human primate.* San Francisco: Freeman.

Pepperberg, I. M. (1994). Vocal learning in African grey parrots: Effects of social interaction. *Auk, 111*, 300–313.

Peters, R. P., & Mech, L. D. (1975). Scent-marking in wolves. *American Scientist, 63*, 628–637.

Petrill, S. A. (1997). Molarity versus modularity of cognitive functioning? A behavioral genetic perspective. *Current Directions in Psychological Science, 6*, 96–99.

Pilbeam, D. (1984). The descent of the hominoids and the hominids. *Scientific American, 250*(3), 84–96.

Pinker, S. (1994). *The language instinct: How the mind creates language.* New York: William Morrow & Co.

Platel, R. (1979). Brain weight – body weight relationships. In C. Gans, R. G. Northcutt, & P. Ulinski (Eds.), *Biology of the reptilia* (Vol. 9, pp. 147–171). New York: Academic Press.

Polyak, S. (1957). *The vertebrate visual system.* H. Kluver (Ed.). Chicago: University of Chicago Press.

Posner, M. I. (1994). *Images of mind.* New York: Scientific American Library.

Ridet, J. M., & Bauchot, R. (1990). Analyse quantitative de l'encéphale des Téléostéens: Charactres évolutifs et adaptifs de l'encéphalization. III. Analyze multivarieé des indices encéphaliques. *Journal für Hirnforschungen, 33*, 383–393.

Rockel, A. J., Hiorns, R. W., & Powell, T. P. S. (1980). The basic uniformity in structure of the neocortex. *Brain, 103*; 221–244.

Roth, G. (1987). *Visual behavior in salamanders.* New York: Springer-Verlag.

Rumbaugh, D. M. (1997). Competence, cortex, and primate models: A comparative primate perspective. In N. A. Krasnegor, G. R. Lyon, & P. S. Goldman-Rakic, (Eds.), *Development of the prefrontal cortex: Evolution, neu-*

robiology, and behavior (pp. 17–139). Baltimore: Paul H. Brookes Publishing Co.

Rushton, J. P. (1995). *Race, evolution, and behavior: A life history perspective.* New Brunswick, NJ, Transaction Publishers.

Savage, R. J. G., & Long, M. R. (1986). *Mammal evolution: An illustrated guide.* London: British Museum (Natural History).

Savage-Rumbaugh, E. S., Murphy, J., Sevcik, R. A., Brakke, K. E., Williams, S. L., & Rumbaugh, D. M. (1993). Language comprehension in ape and child. *Monographs of the Society for Research in Child Development, 58* (3–4); 1–254.

Schopf, J. W. (Ed.). (1992). *Major events in the history of life.* Boston: Jones and Bartlett.

Schüz, A., & Demianenko, G. P. (1995). Constancy and variability in cortical structure: A study on synapses and dendritic spines in hedgehog and monkey. *Journal für Hirnforschung, 36*, 113–122.

Semendeferi, K., Damasio, H., Frank, R., & Van Hoesen, G. W. (1997). The evolution of the frontal lobes: A volumetric analysis based on three dimensional reconstructions of magnetic resonance scans of human and ape brains. *Journal of Human Evolution, 32*, 375–388.

Simpson, G. G. (1970). Uniformitarianism: An inquiry into principle, theory, and method in geohistory and biohistory. In M. K. Hecht & W. C. Steere (Eds.), *Essays in evolution and genetics in honor of Theodosius Dobzhansky* (pp. 43–96). Amsterdam: North-Holland.

Skinner, B. F. (1957). The experimental analysis of behavior. *American Scientist, 45*, 343–371.

Slotnick, B. M., & Katz, H. M. (1974). Olfactory learning-set formation in rats. *Science, 185*, 796–798.

Squire, L. R. (1987). *Memory and the brain.* Oxford: Oxford University Press.

Stensiö, E. (1963). The brain and cranial nerves in fossil, lower craniate vertebrates. *Skrifter Utgitt Av Det Norske Videnskaps-Akademi I Oslo I. Mat.-Naturv. Klasse. NY Series.* No. 13, pp. 1–120.

Stephan, H., Frahm, H., & Baron, G. (1981). New and revised data on volumes of brain structures in insectivores and primates. *Folia Primatologica, 35*, 1–29.

Sternberg, R. J. (1985). Cognitive approaches to intelligence. In B. Wolman (Ed.), *Handbook of intelligence.* New York: Wiley.

Sternberg, R. J. (1988). *The triarchic mind: A new theory of human intelligence.* New York: Penguin Books.

Stevens, S. S. (1946). On the theory of scales and measurement. *Science, 103*, 677–680.

Stevens, S. S. (Ed.). (1951). *Handbook of experimental psychology.* Wiley: New York.

Swets, J. A. (Ed.). 1964. *Signal detection and recognition by human observers.* New York: Wiley.

Thireau, M. (1975). L'allométrie pondérale encéphalosomatique chez lez urodèles. II. Relations interspécifiques. *Bulletin du Muséum National d'Histoire Naturelle, 207*, 483–501.

Tobias, P. V., & Clarke, R. J. (1996). Faunal evidence and Sterkfonetein Member 2 footbones of early hominid: Response to J. K. McKee. *Science, 271*, 1301–1302.

Trinkaus, E., & Shipman, P. (1993). *The Neandertals: Changing the image of mankind.* New York: Alfred A. Knopf.

Tully, T., Preat, T., Boynton, S. C., & Del Vecchio, M. (1994). Genetic dissection of consolidated memory in drosophila. *Cell, 79*, 35–47.

Uylings, H. B. M., & Van Eden, C. G. (1990). Qualitative and quantitative comparison of the prefrontal cortex in rats and in primates, including humans. In H. B. M. Uylings, C. G. Van Eden, J. P. C. De Bruin, M. A. Corner, & M. G. P. Feenstra (Eds.), *Progress in brain research* (Vol. 85, pp. 31–62). Amsterdam: Elsevier.

Van Essen, D. C. (1997). A tension-based theory of morphogenesis and compact wiring in the central nervous system. *Nature, 385*:313–318.

von Uexküll, J. (1934). *Streifzüge durch die Umwelten von Tieren und Menschen.* Berlin: Springer-Verlag. Translated as "A stroll through the worlds of animals and men" In C. H. Schiller (Ed.). (1957). Instinctive behavior: The development of a modern concept (pp. 5–80). New York: International Universities Press.

Weiner, J. S. (1955). *The Piltdown forgery.* London: Oxford University Press.

Weiskrantz, L. (Ed.). (1985). *Animal intelligence.* Oxford: Clarendon Press.

Welker, W. I. (1990). Why does cerebral cortex fissure and fold? A review of determinants of gyri and sulci. In E. G. Jones & A. Peters (Eds.), *Cerebral cortex* (Vol. 8B, pp. 1–132). New York: Plenum Press.

Wever. E. G. (1978). *The reptile ear: Its structure and function.* Princeton: Princeton University Press.

Willerman, L., Schultz, R., Rutledge, J. N., & Bigler, E. D. (1991). In vivo brain size and intelligence. *Intelligence, 15*, 223–228.

Wilson, E. O. (1975). *Sociobiology: The new synthesis.* Cambridge: Harvard University Press.

Wilson, E. O. (1978). *On human nature.* Cambridge: Harvard University Press.

Worthy, G. A. J., & Hickie, J. P. (1986). Relative brain size in marine mammals. *American Naturalist, 128*, 445–459.

Young, J. Z. (1962). *The life of vertebrates* (2nd ed.). New York: Oxford University Press.

Zangerl, R., & Case, G. R. (1976). *Cobelodus aculeatus* (Cope), an anacanthous shark from Pennsylvanian black shales of North America. *Palaeontographica A, 154*, 107–157.

Zeki, S. (1993). *A Vision of the brain.* London: Blackwell.

CHAPTER TWELVE

The Neuropsychology and Psychophysiology of Human Intelligence

PHILIP A. VERNON, JOHN C. WICKETT, P. GORDON BAZANA, AND ROBERT M. STELMACK

Since the time of Sir Francis Galton and throughout the 20th century, numerous researchers interested in human intelligence have attempted to identify its biological bases. Some of these attempts have seemed promising at first but have either failed to replicate or have not been pursued for one reason or another; others have yielded a more consistent and reliable pattern of results.

In this chapter, four approaches to the investigation of biological correlates of intelligence* are described covering (1) anatomical or structural head size and brain volume estimates, (2) psychophysiological event-related potentials, (3) nerve conduction velocity, and (4) cerebral glucose metabolic rates. These are not the only approaches that have been taken to investigate the biology of intelligence, but their description should suffice to give an introduction to the area; coverage of such additional topics as biochemical factors and molecular genetic studies of quantitative trait loci may be found in Vernon (1993a, 1997).

One of the most interesting findings from studies in these areas is the extent to which completely noncognitive measures correlate with performance on complex problem-solving and intelligence tests. Offsetting these encouraging empirical results, however, has been a relative dearth of sound theory development. A substantial amount is currently

known about *which* biological and physiological measures and mechanisms correlate with intelligence, but the functional significance of many of these correlations largely remains unclear. One of the central challenges for scientists who pursue the search for the biological bases of human intelligence will be to integrate their findings into a cohesive explanatory framework that goes beyond the correlational and incorporates causational and theoretically compelling substance.

HEAD SIZE, BRAIN VOLUME AND INTELLIGENCE

Interest in the possible relation between the size of the brain and intelligence dates back at least to the time of Broca (1861) and was brought into the realm of psychology with the work of Galton (1888). This early research, however, was hampered by the absence of appropriate statistical techniques (for example, the correlation coefficient had not yet been developed) and by the absence of reliable means of measuring intelligence. Also missing in these early years were means of assessing brain volume in a living human being, and so many studies focused on head size instead. As it turns out, the assumption that external head size can serve as a proxy for brain volume is not unreasonable: Correlations between the two are about .60 in adults (Hoadley, 1929; Wickett, Vernon, & Lee, 1999; though see Wickett, Vernon, & Lee, 1994 for a lower estimate) and above .90 in infants and children (Bray, Shields, Wolcott, & Madsen, 1969; Dobbing & Sands, 1978; Lemons, Schreiner, & Gresham, 1981).

---

* Although there is undoubtedly more to human intelligence than is captured by an IQ test score, the terms *intelligence* and *IQ* are used more or less interchangeably in this chapter to reflect the fact that the majority of the studies reviewed here have operationally defined intelligence as performance on IQ or similar tests.

Table 12.1 summarizes the key findings of all published studies dating from 1906 to 1998 that have reported correlations between head size and one or more estimates of mental ability. To avoid reporting multiple values from the same sample, only one estimate from each sample was chosen. However, when studies reported correlations from independent samples (e.g., separately for males and females), these are included in Table 12.1. Where several measures of cognitive ability were reported, standardized IQ test scores were chosen first. In the absence of an IQ score, a test of vocabulary or language

TABLE 12.1. Key Findings in the Head Size and IQ Literature

Study	n Sample	Size Measure	IQ Measure	r[a]
Pearl (1906)	935 soldiers ♂	Perimeter	Officers' estimate	.14
Pearson (1906)	1,011 Cambridge graduates ♂	Length	University grades	.11
Pearson (1906)	2,398 age 4 to 20 ♂	Length	Teachers' estimate	.14*
Pearson (1906)	2,188 age 3 to 20 ♀	Length	Teachers' estimate	.08*
Murdoch & Sullivan (1923)	291 age 6 to 18 ♂	Diameter	Various IQ tests	.20
Murdoch & Sullivan (1923)	305 age 6 to 18 ♀	Diameter	Various IQ tests	.27
Reid & Mulligan (1923)	449 medical students ♂	Capacity	University grades	.08
Sommerville (1924)	105 university students ♂♀	Capacity	Thorndike	.08
Estabrooks (1928)	172 age 7 ♂	Capacity	Dearborn A	.23
Estabrooks (1928)	207 age 7 ♀	Capacity	Dearborn A	.16
Wrzosek (1931)[b]	160 medical students ♂	Capacity	Baley	.14
Porteus (1937)	200 children	Perimeter	Porteus Maze	.20
Clark et al. (1961)[c]	36 age 12 to 20 ♂	Perimeter	Raven's Matrices	.18
Clark et al. (1961)[c]	43 age 12 to 20 ♀	Perimeter	Raven's Matrices	.05
Robinow (1968)[d]	300 age 3 to 13 ♂♀	Perimeter	Various IQ tests	.18*
Schreider (1968)	80 adult Otomi Indians	Perimeter	Form Board	.39
Schreider (1968)	158 French farmers	Perimeter	Raven's Matrices	.23
Nelson & Deutschberger (1970)[c]	1,511 age 4 ♂♀ (W)	Perimeter	Stanford–Binet	.14
Nelson & Deutschberger (1970)[c]	1,903 age 4 ♂♀ (B)	Perimeter	Stanford–Binet	.16
Klein et al. (1972)	172 age 3 to 6 ♂	Perimeter	Language Tests	.23
Klein et al. (1972)	170 age 3 to 6 ♀	Perimeter	Language Tests	.29
Susanne & Sporcq (1973)	2,071 Belgian conscripts ♂	Perimeter	Raven's Matrices	.19
Weinberg et al. (1974)	334 age 8 to $9\frac{1}{2}$ ♂	Perimeter	WISC	.35
Passingham (1979)	415 adult English villagers ♂♀	Capacity	WAIS	.13
Pollitt et al. (1982)	91 age 3 to 6 ♂♀	Perimeter	Stanford–Binet	.23
Swan et al. (?)[e]	547 children	Perimeter	Various IQ Tests	.11*
Swan & Miszkiewicz (?)[f]	843 age 5 to 18	Perimeter	PMA	.08*
Majluf (1983)	120 age 8 to 20 mo. ♂♀	Perimeter	Bayley MDI	.35
Ounsted et al. (1984)	214 age 4 ♂♀	Perimeter	Language Test	.06[‡]
Ounsted et al. (1984)	167 age 4 ♂♀	Perimeter	Language Test	.07[‡]
Henneberg et al. (1985)	151 medical students ♂	Capacity	Baley	.09
Henneberg et al. (1985)	151 medical students ♀	Capacity	Baley	.19
Sen et al. (1986)	150 age 16 to 18 ♂♀	Perimeter	Raven's Matrices	.02
Sen et al. (1986)	150 age 16 to 18 ♂♀	Perimeter	Raven's Matrices	.54
Broman et al. (1987)	17,232 age 7 ♂♀ (W)	Perimeter	WISC	.24
Broman et al. (1987)	18,907 age 7 ♂♀ (B)	Perimeter	WISC	.19
Ernhart (1987)	257 age 3 ♂♀	Perimeter	Stanford–Binet	.12
Bogaert & Rushton (1989)	216 university students ♂♀	Perimeter	MAB	.14
Lynn (1989)	161 age 9 to 10 ♂	Perimeter	PMA	.15
Lynn (1989)	149 age 9 to 10 ♀	Perimeter	PMA	.23
Lynn (1990)	205 age 9 ♂♀	Perimeter	Raven's Matrices	.26
Lynn (1990)	91 age 9 ♂♀	Perimeter	Raven's Matrices	.26
Osborne (1992)	106 age 12 to 18 ♂ (W)	Perimeter	Test Battery	.16
Osborne (1992)	84 age 12 to 18 ♂ (B)	Perimeter	Test Battery	.34

Study	n Sample	Size Measure	IQ Measure	r^a
Osborne (1992)	118 age 12 to 18 ♀ (W)	Perimeter	Test Battery	.23
Osborne (1992)	168 age 12 to 18 ♀ (B)	Perimeter	Test Battery	.13
Rushton (1992)	73 university students ♂♀ (O)	Perimeter	MAB	.14
Rushton (1992)	211 university students ♂♀ (W)	Perimeter	MAB	**.21**
Lynn & Jindal (1993)	100 age 8½ to 10½ ♂	Perimeter	Raven's Matrices	.14
Lynn & Jindal (1993)	100 age 8½ to 10½ ♀	Perimeter	Raven's Matrices	.25
Reed & Jensen (1993)	211 college/university ♂	Capacity	Raven's Matrices	.02
Wickett et al. (1994)	40 random adult sample ♀	Perimeter	MAB	.11
Rushton (in press)	98 age 7 ♂♀ (O)	Perimeter	WISC	.21
Wickett et al. (1999)	68 random adult sample ♂	Perimeter	MAB	.18

Adult Populations:	Child/Adolescent Populations:	All Populations:
17 samples	37 samples	54 samples
$N = 6,505$	$N = 50,288$	$N = 56,793$
Unweighted Mean $r = .151$	Unweighted Mean $r = .195$	Unweighted Mean $r = .181$
n-Weighted Mean $r = .149$	n-Weighted Mean $r = .197$	n-Weighted Mean $r = .191$

Note: Correlations printed in bold are significant at least at the $\alpha = .05$ level (two-tailed). Where information is not specified, it was also missing in the source. Abbreviations are as follows: ♂ (males), ♀ (females), ♂♀ (males and females), **W** (Whites—if indicated in the study), **B** (Blacks—if indicated in the study), **O** (Orientals—if indicated in the study), **diameter** ($\frac{1}{2}$ of length plus width), **capacity** (brain volume estimated by formula based on external head measurements), **WISC** (Wechsler Intelligence Scale for Children), **WAIS** (Wechsler Adult Intelligence Scale), **PMA** (Primary Mental Abilities), **MAB** (Multidimensional Aptitude Battery).

[a] Unless otherwise noted (with a superscript), all correlations are unadjusted Pearson product moment correlations between the head measure and the IQ measure. Variables partialled out of correlations are referred to as follows: *age, †sex, ‡social class.

[b] Cited in Henneberg et al. (1985, Table 4, p. 213).

[c] Correlations are derived from tabular data provided in the source.

[d] Cited in Jensen and Sinha (1993, Table 4.10, p. 196).

[e] Cited as Swan, Haskins and Douglas (in press) in Cattell (1982, Table 2.10, p. 38).

[f] Cited as unpublished paper in Jensen and Sinha (1993, Table 4.10, p. 196).

comprehension was selected before tests of other abilities. Only when no other measures were reported were ratings of ability (such as teachers' ratings) used. When more than one measure of head size was reported, the perimeter was preferred (being the most frequently reported), followed by capacity and then length. Corrections for body size are not included because most studies do not include this information; however, when corrections for age or sex were reported, these have been included. In total, the results from 35 studies, comprising 54 independent samples and 56,793 subjects, are summarized.

The most striking finding in Table 12.1 is the absence of a single negative head size–ability correlation among the 54 reported. Across all samples, correlations range from .02 to .54 with an n-weighted mean of .19. Thirty-six of the 54 correlations are statistically significant beyond the .05 level, and the

average correlation of .19 yields $Z = 46.27$ ($p < 1 \times 10^{-466}$). Among 17 adult samples (total $n = 6,505$), the n-weighted correlation is .15; among 37 child and adolescent samples (total $n = 50,288$), the n-weighted correlation is .20. It is probable that the samples of children represented a broader range of ability than the adults, and this likely contributes to the higher correlation among the children. Given that none of the correlations in Table 12.1 have been corrected for attenuation owing to unreliability or for restriction of range, it does not seem unreasonable to propose that the true population correlation between head size and intelligence in humans is no less than .20.

With the advent of computerized axial tomography (CT) and magnetic resonance imaging (MRI) it became possible to obtain in vivo estimates of brain volume. Table 12.2 summarizes the key results of 14 studies conducted to date, comprising 16 samples

TABLE 12.2. Key Findings in the Brain Volume and IQ Literature

Study	n Sample	Age Range[a]	Brain Measure	Cognitive Measure	r[b]
Yeo et al. (1987)	41 outpatients ♂♀	18 to 70	CT–brain	WAIS FSIQ	.07*
DeMyer et al. (1988)	23 local ♂♀	18 to 44	MRI–two slices	WAIS VIQ	.11[c]
Pearlson et al. (1989)	84 staff, visitors, local ♂♀	19 to 59	CT–one slice	SES	**.35**[d]
Willerman et al. (1991)	20 undergraduates ♂	18 to 21	MRI–brain	WAIS-R FSIQ	**.51**
Willerman et al. (1991)	20 undergraduates ♀	18 to 21	MRI–brain	WAIS-R FSIQ	.33
Andreasen et al. (1993)	37 local ♂	18 to 75	MRI–brain	WAIS-R FSIQ	**.40**[†]
Andreasen et al. (1993)	30 local ♀	18 to 75	MRI–brain	WAIS-R FSIQ	**.44**[†]
Raz et al. (1993)	29 unspecified ♂♀	18 to 78	MRI–brain	CFIT	**.43**
Castellanos et al. (1994)	46 local children ♂	5 to 18	MRI–brain	WISC-R Vocabulary	**.33**
Egan et al. (1994, 1995)	40 military ♂♀	18 to 35	MRI–brain	WAIS-R FSIQ	**.31**
Harvey et al. (1994)	34 staff, local ♂♀	19 to 49	MRI–brain	Premorbid IQ[e]	**.69**
Jones et al. (1994)	67 staff, local ♂♀	18 to 50	CT–four slices	Verbal IQ[f]	**.25**
Wickett et al. (1994)	40 local ♀	20 to 30	MRI–brain	MAB FSIQ	**.40**
Kareken et al. (1995)	68 unspecified ♂♀	18 to 45	MRI–brain	Verbal Tests	**.24**
Reiss et al. (1996)	69 local children ♂♀	5 to 17	MRI–brain	Unspecified IQ Test	**.45**[g]
Wickett et al. (1999)	68 local siblings ♂	20 to 35	MRI–brain	MAB FSIQ	**.35**

All studies:[h]

15 samples
$N = 647$
Unweighted Mean $r = .347$
n-Weighted Mean $r = .334$

Studies with explicitly normal populations and full brain measure:[h]

11 samples
$N = 432$
Unweighted Mean $r = .403$
n-Weighted Mean $r = .381$

Note: Correlations printed in bold are significant at least at the $\alpha = .05$ level (two-tailed). Abbreviations are as follows: **local** (volunteers from local population), **staff** (hospital employees), **visitors** (hospital visitors), ♂ (males), ♀ (females), ♂♀ (males and females), **CT** (computerized axial tomography), **MRI** (magnetic resonance imaging), **brain** (brain volume), **WAIS** (Wechsler Adult Intelligence Scale), **SES** (socioeconomic status), **WAIS-R** (Wechsler Adult Intelligence Scale – Revised), **CFIT** (Cattell Culture Fair Intelligence Test), **WISC-R** (Wechsler Intelligence Scale for Children – Revised), **MAB** (Multidimensional Aptitude Battery).

[a] Age range in years is either as presented in the original article or a rough approximation based on the mean and standard deviation presented in the original article.

[b] Unless otherwise noted (with a superscript), all correlations are unadjusted Pearson product moment correlations between the volume measure and the IQ measure. Variables partialled out of correlations are referred to as follows: *number of slices, [†]height.

[c] Mean of four correlations (left and right hemisphere on each slice).

[d] Value is η derived from F-test.

[e] New Adult Reading Test.

[f] New Adult Reading Test or Verbal subtests of the Wechsler Adult Intelligence Scale.

[g] Value is R based on regression equation, including a quadratic component, with sex effects removed before regression.

[h] The Reiss et al. (1996) multiple correlation value is excluded from these computations.

and 716 subjects, that have correlated CT or MRI brain volume estimates with IQ scores. Note that, in contrast to most of the head size studies reported in Table 12.1, the majority of the Table 12.2 studies not only measured brain volume directly but also entailed administering standardized IQ tests.

Brain volume–IQ correlations in Table 12.2 range from .07 to .69 and yield an *n*-weighted mean of

.35. Thirteen of the 16 correlations are significant beyond the .05 level. Focusing just on those studies that tested explicitly normal populations (as compared with samples of patients, for example) and that obtained full brain measures, yields 11 samples comprising 432 subjects from which the *n*-weighted average brain volume–IQ correlation is .38. Unless noted otherwise in Table 12.2, corrections for body size have *not* been made; contrary to what is sometimes claimed, no study of brain volume (or head size) has shown a substantial decrement in correlation after partialling out either height or weight (or both), and some studies have actually reported higher brain volume–IQ correlations after controlling for body size (e.g., Willerman, Schultz, Rutledge, & Bigler, 1991). Corrections for restriction of range in IQ have also not been applied to any of the correlations in Table 12.2; if they had been, it seems likely that the true population brain volume–IQ correlation would have been no less than .40.

Additional findings from the Table 12.2 studies are also of interest. For example, the brain volume–IQ correlation is equally strong in males and in females (e.g., Andreasen et al., 1993; Wickett et al., 1994, 1999; Willerman et al., 1991). Age, although it plays a role in brain size and in intelligence, does not confound the results; studies using a narrow age range have shown the same magnitude of correlation (e.g., Egan, Chiswick, Santosh et al., 1994; Wickett et al., 1994, 1999; Willerman et al., 1991). Most studies have been conducted with adults, but two have shown a brain volume–IQ correlation among children (Castellanos et al., 1994; Reiss, Abrams, Singer, Ross, & Denckla, 1996). Several studies have examined whether different regions of the brain would show differential correlations with IQ; these studies appear to show that the size effects are manifest throughout the brain and not just in any particular region(s) (Andreasen et al., 1993; Egan et al., 1994; Reiss et al., 1996). With the exception of Wickett et al. (1999), there has not been a systematic examination of which types of abilities are most correlated with brain volume. Wickett et al. (1999) show that brain volume correlates most highly with *g*, fluid abilities, and memory but less (and not significantly) with crystallized ability. This is consistent with data on normal aging that indicates a decline in brain volume and in fluid ability but no change in crystallized ability with advancing years.

In Wickett et al. (1999), 34 pairs of adult male siblings (68 subjects) were administered an extensive battery of 22 paper-and-pencil or computerized intelligence, ability, and cognitive tests in addition to undergoing MRI scans to assess right and left hemi-sphere and overall brain volume. Brain volume and full-scale IQ correlated .35 in this study; this correlation rose to .51 after correction for restriction of range in IQ. Verbal and performance IQs (VIQ and PIQ, respectively) were equally highly correlated with left- and right-hemisphere volume; that is, no differential pattern of correlation emerged favoring PIQ and right hemisphere size or VIQ and left hemisphere size. Brain volume was also significantly correlated with digit span memory tests ($r = .41$ [forward span] and .27 [backward span]), a test of verbal closure ($r = .27$), a trail-making test (the ZVT; Oswald & Roth, 1978; $r = .32$), and reaction time measures of speed of information-processing in short-term ($r = -.35$) and in long-term memory ($r = -.42$) but correlated nonsignificantly with tests of visualization, spatial rotation, perceptual speed, and flexibility of closure. Scores on factors extracted from the 22 cognitive tests revealed a very interesting pattern of results: There was a high positive correlation ($r = .59$) between the *g*-loadings of the tests and the degree to which the tests correlated with brain volume. The same was true for the tests' loadings on a fluid ability factor ($r = .49$) and on a memory factor ($r = .45$). The tests' loadings on a spatial ability factor, however, were strongly *negatively* correlated with their correlations with brain volume ($r = -.84$). Thus, the more *g*-loaded, fluid ability-loaded, or memory-loaded a test, the higher its correlation with brain volume, but the more spatially-loaded a test, the lower its correlation with brain volume. If this finding replicates in future studies, it would be of considerable interest from a psychological and an evolutionary perspective, suggesting as it does, that the size of the brain has developed differentially with respect to the characteristics or demands of different tasks.

To what may a brain volume–IQ correlation be attributed? Notwithstanding the important work of Greenough (e.g., Comery, Shah, & Greenough, 1995; Fuchs, Montemayor, & Greenough, 1990; Jones & Greenough, 1996), Diamond (e.g., Bennett, Diamond, Krech, & Rosenzweig, 1964; Diamond, Ingham, Johnson, Bennett, & Rosenzweig, 1976), and others showing experience-related increases among rats in brain weight, cortical thickness, synapse number, and cortical microvasculature, it also does not seem unreasonable to postulate that a larger brain will result in higher IQs. It is possible that both brain size and intelligence could be affected by a third variable, such as nutrition, although Wickett et al. (1999) reported that brain volume and IQs showed both within- as well as between-family correlations. A positive within-family correlation indicates that, on average, the sibling in a family with the larger brain also has the higher IQ. This, in turn, makes it less likely that environmental factors (such as nutritional differences) are responsible for the between-family correlation.

Larger brains are known to have more neurons (Pakkenberg & Gunderson, 1997), and this may lead to higher intelligence through a larger number of synaptic connections and a correspondingly greater cognitive capacity. At the same time, however, Pakkenberg and Gunderson (1997) reported an average 4 billion (or 16%) neuron difference between males and females that does not appear to result in any male–female IQ difference, and thus an increased number of neurons per se is not sufficient to account for the brain volume–IQ correlation. Miller (1994) has suggested that individual differences in myelin, which affect neural transmission rates, may be the basis of the brain volume–IQ correlation. Although this hypothesis cannot be ruled out, it will be seen later in this chapter that there is a low correlation between neural speed and mental speed, suggesting that some other mechanisms must be involved. As was indicated at the beginning of this chapter, the functional significance of the reliable correlation between brain volume and intelligence – the best estimate of which appears to be about .40 – remains to be explicated.

INTELLIGENCE AND EVENT-RELATED POTENTIALS

Event-Related Potentials

Electroencephalographic (EEG) waveforms record the ongoing bioelectric activity of the brain. Event-related potentials (ERPs) are derived by averaging EEG activity that is time-locked to a series of repetitive stimulus presentations. These ERPs are used to provide electrophysiological indices of neuronal cognitive processes. By averaging EEG activity during stimulus events, the bioelectric activity that is not related to the processing of the stimulus is removed.

The resulting waveform is a composite of negative and positive peaks that are identified by their polarity and latency. Amplitude, measured in microvolts, is defined as the vertical deviation of the waveform from a baseline index. Latency is defined as the time in milliseconds from the presentation of the stimulus to the component's peak amplitude. The N100 component, for example, is a negative-going peak with an average latency of 100 ms after stimulus onset. Although both base-to-peak and peak-to-peak measures are possible, base-to-peak indices are more commonly used.

Sensory and Cognitive Components of the ERP Waveform

SENSORY ERP WAVEFORMS. Sensory or exogenous ERP waves are elicited by repetitive stimulation of visual, auditory, and somatosensory modalities (Angel, Boylls, & Weinrich, 1984; Eisen & Elleker, 1980). Simple reversals of visual pattern can also generate exogenous ERPs (Cobb & Dawson, 1960; Harter & White, 1970). The amplitude and latency of the resultant waveforms, which develop in the 100- to 200-ms range, are influenced by physical characteristics of the external eliciting stimuli (Coles, Gratton & Fabiani, 1990; Donchin, Ritter, & McCallum, 1978).

SENSORY ERP WAVES AND INTELLIGENCE. Ertl (Barry & Ertl, 1966; Chalke & Ertl, 1965; Ertl & Schafer, 1969), along with other researchers (e.g., Shucard & Horn, 1972; Perry, McCow, Cunningham, Falgout, & Street, 1976) found negative correlations of about .30 between the latency of ERP waves elicited by punctate visual stimuli and intelligence. Attempts at replication have met with failure (Barrett & Eysenck, 1994; Davis, 1971; Dustman & Beck, 1972; Shucard & Callaway, 1973; Rhodes, Dustman, & Beck, 1969; Widaman, Carlson, Saetermore, & Galbraith, 1993) more often than with success (Federico, 1984; Josiassen, Shagass, Roemer, & Slepner, 1988; Robinson, Haier, Braden, & Krengel, 1984).

Other proposed relations between ERP components and intelligence have included counting the number of times the ERP trace crosses the zero-point within a particular time epoch (Weiss, 1986) and measuring the slope of waveform components

(Morris & Alcorn, 1995). A proposed association between intelligence and N140–P200 peak-to-peak amplitude has also been studied with largely inconclusive results (Haier, Robinson, Braden, & Williams, 1983; Robinson et al., 1984; Stough, Nettlebeck, & Cooper, 1990). Widely disparate results are common, even when apparently identical measures and procedures are used (e.g., Barrett & Eysenck, 1994; Bates & Eysenck, 1993; Shagass, Roemer, Straumanis, & Josiassen, 1981; Vogel, Kruger, Schalt, Schnobel, & Hassling, 1987).

The string measure (A. E. Hendrickson, 1982; D. E. Hendrickson, 1982; Blinkhorn & Hendrickson, 1982; Stough et al., 1990), a measure of waveform complexity, has also received considerable attention and is considered a measure of neural efficiency. Hendrickson et al. posit that higher ability subjects have lower error rates when information is coded and processed. They speculate that neuronal circuitry allowing a high degree of stimulus fidelity is concurrent with error-free information transmission and memory storage. Individuals with neural circuits of higher integrity would be better equipped to process, store, and access information and would do so more rapidly. Ostensibly this results in more complex components because the large number of waveforms required for the averaging process have more pronounced and stable peaks and troughs. Attempts at replication have been indeterminate, however, with smaller correlations found upon reanalysis of Blinkhorn and Hendrickson's data (Haier, Robinson et al., 1983), no consistent relationship found (Robinson, 1997; Vogel et al., 1987), and opposite relations evident (Vetterli & Furedy, 1985). Correlations between the string measure and verbal indices of IQ, apparent in some studies, are absent in others; the same effect is observed with Raven's Progressive Matrices, for significant correlations are present in only some investigations (Eysenck, 1993).

Moreover, and more important, the functional significance of the Hendrickson string measure is far from clear. String measures are obtained in conditions under which no intellectual demands are placed on the subject. A compelling explication of why higher ability subjects should exhibit waveforms with lower complexity (particularly when no cognitive processing is being performed by the subject) has yet to be provided.

Overall, the relation between early sensory components and intelligence is doubtful (Stelmack & Houlihan, 1995).

COGNITIVE COMPONENTS OF THE ERP WAVEFORM. In contrast to exogenous sensory ERP waveforms that are determined primarily by external physical stimulation, endogenous cognitive components are determined primarily by intrinsic psychological activity (e.g., stimulus evaluation or classification, short-term or long-term memory scanning). They may be obtained by involving the subject in a memory task or any task that requires cognitive information processing on the part of the subject (Duncan-Johnson & Donchin, 1982) and can also be elicited by the absence of expected stimuli (Sutton, Braren, Zubin, & John, 1965).

A standard procedure in research relating ERP waves and intelligence involves correlating amplitude and latency measures with intelligence test and subtest scores. Elementary cognitive tasks (ECTs) are performed concurrently with ERP recording, whereas mental ability is assessed independently and then correlated with the ERP components at a later time. Deary and Caryl (1994), in a review of the literature, concluded that P300 latency and P300 amplitude show the most consistent association with intelligence. Deary et al. (Deary, Head, & Egan, 1989) posited three main indices of speed of cognitive processing: inspection time (IT), reaction time (RT), and ERP latency. Both RT and IT have significant correlations with IQ measures (Brand & Deary, 1982; Kranzler & Jensen, 1989; Nettelbeck, 1987; Vernon, 1983), as do some ERP components.

The P300 component of the ERP waveform has been shown to be a reliable index of the detection, recognition, and classification of target stimuli (Polich & Kok, 1995; Segalowitz, Unsal, & Dywan, 1992). More specifically, the P300 component indexes the speed of stimulus classification and decision-making processes (Kutas, McCarthy, & Donchin, 1977; Magliero, Bashore, Coles, & Donchin, 1984). Test–retest reliability of the P300 across various time intervals is high, and one study shows a reliability index of .74 across 2 years (Segalowitz & Barnes, 1993). Within-study reliability indices are in the .80 to .90 range (Fabiani, Gratton, Karis, & Donchin, 1987). The P300 component has also been shown to have high heritability (Katsanas, Iacono, McGue, & Carlson, 1997). Though consensus on the underlying neural generators varies, it is now generally agreed that the medial temporal lobe (particularly the temporal–parietal junction in the case of auditory stimuli [Knight, Scabini, Woods, & Clayworth, 1989]) and hippocampus are involved in its production (McCarthy, Wood, Williamson, & Spencer, 1989).

A number of intelligence studies have utilized the auditory oddball task, a standard, widely utilized procedure for eliciting the P300 component. The technique involves presenting a series of tones along with a discrepant "oddball" tone inserted in the stream of stimuli at various intervals. A cognitive operation comparing standard and deviant tones is performed with subjects responding when a deviant tone is detected. Latency increases systematically with task difficulty (Polich & Martin, 1992). Responses can also be elicited by the absence of the stimuli, that is, when expected tones are omitted from the train of stimuli. When elicited by this task, P300 typically appears as a prominent component that is maximal centroparietally (Falkenstein, Hohnsbein, & Hoorman, 1995). Though its modal latency is 300 ms, P300 is frequently observed 200–300 ms later than this for more difficult discriminations.

Functional Significance of P300 Correlates of Intelligence: RT and P300 Latency

A substantial body of evidence identifies RT as an index of speed of processing (Vernon, 1987). A similar role has been posited for P300 latency. Both P300 latency and RT increase with increasing task difficulty (McGarry-Roberts, Stelmack, & Campbell, 1992). Furthermore, P300 latency and RT have both been shown to increase with increasing set size in the Sternberg (1969) memory scanning task (McGarry-Roberts et al., 1992). Because P300 latency is considered an index of speed of cognitive processing in general and speed of categorization or stimulus evaluation time in particular, the conceptual relation to RT is evident (McCarthy & Donchin, 1983). It is reasonable to posit that both index some related, covarying aspect of speed of information processing. One author (Miller, 1994) openly refers to P300 latency as "a speed measure," noting that "faster reaction times . . . and shorter la-

tencies . . . represent doing the same things faster" (p. 808). By virtue of this RT–ERP latency relationship, the functional significance of ERP research on P300 latency sets it apart from other attempts to relate physiological processes to intelligence.

One important caveat, however, is that RT and P300 latency index independent though covarying processes. Verleger (1997) reviewed the effects of a wide variety of experimental manipulations in P300 latency and RT using the ratio of change in P300 latency to change in RT as an index of relative sensitivity. He found that manipulations that influenced stimulus evaluation and classification (e.g., auditory degradation, attenuation of visual and auditory intensity, and increase in number of irrelevant stimuli while randomly varying location of relevant stimuli) all strongly influenced P300 latency but had relatively small effects on RT. The P300 latency was insensitive to manipulations that delayed response execution (mental rotation, mental arithmetic, response complexity, and Stroop task). Thus, although P300 latency indexes aspects of stimulus-evaluation time, it is, unlike RT, largely independent of response selection and production (Howard & Polich, 1985).

In a study of stimulus and response compatibility, Ragot (Ragot & Renault, 1981; Ragot, 1984) presented stimuli on either the left or right side of a screen. In one condition, subjects responded to stimuli presented on the right side with their right hand; in another condition, left-hand responses were required for stimuli on the right side. When the stimulus and the appropriate response were on opposite sides, RT and P300 latency increased (as compared with the same-side condition). However, when subjects were required to cross their hands over one another, only RT increased. These results indicate that although RT and P300 latency are implicated in the decision-making process, only RT is involved in actual response production. In a pharmacological manipulation, administration of methylphenidate (a stimulant with cognitive effects) decreased mean RT and standard deviation for RT but only decreased standard deviation of P300 latency (Brumaghim, Klorman, Strauss, Lewine, & Goldstein, 1987). Finally, P300 latency has been shown to correlate more highly with reaction time when accuracy rather than speed instructions are given (Donchin et al., 1979).

Functional Significance of P300 Correlates of Intelligence: P300 Amplitude

The relation between P300 amplitude and intelligence is considerably less clear. The P300 amplitude indexes the amount of information extracted by the subject during cognitive processing (Johnson, 1986, 1988). Because higher amplitude is suggestive of greater information extraction (Johnson, 1986, 1988), it may be posited that higher ability subjects will have higher amplitudes than lower ability individuals overall. It can also be possible, however, that subjects with higher intelligence may use their cognitive resources more efficiently, thereby reducing P300 amplitude in some conditions. This issue remains unresolved in the literature.

Early attempts at explaining the relationship between ERP amplitude measures in general, as they relate to intelligence, have been inconclusive (for discussions of neural efficiency see A. E. Hendrickson, 1982; D. E. Hendrickson, 1982; and Blinkhorn & Hendrickson, 1982; on neural adaptability, see Schafer, 1979, 1982). Neural adaptability (Jensen, Schafer, & Crinella, 1981; Schafer, 1982) is reflected in the tendency for the amplitude of ERPs to be large in response to unexpected stimuli and small in response to stimuli that are expected. An early study (Schafer & Marcus, 1973) found that when subjects determined when a stimulus would be delivered themselves, consistently smaller ERP amplitudes were produced. The study demonstrated that these effects were more pronounced with subjects of higher intelligence. Results were interpreted as indexing the greater adaptability of more intelligent subjects. It was argued that less neuronal energy was invested in predictable stimuli, whereas more was invested in novel events and that the more highly intelligent individuals recruited fewer neurons for predictable stimuli than the less intelligent. Greater amplitudes in the studies of Schafer et al. were found in *all* ERP components. Given the difficulties in interpretation, however, this paradigm has been largely abandoned.

Overall, conclusions regarding the functional significance of P300 amplitude are still pending. Conclusions regarding the functional significance of P300 latency, construed as a speed-of-information-processing index complementary to RT, seem fairly well-established.

P300, Intelligence, and Inspection Time

Inspection time (Nettlebeck & Lally, 1976; Vickers, 1970, 1979; Vickers, Nettlebeck, & Willson, 1972) is defined as the threshold exposure duration required for a stimulus to be encoded to a degree sufficient to enable a discrimination task to be successfully performed. Typically, two lines of varying length are presented for very brief durations and the subject is required to identify the longer line correctly; accuracy rather than speed instructions are emphasized. A backward-masking stimulus immediately following the stimulus presentation limits postpresentation processing (Nettlebeck, 1987). Target exposure duration, that is, the duration between target onset and mask onset (also referred to as stimulus onset asynchrony [SOA]) is varied until response accuracy falls below a predefined level (typically 97.5%). Inspection time paradigms using visual, auditory, and tactile modalities are possible (Kranzler & Jensen, 1989).

Alcorn and Morris (1996) recorded ERPs concurrently with IT tasks. Results were then correlated with scores from the Raven's Progressive Matrices. They hypothesized that as SOAs became smaller, corresponding increases in P300 latency and decreases in P300 amplitude would result. As discriminations became increasingly difficult (i.e., as SOAs decreased from 100 to 84, 67, 50, 34, and 17 ms over the course of the experiment), significant effects were observed for P300 amplitude but not for latency. Zhang, Caryl, & Deary (1989a, 1989b), using three SOAs, also found no significant P300 latency effects, though P300 amplitude increased significantly with task difficulty. Caryl (1994) also found a significant correlation between intelligence and P300 amplitude (.28). Similar results were found with respect to P300 latency ($r = -.27$).

AUDITORY ODDBALL. As described earlier, the auditory oddball task involves presenting a sequence of "standard" tones with a certain frequency of occurrence (e.g., 85%). "Rare" tones (e.g., those with 15% frequency of occurrence) occur randomly within this stream of standards. These rare tones are the "oddballs." The subjects' task is to discriminate the oddballs from the standards by some overt response.

Polich et al. (Ladish & Polich, 1989; Polich, Ehlers, Otis, Mandrell, & Bloom, 1986; Polich, Howard, &

Starr, 1985; Polich & Martin, 1992), in a series of experiments employing the oddball paradigm, found consistent latency effects across different indices of intelligence with correlations in the −.35 to −.45 range (e.g., −.359 for P300 latency and grade point average; Polich & Martin, 1992). O'Donnell, Friedman, Swearer, and Drachman (1992) assessed concordance between P300 latency in an oddball task and psychometric performance on a battery of tests. The P300 latency was correlated with general intelligence and concentration in an active oddball paradigm (i.e., the oddball task as described above wherein subjects actively respond to the deviant stimuli). In a passive oddball condition, wherein the subject does not make an overt response, P300 latency was found to correlate with verbal learning, narrative recall, and verbal fluency. Overall, correlations were higher in the active condition, the passive format requiring less cognitive processing on the part of the subject. Most notably, the correlation between latency and general intelligence was −.44, which was significant at the .01 level of probability.

Segalowitz, Unsal, and Dywan (1992), using a group of bright 12-year-old children as subjects (minimum IQ of 135 on the WISC-R instrument) found no significant P300 latency differences compared with normal child controls on an auditory oddball task. However, variability of P300 latency and amplitude, as indexed by the coefficient of variation (SD/M), was larger for child controls, though values failed to reach significance. Another study using child subjects and the oddball paradigm (Robaey, Cansino, Dugas, & Renault, 1995) assessed P300 latency and amplitude measures at the parietal–occipital site. Correlations between four categorization tasks derived from the WISC-R (1981) and P300 components were in the −.30 to −.50 range (latency) and −.37 to −.43 range (amplitude). When scaled scores were used, however, only P300 amplitudes to targets were significant. It is important to note that, as in the study by Robaey et al. (1995), all subjects referred to as normal were of average ability; IQ score range was not given. Stauder et al. (Stauder, van der Molen, & Molenaar, 1995), also using a sample of children in an auditory oddball procedure, found that amplitude effects for a late-occurring P300 just failed to reach significance. No latency effects were reported.

DIGIT SPAN. Although an early demonstration of concordance between memory capacity and P300 latency (Polich, Howard, & Starr, 1985) was criticized for failing to control correctly for effects of age (Surwillo, 1984), two subsequent studies (Howard & Polich, 1985; Polich, Ladish, & Burns, 1990) replicated and extended the previous findings. These results indicate a high degree of concordance between the ability to acquire and store information in short-term memory (STM) and intelligence, on the one hand, and P300 latency, on the other.

MORE COMPLEX ECTS. Egan et al. (1994) found significant correlations between P300 latency and digit symbol, digit span, auditory verbal learning (immediate and delayed recall), word fluency, and two indices of trail-making (absolute values between .25 to .41). Concordance between amplitude and six intelligence subscales, namely similarities, arithmetic, verbal intelligence, logical memory (immediate and delayed recall), and one index of trail-making varied between .30 and .41 (absolute values). Full-scale IQ correlated −.28 with amplitude; no relationship between IQ (verbal, performance, or full-scale) and latency was detected. It is interesting to note that, of the 3 ERP components (N1, P2, and P3) assessed in this study, 14 of the 18 correlations to reach significance were for the P300 component, supporting the position that only later cognitive components will show concordance with intelligence (Deary & Caryl, 1994). Of these, nine were significant at probability values below .05 (five at .025, two at .005, and two at .01). An earlier study by Egan et al. (Egan, Chiswick, Brettle, & Goodwin, 1993) using HIV-positive subjects found similar overall results.

The Sternberg STM scanning task (S. Sternberg, 1966, 1969, 1975), exploited in several experimental paradigms, has also been used in ERP studies. Developed to explore the structure of information held in short-term memory (STM), the technique assesses the timing of STM searches. In the simplest format, the subject first encodes a memory set of, typically, digits. A probe item is then presented, and the subject must indicate whether the probe was present in the memory set. In the auditory version, recordings of spoken digits are presented sequentially through headphones or speakers. They are followed, after a brief pause, by the spoken probe digit.

Pelosi et al. (1992a, 1992b), using auditory Sternberg tasks, found decreasing P300 amplitude to the probe stimuli associated with higher intelligence. No latency effects were uncovered, however. McGarry-Roberts et al. (1992), in a study employing the Sternberg task and five other ECTs, assessed RT and P300 latency simultaneously. Correlations of −.38 and −.32 were found for the category-matching task (which assesses speed of retrieval from long-term memory (LTM) and the Sternberg (STM digit-recognition) task, respectively. Except for the semantic similarity task (a measure of linguistic processing efficiency that assesses speed of retrieval from LTM; Posner, Boies, Eichelman, & Taylor, 1969), no amplitude effects were found.

In summary, results indicate a consistent and replicable negative relationship between P300 latency and intelligence. Results of paradigms exploring amplitude effects are more equivocal, and studies indicating positive correlations are reported as often as those reporting negative concordance or no relationship. Though the latency results accord with expectations, the discrepancy between studies on amplitude effects is difficult to account for.

Conclusion

As mentioned previously, the functional significance of P300 amplitude as it relates to intelligence is somewhat vague; results too are equivocal. Conversely, the functional significance of P300 latency is clearer, for results are more consistent across studies and experimental paradigms. Taken together, these studies indicate that highly intelligent individuals are able to make decisions more rapidly than those of lower ability. This, in turn, provides support for the argument that higher mental ability is, at least in part, determined by speed of information processing. Even on small time scales, such as those used in ERP studies, information accrues more rapidly for the subject with higher intelligence. Extrapolated over months and years, substantial differences in crystallized intelligence and accomplishment may result (Eysenck, 1993). This may represent a possible link between such global constructs as g and its various real-world correlates. Because much of the debate in the intelligence literature centers on the distinction between the underlying physiology of intelligence and the expression of intelligence in social and academic domains, such a link would be of

tremendous value, both in the theoretical and applied spheres. Studies employing endogenous components of the ERP waveform to uncover these relationships promise to contribute substantially to advancement of knowledge in this area.

NERVE CONDUCTION VELOCITY AND INTELLIGENCE

Nerve conduction velocity (NCV) refers to the speed with which electrical impulses are transmitted along nerve fibers and across synapses. Reed (1984) proposed that individual differences in NCV may be attributable to genetic differences in the structure and amount of transmission proteins which, in turn, set limits on information-processing rates. Thus, faster NCV would be expected to correlate with faster RTs and higher intelligence.

Since Reed's 1984 paper, nine studies have investigated relationships between NCV, RTs, and IQ. The key findings of these studies are presented in Table 12.3, where it will be seen that there has been little agreement in the results. Vernon and Mori (1992), for example, reported significant correlations between IQs, RTs, and peripheral NCVs (measured in the median nerve of the arm) in two samples of university students. The NCV–IQ correlations were .42 and .48; NCV–RT correlations were −.28 and −.18. Thus, as expected, faster NCVs were associated with higher IQs and faster speed of information-processing. Wickett and Vernon (1994), however, failed to replicate these results despite using the same procedure to measure NCV. In their study, two measures of NCVs correlated −.12 and .02 with IQs and .02 and .01 with RTs.

Other investigators have also failed to find any correlation between IQs and NCV. These include Reed and Jensen (1991), Barrett, Daum, and Eysenck (1990), and Rijsdijk, Boomsma, and Vernon (1995). This latter study, however, did report that peripheral NCV in humans is a substantially heritable trait ($h^2 = .77$), and Rijsdijk and Boomsma (1997) not only found significant positive peripheral NCV–IQ correlations, of the order of approximately .15, but also reported that these phenotypic NCV–IQ correlations were entirely mediated by common genetic factors. Moreover, although Reed and Jensen (1991) did not find a significant correlation between *peripheral* NCV and IQ, Reed and Jensen (1993) reported

TABLE 12.3. Key Findings in the Nerve Conduction Velocity and IQ Literature

Study	n Sample	Age Range[a]	NCV Pathway	Cognitive Measure	r[a]
Vernon & Mori (1989, 1992)[b]	40 undergraduates ♂	18 to 42	Fingers to axilla[c]	MAB g	**.62**
Vernon & Mori (1989, 1992)[b]	45 undergraduates ♀	18 to 42	Fingers to axilla[c]	MAB g	.28
Vernon & Mori (1989, 1992)[b]	38 undergraduates ♂	17 to 39	Wrist to fingers	MAB g	**.54**
Vernon & Mori (1989, 1992)[b]	50 undergraduates ♀	17 to 39	Wrist to fingers	MAB g	**.37**
Barrett et al. (1990)[b]	42 local, inpatients? ♂ ♀	18 to 41	Fingers to wrist	Raven's Matrices	.00[e]
Reed & Jensen (1991)	112 undergraduates ♂	18 to 25	Wrist to elbow	Raven's Matrices	.04
Reed & Jensen (1991)	88 community college ♂	18 to 25	Wrist to elbow	Raven's Matrices	−.07
Wickett & Vernon (1994)	38 local ♀	20 to 30	Fingers to elbow	MAB FSIQ	−.05[f]
Rijsdijk et al. (1995)	312 twin registry ♂ ♀	14 to 18	Wrist to elbow	Raven's Matrices	−.02[g]
Tan (1996)	43 unspecified ♂	18 to 21	Forearm to fingers	CFIT	**.54**[h]
Tan (1996)	33 unspecified ♀	18 to 21	Forearm to fingers	CFIT	**−.61**[i]
Rijsdijk & Boomsma (1997)[j]	346 twin registry ♂ ♀	16 to 20	Wrist to elbow	WAIS FSIQ	**.15**
Wickett et al.	47 local ♂	20 to 35	Axilla to wrist	MAB FSIQ	**.29**[k]

Male Populations:	Female Populations:	All Populations:[l]
6 samples	4 samples	12 samples
$N = 368$	$N = 166$	$N = 922$
Unweighted Mean $r = .327$	Unweighted Mean $r = -.003$	Unweighted Mean $r = .175$
n-Weighted Mean $r = .219$	n-Weighted Mean $r = .055$	n-Weighted Mean $r = .153$

Note: Correlations printed in bold are significant at least at the $\alpha = .05$ level (two-tailed); where a mean correlation is presented, that value is tested for significance (if significant, at least one of the contributing values must also be significant). Abbreviations are as follows: local (volunteers from local population), ♂ (males), ♀ (females), ♂ ♀ (males and females), **MAB** (Multidimensional Aptitude Battery), **CFIT** (Cattell Culture Fair Intelligence Test), **WAIS** (Wechsler Adult Intelligence Scale − Dutch translation), **FSIQ** (Full-Scale IQ).

[a] Unless otherwise noted (with a superscript), all correlations are unadjusted Pearson product moment correlations between the volume measure and the IQ measure.

[b] The values for males and females separately were reported in Wickett and Vernon (1994).

[c] Aggregate of eight NCV measures based on wrist to fingers, wrist to elbow, and elbow to axilla.

[d] The exact n for these analyses is unknown. The authors indicate that the n varied from 40 to 44.

[e] Mean of four correlations (all between −.04 and .04) for both hands and two recording locations at the wrist.

[f] Mean of two correlations (−.12 and .02) for wrist to fingers and wrist to elbow, respectively.

[g] Value reported in Rijsdijk and Boomsma (1997).

[h] Mean of two correlations (.63 and .44) for wrist to thumb and forearm to fingers, respectively. The correlations were derived with two scores entered for each subject, one for the left hand and one for the right.

[i] Mean of two correlations (−.67 and −.55) as in Note h above.

[j] This sample appears to be the same as the Rijsdijk et al. (1995) sample, except 2 years older.

[k] Mean of two correlations (.37 and .22) for axilla to elbow and elbow to wrist, respectively. Spine to axilla was also measured but showed what was considered extreme variation (five outliers); the correlation with IQ was .00.

[l] Omitting Rijsdijk et al. (1995). The older sample is more directly comparable to the other samples that make up the mean correlations.

a significant correlation between IQ and NCV in a *brain* nerve pathway.

Procedural differences between studies may account for some of the discrepancies between the results of different studies. In addition, Wickett and Vernon's (1994) reanalysis of Vernon and Mori's (1992) data suggested that higher IQ–NCV correlations occur in males than in females. As noted in Table 12.3, the mean unweighted IQ–NCV correlation among male samples is .327 ($Z = 4.47$, $p < .001$), whereas among female samples the mean unweighted correlation is −.003 ($Z = .59$, ns). In the most extreme case, Tan (1996) reported an IQ–NCV correlation of +.54 among males and of −.61 among females. The implications of these results are unclear but perhaps indicate a sex difference in problem-solving strategies with males relying more strongly on neural speed. Although speculative, it is possible that faster neural speed in females causes more errors of processing, offsetting the expected advantages of faster conduction and causing them to rely more heavily on strategies that are less directly speed oriented such as more effective encoding of information.

Rijsdijk and Boomsma (1997) proposed another factor that may contribute to differences in the magnitude of IQ–NCV correlations across studies. In this study, the 18-year-old 159 twin pairs who had previously been tested 2 years earlier showed a WAIS IQ–NCV correlation of .15. Two years earlier, the same subjects' (16-year-old) Raven IQ scores and NCVs correlated nonsignificantly at −.02, but Raven IQs obtained at 16 years of age correlated .17 with the NCVs obtained at 18 years. Rijsdijk and Boomsma suggested a maturation hypothesis whereby NCVs and IQs will only correlate after NCV has fully matured and reached its highest value. Support for this hypothesis was shown by a low and nonsignificant IQ–NCV correlation ($r = .08$) among 104 subjects whose NCVs had not fully matured in comparison with an IQ–NCV correlation of .21 among 189 subjects whose NCVs had fully matured.

In the most recent NCV–IQ study to date, Wickett, Vernon, Brown, and Broome (1999) obtained multiple measures of peripheral NCV (e.g., from elbow-to-wrist, spine-to-wrist, and axilla-to-elbow), a measure of central nervous system (CNS) latency, reaction times, and IQs from 47 adult males (these subjects were part of the sample cited in Wickett et al. (1999) who also underwent MRI testing). Unfortunately, the results from Wickett et al. (1999) do little to clarify the inconsistencies of previous studies: spine-to-wrist peripheral NCVs correlated close to zero with IQs, axilla-to-elbow NCVs correlated significantly ($r = .37$), and CNS latency, which would have been predicted to show the largest correlations, not only correlated nonsignificantly with IQ but in the wrong direction. Moreover, none of the NCV measures correlated significantly with reaction-time measures, indicating that the physiological measures of neural conduction speed are unrelated to the behavioral measures of information-processing speed.

In sum, the evidence for an NCV–IQ correlation is weak and mixed. Even if it is granted that NCVs and IQ are intercorrelated (and at this point this cannot be considered established), the *pattern* of the relationship between them does not appear to follow predictions. Vernon and Mori (1992), for example, predicted that the partial correlation between IQs and RTs, controlling for NCV, should be substantially smaller than their zero-order correlation, but this was not supported. Anderson (1994) also suggested that relationships between IQs and RTs cannot be attributed to speed of neuron conduction. At present, the IQ–NCV studies that have been conducted have probably raised more questions than they have answered, but this is neither necessarily a bad thing, provided that the questions that are raised are testable, nor unique to these particular variables.

INTELLIGENCE AND CEREBRAL GLUCOSE METABOLISM

Like any physical organ, the active brain consumes energy. Thus, when individuals are engaged in a task that requires cognitive activity, an index of the extent to which their brain is "working" is the rate at which it metabolizes glucose to compensate for its expenditure of energy. Cerebral glucose metabolic rate (CGMR) can be measured via positron emission tomography (PET) scans, which trace the concentration of a positron-emitting radioactive analog that has been intravenously administered to a subject and that is taken up into the brain over a period of seconds or minutes. The isotope concentrations measured by the PET scans are then converted into estimates of CGMR.

Several early PET scan studies involved Alzheimer's patients or subjects with other forms of dementia. Chase et al. (1984), for example, obtained WAIS IQs from 17 Alzheimer's disease patients and 5 controls of normal intelligence and then measured their CGMRs while they were at rest. These CGMRs correlated .61, .56, and .68 with verbal, performance, and full-scale IQs, respectively. More recently, DeCarli et al. (1996) also reported a positive correlation ($r = .64$) between WAIS IQ scores and metabolism in the association cortex among 14 probable Alzheimer's disease patients. These authors also reported a lower and statistically nonsignificant IQ–metabolism correlation ($r = .46$) in a different sample of 12 probable Alzheimer patients with severe abnormalities of white matter. Other studies have reported a decline in the CGMRs of Alzheimer's disease patients (e.g., Benson, 1982; Benson, Metter, Kuhl, & Phelps, 1982; de Leon et al., 1983; Martin et al., 1986), and Alavi et al. (1980) reported that the CGMRs of six senile dementia patients were approximately 20 to 30% lower than those of four age-matched normal controls whose CGMRs were themselves some 50% lower than those of eight young normal subjects.

When subjects are engaged in some cognitive task during the tracer uptake period, a different pattern of results emerges. Haier et al. (1988), for example, engaged 30 normal subjects in either a continuous performance task (CPT) or the Advanced Raven Matrices and then obtained PET scans. Subjects who had worked on the Raven showed greater relative CGMRs than the CPT subjects: thus, as expected, the heavier cognitive demands of the more challenging Raven resulted in a greater expenditure of energy. Within the Raven subjects, however, high *negative* correlations, between $-.44$ and $-.84$, were found between Raven scores and absolute CGMRs, indicating that subjects who obtained the highest Raven scores actually consumed the least amount of energy. These results should be interpreted with caution because of the small sample size. The results have, however, been replicated: Parks et al. (1988) reported correlations of approximately $-.50$ between relative CGMRs and verbal fluency test scores in a sample of 16 normal subjects; Haier et al. (1995) reported a correlation of $-.58$ between whole-brain CGMRs and WAIS-R IQs among samples of mildly mentally retarded, Down's syndrome, and normal subjects; and Berent et al. (1988) and Boivin et al. (1992) also reported negative correlations between CGMRs and tests of cognitive function.

Taken together, the PET scan studies provide compelling evidence that, at rest, when subjects can engage in any mental activity they wish, those subjects with higher IQs demonstrate increased brain activity but, when they are required to perform an assigned cognitive task, subjects with higher IQs are able to accomplish the task with a lower consumption of energy. Subjects of higher IQ can thus be characterized as having greater "brainpower" at their disposal

and at the same time as being able to use their brainpower more efficiently when called upon to do so (though see Larson, Haier, LaCasse, & Hazen, 1995). The use of PET scans remains an expensive undertaking – Haier (1990) stated that an eight-subject PET scan study may cost as much as $20,000 – but this is offset by the tremendous potential that these studies have to yield information about the biological basis of intelligence.

CONCLUSIONS

The goals of this chapter were threefold. First, to illustrate that a number of anatomical and physiological correlates of intelligence have been identified and replicated sufficiently often to be considered reliably established. This includes estimates of head and brain size, some parameters of event-related potentials, notably P300 latency, and cerebral glucose metabolic rates. A second goal, however, was to show that not all measures that have been claimed to be biological correlates of intelligence have met with similar replicability or consistency of results. This includes such other ERP parameters as P300 amplitudes and nerve conduction velocity. The third goal was to stress the need for the further development of theories regarding the functional significance of biological correlates of intelligence and for future research in this area to be more theoretically driven.

It would be overstating the case to imply that no theories have been proposed to account for the results of biological investigations. As early as 1927, Spearman suggested that individual differences in g were attributable to differences in people's "mental energy." More recently, others have proposed a similar theory of "neural efficiency" (e.g., Vernon, 1993a), which argues that individual differences in the speed and efficiency with which the brain and neural system can execute the information processing required by cognitive tasks contributes to the success with which the task is performed. Other psychologists (e.g., Eysenck, 1993) have developed a biological theory that focuses on the probability of error of transmission of impulses across synapses (more error-free processing allows faster information-processing speed and higher intelligence), and other biologically oriented theories of intelligence include Schafer's (1982) theory of "neural adaptability" mentioned in the section on ERPs and Robinson's (1996) "arousability theory."

These examples notwithstanding, it is evident that biological theories of intelligence lag well behind empirical demonstrations of correlations between intelligence and biological measures. It is also the case that many more purely psychological theories of intelligence continue to overlook the biological work. The time is ripe for both of these unnecessary situations to be rectified.

REFERENCES

Alavi, A., Ferris, S., Wolf, A., Reivich, M., Farkas, T., Dann, R., Christman, D., MacGregor, R. R., & Fowler, J. (1980). Determination of cerebral metabolism in senile dementia using F-18 deoxyglucose metabolism and positron emission tomography. *Journal of Nuclear Medicine, 21,* 21.

Alcorn, M. B., & Morris, G. L. (1996). P300 correlates of inspection time. *Personality and Individual Differences, 20*(5), 619–627.

Anderson, R. (1994). Speed of neuron conduction is not the basis of the IQ-RT correlation: Results from a simple neural model. *Intelligence, 19,* 317–323.

Andreasen, N. C., Flaum, M., Swayze, V., II, O'Leary, D. S., Alliger, R., Cohen, G., Ehrhardt, J., & Yuh, W. T. C. (1993). Intelligence and brain structure in normal individuals. *American Journal of Psychiatry, 150,* 130–134.

Angel, R. W., Boylls, C. C., & Weinrich, M. (1984). Cerebral evoked potentials and somatosensory perception. *Neurology, 34,* 123–126.

Barrett, P. T., Daum, I., & Eysenck, H. J. (1990). Sensory nerve conduction and intelligence: A methodological study. *Journal of Psychophysiology, 4,* 1–13.

Barrett, P. T., & Eysenck, H. J. (1994). The relationship between evoked potential component amplitude, latency, contour length, zero-crossings, and psychometric intelligence. *Personality and Individual Differences, 16,* 3–32.

Barry, W., & Ertl, J. (1966). Brain waves and human intelligence. In F. B. Davis (Ed.), *Modern educational developments: Another look* (pp. 191–197). New York: Educational Records Bureau.

Bates, T., & Eysenck, H. J. (1993). String length, attention, and intelligence: Focused attention reverses the string length–IQ relationship. *Personality and Individual Differences, 15*(4), 363–371.

Bennett, E. L., Diamond, M. C., Krech, D., & Rosenzweig, M. R. (1964). Chemical and anatomical plasticity of brain. *Science, 146,* 610–619.

Benson, D. F. (1982). The use of positron emission scanning techniques in the diagnosis of Alzheimer's disease. In S. Corkin, K. L. Davis, J. H. Growdon, E. Vodin, & R. J. Wurtman (Eds.), *Alzheimer's disease: A review of progress in research.* New York: Raven Press.

Benson, D. F., Metter, E. J., Kuhl, D. E., & Phelps, M. E. (1982). Positron computed tomography in neurobehavioral problems. In A. Kertesz (Ed.), *Localization in neuropsychology.* New York: Academic Press.

Berent, S., Giordani, B., Lehtinen, S., Markel, D., Penney, J., Buchtel, H., Starosta-Rubinstein, S., Hichwa, R., & Young, A. (1988). Positron emission tomographic scan investigations of Huntington's disease: Cerebral metabolic correlates of cognitive function. *Annals of Neurology, 23,* 541–546.

Blinkhorn, S. F., & Hendrickson, D. E. (1982). Average evoked responses and psychometric intelligence. *Nature, 295,* 596–597.

Bogaert, A. F., & Rushton, J. P. (1989). Sexuality, delinquency and *r/K* reproductive strategies: Data from a Canadian university sample. *Personality and Individual Differences, 10,* 1071–1077.

Boivin, M. J., Giordani, B., Berent, S., Amato, D. A., Lehtinen, S., Koeppe, R. A., Buchtel, H., Foster, N., & Kuhl, D. (1992). Verbal fluency and positron emission tomographic mapping of regional cerebral glucose metabolism. *Cortex, 28,* 231–239.

Brand, C. R., & Deary, I. J. (1982). Intelligence and 'inspection time'. In H. J. Eysenck (Ed.), *A model for intelligence* (pp. 133–148). NY: Springer-Verlag.

Bray, P. F., Shields, W. D., Wolcott, G. J., & Madsen, J. A. (1969). Occipitofrontal head circumferences – An accurate measure of intracranial volume. *Journal of Pediatrics, 75,* 303–305.

Broca, P. (1861). Sur le volume et al forme du cerveau suivant les individus et suivant les races. *Bulletins et mémoires de la Société d'Anthropologie de Paris, 2,* 139–207, 301–321, 441–446.

Broman, S., Nichols, P. L., Shaughnessy, P., & Kennedy, W. (1987). *Retardation in young children: A developmental study of cognitive deficit.* Hillsdale, NJ: Lawrence Erlbaum Associates.

Brumaghim, J. T., Klorman, R., Strauss, J., Lewine, J. D., & Goldstein, M. G. (1987). Does methylphenidate affect information processing? Findings from two studies on performance and P3b latency. *Psychophysiology, 24*(3), 361–373.

Caryl, P. G. (1994). Early event-related potentials correlate with inspection time and intelligence. *Intelligence, 18,* 15–46.

Castellanos, F. X., Giedd, J. N., Eckburg, P., Marsh, W. L., Vaituzis, A. C., Kaysen, D., Hamburger, S. D., & Rapoport, J. L. (1994). Quantitative morphology of the caudate nucleus in attention deficit hyperactivity disorder. *American Journal of Psychiatry, 151,* 1791–1796.

Chalke, F., & Ertl, J. (1965). Evoked potentials and intelligence. *Life Sciences, 4,* 1319–1322.

Chase, T. N., Fedio, P., Brooks, R., Di Chiro, G., & Mansi, L. (1984). Wechsler Adult Intelligence Scale performance: Cortical localization by fluorodeoxyglucose

F18-positron emission tomography. *Archives of Neurology, 41*, 1244–1247.

Clark, P. J., Vandenberg, S. G., & Proctor, C. H. (1961). On the relationship of scores on certain psychological tests with a number of anthropometric characters and birth order in twins. *Human Biology, 33*, 163–180.

Cobb, W. A., & Dawson, G. D. (1960). The latency and form in man of the occipital potentials evoked by bright flashes. *Journal of Physiology, 152*, 108–121.

Coles, M. G. H., Gratton, G., & Fabiani, M. (1990). Event-related brain potentials. In J. T. Cacioppo, & L. G. Tassinary (Eds.), *Principles of psychophysiology: Physical, social, and inferential elements* (pp. 413–455). New York: Cambridge University Press.

Comery, T. A., Shah, R., & Greenough, W. T. (1995). Differential rearing alters spine density on medium-sized spiny neurons in the rat corpus striatum: Evidence for association of morphological plasticity with early response gene expression. *Neurobiology of Learning and Memory, 63*, 217–219.

Davis, F. B. (1971). *The measurement of mental capability through evoked-potential recordings*. Greenwich, CT: Educational Records Bureau.

Deary, I. J., & Caryl, P. G. (1994). Intelligence, inspection time, and cognitive strategies. In P. A. Vernon (Ed.), *Biological approaches to the study of human intelligence*. Norwood, NJ: Ablex.

Deary, I. J., Head, B., & Egan, V. (1989). Auditory inspection time, intelligence, and pitch discrimination. *Intelligence, 13*, 135–147.

DeCarli, C., Grady, C. L., Clark, C. M., Katz, D. A., Brady, D. R., Murphy, D. G. M., Haxby, J. V., Salerno, J. A., Gillette, J. A., Gonzalez-Aviles, A., & Rapoport, S. I. (1996). Comparison of positron emission tomography, cognition, and brain volume in Alzheimer's disease with and without severe abnormalities of white matter. *Journal of Neurology, Neurosurgery and Psychiatry, 60*, 158–167.

de Leon, M. J., Ferris, S. H., George, A. E., Christman, D. R., Fowler, J. S., Gentes, C., Reisberg, B., Gee, B., Emmerich, M., Yonekura, Y., Brodie, J., Kricheff, I. I., & Wolf, A. P. (1983). Positron emission tomographic studies of aging and Alzheimer disease. *American Journal of Neuroradiology, 4*, 568–571.

DeMyer, M. K., Gilmor, R. L., Hendrie, H. C., DeMyer, W. E., Augustyn, G. T., & Jackson, R. K. (1988). Magnetic resonance brain images in schizophrenic and normal subjects: Influence of diagnosis and education. *Schizophrenia Bulletin, 14*, 21–32.

Diamond, M. C., Ingham, C. A., Johnson, R. E., Bennett, E. L., & Rosenzweig, M. R. (1976). Effects of environment on morphology of rat cerebral cortex and hippocampus. *Journal of Neurobiology, 7*, 75–85.

Dobbing, J., & Sands, J. (1978). Head circumference, biparietal diameter and brain growth in fetal and postnatal life. *Early Human Development, 2*, 81–87.

Donchin, E., Ritter, W., & McCallum, W. C. (1978). Cognitive psychophysiology: The endogenous components of the ERP. In E. Callaway, P. Teuting, & S. H. Koslow (Eds.), *Event-related brain potentials in man* (pp. 349–441). New York: Academic Press.

Duncan-Johnson, C. C., & Donchin, E. (1982). The P300 component of the event-related brain potential as an index of information processing. *Biological Psychology, 14*, 1–52.

Dustman, R. E., & Beck, E. C. (1972). Relationship of intelligence to visually evoked potentials. *Electroencephalography and Clinical Neurophysiology, 33*, 254.

Egan, V. G., Cheswick, A., Brettle, R. P., & Goodwin, G. M. (1993). The Edinburgh cohort of HIV-positive drug users: The relationship between auditory P3 latency, cognitive function, and self-rated mood. *Psychological Medicine, 23*, 613–622.

Egan, V. G., Cheswick, A., Santosh, C., Naidu, K., Rimmington, J. E., & Best, J. J. K. (1994). Size isn't everything: A study of brain volume, intelligence, and auditory evoked potentials. *Personality and Individual Differences, 17*(3), 357–367.

Egan, V., Wickett, J. C., & Vernon, P. A. (1995). Brain size and intelligence: Erratum, addendum, and correction. *Personality and Individual Differences, 19*, 113–115.

Eisen, A., & Elleker, G. (1980). Sensory nerve stimulation and evoked cerebral potentials. *Neurology, 30*, 1097–1105.

Ernhart, C. B., Marler, M. R., & Morrow-Tlucak, M. (1987). Size and cognitive development in the early preschool years. *Psychological Reports, 61*, 103–106.

Ertl, J. P., & Schafer, E. W. P. (1969). Brain response correlates of psychometric intelligence. *Nature, 223*, 421–422.

Estabrooks, G. H. (1928). The relation between cranial capacity, relative cranial capacity and intelligence in school children. *Journal of Applied Psychology, 12*, 524–529.

Eysenck, H. J. (1993). The biological basis of intelligence. In P. A. Vernon (Ed.), *Biological approaches to the study of human intelligence* (pp. 1–32). Norwood, NJ: Ablex.

Eysenck, H. J. (1994). A biological theory of intelligence. In D. K. Detterman (Ed.), *Current topics in human intelligence: Vol. 4. Theories of intelligence* (pp. 117–149). Norwood. NJ: Ablex.

Fabiani, M., Gratton, G., Karis, D., & Donchin, E. (1987). The definition, identification, and reliability of the P300 component of the event-related brain potential. In P. K. Ackles, J. R., Jennings, & M. G. H. Coles (Eds.), *Advances in psychophysiology* (Vol. 2, pp. 1–78). Greenwich, CT: JAI Press.

Falkenstein, M., Hohnsbein, J., & Hoorman, J. (1995). Analysis of mental workload with ERP indicators of processing stages. In G. Karmos, M. Molnàr, V. Csèpe, I. Czigler, & J. E. Desmedt (Eds.), *Perspectives on event-related potentials research* (EEG Supplement 44, pp. 190–196). NY: Elsevier Science.

Federico, P.-A. (1984). Event-related potential (ERP) correlates of cognitive styles, abilities, and aptitudes. *Personality and Individual Differences, 5*(5), 575–585.

Fuchs, J. L., Montemayor, M., & Greenough, W. T. (1990). Effect of environmental complexity on size of the superior colliculus. *Behavioral and Neural Biology, 54*, 198–203.

Galton, F. (1888). Head growth in students at the University of Cambridge. *Nature, 38*, 14–15.

Haier, R. J. (1990). The end of intelligence research. *Intelligence, 14*, 371–374.

Haier, R. J., Chueh, D., Touchette, P., Lott, I., Buchsbaum, M. S., MacMillan, D., Sandman, C., LaCasse, L., & Sosa, E. (1995). Brain size and cerebral glucose metabolic rate in nonspecific mental retardation and Down syndrome. *Intelligence, 20*, 191–210.

Haier, R. J., Robinson, D. L., Braden, W., & Williams, D. (1983). Electrical potentials of the cerebral cortex and psychometric intelligence. *Personality and Individual Differences, 4*(6), 591–599.

Haier, R. J., Siegel, B. V., Nuechterlein, K. H., Hazlett, E., Wu, J. C., Peak, J., Browning, H. L., & Buchsbaum, M. S. (1988). Cortical glucose metabolic rate correlates of abstract reasoning and attention studied with positron emission tomography. *Intelligence, 12*, 199–217.

Harter, M. R., & White, C. T. (1970). Evoked cortical responses to checkerboard patterns: Effect of check-size as a function of visual acuity. *Electroencephalography and Clinical Neurology, 28*, 48–54.

Harvey, I., Persaud, R., Ron, M. A., Baker, G., & Murray, R. M. (1994). Volumetric MRI measurements in bipolars compared with schizophrenics and healthy controls. *Psychological Medicine, 24*, 689–699.

Hendrickson, A. E. (1982). The biological basis of intelligence. Part I: Theory. In H. J. Eysenck (Ed.), *A model for intelligence* (pp. 151–196). Berlin: Springer-Verlag.

Hendrickson, D. E. (1982). The biological basis of intelligence. Part II: Measurement. In H. J. Eysenck (Ed.), *A model for intelligence* (pp. 197–228). Berlin: Springer-Verlag.

Henneberg, M., Budnik, A., Pezacka, M., & Puch, A. E. (1985). Head size, body size, and intelligence: Intraspecific correlations in *Homo sapiens*. *Homo, 36*, 207–218.

Hoadley, M. F. (with Pearson, K.). (1929). On measurement of the internal diameters of the skull in relation: I. To the prediction of its capacity; II. To the "preeminence" of the left hemisphere. *Biometrika, 21*, 85–123.

Howard, L., & Polich, J. (1985). P300 latency and memory span development. *Developmental Psychology, 21*, 283–289.

Jensen, A. R., Schafer, E. W. P., & Crinella, F. M. (1981). Reaction time, evoked brain potentials, and psychometric *g* in the severely retarded. *Intelligence, 5*, 179–197.

Jensen, A. R., & Sinha, S. N. (1993). Physical correlates of human intelligence. In P. A. Vernon (Ed.), *Biological approaches to the study of human intelligence.* Norwood, NJ: Ablex.

Johnson, R., Jr. (1986). A triarchic model of P300 amplitude. *Psychophysiology, 23*, 367–384.

Johnson, R., Jr. (1988). The amplitude of the P300 component of the event-related potential: Review and synthesis. In P. K. Ackles, J. R. Jennings, & M. G. H. Coles (Eds.), *Advances in psychophysiology: A research manual* (Vol. 3, pp. 69–138). Greenwich, CT: JAI Press.

Jones, P. B., Harvey, I., Lewis, S. W., Toone, B. K., Van Os, J., Williams, M., & Murray, R. M. (1994). Cerebral ventricle dimensions as risk factors for schizophrenia and affective psychosis: An epidemiological approach to analysis. *Psychological Medicine, 24*, 995–1011.

Jones, T. A., & Greenough, W. T. (1996). Ultrastructural evidence for increased contact between astrocytes and synapses in rats reared in a complex environment. *Neurobiology of Learning and Memory, 65*, 48–56.

Josiassen, R. C., Shagass, C., Roemer, R. A., & Slepner, S. (1988). Evoked potential correlates of intelligence in nonpatient subjects. *Biological Psychology, 27*, 207–225.

Kareken, D. A., Gur, R. C., Mozley, P. D., Mozley, L. H., Saykin, A. J., Shtasel, D. L., & Gur, R. E. (1995). Cognitive functioning and neuroanatomic volume measures in schizophrenia. *Neuropsychology, 9*, 211–219.

Katsanis, J., Iacono, W. G., McGue, M. K., & Carlson, S. R. (1997). P300 event-related potential heritability in monozygotic and dizygotic twins. *Psychophysiology, 34*, 47–58.

Klein, R. E., Freeman, H. E., Kagan, J., Yarbrough, C., & Habicht, J. P. (1972). Is big smart? The relation of growth to cognition. *Journal of Health and Social Behavior, 13*, 219–225.

Knight, R. T., Scabini, D., Woods, D., & Clayworth, C. (1989). Contributions of temporal-parietal junction to the human auditory P3. *Brain Research, 502*, 109–116.

Kranzler, J. H., & Jensen, A. J. (1989). Inspection time and intelligence: A meta-analysis. *Intelligence, 13*, 329–347.

Kutas, M., McCarthy, G., & Donchin, E. (1977). Augmenting mental chronometry: The P300 as a measure of stimulus evaluation time. *Science, 197*, 792–795.

Ladish, C., & Polich, J. (1989). P300 and probability in children. *Journal of Experimental Child Psychology, 48*, 212–223.

Larson, G. E., Haier, R. J., LaCasse, L., & Hazen, K. (1995). Evaluation of a "mental effort" hypothesis for correlations between cortical metabolism and intelligence. *Intelligence, 21*, 267–278.

Lemons, J. A., Schreiner, R. L., & Gresham, E. L. (1981). Relationship of brain weight to head circumference in early infancy. *Human Biology, 53*, 351–354.

Lynn, R. (1989). A nutrition theory of the secular increases in intelligence. Positive correlations between height, head size and IQ. *British Journal of Educational Psychology, 59*, 372–377.

Lynn, R. (1990). New evidence on brain size and intelligence: A comment on Rushton and Cain and

Vanderwolf. *Personality and Individual Differences, 11*, 795–797.

Lynn, R., & Jindal, S. (1993). Positive correlations between brain size and intelligence: Further evidence from India. *Mankind Quarterly, 34*, 109–115.

Magliero, A., Bashore, T. R., Coles, M. G. H., & Donchin, E. (1984). On the dependence of P300 latency on stimulus evaluation processes. *Psychophysiology, 21*, 171–186.

Majluf, A. (1983). Desarrollo mental, postural y somatico de infantes de 8, 14 y 20 meses de edad, de clase socio-economica media y baja de Lima. *Revista Latinoamericana de Psicologia, 15*, 369–386.

Martin, A., Brouwers, P., Lalonde, F., Cox, C., Teleska, P., Fedio, P., Foster, N. L., & Chase, T. N. (1986). Towards a behavioral typology of Alzheimer patients. *Journal of Clinical and Experimental Neuropsychology, 8*, 594–610.

McCarthy, G., & Donchin, E. (1983). Chronometric analysis of human information processing. In A. W. K. Gaillard & W. Ritter (Eds.), Tutorials in ERP research: *Endogenous components* (pp. 251–267). New York: North-Holland.

McCarthy, G., Wood, C. C., Williamson, P. D., & Spencer, D. (1989). Task-dependent field potentials in human hippocampal formation. *Journal of Neuroscience, 9*, 4235–4268.

McGarry-Roberts, P. A., Stelmack, R. M., & Campbell, K. B. (1992). Intelligence, reaction time, and event-related potentials. *Intelligence, 16*, 289–313.

Miller, E. M. (1994). Intelligence and brain myelination: A hypothesis. *Personality and Individual Differences, 17*, 803–832.

Morris, G. L., & Alcorn, M. B. (1995). Raven's progressive matrices and inspection time: P200 slope correlates. *Personality and Individual Differences, 18*, 81–87.

Murdoch, K., & Sullivan, L. R. (1923). A contribution to the study of mental and physical measurements in normal children. *American Physical Education Review, 28*, 209–215, 276–280, 328–330.

Nelson, K. B., & Deutschberger, J. (1970). Head size at one year as a predictor of four-year IQ. *Developmental Medicine and Child Neurology, 12*, 487–495.

Nettlebeck, T. (1987). Inspection time and intelligence. In P. A. Vernon (Ed.), *Speed of information-processing and intelligence* (pp. 295–346). Norwood, NJ: Ablex.

Nettlebeck, T., & Lally, M. (1976). Inspection time and measured intelligence. *British Journal of Psychology, 67*, 17–22.

O'Donnell, B. F., Friedman, S., Swearer, J. M., & Drachman, D. A. (1992). Active and passive P3 latency and psychometric performance: Influence of age and individual differences. *International Journal of Psychophysiology, 12*, 187–195.

Osborne, R. T. (1992). Cranial capacity and IQ. *Mankind Quarterly, 32*, 328–330.

Oswald, W. D., & Roth, E. (1978). *Der Zahlen-Verbindungs-Test (ZVT)*. (The number connecting test). Gottingen, Germany: Hogrefe.

Ounsted, M., Moar, V. A., & Scott, A. (1984). Associations between size and development at four years among children who were small-for-dates and large-for-dates at birth. *Early Human Development, 9*, 259–268.

Pakkenberg, B., & Gundersen, H. J. G. (1997). Neocortical neuron number in humans: Effect of sex and age. *The Journal of Comparative Neurology, 384*, 312–320.

Parks, R. W., Loewenstein, D. A., Dodrill, K. L., Barker, W. W., Yoshii, F., Chang, J. Y., Emran, A., Apicella, A., Sheramata, W. A., & Duara, R. (1988). Cerebral metabolic effects of a verbal fluency test: A PET scan study. *Journal of Clinical and Experimental Neuropsychology, 10*, 565–575.

Passingham, R. E. (1979). Brain size and intelligence in man. *Brain, Behaviour and Evolution, 16*, 253–270.

Pearl, R. (1906). On the correlation between intelligence and the size of the head. *Journal of Comparative Neurology and Psychology, 16*, 189–199.

Pearlson, G. D., Kim, W. S., Kubos, K. L., Moberg, P. J., Jayaram, G., Bascom, M. J., Chase, G. A., Goldfinger, A. D., & Tune, L. E. (1989). Ventricle-brain ratio, computed tomographic density, and brain area in 50 schizophrenics. *Archives of General Psychiatry, 46*, 690–697.

Pearson, K. (1906). On the relationship of intelligence to size and shape of head, and to other physical and mental characters. *Biometrika, 5*, 105–146.

Pelosi, L., Holly, M., Slade, T., Hayward, M., Barrett, G., & Blumhardt, L. D. (1992a). Wave form variations in auditory event-related potentials evoked by a memory-scanning task and their relationship with tests of intellectual function. *Electroencephalography and Clinical Neurophysiology, 84*, 344–352.

Pelosi, L., Holly, M., Slade, T., Hayward, M., Barrett, G., & Blumhardt, L. D. (1992b). Event-related potential (ERP) correlates of performance of intelligence tests. *Electroencephalography and Clinical Neurophysiology, 84*, 515–520.

Perry, N. W., McCow, J. G., Cunningham, W. R., Falgout, J. C., & Street, W. J. (1976). Multivariate visual evoked response correlates of intelligence. *Psychophysiology, 13*, 323–329.

Polich, J., Ehlers, C. L., Otis, S., Mandell, A. J., & Bloom, F. E. (1986). P300 latency reflects the degree of cognitive decline in dementing illness. *Electroencephalography and Clinical Neurophysiology, 63*, 138–144.

Polich, J., Howard, L., & Starr, A. (1985). Stimulus frequency and masking as determinants of P300 latency in event-related potentials from auditory stimuli. *Biological Psychology, 21*, 309–318.

Polich, J., & Kok, A. (1995). Cognitive and biological determinants of P300: An integrative review. *Biological Psychology, 41*, 103–146.

Polich, J., Ladish, C., & Burns, T. (1990). Normal variation of P300 in children: Age, memory span, and head size. *Electroencephalography and Clinical Neurophysiology, 9*, 237–248.

Polich, J., & Martin, S. (1992). P300, cognitive capability, and personality: A correlational study of university undergraduates. *Personality and Individual Differences, 13,* 533–543.

Pollitt, E., Mueller, W., & Leibel, R. L. (1982). The relation of growth to cognition in a well-nourished preschool population. *Child Development, 53,* 1157–1163.

Porteus, S. D. (1937). *Primitive intelligence and environment.* New York: Macmillan.

Posner, M. I., Boies, S. J., Eichelman, W. H., & Taylor, R. L. (1969). Retention of visual and name codes of single letters. *Journal of Experimental Psychology Monographs, 81,* 10–15.

Ragot, R. (1984). Perceptual and motor space representation: An event-related potential study. *Psychophysiology, 21,* 159–170.

Ragot, R., & Renault, B. (1981). P300 as a function of S–R compatibility and motor programming. *Biological Psychology, 13,* 289–294.

Raz, N., Torres, I. J., Spencer, W. D., Millman, D., Baertschi, J. C., & Sarpel G. (1993). Neuroanatomical correlates of age-sensitive and age-invariant cognitive abilities: An *in vivo* MRI investigation. *Intelligence, 17,* 407–422.

Reed, T. E. (1984). Mechanism for heritability of intelligence. *Nature, 311,* 417.

Reed, T. E., & Jensen, A. R. (1991). Arm nerve conduction velocity (NCV); brain NCV, reaction time, and intelligence, *Intelligence, 15,* 33–47.

Reed, T. E., & Jensen, A. R. (1993). Cranial capacity: New Caucasian data and comments on Rushton's claimed Mongoloid–Caucasoid brain-size differences. *Intelligence, 17,* 423–431.

Reid, R. W., & Mulligan, J. H. (1923). Relation of cranial capacity to intelligence. *Journal of the Royal Anthropological Institute, 53,* 322–331.

Reiss, A. L., Abrams, M. T., Singer, H. S., Ross, J. L., & Denckla, M. B. (1996). Brain development, gender and IQ in children. A volumetric imaging study. *Brain, 119,* 1763–1774.

Rijsdijk, F. V., & Boomsma, D. I. (1997). Genetic mediation of the correlation between peripheral nerve conduction velocity and IQ. *Behavior Genetics, 27,* 87–98.

Rijsdijk, F. V., Boomsma, D. I., & Vernon, P. A. (1995). Genetic analysis of peripheral nerve conduction velocity in twins. *Behavior Genetics, 25,* 341–348.

Rhodes, L., Dustman, R., & Beck, E. (1969). The visual evoked response: A comparison of bright and dull children. *Electroencephalography and Clinical Neurophysiology, 27,* 367–372.

Robaey, P., Cansino, S., Dugas, M., & Renault, B. (1995). A comparative study of ERP correlates of psychometric and Piagetian intelligence measures in normal and hyperactive children. *Electroencephalography and Clinical Neurophysiology, 96,* 56–75.

Robinson, D. L. (1996). *Brain, mind, and behaviour.* Westport, CT: Praeger Press.

Robinson, D. L. (1997). A test of the Hendrickson postulate that reduced EEG response variance causes increased AEP contour length: Implications for the "neural transmission errors" theory of intelligence. *Personality and Individual Differences, 22*(2), 173–182.

Robinson, D. L., Haier, R. J., Braden, W., & Krengel, M. (1984). Psychometric intelligence and visual evoked potentials: A replication. *Personality and Individual Differences, 5*(4), 487–489.

Rushton, J. P. (1992). Life-history comparisons between oriental and whites at a Canadian university. *Personality and Individual Differences, 13,* 439–442.

Rushton, J. P. (in press). Cranial size and IQ in Asian Americans from birth to age seven. *Intelligence.*

Schafer, E. W. P. (1979). Cognitive neural ability: A biological basis for individual differences in intelligence. *Psychophysiology, 16,* 199.

Schafer, E. W. P. (1982). Neural adaptability: A biological determinant of behavioral intelligence. *International Journal of Neuroscience, 17,* 183–191.

Schafer, E. W. P., & Marcus, M. M. (1973). Self-stimulation alters human sensory brain responses. *Science, 181,* 175–177.

Schreider, E. (1968). Quelques corrélations somatiques des tests mentaux. *Homo, 19,* 38–43.

Schucard, D. W., & Callaway, E. (1973). Relationship between human intelligence and frequency of analysis of cortical evoked responses. *Perceptual and Motor Skills, 36,* 147–151.

Segalowitz, S. J., & Barnes, K. L. (1993). The reliability of ERP components in the auditory oddball paradigm. *Psychophysiology, 30,* 451–459.

Segalowitz, S. J., Unsal, A., & Dywan, J. (1992). Cleverness and wisdom in 12-year-olds: Electrophysiological evidence for late maturation of the frontal lobe. *Developmental Neuropsychology, 8*(2 & 3), 279–298.

Sen, A. K., Phulia, S. S., & Wasnik, B. K. (1986). Physical growth and intellectual level: A comparative study between scheduled caste and general caste students. *Indian Journal of Current Psychological Research, 1,* 101–106.

Shagass, C., Roemer, R. A., Straumanis, J. J., & Josiassen, R. C. (1981). Intelligence as a factor in evoked potential studies in psychopathology. *Biological Psychiatry, 11,* 1007–1029.

Shucard, D. W., & Horn, J. L. (1972). Evoked cortical potentials and measurement of human abilities. *Journal of Comparative and Physiological Psychology, 78,* 59–68.

Sommerville, R. C. (1924). Physical, motor and sensory traits. *Archives of Psychology, 12*(75), 1–108.

Spearman, C. (1927). *The abilities of man,* New York: Macmillan.

Stauder, J. E. A., van der Molen, M. W., & Molenaar, P. C. M. (1995). Event related brain potentials and transitions in the level of cognitive development during childhood. In G. Karmos, M. Molnár, V. Csèpe, I. Czigler, & J. E. Desmedt (Eds.), *Perspectives on event-related potentials research (EEG Supplement, 44)* (pp. 339–346). New York: Elsevier Science.

Stelmack, R. M., & Houlihan, M. (1995). Event-related

potentials, personality, and intelligence. In D. H. Saklofske, & M. Zeidner (Eds.), *International handbook of personality and intelligence* (pp. 349–365). New York: Plenum Press.

Sternberg, S. (1966). High speed scanning in human memory. *Science, 153,* 421–457.

Sternberg, S. (1969). Memory scanning: Mental processes revealed by reaction time experiments. *American Scientists, 57,* 421–457.

Sternberg, S. (1975). Memory scanning: New findings and current controversies. *Quarterly Journal of Experimental Psychology, 27,* 1–32.

Stough, C. K. K., Nettelbeck, T., & Cooper, C. J. (1990). Evoked brain potentials, string length, and intelligence. *Personality and Individual Differences, 11*(4), 401–406.

Surwillo, W. W. (1984). P300 latency and digit span. *Psychophysiology, 21*(6), 708–709.

Susanne, C., & Sporcq, J. (1973). Etude des correlations existant entre des tests psycho-techniques et des mensurations cephaliques. *Bulletin de la Société Royale Belge d'Anthropologie et de Préhistoire, 84,* 59–69.

Sutton, S., Braren, M., Zubin, J., & John, E. R. (1965). Evoked-potential correlates of stimulus uncertainty. *Science, 150,* 1187–1188.

Tan, Ü. (1996). Correlations between nonverbal intelligence and peripheral nerve conduction velocity in right-handed subjects: Sex-related differences. *International Journal of Psychophysiology, 22,* 123–128.

Verleger, R. (1997). On the utility of P3 latency as an index of mental chronometry. *Psychophysiology, 34,* 131–156.

Vernon, P. A. (1983). Speed of information processing and general intelligence. *Intelligence, 7,* 53–70.

Vernon, P. A. (Ed.). (1987). *Speed of information-processing and intelligence.* Norwood, NJ: Ablex.

Vernon, P. A. (Ed.). (1993a). *Biological approaches to the study of human intelligence.* Norwood, NJ: Ablex.

Vernon, P. A. (1993b). Intelligence and neural efficiency. In D. K. Detterman (Ed.), *Current topics in human intelligence, Vol. 3.* Norwood, NJ: Ablex.

Vernon, P. A. (1997). Behavioral genetic and biological approaches to intelligence. In H. Nyborg (Ed.), *The scientific study of human nature: Tribute to Hans J. Eysenck at eighty.* Oxford: Elsevier Science Ltd.

Vernon, P. A., & Mori, M. (1989). Intelligence, reaction times, and nerve conduction velocity. *Behavior Genetics (abstracts), 19,* 779.

Vernon, P. A., & Mori, M. (1992). Intelligence, reaction times, and peripheral nerve conduction velocity. *Intelligence, 16,* 273–288.

Vetterli, C. F., & Furedy, J. J. (1985). Evoked potential correlates of intelligence: Some problems with Hendrickson's string measure of evoked potential complexity and error theory of intelligence. *International Journal of Psychophysiology, 3,* 1–3.

Vickers, D. (1970). Evidence for the accumulator model of psychophysical discrimination. *Ergonomics, 13,* 37–58.

Vickers, D. (1979). *Decision processes in visual perception.* London: Academic Press.

Vickers, D., Nettlebeck, T., & Willson, R. J. (1972). Perceptual indices of performance: The measurement of "inspection time" and "noise" in the visual system. *Perception, 1,* 263–295.

Vogel, F., Kruger, J., Schalt, E., Schnobel, R., & Hassling, L. (1987). No consistent relationship between oscillations and latencies of visually and auditory evoked EEG potentials and measures of mental performance. *Human Neurobiology, 6,* 173–182.

Weinberg, W. A., Dietz, S. G., Penick, E. C., & McAlister, W. H. (1974). Intelligence, reading achievement, physical size, and social class. *The Journal of Pediatrics, 85,* 482–489.

Weiss, V. (1986). From memory span and mental speed toward the quantum mechanics of intelligence. *Personality and Individual Differences, 7*(5), 737–749.

Wickett, J. C. (1999). Head size, brain volume, and intelligence: 100 years of research. *Personality and Individual Differences.* Manuscript submitted for publication.

Wickett, J. C., & Vernon, P. A. (1994). Peripheral nerve conduction velocity, reaction time, and intelligence: An attempt to replicate Vernon and Mori (1992). *Intelligence, 18,* 27–131.

Wickett, J. C., Vernon, P. A., & Lee, D. H. (1994). *In vivo* brain size, head perimeter, and intelligence in a sample of healthy adult females. *Personality and Individual Differences, 16,* 831–838.

Wickett, J. C., Vernon, P. A., Brown, J. D., & Broome, R. (1999). Nerve conduction velocity predicts intelligence, but not reaction time. *Intelligence.* Manuscript submitted for publication.

Wickett, J. C., Vernon, P. A., & Lee, D. H. (1999). The relationships between the factors of intelligence and brain volume. *Personality and Individual Differences.* Manuscript submitted for publication.

Widaman, K. F., Carlson, J. S., Saetermoe, C. L., & Galbraith, G. C. (1993). The relationship between auditory evoked potentials to fluid and crystallized intelligence. *Personality and Individual Differences, 15*(2), 205–217.

Willerman, L., Schultz, R., Rutledge, J. N., & Bigler, E. D. (1991). *In vivo* brain size and intelligence. *Intelligence, 15,* 223–228.

Yeo, R. A., Turkheimer, E., Raz, N., & Bigler, E. D. (1987). Volumetric asymmetries of the human brain: Intellectual correlates. *Brain and Cognition, 6,* 15–23.

Zhang, Y., Caryl, P. G., & Deary, I. J. (1989a). Evoked potential correlates of inspection time. *Personality and Individual Differences, 10*(4), 379–384.

Zhang, Y., Caryl, P. G., & Deary, I. J. (1989b). Evoked potentials, inspection time, and intelligence. *Personality and Individual Differences, 10*(10), 1079–1094.

PART V

INTELLIGENCE AND INFORMATION PROCESSING

CHAPTER THIRTEEN

Simple Information Processing and Intelligence

IAN J. DEARY

INTRODUCTION

To have accepted the invitation to write a chapter with this title is to accept a poisoned chalice. The poison is in the word "simple." "Apparently simple" will be the otherwise unspoken assumption of the rest of this chapter. What will be presented as simple are those tasks the researchers thought were directly or indirectly assessing a single, basic limitation in the processing of information. Therefore, consigned to "complexity" are those experimental psychology tasks from which information processing parameters may be distilled. These include reaction time procedures such as the Hick and Posner tasks, and S. Sternberg's rapid memory scanning task. A review of these tasks and their relevance to "mental speed" concepts of intelligence is available elsewhere (Neubauer, 1997, which also includes R. Sternberg's reaction–time-based studies of the components of analogical and other types of reasoning). For a brief evaluation of this research, see Deary (1997). Thus, the data presented here will not cover most tasks borrowed from experimental–cognitive psychology; a lower level is addressed. Now that what is too complex for inclusion has been indicated, what is considered too simple? Not covered here are those correlates of intelligence that are arguably more biological, such as nerve conduction velocity, brain-evoked potentials, brain anatomy, and functional brain scanning. The association between these indicators of brain integrity and psychometric intelligence is reviewed by Deary & Caryl (1997a) and Vernon (1993). These types of techniques and the variables inferred from them are highly relevant to the processing of information – and it is possible that any account of human intelligence differences will be unsatisfying until articulated in biological terms – but the tasks and constructs considered here will be at a level somewhat above physiology and biology. To a large extent the material considered here will address the processing of sensory information and its relation to psychometric intelligence. To understand the motivation for the type of research described herein it is useful to be aware of the two streams of intelligence research that began with Galton and Spearman on the one hand, and with Binet on the other.

Binet first. Among other notable contributions he devised the first test of what we would now call general mental abilities. The aim of devising this test was practical: to predict the likelihood of pupils' benefiting from normal schooling. The uptake of the Binet–Simon test and the devising of other tests and the many applications to which mental tests were put demonstrate the popularity of psychometric ability tests of mental abilities. Recent summaries of a large body of research suggest that psychometric measures of intelligence can be described using a hierarchy of abilities from general intelligence down to very specific abilities, are stable across many years, are substantially heritable, and predict real-life outcomes in education, employment, and quality of life (Neisser et al., 1996; Neisser, 1997).

Despite these indicators of the validity of psychometric intelligence, it is widely recognized that we still do not know what it means in terms of brain mechanisms to be more or less intelligent. The so-called intelligence-testing "industry" has a parallel industry of critics of intelligence, and one of the latter's persistent complaints has been that the measurement of intelligence is based on no theory or understanding of the nature of intelligence (Howe, 1988). Thus was prompted Boring's (1923) quip that intelligence is what the tests test and Sternberg's (1990) portrayal of intelligence research as a series of elaborate metaphors. The answer to these proper criticisms is to provide an account of human intelligence differences in terms of parameter differences in a model of human information processing. In our present state of knowledge we do not know enough to specify the level of description that is best suited to articulating such a model. The more intelligent brain may be one that metabolizes more efficiently, has a more elaborate network of dendrites, or transmits neural signals with fewer errors or more speed. On the other hand, the more intelligent brain may be one that has more elaborate cognitive strategies, better working memory, or more attentional resources. The first and second set of possibilities are not exclusive, but contrasting them emphasizes the scale of the explanatory problem. Elsewhere, it has been said that efforts to explain the nature of human intelligence have appealed to constructs at the psychometric, cognitive, psychophysical, physiological, biochemical, and genetic levels (Deary, 1999).

Galton and Spearman are often seen as the founders of a loose body called the London School of Psychology. Jensen (1998) has stated that a characteristic of the London school's approach to mental phenomena is its reductionism: "it aims theoretically to explain complex phenomena in terms of simpler, more elemental processes." Thus, in addition to an interest in quantifying human intelligence differences, Galton and Spearman wanted to explain them in terms of variance in lower level constructs. Their efforts to do this failed to generate a substantial program of continued research. After Spearman's research in this area, it was not until the 1970s – and the growth of cognitive psychology – that an area of research could be identified that was studying intelligence differences in information processing terms (Deary, 1997).

In describing the research effort that tries to account for some of the variance in human intelligence in terms of lower level, simple processing differences there will be a division into direct and indirect methods. Direct methods are those instances in which a test is thought to be a proximal measure of a construct; that is, one's score on the test is a measure of one's limitations in a basic processing construct. Indirect methods are those instances in which simple processing constructs are inferred from more complex tasks.

DIRECT METHODS
Sensory Discrimination
Historical

Galton thought that the basis of individual differences in higher manifestations of intelligence was in the senses (1883). His hypothesis was that brighter people are able to make finer sensory discriminations among colors, tones, and weights than people of lower intelligence. The evidence he collected in his anthropometric laboratory was inconclusive, and Galton's favored evidence in his popular accounts was anecdotal. Thus, he observed, woolsorters, tea tasters, and piano tuners were bright and were men, allowing him to support the sensory discrimination theory of intelligence and his view that men are, on average, more intelligent than women. Galton's contribution was the hypothesis of the link between intelligence and sensory discrimination; he did not leave any data that are conclusive (Deary, 1994a).

The idea was developed empirically by Spearman (1904). He tested schoolchildren's sensory discrimination and correlated their scores with either estimates of intelligence or school subject performance. He found universally positive and substantial correlations among the school subject test scores. The arrangement of these correlations in the matrix he found to be hierarchical, and this led to his discovery of general intelligence or g. He found that there were positive correlations, too, among the tests of sensory discrimination. Moreover, there were positive correlations between the tests of sensory discrimination and estimates of intelligence (average correlation = .39, range = .25 to .47) and school subject scores. It was this result that influenced Spearman's ideas about the nature of intelligence differences for decades; he believed that the basis of human intelligence is the ability to discriminate difference, whether those differences are at the sensory or a much higher cognitive level.

At about the same time, Thorndike, Lay, and Dean (1909) and Burt (1909/1910) found similar results to those of Spearman; that is, modest associations among measures of sensory discrimination and estimates of higher level cognitive abilities. However, their differences in interpretation are of interest. Thorndike argued that one could not rule out some common test-taking variable as the basis for the correlation. Such an argument reminds us to consider the sources of variance in a test score. For Spearman (1904), scores on tests of sensory acuity contained variance attributable to sensory acuity and error. For Thorndike, the tests also contained more nebulous variance related to doing well in tests in general, and he argued that that might be the source of variance accounting for the correlation with intelligence estimates. For example, both tests require attention to instructions and a willingness to try one's best, have a potential to induce performance anxiety, and so forth. Thorndike's suggestion, as we shall see, persists in this field of research and continually proves difficult to confirm or refute.

Burt (1909/1910) also found modest correlations between scores on measures of sensory discrimination and test scores of higher cognitive functions and estimates of intelligence. Though he is usually considered to be Spearman's successor in the London School, his interpretation of his results is interestingly different from Spearman's (1904). Burt was impressed by finding that tests of higher cognitive functions were more closely related to intelligence, and his advocacy of such tests puts him closer to Binet than to Spearman. He considered sensory discrimination measures to be of little use in the testing of intelligence, and he noted that visual and auditory, but not tactile, discrimination were related to intelligence estimates. Burt's reflections on his results begin to build a recognizable picture of the structure of human abilities. He viewed these as a hierarchical continuity from the simplest acts of cognition – sensory discrimination – through more integrated functions to that which is called general intelligence. His construing mental ability in this fashion was not dissimilar to R. Sternberg's (1985) description of ability in terms of components and higher level metacomponents. Burt's view was that one could expect only mod-

est correlations between simple processing measures and psychometric intelligence because the two measures are much separated in the hierarchy of human abilities.

Further confirmation of Spearman's ideas about associations between intelligence and sensory discrimination came from his graduate students before and during World War I. Abelson (1911) and Carey (1914/1915), testing low IQ and more normal children, respectively, administered sensory discrimination measures and psychometric ability tests to larger samples than had Spearman or Burt. The results of these studies show the same modest correlations between sensory discrimination measures and higher level mental ability test scores and that the sensory discrimination measures have substantial loadings on the general factor obtained from the correlation matrix of mental ability tests (Deary, 1994a).

Therefore, before 1920, there was a fair body of research that had found correlations between measures of sensory discrimination – in the visual and auditory modalities – and higher level ability. It is somewhat odd that many who have written the history of this research have concluded the opposite; that is, that no such associations were obtained. In support of this counterclaim they often cite studies by Sharp (1898/1899) and Wissler (1901), neither of whom studied sensory discrimination, the latter having conducted tests on only seven postgraduate students. More details on all of the preceding studies and the inaccuracy of the histories of the period are given by Deary (1994a).

Modern

If individual differences in sensory discrimination are related to psychometric intelligence differences, then the result may be informative about the nature of intelligence. Tests of musical ability often include within them tests of pitch discrimination. These subtests of pitch discrimination have modest correlations with psychometric ability test scores (Bentley, 1963; Lynn, Wilson, & Gault, 1989). The studies tend to examine schoolchildren. We need only refer to the hypothesis of Thorndike et al. (1909) stated earlier to remind us of the possibility that some source of variance other than pitch discrimination could account for the association. However, despite a quiescent period between the historical and more modern research, there are now some better studies that are replicating the same association.

Using Seashore's Measures of Musical Talent it was (Deary, Caryl, Egan, & Wight, 1989; Deary, 1994b) found that pitch discrimination correlated significantly at about .3 with psychometric intelligence in 11- and 13-year-olds but not in university undergraduates. Watson employed the Test of Basic Auditory Capabilities and found that various simple auditory processing measures, including pitch discrimination, correlated significantly with psychometric test scores in learning disabled and student samples at levels of r between .3 and .5. Raz, Willerman, and Yama (1987) used a pitch discrimination test and found substantial – around .5 – correlations with intelligence test scores. These authors were some of the few to develop a theory of such associations, arguing that intelligence lies partly in the ability to represent stimuli in an error-free, faithful way. They averred in addition that such a basic ability could explain some phenomena that have been interpreted as suggesting that intelligence is related to "mental speed," and that Galton was correct in associating intelligence and the senses.

A summary of historical and modern studies reporting correlations between sensory discrimination and psychometric intelligence is given in Table 13.1.

Modern, adequate studies in this field are few, and fewer contain both adequate psychophysical tests and samples of the normal population. It is obvious that validated tests of sensory discrimination are required. However, the nature of the sample is important too. Samples of children are likely to introduce more error of measurement and perhaps more confounding variables (such as attention and motivation) than young adult samples. In older-aged samples there are quite strong correlations between measures of visual and auditory acuity and psychometric test scores. For example, Lindenberger & Baltes (1994) found that "visual and auditory acuity accounted for 49.2% of the total and 93.1% of the age-related reliable variance in intelligence." Over the young-adult age span, from 25 to 69 years, Baltes & Lindenberger (1997) reported 11% of the variance in intelligence being accounted for by visual and auditory acuity. One interpretation of these findings is what Baltes and Lindenberger called "common cause." This hypothesis suggests that, in aging, there are several systems

TABLE 13.1. A Summary of Historical and Modern Studies Reporting Correlations Between Sensory Discrimination and Psychometric Intelligence

Study	Auditory (Pitch) Discrimination	Visual Discrimination	Tactile Discrimination	Sample
Seashore (1899)	.24[a]	—	—	—
Spearman (1904)	.38	.25 to .47	—	Schoolchildren
Burt (1909/1910)	.40	.29	near to zero	Schoolchildren
	.37	.30		
Thorndike et al. (1909)	—	.08 to .23 (median .21)	−.01 to .25 (median .09)	Schoolchildren
Abelson (1911)	—	.30 (girls) .28 (boys)	—	"Backward" children
Carey (1914/1915)	.23	.32	.02	Schoolchildren
Bentley (1963)	.30	—	—	Schoolchildren
Raz et al. (1987)	.42 to .54	—	—	Students
Lynn et al. (1989)	.49[b]	—	—	—
Deary, Head et al. (1989)	near zero	—	—	Students
Watson (1991)	.36 to .57	—	—	Learning disabled
Watson (1991)	.14 & .35	—	—	Students
Deary (1994b)	.29 & .34	—	—	Schoolchildren

Notes: [a] As reported in Spearman (1904). [b] This paper reported the loading on the g factor. All other figures are correlations.

that are in decline and that cognitive function and sensory function are two indicators of general brain integrity. Therefore, rather than sensory performance decline causing intelligence decline, both may be declining because of some general change in the nervous system or body as a whole. Interestingly, Spearman wrote a footnote in Burt's (1909/1910) first published paper in which he indicated a similar idea: that superiority in sensory discrimination tasks and in higher level cognitive ability tasks may both be a reflection of some third variable.

In summary, there is still some life in Galton and Spearman's idea that there is a link between intelligence and the senses. There are some modest associations that become larger when older people are tested. The reasons for any correlations in samples of young subjects may not be the same as those in older examinees in whom a decline in general brain integrity may be the cause. The definitive answer to any connection between intelligence and sensory discrimination awaits new research studies with validated tests of sensory discrimination in normal samples of the population involved in longitudinal studies.

Inspection Time and Related Tasks

We move now to a set of tasks that is often placed under the umbrella term ''mental speed'' (Neubauer, 1997). References to mental speed are met frequently in accounts of the nature of human intelligence. Among laypeople and professionals it is common to hear intelligence explained in part as some form of mental speed (Berger, 1982). Thus, Hobbes (1651/1885) thought intelligence was the speed with which one thought followed on from another. There was much study of reaction time as a basis for intelligence in the early years of the 20th century (Beck, 1933) and again since the 1970s (Deary, 1997). However, whereas mental speed is a useful intuitive term and may even be useful in categorising a series of approaches, it is positively harmful when it comes to be used as a serious explanatory construct. It can encourage the thoughtless use of a task as an indicator of mental speed or of speed of processing. To use this general term to apply to tests that range in type from psychometric (e.g., the digit symbol test from the WAIS–R; Kail & Salthouse, 1994) to biological (e.g., nerve conduction velocity and the latency of the P300 peak in the event-related brain

potential; Deary & Caryl, 1997a) via experimental (various reaction times; e.g., Kranzler, Whang, & Jensen, 1994) and psychophysical (e.g., inspection time; Nettelbeck, 1987) is to make the empirically and as yet unsubstantiated assumption that they all share a major proportion of variance. Some results point to the opposite conclusion: When variance in nerve conduction velocity is removed from the reaction time–psychometric intelligence correlation, the strength of association does not alter (Reed & Jensen, 1993). Bowling and Mackenzie (1996) and Bates and Eysenck (1993) found only limited or zero associations among various measures of speed of mental processing. With mental speed being used to refer to so many different tasks and parameters at different levels of analysis, it is little wonder that some have written forcibly against conceptualizing intelligence in terms of mental speed (Rabbitt, 1996a; Stankov & Roberts, 1997).

Therefore, in studying measures that involve temporal limitations on processing we need to be open to the possibilities that

1. some of the speed variance assessed by a task may be shared with other tasks at different levels of analysis and some may be specific to the measure itself;
2. there may be multiple brain systems for which there are temporal limitations; some of these may be associated with psychometric intelligence and some not;
3. different forms of temporal limitations on information processing may be associated with different types of cognitive ability; some of these may be related to general ability and some to more specific abilities; and
4. the biological foundation of the apparent differences in speed may be some other feature which, though it subserves speed differences at a psychological level, is not a speed measure itself.

Visual

The preceding comments notwithstanding, the idea for inspection time arose from a question of speed. Vickers developed a theory of visual inspection time assuming that human visual perception takes place in quanta and that there are individual differences in these quanta (Vickers, Nettelbeck, & Wilson, 1972). Thus, given a very easy visual discrimination, it should be possible to describe a person's visual processing efficiency in terms of a graph

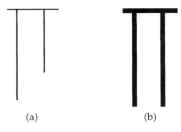

FIGURE 13.1. A stimulus (a) and mask (b) for the inspection time task.

plotting stimulus duration versus the probability of a correct decision. The task Vickers devised to assess this limitation in visual processing is illustrated in Figure 13.1. After a cue, the subject is shown one of two stimuli and must decide which one was the stimulus on a given trial. As shown, the discrimination is an easy one, and the subject merely has to say which of two vertical lines of markedly different lengths is longer; the longer line may appear on the left or the right. To assess the subject's limitations in this easy task, the stimulus durations are varied, and the stimulus is masked to ensure an end to information processing at a defined time. In the inspection-time task there is no speeded response; the measure taken is an indicator of how much stimulus display time was needed for the subject to achieve a given probability of a correct response. In essence, the task is a tachistoscopic presentation one rather like many others in the field of iconic memory, though it has had a rather isolated development largely outside of mainstream psychophysics (White, 1993, 1996).

Individual differences in the inspection-time task correlate significantly with psychometric intelligence test scores. That is, the psychometric function of inspection time in people who score better on IQ-type tests is shifted to the left. This was first discovered by Nettelbeck and Lally in 1976 and has been established in reviews (Brand and Deary, 1982; Deary and Stough, 1996), semiquantitative reviews (Nettelbeck, 1987), a meta-analysis (Kranzler & Jensen, 1989), and some single, larger studies (Deary, 1993; Crawford, Deary, Allan, & Gustafsson, 1998). The correlation between inspection time and performance–fluid-type tests is about .4 to .5, and with verbal tests is smaller (probably around .2 in young adults). Now that this associ-

ation has been established in many independent studies there have been increasing numbers of studies aimed at discovering why the association between some types of psychometric intelligence and inspection time should occur.

DOES THE ASSOCIATION HOLD FOR ALL TYPES OF MENTAL TEST? It was stated above that the association between inspection time and intelligence is stronger for performance-type rather than verbal-type cognitive tasks (Nettelbeck, 1987; Kranzler & Jensen, 1989). Three studies to date have examined the association between inspection time and the Wechsler Adult Intelligence Scale–Revised (WAIS–R) and used structural equation modelling techniques to apportion the variance from inspection time to various WAIS–R factors (Deary, 1993; McGeorge et al., 1996; Crawford et al., in press). Inspection time has a stronger association with the performance or perceptual–organizational factor from the WAIS–R than it does with the g, verbal, or attention–concentration factors. The best model of inspection time's association with the WAIS–R battery appears to be one that involves associations with the perceptual–organizational factor and the general (g) factor. The strongest subtest loadings on the perceptual–organizational factor are block design and object assembly, which have a spatial content, involve combining stimulus fragments into correct spatial orientation, and require work at speed. Therefore, further research with more extensive factor-referenced batteries of mental tests is needed to establish the web of inspection time's psychometric associations and whether these differ in different subject samples (e.g., in different age groups).

One view of information-processing measures and other basic correlates of intelligence is encapsulated by Jensen's (1998) method of correlated vectors. This method examines the correlation between the vector of subtests' loadings on the g factor from a test battery and the vector of correlations between the subtests and the measure in question (e.g., reaction time). Jensen has found, with many measures, that the correlation between such vectors is positive and substantial. This has led Jensen to conclude that associations between biological (e.g., the pH of the brain) and information-processing measures (e.g., reaction times) and tests of cognitive ability is largely accounted for by *g* (e.g., Jensen, 1993). However, the opposite is true for inspection time, which, in three large samples (as above, using the WAIS–R subtests), shows sizable negative correlations using the method of correlated vectors (Deary & Crawford, 1998). One possible reason for this is that, in the WAIS–R battery, the verbal tests predominate in number and have the highest *g* loadings. Therefore, if inspection time provides some explanation for psychometric ability, it may not principally be an explanation of *g* but rather for some group factor of intelligence and less powerfully for *g*. This conclusion may alter when more extensive batteries of cognitive tests – ideally based upon the three-stratum model of psychometric intelligence (Carroll, 1993) – are utilized to examine inspection time.

IS THE ASSOCIATION CAUSED BY STIMULUS ARTIFACTS OF COGNITIVE STRATEGIES? Early on in the study of inspection time–intelligence associations it occurred to researchers that the explanation for the association might be that inspection time was drawing upon individual differences in some high-level performance that was also found in psychometric ability tests (Egan, 1986). Thus, general factors like attention, motivation, personality and test anxiety were hypothesized as the engines of correlation between inspection time and psychometric intelligence rather than the perceptual aspects of inspection time (Howe, 1988). Studies to date suggest that attention (Langsford, Mackenzie, & Maher, 1994; Hutton, Wilding, & Hudson, 1997; Crawford et al., 1998), motivation (Larson, Saccuzzo, & Brown, 1994) and personality (Stough et al., 1996) do not substantially account for the association between inspection time and intelligence.

A related suggestion to the foregoing was that high-ability subjects are more able to find artifacts in the stimulus–mask arrangements that constitute inspection-time tests and that the adoption of these strategies was the cause of the association. It is true that some of the inspection-time setups do produce artifacts, the best known being the apparent movement seen by some subjects in the transition from stimulus to mask (Chaiken & Young, 1993), especially when computer displays or primitive seven-segment light emitting diode displays are used. The

presence of these artifacts has prompted researchers to develop better backward masks (Simpson & Deary, 1997). In addition, detailed study of the types of people who report using apparent movement and other strategies suggests that, although strategy users can attain faster inspection times, they do not have higher IQ-type scores (Egan, 1994). There is no strong evidence to date to suggest that cognitive strategies or stimulus-mask artifacts account for the correlations between inspection times and psychometric intelligence; if anything, the correlations are lowered in the presence of such phenomena (Mackenzie & Bingham, 1985; Egan & Deary, 1992; Chaiken & Young, 1993; Egan, 1994).

ARE THERE PSYCHOPHYSIOLOGICAL, PSYCHOPHARMACOLOGICAL, OR NEUROPSYCHOLOGICAL RESULTS THAT CAN CLARIFY THE RELATIONSHIP? One route to gaining more understanding of the association between inspection time and psychometric intelligence is to examine associations between these variables and physiological performance parameters. This offers the possibility of triangulation: If inspection time and psychometric intelligence relate to a physiological variable, then this may be the source of their shared variance, and we come closer to explaining the inspection time–intelligence association and the nature of intelligence differences.

In a series of studies by Caryl et al. (Zhang, Caryl, & Deary, 1989a,b; Caryl, 1994) it was found that performance on inspection-time tasks is correlated with event-related brain potentials collected while the subject performs the inspection-time discriminations. Specifically, subjects with superior performance on inspection-time tasks tend to have a steeper slope in the epoch at which the negative trough of the event-related potential at about 140 ms after stimulus onset moves to a peak at about 200 ms. Interestingly, the same event-related potential differences were found between high- and low-IQ subjects. Whereas Caryl and colleagues examined the event-related potentials evoked by inspection time stimuli themselves, others have confirmed significant correlations between inspection-time performance and time to reach the P200 peak derived from auditory oddball techniques (Colet, Piera, & Pueyo, 1993). Caryl,

Golding, & Hall (1995) have extended their work to suggest that the gradient of the N140–P200 excursion is related to the necessity to perform a speeded discrimination whether it is in the visual or auditory modality. Caryl's results have been extended by Morris and Alcorn (1995), who found significant correlations between the P200 slope evoked by inspection-time stimuli and scores on Raven's Progressive Matrices. The correlations were highest in the frontal and temporo–occipital areas.

There are sufficient data from independent laboratories to conclude that inspection-time performance has a correlate in the event-related potential and that the specific epoch at which this occurs is the sweep from the negative trough occurring about 100–140 ms after stimulus onset to the positive peak at about 200 ms after stimulus onset. There is more limited evidence to suggest that individual differences in this event-related potential locus also account for some of the variance in psychometric intelligence. This is arguably the most promising area for inspection-time research at present. In future, apart from more replications of this triangulation of psychometrics, psychophysics and psychophysiology, there must be studies using more detailed montages of electrodes to describe more fully the brain localization of these phenomena. In addition, future work will inevitably examine the brain activity induced by inspection-time and psychometric tests using magnetic resonance imaging.

Event-related potentials and functional brain imaging are two ways of assessing brain activity during task performance; they provide parameters related to the brain's electrical activity and metabolism, respectively. Another method of assessing the brain's functional integrity is the use of specific drugs to affect known brain transmitter-receptor systems. One of the most studied systems is the cholinergic, which is known to be of reduced function in Alzheimer's disease. People with Alzheimer's dementia have reduced inspection times when compared with controls and those with Korsakoff's dementia, suggesting that the cholinergic system may be involved in inspection time performance (Deary, Hunter, Langan, & Goodwin, 1991). Another approach to the cholinergic system is to use nicotine, often in the form of smoking. The results here have been contradictory. Petrie and Deary (1989) found that smoking had no effect on inspection time, though

Stough and colleagues (Stough et al., 1995; Stough, Mangan, Bates, & Pellet, 1995) reported that smoking improved inspection time and psychometric intelligence as assessed using Raven's Matrices.

Another approach to discovering the brain bases of inspection time has been to study the differential performance of the two cerebral hemispheres in inspection time. This is done by presenting inspection-time stimuli to one visual field – the subject does not know in advance which one – and masking in both visual fields. Again, we find contradictory results. Nicholls and Atkinson (1993) reported a right visual field–left hemisphere advantage in inspection time and suggested that, in general, the left hemisphere is a faster temporal processor than the right in right-handed subjects. By contrast, Sadler and Deary (1996) found no difference in inspection time in the two hemispheres, though their data suggest that the right hemisphere may benefit more from sustained practice over several days.

IS THERE A SATISFACTORY MECHANISTIC MODEL OF INSPECTION-TIME PERFORMANCE? When Vickers conceived of and developed the inspection-time procedure, the name *inspection time* became applied to more than one thing. Inspection time was the name of the task that involved stating which side of the stimulus had the longer line. Inspection time was also the value attributed to a subject when the task was performed; that is, it was also an individual difference measure. Of more theoretical moment was that inspection time was hypothesized to be the key limitation measured by the task. That is, inspection-time task performance was limited by a single biological parameter, a subject's inspection time. Whereas most psychological tasks are acknowledged to be conglomerates of heaven-knows-how-many performance parameters, the inspection time was supposedly measuring a single limitation in a single parameter. One attraction of the inspection-time procedure as a tool with which to study intelligence was this stark simplicity of the task structure.

More recently, Vickers and others have evinced doubts about the theory behind inspection time. Vickers and Smith (1986) reassessed the rationale for inspection-time theory, but the first substantial criticisms came from Levy (1992), who argued that inspection time theory was never satisfactorily developed and that the evidential (psychophysical) basis for the task was meager. Soon after this there were empirical studies suggesting that inspection-time performance might comprise the working of more than one parameter. Various other parameters have been suggested such as distraction and memory strength; Chaiken (1993) found that models of inspection-time performance could only be fitted well when three parameters were used, leading him to state that "the portrayal of IT [inspection time] as a relatively simple and homogeneous task is false." The amount of information contained in the inspection-time stimulus has been shown to alter subjects' inspection times, and the type of information in the inspection-time stimuli may affect the correlations with specific cognitive abilities; Mackenzie, Molloy, Martin, Lovegrove, & McNicol (1991) concluded from these results that inspection time is not an "atom" of intelligence but rather a "scalpel" that may be used to investigate intelligence.

One basis of the original inspection-time theory is that it tapped into a biological limitation to information processing. If so, then a practiced subject's performance on an inspection–time task should, as suggested by Vickers et al. (1972), be described by a stable, cumulative normal ogive when stimulus duration is plotted against the probability of a correct response. Until 1993 there were no studies of this key psychophysical claim that had examined single-subject data. Earlier, Levy (1992) had demonstrated how misleading combining data from different subjects might be in this regard; convincing-looking psychometric curves can be obtained from combined data when few or none of the subjects' performances adhere to the theoretical expectations. Deary, Caryl, & Gibson (1993) reported extensive inspection-time data taken from two subjects who had each performed over 38,000 trials over a period of months. Contrary to the fixed-parameter model of the inspection-time task, both subjects demonstrated long-term nonstationarity in their task performances. One subject showed long-term practice effects. The other subject had improvements and decrements at specific duration over long periods; interestingly, durations as little as 1 ms apart showed improvement and decrement, respectively, in the same time periods. These

data suggest that, even with long periods of familiarity with the task, there are higher level influences on inspection-time performance, especially at very brief durations. Another suggestion by Vickers et al. (1972) was that information is available even in the shortest durations of the inspection-time task. Burns, Nettelbeck, & White (1998) have shown, to the contrary, that there may be durations below which no information is available. This suggests at least two parameters are involved in the performance of the inspection-time task: the duration of the stimulus below which no information is available (T_{lag}; Muise, Le Blanc, Lavoie, & Arsenault, 1991) and the duration needed by the subject to achieve some predetermined probability of correct responding (inspection time). However, Burns et al. (1998) have found that inspection times are similar for different stimulus configurations and have suggested that (a) inspection time is a measure of speed of temporal resolution in the visual system and (b) the inspection-time–psychometric intelligence association may generally be found across pattern-backward masking tasks. Others, such as Nicholls and Atkinson (1993) agree with (a), and (b) is supported by data from McGeorge, Crawford, and Kelly (1997) and Deary and colleagues (Deary, McCrimmon, & Bradshaw, 1997; Deary, Parker, Campbell, & Nicolson, 1997).

It is to be hoped that more research will continue in this vein. The importance of the association between inspection time and psychometric intelligence is limited by our understanding of what brain processes are tested by inspection-time tasks. At present, a theoretical rethink is under way, and suitable psychophysical studies are beginning to examine the claims made by the original inspection-time theory.

IS THERE ANYTHING PRIVILEGED ABOUT THE INSPECTION TIME PROCEDURE PER SE? The question links this and the previous sections. Thus, one way to proceed in trying to understand the nature of inspection time is to conduct more detailed psychophysical studies of inspection time and to reexamine the theory. Another way forward, articulated by White (1993, 1996), is to recognize that a shortsighted concern with the inspection time alone may not be helpful. Inspection time is a backward-masking procedure, and it is noticeable that there has been relatively little effort on the part of differential psychologists using inspection time to integrate their findings with other psychophysical, backward-masking techniques. Although the commonest stimulus used in inspection-time studies is the "pi figure" devised by Vickers et al. (1972), the structure of the association between inspection time and a battery of psychometric intelligence tests remains almost identical when alphanumerical stimuli are used in a more familiar tachistoscopic, backward-masking setup (McGeorge et al., 1996), although this runs contrary to the finding of Mackenzie et al. (1991). Equivocal findings notwithstanding, the inspection-time–psychometric intelligence result is one to look out from as well as to stare into.

White's (1993, 1996) recommendations to explore other psychophysical tasks to clarify the inspection-time–cognitive ability association were taken up by Deary et al. (1997a). They assembled a battery of three visual-processing tasks hypothesized to test the subject's limitations in temporal processing of visual information. In addition to a standard pi-figure inspection-time task, they employed tests of visual change and movement detection that were devised by Phillips and Singer (1974). These latter tasks, in common with inspection time, varied the stimulus duration of the target stimulus, and performance on these tasks was described by an ogive similar to that found with inspection time. By contrast to inspection time, visual change- and movement-detection tasks required no backward mask, and their targets were single stimuli within a large array of identical stimuli. Thus, the attempt was to bring together visual-processing tasks that differed in as many respects as possible but shared the demand for processing under limitations on stimulus duration. To provide discriminant validity, and to control for the general demands of the visual tasks, a further visual-processing task was added, one that did not include limitations on stimulus duration. This was a test of contrast sensitivity in which a forced choice must be made by the subjects who indicated which of two stimuli contained a grating. Difficulty level was manipulated by lowering the contrast level of the grating. The hypothesis tested was that a general factor extracted from the three stimulus-duration-limited visual processing tasks would be associated with psychometric intelligence. Further, it was hypothesised that contrast sensitivity, though

a difficult two-alternative, forced-choice visual processing task, would have a nonsignificant association with psychometric intelligence and with the other visual tasks. These hypotheses were largely borne out. The three visual-processing tasks involving limitations of stimulus duration showed intercorrelations above .4 and had correlations with nonverbal psychometric intelligence between .45 and .52. Correlations with verbal intelligence were lower and nonsignificant in some cases. Further, using structural equation modeling, the general factor from the three visual tasks correlated .46 with the general factor from the three psychometric intelligence test scores (Alice Heim 4 parts I and II and the National Adult Reading Test). The only additional association was one of .4 between the general factor from the three visual tests and nonverbal ability. Contrast sensitivity had no significant associations with any of the other visual-processing tests or with the psychometric intelligence tests. Deary, McCrimmon et al. (1997) have suggested that studies using this type of approach can be useful in understanding the reason for the inspection-time–psychometric intelligence correlation because they are informative about which aspects of simple processing tests preserve and which eliminate the correlation. This single study suggests that the requirement for processing under limitations of time – temporal resolution according to Burns et al. (1998) – is responsible for the correlations with psychometric intelligence. Further, new developments in thinking about the mechanisms for the association become possible because there are physiological correlates of visual-change-detection task performance (Singer & Phillips, 1974).

Vickers has also looked to new visual processing tasks to explore the supposedly simple processes tapped by inspection time and its association with cognitive ability test scores. Thus, the expanded judgement task (Vickers, Foreman, Nicholls, Innes, & Gott, 1989) and the frequency accrual speed test (FAST; Vickers, 1995) were developed as alternative tests of speed of simple mental processes. The FAST task has significant correlations with psychometric intelligence (Vickers & McDowell, 1996), and Vickers et al. (1995) have suggested that data from the FAST task imply that the interpretation of inspection time in terms of speed of processing may be incorrect. The FAST task requires a subject to indicate which of two series of light flashes on adjacent panels had more flashes. Deary and Caryl (1997b) argued that the FAST task is a high-level, supraspan memory task and that the data from it are not relevant to inspection time.

The clear message from this section is that the interesting finding of a correlation between inspection time and psychometric intelligence must be broadened to other backward-masking tasks and to psychophysical tasks more generally. By observing which task characteristics promote and prevent the processing task–cognitive test score association we will come to a better understanding of the nature of intelligence. It may be thought that too much space has been devoted to discussing a single task. The answer to this potential criticism is that visual inspection time has a bulk of research literature that dwarfs any other visual-processing task. For example, there are very few studies of critical flicker frequency and intelligence, and they tend to report null results (e.g., Jensen, 1983). For a critical view of current research on inspection time and psychometric intelligence, see Sternberg (1997).

INTELLIGENCE AND AUDITORY PROCESSING

Outside the domain of intelligence differences there have been suggestions that the speed with which humans process information is general, as demonstrated by cross-modality limitations. Thus Poppel (1994) has argued that, across the senses, there is a 30–40 ms time window within which any two sensory events will appear to have occurred simultaneously.

The decision process seems to be dependent on an underlying neuronal process that is characterized by sequential quanta of approximately 30 msec duration.

It was also suggested that auditory information-processing speed or efficiency may be related to psychometric intelligence differences on the basis of similar limitations in the visual and auditory senses (Brand & Deary, 1982; Deary, Caryl et al., 1989; Deary, Caryl, Egan, & Wight, 1989). Although tests in the auditory domain have been named inspection-time tests, the relation between visual and auditory so-called inspection-time tests is hypothetical rather than established. Until more evidence is available about the comparability of the information-processing limitations tested by visual and auditory inspection-time tests, the auditory data should be studied as a separate phenomenon.

Most studies to date in the auditory modality have used a pitch discrimination as the basis for their assessment of temporal processing. In what must be considered only as a pilot study, Brand and Deary (1982) constructed a test in which two consecutive tones, separated in pitch by 110 Hz, were played to subjects and then masked by white noise. The duration of the two tones was identical and variable. As expected, briefer tones made the discrimination harder. There was some evidence from this small study that subjects who scored better on psychometric intelligence tests required less stimulus duration to make accurate pitch discriminations. Further research with this type of task revealed small to moderate significant associations with measures of psychometric intelligence (Deary, Caryl et al., 1989; Deary, Head et al., 1989; Irwin, 1984). Other researchers using more standard psychoacoustic tasks in groups of students found more substantial associations, around .5, between tests of auditory discrimination and cognitive test scores (Raz, Willerman, Ingmundson, & Hanlon, 1983; Raz & Willerman, 1985). Typically these latter studies would retain the same stimulus durations throughout but would vary the interstimulus interval to discover the temporal limits of the subject's ability to make a pitch discrimination. Therefore, there are several studies that appeared to indicate that the stimulus duration subjects required to make a simple pitch discrimination is related to psychometric intelligence. In a longitudinal study Deary (1995) tested competing structural equation models of the cross-lagged associations between psychometric intelligence and auditory processing in 13-year-old children and concluded that low-level processing might be partly causal to later intelligence differences. A review of auditory processing and intelligence is given by Deary (1994b).

Originally intended as a simple measure of processing speed analogous to the visual inspection-time task, there are several lines of debate within the auditory, so-called inspection-time field.

1. There is still no adequate study of the association between visual and auditory inspection time and

intelligence that might settle the issue of whether they are tapping a source of shared variance. Those studies that have examined this topic have been performed on students, and the visual correlations range from near zero (Langsford et al., 1994) to .2 to about .5 with large confidence intervals and a median of about .25 to .3 (Deary, Caryl et al., 1989; Nettelbeck, Edwards, & Vreugdenhil, 1986). Therefore, the issue of the cross-modal source of temporal processing limitations is moot.

2. There have been suggestions that the auditory inspection-time task taps, to a greater or lesser degree, pitch discrimination ability rather than temporal-processing limitations (Langsford et al., 1994). Some have taken the view that this is true and that it is the ability to make fine discrimination that is the source of correlation with psychometric intelligence (Raz et al., 1987, as discussed above). Others have provided evidence that temporal-processing limitations and pitch discrimination ability contribute to auditory test performance and that both are related to cognitive ability test scores, although the temporal aspect makes the larger contribution (Deary, 1994b). Some have found that, using student subject samples, neither auditory inspection time nor pitch discrimination relates significantly to psychometric intelligence (Langsford et al., 1994). There is countering evidence that performance on several basic auditory tasks relates to cognitive test scores. Watson (1991) found that several tasks from the Test of Basic Auditory Capabilities related significantly to mental ability test scores in learning disabled and student samples. Deary (1999) reanalyzed the data from Deary (1994) and found that a general factor from three different auditory tasks correlated with a general factor from three cognitive tests; the auditory tasks had been selected to reflect speed and pitch discrimination to different degrees. Caryl et al. (1995) supported the processing-speed interpretation of the auditory inspection–time task by showing that visual and auditory inspection-time task thresholds were correlated with brain-evoked potentials in the rising phase of the P200. On the other hand, they found that threshold-related differences in pitch discrimination were found later, between 200–300 ms after stimulus onset, in the event-related potential. To date, there is no satisfactory resolution to the question of whether, if psychometric intelligence relates to simple auditory processing, this is due to speed of processing of fineness of auditory discrimination, or both, or neither.

3. Even with a large pitch difference between tone pairs, there remains a significant minority of adult subjects who cannot perform the pitch discrimination at any duration (e.g., Irwin, 1984; Deary, Caryl et al., 1989; Deary, Head et al., 1989). The percentage is slightly higher in children. This has led to various procedures for ensuring that measures of auditory processing speed are not contaminated by pitch discrimination differences, such as leaving out subjects who do not attain a threshold performance on the auditory processing task, or covarying out pitch discrimination ability.

Therefore, studies in the auditory domain do not allow us to conclude that either speed of processing or fineness of discrimination is the simple construct that accounts for the associations between auditory processing variables and psychometric intelligence. Some of the difficulty in concluding from this area can be traced to the small number of studies and the inadequate tasks that have been used to date, not to mention the relatively small and ability-restricted samples of subjects. The inadequacy of the tasks is in part the result of the inevitable confounding of temporal processing and pitch discrimination.

Progress in the field of auditory processing will in part be associated with the development of new tasks that use something other than pitch discriminations. For example, Parker has developed a task that uses tone direction rather than pitch (Deary, Parker et al., 1997b). In this task two identical sine wave tones are phase shifted and played simultaneously over headphones, making it appear to the subject that a single sound is emerging from a place off the midline. The duration of these tones is variable, and the masking sound is a midline, louder square wave tone. The subject's task is to indicate whether the first sound (the one before the masking sound) appeared on the left or the right. This task has the advantage over the pitch-based auditory task of involving a spatial judgment, making it more comparable to the visual inspection-time test. Initial results from Parker's laboratory suggest that this task has moderate correlations with both visual inspection times and with psychometric intelligence. A further development in the auditory domain is the use of a loudness-based auditory discrimination instead of a pitch discrimination (Olsson, Bjorkman, Haag & Juslin, 1998).

The number of studies conducted on simple auditory processing is much smaller than in the visual modality. The research is buoyed up by the fact that the associations between auditory processing and psychometric intelligence are at about the same level as those found in visual inspection-time research. The main task for researchers will be to discover better auditory tasks that make more specific demands on the subject and to include visual and auditory processing tasks in the same study.

INFERENCE METHODS

In most of the techniques described in this chapter the investigators have used what they considered to be "simple" processing measures. Simple can mean different things. At one extreme, as in the original theory of inspection time, it can mean that the investigator's view of the task is that it taps a single psychological process or a basic biological limitation. In the field of physiology, nerve conduction velocity provides a comparator: a variable whose interpretation is fairly unequivocal. Vickers and Smith (1986) suggested that some researchers had approached inspection time as the human equivalent of benchmark tests of processing speed in a digital computer. The tasks described herein have at least some face validity with respect to their simplicity; as a group, they appear to draw on fewer domains of ability than do psychometric tasks or experimental psychology tasks that typically involve more complex judgments and physical responses. Other tasks could also be called simple because they purport to tap a basic limitation in processing by capitalizing on some bottleneck in processing. Thus, although the tasks may appear complex, the argument is that they in fact can be interpreted as being simple because performance depends primarily on a few or even one individual difference parameter.

Novelty Preference and Habituation in Infants

Testing mental ability in very young children is difficult because they lack language skills. Tests have tended to include more motor skills at young ages and to be relatively poor in predicting later intelligence. A substantial change has come with the advent of measures of infants' looking behaviors. In these measures infants will be shown stimuli – sometimes faces – many times. The difference between the mean of the looking times for the last two looks and the first two looks can give a measure of the degree to which the infant has habituated to the stimulus (see, e.g., Bornstein & Sigman, 1986; Slater, 1995). Another task has the infant presented with a stimulus that has been seen before and a novel stimulus, and the degree to which the novel stimulus is looked at again may be used to indicate the degree to which the nonnovel face has been processed; this has been called visual recognition memory (Rose & Feldman, 1995). Surprisingly, these measures at an early age have modest correlations with IQ-type scores some years later surpassing previous measures of infant mental ability in their predictive validity. The validity coefficients are all the more surprising given the modest reliability of such measures in infancy. For example, visual recognition memory differences at 7 months of age correlated .45 with Wechsler Full-Scale IQ's at 11 years (Rose and Feldman, 1995). Slater (1995) reckoned that the usual strength of association between infancy measures and later IQs is in the range .3 to .5.

Among the cognoscenti in this field of research there is of course much interest in the reason for the correlations. It is this aspect of the research that makes these studies of interest here. One hypothesis – there are others – is that habituation and novelty preference are to a large degree reflections of speed of information processing. That is, infants who can process stimuli more quickly will learn what is to be learned from them faster than slower infants and will consequently habituate faster and prefer a novel face more readily. Therefore, one hypothesis from this research is that the continuity between habituation and novelty preference measures and later scores on psychometric intelligence tests arises because a basic underlying construct – speed or efficiency of information processing – accounts for some part of the individual differences in both measures. Rose and Feldman (1995) suggested that the linking construct between infancy and later intelligence levels might be perceptual speed, stating that their results "support speculations that speed of processing is a pervasive factor underlying individual and developmental differences in many aspects of cognition" (p. 693). For a true test of this hypothesis an independent measure of speed of processing should be developed; otherwise, it is difficult to prove the inference that this convert variable is the cause of the time-lagged correlation. Slater (1995) offers a detailed discussion of possible mechanisms at work in these remarkable studies. The message for this chapter from these studies is that it is tempting to infer some simple processing continuity to explain such correlations, but demonstrating the existence of such a construct is problematic.

Brinley Ratios and the Theory of General Information Processing Speed

At both ends of the age spectrum a seemingly similar conclusion has been reached: that changes in mental abilities with age may be caused by a single (simple?) general slowing of the processing of information. Kail's (1991) review of a large number of studies of reaction times in children and adolescents led to his concluding that one possibility is that the development of cognitive functions is dependent upon the change in a single index of processing speed:

If two computers have identical software but one machine has a slower cycle time (i.e., the time for the central processor to execute a single instruction), that machine will execute all processes more slowly by an amount that depends on the total number of instructions to be executed. The human analog to cycle time might be the time to scan the productions (i.e., condition-action instructions) in working memory, or it might refer to the time to execute the action side of a production. . . . In either case, a developmental increase in the human cognitive cycle time would be associated with decreased time to complete cognitive operations (p. 499).

Kail and Salthouse (1994) provided a similar type of explanation for much of the change in cognitive function in aging. Influential in this field has been the study by Cerella (1985) in which it was found that, for many tasks of different levels of complexity, performance by old people was simply a multiplier of young people's performance. In many cases the percentage of variance of age changes explained by the assumption of a single slowing factor of information processing was over 98%. The use of such "Brinley functions" was criticized by Rabbitt

(1996b), who suggested that there was room to include the slowing of local as well as general information processing with age. Rabbitt also pointed out that such slowing of cognitive functions with age, and the slowing of processing that is found between groups of high and low psychometric intelligence, could not be accounted for by low-level physiological parameters: The variation that would be required to explain the differences simply does not exist at the physiological level. Instead, he suggested that some cognitive slowing must be accounted for by "higher order prediction and control."

COMMENTS

The findings in infants, children and old people involving complex procedures from which speed of information processing as a general entity is inferred provide an interesting foil to the research that begins with putatively simple measures of processing speed and looks for correlations with mental ability test scores and aging. There is thus a range of circumstances in which processing speed has been a useful hypothesis, and there are many supposed measures of speed at different levels of description. The key question in this field is, What is a simple process and what does processing speed mean when it comes to the functioning of the brain? At present we are not in a position to rule much out. Therefore, speed of processing may in part be due to basic physiological differences in the structure and functioning of nerve cells and their connections. On the other hand, we need also to consider that speed may be a high-level phenomenon emerging from the connectivity of neural network and even higher level cognitive control processes. In addition, as Rabbitt (1996b) suggested, there may be a need to consider both general and domain-specific processing speed functions. With regard to simple processing, the use of simple refers to a specific level of description. Therefore, in comparing, say inspection time and digit symbol performance (the WAIS–R subtest) as measures of speed of processing, we would be tempted to state that inspection time is clearly the simpler of the two tasks. When we turn to the psychophysical level, however, inspection time suddenly appears quite complex.

There is no art to read the brain's information processing construction in the data we have at present.

Associations between various tasks and psychometric intelligence have led us to posit that some relatively basic processes have a part to play in accounting for human intelligence differences. As molecular genetic studies and functional imaging investigations of the nervous system gather strength, we may find that the uses of processing constructs at the cognitive and psychophysical levels will be reduced and that we can go straight to biological concepts to account for what we can at present describe in only vague terms.

REFERENCES

Abelson, A. R. (1911). The measurement of mental ability of backward children. *British Journal of Psychology, 4,* 268–314.

Bates, T. C., & Eysenck, H. J. (1993). Intelligence, inspection time and decision time. *Intelligence, 17,* 523–531.

Baltes, P. B., & Lindenberger, U. (1997). Emergence of a powerful connection between sensory and cognitive functions across the lifespan: A new window to the study of cognitive aging? *Psychology and Aging, 12,* 12–21.

Beck, L. F. (1933). The role of speed in intelligence. *Psychological Bulletin, 30,* 169–178.

Bentley, A. (1963). *Musical ability in children and its measurement.* London: Harrap.

Berger, M. (1982). The "scientific approach" to intelligence: An overview of its history with special references to mental speed. In H. J. Eysenck (Ed.), *A model for intelligence* (pp. 13–43). Berlin: Springer-Verlag.

Boring, E. G. (1923). Intelligence as the tests test it. *New Republic, 35,* 35–37.

Bornstein, M. H., & Sigman, M. D. (1986). Continuity in mental development from infancy. *Child Development, 57,* 251–274.

Bowling, A. C., & Mackenzie, B. D. (1996). The relationship between speed of information processing and cognitive ability. *Personality and Individual Differences, 20,* 775–780.

Brand, C. R., & Deary, I. J. (1982). Intelligence and "inspection time". In H. J. Eysenck (Ed.), *A model for intelligence,* (pp. 133–148). Berlin: Springer-Verlag.

Burns, N. R., Nettelbeck, T., & White, M. (1998). Testing the interpretation of inspection time as a measure of speed of sensory processing. *Personality and Individual Differences, 24,* 25–39.

Burt, C. (1909/1910). Experimental tests of general intelligence. *British Journal of Psychology, 3,* 94–177.

Carey, N. (1914/1915). Factors in the mental processes of schoolchildren. *British Journal of Psychology, 7,* 453–490.

Carroll, J. B. (1993). *Human cognitive abilities: A survey of factor-analytic studies.* Cambridge, England: Cambridge University Press.

Caryl, P. G. (1994). Early event-related potentials correlate with inspection time and intelligence. *Intelligence, 18,* 15–46.

Caryl, P. G., Golding, S. J. J., & Hall, B. J. D. (1995). Interrelationships among auditory and visual cognitive tasks: An event-related potential (ERP) study. *Intelligence, 21,* 297–326.

Cerella, J. (1985). Information processing rates in the elderly. *Psychological Bulletin, 98,* 67–83.

Chaiken, S. R. (1993). Two models for an inspection time paradigm: Processing distraction and processing speed versus processing speed and asymptotic strength. *Intelligence, 17,* 257–283.

Chaiken, S. R., & Young, R. K. (1993). Inspection time and intelligence: Attempts to reduce the apparent motion strategy. *American Journal of Psychology, 106,* 191–210.

Colet, A. V., Piera, P. J. F., & Pueyo, A. A. (1993). Initial stages of information processing and inspection time: Electrophysiological correlates. *Personality and Individual Differences, 14,* 733–738.

Crawford, J. R., Deary, I. J., Allan, K. M., & Gustafsson, J. E. (1998). Evaluating competing models of the relationship between inspection time and psychometric intelligence. *Intelligence, 26,* 27–42.

Deary, I. J. (1993). Inspection time and WAIS–R IQ subtypes: A confirmatory factor analysis study. *Intelligence, 17,* 223–236.

Deary, I. J. (1994a). Sensory discrimination and intelligence: Postmortem or resurrection? *American Journal of Psychology, 107,* 95–115.

Deary, I. J. (1994b). Intelligence and auditory discrimination: Separating processing speed and fidelity of stimulus representation. *Intelligence, 18,* 189–213.

Deary, I. J. (1995). Auditory inspection time and intelligence: What is the direction of causation? *Developmental Psychology, 31,* 237–250.

Deary, I. J. (1997). Intelligence and information processing. In H. Nyborg (Ed.), *The scientific study of human nature: Tribute to Hans Eysenck at eighty* (pp. 282–310). New York: Pergamon.

Deary, I. J. (1999). Intelligence and visual and auditory information processing. In P. L. Ackerman, P. C. Kyllonen, & R. D. Roberts (Eds.), *The future of learning and individual differences research: Processes, traits and content* (pp. 111–130). Washington, DC: American Psychological Association.

Deary, I. J., & Caryl, P. G. (1997a). Neuroscience and human intelligence differences. *Trends in Neurosciences, 20,* 365–371.

Deary, I. J., & Caryl, P. G. (1997b). Not so F.A.S.T., Dr Vickers! *Intelligence, 24,* 397–404.

Deary, I. J., Caryl, P. G., Egan, V., & Wight, D. (1989). Visual and auditory inspection time: Their interrelationship and correlations with IQ in high ability subjects. *Personality and Individual Differences, 10,* 525–533.

Deary, I. J., Caryl, P. G., & Gibson, G. J. (1993). Nonstationarity and the measurement of psychophysical response in a visual inspection time task. *Perception, 22,* 1245–1256.

Deary, I. J., & Crawford, J. R. (1998). A triarchic theory of Jensenism: Persistent, conservative reductionism. *Intelligence, 26,* 273–282.

Deary, I. J., Head, B., & Egan, V. (1989). Auditory inspection time, intelligence and pitch discrimination. *Intelligence, 13,* 135–147.

Deary, I. J., Hunter, R., Langan, S. J., & Goodwin, G. M. (1991). Inspection time, psychometric intelligence and clinical estimates of cognitive ability in presenile Alzheimer's disease and Korsakoff's psychosis. *Brain, 114,* 2543–2554.

Deary, I. J., McCrimmon, R. J., & Bradshaw, J. (1997). Visual information processing and intelligence. *Intelligence, 23,* 461–479.

Deary, I. J., Parker, D. M., Campbell, L. J., & Nicolson, C. (July 1997). *Intelligence and visual and auditory inspection times: Two independent studies.* Paper presented at the 8th Biennial Conference of the International Society for the Study of Individual Differences, Aarhus, Denmark.

Deary, I. J., & Stough, C. (1996). Intelligence and inspection time: Achievements, prospects and problems. *American Psychologist, 51,* 599–608.

Egan, V. (1986). Intelligence and inspection time: Do high-IQ subjects use cognitive strategies. *Personality and Individual Differences, 7,* 695–700.

Egan, V. (1994). Intelligence, inspection time and cognitive strategies. *British Journal of Psychology, 85,* 305–316.

Egan, V., & Deary, I. J. (1992). Are specific inspection time strategies prevented by concurrent tasks? *Intelligence, 16,* 151–167.

Galton, F. (1883). *Inquiries into human faculty and its development.* London: Dent.

Hobbes, T. (1885, originally published 1651). *Leviathan.* London: Routledge.

Howe, M. J. A. (1988). Intelligence as an explanation. *British Journal of Psychology, 79,* 349–360.

Hutton, U., Wilding, J., & Hudson, R. (1997). The role of attention in the relationship between inspection time and IQ in children. *Intelligence, 24,* 445–460.

Irwin, R. J. (1984). Inspection time and its relation to intelligence. *Intelligence, 8,* 47–65.

Jensen, A. R. (1983). Critical flicker frequency and intelligence. *Intelligence, 7,* 217–225.

Jensen, A. R. (1993). Spearman's hypothesis tested with chronometric information-processing tasks. *Intelligence, 17,* 47–77.

Jensen, A. R. (1998). Jensen on "Jensenism." *Intelligence, 26,* 181–208.

Kail, R. (1991). Developmental change in speed of processing during childhood and adolescence. *Psychological Bulletin, 109,* 490–501.

Kail, R., & Salthouse, T. A. (1994). Processing speed as a mental capacity. *Acta Psychologica, 86,* 199–225.

Kranzler, J. H., & Jensen, A. R. (1989). Inspection time and intelligence: A metaanalysis. *Intelligence, 13,* 329–347.

Kranzler, J. H., Whang, P. A., & Jensen, A. R. (1994). Task complexity and the speed and efficiency of elemental information processing: Another look at the nature of intellectual giftedness. *Contemporary Educational Psychology, 19,* 447–459.

Langsford, P. B., Mackenzie, B. D., & Maher, D. P. (1994). Auditory inspection time, sustained attention, and the fundamentality of mental speed. *Personality and Individual Differences, 16,* 487–497.

Larson, G. E., Saccuzzo, D. P., & Brown, J. (1994). Motivation: Cause or confound in information processing/ intelligence correlations? *Acta Psychologica, 85,* 25–37.

Levy, P. (1992). Inspection time and its relation to intelligence: Issues of measurement and meaning. *Personality and Individual Differences, 13,* 989–1002.

Lindenberger, U., & Baltes, P. B. (1994). Sensory functioning and intelligence in old age: A strong connection. *Psychology and Aging, 9,* 339–355.

Lynn, R., Wilson, R. G., & Gault, A. (1989). Simple musical tests as measures of Spearman's *g. Personality and Individual Differences, 10,* 25–28.

McGeorge, P., Crawford, J. R., & Kelly, S. W. (1996). The relationship between WAIS–R abilities and speed of processing in a word identification task. *Intelligence, 23,* 175–190.

Mackenzie, B., & Bingham, E. (1985). IQ, inspection time and response strategies in a university population. *Australian Journal of Psychology, 37,* 257–268.

Mackenzie, B., Molloy, E., Martin, F., Lovegrove, W., & McNicol, D. (1991). Inspection time and the content of simple tasks: A framework for research on speed of information processing. *Australian Journal of Psychology, 43,* 37–43.

Morris, G. L., & Alcorn, M. B. (1995). Raven's Progressive Matrices and inspection time: P200 slope correlates. *Personality and Individual Differences, 18,* 81–87.

Muise, J. G., LeBlanc, R. S., Lavoie, M. E., & Arsenault, A. S. (1991). Two stage model of visual backward masking: Sensory transmission and accrual of effective information as a function of target intensity and similarity. *Perception and Psychophysics, 50,* 197–204.

Neisser, U. (1997). Never a dull moment. *American Psychologist, 52,* 79–81.

Neisser, U., Boodoo, G., Bouchard, T. J., Boykin, A. W., Brody, N., Ceci, S. J., Halpern, D. F., Loehlin, J. C., Perloff, R., Sternberg, R. J., & Urbina, S. (1996). Intelligence: knowns and unknowns. *American Psychologist, 51,* 77–101.

Nettelbeck, T. (1987). Intelligence and inspection time. In P. A. Vernon (Ed.), *Speed of information processing and intelligence.* Norwood, NJ: Ablex.

Nettelbeck, T., Edwards, C., & Vreugdenhil, A. (1986). Inspection time and IQ: Evidence for a mental speed–ability association. *Personality and Individual Differences, 7,* 633–641.

Nettelbeck, T., & Lally, M. (1976). Inspection time and measured intelligence. *British Journal of Psychology, 67,* 17–22.

Neubauer, A. C. (1997). The mental speed approach to the assessment of intelligence. In J. Kingma & W. Tomic (Eds.), *Advances in Cognition and Educational Practice* (pp. 149–174). Greenwich, CT: JAI Press.

Nicholls, M. E. R., & Atkinson, J. (1993). Hemispheric asymmetries for an inspection time task: A general left hemisphere temporal advantage? *Neuropsychologia, 31,* 1181–1190.

Olsson, H., Bjorkman, C., Haag, K., & Juslin, P. (1998). Auditory inspection time: on the importance of selecting the appropriate sensory continuum. *Personality and Individual Differences, 25,* 627–634.

Petrie, R. X. A., & Deary, I. J. (1989). Smoking and human information processing. *Psychopharmacology, 99,* 393–396.

Phillips, W. A., & Singer, W. (1974). Function and interaction of On and Off transients in vision. I. Psychophysics. *Experimental Brain Research, 19,* 493–506.

Poppel, E. (1994). Temporal mechanisms in perception. *International Review of Neurobiology, 37,* 185–202.

Rabbitt, P. (1996a). Intelligence is not just mental speed. *Journal of Biosocial Science, 28,* 425–449.

Rabbitt, P. (1996b). Do individual differences in speed reflect "global" or "local" differences in mental abilities? *Intelligence, 22,* 69–88.

Raz, N., & Willerman, L. (1985). Aptitude-related differences in auditory information processing: Effects of selective attention and tone duration. *Personality and Individual Differences, 6,* 299–304.

Raz, N., Willerman, L., Ingmundson, P., & Hanlon, M. (1983). Aptitude-related differences in auditory recognition masking. *Intelligence, 7,* 71–90.

Raz, N., Willerman, L., & Yama, M. (1987). On sense and senses: Intelligence and auditory information processing. *Personality and Individual Differences, 8,* 201–210.

Reed, T. E., & Jensen, A. R. (1993). Choice reaction time and visual pathway nerve conduction velocity both correlate with intelligence but appear not to correlate with each other: Implications for information processing. *Intelligence, 17,* 191–203.

Rose, S. A., & Feldman, J. F. (1995). Prediction of IQ and specific cognitive abilities at 11 years from infancy measures. *Developmental Psychology, 31,* 685–696.

Sadler, A. J., & Deary, I. J. (1996). Cerebral asymmetries in inspection time? *Neuropsychologia, 34,* 283–295.

Sharp, S. E. (1898/1899). Individual psychology: A study in psychological method. *American Journal of Psychology, 10,* 329–391.

Simpson, C. R., & Deary, I. J. (1997). Strategy use and feedback in inspection time. *Personality and Individual Differences, 23,* 787–797.

Singer, W., & Phillips, W. A. (1974). Function and interaction of On and Off transients in vision II. Neurophysiology. *Experimental Brain Research, 19,* 507–521.

Slater, A. (1995). Individual differences in infancy and later IQ. *Journal of Child Psychology and Psychiatry, 36,* 69–112.

Spearman, C. (1904). "General intelligence," objectively determined and measured. *American Journal of Psychology, 15,* 201–293.

Stankov, L., & Roberts, R. D. (1997). Mental speed is not the "basic" process of intelligence. *Personality and Individual Differences, 22,* 69–84.

Sternberg, R. J. (1985). *Beyond IQ: A triarchic theory of human intelligence.* Cambridge, England: Cambridge University Press.

Sternberg, R. J. (1990). *Metaphors of mind.* Cambridge, UK: Cambridge University Press.

Sternberg, R. J. (1997). Inspection time for inspection time: Reply to Deary and Stough. *American Psychologist, 52,* 1144–1150.

Stough, C., Brebner, J., Nettelbeck, T., Cooper, C. J., Bates, T., & Mangan, G. L. (1996). The relationship between intelligence, personality and inspection time. *British Journal of Psychology, 81,* 255–268.

Stough, C., Mangan, G., Bates, T., Frank, N., Kerkin, B., & Pellett, O. (1995). Effects of nicotine on perceptual speed. *Psychopharmacology, 119,* 305–310.

Stough, C., Mangan, G., Bates, T., & Pellett, O. (1995). Smoking and Raven IQ. *Psychopharmacology, 116,* 382–384.

Thorndike, E. L., Lay, W., & Dean, P. R. (1909). The relation of accuracy in sensory discrimination to general intelligence. *American Journal of Psychology, 20,* 364–369.

Vernon, P. A. (Ed.). (1993). *Biological approaches to the study of human intelligence.* Norwood, NJ: Ablex.

Vickers, D. (1995). The frequency accrual speed test (FAST): A new measure of "mental speed"? *Personality and Individual Differences, 19,* 863–879.

Vickers, D., Foreman, E. A., Nicholls, M. E. R., Innes, N. J., & Gott, R. E. (1989). Some experimental tests of the application of an interval of uncertainty model to a time-limited expanded judgement task. In D. Vickers, & P. L. Smith (Eds.), *Human information processing: Measures, mechanisms and models* (pp. 253–265) Amsterdam: North-Holland.

Vickers, D., & McDowell, A. (1996). Accuracy in the frequency accrual speed test (FAST), inspection time and psychometric intelligence in a sample of primary school children. *Personality and Individual Differences, 20,* 463–469.

Vickers, D., Nettelbeck, T., & Willson, R. J. (1972). Perceptual indices of performance: The measurement of "inspection time" and "noise" in the visual system. *Perception, 1*, 263–295.

Vickers, D., Pietsch, A., & Hemingway, T. (1995). Intelligence and visual and auditory discrimination: Evidence that the relationship is not due to the rate at which sensory information is sampled. *Intelligence, 21*, 197–224.

Vickers, D., & Smith, P. L. (1986). The rationale for the inspection time index. *Personality and Individual Differences, 7*, 609–624.

Watson, B. U. (1991). Some relationships between intelligence and auditory processing. *Journal of Speech and Hearing Research, 34*, 621–627.

White, M. (1993). The inspection time rationale fails to demonstrate that inspection time is a measure of the speed of post-sensory processing. *Personality and Individual Differences, 15*, 185–198.

White, M. (1996). Interpreting inspection time as a measure of the speed of sensory processing. *Personality and Individual Differences, 20*, 351–363.

Wissler, C. (1901). The correlation of mental and physical tests. *Psychological Review*, Monograph No. 3.

Zhang, Y., Caryl, P. G., & Deary, I. J. (1989a). Evoked potential correlates of inspection time. *Personality and Individual Differences, 10*, 379–384.

Zhang, Y., Caryl, P. G., & Deary, I. J. (1989b). Evoked potentials, inspection time and intelligence. *Personality and Individual Differences, 10*, 1079–1094.

CHAPTER FOURTEEN

Complex Information Processing and Intelligence

DAVID F. LOHMAN

Theories of human intelligence must explain those complex human behaviors that are most commonly understood as its indicants. Thus, the central facts to be explained by a theory of intelligence must go beyond faster or more efficient processing of elementary tasks, for example, or the efficiency of biological processes and inherited structures, or the influence of other individuals, environments, or even cultures on abilities. Rather, a theory of intelligence must explain the writing of novels, the solving of complex mathematical problems, the designing of skyscrapers and microchips, and the myriad other forms of complex cognition valued by society. In short, an understanding of how individuals solve complex tasks and an explanation of why they differ so markedly in their ability to do so are in fact central to any theory of intelligence.

COGNITIVE TESTS AS COGNITIVE TASKS

But where to begin? There are many thousands of complex tasks, each of which may be considered an indicant of intelligence (especially by those who excel in accomplishing the task!). Correlational studies of human abilities offer a reasonable starting place because they have identified groups of tasks that consistently measure abilities viewed as indicants of intelligence – both by psychologists and lay persons. Estes (1974) argued as follows that we start by examining intelligence tests:

Rather than looking to learning or physiological theory or some correlate of intelligence, I should like to focus attention on intellectual activity itself. By bringing the concepts and methods of other disciplines to bear on

the analysis of intellectual behavior we may come to understand how the conditions responsible for the development of its constituent processes and the manner of their organization lead to variations in effectiveness of intellectual functioning. If this approach has appeal in principle, we need next to consider just what behaviors to analyze in order to be sure that the activity we are dealing with is closely related to that involved in the measurement of intelligence. The simplest and most direct approach, it seems, is to begin with the specific behaviors involved in responding to items on intelligence tests (pp. 742–743).

The vast majority of research on individual differences in intelligence as it relates to behavior on complex tasks has followed Estes' suggestion, even though some have questioned the wisdom of this decision. In this chapter, then, I will examine research on test-like tasks modeled after item-types commonly used on intelligence tests. I focus especially on measures of reasoning, particularly inductive reasoning, in part because reasoning tests have been studied extensively and in part because inductive reasoning is the primary ability most commonly associated with G. Gustafsson (1988 claims, for example, that general mental ability (G) can be equated with general fluid ability (Gf), which, in turn, can be equated with inductive reasoning (I). Sternberg (1986) makes a similar point:

An interesting finding that emerges from the literature attempting to relate cognitive task performance to psychometrically measured intelligence is that the correlations of task performance and IQ seem to be a direct function of the amount of reasoning involved in a given task, independent of the paradigm or label given to the paradigm.... Thus, reasoning ability appears to be central to intelligence (pp. 309–310).

Even those who believe that there is more to *G* than inductive reasoning would agree that reasoning is a crucial aspect of any understanding of human intelligence.

Although many different tasks have been used to measure inductive reasoning, a few are used much more commonly than others: analogies, matrix problems, series completions, and classification. Some reasoning batteries also contain tests that measure verbal reasoning through sentence completion tests, sentence comprehension tests, and even vocabulary. Others include more specific spatial tasks, such as form boards or paper-folding tests. And others use quantitative tests that require examinees to make relational judgments (such as greater than or less than) between quantitative concepts, or to determine how numbers and mathematical operators can be combined to generate a product. Examples of these different item types are shown in Figure 14.1.

In addition to the identification of clusters of tasks that define particular ability constructs, correlational studies show how these tests and the factors they define are related to one another. There is now broad consensus that these relations can be represented hierarchically (Carroll, 1993; Gustafsson, 1988). Even more suggestive for the present discussion, however, was the demonstration that hierarchical factor models are conformable with a radex model. The radex is produced by treating test intercorrelations as distances, which are then scaled in two or three dimensions using nonmetric, multidimensional scaling. The resultant scalings show three important features, all of which are illustrated in the idealized scaling shown in Figure 14.2 (from Snow, Kyllonen, & Marshalek, 1984). First, tests cluster by content, which typically appear as verbal, spatial, and symbolic–quantitative slices of a two-dimensional radex. Second, tests and test clusters that define broad factors tend to fall near the center of the radex. More specific primaries fall near the periphery. Indeed, in a well-balanced battery of tests, tests that define *G* fall near the center of the plot. Third, task complexity is roughly related to distance from the center (or *G*). This suggests that one key to a theory of *G*, then, may be an understanding of the complexity gradients that emanate from *G* to more peripheral or specific abilities.

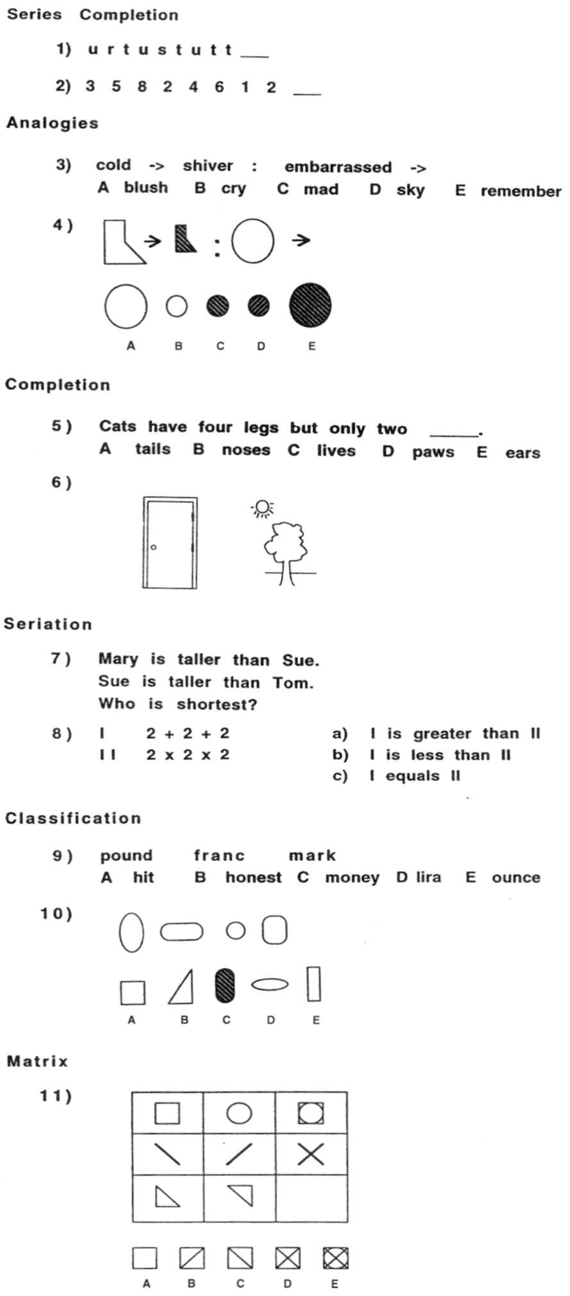

FIGURE 14.1. Examples of inductive reasoning tasks: (1) letter series (answer = "u"), (2) number series (answer = "3"), (3) verbal analogies (answer = A), (4) figural analogies (answer = C), (5) sentence completion (answer = E), (6) picture completion (answer = bottom hinge in first picture, shadow in second picture), (7) three-term series (answer = "Tom"), (8) quantitative relations (answer = b), (9) verbal classification (answer = D), (10) figure classification (answer = D), and (11) figural matrices (answer = C).

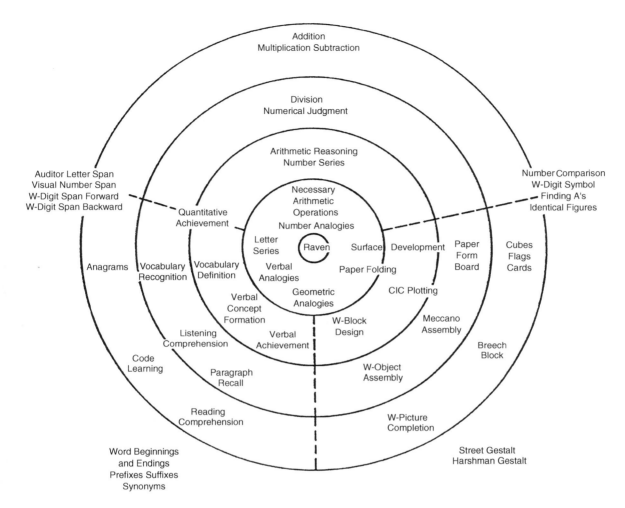

FIGURE 14.2. Hypothetical radex map showing suggested ability and learning simplexes and the content circumplex. "W" identifies subtests of the Wechsler Adult Intelligence Scale (after Snow, Kyllonen, & Marshalek, 1984).

In short, correlational studies of human abilities have guided investigations of the processes that generate intelligent behavior through (a) the identification of ability constructs that are broadly predictive of performance in nontest situations, (b) the isolation of tests that consistently measure these abilities and thus may constitute interesting cognitive tasks, and (c) the display of interconstruct and intertask relationships (such as the centrality of *G* and the apparent complexity gradients) that need to be explained by a theory of intelligence.

COMPLEXITY

But what is complexity? How might it be defined and measured? In the history of research on human intelligence, the "simple" reaction time and perceptual–motor tasks used by Galton and J. McK.

Cattell were distinguished from the more complex tasks used by Binet. "The early mental tasks were predominantly sensori-motor or very simple in nature.... [Then, as now,] complex mental processes were believed to be best understood by analyzing them into their elementary components, usually of a sensory nature" (Anastasi & Foley, 1949, pp. 14–15). However, Binet and Henri (1896) argued that more complex tests were needed to measure intelligence. The battery they proposed included tests of memory, mental imagery, imagination, attention, comprehension, suggestibility, aesthetic appreciation, moral feelings, muscular force and force of will, and motor ability and visual discrimination. The success of Binet's test and the seeming failure of the Galton–Cattell approach (Sharp, 1898/1899) established a working definition of task complexity for differential psychologists for the next 70 years: complex tasks are those that require comprehension, judgment, and reasoning, like Binet's tests; simple tasks are those that measure basic sensory and motoric processes. It was not until the advent of modern cognitive psychology – particularly the information-processing paradigm – that more precise definitions were offered.

INFORMATION PROCESSING

Information processing does not label a unified approach but rather a spectrum of researchers and theorists who use a variety of methods to study an equally diverse array of problems. In this view, cognitive tasks, including psychological tests, can be analyzed to reach deeper understanding of the mental processes and content knowledge that constitute complex performance. In all information-processing models of thought one or more sequences of processing steps or stages are posited in which cognitive operations are performed on incoming or stored information. The once fuzzy notion of "cognitive process" is thus concretely operationalized as a particular cognitive transformation performed on a particular mental representation. Some information-processing models are simple constructions with only one or two parameters to reflect the functioning of different processing stages in performance on paradigmatic laboratory tasks. Others are mathematical models of more complex tasks that appear important in their own right outside the laboratory. Some take the form of computer programs for complex tasks that reach a level of detail far more explicit than most mathematical models (Anderson, 1983, 1993; Newell & Simon, 1972). This detail can be overwhelming, however, unless one has some way of discovering generalizations that hold across time, task, and persons. In other words, suppose one starts with a full accounting of how a particular person solves a particular task on one occasion. Some of these processes may not occur if the same task were administered at another time (even if no specific memory of the first solution is assumed). More important, even those processes that are common

across occasions may not generalize to other tasks or to other persons. Indeed, the subset of processes that produce individual differences that generalize over time and tasks is likely to be but a tiny fraction of the processes required to specify the behavior of a single individual on one task on one occasion. It is important, therefore, to find a level of detail that explicates but does not overwhelm, that can capture useful generalizations that hold across families of tasks, and above all, that can represent individual differences in success in solving problems on these tasks.

General Features of Information-Processing Models

There is a trade-off between process and structure in all cognitive models. Models that specify many structures require fewer processes, and the converse. Of the many structural features of information-processing models that could be discussed, three seem particularly important for any discussion of relations between complex information processing and intelligence. First is the distinction between different memory systems – particularly working memory and long-term memory. Second is the distinction among different types of knowledge representations – particularly between declarative knowledge and procedural knowledge, but also among different types of declarative knowledge codes. And third is the distinction between controlled and automatic processing.

MEMORY SYSTEMS. The earliest information-processing models consisted of one or more sensory buffers, a limited-capacity short-term memory, and an unlimited long-term memory. However, the old notion of a relatively passive, limited-capacity short-term memory has been replaced by a more active working-memory system that not only holds and manipulates information (Daneman & Carpenter, 1980) but also attends selectively to one stimulus while inhibiting another, coordinates performance on tasks, and switches strategies (Baddeley, 1996). In fact, the characteristics Baddeley now posits for supervisory attentional system in working memory look much like the sort of executive processes Snow (1978) and Sternberg (1977) hypothesized as essential features of intelligence.

Oberauer, Süß, Schulze, Wilhelm, & Wittmann (1996) summarize these processes as (1) simultaneous storage and processing, (2) supervision or monitoring, and (3) coordination. Although there is substantial agreement on the first function (simultaneous storage and processing), there is disagreement whether storage and processing share common resources (Just & Carpenter, 1992), or draw on separate resources (Halford, Maybery, O'Hare, & Grant, 1994). Supervisory functions in most models include not only a monitoring function but also an inhibition function (which was also the central component in Thurstone's, 1924, earliest theory of intelligence). Finally, at least three aspects of coordination have been proposed: (1) information coordination across sensory modalities (Law, Morrin, & Pellegrino, 1995), (2) coordination of successive mental operations into a sequence (Hagendorf & Sá, 1995), and (3) coordination of elements into a coherent structure or mental model (Johnson-Laird, 1983; Oberauer, 1993).

Baddeley (1986) also claimed that different memory systems are employed for verbal and spatial tasks. Some have also attempted to separate numerical from verbal content in keeping with the long-established distinctions among verbal, numerical–symbolic, and spatial abilities.

DECLARATIVE AND PROCEDURAL KNOWLEDGE. A second important distinction is between declarative and procedural knowledge, or more simply, between content knowledge and process knowledge (Anderson, 1976, 1983, 1993; Greeno, 1978; Ryle, 1949). *Declarative knowledge* is factual knowledge about the meaning or perceptual characteristics of things, from anecdotal memories about daily events to the highly organized conceptual knowledge of some subject matter. A novice's knowledge of a newly learned theorem of geometry, for example, is declarative knowledge. Anderson (1983, 1993) also distinguishes between two types of declarative knowledge representations: a meaning-based memory code (abstract propositions) and a variety of perception-based codes (linear orders, images, etc.). The dominance of the meaning-based code parallels the ubiquitous *G* factor in individual differences research, whereas the specialized codes correspond to at least some of the major primary ability factors, particularly verbal fluency and spatial ability.

Procedural knowledge is knowledge of how to do something, from pronouncing a word or driving a car, to transforming and rehearsing information in working memory, to assembling new methods for solving problems and monitoring the effectiveness with which these methods are implemented. Organizing words into a sequence to express a particular idea, for example, requires procedural knowledge, as does the mental rotation of a figure into a new orientation.

All cognitive tasks require declarative and procedural knowledge, and in the abstract the two can be seen as one (Greeno, 1978; Winograd, 1972, 1975). Procedural knowledge can often be stated declaratively and declarative knowledge can become proceduralized with practice. Nevertheless, tasks differ in the demands they place on one or the other type of knowledge. For example, tests that sample factual knowledge in a domain place heavy demands on the examinee's store of declarative knowledge, its organization, and its retrievability. On the other hand, tests of inductive reasoning or spatial visualization ability place heavier demands on the examinee's execution of certain cognitive procedures or skills. Some tasks require complex mixtures of factual knowledge and cognitive skill (e.g., mathematical reasoning tests).

CONTROLLED AND AUTOMATIC PROCESSING. The controlled versus automatic processing distinction refers to the degree to which a knowledgeable or skillful performance requires conscious attentional resources for successful operation. Automatization occurs when cognitive tasks are consistent in their information-processing demands such that a transition from controlled to automatic processing can occur with practice. Using arithmetic facts is a controlled process for a child. For the practiced adolescent, their use has become automatic. Automatization is thought to free attentional resources for other controlled processing. Tasks with inconsistent information-processing requirements remain consciously controlled; automatization is not possible. Tests of ability and achievement may emphasize either type of processing, or some mixture, and a given test may vary on this continuum as a function of where on a learning curve it is administered (Ackerman, 1986). A perceptual speed test, such as Number Comparison, may reflect automatic processing for most adults, but it may reflect controlled processing among children. A test composed of algebra word problems will likely require both kinds of processing. One important characteristic of reasoning problems is that they require controlled processing (Sternberg, 1986).

Information Processing and Task Complexity

The information-processing approach permits much greater specificity in hypotheses about complexity. Nevertheless, even within this paradigm, there is no simple way to distinguish complex information processing from simple information processing. For example, those who study reaction times properly speak of tasks that require a discrimination ("respond only when the red light is lit") as more complex than tasks that do not ("respond when any light is lit"). Clearly, "complexity" is a relative term. Simon (1979) argued that information-processing psychology has been pursued at two levels: at the level of the "immediate processor" and at the level of "relatively complex human performances" (p. xi). Investigations of memory-scanning or sentence-picture verification (see, e.g., Clark and Chase, 1972) characterize the former approach, whereas the Simon and Kotovsky (1963) studies of letter series tasks are typical of the latter. The duration of primitive processes are typically tens or hundreds of milliseconds in studies of the immediate processor, and of seconds – even tens of seconds – in studies of more complex behavior. Thus, although there is more at stake here than the nature of the dependent measure, classification of investigations by the nature of the dependent measure used affords a useful way to parse the domain.

DEPENDENT MEASURES. At the broadest level, one way to distinguish among levels of complexity is to examine the type of dependent measure used to index performance. Figure 14.3 shows such a continuum. At the simplest level, response latency is most useful. Errors are infrequent and may reflect nuisance factors (such as speed–accuracy trade-off or inattention). Next come eye fixations. Again, fixation patterns are generally most informative when tasks are of relatively short duration, especially when comparing the performances of many subjects. However, performance need not be error free. In fact, eye fixation patterns that differentiate between correct and error trials may suggest how errors occurred. Next come protocol analyses. Subjects are asked to think aloud while solving a task. Verbal utterances are then analyzed to infer processes. Next comes a classification or analysis of the response itself, typically across many items or trials. On forced-choice tests, the classification scheme is often simply "correct" or "incorrect," and sometimes "attempted." However, open-ended responses can be classified in many ways. For example, responses on many of the tasks studied by developmental psychologists (such as balance-beam problems) can be classified according to the rule or rules seemingly used to generate the response. At a more complex level, essays can be scored for organizational structure or other emergent features (e.g., Biggs & Collis, 1982).

SOURCES OF DIFFICULTY. To understand why subjects differ on a task, one must first understand what makes items difficult. On a typical reasoning test, the easiest items will be answered correctly by 90% (or more) of the examinees, whereas the most difficult items may be answered correctly by only 30% of the examinees. Items vary not only in difficulty, but also in the particulars of what makes them difficult. By design, a good psychometric test may be a veritable hodgepodge of different sources and levels of difficulty. The first task, then, is to tease these sources apart – typically by designing item pools in which sources of difficulty vary systematically (and orthogonally, if possible). The advent of item response theory (IRT) models (see Chapter 19) in which items from different forms of a test may

FIGURE 14.3. A continuum of dependent measures used in investigations of cognition.

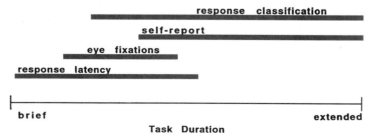

be placed on a common difficulty scale provides other options. Suppose a particular source of difficulty is reflected in only one or two items on one form of the verbal analogies subtest of the SAT (Scholastic Aptitude Test). Placing many forms of the test on the same scale allows one to estimate the effects of that source of difficulty from a much broader sample of items. This is particularly useful on verbal items given the large number of ways in which such items can differ.

Sheehan (1997) studied sources of difficulty on the SAT Verbal Reasoning Test in this way. The dependent measure was an IRT estimate of item difficulty, and the independent variables were various item characteristics hypothesized to influence difficulty. Sheehan (1997) used a tree-based regression procedure to assign items to nonoverlapping clusters. Figure 14.4 shows one set of results for the reading comprehension items. Clusters at the highest level (vocabulary in context, main idea, inference, and application–extrapolation) were specified in advance. Clustering at lower levels was determined by the regression procedure. Some clusters are composed of items of uniform difficulty, whereas items in other clusters vary substantially in difficulty. Not captured in this sort of analysis, of course, is information about the extent to which different subjects or groups of subjects would be equally well characterized by the same clustering solution. Nonetheless, the analysis goes considerably beyond global statements about an undifferentiated item difficulty. Just because items can be nicely ordered on a single scale does not mean that they are psychologically homogeneous.

METHODOLOGY

Introspection, Retrospection, and Think-Aloud

Inferences about mental processes require a rich observation base. The first task of the cognitive scientist is thus to increase the density of observations between stimulus and response. The simplest and oldest method for doing this is to ask participants to introspect on their processing while attempting a problem and, after making a response, to summarize retrospectively their observations of self. However, the retrospective report will usually be an edited account that omits unproductive avenues of

thought, or simply orders events in a more logical manner. In spite of these limitations, retrospective reports have long contributed usefully to inferences about processes (see, e.g., Bloom & Broder, 1950). A more common procedure is to ask the participant to think aloud while solving the problem. The basic assumption is that subjects can do this without altering their problem-solving processes as long as the information that is reported is already in working memory and does not require additional processing (Ericsson & Simon, 1984). This is often a reasonable assumption if subjects are verbally fluent, if the task is one that demands or affords verbal labeling of objects and transformations, and if subjects are well practiced. However, some subjects find a think-aloud protocol intrusive and difficult. Francis Galton spoke for many of these people when he wrote

> It is … a serious drawback to me in writing, and still more in explaining myself, that I do not so easily think in words as otherwise. It often happens that after being hard at work, and having arrived at results that are perfectly clear and satisfactory to myself, when I try to express them in language I feel I must begin by putting myself on another intellectual plane. I have to translate my thoughts into a language that does not run very evenly with them (in West, 1991, p. 179).

In spite of such limitations, introspective, retrospective, and think-aloud reports are such a rich and important source of information on cognition that they are used in studies of complex problem solving – either as a primary dependent measure (as, for example, in comparisons of expert verus novice problem solvers) or a secondary dependent measure (as, for example, in attempts to develop computer programs that simulate human problem solving).

Computer Simulation

One of the best methods for understanding how individuals solve a task is to attempt to simulate their behavior with a computer program. Early claims about the potential of the computational approach to cognition often relied on the success of a particular program in solving items like those found on ability tests. A key distinction in this work was between algorithms and heuristics. An algorithm specifies a series of operations that, if performed correctly, will produce a solution to a problem. For example, children are taught an algorithm that will

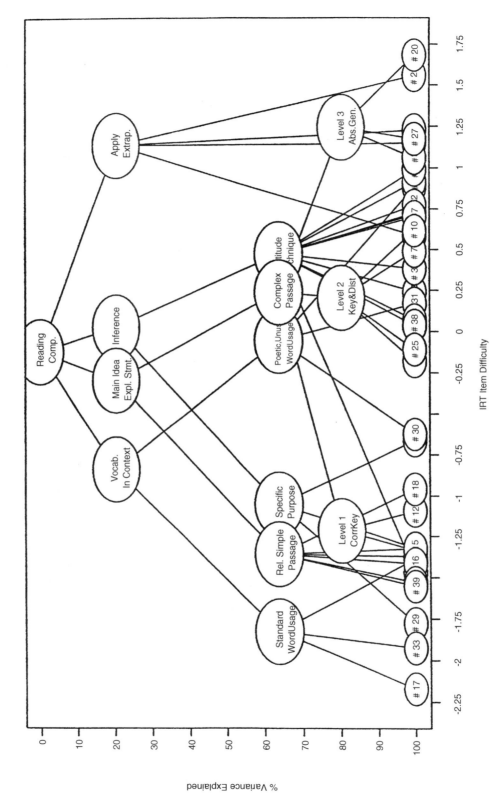

FIGURE 14.4. Clustering of items on the SAT Verbal Reasoning test (after Sheehan, 1997).

allow them to solve long-division problems in arithmetic. A heuristic, on the other hand, is a rule of thumb that specifies a series of steps or operations. Unlike an algorithm, however, the heuristic may or may not lead to a correct solution of the problem. Many of the early attempts to simulate human problem solving sought to develop computer programs that would apply general problem-solving heuristics to a wide range of problems. For example, the General Problem Solver (Newell & Simon, 1961) implemented a means–ends heuristic in which the problem solver determines the current state and the goal state and then selects a path or operation that will effect the greatest reduction in distance between the two. Means–ends analysis is called a working-backward heuristic because the problem solver starts with the goal state and tries to work backward to the present state.

Studies of expertise, however, demonstrated that although novices tended to use working-backward heuristics such as means–ends analyses, experts tended to use working-forward strategies (Simon & Simon, 1978). For example, experts in algebra may begin by rearranging terms without any clear understanding for how such a transformation gets them closer to the goal. However, once the terms are rearranged, another transformation will generally be suggested by the new pattern, and the process is repeated until the problem is solved. Such behavior is better characterized by a series of production rules that are applied automatically and consecutively. It suggests that domain-specific knowledge enters more prominently into the problem-solving behavior of experts than of novices.

Many of the early simulation programs ignored or at least downplayed the issue of knowledge. However, studies of human experts consistently showed that they relied extensively on stored problem patterns, not only in solving artificial problems (such as chess) but also in more natural domains such as language processing (Schank, 1980). The pendulum thus swung from the knowledge-lean programs of Newell and Simon (1961) to knowledge-rich expert systems. Indeed, even the architecture of different expert systems seemed to vary by the type of problem the system was expected to solve (Sternberg, 1990). Nonetheless, there are common structures and processes that differentiate between more- and less-intelligent systems. Sternberg (1990) identifies

six: multiple indexing, higher order knowledge structures, beliefs, inferential logic, levels of understanding, and learning mechanisms. Multiple indexing refers to the need to tag or index new information in many different ways (or simultaneously to store it in many different "places"). Multiple indexing is important because later recall and use of that information depend critically on how elaborately it was processed on input. Higher order knowledge structures refer to scripts or schemes. Schemes are crucial in allowing the system to organize incoming information, to determine which information is central and which is peripheral, and to go beyond the information given in making inferences about the situation. Beliefs are typically implemented as very high-level knowledge structures and thus function like schemes but at a more general level in the system. For human problem solvers, beliefs are often imbued with affect as well (Damasio, 1994).

More intelligent systems are also better able to make good inferences. One way to accomplish this is through high-level knowledge structures such as schemes: unfilled slots in the scheme are filled with default values. Another is through control mechanisms that index the extent to which new information deviates from the normal or expected. Schank (1978) argued that an intelligent system will make good use of such "interesting" information. Schank (1984) also argued that levels of intelligence are related to levels of understanding, from simply making sense of a situation through levels in which systems justify their actions in terms of goals, alternative hypotheses, and knowledge used, to a level of "complete empathy" in which the system's explanation would include an account of its feelings and emotions.

Systems also vary enormously in their ability to learn. Exactly how this occurs varies across systems. At the simplest level, systems learn by adding new knowledge to an existing knowledge base, modifying the strength of association among elements in that base, and reorganizing the knowledge base. Other systems allow for learning of new skills and heuristics and for the conversion of fact knowledge to skill knowledge.

Componential Analysis

A detailed information-processing model is the single most important outcome of a cognitive analysis or computer simulation of a task. In the best methods for reaching this goal, the investigator specifies the details of each component process or stage and how these component processes combine, then finds ways to operationalize the model, then evaluates the model by comparing how well it accounts for variation in the data with that of rival models, and then revises and reevaluates accordingly. This is an important departure from methods in which an investigator attempts to infer a full model from one or two statistically significant effects (see Greeno, 1980, for further discussion).

One of the earliest and most influential methods for accomplishing this sort of task decomposition and model testing was formulated by Sternberg (1977) in a method he called componential analysis. Early experiments examined analogies; in later experiments, the method was applied to a wide range of reasoning tasks. Sternberg proposed that analogy items – such as "doctor:patient::lawyer:(a) client, (b) judge"– require at least five component processes: encoding the various terms (here referred by the letters $A:B::C:D_1,D_2$), inferring the relationship between A and B, mapping the relationship between A and C, applying the A–B relationship to C to generate an answer, comparing the constructed answer with the alternative D answers provided, and responding. By the definition of analogy, however, the nature of the A to B transformation will be the same as that of the C to D transformation. For example, in a verbal analogy, if A is the opposite of B, then C must be the opposite of D. Thus, independent variables representing the type of inference or amount of transformation required in the inference stage would be perfectly correlated with corresponding independent variables for the application stage, and thus only one set of variables could be entered into the regression equation. This is a problem if one wants to test the assertion that two component processes are required, or to estimate the speed or efficiency with which these separate component processes are executed for individual subjects. Perhaps some subjects quickly infer the correct relationship between A and B but have difficulty remembering the relationship and thus have difficulty applying it to C in order to generate an ideal answer D.

Several experimental manipulations have been proposed to unconfound these correlated variables (Sternberg, 1985). One method is called *precuing*.

Here, the subject first examines a part of the problem for as long as necessary and then signals readiness to see the remainder of the item. Two latencies are obtained: time taken to view the precue, called a *cue latency* (which is sometimes discarded), and time taken to solve the remainder of the problem, which is called a *solution latency*. For example, given the analogy

A:B::C:D (true or false?),

one could precue with

A:B :: (measure T_1)

and then present

C:D (true or false)
  (measure T_2 and subject's response).

The precuing time (T_1) would include time for encoding A and B and for inferring the relationship between A and B. The separate solution time (T_2) would include the time for encoding C and D and for the mapping, application, and comparison–response processes. Precuing only the first term (A:) or the first three terms (A:B::C:) would permit separation of other component processes.

Precuing has probably been less frequently used than experimentally decomposing a complex task into two or more consecutively presented steps. Response latencies (and sometimes, response errors) are estimated for each step or subtask. Models are then fitted to each step (e.g., Kyllonen, Lohman, & Woltz, 1984) or to all steps simultaneously (e.g., Sternberg, 1977). When the latter procedure is used, model fits may be inflated because any variable that distinguishes among cue conditions will account for variance in latencies to different items. For details on the modeling procedures, see Sternberg (1977) and Pellegrino and Lyon (1979).

Strategies and Strategy Shifting

The first results from componential analyses were process models for several kinds of reasoning tasks. But the assumption that the same model should fit all subjects on a given task was quickly recognized as a useful first approximation that might be unwarranted on some tasks. Different process models might thus be needed to fit the performance of different individuals. Both Sternberg (1977) and Snow

(1978) had predicted that strategic variations would be an important source of individual differences in complex information processing. Although such differences in strategy are common on complex tasks, they occur on simpler tasks as well. For example, Cooper (1982) distinguished different strategies on a spatial comparison task. She also discovered that individuals sometimes could change strategies if induced to do so.

MacLeod, Hunt, and Mathews (1978) demonstrated a similar divergence of strategies on a sentence verification task. The performance of some subjects was well fit by a linguistic processing model, whereas the performance of other subjects was better described by a spatial processing model. In other words, a linguistic processor might read the presented sentence, encode it in memory linguistically (and also the picture when it appeared), and then compare these linguistic descriptions; a spatial processor might use the sentence to visualize the expected picture and then compare this image with the picture when it appeared. Verbal and spatial ability test profiles for the two groups differ in expected ways, suggesting that strategy choice was systematic. However, it was also clear that a subject could change from one strategy to the other if asked to do so.

Sternberg and Weil (1980) also conducted a training experiment in which linguistic versus spatial strategies were contrasted for reasoning in linear syllogisms. Linear syllogisms are problems such as "Mary is taller than Sue. Sue is taller than Amy. Who is shortest? Mary, Sue, Amy." Componential models were fit to identify four different strategy groups. Correlations with reference ability tests showed strikingly different patterns across groups. Success with the linguistic strategy correlated with verbal but not spatial ability; the opposite pattern occurred with the spatial strategy; and a mixed strategy group showed correlation with both abilities. Those using a fourth strategy, a simplified algorithmic procedure, showed reduced correlation with ability.

Kyllonen, Lohman, and Woltz (1984) next showed how componential models can be generalized to account for cases in which subjects not only use different strategies but shift between them during task performance. Although many investigators had argued that subjects seemed to shift strate-

gies as items became more difficult (Mulholland, Pellegrino, & Glaser, 1980; Bethell-Fox, Lohman, & Snow, 1984), no one had yet tested this within the framework of componential analysis. Kyllonen et al. (1984) identified three kinds of ability–strategy relationships: In a Case I relationship, ability limits strategy selection. In Case II, strategy choice is unrelated to ability, but the effectiveness of implementing a strategy depends on ability. In Case III, ability both limits strategy and predicts performance within strategy groups. Evidence for all three cases was found in componential analyses of a complex form board task that contained three steps. In the first step, subjects were required to memorize a geometric figure. In the second step, they were required to combine this first figure, which was no longer in view, with one or two new shapes displayed on a screen. In the third step, they were shown another figure and asked whether the two or three previously shown shapes would combine (in the order indicated) to form this final shape.

Models for each of the three steps (called encoding, synthesis, and comparison) were constructed from retrospective reports from experimental subjects, introspections of the experimenters, and the literature on spatial cognition. Each was then tested by regressing latencies for each step on independent variables that estimated the amount or difficulty of each hypothesized process. Independent variables were formed by coding objective features of items or by obtaining ratings of the desired characteristic from other subjects. Two types of models were tested: single-strategy models and strategy-shift models. Single-strategy models presume that the subject solves all items in basically the same way. Strategy-shift models, however, presume that the subject uses different strategies to solve different types of items.

The results of fitting these sorts of models to response latencies for each of the three task steps show two important effects. First, for each task step, different subjects solved different items in predictably different ways. Second, solution strategies were systematically related to the profile of scores on reference ability tests. This is shown in Figure 14.5. For example, for the synthesis step, subjects who were best fit by the most complex strategy-shifting model had the highest average ability profile. In other words, high-G subjects showed the most flexibility in making within-task adaptations in their solution strategies. Subjects who followed more restricted strategies had more extreme profiles, either always synthesizing figures (high on spatial but low on verbal ability) or synthesizing only those figures presently in view (very low spatial, but average on verbal ability).

Other studies have supported the utility of strategy-shift models and also have shown that seemingly minor variations in task demands can have a pronounced impact on how subjects solve items on spatial and figural reasoning tasks (Embretson, 1986; Lohman & Kyllonen, 1983; Lohman, 1988). Bethell-Fox et al. (1984) also demonstrated that strategy shifting within persons in geometric analogy tasks could account for differences between previous models offered by Sternberg (1977) and Mulholland, Pellegrino, and Glaser (1980). Furthermore, analyses of eye movements during performance of analogy items added evidence that subtle individual differences in strategy shifting occur not previously incorporated in componential models of reasoning about geometric forms. Although spatial tasks

FIGURE 14.5. Ability profiles for subjects classified as using different strategies on a mental synthesis task. Subjects in the Consistent Synthesis group (open triangles) were best fit by a model that said they always synthesized figures. Subjects in the Backward-Stepping group only synthesized when stimuli were in view. The other two groups synthesized in some trials, but not in others, depending on the complexity of the to-be-synthesized figure. Subjects in the last group (Simultaneous Recovery) evidenced the most flexibility in fitting strategy to item demands. (Gs = general crystallized; Gf = general fluid; Gv = general visualization; CS = closure speed; PS = perceptual speed; VM = visual memory; MS = memory span) (after Kyllonen, Lohman, & Woltz, 1984).

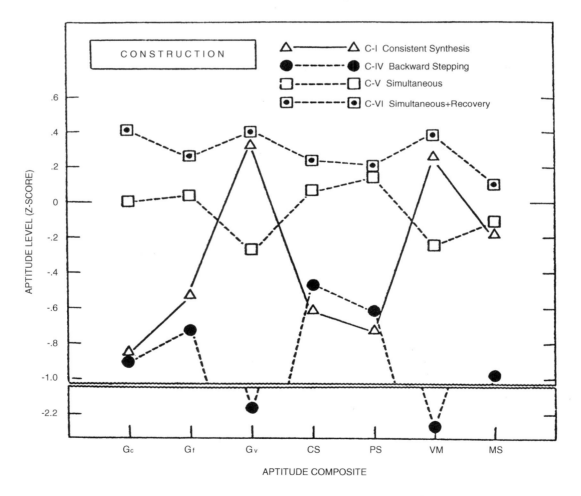

seem particularly susceptible to alternative solution strategies, verbal tasks are not exempt. Marquer and Pereira (1987) have reported that substantial strategy shifting occurs even on the sentence verification task used previously to contrast strategies that were assumed to be stable. For example, more than two thirds of the subjects in their study exhibited nonrandom shifts during performance. It is possible then that strategy shifting is a key aspect of individual differences in verbal as well as spatial and reasoning task performance (see, e.g., Spiro & Myers, 1984).

Strategy shifts can represent noise or substance, depending on the goal of test analysis. They contribute noise if the goal is to estimate a particular set of process parameters (e.g., rate of rotation, speed of lexical access) from a sample of items. They represent substance important for theory if, at some point, a higher level of ability means having a more flexible approach to problem solving. In either case, in interpreting research on abilities, it is incorrect to assume that all items or problems in a task are solved in the same way and that subjects differ only in the speed or power with which they execute a common set of processes. It is also incorrect to assume that subjects may be typed by strategy, or even that they shift strategies in the same way. At least, general abilities such as verbal comprehension, reasoning and spatial visualization appear to be more complex than this. Higher levels of performance in these ability domains seem to involve at least some flexible strategy shifting. On the other hand, it is abundantly clear that ability is much more than strategy. Indeed, the most able subjects often show little evidence of strategy shifting, most probably because they have no need to do so on the problems presented. Thus, although strategies and strategy shifting are important, it is unclear how much of the variation in G can be attributed to such processes and how much it reflects other factors such as differences in attentional resources or knowledge, for example.

Modeling Response Errors

REGRESSION MODELS. Problems on ability tests tend to be hard. Individual differences are reflected in how many problems examinees answer correctly, not how rapidly they finish. For example, time limits on the Cognitive Abilities test (Thorndike &

Hagen, 1993) are such that most students respond to all items in each of the nine subtests. Indeed, complex tests that load highly on G tend to be less speeded than tests that define more specific factors (or fall near the periphery of the radex). This is especially the case for spatial tests (Lohman, 1979). Thus, one of the earliest criticisms of the information-processing studies of abilities was that models that well described how rapidly subjects solved simple tasks might miss important aspects of individual differences in intelligence.

The regression procedures used to model response latencies assume that total response time is the simple sum of the time required to perform each of the hypothesized component processes. When modeling response accuracy, however, a probabilistic model (such as logistic regression) is more appropriate. An additive model makes little sense for response probabilities. A more plausible model would allow for conditional independence between components. In other words, the probability of executing component $n+1$ correctly is independent of the prior n components, but only if they were executed successfully (Embretson, 1995).

Goldman and Pellegrino (1984) provided an excellent introduction to models of response accuracy. They began with the derivation of a fairly simple model for an analogy in which E stimulus elements are subjects to T transformations. They assumed that there is some probability α of misrepresenting individual transformations and a similar probability β of misrepresenting individual elements; then, the general equation for predicting error rate on a given class of problems would be

$$\text{Probability (error)} = 1 - (1 - \alpha)^T (1 - \beta)^E$$

A more complete model separates different aspects of item processing such as the processing of the item stem and the processing of item alternatives. For example, in Alderton, Goldman, and Pellegrino (1985), accuracy of stem processing was estimated by either

1. Presenting the A and B terms of the analogy and asking the subject to generate a relational rule. If the rule was judged to be one that would lead to accurate solution, then *inference* is scored correct (component process: inference).

2. Presenting the A, B, and C terms and asking the subject to generate a response. Response was scored correct if it was the target response or a synonym (component processes: inference, mapping, application).

For alternative processing, the stem and five alternatives were presented.

3. If the subject generated an incorrect relationship or alternative when shown only the stem but then chose the correct alternative when shown the alternatives, then *recognition* was coded.
4. If the subject generated a correct relationship or completion term when shown the stem but then chose an incorrect alternative when shown the full item, then *distraction* was coded.

These separate probabilities were then combined for each subject in a single equation that predicted overall probability of a correct response on forced-choice items as the combined probability of correctly processing the stem (inference, application) and correctly processing the alternatives (recognition, guessing, distraction). The possibility that different subjects use different strategies is directly reflected in the estimated probabilities for each component in the model.

Error models can also be formulated to test for within-subject as well as between-subject shifts in solution strategy. For example, Embretson (1985, 1986; see also Embretson, Schneider, & Roth, 1986) used multicomponent latent-trait models to test the hypothesis that subjects attempt to solve items in more than one way. Embretson proposed that subjects first attempt to solve verbal analogy items using a rule-oriented strategy much like the strategy Sternberg hypothesized: they infer a rule that relates the first and second terms of the analogy, apply this rule to the third term to generate an answer, then compare this answer with the response alternatives. However, subjects switch to a secondary strategy if any part of the rule strategy fails. Three secondary strategies were proposed based on associations, partial rules, and response elimination. In the association strategy, subjects choose the alternative that is most highly associated with the third term; this is sometimes also the keyed answer (Gentile, Kessler, & Gentile, 1969). In the partial-rule strategy, subjects infer only part of the rule that relates the first and second terms, but this partial rule may be sufficient

to eliminate all distractors. In the response elimination strategy, subjects again infer only a partial rule, but this partial rule serves to eliminate only some of the distractors, and thus other item features or guessing must be used. Component scores for exact-rule construction, partial-rule construction, and response elimination were estimated by showing subjects the first two terms of each analogy and asking them to write the rule that described the A-to-B relationship. This procedure is the accuracy analog to the precuing procedure Sternberg used for response latencies. Exact rules stated the keyed relationships; partial rules stated only some of the keyed relationships but served to eliminate all foils; response elimination was scored if the partial rule eliminated only some foils. A rule evaluation component was scored by providing subjects with the exact A–B rule and asking them to select the correct alternative.

Different strategies were then formulated by combining these five component probabilities (plus another variable for overall probability of strategy execution) in different ways. For example, the probability that person j solves the full (T) item i by the rule strategy is given by

$$P_{\text{rule}}(X_{ijT}) = P_a P_{ij1} P_{ik2} \quad \text{where}$$

P_{ij1} is the probability of correctly inferring the exact A–B rule;
P_{ik2} is the probability of correctly applying the exact A–B rule; and
P_a is the probability in the sample of applying the rule strategy.

The multiplicative relationship between component probabilities indicates that component operations are sequentially dependent: a failure on one component leads to a failure of the strategy. Also note that P_a does not vary over persons or items in this model.

Multiple-strategy models were formed by summing the probabilities for individual strategies. For example, the probability of solving an item by first attempting but failing the rule strategy and then selecting the correct response by choosing the alternative most highly associated with the C term is

$$P_{\text{assoc+rule}}(X_{ijT}) = P_{\text{rule}}(X_{ijT}) + P_{\text{assoc}}(X_{ijT})$$

where

$$P_{\text{assoc}}(X_{ijT}) = P_c P_{ij3} (1 - P_{ij1} P_{ij2});$$

P_{ij3} is the probability of choosing the correct answer by simple association;

$(1 - P_{ij1} P_{ij2})$ is the probability that the rule strategy failed; and

P_c is the probability in the sample of applying the association strategy when available.

Adding probabilities for mutually exclusive strategies makes these models compensatory, like the strategy-shift models studied by Kyllonen, Lohman, and Woltz (1984) for response latencies.

Analyses showed that Model III (rule or partial rule strategy) and Model IV (rule strategy or response elimination) both predicted substantially more of the variation in estimated item difficulties than did Model I (rule strategy alone). However, all models were equally good predictors of subject differences. Thus, these models suggest that strategy shifts contributed significantly to item difficulty but not to individual differences in overall performance in the task. This may reflect the fact that the probability of executing each strategy (P_a, P_b, or P_c) could not be separately estimated for each subject.

RULE-SPACE ANALYSES. The rule-space methodology was developed as a method for diagnosing errors (or "bugs") in component skills from observations of complex performances that require combinations of many skills (see Tatsuoka, 1995, 1997 for overviews). Initially the method was applied to computation skills in mathematics. Of late it has been applied to verbal tests as well, such as the Critical Reading, Sentence Completion, and Verbal Analogies subtests of the GRE. Continued refinements and elaborations have resulted in the complex set of procedures shown schematically in Figure 14.6.

The first step in conducting a rule-space analysis is to identify the attributes hypothesized to be required by items on the test. In elementary mathematics, these would be component skills (such as "carry" in multicolumn addition). For more complex problems, attributes are often far less specific ("ability to synthesize information") and sometimes represent different aspects of a common skills (e.g., vocabulary skills are represented by the average word frequency of the five most difficult words and

also by the average word length of words in a passage). The presence or absence of each attribute is then coded for each item on the test (this is the incidence matrix in Figure 14.6). All possible latent knowledge states are then generated from the incidence matrix using a procedure called a Boolean descriptive function. Each of these latent knowledge states corresponds to a particular pattern of scores on the test items. Observed score patterns are then mapped on to these ideal score patterns with some allowance for "slips" or model misfit. Finally, for each subject classified in one of the knowledge states, the probability that the subject has mastered each attribute specified in the original list of attributes is computed.

In typical study, the procedure is applied iteratively – usually beginning with a long list of attributes that is reduced over iterations. Success of the model has been indexed by the percentage of test takers classified in one of the latent knowledge states specified in the model (which typically number in the thousands) and by the regression of total score on the test on the set of attribute mastery scores. More convincing indices would be the probability that an individual is classified in a similar knowledge state on a parallel test and the demonstration that attribute mastery scores generalize across test forms and show convergent and discrimant correlations with external measures of the same or similar constructs.

This brief summary cannot begin to explain the rule-space method. It is introduced here, however, as an illustration of a larger trend in research on individual differences in complex information processing. Limitations of the methods that were used to model performance on relatively simple testlike tasks have become more apparent over the years. More complex statistical methods have been developed in an effort to model better the enormous diversity of processing that occurs on complex tests such as the GRE and also to take advantage of advances in measurement (such as IRT-based scales) that had been ignored in earlier efforts. There is a great paradox here, however, in that diversity at one level is purchased at the price of uniformity at another level. For example, the basic assumption of the rule-space procedure is that items can be unambiguously characterized as requiring or not requiring a particular skill. Thus, each column in the incidence

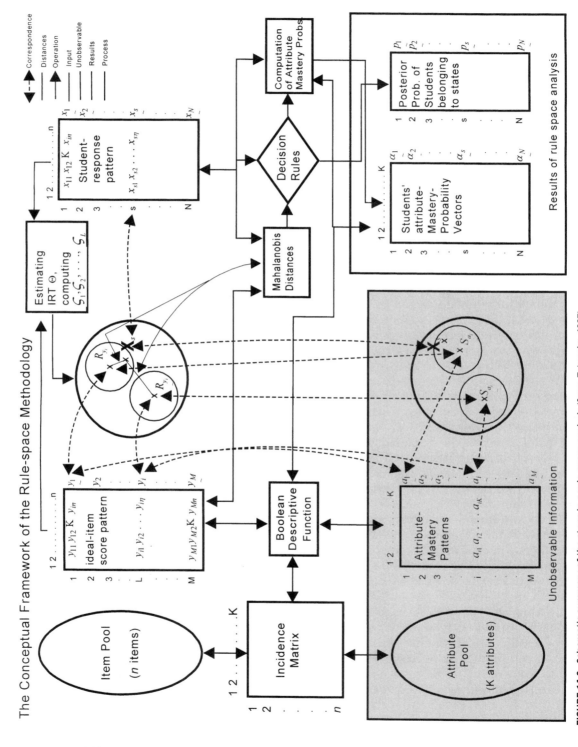

FIGURE 14.6. Schematic summary of the steps in a rule-space analysis (from Tatsuoka, 1997).

300

matrix represents a strong statement about how all subjects must solve that item. Alternative strategies or compensatory mechanisms are not allowed. A person is expected to solve the item only if he or she has mastered all of the component skills that are specified in the matrix. It may well be that such strong models can work when attributes are specified at a global level (e.g., "can synthesize information" or "can apply general background knowledge"). Such attributes are perhaps better seen as category labels for task demands ("can do X somehow") rather than specific cognitive processes ("does X at Y rate"). Indeed, whether test takers can be classified into one or more knowledge states specified by the procedure may be less important for theory than the fact that collections of items used in these tests are being scrutinized for the demands they place on test takers.

PROCESS MODELS OF REASONING TASKS

Hypotheses about Processing Complexity

Returning to the radex example in Figure 14.2, researchers working within the information-processing paradigm have offered several hypotheses to explain how tasks increase in complexity along these spokes: (a) an increase in the number of component processes involved in task performance; (b) an increase in the involvement of one or more particular components (such as inference); (c) an increase in demands on working memory or attentional resources; and (d) an increase in demands on adaptive functions, including executive or metacognitive controls (Snow, Kyllonen, & Marshalek, 1984).

Investigations of particular reasoning tasks sometimes address one of these hypotheses but more commonly cut across them. Thus, although I will use these hypotheses to organize the discussion, the initial presentation of research is by necessity more task based. I begin with the early simulation of reasoning on series completion problems and then move to analogies, sentence completion, classification tasks, seriation tasks, and matrix tasks. I then summarize more general theories of reasoning that cut across task boundaries.

Series Completion

Series completion problems require the test taker to extrapolate the next member of a series of stimuli such as letters, numbers, or geometric figures. For example, one might be required to identify the next number in the series 1, 3, 6, 10, ___ or the next letter in the series b, c, x, d, e, y, ___.

Simon and Kotovsky (1963) proposed a computer simulation model for letter series problems of this sort. Their model contained two basic routines: a pattern generator and a sequence generation. The first corresponds to Spearman's "education of relations" and the second to his "education of correlates." The pattern generator was composed of subroutines for (a) detection of the interletter relations, (b) identification of period length of the pattern, and (c) generation of a description or rule integrating these two aspects of the problem. Subsequent investigators often subdivided this last component into pattern description and extrapolation. In the Simon and Kotovsky (1963) theory, the rule or pattern description output by the pattern generator module served as input to the sequence generator module, which applied the pattern description to the problem to generate elements that would come next in the problem. The knowledge base assumed by the program was limited to forward and backward knowledge of the alphabet and the relational concepts identity next, and backwards-next (or reverse order).

Each of these aspects of problem description was shown to be related to problem difficulty. *Identity* relations were easier than *next* relations, which were easier than *backwards-next* relations. As in most problems that contain multiple sources of difficulty, however, the relative difficulty of different nonidentity relations depends on the location of the relation within the period. In particular, the difficulty of a *next* relation increases as it is further embedded in the pattern. In general, the longer the pattern description and the greater the demands presumably placed on working memory in the identification of the rule, the more difficult the problem (Simon & Kotovsky, 1963; Holzman, Glaser, & Pellegrino, 1976). However, contrary to the model, period length does not appear to be related to solution accuracy.

Butterfield, Nielsen, Tangen, and Richardson (1985) revised and elaborated on the model to account for item difficulty in all possible series items, not for just the samples of items that might happen to appear on some particular test. They argued that a good theory of how people solve series problems and of what makes such problems easy or difficult to solve must apply to representative samples of items from a defined universe that includes all known item attributes. Because some attributes are over- or underrepresented in the sample of items studied, the resulting theory of solution processes or item difficulty will be distorted and will vary unpredictably from study to study. Their theory discards period length as important in the representation stage, setting forth several levels of knowledge about what are called *moving strings* and predicting that item difficulty is determined by the string that is most difficult to represent. It also subdivides the memory load aspect of the continuation stage of performance. The theory accounts well for the data from the earlier work and from several new experiments.

LeFevre and Bisanz (1986) sought to provide a more detailed account of the processes involved in the "detection of relations" component and to determine the extent to which individual differences in tasks designed to measure this component predicted performance in the number series subtest of the Lorge–Thorndike Test of Intelligence (Lorge & Thorndike, 1957). LeFevre and Bisanz (1986) hypothesized that three procedures were used for detecting relations among numbers: recognition of memorized numerical series (e.g., 2 4 6 8), calculation (e.g., computing the interelement differences in a series such as 1 2 4 7 11), and checking (e.g., determining whether the last digit in "2 5 8 11 13" was encoded or calculated incorrectly or instead marks the boundary between two periods). These hypotheses were investigated on very simple problems that combined procedures in different ways. Results showed that high-ability subjects used recognition of memorized sequences on a wider range of problems and calculated more efficiently than did low-ability subjects. High- and low-ability subjects did not differ on checking, although this may have been due to the low error rate (2.8% overall).

These studies of series completion tasks illustrate the range of analytic procedures used to infer process. The early studies of Simon and Kotovsky relied heavily on introspection and think-aloud protocols for theory generation. However, the test of the theory was the ability of the computer simulation to solve problems successfully and also to account

for sources of difficulty in the task. The later work of Butterfield et al. (1984) and LeFevre and Bisanz (1986) focused on the analysis of response latencies and errors. Although simulation models continue to be an important source of evidence (e.g., Carpenter, Just, & Shell, 1990), methods for testing processing models against error and latency data have become much more popular. One reason has been the success of a set of methods for latency and error modeling known collectively as componential analysis, which is perhaps best illustrated in the research on analogical reasoning.

Models of Analogical Reasoning

Sternberg (1977) reported several investigations into the processes subjects use to solve analogies. Figure 14.7 shows flowcharts for four alternative models of analogy performance he hypothesized. Component processes are identified inside the boxes; parameters reflecting the operation of each component are listed at the side of each box.

In Model I, the inference, mapping, and application components are all exhaustively applied, that is, all attributes of the terms of the analogy are compared. In Model II, the application component is self-terminating, that is, after D is encoded, attributes are tested one at a time until a correct attribute is found for response. In Model III, both mapping and application are self-terminating. In Model IV, inference also becomes self-terminating. Model III best fitted the data in Sternberg's (1977) first experiments, accounting for 92, 86, and 80% of the variance in the latency for schematic-people, verbal, and geometric analogies data, respectively. A subsequent experiment with schematic-people analogies confirmed this order.

GEOMETRIC ANALOGIES. Mulholland et al. (1980) proposed a somewhat different model for geometric analogies. Borrowing from Evans (1968), they argued that subjects *infer* the relationship between A and B, *infer* the relationship between C and D, and then *compare* the two sets of relationships. Mulholland et al. (1980) refer to Sternberg's hypothesis as an infer-apply-test model and to their own as an infer-infer-compare model. Importantly, they studied true-false analogies in which an infer-infer-compare strategy would make more sense than in the two alternative items Sternberg (1977)

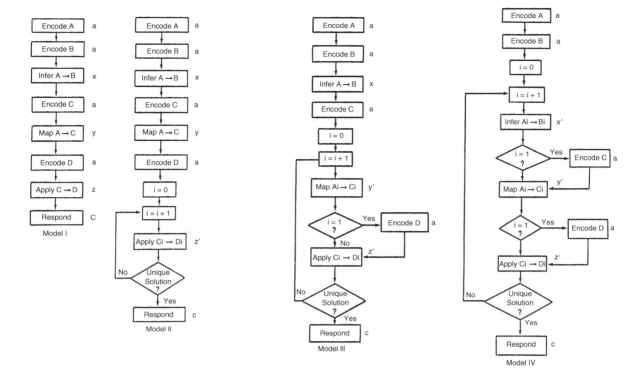

FIGURE 14.7. Alternative models of analogical reasoning (after Sternberg, 1977).

studied or the four alternative items Bethell-Fox et al. (1984) studied. Probably the most important result of their study, however, was the finding of a small but significant interaction between the number of elements or figures and the number of transformations (size change, rotation, doubling, etc.). Problems requiring multiple transformations on a single element were much harder than problems that required the same number of transformations on single elements. They argued that such items further burdened an already taxed working memory by requiring participants to retain the element in memory while operating on the intermediate products of a transformation. (They also noted that the solution of "ambiguous" items [i.e., items in which the A-to-B transformation was nonobvious], although common on psychometric tests, were not included in their study.) They also speculated that strategic flexibility may be particularly important when attempting complex items.

The hypothesis that more complex items induce subjects to alter their strategies was addressed in a study by Bethell-Fox et al. (1984). Bethell-Fox et al. (1984) presented both two-alternative items (as in

Sternberg) and four-alternative items (as on some mental tests). They also recorded eye fixations and administered an extensive battery of reference ability measures.

Several of their results were particularly noteworthy. First, unlike Sternberg (1977), they included a comparison component in all of their componential models. With the addition of this component, Sternberg's Models I through IV (see Figure 14.7) all fit the data equally well ($r^2 = .911$ to $.917$ for two-alternative items, and $r^2 = .938$ to $.941$ for four-alternative items). Mapping was a trivial component and was dropped, and two new components were added: spatial inference and spatial application. These components were only implicated on items involving spatial transformations. In other words, subjects appeared to activate and deactivate these processes across items.

Bethell-Fox et al. (1984) also followed up on Mulholland et al.'s (1980) suggestion to include items in which the nature of the A-to-B transformation was not immediately apparent (i.e., the most obviously correct answer did not appear among the response alternatives). The component Sternberg (1977) called justification accounted for approximately 25% of the variance in both latency and error data on these ambiguous items but was not significant for nonambiguous items.

Analyses of eye fixations, however, showed that subjects often looked back to the A and B terms after inspecting C and the alternatives. Such lookbacks were particularly common on difficult, four-alternative items. This suggests that lookbacks were an integral part of solution strategy. Other results suggested that as problems increased in difficulty, subjects shifted from a strategy of constructing an ideal answer and comparing it to alternatives, to a more iterative, systematic examination of stem and alternatives. Lower-ability subjects transited to this strategy sooner than their high-ability counterparts.

VERBAL ANALOGIES. The declarative knowledge necessary to solve a geometric analogy is relatively easy to specify. Although the set of rules that transforms one element into another is not small, it is not large either. Most items are constructed by applying one or more simple transformations (size change, rotation, shading change) to specific elements to produce specific products. However, in verbal analogies, the transformation rules are often subtler and the elements far more variable. Further, variables hy-

pothesized to index these relationships must often be obtained from ratings rather than from codings of objective features of stimuli.

Several classification schemes have been proposed for classifying verbal analogies by the type of semantic relations represented in the stem. These include class membership, function, location, conversion, part–whole, order-in-time, and property (Pellegrino & Glaser, 1982; Whitely, 1976). Location and function relations tend to be easier than others. Nevertheless, Pellegrino and Glaser (1982) argued that classification schemes do not predict difficulty because they capture only the most salient relational feature. The ease or likelihood of identifying a relation varies enormously across items within each category. For example, in one study, a group of undergraduates generated responses to 150 stems (A:B::C:?). The probability associated with the most frequently generated response ranged from .10 to .90, indicating substantial variability in the typicality of generated answers, most of which were semantically appropriate (e.g., for "antler:deer::tusk," the most frequent response was "elephant," with "walrus" a distant second). As would be expected, items in which the constraints imposed by the stem restrict alternatives tend to be easier.

Building on the earlier work of Whitely (1976) and Chaffin and Herrmann (1984), Bejar, Chaffin, and Embretson (1991) proposed a more elaborate taxonomy of semantic relations. As shown in Table 14.1, the 10 categories in their taxonomy are grouped into two higher order categories of intensional and pragmatic relations. Intensional relations are said to be based solely on the meanings of the two words and require an evaluation of the overlap or contrast of attributes of the two concepts. Pragmatic relations, in contrast, require knowledge of the world that goes beyond the meaning of the two words.

In an analysis of 179 GRE verbal-analogy items, Bejar et al. (1991) found differences in the average difficulty of items in each of the 10 categories. With one exception (Contrast Relations), the easier items were all classfied as pragmatic relations. However, a follow-up study by

---

TABLE 14.1. A Taxonomy of Semantic Relations

Semantic Type	Semantic Class	Example
Intensional	Class Inclusion	robin:bird
	Similarity	breeze:gale
	Attribute	beggar:poor
	Contrast	stutter:speech
	Nonattribute	harmony:discordant
Pragmatic	Event	tailor:suit
	Cause-purpose	virus:illness
	Space-time	judge:courthouse
	Part-whole	engine:car
	Representation	building:blueprint

Source: From *Cognitive and psychometric analysis of analogical problem solving* (p. 71), by I. I. Bejar, R. Chaffin & S. Embretson, 1991, New York: Springer-Verlag.

Diones, Bejar, and Chaffin (1996) failed to replicate this finding on SAT items. More importantly, mean difficulty in the earlier Bejar et al. (1991) study was inversely related to mean item discrimination (*r*-biserial with GRE verbal composite). The authors showed that this relationship between difficulty and discrimination can be eliminated by estimating discrimination using a coefficient that takes into account the differential attractiveness of different alternatives to examinees of different levels of ability. Put differently, one of the features of difficult analogy items is that they require careful discrimination among two (or more) plausible alternatives.

Buck, VanEssen, Tatsuoka, Kostin, Lutz, & Phelps (1998a) investigated SAT verbal analogies using Tatsuoka's (1995) rule space methodology. The first step in this analysis requires the identification of attributes that are hypothesized to affect performance on the items. They identified a large number of variables, most of which indexed different aspects of vocabulary difficulty and semantic or conceptual complexity. These are shown in Table 14.2. The major determinants of semantic complexity were whether a word had multiple meanings and whether it referred to an abstract concept. Attributes of the relationship between concepts were the ability to recognize a negative rationale, a complex rationale, and those that required the processing of concepts from different discourse domains. Several of these attributes are particularly interesting in that they suggest that at least some items require a flexibility or fluidity of thought, especially the ability to sort through multiple meanings and to make inferences across domains. Pellegrino and Glaser (1982) argued that ambiguity in the relationship between the A and B terms was one of the major sources of difficulty on the analogy items they examined.

Pellegrino and Glaser (1982) proposed that subjects solve verbal analogies by first abstracting (i.e., inferring) semantic relationships from the stem of the item, and then evaluating the alternatives in a generate and test mode. But for more difficult

---

TABLE 14.2. Attributes Hypothesized to Influence Performance on SAT Verbal Analogy Items

Processing Difficult Vocabulary

01a	The ability to process low-frequency vocabulary in the stem.
01b	The ability to process low-frequency vocabulary in the key.
01e	The ability to process low-frequency vocabulary in the four distractors.
14	The ability to process longer words in the key.
15	The ability to process longer words in the distractors.
18	The ability to process longer words in the stem.
02	The ability to process vocabulary out of its usual context.

Processing Complex Concepts and Relationships

03a	The ability to process multiple meanings due to semantic ambiguity.
03b	The ability to process multiple meanings due to syntactic ambiguity.
07	The ability to process a negative rationale.
08	The ability to process a complex rationale.
25	The ability to analyze and contrast concepts.

Deploying Background Knowledge

09	The ability to process scientific topics.
10	The ability to discount the influence of emotive language.

Note: The following interaction attributes were also retained in the final model: 14×18, $01b \times 10$, 14×05, $01b \times 22b$, $01b \times 02$, and $03b \times 22b$.

Source: Development, selection and validation of cognitive and linguistic attributes for the SAT I Verbal: Analogy section, by G. Buck, T. VanEssen, K. Tatsuoka, I. Kostin, D. Lutz, & M. Phelps, 1998a. Research Rep. No. 98-19. Princeton, NJ: Educational Testing Service.

problems, they argued that subjects must use information in options to guide the search for the appropriate A–B relationship. Key sources of difficulty, then, are the abstractness or complexity or precision of the rule that must be generated and the variability or initial ambiguity in the rules that may be inferred. They hypothesized that this *representational variability* is a key source of problem difficulty, especially on verbal analogies.

The claim that subjects use information in the alternatives to constrain the inference process on difficult analogies was strongly supported in a study by Alderton, Goldman, and Pellegrino (1985). Alderton et al. (1985) obtained separate estimates for the accuracy of stem processing and alternative processing on verbal analogy problems (considered here) and verbal classification problems (considered below). The goal was to obtain separate estimates of the probability that subjects used information in the stem to "reason forward" to the answer (which was selected from the set provided), or to "reason backward" from the alternatives to stem. Reasoning from alternatives to stem could lead to a successful solution in that the alternatives could be used to constrain the search for relationships among terms in the stem, thereby allowing recognition of an alternative that would not have been selected on the basis of initial stem processing. (Whitely (1980) refers to this as "event recovery.") But analysis of alternatives could also be a source of error such as when an incorrect but plausible distractor was chosen even though stem processing had been accurate. Previous work with children showed that distraction was a major source of error for children (Goldman, Pellegrino, Parseghian, & Sallis, 1982).

Results showed that recognition was more important than stem processing in predicting overall problem-solving success – substantially so in one sample and moderately so in another. Distraction, although generally not as important for adults (4% of items) as for children (36% and 27% of items for third and fifth graders, respectively, in Goldman et al., 1982), was a significant predictor of overall accuracy for low-scoring subjects but not for high-scoring subjects. Thus, the assumption that adults engage in exhaustive encoding of the A–B terms in an analogy may apply only to simple problems. For more difficult problems, successful analogy

solvers used both feed-forward and feed-backward strategies.

Several other studies confirm the hypothesis that more complex models are needed to characterize the behavior of subjects on difficult items. Gitomer, Curtis, Glaser, and Lensky (1987) studied subject's eye fixation patterns on verbal analogy items that varied widely in difficulty. Results for easy problems replicated Sternberg's (1977) finding that high-ability subjects spend proportionately more time processing the stem (encoding, inferring, mapping) than low-ability subjects. The pattern was reversed on difficult problems. Highs actually spent more time processing stem words after, rather than before, looking at answer options. In addition, highs were much more likely than lows to consider all answer choices on difficult problems. Gitomer et al. (1987) interpreted their results as supporting the claim of Bethell-Fox et al. (1984) that explanations of individual differences on analogies of nontrivial difficulty must include an explanation of this differential flexibility of subjects in using different solution strategies as items increase in difficulty. They suggested that the important metacognitive skill may be the ability to monitor the success of each processing step – particularly the crucial step of ensuring that the A–B relation maps on to the C–D relation. They cautioned, however, that processing flexibility may be only one aspect of observed ability differences, given the importance of vocabulary knowledge in predicting difficulty of verbal analogies.

But vocabulary knowledge is a slippery variable. Increasing difficulty by using infrequent words may actually introduce construct-irrelevant variance – at least if the goal is to measure Gf rather than Gc. Horn (1972) showed this in a study in which he presented two types of analogies, which he called esoteric word analogies and common word analogies. Esoteric analogies used infrequent words about a topic unfamiliar to most adults. A test of the former loaded on a Gc factor (along with vocabulary), whereas a test of the latter split its variance between a Gc and a Gf factor. Marshalek (1981) made a similar observation about tests of vocabulary knowledge: correlations with reasoning (Gf) increased as vocabulary items emphasized precise understanding of common concepts and declined as items required vague understanding of common concepts or knowledge of infrequent words.

Sentence Completion

The sentence completion test is one of the oldest mental tests. In the late 1890s, Ebbinghaus was using sentences from which one or more words had been deleted to study learning and memory. From this work, Ebbinghaus concluded that the ability to combine information is a major component of intelligence (Ebbinghaus, 1913/1985).

As with other verbal tasks, incomplete sentences can be constructed to emphasize different aspects of verbal knowledge and reasoning. Consider the following:

1. Children who do not mind their parents are said to be ___.
   disrespectful   unkind   disobedient
2. Yesterday, Tom ___ on a trip to Mississippi.
   go   went   gone
3. The ice will ___ when the sun comes out.
   freeze   melt   evaporate
4. Even though I am older than Bob, Bob is ___ than I am.
   younger   shorter   taller

The first sentence emphasizes vocabulary knowledge; the second, knowledge of grammar (syntax); the third, general word knowledge; and the fourth, reasoning.

Other than a few isolated studies of cloze tests in reading, sentence completion tests have received little attention as measures of reasoning ability. One notable exception is the work of Buck et al. (1998b) with sentence completion items on the SAT. Buck et al. treated sentence completion items as mini-reading comprehension tests. They coded four different types of attributes for each item: vocabulary knowledge in both stem and options (e.g., word length, word frequency); syntactic complexity (e.g., number of words in sentence, use of negation); rhetorical and semantic structure (e.g., two missing words in item, opposite meanings, connections or relationships between ideas); and content (e.g., unfamiliar topics, scientific topics). The final rule-space analysis retained 20 of these attributes and 3 interactions among them. All of these attributes correlated significantly with total score ($r = .18$ to $.62$)

and had significant beta weights in the regression of total score on attributes. Some of the attributes identify aspects of items that can be directly mapped onto cognitive skills; others require unpacking. Further, although total score is a useful first criterion, relationships between attributes and a more finely differentiated set of reference constructs would be even more informative. For example, do some attributes show stronger relationships with reasoning? with verbal fluency? As suggested in the sample sentences above, incomplete sentences can be constructed that emphasize different abilities. Clearly, more work needs to be done, although the Buck et al. report provides an excellent overview of variables that influence processing on the type of sentence completion items used on the SAT.

Classification Problems

Although classification problems are commonly used as measures of inductive reasoning, they have not been the object of much experimental effort. In a typical classification problem, the subject sees three or more words or figures and must decide which of a set of alternatives belongs in the same set. Sternberg and Gardner (1983) studied problems of the form A B, C D : E in which the subject's task is to decide whether E fits better with A and B or with C and D. The model for these problems contained the same component processes specified for analogies and series problems. However, classification problems on ability tests typically take a different form. The problem stem contains three or more elements that are alike in some way. The subject's task is to decide which of four or five alternatives also belongs in the set. For example, the stem might present the words: POUND GUILDER FRANC. The stem here appears to be "currencies" or perhaps "foreign currencies" or even "Western European currencies." Because the number of elements in even the most restrictive set is quite large, it is unlikely that the subject will correctly generate the desired answer without examining the alternatives. Analogy items differ in that the set of acceptable alternatives is typically much smaller. Alderton et al. (1985) used the procedures previously described to estimate the probability that adult subjects inferred the correct relation rule for the stem elements, applied this rule to generate the target alternative, could recognize the correct alternative even if the inferred rule would not have included the keyed answer, and would select an incorrect alternative even if correct rule or category had been generated in stem processing. Thus, four process-outcome scores were estimated for each subject: inference, application, recognition, and distraction.

Results showed that low-scoring subjects were much more likely to be fit by the model that included a component for distraction than were high-scoring subjects. Recognition (weighted positively) and distraction (weighted negatively) were better predictors of total score than were inference and application. Other studies (see Goldman & Pellegrino, 1984) suggest that inference is a more important predictor of success on classification problems for children. Thus, adults seem to make better use of the alternatives to reason about the problem than do children. Classification problems thus differ in interesting ways from analogy and series completion problems. Future studies may investigate performance on figural classification problems (see Figure 14.1). It would also be interesting to separate the rule or category inferencing step (which is the only operation on tests such as Similarities in the Wechsler, 1991, scales) from the recognition process, which is emphasized on verbal classification problems.

Seriation Problems

Seriation problems or linear syllogisms are commonly used in tests of reasoning abilities. Figure 14.1 shows examples from the CogAT (Thorndike & Hagen, 1993) that use numerical content such as the following:

I. 1 dime + 2 nickels I is worth more than II.
II. 25 pennies   I is worth less than II.
                     I is worth the same
                       amount as II.

Series problems can present any number of elements to be arranged. The quantitative example above uses only two terms; verbal series problems typically use three terms. Difficulty of problems can be predicted from the number of terms, the order of presentation of elements, the use of negations, and the presence of marked adjectives (Wright & Dennis, 1999). In particular, items are easier if they have fewer

terms, if the first premise refers to the first or last term rather than the middle term (Huttenlocher, 1968), and if the premises are worded positively and use unmarked adjectives (e.g., "better" rather than "worse"). Wright and Dennis (1999) showed that one could construct a test of linear syllogistic reasoning of known difficulty by systematically varying these facets of item difficulty.

Theorists differ, though, in explanations of how subjects represent and solve such problems. Huttenlocher (1968) argued that subjects create a visual mental model of the elements. Clark (1969) argued instead that subjects represent premises linguistically and compare them. Johnson-Laird (1972) proposed that subjects use both types of processes: a spatial representation early in problem solution and a linguistic representation later on. Sternberg (1980) also argued that both linguistic and spatial representations are used, but on different problems. Johnson-Laird (1985) seems to agree: He notes that several experiments suggest that in processing many linear syllogisms, different subjects employ different strategies and that some subjects can be induced to change their strategies.

Sternberg (1986) argued that the primary sources of individual differences on such problems are encoding and combining the premises. Encoding requires that the subject apply a fairly complex set of procedural rules (e.g., for processing negations, marked adjectives). Combining premises requires the construction of some sort of representation or model in working memory that can be coordinated with the premises as they are encoded. Several working-memory functions are thus required, which include but go considerably beyond simultaneous storage and processing. Working memory requirements can be even more substantial when premises are presented sequentially and singly (see, e.g., the grammatical reasoning test in Kyllonen and Christal, 1990).

Matrix Tests

Matrix tests – particularly the Progressive Matrices test of Raven (1938/1965) – have long been used as a marker for *Gf* (see, e.g., Figure 14.1). Several analyses of this test have been reported (Jacobs & Vandeventer, 1972; Hunt, 1974), including an extensive investigation by Carpenter, et al. (1990). The Carpenter et al. report is particularly noteworthy because the authors used a variety of methods – including task analysis, protocol analysis, and computer simulations, and an equally diverse array of dependent measures – retrospective reports, eye fixations, response errors and response latencies, and success (or failure) of the simulation programs.

Carpenter et al. (1990) began with a task analysis of the progressive matrices test, which suggested that five different types of rules were used to solve items on the test. Ordered from simple to complex, the rules were (a) identity relations, in which an element is the same across all rows or columns; (b) pairwise progression, in which an element changes systematically from cell to cell (e.g., decreases in size across columns); (c) figure addition or subtraction, in which the first two entries combine to make the last entry; (d) distribution of three relations, in which an object or attribute appears once in each row or column; and (e) distribution of two relations, in which one of the elements in the distribution of three rule has a null or nonmatching value. Some progressions could be described by more than one rule, and some rules could be described differently. In particular, the difficult "distribution of two values" rule could be represented perceptually as "add (or synthesize) elements of figures, but two identical elements cancel." In problems with multiple rules, subjects must discover which elements in three entries in a row are governed by the same rule – a process Carpenter, Just, and Shell call *correspondence finding*. To do this, subjects must focus on one attribute (shape, number, orientation, shading) and determine if the chosen attribute for each pair of entries in a row matches one of the known rules. To further complicate matters, entries in columns 1 and 2 may follow a rule, but entries in columns 2 and 3 may not. Significantly, Simon and Kotovsky (1963) argued that solving series completion problems also requires correspondence finding, pairwise comparison of adjacent elements, and the induction of rules based on patterns of similarities and differences. Thus, the first source of individual differences on the matrix test was hypothesized to be the ability to infer these sorts of abstract relations.

Some subjects (12 students) were asked to think aloud while they solved problems and their eye fixations were recorded. Other subjects (22 adults) worked silently and then described the rules that motivated their response. "The most striking feature of the eye fixations and verbal protocols was the...incremental nature of the processing"(p. 411). In other words, subjects appeared to solve problems by decomposing them into smaller subproblems, which were then solved. Thus, it was hypothesized that the second major source of individual differences was the ability to generate subgoals in working memory, to monitor progress toward attaining them, and to set new subgoals as others are attained.

SIMULATION MODELS. Hypotheses about the processes used to solve items were tested in two simulation programs: FAIRAVEN, which performed at the level of the median college student in the sample, and BETTERAVEN which performed at the level of the best subjects in the sample.

FAIRAVEN consisted of 121 production rules in 3 categories: perceptual analyses (48%), conceptual analyses (40%), and response generation and selection (12%). The point–biserial correlation between the average error rate for 12 subjects and FAIRAVEN's success or failure was $r (32) = .67$, indicating a reasonable correspondence. A comparison with error rates for larger, more representative samples used in norming the test was not reported.

FAIRAVEN's limitations were (a) it could not "induce" more complex rules, (b) it had no way to backtrack if a hypothesized correspondence was incorrect and thus it had difficulty where correspondence was based on texture or location, and (c) too many high level goals at once overwhelmed the concurrent processing of goals.

BETTERAVEN was designed to overcome these limitations. Differences are shown schematically in Figure 14.8. In particular, it exercised more direct strategic control over its own processes through the addition of a goal monitor. BETTERAVEN also could induce (i.e., "knew") more "abstract" rules, such as the "distribution of two" rule. The goal monitor consisted of 15 new productions that set main goals and subgoals. The main purposes of the goal monitor were (a) to ensure higher level processes would occur serially (do one thing at a time), (b) to provide an order for inducing rules (conflict resolution), and (c) to maintain an account of the model's progress toward its goals. With these enhancements, BETTERAVEN performed at the same level as the best college students in the sample. Carpenter et al.

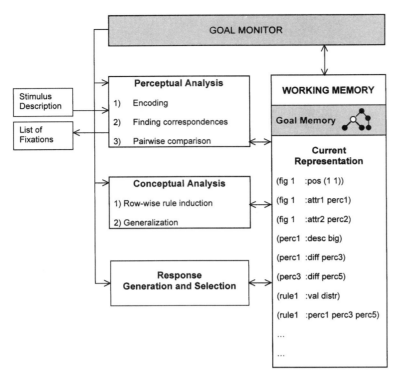

FIGURE 14.8. Production rules in the simulation BETTERAVEN. (The distinction from FAIRAVEN visible from the block diagram is the inclusion of a goal monitor that generates and keeps track of progress in a goal tree in working memory. These boxes are shaded in the figure. (fig = figure; pos = position; attr = attribute; perc = percept; desc = description; diff = different; val = value; distr = distribution) (after Carpenter et al., 1990).

(1990) concluded that what matrix tests such as the Progressive Matrices measure is the "common ability to decompose problems into manageable segments and iterate through them, the differential ability to manage the hierarchy of goals and subgoals generated by this decomposition, and the differential ability to form higher level abstractions" (p. 429).

A THEORY-BASED MATRIX TEST. Embretson (1998) used the Carpenter et al. (1990) theory to specify templates for 30 matrix items. Twenty-four templates were identical to item structures studied by Carpenter et al., although two item structures that contained the "distribution of two" rule were reclassified as solvable by an easier figure combina-

tion rule. Six new structures, consisting primarily of pairwise or "distribution of three" relationships, were added. A list of 22 objects (such as square, cross) and seven attributes (such as "increases in size") was combined with the item templates to generate items. Finally, seven distractors were created for each item to contain one or more inappropriate attributes or objects. Items were then administered on a computer.

As expected, the best predictor of item difficulty and response time was a variable that summed the relational level of the rules used to construct the item (i.e., identity = 1, pairwise progression = 2, combination = 3, distribution of three = 4, and distribution of two = 5). This variable was hypothesized to represent working memory load (including executive processes for goal setting and strategy monitoring) but also represents difficulty (or abstractness) of inference. It correlated $r = .71$ with difficulty for 150 generated items. A second study showed that a test composed of 34 of these items correlated $r = .78$ with the 48-item progressive matrices test, and both had similar patterns of correlations with subtests of the Armed Services Vocational Aptitude Battery.

There are many ways one can test the adequacy of a theory of a test, one of which is to use the theory to generate new items. If these items behave like items on the source test, then confidence is raised in the theory, at least as it describes sources of difficulty that have an impact on individual differences in the construct measured by the test (Embretson, 1998; Nichols, 1994). However, identifying sources of difficulty is not the same as identifying individual differences in processes that are influenced by those variables. Another study by Embretson (1995) illustrates this point.

This study once again examined performance on the 150 matrix items used in the previous study. The goal of this study, however, was to estimate the relative contributions of individual differences in general control processing and in working memory capacity to individual differences in performance on these matrix items. Some have emphasized the importance of executive functions (such as assembling performance programs, monitoring their implementation, etc.) in understanding individual differences in intelligence (e.g., Belmont & Butterfield, 1971; Sternberg, 1977, 1985; Snow, 1981), whereas others have emphasized the role of working memory (Pellegrino & Glaser, 1980; Carpenter et al., 1990). Indeed, Kyllonen and Christal (1990) found that reasoning ability correlated approximately $r = .8$ with working-memory ability in a series of larger studies. Embretson (1995) attempted to distinguish these hypotheses using a multicomponent latent-trait model. She posited in the model that two latent variables were responsible for individual differences on the task: working memory capacity (the influence of which varied according to the memory load of the item) and control processing (assumed to be required equally by all items). Thus, although the second factor was interpreted as reflecting control processes, it could reflect these processes or any other processes required by all items. Others have argued that control processes are most strongly engaged when tasks are perceived to be of moderate difficulty (Belmont & Mitchell, 1987) and thus would not be required equally by all items. In any event, results showed that the two latent variables accounted for 92% of the variation in total score and that the "control process" latent variable accounted for more variance than the "working-memory" latent variable.

Analyses of matrix problems provide the strongest evidence to date for the importance of control processes for high levels of performance on difficult reasoning tasks. But as Embretson's (1995) study shows, working memory or attentional resources also play an important role. Further, control and assembly processes are probably best understood as aspects of a working-memory system rather than as alternatives to it (Baddeley, 1996).

Theories of Reasoning that Span Several Tasks

Cognitive psychology – particularly the information-processing branch of it – has been characterized as task-bound (Newell, 1980). This criticism is amply demonstrated in many of the studies reviewed to this point. Most reflect intensive analyses of particular tasks. Although such analyses are a useful first step in developing a theory of reasoning or intelligence, ultimately one must identify commonalities across tasks. There are two aspects to be considered, which are nicely captured in Embretson's (1983) distinction between construct representation and nomothetic span. Construct representation refers to the identification of psychological constructs (e.g., component processes, strategies, structures) that are involved in responding to items on tests. Processes of most interest are those that are common across families of tests that collectively define individual difference constructs, such as inductive reasoning ability, or those that fall along one of the spokes of a radex.

Nomothetic span, on the other hand, concerns the correlates of individual differences on tests. Of the many processes that are involved in performance on a particular task, only some will be shared with other tasks, and of these common processes an even smaller subset will be responsible for individual differences that are common across tasks. In other words, even processes and structures that are common to all tests in a family of reasoning tasks may contribute little or not at all to individual differences in inductive reasoning.

With these caveats in mind, then, I examine proposals for theories of reasoning that cut across task boundaries. In the final section, I reconsider hypotheses about which processes and structures are most responsible for individual differences in $I = Gf = G$.

PELLEGRINO'S SUMMARY. Pellegrino (1985; see also Goldman & Pellegrino, 1984) argued that inductive reasoning tasks such as analogies, series completions, and classifications all require four types of processes: encoding or attribute discovery, inference or attribute comparison, relation or rule evaluation, and decision and response.

Encoding processes create mental representations of stimuli on which various inference or attribute-comparison processes operate, the nature of which varies across tasks. In an analogy, the inference process must determine how various terms (particularly the A and B terms) are related to each other. In classification problems, the inference process must identify a rule or category that is shared by all the terms. In series problems, the inference process must identify the pattern in a sequence of letters or numbers. Inference processes are not sufficient for problem solution, however. The problem solver must also determine relationships among two or more first-order relationships in the problem. In an analogy, for example, the relationship between A and B must be identical to the relationship between C and D. In a matrix problem, the relationship among elements in one row must be the same in the other two rows. Pellegrino (1985) argued that one of the most important aspects of inductive reasoning is the ability to create two or more of these complex relationship structures in memory and to determine their consistency. Errors occur when working-memory resources are exceeded.

STERNBERG–GARDNER THEORY. One of the more ambitious attempts to generalize across analogies, series completion, and classification problems was made by Sternberg and Gardner (1983). Analogy items were of the form A:B::C: (D_1, D_2), i.e., A is to B as C is to which of two given D alternatives. Series completion items were of the form A B C ::D: (E_1, E_2), where the series ABC must be carried to D and then extended to one of two given E alternatives. Classification items were of the form A B, C D :E, where subjects decide whether E fits better with class AB or class CD. The claim here is that a common information-processing model can be identified that applies to all three item types.

Sternberg and Gardner argue that solving such items requires seven different component processes: encoding, inference, mapping, application, comparison, justification, and response. Encoding refers to the process of activating information in long-term memory on the basis of information received through the senses. What is activated depends on the contents and organization of information in memory, as well as on the perceived demands of the task and on residual activation from previously encoded items. Inference refers to the process of discovering relationships between two concepts activated by encoding processes. For verbal analogies, this may be modeled as the attempt to discover whether two concepts are related in semantic memory, and if so, what the nature of that relationship may be. A weak knowledge base may support the inference that two concepts are somehow associated but may not contain information on the nature of that association. Some relationships seem to be pre-stored, whereas others must be determined by comparing attributes of the terms or by comparing their labeled relationships with other terms in memory. The inference step can also require the finding of relationships between relationships. For example, the pairs up-down and black-white are both opposites, and thus the relationship between the relationships is one of identity. Mapping and application are similar. Mapping refers to the process of inferring the relationship between the A and C terms. Application refers to the process of generating a term that is related to C in the same way that A was inferred to be related to B. Comparison or evaluation refers to the process of comparing the internally generated answer (D) to the D options provided to determine which is most nearly correct. If none of the available options meets the individual's criterion for acceptability, then the individual may recycle through some or all of the previous model steps, a process sometimes called justification. True–false analogies in which a single answer option is presented do not require this step. Response is not estimated as a separate component but is assumed to be combined with preparatory and other unspecified sources of variance and reflected in the catchall intercept parameter.

Sternberg and Gardner tested their theory in a series of three experiments in which 18 subjects solved a total of 1,440 analogy, series completion, and classification tasks. All tasks used a common set of animal-name stimuli. Although this limited

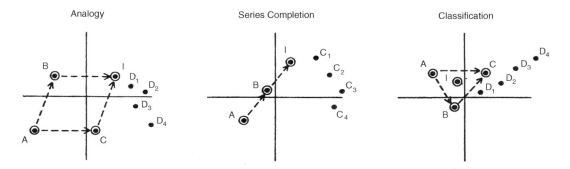

FIGURE 14.9. Schematic diagrams showing rules for arriving at ideal point, I, in each of the three induction tasks. (In analogies, I is located as the fourth vertex in a parallelogram having A, B, and C as three given vertices. In series completions, I is located as the completion of a line segment that is at the same vector distance from B that B is from A. In classifications, I is the centroid of the triangle with A, B, and C as vertices. The rules can be extended to *m* dimensions by assuming *m*-dimensional analogues to the two-dimensional figures depicted. In each type of problem, four answer options are presented at successively greater Euclidean distances from the I) (from Sternberg and Gardner, 1983).

generalizability, it allowed the authors to use previous multidimensional scalings of similarity judgments on these stimuli to make predictions about the difficulty of inducing rules in each of the three tasks. Following Rumelhart and Abrahamson (1973) and Henly (1969), it was assumed that the difficulty of inferring relations between concepts is a monotonic function of the similarity between them. To operationalize the measurement of this distance, it was assumed that (a) memory structure may be represented as a multidimensional Euclidean space, and (b) judged similarity between concepts is inversely related to distance in this space. To solve various induction problems, it is assumed that the individual must evaluate the distance between an ideal answer and each of the alternatives. The location of the ideal point varies across different item formats, as shown in Figure 14.9. For example, in an analogy problem, the ideal point coincides with the fourth vertex of a parallelogram, whereas for a classification problem, it falls at the centroid of the *n* terms that define the stem.

VALIDATION OF COMPONENT SCORES. Individual differences in the speed of performing component processes on one task were expected to show correlations with similarly named component scores on other tasks and also with external reference-ability tests, especially reasoning tests. Early studies (Sternberg, 1977) found generally small and inconsistent relationships among component scores and between component latencies and reference tests. The strong correlations with reasoning tests came from the preparation-response parameter. However, samples were often too small for correlational analyses (*n* = 16 or 24 in each of Sternberg's three experiments). Sternberg and Gardner (1983) did find significant correlations between inference

and comparison components and reference reasoning tests. Nevertheless, Brody (1992) criticized the Sternberg–Gardner theory because correlations among component scores showed only weak evidence of convergent and discriminant validity. For example, the average correlation (across tasks) for components with the same label was $r = .32$, which was only slightly higher than the average correlation among components with different names of $r = .24$. Once again, though, sample size (*n* = 18 Yale undergraduate students) required cautious interpretation.

Melis (1997) also examined the correlates of component scores. He administered 3 figural, 3 verbal tasks, and 6 reference tests to 72 undergraduate students. Two experimental tasks emphasized encoding (verbal or figural); two emphasized reasoning (with verbal or figural stimuli); and two, evaluation (again with verbal or figural stimuli). Precuing was used to unconfound component scores. Componential models showed excellent internal validity. Furthermore, a multidimensional scaling of component scores across tasks showed a tendency for like-named components to cluster together. However, only 14 of the 114 correlations between reference tests and component scores were statistically significant, and some of these in the "wrong" direction.

Several other studies have estimated correlations between same-named components on different tasks. In the Alderton et al. (1985) study of verbal classification and verbal analogy, accuracy scores were estimated for stem and option processing. Significant cross-task correlations were obtained for inference scores ($r = .47$) and recognition scores ($r = .42$). On the other hand, Whitely (1980) failed to obtain significant correlations among common components for analogy and classification tests. In the spatial domain, Mumaw, Pellegrino, Kail, and Carter (1984) reported convergent and discriminant validity for component scores on two spatial tasks. Thus, the evidence supporting the convergent and discriminant validity of individual differences in component scores is mixed.

Although such correlations do address the issue of the validity of component scores as individual difference measures, nonsignificant correlations among similar components should not be viewed as indictments of the information-processing models themselves. The problem is that individual differences that are consistent across trials within a task are removed when component scores are estimated for individuals.

Other evidence can be offered to support the claim of process congruence or identity across tasks. For example, Sternberg and Gardner (1983) compared estimated values for encoding, comparison, and response components across tasks and found them to be equivalent. More important would be the demonstration that components with the same name on two tasks are similarly influenced by the same set of independent variables (see Cronbach, 1957, for an example comparing "treatments" and Pieters, 1983, for a discussion of process congruence and independence in the additive factors method).

The important point for this discussion, however, is that degree of correlation between component scores and reference tests is less important than is the identification of information-processing models that describe how subjects solve tasks. Validation of individual difference measures might better proceed through subtask scores that do not require subtraction.

DEVELOPMENTAL DIFFERENCES. Scattered other studies also suggest processes that are common across tasks. For example, developmental changes in analogical reasoning have been studied by several investigators with interesting results. In one study of pictorial analogies, 8-year-olds appeared not to use a mapping process (Sternberg & Rifkin, 1979). In another study using verbal analogies, preadolescents appeared to shift strategies as item complexity increased, changing from an analogical reasoning strategy to a strategy in which responses were chosen on the basis of their associative relatedness to the C term. Adolescents and adults continued to use analogical reasoning even on the more difficult items. Heller (1979) reported similar ability-related differences among high-school students, characterized by low-verbal subjects more often using the associative strategy. Goldman, Pellegrino, Parseghian, and Sallis (1982) also found that older children (10-year-olds) were less likely to be distracted by foils that were associates of the C term than were younger children (8-year-olds). Retrospective reports suggested even more substantial differences in processing strategy. Older children were more likely to understand that the C to D relationship had to mirror the relationship between A and B. Pellegrino (1985) argued that younger and less-able students have particular difficulty in remembering and comparing multiple relationships, possibly because they do not understand the "rules of the game" or because problem complexity exceeds mental resources.

Distractors also function differently for adults and children and for subjects of high and low ability. Bethell-Fox et al. (1984) found that four alternative items like those found in many mental tests were solved differently than otherwise similar two-alternative items. Other data (see Pellegrino, 1985, p. 212) suggest that high-ability subjects are better able to recognize the correct answer on a forced-choice analogy test even when they have processed the stem incorrectly. Snow (1980b) and Whitely and Barnes (1979) reported similar evidence for subjects working backward from the options provided. By combining analyses of eye fixation and componential models of latencies and errors, Bethell-Fox et al. also found evidence that lower ability adolescent subjects shifted strategies on difficult items, changing from one in which they constructed a response and compared it with the alternatives to one in which they attempted to eliminate response alternatives. High-ability subjects, however, showed little evidence of strategy shifting, probably because most items were relatively easy for them.

STERNBERG'S UNIFIED THEORY OF REASONING. Sternberg (1986) claimed that there are three kinds of reasoning processes, any one of which defines a task as a reasoning task. The three processes are (a) selective encoding (distinguishing relevant from irrelevant information), (b) selective comparison (deciding what mentally stored information is relevant for solving a problem), and (c) selective combination (combining selectively encoded or compared information in working memory). Furthermore, the three processes define a reasoning situation only to the extent that they are executed in a controlled rather than in an automatic fashion. This implies that the extent to which a task measures reasoning depends on the relative novelty of the task for the individual.

These processes are implemented by various sorts of inferential rules. Procedural rules include operations called performance components in earlier theories (e.g., inference, mapping, application). Declarative rules vary by problem content and specify the type of semantic relations allowed in a problem. (For verbal analogy problems, for example, the set of possible semantic relations includes equality, set-subset, set-superset, static properties, and functional properties). Not all rules are rules of reasoning; reasoning rules are those that serve the functions of selective encoding, selective comparison, and selective combination. Thus, mnemonic strategies and computation algorithms are not reasoning rules.

The theory also claims that the probability that particular inferential rules will be used in the solution of a reasoning problem will be influenced by mediating variables, such as the individual's subjective estimate of the likelihood of the occurrence of a rule, the individual's prior knowledge, working-memory capacity, and ability to represent certain types of information (e.g., spatial versus linguistic).

Sternberg claims that the major difference between inductive and deductive reasoning is that the difficulty of the former derives mainly from the selective encoding and comparison processes, whereas the difficulty of the latter derives mainly from the selective combination process. Thus, for verbal analogies, the primary difficulty is determining which of the many features of the A term are relevant to the B term as well. For example, in the analogy paper:tree::plastic:?, one must decide which of the many attributes of the word *paper* (that we write on it, that it sometimes comes in tablets, that printers use it, that it is a short form of the word "newspaper," that it is made from wood, etc.) also overlap with what one knows about the word *tree*. In contrast, figural analogies tend to emphasize selective encoding. A key difficulty of problems such as those shown in Figure 14.1 is deciding which features of the stimuli to attend to in the first place.

Series completion problems not only require many of the same processes as analogies (Greeno, 1978; Pellegrino & Glaser, 1980; Sternberg & Gardner, 1983) but also emphasize selective comparison. In a typical series problem, there are many possible relations that could be obtained between successive pairs of numbers or letters. For example, in the series 1, 3, 6, 10,..., the relation between the first two digits could be plus 2, times 3, next odd number, and so on. The relation between 3 and 6 could be plus 3, times 2, and so on. Problem difficulty is highly related to the obscurity of the rule. However, when multiple rules account for a series, the "best" rule is typically the most specific rule. A similar set of arguments applies to the analysis of classification problems.

For deductive reasoning tasks such as categorical syllogisms, however, the main source of difficulty is not in encoding the terms or even in selectively comparing relations among them but rather in keeping track of the ways in which terms can be combined. Consider, for example, a categorical syllogism such as "Some A are B. All B are C." Is the conclusion "Some A are C" valid? Information-processing models of syllogistic reasoning all share four stages of information processing, which Sternberg (1986) calls encoding, combination, comparison, and response. In the encoding stage, the individual must create a mental representation of each premise that is amenable to mental transformation. Some have argued that this representation is imagistic or at least like a Euler diagram (Erickson, 1978). Others claim it is propositional (Johnson-Laird & Steedman, 1978). Regardless of the nature of the representation, the important aspect of this encoding is that it is not particularly selective. In other words, all "All A are B." statements should be translated into the same representation, regardless of their context. Indeed, there are four forms of statement permissible for each premise and the conclusion, and four different sets of mental representations, one for each of these four forms. However, for inductive reasoning problems such as series completions, classifications, or analogies, there are a vast number of possible representations.

It is the large number of combinations between representations of premises that taxes processing resources. For example, the problem "Some B are C. Some A are B." involves 16 combinations (4 for each of the 2 premises). Further, the exact inferential rule used also appears to be a major source of difficulty, although there is controversy as to exactly what these rules are. For example, Erickson (1974) specified rules for mapping premises on to Euler diagrams but claimed that the mapping is stochastic rather than deterministic. More important, however, has been the recurring finding that many other factors (what Sternberg calls mediators) influence performance as categorical syllogisms. For example, subjects show flagrant biases in solving such problems as a function of the emotionality of the premise, subjects' agreement with the content of the premises, abstractness of the content, and even the form in which the problems are presented. This suggests that, although such problems may be interesting candidates for research, they are probably not good candidates for assessments of individual differences in reasoning abilities.

Another type of deductive reasoning task that has been extensively studied is the linear syllogism. These are problems of the sort "Bill is taller than Mary. Mary is taller than Sue. Who's tallest?" On tests of inductive reasoning, problems of this sort have anywhere from two to four terms, but the most typical number is three.

Different theories of how such problems are solved have been proposed. Clark (1969) argued that solvers code the premises linguistically, Huttenlocher (1968) argued that premises are coded spatially, and Sternberg (1980) argued that both types of representation are used. As in other deductive reasoning problems, the major source of difficulty is not in encoding the terms or in comparing them (for example, to know that "short" is the opposite of "tall") but rather to combine the information in the premises into a single mental model. Unlike linear syllogisms, however, there are fewer

content-induced biases to cloud performance. Indeed, the most likely bias occurs when the premise contradicts one's personal knowledge, such as when one knows that Mary is shorter than Sue, whereas the problem asks one to envision the opposite. Such contrafactual reasoning can be deliberately introduced into problems (e.g., "imagine that mice are larger than elephants," etc.).

VERBAL AND SPATIAL ABILITIES

Although reasoning or *Gf* abilities are the focus of this chapter, any discussion of complex information processing and intelligence would be incomplete without at least some overview of the research on verbal and spatial abilities. One may also discuss quantitative or symbolic reasoning abilities as well, although individual differences in such tasks are often completely subsumed in the *Gf* factor. This is not the case for verbal and spatial abilities. Both a broad verbal factor (*Gc*) and a broad spatial factor (*Gv*) can be identified that are at least somewhat independent of *Gf*. The objectives of this section, then, are to explore the overlap and the uniqueness, that is, to explain (a) why verbal comprehension or spatial visualization is primarily a measure of *G* or *Gf* and (b) why each measures something unique.

Verbal Abilities

Verbal abilities are central to all theories of intelligence. Spearman (1927) noted that a verbal factor was one of the first to be identified among the residual correlations in a matrix after *G* had been removed. Thurstone (1938) identified two factors that he called *verbal relations*, which roughly corresponded to the factor Spearman had identified, and a second factor that he called *word fluency*. This distinction, or something like it, persists in modern summaries. Carroll (1993) claimed that the major factor distinction within the verbal domain is between *Gc* (general crystallized verbal abilities) and *Gi* (general idea production). Thus, the first task for a cognitive theory of verbal abilities is to explain this distinction. The second task is to explain the high correlation between general reasoning abilities (*G* or *Gf*) and verbal comprehension and vocabulary test. The overlap is more understandable for comprehension tests than for vocabulary tests, which appear to represent little more than the number of words the examinee has learned through instruction or exposure.

VERBAL COMPREHENSION VERSUS WORD FLUENCY. Verbal comprehension abilities are typically assessed by tests of oral and written comprehension, sentence completion, verbal information, and vocabulary (including defining words, selecting or generating synonyms and antonyms). Verbal fluency, on the other hand, refers to the speed and ease with which ideas, words, sentences, and other linguistic responses can be generated, often on the basis of perceptual cues such as the first letter of a word or its final phoneme. It is not one but a loose collection of many abilities (Carroll 1941, 1993).

The same task can require both fluency and comprehension abilities. For example, Janssen, DeBoek, and Vander Steene (1996) showed that an open synonym task, in which participants were required to generate synonyms for a given word, could be decomposed into a generation component and an evaluation component. Individual differences in a generation subtask were primarily related to verbal fluency, whereas individual differences on an evaluation task were primarily related to verbal comprehension.

Word fluency abilities would seem to be dependent upon verbal comprehension abilities: words must be understood before they can be generated (Sincoff & Sternberg, 1987). On the other hand, the literature on savants provides examples of individuals who can retain and reproduce much oral language while understanding little or none of it.

Verbal comprehension tests emphasize semantic processing and show high correlations with general reasoning measures. Verbal tests that show relatively low correlations with reasoning are more diverse. Such tasks are usually simpler; emphasize speed of response; require knowledge of linguistic conventions (e.g., grammar); require phonological or articulatory processing; or require memory for the exact order of events, words, letters, or sounds. Conversely, correlations between verbal tasks and reasoning increase as tasks require (a) more inferencing; (b) the integration of information (across words, sentences, or paragraphs; or with prior knowledge);

(c) knowledge of abstract words; or (d) precise understandings of common words and concepts. Sex differences are also inversely related to the correlation of the task with G. The female advantage is large on many of the more specific verbal tests and factors, but small or nonexistent on verbal comprehension and vocabulary tests.

Research in the information-processing paradigm has suggested several hypotheses about this contrast. One possible difference between tasks that show high correlations with reasoning and tasks that define more specific verbal abilities such as fluency or spelling may be the nature of the memory code on which performance is based. Verbal comprehension and vocabulary tests may estimate facility in creating, retaining, and transforming information coded in a way that preserves meaning (e.g., abstract propositions). More specific verbal (and spatial) measures may estimate how well and how fast one can create, retain, and transform information coded in one of several perception-based codes. A string code would preserve order information for sounds, letters, words, and other stimuli. An image code would preserve configural information for spatial arrays. Specific phonological, articulatory, or other codes seem highly likely as well, but have not been much studied (see Anderson, 1983, 1985).

A second hypothesis is that more highly G-loaded tasks place greater demands on working memory (Kyllonen & Christal, 1990). In this view, verbal tasks such as comprehending and inferencing are more highly G-loaded than tasks such as rhyming and spelling because they place greater demands on working memory, particularly for simultaneous storage and processing of information, but also on monitoring and inhibition functions. This leads directly to the second problem: the overlap between measures or reasoning, comprehension, and vocabulary.

REASONING, COMPREHENSION, AND VOCABULARY. The relationship between reasoning ability and verbal ability is perhaps best understood by examining how people understand text that contains unfamiliar or ambiguous words, or conversely, how they come to understand new words.

Word meanings are learned in two ways: by explicit definition and through contextual inference, that is, through the process of inferring the meaning of a word from context (Werner & Kaplan, 1952; Johnson-Laird, 1983). Van Daalen-Kapteijns and Elshout-Mohr (1981) used verbal protocols to study the process of abstracting word meanings from contexts. They proposed that subjects first generate a schema or hypothesis for the meaning of an unfamiliar word based on their best interpretation of its meaning in the first sentence in which it occurs. The schema has slots that can then either be confirmed or contradicted by new evidence. This can lead to adjustment or complete reformation of the schema. Ideally, the initial schema would be sufficiently well-articulated to permit an active search for information to confirm it. In their research, low-verbal subjects were less likely to use this strategy of schema-guided search, possibly because they did not have or were not able to activate the appropriate knowledge schema for the neologisms.

Rumelhart (1980) proposed an almost identical model for the process of comprehending written prose. In a series of experiments, Rumelhart presented subjects with a series of somewhat ambiguous sentences describing an event. After each sentence, subjects were asked to tell what they thought the passage was about. Subjects typically had multiple hypotheses about the meaning of the passage after reading the first sentence. Most entertained different hypotheses as new sentences were presented, and eventually all inferred the intended scheme.

Although Rumelhart (1980) did not investigate individual differences in his experiments, Frederiksen (1981) has found that subjects differ in the extent to which they use contextual cues when reading; skilled readers prime a wider range of relevant concepts in memory for a given set of contextual cues than do less-skilled readers.

Sternberg and Powell (1983) have also presented a process theory of verbal comprehension that is based on learning from context. Their theory has three parts: context cues, mediating variables, and processes of verbal learning. Context cues are hints about the meaning of the unknown word contained in the passage. Mediating variables (e.g., "variability of context") attempt to specify how contextual cues may help or hinder the inference process in any particular situation. Three verbal learning processes are hypothesized in the theory: selective encoding, selective combination, and selective comparison (see Sternberg & Powell, 1983, for details). Selectivity in encoding, combination, and comparison in part reflects the contribution of well-structured knowledge. Experts in medical diagnosis, for example, selectively attend to certain symptoms because their thinking is guided by their declarative knowledge of diseases (see Lesgold, 1984). Nevertheless, declarative knowledge cannot be the only difference between high- and low-ability subjects because one then could not explain how some individuals acquire more precise and useful knowledge in the first place. One possibility is that learners differ in their use of certain metacognitive or performance processes when learning, such as systematically testing alternative interpretations in unfamiliar situations, that then lead to a richer and more usefully organized knowledge base to guide new learning (see, e.g., Robinson & Hayes, 1978).

Parts of the Sternberg–Powell theory were tested in an experiment in which subjects were asked to read passages containing one to four extremely low-frequency words. These words were presented with different frequencies and with different contextual cues. Students then attempted to define the words, and their definitions were rated for quality. These ratings were then regressed on independent variables coded to estimate variables hypothesized in the model. When averaged over four types of passages, the model variables accounted for 67% of the variance in the ratings. Rated quality of definition for individuals correlated approximately $r = .6$ with IQ as well as vocabulary and reading comprehension tests. This is consistent with Marshalek's (1981) claim that the ability to infer word meanings from the contexts in which they occur is the cause of high correlation typically observed between vocabulary and reasoning tests.

Sternberg and McNamara (1985) attempted to incorporate these and other findings into a model of verbal comprehension. Their model includes the representation of word meaning and the nature and speed of word processing in verbal comparison tasks. They showed that overall latency scores on their tasks correlated significantly with a combination of rate and comprehension scores from conventional reading comprehension tests. The multiple correlation was not strikingly high ($R = .47$), but samples were small.

Their two-stage componential model first compared alternative possibilities for word representation by contrasting defining attribute models and characteristic attribute models. In the former, word meaning depends on a stored list of semantic features that are both necessary and sufficient for a word to refer to an object or concept. In the latter, attributes are neither necessary nor sufficient but rather combine to characterize the referent as in family-resemblance models of concepts (Rosch & Mervis, 1975). The best fit to data was obtained with a mixed model that assumed defining attributes and a weighted sum of characteristic attributes specifying a word referent. Then, various alternative models were compared to determine whether processing of word attributes, answer options, or both, was performed in an exhaustive or self-terminating mode. Modeling suggested that subjects always process answer options exhaustively, that is, they search all answer options given and apparently also always use defining and characteristic information about the stimulus words in doing so.

The Sternberg–McNamara theory thus supports a view of verbal ability in which the acquisition of word meanings from contexts using contextual and other cues to guide selective encoding, combination, and comparison processes to produce schemata is assumed. These, in turn, drive further search and hypothesis-testing processes. Such schemata have slots for definitions and characteristic attributes of words and are used exhaustively in tasks requiring the demonstration of verbal comprehension.

To recapitulate, the high correlation between vocabulary knowledge and reasoning seems to reflect primarily the fact that word meanings are generally inferred from the contexts in which they are embedded. But there is a synergism here in that vocabulary knowledge allows comprehension and expression of a broader array of ideas, which in turn facilitate the task of learning new words and concepts. Thus, language functions as a vehicle for the expression, refinement, and acquisition of thought. The humble vocabulary test masks an enormous amount of reasoning and remembering.

Spatial Abilities

Spatial ability may be defined as the ability to generate, retain, retrieve, and transform well-structured visual images (Lohman, 1988). It is not a unitary construct. There are, in fact, several spatial abilities, each emphasizing different aspects of the process of image generation, storage, retrieval, and transformation.

Reviews of factor-analytic studies of spatial abilities (Anderson, Fruchter, Manuel, & Worchel, 1954; Carroll, 1993; Lohman, 1979; McGee, 1979), show a broad array of spatial factors that can be organized hierarchically. A general visualization factor (Gv or Vz) appears at or near the top of this hierarchy (Carroll, 1993) usually defined by complex spatial tests such as paper form board, paper folding, and surface development (see Ekstrom, French, & Harman, 1976). However, the Vz factor is often difficult to separate from a Gf, or reasoning, factor (Guilford & Lacey, 1947; Lohman, 1979; Marshalek, Lohman, & Snow, 1983). Indeed, Vz tests appear to be primarily measures of G or Gf, secondarily measures of task-specific functions, and thirdly measures of something that covaries uniquely with other Vz tests. A spatial orientation (SO) factor can sometimes be distinguished from Vz. Spatial orientation tests require subjects to imagine how an array would appear from a different perspective and then to make a judgment from that imaged perspective. A speeded rotation (SR) factor emerges if two or more simple, highly speeded rotation tasks are included in a test battery. Complex, three-dimensional rotation tasks (such as the Vandenberg–Kruse, 1978, adaptation of the Shepard–Metzler, 1971, figures) generally split their variance between SR and Vz factors. Other distinguishable visual–spatial abilities include flexibility of closure, speed of closure, perceptual speed, visual memory, serial integration, and kinesthetic factors (see Carroll, 1993; Lohman, 1988).

As with verbal abilities, the major tasks for understanding spatial abilities are to explain (a) the systematic individual difference variance that is uniquely spatial and (b) the much larger portion of the variation on such tasks that is shared with general reasoning abilities.

INDIVIDUAL DIFFERENCES IN SPATIAL COGNITION. Cognitive psychology has contributed importantly to understanding the uniquely spatial variance on figural tasks through its investigations of how subjects encode, remember, and transform visual images. Seminal research here was that of Roger Shepard and his students on mental rotation (see Shepard & Cooper, 1982, for a summary).

The basic finding was that the time required to determine whether two figures could be rotated into congruence was a linear function of the amount of rotation required. On the basis of this and other evidence, Shepard claimed that mental rotation is an analog process that shows a one-to-one correspondence with physical rotation. The second claim was that this rotation process is performed on a mental representation that somehow preserves information about structure at all points during the rotation transformation.

However, most theorists argue than spatial knowledge can be represented in more than one way. One representation (sometimes called an image code) is thought to be more literal (Kosslyn, 1980) or at least more structure- or configuration-preserving (Anderson, 1983). This is the sort of representation that Shepard thought necessary to explain mental rotation. Another representation is more abstract and more meaning- or interpretation-preserving (Kosslyn, 1980; Anderson, 1983; Palmer, 1977) and is usually modeled by the same propositional structures used to represent meaningful verbal knowledge. Some of the confusion in understanding spatial abilities can be traced to whether spatial abilities are restricted to image-coded memories and the analog processes that operate on them or whether proposition-coded memories and the general procedural knowledge that operate on them are also considered part of the term.

Although research and theory in cognitive psychology and artificial intelligence suggest much about the nature of spatial knowledge and processes, they do not explicitly address the source of individual differences in spatial processing. Research on this question has followed four hypotheses: that spatial abilities may be explained by individual differences in (a) speed of performing analog transformations, (b) skill in generating and retaining mental representations that preserve configural information, (c) the amount of visual–spatial information that can be maintained in an active state, or (d) the sophistication and flexibility of strategies available for solving such tasks.

The most popular hypothesis has been that spatial abilities may be explained by individual differences in the speed with which subjects can accurately perform analog mental transformations, particularly

rotation. However, correlations between estimated rate of rotation and spatial ability vary from highly negative (e.g., Lansman, 1981) to moderately positive (e.g., Poltrock & Brown, 1984). Correlations are generally somewhat higher for three-dimensional rotation problems than for two-dimensional problems (Pellegrino & Kail, 1982; Cooper & Regan, 1982), and for practiced than for nonpracticed subjects (Lohman & Nichols, 1990). However, even moderate correlations between the slope measure and other variables are difficult to interpret. The slope is heavily influenced by the amount of time taken on trials requiring the most rotation. Some subjects make more than one attempt to rotate stimuli on such problems. Therefore, at least for these subjects, the slope better reflects the number of attempts made to solve a problem or simply the time taken to solve these most difficult problems and not rate of rotation per se. More important, the slope measure ignores individual differences on the task that are consistent across different trial types. These individual differences are captured in the mean or in the intercept scores (Lohman, 1994). On the other hand, correlations between overall error rates and spatial reference tests are often quite high. Indeed, although the rate of information processing on rotation tasks and accuracy levels achieved under liberal time allotments are necessarily confounded, differences between high- and low-spatial subjects are much greater on the accuracy score than on a rate of information-processing score (Lohman, 1986). One interpretation of this finding is that the amount of information that can be maintained in an active state while it is being transformed is more important than the rate of executing that transformation in accounting for individual differences in spatial ability.

The second hypothesis is that high spatial subjects have superior spatial working-memory resources. Baddeley (1986), in his model of working memory, hypothesizes a central executive and two slave systems: an articulatory loop and a visual–spatial scratch pad. Perhaps high-spatial subjects can maintain more information in this scratch pad. Kyllonen's (1984) study of ability differences in types and number of errors made on a paper-folding task supports this hypothesis. His study showed that high- and low-spatial subjects differed not so much in the type of error committed but in the number of errors committed. Because of this, Kyllonen (1984) concluded that the main difference between the performance of high- and low-spatials on a paper-folding task was that lows were more likely to forget a fold and then either not perform it or substitute an incorrect fold for the forgotten one. Other theorists (e.g., Just & Carpenter, 1992) emphasized the trade-off between storage and transformation functions in a unitary working-memory system. By this account, mental rotation problems are good measures of spatial ability because they place substantial demands on storage and transformation functions and require subjects to manage the trade-off between them. Other evidence in support of this view comes from verbal problems that require imagery for their solution, such as Binet's "It is 12:15. If we switch the hands on the clock, what time will it be?" Tests constructed on such problems often show high predictive validities but are not factorially pure (Ackerman & Kanfer, 1993).

The third hypothesis focuses on the nature of the representation. Several investigators have sought to determine whether high- and low-spatial subjects differ in the type of mental representations they create (see, e.g., Cooper, 1982; Lohman, 1988). Individual differences in memory for random forms show no relationship with performance on other spatial tests (Christal, 1958). Thus, it is not so much the ability to remember stimuli but the ability to remember systematically structured stimuli that distinguishes between subjects high and low in spatial ability. Low-spatial subjects seem to have particular difficulty in constructing systematically structured images. High-spatial subjects appear to be able to construct images that can be compared holistically with test stimuli. Differences between high- and medium-spatial subjects are often small in this respect. It is the very-low-spatial subjects who appear qualitatively different (Pellegrino & Kail, 1982; Lohman, 1988).

The fourth explanation emphasizes the role of strategies. It has long been noted that spatial tasks may be solved in more than one way and that some strategies place greater demands on analog processing than others. Several studies have now shown that the strategies subjects employ on form-board tasks are systematically related to their ability profiles (Kyllonen, Lohman, & Woltz, 1984; Lohman,

1988). The major distinction is between spatial and nonspatial strategies. Subjects using the spatial strategy remember complex polygons by decomposing them into simpler geometric shapes. When they are required to assemble figures mentally, their performance is more influenced by the characteristics of the to-be-assembled figure than by that of the component figures. Time to perform this assembly operation is usually negatively correlated with reference spatial tests. On the other hand, subjects using the nonspatial strategy try to remember complex polygons by associating the figure with another concrete, easily labeled object. When they are asked to assemble figures mentally, their performance is strongly influenced by the complexity of the component figures rather than that of the to-be-assembled figure. Further time to perform the assembly often shows higher correlations with tests of verbal ability than with tests of spatial ability.

Rotation tasks are also solved in different ways by different subjects. Bethell-Fox and Shepard (1988) found that rotation times for unfamiliar stimuli were generally influenced by the complexity of the stimulus. With practice, most subjects learned to rotate all stimuli at the same rate. However, some subjects continued to show effects for stimulus complexity even after much practice. Bethell-Fox and Shepard (1988) argued that these subjects rotated stimuli piece by piece, whereas after practice others rotated them holistically. Carpenter and Just (1978) argued that even practiced subjects do not rotate an image of an entire three-dimensional object but rather only a skeletal representation of it. In experiments on a cube-rotation task, they found that subjects used different strategies, presumably related to the coordinate system the subject adopted. Low-spatial subjects appeared to rotate the cube iteratively along standard axes, whereas high-spatial subjects were able to use the shorter trajectory defined by a single transformation through both axes (Just & Carpenter, 1985).

Thus, subjects of different ability levels and profiles often solve spatial tests in predictably different ways. However, flexibility of strategy in solving such tasks seems to be more related to G or Gf than to spatial ability (Kyllonen et al., 1984). Indeed, subjects high in spatial but low in verbal abilities have been found to apply the same "spatial" strategy to all problems. Perhaps they have no need to switch to other strategies.

SPATIAL ABILITY AND *Gf*. In addition to explaining the uniquely spatial variation on spatial tasks, a theory of spatial ability must also explain the substantial overlap between spatial and reasoning abilities. These explanations have taken several forms. Some have argued that the overlap stems from most complex spatial tests being solvable at least in part through the application of reasoning abilities. For example, when a piece of paper is folded in half, then in half again, and a hole is punched through the quarter-folded paper, one need not envision the unfolding process to infer that the unfolded paper must have four symmetrically arrayed holes, one of which must coincide with the hole that was punched. Such reasoning is facilitated when tasks show where and how the folds are made. A second explanation focuses on the nature of the mental representation. Much spatial knowledge seems to be represented in the same propositional format that some argue is also used to represent abstract verbal knowledge. Both Palmer (1977) and Kosslyn (1980) claimed that only a subset of spatial knowledge is represented in a more literal code that is processed analogically. It is the literal code that represents the uniquely spatial knowledge and processes, whereas the propositional code is common to all meaning-making tasks. A third explanation for the overlap focuses on working-memory demands. Spatial tasks are process intensive, thereby placing substantial demands on working memory for the simultaneous storage and processing of information. If reasoning ability is "little more than working memory" (Kyllonen & Christal, 1990), then spatial tasks would be little more than reasoning tasks. A fourth explanation also involves working memory but emphasizes the coordination of different mental models. In this view, individuals often construct different types of mental models when listening, reading, or thinking. For example, Kintsch and Greeno (1985) argued that individuals typically must create and coordinate two types of mental models when solving word problems in mathematics. One model is more text or proposition based, and the other is more image or situation based. Understanding requires not only the construction, but also the active coordination of the two models. The finding that verbally presented spatial problems (such as the paper-folding problem previously described) load on both *Gv* and *Gf* supports such an interpretation.

COMPLEXITY CONTINUUM REVISITED

In their discussion of evidence from correlational studies concerning the nature of *G*, Snow et al. (1984) argued that the complexity continua in the radex is an important – if not *the* most important – feature to be explained by a theory of intelligence. Tests that load heavily on the *G* or *Gf* typically fall near the center of the radex, whereas seemingly simpler tasks are distributed around the periphery. Moving from the periphery to the center, one steps from task to task along spokes where tasks sometimes seem to build systematically on one another and sometimes increase in complexity in less obvious ways. But what is the nature of this complexity? We are now in a position to examine this question.

Several hypotheses have been advanced to explain how processing complexity increases along the various spokes that run from periphery to *G*: (1) an increase in the number of component processes; (2) an accumulation of differences in speed of component processing; (3) increasing involvement of one or more critically important performance components, such as inferencing processes; (4) an increase in demands on limited working memory or attention; and (5) an increase in demands on adaptive functions, including assembly, control, and monitor functions. Clearly these explanations are not independent. For example, it is impossible to get an accumulation of speed differences over components (Hypothesis 1) without also increasing the number of component processes required (Hypothesis 2). In spite of this overlap, these hypotheses provide a useful way to organize the discussion.

More Component Processes

Even the most superficial examination of tasks that fall along one of the spokes of the radex reveals that more central or *G*-loaded tasks require subjects to do more than the more peripheral tests. Many years ago, Zimmerman (1954) demonstrated that a form-board test could be made to load more on perceptual speed, spatial relations, visualization, and reasoning factors, in that order, by increasing the complexity of the items. Snow et al.'s (1984) re-analyses of old learning-task and ability-test correlation matrices showed similar continua. Spilsbury (1992) argued that the crucial manipulation here is an increase in the factorial complexity of a task. However, increases in the number or difficulty of task steps beyond a certain point can decrease the correlation with G (Crawford, 1988; Raaheim, 1988; Swiney, 1985). For example, Crawford (1988) reported a decrease in correlation with G for a mental counting task as task complexity increased. Correlations were slightly higher for 8–9 element items than for 11–12 element items. Although both string lengths are supraspan for most individuals, the latter are probably supraspan for all unpracticed participants. Thus, one does not automatically increase the relationship with G simply by making problems harder or even by increasing the factorial complexity of a task – unless, of course, the added dimension reflects a type of processing or capacity limitation that is central to G. Indeed, there are many hard problems (e.g., memorizing lists of randomly chosen numbers or words) that are not particularly good measures of G. Furthermore, even for problems that do require the type of processing that causes the test to measure G, problems must be of the appropriate level of difficulty for subjects, or in what Elshout (1985) has called the "zone of tolerable problematicity."

Speed or Efficiency of Elementary Processing

This hypothesis has taken several forms. Because this work is reviewed in detail elsewhere in this handbook, only a few points will be made here. In its strongest form, the assertion has been that individuals differ in the general speed or efficiency with which they process information (Jensen, 1980, 1982, 1987, 1998). In principle, processing speed could be estimated on any elementary cognitive task that minimizes the import of learning, motivation, strategy, and other confounding variables. Although disattenuated correlations between RT and G can be substantial when samples vary widely in ability (even, for example, including mentally retarded participants), samples more typical of those used in other research on abilities yield correlations between RT and G in the $r = -.1$ to $r = -.4$ range (Jensen, 1982; Roberts, 1995; Sternberg, 1985;

Deary & Stough, 1996). Furthermore, response latencies on many tasks show a pattern of increasing correlation with an external estimate of G as task complexity is *decreased*. In other words, response latencies for simpler tasks typically show higher correlations with G than do response latencies for more complex tasks. But this is unsurprising. The more complex the task, the more room there is for subjects to use different processes or even to be inconsistent in the execution of a common set of processes. Indeed, for the most complex task, latency becomes more a measure of persistence than ability, which is instead reflected in the quality of the response given.

Others argue that more able individuals refresh memory traces more rapidly and thus are better able to hold information in working memory – especially when required to effect transformations on that information as well. This is a good example of the inevitable trade-off between process and structure in cognitive models, because speed of refreshing memory traces would generally be indistinguishable from the strength or persistence of those traces. Put differently, what one theorist interprets as a speed of processing difference may be interpreted as a processing capacity difference by another theorist.

In its weak form, the hypothesis has been that, although speed of processing on any one task may be only weakly correlated with more complex performances, such small differences cumulate over time and tasks. Thus, Hunt, Frost and Lunneborg (1973) noted that, although latency differences in the retrieval of overlearned name codes correlated only $r = -.3$ with verbal ability, such small differences on individual words cumulate to substantial differences in the course of a more extended activity. Determan (1986) emphasized the cumulation across different component processes rather than across time. He showed that although individual component processes were only weakly correlated with G, their combined effect was more substantial.

Although individual differences in speed of processing are an important aspect of G, G is more than rapid or efficient information processing. Furthermore, the strength of the relationship between speed of processing and G varies considerably across domains, being strongest ($r \approx -.4$) in verbal domain and weakest ($r \approx -.2$) in the spatial domain. Indeed, for complex spatial tasks, the speed with which individuals perform different spatial operations is usually much less predictive of overall performance than the richness or quality of the mental representations they create (Lohman, 1988; Salthouse, Babcock, Mitchell, Palmon, & Skovronek, 1990).

More Involvement of Central Components

If *G* is not simply a reflection of more or faster processing, might it be the case that *G* really reflects the action of particular mental processes? Spearman (1927) was one of the first to argue for this alternative. For him, the essential processes were the "eduction of relations," which Sternberg calls *inference*, and the "eduction of correlates," which Sternberg calls *mapping* and *application*. Evidence favoring this hypothesis is substantial. A common characteristic of tests that are good measures of *Gf* – such as the matrices, series completion, analogies, and classification reviewed in this chapter – is that they are all measures of reasoning, particularly inductive reasoning. Many school learning tasks, particularly in science and mathematics, bear formal similarity to *Gf* tests. Greeno (1978) referred to such tasks collectively as problems of inducing structure. Indeed, the problem of inducing structure in instruction is probably why reasoning tests correlate with achievement tests (Snow, 1980a). But to describe the overlap in this way is not to explain it.

Evidence supporting the hypothesis that particular component processes are central to *G* has been surprisingly difficult to obtain. Sternberg's (1977) investigations of analogical reasoning found little generalizability of component scores for inference across tasks and at best inconsistent correlations with reference reasoning tests. Rather it was the intercepts that showed more consistent correlations with reference abilities. We now know that this was in large measure an inevitable consequence of the way component scores are estimated (Lohman, 1994). Individual differences that are consistent across items requiring different amounts of a particular component process will appear in the intercept rather than in the component scores. Put differently, if examinees who are fast in making easy inferences are also fast in making more difficult inferences, then most of the reliable individual difference variance in speed of making inferences will be removed through subtraction. In addition, if those who are faster making inferences are also faster in general in solving items, then these differences will be reflected in the intercepts. Indeed, the conditions under which component scores will show strong and consistent correlations with other variables are exactly the same as those that lead to more reliable difference scores: low correlation between the two scores that are subtracted and an increase in variance across scores. Therefore, low or inconsistent correlations between component scores for inferencing and other variables do not provide much evidence against the hypothesis that these processes are particularly important.

A second line of evidence on the centrality of particular component processes comes from demonstrations that certain types of task manipulations are more likely than others to increase the *Gf* loading of a task (Pellegrino, 1985; Sternberg, 1986). Sternberg (1986) called these *selective encoding*, that is, the requirement to attend selectively to information and to encode only that subset that is likely to be needed for solving a problem; *selective comparison*, that is, to retrieve only information that is relevant to a problem, especially when the set of potentially relevant information in memory is vast; and *selective combination*, that is, to assemble in working memory information already selected as relevant. Selective encoding depends heavily on the individual's store of prior knowledge (schema) and its attunement to the affordances of the situation. It also means the ability to resist the distractions of salient but irrelevant information, or, when solving items on mental tests, to look ahead to the alternatives before studying the stem (Bethell-Fox et al., 1984). Selective comparison also depends heavily on the store of knowledge, but also on its organization and accessibility, especially the ability to search rapidly through memory for overlap between two concepts. This is the essential feature of inference or abstraction problems: finding ways in which concepts A and B are not merely associated with each other but rather finding the rules or relations that most specifically characterize their association. Problems in inductive reasoning emphasize selective encoding and comparison. Problems in deductive reasoning, on the other hand, emphasize selective combination. For example, syllogistic reasoning problems are difficult not because it is difficult to discern the relevant information in statements such as "all A are B" or in the understanding of the relations between words such as "all" and "some" (although this is a source of confusion for some); rather, the main difficulty is in keeping track of all of the ways in which the premises can be combined. This taxes both working memory and the ability to manipulate symbols. Thus, although certain processes may be central to intelligent thinking, individual differences in those processes may be in part due to other system limitations such as working-memory resources.

Attention and Working-Memory Capacity

In information-processing models of memory and cognition, a limited-capacity working memory system functions not only as a central processor but also as a bottleneck in the system. Some interpret working memory in terms of capacity limitations; others view it in terms of attentional resources. Hunt and Lansman (1982) and Ackerman (1988) argued that tasks that show higher correlations with G require more attentional resources. Attempts to manipulate the attentional demands of tasks often use a dual-task paradigm. Here, participants are required to do two things simultaneously such as searching for a particular stimulus in a visual display while simultaneously listening for a specified auditory stimulus. Although the effect is often not observed, differences between more and less able subjects are typically greater in the dual task than in the single task condition. However, interpretation of this finding is problematic. For example, in one study, Stankov (1988) found that correlations with both Gc and Gf, but especially Gf, were higher for dual tasks than for single tasks. However, high levels of performance in the dual-task situation were due to a strategy of momentarily ignoring one task while attending to the other. Thus, what on the surface seemed to implicate attentional resources on closer inspection implicated self-monitoring and the shifting of attentional resources.

Attentional requirements of tasks vary according to an individual's familiarity with the task and to the susceptibility of the task to automatization. Tasks – or task components – in which there is a consistent mapping between stimulus and response can be automatized in this way. Individuals who recognize the consistencies can automatize task components more rapidly than those who are not so at-

tuned. Thus, explanations of ability differences in terms of differences in attentional resources must account not only for attention shifting in dual tasks but also differences in the extent to which task steps are or become automatized.

The explanation of differences in reasoning as reflecting differences in working-memory capacity parallels the attentional explanation. Many researchers have claimed that a major source of individual differences on reasoning tasks lies in how much information one must maintain in working memory, especially while effecting some transformation of that information (Holzman, Pellegrino, & Glaser, 1980). For example, as Kyllonen and Christal (1990) noted, most performance processes (such as encoding and inference) and executive processes (such as goal setting, goal management, and monitoring) are presumed to occur in working memory. Thus, even though, say, the inference process may be effective, it must be performed within the limits of the working-memory system. Therefore, although many different processes may be executed in the solution of a task, individual differences in them may primarily reflect *individual differences* in working-memory resources.

Newer theories of working memory also differ importantly from the older concept of short-term memory. Indeed, one of the major differences lies in the relative emphasis on passive storage functions in older theories of short-term memory versus more effortful, controlled processing of information that is also being maintained in an active state in newer theories of working memory. Some see this in terms of a trade-off between processing capacity and storage capacity (Daneman & Carpenter, 1980), whereas others view it in terms of different memory systems. For example, Baddeley (1986) posited a working memory with a passive storage component and a separate executive (or supervisory attentional system) that attends selectively to one stimulus while inhibiting another, coordinates performance in tasks, and switches strategies (Baddeley, 1996). When working memory is interpreted in this way, studies that find high correlation between working memory and reasoning seem less astonishing. For example, Kyllonen and Christal (1990) found that latent variables for reasoning ability and working memory correlated approximately $r = .8$ in four large studies. Their working memory tasks were specifically designed to reflect Baddeley's theory and thus required both storage and transformation (although the former was presumed to be more difficult). Critics of the Kyllonen–Christal studies have argued that some of the tasks they used to measure working memory mirror common reasoning tasks. The criticism is not without merit. The same task was used as a working-memory test in one study and as a reasoning test in another study.

Oberauer et al. (1996) sought to address this problem. They administered 26 tasks designed to measure one or more of the three putative functions of working memory (storage and processing, monitoring, or coordination) on three contents (verbal, numerical, or figural) and the Berlin Intelligence test to a sample of 113 young adults. The Berlin Intelligence Scale is a faceted test that crosses operation (speed, memory, creativity, and reasoning) with content (verbal, figural, numeric). Scores on the intelligence test and the working-memory battery were aggregated in different ways (for example, by content or by operation) and to different levels (for example, to the level of test, the level of content or operation, or to the level of a single score). Analyses then focused on the utility of different parsings in accounting for relations between the working-memory tests and the intelligence test. Results showed that at the highest level of aggregation, latent factors from the working-memory battery and the intelligence test were highly related (estimated disattenuated correlation was approximately $r = .92$). However, differentiations of working memory into two functions (a first function of storage, processing, and coordination; a second function of supervision) and the test battery into subtests grouped by operation (speed, memory, creativity, and reasoning) led to a significant improvement in model fit. Other analyses showed that, although the division between verbal–numerical content and spatial content was useful for the working-memory measures, the hypothesized three-way split into verbal, numerical, and spatial contexts was not.

In short, although the Oberauer et al. (1996) study supports the Kyllonen and Christal (1990) claim that individual differences in working memory are largely redundant with individual differences in reasoning ability, the study also suggests that working memory may usefully be broken down into at least two subprocesses (storage–processing and su-

pervision) that operate with different effectiveness on two types of content (verbal–numerical and spatial). The argument is reminiscent of the earlier debate between Spearman and his American critics (first Thorndike, then Thurstone) as to whether the central processes of intelligence (which he identified with g) were unitary or multiple. And, as in the earlier debate, the argument seems to hinge upon the relative value of psychological meaningfulness of constructs (which usually favors decomposition) versus predictive ability (which usually favors aggregation).

Adaptive Processing

Although acknowledging that individual differences in G reflected differences in all of these levels – in the speed and efficacy of elementary processes, in attentional or working memory resources, in the action of processes responsible for inference and abstraction (which includes knowledge, skill, and attunement to affordances in the task situation) – several theorists have argued that more is needed. Sternberg (1985) claimed that intelligent action requires the application of meta-components – that is, control processes that decide what the problem is, select lower order components and organize them into a strategy, select a mode for representing or organizing information, allocate attentional resources, monitor the solution process, and attend to external feedback. Marshalek et al. (1983) emphasized the importance of assembly and control processes. They hypothesized that

more complex tasks may require more involvement of executive assembly and control processes that structure and analyze the problem, assemble a strategy of attack on it, monitor the performance process, and adapt these strategies as performance proceeds, within as well as between items in a task, and between tasks (Marshalek, 1983, p. 124).

The Carpenter et al. (1990) analysis of the Raven test supports and extends this hypothesis. In their simulation, the crucial executive functions were (a) the ability to decompose a complex problem into simpler problems and (b) the ability to manage the hierarchy of goals and subgoals generated by this decomposition.

The claim is *not* that more able problem solvers are always more strategic or flexible or reflective in their problem solving (cf. Alderton & Larson, 1994). Indeed, as previously noted in the discussion of strategies and stategy shifting, subjects who are most able to solve items often show little evidence of strategy shifting. For example, in the Kyllonen, Lohman, and Woltz (1984) study of a spatial synthesis task, subjects very high in spatial ability (but low in verbal ability) were best described by a model that said that they always mentally synthesized stimuli. These subjects probably did not have to resort to other strategies. Rather, it was the subjects who had less extreme scores profiles but relatively high scores on G that showed the most strategy shifting. The authors' interpretation was that, for this latter group of subjects, the pure "spatial" strategy of mentally combining figures exceeded working memory resources as problem difficulty increased. Subjects then switched to other strategies, as necessary, to solve problems. This required the ability to monitor one's problem solving as it proceeded, to assemble a new strategy when necessary, and to make these adaptations as item demands varied. Indeed, the models they tested could be fit only to the extent that subjects *systematically* altered their solution strategies in response to observable features of items.

One can provide a stronger test of the hypothesis by turning the problem around. In other words, if fluid reasoning requires flexible adaptation, then it should be possible to manipulate the extent to which items require such processing and thereby alter their relationship with G. This was the approach taken by Swiney (1985) and by Chastain (1992). Swiney sought to test the hypothesis that correlations between performance on geometric analogies and G would increase as more flexible adaptation was required, at least for easy and moderately difficult problems. Correlations with G were expected to decline if task difficulty was too great. Adaptation was manipulated by grouping items in different ways. In the blocked condition, interitem variation was minimized by grouping items with similar processing requirements (estimated by the number of elements and the number and type of transformations). In the mixed condition, items were grouped to be as dissimilar as possible.

Two experiments were conducted. In the first study, 20 subjects selected to represent the full range of ability in a pool of 146 high school students were administered geometric analogy items that varied in difficulty (low versus high), condition (blocked or mixed), phase (rule learning, rule identification, rule application), and order (blocked or mixed first). In the rule-learning phase, participants solved a series of five geometric analogies and verbalized the rule common to the set. Those who did not identify the rules were taught them. In the identification phase, subjects were required to determine which analogy stem differed from the others in a set of four stems. Rules used to construct the stems had been taught in the learning phase. The application phase was identical to the rule identification phase except that subjects were given the correct rule(s) prior to the presentation of the item.

In the second experiment, 50 subjects representing the full range of G in another pool of high school students performed the same task with the addition of a rule-discovery phase and items from sets C, D, and E of the Raven progressive matrices. In the discovery phase, subjects were first given practice on rules not used in the experiment and then attempted 18 items. Raven items were split into 18 odd- and 18 even-numbered items. Items in the blocked condition were administered in this order; items in the mixed condition were reordered by interspersing the hardest items throughout the 18-item test.

Results of the first experiment showed that low-ability subjects were more adversely affected by mixing items than were high-ability subjects, regardless of treatment order. Effects were similar for the Raven in Experiment 2, but smaller. Relationships between task accuracy and G for the different item sets in Experiment 2 is shown in Figure 14.10. Clearly, relationship with G varies systematically as a function of item difficulty and task requirements. Strongest relationships were observed for identifying (i.e., inferring) and applying difficult rules. Weakest relationships were observed for applying easy rules or discovering difficult rules, especially in the mixed condition.

Retrospective reports supported the conclusion that high-G subjects were better able to adapt their strategy's flexibly to meet changing task demands. Low-G subjects reported a preference for holistic strategies such as trying to "see" the answer; high-G subjects reported switching to more analytic strategies as item difficulty increased. In contrast, low-G subjects were more likely to report just

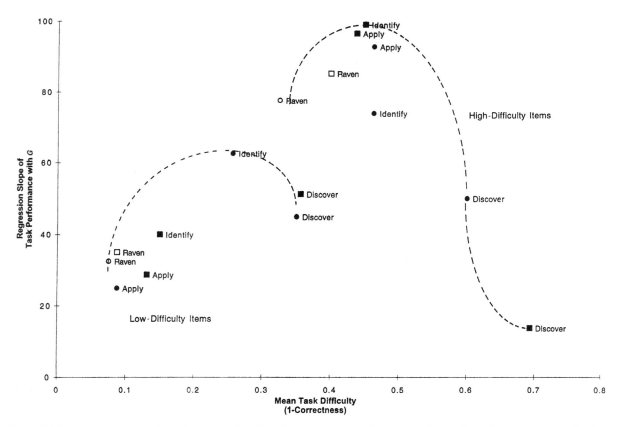

FIGURE 14.10. Plots of regressions slopes of subtask performance on *G* by subtask difficulty for rule discovery, rule identification, and rule application phases for items in Blocked (filled circles) and Mixed (filled squares) item orders. Raven matrices items shown in open circles. (*n* = 50) (after Swiney, 1985).

"trying harder" on more difficult problems. Swiney also found that low-*G* subjects overestimated their performance on highly difficult items; they also consistently underestimated the difficulty of problems. This suggests differences in monitoring and evaluation processes.

Chastain (1992) reported three additional studies contrasting blocked versus mixed item presentations. Experiments 1 and 2 used items from the Wonderlic Personnel Test, a 50-item test that samples a broad range of item formats. The third experiment used a figural encoding task and a dynamic spatial task. In all studies, flexible adaptation was estimated by a simple difference score (mixed minus blocked) and by a residual score (regression of mixed on blocked). Correlations between these two

scores, reference tests, and performance on a logic-gates learning task were small but generally in the expected direction.

Gustafsson (1999) reports a study by Carlstedt that challenges this interpretation of the blocked–mixed contrast. Carlstedt administered three kinds of inductive reasoning problems to groups of Swedish military recruits: figure series completion (*series*), figure classification (*groups*), and a task called *opposite groups* (identify the feature that unites the figures in one group and differentiates the group from the other group). Items were combined in different ways to form two test forms: heterogeneous (HET) and homogeneous (HOM). In the HET forms, subjects first attempted one groups item, then one opposite groups item, and then one series item, after which the sequence was repeated. In the HOM form, groups items were presented first, then all series items, and then all opposite groups items.

Unexpectedly, Carlstedt found that *G* loadings were higher in the HOM condition than in the HET condition. He argues that the homogeneous arrangement affords better possibilities for learning and transfer across items. Different principles are introduced successively and combined in the more complex items. Gustafsson (1999) claims that the efficiency of a test as a measure of G is thus partly a function of dependence among the items. Such dependencies violate a basic assumption of IRT methods for scaling responses, once again illustrating the conflict between psychological and psychometric theories of test performance (Snow & Lohman, 1989).

To summarize the discussion to this point: As one moves from periphery to center in a two- (or even three-)dimensional radex, tasks increase in apparent complexity. Tasks near the center typically require more steps or component processes and emphasize accuracy rather than speed of response. But this does not mean that speed of processing is unimportant or that the addition of any type of process will increase the correlation with G. Increasing the demand on certain types of processing, which Sternberg describes as selective encoding, comparison, and combination, also increases the correlation with G. Importantly, though, such processes require controlled, effortful processing and place heavy demands on working-memory resources. They also require subjects to be more strategic or flexible or adaptive in their problem solving or to learn rules from easy items that will be needed in combination to solve hard items.

Limitations and Future Directions

The information-processing paradigm has enormously enriched our understanding of cognitive tests and the ability constructs they estimate. We have moved from trait labels and vague notions of "process" to the rich and detailed models of thinking sampled in this chapter. All paradigms are inadequate in some respects, and the information-processing approach is no exception. Two shortcomings are particularly salient: (a) the neglect of affect and conation, and (b) the failure to understand the contextual specificity of abilities.

AFFECT AND CONATION. Although theorizing about the influence of affect (or feeling) and conation (or willing) on cognition dates back to the Greek philosophers, it is only recently that investigators have attempted to study their complex and reciprocal influences on each other. Although many promising leads have been identified (see Snow, Corno, & Jackson, 1996; Boekaerts, 1995; Kuhl & Kraska, 1989; Corno & Kanfer, 1993; Schunk & Zimmerman, 1994), there is no simple way to summarize the enormous diversity of paradigms and findings. Nonetheless, it is clear that persons who do well on ability tests expend effort differently from persons who score poorly. In general, those who score well retrieve information from memory with greater ease and rapidity and are better able to maintain that information in working memory while executing other processes. The difference is most striking in comparisons of experts and novices in skill domains such as reading. Experts expend their efforts on high-level processes (that include, but go beyond comprehension), whereas novices struggle to identify words and the sentences they create. Affect enters not only as anxiety and frustration, which further constrict cognition, but also as interest and surprise, which enhance and direct cognition. In particular, those who adopt a constructive, motivational orientation towards a task will tend to exhibit more and better self-regulation than individuals who adopt a less constructive or even defensive orientation. Situations differentially elicit these conative and affective resources. Indeed, understanding the role of affect in cognition seems to demand a mode of theorizing and experimentation that attends not only to persons or to situations but also to the attunement of particular individuals to particular aspects of situations.

INCLUDING SITUATIONS AND THEIR AFFOR-DANCES. A theory of G must explain individual differences in problem solving not only on tests but in school and other everyday contexts. Although occasionally nodding to the role of culture, cognitive theories of abilities have not taken seriously the fact that cognition is situated. Snow (1994) argues that a theory of G needs to start with the proposition that abilities are situated. In his view, this means that abilities are reflected in the tuning of particular persons to the particular demands and opportunities of situations and thus reside in the union of person in situation, not "in the mind" alone.

The situation contains some pieces of what the person needs or can use to accomplish a given task. But persons must be tuned to perceive and use these pieces, and also to supply needed pieces from their own learning histories. Some persons are prepared to perceive these affordances, to use the pieces provided by the situation, and to complement these with pieces they provide, but some are not. Among those who are so tuned, each may use and supply slightly different pieces; there is functional equivalence despite idiosyncrasy. The result is that some persons succeed in learning in a given situation; they are in *harmony* with it. Others do not, because they are not tuned to use the opportunities the situation provides or to produce what it demands (Snow, 1994, p. 31–32).

The idea of affordances brings back not only the physical and social environment but also the particular couplings or attunements to aspects of that environment that arise through the long history of the evolution of the species or the short history of the development of the individual. Put differently, the notion of affordances in the situation and propensities in the individual provides one way to reason about the selectivity in encoding exhibited by more able individuals (cf. Sternberg, 1986).

A SUMMARY HYPOTHESIS. Elshout (1985) defined a problem as the state of a particular person in a particular task situation such that, should the person succeed, any explanation of the event based only on the person's experience in that particular situation is excluded beforehand. Tasks that can be accomplished using stored routines do not, in Elshout's view, count as problems. Sternberg (1986) makes a similar but less radical distinction when he claims that processes used to solve problems must be executed in a controlled, rather than an automatized, fashion if reasoning is required. Likewise, Belmont and Mitchell (1987) contended that learners will generally be most strategic on tasks they perceive to be of moderate difficulty. This is because strategy use is presumed to require effort and people are unlikely to invest effort when it is unnecessary or unlikely to be unrewarded.

Snow (1989) offered the following summary hypothesis. Imagine tasks as scaled along a continuum of difficulty or complexity. Elshout argued that there is a threshold for each person along such a continuum. Below the threshold, performance follows directly from routines the person already has in store for the task; the flow of activity is relatively automatic and algorithmic. Errors come mostly from cognitive slips and inattention rather than from inadequacies in the system. In the language of Cattell (1963), these are crystallized abilities and skills. Above the threshold, however, the person must increasingly operate in a heuristic, improvisational, controlled, and achievement-motivated mode. Here, errors occur because the previously stored routines and knowledge are inadequate, or poorly applied, or are not tuned to the specific task at hand, or because motivation flags prematurely. Furthermore, the farther above one's threshold one is forced to work, the more likely that heuristic processing and improvising degrade into helpless, even anxious, muddling; errors become more conceptual and strategic. What have been here called fluid reasoning abilities would be measured for most individuals in the lower end of this range. Novices are thus to be seen as persons who must work at or above their thresholds in tasks of a given type, whereas experts are those who can work well below their thresholds in that task type. The contrast is also seen in the pattern of declining correlations with G and increasing correlations with more specific abilities as participants acquire a new skill (Ackerman, 1986, 1988). The goal of instruction is to move a person's threshold up in each type of task that society and the person values. Raising the threshold means making more and more difficult or complex instances of the task type nonproblematical and automatic. To measure reasoning, however, problems must be perceived by the individual as falling somewhere above the lower threshold and below the upper threshold, i.e., within the zone of tolerable problematicity.

CONCLUSIONS AND IMPLICATIONS
Desiderata for a Theory of Complex Information Processing

Any theory of intelligence that purports to explain the sort of complex information processing discussed in this chapter must accommodate several facts. First, the theory must explain the repeatedly demonstrated finding that human abilities are organized hierarchically (Carroll, 1993; Gustafsson & Undheim, 1996). Thus, theories in which only a series of abilities arranged nonhierarchically are posited (e.g., Thurstone, 1938; Gardner, 1983) are fundamentally inadequate. Second, the theory must explain the clustering of abilities by content, especially verbal, spatial, and numerical–symbolic. Thus, theories in which only one individual-difference dimension is posited (such as *g*) or claim that intelligence is reflected in the action of a single cognitive structure or process (such as attention or working memory) are also inadequate. Third, the theory must give some principled account of processing complexity and how it is related to the loading of a task on the general factor. Thus, theories that do not distinguish among levels of processing complexity are inadequate. Fourth, and perhaps most important, the theory must coordinate the findings of differential psychology with general theories of human information processing. Theories of cognition that ignore the literature on individual differences are unlikely to provide a full accounting of the individual-difference construct of intelligence. Conversely, theories of individual differences that ignore the literature on human cognition are unlikely to evolve measures that are psychologically transparent or that represent in a systematic way different features of the human cognitive system.

Theory-Based Tests and Testing

This chapter shows how information-processing psychology can be applied to existing ability tests and constructs in order better to understand them. But the problem can be turned around, and information-processing theories of cognition can be used to guide the development of new tests. Although Sternberg's (1985) triarchic theory of intelligence is in part rooted in the information-processing paradigm, an operational test that embodies all aspects of the triarchic theory has not been developed. Indeed, the main implication for assessment seems to be in the measurement of practical intelligence rather than in refined measures of fluid and crystallized abilities. The most extensive effort to date to develop an ability testing battery grounded in information-processing psychology has been the Cognitive Abilities Measurement (CAM) program in the United States Air Force (Kyllonen, 1993, 1994). The CAM framework consists of a 4 × 3 grid with four "sources" and three "contents." The sources are processing speed, working memory, declarative knowledge, and procedural knowledge. The three contents are verbal, quantitative, and spatial. Empirical tests of the model confirm that content and source (or process) can be distinguished

and also show that a hierarchical model fits the data slightly better than a flat or nonhierarchical model (Kyllonen, 1993).

The CAM framework is tied to theories of cognition in two ways: (1) through the structure of the framework itself, particularly the four sources, and (2) through the tasks used to represent different cells in the model. For example, working-memory tasks were based on Baddeley's (1986) theory of working memory and in some cases directly modeled after tasks used in his research program or that of other researchers (e.g., Daneman & Carpenter, 1980). It is much easier to elaborate ties to cognitive processes and to address the construct validity of tasks when theory is used in this way to guide test construction rather than post hoc to guide interpretation of investigations of otherwise ambiguous tasks. On the other hand, tests for some cells in the model were not constructed, and tests for other cells were selected on the basis of availability or apparent match to the somewhat vague source definitions. Further work is needed to establish the validity of task selection and assignment to cells in the framework – perhaps, for example, by panels of judges. The CAM battery is also interesting for what it tells us about how best to measure processes. Early in the project, much effort was devoted to examining the correlates of various "process" measures estimated by individual regression coefficients or simple difference scores. None of these measures were retained in the final battery. Instead, individual performance is summarized in various total (or part) scores on tasks designed to emphasize a particular aspect of individual differences in processing. Once again, it seems that information-processing models – although extremely useful for the internal validation of tasks – are not particularly helpful when it comes to the practical task of specifying dependable individual scores with stable external correlates.

The CAM battery uses theory at a fairly global level to guide task selection. Other efforts to use theory to guide test construction have generally used process models of particular tasks to guide the development of items for new tests (see, e.g., Embretson, 1998; Bejar, 1985; Irvine, Dann, & Anderson, 1990; Nichols, 1994). Theory-based tests offer many advantages, including the possibility of constructing items with predictable characteristics "on the fly," which is an especially attractive option in computer adaptive testing. There are also advantages for creation of paper-and-pencil tests. For example, estimating the difficulty of an item without first administering it can eliminate an entire cycle in test development. There are drawbacks, however. Verbal reasoning items have proven vastly more difficult to generate in this way. The substantial effort of Bejar et al. (1991) to generate verbal analogy items for the SAT did not succeed. The more recent efforts of Buck et al. (1998) using Tatsuoka's (1995) methods may be more successful, at least in identifying more of the many item attributes that influence performance on verbal analogies. A less obvious difficulty with theory-based tests lies in the relatively constricted set of items that are generated by a particular set of rules. The hodgepodge of items on many well-constructed ability tests may actually require more flexibility from test takers and may also be less amenable to coaching or simple practice effects than pools of items generated by more restricted sets of rules. These concerns apply primarily to *Gf* measures rather than to measures of more specialized abilities such as perceptual speed or even working-memory capacity.

Sources of Difficulty, Sources of Individual Differences

Understanding what makes a task difficult is not the same as understanding how participants solve items on the task, but it is a useful place to start. Indeed, although there are often many different ways to solve a task that would conform with the observation that some types of items are more difficult than others, there is a much larger set of processing models excluded by an observed ordering of items according to difficulty. More important, though, is the realization that understanding how participants solve items on a task is not an understanding of individual differences – except in the rare instance in which individual differences are entirely reflected in how the task is solved. Manipulations that make tasks difficult will, in general, make people differ. But making a task difficult is like making an object heavy – there are many, many ways to make something heavy. Some of these manipulations introduce construct-relevant variance (making a bucket of water heavier by adding more water); some introduce construct-irrelevant variance (making the bucket out of lead). An analysis that parti-

tions variation into stimulus (or task) variance and individual difference (or subject) variance can help clarify these relationships (see Embretson, 1985; this volume). Indeed, one of the major contributions of cognitive process analyses of ability tests to the practical business of measurement has been to identify irrelevant sources of difficulty in tasks and conditions in which they are eliminated (Embretson, 1985; Snow & Lohman, 1989). However, even individual difference variance may be construct irrelevant, as was shown in the examples in which increases in task difficulty beyond some point caused a decrease in correlation with the target construct, and an increase in correlation with some other construct. The main point, however, is that isolated analyses of particular tasks – no matter how well selected – cannot support a theory of an individual difference construct. For this reason, Sternberg and his colleagues, Pellegrino and his colleagues, and Snow and his colleagues all sought to study families of related tasks. There seems to be no other way to discover which portions of the individual-difference variance are task-specific and which portions generalize to other tasks.

We now also know that understanding individual differences on tasks used to measure general reasoning abilities requires the investigation of items that are not only complex in the sense of requiring multiple processes but also difficult. In other words, conclusions about process differences between high- and low-ability subjects depend importantly on the difficulty of the task. In particular, recent studies of individual differences in inductive reasoning replicate earlier findings that high-ability subjects spend more time encoding and less time on inference and application and are more likely to engage in exhaustive processing. However, these studies also show quite different, even contrary, patterns on difficult problems.

Items contain options, not just stems. How subjects use information in options to reason about the problem posed in the stem is an important aspect of how they solve difficult reasoning items – especially classification problems. Younger and less-able subjects are often misled or distracted by foils. Older and more-able subjects show evidence of both working backward and working forward on such problems. What may appropriately be described as "justification" or cycling through the stem a second time on simple problems requires a far more extensive set of processes on complex problems. Complex problems also require a level of task decomposition, goal setting, and monitoring unlike that required for simple problems (Carpenter et al., 1990). Once again, early suspicions that complex problem solving requires a level of planning (or "assembly") and monitoring (or "control") processes have been confirmed. Some have argued that there are affective and volitional states and processes to be considered as well (Snow et al., 1996).

On the other hand, we have learned that the lion's share of individual differences in inductive reasoning is shared with working memory. This is an extremely important finding. Importantly, though, working memory is represented by tasks that require a good deal of higher order or executive processes (Baddeley, 1996).

Do Cognitive Tests Make Good Cognitive Tasks?

Most of the research reviewed in this chapter has followed Estes' (1974) argument that the best way to understand intelligence is to understand how individuals solve items on intelligence and other ability tests. This was certainly a reasonable place to start. But ability tests are limited in at least two ways. First, some argue that the abilities sampled by such tests are an unrepresentative sample of the full range of human competencies that properly fall under the rubric of intelligent behavior. These critics argue that measures of musical abilities, social intelligence, practical intelligence, everyday reasoning, participatory skills, and so forth, should be studied as well. As long as we have no agreed-upon definition of the universe of competencies that qualify as "intelligent," then there will always be reasonable (as well as unreasonable) criticisms of this sort.

Ability tests are limited in another respect, however. Indeed, even if such tests were thought to constitute a fair and representative sample of the behavior considered intelligent, one might still argue that psychometric tests do not constitute the best or most revealing way to study the processes that generate such behaviors. The claim here is that although psychometric tests often constitute efficient ways to measure individual differences in abilities, they often are not very informative vehicles for understanding what those abilities might

be. For example, although a multiple-choice vocabulary test is an excellent measure of both verbal ability and general ability, even the most careful information-processing analysis of how subjects respond to items on such tests reveals little about the nature of either verbal or general ability. Because of this, some have sought instead to understand abilities by correlating ability test scores with scores derived from laboratory tasks (e.g., Hunt, Frost, & Lunneborg, 1973) or from learning tasks (e.g., Ackerman, 1988). Process models of any of these tasks – whether based on ability tests or laboratory tasks, or learning tasks – are often most informative when subjects who differ in ability differ systematically in *how* they process information. Such qualitative differences have been pivotal in investigations of cognitive development (e.g., Piaget, 1963). In this view, then, a process understanding of ability requires the invention or selection of tasks that elicit qualitative differences in processing between individuals who differ in ability. Scores on cognitive tests provide an important external reference point but may not be themselves the most informative objects of inquiry into the nature of abilities. This is particularly the case for ability tests and constructs that primarily reflect the efficacy of *past* processing (e.g., a test of verbal knowledge) rather than of present processing (e.g., a test of figural analogical reasoning).

Methodology

Methodology matters. The seemingly straightforward task of estimating process scores for individuals by subtracting latency in one condition from latencies in another turned out to be far more troublesome than initially envisioned. What should be done about error-response latencies? The experimenter not interested in individual differences often eliminates subjects who err too often and does not worry if all remaining participants are equated on speed–accuracy trade-off. Not so when individual differences are the object of investigation. Further, on any but the simplest *RT* task, multiple processes must be used. Thus, subtraction gave way to more complex regression procedures, which estimated scores for several components simultaneously and also gave some indication of overall model fit. Attempts to account for both error and latency led some to use canonical correlation and others to control exposure latencies experimentally and to fit nonlinear regression models. Others sought to improve the scaling of accuracy and latency data through transformations, signal-detection theory, and latent-trait models (as in Embretson's multicomponent latent-trait models). Tatsuoka's rule-space procedure (see Figure 14.6) shows the current state of one effort to solve some of these problems.

Thus, methodology matters, perhaps as much for how every attempt to solve one problem has created others. Both researchers and outsiders have been led down more than one blind alley by the failure to understand the sometimes not-so-obvious limitations of their favorite methodology.

What does the future hold? If the recent past is any guide, we will see the further development of sophisticated methodologies for modeling performance on complex tasks. But it is unlikely that such procedures will be widely used. If Sternberg's (1977) componential methods, which were based on relatively straightforward regression procedures, were too daunting for many, how will multicomponent latent-trait theory or the rule-space methodology fare? On the bright side, confirmatory factor analyses and modeling techniques have shown structure where chaos once ruled (see especially Gustafsson, 1988); new scaling procedures in psychometrics allow comparisons of items across samples (Embretson, 1985; Sheehan, 1997) and the development of intelligent systems for creating items and scoring complex constructed responses (Bennett, 1998). These and other developments will continue to inform and reform assessment of complex information processing. Thus, the future will bring continued innovations but few that are simple. Whether the constructs of the future will look radically different from those of the past is more difficult to say. In spite of repeated arguments against G and in favor of one or another system of multiple abilities, data routinely support not so much the existence of G as its utility. Thus, it is a fair bet that, whatever the future holds, tests of G – especially Gf and particularly I – will be a part of it.

REFERENCES

Ackerman, P. L. (1986). Individual differences in information processing: An investigation of intellectual abilities and task performance during practice. *Intelligence, 10,* 101–139.

Ackerman, P. L. (1988). Determinants of individual differences during skill acquisition: A theory of cognitive abilities and information processing. *Journal of Experimental Psychology: General, 117,* 299–329.

Ackerman, P. L., & Kanfer, R. (1993). Integrating laboratory and field study for improving selection: Development of a battery for predicting air traffic controller success. *Journal of Applied Psychology, 78,* 413–432.

Alderton, D. L., & Larson, G. E. (1994). Cross-task consistency in strategy use and the relationship with intelligence. *Intelligence, 18,* 47–76.

Alderton, D. L., Goldman, S. R., & Pellegrino, J. W. (1985). Individual differences in process outcomes for verbal analogy and classification solution. *Intelligence, 9,* 69–85.

Anastasi, A., & Foley, J. P. (1949). *Differential psychology* (rev. ed.). New York: Macmillan.

Anderson, G. V., Fruchter, B., Manuel, H. T., & Worchel, P. (1954). *Survey of research on spatial factors* (Research Bulletin AFPTRC-TR-54-84). San Antonio, TX: Lackland AFB.

Anderson, J. R. (1976). *Language, memory, and thought.* Hillsdale, NJ: Erlbaum.

Anderson, J. R. (1983). *The architecture of cognition.* Cambridge, MA: Harvard University Press.

Anderson, J. R. (1985). *Cognitive psychology and its implications* (2nd ed.). New York: W. H. Freeman.

Anderson, J. R. (1993). *Rules of the mind.* Hillsdale, NJ: Erlbaum.

Baddeley, A. D. (1986). *Working memory.* Oxford: Clarendon Press.

Baddeley, A. D. (1996). Exploring the central executive. *The Quarterly Journal of Experimental Psychology, 49A*(1), 5–28.

Bejar, I. I. (1985). Speculations on the future of test design. In S. E. Embretson (Ed.), *Test design: Developments in psychology and psychometrics* (pp. 279–294). New York: Academic Press.

Bejar, I. I., Chaffin, R., & Embretson, S. (1991). *Cognitive and psychometric analysis of analogical problem solving.* New York: Springer-Verlag.

Belmont, J. M., & Butterfield, E. C. (1971). Learning strategies as determinants of memory deficiencies. *Cognitive Psychology, 2,* 411–420.

Belmont, J. M., & Mitchell, D. W. (1987). The general strategy hypothesis as applied to cognitive theory in mental retardation. *Intelligence, 11,* 91–105.

Bennett, R. E. (1998). *Reinventing assessment: A policy information perspective.* Princeton, NJ: Educational Testing Service, Policy Information Center, Research Division.

Bethell-Fox, C. E., Lohman, D. F., & Snow, R. E. (1984). Adaptive reasoning: Componential and eye movement analysis of geometric analogy performance. *Intelligence, 8,* 205–238.

Bethell-Fox, C. E., & Shepard, R. N. (1988). Mental rotation: Effects of stimulus complexity, familiarity, and individual differences. *Journal of Experimental Psychology: Human Perception and Performance, 14*, 12–23.

Biggs, J. B., & Collis, K. F. (1982). *Evaluating the quality of learning: The SOLO Taxonomy.* New York: Academic Press.

Binet, A., & Henri, V. (1896). La psychologie individuelle [Individual psychology]. *Année psychologique, 11*, 191–465.

Bloom, B. S., & Broder, L. J. (1950). Problem-solving processes of college students. *Supplementary Educational Monographs, 73.*

Boekaerts, M. (1995). The interface between intelligence and personality as determinants of classroom learning. In D. H. Saklofske & M. Zeidner (Eds.), *International handbook of personality and intelligence* (pp. 161–183). New York: Plenum Press.

Brody, N. (1992). *Intelligence* (2nd ed.). San Diego, CA: Academic Press.

Buck, G., VanEssen, T., Tatsuoka, K., Kostin, I., Lutz, D., & Phelps, M. (1998a). *Development, selection and validation of a set of cognitive and linguistic attributes for the SAT I Verbal: Analogy section.* (Research Rep. No. 98-19). Princeton, NJ: Educational Testing Service.

Buck, G., VanEssen, T., Tatsuoka, K., Kostin, I., Lutz, D., & Phelps, M. (1998b). *Development, selection and validation of a set of cognitive and linguistic attributes for the SAT I Verbal: Sentence Completion section.* (Research Rep. No. 98-23). Princeton, NJ: Educational Testing Service.

Butterfield, E. C., Nielsen, D., Tangen, K. L., & Richardson, M. B. (1985). Theoretically based psychometric measures of inductive reasoning. In S. E. Embretson (Ed.), *Test design: Developments in psychology and psychometrics* (pp. 77–148). New York: Academic Press.

Carpenter, P. A., & Just, M. A. (1978). Eye fixations during mental rotation. In J. W. Senders, D. F. Fisher, & R. A. Monty (Eds.), *Eye movements and the higher psychological functions.* Hillsdale, NJ: Erlbaum.

Carpenter, P. A., Just, M. A., & Shell, P. (1990). What one intelligence test measures: A theoretical account of the processing in the Raven Progressive Matrices test. *Psychological Review, 97*, 404–431.

Carroll, J. B. (1941). A factor analysis of verbal abilities. *Psychometrika, 6*, 279–307.

Carroll, J. B. (1993). *Human cognitive abilities. A survey of factor-analytic studies.* Cambridge, UK: Cambridge University Press.

Cattell, R. B. (1963). Theory of fluid and crystallized intelligence: A critical experiment. *Journal of Educational Psychology, 54*, 1–22.

Chaffin, R., & Herrmann, D. J. (1984). The similarity and diversity of semantic relations. *Memory & Cognition, 12*, 134–141.

Chastain, R. L. (1992). *Adaptive processing in complex learning and cognitive performance.* Unpublished doctoral dissertation, Stanford University, Stanford, CA.

Christal, R. E. (1958). Factor analytic study of visual memory. *Psychological Monographs, 72* (13: Whole No. 466).

Clark, H. H. (1969). The influence of language in solving three-term series problems. *Journal of Experimental Psychology, 82*, 205–215.

Clark, H. H., & Chase, W. G. (1972). On the process of comparing sentences against pictures. *Cognitive Psychology, 3*, 472–517.

Cooper, L. A. (1982). Strategies for visual comparison and representation: Individual differences. In R. J. Sternberg (Ed.), *Advances in the psychology of human intelligence* (Vol. 1, pp. 77–124). Hillsdale, NJ: Erlbaum.

Cooper, L. A., & Regan, D. T. (1982). Attention, perception, and intelligence. In R. J. Sternberg (Ed.), *Handbook of human intelligence* (pp. 123–169). Cambridge, UK: Cambridge University Press.

Corno, L., & Kanfer, R. (1993). The role of volition in learning and performance. In L. Darling-Hammond (Ed.), *Review of research in education* (Vol. 19, pp. 3–43). Washington, DC: American Educational Research Association.

Crawford, J. (1988). *Intelligence, task complexity and tests of sustained attention.* Unpublished doctoral dissertation, University of New South Wales, Sydney, Australia.

Cronbach, L. J. (1957). The two disciplines of scientific psychology. *American Psychologist, 12*, 671–684.

Damasio, A. (1994). *Descartes' error: Emotion, reason, and the human brain.* New York: Putnam.

Daneman, M., & Carpenter, P. A. (1980). Individual differences in working memory and reading. *Journal of Mathematical Behavior, 19*, 450–466.

Deary, I. J., & Stough, C. (1996). Intelligence and inspection time: Achievements, prospects, and problems. *American Psychologist, 51*, 599–608.

Detterman, D. K. (1986). Human intelligence is a complex system of separate processes. In R. J. Sternberg, & D. K. Detterman (Eds.), *What is intelligence?* (pp. 57–61). Norwood, NJ: Ablex.

Diones, R., Bejar, I., & Chaffin, R. (1996). *The dimensionality of responses to SAT analogy items* (Research Report 96-1). Princeton, NJ: Educational Testing Service.

Ebbinghaus, H. (1985). *Memory: A contribution to experimental psychology* (H. A. Ruger & C. E. Bussenues, Trans.). New York: Teachers College Press. (Original work published 1913).

Ekstrom, R. B., French, J. W., & Harman, H. H. (1976). *Kit of factor-referenced cognitive tests.* Princeton, NJ: Educational Testing Service.

Elshout, J. J. (1985, June). *Problem solving and education.* Paper presented at the meeting of the American Educational Research Association, San Francisco.

Embretson, S. E. (1983). Construct validity: Construct representation versus nomothetic span. *Psychological Bulletin, 93*, 179–197.

Embretson, S. E. (1985). Multicomponent latent trait models for test design. In S. E. Embretson (Ed.), *Test design: Developments in psychology and psychometrics* (pp. 195–218). New York: Academic Press.

Embretson, S. E. (1986). Intelligence and its measurement: Extending contemporary theory to existing tests. In R. J. Sternberg (Ed.), *Advances in the psychology of human intelligence* (Vol. 3, pp. 335–368). Hillsdale, NJ: Erlbaum.

Embretson, S. E. (1995). The role of working memory capacity and general control processes in intelligence. *Intelligence, 20,* 169–189.

Embretson, S. E. (1998). A cognitive design system approach to generating valid tests: Application to abstract reasoning. *Psychological Methods, 3,* 380–396.

Embretson, S. E., Schneider, L., & Roth, D. (1986). Multiple processing strategies and the construct validity of verbal reasoning tests. *Journal of Educational Measurement, 23,* 13–32.

Erickson, J. R. (1974). A set analysis theory of behavior in formal syllogistic reasoning tasks. In R. Solso (Ed.), *Loyola symposium on cognition* (Vol. 2, pp. 305–329). Hillsdale, NJ: Erlbaum.

Erickson, J. R. (1978). Research on syllogistic reasoning. In R. Revlin & R. E. Mayer (Eds.), *Human reasoning* (pp. 39–50). Washington, DC: Winston.

Ericsson, K. A., & Simon, H. A. (1984). *Protocol analysis: Verbal reports as data.* Cambridge, MA: MIT Press.

Estes, W. K. (1974). Learning theory and intelligence. *American Psychologist, 29,* 740–749.

Evans, T. G. (1968). A program for the solution of geometric-analogy intelligence test questions. In M. Minsky (Ed.), *Semantic information processing.* Cambridge, MA: MIT Press.

Frederiksen, J. R. (1981). Sources of process interaction in reading. In A. M. Lesgold & C. A. Perfetti (Eds.), *Interactive processes in reading* (pp. 361–386). Hillsdale, NJ: Erlbaum.

Gardner, H. (1983). *Frames of mind: The theory of multiple intelligences.* New York: Basic Books.

Gentile, J. R., Kessler, D. K., & Gentile, P. K. (1969). Process of solving analogy items. *Journal of Educational Psychology, 60,* 494–502.

Gitomer, D. H., Curtis, M. E., Glaser, R., & Lensky, D. B. (1987). Processing differences as a function of item difficulty in verbal analogy performance. *Journal of Educational Psychology, 79,* 212–219.

Goldman, S. R., & Pellegrino, J. W. (1984). Deductions about induction: Analyses of developmental and individual differences. In R. J. Sternberg (Ed.), *Advances in the psychology of human intelligence* (Vol. 2, pp. 149–197). Hillsdale, NJ: Erlbaum.

Goldman, S. R., Pellegrino, J. W., Parseghian, P. E., & Sallis, R. (1982). Developmental and individual differences in verbal analogical reasoning by children. *Child Development, 53,* 550–559.

Greeno, J. G. (1978). A study of problem solving. In R. Glaser (Ed.), *Advances in instructional psychology* (Vol. 1, pp. 13–75). Hillsdale, NJ: Erlbaum.

Greeno, J. G. (1980). Psychology of learning, 1960–1980: One participant's observations. *American Psychologist, 35,* 713–728.

Guilford, J. P., & Lacey, J. I. (Eds.). (1947). Printed classification tests. *Army Air Forces aviation psychology research program* (Report No. 5). Washington, DC: Government Printing Office.

Gustafsson, J.-E. (1988). Hierarchical models of individual differences in cognitive abilities. In R. J. Sternberg (Ed.), *Advances in the psychology of human intelligence* (Vol. 4, pp. 35–71). Hillsdale, NJ: Erlbaum.

Gustafsson, J.-E. (1999). Measuring and understanding *G*: Experimental and correlational approaches. In P. L. Ackerman, P. C. Kyllonen, & R. D. Roberts (Eds.), *Learning and individual differences: Process, trait, and content determinants* (pp. 275–292). Washington, DC: American Psychological Association.

Gustafsson, J.-E., & Undheim, J. O. (1996). Individual differences in cognitive functions. In D. C. Berliner & R. C. Calfee (Eds.), *Handbook of educational psychology* (pp. 186–242). New York: Simon & Schuster Macmillan.

Hagendorf, H., & Sá, B. (1995). Koordinierungsleistungen im visuellen Arbeitsgedächtnis [Coordination in visual working memory]. *Zeitschrift für Psychologie, 203,* 53–72.

Halford, G. S., Maybery, M. T., O'Hare, A. W., & Grant, P. (1994). The development of memory and processing capacity. *Child Development, 65,* 1338–1356.

Heller, J. I. (1979). Cognitive processing in verbal analogy solution. (Doctoral dissertation, University of Pittsburgh, 1979). *Dissertation Abstracts International, 40,* 2553A.

Henley, N. M. (1969). A psychological study of the semantics of animal terms. *Journal of Verbal Learning and Verbal Behavior, 8,* 176–184.

Holzman, T. G., Pellegrino, J. W., & Glaser, R. (1982). Cognitive dimensions of numerical rule induction. *Journal of Educational Psychology, 74,* 360–373.

Horn, J. L. (1972). The structure of intellect: Primary abilities. In R. M. Dreger (Ed.), *Multivariate personality research.* Baton Rouge, LA: Claitor.

Hunt, E. B. (1974). Quote the Raven? Nevermore! In L. W. Gregg (Ed.), *Knowledge and cognition* (pp. 129–158). Hillsdale, NJ: Erlbaum.

Hunt, E. B., Frost, N., & Lunneborg, C. (1973). Individual differences in cognition: A new approach to intelligence. In G. Bower (Ed.), *The psychology of learning and motivation: Vol. 7* (pp. 87–122). New York: Academic Press.

Hunt, E., & Lansman, M. (1982). Individual differences in attention. In R. J. Sternberg (Ed.), *Advances in the psychology of human abilities* (Vol. 1, pp. 207–254). Hillsdale, NJ: Erlbaum.

Huttenlocher, J. (1968). Constructing spatial images: A strategy in reasoning. *Psychological Review, 75,* 550–560.

Irvine, S. H., Dann, P. L., & Anderson, J. D. (1990). Towards a theory of algorithm-determined cognitive test construction. *British Journal of Psychology, 81,* 173–195.

Jacobs, P. I., & Vandeventer, M. (1972). Evaluating the teaching of intelligence. *Educational and Psychological Measurement, 32*, 235–248.

Janssen, R., De Boeck, P., & Vander Steene, G. (1996). Verbal fluency and verbal comprehension abilities in synonym tasks. *Intelligence, 22*, 291–310.

Jensen, A. R. (1980). *Bias in mental testing*. New York: Free Press.

Jensen, A. R. (1982). The chronometry of intelligence. In R. J. Sternberg (Ed.), *Advances in the psychology of human intelligence* (Vol. 1, pp. 255–310). Hillsdale, NJ: Erlbaum.

Jensen, A. R. (1987). Process differences and individual differences in some cognitive tasks. *Intelligence, 11*, 107–136.

Jensen, A. R. (1998). *The g factor: The science of mental ability*. Westport, CT: Praeger.

Johnson-Laird, P. N. (1972). The three-term series problem. *Cognition, 1*, 57–82.

Johnson-Laird, P. N. (1983). *Mental models: Towards a cognitive science of language, inference and consciousness*. Cambridge, MA: Harvard University Press.

Johnson-Laird, P. N. (1985). Deductive reasoning ability. In R. J. Sternberg (Ed.), *Human abilities: An information-processing approach* (pp. 173–194). New York: W. H. Freeman.

Johnson-Laird, P. N., & Steedman, M. (1978). The psychology of syllogisms. *Cognitive Psychology, 10*, 64–99.

Just, M. A., & Carpenter, P. A. (1985). Cognitive coordinate systems: Accounts of mental rotation and individual differences in spatial ability. *Psychological Review, 92*, 137–172.

Just, M. A., & Carpenter, P. A. (1992). A capacity theory of comprehension: Individual differences in working memory. *Psychological Review, 99*, 122–149.

Kintsch, W., & Greeno, J. G., (1985). Understanding and solving word arithmetic problems. *Psychological Review, 92*, 109–129.

Kosslyn, S. M. (1980). *Image and mind*. Cambridge, MA: Harvard University Press.

Kuhl, J., & Kraska, K. (1989). Self-regulation and metamotivation: Computational mechanisms, development, and assessment. In R. Kanfer, P. L. Ackerman, & R. Cudeck (Eds.), *Abilities, motivation, and methodology* (pp. 343–374). Hillsdale, NJ: Erlbaum.

Kyllonen, P. C. (1984). Information processing analysis of spatial ability (Doctoral dissertation, Stanford University, 1984). *Dissertation Abstracts International, 45*, 819A.

Kyllonen, P. C. (1993). Aptitude testing inspired by information processing: A test of the Four-Sources model. *Journal of General Psychology, 120*, 375–405.

Kyllonen, P. C. (1994). CAM: A theoretical framework for cognitive abilities measurement. In D. Detterman (Ed.), *Current topics in human intelligence: Vol. 4. Theories of intelligence* (pp. 307–359). Norwood, NJ: Ablex.

Kyllonen, P. C., & Christal, R. E. (1990). Reasoning ability is (little more than) working-memory capacity?! *Intelligence, 14*, 389–433.

Kyllonen, P. C., Lohman, D. F., & Woltz, D. J. (1984). Componential modeling of alternative strategies for performing spatial tasks. *Journal of Educational Psychology, 76*, 1325–1345.

Lansman, M. (1981). Ability factors and the speed of information processing. In M. P. Friedman, J. P. Das, & N. O'Connor (Eds.), *Intelligence and learning* (pp. 441–457). New York: Plenum Press.

Law, D. J., Morrin, K. A., & Pellegrino, J. W. (1995). Training effects and working memory contributions to skill acquisition in a complex coordination task. *Learning and Individual Differences, 7*, 207–234.

LeFevre, J.-A., & Bisanz, J. (1986). A cognitive analysis of number-series problems: Sources of individual differences in performance. *Memory & Cognition, 14*, 287–298.

Lesgold, A. M. (1984). Acquiring expertise. In J. R. Anderson & S. M. Kosslyn (Eds.), *Tutorials in learning and memory* (pp. 31–60). New York: W. H. Freeman.

Lohman, D. F. (1979). *Spatial ability: A review and reanalysis of the correlational literatures* (Tech. Rep. No. 8). Stanford, CA: Stanford University, Aptitude Research Project, School of Education. (NTIS No. AD-A075 973).

Lohman, D. F. (1986). The effect of speed-accuracy trade-off on sex differences in mental rotation. *Perception and Psychophysics, 39*, 427–436.

Lohman, D. F. (1988). Spatial abilities as traits, processes, and knowledge. In R. J. Sternberg (Ed.), *Advances in the psychology of human intelligence* (Vol. 4, pp. 181–248). Hillsdale, NJ: Erlbaum.

Lohman, D. F. (1994). Component scores as residual variation (or why the intercept correlates best). *Intelligence, 19*, 1–11.

Lohman, D. F., & Kyllonen, P. C. (1983). Individual differences in solution strategy on spatial tasks. In R. F. Dillon & R. R. Schmeck (Eds.), *Individual differences in cognition* (Vol. 1, pp. 105–135). New York: Academic Press.

Lohman, D. F., & Nichols, P. D. (1990). Training spatial abilities: Effects of practice on rotation and synthesis tasks. *Learning and Individual Differences, 2*, 69–95.

Lorge, I., & Thorndike, R. L. (1957). *The Lorge–Thorndike intelligence test, levels A–H*. Boston: Houghton Mifflin.

Macleod, C. M., Hunt, E. B., & Mathews, N. N. (1978). Individual differences in the verification of sentence–picture relationships. *Journal of Verbal Learning and Verbal Behavior, 17*, 493–508.

Marquer, J., & Pereira, M. (1987, April). *Individual differences in sentence-picture verification*. Paper presented at the meeting of the American Educational Research Association, New York.

Marshalek, B. (1981). *Trait and process aspects of vocabulary knowledge and verbal ability* (Tech. Rep. No. 15). Stanford, CA: Stanford University, Aptitude Research Project, School of Education. (NTIS No. AD-A102 757).

Marshalek, B., Lohman, D. F., & Snow, R. E. (1983). The

complexity continuum in the radex and hierarchical models of intelligence. *Intelligence, 7*, 107–128.

McGee, M. (1979). *Human spatial abilities: Sources of sex differences.* New York: Praeger.

Melis, C. (1997). *Intelligence: A cognitive-energetic approach.* Wageningen, The Netherlands: Ponsen & Looijen BV.

Mulholland, T. M., Pellegrino, J. W., & Glaser, R. (1980). Components of geometric analogy solution. *Cognitive Psychology, 12*, 252–284.

Mumaw, R. J., Pellegrino, J. W., Kail, R. V., & Carter, P. (1984). Different slopes for different folks: Process analysis of spatial aptitude. *Memory & Cognition, 12*, 515–521.

Newell, A. (1980). Resoning, problem-solving, and decision processes: The problem space as a fundamental category. In R. Nickerson (Ed.), *Attention and performance VIII* (pp. 693–718). Hillsdale, NJ: Erlbaum.

Newell, A., & Simon, H. A. (1961). GPS, a program that simulates human thought. In E. A. Feigenbaum & J. Feldman (Eds.), *Computers and thought* (pp. 279–296). New York: McGraw-Hill.

Newell, A., & Simon, H. A. (1972). *Human problem solving.* Englewood Cliffs, NJ: Prentice Hall.

Nichols, P. D. (1994). A framework for developing cognitively diagnostic assessment. *Review of Educational Research, 64*, 575–603.

Oberauer, K. (1993). Die Koordination kognitiver Operationen – eine Studie zum Zusammenhang von Intelligenz und "working memory" [The coordination of cognitive operations – A study on the relation between intelligence and working memory]. *Zeitschrift für Psychologie, 201*, 57–84.

Oberauer, K., Süß, H.-M., Schulze, R., Wilhelm, O., & Wittmann, W. W. (1996). *Working memory capacity – Facets of a cognitive ability construct.* (Berichte des Lehrstuhls Psychologie II, Universität Mannheim [University of Mannheim Department of Psychology II Reports] Heft 7, Jahrgang 1996) Mannheim, Germany: University of Mannheim, Lehrstuhl für Psychologie II [Department of Psychology].

Palmer, S. E. (1977). Hierarchical structure in perceptual representation. *Cognitive Psychology, 9*, 441–474.

Pellegrino, J. W. (1985). Inductive reasoning ability. In R. J. Sternberg (Ed.), *Human abilities: An information-processing approach* (pp. 195–225). New York: W. H. Freeman.

Pellegrino, J. W., & Glaser, R. (1980). Components of inductive reasoning. In R. E. Snow, P.-A. Federico, & W. E. Montague (Eds.), *Aptitude, learning, and instruction: Vol. 1. Cognitive process analyses of aptitude* (pp. 177–218). Hillsdale, NJ: Erlbaum.

Pellegrino, J. W., & Glaser, R. (1982). Analyzing aptitudes for learning: Inductive reasoning. In R. Glaser (Ed.), *Advances in instructional psychology* (Vol. 2, pp. 269–345). Hillsdale, NJ: Erlbaum.

Pellegrino, J. W., & Kail, R. (1982). Process analyses of spatial aptitude. In R. J. Sternberg (Ed.), *Advances in the*

psychology of human intelligence (Vol. 1, pp. 311–366). Hillsdale, NJ: Erlbaum.

Pellegrino, J. W., & Lyon, D. R. (1979). The components of a componential analysis [Review of the book *Intelligence, information processing and analogical reasoning: The componential analysis of human abilities*]. *Intelligence, 3*, 169–186.

Piaget, J. (1963). *The psychology of intelligence.* New York: International Universities Press.

Pieters, J. P. M. (1983). Sternberg's additive factor method and underlying psychological processes: Some theoretical considerations. *Psychological Bulletin, 93*, 411–426.

Poltrock, S. E., & Brown, P. (1984). Individual differences in visual imagery and spatial ability. *Intelligence, 8*, 93–138.

Raaheim, K. (1988). Intelligence and task novelty. In R. J. Sternberg (Ed.), *Advances in the psychology of human intelligence* (Vol. 4, pp. 73–97). Hillsdale, NJ: Erlbaum.

Raven, J. C. (1938/1965). *Progressive matrices.* New York: The Psychological Corporation.

Roberts, R. D. (1995). *Speed of processing within the structure of human cognitive abilities.* Unpublished doctoral dissertation, University of Sydney, Australia.

Robinson, C. S., & Hayes, J. R. (1978). Making inferences about relevance in understanding problems. In R. Revlin & R. E. Mayer (Eds.), *Human reasoning* (pp. 195–206). Washington, DC: V. H. Winston.

Rosch, E. R., & Mervis, C. B. (1975). Family resemblances: Studies in the internal structure of categories. *Cognitive Psychology, 7*, 573–605.

Rumelhart, D. E. (1980). *Understanding understanding.* (Tech. Rep. 8101). San Diego: University of California, Center for Human Information Processing.

Rumelhart, D. E., & Abrahamson, A. A. (1973). A model for analogical reasoning. *Cognitive Psychology, 5*, 1–28.

Ryle, G. (1949). *The concept of mind.* London: Hutchinson's University Library.

Salthouse, T. A., Babcock, R. L, Mitchell, D. R. D., Palmon, R., & Skovronek, E. (1990). Sources of individual differences in spatial visualization ability. *Intelligence, 14*, 187–230.

Schank, R. C. (1978). *Interestingness: Controlling inferences* (Computer Science Research Report No. 145). New Haven, CT: Yale University.

Schank, R. C. (1980). How much intelligence is there in artificial intelligence? *Intelligence, 4*, 1–14.

Schank, R. C. (1984). *The explanation game* (Computer Science Research Report No. 307). New Haven, CT: Yale University.

Schunk, D. H., & Zimmerman, B. J. (Eds.). (1994). *Self-regulation of learning and performance: Issues and educational applications.* Hillsdale, NJ: Erlbaum.

Sharp, S. E. (1898/1899). Individual psychology: A study in psychological method. *American Journal of Psychology, 10*, 329–391.

Sheehan, K. M. (1997). *A tree-based approach to proficiency scaling and diagnostic assessment* (Research Report 97-9). Princeton, NJ: Educational Testing Service.

Shepard, R. N., & Cooper, L. A. (1982). *Mental images and their transformation*. Cambridge, MA: MIT Press.

Shepard, R. N., & Metzler, J. (1971). Mental rotation of three-dimensional objects. *Science, 171*, 701–703.

Simon, D. P., & Simon, H. A. (1978). Individual differences in solving physics problems. In R. S. Siegler (Ed.), *Children's thinking: What develops?* (pp. 325–348). Hillsdale, NJ: Erlbaum.

Simon, H. A. (1979). *Models of thought*. New Haven, CT: Yale University Press.

Simon, H. A., & Kotovsky, K. (1963). Human acquisition of concepts for sequential patterns. *Psychological Review, 70*, 534–546.

Sincoff, J. B., & Sternberg, R. J. (1987). Two faces of verbal ability [editorial]. *Intelligence, 11*, 263–276.

Snow, R. E. (1978). Theory and method for research on aptitude processes. *Intelligence, 2*, 225–278.

Snow, R. E. (1980a). Aptitude and achievement. *New Directions for Testing and Measurement, 5*, 39–59.

Snow, R. E. (1980b). Aptitude processes. In R. E. Snow, P.-A. Federico, & W. E. Montague (Eds.), *Aptitude, learning, and instruction: Vol. 1. Cognitive process analyses of aptitude* (pp. 27–64). Hillsdale, NJ: Erlbaum.

Snow, R. E. (1981). Toward a theory of aptitude for learning: Fluid and crystallized abilities and their correlates. In M. P. Friedman, J. P. Das, & N. O'Connor (Eds.), *Intelligence and learning* (pp. 345–362), New York: Plenum.

Snow, R. E. (1989). Aptitude-treatment interaction as a framework for research on individual differences in learning. In R. J. Sternberg & R. Glaser (Eds.), *Learning and individual differences: Advances in theory and research* (pp. 13–59). New York: W. H. Freeman.

Snow, R. E. (1994). Abilities in academic tasks. In R. J. Sternberg & R. K. Wagner (Eds.), *Mind in context: Interactionist perspectives on human intelligence* (pp. 3–37). Cambridge, UK: Cambridge University Press.

Snow, R. E., & Lohman, D. F. (1989). Implications of cognitive psychology for educational measurement. In R. Linn (Ed.), *Educational measurement* (3rd ed., pp. 263–331). New York: Macmillan.

Snow, R. E., Corno, L., & Jackson, D., III. (1996). Individual differences in affective and conative functions. In D. C. Berliner & R. C. Calfee (Eds.), *Handbook of educational psychology* (pp. 243–310). New York: Simon & Schuster Macmillan.

Snow, R. E., Kyllonen, P. C., & Marshalek, B. (1984). The topography of ability and learning correlations. In R. J. Sternberg (Ed.), *Advances in the psychology of human intelligence* (Vol. 2, pp. 47–104). Hillsdale, NJ: Erlbaum.

Spearman, C. E. (1927). *The abilities of man*. London: Macmillan.

Spilsbury, G. (1992). Complexity as a reflection of the dimensionality of a task. *Intelligence, 16*, 31–45.

Spiro, R. J., & Myers, A. (1984). Individual differences and underlying cognitive processes. In P. D. Pearson, R. Bar, M. L. Kamil, & P. Mosenthal (Eds.), *Handbook of reading research* (pp. 471–501). New York: Longman.

Stankov, L. (1988). Single tests, competing tasks and their relationship to broad factors of intelligence. *Personality and Individual Differences, 9*, 25–33.

Sternberg, R. J. (1977). *Intelligence, information processing, and analogical reasoning: The componential analysis of human abilities*. Hillsdale, NJ: Erlbaum.

Sternberg, R. J. (1980). Representation and process in linear syllogistic reasoning. *Journal of Experimental Psychology: General, 109*, 119–159.

Sternberg, R. J. (1985). *Beyond IQ: A triarchic theory of human intelligence*. Cambridge, UK: Cambridge University Press.

Sternberg, R. J. (1986). Toward a unified theory of human reasoning. *Intelligence, 10*, 281–314.

Sternberg, R. J. (1990). *Metaphors of mind: Conceptions of the nature of intelligence*. Cambridge, UK: Cambridge University Press.

Sternberg, R. J., & Gardner, M. K. (1983). Unities in inductive reasoning. *Journal of Experimental Psychology: General, 112*, 80–116.

Sternberg, R. J., & McNamara, T. P. (1985). The representation and processing of information in real-time verbal comprehension. In S. E. Embretson (Ed.), *Test design: Developments in psychology and psychometrics* (pp. 21–43). New York: Academic Press.

Sternberg, R. J., & Powell, J. S. (1983). Comprehending verbal comprehension. *American Psychologist, 38*, 878–893.

Sternberg, R. J., & Rifkin, B. (1979). The development of analogical reasoning processes. *Journal of Experimental Child Psychology, 27*, 195–232.

Sternberg, R. J., & Weil, E. M. (1980). An aptitude-strategy interaction in linear syllogistic reasoning. *Journal of Educational Psychology, 72*, 226–234.

Swiney, J. F. (1985). A study of executive processes in intelligence. Unpublished doctoral dissertation, Stanford University, Stanford, CA.

Tatsuoka, K. (1995). Architecture of knowledge structures and cognitive diagnosis: A statistical pattern recognition and classification approach. In P. D. Nichols, S. F. Chipman, & R. L. Brennan (Eds.), *Cognitively diagnostic assessment* (pp. 327–360). Hillsdale, NJ: Erlbaum.

Tatsuoka, K. (1997). Rule-space methodology. Unpublished paper. Princeton, NJ: Educational Testing Service.

Thorndike, R. L., & Hagen, E. P. (1993). *The Cognitive Abilities Test*. Itasca, IL: Riverside Publishing.

Thurstone, L. L. (1924). *The nature of intelligence*. New York: Harcourt, Brace.

Thurstone, L. L. (1938). Primary mental abilities. *Psychometric Monographs, 1*.

van Daalen-Kapteijns, M. M., & Elshout-Mohr, M. (1981). The acquisition of word meanings as a cognitive learning process. *Journal of Verbal Learning and Verbal Behavior, 20,* 386–399.

Vandenberg, S. G., & Kruse, A. R. (1978). Mental rotations: Group tests of three-dimensional spatial visualization. *Perceptual and Motor Skills, 47,* 599–604.

Wechsler, D. (1991). *Manual for the Wechsler Intelligence Scale for Children – III.* San Antonio, TX: The Psychological Corp.

Werner, H., & Kaplan, E. (1952). The acquisition of word meanings: A developmental study. *Monographs of the Society for Research in Child Development* (No. 51).

West, T. G. (1991). *In the mind's eye.* Buffalo, NY: Prometheus Books.

Whitely, S. E. (1976). Solving verbal analogies: Some cognitive components of intelligence test items. *Journal of Educational Psychology, 68,* 234–242.

Whitely, S. E. (1980). Modeling aptitude test validity from cognitive components. *Journal of Educational Psychology, 72,* 750–769.

Whitely, S. E., & Barnes, G. M. (1979). The implication of processing event sequences for theories of analogical reasoning. *Memory & Cognition, 7,* 323–331.

Winograd, T. (1972). Understanding natural language. *Cognitive Psychology, 3,* 1–191.

Winograd, T. (1975). Frames and the declarative-procedural controversy. In D. G. Dobrow & A. Collins (Eds.), *Representation and understanding: Studies in cognitive science* (pp. 185–210). New York: Academic Press.

Wright, D., & Dennis, I. (1999). Exploiting the speed-accuracy trade-off. In P. L. Ackerman, P. C. Kyllonen, & R. D. Roberts (Eds.), *Learning and individual differences: Process, trait, and content determinants* (pp. 231–243). Washington, DC: American Psychological Association.

Zimmerman, W. S. (1954). The influence of item complexity upon the factor composition of a spatial visualization test. *Educational and Psychological Measurement, 14,* 106–119.

CHAPTER FIFTEEN

Artificial Intelligence

ROGER C. SCHANK AND BRENDON TOWLE

INTRODUCTION: WHAT ARTIFICIAL INTELLIGENCE IS NOT

What is artificial intelligence (AI)? You almost certainly have some ideas. Maybe you think that AI is the quest to build HAL. Maybe you think that AI is the quest to build Deep Blue. Maybe you think that AI is a grand waste of time, or impossible, or a bad idea.

These perspectives are indicative of a wide range of thinking about AI. The field of AI itself includes a similarly wide range of thinking about both what AI is and about how it should be achieved. A brief catalog of research areas that are typically included under the heading of AI includes the following:*

- Robotics
- Natural Language Processing
- Planning
- Neural Nets
- Computer Vision
- Machine Learning
- Computer Game Playing
- Rule-based Systems
- Case-based Reasoning, and many more.

Concisely defining a field that includes such diverse research areas is a nearly impossible task. Computer game playing, for example, shares little if anything with natural language processing, and yet these are both lumped under the title of AI. Any defi-

nition that would include both of those fields might well be so inclusive as to be meaningless.

On the surface, this chapter will be taking on not only that impossible task but two others as well: summarizing the history of AI and the current state of the field. Our hope is not to succeed comprehensively at any one of those tasks, although this chapter will certainly work in those directions. Instead, our hope is that this chapter will provide an insight into some of the reasons we, and generations of AI researchers before and after us, find, and will find, AI such an exciting and interesting field. Further, we hope that this chapter will provide useful points of reference for examining and evaluating further AI contributions, allowing the reader to make intelligent judgments about what is good and bad AI.

Noted science fiction author and critic Damon Knight, when asked, "What is science fiction?" is supposed to have responded with, "Science fiction is what we point at when we say 'That's science fiction.'" Although somewhat circular and insular, the analogous definition may be the most accurate for the AI community as well. Artificial intelligence is composed of those things that the AI community has collectively identified as AI. Typically, these things have involved attempting to get computers to solve problems that are ill-defined, extremely complicated, or seemingly require a human, as is the case in many of the items on the list above.

Many of the problems that AI has attempted to solve are computing problems that are *computationally intractable*; no algorithm, no matter how well written and efficiently executed, can hope to solve them consistently. This would seem to pose an

---

* Those familiar with the field will note that we have mixed techniques and goals in this particular list.

341

insoluble problem for AI: How can you use a computer to solve a problem if there are no algorithms for solving it? The answer lies in how AI programs use knowledge about the world to help in their problem solving.

Artificial intelligence programs often use *heuristics* to help find the solution. A heuristic is essentially a rule of thumb – a comment about certain kinds of problems that will often help to find the correct solution quickly but will occasionally be completely wrong. Clever use of heuristics can turn intractable computational problems into merely difficult ones. However, clever use of heuristics depends on having a proper analysis of the domain and having appropriately represented the knowledge about the domain so that the computer can use it. This task of analyzing the domain and determining how to embody knowledge about that domain into a useful form in a computer program is called *knowledge representation*.

One of the major trends in knowledge representation over the past 20 years has been the "flight from syntax"; the tendency to move away from rules and knowledge about the *form* of objects or statements in the world towards rules and knowledge about the *content* of objects in the world. This has often also involved determining what people know about a given subject or task that allows them to perform it and attempting to get that knowledge into the computer in a usable form. As you read the descriptions of AI programs in the rest of the chapter, you should ask yourself what sorts of knowledge representation they seem to use and if it seems plausible that people use the same sort of knowledge.

AI BACKGROUND: MAKING SENSE OF IT ALL

Any discussion of AI will make more sense with some background information. One important distinction to make immediately is the difference between "strong" AI and "weak" AI. Strong AI is the attempt to make computer programs that think in the same manner and with the same depth and richness that humans do; that is, process information in the same way, reach the same sorts of conclusions, and so forth. This is the conception of AI that most philosophical arguments about it are concerned with. The strong AI hypothesis is that such computer programs are possible. Weak AI is simply the attempt to use human or potentially human processing techniques to get computers to solve hard problems; no claim is made that the computer is intelligent or necessarily an accurate simulation of human thought but merely that it solves some hard problem. Very little current AI research is truly strong. Although models are presented as psychological models, and AI programs use techniques that are inspired by human performance and methods, very few AI researchers claim that their programs are actually thinking like people.

From here, we would like to cover four major areas of background information. First, we will present the distinction between symbolic and connectionist approaches to AI, which have essentially polarized the field. Virtually every current AI project can be categorized as taking either a connectionist approach, a symbolic approach, or trying to merge the two. Second, two of the most persistent critiques of AI will be addressed, both of which continue to mislead people about the nature and goals of AI. Third, we will discuss some of the common misconceptions about the mechanics of AI and how those misconceptions have influenced AI research. Finally, this section will conclude with a short discussion about the mechanics of AI.

Different Approaches to the Hard Problems

As already discussed, AI is a large field, and many different approaches are being taken in research.* However, we would be remiss if we did not comment on the major difference that has dominated AI research for almost the past 20 years: the distinction between *symbolic* AI and *connectionist* AI.

Symbolic AI is rooted in the idea of a *physical symbol system* presented by Newell and Simon (1976). In a physical symbol system, a symbol is simply a token that is taken to stand for something in the world outside the system. It need not have any meaning or content to an outside observer, but within the system it is understood to represent something outside the system. A physical symbol system processes these symbols in accordance with rules in the system. The physical symbol system's hypothesis is that

---

* Readers who are interested in a further discussion of the different approaches are invited to investigate, for example, the many flavors of machine learning as described in Buchanan and Wilkins (1993).

a physical symbol system is sufficient to account for intelligent human reasoning.

As an example, consider a robot whose task is to arrange blocks on a table according to the instructions given to it by a human.* Given a set of alphabet blocks with the letters A, B, and C, the human might tell the robot to make a tower that has block A on top of block B on top of block C. This robot would need to have knowledge about the relationships among blocks in the world, about the actions available to it, about the results of its actions, about the conditions necessary for it to take actions, and about how to sequence actions to achieve certain goals.

To take just one example, the robot would need to know that one result of picking up a block is that the robot is now holding the block.† The robot would "know" this, of course, because it had been programmed with a bit of computer data that allowed it to know this. Taken individually, any given piece of knowledge in a symbolic AI program looks silly and obvious; *of course* the result of picking up a block is that the robot is holding the block. However, the robot does not know that (or anything else) when we start; all of the knowledge has to be put in by the programmers. (As will be discussed shortly, there are no magic bullets.) Further, having a collection of knowledge such as this, if the knowledge base is large enough, can allow the robot to perform actions toward a goal in the blocks world. In addition to the piece of knowledge given above, the robot would know, for example, that if the result of an action matches a goal currently held by the robot, that action is an appropriate action to consider taking.

Connectionist AI (popularly known as "neural nets," among other things) has its roots in the idea of *perceptrons* (Minsky & Papert, 1969) and is codified in Parallel Distributed Processing (Rumelhart, McClelland, & the PDP Research Group, 1986). Consider, for a moment, a neuron. Simplified to an enormous degree, a neuron is essentially a device with some large number of inputs that fires an output when the total input exceeds some threshold. Now, true neurons are not digital devices, but we can imagine a low-fidelity simulation of a neuron that simply takes a function over all of the inputs and computes a digital output based on that function. Generally, for simplicity, each input is assumed to be either $+1$ or -1, and the function computed is simply a weighted sum of the inputs, which is then normalized back to either $+1$ or -1.

A connectionist network, in its most basic form, is a set of these simulated neurons connected as follows: A layer of neurons is connected to the input from the outside world. This layer is then connected to one or more *hidden layers*, which are then connected to the output layer, which then could be connected to effectors or used as indicators of the state of the world.

One fairly standard use of a connectionist network of this sort is in computer vision in which the task is to identify a given picture as one of a discrete set of elements. (For example, we might want to identify a printed letter as one of the capital letters A–Z.) In this case, the typical approach is to have one input node for each pixel in the picture being considered and one output node for each potential result.

Note that it is relatively difficult to talk about the meaning of the knowledge representation in a connectionist program. Each individual node in the network certainly has some influence on the final output, and it seems plausible that a given node might, for the letter recognition task given above, have some meaning like "if my output is positive, the letter has a horizontal crossbar; if my output is negative, the letter has no horizontal crossbar." However, there is no good way to determine what these meanings might be for any given connectionist network.

DIFFERENT TOOLS FOR DIFFERENT JOBS. Which of these perspectives (symbolic and connectionist) is right? Well, both of them, and neither of them. There is certainly cognitive evidence to suggest that some forms of symbolic AI are an accurate description of human reasoning; see, for example, Bower et al.'s work on scripts (Bower, Black, & Turner, 1979). Equally certain, however, is that the brain is a neural architecture, and although we may not have arrived at a useful neural model yet, there ought to be one, at least in theory. However, deciding which method should be used to solve a

---

* This domain, known as *blocks world*, is one of the most frequent domains used in early AI programs. Although it has many problems as far as generating useful AI theories is concerned (the real world is much more complicated than a set of blocks on a table), it does make for a useful domain in which to provide examples.

† This is only one result of that action; the robot would need to have separate knowledge about the fact that the block is no longer where it was.

given AI problem, in general, is more a question of choosing the right tool for the problem rather than choosing the best tool. Symbolic methods have proven useful for solving problems in which the representation of the problem is well defined, whereas connectionist methods have proven useful for solving problems such as vision or speech recognition in which the representation is less clear.

Critiques of AI

Artificial intelligence, particularly "strong" AI, has been a target of philosophers ever since Lady Lovelace observed that Babbage's Analytical Engine might be used to compose music. Many of these critiques revolve around religious conceptions of "soul," or are made by people whose understanding of AI is incomplete or inaccurate. Two particularly pernicious critiques, however, are those leveled by Searle and Penrose; it is worth discussing these briefly.

SEARLE'S CHINESE ROOM. In what may be the most influential thought experiment in the history of AI, Searle (Searle, 1980) proposed what has come to be called the Chinese room experiment. Imagine building a set of rules (written in English) that associate Chinese characters with other Chinese characters. Now, imagine that these rules describe completely the process by which a particular individual might have a conversation in Chinese, with the first set of Chinese glyphs in each rule corresponding to the query, and the second set of Chinese glyphs corresponding to the response. Finally, imagine a man who speaks only English in a closed room. We pass a paper containing Chinese glyphs into the room. He looks through the rules until he finds the rule that matches the glyphs passed in, copies the response from the rule onto another sheet of paper, and passes that paper out.

If the rules are properly written, it will look to observers outside the room as if the room understands Chinese because it can hold a written conversation in Chinese. Searle's argument, roughly stated, goes as follows:*

- Clearly the room does not (and cannot) understand Chinese, because it is just a room;
- Equally clearly, the book does not (and cannot) understand Chinese;
- The man in the room does not (and cannot)* understand Chinese because all he is doing is following the rules provided by the book;
- Because none of the components of the room are capable of understanding Chinese and because these components are structurally identical to the components of a computer (an input–output device, a set of rules, and a means of executing those rules), computers are incapable of understanding language, and thus AI is impossible.

For those who believe (as we do) that strong AI is at least a theoretical possibility, there are two main responses to Searle's argument. First, although none of the components of the system understand Chinese, the system taken as a whole can be said to understand Chinese. We empathize with the man in the room because we are people. However, nobody really expects a single neuron or cluster of neurons to "understand" what the entire brain is doing or to "know" what we know; equating the understanding of the person in the room with the understanding of the entire system is the same kind of mistake.

Second, Searle minimizes the amount of knowledge and work that goes into the book of rules. Earlier we mentioned the centrality of knowledge representation in AI efforts. Knowledge representation is a difficult and time-consuming task, even for experts in the field. In our discussion of Eliza later in this chapter we will describe a small program that uses conversational rules to carry on a poor facsimile of a conversation in a limited domain – and not even very well, but this program required a substantial amount of work.

To illustrate the difficulty of writing these rules, imagine the effort it would take to write the rules that you use for conversations with only a single person on only a single topic; for the sake of argument, let us pick conversations with your mother about what to have for dinner. To do this, you would

---

* Searle also spends some time discussing whether a computer could have *intentionality* (roughly, the quality of being able to want to do something); we will ignore that part of the discussion here.

* Searle does not claim that the man is necessarily incapable of learning to understand Chinese but merely that the setup of the problem requires that he cannot understand Chinese in the current situation.

need to know about your own personal likes and dislikes, about your mother's likes and dislikes, about the kinds of foods that typically are served for dinner, about the kinds of food combinations that work and do not work, about what things are and are not food, and much much more. Building a set of rules that would allow the man in the room to appear to be holding a conversation in Chinese (with any person, on any topic) would embody a complete and fantastic understanding of both Chinese and of the person whose desires and knowledge were being simulated by the rules. This kind of detailed knowledge representation, although "just a set of rules," is much more useful and difficult than that characterization would let on.

PENROSE'S GÖDEL ARGUMENT. Penrose, in a series of popular scientific books (Penrose, 1989, 1994) has also produced an argument against the possibility of strong AI, which goes roughly as follows:

- Gödel's theorem states that every sufficiently complex mathematical system will contain propositions that are true but unprovable within that system;
- Human mathematicians are able to evaluate the truth of certain classes of unprovable propositions;
- Therefore, human mathematicians must be using something other than formal mathematics to evaluate mathematical truth; thus, human thinking is fundamentally nonmathematical in nature and strong AI is impossible to produce with any mathematical system.

Essentially, this is a claim that mathematical intuition is inherently nonalgorithmic; that whatever we do to attempt to reproduce intelligence on a computer (or any other mathematically based device) is doomed to miss that portion of human intelligence.

Again, there are essentially two arguments against Penrose's. The first is the mathematical argument. Gödel's theorem speaks about the unprovability of propositions *within the system that contains them*; it says nothing about the provability of those propositions in different formal systems that *contain* the original formal system. In fact, many propositions that cannot be proven within the smallest formal system containing them can, in fact, be proven within a larger formal system. So, all that is necessary for human mathematicians to be using formal mathematics to decide truth is for them to be using a different formal system than the one they are analyzing.

The second argument is an intuitive one. The claim that intuition is nonalgorithmic is a claim that is relatively easy to sympathize with – we do not know what we do when we have intuitions or gut feelings about a situation, and thus it is easy to assume that there is some sort of magic going on. However, the reason that intuition appears so magical is simply that the processes that drive it are unavailable for conscious introspection. We can easily imagine, for example, a system that reproduced intuitive responses purely algorithmically by remembering past events according to some set of features and by responding according to whatever past event seemed most similar to the current event.[*] Although this does not mean that intuition is necessarily an algorithmic process, it does suggest that it could be.

Also, do not be confused by the fact that heuristics are described as an AI technique to avoid intractable algorithms; this does not mean that intelligence is inherently nonalgorithmic. Heuristics are used in places where the algorithm that is guaranteed to be correct is intractable. The process of using heuristics on a computer still involves an algorithm; every computer program does. However, the algorithm that uses the heuristics (or the algorithm that remembered the past events described above) would not be guaranteed to reach the correct answer. This actually fits well with what we know about human intuition; it often reaches correct conclusions based on little evidence but also can reach incorrect conclusions.

The Mechanics: What AI Does Not Mean

Within the programming community, one question frequently asked about AI programs, particularly programs that use AI techniques to solve hard problems, is, Where is the AI? This question is often based on a misconception of what it means for a program to be an AI program; if the program does not look like one of the classical "AI things," then it must not be AI. To combat this, we will discuss three of the most common misconceptions about the

---

[*] This, in fact, is exactly how case-based reasoning programs work; see below.

nature of the mechanics of AI (these are three of the four perspectives discussed in Schank, 1991).

The first misconception is that AI means magic bullets, that is, somehow getting the computer, with the help of some new technology, to solve the problem for us (i.e., become intelligent on its own). The second misconception is that AI means getting a computer do to whatever currently seems impossible for computers to do. The third misconception is that AI means machine learning, that is, getting the computer to learn things on its own given some starting method of learning.

AI DOES NOT MEAN MAGIC BULLETS. The "magic bullet" perspective on AI says that much of the hard work in knowledge representation is actually unnecessary. Because the work is so hard, this view says, Why not let the computer do all the work? If we make the machine efficient enough so that it can make all the connections between the things that are related, intelligence will just emerge for free as a byproduct of these connections. Proponents of this view usually also claim that the machine will make connections that we have previously been unable to see.

The reason this is called the "magic bullet" view of AI is that there is the assumption that we are missing one crucial piece of the puzzle. Just as the invention of the transistor produced radical changes in what was technologically feasible in electronic devices, this view assumes that when the new breakthrough comes, AI will become a simple problem.

This analogy illustrates exactly how this view misses the point, however. All that the transistor did for electronic devices was to replace the vacuum tube with something that performed the same function but was much smaller and cooler. In principle, anything built with transistors today could have been built with vacuum tubes; it might be substantially bigger than New York and take more power to run than all of the energy available in the United States, but it would be possible in principle.

This view is not a view of AI that will result in any long-term success. In AI, as in most fields of intellectual endeavor, there are no magic bullets and no substitute for hard work and understanding. If we are to get AI to work, it will be simply by understanding intelligence and programming the computer to do that rather than by having some magic invention do all the work for us. This understanding and programming, of course, will take a fantastic amount of work. The Cyc project (Lenat & Guha, 1990) is aimed at codifying human commonsense knowledge in a form that a computer can use. Although attacking tasks of this magnitude is an important goal for AI research, Cyc lacks a task focus to guide the knowledge representation. The magnitude of the task forces Cyc to make many assumptions about the eventual use of the knowledge, and the lack of a task focus makes it more difficult to get those assumptions right.

AI DOES NOT MEAN DOING THE IMPOSSIBLE. The best chess player in the world is a computer. At one time, this was thought to be impossible; expert game playing was "obviously" the domain of humans, and machines would never be able to approach human competence, even in relatively constrained aspects of chess such as endgames. The "doing the impossible" view of AI is the perspective that says that AI means getting a computer to do whatever it is that computers cannot do. This is how machine chess would have been viewed as AI in the 1960s, but it is not today because we have done it. Under this perspective, a good computer Go player is still AI, as is conversational-level natural language processing on arbitrary topics, as is visual recognition of arbitrary objects.

This perspective has the hazard that it ignores the little steps that lead up to the seemingly impossible. Deep Blue defeated Kasparov recently, but GNU Chess, freely available for years, is good enough to beat most human players when put on its most advanced setting; surely, if chess playing is intelligent,[*] GNU Chess is nearly as intelligent as Deep Blue. Further, "the impossible" is a floating target; under this view, as soon as a computer can do something, that something does not require a substantial amount of intelligence anymore.

AI DOES NOT MEAN MACHINE LEARNING. This final perspective is actually a bit backwards, for building any strong AI program would, in fact,

---

[*] Chess playing as humans play chess is probably a sign of intelligence, but that is irrelevant to this particular example.

involve machine learning. When dealing with people, whom we expect to be intelligent, we often consider them dumb if they do not learn from their environment. For example, when Hofstadter comments on the description of a certain kind of wasp that engages in repetitive and unnecessary behavior (Hofstadter, 1979), everyone agrees that the wasp is pretty stupid. Why? Because it did not learn anything from the events going on around it. Under this view, AI would involve building computer systems that learn from the world around them, and in fact, a computer system that learned something about the world in which it was acting would be truly intelligent.

For the computer to learn something, however, it would have to be engaged in a real-world task of some sort. Human learning only occurs when we are surprised by something in the world; we have expectations about what we are doing or what will happen, and they fail in some way, thus allowing us to learn something new about the world (Schank, 1982; Schank, 1986). However, the world surprises us because there is a lot going on in it. In the world of a typical AI system, very little is going on; the possibilities for surprise are few. Further, the typical AI system is not interacting with the world in a way that would allow it to have failed expectations.

Because very few AI systems are actually engaged in a task from which they might learn something, and because funders of AI research typically want a system that works immediately, not one that will work as soon as it has learned how to solve the problem, defining AI as machine learning would make AI research difficult to achieve. Further, although any strong AI program would, in fact, do machine learning, it is possible to do useful AI research without machine learning, as the rest of this chapter will illustrate.

AI Research in Practice

Given the preceding description of what AI is not and our emphasis on knowledge representation mentioned earlier, it might be expected that AI in practice involves extensive investigation of human intelligence. Although some AI research does involve this (see, for example, the descriptions of SAM and CHEF below), the unfortunate truth is that the practical side of AI research often looks

very different from cognitive science and human intelligence.* Artificial intelligence programs often do what is called problem solving. Although this term has many different meanings in different academic communities, a generally accepted meaning within the AI community is the following:

The process of taking the description of a start state and a goal state and producing from them a list of operators (alternately called a solution or a plan) that, taken in order, will change the start state into the goal state.

An example from the blocks world might be that to change the start state {(ON X TABLE) (ON Y TABLE)} into the goal state {(ON X Y) (ON Y TABLE)}, the plan ((PICKUP X) (PUT-ON X Y)) will suffice.

Statespace search (often just called search) is the process of enumerating and examining the potential states that a system could be in. So, for example, one very simple way of finding the plan given above would be to list the result of applying every operator available to the system to the start state. If any of those are equivalent to the goal state, then that action composes the entire plan; otherwise, try applying every action to each of the resulting states. This process of simply generating every possible state of the system and examining them all is often called *brute-force* search.

A brief examination of the brute-force search process described above will indicate that, for all but the most simple of systems and the shortest of plans, the system will spend an inordinate amount of time doing fruitless or wasteful searching. Further, this search process is subject to the "combinatorical explosion" problem; the size of the search space grows exponentially with the number of steps in the plan under consideration, which results in a search space that is completely unsearchable for even relatively small plans. Much of the historical work in AI has consisted of finding ways of improving this process.

However, this emphasis on search completely overlooks the importance of knowledge representation and the fact that people solve problems in

* We say "unfortunately" not because these methods do not work or are not useful but because they are not (to us) as interesting as methods that attempt to reproduce human behavior.

a context. When a person builds a block tower, or writes a paper, or plans to go somewhere, he or she has a substantial amount of knowledge about the world that will be used in the task as well as a substantial amount of experience and knowledge about the task itself. Focusing on the search process as an end in and of itself will not help without appropriate knowledge representations to search through.

HISTORICAL AI RESEARCH

To this point, we have merely given an overview of the philosophical and practical issues involved in AI as well as a roundabout answer to the question: What is AI? Now, we will describe some of the most famous and important programs in the history of AI. The point here is not to provide a general introduction to the practice of AI; that would take a book in itself, and interested readers are encouraged to examine, for example, the book by Russell and Norvig (1995). Instead, the point is to use several of the programs from the early history of AI to illustrate current problems in building or evaluating AI programs.* We will look at programs in two of the areas that have tantalized AI researchers from the beginning: planning and game playing, and natural language processing (NLP).

Planning and Game-Playing Programs

We lump planning and game playing together because they are in some sense similar; planning (as historically practiced within the AI community) is determining what to do in the case in which the world is unchanging, and game playing is determining what to do in the case in which the world is changing – specifically, changing because of the actions of an adversary. We will discuss three programs from the early history of planning here: Samuel's checkers program, which is the first game playing program; GPS, the first serious attempt at a computer-based cognitive theory of human problem solving; and CHEF, a planner whose methods were largely a response to the methods started by GPS.

SAMUEL'S CHECKERS. Samuel's checkers program (Samuel, 1963) is often given credit as being the first serious AI program and the first game-playing program. As the intellectual ancestor of Deep Blue, it deserves some attention.

The program actually did machine learning, which is a rarity even among game-playing programs today. The program had a function that evaluated the strength of board positions in terms of factors such as the number of kings, the number of potential kings, the piece advantage, and so on. Each of these factors was given a weight, and the sum of all the weighted factors was taken as the strength of a board position. The program would check what the strength of the board would be after each of its possible moves and make the move that resulted in the strongest board.*

Obviously, the success of this program is completely dependent on the exact details of the evaluation function used by the program; if the function accurately reflects the "goodness" of a board position, then the program will be very successful; if not, the program will be very unsuccessful. This is not an equation that even expert checker players are likely to be able to fill in accurately; experts are often unable to express their knowledge in a form that is usable by a machine.

Samuel solved this problem by simply starting with a function that looked like it might be close and building into the program the ability to change the function (i.e., learn) based on the results of games. The basic idea is simple; if a component of the function contributed to making a good move, make it slightly stronger; if a component contributed to making a bad move, make it slightly weaker. Of course, getting exact definitions of good and bad moves, as well as discovering which components led to good moves are both hard problems. In addition, a component that contributed to making a good move at one point in the game might also contribute to making a bad move later in the game. However, if the function is close enough, it can be used to provide feedback on itself; Samuel had the program play itself with only one copy learning. If

---

* Historical AI programs are good for this because they tend to focus on simpler domains and are easier to illustrate with simple examples. These same problems exist in current AI programs, however, which is why this analysis is worthwhile.

* Samuel's program actually did some lookahead and considered board positions that might result several turns later in the game; we will ignore that fact for purposes of this discussion.

the learning copy won, then its version of the function was kept.

In addition to being the first game-playing program in AI, Samuel's checkers program illustrates one of the great problems in AI programs; the problem of *scaleup*. The checkers program worked only because the domain is simple enough to allow the construction of a reasonable function for evaluating board positions and because the number of moves on any given turn is small enough so that brute-force lookahead can be done a fair number of turns in advance. Even so, this function was fairly complex, taking into account 16 different components of the board, and the program did not look ahead very many turns.

Consider for a moment a game like chess (or worse yet, Go) in which the board is much more complicated and the number of potential moves at any turn is much greater. Although we might be able to write an equation that described the strength of board positions in chess, we would be very unlikely to get it close enough so that it could be used to reinforce itself. Further, brute-force lookahead is just not feasible in chess; the number of possible moves makes it difficult to look ahead enough turns to matter. This suggests that writing a successful chess-playing program will take more than just lookahead (and indeed, the techniques used to build Deep Blue involved much more).

GENERAL PROBLEM SOLVER. Newell and Simon's General Problem Solver (GPS; Newell & Simon, 1961) was one of the earliest attempts at a general-purpose AI program and was influential in the formation of the physical symbol system hypothesis (see above). The GPS also pioneered the use of *means–ends analysis* as an AI technique for reducing the amount of search that a planning program needed to do.

The core idea of means–ends analysis is to consider the differences between the goal state and the start states and for the system to know what differences each available operator is good at reducing. Given a difference between the goal state and the current state, the system should choose the operator that reduces that difference by the greatest amount. Then, given the preconditions for each available operator, subgoals can be set up that would allow each operator to be used.

For example, assume that a robot is in Chicago (the start state), and that the goal state is to be in San Francisco. Further assume that the available operators are WALK, DRIVE, and TAKE-PLANE. TAKE-PLANE is the operator that creates the most change in location, and thus the system will choose that first, resulting in a plan that looks like (... TAKE-PLANE...),* where the ellipses represent uncompleted portions of the plan. However, TAKE-PLANE has a precondition of being at the airport. Given that, the system will produce a subgoal of being at the airport. DRIVE is the operation that is next most effective at changing location, and thus the system will now have a plan that looks like (... DRIVE TAKE-PLANE...). Finally DRIVE has a precondition that the robot be at the car, which WALK can be used to fulfill, resulting in a plan that looks like (WALK DRIVE TAKE-PLANE...). A similar process can be used to fill in the empty space at the end of the plan.

Means–ends analysis was certainly an improvement over existing methods of search, both functionally (seeming to work for more complex search processes) and philosophically (using more knowledge about the domain to guide search). However, this is still an impractical algorithm for extremely complex domains for two reasons. First, the search process is subject to the same exponential explosion that was discussed in the section on search. Second, incremental planning like this often has the problem that later parts of the plan undo things that have been accomplished in early parts of the plan. The simplest version of this problem is known as the Sussman anomaly† (Sussman, 1975), but it is a problem in many more subtle and complicated ways.

The most fundamental problem with GPS, however, is that it was proposed as a cognitive theory of human problem solving, yet it does not seem to

---

* A fully functional implementation of this algorithm would need to have many more details about the plan and would need to store the parameters of the operators as well; for example, (TAKE-PLANE OHARE SAN FRANCISCO). We will ignore these details for the purposes of illustration.

† The Sussman anomaly concerns building a tower of three blocks. Under certain conditions, certain planners will put the top block on the middle block first, which then requires them to take the top block off so that the middle block can be placed on the bottom block.

reflect what people actually do when solving a problem such as getting from Chicago to San Francisco. Any adult who has gone to the airport before (or indeed, taken any kind of a trip) will know that he or she has taken planes before and will remember the process of having gotten to the airport before; thus, he or she will not need to spend any cognitive energy planning the trip from first principles. GPS, however, suggests that every time a person comes upon a problem, he or she solve the problem from scratch.

CHEF. CHEF (Hammond, 1986) was a program that planned how to cook a new recipe by modifying old recipes according to a body of knowledge about how to modify old plans to apply in new situations. This embodies an approach to AI known as case-based reasoning (CBR) (Leake, 1996; Riesbeck & Schank, 1989), which is a cognitive theory that suggests that when solving a problem people simply remember an old problem that was similar to the current problem and adapt (or just reuse) the solution to that problem. These two parts of the CBR process are generally referred to as *retrieval* and *adaptation*.

Case-based reasoning was created largely as a response to the tendency in the AI community to write programs that reason from first principles. Obviously, when a human expert in a domain such as cooking is given a new stir-fry request, he or she does not need to think about whether or not to chop the meat; it is just a part of the standard procedure. Similarly, human experts in many domains use past experiences as an integral part of their reasoning processes.

CHEF worked by finding an old recipe similar to the recipe currently being requested and modifying that recipe according to rules about, among other things, the similarity of ingredients. For example, the user might come to CHEF with a request for a stir-fry containing beef and broccoli. In searching through its case memory, CHEF finds no stir-fry recipes that contain beef and broccoli, but it knows that beef and chicken are both meats, and broccoli and green peppers are both vegetables, and it finds a recipe for a chicken and green pepper stir-fry. It then substitutes the beef for the chicken, the broccoli for the green pepper, makes some changes to the cooking times and other ingredients based on knowledge about the differences between beef and chicken, and produces a recipe.*

The knowledge used by CHEF to adapt old cases to new problems was very domain-specific and programmed into the system in advance. As an early CBR program, it served more to demonstrate that CBR was possible in a particular domain than to advance any particular theory of case adaptation, but it is clear that any successful theory of CBR must have a strong way to adapt old cases. Early CBR systems such as CHEF typically used a library of case-adaptation rules to accomplish case adaptation; recent research (Leake, Kinley, & Wilson, 1996) has focused on the possibility of making case adaptation itself the subject of a CBR process.

Natural Language Processing Programs

Natural language processing (NLP) (and understanding) has been another domain that has enticed AI researchers from the beginning. The idea that a computer or other machine could somehow "understand" written natural language has been an attractive one for generations. We will discuss three NLP programs in this section: Eliza, one of the first programs to respond to natural language in a seemingly intelligent manner; SHRDLU, which took some of the ideas from Eliza and implemented them in a domain with some goals and other processing; and SAM, which took a completely different approach to the problem based on our understanding of how people understand natural language. Again, these programs are chosen to be representative of larger problems and issues in the field; you should look at them as examples and think about how the approach to knowledge representation compares with the knowledge that people have.

ELIZA. Eliza (Weizenbaum, 1966) is barely an AI program but is illustrative of some of the problems in evaluating AI programs. The premise of Eliza was that the program was a psychiatrist implemented on the computer; a user could come to the program and start talking about the problems he or she was having, and Eliza would respond and carry on a discussion with the user.

---

* CHEF actually had the additional capability of dealing with failures in the new recipes. However, the essential ideas of CBR are illustrated by this example.

People have been completely fooled by Eliza; they were convinced that they were talking to a real person. However, not even the designers of Eliza would claim that there is any intelligence in the program. In a structure reminiscent of Searle's Chinese Room experiment,* Eliza is simply a set of conversational rules, like the ones described below.

- If the user inputs a sentence containing the word "mother" or "mom," reply with "Tell me about your mother."
- If the user inputs a sentence of the form "I need X," reply with "How would it help you to have X?"

By searching through the rules to find the appropriate response to the user, and by having appropriate defaults in case no matching response is found, Eliza can appear intelligent to the user *as long as the user is playing along*. This is a problem in general when discussing AI programs; people tend to anthropomorphize the objects in their world, and anthropomorphizing an AI program tends to give it much more credit for intelligence than it probably deserves. There is just the barest minimum of intelligence in Eliza, but it can look remarkably intelligent to a user who's willing to play along.

SHRDLU. SHRDLU (Winograd, 1972) was a natural language understanding program in the blocks world domain. It maintained a simulation of a relatively complex blocks world (as these things go), and had a simulated robot that could move things around in the world in response to user commands expressed in natural language. So, you could ask SHRDLU "Where is the blue pyramid?," and it would reply with "The blue pyramid is on the table." After telling it, "Put the blue pyramid on the red cube," it would then know that the blue pyramid was on the red cube. It also had knowledge about clearing blocks so that other blocks could be stacked on top of them, and knowledge about which blocks had flat surfaces so that something could be stacked on top of them, and so forth.

In one sense, this was a landmark program; the simulated robot could do any of a number of things with the blocks, and explain why it did them, all in

natural language. Further, you could actually type in a command, and the simulated robot would execute that command in the simulated world, and then report back to you on the new state of the world.

However, the implementation of the natural language recognizer in SHRDLU was through a set of templates, each configured to match a particular command expected by the designers. In this respect, it was similar to Eliza, and not particularly an advance in language processing, especially not human language processing; people clearly can understand sentences even when they have not heard a similar sentence before.

SAM. SAM (Cullingford, 1978) was in many ways a response to the natural language approach taken by programs like SHRDLU and Eliza. The idea of SAM went as follows: People understand common everyday events (such as what happens in a restaurant) because they have a memory structure (which we shall call a *script*) that allows them to make helpful predictions about the events that will take place. So, for example, when you hear a short story that "Jack went into a restaurant and ordered a hamburger. He paid the bill and left," you are able to infer that Jack did in fact eat the hamburger even though that information is nowhere in the story.

SAM was built with scripts for restaurants, earthquakes, and terrorist attacks, and could answer questions accurately about a story – even about information that was not in the story directly. In this respect, it was a substantial advance over the previous methods of natural language understanding. The problem with SAM was actually getting the scripts into the machine in the first place; it was difficult and time consuming to program in the scripts, and even then the results needed much fine-tuning. This has been described elsewhere (Buchanan & Shortliffe, 1984; Buchanan, Sutherland, & Feigenbaum, 1970) as the *knowledge acquisition bottleneck*: the idea that when building an AI program, actually writing the algorithms is not the difficult part; defining and building accurate knowledge structures for those algorithms to work with is.

Another way of looking at the knowledge acquisition problem in SAM is by contrast with GPS. In GPS, the program does a lot of work at runtime to figure out the solution to whatever problem it is confronted with, and this work is considered to

---

* Eliza actually predated the Chinese room; the reminding is for readers who have been reading this chapter in order.

be the intelligence in GPS. In SAM, however, most of the work has been done in the preparation of the scripts before the program ever runs, and the program does very little at runtime. This is analogous to human problem solving; the more you know, the less work you have to do to solve a given problem.

CURRENT AI RESEARCH

Completely summarizing the current state of AI research is also an impossible task for a chapter of this size. The proceedings from the AAAI conference in 1996, for example, run to 1,600 pages, and that is just one of many conferences dealing with AI, not to mention the numerous journals related to the field. Thus, this section will not attempt to be comprehensive about the current state of AI. Instead, it will illustrate some of the issues involved in AI research as well as some of the reasons that AI research can be an exciting and interesting field by examining a couple of the more interesting or potentially useful recent (post-1990) works in the field.*

These works are chosen to emphasize and illustrate the different approaches and styles of AI discussed earlier in the chapter. Some questions to think about regarding these works are: Is it based on an accurate (or potentially accurate) model of human thinking? Does it claim to be? If the technique works for some small set of examples, how might it scale up to larger sets of examples? How would getting the program to work in one domain contribute to getting it to work in a different domain?

Agents

The idea of an agent has been around for quite some time. Simply, an agent is a software "entity" that performs some tasks for its user. Often these are information management or filtering tasks; any task that involves sorting through more information than a person can reasonably be expected to handle is a good candidate task for an agent. Also, these

agents have often taken the form of helpers; a complex piece of software might have embedded agents that could help the user to perform some complex task within the software.*

One of the most fertile areas for agent research, at this writing, is the Internet. The Internet puts a tremendous amount of information at the fingertips of the average person; however, this is not necessarily an advantage. Trying to get useful information from the Internet has been compared with trying to drink from a firehose; it may be possible, but it can be a lot of work without some additional tools, and it is as likely to cause people to become overwhelmed as it is to help them actually get anything useful. Agents are potentially an ideal solution to this problem; if an agent knew what a given user would find interesting, it could filter the tremendous amount of information coming in, leaving only the interesting bits. Similarly, if an agent knew where information was located, it could find it for the user in response to a query.

There are two current approaches to these agent problems roughly corresponding to these two problems of information filtering and information location. The approaches also roughly correspond to the GPS-like idea of solving the problem at runtime and the SAM-like idea of solving the problem before the user ever arrives at the computer.

INFORMATION FILTERING: RUNTIME DECISIONS. Syskill and Webert (Pazzani, Muramatsu, & Billsus, 1996) is a system that uses a feature-based analysis of Web pages to learn what a user is interested in and then offers predictions as to how interesting a user will find new pages. The essential idea is to analyze the different features (in the case of WWW pages, the features are words) present in the WWW pages and determine which features and sets of features are likely to be associated with pages that the user will either like or not like. Given that information, the system can then predict whether the user will like a new web page or not and make recommendations as to which links to follow.

INFOS (Mock, 1996) is a similar system for the classification of USENET articles. In addition to a

---

* Readers who are interested in a more complete (although also more detailed and technical) overview of the current state of AI can examine, for example, the AAAI conference proceedings, or *AI Magazine*, the quarterly publication of the AAAI. *Artificial Intelligence* also provides a good review of current research in the field.

* One example of an attempt to do this might be the Wizards used by many of the Microsoft programs to assist users in preparing a presentation, formatting a document, and so on.

feature-based analysis of the articles, INFOS uses WordNet (Miller, 1995), a database of English word meanings, to enhance the classification process, and also uses a CBR system to provide additional justification for the rating of the article based on the past ratings of articles by the user. However, INFOS does not use any juxtaposition of features to inform its decision making; an article is simply given a rating based on a weighted sum of the individual features present in it and then accepted or rejected based on that weighted sum.

Although both of these approaches have their advantages, neither of them seems to have the potential for long-term success. INFOS is plagued by its inability to consider conjunctions of features. The author mentioned the need to make the model something that the users of the system could modify but then did not discuss how or why that was important. Syskill and Webert, on the other hand, use a fairly sophisticated set of feature analyses, but the system has no way of even knowing, for example, that the words "protein" and "proteins" refer to the same thing; these words would be considered to be two separate features, and they would be analyzed separately.* A system that used the feature analysis from Syskill and Webert along with the case memory and linguistic analysis from INFOS would seem to have a much greater chance of success.

Again, the issue is not so much the algorithms used as the representation that the system uses to help it determine what a "good" article is. It is entirely possible, for example, that if a system understood that people often browse USENET or the WWW for different reasons (work, research, pleasure) and that the criteria for goodness are different depending on the reason, the system could make much more accurate predictions about whether or not the browser would like any particular article. Knowledge about the task and situating the task in its real-world context almost always make the job of an AI program much easier.

Information Location: Resource Compilation

Anyone familiar with USENET has seen references to the FAQ or FAQ list; a list of questions relevant to the domain of a particular newsgroup that come up so frequently that they (and their answers) have been compiled into a list. FAQFinder (Burke & Hammond, 1997; Burke, Hammond, Kulyikin, Lytinen, Tomuro, & Schoenberg, 1997) is a program that allows the user to type in a question and then tries to find an answer among the FAQs that the system has on file.

The core idea of FAQFinder is simple; treat each question as a case in a case-based retrieval process, in which each case in memory is a single question and answer pair and find the pair whose question most closely matches the input question. FAQFinder uses a feature vector composed of semantically important words from the question as the basis for the retrieval algorithm.

In order to work, FAQFinder makes several assumptions about the format of the FAQ files. These assumptions are both what makes it possible for FAQFinder to work and its Achilles' heel. FAQFinder assumes that the file is composed solely (other than some preliminary heading information) of question and answer pairs, that each question is completely self-contained, and that the question and answer pairs follow some standard formatting conventions. Although this is often the case, FAQs are not always so cooperative. When the FAQ is formatted differently, FAQFinder can fail to find an answer even if the user's question is a direct quote from one of the FAQs.*

This is not necessarily a failing of FAQFinder, for it is still possible to find the answers to many questions by using the FAQFinder system. Nor is this a phenomenon restricted exclusively to FAQFinder. Artificial intelligence researchers use the term *brittle* to describe a program likely to break if even slightly unexpected variations in working conditions occur. In general, an AI program that is extremely sensitive

---

* To be fair, the authors address this particular example in their plans for future work; however, they plan to use stemming (reducing all words to their identifying word stem, such as "protein" to catch all noun forms of proteins, or "observ" to catch all forms of the verb observe) as the solution. Although that will help address this particular problem, it will not address more complicated linguistic features such as synonyms.

* For example, the FAQFinder system as of November 1997 failed to find the answer to the question What is the difference between science fiction and fantasy?, despite that question's being a direct quote from the rec.arts.sf.written FAQ — one of the FAQs supported, but a FAQ that uses a relatively nonstandard format.

to the format (or other detailed characteristics) of its input will tend to be very brittle under those circumstances when the input does not conform to expectations. However, successfully determining regularities in the input and exploiting knowledge of those regularities are among the most potentially successful AI techniques. Any AI program that actually does something (as opposed to demonstrating some neat theoretical technique) will be operating in an environment that has regularities; the world is fairly consistent in very useful ways. Artificial intelligence programs that know what task they are performing and exploit that knowledge are much more likely to be successful in the real world.

Computer Vision: Applications

Computer vision was first used in the first blocks world programs; there were actual blocks on a table, and a camera hooked up to the computer provided the input for the program to construct plans. Since then, computer vision has become a field of its own within AI, drawing much attention and research. Although many of the advances in computer vision have been in the mathematical mechanics used to analyze the input stream from the camera, we choose not to concentrate on those here. Instead, we will concentrate on one of the potentially more interesting applications of computer vision: autonomous mobile robots.

AUTONOMOUS MOBILE ROBOTS. Building C3PO, or something very similar, could be said to be the ultimate goal of AI in general, and of robotics in particular. The builders of a mobile robot face many challenges in getting their robot to function properly; accurately sensing the characteristics of the environment, distinguishing shadows on the floor from walls, designing workable grasping devices, and building an ambulatory system that will work for their domain are just a few examples. However, for the purposes of this chapter, we will focus on just one: the issue of mapping the environment and remembering where the robot is in that environment. There are two philosophically distinct approaches to this, each roughly embodied in a recent paper.

Thrun and Bücker (Thrun & Bücken, 1996) presented a system for combining two forms of map-

making; grid-based and topological. These systems of mapping are exactly what they might seem: A grid-based map is one that is mostly concerned with locating objects in the world on a reference grid, whereas a topological map is mostly concerned with discovering what areas of the world are connected to other areas of the world by a path that the robot can follow. These authors presented a system that combined these two forms of mapmaking with impressive results in performance for shortest-path determination. They presented no task for the robot; mapmaking was presented as a general purpose module, and the object for this module was to make a map as detailed and as accurate as possible. The accurate map is seen as the natural end goal of the module.

Fu et al. (Fu, Hammond, & Swain, 1996) presented a system in which a robot* is given the task of finding items in a grocery store. Their system, SHOPPER, used a topological mapping system merely to track places of interest and exploit many of the features of the environment to make object recognition and mapmaking easier; for example, the light will always be coming from above, and the item that the robot is looking for can be safely assumed to be found on a shelf with the label facing the robot. In this view, mapmaking is a necessary and integrated part of the greater task of finding objects in the store; the object of mapmaking is to make the greater task easier. Mapmaking has moved from an end in itself to a means to a greater end.

Although having a detailed map of the world may seem like a good idea, creating it (and remembering the landmarks that go along with it) is a lot of work that will often go for naught. Any robot that is performing a task in the real world will be dealing with a dynamic environment, and any map that the robot creates will become out of date – sometimes quickly, sometimes slowly, but the map will certainly become inaccurate. SHOPPER manages to accomplish a task in the world without going through all that wasted work, thus freeing up both processing power that the robot can use for other things and human research power that can be used to solve greater problems.

---

* Actually, a simulated robot, but they use actual color photographs from their domain as input to their simulator.

CONCLUSIONS

This chapter has introduced some of the basic techniques and building blocks of AI research and has discussed a history of AI programs, both early and recent, and how these programs embodied the mistakes that are so easy to make in AI research. It has also presented our philosophy on AI: that a truly successful AI program will need to be doing some task in the world that requires intelligence, and that the best approaches to AI incorporate knowledge about the tasks being performed. Further, any component of that task should not be treated as an end in and of itself; components should be measured on how they contribute to the task at hand.

Every graduate student in AI comes in with the dream of building HAL, or something very like HAL – a truly intelligent machine that can converse with people, pilot spaceships, and solve the problems facing humanity. HAL and his cousins remain a distant dream for the AI community, but progress is being made in many areas. Although we do not have C3PO or R2–D2, we do have robots that can give tours of laboratories (Horswill, 1994), collect soda cans for recycling (Connell, 1989), or play soccer (Veloso, Stone, Han, & Achim, 1997). Although we do not have programs that can converse with people like HAL, we do have commercially available grammar checkers, and programs that can translate languages within narrow domains (Nyberg & Mitamura, 1992).

It remains to be seen whether HAL is a possibility. However, the accomplishments that are being made along the road to HAL are exciting enough in their own right to ensure that AI research will continue.

REFERENCES

Bower, G. H., Black, J. B., & Turner, T. J. (1979). Scripts in memory for text. *Cognitive Psychology, 11*, 177–220.

Buchanan, B. G., & Shortliffe, E. H. (Eds.). (1984). *Rule-based expert systems: The MYCIN experiments of the Stanford Heuristic Programming Project*. Menlo Park, CA: Addison-Wesley.

Buchanan, B. G., Sutherland, G., & Feigenbaum, E. A. (1970). Rediscovering some problems of artificial intelligence in the context of organic chemistry. In B. Meltzer & D. Michie (Eds.), *Machine Intelligence 5*. Edinburgh, UK: Edinburgh University Press.

Buchanan, B. G., & Wilkins, D. C. (Eds.). (1993). *Readings in knowledge acquisition and learning*. San Mateo, CA: Morgan Kaufmann.

Burke, R., & Hammond, K. (1997). FAQFinder [Computer program]. <http://faqfinder.cs.uchicago.edu>.

Burke, R., Hammond, K., Kulyikin, V., Lytinen, S., Tomuro, N., & Schoenberg, S. (1997, Summer 1997). Question answering from frequently asked question files: Experiences with the FAQFinder system. *AI Magazine, 18*(2), 57–66.

Connell, J. (1989). *A colony architecture for an artificial creature* (Technical Report No. AITR 1151). MIT Artificial Intelligence Laboratory.

Cullingford, R. E. (1978). *Script application: Computer understanding of newspaper stories*. Unpublished doctoral dissertation, Yale University.

Fu, D. D., Hammond, K. J., & Swain, M. (1996). Navigation for everyday life. *Proceedings AAAI–96*, 902–908.

Hammond, K. (1986). CHEF: A model of case-based planning. *Proceedings AAAI–86*, 267–271.

Hofstadter, D. R. (1979). *Gödel, Escher, Bach: An eternal golden braid*. New York: Basic Books.

Horswill, I. (1994). *Specialization of perceptual processes* (Technical Report No. AITR 1511). MIT Artificial Intelligence Laboratory.

Leake, D. B. (Ed.). (1996). *Case-based Reasoning: Experiences, lessons, and future directions*. Cambridge, MA: The MIT Press.

Leake, D. B., Kinley, A., & Wilson, D. (1996). Acquiring case adaptation knowledge: A hybrid approach. *Proceedings AAAI–96*, 684–689.

Lenat, D. B., & Guha, R. B. (1990). *Building large knowledge-based systems*. Reading, MA: Addisson-Wesley.

Miller, G. A. (1995). WordNet: A lexical database for English. *Communications of the ACM, 38*(11), 39–41.

Minsky, M., & Papert, S. (1969). *Perceptrons*. Cambridge, MA: MIT Press.

Mock, K. J. (1996). Hybrid hill-climbing and knowledge-based methods for intelligent news filtering. *Proceedings AAAI–96*, 48–53.

Newell, A., & Simon, H. A. (1961). GPS, a program that simulates human thought. Reprinted in E. A. Feigenbaum & J. Feldman (Eds.) (1963), *Computers and thought* (pp. 279–293). New York: McGraw-Hill.

Newell, A., & Simon, H. A. (1976). Computer science as empirical inquiry: Symbols and search. *Communications of the ACM, 19*(3), 113–126.

Nyberg, E. & Mitamura, T. (1992). The KANT system: Fast, accurate, high-quality translation in practical domains. *Proceedings of COLING–92*.

Pazzani, M. J., Muramatsu, J., & Billsus, D. (1996). Syskill and Webert: Identifying interesting Web sites. *Proceedings AAAI–96*, 54–61.

Penrose, R. (1989). *The emperor's new mind*. New York: Penguin Books.

Penrose, R. (1994). *Shadows of the mind*. Oxford: Oxford University Press.

Riesbeck, C. K., & Schank, R. C. (1989). *Inside case-based reasoning*. Hillsdale, NJ: Erlbaum.

Rumelhart, D. E., McClelland, J. L., & the PDP Research Group (Eds.). (1986). *Parallel distributed processing*. Cambridge, MA: MIT Press.

Russell, S. J., & Norvig, P. (1995). *Artificial intelligence: A modern approach*. Englewood Cliffs, NJ: Prentice Hall.

Samuel, A. L. (1963). Some studies in machine learning using the game of checkers. In E. A. Feigenbaum & J. Feldman (Eds.), *Computers and thought*. New York: McGraw-Hill.

Schank, R. C. (1982). *Dynamic memory*. Cambridge: Cambridge University Press.

Schank, R. C. (1986). *Explanation patterns*. Hillsdale, NJ: Erlbaum.

Schank, R. C. (1991). Where's the AI? *AI Magazine* (Winter 1991), *12*(4), 38–49.

Searle, J. R. (1980). Minds, Brains, and Programs. *The Behavioral and Brain Sciences, 3*(3), 417–457.

Sussman, G. J. (1975). *A computer model of skill acquisition*. Cambridge, MA: MIT Press.

Thrun, S., & Bücken, A. (1996). Integrating grid-based and topological maps for mobile robot navigation. *Proceedings AAAI–96*, 944–950.

Veloso, M., Stone, P., Han, K., & Achim, S. (1997). CMUnited: A team of robotic soccer agents collaborating in an adversarial environment. *IJCAI–97*.

Weizenbaum, J. (1966). ELIZA – A computer program for the study of natural language communication between man and machine. *Communications of the ACM, 9*(1), 36–44.

Winograd, T. (1972). *Understanding natural language*. New York: Academic Press.

PART VI

KINDS OF INTELLIGENCE

CHAPTER SIXTEEN

Social Intelligence

JOHN F. KIHLSTROM AND NANCY CANTOR

The capacity to know oneself and to know others is an inalienable a part of the human condition as is the capacity to know objects or sounds, and it deserves to be investigated no less than these other "less charged" forms.

Howard Gardner (1983, p. 243)
Frames of Mind

Intelligence, as defined in standard dictionaries, has two rather different meanings. In its most familiar meaning, intelligence denotes the individual's ability to learn and reason. It is this meaning that underlies common psychometric notions such as *intelligence testing*, the *intelligence quotient*, and the like. In its less common meaning, intelligence refers to a body of information and knowledge. This second meaning is implicated in the titles of certain government organizations such as the Central Intelligence Agency in the United States and its British counterparts MI–5 and MI–6. Similarly, both meanings are invoked by the concept of social intelligence. As originally coined by E. L. Thorndike (1920), the term referred to the person's ability to understand and manage other people and to engage in adaptive social interactions. More recently, however, Cantor and Kihlstrom (1987) redefined social intelligence as the individual's fund of knowledge about the social world.

THE PSYCHOMETRIC VIEW

The psychometric view of social intelligence has its origins in E. L. Thorndike's (1920) division of intelligence into three facets: the ability to understand and manage ideas (abstract intelligence), concrete objects (mechanical intelligence), and people (social intelligence). In his classic formulation: "By social intelligence is meant the ability to understand and manage men and women, boys and girls – to act wisely in human relations" (p. 228). Similarly, Moss and Hunt (1927) defined social intelligence as the "ability to get along with others" (p. 108). Vernon (1933) provided the most wide-ranging definition of social intelligence as the person's "ability to get along with people in general, social technique or ease in society, knowledge of social matters, susceptibility to stimuli from other members of a group, as well as insight into the temporary moods or underlying personality traits of strangers" (p. 44).

By contrast, Wechsler (1939, 1958) gave scant attention to the concept. He did acknowledge, however, that the Picture Arrangement subtest of the WAIS might serve as a measure of social intelligence because it assesses the individual's ability to comprehend social situations (see also Rapaport, Gill, & Shafer, 1968; Campbell & McCord, 1996). In his view, however, "social intelligence is just general intelligence applied to social situations" (1958, p. 75). This dismissal is repeated in Matarazzo's (1972, p. 209) fifth edition of Wechsler's monograph, in which "social intelligence" was deleted as an index term.

Defining social intelligence seems easy enough, especially by analogy to abstract intelligence. When it came to *measuring* social intelligence, however, E. L. Thorndike (1920) noted somewhat ruefully that convenient tests of social intelligence are hard to devise.... Social intelligence shows itself abundantly in the nursery, on the playground, in barracks and factories and salesroom (*sic*), but it eludes the formal standardized conditions of the testing laboratory. It requires human beings to respond to, time to adapt its responses, and face, voice, gesture, and mien as tools (p. 231).

Nevertheless, true to the goals of the psychometric tradition, the abstract definitions of social intelligence were quickly translated into standardized laboratory instruments for measuring individual differences in social intelligence (for additional reviews, see Taylor, 1990; Taylor & Cadet, 1989; Walker & Foley, 1973).

The George Washington Social Intelligence Test

The first of these was the George Washington Social Intelligence Test, (GWSIT; Hunt, 1928; Moss, 1931; Moss & Hunt, 1927; Moss, Hunt, Omwake, & Ronning, 1927; for later editions, see Moss, Hunt, & Omwake, 1949; Moss, Hunt, Omwake, & Woodward, 1955). Like the Stanford–Binet Intelligence Test or Wechsler Adult Intelligence Scale, the GWSIT was composed of a number of subtests, that can be combined to yield an aggregate score. The subtests are as follows:

Judgment in Social Situations
Memory for Names and Faces
Observation of Human Behavior
Recognition of the Mental States Behind Words
Recognition of Mental States from Facial Expression
Social Information
Sense of Humor.

The first four subtests were employed in all editions of the GWSIT. The Facial Expression and Social Information subtests were dropped, and the Humor subtest was added, in later editions.

Hunt (1928) originally validated the GWSIT through its correlations with adult occupational status, the number of extracurricular activities pursued by college students, and supervisors' ratings of employees' ability to get along with people. However, some controversy ensued about whether social intelligence should be correlated with personality measures of sociability or extraversion (e.g., Strang, 1930; R. L. Thorndike & Stein, 1937). Most important, however, the GWSIT came under immediate

criticism for its relatively high correlation with abstract intelligence. Thus, Hunt (1928) found that aggregate GWSIT scores correlated $r = .54$ with aggregate scores on the George Washington University Mental Alertness Test (GWMAT), an early IQ scale (see also Broom, 1928). A factor analysis by R. L. Thorndike (1936) indicated that the subtests of the GWSIT loaded highly on the same general factor as the subtests of the GWMAT. Woodrow (1939), analyzing the GWSIT with a much larger battery of cognitive tests, found no evidence for a unique factor of social intelligence. R. L. Thorndike and Stein (1937) concluded that the GWSIT "is so heavily loaded with ability to work with words and ideas, that differences in social intelligence tend to be swamped by differences in abstract intelligence" (p. 282).

The inability to discriminate between the social intelligence and IQ, coupled with difficulties in selecting external criteria against which the scale could be validated, led to declining interest in the GWSIT, and indeed in the whole concept of social intelligence as a distinct intellectual entity. Of course, Spearman's (1927) model of *g* afforded no special place for social intelligence.* Nor is social intelligence included, or even implied, in Thurstone's (1938) list of primary mental abilities.

Social Intelligence in the Structure of Intellect

After an initial burst of interest in the GWSIT, work on the assessment and correlates of social intelligence fell off sharply until the 1960s (Walker & Foley, 1973), when this line of research was revived within the context of Guilford's (1967) Structure of Intellect model. Guilford postulated a system of at least 120 separate intellectual abilities based on all possible combinations of five categories of

---

* Nevertheless, Spearman did sponsor a 1933 doctoral dissertation by Wedeck (cited in Wedeck, 1947) that documented "verbal" and "psychological" abilities separate from general abstract intelligence. Wedeck's findings were confirmed using more modern methods of factor analysis (O'Sullivan et al., 1965). Jensen (1998), operating squarely within the tradition of *g* founded by Spearman, also noted that measures of social intelligence "show remarkably low correlations with psychometric abilities, both verbal and quantitative" (p. 576), indicating that social intelligence is distinct from *g*. However, Jensen preferred to label these abilities *social competence* — perhaps to preserve the unity of general intelligence.

operations (cognition, memory, divergent production, convergent production, and evaluation), with four categories of content (figural, symbolic, semantic, and behavioral) and six categories of products (units, classes, relations, systems, transformations, and implications). Interestingly, Guilford considered his system to be an expansion of the tripartite classification of intelligence originally proposed by E. L. Thorndike. Thus, the symbolic and semantic content domains correspond to abstract intelligence, the figural domain to practical intelligence, and the behavioral domain to social intelligence.

Within Guilford's (1967) more differentiated system, social intelligence is represented as the 30 (5 operations × 6 products) abilities lying in the domain of behavioral operations. In contrast to its extensive work on semantic and figural content, Guilford's group addressed issues of behavioral content only very late in their program of research. Nevertheless, of the 30 facets of social intelligence predicted by the Structure of Intellect model, actual tests were devised for six cognitive abilities (O'Sullivan, Guilford, and deMille, 1965; Hoepfner & O'Sullivan, 1969) and six divergent production abilities (Hendricks, Guilford, & Hoepfner, 1969).

O'Sulivan et al. (1965) defined the category of behavioral cognition as representing the "ability to judge people" (p. 5) with respect to "feelings, motives, thoughts, intentions, attitudes, or other psychological dispositions which might affect an individual's social behavior" (O'Sullivan et al., p. 4). They made it clear that one's ability to judge individual people is not the same as his or her comprehension of people in general, or "stereotypic understanding" (p. 5), and bears no a priori relation to one's ability to understand oneself. Apparently, these two aspects of social cognition lie outside the standard Structure of Intellect model.

In constructing their tests of behavioral cognition, O'Sullivan et al. (1965) assumed that "expressive behavior, more particularly facial expressions, vocal inflections, postures, and gestures, are the cues from which intentional states are inferred" (p. 6). While recognizing the value of assessing the ability to decode these cues in real-life contexts with real people serving as targets, economic constraints forced the investigators to rely on photographs, cartoons, drawings, and tape recordings (the cost of film was prohibitive); verbal materials were avoided wherever possible, presumably in order to avoid contamination of social intelligence by verbal abilities. In the final analysis, O'Sullivan et al. developed at least three different tests within each product domain, each test consisting of 30 or more separate items – by any standard, a monumental effort at theory-guided test construction. The following are the six cognitive abilities defined by O'Sullivan et al.:

> *Cognition of behavioral units*: the ability to identify the internal mental states of individuals;
> *Cognition of behavioral classes*: the ability to group other people's mental states on the basis of similarity;
> *Cognition of behavioral relations*: the ability to interpret meaningful connections among behavioral acts;
> *Cognition of behavioral systems*: the ability to interpret sequences of social behavior;
> *Cognition of behavioral transformations*: the ability to respond flexibly in interpreting changes in social behavior; and
> *Cognition of behavioral implications*: the ability to predict what will happen in an interpersonal situation.

After devising these tests, O'Sullivan et al. (1965) conducted a normative study in which 306 high-school students received 23 different social intelligence tests representing the 6 hypothesized factors along with 24 measures of 12 nonsocial ability factors. A principal factor analysis with orthogonal rotation yielded 22 factors, including the 12 nonsocial reference factors and 6 factors clearly interpretable as cognition of behavior. In general, the six behavioral factors were not contaminated by nonsocial semantic and spatial abilities. Thus, O'Sullivan et al. apparently succeeded in measuring expressly social abilities that were essentially independent of abstract cognitive ability. However, echoing earlier findings with the GWSIT, later studies found substantial correlations between IQ and scores on the individual Guilford subtests as well as various composite social intelligence scores (Riggio, Messamer, & Throckmorton, 1991; Shanley, Walker, & Foley, 1971). Still Shanley et al. conceded that the correlations obtained were not strong enough to warrant the conclusion (e.g., Wechsler, 1958) that social intelligence is nothing more than general intelligence applied in the social domain.

In one of the last test-construction efforts by Guilford's group, Hendricks et al. (1969) attempted to develop tests for coping with other people, not just understanding them through their behavior – what they referred to as "basic solution-finding skills in interpersonal relations" (p. 3). Because successful coping involves the creative generation of many diverse behavioral ideas, these investigators labeled these divergent-thinking abilities *creative social intelligence*. The following six divergent production abilities were defined by Hendricks et al.:

> *Divergent production of behavioral units*: the ability to engage in behavioral acts that communicate internal mental states;
> *Divergent production of behavioral classes*: the ability to create recognizable categories of behavioral acts;
> *Divergent production of behavioral relations*: the ability to perform an act that has a bearing on what another person is doing;
> *Divergent production of behavioral systems*: the ability to maintain a sequence of interactions with another person;
> *Divergent production of behavioral transformations*: the ability to alter an expression or a sequence of expressions; and
> *Divergent production of behavioral implications*: the ability to predict many possible outcomes of a setting.

As with the behavioral cognition abilities studied by O'Sullivan et al. (1965), the very nature of the behavioral domain raised serious technical problems for test development in the behavioral domain, especially with respect to contamination by verbal (semantic) abilities. Ideally, of course, divergent production would be measured in real-world settings in terms of actual behavioral responses to real people. Failing that, testing could rely on nonverbal behaviors such as drawings, gestures, and vocalizations, but such tests could well be contaminated by individual differences in drawing, acting, or public-speaking ability that have nothing to do with social intelligence per se.

Still, in accordance with the pattern of O'Sullivan et al. (1965), a battery of creative social intelligence tests, 22 for divergent production of behavioral products and another 16 representing 8 categories of (convergent) cognition of behavior and divergent production in the semantic domain, was administered to 252 high school students. As might be expected, scoring divergent productions proved considerably harder than scoring cognitions, for in the former case there is no one best answer, and the subject's responses must be evaluated by independent judges for quality as well as quantity. Principal-components analysis yielded 15 factors, 6 of which were clearly interpretable as divergent production in the behavioral domain. Again, the divergent production abilities in the behavioral domain were essentially independent of divergent semantic production and (convergent) cognition in the behavioral domain.

A later study by Chen and Michael (1993), employing more modern factor-analytic techniques, essentially confirmed these findings. In addition, Chen and Michael extracted a set of higher order factors that largely conformed to the theoretical predictions of Guilford's (1981) revised Structure of Intellect model. A similar reanalysis of the O'Sullivan et al. (1965) data has yet to be reported.

In summary, Guilford and his colleagues were successful in devising measures for two rather different domains of social intelligence: understanding the behavior of other people (cognition of behavioral content), and coping with the behavior of other people (divergent production of behavioral content). These component abilities were relatively independent of each other within the behavioral domain, and each was also relatively independent of the nonbehavioral abilities, as predicted (and required) by the structure of intellect model.

Despite the huge amount of effort that the Guilford group invested in the measurement of social intelligence, it should be understood that the studies of O'Sullivan et al. (1965) and Hendricks et al. (1969) went only part of the way toward establishing the construct validity of social intelligence. Their studies described essentially established convergent and discriminant validity by showing that ostensible tests of the various behavioral abilities hung together as predicted by the theory and were not contaminated by other abilities outside the behavioral domain. As yet, there is little evidence for the ability of any of these tests to predict external criteria of social intelligence.

Tests of the remaining three structures of intellect domains (memory, convergent production, and evaluation) had not developed by the time the Guilford program came to a close. Hendricks et al. (1969) noted that "these constitute by far the greatest number of unknowns in the [structure of intellect] model" (p. 6). However, O'Sullivan et al. (1965) did sketch out how these abilities were defined. *Convergent production* in the behavioral domain was defined as "doing the right thing at the right time" (p. 5) and presumably might be tested by a knowledge of etiquette. *Behavioral memory* was defined as the ability to remember the social characteristics of people (e.g., names, faces, and personality traits), whereas *behavioral evaluation* was defined as the ability to judge the appropriateness of behavior.

Convergent and Discriminant Validity in Social Intelligence

Following the Guilford studies, several investigators continued the attempt to define social intelligence and determine its relation to general abstract intelligence. Most of these studies explicitly employed the logic of the multitrait–multimethod matrix (Campbell & Fiske, 1959), using multiple measures of social and nonsocial intelligence and examining the convergent validity of alternative measures within each domain and their discriminant validity across domains (e.g., Sechrest & Jackson, 1961).

For example, Keating (1978) measured social intelligence with a battery of instruments including Rest's (1975) Defining Issues Test, derived from Kohlberg's (1963) theory of moral development; Chapin's (1942) Social Insight Test, which asks the subject to resolve various social dilemmas; and Gough's (1966) Social Maturity Index, a self-report scale derived from the California Psychological Inventory measuring effective social functioning (see also Sipps, Berry, & Lynch, 1987). Applying a multitrait–multimethod analysis, Keating found no evidence that social intelligence, so defined, was discriminable from academic intelligence. Thus, the average correlation between tests within each domain was actually *lower* than the corresponding average across domains. Although a factor analysis produced two factors, each of these factors consisted of a mix of the two types of intelligence test. Finally, Keating found that the three measures of abstract intelligence were actually better predictors of Gough's (1966) Social Maturity Index than were the remain-

ing two measures of social intelligence. However, it should be noted that Keating's putative measures of social intelligence are highly verbal in nature, and thus some contamination by abstract verbal and reasoning ability may be expected.

In response to Keating's (1978) study, Ford and Tisak (1983) conducted an even more substantial study involving over 600 high school students. Four measures of verbal and mathematical ability were derived from school records of grades and standardized test scores. Social intelligence was measured by self-, peer-, and teacher-ratings of social competence, Hogan's (1969) empathy test, self-reports of social competence, and a judgment based on an individual interview. In contrast to Keating's (1978) results, Ford and Tisak found that the measures of academic and social intelligence loaded on different factors. Moreover, the three ratings of social competence and Hogan's empathy scale were more highly predictive of the interview ratings of social competence than were the academic measures. Ford and Tisak attributed these results to the selection of social intelligence measures according to a criterion of behavioral effectiveness in social situations rather than cognitive understanding of them. Put another way, measures of verbal ability, including standard measures of IQ, are likely to correlate highly with verbal, but not nonverbal measures of social intelligence.

Similar findings were obtained by several other investigators (e.g., Brown & Anthony, 1990), including Marlowe (1986; Marlowe & Bedell, 1982), who assembled a large battery of personality measures ostensibly tapping various aspects of social intelligence. Factor analysis of these instruments yielded five dimensions of social intelligence: interest and concern for other people, social performance skills, empathic ability, emotional expressiveness and sensitivity to others' emotional expressions, and social anxiety and lack of social self-efficacy and self-esteem. Factor scores on these dimensions of social intelligence were essentially unrelated to measures of verbal and abstract intelligence.

In evaluating studies like Marlowe's (1986), however, it should be noted that the apparent independence of social and general intelligence may be at least partially an artifact of method variance. Unlike the GWSIT and the batteries of cognitive and divergent production measures devised by the Guilford group, Marlowe's ostensible measures of social intelligence are all self-report scales, whereas his measures of verbal and abstract intelligence were the usual sorts of objective performance tests. The difference in data collection methods alone may explain why the social and verbal–abstract dimensions lined up on different factors. In any event, the measurement of individual differences in social intelligence by means of self-report scales is a major departure from the tradition of intelligence testing, and it seems important to confirm Marlowe's findings using objective performance measures of the various facets of social intelligence.[*]

For example, Frederickson, Carlson, and Ward (1984) employed an extensive behavioral assessment procedure along with a battery of performance tests of scholastic aptitude and achievement and medical and nonmedical problem solving. In addition, each subject conducted 10 interviews with simulated medical patients and nonmedical clients. On the basis of codings of their interview behavior, each subject received ratings for organization, warmth, and control. None of the measures of aptitude, achievement, or problem-solving behavior correlated substantially with any of the interview-based ratings of social intelligence. Lowman and Leeman (1988), employing a number of performance measures, obtained evidence for three dimensions of social intelligence: social needs and interests, social knowledge, and social ability. Interestingly, the correlations of all three dimensions with grade point average, a proxy for academic intelligence, were either null or negative.

On the other hand, Stricker and Rock (1990) administered a battery of performance measures of social intelligence and found that subjects' accuracy in judging a person and a situation portrayed in a videotaped interview was correlated with verbal ability. Wong, Day, Maxwell, and Meara (1995) constructed measures of social perception (accuracy in decoding verbal and nonverbal behavior), social insight (accuracy in interpreting social behavior), and social knowledge (awareness of the rules of etiquette). Factor analysis showed that social percep-

tion and insight were closely related, neither of these dimensions was closely related to social knowledge, and none of the social abilities was related to traditional academic ability.

Expanding on the study by Wong et al., Jones and Day (1997) based their analysis on Cattell's (1971) distinction between fluid and crystallized intelligence. In the social domain, crystallized intelligence reflects the individual's accumulated fund of knowledge about the social world, including his or her vocabulary for representing social behaviors and situations; fluid intelligence, by contrast, reflects the individual's ability to solve problems posed by novel social situations quickly and accurately. Jones and Day assembled four measures of each kind of ability, including verbal and pictorial performance measures, self-ratings, and teacher ratings. They also had multiple measures of academic ability. Confirmatory factor analyses testing various specific models of the relations between social and academic intelligence indicated that crystallized social intelligence was discriminable from fluid social intelligence but not from academic intelligence.

Clearly, more studies employing performance-based measures are needed before any definitive conclusions can be drawn about the relations among various aspects of social intelligence (convergent validity) and the relations between social intelligence and other intellectual abilities (discriminant validity).

Social Intelligence as a Cognitive Module

An exception to the general rule that social intelligence plays little role in scientific theories of intelligence is the theory of *multiple intelligences* proposed by Gardner (1983, 1993). Unlike Spearman (1927) and other advocates of general intelligence (e.g., Jensen, 1998), Gardner has proposed that intelligence is not a unitary cognitive ability but that there are seven (and perhaps more) quite different kinds of intelligence, each hypothetically dissociable from the others, and each hypothetically associated with a different brain system. Although most of these proposed intelligences (linguistic, logical–mathematical, spatial, musical, and bodily–kinesthetic) are "cognitive" abilities somewhat reminiscent of Thurstone's primary mental abilities, two are explicitly personal and social in nature. Gardner defines *intrapersonal intelligence* as the

---

[*] By contrast, two of Keating's (1978) three measures of social intelligence were performance measures. Ford and Tisak (1983) employed a mix of self-ratings and judgments by other people.

person's ability to gain access to his or her own internal emotional life and *interpersonal intelligence* as the individual's ability to notice and make distinctions among other individuals.

Although Gardner's (1983) multiple intelligences are individual differences constructs in which some people, or some groups, are assumed to have more of these abilities than others, Gardner does not rely on the traditional psychometric procedures – scale construction, factor analysis, multitrait–multimethod matrices, external validity coefficients, and so on – for documenting individual differences. Rather, his preferred method is a somewhat impressionistic analysis based on a convergence of signs provided by eight different lines of evidence.

Chief among these signs are *isolation by brain damage* (such that one form of intelligence can be selectively impaired, leaving other forms relatively unimpaired) and *exceptional cases*, individuals who possess extraordinary levels of ability in one domain against a background of normal or even impaired abilities in other domains (alternatively, a person may show extraordinarily *low* levels of ability in one domain against a background of normal or exceptionally high levels of ability in others). So, for example, Gardner (1983) argued from neurological case studies that damage to the prefrontal lobes of the cerebral cortex can selectively impair personal and social intelligence, leaving other abilities intact. The classic case of Phineas Gage may serve as an example (Macmillan, 1986). The opposite phenomenon is illustrated by Luria's (1972) case of Zazetsky, "the man with a shattered world," who sustained damage in the occipital and parietal lobes that severely impaired most of his intellectual capacities but left his personal and social abilities relatively intact. Gardner also noted that, although Down's syndrome and Alzheimer's disease have severe cognitive consequences but little impact on the person's ability to get along with other people, Pick's disease spares at least some cognitive abilities while severely impairing the person's ability to interact with others. In related work, Taylor and Cadet (1989) have proposed that three different brain systems provide the neurological substrate of social intelligence: a balanced or integrated cortical subsystem that relies on long-term memory to make complex social judgments; a frontal-dominant subsystem that organizes and generates social behaviors; and a limbic-dominant subsystem that rapidly produces emotional responses to events. However, it should be noted that, with the exception of emotion (for an authoritative summary, see LeDoux, 1996; see also Kihlstrom, Mulvaney, Tobias, & Tobis, 1999), research on the neurological underpinnings of social cognition and behavior is highly impressionistic and speculative (for a review of neuropsychological approaches to social cognition and social intelligence, see Klein & Kihlstrom, 1998).

With respect to exceptional individuals, Gardner offered Sigmund Freud and Marcel Proust as "prodigies" in the domain of intrapersonal intelligence, and Mohandas Gandhi and Lyndon Johnson as their counterparts in the domain of interpersonal intelligence. Each of these individuals, Gardner claimed, displayed high levels of personal and social intelligence against a background of more "normal" abilities in other domains. On the negative side, Gardner noted that infantile autism (Kanner's syndrome, Williams' syndrome, etc.) severely impairs the individual's ability to understand other people and navigate the social world.

In addition, Gardner postulated several other signs suggesting different types of intelligence. Among these are *identifiable core operations*, coupled with *experimental tasks* that permit analysis of these core operations and *psychometric tests* that reveal individual differences in ability to perform them. With respect to social intelligence, of course, the core operations are those that form the core of research on social cognition: person perception and impression formation, causal attribution, person memory, social categorization, impression management, and the like. The social cognition literature offers numerous paradigms for studying these operations, of course, and sometimes these experimental procedures have been translated into techniques for the analysis of individual differences (e.g., Kihlstrom & Nasby, 1981; Nasby & Kihlstrom, 1986). For example, Kaess and Witryol (1955) studied memory for names and faces; Sechrest and Jackson (1961) examined individual differences in the ability to predict other people's behavior in various kinds of situations; and Sternberg and his colleagues (Barnes & Sternberg, 1989; Sternberg & Smith, 1985) have assessed individual differences in the ability to decode nonverbal communications.

Whether the core operations involved in social cognition differ qualitatively from those involved in nonsocial cognition is, however, an open question. Although perceiving emotion in a face may appear to differ qualitatively from mentally rotating an image of the letter **R**, a working assumption in most social cognition research is that the underlying mental processes are the same as those deployed in nonsocial cognition. Thus, for example, Cantor and Mischel's (1979) research on prototypes in person perception was intended as a fairly direct translation of Rosch's (1978) pioneering work on fuzzy-set approaches to nonsocial categories. And although it is quite plausible to suggest that the perception of faces, those most social of stimuli, follows special rules and is mediated by a special brain area (e.g., Farah, 1996), recent experimental and neuroimaging evidence indicates that face recognition is simply an instance of a broader expertise for identifying objects at subordinate levels of categorization (Gauthier, 1998).

One potentially important difference between the social and nonsocial domains, of course, is that in social cognition the object (i.e., the person) represented in the observer's mind is intelligent and conscious. Thus, the person being perceived may try to control the impression formed by the perceiver through a variety of impression-management strategies (Goffman, 1959; Jones and Pittman, 1982). To complicate things further, the perceiver may well be aware of the possibility of strategic self-presentation and thus adjust his or her perceptions accordingly, and the person being perceived may modulate his or her impression-management activities so as to minimize these corrections. Such *interaction rituals* (Goffman, 1967) are not likely to occur in nonsocial perception and cognition.

In addition to experimental and psychometric evidence, Gardner (1983) also assumed that qualitatively different forms of intelligence will show *distinctive developmental histories*. From an *ontogenetic* point of view, then, the hypothesis is that the acquisition and mastery of competencies in the social domain follows a different developmental trajectory, from infancy through adolescence and adulthood to old age, than other abilities.* Similarly, from a *phylogenetic* point of view, the hypothesis would be that personal and interpersonal abilities trace different evolutionary pathways as well.* Thus, Gardner (1983) cites Gallup's (1970, 1998; Gallup, Marino, & Eddy, 1997) finding that humans and chimpanzees, but not other primates (and not other mammals), pass the mirror-image test of self-recognition.

Finally, Gardner argued that each form of intelligence is encoded in a *unique symbol system* by which the ability in question can be manipulated and transmitted by a culture. For some of his proposed intelligences, the existence of the symbol system is fairly obvious: written language, mathematical symbols, and musical notation are clear examples. As evidence suggestive of special personal symbol systems, Gardner cited Geertz's (1975) ethnographic work in Java, Bali, and Morocco, which revealed considerable cultural diversity in the means by which people maintain a sense of self and the rules that govern their social relations – personal and social intelligence that is acquired through socialization. Certainly, the English language contains a large vocabulary of words – 17,953 by one count (Allport & Odbert, 1937) – which can represent people's cognitive, emotional, and motivational states, behavioral dispositions, and other psychosocial characteristics. And within Western culture, structures like the classic fourfold classification of temperament (melancholic, phlegmatic, choleric, and sanguine; Kant, 1798/1978) and the Big Five personality dimensions (neuroticism, extraversion, agreeableness, conscientiousness, and openness to experience; John, 1990) are commonly employed to

---

* See the concluding section on the development of social intelligence.

* A similar notion has been promoted by Byrne and Whiten (1988; Whiten & Byrne, 1997) in their concept of Machiavellian intelligence. Following Humphrey (1976), these authors have proposed that the special demands of cooperation and competition have led social animals (especially primates) to evolve forms of intelligence that are not found in nonsocial species. In fact, Whiten and Byrne (1997) have gone so far as to suggest that social intelligence evolved in advance of "object intelligence," or the ability to deal with the nonsocial physical world, and that the evolution of general intellectual abilities was driven by natural selection for manipulative social expertise within groups. In a very real sense, the notion of Machiavellian intelligence reverses Wechsler's doctrine that social intelligence is just general intelligence applied to social problems. According to Whiten and Byrne, general intelligence is derived from social intelligence. See also Premack and Woodruff (1978) and Worden (1996).

capture and communicate the gist of another person's personality.

The Prototype of Social Intelligence

Although social intelligence has proved difficult for psychometricians to operationalize, it does appear to play a major role in people's naive, intuitive concepts of intelligence. Following up on earlier work by Rosch (1978), Cantor (Cantor & Mischel, 1979; Cantor, Smith, French, & Mezzich, 1980), and Neisser (1979), Sternberg and his colleagues asked subjects to list the behaviors they considered characteristic of intelligence, academic intelligence, everyday intelligence, and unintelligence; two additional groups of subjects rated each of 250 behaviors from the first list in terms of how "characteristic" each was of the ideal person possessing each of the three forms of intelligence (Sternberg, Conway, Ketron, & Bernstein, 1981). Factor analysis of ratings provided by laypeople yielded a factor of "social competence" in each context. Prototypical behaviors reflecting social competence were the following:

Accepts others for what they are;
Admits mistakes;
Displays interest in the world at large;
Is on time for appointments;
Has social conscience;
Thinks before speaking and doing;
Displays curiosity;
Does not make snap judgments;
Makes fair judgments;
Assesses well the relevance of information to a problem at hand;
Is sensitive to other people's needs and desires;
Is frank and honest with self and others; and
Displays interest in the immediate environment.

Interestingly, a separate dimension of social competence did not consistently emerge in ratings made by a group of experts on intelligence. Rather, the experts' dimensions focused on verbal intelligence and problem-solving ability, and social competence expressly emerged only in the ratings of the ideal "practically intelligent" person. Perhaps these experts shared Wechsler's (1939) dismissive view of social intelligence.

A similar study was performed by Kosmitzki and John (1993). On the basis largely of prior research by Orlik (1978), these investigators assembled a list of 18 features that make up people's implicit concept of social intelligence. When subjects were asked to rate how necessary each feature was to their own personal understanding of social intelligence, the following dimensions emerged as most central to the prototype:

Understands people's thoughts, feelings, and intentions well;
Is good at dealing with people;
Has extensive knowledge of rules and norms in human relations;
Is good at taking the perspective of other people;
Adapts well in social situations;
Is warm and caring; and
Is open to new experiences, ideas, and values.

In another part of the study, subjects were asked to rate someone they liked on each of these attributes. After statistically controlling for differential likability of the traits, a factor analysis yielded a clear dimension of social intelligence defined by the attributes listed above. The remaining two factors were named social influence and social memory.

A recent psychometric study of social intelligence used a methodology similar to that employed by Sternberg et al. (1981) and Kosmitzki and John (1993). Schneider, Ackerman, and Kanfer (1996) asked subjects to generate descriptions of socially competent behavior. These descriptors were then collated and reduced to form a Social Competence Questionnaire on which subjects were asked to rate the extent to which each item described their typical social behavior. A factor analysis revealed seven dimensions of social competence: extraversion, warmth, social influence, social insight, social openness, social appropriateness, and social maladjustment. Composite scores on these dimensions were essentially uncorrelated with measures of quantitative and verbal reasoning ability. On the basis of these findings, Schneider et al. concluded that "it is time to lay to rest any residual notions that social competence is a monolithic entity, or that it is just general intelligence applied to social situations"(p. 479). As with Marlowe's (1986) study, however, the reliance on self-report measures of social intelligence compromises this conclusion, which remains to be confirmed using objective performance measures of the various dimensions in the social domain.

Sternberg et al. (1981) have noted that in contrast to explicit theories of intelligence, which attempt to explain what intelligence is, implicit theories attempt to capture people's views of what the word *intelligence* means. Social intelligence played little role in Sternberg's early componential view of human intelligence (Sternberg, 1977, 1980; but see Sternberg, 1984b), which was intended to focus on reasoning and problem-solving skills as represented by traditional intelligence tests. However, social intelligence is explicitly represented in Sternberg's more recent *triarchic* view of intelligence (Sternberg, 1984a, 1985, 1988). According to the triarchic theory, intelligence is composed of analytical, creative, and practical abilities. Practical intelligence is defined in terms of problem solving in everyday contexts and explicitly includes social intelligence (Sternberg & Wagner, 1986). According to Sternberg, each type of intelligence reflects the operation of three different kinds of component processes: performance components, which solve problems in various domains; executive metacomponents, which plan and evaluate problem solving; and knowledge-acquisition components by which the first two components are learned. To complicate things further, Sternberg (1985, 1988) argued that the measurement of all forms of intelligence is sensitive to the context in which it is assessed. This may be especially the case for practical and social intelligence; for example, the correct answer to a question of social judgment may well be different if it is posed in a corporate (Wagner & Sternberg, 1985) or military (Legree, 1995) context.

For Sternberg, these abilities, and thus their underlying components, may well be somewhat independent of each other. There is no implication, for example, that a person who is strong on analytical intelligence will also be strong in creative and practical intelligence. In any event, the relation among various intellectual abilities is an empirical question. Answering this question, of course, requires that we have adequate instruments for assessing social intelligence – tests that adequately sample the domain in question in addition to being reliable and valid. At present, these instruments do not appear to exist. However, future investigators who wish to make the attempt may be well advised to begin with the intuitive concept of social intelligence held in the mind of the layperson. After all, social intelligence is a social construct, not just an academic one.

PERSONALITY AS SOCIAL INTELLIGENCE

In contrast to the psychometric approaches reviewed above, the social intelligence view of personality (Cantor & Kihlstrom, 1987, 1989; Cantor & Fleeson, 1994; Cantor & Harlow, 1994; Kihlstrom & Cantor, 1989; see also Cantor & Kihlstrom, 1982; Cantor & Zirkel, 1990; Snyder & Cantor, 1998) does not conceptualize social intelligence as a trait, or group of traits, on which individuals can be compared and ranked on a dimension from low to high. Rather, the social intelligence view of personality begins with the assumption that social behavior is *intelligent* – that it is mediated by cognitive processes of perception, memory, reasoning, and problem solving rather than being mediated by innate reflexes, conditioned responses, evolved genetic programs, and the like. Accordingly, the social intelligence view construes individual differences in social behavior – the public manifestations of personality – to be the product of individual differences in the knowledge that individuals bring to bear on their social interactions. Differences in social knowledge cause differences in social behavior, but it does not make sense to construct measures of social IQ. The important variable is not *how much* social intelligence the person has but rather *what* social intelligence he or she possesses.

The Evolution of Cognitive Views of Personality

The social intelligence view of personality has its origins in the social–cognitive tradition of personality theory in which construal and reasoning processes are central to issues of social adaptation. Thus, Kelly (1955) characterized people as naive scientists generating hypotheses about future interpersonal events based on a set of personal constructs concerning self, others, and the world at large. These constructs were idiographic with respect to both content and organization. Individuals might be ranked in terms of the complexity of their personal construct systems, but the important issue for Kelly was knowing what the individual's personal constructs were. Beyond complexity, the idiosyncratic nature of personal construct systems precluded much nomothetic comparison.

Although Kelly's theory was somewhat iconoclastic, similar developments occurred in the evolution of social learning theories of personality. The initial formulation of social learning theory (Miller & Dollard, 1941), a combination of Freudian psychoanalysis and Hullian learning theory, held that personality is largely learned behavior and that understanding personality requires understanding the social conditions under which it was acquired. However, the slow rise of cognitive theories of learning (e.g., Tolman, 1932) soon lent a cognitive flavor to social learning theory itself. Thus, habit and drive played little role in Rotter's (1954) cognitive social learning theory. In contrast to earlier behaviorist conceptions of organismal responses to environmental stimuli controlled by objective contingencies of reinforcement (e.g., Skinner, 1953; Staats & Staats, 1963), Rotter argued that people's behavior reflects choices that follows from their *goals* in a particular situation and their *expectations* of the outcomes of their behavior. Similarly, Bandura (Bandura & Walters, 1963; Bandura, 1973) argued for the acquisition of social knowledge through precept and example rather than the direct experience of rewards and punishment and later (1986) distinguished between the outcome expectancies emphasized by Rotter (1954) and expectancies of self-efficacy – the individual's judgment of belief concerning his or her ability to carry out the actions required to achieve control over the events in a situation. Self-efficacy provides the cognitive basis for motivation, but it should be understood that judgments of self-efficacy are highly context specific. Although Rotter (1966) proposed an individual difference measure of internal versus external locus of control, it would never occur to Bandura to propose a nomothetic instrument for measuring individual differences in generalized self-efficacy expectations. The important consideration is not whether an individual is relatively high or low in self-perceptions of competence but rather whether the person feels competent to perform a particular behavior in some particular situation.

The immediate predecessor to the social intelligence view of personality is Mischel's (1968, 1973) cognitive social-learning reconceptualization of personality. Although sometimes couched in behaviorist language, Mischel's (1968) provocative critique of the trait approach to personality was explicitly cognitive in nature: "[O]ne must know the ... meaning that the stimulus has acquired for the subject. Assessing the acquired meaning of stimuli is the core of social behavior assessment" (p. 190). Thus, understanding individual differences in social behavior requires understanding individual differences in the meaning given to behavior, its outcome, and the situation in which it takes place.

This emphasis on the *subjective meaning* of the situation marked Mischel's early theory as cognitive in nature. Since that time, Mischel (1973) has broadened his conceptualization of personality to include a wide variety of different constructs, some derived from the earlier work of Kelly, Rotter, and Bandura, and others reflecting the importation into personality theory of concepts originating in the laboratory study of human cognitive processes. All are construed as modifiable individual differences, products of cognitive development and social learning that determine how features of the situation will be perceived and interpreted. Thus, they contribute to the construction of the meaning of the stimulus situation – in other words, to the cognitive construction of the situation itself – to which the person ultimately responds.

From Mischel's (1973) point of view, the most important product of cognitive development and social learning is the individual's repertoire of *cognitive and behavioral construction competencies* – the ability to engage in a wide variety of skilled, adaptive behaviors, including overt action and covert mental activities. These construction competencies are as close as Mischel gets to the psychometric notion of social (or, for that matter, *non*social) intelligence.

The importance of perception and interpretation of events in Mischel's system calls for a second set of person variables having to do with *encoding strategies* governing selective attention and *personal constructs* – Kelly-like categories that filter people's perceptions, memories, and expectations. Then, of course, following Rotter and Bandura, Mischel also stressed the role of stimulus-outcome, behavior-outcome, and self-efficacy *expectancies* concerning the outcomes of environmental events and personal behaviors as well as self-efficacy expectancies. Also in line with Rotter's theory, Mischel noted that behavior will be governed by the *subjective values* associated with various outcomes. A final set of relevant variables consists of *self-regulatory systems and plans*, self-defined goals and consequences that govern behavior in the absence (or in spite) of social monitors and external constraints.

The Intelligence Model

From a cognitive point of view, Mischel's "cognitive-social learning person variables" all represent the person's knowledge and expertise – *intelligence* – concerning him- or herself and the surrounding social world. Following Winograd (1975) and Anderson (1976), this social intelligence (Cantor & Kihlstrom, 1987) is classified into two broad categories: *declarative knowledge*, consisting of abstract concepts and specific memories, and *procedural knowledge*, consisting of the rules, skills, and strategies by which the person manipulates and transforms declarative knowledge and translates knowledge into action. The individual's fund of declarative knowledge, in turn, can be broken down further into context-free *semantic* memory about the world in general and *episodic* memory for the events and experiences, each associated with a unique spatiotemporal context, that make up the person's autobiographical record (Tulving, 1983). Similarly, procedural knowledge can be subclassified in terms of cognitive and motor skills. These concepts, personal memories, interpretive rules, and action plans are the cognitive structures of personality. Together, they constitute the expertise that guides an individual's approach to solving the problems of social life.

The cognitive architecture of social intelligence will be familiar from the literature on social cognition (for overviews, see Cantor & Kihlstrom, 1982; Fiske & Taylor, 1991; Kihlstrom & Hastie, 1997) – a literature which, interestingly, had its beginnings in early psychometric efforts to measure individual differences in social intelligence. Thus, for Vernon (1933) one of the characteristics of a socially intelligent person was that he or she was a good judge of personality – a proposition that naturally led to inquires into how people form impressions of personality (Asch, 1946) or engage in person perception (Bruner & Tagiuri, 1954) as well as to the implicit theories of personality (Bruner & Tagiuri, 1954; Cronbach, 1955) that lie at the base of such impressions and perceptions. Specifically, Cronbach argued that one's implicit theory of personality consists of his or her knowledge of "the generalized Other" (1955, p. 179): a mental list of the important dimensions of personality, and estimates of the mean and

variance of each dimension within the population, as well as estimates of the covariances among the several dimensions. Cronbach argued that this intuitive knowledge might be widely shared and acquired as a consequence of socialization and acculturation processes, but he also assumed that there would be individual and cultural differences in this knowledge, leading to individual and group differences in social behavior. Studies of impression formation, implicit personality theory, and, later, causal attributions (e.g., Kelley, 1967), social categories (Cantor & Mischel, 1979; Cantor, Mischel, & Schwartz, 1982b), and scripts (Schank & Abelson, 1977), and person memories (Hastie et al., 1980) provided the foundation for the social intelligence analysis of personality structures and processes.

Following Kelly (1955) and Mischel (1973), Cantor and Kihlstrom (1987) accorded *social concepts* a central status as cognitive structures of personality. If the purpose of perception is action, and if every act of perception is an act of categorization (Bruner, 1957), the particular categories that organize the people's perception of themselves, others, interpersonal behavior, and the social world in which behavior takes place assume paramount importance in a cognitive analysis of personality. Some of these concepts concern the world of other people and the places we encounter them: knowledge of personality types (e.g., achievers and altruists; Cantor & Mischel, 1979) and social groups (e.g., women and WASPS; Hamilton, 1981), and situations (e.g., blind dates and job interviews; Cantor, Mischel, & Schwartz, 1982a). Other concepts concern the personal world: knowledge of the kind of person we are, both in general and in particular classes of situations (e.g., an achiever at work but an altruist at home; Kihlstrom & Klein, 1994; Kihlstrom, Marchese, & Klein, 1997), and our theories of how we got that way (e.g., an adult child of alcoholics or a survivor of child sexual abuse; Ross, 1989). On the basis of studies of categorization in nonsocial domains (e.g., Rosch, 1978; Ross & Spalding, 1994), social concepts may be viewed as being structured as fuzzy sets around summary prototypes, perhaps along with representative exemplars that epitomize the category, and as being related to each other through tangled hierarchies reflecting conceptual relations. Some of these conceptual relations may be universal, and others may be highly consensual within the individual's culture; but, as Kelly (1955) argued, some may be quite idiosyncratic. Regardless of whether they are shared with others, the individual's conceptual knowledge about the social world forms a major portion of his or her declarative social intelligence.

Another important set of declarative social knowledge structures represents the individual's autobiographical memory (Conway, 1990; Rubin, 1996; Thompson, 1996, 1998). In the context of social intelligence, autobiographical memory includes a narrative of the person's own actions and experiences, but it also includes what he or she has learned through experience about the actions and experiences of specific other people (Hastie et al., 1980), and the events that have transpired in particular situations. Although social concepts constitute more or less abstract and context-free *semantic* memory, autobiographical memory is *episodic* memory – each piece of the narrative is tied to a specific location in space and time (Tulving, 1983). In addition, every piece of conscious autobiographical memory is linked to a mental representation of the self as the agent or patient of some action or the stimulus or experiencer of some state (Kihlstrom, 1997). As part of this connection to the self, each fragment of autobiographical memory is, at least in principle, also connected to knowledge about the person's emotional and motivational states at the time of the event in question. Thus, autobiographical memory is rich in content and complicated in structure – so rich and complicated that it is no wonder that most cognitive psychologists fall back on laboratory tasks involving memory for words and pictures.

On the procedural side, a substantial portion of the social intelligence repertoire consists of interpretive rules for making sense of social experience: for inducing social categories and deducing category membership, making attributions of causality, inferring other people's behavioral dispositions and emotional states, forming judgments of likability and responsibility, resolving cognitive dissonance, encoding and retrieving memories of our own and other people's behavior, predicting future events, and testing hypotheses about our social judgments. Some of these procedures are algorithmic, whereas others are heuristic shortcuts (Nisbett & Ross, 1980). Some are enacted deliberately, whereas others are enacted automatically without much atten-

tion and cognitive effort on our part (for summaries, see Bargh, 1994; Kihlstrom, 1987, 1996a, 1996b; Wegner & Bargh, 1998). But they are all part of the procedural repertoire of social intelligence.

Given this summary, it should be clear that, from the point of view of the social intelligence theory of personality, the assessment of social intelligence has quite a different character than it does from the psychometric point of view. From a psychometric point of view, the questions posed have answers that are right or wrong: Are smart people also friendly? How do you know when a person is happy or sad? Is it proper to laugh at a funeral? In this way, it is possible, at least in principle, to evaluate the accuracy of the person's social knowledge and the effectiveness of his or her social behaviors. However, as noted at the outset, the social intelligence approach to personality abjures such rankings of people. Rather than asking how socially intelligent a person *is*, compared with some norm, the social intelligence view of personality asks what social intelligence a person *has* with which he or she can guide his or her interpersonal behavior. In fact, the social intelligence approach to personality is less focused on assessing the individual's repertoire of social intelligence than in seeking to understand the general cognitive structures and processes out of which individuality is constructed, how these develop over the life course of the individual, and how they play a role in ongoing social interactions. For this reason, Cantor and Kihlstrom (1987, 1989; Kihlstrom & Cantor, 1989) have not proposed any individual difference measures by which a person's social intelligence can be assessed.*

Social Intelligence in Life Tasks

Although the social intelligence view of personality diverges from the psychometric approach to social intelligence on the matter of assessment, it agrees with some contemporary psychometric

---

* One exception to this rule is PERSPACE, a microcomputer software system designed for the assessment of the individual's context-specific self-concepts and other aspects of interpersonal space (Kihlstrom & Cunningham, 1991; Kihlstrom et al., 1997). However, like Kelly's (1955) Role Construct Repertory Test, PERSPACE is intended as a purely ideographic instrument and cannot be used to rank individuals or compare them with normative standards of performance.

views that intelligence is context-specific. Thus, in Sternberg's (1985, 1988) triarchic theory, social intelligence is part of a larger repertoire of knowledge by which the person attempts to solve the practical problems encountered in the physical and social world. According to Cantor and Kihlstrom (1987), social intelligence is specifically geared to solving the problems of social life, and in particular managing the *life tasks, current concerns* (Klinger 1977) or *personal projects* (Little, 1989) the person selects for him- or herself or that other people impose on him or her from outside. Put another way, one's social intelligence cannot be evaluated in the abstract but only with respect to the domains and contexts in which it is exhibited and the life tasks it is designed to serve. And even in this case, "adequacy" cannot be judged from the viewpoint of the external observer but rather from the point of view of the subject whose life tasks are in play.

Life tasks provide an integrative unit of analysis for the analysis of the interaction between the person and the situation. They may be explicit or implicit, abstract or circumscribed, universal or unique, enduring or stage-specific, rare or commonplace, ill-defined or well-defined problems. Whatever their features, they give meaning to the individual's life and serve to organize his or her daily activities. They are defined from the subjective point of view of the individual: they are the tasks which the person perceives him- or herself as "working on and devoting energy to solving during a specified period in life" (Cantor & Kihlstrom, 1987, p. 168).* First and foremost, life tasks are articulated by the individual as self-relevant, time-consuming, and meaningful. They provide a kind of organizing scheme for the individual's activities and are embedded in the individual's ongoing daily life. And they are responsive to the demands, structure, and constraints of the social environment in which the person lives. Many life tasks are normative for a particular life period

(e.g., retirement) or other life content (e.g., divorce), and the ways in which they are approached may be constrained by sociocultural factors. However, unlike the stage-structured views of Erikson (1950) and his popularizers (e.g., Levinson, 1978; Sheehy, 1976), the social intelligence view of personality does not propose that everyone at a particular age is engaged in the same sorts of life tasks. Instead, periods of transition in which the person is entering into new institutions are precisely those times when individual differences in life tasks become most apparent.

For example, Cantor and her associates have chosen the transition from high school to college as a particularly informative period in which to investigate life tasks (Cantor, Acker, and Cook-Flanagan, 1992; Cantor & Fleeson, 1991, 1994; Cantor & Harlow, 1994; Cantor & Langston, 1989; Cantor & Malley, 1991; Cantor et al., 1991; Cantor, Norem, Niedenthal, Langston, & Brower, 1987; Zirkel & Cantor, 1990). Freshman year is more than just convenient for academic researchers to study: The transition from high school to college and adulthood is a critical developmental milestone in which many individuals leave home for the first time to establish various independent habits and lifestyles. And although the decision to attend college may have been made for them (or may not have been a *decision* at all but just a fact of life), students still have a great deal of leeway to decide for themselves what they are going to do with the opportunity – what life tasks will occupy them for the next 4 years. Accordingly, when college students are asked to list their life tasks, they list social life tasks (e.g., *making friends* or *being on my own*) as often as they list academic ones (e.g., *getting good grades* or *carving a future direction*). And although the majority of students' life tasks could be slotted into a relatively small number of common categories, their individual construals of these tasks were quite unique and led to equally unique strategies for action.*

The intelligent nature of life-task pursuit is clearly illustrated by the strategies deployed in its service.

---

* A friend of ours once laid out her life tasks candidly and explicitly: "First I'll get tenure, and then I'll get married." This was probably not her life task as a child, nor even, perhaps, in college or graduate school; and once she got tenure and married, no doubt she would take up some other life task. Her age peers among university junior faculty may have had one task or the other, or neither, or had both tasks but reversed the order in which they were to be accomplished, or added other tasks (like bearing and raising children, or taking care of aged or infirm parents) to the mix.

* College students, of course, are not the only ones who have life tasks. Harlow and Cantor (1996) found that participation in life tasks such as *serving the community* and *having a social life* were important predictors of life satisfaction after retirement — especially for men who, in this cohort, had left behind the life tasks involved with work and career.

People often begin to comprehend the problem at hand by simulating a set of plausible outcomes and relating them to previous experiences stored in autobiographical memory. They also formulate specific plans for action and monitor their progress toward the goal, taking special note of environmental factors that stand in the way and determining whether the actual outcome meets their original expectations. Much of the cognitive activity in life-task problem solving involves forming causal attributions about outcomes and in surveying autobiographical memory for hints about how things might have gone differently. Particularly compelling evidence of the intelligent nature of life-task pursuit comes when, inevitably, plans go awry or some unforeseen event frustrates progress. Then, the person will map out a new path toward the goal or even choose a new goal compatible with a superordinate life task. Intelligence frees us from reflex, tropism, and instinct in social life as in nonsocial domains.

THE DEVELOPMENT OF SOCIAL INTELLIGENCE

Although the psychometric and personality views of social intelligence are opposed on many important points, such as the matter of comparative assessment of individuals, they come together nicely in recent work on the development of social intelligence (for reviews, see Greenspan, 1979; Greenspan & Love, 1997). Of course, social intelligence has always played a role in the concept of mental retardation. This psychiatric diagnosis requires not only evidence of subnormal intellectual functioning (i.e., IQ < 70) but also demonstrated evidence of impairments in "communication, self-care, home living, social and interpersonal skills, use of community resources, self-direction, functional academic skills, work, leisure, health, and safety" (American Psychiatric Association, 1994, p. 46). In other words, the diagnosis of mental retardation involves deficits in social as well as academic intelligence. Furthermore, the wording of the diagnostic criteria implies that social and academic intelligence are not highly correlated; the diagnosis requires positive evidence of *both* forms of impairment, meaning that the presence of one cannot be inferred from the presence of the other.

Although the conventional diagnostic criterion for mental retardation places primary emphasis on

IQ and intellectual functioning, Greenspan (1979) has argued that it should emphasize social and practical intelligence instead. To this end, Greenspan proposed a hierarchical model of social intelligence. In this model, social intelligence consists of three components: *social sensitivity*, reflected in role taking and social inference; *social insight*, including social comprehension, psychological insight, and moral judgment; and *social communication*, subsuming referential communication and social problem solving. Social intelligence, in turn, is only one component of *adaptive intelligence* (the others being *conceptual intelligence* and *practical intelligence*), which, in turn joins *physical competence* and *socioemotional adaptation* (temperament and character) as the major dimensions of personal competence broadly construed. Greenspan did not propose specific tests for any of these components of social intelligence but implied that they could be derived from experimental procedures used to study social cognition in general.

All this is well and good, but while the criterion for impaired intellectual functioning is clearly operationalized by an IQ threshold, there is as yet no standard by which impaired social functioning – impaired *social intelligence* – can be determined. The Vineland Social Maturity Scale (Doll, 1947) was an important step in this direction: this instrument, which yields aggregate scores of *social age* (analogous to mental age) and *social quotient* (by analogy to the intelligence quotient, calculated as social age divided by chronological age). However, it is a telling point that this instrument for evaluating social intelligence and other aspects of adaptive behavior was introduced almost a half century after the first IQ scale was introduced by Binet and Simon.* The Vineland has been recently revised (Sparrow, Balla, & Cicchetti, 1984), but its adequacy as a measure of social intelligence is compromised because linguistic functions, motor skills, occupational skills, and self-care and self-direction

---

* It is also a telling point that despite the fact that adaptive behavior has played a role in the diagnosis of mental retardation at least since the 1950s (Heber, 1961), the first edition of Ellis's (1963) *Handbook of Mental Deficiency, Psychological Theory, and Research*, a standard text in the field, had no chapter devoted to social intelligence — an omission corrected in subsequent editions by Greenspan (1979) and Greenspan and Love (1997).

are assessed as well as social relations. As an alternative, Taylor (1990) has proposed a semistructured social intelligence interview covering such domains as social memory, moral development, recognition of and response to social cues, and social judgment. However, Taylor concedes that such an interview, being ideographically constructed to take account of the individual's particular social environment, cannot easily yield numerical scores by which individuals can be compared and ranked. More important than ranking individuals, from Taylor's point of view, is identifying areas of high and low functioning within various environments experienced by the individual and determining the goodness of fit between the individual and the environments in which he or she lives. This latter goal, of course, is a primary thrust of the social intelligence view of personality espoused by Cantor and Kihlstrom (1987).

A further step away from the psychometric emphasis on ranking toward the social–cognitive emphasis on general processes is illustrated by recent trends in research on autism. Specifically, it has been proposed by Leslie (1987) and Baron-Cohen (1995), among others, that autistic children and adults lack a "theory of mind" (Premack & Woodruff, 1978; see also Flavell, Green, & Flavell, 1995; Gopnik & Meltzoff, 1997; Wellman, 1990) by which they can attribute mental states to other people and reflect on their own mental life (for a summary review, see Klein & Kihlstrom, 1998). For example, Baron-Cohen, Leslie, and Frith (1985) suggested that the core deficit in autism is that the affected children are unable to appreciate that other people's beliefs, attitudes, and experiences may differ from their own. This hypothesis brought the problem of assessing social intelligence in disabled populations (including mental retardation and learning disability as well as autism; see Greenspan & Love, 1997) directly in contact with a literature on the development of social cognition in normal children that had been emerging since the 1970s (Flavell, 1974; Flavell & Ross, 1981; Shantz, 1975). In this way, scientific understanding of social cognition *in general* began to influence research and theory on individual differences in social cognition.

Still, the problem remains. Is the core deficit in autism one of social intelligence, as Baron-Cohen (1995) claims? In this respect, it is interesting to note, along with Gardner (1983), that autistic individuals can show an impaired ability to understand others' mental states but retain abilities to deal cognitively with nonsocial objects and events as well as to comprehend social situations in which they are not required to understand another person's knowledge, belief, feelings, and desires. On the other hand, Bruner and Feldman (1993) have proposed that these deficits in social cognition are secondary to deficits in general cognitive functioning. Thus, although research on normal and abnormal development is more closely in contact with general social–cognitive theory than before, the fundamental questions endure: Is social cognition a separate faculty from nonsocial cognition? Is social intelligence anything different from general intelligence applied to the social domain?

As psychologists are fond of saying, further research is needed to answer these questions. However, we can hope that future research on social intelligence will have a different character than it has had in the past. One of the most salient, and distressing, features of the history of intelligence is how little contact there has been between the instruments by which we assess individual differences in intellectual ability and our understanding of the processes that supply the cognitive substrate of intellectual ability (Sternberg, 1977). The IQ test, once touted as "psychology's most telling accomplishment to date" (Herrnstein, 1973, p. 62), is almost entirely atheoretical, having been pragmatically constructed to model the sorts of things children do in school. So too with social intelligence, which all too often has been conceptualized informally and assessed by means of a jury-rigged assortment of tests (Walker & Foley, 1973). Perhaps new theoretical approaches, such as the social-intelligence view of personality and the "theory of mind" view of development, will change this situation so that future reviews of this sort will be able to describe assessments of social intelligence grounded in an understanding of the general social–cognitive processes out of which individual differences in social behavior emerge.

ACKNOWLEDGMENT

The point of view represented in this chapter is based on research supported by Grant MH-35856 from the National Institute of Mental Health and Grants BNS-84-11778 and BNS-87-18467 from the National Science Foundation. We wish to acknowledge our collaboration with the following individuals, whose ideas and research have greatly influenced our own: Jennifer Beer, William Fleeson, Jack Glaser, Robert Harlow, Christopher Langston, Julie Norem, Lillian Park, and Sabrina Zirkel.

REFERENCES

Allport, G. W., & Odbert, H. S. (1937). Trait-names: A psycho-lexical study. *Psychological Monographs, 47* (Whole No. 211).

American Psychiatric Association. (1994). *Diagnostic and statistical manual of mental disorders*, 4th ed. Washington, DC: American Psychiatric Association.

Anderson, J. R. (1976). *Language, memory, and thought.* Hillsdale, NJ: Erlbaum.

Asch, S. E. (1946). Forming impressions of personality. *Journal of Abnormal & Social Psychology, 41*, 258–290.

Bandura, A. (1973). *Aggression: A social learning analysis.* Englewood Cliffs, NJ: Prentice Hall.

Bandura, A. (1986). *Social foundations of thought and action: A social cognitive theory.* Englewood Cliffs, NJ: Prentice Hall.

Bandura, A., & Walters, R. H. (1963). *Social learning and personality development.* New York: Holt, Rinehart, & Winston.

Bargh, J. A. (1994). The four horsemen of automaticity: Awareness, intention, efficiency, and control in social cognition. In R. S. Wyer & T. K. Srull (Eds.), *Handbook of social cognition*, 2nd ed. (Vol. 1, pp. 1–40). Hillsdale, NJ: Erlbaum.

Barnes, M. L., & Sternberg, R. J. (1989). Social intelligence and decoding of nonverbal cues. *Intelligence, 13*, 263–287.

Baron-Cohen, S. (1995). *Mindblindness: An essay on autism and theory of mind.* Cambridge, MA: MIT Press.

Baron-Cohen, S., Leslie, A. M., & Frith, U. (1985). Does the autistic child have a "theory of mind"? *Cognition, 21*, 37–46.

Baron-Cohen, S., Tager-Flusberg, H., & Cohen, D. J. (Eds.). *Understanding other minds: Perspectives from autism.* Oxford, UK: Oxford University Press.

Broom, M. E. (1928). A note on the validity of a test of social intelligence. *Journal of Applied Psychology, 12*, 426–428.

Brown, L. T., & Anthony, R. G. (1990). Continuing the search for social intelligence. *Personality & Individual Differences, 11*, 463–470.

Bruner, J. S. (1957). On perceptual readiness. *Psychological Review, 64*, 123–152.

Bruner, J. S., & Feldman, C. (1993). Theories of mind and the problem of autism. In S. Baron-Cohen, H. Tager-Flusberg, & D. J. Cohen (Eds.), *Understanding other minds: Perspectives from autism* (pp. 267–291). Oxford: Oxford University Press.

Bruner, J. S., & Tagiuri, R. (1954). The perception of people. In G. Lindzey (Ed.), *Handbook of social psychology* (Vol. 2, pp. 634–654). Reading, MA: Addison-Wesley.

Byrne, R., & Whiten, A. (Eds.). (1988). *Machiavellian intelligence: Social expertise and the evolution of intellect in monkeys, apes, and humans.* Oxford: Clarendon Press.

Campbell, D. T., & Fiske, D. W. (1959). Convergent and discriminant validation by the multitrait-multimethod matrix. *Psychological Bulletin, 56*, 81–105.

Campbell, J. M., & McCord, D. M. (1996). The WAIS–R Comprehension and Picture Arrangement subtests as measures of social intelligence: Testing traditional interpretations. *Journal of Psychoeducational Assessment, 14*, 240–249.

Cantor, N., Acker, M., & Cook-Flanagan, C. (1992). Conflict and preoccupation in the intimacy life task. *Journal of Personality & Social Psychology, 63*, 644–655.

Cantor, N., & Fleeson, W. (1991). Life tasks and self-regulatory processes. In M. Maehr & P. Pintrich (Eds.), *Advances in motivation and achievement* (Vol. 7, pp. 327–369). Greenwich, CT: JAI Press.

Cantor, N., & Fleeson, W. (1994). Social intelligence and intelligent goal pursuit: A cognitive slice of motivation. In W. D. Spaulding (Ed.), *Integrative views of motivation, cognition, and emotion. Nebraska Symposium on Motivation, 41*, 125–180.

Cantor, N., & Harlow, R. (1994). Social intelligence and personality: Flexible life-task pursuit. In R. J. Sternberg & P. Ruzgis (Eds.), *Personality and intelligence* (pp. 137–168). Cambridge, UK: Cambridge University Press.

Cantor, N., & Kihlstrom, J. F. (1982). Cognitive and social processes in personality. In G. T. Wilson & C. M. Franks (Eds.), *Contemporary behavior therapy: Conceptual and empirical foundations* (pp. 142–201). New York: Guilford.

Cantor, N., & Kihlstrom, J. F. (1987). *Personality and social intelligence.* Englewood Cliffs, NJ: Prentice Hall.

Cantor, N., & Kihlstrom, J. F. (1989). Social intelligence and cognitive assessments of personality. In R. S. Wyer & T. K. Srull (Eds.), *Advances in social cognition* (Vol. 2, pp. 1–59). Hillsdale, NJ: Erlbaum.

Cantor, N., & Langston, C. A. (1989). "Ups and downs" of life tasks in a life transition. In L. A. Pervin (Ed.), *Goal concept in personality and social psychology* (pp. 127–168). Hillsdale, NJ: Erlbaum.

Cantor, N., & Malley, J. (1991). Life tasks, personal needs, and close relationships. In G. J. O. Fletcher & F. D. Fincham (Eds.), *Cognition in close relationships* (pp. 101–125). Hillsdale, NJ: Erlbaum.

Cantor, N., & Mischel, W. (1979). Prototypes in person perception. In L. Berkowitz (Ed.), *Advances in experimental social psychology* (Vol. 12, pp. 3–52). New York: Academic Press.

Cantor, N., Mischel, W., & Schwartz, J. (1982a). A prototype analysis of psychological situations. *Cognitive Psychology, 14*, 45–77.

Cantor, N., Mischel, W., & Schwartz, J. (1982b). Social knowledge: Structure, content, use and abuse. In A. H. Hastorf & A. M. Isen (Eds.), *Cognitive social psychology* (pp. 33–72). New York: Elsevier North-Holland.

Cantor, N., Norem, J., Langston, C., Zirkel, S., Fleeson, W., & Cook-Flanagan, C. (1991). Life tasks and daily life experiences. *Journal of Personality, 59*, 425–451.

Cantor, N., Norem, J. K., Niedenthal, P. M., Langston, C. A., & Brower, A. M. (1987). Life tasks, self-concept ideals, and cognitive strategies in a life transition. *Journal of Personality & Social Psychology, 53*, 1178–1191.

Cantor, N., Smith, E. E., French, R., & Mezzich, J. (1980). Psychiatric diagnosis as prototype categorization. *Journal of Abnormal Psychology, 89*, 181–193.

Cantor, N., & Zirkel, S. (1990). Personality, cognition, and purposive behavior. In L. Pervin (Ed.), *Handbook of personality: Theory and research* (pp. 125–164). New York: Guilford.

Cattell, R. B. (1971). *Abilities: Their structure, growth, and action*. Boston: Houghton Mifflin.

Chapin, F. S. (1942). Preliminary standardization of a social impact scale. *American Sociological Review, 7*, 214–225.

Chen, S. A., & Michael, W. B. (1993). First-order and higher-order factors of creative social intelligence within Guilford's structure-of-intellect model: A reanalysis of a Guilford data base. *Educational & Psychological Measurement, 53*, 619–641.

Conway, M. A. (1990). *Autobiographical memory: An introduction*. Milton Keynes, UK: Open University Press.

Cronbach, L. J. (1955). Processes affecting scores on "understanding of others" and "assumed similarity". *Psychological Bulletin, 52*, 177–193.

Doll, E. A. (1947). *Social maturity scale*. Circle Pines, MN: American Guidance Service.

Ellis, N. R. (Ed.). (1979). *Handbook of mental deficiency: Psychological theory and research*, New York: McGraw-Hill.

Erickson, E. H. (1950). *Childhood and society*. New York: Norton.

Farah, M. (1996). Is face recognition "special"? Evidence from neuropsychology. *Behavioural Brain Research, 76*, 181–189.

Fiske, S. T., & Taylor, S. E. (1991). *Social cognition*, 2nd ed. Reading, MA: Addison-Wesley.

Flavell, J. H. (1974). The development of inferences about others. In T. Mischel (Ed.), *Understanding other persons* (pp. 66–116). Oxford: Blackwell, Basil, & Mott.

Flavell, J. H., Green, F. L., & Flavell, E. R. (1995). Young children's knowledge about thinking. *Monographs of the Society for Research in Child Development, 60*, Whole No. 1.

Flavell, J. H., & Ross, L. (1981). *Social and cognitive development: Frontiers and possible future*. New York: Cambridge University Press.

Ford, M. E., & Tisak, M. S. (1983). A further search for social intelligence. *Journal of Educational Psychology, 75*, 196–206.

Fredrickson, N., Carlson, S., & Ward, W. C. (1984). The place of social intelligence in a taxonomy of cognitive abilities. *Intelligence, 8*, 315–337.

Gallup, G. G. (1970). Chimpanzees: Self-recognition. *Science, 167*, 86–87.

Gallup, G. G. (1998). Self-awareness and the evolution of social intelligence. *Behavioural Processes, 42*, 239–247.

Gallup, G. G., Marino, L., & Eddy, T. J. (1997). Anthropomorphism and the evolution of social intelligence: A comparative approach. In R. W. Mitchell, N. S. Thompson, & H. L. Miles (Eds.), *Anthropomorphism, anecdotes, and animals* (pp. 77–91). Albany: State University of New York Press.

Gardner, H. (1983). *Frames of mind: The theory of multiple intelligences*. New York: Basic Books.

Gardner, H. (1993). *Multiple intelligences: The theory in practice*. New York: Basic Books.

Gauthier, I. (1998). *Dissecting face recognition: The role of categorization level and expertise in visual object recognition*. Unpublished doctoral dissertation, Yale University.

Geertz, C. (1975). On the nature of anthropological understanding. *American Scientist, 63*, 47–53.

Goffman, E. (1959). *The presentation of self in everyday life*. Garden City, NY: Doubleday Anchor.

Goffman, E. (1967). *Interaction ritual: Essays in face-to-face behavior*. Chicago: Aldine.

Gopnik, A., & Meltzoff, A. N. (1997). *Words, thoughts, and theories*. Cambridge, MA: MIT Press.

Gough, H. G. (1966). Appraisal of social maturity by means of the CPI. *Journal of Abnormal Psychology, 71*, 189–195.

Greenspan, S. (1979). Social intelligence. In N. R. Ellis (Ed.), *Handbook of mental deficiency: Psychological theory and research*, 2nd ed. (pp. 483–532). Hillsdale, NJ: Erlbaum.

Greenspan, S., & Love, P. F. (1997). Social intelligence and development disorder: Mental retardation, learning disabilities, and autism. In W. E. MacLean (Ed.), *Ellis' handbook of mental deficiency: Psychological theory and research*, 3rd ed. (pp. 311–342). Mahwah, NJ: Erlbaum.

Guilford, J. P. (1967). *The nature of intelligence*. New York: McGraw-Hill.

Guilford, J. P. (1981). Higher-order structure-of-intellect abilities. *Multivariate Behavioral Research, 16*, 411–435.

Hamilton, D. (1981). *Cognitive processes in stereotyping and intergroup behavior*. Hillsdale, NJ: Erlbaum.

Harlow, R. E., & Cantor, N. (1996). Still participating after all these years: A study of life task participation in later life. *Journal of Personality & Social Psychology, 71*, 1235–1249.

Hastie, R., Ostrom, T., Ebbesen, E., Wyer, R. S., Hamilton, D., & Carlston, D. E. (1980). *Person memory: The cognitive basis of social perception*. Hillsdale, NJ: Erlbaum.

Heber, R. A. (1961). A manual on terminology and classification in mental retardation, 2nd ed. *American Journal of Mental Deficiency, 65*, Monograph Supplement.

Hendricks, M., Guilford, J. P., & Hoepfner, R. (1969). Measuring creative social intelligence. *Reports from the Psychological Laboratory, University of Southern California*, No. 42.

Herrnstein, R. J. (1973). *IQ in the meritocracy*. Boston: Atlantic-Little, Brown.

Hoepfner, R., & O'Sullivan, M. (1969). Social intelligence and IQ. *Educational & Psychological Measurement, 28*, 339–344.

Hogan, R. (1969). Development of an empathy scale. *Journal of Consulting & Clinical Psychology, 33*, 307–316.

Humphrey, N. (1976). The social functions of intellect. In P. P. G. Bateson & R. A. Hinde (Eds.), *Growing points in ethology* (pp. 303–317). Cambridge: Cambridge University Press.

Hunt, T. (1928). The measurement of social intelligence. *Journal of Applied Psychology, 12*, 317–334.

Jensen, A. R. (1998). *The g factor: The science of mental ability*. Westport, CT: Praeger.

John, O. P. (1990). The "big five" factor taxonomy: Dimensions of personality in the natural language and in questionnaires. In L. Pervin (Ed.), *Handbook of personality: Theory and research* (pp. 66–100). New York: Guilford.

Jones, E. E., & Pittman, T. S. (1982). Toward a general theory of strategic self-presentation. In J. Suls (Ed.), *Psychological perspectives on the self* (pp. 231–262). Hillsdale, NJ: Erlbaum.

Jones, K., & Day, J. D. (1997). Discrimination of two aspects of cognitive–social intelligence from academic intelligence. *Journal of Educational Psychology, 89*, 486–497.

Kaess, W. A., & Witryol, S. L. (1955). Memory for names and faces: A characteristic of social intelligence? *Journal of Applied Psychology, 39*, 457–462.

Kant. I. (1798/1978). *Anthropology from a pragmatic point of view*. Carbondale, II: Southern Illinois University Press. (Originally published 1798).

Keating, D. K. (1978). A search for social intelligence. *Journal of Educational Psychology, 70*, 218–233.

Kelley. H. L. (1967). Attribution theory in social psychology. In D. Levine (Ed.), *Nebraska symposium on motivation* (Vol. 15, pp. 192–238). Lincoln: University of Nebraska Press.

Kelly, G. (1955). *The psychology of personal constructs*. New York: Norton.

Kihlstrom, J. F. (1987). The cognitive unconscious. *Science, 237*, 1445–1452.

Kihlstrom, J. F. (1996a). Conscious and unconscious cognition. In R. J. Sternberg (Ed.), *The concept of cognition* (pp. 173–203). Cambridge, MA: MIT Press.

Kihlstrom, J. F. (1996b). Unconscious processes in social interaction. In S. Hameroff, A. W. Kaszniak, & A. C. Scott (Eds.), *Toward a science of consciousness: The 1st Tucson discussions and debates* (pp. 93–104). Cambridge, MA: MIT Press.

Kihlstrom, J. F. (1997). Consciousness and me-ness. In J. Cohen & J. Schooler (Eds.), *Scientific approaches to the question of consciousness* (pp. 451–468). Mahwah, NJ: Erlbaum.

Kihlstrom, J. F., & Cantor, N. (1989). Social intelligence and personality: There's room for growth. In R. S. Wyer & T. K. Srull (Eds.), *Advances in social cognition* (Vol. 2, pp. 197–214). Hillsdale, NJ: Erlbaum.

Kihlstrom, J. F., & Cunningham, R. L. (1991). Mapping interpersonal space. In M. Horowitz (Ed.), *Person schemas and interpersonal behavior patterns* (pp. 311–336). Chicago: University of Chicago Press.

Kihlstrom, J. F., & Hastie, R. (1997). Mental representations of persons and personality. In S. R. Briggs, R. Hogan, & W. H. Jones (Eds.), *Handbook of personality psychology* (pp. 711–735). San Diego, CA: Academic Press.

Kihlstrom, J. F., & Klein, S. B. (1994). The self as a knowledge structure. In R. S. Wyer & T. K. Srull (Eds.), *Handbook of social cognition*, 2nd ed. (Vol. 1, pp. 153–208). Hillsdale, NJ: Erlbaum.

Kihlstrom, J. F., Marchese, L. A., & Klein, S. B. (1997). Situating the self in interpersonal space. In U. Neisser & D. A. Jopling (Eds.), *The conceptual self in context: Culture, experience, self-understanding* (pp. 154–175). New York: Cambridge University Press.

Kihlstrom, J. F., Mulvaney, S., Tobias, B. A., & Tobis, I. P. (1999). The emotional unconscious. In E. Eich, J. F. Kihlstrom, G. H. Bower, J. P. Forgas, & P. M. Niedenthal, *Counterpoints: Cognition and emotion*. New York: Oxford University Press.

Kihlstrom, J. F., & Nasby, W. (1981). Cognitive tasks in clinical assessment: An exercise in applied psychology. In P. C. Kendall & S. D. Hollon (Eds.), *Cognitive-behavioral interventions: Assessment methods* (pp. 287–317). New York: Academic Press.

Klein, S. B., & Kihlstrom, J. F. (1998). On bridging the gap between social-personality psychology and neuropsychology. *Personality & Social Psychology Review*, 228–242.

Klinger, E. (1977). *Meaning and void: Inner experience and the incentives in people's lives*. Minneapolis: University of Minnesota Press.

Kohlberg, L. (1963). The development of children's orientations toward a moral order: I. Sequence in the development of moral thought. *Vita Humana, 6*, 11–33.

Kosmitzki, C., & John, O. P. (1993). The implicit use of explicit conceptions of social intelligence. *Personality & Individual Differences, 15*, 11–23.

LeDoux, J. (1996). *The emotional brain: The mysterious underpinnings of emotional life*. New York: Simon & Schuster.

Legree, P. J. (1995). Evidence for an oblique social intelligence factor established with a Likert-based testing procedure. *Intelligence, 21*, 247–266.

Leslie, A. M. (1987). Pretense and representation: The origins of "theory of mind." *Psychological Review, 94*, 412–426.

Levinson, D. (1978). *The seasons in a man's life*. New York: Balantine.

Little, B. (1989). Personal projects analysis: Trivial pursuits, magnificent obsessions, and the search for coherence. In D. Buss and N. Cantor (Eds.), *Personality psychology: Recent trends and emerging directions* (pp. 15–31). New York: Springer-Verlag.

Lowman, R. L., & Leeman, G. E. (1988). The dimensionality of social intelligence: Social abilities, interests, and needs. *Journal of Psychology, 122,* 279–290.

Luria, A. R. (1972). *The man with a shattered world: The history of a brain wound.* New York: Basic Books.

Macmillan, M. B. (1986). A wonderful journey through skull and brains: The travels of Mr. Gage's tamping iron. *Brain & Cognition, 5,* 67–107.

Marlowe, H. A. (1986). Social intelligence: Evidence for multidimensionality and construct independence. *Journal of Educational Psychology, 78,* 52–58.

Marlowe, H. A., & Bedell, J. R. (1982). Social intelligence: Evidence for independence of the construct. *Psychological Reports, 51,* 461–462.

Matarazzo, J. D. (1972). *Wechsler's measurement and appraisal of adult intelligence,* 5th ed. Baltimore, MD: Williams & Wilkins.

Miller, N. E., & Dollard, J. H. (1941). *Social learning and imitation.* New Haven: Yale University Press.

Mischel, W. (1968). *Personality and assessment.* New York: Wiley.

Mischel, W. (1973). Toward a cognitive social learning reconceptualization of personality. *Psychological Review, 80,* 252–283.

Moss, F. A. (1931). Preliminary report of a study of social intelligence and executive ability. *Public Personnel Studies, 9,* 2–9.

Moss, F. A., & Hunt, T. (1927). Are you socially intelligent? *Scientific American, 137,* 108–110.

Moss, F. A., Hunt, T., & Omwake, K. T. (1949). *Manual for the social intelligence test, Revised form.* Washington, DC: Center for Psychological Service.

Moss, F. A., Hunt, T., Omwake, K. T., & Ronning, M. M. (1927). *Social intelligence test.* Washington, DC: Center for Psychological Service.

Moss, F. A., Hunt, T., Omwake, K. T., & Woodward, L. G. (1955). *Manual for the George Washington University series social intelligence test.* Washington, DC: Center for Psychological Service.

Nasby & Kihlstrom. (1986). Cognitive assessment in personality and psychopathology. In R. E. Ingram (Ed.), *Information processing approaches to psychopathology and clinical psychology* (pp. 217–239). New York: Academic Press.

Neisser, U. (1979). The concept of intelligence. *Intelligence, 3,* 217–227.

Nisbett, R. E., & Ross, L. (1980). *Human inference: Strategies and shortcomings in social judgment.* Englewood Cliffs, NJ: Prentice Hall.

Orlik, P. (1978). [Social intelligence.] In K. J. Klauer (Ed.), [*Handbook of pedagogical diagnosis*] (pp. 341–354). Dusseldorf: Schwann.

O'Sullivan, M., Guilford, J. P., & deMille, R. (1965). The measurement of social intelligence. *Reports from the Psychological Laboratory, University of Southern California,* No. 34.

Premack, D., & Woodruff, G. (1978). Does the chimpanzee have a theory of mind? *Behavioral & Brain Sciences, 1,* 515–526.

Rapaport, D., Gill, M. M., & Schafer, R. (1968). *Diagnostic psychological testing,* Rev. ed. New York: International Universities Press.

Rest, J. R. (1975). Longitudinal study of the Defining Issues Test of moral judgment: A strategy for analyzing developmental change. *Developmental Psychology, 11,* 738–748.

Riggio, R. E., Messamer, J., & Throckmorton, B. (1991). Social and academic intelligence: Conceptually distinct but overlapping constructs. *Personality & Individual Differences, 12,* 695–702.

Rosch, E. (1978). Principles of categorization. In E. Rosch, & B. B. Lloyd (Eds.), *Cognition and categorization* (pp. 27–48). Hillsdale, NJ: Erlbaum.

Ross, B. H., & Spalding, T. L. (1994). Concepts and categories. In R. J. Sternberg (Ed.), *Thinking and problem solving* (pp. 119–148). San Diego, CA: Academic Press.

Ross, M. (1989). Relation of implicit theories to the construction of personal histories. *Psychological Review, 96,* 341–357.

Rotter, J. B. (1954). *Social learning and clinical psychology.* Englewood Cliffs, NJ: Prentice Hall.

Rotter, J. B. (1966). Generalized expectancies for internal versus external control of reinforcement. *Psychological Monographs, 80*(1, Whole No. 609).

Rubin, D. C. (Ed.). (1996). *Remembering our past: Studies in autobiographical memory.* Cambridge, UK: Cambridge University Press.

Schneider, R. J., Ackerman, P. L., & Kanfer, R. (1996). To "act wisely in human relations": Exploring the dimensions of social competence. *Personality & Individual Differences, 21,* 469–482.

Sechrest, L., & Jackson, D. N. (1961). Social intelligence and the accuracy of interpersonal predictions. *Journal of Personality, 29,* 167–182.

Schank, R., & Abelson, R. (1977). *Scripts, plans, goals, and understanding.* Hillsdale, NJ: Erlbaum.

Shanley, L. A., Walker, R. E., & Foley, J. M. (1971). Social intelligence: A concept in search of data. *Psychological Reports, 29,* 1123–1132.

Shantz, C. V. (1975). The development of social cognition. In E. M. Hetherington (Ed.), *Review of child development research* (Vol. 5, pp. 257–323). Chicago: University of Chicago Press.

Sheehy, G. (1976). *Passages: Predictable crises of adult life.* New York: Dutton.

Sipps, G. J., Berry, G. W., & Lynch, E. M. (1987). WAIS–R and social intelligence: A test of established assumptions that uses the CPI. *Journal of Clinical Psychology, 43,* 499–504.

Skinner, B. F. (1953). *Science and human behavior.* New York: Macmillan.

Snyder, M., & Cantor, N. (1998). Understanding personality and social behavior: A functionalist strategy. In D. T. Gilbert & S. T. Fiske (Eds.), *Handbook of social psychology,* 4th ed. (Vol. 2, pp. 635–679). Boston: McGraw-Hill.

Sparrow, S. S., Balla, D. A., & Cicchetti, D. V. (1984). *Vineland adaptive behavior scale.* Circle Pines, MN: American Guidance Service.

Spearman. C. (1927). *The abilities of man.* New York: Macmillan.

Staats, A. W., & Staats, C. K. (1963). *Complex human behavior: A systematic extension of learning principles.* New York: Holt, Rinehart, & Winston.

Sternberg, R. J. (1977). *Intelligence, information processing, and analogical reasoning: The componential analysis of human abilities.* Hillsdale, NJ: Erlbaum.

Sternberg, R. J. (1980). Sketch of a componential subtheory of human intelligence. *Behavioral & Brain Sciences, 3,* 573–614.

Sternberg, R. J. (1984a). Toward a triarchic theory of human intelligence. *Behavioral & Brain Sciences, 7,* 269–315.

Sternberg, R. J. (1984b). Metacomponents and microcomponents of education: Some proposed loci of mental retardation. In P. H. Brooks, R. Sperber, & C. McCauley (Eds.), *Learning and cognition in the mentally retarded* (pp. 89–114). Hillsdale, NJ: Erlbaum.

Sternberg, R. J. (1985). *Beyond IQ: A triarchic theory of human intelligence.* New York: Cambridge University Press.

Sternberg, R. J. (1988). *The triarchic mind: A new theory of intelligence.* New York: Viking.

Sternberg, R. J., Conway, B. E., Ketron, J. L., & Bernstein, M. (1981). People's conceptions of intelligence. *Journal of Personality & Social Psychology, 41,* 37–55.

Sternberg, R. J., & Smith, C. (1985). Social intelligence and decoding skills in nonverbal communication. *Social Cognition, 3,* 168–192.

Sternberg, R. J., & Wagner, R. (Eds.). (1986). *Practical intelligence: Nature and origins of competence in the everyday world.* Cambridge, UK: Cambridge University Press.

Strang, R. (1930). Measures of social intelligence. *American Journal of Sociology, 36,* 263–269.

Stricker, L. J., & Rock, D. A. (1990). Interpersonal competence, social intelligence, and general ability. *Personality & Individual Differences, 11,* 833–839.

Taylor, E. H. (1990). The assessment of social intelligence. *Psychotherapy, 27,* 445–457.

Taylor, E. H., & Cadet, J. L. (1989). Social intelligence, a neurological system? *Psychological Reports, 64,* 423–444.

Thompson, C. P. (1996). *Autobiographical memory: Remembering what and remembering when.* Mahwah, NJ: Erlbaum.

Thompson, C. P. (1998). *Autobiographical memory: Theoretical and applied perspectives.* Mahwah, NJ: Erlbaum.

Thorndike, E. L. (1920). Intelligence and its use. *Harper's Magazine, 140,* 227–235.

Thorndike, R. L. (1936). Factor analysis of social and abstract intelligence. *Journal of Educational Psychology, 27,* 231–233.

Thorndike, R. L., & Stein, S. (1937). An evaluation of the attempts to measure social intelligence. *Psychological Bulletin, 34,* 275–285.

Thurstone, L. L. (1938). *Primary mental abilities.* Chicago: University of Chicago Press.

Tolman, E. C. (1932). *Purposive behavior in animals and men.* New York: Appleton-Century-Crofts.

Tulving, E. (1983). *Elements of episodic memory.* New York: Oxford University Press.

Vernon, P. E. (1933). Some characteristics of the good judge of personality. *Journal of Social Psychology, 4,* 42–57.

Wagner, R. K., & Sternberg, R. J. (1985). Practical intelligence in real-world pursuits: The role of tacit knowledge. *Journal of Personality & Social Psychology, 49,* 436–458.

Walker, R. E., & Foley, J. M. (1973). Social intelligence: Its history and measurement. *Psychological Reports, 33,* 839–864.

Wechsler, D. (1939). *The measurement and appraisal of adult intelligence.* Baltimore: Williams & Wilkins.

Wechsler, D. (1958). *The measurement and appraisal of adult intelligence,* 4th ed. Baltimore: Williams & Wilkins.

Wedeck, J. (1947). The relationship between personality and psychological ability. *British Journal of Psychology, 36,* 133–151.

Wegner, D. M., & Bargh, J. A. (1998). Control and automaticity in social life. In D. T. Gilbert & S. T. Fiske (Eds.), *Handbook of social psychology,* 4th ed. (Vol. 2, pp. 446–496). Boston: McGraw-Hill.

Wellman, H. M. (1990). *The child's theory of mind.* Cambridge, MA: MIT Press.

Whiten, A., & Byrne, R. (Eds.). (1997). *Machiavellian intelligence II: Extensions and evaluations.* Cambridge: Cambridge University Press.

Winograd, T. (1975). Frame representations and the procedural-declarative controversy. In D. Bobrow & A. Collins (Eds.), *Representation and understanding: Studies in cognitive science* (pp. 185–210). New York: Academic Press.

Wong, C.-M. T., Day, J. D., Maxwell, S. E., & Meara, N. M. (1995). A multitrait-multimethod study of academic and social intelligence in college students. *Journal of Educational Psychology, 87,* 117–133.

Woodrow, H. (1939). The common factors in 52 mental tests. *Psychometrika, 4,* 99–108.

Worden, R. P. (1996). Primate social intelligence. *Cognitive Science, 20,* 579–616.

Zirkel, S., & Cantor, N. (1990). Personal construal of life tasks: Those who struggle for independence. *Journal of Personality & Social Psychology, 58,* 172–185.

CHAPTER SEVENTEEN

Practical Intelligence

RICHARD K. WAGNER

PRACTICAL INTELLIGENCE

Among the most interesting and important pages of any handbook are the few pages devoted to the table of contents. More than simply an aid to finding a page number of interest, the table of contents provides at least one view – the editor's – of *what constitutes a field at a given time*. At a point early in the process of editing a handbook, the editor must put together a proposed table of contents. In doing so, a snapshot of the landscape that makes up a field as it exists in the mind of the editor is created. When more than one handbook or other similarly comprehensive reference work targets the same field at different points in time, comparing tables of contents can provide clues to identifying which issues and areas of inquiry are old and which are new.

Comparing the table of contents of the present edition to that of the former *Handbook of Human Intelligence* (Sternberg, 1982) is informative about the location of practical intelligence in the landscape of human intelligence, at least as revealed by two snapshots taken almost two decades apart by the same editor. Simply put, the former handbook did not devote a chapter to practical intelligence, although related issues such as the contextual basis of intelligence are evident. In fact, practical intelligence is not even an entry in the index of the previous work. What has changed in the field of intelligence over the past two decades that warrants an entire chapter devoted to a topic that did not even appear in the index of the previous volume?

This chapter is an attempt to answer this question. The chapter is divided into two major parts. The first part addresses the nature of practical intelligence as distinct from traditional or other forms of intelligence. The section contains a review of empirical studies that chronicle a divergent effort to identify and define a practical kind of intelligence different from the more academic kind of intelligence represented by the ubiquitous IQ test. The fundamental question this work attempts to answer is, What is practical intelligence? The second part of the chapter addresses the primary challenge for the future. After establishing that practical intelligence is distinct from other kinds of intelligence, what is required is a convergent effort that examines the interface between practical, academic, and possibly other kinds of intelligence. The fundamental question to be answered by this effort is, How is practical intelligence related to other kinds of intelligence? The goal is nothing less than a comprehensive account of human intelligence.

WHAT IS PRACTICAL INTELLIGENCE?

Definitions of intelligence have not proved to be either easy to agree on or particularly useful. In 1921, when the *Journal of Educational Psychology* asked 17 leading researchers to define intelligence, the responses amounted to 14 different definitions and 3 nonreplies. When leading researchers were asked to respond to the same question 65 years later, the responses again showed remarkable variability (Sternberg & Detterman, 1986). When definitions presented in 1921 and 1986 were analyzed, 27 different attributes were identified (Sternberg &

Berg, 1986). Nevertheless, an analysis of working definitions of practical intelligence proves useful in a first attempt to describe what is meant by practical intelligence.

Exclusionary Definitions

An exclusionary definition defines something by cataloging what it is not. For example, learning disabilities are defined by the exclusionary definition of poor achievement that cannot be attributed to sensory impairment, mental retardation, or lack of opportunity to learn. A similar approach has been taken for practical intelligence.

Frederiksen (1986) described practical intelligence as being reflected in our cognitive responses to almost everything that happens outside the school setting. Frederiksen's interest was in practical intelligence as manifested in the domain of business management. He popularized research using the in-basket task. He asked managers to sit at a desk and work their way through an in-basket of simulated memos, phone messages, and tasks that required handling. Performance was analyzed by having observers classify what the managers did in categories such as "seeks additional information," "asks for advice," and "delegates task to subordinate." Studies using the in-basket technique were carried out over the years in various domains such as government administration, administration in the Air Force, and school administration. Effective performance on the in-basket task was found to depend primarily on two things. The first was the amount of domain knowledge of the particular problems found in the in-basket. Managers who had previously handled the task or problem or one similar to it in their jobs were able to apply what they learned to the in-basket version. The second was ideational fluency, which Frederiksen defined in the context as the number of relevant ideas and information produced by the manager.

If practical intelligence is demonstrated in our cognitive responses to problems that occur outside the school setting, how do such problems differ from school-based ones? Problems found in the classroom, as well as on IQ tests, tend to (a) be well-defined, (b) be formulated by others, (c) come with all information required for problem solution, (d) have one correct answer, (e) have one or at most several methods for obtaining the correct answer,

and (f) be unrelated to everyday experience (Neisser, 1976; Wagner & Sternberg, 1985). In contrast, the more practical problems of everyday life, including many of the problems encountered in diverse careers, often are (a) defined poorly; (b) formulated by the problem solver; (c) missing information essential to solution; (d) characterized by having multiple solutions, each associated with liabilities and assets; (e) characterized by having multiple methods of obtaining each solution; and (f) related to everyday experience.

Given characteristics such as being ill-defined, lacking in essential information, and having no single correct answer, it would seem that practical problems would be nearly impossible to solve. Yet, ordinary people often do quite well at solving practical problems, and, as will be described subsequently, older individuals may be better at solving practical problems than academic ones. What appears key is the final characteristic of being related to everyday experience. Individuals often have a great deal of specific knowledge they can apply to practical problems, and as has become clear from countless studies, domain-specific knowledge is extraordinarily powerful for successful problem solving. Recall that the amount of relevant domain knowledge was a potent predictor of performance in Frederiksen's in-basket studies. In contrast, academic problems tend to be disembedded from everyday experience. If you do not possess the precise knowledge of facts and permissible strategies and operations, no amount of practical information will be sufficient for correct solution.

One source of empirical evidence relevant to the claim that important differences exist between the practical problems of the everyday world and the academic problems found in the classroom and on IQ tests is provided by studies of the predictive power of IQ scores for real-world criteria. The degree to which IQ test scores predict real-world performance criteria, such as job performance, has been an area of controversy. Opinions about the usefulness of IQ test scores for job selection range from the view that little or no justification exists for use of IQ test scores in selection (McClelland, 1973) to the view that IQ tests are valid predictors of job performance for all jobs (Schmidt & Hunter, 1981). Others have taken the middle ground by asserting that IQ test scores provide useful yet incomplete information for selecting individuals for many jobs (Sternberg, Wagner, Williams, & Horvath, 1995; Wagner, 1997; see also Barrett & Depinet, 1991; Gottfredson, 1991; Hawk, 1986).

Nevertheless, some basic facts about the predictive validity of IQ tests for job selection are indisputable, even if their implications and appropriate interpretation remain controversial. For example, the average observed validity coefficient between IQ scores and job performance falls at about the .2 level (Hartigan & Wigdor, 1989; Wigdor & Garner, 1982). This indicates that IQ predicts only about 4% of the variance in job performance. However, the average observed validity coefficient between IQ scores and performance in job training programs rises to about the .4 level, and IQ now accounts for about 16% of the variance in training performance. Thus, the more schoollike the criterion measure to be predicted, the greater the predictive validity of IQ test scores.

Observed validity coefficients may not provide accurate estimates of the importance of IQ test scores for selecting individuals for jobs or other out-of-school settings for several reasons, some of which suggest that observed validity coefficients are smaller than they should be, others of which suggest just the opposite. Examples of reasons why observed validity coefficients are smaller than they should be include the facts that observed validity coefficients are affected by restriction of range and measurement error. Restriction of range refers to the fact that the samples used in most predictive validity studies are limited to individuals who previously had been hired by a company. Had they not been hired, job performance data would not be available for them to be used as a criterion measure to be predicted. But if companies hire only applicants who score relatively highly on the tests used for selection, the range of test scores of individuals who were hired will be less than that of individuals who make up the applicant pool. The size of a correlation coefficient depends upon the amount of variability in the data. Less variability means smaller validity coefficients.

Observed validity coefficients are also affected by measurement error. Unreliability in either the test or the criterion to be predicted reduces the magnitude of the observed validity coefficient. When observed validity coefficients are corrected statisti-

cally for restriction of range and measurement error, the average validity coefficient increases to about the .5 level (Schmidt & Hunter, in press). Restriction of range effects would also raise the average validity coefficient for training outcomes, as would measurement error, although perhaps to a lesser degree than for job performance because training performance may be measured more reliably through paper-and-pencil tests than actual job performance. It remains likely, therefore, that the average validity coefficient for job training will exceed that for job performance even after both validity coefficients are corrected for restriction of range and measurement error.

Validity coefficients may overestimate the importance of using IQ test scores in prediction because validity coefficients do not take into account the role of other predictors. A validity coefficient is, by definition, a simple correlation between a test score and a criterion measure. Because of this, the validity coefficient commonly will overestimate the unique predictive power of IQ scores when multiple sources of information are used to select individuals for jobs, and these sources are also related to the criterion measure of job performance (Wagner, 1997). Validity coefficients only indicate what would happen if the test were used as the sole source of information, ignoring overlap with other sources of information. In actual selection situations, multiple sources of information are used routinely. College students are selected on the basis of high school grades, biographical statements, and perhaps interviews, in addition to SAT or ACT scores. Job applicants are selected on the basis of previous experience, educational background, and letters of recommendation in addition to scores on IQ or other employment tests.

In conclusion, a strength of a working definition of practical intelligence based on exclusion is its breadth. Because of its breadth, it is not likely that an important aspect of practical intelligence would be ruled out of consideration a priori. However, the price of such breadth is that a working definition based on exclusion provides little specific guidance about what one should attempt to study. In the following sections, studies based on more inclusionary working definitions of practical intelligence will be reviewed, beginning with working definitions based on the construct of practical know-how.

Practical Know-How

Berry and Irvine's (1986) cross-cultural studies of practical know-how provide intriguing examples of practical intelligence manifested in various cultures, particularly cultures viewed as "primitive" by Western standards. An example is provided by individuals who make a living repairing machines and appliances in situations in which sophisticated diagnostic tools and replacement parts are not available. If you live in a modern Western country and the engine in your automobile stops running, a mechanic is likely to hook up your engine to a diagnostic computer that will identify the module or component that is not functioning properly. The mechanic will swap the defective module or component with a new one, and in most cases, the problem will have been solved. In contrast, when one travels to poorer countries, one sees old automobiles that are kept in running order by mechanics who lack modern test equipment and even access to replacement parts. Berry and Irvine adopted the concept of the *bricoleur* to describe such individuals. Levi-Strauss (1966) originally introduced the term *bricolage* to refer to work of an odd-job sort. A bricoleur is someone who completes jobs by adapting whatever resources are at hand – as opposed to the skilled craftsman or repairman who relies on technical manuals and specialized tools. The bricoleur will size up the situation and the available materials and then improvise a solution.

Gladwin (1970) studied ocean navigation among the Puluwat people of Micronesia. The Puluwat travel among islands in large canoes. Navigation is based on an abstract system in which the islands, rather than the canoe, are considered to be moving. This view defies conventional wisdom but is understandable when one considers that, from the point of view of the navigator in the canoe, the islands appear to move toward, away, or by the canoe on the voyage. The journey is divided by the navigator into three phases. The first phase consists of selecting the destination and the initial course to be followed. Selecting the destination involves evaluating the weather, wind, and season. Once the canoe is out in the harbor, the initial course is established by drawing an imaginary line from the canoe to points on the departure island that are known to indicate the approximate direction to the target island. The second phase consists of navigating to maintain the correct course. Maintaining the correct course is accomplished in a variety of ways. Direction is maintained with reference to the stars at night, the sun during the day, the direction of the wind and waves, and by etak. Etak is a system of navigation in which the journey is divided into sectors based on extensions of imaginary lines drawn between a known reference island that is encountered along the way and stars above it. Position information is maintained by the use of dead reckoning (i.e., keeping track of direction and estimated distance covered since the last known location) and by identifying reefs and islands encountered along the way. The third and final phase entails locating the destination island. Techniques used in this last phase include observing birds at dusk that are known to roost on land at night; being alert at night for odors, sounds, and changes in wind velocity and direction associated with being in the lee of a land mass; and adopting a zigzag search pattern.

Many other examples of cross-cultural studies of intellectual performance are available (see, e.g., Berry et al., 1986; Blurton, Jones, & Konner, 1976; Cole, Gay, Glick, & Sharp, 1971; Laboratory of Comparative Human Cognition, 1982; Levy-Strauss, 1966; Scribner & Cole, 1981). In general, even unschooled individuals in "primitive" cultures exhibit logical thinking, but mostly in the context of solving practical problems. When presented with tasks to perform, performance is greatly affected by the specific materials and procedures employed and other aspects of the experimental context (Berry & Irvine, 1986).

In a series of studies, Wagner and Sternberg have studied practical know-how in the form of *tacit knowledge* (Sternberg, Wagner, Williams, & Horvath, 1995; Wagner, 1987; Wagner & Sternberg, 1985; see Jensen, 1993, and Schmidt & Hunter, 1993, for critiques of this approach). Tacit knowledge refers to practical know-how that rarely is formally described or taught directly (Wagner, 1987). Tacit knowledge has been measured by presenting individuals with scenarios depicting real-world situations and then having them rate the quality of various courses of action. Studies of tacit knowledge have been carried out in diverse domains ranging from business management, sales, academic psychology, and schooling (see Sternberg et al., 1995, for a review of this research).

Several consistent findings have emerged from these studies. For example, tacit knowledge is a robust predictor of success in real-world pursuits. In a study of 80 psychology department faculty members from around the country, correlations were obtained between tacit knowledge and various indices of career performance as an academic psychologist. The correlation between tacit knowledge and rated quality of departmental faculty members was .48 ($p <$ .001). Perhaps the single best measure of scholarly productivity is citation count. Citation count refers to the number of times other researchers cite one's work in articles they have published and is regarded as an index of the extent to which one's research has influenced the field of science in a particular area. The correlation between tacit knowledge and citation count was .44 ($p < $.001). Correlations of similar magnitude have been found between tacit knowledge and career performance in other domains, including business management and sales. These correlations are about double those typically found between IQ test scores and these same measures of career performance.

Tacit knowledge predicts real-world performance independently of IQ and personality measures. Scores on measures of tacit knowledge rarely correlate significantly with IQ. For example, Wagner and Sternberg (1985) reported nonsignificant correlations between tacit knowledge and the Verbal Reasoning subtest of the Differential Aptitude Tests of .16 and .12 for samples of 22 and 60 undergraduates, respectively. The correlation between tacit knowledge and IQ for a sample of 45 managers who participated in a leadership development program at the Center for Creative Leadership in Greensboro, North Carolina, was .14.

One limitation of these studies involving students or business managers is that such samples are characterized by a limited range of IQ relative to the general population and perhaps even a limited range in tacit knowledge as well. A limited range of IQ might limit the size of the correlation between IQ and tacit knowledge. However, near-zero correlations between IQ and tacit knowledge have been reported even for more general samples. Eddy (1988) obtained scores on a tacit knowledge inventory for business management and on the Armed Services Vocational Aptitude Battery (ASVAB) for a sample of 631 Air Force recruits. The ASVAB is a multiple-aptitude battery used by the armed services to select recruits for all branches of the United States Armed Forces. Prior studies of the ASVAB have shown that it is a typical measure of cognitive ability. Correlations between the ASVAB and other cognitive ability tests are about .7, and factor analytic studies show that the ASVAB measures the same verbal, quantitative, and mechanical abilities that are measures by the Differential Aptitude Tests and the same verbal and mathematical abilities measured by the California Achievement Tests.

The median correlation between tacit knowledge and the ASVAB subtests was .07, with a range of $-$.06 to .15. Of the 10 correlations examined, only 2 were significantly different from 0 despite the power provided by a sample size of over 600 individuals. Factor analysis of these data yielded the usual ASVAB factors and a separate tacit knowledge factor. The loading of the tacit knowledge measure was .99 on the tacit knowledge factor, whereas the maximum loading of the tacit knowledge measure on the ASVAB factors was only .06. The use of oblique rotation of factors permitted estimates of the correlations among the ASVAB and tacit knowledge factors. The ASVAB factors were moderately correlated among themselves, as would be expected, but the correlations between the tacit knowledge factor and the four ASVAB factors were minimal (.075, .003, .096, and .082).

We will now turn to relations between tacit knowledge and personality. Participants in the Center for Creative Leadership study just mentioned completed a battery of personality and interest inventories, including the California Psychological Inventory, the Myers–Briggs Type Indicator, the Fundamental Interpersonal Relations Orientation-Behavior, and the Kirton Adaptation Innovation Inventory, among others. Managerial performance was quantified in terms of ratings of performance in several small-group simulations that involved working together to solve fictitious business problems.

Tacit knowledge was the best predictor of managerial performance in small-group simulations ($r =$ .61, $p < $.001). Hierarchical multiple regression was used to determine whether the relation between tacit knowledge and managerial performance was independent of relations between personality variables and managerial performance. Tacit knowledge was added last to various batteries of predictors that represented combinations of the various personality variables, interest variables, and IQs that were available. Regardless of which predictors already were in the model, tacit knowledge added significant and substantial predictive power. These results indicate that relations between tacit knowledge and career performance are not subsumed by personality constructs – at least when measured by common personality inventories.

Tacit knowledge appears to be relatively general within and across career domains. Wagner (1987) used confirmatory factor analysis to test alternative models of relations between tacit knowledge scenarios that measured practical know-how important for managing others, oneself, and one's tasks. The results supported a single general factor. This suggests that people who have a lot of tacit knowledge about one aspect of domain performance, such as knowing how to manage others effectively, also tend to have a lot of tacit knowledge about other aspects of domain performance, such as knowing how to maximize their own productivity and how to do tasks that are important to doing their jobs well.

When undergraduates were given tacit knowledge measures for different domains (e.g., business management and academic psychology), correlations of scores across domains were in the .5 to .6 range. Thus, individuals who scored well on a tacit knowledge measure for one domain tended to score well on a tacit knowledge measure for another domain.

Practical Mathematics

Mathematics is an example of a domain that is interesting with respect to issues of practical intelligence because it is taught formally in schools and used less formally in everyday lives.

Nunes, Schliemann, and Carraher (1993) describe a number of examples of "street mathematics," or math used for everyday purposes. For example, they studied the sons and daughters of street vendors in the Brazilian city of Recife. Children from about 8 years of age commonly help out in their parents' street vendor businesses, including carrying out transactions with customers while their parents are occupied with another customer or an errand. Doing so requires solving mathematics problems, usually without relying on paper and pencil. Examples of such problems include the following: If one coconut costs X, how much are four coconuts? and

If the customer pays for her produce by giving the vendor 500 cruzieros, and the cost is 375 cruzieros, how much change should she be given? In one study, accuracy of computations was compared in three contexts (Carraher, Carraher, & Schliemann, 1985). An informal context consisted of having the children carry out real transactions at work. The accuracy level in this context was 98% correct. A formal word-problem context consisted of having the children solve word problems that provided some descriptive context using paper and pencil. The numbers and operations required were identical to those from the informal context. Accuracy dropped to 74%. Finally, a formal arithmetic operations context consisted of simply presenting math problems (e.g., $4 \times 35 = ?$) again involving the identical numbers and operations. Under these conditions, the accuracy level was only 37% correct. Thus, performance on identical problems was better when presented in a practical context as opposed to academic ones.

Lave, Murtaugh, and de la Roche (1984) studied the everyday mathematics used by California grocery shoppers. The shoppers sought to obtain the best value when buying products that were available in different-sized containers. Note that these studies were carried out before the advent of posting cost per unit quantity. Although the largest size often is the most economical purchase, this is not always the case. In fact, the largest size was not the most economical for about a third of the items purchased by the shoppers. What the shoppers were observed to do was to use mental shortcuts that were not completely accurate but nevertheless were accurate enough to determine the most economical size. Consider an example in which oatmeal can be purchased in a 10-ounce box for $.98 or a 24-ounce box for $2.29. Shoppers translated $.98 for 10 ounces of oatmeal into about 10 cents per ounce. Thus, a comparable price for 24 ounces would be about $2.40. Because the price of $2.29 for the 24-ounce box was noticeably less than $2.40, it was selected as the better buy. Interestingly, accuracy at picking the best buys was unrelated to performance on the M.I.T. test of mental arithmetic.

Scribner (1984) studied how workers at a milk processing plant filled orders. The workers she studied are called assemblers. Their job is to assemble orders of cases that vary in quantity (e.g., pints, quarts, and gallons) and product (e.g., whole milk, low-fat milk, and buttermilk). The workers were found to fill orders by combining partially filled cases in a manner that minimized the numbers of moves required. Doing so required calculating quantities involving different base number systems in their heads. They were able to do so despite being the least educated workers in the plant. Their performance at filling orders was unrelated to IQ, arithmetic test scores, or school grades, and exceeded the performance of more highly educated white-collar workers who sometimes substituted when assemblers were absent.

A final example of everyday mathematics is provided by Ceci and Liker's (1988) study of expert racetrack handicappers. Ceci and Liker studied the strategies that handicappers used to predict post-time odds at the racetrack. Expert handicappers were found to use a complex algorithm that involved interactions among multiple pieces of information. For example, one predictor of a horse's odds is the horse's quarter-mile times posted in its last race. Rather than just using straight times, however, the expert handicappers adjusted the times on the basis of whether the horse was attempting to pass other horses on the outside, the speed of the other horses, and where the attempted passes took place. The reason for the adjustment is that a horse attempting an outside pass of other horses on a curve necessarily will run away from the rail. Running away from the rail on a curve means running greater distance, which affects quarter-mile times. Ceci and Liker found that use of an interactive strategy was related to accuracy of predicting post-time odds but was unrelated to the handicappers' IQs.

Practical Planning

For Goodnow (1986), practical intelligence is manifested in how we organize our everyday activities to accomplish what we must and in how we reorganize when something goes awry. The task of getting ready for school can be viewed as an everyday example of a planning task in which a number of activities must be completed in a sensible sequence over a limited period of time. Activities may include taking a shower, getting dressed, eating breakfast, brushing teeth, feeding animals, collecting school materials, and walking down the street to the bus stop. Individual and developmental differences are

readily observed in children's ability to accomplish this task in an organized manner. As important, if not more important, is the ability to reorganize a task when necessary. An example of the importance of reorganization is handling the situation when an alarm fails to go off and a child gets up a half-hour late.

Berg (1989) studied children's and adolescents' knowledge about effective plans and strategies for dealing with everyday problems. The nature of everyday problems varies developmentally based on an analysis of responses when children and adults were asked to report a recent problem they had experienced (Berg & Calderone, 1994). For 5- and 6-year-olds, everyday problems primarily involve relations with family members (e.g., fighting with a sibling) and accomplishing household chores. For 11- and 12-year-olds, everyday problems involved tasks at school (e.g., completing an assignment) and problems associated with free-time activities such as sports and hobbies. For college students, the reported problems were widely distributed across interpersonal, school, and work domains. For older adults, everyday problems concerned health and family issues.

Berg presented students with everyday problems and asked them to rate the effectiveness of the following six courses of action: plan to take action in the future; seek more information; change one's perception of the problem; adapt to the problem; shape the environment to change the problem situation; and select another environment, thereby removing oneself from the problem. An example of an everyday problem is that you and your friends want to go out to a movie on Friday night that will be over at 11 o'clock, meaning you will not be home until 11:30, but your parents insist that you come home by 10:30 on Friday and Saturday nights. The movie will be playing at the theater for one more week. Students were asked to rate the quality of strategies such as waiting to see the movie until Saturday afternoon, trying to persuade their parents to make an exception to their curfew, or staying overnight at the house of a friend who has a later curfew. The results were that some strategies were deemed to be more effective than others overall. However, this result was qualified by an interaction between strategy effectiveness and whether the context of the problem was in school or out of school.

Practical Presupposition

Concept learning has been of keen interest to experimental and educational psychologists for many years (Estes, 1982). Concept learning also has been of interest to comparative psychologists because similar or even identical tasks can be given to both humans and lower animals. In a typical concept-learning task, the participant is given repeated trials in which stimuli such as geometric shapes of various colors are presented. The concept to be identified might be the color green or the geometric shape triangle. Over trials, the participant guesses whether the concept is represented in the presented trial and then is told whether the guess is correct or not. The trials may continue until the participant identifies the concept or reaches a criterion number of trials without success.

Through countless studies, theories of learning emerged that accounted for performance on these kinds of concept-learning tasks. A similar kind of concept learning takes place in everyday situations, making it possible for us to discover regularities in the behavior of others and in other aspects of our environment. One key difference between concept learning in everyday situations and that exhibited in laboratory tasks is in the possible role of presupposition. Presupposition refers to assumptions, suppositions, and biases that are brought to the learning situation. In a laboratory concept-learning task, the role of presupposition is minimized if not eliminated entirely because of the arbitrary nature of the concepts to be learned (e.g., red triangle). In contrast, individuals bring considerable world knowledge in the form of presuppositions to everyday learning situations.

For example, in a series of studies, Wagner (1990) presented a practical concept-learning task to participants. Each problem began with a description of a fictitious individual whose stated intention was to do one of three things, depending on the problem: purchase an automobile, select an apartment, or choose a roommate. This description was followed by a series of cases, each of which described a particular automobile, apartment, or roommate, depending on the problem. A sample case for the automobile problem follows:

This car seats six comfortably. It has few options and is priced well below average for a car of this size. It is equipped with a standard transmission. There is adequate luggage space, and the fuel tank is located near the rear axle to avoid rupture. The car has 50,000 miles on the odometer. Insurance rates are low for this model. Labor charges for repair work are also low.

The participants' task was to predict, using a 5-point scale, how much the fictitious individual would like the item or individual described in the case. After making a prediction, the same scale was used to inform participants of the true rating (i.e., the extent to which the fictitious individual liked what was described in the case). The true ratings were based on the degree to which the case represented the prototype for that particular problem.

Participants' presuppositions were manipulated merely by altering a brief description of the fictitious individual who was presented before each problem. In a congruent presupposition condition, the description was of an individual who would be expected to like the case to be rated. For example, a congruent description for the family car problem was "Jim Smith is 43 years old. He is married and the father of four children, ages 5, 7, 10, and 15. The Smiths have two dogs and a cat and enjoy activities as a group." In an incongruent presupposition condition, the description was of an individual who would not be expected to like the exemplar to be rated: "Jim Smith is a freshman at UCLA. He is more interested in his social life than in his academic studies. In fact, he chose UCLA over USC because he heard it was the better party school." Descriptions for a neutral presupposition condition were written to be irrelevant with regard to whether the individual would like the exemplar to be rated: "Jim Smith was born in Pennsylvania. His favorite colors are red and yellow. He considers himself to be a good person, though one who has had perhaps more than his share of luck."

Task performance was quantified in terms of the absolute value of the difference between the predicted and actual rating values with smaller differences indicating better performance. Planned comparisons indicated that performance on the congruent presupposition condition exceeded that of the neutral presupposition condition, and performance on the neutral presupposition condition exceeded that of the incongruent presupposition condition. Even after 10 learning trials in which feedback was provided, the performance of the incongruent condition was as bad or worse as that of the other two groups on *their first learning trial*. Yet, world knowledge in the form of presupposition and biases routinely is not studied in concept-learning studies, and, in fact, materials are carefully chosen to eliminate such effects entirely. Finally, task performance was unrelated to verbal reasoning performance, both for the entire sample and for the separate groups. In related studies with fourth-grade, seventh-grade, and college subjects, task performance again was not related to verbal ability.

Ceci and Bronfenbrenner (1985) have carried out a related set of studies in which children were asked to perform the same essential task in two or more contexts. For example, 10-year-olds were asked to predict where a geometric shape would move on a computer screen by moving a cursor to the predicted location. An algorithm that was not revealed to the child determined movement. Thus, shape might indicate horizontal direction of movement (e.g., square = right, circle = left, triangle = no horizontal movement), color might indicate vertical direction of movement (e.g., dark = upward, light = downward), and size might indicate distance (e.g., large = short; small = far). A large dark circle then would move up and left a short distance. Performance remained near chance after 750 trials of training. However, performance improved dramatically when the identical task was presented in the context of a video game. Instead of placing the cursor at the predicted spot a circle, square, or triangle would move to, the child's task was to capture birds, bees, and butterflies with a representation of a net. The algorithm was identical to that used in the previous condition. In this context, performance approached the ceiling of near perfect performance after about half as many training trails.

Social Judgment

Most definitions of general intelligence include some aspect of adapting to one's environment. Given the importance of others in human affairs, it is not surprising that social judgment or competence is featured in some working definitions of practical intelligence. For example, practical intelligence is considered to be synonymous with social competence by Mercer, Gomez-Palacio, and Padilla (1986). Social competence is defined as the extent to which

an individual is able to meet the normative expectations of others in six kinds of social roles: family roles, peer roles, community roles, earner–consumer roles, self-maintenance roles, and nonacademic school roles. A wide range of behaviors is included for each social role. Thus, family roles range from interpersonal skills used in dealing with family members to helping to repair family possessions. Note also the emphasis on normative expectations and the implication that normative expectations are likely to vary across cultures and subcultures.

Ford (1986) also emphasized social competence in his conceptualization of practical intelligence. He considered practical intelligence to be reflected in the attainment of important transactional (i.e., dealing with effects outside the person) goals. Given the social nature of human beings, many of these transactional goals involve social competence.

Prototypes of Practical Intelligence

Neisser (1979) has suggested that it is impossible to define intelligence as any one thing. Rather, the best we can do is to view the concept of intelligence in terms of Rosch's theory of concepts (1978). Practical intelligence then is defined with reference to a prototype that characterizes an ideal exemplar of the target concept. In the case of practical intelligence, an individual would be said to possess practical intelligence to the extent that he or she resembles the prototypic, practically intelligent individual. With this view, the task then becomes identification of the prototype.

An example of this approach was provided by Sternberg, Conway, Ketron, and Bernstein (1981), who asked laypersons and experts to rate how characteristic 250 descriptions were of an (a) ideally intelligent person, (b) academically intelligent person, and (c) everyday intelligent person. The results of interest in the present context are those of the factor analyses of the everyday intelligent person ratings. For laypersons, the results yielded four interpretable factors: practical problem-solving ability, social competence, character, and interest in learning and culture. For experts, the results yielded three interpretable factors: practical problem-solving ability, adaptive behavior, and social competence. Ford and Miura (1983) used a similar approach to identifying characteristics of the prototypic socially competent individual. The results provided support for four facets of social competence: prosocial skills (i.e., sensitivity to the needs of others), social-instrumental skills (i.e., knowledge of how to get things done), social ease (i.e., comfort in social activities), and self-efficacy (i.e., a positive self-concept).

HOW IS PRACTICAL INTELLIGENCE RELATED TO OTHER KINDS OF INTELLIGENCE?

Given its relatively recent growth, much of the existing research on practical intelligence consists of presenting examples of practical intelligence and perhaps providing evidence that the examples represent something other than intelligence traditionally defined.

If we accept the premise that much of the traditional literature on intelligence is incomplete by virtue of ignoring practical intelligence, what is the origin of this omission? Surely prior theorists and researchers did not intentionally set out to study *impractical* intelligence. Is the constraint on previous work a result of limited theory and conceptualization or of measurement? The answer to this question may help point out the most critical remaining work that needs to be done (e.g., Do we need broader conceptualizations or different measures?). More importantly, how can the constructs of traditional academic and practical intelligence be integrated in a comprehensive account of human intelligence?

Limited Conceptualizations?

Are limitations in conceptualizations of intelligence responsible for the relatively short shrift given practical intelligence over the years relative to academic intelligence? Sternberg and Berg's (1986) analysis of the definitions presented in the 1921 *Journal of Educational Psychology* symposium and those presented 65 years later suggest the answer to this question to be a resounding no. Sternberg and Berg were able to identify 27 core attributes of the contributors' definitions of intelligence. Their analysis of the 1921 and 1986 data indicates that existing conceptualizations of intelligence are quite compatible with notions about practical intelligence. Of the 27 attributes, 19 are effectively neutral about whether the nature of the manifestation of intelligence is academic or practical (e.g., metacognition, knowledge, speed of mental processing). Thus,

metacognition could be used to monitor one's performance in solving a mathematics problem or a problem with a coworker. Knowledge can be practical or academic, and speed of mental processing can be as important when hunting food for survival as it is when answering questions on the SAT. Six of the attributes were clearly associated with practical intelligence (adaptation to meet the demands of the environment effectively; real-world manifestations; that which is valued by culture; emotional, motivational constructs; individual differences in mental competence; and overt behavioral manifestations–effective, successful responses). In fact, only 2 attributes would seem to preclude aspects of practical intelligence (*g*; restricted to academic–cognitive abilities).

Limited Measures?

IQ tests have changed remarkably little from Alfred Binet's efforts to devise a test that would identify children with mental retardation who were thought at the time to be incapable of profiting from public education. Given Binet's original purpose, and the similarity between current IQ tests and the earliest ones, is it possible that the problem simply is that IQ tests do not assess important aspects of practical intelligence? Recall the differences described earlier between academic and practical problems, such as having all necessary information available and a single correct answer (Neisser, 1976; Wagner & Sternberg, 1985).

An analysis of changing relations between IQ and measures of practical intelligence as a function of the nature of the practical intelligence task that is used suggests that the format of IQ tests may limit their sensitivity to assessing more practical aspects of intelligence. An edited book on practical intelligence (Sternberg & Wagner, 1986) included reports of relations between IQ tests and a wide variety of measures of practical intelligence. For the most part, relations between IQ and practical intelligence were reported as being small or nonexistent. However, there was at least one noticeable exception. Willis and Schaie (1986) reported correlations in the range of .6 to .7 between their measure of practical intelligence and both fluid and crystallized intelligence. However, whereas other studies had devised hands-on or simulation-based measures, Willis and Schaie's measure of practical intelligence was the Basic Skills Test (Educational Testing Service, 1977), a paper-and-pencil psychometric test that required, among other things, comprehending newspaper stories, reading a street map, filling out forms, and reading labels. In fact, the test originally was devised to assess the real-life application of what high school seniors had learned in school. An analysis of relations between IQ and measures of practical intelligence led to the following generalization:

Looking across the studies reported in this volume, the correlation between measures of practical and academic intelligence varies as a function of the format of the practical intelligence measure: Correlations are large when the practical intelligence measure is test-like, and virtually nonexistent when the practical intelligence measure is based on simulation (Wagner, 1986, p. 372).

INTEGRATING PRACTICAL AND ACADEMIC INTELLIGENCE IN A COMPREHENSIVE FRAMEWORK

Most of the effort of researchers who study practical intelligence has been directed toward a divergent aim: to show that a practical kind of intelligence exists and that it can be differentiated from the kind of intelligence measured by traditional IQ tests. Now that researchers have largely succeeded in accomplishing this aim, the next challenge has a more convergent aim: to show how practical, academic, and perhaps other kinds of intelligence can be integrated into a comprehensive account. This is an ambitious agenda to be sure, but some progress already has been made. Consider several examples.

life-Span Developmental Models

Life-span models of cognitive development provide examples of comprehensive accounts of human abilities that encompass practical as well as academic aspects. Three such accounts will be described.

FLUID AND CRYSTALLIZED ABILITIES. Horn and Cattell (1966) described two fundamental kinds of mental abilities that have different life-span developmental functions. Fluid abilities are abilities that are required to deal with novelty in a testing situation, as when inducing the next number in the number series 1, 5, __, 13. Crystallized abilities represent acculturated knowledge, as in defining the

meanings of words on a vocabulary test. Fluid abilities appear to reach their maximum level in the late teens, and begin a gradual decline thereafter. Crystallized abilities are maintained at high levels through adulthood, and appreciable decline is evident only in the elderly (Dixon & Baltes, 1986; Horn, 1982; Schaie, 1977/1978). On the basis of an analysis of the different characteristics of academic and practical problems, Sternberg et al. (1995) reasoned that fluid abilities are more important for solving academic problems than practical ones, and conversely, that crystallized abilities are more important for solving practical problems than academic ones. They also speculated that maintenance of practical abilities through adulthood may reflect the greater contribution of crystallized abilities in solving practical, everyday problems, relative to the role of fluid abilities.

Some support for these speculations comes from life-span developmental studies. Older adults typically believe that their reasoning abilities have either been maintained or even further developed through adulthood, despite evidence of decline in academic abilities. For example, Williams, Denney, and Schadler (1983) interviewed adults over the age of 65 about their perceptions of changes in their ability to solve problems, think, and reason as they aged. Fully 76% of participants believed that their ability had increased as they aged, 20% believed that their ability had not changed, and only 4% believed that their ability had declined. When participants were informed that performance on many cognitive ability tests declines upon completion of formal schooling, they replied that they were not referring to the kinds of problems found on IQ tests. Rather, they were referring to performance on "everyday" problems such as financial ones. The Williams et al. study dealt with older adults' self-perceptions. What evidence is there about the accuracy of these self-perceptions?

Denney and Palmer (1981) gave a cross-section of adults aged 20- to 79-years-old two kinds of reasoning problems. Practical reasoning problems consisted of real-life situations such as the following: "If you were traveling by car and got stranded out on an interstate highway during a blizzard, what would you do?" and "Now let's assume that you lived in an apartment that didn't have any windows on the same side as the front door. Let's say that at 2:00 a.m., you heard a loud knock on the door and someone yelled, 'Open up. It's the police!' What would you do?" Academic problems consisted of a 20-question task. Denney and Palmer plotted performance on the two kinds of problems as a function of age. For academic problems, performance decreased linearly after age 20. In contrast, performance on the practical problem-solving task increased to a peak for the 40- and 50-year-olds and then declined thereafter.

Cornelius and Caspi (1987) considered relations between everyday problem solving, fluid intelligence, and crystallized intelligence in a study of adults aged 20 to 78. The everyday problem-solving tasks consisted of problems sampling domains such as consumer problems (e.g., what do to about a landlord who refuses to make repairs), information seeking (e.g., filling out a complicated form that requires finding additional information), personal concerns (e.g., deciding what to do about attending a concert you want to go to, but you are unsure about whether it is safe to go), family problems (e.g., responding to criticism from a child or parent), problems with friends (e.g., convincing a friend to visit you more often), and problems at work (e.g., not getting a deserved promotion). The measure of fluid ability was letter series completion, and the measure of crystallized ability was defining vocabulary words. Performance on the everyday problem-solving task and the measure of crystallized ability increased up to age 70. In contrast, performance on the measure of fluid ability increased only through age 30, remained stable through age 50, and then declined thereafter. Performance on the everyday reasoning task was moderately correlated with both fluid ($r = .29$, $p < .01$) and crystallized abilities ($r = .27$, $p < .01$). Although everyday problem solving and crystallized ability shared similar life-span developmental functions, crystallized ability was not more correlated with everyday problem solving than was fluid ability.

PRAGMATICS AND MECHANICS OF INTELLIGENCE. Baltes and colleagues (Baltes, Dittmann–Kohli, & Kliegl, 1984) proposed a model of life-span intellectual development that encompasses both everyday and academic aspects of intelligence. It represents an extension of Horn and Cattell's (1966) distinction between fluid and crystallized abilities.

Intellectual functioning is divided into two interrelated domains. The first domain, called the mechanics of intelligence, represents the content-free architecture of information processing and problem solving. The second domain, called the pragmatics of intelligence, includes accumulated knowledge and skill as well as other specialized aspects of intelligence. According to the model, intellectual aging displays aspects of growth, stabilization, and decline. A decline in the mechanics of intelligence is normally associated with aging. In contrast, pragmatic aspects of intelligence can be maintained, and even enhanced, in selected areas. Successful aging involves selecting goals and trajectories for which internal and external conditions are supportive. The interface between the mechanics and pragmatics of intelligence gives rise to selective optimization with compensation. Accumulated knowledge and skills allow for intellectual performance to be optimal in selected domains and for compensation for a more global decline in the mechanics of intelligence.

COGNITIVE APPRENTICESHIP. Rogoff (1990) viewed children's cognitive development as an apprenticeship in which guided participation provided to a child by his or her caregivers and companions results in an expansion of the child's understanding and mastery of the tools of the child's culture. Rogoff viewed thinking as intellectual activity directed toward solving problems in the everyday interpersonal and physical worlds. The child's developmental task is to learn to identify and solve such problems using intellectual tools inherited from previous generations and social resources provided by others. Note that, although Rogoff's emphasis is on learning to solve the problems of everyday life, cognitive apprenticeship is viewed by many as the preferable model of school learning.

Other Comprehensive Models

Several recent conceptualizations of intelligence attempt to expand the kinds of intellectual abilities that are included beyond those assessed by IQ tests (Neisser et al., 1996). Three such examples will be described briefly. The interested reader is encouraged to consult the primary sources directly for more information.

TRIARCHIC THEORY OF HUMAN INTELLIGENCE. Sternberg's (1985) triarchic theory of human intelligence proposes three key aspects of intelligence. Analytic intelligence is what is measured for the most part by traditional IQ tests. Creative and practical intelligence, the other two key aspects, are equally important yet have been neglected relative to the effort that has been applied to the study of analytic intelligence. The importance of tacit knowledge and other forms of practical know-how is consistent with the theory. Tacit knowledge is viewed as the product of knowledge acquisition components (one of several kinds of components proposed by the theory) applied to everyday contexts, including that of employment.

Sternberg's theory has recently been extended in a way that makes it more applicable to understanding relations between practical and academic kinds of intelligence. A recurring theme in accounts of practical intelligence is that competence in solving everyday problems depends on the application of highly developed practical knowledge and forms of expertise. Considerable prior experience is available to problem solvers that may be applied to many everyday problems they confront. In contrast, academic problems of the sort found on IQ tests tend to be more novel, and hence their solution often depends more on the use of broadly applicable problem-solving strategies and a limited amount of specialized academic knowledge. Sternberg's (1998) extension provides a framework that unites traditional abilities and expertise in which abilities are viewed as forms of developing expertise.

MULTIPLE INTELLIGENCES. According to Gardner's (1983) theory, human intelligence consists of a small set of human intellectual potentials that relate to different cultural domains: linguistic, musical, logical–mathematical, spatial, bodily–kinesthetic, intrapersonal, and interpersonal. Linguistic intelligence refers to sensitivity to spoken and written languages, including being aware of subtle shades of meaning and interactions among linguistic connotations. Musical intelligence refers to sensitivity to rhythm, pitch, and timbre. Logical–mathematical intelligence refers to facility with numbers, hypothetical statements, and exploration of relations among hypothetical statements. Spatial intelligence refers to sensitivity to visual–spatial elements and facility in transforming one visual–spatial element into another. Bodily–kinesthetic intelligence refers

to sensitivity to, and control over, actions of one's body. Intrapersonal intelligence refers to our understanding of one's personal strengths, weaknesses, and feelings and is relied on for making informed personal decisions. Finally, interpersonal intelligence refers to sensitivity to the intentions and desires of others and the ability to influence others in desired ways.

Gardner's multiple intelligences span both academic and practical domains. Linguistic, logical–mathematical, and spatial intelligences represent largely academic abilities that commonly are measured by IQ tests. Intrapersonal and interpersonal intelligences represent more practical abilities that are applied in everyday contexts. Musical and bodily-kinesthetic intelligences perhaps fall somewhere in between. Regarding relations among the multiple intelligences, Gardner argued that the core set of intellectual potentials reflected in the various contexts are independent of one another.

INTELLIGENCE, KNOWLEDGE, AND PERSONALITY. Ackerman (1996) argued that IQ tests are not particularly useful for understanding adult intelligence beyond identifying individuals at either extreme end because they the tests do not address the importance of knowledge – including practical knowledge. Most conceptions of intelligence have focused on traits or processes to the neglect of knowledge.

In addition to emphasizing knowledge, Ackerman and Heggestad (1997) sought to integrate personality and interests into a global framework of adult intellectual competence. A distinction between maximal and typical performance figures prominently in this effort and has implications for relating academic and practical abilities. IQ tests are designed to measure maximal performance – the best one is capable of doing. The argument for seeking to measure maximal performance is that it is assumed to be more stable than performance obtained under everyday circumstances. In contrast, personality tests are designed to measure typical performance – what one is most likely to do. Ackerman and Heggestad argued for measurement of typical intellectual performance, believing that typical intellectual performance in likely to be a better predictor of daily intellectual efforts in everyday contexts than is maximal performance.

In conclusion, one of the most interesting and important developments in the field of intelligence over the past two decades has been interest in practical intelligence. Using ingenious means, the *bricoleurs*, whose work has been described in this chapter, have succeeded at what was believed by many to be nearly impossible: to show that there is indeed something beyond IQ. The harder part will be further developing a comprehensive framework of human intelligence that integrates academic, practical, and perhaps other forms of intelligence.

REFERENCES

Ackerman, P. J. (1996). A theory of adult intellectual development: Process, personality, interests, and knowledge. *Intelligence, 22,* 229–259.

Ackerman, P. J., & Heggestad, E. D. (1997). Intelligence, personality, and interests: Evidence for overlapping traits. *Psychological Bulletin, 121,* 219–245.

Barrett, G. V., & Depinet, R. L. (1991). A reconsideration of testing for competence rather than for intelligence. *American Psychologist, 46,* 1012–1024.

Baltes, P. B., Dittmann-Kohli, F., & Kliegl, R. (1984). New perspectives on the development of intelligence in adulthood: Toward a dual-process conception and a model of selective optimization with compensation. In P. B. Baltes & O. G. Brim (Eds.), *Life-span development and behavior* (pp. 33–76). New York: Academic Press.

Berg, C. A. (1989). Knowledge of strategies for dealing with everyday problems from childhood through adolescence. *Developmental Psychology, 25,* 607–618.

Berg, C. A., & Calderone, K. S. (1994). The role of problem interpretations in understanding the development of everyday problem solving. In R. J. Sternberg & R. K. Wagner (Eds.), *Mind in context: Interactionist perspectives on human intelligence* (pp. 105–132). New York: Cambridge University Press.

Berry, J. W., & Irvine, S. H. (1986). Bricolage: Savages do it daily. In R. J. Sternberg & R. K. Wagner (Eds.), *Practical intelligence: Nature and origins of competence in the everyday world* (pp. 271–306). New York: Cambridge University Press.

Berry, J. W., van de Koppel, J., Senechal, C., Annis, R., Bahuchet, S., Cavalli-Sforza, L. L., & Witkin, H. A. (1986). *On the edge of the forest.* Lisse: Swets and Zeitlinger.

Bluton Jones, N., & Konner, M. (1976). Kung knowledge of animal behavior. In R. B. Lee & I. DeVore (Eds.), *Kalahari hunter-gatherers* (pp. 326–348). Cambridge, MA: Harvard University Press.

Carraher, T. N., Carraher, D. W., & Schliemann, A. D.

(1985). Mathematics in the streets and in schools. *British Journal of Developmental Psychology, 3,* 21–29.

Ceci, S. J., & Bronfenbrenner, U. (1985). Don't forget to take the cupcakes out of the oven: Strategic time-monitoring, prospective memory and context. *Child Development, 56,* 175–190.

Ceci, S. J., & Liker, J. (1988). Stalking the IQ-expertise relationship: When the critics go fishing. *Journal of Experimental Psychology: General, 117,* 96–100.

Cole, M., Gay, J., Glick, J., & Sharp, D. (1971). *The cultural context of learning and thinking.* New York: Basic.

Cornelius, S. W., & Caspi, A. (1987). Everyday problem solving in adulthood and old age. *Psychology and Aging, 2,* 144–153.

Denney, N. W., & Palmer, A. M. (1981). Adult age differences on traditional and practical problem-solving measures. *Journal of Gerontology, 36,* 323–328.

Dixon, R. A., & Baltes, P. B. (1986). Toward life-span research on the functions and pragmatics of intelligence. In R. J. Sternberg & R. K. Wagner (Eds.), *Practical intelligence: Nature and origins of competence in the everyday world* (pp. 203–235). New York: Cambridge University Press.

Eddy, A. S. (1988). *The relationship between the Tacit Knowledge Inventory for Managers and the Armed Services Vocational Aptitude Battery.* Unpublished master's thesis, St. Mary's University, San Antonio, TX.

Educational Testing Service (1977). *Basic Skills Assessment Test: Reading.* Princeton, NJ: Educational Testing Service.

Estes, W. K. (1982). Learning, memory, and intelligence. In R. J. Sternberg (Ed.), *Handbook of human intelligence* (pp. 170–224). New York: Cambridge University Press.

Ford, M. E. (1986). For all practical purposes: Criteria for defining and evaluating practical intelligence. In R. J. Sternberg & R. K. Wagner (Eds.), *Practical intelligence: Nature and origins of competence in the everyday world* (pp. 183–200). New York: Cambridge University Press.

Ford, M. E., & Miura, I. (1983, August). *Children's and adults' conceptions of social competence.* Paper presented at the meeting of the American Psychological Association, Anaheim, CA.

Frederiksen, N. (1986). Toward a broader conception of human intelligence. In R. J. Sternberg & R. K. Wagner (Eds.), *Practical intelligence: Nature and origins of competence in the everyday world* (pp. 84–116). New York: Cambridge University Press.

Gardner, H. (1983). *Frames of mind.* New York: Basic Books.

Gladwin, T. (1970). *East is a big bird: Navigation and logic on the Puluwat atoll.* Cambridge, MA: Harvard University Press.

Goodnow, J. J. (1986). Some lifelong everyday forms of intelligent behavior: Organizing and reorganizing. In R. J. Sternberg & R. K. Wagner (Eds.), *Practical intelligence: Nature and origins of competence in the everyday world* (pp. 143–162). New York: Cambridge University Press.

Gottfredson, L. S. (1991). The evaluation of alternative

measures of job performance. In A. K. Wigdor & B. F. Green, Jr. (Eds.), *Performance assessment in the workplace* (Vol. 1, pp. 75–126). Washington, DC: National Academy Press.

Hartigan, J. A., & Wigdor, A. K. (1989). *Fairness in employment testing.* Washington, DC: National Academy Press.

Hawk, J. (1986). Real world implications of *g. Journal of Vocational Behavior, 29,* 411–414.

Horn, J. L. (1982). The theory of fluid and crystallized intelligence in relation to concepts of cognitive psychology and aging in adulthood. In F. I. M. Craik & A. Trehub (Eds.), *Aging and cognitive processes* (pp. 237–278). New York: Plenum.

Horn, J. L., & Cattell, R. B. (1966). Refinement and test of the theory of fluid and crystallized intelligence. *Journal of Educational Psychology, 57,* 253–270.

Jensen, A. R. (1993). Test validity: *g* versus "tacit knowledge." *Current Directions in Psychological Science, 2,* 9–10.

Laboratory of Comparative Human Cognition. (1982). Culture and intelligence. In R. J. Sternberg, R. J. (Ed.), *Handbook of human intelligence* (pp. 642–719). New York: Cambridge University Press.

Lave, J., Murtaugh, M., & de la Roche, O. (1984). The dialectic of arithmetic in grocery shopping. In B. Rogoff & J. Lace (Eds.), *Everyday cognition* (pp. 67–94). Cambridge, MA: Harvard University Press.

Levi-Strauss, C. (1966). *The savage mind.* London: Weidenfield & Nicholson.

McClelland, D. C. (1973). Testing for competence rather than for "intelligence." *American Psychologist, 28,* 1–14.

Mercer, J. R., Gomez-Palacio, M., & Padilla, E. (1986). The development of practical intelligence in cross-cultural perspective. In R. J. Sternberg & R. K. Wagner (Eds.), *Practical intelligence: Nature and origins of competence in the everyday world* (pp. 307–337). New York: Cambridge University Press.

Neisser, U. (1976). General, academic, and artificial intelligence. In L. Resnick (Ed.), *Human intelligence: Perspectives on its theory and measurement* (pp. 179–189). Norwood, NJ: Ablex.

Neisser, U. (1979). The concept of intelligence. In R. Sternberg & D. Detterman (Eds.), *Human intelligence: Perspectives on its theory and measurement* (pp. 179–189). Norwood, NJ: Ablex.

Neisser, U., Boodoo, G., Bouchard, T. J., Boykin, A. W., Brody, N., Ceci, S. J., Halpern, D. F., Loehlin, J. C., Perloff, R., Sternberg, R. J., & Urbina, S. (1996). Intelligence: Knowns and unknowns. *American Psychologist, 51,* 77–101.

Nunes, T., Schliemann, A. D., & Carraher, D. W. (1993). *Street mathematics and school mathematics.* New York: Cambridge University Press.

Rogoff, B. (1990). *Apprenticeship in thinking.* New York: Oxford University Press.

Rosch, E. R. (1978). Human categorization. In N. Warren (Ed.), *Studies in cross-cultural psychology* (pp. 1–47). London: Academic Press.

Schaie, K. W. (1977/1978). Toward a stage theory of adult cognitive development. *International Journal of Aging and Human Development, 8,* 129–138.

Schmidt, F. L., & Hunter, J. E. (1981). Employment testing: Old theories and new research findings. *American Psychologist, 36,* 1128–1137.

Schmidt, F. L., & Hunter, J. E. (1993). Tacit knowledge, practical intelligence, general mental ability, and job knowledge. *Current Directions in Psychological Science, 1,* 8–9.

Schmidt, F. L., & Hunter, J. E. (in press). Measurable personnel characteristics: Stability, variability, and validity for predicting future job performance. In M. Kleinmann & B. Strauss (Eds.), *Instruments for potential assessment and personnel development.* Göttingen, Germany: Hogrefe.

Scribner, S. (1984). Studying working intelligence. In B. Rogoff & J. Lace (Eds.), *Everyday cognition* (pp. 9–40). Cambridge, MA: Harvard University Press.

Scribner, S., & Cole, M. (1981). *The psychology of literacy.* Cambridge, MA: Harvard University Press.

Sternberg, R. J. (Ed.) (1982). *Handbook of human intelligence.* New York: Cambridge University Press.

Sternberg, R. J. (1985). *Beyond IQ: A triarchic theory of human intelligence.* New York: Cambridge University Press.

Sternberg, R. J. (1998). Abilities are forms of developing expertise. *Educational Researcher, 27,* 11–20.

Sternberg, R. J., & Berg, C. A. (1986). Quantitative integration: Definitions of intelligence: A comparison of the 1921 and 1986 symposia. In R. J. Sternberg & D. K. Detterman (Eds.), *What is intelligence?* (pp. 155–162). Norwood, NJ: Ablex.

Sternberg, R. J., Conway, B. E., Ketron, J. L., & Bernstein, M. (1981). People's conceptions of intelligence. *Journal of Personality and Social Psychology, 41,* 37–55.

Sternberg, R. J., & Detterman, D. K. (Eds.) (1986). *What is intelligence?* Norwood, NJ: Ablex.

Sternberg, R. J., & Wagner, R. K. (Eds.). (1986). *Practical intelligence: Nature and origins of competence in the everyday world.* New York: Cambridge University Press.

Sternberg, R. J., Wagner, R. K., Williams, W. M., & Horvath, J. A. (1995). Testing common sense. *American Psychologist, 50,* 912–927.

Wagner, R. K. (1986). The search for intraterrestrial intelligence. In R. J. Sternberg & R. K. Wagner (Eds.), *Practical intelligence: Nature and origins of competence in the everyday world* (pp. 361–378). New York: Cambridge University Press.

Wagner, R. K. (1987). Tacit knowledge in everyday intelligent behavior. *Journal of Personality and Social Psychology, 52,* 1236–1247.

Wagner, R. K. (1990). Products and processes of practical reasoning. *International Journal of Research in Education, 14,* 437–454.

Wagner, R. K. (1997). Intelligence, training, and employment. *American Psychologist, 52,* 1059–1069.

Wagner, R. K., & Sternberg, R. J. (1985). Practical intelligence in real-world pursuits: The role of tacit knowledge. *Journal of Personality and Social Psychology, 49,* 436–458.

Wigdor, A. K., & Garner, W. R. (Eds.). (1982). *Ability testing: Uses, consequences, and controversies.* Washington, DC: National Academy Press.

Williams, S. A., Denney, N. W., & Schadler, M. (1983). Elderly adults' perception of their own cognitive development during the adult years. *International Journal of Aging and Human Development, 16,* 147–158.

Willis, S. L., & Schaie, K. W. (1986). Practical intelligence in later adulthood. In R. J. Sternberg & R. K. Wagner (Eds.), *Practical intelligence: Nature and origins of competence in the everyday world* (pp. 236–268). New York: Cambridge University Press.

CHAPTER EIGHTEEN

Models of Emotional Intelligence

JOHN D. MAYER, PETER SALOVEY, AND DAVID CARUSO

COMPETING MODELS OF EMOTIONAL INTELLIGENCE

Studies of emotional intelligence initially appeared in academic articles beginning in the early 1990s.* By middecade, the concept had attracted considerable popular attention, and powerful claims were made concerning its importance for predicting success. Emotional intelligence is the set of abilities that accounts for how people's emotional reports vary in their accuracy and how the more accurate understanding of emotion leads to better problem solving in an individual's emotional life. More formally, we define emotional intelligence as the ability to perceive and express emotion, assimilate emotion in thought, understand and reason with emotion, and regulate emotion in the self and others (Mayer & Salovey, 1997). As of now, the academic concept has been developed over several theoretical articles (e.g., Mayer & Salovey, 1997; Salovey & Mayer,

* The term *emotional intelligence* has been used for several decades at least before the present set of articles. Some use of the term stems from a Piagetian tradition (e.g., his book on affect and intelligence). Articles focused on Piaget's work, although noteworthy, are generally focused on a Piagetian stage or concept relatively unrelated to the present work (e.g., Leuner, 1966; Greenspan, 1989). Probably the most interesting development before 1990 was in a dissertation by Payne (1986) who wrote, in his abstract, that "the mass suppression of emotion throughout the civilized world has stifled our growth emotionally," and who reported the development of a rigorous theoretical and philosophical framework to explore and address this problem. To the best of our knowledge, however, the research we cite from 1990 forward marks the first development of the concept as an empirical research area of study.

1990) and is based on a growing body of relevant research (e.g., Averill & Nunley, 1992; Buck, 1984; Lane, Sechrest, Reidel et al., 1996; Mayer, DiPaolo, & Salovey, 1990; Mayer & Geher, 1996; Mayer & Stevens, 1994; Rosenthal, Hall, DiMatteo, Rogers, & Archer, 1979; Salovey, Mayer, Goldman, Turvey, & Palfai, 1995; see also, Salovey & Sluyter, 1997).

Shortly after the academic work began, a popular book on the subject appeared (Goleman, 1995a). The book covered much of the literature reviewed in the aforementioned articles as well as considerable additional research on emotions and the brain, emotions and social behavior, and school-based programs designed to help children develop emotional and social skills. The book emphasized earlier comments we had made concerning how people with emotional intelligence might be more socially effective than others in certain respects (Salovey & Mayer, 1990). Particularly strong claims were made about emotional intelligence's contribution to the individual and society (Goleman, 1995a, p. xii). This combination of science and human potential attracted extensive media coverage, culminating, perhaps, when *Time* magazine asked the question "What's your EQ?," on its cover, and stated, "It's not your IQ. It's not even a number. But emotional intelligence may be the best predictor of success in life, redefining what it means to be smart" (*Time*, 1995).

In short order, the general notion of emotional intelligence became widely known, appearing in many magazine and newspaper articles (e.g., Bennetts, 1996; Henig, 1996; Peterson, 1997), popular books (e.g., Cooper & Sawaf, 1997; Gottman, 1997; Salerno, 1996; Segal, 1997; Shapiro, 1997;

Simmons & Simmons, 1997; Steiner & Perry, 1997; Weisinger, 1997), and even two popular comic strips, "Dilbert" (Adams, 1997) and "Zippy the Pinhead" (Griffith, 1996).*

The first portion of this chapter will review several competing concepts of emotional intelligence. Some attention will be paid to what is meant by the terms *emotion, intelligence,* and *emotional intelligence.* A distinction will be drawn between models of emotional intelligence that focus on mental abilities and those that mix mental abilities with personality attributes such as persistence, zeal, and optimism. Measures of emotional intelligence will be examined in the chapter's second section. Research work increasingly supports the existence of a mental-ability emotional intelligence that is somewhat distinct from standard analytical intelligence. Research work on mixed models of emotional intelligence is more preliminary to date but shows some progress. In the discussion section we will address in greater detail the claims about what emotional intelligence may predict and discuss the opportunities, real and imagined, that exist more generally in the fields of intelligence and personality for studying an individual's success.

THEORETICAL CONSIDERATIONS REGARDING EMOTIONAL INTELLIGENCE

The Terms Emotion and Intelligence

Theories should be internally consistent, make meaningful use of technical language, and make important predictions. One issue in studying emotional intelligence is that some theories under that name pertain to emotions and intelligence, whereas others seem far broader. Therefore, it is worth examining the constituent terms, emotion, intelligence, and their combination at the outset.

Conceptions of Emotion

Emotions are recognized as one of three or four fundamental classes of mental operations. These

classes include motivation, emotion, cognition, and (less frequently) consciousness (Bain, 1855/1977; Izard, 1993; MacLean, 1973; Mayer, 1995a, 1995b; Plutchik, 1984; Tomkins, 1962; see Hilgard, 1980; and Mayer, Chabot, & Carlsmith, 1997, for reviews). Among the triad of motivation, emotion, and cognition, basic motivations arise in response to internal bodily states and include drives such as hunger, thirst, need for social contact, and sexual desires. Motivations are responsible for directing the organism to carry out simple acts to satisfy survival and reproductive needs. In their basic form, motivations follow a relatively determined time course (e.g., thirst rises until quenched) and are typically satisfied in a specific fashion (e.g., thirst is satisfied by drinking).

Emotions form the second class of this triad. Emotions appear to have evolved across mammalian species so as to signal and respond to changes in relationships between the individual and the environment (including one's imagined place within it). For example, anger arises in response to threat or injustice; fear arises in response to danger. Emotions follow no rigid time course but instead respond to external changes in relationships (or internal perceptions of them). Moreover, each emotion organizes several basic behavioral responses to the relationship; for example, fear organizes fighting or fleeing. Emotions are therefore more flexible than motivations, though not quite so flexible as cognition.

Cognition, the third member of the triad, allows the organism to learn from the environment and to solve problems in novel situations. This is often in service to satisfying motives or keeping emotions positive. Cognition includes learning, memory, and problem solving. It is ongoing and involves flexible, intentional information processing based on learning and memory (see Mayer et al., 1997, for a review of these concepts). These three basic classes of personality components are illustrated in the lower portion of Figure 18.1.

The next level up in Figure 18.1 depicts the interaction between motivation and emotion (on the left) and emotion and cognition (on the right). A great deal of research addresses how motivations interact with emotions and how emotions interact with cognition. For example, motives interact with emotion when frustrated needs lead to increased

---

* We entered the popular arena as well with an educational CD–ROM version of an emotional intelligence test. We experienced first hand the lengths marketers will go to to capture people's attention. Our publisher put the quote, "The true measure of intelligence!" from Gibbs' (1995) *Time* magazine article on the box even though (as the CD–ROM itself makes clear) we do not view this as accurate.

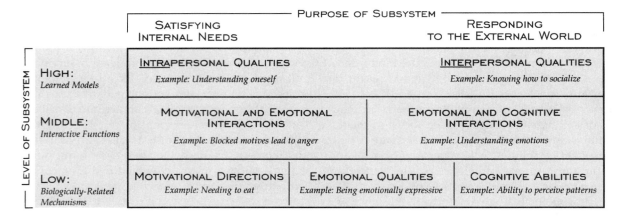

FIGURE 18.1. *An Overview of Personality and Its Major Subsystems.* A representation of personality components primarily according to lower versus higher-levels of processing (adapted from Mayer, 1995a; 1998b). Components at lower levels are generally divisible into motivational, emotional, and cognitive groups. For example, an urge to eat is motivational, whereas a feeling of generalized fear is emotional. Mid-level components, such as emotional intelligence, involve the interaction between lower level groups, such as the interactions between internal emotional feelings and cognitive understanding. High level components, such as self-esteem, are representations of the personal and social worlds that synthesize the lower-levels of processing in more complex, integrated fashions.

anger and aggression. Emotion interacts with cognition when good moods lead a person to think positively. One would expect that the interaction of emotion and cognition would also give rise to emotional intelligence.

It makes sense to distinguish among basic motivation, emotion, and cognition and their interactions. The three areas are integrated in more complex personality functioning, however, so we no longer speak of emotional, motivational, or cognitive elements separately. Rather, the focus turns to more general personality or social processes, which blend the three. For example, the self-concept entails a blended representation of oneself involving all three areas or modes of processing. The top of Figure 18.1 includes components that focus on these more general intra- and interpersonal qualities.

The term *emotional intelligence*, then, implies something having to do with the intersection of emotion and cognition. From our perspective, evaluating theories of, and related to, emotional intelligence requires an assessment of the degree to which the theory pertains to this intersection.

Conceptions of Intelligence

An intelligence researcher was invited mistakenly to a conference on military intelligence by someone who noticed he was an expert on intelligence but did not take note of the kinds of intelligence he studied. Gardner (1999) used this true story about himself to make the point that *intelligence* is used differently by different people.* Although we acknowledge different meanings of the term, we also believe intelligence possesses a core meaning in the sciences. Artificial intelligence, human intelligence, Offices of Military Intelligence, all imply gathering information, learning about that information, and reasoning with it – they all imply mental ability associated with the cognitive operations. The mental ability model was represented in pure form by Terman (1921, p. 128), who stated that, "An

---

* The problem of intelligence's meaning is an old one in the field and should not discourage us. Spearman (1927, p. 24) noted the following:

> The most enthusiastic advocates of intelligence become doubtful of it themselves. From having naively assumed that its nature is straightway conveyed by its name, they now set out to discover what this nature really is. In the last act, the truth stands revealed, that the name really has no definite meaning at all; it shows itself to be nothing more than a hypostatized word, applied indiscriminately to all sorts of things.

individual is intelligent in proportion as he is able to carry on abstract thinking." In fact, symposia on intelligence over the years repeatedly conclude that the first hallmark of intelligence is high-level mental ability such as abstract reasoning (Sternberg, 1997).

Intelligence, conceptualized as abstract thinking, has often been demonstrated to predict one or another type of success, particularly academic success. But although it is a potent predictor, it is far from a perfect one, leaving the vast amount of variance unexplained. As Wechsler (1940, p. 444) put it, "individuals with identical IQs may differ very markedly in regard to their effective ability to cope with the environment." One way to regard this limitation is to view human life as naturally complex and subject both to chance events and complicated interactions. A second approach is to search for better ways to assess intelligence (e.g., Sternberg, 1997). A third approach is to attribute the difference to a combination of factors, such as non-intellective personality traits. These approaches are all complementary and have all been used with different degrees of effectiveness in enhancing psychological predictions of positive outcomes.

A fourth alternative to dealing with IQ's limited predictive ability is to redefine intelligence itself as a combination of mental ability and non-intellective personality traits. Thus, Wechsler (1943, p. 103) wondered, "whether non-intellective, that is, affective and conative [motivational] abilities are admissible as factors in general intelligence." In his next sentence, he concluded they were. A few sentences thereafter, however, he qualifies the notion: they predict intelligent *behavior* (as opposed to being a part of intelligence). Wechsler remained straddling the fence, as it were. On the one hand, he at times defined intelligence as involving "...the aggregate or global capacity of the individual to act purposefully, to think rationally and to *deal effectively with his environment.*" (italics added; Wechsler, 1958, p. 7). On the other hand, the intelligence tests that carried his name focused on measuring mental ability.

Although most (if not all) intelligence researchers agree that traits other than intelligence predict success, many are quite vocal in their objections to considering those other characteristics *to be* intelligence. As noted above, there is a long theoretical tradition that distinguishes mental ability (i.e., cognition) from motivation and emotion. Labeling

nonintellectual characteristics intelligence potentially obscures their meaning (cf., Salovey & Mayer, 1994; Sternberg, 1997). Goodness in human relationships, athletic ability (i.e., kinesthetic ability), and certain talents in music, dance, and painting, have all been labeled intelligence at one time or another. Scarr (1989, p. 78) cautions, however, that "[t]o call them intelligence does not do justice either to theories of intelligence or to the personality traits and special talents that lie beyond the consensual definition of intelligence." Empirical findings illustrate repeatedly that mental abilities are generally unrelated to (i.e., uncorrelated with) other personality traits in any simple, strong fashion (although some modest and more complex connections are found; see, for example, Mayer, Caruso, Zigler, & Dreyden, 1989; Sternberg & Ruzgis, 1994).

Some models of emotional intelligence covered in this chapter do define emotional intelligence as a mixture of abilities and other personality dispositions and traits. The motivation for this appears to be the desire to label as a single entity what appear to be, in fact, a diverse group of things that predict success. Although we realize we cannot prevent such usage, it presents considerable difficulty for us. For example, does it make sense to label a trait such as optimism an "intelligence" because it predicts success (like intelligence)? We wonder whether this makes any more sense than labeling sleepiness an "alcoholic beverage" because, like alcohol, it leads to traffic accidents. Despite such reservations, we will cover all noteworthy models that use the term emotional intelligence. We will distinguish, however, between *ability models* of emotional intelligence, which focus on the interplay of emotion and intelligence as traditionally defined, and *mixed models*, which describe a compound conception of intelligence that includes mental abilities, and other dispositions and traits.

COMPETING MODELS LABELED "EMOTIONAL INTELLIGENCE"

Ability Models of Emotional Intelligence

In Western history and in psychology, emotions and reasoning sometimes have been viewed in opposition to one another (e.g., Schaffer, Gilmer, & Schoen, 1940; Payne, 1986; Publilius Syrus, 100 B.C.E./1961; Woodworth, 1940; Young, 1936). The contemporary view that emotions convey information about relationships however, suggests that emotions and intelligence can work hand in hand. Emotions reflect relationships between a person and a friend, a family, the situation, a society, or more internally, between a person and a reflection or memory. For example, joy may indicate one's identification with a friend's success; sadness may indicate disappointment with one's self. Emotional intelligence refers in part to an ability to recognize the meanings of such emotional patterns and to reason and solve problems on the basis of them (Mayer & Salovey, 1997; Salovey & Mayer, 1990).

The domain of emotional intelligence describes several discrete emotional abilities. As we now view it,* these emotional abilities can be divided into four classes or branches, as shown in Table 18.1, Column 1. (The specific skills listed in Column 1 are meant to be representative; there are other skills that could be included on each branch as well as the ones shown). The most basic skills involve the perception and appraisal of emotion. For example, early on, the infant learns about facial expressions of emotion. The infant watches its cries of distress, or joy, mirrored in the parent's face, as the parent empathically reflects those feelings. As the child grows, he or she discriminates more finely among genuine versus merely polite smiles and other gradations of expression. Also important is that people generalize emotional experience to objects, interpreting the expansiveness of a dining hall, or the stoicism of a Shaker chair (cf., Arnheim, 1974).

The second set of skills involves assimilating basic emotional experiences into mental life, including weighing emotions against one another and against other sensations and thoughts and allowing emotions to direct attention. For example, we may hold an emotional state in consciousness so as to compare it with a similar sensation in sound, color, or taste.

The third level involves understanding and reasoning about emotions. The experience of specific emotions – happiness, anger, fear, and the like – is rule-governed. Anger generally rises when justice is denied; fear often changes to relief; dejection may separate us from others. Sadness and anger move according to their own characteristic rules, just as the knight and bishop on a chessboard move in different ways. Consider a woman who is extremely angry and an hour later ashamed. It is likely that only certain events may have intervened. For example, she may have expressed her anger inappropriately or discovered she falsely believed that a friend betrayed her. Emotional intelligence involves the ability to recognize the emotions, to know how they unfold, and to reason about them accordingly.

The fourth, highest level, of emotional intelligence involves the management and regulation of emotion in oneself and others such as knowing how to calm down after feeling angry or being able to alleviate the anxiety of another person. Tasks defining these four levels are described in greater detail in the section concerning scale development below.

The mental ability model of emotional intelligence makes predictions about the internal structure of the intelligence and also its implications for a person's life. The theory predicts that emotional intelligence is, in fact, an intelligence like other intelligences in that it will meet three empirical criteria. First, mental problems have right or wrong answers, as assessed by the convergence of alternative scoring methods. Second, the measured skills correlate with other measures of mental ability (because mental abilities tend to intercorrelate) as well as with self-reported empathy (for more complex reasons; see Mayer, DiPaolo, & Salovey, 1990). Third, the absolute ability level rises with age.

The model further predicts that emotionally intelligent individuals are more likely to (a) have grown up in biosocially adaptive households (i.e., have had emotionally sensitive parenting), (b) be nondefensive, (c) be able to reframe emotions effectively (i.e., be realistically optimistic and appreciative), (d) choose good emotional role models, (e) be able to communicate and discuss feelings, and (f) develop expert knowledge in a particular emotional area such as aesthetics, moral or ethical

---

* For example, since our original theory was proposed we have more carefully distinguished between the intelligence and human effectiveness portions of our model, and each has been developed in important ways. The intelligence model has been clarified by (a) describing how and in what sense emotions convey information and by (b) adding explicit discussion of the fact that a central portion of emotional intelligence involves reasoning with or understanding of emotion (neither our own nor any other theory had mentioned this until recently; Mayer & Salovey, 1995). In addition, we have focused our social adaptiveness model so that it deals specifically with emotional effectiveness.

TABLE 18.1. Three Competing Models, all Labeled "Emotional Intelligence"

Mayer & Salovey (1997)	Bar-On (1997)	Goleman (1995a)
Overall Definition	Overall Definition	Overall Definition(s)
"Emotional intelligence is the set of abilities that account for how people's emotional perception and understanding vary in their accuracy. More formally, we define emotional intelligence as the ability to perceive and express emotion, assimilate emotion in thought, understand and reason with emotion, and regulate emotion in the self and others" (after Mayer & Salovey, 1997).	"Emotional intelligence is . . . an array of noncognitive capabilities, competencies, and skills that influence one's ability to succeed in coping with environmental demands and pressures." (Bar-On, 1997, p. 14).	"The abilities called here *emotional intelligence*, which include self-control, zeal and persistence, and the ability to motivate oneself." (Goleman, 1995a, p. xii). [. . .and. . .] "There is an old-fashioned word for the body of skills that emotional intelligence represents: *character*" (Goleman, 1995a, p. 28).
Major Areas of Skills and Specific Examples	Major Areas of Skills and Specific Skills	Major Areas of Skills and Specific Examples

Perception and Expression of Emotion
    *Identifying and expressing emotions in one's physical states, feelings, and thoughts.
    *Identifying and expressing emotions in other people, artwork, language, etc.
Assimilating Emotion in Thought
    *Emotions prioritize thinking in productive ways.
    *Emotions generated as aids to judgment and memory.
Understanding and Analyzing Emotion
    *Ability to label emotions, including complex emotions and simultaneous feelings.
    *Ability to understand relationships associated with shifts of emotion.
Reflective Regulation of Emotion
    *Ability to stay open to feelings.
    *Ability to monitor and regulate emotions reflectively to promote emotional and intellectual growth (after Mayer & Salovey, 1997, p. 11).
	Intrapersonal Skills:
	    *Emotional self-awareness,
	    *Assertiveness,
	    *Self-Regard
	    *Self-Actualization,
	    *Independence.
	Interpersonal Skills:
	    *Interpersonal relationships,
	    *Social responsibility,
	    *Empathy.
	Adaptability Scales:
	    *Problem solving,
	    *Reality testing,
	    *Flexibility.
	Stress-Management Scales:
	    *Stress tolerance,
	    *Impulse control.
	General Mood:
	    *Happiness,
	    *Optimism.
		Knowing One's Emotions
		    *Recognizing a feeling *as it happens*.
		    *Monitoring feelings from moment to moment.
		Management Emotions
		    *Handling feelings so they are appropriate.
		    *Ability to soothe oneself.
		    *Ability to shake off rampant anxiety, gloom, or irritability.
		Motivating Oneself
		    *Marshalling emotions in the service of a goal.
		    *Delaying gratification and stifling impulsiveness.
		    *Being able to get into the "flow" state.
		Recognizing Emotions in Others
		    *Empathic awareness.
		    *Attunement to what others need or want.
		Handling Relationships
		    *Skill in managing emotions in others.
		    *Interacting smoothly with others

Model Type *Ability*	Model Type *Mixed*	Model Type *Mixed*

feeling, social problem solving, leadership, or spiritual feeling (Mayer & Salovey, 1995).

Mixed Models of Emotional Intelligence

Mixed models of emotional intelligence are substantially different than the mental ability models. In one sense, both kinds of models were proposed in the first academic articles on emotional intelligence (e.g., Mayer, DiPaolo, & Salovey, 1990; Salovey & Mayer, 1990). Although these articles set out a mental ability conception of emotional intelligence, they also freely described personality characteristics that might accompany such intelligence. Thus, emotional intelligence was said to distinguish those who are "genuine and warm...[from those who] appear oblivious and boorish." Emotionally intelligent individuals were also said to "generate a larger number of future plans...and [better]...take advantage of future opportunities (p. 199)..., exhibit "...persistence at challenging tasks...," (p. 200); and have "positive attitudes toward life...that lead to better outcomes and greater rewards for themselves and others..." (Salovey & Mayer, 1990, pp. 199–200).

Almost immediately after these initial articles on emotional intelligence appeared, we recognized that our own theoretical work would be more useful if we constrained emotional intelligence to a mental ability concept and separated it from the very important traits of warmth, outgoingness, and similarly desirable virtues. By keeping them separate, it would be possible to analyze the degree to which they independently contributed to a person's behavior and general life competence. Although traits such as warmth and persistence are important, we believe they are better addressed directly and as distinct from emotional intelligence (Mayer & Salovey, 1993, 1997).

In contrast to honing this core conception of emotional intelligence, others expanded the meaning of emotional intelligence by explicitly mixing in nonability traits. For example, Bar-On's (1997) model of emotional intelligence was intended to answer the question, "Why are some individuals more able to succeed in life than others?" Bar-On reviewed the psychological literature for personality characteristics that appeared related to life success and identified five broad areas of functioning relevant to success. These are listed in Column 2 of Table 18.1, and include (a) intrapersonal skills, (b) interpersonal skills, (c) adaptability, (d) stress management, and (e) general mood. Each broad area is further subdivided. For example, intrapersonal skills are divided into emotional self-awareness, assertiveness, self-regard, self-actualization, and independence. Bar-On offered the following rationale for his use of the term emotional intelligence:

Intelligence describes the aggregate of abilities, competencies, and skills...that...represent a *collection of knowledge used to cope with life effectively*. The adjective *emotional* is employed to emphasize that this specific type of intelligence differs from cognitive intelligence...(Bar-On, 1997, p. 15).

Bar-On's theoretical work combines what may qualify as mental abilities (e.g., emotional self-awareness) with other characteristics that are considered separable from mental ability, such as personal independence, self-regard, and mood; this makes it a mixed model. (There is generally no consistent correlation between mood and intelligence, for example; Watson, 1930; Wessman & Ricks, 1966, p. 123).

Despite the breadth of his model, Bar-On (1997) is relatively cautious in his claims for his model of emotional intelligence. Although his model predicts success, this success is "the end-product of that which one strives to achieve and accomplish..." Moreover, his Emotional Quotient Inventory (EQ_i, reviewed below) relates to "the potential to succeed rather than success itself." At a broader level, he believes that EQ, along with IQ, can provide a more balanced picture of a person's general intelligence (Bar-On, 1997, p. 19).

A third view of emotional intelligence was popularized by Goleman (1995a). Goleman created a model that also was mixed and was characterized by the five broad areas depicted in Column 3 of Table 18.1, including (a) knowing one's emotions, (b) managing emotions, (c) motivating oneself, (d) recognizing emotions in others, and (e) handling relationships. His list of specific attributes under motivation, for example, include, marshalling emotions, delaying gratification and stifling impulsiveness, and entering flow states (Goleman, 1995a, p. 43). Goleman recognized that he was moving from emotional intelligence to something far broader. He states that "'ego resilience,'...is quite similar to [this model of] emotional intelligence" in that it includes social (and emotional) competencies (Goleman, 1995a, p. 44). He goes so far as to note that, "There is an old-fashioned word for the body of skills that emotional intelligence represents: *character*." (Goleman, 1995a, p. 285).

Goleman (1995a; 1998a,b) makes extraordinary claims for the predictive validity of his mixed model. He states that emotional intelligence will account for success at home, at school, and at work. Among youth, he says, emotional intelligence will lead to less rudeness or aggressiveness, more popularity, improved learning (Goleman, 1995a, p. 192), and better decisions about "drugs, smoking, and sex" (Goleman, 1995a, p. 268). At work, emotional intelligence will assist people "in teamwork, in cooperation, in helping learn together how to work more effectively." (Goleman, 1995a, p. 163). More generally, emotional intelligence will confer "an advantage in any domain in life, whether in romance and intimate relationships or picking up the unspoken rules that govern success in organizational politics"(Goleman, 1995a, p. 36).

Goleman notes that "At best, IQ contributes about 20% to the factors that determine life success, which leaves 80% to other factors." (Goleman, 1995a, p. 34). That 20% figure, with which we agree, is obtained (by mathematical means) from the fact that IQ correlates with various criteria at about the $r = .45$ level.[*] "[W]hat data exist," Goleman writes of emotional intelligence, "suggest it can be as powerful, and at times more powerful, than IQ." (Goleman, 1995, p. 34) With this statement and others even stronger, (e.g., Goleman, 1998a, p. 94; 1998b, p. 31) Goleman suggests that emotional intelligence should predict success at many life tasks at levels higher than $r = .45$. It is hard not to conclude that at least part of the popular excitement surrounding emotional intelligence is due to these very strong claims. If there were truly a single psychological entity that could predict widespread success at such levels, it would exceed any finding in a century of research in applied psychology.[†]

Summary

There are both mental ability models and mixed models of emotional intelligence. The mental ability model focuses on emotions themselves and their interactions with thought (Mayer & Salovey, 1997; Salovey & Mayer, 1990). The mixed models treat mental abilities and a variety of other characteristics such as motivation, states of consciousness (e.g.,

"flow") and social activity as a single entity (Bar-On, 1997; Goleman, 1995a). Figure 18.2 projects the different makeup of emotional intelligence as described by these models onto the earlier diagram of personality components. There, as in Figure 18.1, personality components are divided among those primarily concerned with lower level, specific processing (motivation, emotion, cognition), midlevel functioning that concerns interactions between the lower level areas, and those that represent upper-level synthetic models of the intrapersonal self and interpersonal social world.

In this diagram, the three models represent emotional intelligence in different ways. Both the Bar-On (1997) and Goleman (1995a) models are distributed across the various levels. For example, Bar-On's adaptability skills (problem-solving, reality testing, and flexibility) primarily represent cognitive skills (lower right), whereas his interpersonal skills (interpersonal relationships, social responsibility, and empathy) primarily represent more synthetic interpersonal relatedness (upper right). By way of contrast, the Mayer & Salovey (1997) model fits within the emotion and cognitive interactions area. The diagram shows in yet another way that a central difference among models is that the mental ability models operate in a region defined by emotion and cognition, whereas mixed models label a multitude of components as emotional intelligence.

OTHER-NAMED CONCEPTS RELATED TO EMOTIONAL INTELLIGENCE

The mental ability and mixed models of emotional intelligence overlap to some degree with other concepts. The ability model of emotional intelligence overlaps with several other hypothesized intelligences. Mixed models, because of their breadth, overlap with dozens of other concepts.

Concepts Primarily Related to the Mental Ability Model of Emotional Intelligence

Some concepts related to the mental ability emotional intelligence focus on one or another of its specific skills such as nonverbal perception (e.g., Buck, 1984; Rosenthal et al., 1979) or empathic accuracy (Ickes, 1997). Other related concepts appear to be similar or complementary to emotional intelligence. For example, Saarni's emotional competence (Saarni, 1990; 1997; 1999) is

---

[*] The correlation is the square root of the proportion of variance accounted for (i.e., $r = .447$ is the square root of .20 or 20% of the variance) under standard assumptions of statistical theory.

[†] After reviewing a draft of this manuscript, Dr. Goleman wished to clarify his position by stating that his general point has been that "...in some life domains emotional intelligence seems to be more highly correlated with a positive outcome than is a measure of IQ. The domains where this can occur are "soft"—those where, e.g., emotional self-regulation or empathy may be more salient skills than purely cognitive abilities, such as health or marital success." That is, he noted, "In those cases where EI is more salient than IQ, the predicative power for IQ would be lower than usual (D. Goleman, Personal communication, July 22 and 27, 1999).

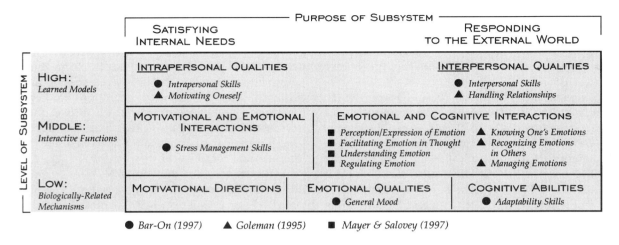

FIGURE 18.2. *An Overview of Personality and Its Major Subsystems with Three Models of Emotional Intelligence Embedded Within It.* Figure 2 retains the general arrangement of personality components depicted in Figure 1. Added to the picture, however, are specific personality components said (by three different theories) to be a part of emotional intelligence. Bar-On's (1997) five-part model is divided among intrapersonal qualities (e.g., intrapersonal skills), emotional states (e.g., general mood), and other areas. Goleman's (1995a) five-part model is split between both intrapersonal and interpersonal qualities (e.g., motivating oneself; handling relationships) as well as interactions between emotion and cognition (e.g., recognizing emotions in others). Mayer & Salovey's (1997) four-part model is located entirely within the area of emotional-cognitive interactions (e.g., perceiving emotions; understanding emotions).

defined as the demonstration of capacity and skills in emotion-eliciting social transactions (e.g., Saarni, 1997, p. 38). Emotional creativity (Averill & Nunley, 1992) emphasizes the divergent, unexpected, creative elements in thinking about feelings. Finally, there are intelligences defined in such a way as to overlap emotional intelligence partially. These include personal intelligence (Gardner, 1993), social intelligence (Cantor & Kihlstrom, 1987; Sternberg, 1988; Sternberg & Smith, 1985; Thorndike & Stein, 1937), and even Jung's feeling function (Jung, 1921/1971, p. 354).

Of the partly overlapping intelligences, only social intelligence has been operationalized satisfactorily as a mental ability (e.g., Legree, 1995; Sternberg & Smith, 1985; Wong, Day, Maxwell, & Meara, 1995). Others among the foregoing concepts have

been operationalized in more limited fashion, such as emotional creativity (Averill & Nunley, 1992). Still other intelligences, such as Gardner's (1993) personal intelligences or Jung's (1921, 1971, p. 354) feeling function have been left virtually unoperationalized as mental abilities (Sternberg, 1994).

Given the partial theoretical overlap among some of these concepts, there is likely to be some empirical overlap among them as well. The key to selecting which of these intelligences is "best" is to some degree a matter of personal theoretical preference. Ultimately, each may do the job of describing abilities that presently are omitted from intelligence tests. Emotional intelligence (as a mental ability) is our preferred theory because we believe it is theoretically defined as more distinct from traditional (i.e., verbal and performance) intelligences than some of these alternatives. For example, compared with social intelligence, emotional intelligence is broader in including internal, private emotions that are important for personal (as opposed to social) growth. On the other hand, emotional intelligence is also more focused than social intelligence in pertaining primarily to the emotional (as opposed to the social or political) aspects of problems. This makes it distinct from the social knowledge questions already found in many of today's tests of verbal intelligence (e.g., "Who was President Kennedy?"), although admittedly, social intelligence shows good psychometric distinctness from traditional intelligence measures (e.g., Sternberg & Smith, 1985). This increased theoretical breadth and focus of emotional intelligence means that it may make a very good counterpart to traditional measurement scales when compared with the alternatives.

Concepts Related to the Mixed Models of Emotional Intelligence

The family of overlapping concepts for the mixed models of emotional intelligence is larger than that of the mental ability model. Like the mental ability model, the mixed models are a member of a family of concepts (e.g., Davies, Stankov, & Roberts, 1998; Feist, 1996; Goleman, 1995a). There are, first of all, often vast literatures on each of the parts of mixed models of emotional intelligence. These include literatures on achievement motivation (McClelland, Atkinson, Clark, & Lowell, 1953), alexithymia (Bagby, Parker, & Taylor, 1994), emotional-responsiveness empathy (Mehrabian & Epstein, 1972), openness (Costa & McCrae, 1985), optimism (Scheier & Carver, 1985), pleasant–unpleasant affectivity (Green, Goldman, & Salovey, 1993; Mayer & Gaschke, 1988; Russell, 1979), practical intelligence (Sternberg & Caruso, 1985; Sternberg, Wagner, Williams, & Horvath, 1995; Wagner & Sternberg, 1985), self-esteem (e.g., Blascovich & Tomaka, 1991), and subjective well-being (Andrews & Robinson, 1991).

Other concepts partially overlap the mixed models of emotional intelligence because, like them, they are composites of many characteristics thought to lead to life success. Recall that Goleman (1995a) acknowledged that his model is little different than Block and Block's (1980) model of ego strength. Other related concepts include general intelligence itself and also practical and creative intelligence (e.g., Sternberg, 1997; Sternberg & Caruso, 1985; Sternberg & Lubart; 1995a; 1995b; Wagner & Sternberg, 1985), constructive thinking (Epstein & Meier, 1989), the aforementioned ego strength (Block & Block, 1980), the motivation toward social desirability, (Paulhus, 1991) and social insight (Chapin, 1967). Moreover, the individual aspects of the mixed models overlap considerably with the specific areas of the Big Five personality dimensions (e.g., McCrae & Costa, 1985), including such Big Five subscales as warmth, assertiveness, trust, self-discipline, and others. (This overlap tells us a great deal about the mixed models' potential for predicting success, which will be considered in the discussion section). It will be desirable in the future for the mixed model theorists to compare and distinguish their own versions of emotional intelligence from these related concepts.

THE MEASUREMENT OF EMOTIONAL INTELLIGENCE

Mental ability models of emotional intelligence, as well as mixed models, have prompted the construction of instruments to measure emotional intelligence. These measures will be examined in this section of the chapter. Mental ability models of emotional intelligence are most directly assessed by ability measures, but self-reported ability provides an alternative approach. Ability measures have the advantage of representing an individual's performance level on a task. By contrast, self-report measures are filtered through a person's self-concept and impression management motives. For example, a bright student with low self-esteem may believe he or she is not very smart, and a not-so-bright student who needs to impress others may claim to be quite smart. Mental ability measures are typically both reliable and valid and often intercorrelate at the $r = .80$ level or better. Self-report measures seem far less valid, correlating rather poorly with actual performance levels. For example, in one study, people's scores on a self-report scale of problem-solving skills (e.g., "When trying to solve a problem, I look at each possibility and then decide on the best way") correlated only $r = .15$ with an actual test of mental ability (Bar-On, 1997, p. 138).[*] We begin by examining the ability measures of emotional intelligence, move to the self-report, and then look at the relation between the two.

Emotional Intelligence as a Mental Ability Measured with Ability Measures
Emotional Intelligence Measurement before Emotional Intelligence Theory

Recall that emotional intelligence, as we define it, consists of four broad areas of specific tasks: emotional perception, assimilation, understanding, and management. As of 1990, there were several studies describing measures of emotional (or, more accurately, nonverbal) perception but fewer or

---

[*] This correlation may underestimate the relation a bit because it did not directly ask people how intelligent they believed themselves to be.

no ability-task studies related to the other areas. Concerning such emotional perception tests, the Affect Sensitivity Test presented videotaped interactions between pairs of individuals; respondents indicated the emotions and thoughts being expressed by the targets (Campbell, Kagan, & Krathwohl, 1971; Kagan, 1978). Other tests existed as well (e.g., the Profile of Nonverbal Sensitivity, PONS; Rosenthal et al., 1979; the CARAT; Buck, 1976).

Three methods were commonly employed to assess the participants' responses to these tests. The first, consensus method, compared a participant's answers to the remainder of the group (or to a prior criterion sample), and individuals received credit according to their agreement with the group consensus. The second, expert method, compared participants' answers to an expert criterion (e.g., Ekman's Facial Coding System). The third criterion, target method, compared participants' answers with those of the target they were judging. For example, members of a couple might be asked to identify what their partners reported feeling during videotaped conversation (Ickes, Stinson, Bissonette, & Garcia, 1990); other participants have been asked to predict what emotion an actor had been asked to portray (Buck, Miller, & Caul, 1974).

These early scales provided little evidence for an actual emotional intelligence. The scales themselves seemed to be unrelated to one another; the tests intercorrelated only slightly, leading one reviewer to conclude that either the early tests were sensitive to different aspects of nonverbal receiving ability, or nonverbal receiving ability was not a unidimensional construct (Buck, 1984, pp. 277, 282–283). Some interesting patterns emerged, however, including the existence of low correlations among socioemotional perception, intelligence scales, and self-reports of empathy, as well as the finding that women sometimes performed slightly better than men.

Early Research Explicitly Directed Toward Emotional Intelligence

In our initial work on measuring aspects of emotional intelligence, we suggested that emotional perception might be similar across a variety of stimuli that had been studied before in isolation (faces, abstract designs, and colors) and that prior tests may have masked a general emotion perception factor by using overly simplistic response scales (Mayer, DiPaolo, & Salovey, 1990). For example, on the PONS, participants viewed a brief videotape and then were asked only one or two questions such as how pleasant or unpleasant the video character was. We reasoned that scales would be more reliable if the response alternatives were increased in number and specificity. For example, given a face, how angry is it? . . . sad? . . . happy? and so on. One hundred thirty-nine participants judged the specific emotional content of 18 stimuli including faces, abstract designs, and colors. Consensual accuracy in identifying emotion was reliable, and there was a single factor of emotional perception common to all those stimuli.

Davies, Stankov, and Roberts (1998, Study 1) replicated and extended these findings. They correlated four emotion perception measures: faces, colors, music, and sound intervals, and found they were unifactorial. In their study, emotional perception showed nonsignificant positive correlations with measures of analytical intelligence (crystalized intelligence, $r = .05$, fluid intelligence, $r = .15$), as measured by Cattell's matrices and letter cancellation tasks (Roberts, Beh, Spilsbury, & Stankov, 1991). Davies et al., also expressed serious reservation about the reliability of these individual performance tasks. This criticism has been addressed in more recent measures, as will be seen below.

The early 1990s also saw work related to the higher level skills of emotional intelligence: understanding emotions and managing them. For example, Mayer & Geher (1996) studied emotional perception in story passages. Preliminary to the main study, eight target individuals each described their thoughts in a brief passage. For example, one target wrote:

> My best friend's father died this weekend. He had diabetes for a long time, and as he got older his health grew worse and worse. I went to his funeral on Monday. Many of my friends from high school were also there because we all wanted to be there for our friend and because we all knew and liked her father. It made me realize how lucky I am to have younger, healthy parents when I saw my friend standing there crying. Just watching her huge family come pouring into the synagogue also made me sad. (Mayer & Geher, 1996, p. 98).

Participants in the main study were asked to identify the targets' emotions or emotion-related thoughts in the passage by making a series of forced choices between two alternatives (e.g., be by my-self–kick something; fearful–apart from others.) Skill at this task, measured by agreement with the group consensus, correlated significantly with self-reported SAT scores (a proxy measure of verbal intelligence), and with self-reports of trait empathy. Target agreement showed similar but weaker results. A closely related task was developed by Lane et al. (1996). In that study, participants read a sentence (e.g., "I want to hit someone") and were asked to match it to one of seven emotion words (e.g., happiness, sadness, fear, anger, surprise, disgust, and neutral).* In other parts of the task, they matched sentences to emotional faces, or emotional faces to emotion words, and so forth. Regrettably, no measures of intelligence or empathy were included in the latter study. A study using similar tasks to Lane et al.s', however, did find a correlation between task performance and intelligence among a group of mentally retarded adults (Simon, Rosen, & Ponpipom, 1996).

In another test of emotional understanding, Averill & Nunley (1992) presented participants with three emotions and asked them to write a brief description of a situation in which they would feel the three emotions together. For example, in response to the emotional triad "joy/relief/distress"; one participant wrote about the joy of being on a mountaintop, the distress at imagining falling off, and the relief of not actually falling. Scoring was according to an expert criterion. Success at this task appears moderately correlated with general intelligence as well as with measures of creativity.

Another task that measured something between understanding and management (or at least, awareness) was also designed by Lane, Quinlan, Schwartz, Walker, and Zeitlin (1990). In this test, participants read stories such as

You and your best friend are in the same line of work. There is a prize given annually to the best performance of the year. The two of you work hard to win the prize. One night the winner is announced: your friend. How would you feel?

The test-taker provides an open-ended response that is then compared, and matched, if possible, with

---

* No examples are presented in the original study; we infer the sentences were similar to this.

various alternatives. For example, a low-awareness response to the preceding scenario is "I'd probably feel bad about it for a few days and try to figure out what went wrong. I'm sure my friend would be feeling really good." A high awareness response, by contrast, is "I'd feel disappointed that I didn't win but glad that if someone else did, that person was my friend. My friend probably deserved it! My friend would feel happy and proud but slightly worried that my feelings might be hurt."

Better performance at this task correlated positively with the emotional perception task developed by the same authors (see above), and negatively with the Toronto Alexithymia Scale (Taylor, Ryan, & Bagby, 1985), a self-report measure of difficulty at expressing emotion.

More Recent Measurement Work With Emotional Intelligence

THE MULTIFACTOR EMOTIONAL INTELLIGENCE SCALE (MEIS) STUDY. Our current research program has been devoted primarily to developing a full-fledged test of emotional intelligence as a set of mental abilities (Mayer, Caruso, & Salovey, in press). We have designed a Multifactor Emotional Intelligence Scale (MEIS) that consists of 12 ability measures of emotional intelligence divided into 4 classes or "branches" of abilities, including (a) perceiving, (b) facilitating, (c) understanding, and (d) managing emotion (Mayer & Salovey, 1997; Mayer, Caruso, & Salovey, in press; Mayer, Salovey, & Caruso, 1997). Branch 1 tasks measure emotional perception in Faces, Music, Designs, and Stories. The first three of these were similar to the emotional perception tasks described above (Mayer, DiPaolo, & Salovey, 1990), and the fourth Stories task, which is equally an understanding task was also discussed above (Mayer & Geher, 1996). The second, Facilitation branch, contains two tests that measure Synesthesia Judgments (e.g., "How hot is anger?") and Feeling Biases. Briefly, these taks were expected to measure emotion's facilitation of cognition but resulted in a weaker factor than the others and may be dropped for some purposes. Branch 3's four tasks examine the understanding of emotion. For example, one question asks, "Optimism most closely combines which two emotions?" and a participant has to choose "pleasure and anticipation" over less specific alternatives such as "pleasure and joy."

Branch 4's two tests measure Emotion Management in (a) the Self and (b) Others. These tasks ask participants to read a scenario such as the following and then rate five reactions to it according to how good they were:

One of your colleagues at work looks upset and asks if you will eat lunch with him. At the cafeteria, he motions for you to sit away from the other diners. After a few minutes of slow conversation he says that he wants to talk to you about what's on his mind. He tells you that he lied on his resume about having a college degree. Without the degree, he wouldn't have gotten the job.

(Please judge the value of the following reaction:)

Ask him how he feels about it so you can understand what's going on. Offer to help him, but don't push yourself on him if he really doesn't want any of your help.

Five hundred and three adults completed all the tasks as well as several criterion scales. An additional 229 adolescents also completed a slightly abbreviated version of the scales.

FINDINGS WITH THE MEIS. Work with the MEIS yielded a number of important findings (Mayer, Caruso, & Salovey, in press). First, consensus, expert, and target scoring methods for the same tasks converged on correct answers to a degree anticipated by theory. This adds confidence to any of the scoring approaches. Of these, consensus scoring appeared to be the best all-around method. As noted earlier, Davies et al. (1998) worried about early mental ability tasks in the area because they exhibited only modest reliabilities. The MEIS achieved a full-scale alpha reliability of $r = .96$.

The second major finding concerned the structure of emotional intelligence as represented by these 12 tasks. First, the tasks were generally positively intercorrelated with one another. A study of the test's factorial structure recommended two equally viable factorial models. The first was a three-factor solution that separated out factors of (a) emotional perception, (b) emotional understanding, and (c) emotional management. (An alternative, four factor model, including a weaker (d) Facilitation factor was also possible). The second factorial model involved a hierarchical factor analysis based on those three (or four) factors (equally well represented by the first unrotated factor of the whole test) that describes a general factor of emotional intelligence, g_{ei}.

The same study indicated that general emotional intelligence, g_{ei}, correlated both with measures of verbal intelligence ($r = .36$) and with measures of self-reported empathy ($r = .33$). Few other criterion scales were administered, but the same general factor also correlated with parental warmth ($r = .23$). The fourth major finding was that ability at emotional intelligence was age dependent, increasing between young adolescence and early adulthood.

Findings from the MEIS indicate that emotional intelligence may qualify as a conventional intelligence operationalized as a mental ability (Mayer & Salovey, 1993; Neisser, Boodoo, Bouchard, Boykin, Brody, Ceci, Halpern, Loehlin, Perloff, Sternberg, & Urbina, 1996; Scarr, 1989). Emotional intelligence, like other well-operationalized intelligences, show convergence among criteria for scoring correct answers. Emotional intelligence also "looks like" other intelligences, in that its tasks are intercorrelated. Findings also indicate that emotional intelligence is related to more traditional intelligence (i.e., analytical intelligence), but sufficiently distinct from it to represent new and unique variance. And finally, emotional intelligence, like other standard intelligences, develops with age (Binet & Simon, 1905/1916, pp. 320–321; Brown, 1997; Fancher, 1985, p. 71). Certain of these findings have now been replicated in other laboratories (Ciarrochi, Chan, & Caputi, in press).

EMOTIONAL INTELLIGENCE AS A MENTAL ABILITY BUT MEASURED WITH SELF-REPORT MEASURES

The mental ability model of emotional intelligence can be measured by self-report scales as well as by mental ability tasks. Self-report is a less direct way of assessing performance. It has its own merits, though, including being relatively easy to administer, tapping internal experiences difficult to obtain with performance measures, and assessing ongoing conscious processes related to emotional thinking. As with ability measures, there are several self-report scales that examine individual aspects of emotional intelligence, particularly Branch 1 (perception) and Branch 4 (management).

One of the most original and interesting approaches to measuring emotional perception (Branch 1) is the "BB" (based on body) scale of Bernet's (1996) Style in the Perception of Affect Scale (SIPOAS). The BB scale is intended to assess real connectedness to the (sometimes) slight bodily changes that accompany feelings and emotions. It is contrasted to two other ways of thinking about emotion. The "Emphasis on Evaluation" (EE) scale reflects effortful attempts to understand one's own emotions in terms of outsiders, ideals, or expectations and is related to neuroticism. The "Looking to Logic" (LL) scale involves favoring intellect and avoiding feeling. Bernet (1996) has found that (self-reported) gains in psychotherapy are highest among high BB scorers who experience a variety of treatment modalities, including talking therapies, but also physically-oriented therapies and spiritual approaches to difficulties. The exact relation of the SIPOAS scores to emotional intelligence is not yet clear, but it appears to be an interesting measure worthy of further study.

Many scales also measure the management of emotion (Branch 4). Mayer & Gaschke (1988) described a reflective experience of mood they termed meta-experience. This reflective experience is measured with such statements as, "I know exactly how I am feeling," or "I am confused about how I feel." Since then, a large number of both state and trait measures of emotional meta-experience have been developed and studied. Findings with such scales indicate, for example, that people higher in mood attention and clarity are better able to reduce their rumination over negative material (Salovey et al., 1995). Further details on the measurement properties and results obtained with such scales may be found in several recent articles and chapters (e.g., Mayer & Stevens, 1994; Salovey et al., 1995; Salovey, Bedell, Detweiler, & Mayer, in press). For that reason we will not repeat those reviews here. Instead, we will focus on a full self-report operationalization of the emotional intelligence model.

Tett and his colleagues (Tett, Wang, Fisher, Martinez, Griebler, & Linkovich, 1997; Tett, Wang, Gribler, Thomas, & Martinez, 1997) developed 10 scales based on the original model of emotional intelligence (Salovey & Mayer, 1990). Emotional appraisal was divided into four scales: (a) Emotional Perception of the Self–Verbal, (b) Emotional Perception in the Self–Nonverbal, (c) Emotion in Others–Nonverbal, and (d) Empathy. The regulation of emotion was divided into two: (e) Regulation of Emotion in the Self, and (f) Regulation of Emotion in Others. Lastly, the utilization of emotion was divided into four additional scales: (g) Flexible Thinking, (h) Creative Thinking, (i) Mood Redirected Attention, and (j) Motivating Emotions. Each of the scales was internally consistent, and coefficient alphas ranged between $\alpha = .60$ and .86. A factor analysis of these scales yielded four factors: (a) recognition and regulation of emotion in others, (b) the recognition of emotion in the self and the expression of emotion, (c) emotional stability, and (d) high self-reported intuition coupled with poor delay of gratification. This self-report measure plainly yielded results somewhat different from those obtained with the MEIS. The Tett et al. measures have not yet been correlated with other criteria.

EMOTIONAL INTELLIGENCE AS A MIXED MODEL MEASURED BY SELF-REPORT

Just as the ability model of emotional intelligence can be operationalized and measured, so too can the mixed models. To date, all mixed models have been measured via self-report approaches. A first test of mixed-model emotional intelligence drew its organization from Salovey & Mayer (1990). Schutte, Malouff, Hall, Haggerty, Cooper, Golden, & Dornheim (1998) purposefully interpreted the 1990 model as a mixed model so that it would include diverse attributes defined as emotional intelligence in popular works (specifically, Cooper & Sawaf, 1997; Goleman, 1995a). Using factor analytic techniques, the authors extracted 4 factors from 62 initial test items they examined but settled on a single factor solution because their factors 2 through 4 loaded few of those items. Items from all the areas of the 1990 model were fairly evenly represented on this single first, factor, which had an alpha coefficient of $\alpha = .90$ and a test-retest reliability of $r = .78$.

A correlational analysis between their final 33-item scale and other measures suggested its overlap with positive affectivity and openness (Schutte et al., 1998). For example, the scale correlated highly (and negatively) with the Toronto Alexithymia Scale $(r(24) = -.65)$ and positively with attention and clarity subscales of the Trait Meta-Mood Scale

$(r(47) = .63, .52$, respectively), as well as in expected directions with several scales that overlap with generally positive affect (e.g., Life Orientation Test–Pessimism, $r(23) = -.43$, Zung Depression, $r(37) = -.37$, Trait Meta-Mood Mood–Repair, $r(47) = .68$. It also correlated $r(22) = .54$ with Openness on the NEO scale (and at lower levels, positively with Extraversion and negatively with Neuroticism).

The work by Schutte et al. (1998) tested a uniquely important behavioral prediction. In their studies, 64 first-year college students completed the 33-item emotional intelligence scale at the outset of the academic year; SAT or ACT scores were also available for 42 of the participants. The emotional intelligence scale predicted end-of-year GPA for the students ($r(63) = .32$) even though scores on the emotional intelligence scale were not related to SATs ($r(41) = -.06$). This study provides some initial support for the idea that mixed models of emotional intelligence may predict academic success beyond that of general cognitive measures. Other research, however, has indicated that happier college students obtain higher grades in general (Wessman & Ricks, 1966, p. 123). Because the Schutte et al. scale (and other self-report measures of emotional intelligence) correlate highly with positive affect, future research will need to partial out the influence of general mood level from those self-report scales.

Bar-On's mixed model of emotional intelligence was designed and operationalized as his Emotional Quotient Inventory (EQ_i). A factor analysis of his EQ_i scale (Bar-On, 1997, pp. 98–108) yielded 13 factors more or less consistent with the individual attributes listed in Table 18.1 (Column 3) of this chapter. For example, a first, self-contentment factor, was measured by such items as "I feel sure of myself in most situations." The second, social responsibility factor was measured by such items as "I like helping people," and a third impulse control factor was measured by the statement "When I start talking it is hard to stop." The first three factors represented about 23, 5, and 4% of the variance, respectively. The remaining factors explained from between 3 to 1% of the test variance. The 13 subscales have intercorrelations hovering around $r = .50$, and not surprisingly, given such interdependence, a one-factor solution of the test is also possible (Bar-On, 1997).

The overall test correlates negatively and highly (in the $r = .50$ to .75 range) with measures of

negative affect such as the Beck Depression Inventory and the Zung Self-Rating Depression Scale. It also correlates positively with traits related to positive affect. A cross-national administration of the Bar-On and the 16PF indicated that the Bar-On was consistently positively correlated (mostly between $r = .40$ and .60) with emotional stability and with components of extraversion, including social boldness and social warmth (Bar-On, 1997, pp. 110–111). Notably, neither the overall scale, nor any of its subscales ever showed a significant correlation with the mental ability intelligence test – Scale B – embedded in the 16PF. Consistent with that, a study correlating the EQ_i with the WAIS–R yielded a negligible correlation of $r = .12$ (Bar-On, 1997, pp. 137–138).

The EQ_i has been correlated with several other scales as well (see Bar-On, 1997), but there are few reported predictions of actual behavioral outcomes. The closest to such a study concerns job performance and work satisfaction in which the EQ_i predicted a self-report measure of "sense of competence" on the job ($r = .51$). It is difficult to interpret this finding because the EQ_i and sense of competence scale were given at the same time and would seem to share content and error variance. Hence, the correlation could reflect a general sense of positive affectivity and self-esteem at the time of testing; on the other hand, something more might be involved. Further research is needed in order to clarify the findings.

Finally, Goleman (1995b) also compiled a test of emotional intelligence for an article in the Utne Reader. The Goleman scale is composed of 10 items; for each item, people must state their response to a hypothetical situation. One item, for example, reads as follows:

Assume you're a college student who had hoped to get an A in a course, but you have just found out you got a C– on the midterm. What do you do?

a. Sketch out a specific plan for ways to improve your grade and resolve to follow through on your plans.

b. Resolve to do better in the future.

c. Tell yourself it really doesn't matter much how you do in the course and concentrate instead on other classes where your grades are higher.

d. Go to see the professor and try to talk her into giving you a better grade.

We doubted Goleman ever intended that this scale would be used for serious purposes, which he recently confirmed for us (D. Goleman, personal communication, July 22, 1999). Nonetheless, Goleman's scale does bear some content overlap with the third factor of the MEIS (which loads emotional management tasks) and has been studied by Davies, Stankov, & Roberts (1998). Goleman's scale, like the third MEIS factor, correlates highly with self-reported empathy (Davies, Stankov, & Roberts, 1998). Davies et al. found that the Goleman scale also correlated with a measure of emotional control (Roger & Najarian, 1989). The same authors also concluded, however, that the Goleman test has unacceptably low reliability ($\alpha = .18$; Davies, Stankov, & Roberts, 1998, pp. 33, 55).

Summary

Several self-report measures of the mixed models of emotional intelligence exist. As a group, the scales tend to be strongly related to both positive affect (and negatively to negative affect), as well as to emotional openness. Whether these self-report scales of emotional intelligence add unique variance above and beyond already-existing measures of personality has not yet been answered, but their item content seems sufficiently distinct that it is possible they do. In this regard, the findings by Schutte et al. (1998) that their measure may predict academic achievement independently of traditional measures of analytic intelligence is provocative.

DISCUSSION

This chapter first covered several competing models of emotional intelligence and compared them. The concepts of "emotion," "intelligence," and their combination were examined. A distinction was made between mental ability conceptions of emotional intelligence and mixed conceptions that combine abilities with nonability components of personality.

The chapter next reviewed some of the current research on emotional intelligence, which was quite supportive of the mental ability model of emotional intelligence. Some key findings include that (a) different methods for finding the correct answers to emotional intelligence questions appear to converge, (b) there is a clear general factor of emo-

tional intelligence, and (c) this general factor breaks down into three specific subfactors concerned with emotional perception, understanding, and management. Moreover, (d) findings from several different laboratories indicate that emotional intelligence correlates (low-to-moderately) with general intelligence and empathy. Finally, (e) the abilities involved appear to grow with age. There are further hints that emotional intelligence is related to self-report of warm parenting.

Matters with the mixed models are less clear. The Schutte et al. (1998) report suggests that emotional intelligence measured by their scale might predict the grades obtained by incoming college students somewhat independently of predictions made from SAT scores. The Bar-On EQ_i has been normed, factor analyzed, and correlated with many tests, but its predictions of academic or career success have not yet been ascertained. The Goleman scale has not been used much by researchers, and it appears to be unreliable.

Several issues remain to be concluded. A very central issue is whether, as some have claimed, emotional intelligence is a better predictor of success than intelligence. Is this claim serious and can it be supported? If not, what is the real excitement of emotional intelligence? What are its challenges (if any) to contemporary approaches to intelligence. And, finally, what will future research tell us?

Excitement over Emotional Intelligence: What Is Real and What Is Unreal?

At the outset of this chapter, we noted that emotional intelligence had attracted a great deal of attention and had generated a great deal of excitement. Although we are great fans of emotional intelligence, and we believe some of the enthusiasm is deserved, we must also say that some of the enthusiasm appears to be misplaced.

Misplaced Excitement over Emotional Intelligence

Earlier in the chapter, for example, we considered the popular claim that emotional intelligence predicts a variety of successful behaviors among children, at home, and at work at a level at or exceeding that of general intelligence. Such a claim appears misleading in several ways. The first way it is misleading is with respect to how strong a prediction can be made. According to popular writing, if intelligence predicts 20% of the variance of some success, emotional intelligence can help fill in the 80% gap. To the unsophisticated reader, bringing up the "80% unaccounted-for variance" figure suggests that there may indeed be a heretofore overlooked variable that truly can predict huge portions of life success. Although that is desirable, no variable studied in a century of psychology has made much such huge contributions.

The unexplained 80% of success appears to be in large part the consequence of complex, possibly chaotic interactions among hundreds of variables playing out over time. Predicting a person's future success shares much in common with intermediate or long-range forecasts of such outcomes as earthquakes, hurricanes, stock market rallies, election outcomes, and geopolitics. For example, a person's career success is a product not only of personality components themselves but also economic forces (e.g., real estate booms), political forces (e.g., pork-barrel projects), scientific advances (e.g., automation of customer service), and swings in public sentiment (e.g., demand for Peruvian coffee). We can predict such outcomes at levels that are recognizably greater than chance but far less than certainty. For these reasons, a new variable's value for predicting success is more realistically compared with how much variance new variables typically explain rather than how much unexplained variance is yet to be explained. The best new variables typically increase predictions, for instance, of job performance by between 1 and 4%. That 1 to 4% can mean great savings when scientific methods of selection are employed for thousands of people, but it is far different than what was claimed for emotional intelligence.

A second way that such popular claims are misleading is that they suggest there is an integrated, single, psychological entity that combines such entities as "persistence," "zeal," "emotional perceptiveness," and "good social skills." There is nothing wrong with studying such assorted variables together and seeing how they collectively predict some criterion. But to call them a single entity, i.e., "emotional intelligence,"– or even parts of a single entity, leaves the mistaken impression that all those different attributes come together as a package

when, in fact, they are more-or-less independent entities (recall how they are spread out in Figure 18.2). In addition, calling them a single entity suggests that the "package" is somehow new and mysteriously powerful when, indeed, many of its elements have been studied for years and have no special predictive powers. Finally such claims suggest that this highly desirable package can be acquired or learned as a whole when, in fact, it consists of many different – perhaps even opposing – qualities.

Consider this analogy: It is perfectly acceptable, and even desirable, to study variables that, acting together, cause car accidents: alcoholism, poor eyesight, suicide-proneness, lead-footedness, and sleep deprivation. It is also justifiable to create mathematical composites of such variables to predict car accidents. To claim, however, that alcoholism, poor eyesight, suicide-proneness, and so forth are all part of a *unitary syndrome* of "car-accident-proneness" that some unfortunate people have and some lucky ones do not, is misrepresentation. Poor eyesight, alcoholism, and other unrelated variables each arise from different causes and are treated by different methods. Claiming that they are a single syndrome that defines a radical new understanding of driving skill is sensationalism, not science.

Finally, the most serious way that these popular claims are misleading is in seeming to present scientific studies that support their powerful claims but in fact fail to do so. For instance, Goleman (1995a; 1995c) referred to a study of Bell Laboratory engineers in which the top performers were equivalent in IQ to other engineers. The key difference, he claims, is that the top performers were more emotionally intelligent than were their peers. Unfortunately, this is conjecture, because the engineers were not tested for emotional intelligence explicitly using either mental ability or mixed model approaches to measurement (see Kelley & Caplan, 1993).

Extravagant claims as to the power of emotional intelligence to predict success in the workplace appear to fly in the face of our existing research base. For instance, Barrick and Mount (1991) conducted a meta-analysis of 117 criterion-related validity studies of how the Big Five personality dimensions predict job behavior. The 117 studies yielded 162 samples with a total N of 23,994 individuals. The Big Five dimensions include emotionality, extraversion, openness, agreeableness, and neuroticism. Each dimension is a composite that itself includes several highly correlated subfactors or facets. Interestingly, many of these factors overlap with what Goleman and Bar-On described as emotional intelligence. For example, agreeableness overlaps in part with such mixed models in its facets of (a) trust, (b) straightforwardness, (c) altruism, (d) compliance, (e) modesty, and (f) tender-mindedness. What did agreeableness predict among the 23,994 individuals who were studied? Agreeableness, the authors concluded, "is not an important predictor of job performance, even in those jobs containing a large social component (e.g., sales or management)" (Barrick & Mount, 1991, p. 21).

Extraversion also contains mixed-model elements such as (a) warmth, (b) gregariousness, (c) assertiveness, (d) activity, (e) excitement-seeking, and (f) positive emotions. Extraversion fared a bit better, validly predicting success for people in management and sales, although not for those in professions (e.g., lawyers, accountants, teachers), in police work, or in skilled or semiskilled occupations (e.g., plumbers, farm workers, factory workers). And, a third dimension, conscientiousness, overlaps with mixed models a bit as well, including (a) competence, (b) order, (c) dutifulness, (d) achievement striving, (e) self-discipline, and (f) deliberation. Conscientiousness was found to be the best predictor, showing consistent predictions across all occupational groups (Barrick & Mount, 1991, pp. 17–18). What was the strength of such predictions? The overall correlations topped out at $r = .15$, or 2 to 3% of the variance – rather less than the 20 to 80% suggested in popular writings.

Justifiable Excitement over Emotional Intelligence

REAL EXCITEMENT INTRINSIC TO EMOTIONAL INTELLIGENCE. If emotional intelligence is not what Gibbs (1995, p. 60) referred to as the "true measure of intelligence," is it worth getting excited about? We certainly think so. The rigorous search for new intelligences can result in important, incremental predictive power over current measures of intelligence. We believe that emotional intelligence – as mental ability – identifies a previously overlooked area of ability critical to certain human functioning. These emotionally intelligent skills lay hidden in the boundary area between mental ability and noncognitive dispositions. Many intelligence researchers were relieved when Scarr (1989) came to the defense of traditional intelligence with the statement that "human virtues . . . such as goodness in human relationships, and talents in music, dance, and painting" should not be called intelligent. Yet there is a borderland between the two. Musical ability, after all, is related to mathematical ability. Bar-On's (1997) search for "noncognitive competencies" represents this intuition that ability sometimes lurks amidst everyday traits and tendencies. Our own intuition was that there is something more than simple hyperemotionality among those sometimes labeled as touchy–feely, bleeding hearts, sensitive, or empathic souls. Emotional intelligence is the mental ability that lurks amidst the emotions.

"There is no right way to feel," is a battle cry of the human potential movement, and it obscures the fact that there may indeed by right ways to feel. Emotions are certainly evolved as a part of natural selection; consistent signal systems provide evolutionary advantages to those organisms that develop them over others (Darwin, 1872/1965; Ekman, 1973). Once evolved, these emotions are modified by culture as necessary. Thus, the correct feeling(s) to have at a funeral or elsewhere are the joint product of evolutionary developments in emotion and socially constructed rules of how to feel and behave.

A mental ability test of emotional intelligence will be the optimal tool for identifying people who truly understand emotions. Mental ability tests best distinguish between the person who is aesthetically minded but does not really understand feelings and the person who does really understand. Ability-based emotional intelligence measures can distinguish best the people who truly understand their own emotions from those who get lost in them. It is such ability-based emotional intelligence measures that can identify optimally those who may be mismatched with a given career (e.g., counseling and psychotherapy) because they lack the understanding of feelings necessary to listen empathically and to behave sensitively.

There is a social implication of this finding as well as an individual differences–career selection implication. Scarr (1989) believed that identifying an intelligence adjusts social behavior so as to value the entity more than before. She suspects this is one reason some have labeled nonintelligences such as warmth, as intelligence. Identifying an actual intelligence, therefore, may readjust values. For example, people who have different skills and know it often can communicate more smoothly about their abilities and limitations. We have often noticed that people in cars readily say, "Oh, I can't read maps; you tell me where to go" (low spatial intelligence) and pass the map over to someone else. We look forward to the day when, rather than dismissing someone else as a "bleeding heart," or a "touchy feely type," or "oversensitive," a person will feel comfortable to exclaim, "Oh, I can't read emotions; you help me understand how to make my spouse feel better." Passing the job of emotional reading over to the individual who can perform it would be readjusting social values in a way that might make good sense for both parties.

REAL EXCITEMENT ABOUT EMOTIONAL INTELLIGENCE AND SUCCESS. The concept of emotional intelligence has also raised the issue of how success might be predicted. Although success may not be optimally predicted by emotional intelligence alone, the prediction of success is a relevant aspect of intelligence research, and more generally, personality psychology (Ford, 1994; Sternberg, 1996). A headlong rush to predict success was unleashed by the concept of emotional intelligence. Thus far, the science of prediction has been overwhelmed by wild claims and popular self-help writings. If this interest in success can be channeled more seriously, however, much good may come of the enthusiasm.

To us, studying personal success involves collecting measurable characteristics of personality and using them to predict measurable outcomes. Within the realm of cognition this may mean measuring a broader variety of intelligences than has been the case (e.g., Gardner, 1993; Sternberg, 1996); more generally, it means examining any part of personality that may contribute to a good life—as well as better defining what a successful life is. To some extent, the mixed models of emotional intelligence have initiated such a search. If we superimpose the predictive elements of these mixed models on a generic model of personality, as was done in Figure 18.2, however, it is apparent that the features selected do not cover intelligence or personality in a comprehensive or balanced fashion. Those studying success, in other words, may do better to sample variables from a broader and more balanced fashion across the personality system. Over 400 parts of personality are commonly discussed in personality psychology (Mayer, 1995b), and these are unevenly sampled by mixed emotional intelligence models: Once variables are collected, it is necessary to remember that a systems' elements have unexpected and nonlinear relations with one another. High self-esteem may seem perfectly wonderful in itself, but in some personalities that are disconnected from normal human relations (e.g., Adolph Hitler, Joseph Stalin) such self-esteem may promote evil behavior (Baumeister, 1997; Mayer, 1993).

In addition to better variable selection, more attention needs to be paid to what kind of success we are talking about. There are many different sorts of success, which is a point that can be made quite clearly if we represent personality amidst its neighboring systems. Placing personality in context has been a major focus of contemporary integrations of personality psychology (Mayer, 1998). Personality and its neighboring systems can be arranged according to the two dimensions we employed earlier to arrange its internal components: the molecular–molar dimension, which separates basic level emotional and cognitive processing from more synthetic processing, and the internal–external dimension, which separates the intrapersonal from the interpersonal. Extending these two dimensions, as in Figure 18.3, we see personality surrounded by its own neurological underpinnings (below), its external situation (to the right), and the groups to which it belongs (above; Mayer, 1995a; 1998).

Looked at this way, success depends upon which system we are observing. Internal personality may attain success in the form of happiness or other private positive feelings. Biological success involves good health and longevity, situational success involves being treated well, and group-based success involves being a well-accepted member of a loving family and other desirable social organizations. Looked at this way, it seems unlikely that there will be a one-personality-fits-all sort of success. Rather, some personality features will assist with some sorts of success and other features will assist with other sorts of success. We share the desire with others to understand what leads to human success—that is one motive (among several) that turned us to the study of emotional intelligence in the first place.

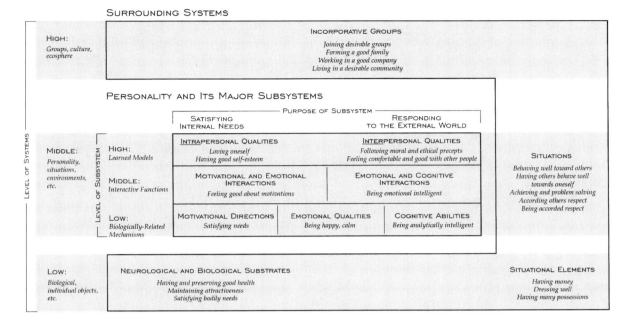

FIGURE 18.3. *Personality and Its Surrounding Systems With Examples of Success Relevant to Each System*. In Figure 3, personality is placed amidst its neighboring systems: biology (below), situations (to the right), and groups (above) so as to illustrate the multifaceted nature of success (modified from Mayer, 1998). Personal success is an aspect of personality and all its adjoining systems. For example, personal success might include good health (biology), a calm, happy mood (internal emotions), plenty of money (situational elements), or respect from others (situations), as well as success in forming a rewarding family environment (social groups).

There is no reason that good scientific research should not have important practical applications in that regard, but it needs to take a more thoughtful turn than has been the case thus far.

Charting New Ground

Once upon a time in our discipline, there was a fairly active search for characteristics other than traditional analytical intelligence that predict success in life (e.g., McClelland et al., 1953). Some of these searches yielded mixed results but were forgotten; many other searches failed, or appeared to do so. To avoid unnecessary disappointments, we must look at what will be realistic and worthwhile; additional prediction over existing constructs in the 1–5% range should satisfy us for the time being. If we find variables that predict somewhat above that, all the better.

We must define success, and then we must develop good criteria for success carefully. As we only have come to understand in the last decade, measures of traditional intelligence look like wonderful predictors in part because the school performance they predict so well is a powerful criterion. People care about school performance, of course, but school performance is also unique as a variable because it aggregates so many behavioral observations. Consider that a person's grade point average is a reflection of her or his behavior over hundreds of days, over hundreds of quizzes, tests, and other assignments, as assessed by multiple independent observers (teachers). We now know that it is far more possible to predict records of aggregated behavior than it is to predict individual instances of behavior (Epstein, 1979).

What will be the aggregated criteria for emotional intelligence or other types of success? We need to find new such criteria to chart the predictors of success. There will be many directions to pursue.

Perhaps certain emotional disorders (i.e., psychiatric diagnoses) will distinguish otherwise emotionally intelligent individuals from the emotionally unintelligent. Perhaps the quality of social networks will be an important criterion, or retrospective reports of parenting. To aggregate such outcomes, some personality psychologists have been working on scales that aggregate external, behavioral, or life-space measures (e.g., Buss & Craik, 1983; Mayer, Carlsmith, & Chabot, 1998; Stokes, Mumford, & Owens, 1994). For example, life-space scales are basically a means of aggregating a wide variety of outcome variables, all external to personality, (e.g., "How many jars of vitamins do you own?" "Do you belong to the Young Republicans?") so as to create new, more powerful descriptions of a person's environment and, for those interested in it, new measures of their success.

So, there are reasons to be excited both about emotional intelligence and the search for variables that predict success. Naive approaches will, we suspect, run headlong into the disappointments of predicting success that have arisen in the past. There is, however, room for further sophisticated studies of intelligence, personality, and their predictions of success.

CONCLUSION

There now are two general models of emotional intelligence: a mental ability model and a mixed model that includes various personality dispositions. The mental ability model is probably the only one that is aptly called emotional intelligence. The other is somewhat more general than the meanings of "emotional" and "intelligence" would suggest. The use of the term "intelligence" to depict all varieties of human endeavor aside from mental ability is not new, however, and has merely reasserted itself in the present context.

Current research suggests that mental ability models of emotional intelligence can be described as a standard intelligence and empirically meet the criteria for a standard intelligence. This means that certain people previously called emotional may be carrying out sophisticated information processing. Emotional intelligence, carefully considered, also illuminates a boundary between cognitive intelligence and nonintellective dispositions. For

example, emotional intelligence makes clear that socializing involves intellective and nonintellective aspects; only the intellective, we argue, should be referred to as intelligent.

The concept of emotional intelligence as ability is distinct from mixed models of emotional intelligence. Both may be useful in the study of human effectiveness and success in life. We believe it is useful to take a reasoned, thoughtful approach to studying human effectiveness under various conditions, and indeed much research does so. Calling any human variable related to personal success, "emotional intelligence," however, is likely to impede rather than promote progress in either area. More serious undertakings than can be orchestrated from the popular press are required.

The first mental ability measures of emotional intelligence now exist, and they appear reliable, content valid, and structurally valid. To some extent, the fate of emotional intelligence measures is connected to advances in personality psychology wherein better criteria of life activities (including success) are specified. There are few ready-made real-life criteria with which to correlate emotional intelligence at present. Questions such as What is an effective emotional life? or What is an effective, successful life? have only begun to be addressed in measurement psychology. Answering such questions will require a great deal of ingenuity on the part of both theorists and researchers. Clarification of the spheres of life activity will profit not only research on emotional intelligence but research on the intelligences and personality psychology more broadly.

ACKNOWLEDGMENTS

The authors wish to acknowledge the others who assisted us with this chapter. Tamara L. Bress, & Tracey A. Martin conducted library research that greatly enriched this review. Tracey A. Martin & Sherry Palmer critiqued and helped clarify the figures. Sherry Palmer generated the computer figures. We are grateful for all their help.

Preparation of this manuscript was supported in part by a University of New Hampshire Faculty Scholar Award to John D. Mayer and by the grants SBR-9058020 from NSF, PBR-84B from ACS, and R01-CA68427 and P01-MH/DA56826 from NIH to Peter Salovey.

Correspondence regarding this chapter may be sent to John D. Mayer, Department of Psychology, University of New Hampshire, Durham, NH 03824; e-mail: jack.mayer@unh.edu.

REFERENCES

Adams, S. (April 7, 1997). Dilbert. In *The Boston Globe*. Boston, MA.

Andrews, F. M., & Robinson, J. P. (1991). Measures of subjective well-being. In J. P. Robinson, P. R. Shaver, & L. S. Wrightsman (Eds.). *Measures of personality and social psychological attitudes* (pp. 61–114). New York: Academic Press/Harcourt Brace Jovanovich.

Arnheim, R. (1974). *Art and visual perception (The new version)*. Berkeley, CA: University of California Press.

Averill, J. R., & Nunley, E. P. (1992). *Voyages of the heart: Living an emotionally creative life*. New York: Free Press.

Bagby, R. M., Parker, J. D., & Taylor, G. J. (1994). The twenty-item Toronto Alexithymia Scale–I. Item selection and cross-validation of the factor structure. *Journal of Psychosomatic Research, 38*, 23–32.

Bain, A. (1855/1977). *The senses and the intellect*. London: John W. Parker & Son. Reprinted in D. N. Robinson (Ed.), *Significant contributions to the history of psychology: 1750–1920. Series A: Orientations; Vol. 4*. Washington, DC: University Publications of America.

Bar-On, R. (1997). *The Emotional Quotient Inventory (EQ-i): Technical Manual*. Toronto: Multi-Health Systems.

Barrick, M. R., & Mount, M. K. (1991). The Big Five personality dimensions and job performance: A meta-analysis. *Personnel Psychology, 44*, 1–26.

Baumeister, R. F. (1997). *Evil: Inside human violence and cruelty*. New York: W. H. Freeman & Company.

Bennetts, L. (1996, March). Emotional Savvy. *Parents, 71*, 56–61.

Bernet, M. (1996). *Emotional intelligence: Components and correlates*. In Symposium #4057, Emotional health and emotional intelligence. Presentation at the 104th Annual Convention of the American Psychological Association. Toronto, Canada, August 9–13th.

Binet, A., & Simon, T. (1916). Application of the new methods to the diagnosis of the intellectual level among normal and subnormal children in institutions and in primary schools. In A. Binet, & T. Simon (E. S. Kite, Trans.) *The development of intelligence in children*. Baltimore: Wilkins & Wilkins. [Authorized facsimile, 1970, University Microfilms, Ann Arbor, MI] [Translation of the original 1905 work, Applications des méthodes nouvelles au diognostic du niveau intellectuel chez des enfants normaux et anormaux d'hospice et d'école primaire. *L' Année Psychologique, 11*, 245–336].

Blascovich, J., & Tomaka, J. (1991). Measures of self esteem. In J. P. Robinson, P. R. Shaver, & L. S. Wrightsman (Eds.), *Measures of personality and social psychological attitudes* (pp. 115–160). New York: Academic Press/Harcourt Brace Jovanovich.

Block, J., & Block, J. H. (1980). The role of ego-control and ego resiliency in the organization of behavior. In W. A. Collins (Ed.), *The Minnesota symposium on child psychology* (Vol. 13, pp. 33–101). Hillsdale, NJ: Erlbaum.

Brown, B. (1997, June). Raw scores of cognitive ability are real psychological variables: IQ is a hyperspace variable. In V. C. Shipman (Chair), *IQ or cognitive ability?* Symposium presented to the 95th annual convention of the American Psychological Society, Washington, DC.

Buck, R. (1976). A test of nonverbal receiving ability: Preliminary studies. *Human Communication Research, 2*, 162–171.

Buck, R. (1984). *The communication of emotion*. New York: The Guilford Press.

Buck, R., Miller, R. E., & Caul, D. F. (1974). Sex, personality, and physiological variables in the communication of emotion via facial expression. *Journal of Personality and Social Psychology, 30*, 587–596.

Buss, D. M., & Craik, K. H. (1983). The act frequency approach to personality. *Psychological Review, 90*, 105–126.

Campbell, R. J., Kagan, N. I., & Krathwohl, D. R. (1971). The development and validation of a scale to measure affective sensitivity (empathy). *Journal of Counseling Psychology, 18*, 407–412.

Cantor, N., & Kihlstrom, J. F. (1987). *Personality and social intelligence*. Englewood Cliffs, NJ: Prentice Hall.

Chapin, F. S. (1967). *The social insight test*. Palo Alto, CA: Consulting Psychologists Press.

Ciarrochi, J. V., Chan, A. Y. C., & Caputi, P. (in press). A critical evaluation of the emotional intelligence construct. *Personality and Individual Differences*.

Costa, P. T., & McCrae, R. R. (1985). *The NEO Personality Inventory Manual*. Odessa, FL: Psychological Assessment Resources, Inc.

Cooper, R. K., & Sawaf, A. (1997). *Executive EQ: Emotional intelligence in leadership and organizations*. New York: Grosset/Putnum.

Davies, M., Stankov, L., & Roberts, R. D. (1998). Emotional intelligence: In search of an elusive construct. *Journal of Personality and Social Psychology, 75*, 989–1015.

Darwin, C. (1872/1965). *The expression of emotions in man and animals*. Chicago: University of Chicago Press.

Ekman, P. (1973). *Darwin and facial expression: A century of research in review*. New York: Academic Press.

Epstein, S. (1979). The stability of human behavior: On predicting most of the people most of the time. *Journal of Personality and Social Psychology, 37*, 179–184.

Epstein, S., & Meier, P. (1989). Constructive thinking: A broad coping variable with specific components. *Journal of Personality and Social Psychology, 54*, 332–350.

Fancher, R. E. (1985). *The intelligence men: Makers of the IQ controversy*, New York: W. W. Norton.

Feist, G. J. (1996, June). *Academic versus emotional intelligence as predictors of career success and life satisfaction.* [Poster presented at the 104th annual convention of the American Psychological Society], San Francisco, CA.

Ford, M. E. (1994). A living systems approach to the integration of personality and intelligence. In Sternberg, R. J., & Ruzgis, P. (Eds.). (1994). *Personality and intelligence.* Cambridge, UK: Cambridge University Press.

Gardner, H. (1993). *Frames of Mind (10th Anniversary Edition).* New York: Basic Books.

Gardner, H. (1999). Intelligence reframed. New York: Basic Books.

Gibbs, N. (1995, October 2). The EQ factor. *Time*, pp. 60–68.

Goleman, D. (1995a). *Emotional intelligence.* New York: Bantam Books.

Goleman, D. (1995b). What's your EQ. *The Utne Lens, Utne Reader.* http://www.utne.com/lens/bms/eq.htm/.

Goleman, D. (1995c, September 10). Ideas and trends: The decline of the nice-guy quotient. *New York Times* (Sunday Week in Review), p. 6.

Goleman, D. (1998a). What makes a leader? *Harvard Business Review, 76*, 93–102.

Goleman, D. (1998b). *Working with emotional intelligence.* Bantam Books: New York.

Gottman, J. (1997). *The heart of parenting: How to raise an emotionally intelligent child.* New York: Simon & Schuster.

Green, D. P., Goldman, S. L., & Salovey, P. (1993). Measurement error masks bipolarity in affect ratings. *Journal of Personality and Social Psychology, 64*, 1029–1041.

Greenspan, S. I. (1989). *Emotional intelligence.* In K. Field, B. J. Cohler, & G. Wool (Eds.). *Learning and education: Psychoanalytic perspectives.* Madison, CT: International Universities Press.

Griffith, B. (November 17, 1996). Zippy the pinhead. *The Boston Globe* [comics section]. Boston: MA.

Henig, R. M. (1996, June). Are you smarter than you think? *McCall's* 84–91.

Hilgard, E. R. (1980). The trilogy of mind: Cognition, affection, and conation. *Journal of the History of the Behavioral Sciences, 16*, 107–117.

Ickes, W. (1997). *Empathic accuracy.* New York: Guilford.

Ickes, W., Stinson, L., Bissonette, V., & Garcia, S. (1990). Naturalistic social cognition: Empathic accuracy in mixed-sex dyads. *Journal of Personality and Social Psychology, 54*, 730–742.

Izard, C. E. (1993). Four systems for emotion activation: Cognitive and noncognitive processes. *Psychological Review, 100*, 68–90.

Jung, C. (1921/1971). *Psychological types.* H. G. Baynes (Trans.), R. F. C. Hull (Rev. Trans.). Princeton, NJ: Princeton University Press. [Original work published 1921].

Kagan, N. (1978, August). Affective sensitivity test: Validity and reliability. Paper presented at the 86th meeting of the American Psychological Association, San Francisco.

Kelley, R., & Caplan, J. (1993). How Bell Labs creates star performers. *Harvard Business Review, 71*, 128–139.

Lane, R. D., Quinlan, D. M., Schwartz, G. E., Walker, P. A., & Zeitlin, S. B. (1990). The Levels of Emotional Awareness Scale: A cognitive-developmental measure of emotion. *Journal of Personality Assessment, 55*, 124–134.

Lane, R. D., Sechrest, L., Reidel, R., Weldon, V., Weldon, V., Kaszniak, A., & Schwartz, G. E. (1996). Impaired verbal and nonverbal emotion recognition in alexithymia. *Psychosomatic Medicine, 58*, 203–210.

Legree, P. J. (1995). Evidence for an oblique social intelligence factor established with a likert-based testing procedure. *Intelligence, 21*, 247–266.

Leuner, B. (1966). Emotional intelligence and emancipation. *Praxis der Kinderpsychologie und Kinderpsychiatrie, 15*, 193–203.

MacLean, P. D. (1973). *A triune concept of the brain and behavior.* Toronto: University of Toronto Press.

Mayer, J. D. (1993). The emotional madness of the dangerous leader. *Journal of Psychohistory, 20*, 331–348.

Mayer, J. D. (1995a). The System-Topics Framework and the structural arrangement of systems within and around personality. *Journal of Personality, 63*, 459–493.

Mayer, J. D. (1995b). A framework for the classification of personality components. *Journal of Personality, 63*, 819–877.

Mayer, J. D. (1998). A systems framework for the field of personality psychology. *Psychological Inquiry.*

Mayer, J. D., Caruso, D., Zigler, E., & Dreyden, J. (1989). Intelligence and intelligence-related personality traits. *Intelligence, 13*, 119–133.

Mayer, J. D., Caruso, D., & Salovey, P. (in press). Emotional intelligence meets traditional standards for an intelligence. *Intelligence.*

Mayer, J. D., Chabot, H. F., & Carlsmith, K. M. (1997). Conation, affect, and cognition in personality. In G. Matthews (Ed.), *Cognitive science perspectives on personality and emotion* (pp. 31–63). New York: Elsevier.

Mayer, J. D., Carlsmith, K. M., Chabot, H. F. (1998). Describing the person's external environment: Conceptualizing and measuring the life space. *Journal of Research in Personality, 32*, 253–296.

Mayer, J. D., DiPaolo, M. T., & Salovey, P. (1990). Perceiving affective content in ambiguous visual stimuli: A component of emotional intelligence. *Journal of Personality Assessment, 54*, 772–781.

Mayer, J. D., & Gaschke, Y. N. (1988). The experience and meta-experience of mood. *Journal of Personality and Social Psychology, 55*, 102–111.

Mayer, J. D., & Geher, G. (1996). Emotional intelligence and the identification of emotion. *Intelligence, 22*, 89–113.

Mayer, J. D., & Salovey, P. (1993). The intelligence of emotional intelligence. *Intelligence, 17*, 433–442.

Mayer, J. D., & Salovey, P. (1995). Emotional intelligence and the construction and regulation of feelings. *Applied and Preventive Psychology, 4*, 197–208.

Mayer, J. D., & Salovey, P. (1997). What is emotional intelligence? In P. Salovey & D. Sluyter (Eds.), *Emotional development and emotional intelligence: Implications for educators* (pp. 3–31). New York: Basic Books.

Mayer, J. D., Salovey, P., & Caruso, D. (1997). *Emotional IQ test (CD ROM)*. Needham, MA: Virtual Knowledge.

Mayer, J. D., & Stevens, A. (1994). An emerging understanding of the reflective (meta-) experience of mood. *Journal of Research in Personality, 28*, 351–373.

McClelland, D. C., Atkinson, J. W., Clark, R. W., & Lowell, E. L. (1953). *The achievement motive*. New York: Appleton-Century-Crofts.

McCrae, R. R., & Costa, P. T., Jr. (1985). Updating Norman's "adequate taxonomy": Intelligence and personality dimensions in natural language and in questionnaires. *Journal of Personality and Social Psychology, 49*, 710–721.

Mehrabian, A., & Epstein, N. (1972). A measure of emotional empathy. *Journal of Personality, 40*, 525–543.

Neisser, U., Boodoo, G., Bouchard, T. J., Boykin, A. W., Brody, N., Ceci, S. J., Halpern, D. F., Loehlin, J. C., Perloff, R., Sternberg, R. J., & Urbina, S. (1996). Intelligence: Knowns and unknowns. *American Psychologist, 51*, 77–101.

Paulhus, D. L. (1991). Measurement and control of response bias. In J. P. Robinson, P. R. Shaver, & L. S. Wrightsman (Eds.), *Measures of personality and social psychological attitudes* (pp. 17–60). New York: Academic Press/Harcourt Brace Jovanovich.

Payne, W. L. (1986). A study of emotion: Developing emotional intelligence; Self-integration; relating to fear, pain and desire. *Dissertation Abstracts International, 47*, (01), p. 203A. (University Microfilms No. AAC 8605928).

Peterson, K. S. (February 18, 1997). Signs of intelligence: Do new definitions of smart dilute meaning? *USA Today* Section D, p. 1.

Plutchik, R. (1984). Emotions: A general psychoevolutionary theory. In K. R. Scherer & P. Ekman (Eds.), *Approaches to emotion*. Hillsdale, NJ: Erlbaum.

Publilius Syrus (1961). "Sententiae" in J. W. Duff & A. M. Duff (Eds.), *Minor Latin poets*. Cambridge, MA: Harvard University Press. [Original work published c. 100 B.C.E.].

Roberts, R. D., Beh, H. C., Spilsbury, G., & Stankov, L. (1991). Evidence for an attentional model of human intelligence using the competing task paradigm. *Personality and Individual Differences, 12*, 445–555.

Roger, D., & Najarian, B. (1989). The construction and validation of a new scale for measuring emotional control. *Personality and Individual Differences, 10*, 845–853.

Rosenthal, R., Hall, J. A., DiMatteo, M. R., Rogers, P. L., & Archer, D. (1979). *Sensitivity to nonverbal communication: The PONS Test*. Baltimore, MD: Johns Hopkins University Press.

Russell, J. A. (1979). Affective space is bipolar. *Journal of Personality and Social Psychology, 37*, 1161–1178.

Saarni, C. (1990). Emotional competence: How emotions and relationships become integrated. In R. A. Thompson (Ed.), *Socioemotional development. Nebraska symposium on motivation*. (Vol. 36, pp. 115–182). Lincoln, NE: University of Nebraska Press.

Saarni, C. (1997). Emotional competence and self-regulation in childhood. In P. Salovey & D. J. Sluyter (Eds.), *Emotional development and emotional intelligence* (pp. 35–66). New York: Basic Books.

Saarni, C. (1999). *The Development of emotional competence*. New York: Guilford.

Salerno, J. G. (1996). *The whole intelligence: Emotional quotient (EQ)*. Oakbank, South Australia: Noble House of Australia.

Salovey, P., Bedell, B., Detweiler, J., & Mayer, J. D. (1999). Coping intelligently: Emotional intelligence and the coping process. In C. R. Snyder (Ed.), *Coping: the psychology of what works* (pp. 141–164). New York: Oxford University Press.

Salovey, P., & Mayer, J. D. (1990). Emotional intelligence. *Imagination, Cognition, and Personality, 9*, 185–211.

Salovey, P., Mayer, J. D., Goldman, S., Turvey, C., & Palfai, T. (1995). Emotional attention, clarity, and repair: Exploring emotional intelligence using the Trait Meta-Mood Scale. In J. W. Pennebaker (Ed.), *Emotion, disclosure, and health* (pp. 125–154). Washington, D. C.: American Psychological Association.

Salovey, P., & Mayer, J. D. (1994). Some final thoughts about personality and intelligence. In R. J. Sternberg, & P. Ruzgis (Eds.), *Personality and intelligence* (pp. 303–318). Cambridge, UK: Cambridge University Press.

Salovey, P., & Sluyter, D. J. (1997). *Emotional development and emotional intelligence*. New York: Basic Books.

Scarr, S. (1989). Protecting general intelligence: Constructs and consequences for intervention. In R. L. Linn (Ed.), *Intelligence: Measurement, theory, and public policy*. Urbana, IL: University of Illinois Press.

Schaffer, L. F., Gilmer, B., & Schoen, M. (1940). *Psychology* (pp. xii). New York: Harper & Brothers.

Scheier, M. F., & Carver, C. S. (1985). Optimism, coping, and health: Assessment and implications of generalized outcome expectancies. *Health Psychology, 4*, 219–247.

Schutte, N. S., Malouff, J. M., Hall, L. E., Haggerty, D. J., Copper, J. T., Golden, C. J., & Dornheim, L. (1998). Development and validation of a measure of emotional intelligence. *Personality and Individual Differences, 25*, 167–177.

Segal, J. (1997). *Raising your emotional intelligence*. New York: Holt.

Shapiro, L. E. (1997). *How to raise a child with a high E.Q: A parents' guide to Emotional Intelligence*. New York: HarperCollins Publishers.

Simmons, S., & Simmons, J. C. (1997). *Measuring emotional*

intelligence with techniques for self-improvement. Arlington, TX: Summit Publishing Group.

Simon, E. W., Rosen, M., & Ponpipom, A. (1996). Age and IQ as predictors of emotion identification in adults with mental retardation. *Research in Developmental Disabilities, 17*, 383–389.

Spearman, C. (1927). *The abilities of man.* New York: The Macmillan Company.

Steiner, C., & Perry, P. (1997). *Achieving emotional literacy: A program to increase your emotional intelligence.* New York: Avon.

Sternberg, R. J. (1988). *The triarchic mind: A new theory of human intelligence.* New York: Penguin Books.

Sternberg, R. J. (1994). Commentary: Reforming school reform: Comments on "Multiple intelligences: The theory in practice." *Teachers College Record, 95*, 561–569.

Sternberg, R. J. (1996). *Successful intelligence: How practical and creative intelligence determine success in life.* New York: Simon & Schuster.

Sternberg, R. J. (1997). The concept of intelligence and its role in lifelong learning and success. *American Psychologist, 52*, 1030–1045.

Sternberg, R. J., & Caruso, D. R. (1985). Practical modes of knowing. In E. Eisner (Ed.), *Eighty-fourth Yearbook of the National Society for the Study of Education (Part II)* (pp. 133–158). Chicago: University of Chicago Press.

Sternberg, R. J., & Lubart, T. I. (1995a). An investment perspective on creative insight. In R. J. Sternberg & J. E. Davidson (Eds.), *The nature of insight.* Cambridge, MA: MIT Press.

Sternberg, R. J., & Lubart, T. I. (1995b). *Defying the crowd: Cultivating creativity in a culture of conformity.* New York: Free Press.

Sternberg, R. J., & Ruzgis, P. (1994). *Personality and Intelligence.* New York: Cambridge University Press.

Sternberg, R. J., & Smith, C. (1985). Social intelligence and decoding skills in nonverbal communication. *Social Cognition, 3*, 168–192.

Sternberg, R. J., Wagner, R. K., Williams, W. M., & Horvath, J. A. (1995). Testing common sense. *American Psychologist, 50*, 912–927.

Stokes, G. S., Mumford, M. D., & Owens, W. A. (1994). *Biodata handbook: Theory, research, and use of biographical information in selection and performance prediction.* Palo Alto, CA: Consulting Psychologists Press.

Taylor, G. J., Ryan, D., & Bagby, R. M. (1985). Toward the development of a new self-report alexithymia scale. *Psychotherapy and Psychosomatics, 44*, 191–199.

Terman, L. M. (1921). II. Intelligence and its measurement: A symposium. *Journal of Educational Psychology, 12*, 127–133.

Tett, R., Wang, A., Fisher, R., Martinez, A., Griebler, J., & Linkovich, T. (April 4, 1997). *Testing a model of emotional intelligence.* 1997 Annual Convention of the Southeastern Psychological Association, Atlanta, GA.

Tett, R., Wang, A., Thomas, M., Griebler, J., & Martinez, A. (April 4, 1997). *Development of Self-Report Measures of Emotional Intelligence.* Paper presented at the 1997 Annual Convention of the Southeastern Psychological Association, Atlanta, GA.

Thorndike, R. L., & Stein, S. (1937). An evaluation of the attempts to measure social intelligence. *Psychological Bulletin, 34*, 275–284.

Time (October 2, 1995). [Cover]. New York: Time Warner.

Tomkins, S. S. (1962). *Affect, imagery, consciousness. Vol. 1: The positive affects.* New York: Springer-Verlag.

Wagner, R. K., & Sternberg, R. J. (1985). Practical intelligence in real-world pursuits: The role of tacit knowledge. *Journal of Personality and Social Psychology, 50*, 737–743.

Watson, G. (1930). Happiness among adult students of education. *Journal of Educational Psychology, 21*, 79–109.

Wechsler, D. (1940). Nonintellective factors in general intelligence. *Psychological Bulletin, 37*, 444–445.

Wechsler, D. (1943). Non-intellective factors in general intelligence. *Journal of Abnormal Social Psychology, 38*, 100–104.

Wechsler, D. (1958). *The measurement and appraisal of adult intelligence (4th ed.).* Baltimore, MD: The Williams & Wilkins Company.

Weisinger, H. (1997). *Emotional intelligence at work.* New York: Jossey-Bass.

Wessman, A. E., & Ricks, D. F. (1966). *Mood and personality.* New York: Holt, Rinehart, & Winston, Inc.

Wong, C. T., Day, J. D., Maxwell, S. E., Meara, N. M. (1995). A multitrait–multimethod study of academic and social intelligence in college students. *Journal of Educational Psychology, 87*, 117–133.

Woodworth, R. S. (1940). *Psychology* (4th ed.). New York: Henry Holt.

Young, P. T. (1936). *Motivation of behavior.* New York: John Wiley & Sons.

PART VII

TESTING AND TEACHING INTELLIGENCE

CHAPTER NINETEEN

Psychometric Approaches to Understanding and Measuring Intelligence

SUSAN E. EMBRETSON AND KAREN M. SCHMIDT McCOLLAM

Since the *Handbook of Human Intelligence* appeared in 1982, the "psychometric approach" has changed dramatically. Traditionally, the psychometric approach was synonymous with the factor-analytic approach. Exploratory factor analysis was applied to discover the number and nature of the factors that underlie performance on cognitive tasks. Carroll's (1993) three-stratum model of intellect synthesizes the factors supported across hundreds of studies. Although the studies reported somewhat inconsistent factor patterns, Carroll found consistent support for several factors by reanalyzing their data with common methods of factor analysis.

However, the contemporary psychometric approach differs in three major ways from the traditional psychometric approach: (1) confirmatory approaches predominate over exploratory approaches, (2) structural analysis of items predominates over structural analysis of variables, and (3) item response theory (IRT) models predominate over factor analytic models. Thus, in the contemporary psychometric approach, confirmatory IRT models are applied to understand and measure individual differences. The intelligence construct is elaborated in confirmatory IRT models by comparing alternative models as explaining item responses. Some confirmatory IRT models include parameters to estimate the cognitive processing demands in items. These models permit items to be selected and banked by their cognitive demand features and provide results relevant to understanding what is measured by the items. Other confirmatory IRT models include parameters for person differences on the underlying processes, strategies, or knowledge structures. These models can define new types of individual differences. As will be elaborated below, parameters are included to measure qualitative differences in item responses such as relative success in various underlying cognitive operations, use of different strategies or knowledge structures, and modifiability of ability with intervention.

In this chapter, we will first describe the major historical exploratory factor analytic theories and their implications for measuring and understanding intelligence. Then, several IRT models will be elaborated. Both unidimensional and multidimensional models will be presented. For each IRT model, we will present an overview of the model, describe some key applications, and present one or two elaborated examples to illustrate the potential of the model.

FACTOR ANALYTIC APPROACHES TO MEASURING AND UNDERSTANDING INTELLIGENCE

Factor analysis has been the primary tool for measuring and understanding intelligence for several decades. In this section, we begin with the historical foundations of measurement through factor analysis. Factor analysis has not only been important for understanding the intelligence tests that have been developed but has also provided a rationale for several testing methods. Factor analysis remains influential in testing.

Exploratory Factor Analysis Methods
General Factor Emphasis

SPEARMAN. Spearman (1904) proposed a two-factor theory of intelligence in which performance was determined by a general factor (g), a universal due to a person's general intelligence, and a specific factor (s) due to a unique ability or activity related to a particular test. Spearman (1904) suggested "all branches of intellectual activity have in common one fundamental function (or group of functions), whereas the remaining or specific elements seem in every case to be wholly different from that in all the others" (p. 202). Although both factors are present within each intellectual activity, their relative weight varies from activity to activity (Spearman, 1904, 1927). For example, Spearman's "abilities," originally defined by school subjects, had a greater relative g-to-s ratio for classics than for music study (Spearman, 1927).

On the basis of preparatory school student performance data, Spearman (1904) found an overall pattern of correlations among all of the various intellectual activities, indicating uniformity. The general factor is responsible for two tests being correlated. However, Spearman's two-factor theory holds only if a test battery includes only one of each type of test. Spearman (1927) prescribed this universality of g for application to the measurement of individual differences. For example, by measuring an individual's abilities on a series of tests, g can be determined, explaining much information about some of the abilities, and some about all abilities. Supplemental performance variation would be explained by s. In addition, Spearman's (1927) suggestion for test design was governed by the extent to which the test measures an individual's g or s.

TETRAD DIFFERENCES. Spearman's method of tetrad differences was the result of his observation that the true difference between correlation products of different abilities equals zero. The form of the equation is as follows:

$$(r_{ab} \times r_{cd}) - (r_{ac} \times r_{bd}) = 0.$$

For example, suppose the following four tests, a = French; b = English; c = Music; d = Math, and their correlations are as follows: $r_{ab} = .750$; $r_{cd} = .500$; $r_{ac} = .600$; $r_{bd} = .625$. Of course, the true difference

and the observed difference are not always the same owing to sampling error. If tests are correlated through the specific factors, for example for two memorizing symbols tests, then the tetrad equation becomes invalid.

The meaning of g for Spearman was "objective" because of this tetrad equation. In fact, Spearman (1927) stated, "Eventually, we may or may not find reason to conclude that g measures something that can appropriately be called 'intelligence.' Such a conclusion, however, would still never be the definition of g, but only a 'statement about' it" (p. 76). He originally proposed the psychological meaning of g to be mental energy, concentration, or will power. For the physiological meaning, he hypothesized that neural plasticity or neural energy was important for g (Spearman, 1927). Later, however, Spearman included "agreement and difference" in his psychological characterization of g. For example, the presence of a spatial factor and a g factor together also implies that the absence of a spatial factor entails the absence of g (Spearman & Jones, 1950).

EVIDENCE FOR g. Spearman (1927) presented a variety of evidence concerning g in psychological tests that embody different relationships. Summarizing the correlational patterns of tests with tetrad differences, Spearman concluded that g exists in all types of relationships to the same degree and that cases in which "group factors" contribute to the correlations between tests are rare. However, a closer examination of Spearman's data reveals that the patterns of correlations did not support the two-factor theory so strongly as Spearman's conclusions would indicate. Although Spearman elaborated 10 types of relationships in tests, which he categorized as ideal types (evidence, likeness, and conjunction) and real types (space–time, attribution, identity, constitution, causality, and psychological), evidence was obtained for only 5 relationships. Four of the five types were moderately saturated with g comparable to factor loading magnitudes in the .70s. The remaining type of relationship (time) only weakly supported g with a saturation comparable to a factor loading in the .30s. Further, for only one type of relationship did the evidence clearly support only one common factor. Weak evidence for group factors was obtained for two types of relationships, whereas strong evidence was obtained for two other types of relationships. The inconsistencies in Spearman's own data on the two-factor theory foreshadowed what was to come, namely, the identification of significant group factors.

SPEARMAN'S COGNITIVE THEORY. The general factor *g* in Spearman's psychometric theory is not really an explanatory concept. It is simply a description given to the central factor in a battery of tests or item types. Spearman (1923) also proposed a cognitive theory to explain intelligent thought. The analogy item played a central role in Spearman's cognitive theory, and defined *g* (i.e., it was highly saturated with *g*). Spearman postulated three qualitative principles of cognition to account for intelligent behavior, which he called "noegenetic" thinking. Spearman regarded the analogy as the paradigm of noegenetic thinking because solving analogies depends on all three principles.

Consider first the three principles as elaborated by Spearman (1923). The first principle is *apprehension of experience*. As explained by Spearman (1923, p. 48), "Any lived experience tends to evoke immediately a knowing of its direct attributes and its experiences." Stimuli are meaningful for persons when they have relevant experiences or knowledge of related attributes.

The second principle is the *eduction of relations*. According to Spearman (1923, p. 63), "The presenting of two or more characters tends to evoke immediately a knowing of relation between them." The second principle involves inference. The third principle is the *eduction of correlates*. "The presenting of any character together with a relation tends to evoke immediately a knowing of the correlative character" (Spearman, 1923, p. 91). That is, given a new stimulus and a relationship, a new stimulus that fulfills the relationship can be anticipated.

Sternberg's (1977) theory expanded Spearman's three principles and connected them to contemporary information-processing theory. The first principle is simply an assurance that organisms are able to understand their environment and act intelligently within it. The contemporary cognitive psychology process of encoding is similar to the apprehension of experience. The second and third principles concern the way in which objects, characters, or fundament in the environment are cognitively organized and processed. The second principle, the eduction of relations, is similar to Sternberg's (1977) concept of inference in which a relationship is inferred between pairs of stimuli. The third principle, the eduction of correlates, is similar to Sternberg's (1977) application in which a new stimulus is anticipated to fulfill a relationship that is applied to a stimulus.

To understand how the two processes of eduction are presented in prototypic form in the analogy item, it is necessary to compare the theory with the structure of the analogy item. Figure 19.1 presents a general schematization of Spearman's second and third principles of cognition along with an analogy item. In the part of the drawing labeled Relationship 1, the boxes represent two fundaments, which are given. The left side of the analogy contains two fundaments from which some relationship can be educed. The educed relationship is represented by the circle above the fundament. The right side of the drawing, Relationship 2, represents the eduction of correlates in which one fundament and the relationship are given. Now, for the analogy item below, it can be seen that the only part given on the right side is the fundament. Solving the item then depends on using the relationship educed on the left to educe the correlate on the right side.

If Spearman's (1923) theory is to account for a broad range of behavior, it should be apparent that the fundaments should incorporate a broad range of phenomena. Spearman indicated that the fundaments are not restricted to simple elements. The relationship between two fundaments may define a higher order fundament which, in turn, can be

FIGURE 19.1. Spearman's cognitive theory applied to verbal analogies.

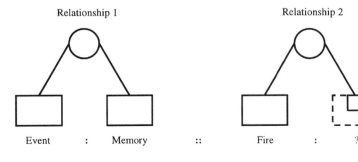

related to another higher order fundament. The relationship between higher order fundaments, so derived, would be a relationship of relationships. Neither the number of levels from which the fundaments are removed from actual objects nor the range of objects has any limits, according to Spearman.

Spearman's cognitive theory gives the *g* concept explanatory power. Of course, the status of Spearman's cognitive theory is questionable because it is quite old and relatively untestable with the methods available to Spearman. Sternberg's (1977) contemporary theory of information processing on analogies incorporated many principles similar to Spearman's cognitive theory. Sternberg's (1977) theory was supported by modern methods of mathematical modeling (see also Sternberg, 1985).

Multiple Factor Emphasis

Other researchers disagreed with Spearman's theory and method. For example, Holzinger and his colleagues (Holzinger & Swineford, 1939; Holzinger & Harman, 1941) found conditions in which the two-factor theory was not applicable, namely, bifactor situations, which they described as both general and secondary group factors necessary for reproducing correlations in complex sets of variables. Others, such as Hotelling (1933) and Kelley (1935) emphasized different methods for extracting factors, such as principal components analysis, in which the first axis has the best possible fit to the entire matrix of scores, and the second axis has the next possible fit, lying perpendicular to the first axis.

KELLY. Kelly (1928), who was interested in the method and content of group factors, carefully analyzed test performance in several age groups. Kelly thoroughly examined test pair bonds to determine their shared nature and to build factors uncontaminated by other factors in order to obtain independent mental trait factors. In seventh-grade, third-grade, and kindergarten populations, Kelly identified verbal facility, number facility, memory, spatial facility, and interest factors, and he identified general and speed factors for the seventh-grade population. Kelly (1928) defined intelligent behavior as "largely the regulation of impulses and the co-operation between adaptability and persistence, while intellect may involve a more abstract analytical capacity besides" (p. 223).

THURSTONE. Thurstone (1938) proposed a theory of primary mental abilities in which 9 independent factors were identified by examining 250 select college students on 56 tests: memory, number, verbal comprehension, induction, deduction, arithmetic reasoning, word fluency, space, and perceptual speed. Later, Thurstone (1941) examined high school students and found the same factors present. In another sample of 700 eighth-grade children, Thurstone (1941) found most of the original factors present, although the factors were correlated in this young age group. In addition, Thurstone believed the obtained second-order general factor was "probably the general factor which Spearman has so long defended" (Thurstone, 1941, p. 111). In addition, verbal comprehension, reasoning, and induction factors had the highest second-order general factor loadings.

GUILFORD. Guilford's structure of intellect model (Guilford, 1967, 1977) is a three-facet model that explains mental operations, stimulus content, and response forms or products. The model contains up to 150 different abilities. Guilford (1967) rejected a general factor. Thirteen studies from an aptitudes project on young adults showed about 17% of all test variable correlations being at or near zero.

Guilford (1948) valued factor analysis in developing tests for personnel selection and classification because it can result in minimally correlated scores that represent different contributors for predicting success. Additionally, Guilford (1948) believed that factor analysis should be applied in a planned experimental investigation rather than as an afterthought for a set of convenient intercorrelations. Guilford (1985) typically extracted a larger number of factors than indicated by the SCREE criterion to make better use of information and to avoid ignoring a potential factor.

HUMPHREYS. Humphreys' (1985) theory of general intelligence was broadly defined. His tests included heterogeneous item types from different varying dimensions. He believed that heterogeneous items preserved predictive validity over reliability. Especially appealing to Humphreys for measuring intelligence were items that shared a particular attribute, such as content, but loaded on different factors. Humphreys' goal was to include one dominant dimension rather than one purely defined, homogeneous dimension. Humphreys' theory of general intelligence measurement included several measurement principles, as follows:

1. Items can be added together to form a total score if they are positively correlated.
2. Items should be as heterogeneous as possible within certain defined parameters.
3. A test should be broadly defined without losing its measurement purpose.
4. Psychometric analyses should be applied to check assumptions but not to make decisions in test construction.
5. The item homogeneity criterion should be used sparingly; tests can be rejected for either too much or too little homogeneity.

Humphreys (1952) believed that abilities should be organized in a hierarchical structure. For example, a set of tests measuring mechanical information about tools would be organized into three different levels: (1) narrow tool group factors, (2) broad mechanical area factors, and (3) a general mechanical information factor. Using orthogonal factor transformation techniques to create a more parsimonious matrix allows one to interpret factors at all levels. However, Humphreys suggested that interpretation be limited to the broad and general levels.

VERNON AND BURT. Vernon (1950) defined ability as g at one level of a hierarchy and then two broad abilities at the next level: $v{:}ed$ (verbal–educational) and $k{:}m$ (practical–mechanical). Under $v{:}ed$, verbal and numerical specific abilities are factored, and under $k{:}m$, spatial and mechanical abilities are factored. Vernon (1961) cautioned that these group factors are infinitely divisible, depending upon the level of detail at which the analysis is performed. A similar hierarchical structure was also proposed by Burt (1949).

CATTELL AND HORN. Cattell and Horn (Cattell, 1963; Horn & Cattell, 1966) organized abilities according to a hierarchical structure as well with g divided into major factors, fluid intelligence (gf) and crystallized intelligence (gc). Fluid intelligence was hypothesized to be more genetically influenced and based on physiological aspects of an individual. Crystallized intelligence was hypothesized

to be experientially determined or acculturated. Tests of fluid intelligence include response to novelty, problem solving, and figural reasoning; tests of crystallized intelligence include, most prominently, knowledge-based tests such as vocabulary and mathematical tests.

CARROLL. Carroll's three-stratum theory of intelligence (Carroll, 1993) was developed through surveying and factor analyzing over 460 prominent datasets in the literature. The stratum theory is also hierarchical. Stratum 1 comprises narrow factors, which are first-order factors to explain the correlation matrix of test items. Stratum 2 comprises broad factors that explain the correlations of the Stratum 1 factors. Stratum 3 is a general factor g, which explains the correlations of the Stratum 2 factors. Carroll's theory extends the theories of Thurstone (1938), Guilford (1967), and Horn and Cattell (1967). However, the three-stratum model also includes several narrowly defined abilities, such as phonetic coding and perceptual illusions, that typically are not included in such models.

The 1921 Symposium on Intelligence and Its Measurement

After Spearman introduced his two-factor theory and others followed with alternatives, a movement for discussion of conceptions of intelligence occurred. Seventeen leading researchers gathered in 1921 to discuss the definition of intelligence and its measurement. Most investigators disavowed the notion of general intelligence and desired that its definition be expanded. It should be noted that Spearman, who was the primary advocate of general intelligence, did not attend the conference.

Among the most outstanding comments made by the investigators were R. L. Thorndike's statement: "The value of a test score is its value in prophesying how well a person will do in other intellectual tasks" (1921 symposium, p. 125). Specifically, Thorndike called for using zero-order and partial correlations of simple and analytical processes with the criterion task to understand their explanatory contributions better.

Terman's view of intelligence involved grasping the significance of adaptive situations and that "An individual is intelligent in proportion as he is able to carry on abstract thinking" (1921 symposium,

p. 128). Terman critiqued the notion of a singular type of test measuring a mental function with the following comments: "...a test does not, at all points, bring the same kind of mental activities into play. Success in the easier part of the test may depend chiefly on the subject's ability to remember what he is told to do; see likeness and differences on the representative level, or even to a considerable extent on eye–hand coordination in the use of a pencil" (1921 symposium, p. 131). Hence, Terman viewed intelligence as multifaceted and operating jointly at different levels.

Colvin suggested that "An individual possesses intelligence in so far as he has learned, or can learn to adjust himself to his environment" (1921 symposium, p. 136). He recommended that testing proceed by focusing on analysis, synthesis, and attention span and disregarding speed. In contrast, Thurstone's definition of intelligence contained three components: (a) inhibitive capacity, (b) analytical capacity, and (c) perseverance. Inhibitive capacity involves substituting instinctive, environmental, and social pressure with conceptual thinking. Analytical capacity involves inhibiting instinctive pressure to ensure response flexibility. Perseverance involves volitional energy.

Perhaps most striking is the diversity of definitions and qualities of intelligence noted by these researchers. A much more recent survey of researchers in intelligence (Sternberg & Detterman, 1986) found similar divergence of views and many similar beliefs. Overall, the researchers agreed upon continued investigations for the improvement of measurement and expansion of knowledge about intelligence. It is noteworthy that decades of research have not led to convergence of theoretical views, however.

Confirmatory Factor Analysis

Joreskog and Sorbom's confirmatory factor analytic work has made an enormous impact on the field of psychometrics (Joreskog, 1969; Joreskog & Sorbom, 1989). Their LISREL (Joreskog & Sorbom, 1989) methods have allowed researchers to investigate hypothesized models in relation to sample data and alternatives that explain the factor structure of test intercorrelations and underlying processes. Confirmatory factor analysis computer programs are growing in number and becoming more widely available, including EQS (Bentler,

1985), AMOS (Arbuckle, 1993), and Mx (Neale, 1994), allowing for widespread use among social science investigators, including those interested in measuring intelligence constructs.

Confirmatory factor analysis is now applied widely to study intelligence. In fact, it is usually preferred over exploratory factor analysis owing to the massive literature on theoretical factor structure. To illustrate the advantages of confirmatory factor analysis, consider Kyllonen and Christal's (1990) study of the relationship of general intelligence (reasoning) to working memory capacity. In an effort to understand processing, content, and methodological aspects of reasoning and working memory for delineating their relationship, Kyllonen and Christal (1990) examined multiple tests describing these constructs in four large-sample studies. The authors carefully considered experimental and correlational disciplines for defining factors and included speed and knowledge factors in addition to working memory and reasoning. In addition, within reasoning and working memory, they analyzed domain-specific and domain-independent aspects of tests for describing the nature of the factors.

For Study 1, working memory and reasoning factor correlations ranged from .79 to .93 across fitted models. Working memory was found to be general in nature, for both linguistic and quantitative processes of working memory were correlated. For Study 2, testing modalities and domains were varied. The reasoning factor's tests were broadened to eliminate confounding with working memory content, and computer-administered tests were given within both factors. In addition, two reasoning factors were defined to understand method variance better. Fit analyses indicated better fit with the two-factor reasoning model over the one-factor reasoning model. Reasoning was found to be more highly related to knowledge, and working memory with speed. For Study 3, a more broadly defined reasoning factor was defined by including ETS Kit tests (Ekstrom et al., 1976), and similar results were found. For Study 4, the reasoning factor was defined more generally to detect any changes in its correlation with working memory. Across all four studies, the correlations between working memory and reasoning were .82, .88, .80, and .82, respectively, suggesting that differences in working memory capacity are strongly related to executive processes regardless of variation in test content and administration method.

The obvious strengths in using confirmatory factor analysis in Kyllonen and Christal's (1990) approach are (1) multiple tests defining the constructs can be fitted and compared using hypothesized and alternative models, (2) a variety of test content within constructs can be used to test domain specificity, and (3) method variance can be better understood by using different types of administration techniques. The major weakness is that constructs are clearly defined between rather than within factors.

Implications for Measuring and Understanding Intelligence

The factor analytic approaches have had major impact on how intelligence has been measured and understood. We will first elaborate impact on measurement and then elaborate impact on understanding.

Measuring Intelligence

Neither Spearman's (1927) psychometric theory nor Spearman's (1923) cognitive theory was uniquely associated with a test of intelligence. A single-factor test, which includes only a single item type that is highly saturated with g, is most consistent with both Spearman's psychometric theory and cognitive theory. Given the central role of analogies in both theories, one would have expected an analogy test to be developed directly from Spearman's theories. Surprisingly, however, the single factor test that is most closely associated with Spearman consists of matrix problems. John Raven, Spearman's student, developed a matrix completion test that reflects Spearman's principles of eduction of relation and eduction of correlates. Raven's matrix problems (see Raven, 1956) consisted of a three-by-three array of complex figures that varied systematically across the rows and columns. The last element was missing. To find the missing element, relationships among elements had to be educed, and then a correlate to complete the missing entry had to be educed. Spearman is reported to have favored matrix problems for educing relationships, and he had huge displays of matrix problems in his office. Tests with Raven's matrices have been used cross-culturally for several decades to measure general reasoning.

The Raven's Progressive Matrices Tests have recently been updated and remain an important measure of intelligence (Raven, J., Raven, J. C., & Court, 1995).

However, a general intelligence test, with mixed item types, is compatible with Spearman's two-factor theory as well. Because g was postulated to be the only source of correlations between distinct types of items, the dimension measured from a mixed test would be g. The influence of specific factors, balanced over item types, would essentially be cancelled. According to Spearman's view, a test of heterogeneous items, with varying saturations with g, would be inefficient but would still measure g. However, Humphreys' views about item heterogeneity would be well represented by a test of mixed-item types. In any case, many intelligence tests employ mixed-item types. Even the first successful intelligence test, Binet's scales of intelligence, is compatible with these views. The current revision of the Stanford–Binet still renders a global score from mixed-item types (Thorndike, Hagen, & Sattler, 1986). Similarly, many contemporary intelligence tests, such as the Wechsler scales (WAIS–R; Wechsler, 1981; WISC–III; Wechsler, 1991) continue to provide an overall index of intelligence based on mixed-item types.

In contrast, several tests have been directly associated with the multiple factor theories. For example, the Primary Mental Abilities Test (Thurstone & Thurstone, 1941) resulted directly from Thurstone's application of multiple factor analysis. More recently, the Schaie–Thurstone Adult Mental Abilities Test (Schaie, 1985) has updated the original Primary Mental Abilities Test. Similarly, Guilford (1967) developed a battery of tests to represent factors in his theory. In other cases, tests that were developed later were inspired by factor theories. Examples of multiple aptitude tests of separate abilities include the ETS Kit of Factor-Referenced Cognitive Tests (Ekstrom, French, Harman, & Dermen, 1976), the Differential Aptitudes Test (Bennett, Seashore, & Wesman, 1984), and the Armed Services Vocational Aptitude Battery (Moreno, Wetzel, McBride, & Weiss, 1984).

Many contemporary intelligence tests have been influenced by the hierarchical theories of intellect. Scores at different levels are routinely reported in contemporary tests. For example, the Kaufman Adolescent and Adult Intelligence Test (Kaufman & Kaufman, 1993), the Woodcock–Johnson Tests of

Cognitive Ability (Woodcock & Johnson, 1989) and the Differential Ability Scales (Elliott, 1990) provide scores for fluid and crystallized intelligence.

Both exploratory and confirmatory factor analysis are important in determining the scores reported from intelligence tests with mixed-item types. For example, on the Differential Ability Scales (Elliott, 1990), the actual structure of the abilities to be measured at various ages was determined by confirmatory factor analysis.

Understanding Intelligence

Factor theories have also had an impact on how intelligence is understood. Factors are derived from the similarity of persons' responses to items or subtests. Items that are responded to in the same way load on the same factor or factors. The factor analytic method identifies factors that summarize patterns of correlations. The factors are often interpreted as latent variables that underlie test or item performance. The nature of the dimension typically is determined by an inspection of the items that load on it. That is, the dimension is interpreted by comparing features shared by the items.

For a single-factor theory, such as postulated by Spearman (1927), item features are quite diverse because all cognitive tasks depend on g to some extent. Thus, the nature of g must be determined from other considerations. The most prevalent approach has been to correlate measures of g with external variables such as group membership, other tests, criterion variables, and so forth to build a nomological network according to Cronbach and Meehl's concept of construct validity. Thus, the theoretical meaning of g depends on its empirical relationships. Another approach is to develop a theory about the item types that load highly on g. For example, Spearman (1923) postulated processing mechanisms to explain performance on verbal analogies, an item type that was highly saturated with g. The latter approach, termed the construct representation aspect of construct validity (Embretson, 1983), has been applied effectively only in the last two decades (e.g., Sternberg, 1977). Further, the processing mechanisms underlying the items that appear on existing tests have rarely been examined empirically.

For multiple factor theories, items or subtests that load on the same factor often share obvious features such as verbal comprehension or spatial visualization. These shared features give rise to interpretations. However, the shared features are often quite global so that further understanding must be provided from outside considerations like understanding g. The most prevalent approach has been to elaborate empirical relationships with other variables. Confirmatory factor analysis (e.g., Kyllonen & Christal, 1990), along with structural equation modeling, has been particularly effective in expanding nomological networks for multiple factors. However, the mechanisms underlying item performance are not necessarily elaborated by empirical correlates with other variables. Unless the other variables represent theoretically singular dimensions, it is difficult to pinpoint the source of the correlation.

ITEM RESPONSE THEORY MODELS FOR MEASURING AND UNDERSTANDING INTELLIGENCE

Both exploratory and confirmatory IRT models are available to measure and understand intelligence. The exploratory models were developed earlier and have been applied more extensively. Unidimensional and multidimensional exploratory IRT models have been applied. We will begin by presenting exploratory models. Although the exploratory IRT models have substantial practical advantages, applying them usually results in measuring aspects of intelligence that are similar to the aspects derived from the factor analytic approaches. Yet, it is valuable to elaborate these models for two reasons: (1) IRT models and their many properties, are unfamiliar to many psychologists and (2) the advantages of the confirmatory models depend directly on the properties of IRT models.

Unidimensional Item Response Theory Models

Item response theory is rapidly replacing classical test theory as the psychometric basis for testing and has many theoretical and practical advantages over classical test theory. The exploratory models mentioned below have become quite routine in testing. Some typical models and some elaborated applications will be discussed to illustrate some properties. More extended treatments are available in textbooks (see Embretson & Reise, in press;

Hambleton, Swaminathan, & Rogers, 1989). The exploratory models do not permit direct incorporation of theory into the estimates that are obtained. The confirmatory IRT models, however, were designed to incorporate theory explicitly in the measurement process.

Exploratory IRT Models
Some Logistic IRT Models

In IRT, persons are measured in the context of a model of the item response process. IRT models are mathematical models of the responses of persons to particular tasks or items. Thus, ability estimates depend not only on persons' responses but also on the properties of the items.

IRT models contain parameters to represent the characteristics of items and persons. The probability that a person solves a particular item depends jointly on ability level and on the item characteristics. In typical IRT models, ability level and item difficulty combine additively to produce the probability that the item is endorsed or passed. Many IRT models are based on the logistic distribution in which the parameters are exponents. For example, the Rasch (1960) model predicts item success from the simple difference between the item's difficulty b_i and the person's ability θ_j as follows:

$$P(X_{ij} = 1 \mid \theta_j, b_i) = \frac{\exp(\theta_j - b_i)}{1 + \exp(\theta_j - b_i)} \quad (19.1)$$

Abilities and item difficulties that are estimated from Equation 19.1 are similar in magnitude to z scores. High values are assigned to high abilities and difficult items.

More complex unidimensional IRT models add parameters to reflect additional item properties. Items, for example, may differ in how well they discriminate between levels of ability and in their vulnerability to guessing. Thus, the simple model in Equation 19.1 can be expanded to include item discrimination a_i and guessing c_i as follows:

$$P(X_{ij} = 1 \mid \theta_j, b_i, a_i)$$
$$= c_i + (1 - c_i)\frac{\exp(a_i(\theta_j - b_i))}{1 + \exp(a_i(\theta_j - b_i))} \quad (19.2)$$

Notice that the impact of the difference between the person's ability and the item's difficulty is proportional to item discrimination, which is the multiplier a_i in Equation 19.2. Notice also that the guessing parameter c_i prevents the response probability from falling to zero, even for the lowest ability levels.

Meaning of the Parameters

Three types of meanings for the parameters estimated from Equation 19.1 or Equation 19.2 may be illustrated: (1) the impact of ability on performance, (2) the impact of item difficulty, and (3) conjoint scaling of persons and items. These meanings are essential to the advantages of IRT over classical test theory. In the examples below, a 30-item test of fluid ability, the Abstract Reasoning Test (ART; Embretson, 1995), was calibrated with the Rasch model (i.e., Equation 19.1) for a sample of 818 young adults.

MEANING OF ABILITY FOR PERFORMANCE. The meaning of a person's ability for item responses is easily shown by *person characteristics curves* (PCCs). Suppose that three persons are selected from the sample with abilities of -1.0, $.00$, and 1.0 (similar in magnitude to z scores), respectively. By inserting item difficulties at various levels in Equation 19.1, a probability for solving each item may be calculated. Figure 19.2 shows the PCCs for the three persons. Item difficulty is represented on the abscissa. Item solving probability is represented on the ordinate. The point of inflection occurs at the probability of .50, which is shown by a reference line from the ordinate axis on Figure 19.2. The item difficulty for the point of inflection is analogous to

FIGURE 19.2. Person characteristics curves.

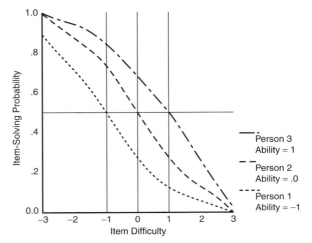

a threshold value. Like a psychophysical threshold, items at a threshold are as likely to be passed as to be failed.

Several meanings for an ability level are shown in Figure 19.2. First, items at the person's threshold may be identified. If the difference between ability and item difficulty is zero, the probability of passing is .50. Three reference lines through the abscissa at the item values that correspond to the three abilities, −1.00, .00, and 1.00, are shown in Figure 19.2. Notice that the reference lines intersect the line through a probability of .50 differently for each PCC. For the PCC at the ability of −1.00, for example, the reference line through the ordinate probability of .50 crosses the reference line from the item difficulty at −1.00. Thus, one meaning for ability is the scale value of items at the person's threshold. Second, diagnostic information about the person's relative success on other items may readily be obtained. If a person's ability exceeds item difficulty, then the difference is positive and Equation 19.1 predicts a probability of success greater than .50. Conversely, if the person's ability falls below item difficulty, then the probability of passing is less than .50. For Person 2, for example, items with difficulties less than .00 are relatively easy, whereas items with difficulties greater than .00 are harder.

Of course, the actual response of the persons to the 30 ART items is known. In what ways do PCCs provide additional information? If the IRT model fits the data, the advantages of the PCC for diagnosing performance include: (1) more detailed descriptions of performance than actual item responses because the latter has only two values, pass or fail; (2) more accurate description of performance because error factors may result in the person's actually failing an easy item and passing a hard item; (3) predictions for items that the person has not been presented, if their item difficulties are known; and (4) possible detection of aberrant response patterns because fit of the person to the model can be checked by comparing actual responses to predictions.

ITEM CHARACTERISTICS CURVES. Diagnostic information about items also can be given by Equation 19.1 predictions. An *item characteristics curve* (ICC) regresses item solving probabilities on ability level. Figure 19.3 shows ICCs for three ART items from Table 19.1. Like the PCCs, the ICCs

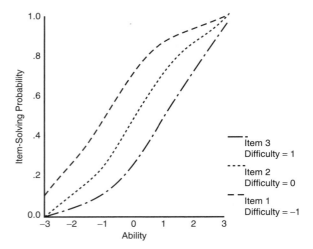

FIGURE 19.3. Item characteristics curves.

are S-shaped. In the middle of the curve, large changes in item-solving probability are observed for small ability changes, whereas at the extremes, item-solving probabilities change very slowly with ability changes.

The three ICCs in Figure 19.3 have the same shape but differ in location. Location is indicated by item difficulty; it is the inflection point at which the item-solving probability is .50. Like the PCCs, location is directly linked to ability level. For example, the ability level that has a probability of .50 for solving Item 1 is −1.00, which is its item difficulty.

In Figure 19.3, all items have the same discrimination and a lower asymptote of zero. If the three-parameter logistic model in Equation 19.2 had been applied to the ART data, items would have differing slopes (item discrimination) and a nonzero lower asymptote (due to guessing).

CONJOINT SCALING. Conjoint scaling means that item difficulty and person ability are placed on a common scale. Figure 19.4 presents a joint frequency distribution of item difficulty and ability on the ART. Notice how items are located on the same scale as persons. Further, the distributions may be compared to determine if the test is appropriately targeted to the sample. In Figure 19.4, item difficulties have the highest frequency near the middle of the ability distribution; thus, most items are appropriate for most persons. However, Figure 19.4

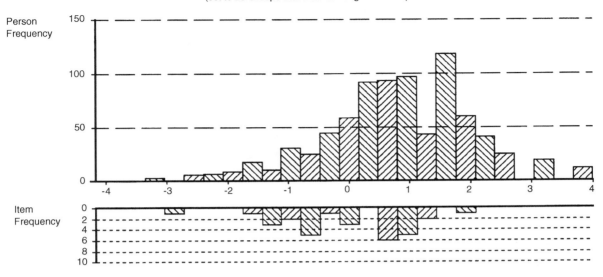

Person–Item Frequency Distribution
(set to 25 Groups with Interval Length of 0.320)

FIGURE 19.4. Conjoint distributions of persons and items.

also shows a noticeable lack of difficult items and many persons with high abilities. Thus, more difficult items are needed to measure these persons optimally.

ADVANTAGES. The theoretical advantages of IRT models include the following:

1. Justifiable interval or ratio-level scaling of persons.
2. Population-invariant item calibrations.
3. Item-invariant meaning for ability.
4. Item-referenced meaning for ability levels.
5. Superior capability for handling missing data (e.g., persons do not receive all the same items).
6. Standard errors of measurement that reflect the appropriateness of items for the various ability levels.

Each of these advantages will be elaborated in turn.

First, conjoint scaling means that persons and items are located on the same continuum, as shown in Figure 19.4. The same increase in item probabilities results from either increasing ability or decreasing item difficulty. Andrich (1988) pointed out that the conjoint additivity criterion for fundamental measurement is met directly by successful scaling with the Rasch model. Thus, interval-

level scaling can be justified by fitting the Rasch. In contrast, classical test theory can be justified as interval-level scaling under only limited conditions (see Embretson, 1996). A practical advantage that derives from interval-level scaling is measuring individual change to reflect treatment or developmental effects. When interval level scaling is not obtained, as is true for tests developed under classical test theory, change scores have paradoxical reliabilities, spurious correlations with initial scores, and nonmonotonic relationships to true change (see Bereiter, 1963). Failing to achieve interval scaling also influences means and variances, which will lead to biased estimates of effects and their significance (see Embretson, 1995; Maxwell & Delaney, 1985). Second, population-invariant item calibrations mean that item properties are unbiased by the population ability distribution. Because ability levels are included in the model, item parameter estimates are implicitly controlled for the abilities of the calibration sample. Very high ability or very low ability samples will yield the same item calibrations (see Hambleton et al., 1991).

Third, abilities have item-invariant meaning in item response theory. The PCCs show that the meaning of ability for performance applies to *any* calibrated item. Further, it can be readily shown that ability differences have invariant implications for item performance differences, regardless of the specific item (i.e., for the Rasch model). Andrich (1988) elaborated this principle. Fourth, item-referenced meaning is possible because ability level may be referenced directly to the items, as shown by the PCCs above. Diagnostic feedback may be given about an ability by direct reference to the items that persons at an ability level find hard or easy. Further, it is often revealing to examine the properties of items that fall at the threshold.

Fifth, handling missing data is a very significant practical advantage of item response theory. In fact, data may be so sparse that two persons do not even receive any common items. Missing data handling capabilities result from the item-invariant meaning of ability. Ability estimates are readily comparable over different item sets, such as from different test forms or from computerized adaptive testing. Because item parameters are included in the model, person ability level estimates are implicitly controlled for the properties of the items that were administered. Sixth, the standard errors of measurement reflect the appropriateness of the items for an individual. The information provided by an item for an ability depends mainly on probability of passing. The smallest standard error of measurement is obtained when many items are near a person's threshold level. Standard errors are also useful in selecting items for optimal precision for a person or a population.

Confirmatory IRT Models

A major advantage of IRT, as shown in the preceding section, is item-referenced meaning for ability. However, the exploratory IRT models do not elaborate the *nature* of the items that correspond to various ability levels. Most ability test items are complex problem-solving tasks that involve multiple processing stages. The unidimensional exploratory IRT model parameters will reflect a confounded composite of these influences, thus yielding parameters with unclear construct representation. Consequently, "enhancing" ability interpretations by

showing representative items that correspond to the ability level will not be effective if the nature of the items cannot be clearly specified.

The confirmatory IRT models include parameters that can represent cognitive theory variables to describe the processing characteristics of the items. Two models will be described below.

Unidimensional Models

LINEAR LOGISTIC LATENT TRAIT MODEL. The linear logistic latent trait model (LLTM; Fischer, 1973) incorporates item stimulus features into the prediction of item success. For example, if the item stimulus features that influence processes are specified numerically (or categorically) for each item, as in a mathematical model of item accuracy, then the impact of processes in each item may be estimated directly as follows:

$$P(X_{ij} = 1 \mid \theta_j, \tau_k) = \frac{\exp(\theta_j - \Sigma_k \tau_m q_{ik})}{1 + \exp(\theta_j - \Sigma_k \tau_k q_{ik})} \quad (19.3)$$

where q_{ik} is the value of stimulus feature k in item I, τ_k is the weight of stimulus feature k in item difficulty, and θ_j is the ability for person j.

To give an example, consider the matrix task in Figure 19.4. The Abstract Reasoning Test (ART; Embretson, 1995) contains matrix items that were designed to reflect Carpenter, Just, and Shell's (1990) theory of processing. Carpenter et al.'s (1990) theory emphasized working memory requirements and abstraction as underlying processing difficulty. Working memory requirements for solving a matrix problem were influenced by the number of relational tokens in a problem. Abstraction was influenced by abstract correspondence among elements (e.g., correspondence due to common properties rather than common objects) or null values.

ART items were generated mechanically by specifying 30 formal structures that defined various combinations of number and type of rules. In addition, some drawing principles were specified. The drawing principles specified whether objects in each position of the matrix were overlaid (objects placed inside other objects), fused (separate object appearing as a single object), or distorted (corresponding objects are perceptually distorted versions of each other). Five clone items that involved the same number and type of rules, but different stimuli and attributes, were generated for each structure.

For the ART item in Figure 19.5, three relationships are involved. Two relationships are pairwise progressions in which the attributes are changing across the rows (orientation of the interior lines) or across the columns (i.e., number of lines). The third relationship is a distribution of three elements in which the oval, diamond, and rectangle are distributed to appear once in every row and column. None of the relationships involve a null value, and correspondence is not based on abstract properties. The drawing principles specified overlay (i.e., the lines are inside the shapes) but show no fusion or distortion.

To operationalize the Carpenter et al. (1990) theory into a mathematical model, each ART item was scored for number of rules and abstract correspondence, which operationalizes working-memory load and abstraction, respectively. Further, each item was also scored on the three drawing principles. Then, the 150 items were placed in 5 forms of 30 items each, with 4 additional items that appeared in every form to link estimates. The 5 forms were randomly assigned to 5 groups of about 250 participants each (see Embretson, 1995, for details).

Table 19.1 presents the LLTM estimates, standard errors, and t values that were obtained. Model fit for LLTM was comparable to a multiple correlation of .76. Although item difficulties are not fully explained by the variables in the model, moderately good prediction was obtained. Table 19.1 shows that the number of rules, which operationalizes working memory, is the most highly significant variable. However, abstract correspondence and two drawing principles were also significant.

An item can be decomposed into its processing contributions by multiplying the value of the stimulus feature q_{ik} times its weight. Thus, for the item in Figure 19.4, item diffi-

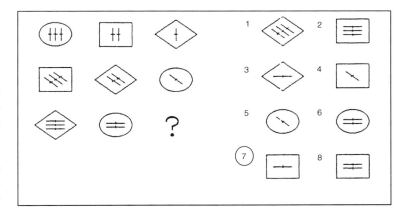

FIGURE 19.5. An item from the Abstract Reasoning Test.

culty is decomposed as follows:

$$= .67(3) + 1.49(0) + .88(0) - .31(0) + .96(1) - 2.39.$$
$$= 2.01 + 0 + 0 + 0 + .96 - 2.39$$
$$= .58. \tag{19.4}$$

Thus, the item is predicted to be moderately difficult (.58), and the primary source of difficulty is working-memory load. Other items, in contrast, could be difficult primarily from other factors, such as abstract correspondence.

TREE-BASED REGRESSION. Sheehan (in press) has applied tree-based regression to enhance the meaning of the ability scale. In this method, clusters of homogeneous items with respect to skill components are located on the common IRT scale for item difficulty and ability. Persons' abilities can be described by the characteristics of the clusters at their

TABLE 19.1. LLTM Estimates for Extended Carpenter et al. Model on ART[a]

Processing Variable	Scored Variable	LLTM Weight τ_m	SE	t
Working Memory Load	Number of Rules	.67	.09	7.14
Abstraction	Abstract Correspondence	1.49	.25	5.99
Drawing Principles	Distortion	.88	.29	3.05
	Fusion	−.31	.24	−1.31
	Overlay	.96	.20	4.73

[a] The model also included dummy variables to represent key position.

level. The item clusters are hierarchically organized; clusters are merged at higher levels based on common global properties. The cluster structure is determined by regressing IRT item difficulty on a set of binary predictors that reflect substantive item properties. As in LLTM analyses, items are scored on independent variables that represent sources of processing difficulty.

For example, Sheehan (in press) has applied tree-based regression to mathematical reasoning items. At the highest level, two clusters of items were formed; thus, items were parsed into two-class concrete versus abstract schemas. The binary variable that represented schema type had the strongest relationship to item difficulty. At the next level, the number of independent equations in the items defined the clusters. Number of independent equations had four levels, which were represented by three binary variables. These clusters for equations are nested within schema. Thus, within concrete schema, for example, items were parsed into clusters with one, two, three, or four equations. Similarly, items were also clustered by number of equations within abstract schema.

All clusters, regardless of hierarchical level, can be located on a common continuum for item difficulty and ability. Thus, for a given ability level, meaning may be enhanced by referring to the properties of the item clusters that correspond to that level.

SOME APPLICATIONS. The confirmatory IRT models described above have been applied to verbal and nonverbal items that measure intelligence. Embretson and Reise (in press) summarize these applications in a chapter on applications of IRT to cognition and life span. For example, applications of LLTM to nonverbal abilities includes studies of basic components in mathematical reasoning, abstract reasoning (i.e., matrix problems), geometric analogies, spatial visualization, and developmental balance problems. Applications of LLTM to verbal measures of ability include verbal comprehension, verbal analogies, and literacy. Applications of tree-based regression are just now appearing but include mathematical reasoning items and reading comprehension items.

IMPLICATIONS FOR MEASURING AND UNDERSTANDING INTELLIGENCE. Applications of both LLTM and tree-based regression can lead to (1) enhanced construct validity, (2) enhanced meaning for ability, and (3) item selection by cognitive properties. Each of these advantages will be elaborated, in turn.

For the first advantage, construct validity is enhanced by explicating the processes involved in item difficulty. The construct representation aspect of construct validity (see Embretson, 1983) is supported by elaborating the theoretical nature of the constructs reflected in test performance. It is most adequately studied by cognitive psychology methods such as mathematical modeling. The prediction model in LLTM and the item bundles in tree-based regression explicate the relative impact of various processes or knowledge structures on item difficulty.

For the second advantage, it should clearly be noted that the confirmatory unidimensional IRT models probably do not result in defining any new dimensions of intelligence. Instead, the IRT property of item-referenced meaning for ability is extended by describing the processing properties of items. Rather than merely show items that correspond to a person's ability, the investigator can show that items can be described by the processes and knowledge structures involved in their solution.

For the third advantage, decomposing items into cognitive components permits items to be selected by their cognitive properties. For example, if the construct to be measured is deemed to require a combination of processes, then these processes can be balanced across item subsets to reflect the desired combinations. For ART items, for example, if both abstraction and working memory are to be reflected in the measured ability, then items that include both sources of processing difficulty can be selected. This advantage can lead to selecting items that are more pure measures of targeted constructs.

Multidimensional Models

If ability test items are complex tasks with multiple processing stages, each stage may require a different ability. Multidimensional IRT models contain two or more abilities for each person. The confirmatory IRT models contain design structures to link items to underlying cognitive variables. The variables in the design structures can be derived from cognitive psychology research to identify processes, strategies, or knowledge structures from item responses.

It should be noted that exploratory IRT models with multiple dimensions are also available. For example, Bock, Gibbons, and Muraki (1987) developed a multidimensional IRT model in which a linear combination of several abilities predicts item-solving probabilities. The exploratory multidimensional IRT models are very similar to factor analysis models. In fact, Bock et al. (1987) described their model as full-information factor analysis. It is full information in the sense that item responses are modeled, and hence the full dataset is used to estimate parameters. In contrast, factor-analysis attempts to model statistics that have been computed on the data; namely, correlations. The exploratory multidimensional IRT models are more appropriate than factor analysis for binary data or for data with discrete categories.

In this section, only confirmatory IRT models will be considered. Although the exploratory multidimensional IRT models are more justifiable for analyzing item level data, the models do not identify dimensions that differ much from factor analysis. Although confirmatory factor analysis models, in some applications, can identify new aspects of individual differences, little attention has been given to measurement from item level data. The confirmatory multidimensional IRT models, however, do have potential for identifying new aspects of individual differences.

In this section, only a few confirmatory IRT models will be presented. Confirmatory IRT modeling is a rapidly expanding area. This section cannot review all these developments, but several models will be mentioned here. The reader is referred to the Embretson (1983) *Handbook of Modern Item Response Theory* for more details on several models.

Models for Independent Processing Components

MLTM AND GLTM. The general component latent trait model (GLTM, Embretson, 1984) measures (1) abilities on covert processing components, (2) item difficulties on processing components, and (3) the relationship of item stimulus features to component processing difficulties. GLTM is a generalization of MLTM (Whitely,[*] 1980) and is a noncompensatory model appropriate for tasks that require correct outcomes on several processing components.

Two types of mathematical models as well as an IRT model are specified by GLTM. The first model in GLTM specifies how component outcomes are related to item solving. In GLTM, item success is assumed to require success on *all* underlying components. If any component is failed, then the item is not successfully solved. Thus, GLTM is a noncompensatory model that gives the probability of success for person j on item I, X_{ijT}, as the product of successes on the underlying components X_{ijm} as follows:

$$P(X_{ijT} = 1) = \Pi_m P(X_{ijm} = 1) \tag{19.5}$$

Although the component outcomes are covert, they may be operationalized by subtasks or by special constraints on the GLTM model without subtasks (see the following paragraphs for details).

The second mathematical model in GLTM specifies how item features influence component difficulty. Essentially, each component item difficulty is modeled by a linear combination of scored item features as in LLTM above. The third model in GLTM is an IRT model. A Rasch model gives the component success probabilities as a combination of ability and item difficulty. These three models are represented in GLTM in the following equation:

$$P(X_{ijT} = 1 | \Theta_j, b_i) = \Pi_m \frac{\exp(\theta_{jm} - \Sigma_k \tau_{km} q_{ikm})}{1 + \exp(\theta_{jm} - \Sigma_k \tau_{km} q_{ikm})}, \tag{19.6}$$

where τ_{km} is the weight of stimulus factor k in component m, q_{ikm} is the score of stimulus factor k on component m for item i, and θ_{jm} is the ability level of person j on component m. Like LLTM, item difficulty is replaced with a linear combination of the item features, which predict item difficulty.

To give an example, Maris (1995) applied MLTM to estimate two components, generation and evaluation, that were postulated to underlie success in synonym items. The results had several implications. First, Maris' results further elaborated the construct

---

[*] S. E. Embretson has published previously as S. E. Whitely.

representation of synonym items; the generation component was much stronger than the evaluation component in contributing to item solving. Second, generation ability and evaluation ability were measured for each person. Thus, diagnostic information about the source of performance may be obtained by comparing the relative strength of the two abilities. Third, the contributions of each component to the difficulty of each item could also be described. Such information is useful for selecting items to measure specified sources of difficulty.

Originally, both MLTM and GLTM required component responses, as well as the total item response, to estimate the component parameters. Now, however, GLTM can be applied to the total item task directly without subtasks if a strong cognitive model of item difficulty is available. That is, if stimulus features are known to predict item difficulty strongly, they may be used to place constraints on the GLTM solution when applied with Maris' (1995) missing-data algorithm. GLTM has been applied to measure individual differences in working-memory capacity versus control processing on abstract reasoning items (Embretson, 1995) and on spatial visualization items (Schmidt McCollam, 1998).

Models for Contrasting Experimental Task Conditions

Several IRT models can identify abilities by contrasting a person's performance over varying conditions. These IRT models interface well with contemporary cognitive experiments that use within-subject designs in which each person receives several conditions. In these experiments, construct impact is estimated by comparing performance across conditions. A similar approach can be applied in testing to measure individual differences in construct impact. Calculating performance differences directly for a person, say by subtracting one score from another, has well-known psychometric limitations (see Bereiter, 1963). Some new confirmatory IRT models, however, can provide psychometrically defensible alternatives. Several general models have been proposed, including Adams and Wilson (1996); DiBello, Stout, and Roussos (1995); and Embretson (1994, 1997). Like all structured IRT models, performance under a certain condition or occasion is postulated to depend on a specified combination of underlying abilities.

Like confirmatory factor analysis, the specification is determined from theory.

These models may be illustrated by elaborating a special case, the multidimensional Rasch model for learning and change (MRMLC; Embretson, 1991), which measures a person's initial ability and one or more modifiabilities from repeated measurements. MRMLC contains a Wiener process design structure (shown below) to relate the items to initial ability and the modifiabilities. The Wiener process structure increases in the number of dimensions involved in performance across time or conditions. Complex cognitive data often have properties that correspond to the Wiener processing design structure, that is, increasing variances and decreasing correlations over time (see Embretson, 1991).

A general structured latent trait model (SLTM; Embretson, 1997) that includes MRMLC is given as follows:

$$P(X_{i(k)j} = 1 \mid \theta_j, b_i) = \frac{\exp(\Sigma_m \lambda_{i(k)m}\theta_{jm} - b_i)}{1 + \exp(\Sigma_m \lambda_{i(k)m}\theta_{jm} - b_i)},$$
(19.7)

where θ_{j1} is initial ability level and $\theta_{j2}, \ldots, \theta_{jm}$ are modifiabilities between successive occasions or conditions, and b_i is difficulty for item i. The weight $\lambda_{i(k)m}$ is the weight of ability m in item i under occasion k. In MRMLC the weight is specified as 0 or 1, depending on the occasion. The Wiener process design structure determines which ability is involved on each occasion. For three occasions the structure, Λ, is specified as follows:

		Ability		
	Occasion	θ_1	θ_2	θ_3
	1	1	0	0
$\Lambda =$	2	1	1	0
	3	1	1	1

Thus, on the first occasion, only initial ability is involved. On the second occasion, both initial ability and the first modifiability are involved.

A recent application of MRMLC appears in Schmidt McCollam (1998). A dynamic test of spatial visualization ability with measures at three time points was analyzed by MRMLC for older and younger adults. Ability was estimated at time 1 (Pretest), after physical analogue training at time 2

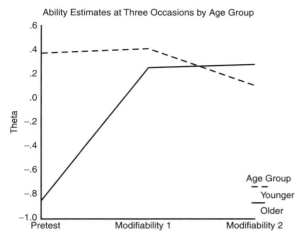

FIGURE 19.6. Means for initial spatial ability and two spatial modifiabilities in young and older adults.

(Modifiability 1), and after verbal-analytic training at time 3 (Modifiability 2) for both age groups. The Age x Occasion interaction was statistically significant, $F(2, 352) = 30.33$, $p < .0005$. It can be seen from Figure 19.6 that, although younger adults' initial pretest ability was greater than that of older adults, neither modifiability differed significantly. Analyses using raw scores failed to show the same trends. Because MRMLC is a Rasch-family model, it does have justifiable interval level measurement. Hence, MRMLC provides a more justifiable index of age group differences.

Equation 19.7 is obviously more general than MRMLC. Other design structures can be developed to represent specific comparisons or contrasts between conditions such as trends or Helmert contrasts and more.

Models for Distinct Classes of Persons

Several IRT models can identify groups of persons that differ qualitatively in their response patterns. On many cognitive tasks, persons have different knowledge bases or apply different strategies for item solving. The relative difficulty of the tasks depends on which knowledge structure or strategy is being applied. For example, in many spatial ability tests, items may be solved by either a spatial or a verbal strategy. Or, for another example, suppose that the source of knowledge for an achievement test differs between persons (e.g., formal education versus practical experience). In both cases, the groups are distinguished by a different pattern of item difficulties.

MIXED RASCH MODEL. The mixed population Rasch model (MIRA; Rost, 1990) has the following properties: (1) latent classes are identified from characteristic response patterns, (2) abilities are estimated for each person within each class, and (3) class membership is estimated for each person. In MIRA, IRT is combined with latent class analysis. The meaning of the ability level depends on the class because the item difficulties are ordered differently. The Mixed Rasch Model is given as follows:

$$P(X_{ij} = 1) = \sum_g \pi_g \frac{\exp(\theta_{jg} + b_{ig})}{1 + \exp(\theta_{jg} + b_{ig})} \quad (19.8)$$

where $\theta_{jg} = \theta$ for person j in group g, $b_{ig} = $ easiness for item I in group g, and $\pi_g = $ the class size parameter or mixing proportion. Note that b_{ig} in this model is designated as item easiness. The b-value has a reverse sign from item difficulty. The constraint

$$\sum_g \pi_g = 1$$

designates the sum of the mixing proportions over all groups as equal to 1.

MIRA analyses enable estimation of class membership based upon different patterns of responses. Advantages of applying MIRA include (1) increased knowledge of construct representation for the test and (2) identification of a possible moderator variable (i.e., the latent class) that influences the prediction of criterion behaviors or other tasks.

An application that illustrates the properties of MIRA is a study by Schmidt McCollam (1998). A spatial visualization test was administered to a sample of adults and then analyzed with MIRA. Because it is well known that spatial solution strategies differ among persons, it was hypothesized that these strategy differences defined distinct latent classes. A goodness of fit test for MIRA indicated a two-class solution best fit the data. In one class, item difficulty patterns were highly related to spatial processing features of the items, whereas in the other it was not. Further, the external correlates of abilities from the two classes further indicated that the classes were spatial processing versus verbal-analytic processing.

An inspection of the mixing proportions indicated that 38% of the sample belonged to a verbal-analytic class and 62% belonged to a spatial processing class.

Thus, these results suggested qualitative as well as quantitative differences between persons. The results not only reflect widely held hypotheses about spatial processing but further allow assessment of individuals for processing strategies.

SALTUS: A DEVELOPMENTAL MODEL. Wilson (1989) designed the Saltus model as a developmental extension of the Rasch (1960) model to measure discontinuous stage changes in persons. Saltus is the Latin word for *leap*. The Saltus model measures state changes by using multiple tasks at each of various developmental levels. Wilson (1989) described the Saltus model in terms of Fischer et al.'s (1984) distinctions between first-order and second-order discontinuities. First-order discontinuities are sudden or abrupt changes in a single ability, whereas second-order discontinuities are these changes occurring in at least two domains. The Rasch model is used for first-order discontinuities, and the Saltus model, which estimates parameters for persons, domains, and levels, is used for second-order discontinuities.

The Saltus model also can be viewed as a refinement of Guttman's scalogram model (1944), which assumes that one item exists per level. A person is assigned to a given level based upon passing all previous items and failing all subsequent items. There are three major shortcomings of the scalogram model: (1) persons are discarded who do not adhere to the ordinal scalogram model, (2) the use of one item per level assumes that the exact nature determining the item's difficulty is known, and relatedly (3) the use of one item per level assumes no replication of task is needed. Wilson (1989) applied Rasch's probabilistic approach and interval scaling in Saltus to resolve the scalogram adherence problem. Further, Wilson (1989) noted that multiple tasks tied to cognitive theory can resolve the nature and replication problems.

A necessary part of first-order discontinuity for Wilson's Saltus model is segmentation, or the differences between difficulty across levels. Segmentation consistent with first-order discontinuity requires the item difficulties between levels be nonoverlapping. The Saltus model, in addition to θ_j and b_i, contains parameters to represent stages for persons and to represent the impact of stages on different types of items. An important aspect of Saltus is its extension of IRT to cognitive task data that otherwise would not fit IRT models. Further, the impact of stages on different types of tasks further elaborates the nature of developmental changes.

COGNITIVE DIAGNOSTIC ASSESSMENT. The rule-space methodology (Tatsuoka, 1983, 1984) classifies persons on the basis on their knowledge states, and measures overall ability level. For example, a person's score on a mathematical test indicates overall performance levels but does not usually diagnose processes or knowledge structures that need remediation. The rule-space methodology provides diagnostic information about the meaning of a person's response pattern. The meaningfulness of the diagnostic assessment depends directly on the quality of the cognitive theory behind the attributes and resulting knowledge states. The rule-space methodology has been applied to ability and achievement tests and to both verbal and nonverbal tests (see Embretson & Reise, in press, for a summary).

A basic rule space is defined by two dimensions, the ability level (namely θ_j from an IRT model), and by a fit index (ζ_j). Ability, of course, represents overall performance, and the fit index measures the typicality of the person's response pattern. For example, passing hard items and failing easy items is an atypical response pattern that would yield an extreme value for a fit index. Fit indices are calculated by comparing the person's response pattern to the predictions given by the IRT model.

Figure 19.7 plots both persons and knowledge states into the rule space from ability level and fit. Persons are classified into knowledge states by the distances of their response patterns from the locations of the knowledge states. Obviously, persons are plotted directly to the rule space because both ability level and fit are estimated. Locating a knowledge state requires some intermediate steps. First, an attribute incidence matrix is scored to reflect which attributes are required to solve each item. This is the first step in which cognitive theory is implemented. Second, knowledge states are defined from patterns of attributes. Knowledge states are extracted empirically by applying a Boolean clustering algorithm to the attribute incidence matrix. Third, an ideal response pattern is generated for each knowledge state; that is, the ideal response pattern specifies the items that are passed and failed by someone in the knowledge state. Like a person, an ideal response pattern can be scored for ability (i.e., from total number of items passed) and for a fit index.

IMPLICATIONS FOR MEASURING AND UNDERSTANDING. Contemporary studies of intelligence have been strongly influenced by cognitive psychological theories. The confirmatory multidimensional IRT models can readily be interfaced with cognitive theory to understand intelligence. Unlike factor analysis, IRT focuses on the basis of item response rather than on decomposition of whole variables. The models include parameters to represent both persons and items.

Several advantages for measuring and understanding intelligence result from interfacing the confirmatory IRT models with cognitive theory. For items, the impact of various cognitive processes on item difficulty can be estimated from models such as LLTM or tree-based regression. In turn, these parameters can be used to select items by their processing demands. Recent research has also shown the potential to generate items from cognitive theory and to anticipate their psychometric properties by confirmatory IRT models (Embretson, in press). For persons, the confirmatory IRT models are more flexible in how abilities may be combined in processing an item. Multiple abilities are not restricted to a compensatory relationship as in factor analysis. In fact, compensatory models, such as linear combinations, do not interface well with contemporary theory in cognitive psychology. Noncompensatory IRT models better represent cognitive processes as independent events that must all be processed successfully.

Perhaps even more important is the potential of confirmatory IRT models to measure new aspects of individual differences. For example, qualitative differences in the basis of item responding can be assessed with the mixed Rasch model or with

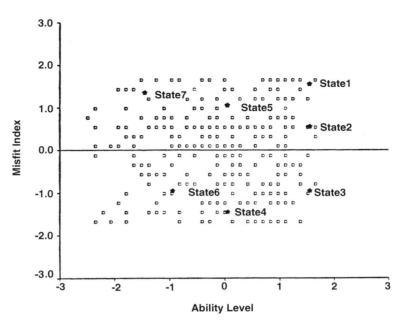

FIGURE 19.7. The rule space of ability level by misfit.

Tatsuoka's cognitive diagnostic assessment method. Further, individual differences in the component resources that underlie test performance can be assessed with the multicomponent latent trait model or the general latent trait model. Last, the differential sensitivity of persons to treatments or conditions that are varied during a testing session may be measured with the structured latent trait model.

These are just a few examples of the rapidly emerging field of confirmatory IRT models. Although such models are not fully implemented in testing as yet, relevant basic research to operationalize these models is expanding. At one major test publisher, Educational Testing Service, applications of diagnostic assessment and tree-based regression are now being considered.

SUMMARY

In this chapter we reviewed two types of psychometric models for impact on measuring and understanding intelligence. Factor analytic models and item response theory models are major psychometric approaches that are being applied to current measures of intelligence.

The factor analytic tradition was reviewed first because it has been the psychometric model with the longest history. Until the mid-1970s, factor analysis was a predominant paradigm for understanding human intelligence. Understanding ability was synonymous with discovering the number and the nature of the underlying factors. Unidimensional and multiple factor models were reviewed for impact on current measurement practice. Although Spearman postulated a central factor in intelligence nearly a century ago, many contemporary intelligence tests provide an index of general intelligence. Similarly, multiple factor theories, such as those proposed by Thurstone and Guilford, have a history of at least one-half century and, again, contemporary tests that involve these factors remain available. Perhaps most influential for current measures of intelligence are the hierarchical factor theories. Many intelligence tests now report several scores at different levels of abstraction. Broad and narrow indices of ability are reported in tests such as the Stanford–Binet IV and the Differential Ability Scales, for example. Cattell and Horn's distinction between fluid and crystallized intelligence has been particularly influential, for many contemporary intelligence tests provide these estimates.

Item response theory methods were developed much more recently. For example, Rasch developed his IRT model in 1960. Currently, IRT is being applied in many contemporary tests to solve practical testing problems such as equating adaptive tests. The advantages of IRT were briefly reviewed, and two popular unidimensional IRT models were presented. Applications of these models have little potential to provide understanding of the nature of intelligence, however, or to define new aspects of individual differences.

However, a family of confirmatory IRT models is rapidly developing. These models have the potential to replace factor analysis as a tool for understanding intelligence. In fact, the exploratory multidimensional IRT models are equivalent to a full information factor analysis for item level data. In general, however, the IRT models are better interfaced with cognitive psychological approaches to understanding intelligence than are the factor analytic models for several reasons. First, it was shown that IRT models are applied to individual task responses like mathematical modeling in cognitive psychology. Second, the confirmatory IRT models utilize similar independent variables for modeling item difficulty as cognitive psychological approaches. The linear logistic latent trait model, for example, can utilize the same stimulus design data as mathematical modeling of response times. Third, confirmatory multidimensional IRT models have the potential to characterize qualitative variables more fully such as differing knowledge states and strategies. For example, the mixed Rasch model and diagnostic assessment can diagnose groups of person whose response patterns differ systematically from other response patterns. Fourth, confirmatory multidimensional IRT models have also been proposed to measure individual sensitivity to various interventions or conditions. Within-subject variations are commonly used in cognitive psychology to test hypotheses about processing mechanisms. Similar task variations can be applied in intelligence measurement to assess individual differences in sensitivity to processing.

If another *Handbook of Intelligence* is published several years from now, we predict that IRT-based approaches will predominate for measuring and understanding intelligence. Further, we anticipate a broad array of new types of individual differences to result from the application of the newer confirmatory IRT models. These new models can assess individual differences in knowledge structures, strategies, processing components, modifiability, and more if applied in the context of well-understood cognitive ability items.

REFERENCES

Adams, R. A., & Wilson, M. (1996). Formulating the Rasch model as a mixed coefficients multinomial logit. In G. Engelhard & M. Wilson (Eds.), *Objective measurement III: Theory into practice.* Norwood, NJ: Ablex.

Andrich, D. (1988). *Rasch models for measurement.* Newbury Park, CA: Sage Publications.

Arbuckle, J. L. (1995). Amos for Windows. Analysis of moment structures (Version 3.5). Chicago: SmallWaters.

Bennett, R. E., Seashore, H. G., & Wesman, A. G. (1984). *Differential aptitude tests: Technical supplement.* San Antonio, TX: Psychological Corporation.

Bentler, P. M. (1985). Theory and implementation of EQS: A structural equations program (manual for version 2.0). Los Angeles: BMDP Statistical Software.

Bereiter, C. (1963). Some persisting dilemmas in the measurement of change. In C. Harris (Ed.), *Problems in measuring change* (pp. 3–20). Madison, WI: University of Wisconsin Press.

Bock, R. D., Gibbons, R., & Muraki, E. J. (1988). Full information item factor analysis. *Applied Psychological Measurement, 12,* 261–280.

Burt, C. (1949). The structure of mind: A review of results of factor analysis. *British Journal of Educational Psychology, 19,* 100–111, 176–199.

Carpenter, P. A., Just, M. A., & Shell, P. (1990). What one intelligence test measures: A theoretical account of processing in the Raven's Progressive Matrices Test. *Psychological Review, 97,* 404–431.

Carroll, J. B. (1993). *Human cognitive abilities: A survey of factor-analytic studies.* New York: Cambridge University Press.

Cattell, R. B. (1963). Theory of fluid and crystallized intelligence: A critical experiment. *Journal of Educational Psychology, 54,* 1–22.

DiBello, L. V., Stout, W. F., & Roussos, L. (1995). Unified cognitive psychometric assessment likelihood-based classification techniques. In P. D. Nichols, S. F. Chipman, & R. L. Brennan (Eds.), *Cognitively diagnostic assessment.* Hillsdale, NJ: Erlbaum Publishers.

Ekstrom, R. B., French, J. W., Harman, H. H., & Dermen, D. (1976). *Manual for kit of factor-referenced cognitive tests.* Princeton, NJ: Educational Testing Service.

Elliot, C. D. (1990). *Differential ability scales.* San Antonio, TX: Psychological Corporation.

Embretson, S. E. (1983). Construct validity: Construct representation versus nomothetic span. *Psychological Bulletin, 93,* 179–197.

Embretson, S. E. (1984). A general multicomponent latent trait model for response processes. *Psychometrika, 49,* 175–186.

Embretson, S. E. (1991). A multidimensional latent trait model for measuring learning and change. *Psychometrika, 56,* 495–516.

Embretson, S. E. (1994a). Application of cognitive design systems to test development. In C. R. Reynolds (Ed.), *Cognitive assessment: A multidisciplinary perspective* (pp. 107–135). New York: Plenum Press.

Embretson, S. E. (1994b, April). *Structured multidimensional IRT models for measuring individual differences in learning or change.* Paper presented at the annual meeting of the American Educational Research Association, New Orleans, LA.

Embretson, S. E. (1995). Working memory capacity versus general control processes in intelligence. *Intelligence, 20,* 169–189.

Embretson, S. E. (1996). Item response theory models and spurious interaction effects in factorial ANOVA designs. *Applied Psychological Measurement, 20,* 201–212.

Embretson, S. E. (1997). Structured ability models in tests designed from cognitive theory. In M. Wilson, G. Engelhard, & K. Draney (Eds.), *Objective Measurement III.* Norwood, NJ: Ablex, pp. 223–236.

Embretson, S. E. (1998). A cognitive design system approach to generating valid tests: Application to abstract reasoning. *Psychological Methods, 3,* 380–396.

Embretson, S. E., & Reise, S. R. (in press). *Item response theory for psychologists.* Matawah, NJ: Erlbaum Publishers.

Fischer, G. H. (1973). Linear logistic test model as an instrument in educational research. *Acta Psychologica, 37,* 359–374.

Fischer, K. W., Pipp, S. L., & Bullock, D. (1984). Detecting discontinuities in development: Methods and measurement. In R. N. Emde & R. Harmon (Eds.), *Continuities and discontinuities in development.* Norwood, NJ: Ablex.

Guilford, J. P. (1948). Factor analysis in a test-development program. *Psychological Review, 55,* 79–84.

Guilford, J. P. (1959). Three faces of intellect. *American Psychologist, 14,* 469–479.

Guilford, J. P. (1967). *The nature of human intelligence.* NY: McGraw-Hill.

Guilford, J. P. (1977). The invariance problem in factor analysis. *Educational and Psychological Measurement, 37,* 11–19.

Guilford, J. P. (1985). A sixty-year perspective on psychological measurement. *Applied Psychological Measurement, 9,* 341–349.

Guttman, L. A. (1944). A basis for scaling qualitative data. *American Sociological Review, 9,* 139–150.

Hambleton, R. K., Swaminathan, H., & Rogers, H. J. (1991). *Fundamentals of item response theory.* Newbury Park, CA: Sage.

Holzinger, K. J., & Harman, H. H. (1941). *Factor analysis: A synthesis of factorial methods*: Chicago: University of Chicago Press.

Holzinger, K. J., & Swineford, F. (1939). A study in factor analysis: The stability of a bifactor solution. *Supplementary Educational Monographs, 48,* xi–91.

Horn, J. L., & Cattell, R. B. (1967). Age differences in fluid and crystallized intelligence. *Acta Psychologica, 26,* 107–129.

Hotelling, H. (1933). Analysis of a complex of statistical variables into principal components. *Journal of Educational Psychology, 24,* 417–441.

Humphreys, L. G. (1952). Individual differences. *Annual Review of Psychology, 3,* 131–150.

Humphreys, L. G. (1985). General intelligence: An integration of factor, test, and simplex theory. In B. B. Wolman (Ed.), *Handbook of intelligence: Theories, measurements, and applications.* NY: Wiley (pp. 201–224).

Intelligence and its measurement: A symposium. (1921). *Journal of Educational Psychology, 12,* 123–147.

Joreskog, K. G. (1971). Simultaneous factor analysis in several populations. *Psychometrika, 36,* 409–426.

Joreskog, K. G., & Sorbom, D. (1983). *LISREL VI: User's guide.* Uppsala: Department of Statistics.

Kaufman, A. S., & Kaufman, N. L. (1993). *Manual for the Kaufman Adolescent and Adult Intelligence Test (KAIT).* Circle Pines, MN: American Guidance Service.

Kelly, T. (1928). *Crossroads in the mind of man*. Stanford, CA: Stanford University Press.

Kelley, T. (1935). *Essential traits of mental life*. Cambridge, MA: Harvard University Press.

Kyllonen, P. C., & Christal, R. E. (1990). Reasoning ability is (little more than) working-memory capacity?! *Intelligence, 14*, 389–433.

Maris, E. M. (1995). Psychometric latent response models. *Psychometrika, 60*, 523–547.

Maxwell, S., & Delaney, H. (1985). Measurement and statistics: An examination of construct validity. *Psychological Bulletin, 97*, 85–93.

Moreno, K. E., Wetzel, C. D., McBride, J. R., & Weiss, D. J. (1984). Relationship between corresponding Armed Services Vocational Aptitude Battery (ASVAB) and computerized adaptive testing (CAT) subtests. *Applied Psychological Measurement, 8*, 155–163.

Neale, M. C. (1994). Mx: Statistical modeling (2nd ed.). Richmond, VA: Author.

Rasch, G. (1960). *Probabilistic models for some intelligence and attainment tests*. Copenhagen: Danmarks Paedagogiske Institut.

Raven, J. C. (1956). *Guide to using progressive matrices*. London: H. K. Lewis.

Raven, J. C., Court, J. H., & Raven, J. (1992). *Manual for Raven's Progressive Matrices and Vocabulary Scale*. San Antonio, TX: The Psychological Corporation.

Rost, J. (1990). Rasch models in latent classes: An integration of two approaches to item analysis. *Applied Psychological Measurement, 14*, 271–282.

Schaie, K. W. (1985). *Schaie–Thurstone Adult Mental Abilities Test*. CA: Consulting Psychologists Press.

Schmidt McCollam, K. M. (1998). Latent trait and latent class models. In G. M. Marcoulides (Ed.), *Modern Methods for Business Research* (pp. 23–46). Hillsdale, NJ: Erlbaum.

Schmidt McCollam, K. M., & Embretson, S. E. (1998). Modifiability of spatial visualization performance in older and younger adults. Unpublished manuscript.

Sheehan, K. M. (1997). A tree-based approach to proficiency scaling and diagnostic assessment. *Journal of Educational Measurement, 34*, 333–354.

Spearman, C. (1904). "General intelligence" objectively determined and measured. *American Journal of Psychology, 15*, 201–293.

Spearman, C. (1923). *The nature of intelligence and the principles of cognition*. London: Macmillan.

Spearman, C. (1927). *The abilities of man*. New York: Macmillan.

Spearman, C., & Jones, L. W. (1950). *Human ability: A continuation of "The abilities of man."* London: Macmillan.

Sternberg, R. J. (1977). *Intelligence, information-processing and analogical reasoning: The componential analysis of human abilities*. Hillsdale, NJ: Erlbaum.

Sternberg, R. J. (1985). *Beyond IQ: A triarchic theory of human intelligence*. New York: Cambridge University Press.

Sternberg, R. J., & Detterman, D. K. (Eds.). (1986). *What is intelligence? Contemporary viewpoints on its nature and definition*. Norwood, NJ: Ablex.

Tatsuoka, K. K. (1983). Rule space: An approach for dealing with misconceptions based on item response theory. *Journal of Educational Measurement, 20*, 34–38.

Tatsuoka, K. K. (1984). Caution indices based on item response theory. *Psychometrika, 49*, 94–110.

Thorndike, R. L., Hagen, E. P., & Sattler, J. M. (1986). *The Stanford–Binet Intelligence Scale: Fourth Edition*. Chicago: Riverside.

Thurstone, L. L. (1938). *Primary mental abilities*. Psychometric Monographs, No. 1.

Thurstone, L. L., & Thurstone, T. G. (1941). Factorial studies of intelligence. *Psychometric Monographs*, No. 2.

Vernon, P. E. (1950). *The structure of human abilities*. New York: Wiley.

Vernon, P. E. (1961). *The structure of human abilities (2nd ed.)*. London: Methuen.

Wechsler, D. (1981). *Wechsler Adult Intelligence Scale-Revised*. San Antonio, TX: Psychological Corporation.

Wechsler, D. (1991). *Wechsler Intelligence Scale for Children-III*. San Antonio, TX: Psychological Corporation.

Whitely, S. E. (1980). Multicomponent latent trait models for ability tests. *Psychometrika, 45*, 479–494.

Wilson, M. (1984). *A psychometric model of hierarchical development*. Unpublished doctoral dissertation, University of Chicago.

Wilson, M. (1989). Saltus: A psychometric model of discontinuity in cognitive development. *Psychological Bulletin, 105*, 276–289.

Woodcock, R. W., & Johnson, M. B. (1989). *Woodcock–Johnson Tests of Cognitive Ability – Revised*. Chicago: Riverside.

CHAPTER TWENTY

Tests of Intelligence

ALAN S. KAUFMAN

HISTORY OF INTELLIGENCE TESTING

Intelligence tests were conceived in a theoretical void and born into a theoretical vacuum. During the last half of the 19th century, first Sir Francis Galton in England (1869, 1883) and then Alfred Binet in France (Binet & Henri, 1895) took turns in developing the leading intelligence tests of the day. Galton, who was interested in men of genius and in eugenics, developed his test from a vague, simplistic theory that people take in information through their senses, and thus the most intelligent people must have the best developed senses. His test included a series of sensory, motor, and reaction-time tasks, all of which produced reliable, consistent results (Galton, the half-cousin of Charles Darwin, was strictly a scientist, and accuracy was essential) but none of them proved to be valid as measures of the construct of intelligence (Cohen, Montague, Nathanson, & Swerdlik, 1988). Galton developed a statistic that was the forerunner of the coefficient of correlation, and that proved to be his own undoing; shortly after his friend and biographer Karl Pearson perfected the statistic, a few studies revealed that the Galton intelligence test was misnamed because it did not correlate meaningfully with pertinent cognitive variables (such as grade point average).

In fact, the research studies that sounded the death knell for Galton's test conducted in the United States around the turn of the century at Galton-inspired laboratories at Columbia and Cornell were as flawed as the test itself (e.g., very small sample size, highly restricted sample of bright sub-jects). Nonetheless, Galton's test, quite appropriately (despite the contentions of some current psychologists such as Jensen, 1985, about the validity of reaction time to measure IQ) was laid to rest. Before the burial, however, his influence had spread throughout Europe and the United States by disciples such as Wundt, Titchener, and James McKeen Cattell (who considered Galton to be the greatest man he ever met; Roback, 1961). Regardless of the persistent grumblings of Binet and his scholarly colleagues, often in the journal that Binet himself founded (*L'Année psychologique*), Galton's notion of intelligence *was* intelligence from the 1880s through the early part of the 20th century.

The Role of Alfred Binet

At that point, Binet seized the opening, and, with the assistance of the Minister of Public Instruction in Paris, who was eager to separate mentally retarded from normal children in the classroom, published the first "real" intelligence test in 1905. Like Galton's test, Binet's instrument had only a vague tie to theory (in this case the notion of intelligence as a single, global ability that people possess in different amounts). In fact, Binet was more influenced by the English philosopher John Stuart Mill than by anyone in the emerging field of psychology. To Binet (1903), Mill was his "only teacher of psychology" (p. 68). Mill (1875) claimed, "The science of human nature...falls far short of the standard of exactness now realized in Astronomy" (p. 432), and that became Binet's credo. In a stance antithetical to Galton's, Binet declared that because intelligence is complex, so, too, must be its measurement. He conceptualized intelligence as one's ability to demonstrate memory, judgment, reasoning, and social comprehension, and he and his colleagues developed tasks to measure these aspects of global intelligence. Binet's contributions included his focus on language abilities (rather than the nonverbal skills measured by Galton) and his introduction of the mental age concept derived from his use of age levels, ranging from 3 to 13 years, in his revised 1908 scale (mental age was the highest age level at which the child had success; the intelligence quotient, or IQ, became the ratio of the child's mental age to chronological age multiplied by 100). Yet, perhaps Binet's biggest contribution was his Mill-inspired insistence that one must be willing to accept a certain degree of *measurement error* to measure human intelligence. Consequently, he was content to include items such as the following in his tests of intelligence, even though some of these items did not lend themselves to purely objective scoring: taking candy out of a paper wrapper; comparing the length of two lines; defining the words *house* and *fork*; repeating from memory a 15-word sentence; constructing a sentence using the words *Paris, gutter*, and *fortune*; and distinguishing between abstract words such as *sadness* and *boredom*.

Terman Brings the Binet to the United States

From the very beginning, when Binet made detailed developmental observations of his young daughters, Madeleine and Alice, his approach was practical rather than theoretical, and that practical perspective persisted when Lewis Terman of Stanford University translated and adapted the Binet–Simon scales in the United States to produce the Stanford–Binet. Terman triumphed over other pretenders to the Binet throne, such as the Goddard–Binet and the Kuhlmann–Binet, because he did more than merely translate Binet's test. Instead, he adapted his Stanford–Binet Intelligence Scale (Terman, 1916) to American culture and used state-of-the-art methodology to introduce the concept of intelligence quotient or IQ. He also understood the importance of standardizing the test on substantial numbers of children at different ages who lived in the United States rather than relying on Binet's placement of tasks at year level IV or IX,

for example, based on data from Paris schoolchildren. When Terman initially published a "tentative" revision of the Binet–Simon scale in 1912, no one used it, and the Goddard–Binet (Goddard, 1908) took a commanding lead. But when Terman published his painstaking, standardized version in 1916, the Stanford–Binet became the undisputed king of intelligence tests. Yet, Terman's theoretical approach never strayed far from a *g* or general-factor approach, and his appreciation of the test's usefulness rarely extended beyond his practical vision of its utility for identifying the "feebleminded" and weeding out the unfit.

The World War I Influence

Nearly coinciding with the Stanford–Binet's birth was a second great influence on the development of IQ tests in the United States: America's entry into World War I in 1917. Once more, practical concerns superseded theoretical issues. Large numbers of recruits needed to be tested quickly, leading to the development of a group IQ test, the Army Alpha, by Terman's student, Arthur Otis (the Otis–Lennon School Ability Test lives on to the present day). Immigrants who spoke English poorly or not at all had to be evaluated with nonverbal measures, spearheading the construction of the nonverbal group test, the Army Beta. Finally, and most importantly in view of current assessment procedures, the individually administered Army Performance Scale Examination was developed "to prove conclusively that a man was weak-minded and not merely indifferent or malingering" (Yoakum & Yerkes, 1920, p. 10). The entire test development endeavor during World War I reflected a huge contribution by the American Psychological Association led by Robert Yerkes. The practical consequences of this focused effort were many: As noted, Binet's individually administered test was transformed into a time-saving group format; nonverbal tests (measuring problem solving, not just Galton-like sensory–motor functions) joined verbal tests as legitimate ways to infer a person's general ability; IQ tests were found to be useful for adults, not just children; IQ tests were perceived to be valuable for high-functioning people, not just the lower extreme (they gained respect as valid tools for selecting officers and placing men in different types of service); data from huge samples (almost two million) were analyzed, demonstrating the IQ test's validity in discriminating officers from recruits; and wild misinterpretations of the data led to controversy, cries of racism and inferiority, and debates about the value of IQ tests and their social implications (Cronbach, 1975; Kaufman, 1990a; Yoakum & Yerkes, 1920).

Front and Center: David Wechsler

The link between the World War I practical innovations and current tests and practices in the clinical assessment of intelligence is summed up by two words: David Wechsler. As the 21-year-old Wechsler awaited induction into the U.S. Army in 1917, he obtained a job with E. G. Boring that required him to score thousands of Army Alpha exams. After induction he was trained to administer individual tests of intelligence such as the new Stanford–Binet and Yerkes' nonverbal tests. From these experiences, Wechsler became keenly aware of the need for fairness regarding the evaluation of people who spoke English poorly and of the necessity of developing adult-oriented tests for adults (Kaufman, in press). These clinical experiences paved the way for his Wechsler series of scales, starting with the Wechsler–Bellevue Intelligence Scale (Wechsler, 1939) and continuing to the present day, long after his death in 1981, with the Wechsler Preschool and Primary Scale of Intelligence-Revised (WPPSI–R; Wechsler, 1989) for ages 3 to 7 years, the Wechsler Intelligence Scale for Children – Third Edition (WISC–III; Wechsler, 1991) for ages 6 to 16 years, and the Wechsler Adult Intelligence Scale – Third Edition (WAIS–III; Wechsler, 1997) for ages 16 to 89 years.

Wechsler borrowed liberally from the Stanford–Binet and Army Alpha to develop his Verbal Scale and from the Army Beta and Army Performance Scale Examination to develop his nonverbal Performance Scale. His creativity came not from his choice of tasks, all of which were already developed and validated, but from his insistence that *everyone* should be evaluated on *both* verbal and nonverbal scales and that profiles of scores on a variety of mental tasks should be provided for each individual to supplement the global or aggregate measure of intelligence. The prevailing belief was that nonverbal tests were fine for new immigrants or for the hearing impaired but that verbal tests were sufficient for the typical person who had to be tested. Indeed,

Wechsler's notions were considered foolish because why would any examiner choose to spend 3 minutes administering a single jigsaw puzzle to be assembled when perhaps 15 or 20 general information questions could be asked during those 3 minutes? And why would anyone choose to interpret a profile of test scores when a single overall score corresponded quite well to the *g* factor that people possessed in varying amounts?

In fact, to his dying day Wechsler was a staunch believer in *g* theory, but he was a clinician at heart who considered his IQ tests to measure an aspect of personality and to be clinical instruments more so than psychometric devices. He was more impressed with how someone solved a problem and the precise words that person used to answer a verbal question (did the response suggest dependence? aggression? anxiety? self-control? low self-esteem?) than with the simple notion of correct versus incorrect answers. He wanted to determine how the person manifested his or her *g* factor in a variety of situations and via different modalities (verbal versus visual–motor). It is true that Wechsler's distinction between Verbal IQ and Performance IQ was subsequently related to neuropsychological theory (Reitan, 1955) and to Sperry's (1968) psychobiological cerebral specialization theory, and thus deficits in Verbal IQ were believed to correspond to damage to the *left* hemisphere of the brain and deficits in Performance IQ were posited to correspond to damage to the *right* hemisphere. It is also true that the Verbal IQ–Performance IQ distinction has been tied in directly to the Horn–Cattell theory of fluid and crystallized intelligence (Horn, 1989; Horn & Hofer, 1992). That theory, which distinguishes between novel problem solving (fluid) and knowledge acquired from schooling and acculturation (crystallized), has been used as a theoretical rationale for Wechsler's series of scales since the early 1970s when Matarazzo (1972) noted the correspondence of Verbal IQ and Performance IQ with crystallized and fluid ability, respectively. In fact, Horn has depended heavily on data from Wechsler's adult scales in applying the Horn–Cattell theory to changes in intellectual ability across the adult life span (Horn & Hofer, 1992; Kaufman, 1990a, chapter 7).

Nonetheless, neither these after-the-fact applications of theory to Wechsler's scales nor Wechsler's (1950, 1975) subsequent theoretical speculations about the nature of intelligence can deny one simple fact: Wechsler developed his scale from a wholly practical and clinical perspective, without regard to theory, and his series of tests does not correspond very well to his articulated theoretical views about the nature of intelligence. As clinical tests, however, the Wechsler scales have successfully met the test author's goals because, when they are interpreted by trained clinicians, they are, indeed, quite valuable for inferring aspects of personality and temperament from a person's test behaviors, both verbal and nonverbal. And Wechsler's scales, notably the ones developed for school-age children and adults, continue to be by far the most widely used tests of intelligence in the world. Finding a publisher for the Wechsler scales was difficult at first because of the deep-seated and widespread belief that the Stanford–Binet could not be challenged. The Binet did reign supreme for years after the Wechsler–Bellevue was published, but Wechsler triumphed during the 1960s and 1970s thanks to two unrelated events. First, the learning disabilities movement gathered steam in the 1960s, and the Wechsler Intelligence Scale for Children (WISC; Wechsler, 1949) was ready and waiting to meet the movement leaders' demand for multiscore tests to afford an examination of learning-disabled children's cognitive strengths and weaknesses instead of having profile fluctuations obscured by a single number. Second, the Stanford–Binet publishers forgot the reason that Terman's Binet emerged victorious over other pretenders in the first place, namely, his patience in obtaining careful standardization data. In 1960, several years after Terman died, the Binet was revised without being restandardized (Terman & Merrill, 1960), and in the early 1970s, the Binet was restandardized without being revised (Terman & Merrill, 1973). In the 1960 version, two forms were merged into one, but the outdated norms from the 1930s were largely retained for the "new" test. That was bad. Even worse, though, was the decision not to revise the test but simply to obtain updated norms for the version that was published in 1973. Children had changed over the generations, and thus children in the 1970s performed better on cognitive tasks than did children in the 1930s and 1940s. Consequently, the Binet age levels were all out of whack; children of 3 years were now passing the items at Level $3\frac{1}{2}$, and

9-year-olds were succeeding at the 10-year level. Mental ages lost their meaning, and IQs no longer made sense. A 4-year-old child who obtained a mental age of 4 should have earned an IQ of 100 whether the old Binet formula or Wechsler's innovation of the Deviation IQ (a standard score that the Binet people began to use with the 1960 edition) was used. In fact, that 4-year-old earned an IQ of 88, which made no sense at all and underscored the failure of the Stanford–Binet to adhere to Terman's initial high standards. The Wechsler takeover of the Binet was complete.

A New Breed of Theory-Based Intelligence Tests

The late 1970s finally produced a major intelligence test that was not a clone of the Binet or Wechsler scales (Woodcock & Johnson, 1977), and it was during the decade of the 1980s that psychological theory was at last applied directly to the development of mental ability tests (Kaufman & Kaufman, 1983a; Thorndike, Hagen, & Sattler, 1986; Woodcock & Johnson, 1989). All of these theory-based instruments are *clinical* tests of intelligence designed to be administered *individually* to children or adults who are referred for psychological evaluation.

Theory has played a smaller role in group-administered tests of the multiple-choice variety. Yet group tests of intelligence are also important to society because of their prevalent use within the educational system, military services, industry, and government service (Anastasi & Urbina, 1997). Such tests have consistently been revised, computerized, and improved substantially by the application of new and sophisticated psychometric procedures; but they have only rarely been impacted by advances in psychological theory. Occasional group tests have been theory based, most notably the S. O. I. Learning Abilities Test (Meeker, Mestyanek, Shadduck, & Meeker, 1975) developed from Guilford's (1967) Structure of Intellect model of intelligence, but these tests have typically not met the psychometric rigors of standardization and validation that characterize most individual tests of intelligence, and their impact has been modest.

The most popular group-administered tests are multilevel batteries that typically span the primary grades through high school and multiple aptitude batteries designed for adolescents and adults and often used for educational and career counseling. Group-administered tests of all sorts are almost always composed of multiple choice items, which are easy to administer and objective to score.

Well-constructed and well-normed multilevel batteries include the Otis–Lennon School Ability Test (OLSAT; Otis & Lennon, 1997) for grades K–12, which is an updated and expanded adaptation of the original Army Alpha that was developed by Terman's student Otis; the Cognitive Abilities Test (CogAT; Thorndike & Hagen, 1993) for grades K–12, which provides separate verbal, quantitative, and nonverbal scores; the Test of Cognitive Skills (TCS/2 *technical report*, 1993) for grades 2–12, which includes four subtests at each level of the test, namely, sequences, analogies, verbal reasoning, and memory; and the Naglieri Nonverbal Ability Test (NNAT; Naglieri, 1997) for grades 2–12, which is a brief nonverbal measure of reasoning ability using figural matrices and designs. All of these tests are notable for the high quality of their test construction procedures, the recency of their latest versions, the size and quality of their standardization samples, their impressive psychometric properties, and – most important – the concurrent standardization at the same grade levels with one or more major multilevel achievement batteries, thereby permitting easy comparison of ability with achievement (Anastasi & Urbina, 1997; Naglieri, 1997). These multilevel group-administered intelligence tests and others like them usually avoid the word "intelligence" in favor of terms such as "school ability," "mental maturity," or "academic potential," but what they measure is, indeed, what historically has been called intelligence. Most multilevel intelligence tests include the same subtests across virtually the entire broad age range. For example, "The upper levels of multilevel batteries, appropriate for *high school students*, do not differ basically from those designed for the elementary school grades except in degree of difficulty" (Anastasi & Urbina, 1997, p. 283).

Two multiple aptitude batteries of note are the Differential Aptitude Tests (DAT; Bennett, Seashore, & Wesman, 1990), for grades 7 to 12 and adults, and the Multidimensional Aptitude Battery (MAB; Jackson, 1994) for adolescents and adults. The DAT is one of the most popular multiple-aptitude batteries, has been popular since its inception in 1947, and is now available in a computerized version (Anastasi & Urbina, 1997). It measures eight separate areas such as Verbal Reasoning, Space Relations, and Spelling. The MAB is essentially a group-administered version of the WAIS–R that includes five verbal and five performance subtests, most with the same names used by Wechsler, and yields verbal, performance, and full-scale IQs. Both the DAT and MAB are of high technical quality and have been useful for counseling purposes (Anastasi & Urbina, 1997).

Group tests of intelligence have several practical advantages, including the feasibility of testing large numbers of individuals simultaneously by personnel with limited training in testing. This particular practical advantage is a cost-saving device that permits the generation of large numbers of items, the selection of items with excellent psychometric properties, and the testing of standardization samples in the kind of large numbers that can only be fantasized by developers of individually administered tests. For example, the NNAT fall and spring norms are based on data from nearly 90,000 students tested in 1995–96 (Naglieri, 1997), and "it is not unusual for the normative samples to number between 100,000 and 200,000" (Anastasi & Urbina, 1997, p. 273).

However, group-administered tests, no matter how large the sample and how exceptional the reliability and validity of the scores they yield, have built-in disadvantages by virtue of the very features that make them so cost efficient. The greatly reduced role of the examiner prevents the professional's accurate interpretation of test scores, especially for those who score poorly on the tests. Was the examinee motivated or bored, distractible or attentive, relaxed or anxious, alert or tired? Did the examinee understand the instructions or were the written directions a mystery because of a reading problem and the oral directions incomprehensible because of an auditory processing or memory problem? Was the examinee able to display his or her knowledge, or did the multiple-choice format impair communication of the examinee's knowledge base and true understanding of the material? Each drawback of the group-administered test makes such instruments of limited usefulness for assessing the children and adults who are referred for evaluation. These individuals often have learning or behavior problems, difficulties in reading, attentional difficulties, and the like, and their test performance is often readily understood only by a highly trained test examiner who is able to integrate test performance with observed test behaviors and who is able to interpret the quality of a person's oral and visual–motor responses.

A further disadvantage of the most popular group intelligence tests, as noted earlier, is their failure to incorporate theories of intelligence in their development or application. Even developmental theory is ignored in the efforts that have been taken by most developers of group tests to include the same subtests for everyone, regardless of age or grade level. Psychometric theories, such as the Rasch latent-trait model and item response theory, have been applied to the development of group tests to ensure, for example, the linkage of one level to another, but theories of intelligence and brain functioning have not impacted the revision of these tests or the development of new group tests. Theories such as Thurstone's (1938) were instrumental in the initial development of multiple aptitude batteries such as the DAT in the late 1940s by virtue of their de-emphasis of the then-hallowed *g* concept. However, such theories merely provided the impetus for the multiple-ability notion, but they did not provide the blueprint for the actual test construction. Those blueprints were defined more by the practicalities of test usage, such as the "growing activities of psychologists in career counseling, as well as the selection and classification of industrial and military personnel" (Anastasi & Urbina, 1997, pp. 287–288).

Group tests have much value in different aspects of life, including mass testing within the educational system. Yet, they suffer the same failings that the Army Alpha and Army Beta did during wartime, the failings that led to the development of the Army Performance Scale Examination, the precursor of Wechsler's clinical tests of nonverbal ability. It is the clinical tests that are the direct descendants of Galton, Binet, Terman, World War I, and Wechsler that have been the subject of intense controversy regarding test bias, heredity versus environment, and placement in school programs (Herrnstein & Murray, 1994; Kaufman, 1990a, chapter 2; Williams, 1974); that have been the subject of thousands of empirical investigations; and that have become the standard of intellectual potential within schools, clinics, hospitals, and private practices worldwide.

And it is the individually administered clinical tests of intelligence, not the group tests of mental ability, that have been on the forefront of the application of psychological theory to test development and test interpretation. It is, therefore, the individual tests to which the rest of this chapter is devoted.

Two tests that began the direct application of theory to test development in the 1980s, the K–ABC and Binet–4, are discussed briefly in the sections that follow.

KAUFMAN ASSESSMENT BATTERY FOR CHILDREN (K–ABC). The K–ABC (Kaufman & Kaufman, 1983a) is a battery of tests measuring intelligence and achievement of children ages 2½ through 12½ years. The K–ABC has been the subject of controversy from the outset, as evident in the strongly pro and con articles written for a special issue of the *Journal of Special Education* devoted to the K–ABC (Miller & Reynolds, 1984). These controversies stemmed primarily from the choice of theoretical foundation for the intelligence portion of the battery, that is, the scale labeled Sequential Processing comprised only short-term memory tests, calling into question the nature of the construct that it measures; the decision to depart from the Wechsler–Binet tradition and segregate language and fact-related tasks onto a separate Achievement Scale that does not contribute to the overall intelligence score; and the finding that IQ differences between Caucasians and minority children (African American, Hispanic, Native American) are considerably smaller than differences found on other, conventional tests of intelligence (Kaufman & Kaufman, 1983b; Vincent, 1991; Whitworth & Chrisman, 1987).

Though the controversies have persisted over time, the K–ABC has remained a popular choice for clinicians in the United States and throughout Europe and Asia; in part because of these controversies, a bulk of research has been conducted on the K–ABC that has added to understanding of cognitive functioning in preschool and elementary school children (Kamphaus, Beres, Kaufman, & Kaufman, 1995). Most important, the K–ABC has two key legacies: It designed a clinical intelligence test on research-based theories, and it demonstrated that it was possible to challenge the Wechsler–Binet monopoly, leading to the development of an impressive array of alternative IQ tests during the past 10 to 15 years and providing clinicians with more choices than ever before for assessing children, adolescents, and adults.

The K–ABC intelligence scales are based on a theoretical framework of sequential and simultaneous information processing, which relates to *how* children solve problems rather than *what* type of problems they must solve (e.g., verbal or nonverbal). The sequential and simultaneous framework for the K–ABC stems from an updated version of a variety of theories (Kamphaus et al., 1995). The foundation lies in a wealth of research in clinical and experimental neuropsychology and cognitive psychology. The sequential and simultaneous theory was primarily developed from two lines of theory: the information processing approach of Luria (1966, 1973, 1980) derived from his neurophysiological observations and empirical research conducted on Luria's model (Das, Kirby, & Jarman, 1975); and the cerebral specialization work of Sperry (1968, 1974), Bogen (1975), Kinsbourne (1978), and Wada, Clarke, and Hamm (1975).

This neuropsychological processing model describes two very distinct types of processes that individuals use to organize and process information received in order to solve problems successfully: successive or sequential, analytic–linear processing versus holistic–simultaneous processing (Levy & Trevarthen, 1976; Luria, 1966). From Sperry's cerebral specialization perspective, these processes represent the problem-solving strategies of the left hemisphere (analytic–sequential) and the right hemisphere (Gestalt–holistic). From Luria's theoretical approach, successive and simultaneous processes reflect the "coding" processes that characterize "Block 2" functions. Regardless of theoretical model, sequential processing refers to the processing of information in a sequential, serial order. The essential nature of this mode of processing is that the system is not totally surveyable at any point in time. Simultaneous processing refers to the synthesis of separate elements into groups such that any portion of the result is, at once, surveyable without dependence on its position in the whole. The model assumes that the two modes of processing information are available to the individual. The selection of either or both modes of processing depends on two conditions: (a) the individual's habitual mode of processing information as determined by social–cultural and genetic factors, and (b) the demands of the task (Das et al., 1975).

One prime goal in the development of the K–ABC was to facilitate the educational translation of test scores. The basic underlying principle is that if clinicians understand how children are best able to process information, then that knowledge can be used to remediate academic deficits (Kaufman & Kaufman, 1983b, chapter 7). Like the debates over the theory underlying the K–ABC, and the degree to which the K–ABC's constructs are direct measures of that theory, there is also controversy over the efficacy of using test scores from the K–ABC or any IQ test for educational intervention (Gresham & Witt, 1997). Interestingly, there is much more acceptance of the K–ABC theory in Europe than in the United States, according to the senior author of the German K–ABC (P. Melchers, personal communication, September 5, 1997).

Nonetheless, comments and criticisms made by colleagues such as Sternberg (1984), Jensen (1984), and Keith (1991) are being given careful consideration as we embark on the process of substantially revising and restandardizing the K–ABC for a release date in 2002 or 2003. Many of the criticisms regarding the choice of theory (Sternberg, 1984), the appropriate interpretation of the major constructs (Keith, 1991), the excess of short-term memory tests (Jensen, 1984; Sternberg, 1984), the minimal inclusion of tests of planning ability (Das, 1984), and the questionable distinction between intelligence and achievement (Anastasi, 1988) have been cogently argued by well-respected psychologists and have compelled us to consider large-scale modifications in the original K–ABC, both in terms of theoretical foundation and scale structure.

THE STANFORD-BINET: FOURTH EDITION (BINET–IV). Like its predecessors, the Binet IV (Thorndike et al., 1986) is based largely on the principle of a general ability factor g rather than on separate abilities, and the scale provides a continuous appraisal of cognitive development from ages 2 years through young adult. Unlike its previous versions, however, the Binet–IV has a decided theoretical basis for its structure, includes discrete subtests (instead of short tasks grouped by age level), and has a healthy dose of nonverbal tests in addition to its traditional emphasis on verbal skills.

The Binet–IV's theoretical foundation is a three-level hierarchical model of the structure of cognitive abilities. A general reasoning factor is at the top level (*g*). The next level consists of three broad factors: crystallized abilities, fluid analytic abilities and short-term memory. The Horn–Cattell (1966, 1967) theory of fluid (*Gf*) and crystallized (*Gc*) intelligence forms a foundation for the test; measures of *Gc* are the school-related Verbal Reasoning and Quantitative Reasoning scales, and the nonverbal, visual–motor Abstract–Visual Reasoning scale constitutes the measure of *Gf*. The third level consists of more specific factors, similar to some of Thurstone's (1938) primary mental factors: verbal reasoning, quantitative reasoning, abstract–visual reasoning, and short-term memory. The selection of these four areas of cognitive abilities came from the authors' research and clinical experience of the kinds of cognitive abilities that correlate with school progress. Taken together, the three levels of the model represent a blend of *g* theory, Horn–Cattell *Gf–Gc* theory, and Thurstone's theory of primary mental abilities. That theoretical foundation for the battery, though in some ways contradictory (Thurstone's theory was developed in opposition to *g* theory), reflects a major contribution of the 1986 Binet over previous Binets and a theoretical contribution to the history of test development.

Unfortunately, the theoretical basis of the Binet–IV was not supported very well by empirical, factor–analytic investigations. Various exploratory and confirmatory techniques did not identify the four hypothesized dimensions (Reynolds, Kamphaus, & Rosenthal, 1988; Sattler, 1988) and also did not provide appropriate support for the Horn–Cattell *Gf–Gc* distinction. In particular, the Binet–IV Quantitative subtests emphasize reasoning ability and join the fluid rather than the hypothesized crystallized dimension; the latter result is not surprising in view of Horn's (1985, 1989, 1991) consistent characterization of quantitative tasks as possessing a healthy dose of *Gf* ability. In addition to the failure of the Binet–IV to demonstrate that it rests on its intended theories, this test has a practical problem. Its standardization sample is heavily weighted with individuals from higher socioeconomic backgrounds (e.g., 46% of the children in the sample had parents in managerial and professional occupations even though the appropriate census figure is 22%; similarly, 44% were at least college graduates, whereas the census percentage is 19). To ad-

just for this discrepancy, a weighting procedure was applied. Although weighting is a legitimate statistical technique, it is more desirable for a standardization sample to include proportionate representation on all key background variables. Reliance on the weighting of data introduces unwanted error into the standardization data, which is what most major test standardization procedures are designed to avoid. Despite the presentation of ample evidence of internal consistency and concurrent validity for its scores, the substantial problems with construct validity, the data collection method, and other difficulties with the Binet–IV led one reviewer to recommend that the battery be laid to rest (Reynolds, 1987): "To the-S–B IV, *Requiescat in pace*" (p. 141).

ORGANIZATION OF REST OF CHAPTER

The preceding portion of this chapter has dealt primarily with the history of IQ testing from the practical factors that shaped its birth to the more recent application of theory to test construction. For the remainder of the chapter, the emphasis will be on describing and discussing six recent tests, all of which were published between 1989 and 1997: the three current Wechsler scales, which remain the most used tests in the United States and abroad, and three instruments that are specifically derived from theory and that have strong empirical support for the match between their scales and the theoretical constructs they were intended to measure. These theory-based tests include the Woodcock–Johnson Psycho-Educational Battery–Revised: Tests of Cognitive Ability (WJ–R; Woodcock & Johnson, 1989), the Kaufman Adolescent and Adult Intelligence Test (KAIT; Kaufman & Kaufman, 1993), and the Das–Naglieri Cognitive Assessment System (CAS) (Naglieri & Das, 1997a). Though the Differential Abilities Scales (DAS; Elliott, 1990) is comparable to these other tests in terms of psychometric quality and popularity, it is not featured in this chapter because it is deliberately not developed from any theoretical base. The DAS is, however, discussed in the later section, Theoretical Critique of Wechsler's Scales, because the scale structure of the DAS permits a greater understanding of the interpretation of the theoretical constructs measured by Wechsler's scales.

The three Wechsler tests and the three theory-driven instruments will each be described in terms of theoretical rationale, the major scales included, and basic psychometric properties (quality of norms, reliability and validity of scores). The tests will be evaluated in terms of quality and the degree to which their theoretical objectives were met. In the case of Wechsler's scales, the theoretical issues will be handled by assessing the degree to which they measure the theoretical constructs that have been posited for its major scores. Readers who are devotees of popular contemporary theories of intelligence (Gardner, 1983; Sternberg, 1985); of the developmental psychology of Jean Piaget; or of the diversity of theories of learning, cognition, and memory will be disappointed to realize that these theories – despite their obvious pertinence to the clinical assessment of intelligence – have barely made a dent in the formulation of current or past IQ tests. Rather, the major theoretical influences by far have come from two sources: the Horn–Cattell theory of fluid and crystallized intelligence and Horn's expansion of that theory, and Luria's (1966) neuropsychological approach to brain functioning. The former theory provides the foundation of the WJ–R and KAIT (and the Binet–IV, as noted earlier), whereas the latter was not only the main inspiration for the K–ABC but also the CAS.

The focus on the importance of theory in this chapter is key because competent interpretation of any IQ test profile depends on providing a suitable theoretical context. Nonetheless, this focus must also be tempered with the decidedly practical uses for IQ tests in contemporary society: *identification* (of mental retardation, learning disabilities, other cognitive disorders, giftedness), *placement* (gifted and other specialized programs), and as a *cognitive adjunct* to a clinical evaluation whose main focus is on personality or neuropsychological evaluation.

The Wechsler scales will be featured first, followed by the theory-based tests. But first, I would like to outline briefly a philosophy of interpretation and use of IQ tests that has been applied to Wechsler's tests (Kaufman, 1979, 1990a, 1994) and my own intelligence tests (Kaufman & Kaufman, 1983a, 1993) but that is broadly applicable to all clinical measures of intellectual ability. I have called this method the "intelligent testing" philosophy, a term initially coined by Wesman (1968). According to Anastasi (1988), this philosophy represents, "A clear illustration of the sophisticated clinical use of intelligence tests, combining psychometric data with qualitative observations [and] . . . with knowledge about human development, personality theory, and other areas of psychological research" (p. 484). And Anastasi and Urbina (1997) observe, concerning Kaufman's basic approach, that, "Even its critics acknowledge that it has become the method of choice for teaching intelligence testing and has guided the creation of much of the software available to aid in the interpretation of intelligence tests" (p. 513).

THE INTELLIGENT TESTING PHILOSOPHY

At the core of the intelligent testing philosophy is the notion that only highly trained scientist-practitioners are legally and ethically permitted to administer and interpret individual intelligence tests, and, therefore, the clinician must occupy a higher rung in the hierarchy than the test itself or the scores it yields. The clinician has accumulated vast stores of classroom knowledge about theories of learning, cognition, personality, development, memory, neuropsychology, special education, and the like; is familiar with the results of a vast array of research investigations in these and related areas; and has received on-site trained supervision in the clinical and behavioral observation of clients of all ages. This knowledge base and clinical experience form the foundation of the interpretation of any test data obtained on the child or adult, and the interpretation, therefore, is unique for every person tested – even if the actual test scores are identical. In essence, when interpreting a Wechsler test or similar scale, "assessment is of the individual, by the individual, and for the individual" (Kaufman, 1994, p. 14). Through research knowledge, theoretical sophistication, and clinical ability, examiners must generate hypotheses about an individual's assets and deficits and then confirm or deny these hypotheses by exploring multiple sources of evidence. Well-validated hypotheses must then be translated into meaningful, practical recommendations. Practitioner-scientists must come well equipped with in-depth understanding of the state-of-the-art instrumentation and select tests that meet exceptional psychometric standards, but good judgment, knowledge of psychology, and clinical training are more important than the particular instrument selected for an evaluation if one is to move beyond the obtained IQs and profile of subtest scores (Kaufman, 1990a, 1994). Each adult and child who comes for an assessment has unique characteristics, a particular way of approaching test items, and may be affected differently by the testing situation than the next individual. Through the use of an integrated interpretation approach, the various dimensions that influence a child can become apparent.

Apart from this general philosophy of test interpretation, the intelligent testing approach is rooted in five basic principles. These have most recently been articulated for the WISC–III (Kaufman, 1994, chapter 1), but they pertain to all of the individual tests of intelligence discussed in this chapter.

1. *The tasks constituting the intelligence tests, whether verbal or nonverbal, measure what the individual has learned.* As such, these tests are like achievement tests in that they measure past accomplishments and are predictive of success in traditional school subjects. Research indicates that intelligence tests consistently prove to be good predictors of conventional school achievement (e.g., Wechsler, 1991, pp. 206–209). Although this connection between the IQ and school achievement is well documented empirically, it should not ultimately be accepted as a statement of fate that if a child earns low IQs he or she will do poorly in school. Instead, constructive interpretation of a test battery can lead to recommendations that may helpfully alter a child's development, and, in effect, kill the prediction by translating test scores to successful educational intervention.

2. *Subtests included in individual IQ tests are samples of behavior and are not exhaustive.* Because the subtests only offer a brief glimpse into a child's overall level of functioning, examiners must be cautious in generalizing the results to performance and behaviors in other circumstances. The WISC–III Full-Scale IQ, for example, "should not be interpreted as an estimate of a child's global or total intellectual functioning; and the WISC–III should be administered along with other measures, and the IQs interpreted in the context of other test scores" (Kaufman, 1994, p. 7). It is important that the actual scores are not emphasized as the bottom line; rather, it is more beneficial to elaborate on what children or adults can do well, relative to their own level of ability, and what causes

them difficulties. However, each IQ test can only include a finite and relatively small number of separate tasks because of practical time constraints. Each test, therefore, can only illustrate aspects of the person's cognitive ability; the likelihood of the test missing important strengths and weaknesses is great, and any obtained global score can never be thought of as truly global. For example, from Sternberg's (1985) triarchic theory, conventional intelligence tests are heavily weighted in measuring analytic abilities but do a poor job of assessing either creative skills or practical, tacit knowledge.

3. *Tasks on IQ tests assess mental functioning under fixed experimental conditions.* Rigid adherence to the standardized procedures for administration and scoring each subtest helps to ensure that all children and adults are measured in an objective manner. However, parts of the standardized procedure make the testing situation very different than a natural setting. For example, it is not very often in everyday life that someone is transcribing virtually every word they say or timing them with a stopwatch. The standardization procedures are important to follow but must be taken into account as limitations when interpreting the scores obtained in the artificial testing situation. The value of the intelligence test is enhanced when the examiner can meaningfully relate observations of the child's or adult's behaviors in the testing situation and specific knowledge about the person's real-life situation to the profile of scores.

4. *Subtests composing an IQ test are optimally useful when interpreted from an information-processing model.* This principle is especially beneficial for helping to hypothesize functional areas of strength and dysfunction. This model suggests examining how information enters the brain from the sense organs (input), how information is interpreted and processed (integration), how information is stored for later retrieval (storage), and how information is expressed linguistically or motorically (output). Through this model, examiners can organize the test data, including fluctuations in subtest scores, into meaningful underlying areas of asset and deficit.

5. *Hypotheses generated from IQ test profiles should be supported with data from multiple sources.* Hypotheses generated solely from profiles of test scores do not hold water unless verified by diverse pieces of data. Such supporting evidence may come from careful observation of a person's behavior during test administration; from the pattern of responses across

various subtests; from background information obtained from parents, teachers, therapists, the client, or from other referral sources; from previous test data; and from the administration of supplemental subtests. The integration of data from all these different sources is critical in obtaining the best and most meaningful clinical interpretation of a test battery.

THE WECHSLER SCALES

First, the theoretical rationale of Wechsler's series of scales is presented. Then, the three most recently revised and restandardized versions, spanning the ages of 3 to 89 years, will be discussed: the 1989 WPPSI–R for preschool and primary-grade children; the 1991 WISC–III for elementary and high school children; and the 1997 WAIS–III for older adolescents through old age. Finally, the series of scales will be evaluated from a theoretical perspective.

Theoretical Rationale

Wechsler (1974) puts forth the definition that "intelligence is the overall capacity of an individual to understand and cope with the world around him [or her]" (p. 5). His tests, however, were not predicated on this definition, as mentioned previously. Tasks developed were not designed from well-researched concepts exemplifying his definition. In fact virtually all of his tasks were adapted from other existing tests. Like Binet's notions, Wechsler's definition of intelligence also subscribes to the conception of intelligence as an overall global entity. He believed that intelligence cannot be tested directly but can only be inferred from how an individual thinks, talks, moves, and reacts to different stimuli. Therefore, Wechsler did not give credence to one task above another but believed that this global entity called intelligence could be ferreted out by probing a person with as many different kinds of mental tasks as one can conjure up. Wechsler did not believe in a cognitive hierarchy for his tasks, and he did not believe that each task was equally effective. He felt that each task was necessary for the fuller appraisal of intelligence.

Wechsler Preschool and Primary Scale of Intelligence – Revised (WPPSI–R)

The WPPSI–R (Wechsler, 1989) is an intelligence test for children aged 3 years, 0 months through 7

years, 3 months. The original version of the WPPSI was developed in 1967 for ages 4 to 6½ years, and the WPPSI–R was revised in 1989. Several changes were made to the revised version of the WPPSI–R. The norms were updated, the appeal of the content to young children was improved, and the age range was expanded.

DESCRIPTION. The WPPSI–R is based on the original Wechsler–Bellevue model of intelligence emphasizing intelligence as a global capacity (and, therefore, providing a Full-Scale IQ) but having Verbal and Performance scales as two methods of assessing this global capacity. The Verbal scale subtests include Information (general factual knowledge, e.g., "What day comes right after Saturday?"), Comprehension (social knowledge and reasoning, e.g., "Why should you keep milk in the refrigerator?"), Arithmetic, Vocabulary, Similarities (verbal analogies and telling how two "things" are alike such as "magazine" and "newspaper"), and Sentences (an optional subtest requiring repetition of a spoken sentence). The Performance scale subtests include Object Assembly (assembling cut-up picture puzzles), Block Design (copying an abstract design with blocks), Mazes, Picture Completion (finding the missing part in a picture, e.g., a ladder missing a rung), Geometric Design (copying abstract designs with paper and pencil), and Animal Pegs (an optional subtest that measures how quickly a child can place a colored peg with the animal that is paired with it).

Like the K–ABC and the DAS, the WPPSI–R allows the examiner to "help" or "teach" the child on early items on the subtests to assure that the child understands what is expected of him or her. Providing this extra help is essential when working with reticent preschoolers (Kamphaus, 1993).

PSYCHOMETRIC PROPERTIES. Like all Wechsler tests, the overall Verbal, Performance, and Full-Scale IQs are standard scores with the mean set at 100 and the standard deviation (*SD*) set at 15. Standard scores, called scaled scores, are provided for the separate subtests (mean = 10, *SD* = 3). The WPPSI–R was standardized on 1,700 children from age 3 through 7 years, 3 months and closely matched 1986 U.S. Census Bureau estimates on the stratification variables of gender, race, geographic region, parental occupation, and parental education.

The WPPSI–R demonstrates good reliability and validity. The internal consistency coefficients average .92 to .96 for the three IQs across age groups and for the Verbal, Performance, and Full-Scale IQs are .95, .92, and .96 respectively. The coefficients for the individual Performance subtests range from .63 for Object Assembly to .85 for Block Design, with a median coefficient of .79; for the individual Verbal subtests, values range from .80 for Arithmetic to .86 for Similarities, with a median coefficient of .84. The test–retest coefficient for the Full-Scale IQ was .91 for 175 children tested twice (interval averaging 4 weeks). Factor analysis provides strong evidence of the division of the subtests into separate Verbal and Performance Scales (Wechsler, 1989).

PSYCHOMETRIC AND CLINICAL CRITIQUE. The WPPSI–R is a thorough revision of the 1967 WPPSI, with an expanded age range, new colorful materials, new item types for very young children, a new icebreaker subtest (Object Assembly), and a comprehensive manual (Kaufman, 1990b). The revision of the test has resulted in an instrument that is more attractive and more engaging and in materials that are easier to use (Buckhalt, 1991; Delugach, 1991). The normative sample is large, provides recent norms, and is representative of the U.S. Census data (Delugach, 1991; Kaufman, 1990b). The split-half reliability of the IQs and most subtests is exceptional, the factor analytic results for all age groups are excellent, and the concurrent validity of the battery is well supported by several excellent correlational studies (Delugach, 1991; Kaufman, 1990b). The manual provides several validity studies, factor analytic results, research overviews, and state-of-the-art interpretive tables that provide the examiner with a wealth of information; the test rests on a solid psychometric foundation (Kaufman, 1990b).

Nonetheless, the WPPSI–R has flaws. It has an insufficient floor at the lowest age levels, which limits the test's ability to diagnose intellectual deficiency in young preschoolers (Delugach, 1991). The directions on some of the Performance subtests are not suitable for young children because they are not developmentally appropriate, and the heavy emphasis on response speed on some nonverbal tests is inappropriate for young children who have not yet internalized the importance of working very quickly (Kaufman, 1990b). However, Delugach (1991) reports that if the directions are too difficult, the test

provides procedures to ensure that the child understands the demands of the task.

Wechsler Intelligence Scale for Children – Third Edition (WISC–III)

The WISC–III (Wechsler, 1991) – geared for children aged 6 years, 0 months through 16 years, 11 months – is a direct descendant of the Wechsler–Bellevue Intelligence Scale, Form II (Wechsler, 1946), WISC (Wechsler, 1949), and WISC–R (Wechsler, 1974).

DESCRIPTION. In addition to yielding Verbal, Performance, and Full-Scale IQs and scaled scores on 13 subtests, the WISC–III offers standard scores (Indexes with mean = 100 and $SD = 15$) on four separate factors: Verbal Comprehension, Perceptual Organization, Freedom from Distractibility, and Processing Speed. The first two factors are composed of Verbal subtests and the last two consist of Performance subtests. Within the WISC–III are 10 mandatory and 3 supplementary subtests. The Verbal scale's 5 mandatory subtests include Information, Similarities, Arithmetic, Vocabulary, and Comprehension; Digit Span (repeating one set of numbers in the same sequence spoken by the examiner and a second set in the reverse sequence) is supplementary. The five required Performance subtests are Picture Completion, Picture Arrangement (arranging cartoonlike pictures in the right order to tell a story), Block Design, Object Assembly, and Coding (rapidly copying symbols that are paired either with other symbols or with numbers). The two supplementary Performance subtests are Mazes and Symbol Search. The latter task, which joins Coding to form the Processing Speed scale, requires children to scan one or two "target" symbols rapidly and then determine whether a target symbol is included in an array of symbols. The Freedom from Distractibility factor is composed of Arithmetic and Digit Span, both of which are extremely susceptible to the influences of distractibility and are dependent on attention, concentration, memory, sequencing ability, and numerical facility.

PSYCHOMETRIC PROPERTIES. The WISC–III was standardized on 2,200 children ranging in age from 6 through 16 years and stratified by age, gender, race–ethnicity, geographic region, and parent education. "Overall, the standardization of the

WISC–III is immaculate...a better – standardized intelligence test does not exist" (Kaufman, 1993b, p. 351). The average reliability, across the age groups, for the IQs and Factor Indexes are .95 for the Verbal IQ, .91 for the Performance IQ, .96 for the Full-Scale IQ, .94 for the Verbal Comprehension Index, .90 for the Perceptual Organization Index, .87 for the Freedom from Distractibility Index, and .85 for the Processing Speed Index (Wechsler, 1991). Exploratory and confirmatory factor analyses offer strong support for the psychological meaningfulness and construct validity of the four factors that underlie the WISC–III (Roid, Prifitera, & Weiss, 1993; Wechsler, 1991).

Although Coding is listed as the regular Performance subtest for computing Performance IQ, Symbol Search is able to be substituted for it. The manual does not specify when it may be substituted, and thus I have recommended that Symbol Search ought always to replace Coding. Whereas Mazes is listed as an accepted replacement for any spoiled Performance subtest, I do not believe it should be given at all. "Symbol Search is an excellent task that should have been included among the five regular Performance subtests instead of Coding. Mazes is an awful task that should have been dropped completely from the WISC–III" (Kaufman, 1994, p. 58); "there's no rational reason for the publisher to have rigidly clung to Coding as a regular part of the WISC–III when the new Symbol Search task is clearly a better choice for psychometric reasons" (p. 59).

PSYCHOMETRIC AND CLINICAL CRITIQUE. Professionals in the field of intelligence testing have described the third edition of the Wechsler Intelligence Scale for Children in a number of different ways. Some critics feel that the WISC–III reflects continuity, the status quo, but makes little progress in the evolution of the assessment of intelligence. Such critics note that despite more than 50 years of advancement in theories of intelligence, the Wechsler philosophy of intelligence (not actually a formal theory), written in 1939, remains the guiding principle of the WISC–III (Shaw, Swerdilik, & Laurent, 1993). One of the principal goals for developing the WISC–III stated in the manual was merely to update the norms, which is "hardly a revision at all" (Sternberg, 1993). If one has chosen to use the WISC–III because he or she is looking for a test of new constructs in intelligence, or merely a new test,

one should look elsewhere (Sternberg, 1993). In contrast to these fairly negative evaluations, I have noted some positives: "The normative sample is exemplary, and the entire psychometric approach to test development, validation, and interpretation reflects sophisticated, state-of-the-art knowledge and competence" (Kaufman, 1993b). On the negative side, I was disappointed to see such a great emphasis given to speed of responding – bonus points are awarded liberally for quick, perfect visual–motor responses on several Performance subtests and were even awarded on Arithmetic, placing too much stress on speed and too little on power. Also disappointing to me was the systematic elimination of many of the clinical items on the test (e.g., Picture Arrangement items involving violence); those were David Wechsler's favorite items and reflected his belief that his IQ tests were primarily clinical instruments designed to evoke emotional as well as cognitive responses.

Wechsler Adult Intelligence Scale – Third Edition (WAIS–III)

The newest member of the Wechsler family of tests is the WAIS–III (The Psychological Corporation, 1997; Wechsler, 1997), for adults ages 16 to 89 years. Its lineage includes the original Wechsler–Bellevue Intelligence Scale, Form I (Wechsler, 1939), WAIS (Wechsler, 1955), and WAIS–R (Wechsler, 1981). The WAIS–III is the first Wechsler adult scale to be normed with a carefully stratified sample above the age of 74.

DESCRIPTION. The new WAIS–III was formatted to be similar to the WISC–III, that is, it includes Verbal, Performance, and Full-Scale IQs and Indexes on four factors, all with mean of 100 and *SD* of 15, and scaled scores on 14 subtests (mean = 10, *SD* = 3), seven Verbal and seven Performance. Three factors have the same names as WISC–III factors – Verbal Comprehension, Perceptual Organization, and Processing Speed – and the fourth factor is called Working Memory. The latter factor resembles the WISC–III Freedom from Distractibility factor but includes a new subtest (Letter–Number Sequencing) in addition to Arithmetic and Digit Span. For this new subtest, the examiner reads series of stimuli that alternate between numbers and letters; the adult has to say the numbers in numerical order, from low to high, and the letters in alphabetic sequence. This new task draws from cognitive research and theory on working memory (e.g., Baddeley, 1986; Woltz, 1988). All three subtests demand auditory processing, however, so the test publishers consider the new task to be more consistent with Richardson's (1996) minimizing of the distinction between verbal and visual working memory than with multicomponent theory (Baddeley, 1986; Logie, 1995) that distinguishes between the storage and processing of verbal and spatial systems (The Psychological Corporation, 1997). Another theoretical advance in the WAIS–III concerns a new subtest, Matrix Reasoning (solving complex abstract analogies), which is a measure of the kind of fluid intelligence that Horn (1989) used to exemplify his fluid construct.

The WAIS–III subtests are organized as follows into the four factors (the number denotes the order of test administration):

VERBAL SUBTESTS	PERFORMANCE SUBTESTS
VERBAL COMPREHENSION FACTOR	PERCEPTUAL ORGANIZATION FACTOR
2. Vocabulary	1. Picture Completion
4. Similarities	5. Block Design
9. Information	7. Matrix Reasoning
WORKING MEMORY FACTOR	PROCESSING SPEED FACTOR
6. Arithmetic	3. Digit Symbol–Coding
8. Digit Span	12. Symbol Search (supplementary subtest that can replace Digit Symbol–Coding if it is spoiled)
13. Letter–Number Sequencing (supplementary Subtest, can replace Digit Span)	
EXCLUDED FROM INDEXES	EXCLUDED FROM INDEXES
11. Comprehension	10. Picture Arrangement
	14. Object Assembly (supplementary subtest that can replace a spoiled Performance subtest for ages 16–74)

The WPPSI–R and WISC–III each include the same number of mandatory Verbal and Performance sub-

tests (five of each). In contrast, the WAIS–III, like its adult predecessors, includes six regular verbal subtests (Vocabulary, Similarities, Arithmetic, Digit Span, Information, and Comprehension), and five mandatory Performance tasks (Picture Completion, Picture Arrangement, Block Design, Matrix Reasoning, and the renamed Digit Symbol-Coding).

PSYCHOMETRIC PROPERTIES. The WAIS–III was standardized on 2,450 adult subjects, selected according to 1995 U.S. Census data, and stratified according to age, sex, race–ethnicity, geographic region, and education level. Subjects were divided into 13 age groups between 16–17 and 85–89 with each age group including 100 to 200 people. In the collection of normative data, an additional 200 African-American and Hispanic individuals were also administered the WAIS–III without discontinue rules: "This over sampling provided a sufficient number of item scores across all items for item bias analyses" (The Psychological Corporation, 1997, p. 20).

Average split-half reliability coefficients across the 13 age groups are as follows: .97 for Verbal IQ, .94 for Performance IQ, and .98 for Full-Scale IQ. The average value for Processing Speed Index was .87 (a test–retest coefficient because split-half is not applicable for highly speeded tasks), and the split-half coefficients averaged .93 to .96 for the other three Indexes. The average individual subtest reliabilities ranged from .93 (Vocabulary) to .70 (Object Assembly) with a median coefficient of .85. Stability coefficients based on 394 adults from four broad age groups tested twice (interval averaging about 5 weeks) were as follows: Verbal IQ (.94–.97), Performance IQ (.88–.92), and Full-Scale IQ (.95–.97).

The WAIS–III Technical Manual (The Psychological Corporation, 1997) reports that numerous factor analytic studies (exploratory and confirmatory) supported the underlying four-factor structure of the WAIS–III for ages 16 to 74 years, thereby offering construct validity support for these ages. For ages 75–89, however, the Perceptual Organization factor was meager (only Matrix Reasoning had a loading above .40), with most Performance subtests joining the Processing Speed Index.

PSYCHOMETRIC AND CLINICAL CRITIQUE. The WAIS–III is likely to follow in the footsteps of the

WAIS–R, which has proven itself as a leader in the field of adult assessment. The new norms and psychometric improvements of the WAIS–III are much welcomed by the assessment community. The WAIS–III has strong reliability and validity for Verbal, Performance, and Full-Scale IQs, as did its predecessor, the WAIS–R. The subtest with the lowest split-half reliability has been removed from the computation of the IQs (Object Assembly). However, Picture Arrangement still exhibits split-half reliability coefficients below .75 at several ages, yet it remains part of the Performance IQ. The WAIS–III standardization sample selection was done with precision, leading to an overall well-stratified sample.

Many visual and practical improvements were made in the development of the WAIS–III. Administration is not difficult with the clear and easy to read WAIS–III manual in addition to the record form with ample space and visual icons (Kaufman & Lichtenberger, 1999). The administration and scoring rules of the WAIS–III were made more uniform throughout the entire test, which reduces chances of examiner error, which is always a problem to be dealt with by examiners of any Wechsler test (Kaufman, 1990a, chapter 4).

The WAIS–III attempted to improve its floor and ceiling in comparison with the earlier version. Several step-down items have been added on each subtest for lower functioning individuals. However, like the WAIS–R, individuals who are extremely gifted or severely retarded cannot be adequately assessed with the WAIS–III because the range of possible Full-Scale IQs is only 45 to 155 (by contrast, the range for the WPPSI–R is 41 to 160, and the range for the WISC–III is 40 to 160). As on the WAIS–R, even if adults earn a raw score of zero on a subtest, they will receive one to five scaled-score points on that subtest.

The WAIS–III predecessors used a reference group (ages 20–34) to determine everyone's scaled scores – a practice that, happily, was dropped for the new test; the WAIS–III computes scaled scores for each individual based solely on his or her chronological age, which is the same procedure used for Wechsler's children's scales. The reference group technique was indefensible because use of this single reference group impaired profile interpretation below age 20 and above 34, with the applicability of norms for ages 20 to 34 becoming extremely questionable for elderly individuals. Also, the WAIS–III manual and record forms themselves provide the beginning to interpretation with clearly laid out tables to calculate score discrepancies and so forth.

The organization of the two scales into four factors on both the WISC–III and WAIS–III represents a departure from Wechsler's clinical, armchair division of subtests into the Verbal and Performance Scales. Wechsler's decision was based on the fact that all Verbal subtests require both verbal comprehension and verbal expression whereas all Performance subtests (though they demand following verbal directions) require nonverbal responding (or permit it on Picture Completion). The use of the four Factor Indexes, however, was an empirical decision based on the results of factor analysis rather than a clinical decision. And just as the use of the four factors represents a psychometric departure from a clinical perspective, so, too, does the shift from the label Freedom from Distractibility (a term that denotes a behavior) to Working Memory reflect a research and theory-based shift. The introduction of four factors, divided equally between the Verbal and Performance Scales, also has a facilitating effect on interpreting the profile of test scores by providing a built-in organization that proceeds from global to specific (IQs to Factor Indexes to scaled scores). Systematic, stepwise approaches to test interpretation have been developed to aid examiners in taking advantage of the new scale structure of the WISC–III (Kaufman, 1994) and WAIS–III (Kaufman & Lichtenberger, 1998, 1999).

The failure to obtain construct validity evidence for all four factors for individuals ages 75 to 89 years is a problem for those who routinely evaluate elderly populations. The Performance IQ seems to be more a measure of visual–motor speed than problem solving for this group, bringing into question the construct validity of the entire Performance Scale and of the Perceptual Organization Index as measures of cognitive ability for those aged 75 and above. In addition, an analysis of age differences in performance on the WAIS–III subtests, factors, and subtests across the broad age span covered by the WAIS–III raises some issues about the interpretation of the Working Memory Index for individuals in their 50s through 80s. Each component subtest has a distinctly different relationship to age: Arithmetic is an ability that is maintained across most of the life span, whereas Digit Span shows the tage-related vulnerability that is characteristic of short-term memory tasks, and Letter–Number Sequencing demonstrates the dramatic decreases in old age that typify measures of fluid reasoning (Kaufman, 1998).

Theoretical Critique of Wechsler's Scales

If one were to evaluate the Wechsler scales from the vantage point of several popular theories of intelligence, they would fall short. For example, Sternberg (1993) has noted, regarding his own triarchic theory, that the WISC–III "is a decent measure of memory–analytic abilities... [but] provides only a poor measure of synthetic–creative and practical–contextual abilities, as is true of virtually all conventional intelligence tests" (p. 162). Sternberg (1993) further indicates that the WISC–III measures only three of Gardner's (1983) multiple intelligences: linguistic, logical–mathematical, and spatial. But these and other cognitive theories have not been shown to provide suitable frameworks for a clinical test of intelligence and are not necessarily the appropriate yardsticks for comparison. In the case of Wechsler's tests, the most relevant theories are the ones that have generated the most pertinent research using Wechsler's subtests or related tasks: cerebral specialization theory and Horn–Cattell *Gf–Gc* theory.

Initial notions of the specialization of the two hemispheres of the brain focused on the verbal nature of the left hemisphere and the nonverbal–spatial nature of the right hemisphere (Reitan, 1955; Sperry, 1968). From that type of "content" interpretation, the Wechsler scales were a natural to reflect a strong theoretical basis. The prediction was obvious in that damage confined to a particular half of the brain should affect only one of the separate IQs, either Verbal or Performance, but not both. The early researchers "validated" this hypothesis (e.g., Reitan, 1955; Dennerll, 1964; Klove, 1959), but subsequent investigators noted methodological flaws in the preliminary research studies and offered results that were less supportive of the link between cerebral specialization theory and the Wechsler scales (e.g., Smith, 1966). An accumulation of studies with the WAIS and WAIS–R with more than 1,400 patients having lesions to either the left or right hemisphere indicated that Performance IQ does seem to be af-

fected negatively by damage to the right hemisphere (10-point decrement) but the Verbal IQ is only trivially affected by left-hemisphere damage ($2\frac{1}{2}$-point decrement) (Kaufman, 1990a, Table 9.7).

The partial validation of the theory, however, may be due more to the failure of the initial theory to reflect the true specialization capacities of the two hemispheres. As more research was conducted by Sperry and his colleagues, the verbal versus nonverbal "content" distinction gave way to an analytic–sequential versus gestalt–holistic "process" distinction between the left and right hemispheres, respectively (Levy & Trevarthen, 1976). Wechsler organized his subtests into two scales based on the content demands of each task, not the process demands, and thus the link between the IQ test and psychological theory was not as intuitive as Reitan and others had believed.

Matarazzo (1972) was probably the first to identify Wechsler's Verbal IQ as a good measure of *Gc* ability and the Performance IQ of *Gf* ability, and that correspondence was accepted almost axiomatically by many researchers, especially those who were investigating IQ changes across the adult life span (Kaufman, 1990a, chapter 7). The original Horn–Cattell theory posited broad fluid and broad crystallized dimensions (Horn & Cattell, 1966, 1967), and most cognitive tasks were readily categorized by these theorists into the fluid arena (if the task demanded new problem solving with minimal dependency on school learning or acculturation) or the crystallized domain (if the task was education dependent).

As Horn (1985, 1989) expanded *Gf–Gc* theory, he shifted his focus to an array of eight to ten abilities that were more "pure" in terms of what they measured. From current Horn theory, tasks are only categorized as *Gf* if they emphasize reasoning ability and as *Gc* if they stress comprehension and knowledge base. Previously, "contamination" with other abilities was acceptable; for example, many *Gf* tasks also depended on memory (short- and long-term), visualization, and speed, whereas numerous *Gc* tasks required short-term memory, auditory processing, quantitative thinking, and fluid reasoning for correct solutions. From the standpoint of Horn's expanded theory, Wechsler's Verbal Scale corresponds to two abilities, *Gc* and short-term apprehension and retrieval (SAR), and the Performance Scale reflects *Gf*, broad visualization (*Gv*), and broad speediness (*Gs*).

One of the current ability tests for ages 2$\frac{1}{2}$–17 years, the individually administered DAS (Elliott, 1990) was developed from tradition and statistical analysis rather than from a theoretical foundation; yet, ironically, its scale structure is such that it has enabled researchers to gain greater insight into the theoretical interpretation of Wechsler's Performance Scale. The DAS is a battery of 17 cognitive and achievement tests, standardized on a representative sample of 3,475 children, that has been reviewed quite positively (Braden, 1992; Sandoval, 1992). Though the DAS is not based on a specific theory of intelligence, Elliott (1990) described his approach to the development of the DAS as "eclectic" and cited researchers and theorists such as Cattell, Horn, Das, Jensen, Thurstone, Vernon, and Spearman as influential in the choices he made. Elliott endorses Thurstone's ideas that the emphasis on intellectual assessment should be on the assessment and interpretation of distinct abilities (Kamphaus, 1993). He also stresses that in the assessment of children with learning and developmental disabilities, clinicians need more fine detail than is provided by a global IQ (Elliott, 1997).

The cognitive portion of the DAS consists of "core" and "diagnostic" subtests designed to assess intelligence at the preschool level and the school-age level. The core subtests measure complex processing and conceptual ability, which are strongly *g*-related. The diagnostic subtests measure less cognitively complex functions, such as short-term memory and processing speed, thereby having less of a *g* saturation (Elliott, 1997). Six of the core subtests at the school-age level are organized into three two-subtest scales – Verbal Ability, Nonverbal Reasoning, and Spatial Ability – which together yield a global measure of intelligence called General Conceptual Ability (GCA).

It is the three core clusters in the DAS that have facilitated a better theoretical understanding of Wechsler's scales. From Horn's expanded theory there are some clear-cut relationships between the three Core scales and theoretical constructs: Horn's (1985, 1989, 1991) concepts of *Gf* and *Gc* are measured quite well by the Nonverbal Reasoning and

Verbal Ability scales, respectively, and the Spatial Ability cluster seems to correspond to *Gv*. Therefore, if Wechsler's scales are jointly analyzed with the DAS Core clusters, researchers will have a better idea of what the Performance Scale measures. Do the Performance subtests align more with the DAS marker of *Gf* (Nonverbal Reasoning) or of *Gv* (Spatial Ability), or do they split up such that some Performance subtests are more associated with *Gf* and others with *Gv*?

Stone (1992) conducted this important study with a sample of 115 normal children tested on both the WISC–R and DAS. He reported the results of a confirmatory factor analysis that clearly showed Wechsler's Performance subtests to be associated only with the factor defined by DAS Spatial Ability subtests and not at all with the DAS Nonverbal Reasoning subtests. The theoretical implication of this finding is that Wechsler's Performance Scale is more a measure of Horn's *Gv* ability than of his *Gf* ability, even though the Performance subtests have almost axiomatically been treated in numerous research investigations as measures of fluid intelligence. Similar factor analyses conducted by Woodcock (1990) with his Woodcock–Johnson cognitive battery reinforced the findings with the DAS, indicating that when scales composed of *Gf* and *Gv* subtests are factor analyzed with Wechsler's Performance Scale, Wechsler's tasks invariably load on factors defined by the visual–spatial *Gv* abilities and not the reasoning-oriented *Gf* abilities.

Some researchers, notably Woodcock (1990) and Flanagan and McGrew (1997), insist that Wechsler's Performance IQ denotes *only* *Gv*, with virtually no *Gf* at all, but that position is arguable. Horn (1989) described *Gv* as requiring mind's-eye rotation of objects in space, or the ability to identify partially completed drawings (Gestalt Completion tasks) without demanding reasoning ability. Horn still considers Wechsler's Performance subtests (except for highly speeded tasks like Digit Symbol–Coding) to measure a blend of *Gf* and *Gv* (Horn & Hofer, 1992), and that interpretation seems more parsimonious with the accumulated research and with clinicians' first-hand observations of the clear-cut problem-solving components of tasks like Block Design and Picture Arrangement (Kaufman, 1994). Overall, Wechsler's tests provide a reasonably good match to the initial *Gf* and *Gc* constructs posited by Horn and Cattell and a moderate match to Horn's expansion of the theory. The only Performance subtest that is an excellent measure of Horn's refined notion of *Gf* – without confounds due to speed, spatial ability, coordination, or memory – is the new WAIS–III Matrix Reasoning task.

THREE RECENT THEORY-BASED IQ TESTS

The next sections delve into the 1989 Woodcock-Johnson Psycho-Educational Battery–Revised: Tests of Cognitive Ability (WJ–R), derived from Horn's expanded *Gf–Gc* theory; the 1993 Kaufman Adolescent and Adult Intelligence Test rooted in the Horn–Cattell *Gf–Gc* theory and, to some extent, in Piaget's and Luria's theories; and the 1997 Das–Naglieri Cognitive Assessment System built to correspond to all three Blocks of Luria's neuropsychological theory.

Woodcock–Johnson Psycho-Educational Battery – Revised: Tests of Cognitive Ability (WJ–R)

The original Woodcock–Johnson Psycho-Educational Battery: Tests of Cognitive Ability (WJ; Woodcock & Johnson, 1977) made a major contribution to test development because of its inclusion of a diversity of novel tasks that represented the first major departure from subtests originally developed by Binet or by World War I psychologists. The WJ, however, was developed from an entirely practical perspective with no apparent emphasis on theory. All that changed with the publication of the WJ–R (Woodcock & Johnson, 1989; Woodcock & Mather, 1989), an expanded and reformulated test battery that is rooted firmly in Horn's modified *Gf–Gc* psychometric theory of intelligence.

DESCRIPTION AND THEORETICAL RATIONALE.
The WJ–R is one of the most comprehensive test batteries available for the clinical assessment of children, adolescents, and adults (Kamphaus, 1993). It is a battery of tests for individuals from ages 2 to 90+ years and is composed of two sections, Cognitive and Achievement. Though the Achievement portion is probably the most widely used individual measure of academic achievement, the focus of this discussion is the Cognitive portion

of the WJ–R. As noted, the WJ–R Cognitive battery is based on Horn's (1985, 1989) expansion of the fluid–crystallized model of intelligence, which encompasses about 8 to 10 separate abilities. The standard cognitive battery (seven subtests, one per Horn ability) and supplemental subtests (an additional 14 tasks) of the WJ–R are aligned with seven of the cognitive abilities isolated by Horn (1985, 1989; Horn & Hofer, 1992): long-term retrieval, short-term memory, processing speed, auditory processing, visual processing, comprehension–knowledge, and fluid reasoning. An eighth ability, quantitative ability (*Gq*), is measured by several subtests on the Achievement portion of the WJ–R. The seven Horn abilities, each measured by two to four WJ–R subtests, are defined as follows:

Long-term retrieval (Glr or TSR) – retrieval of information stored minutes or a couple of days earlier measured with paired-associate learning tasks (learning the names of space creatures and learning a new language in which words are paired with symbols); both tasks have "delayed" versions to assess how many paired associates are retained after several days.

Short-term memory (Gsm or SAR) – storage and retrieval of auditory information, either immediately or within a few seconds, measured by tasks requiring the recall of sentences, words, and numbers in their reversed sequence.

Processing speed (*Gs*) – working quickly on clerical, visual-motor tasks, particularly under pressure to maintain focused attention.

Auditory processing (*Ga*) – demonstrating the ability to perceive patterns fluently among auditory stimuli, e.g., hearing the incomplete word stimulus "kra_er" and responding "cracker."

Visual processing (*Gv*) – demonstrating the visual–spatial ability of perceiving patterns, rotating objects in space, and retaining visual images.

Comprehension–knowledge (crystallized intelligence or *Gc*) – demonstrating the breadth and depth of one's education-related knowledge of a culture, in this instance by one's vocabulary (naming pictured objects, giving antonyms and synonyms of spoken words).

Fluid reasoning (*Gf*) – applying reasoning ability to solve new problems that are not facilitated by one's schooling or acculturation.

Each subtest and cluster score (one per Horn ability) yields standard scores with a mean of 100 and a standard deviation of 15. Though a Broad Cognitive Ability global score is provided, also with mean = 100 and $SD = 15$, it is deemphasized just as Horn has little use for g within his system. Examiners are encouraged to administer whatever portion of the 21 subtests they choose, depending on their assessment goals. One psychometric (i.e., not theoretical) grouping of selected subtests permits the diagnosis of possible learning disabilities by comparing predicted to actual achievement in specific academic areas.

PSYCHOMETRIC PROPERTIES. The WJ–R was normed on a reasonably representative sample of 6,359 individuals selected to provide a cross section of the U.S. population from age 2 to 90+ (Woodcock & Mather, 1989). The sample included 705 preschool children, 3,245 students in grades K–12, 916 college–university students, and 1,493 individuals aged 14 to 90+ who were not enrolled in school. Stratification variables included gender, geographic region, community size, and race. Although representation on important background variables was adequate, it was necessary to use a weighting procedure to adjust the data so it would match U.S. population statistics. The internal consistency estimates for the standard and supplemental battery subtests are good, as median values for ages 2 to 79 ranged from .69 to .93. The Broad Cognitive Ability composite score for the seven standard battery subtests yields a median internal consistency coefficient of .94. Factor-analytic support for the seven Horn abilities is strong (Woodcock, 1990).

PSYCHOMETRIC, CLINICAL, AND THEORETICAL CRITIQUE. The Cognitive battery is quite thorough and, when administered in its entirety, can provide the examiner with a wealth of information about an individual's intellectual functioning and abilities. The test materials and manuals are easy to use and well designed. The administration is fairly simple; however, scoring the test, especially when the Achievement battery is administered as well, can be quite a lengthy and, initially, a difficult process. The scoring, if done by hand, is a nightmare; the easy-to-use computer-scoring software program is essential for a WJ–R user.

Webster (1994) raises issues with the specific psychometric procedures used in developing test items, and I have expressed concerns about the small number of tests that make up each scale (Kaufman, 1990a). Because poor performance on any subtest can be due to attentional, motivational, or emotional variables that have little to do with the specific ability measured by the task, one can never be certain that a test is measuring its intended process. When only one or two subtests are used to define each Horn ability, there is always potential doubt whether the examiner has truly obtained the individual's accurate performance level on each cluster. When several measures of an ability are administered, there is a broader basis for making inferences about skill levels, and, especially, about fluctuations within the seven-cluster profile.

Several standardization procedures were used in the WJ–R that are not typical of those used to create norms for the intelligence tests described in this chapter. First, although the sample was stratified on most of the usual variables, the individual child's parental education level or socioeconomic status level was not directly determined. Instead, children included in the standardization sample were given a socioeconomic status (SES) level based upon the characteristics of the school they attended, not a level reported by their parent or guardian. Therefore, the data at the individual child level are not available to evaluate precisely the SES level of the children included in the WJ–R normative sample. Second, examiners who collected standardization data were mostly substitute teachers and paraprofessionals who were not required to have had prior professional training. Standardization examiners for other major IQ tests have typically had much higher levels of clinical training.

Overall, the WJ–R was a carefully developed instrument that matches its intended theory quite closely. It is a good translation of theory to practice, according to theorist John Horn, based on several conversations I have had with him about the WJ–R during the early 1990s. McGrew, Flanagan, Keith, and Vanderwood (1997) caution that the *Gf–Gc* theory is "largely a product of linear equations (viz., factor analysis)...and is most likely not a good indication of the organization of actual human abilities" (p. 194). Nonetheless, I agree with Esters, Ittenbach, and Han (1997) that, "Quite possibly the best and purest example of *Gf–Gc* theory as operationally defined by an IQ test is the [WJ–R]"(p. 212). The excellent match of the WJ–R to the expanded Horn theory does, though, have a potential downside regarding its clinical utility. By limiting reasoning ability to the *Gf* cluster, a large majority of the skill areas do not have any stress on problem solving. The *Gc* cluster is merely a measure of vocabulary rather than a more broadly defined *Gc* construct, and other clusters (notably *Ga*, *Gv*, and *Gs*) are primarily perceptual or visual–motor scales that seem to lack the complexity and high-level thinking that one may wish for in a test of intelligence. Still, the WJ–R has made an enormous contribution to test development. Even if it is used to supplement other scales, such as Wechsler's, instead of as the comprehensive measure of intelligence, its rich diversity of tasks is valuable for following up clinical hypotheses. In particular, it includes fairly pure measures of *Gf* as well as true learning tasks (such as the *Glr* paired-associate subtests) that are basically excluded from Wechsler's system.

Kaufman Adolescent and Adult Intelligence Test (KAIT)

DESCRIPTION AND THEORETICAL RATIONALE. The Kaufman Adolescent and Adult Intelligence Test (KAIT) (Kaufman & Kaufman, 1993) is an individually administered intelligence test for individuals between the ages of 11 and more than 85 years. It provides Fluid, Crystallized, and Composite IQs, each a standard score with a mean of 100 and a standard deviation of 15. It includes a Core Battery of six subtests (three Fluid and three Crystallized) and an Expanded Battery that also includes alternate Fluid and Crystallized subtests plus measures of delayed recall of information learned earlier in the evaluation during two of the Core subtests. Each subtest (except a supplementary Mental Status task) yields age-based scaled scores with a mean of 10 and a standard deviation of 3. Whenever possible, subtests were designed to be realistic; for example, the Crystallized Auditory Comprehension subtest is a mock news broadcast on cassette. Sample and teaching items are included for most subtests to ensure that examinees understand what is expected of them for each subtest.

The Horn–Cattell theory forms the foundation of the KAIT and defines the constructs believed to be measured by the separate IQs; however, other theories guided the test development process, specifically the construction of the subtests. Tasks were developed from the models of Piaget's formal operations (Inhelder & Piaget, 1958; Piaget, 1972) and Luria's (1973, 1980) planning ability in an attempt to include high-level decision making and more developmentally advanced tasks. Luria's notion of planning ability involves decision making, evaluation of hypotheses, and flexibility and "represents the highest levels of development of the mammalian brain" (Golden, 1981, p. 285).

As noted previously, Horn and Cattell (1966, 1967) postulated a structural model that separates fluid from crystallized intelligence. Fluid intelligence traditionally involves relatively culture-fair novel tasks and taps problem-solving skills and the ability to learn. Crystallized intelligence refers to acquired skill, knowledge, and judgments that have been systematically taught or learned via acculturation. The latter type of intelligence is highly influenced by formal and informal education and often reflects cultural assimilation. Tasks measuring fluid ability often involve more concentration and problem solving than crystallized tasks, which tend to measure retrieval and application of general knowledge.

Piaget's formal operations depict a hypothetical–deductive abstract reasoning system that has as its featured capabilities the generation and evaluation of hypotheses and the testing of propositions. The prefrontal areas of the brain associated with planning ability mature at about ages 11–12 years (Golden, 1981), the same ages that characterize the onset of formal operational thought (Piaget, 1972). The convergence of the Luria and Piaget theories regarding the ability to deal with abstractions is striking; this convergence provided the rationale for having age 11 as the lower bound of the KAIT and for attempting to measure decision making and abstract thinking with virtually every task on the KAIT (Kaufman & Kaufman, 1993). And although abstract thinking was emphasized, visual-motor speed and coordination were deliberately deemphasized.

Within the KAIT framework (Kaufman & Kaufman, 1993), Crystallized intelligence "measures the acquisition of facts and problem-solving ability using stimuli that are dependent on formal schooling, cultural experiences, and verbal conceptual development'' (p. 7). Fluid intelligence ''measures a person's adaptability and flexibility when faced with new problems, using both verbal and nonverbal stimuli''(Kaufman & Kaufman, 1993, p. 7). It is important to note that this Crystallized–Fluid construct split is not the same as Wechsler's verbal-nonverbal split. This was documented in the results of joint factor analyses of WISC–R/KAIT and WAIS–R/KAIT. Both analyses gave the same results (Kaufman & Kaufman, 1993). Three factors defined the abilities measured jointly by the KAIT and Wechsler tests: one factor composed of both KAIT Crystallized and Wechsler Verbal subtests; one composed only of KAIT Fluid subtests; and one composed only of Wechsler's Performance subtests. The conclusion was that the crystallized dimension is the same in both test batteries but that the KAIT Fluid Scale measures an ability quite distinct from the ability measured by Wechsler's Performance Scale. The KAIT Fluid subtests stress reasoning rather than visual–spatial ability, include verbal comprehension or expression as key aspects of some tasks, and minimize the role played by visual–motor speed for correct responding.

The KAIT scales measure what Horn (1989) refers to as broad fluid and broad crystallized abilities rather than the purer and more specific skill areas that have emerged in Horn's expansion and elaboration of the original Horn–Cattell Gf–Gc theory and in Cattell's (1963) earlier work, as discussed previously concerning the WJ–R. The decision to use the broad definitions of the constructs was based on clinical as well as theoretical considerations. Wechsler believed that constructs should be complex and that IQ tests should be based on a small number of broad constructs to obtain comprehensive measurement on these complex dimensions. Too much fragmentation of constructs leads to narrow abilities that are not optimally suited for assessing human intelligence. Because Wechsler was my primary mentor (I worked closely with him in the 1970s during the development and standardization of the WISC–R), his clinical influence is felt in the decision to use the broad Gf–Gc constructs. However, my interest in theory (and that of my wife and coauthor, Nadeen Kaufman) also led to the choice of how to organize the scales. Our research interests in aging and IQ across the life span indicated that Gf–Gc theory is the most pertinent one for explaining ob-

served patterns of growth and decline across the age span covered by the KAIT. A large body of research indicates that Gc abilities are mostly maintained throughout the adult life span, whereas Gf abilities peak in the late teens and early 20s before declining steadily throughout the aging process. And because we used the Piaget and Luria theories as ''entrance'' requirements for a task's inclusion in the KAIT, that ensured that the KAIT would measure broad constructs; for example, the stipulation that virtually each task measure formal operational thought necessitated that each Gc subtest also include a certain amount of reasoning (Gf) ability.

In addition to the broad Gf and Gc abilities measured by the IQ scales, the KAIT offers reasonably pure measurement of another Horn ability when the Expanded Battery is given. The delayed recall subtests are administered without prior warning about 25 and 45 minutes after the administration of the original related subtests. The two delayed recall subtests provide good measure of an ability that Horn (1985, 1989) calls TSR (Long-Term Storage and Retrieval), which is also called Glr in the WJ–R. This long-term memory ability ''involves the storage of information and the fluency of retrieving it later through association'' (Woodcock, 1990, p. 234).

PSYCHOMETRIC PROPERTIES. The KAIT normative sample, composed of 2,000 adolescents and adults between the ages of 11 and 94 years, was stratified on the variables of gender, racial–ethnic group, geographic region, and socioeconomic status (Kaufman & Kaufman, 1993). Mean split-half reliability coefficients for the total normative sample were .95 for Crystallized IQ, .95 for Fluid IQ, and .97 for Composite IQ (Kaufman & Kaufman, 1993). Mean test–retest reliability coefficients, based on 153 identified normal individuals in three age groups (11–19, 20–54, 55–85+), retested after a 1-month interval, were .94 for Crystallized IQ, .87 for Fluid IQ, and .94 for Composite IQ. Mean split-half reliabilities of the four Crystallized subtests ranged from .89 to .92 (median = .90), and mean values for the four Fluid subtests ranged from .79 to .93 (median = .88). Factor analysis, both exploratory and confirmatory, gave strong construct validity support for the Fluid and Crystallized Scales and for the placement of each subtest on its designated scale. Correlational analyses with Wechsler's scales produced high coefficients between KAIT Composite IQ and Wechsler's Full-Scale IQ: .82 with WISC–R for 118 children and adolescents, ages 11–16 years, and .85 with WAIS–R for 343 adults, ages 16–83 years (Kaufman & Kaufman, 1993). For a discussion of other validation studies, consult Kaufman and Kaufman (1997).

PSYCHOMETRIC, CLINICAL, AND THEORETICAL CRITIQUE. Flanagan (1995) states, "The KAIT is a well standardized test of general intellectual functioning that was developed specifically for adolescents and adults... The integration of the developmental (Piaget), neuropsychological (Luria), and experimental–cognitive (Horn–Cattell) models that underlie the KAIT permits interpretation from well-researched theories. The KAIT is easy to administer and score and contains test materials that are well constructed, easy to manipulate, and stimulating to examinees" (p. 530). "The tasks included are interesting and many of them are novel in their approach to the measurement of intelligence" (Keith, 1995, p. 532); also, the manual is well organized and helpful (Dumont & Hagberg, 1994; Flanagan, Alfonso, & Flanagan, 1994; Keith, 1995). The psychometric properties of the KAIT regarding standardization and reliability are excellent and the construct validity evidence that is reported in the manual provides a good foundation for its theoretical underpinnings (Flanagan et al., 1994). Brown (1994) notes that the KAIT represents a reconceptualization of the measurement of intelligence that is more consistent with current theories of intellectual development and adds that the fluid–crystallized dichotomy enhances the richness of the clinical interpretations that can be drawn from this instrument.

The fluid–crystallized dichotomy is based on the original Horn–Cattell theory of intelligence, thus offering a firm and well-researched theoretical framework (Flanagan et al., 1994). Nonetheless, the theoretical framework has been criticized because it is the "original" theory and not Horn's "modern" expansion. Flanagan (1995) emphasized that the Kaufmans' decision to use the two-pronged *Gf–Gc* theory rather than its multiability expanded version "appears to be based on their own clinical experience and not empirical evidence. The differential clinical utility of pure versus mixed measures of ability notwithstanding, the KAIT, one of the newest measures of cognitive functioning in the field of intellectual assessment, appears to be based on an old theory" (p. 528). Keith (1995) added that more construct validity evidence is needed to verify that the KAIT Crystallized and Fluid IQs do, indeed, measure these Horn–Cattell constructs. He also criticized the KAIT for making the final decision about the choice of a theoretical model (i.e., Horn–Cattell), in part, after the analysis of portions of the standardization data: "Thus, it seems likely that the KAIT would adhere to the *Gf–Gc* model less completely than a scale designed explicitly to assess fluid and crystallized intelligence" (Keith, 1995, p. 531).

These theoretical criticisms of the KAIT are well taken. Surely, from a purist's perspective, tests of short-term or long-term memory should be excluded from a Fluid Scale, and fluid reasoning should be eliminated from tests of crystallized ability. Yet the KAIT does include memory as an aspect of fluid intelligence (Rebus Learning, a traditional test of learning ability, is part of the Core Fluid Scale), and fluid reasoning is specifically required for success on the Crystallized Scale. As noted, these choices were by design and represent the integration of clinical with theoretical frameworks. Pure theorists will not be happy with that decision, but we do believe that the KAIT is successful at providing complex measures of intellectual functioning in all of its component tasks, and that would not have been possible with Horn's expanded theory. The complexity is fully consistent with the roles of Luria's and Piaget's theories in providing a framework for the KAIT, even if the match with Horn's modern theory had to suffer. As a *clinical* measure of intelligence, following the Wechsler tradition, these choices are justified. But there is also much empirical and research support for the decision to use a dichotomy for the main scales rather than to include seven or eight scales.

The empirical support comes from the robust results from numerous factor analyses. Keith is correct that the Horn–Cattell theory did not provide a guiding force for task development (that role was served by Luria's and Piaget's theories), but it is hard to see how a better match to the *Gf–Gc* dichotomy could be found. The factor structure offers strong support for the two global KAIT scales across its wide age range, and the integrity of these dimensions remained intact even when the KAIT subtests were jointly factor analyzed with Wechsler's tests (Kaufman & Kaufman, 1993) with a variety of specific tests of Horn abilities (Kaufman, Ishikuma, & Kaufman, 1994) and with the K–ABC (Kaufman, 1993a).

The research support comes from the voluminous research on aging and IQ (Horn & Hofer, 1992; Kaufman, 1990a, chapter 7; Kaufman & Horn, 1996). It is the two constructs, Gf and Gc, for which there is so much research support for differential aging patterns across the adult life span. Support for the additional Horn abilities is much more meager. Furthermore, most of the support is for the "old" notions of global Gf and Gc, not the more specific, pure abilities Horn & Hofer (1992; Kaufman, Kaufman, Chen, & Kaufman, 1996). Thus, Gc has been identified as a "maintained" ability and Gf as a "vulnerable" ability with a preponderance of the evidence "based on the use of the WAIS" (Horn & Hofer, 1992, p. 71). As noted, the Wechsler constructs qualify as global Gf and Gc, not pure or refined constructs. Therefore, the old theory on which the KAIT is partially based is more consistent with the interpretations given to the maintained and vulnerable abilities within the aging literature than is the modern theory. The older theory, therefore, does provide a sensible theoretical framework, especially when viewed in the context of the Piaget and Luria influences, for a test such as the KAIT that extends from preadolescence to old age.

The dependence on the achievement of formal operational thought and the ability to plan effectively for success on many KAIT items may, however, have a downside regarding clinical applications of the KAIT. Brown (1994) has pointed out that the theoretical assumption that formal operations is reached by early adolescence limits that application of the KAIT with certain adolescent and adult populations. If an individual has not achieved formal operations, many of the subtests will be too difficult for him or her and perhaps frustrating and overwhelming. Examiners should be aware of this limitation when working with such individuals in order to maintain rapport. The KAIT can be a useful assessment tool when working with high-functioning, intelligent individuals; however, it can be difficult

to use with borderline individuals and some elderly people (Brown, 1994). Elderly clients' scores on some of the subtests may be negatively impacted by poor reading, poor hearing, and poor memory (Dumont & Hagberg, 1994). Overall, though, the KAIT appears to be well thought out and validated (Dumont & Hagberg, 1994) and represents an advancement in the field of intellectual assessment with its ability to measure fluid and crystallized intelligence from a theoretical perspective and, at the same time, maintain a solid psychometric quality (Flanagan et al., 1994).

Cognitive Assessment System (CAS)

DESCRIPTION AND THEORETICAL RATIONALE. The Das–Naglieri Cognitive Assessment System (CAS; Naglieri & Das, 1997a), for ages 5 to 17 years, is based on, and developed according to, the Planning, Attention, Simultaneous, and Successive (PASS) theory of intelligence. The PASS theory is a multidimensional view of ability that is the result of the merging of contemporary theoretical and applied psychology (see summaries by Das, Naglieri, & Kirby, 1994, and Naglieri & Das, 1997a, 1997b). Naglieri and Das (1997a) linked the work of Luria (1966, 1973, 1980) with the field of intelligence when they suggested that PASS processes are the essential elements of human cognitive functioning. This theory proposes that human cognitive functioning is based on the four essential activities of planning, attention, simultaneous processing, and successive processing that employ and alter an individual's base of knowledge (Naglieri & Das, 1997a). According to this theory, human cognitive functioning includes four components: planning processes that provide cognitive control, utilization of processes and knowledge, intentionality and self-regulation to achieve a desired goal; attentional processes that provide focused, selective cognitive activity over time; and simultaneous and successive information processes that are the two forms of operating on information.

> *Planning:* "Planning is a mental process by which the individual determines, selects, applies, and evaluates solutions to problems" (Naglieri & Das, 1997a, p. 2). Planning processing provides the means to solve problems for which no solution is apparent. It applies to tasks that may involve attention,

simultaneous and successive processes, and acquired knowledge. Success on planning tests should require the child to develop a plan of action or strategy, evaluate the value of the method, monitor its effectiveness, revise or reject an old plan as the task demands change, and control the impulse to act without careful consideration.

Attention: "Attention is a mental process by which the individual selectively focuses on particular stimuli while inhibiting responses to competing stimuli presented over time" (Naglieri & Das, 1997a, p. 3). Successful performance on an attention task requires effort to be focused, selective, sustained, and effortful. Focused attention involves directed concentration toward a particular activity. Selective attention requires the inhibition of responses to some stimuli over others, which may be hard to ignore. Sustained attention refers to the performance over time, which can be influenced by varying amounts of effort required. Attention tests should present children with competing demands on their attention and require sustained focus over time.

Simultaneous Processing: "Simultaneous processing is a mental process by which the individual integrates separate stimuli into a single whole or group..."(Naglieri & Das, 1997a, p. 4). The essence of simultaneous processing is that it allows for the interrelation of elements into a conceptual whole. Simultaneous processing has strong spatial components in nonverbal tasks and in language tasks involving logical–grammatical relationships. The spatial aspect involves both the perception of stimuli as a group and the internalized formation of complex visual images. The logical–grammatical dimension allows for the integration of words into ideas through the comprehension of word relationships to obtain meaning. Thus, simultaneous processes can be important to both nonverbal spatial as well as verbal tasks.

Successive Processing: "Successive processing is a mental process by which the individual integrates stimuli into a specific serial order that forms a chain-like progression" (Naglieri & Das, 1997a, p. 5). Successive processing is involved when parts must follow each other in a specific order such that each element is only related to those that precede it. Successive processing is most important in tasks with serial and syntactic components. The se-

rial aspect involves both the perception of stimuli in sequence and the formation of sounds and movements in order; for example, the serial organization of spoken speech and the synthesis of "separate sounds and motor impulses into consecutive series" (Luria & Tsvetkova, 1990, p. xvi). The syntactic aspect of successive processing allows for the comprehension of the meaning of narrative speech, especially when the "individual elements of the whole narrative always behave as if organized in certain successive series"(Luria, 1966, p. 78). Successive processing activities require perception and reproduction of the serial nature of stimuli, comprehension of sentences based on syntactic relationships, and the articulation of separate sounds in a consecutive series.

The CAS was designed to mirror the PASS theory with subtests organized into four scales designed to provide an effective measure of each of the PASS cognitive processes. Planning subtests require the child to devise, select, and use efficient plans of action to solve the test problems, regulate the effectiveness of the plans, and self-correct when necessary. Attention subtests require the child to attend selectively to a particular stimulus and inhibit attending to distracting stimuli. Simultaneous processing subtests require the child to integrate stimuli into groups to form an interrelated whole, and Successive processing subtests require the child to integrate stimuli in their specific serial order or appreciate the linearity of stimuli with little opportunity for interrelating the parts.

The CAS yields scores for the Planning, Attention, Simultaneous, Successive, and Full-Scale that are normalized standard scores with a normative mean of 100 and standard deviation of 15. All subtests are set at a normative mean of 10 and *SD* of 3. Interpretation of CAS also follows closely from the PASS theory with emphasis on the scale rather than subtest level analyses.

PSYCHOMETRIC PROPERTIES. The CAS was standardized on 2,200 children ranging in age from 5 through 17 years stratified by age, gender, race, ethnicity, geographic region, educational placement, and parent education according to recent U.S. Census reports and closely matches the U.S. population characteristics in the variables used. In addition to administration of the CAS, a representative sample of 1,600 included in the standardization sample were also administered achievement tests from the WJ–R Tests of Achievement (Woodcock & Johnson, 1989). This provided a rich source of validity evidence (e.g., the analysis of the relationships between PASS and achievement) and allowed for the development of predictive difference values needed for interpretation of ability-achievement discrepancies. Finally, 872 children from special populations, including attention deficit, mentally retarded, and learning disabled, for example, were tested for validity and reliability studies.

The internal consistency reliability estimates for the CAS Full Scale are comparable with other tests of its type. The CAS Standard Battery (12 subtests) average scale reliability coefficients for the entire standardization sample of children aged 5–17 years are as follows: Full Scale = .96, Planning = .88; Simultaneous = .93; Attention = .88; and Successive = 93. The average reliability coefficients for all ages in the standardization sample for the 12 subtests range from .75 to .89 (median = .82). The test–retest reliability for the CAS Full Scale = .91, Planning = .85, Simultaneous = .81, Attention = .82, and Successive = .86 for 215 children aged 5–17 years (median interval = 21 days). Confirmatory factor analysis supports the construct validity of the four PASS components. Criterion-related validity was shown by the strong relationships between CAS scores and WJ–R achievement tests, correlations with achievement for special populations, and PASS profiles for children with attention-deficit–hyperactivity disorders, traumatic brain injury, and reading disability. Additionally, the utility of the PASS scores for treatment and educational planning is demonstrated (Naglieri & Das, 1997b).

PSYCHOMETRIC, CLINICAL, AND THEORETICAL CRITIQUE. Carroll (1995) provided two main criticisms of the PASS theory. First, he suggested that Planning is better described as a Perceptual Speed factor, and second he argued that there was insufficient factorial support for the PASS as measures of the constructs. Since the publication of Carroll's review, both of these criticisms have been addressed by data presented in the *CAS Interpretive Handbook* (Naglieri & Das, 1997b), some of which will be summarized here. Naglieri and Das (1997b) provided strong evidence from confirmatory factor analytic investigations using the CAS standardization data that a four-factor PASS configuration of the 12 subtests provided the best fit to the data. Thus, it appears that Carroll's reanalyses of old experimental test data (some of the tests are not in the final version of the CAS) and smaller sample sizes led to the inconsistencies between his results and those provided in the manual. Carroll's second criticism that the Planning subtests really measure speed merits further empirical investigation but is inconsistent with two sources of data.

Naglieri and Das (1997b) showed that about 90% of children in the entire standardization sample used strategies to solve the planning tests. These strategies show developmental changes and are differentially related to success on the subtests. Clearly, tests that have been shown to demand the generation, use, and monitoring of plans of action cannot be described as simple perceptual speed measures. More evidence that planning is not better described as perceptual speed is apparent when the relationship between planning and achievement is considered. Naglieri and Das (1997b) provided considerable information about the relationships between PASS and achievement for a large representative sample of 1,600 children who were administered the WJ–R Tests of Achievement. For example, they showed that the correlations between planning and WJ–R Broad Mathematics and Mathematics Reasoning were substantial (median = .55). The evidence for the use of strategies on planning tests and the strong and consistent correlations between CAS and math achievement do not support Carroll's reinterpretation of planning as speed.

Nonetheless, future research should explore the relationships between CAS Planning subtests with (a) pure perceptual speed tasks that involve minimal decision making and (b) tests of planning ability such as the Piagetian formal operations measures found in the KAIT. The results of such research studies should help clarify the degree to which the highly speeded visual–perceptual and visual–motor CAS Planning subtests are truly measures of Luria's Block 3 planing ability as opposed to perceptual speed, as claimed by Carroll.

Esters, Ittenbach, and Han (1997) stated that "attempts to establish the treatment validity of . . . the

CAS, have met with little success (p. 217)." This statement is inconsistent with evidence summarized by Naglieri and Das (1997) and especially the papers published by Naglieri and Gottling (1995, 1997), who showed the relevance of PASS to math instruction. Naglieri and Gottling demonstrated that children who are poor in planning improved considerably (80% over baseline) in math calculation taken directly from the classroom curriculum when provided an instruction that encouraged their use of strategies or plans. In contrast, children who were good in planning showed modest improvement (about 40% over baseline) when provided exactly the same instruction. No similar relationships were found between Attention, Simultaneous, Successive, or Wechsler IQ scores.

The CAS provides an excellent translation of theory to test development. Although research is needed to clarify the precise construct measured by the Planning Scale, Naglieri and Das have done an exemplary job of assessing the Luria-based constructs and in demonstrating the possible link between theory-based assessment and educational intervention.

OVERVIEW

The history of intelligence testing is deeply rooted in the blend of the practical and psychometric approaches of Binet and World War I psychologists and the clinical and humanistic approach of David Wechsler. That blend still defines IQ testing today because of the continued popularity of the Wechsler scales in today's schools, hospitals, and clinics worldwide. However, the unchanging nature of IQ tests has begun to thaw. For the first three quarters of a century, from Binet's 1905 scale to about 1980, there was the Binet and there was the Wechsler and that was about it. Then came a series of tests that included novel tasks and an attempt to link theory to IQ assessment. Today, clinicians have more choice than ever before, and these choices include a vast spectrum of top-notch psychometric instruments that measure a small number of constructs (such as the KAIT's two), a moderate number (the four measured by the CAS and by the most recent Wechsler revisions), or a large number (the seven Horn abilities measured by the WJ–R,

or eight, counting the Quantitative dimension on its Achievement scale). There is also a choice of theory–namely the Horn–Cattell Gf–Gc, expanded Horn Gf–Gc, and Luria PASS–as well as tests developed from practical and research-based approaches such as the WAIS–III and DAS.

The critics of IQ tests abound, especially among popular and influential theorists such as Sternberg (1984, 1993), and these critics must be heard. It is partly because of the critics that the developers of IQ tests have constantly striven to improve the existing measures and to attempt to bring more theory and research into the development of new tests and the revision of old ones. However, before heeding the advice of strong critics of IQ testing such as Macmann and Barnett (1994), who want to replace conventional IQ tests with alternatives that emphasize real-life problem solving, a few points are worth considering.

Individually administered tests of intelligence are, first and foremost, clinical instruments for understanding aspects (not all) of cognitive functioning, and, more importantly, for interpreting intellect in the context of personality. The effective use of IQ tests depends, to some extent, on how successfully a theory has been translated to practice and whether the theory chosen is the "best" or most complete theory, but it also depends on a plethora of additional variables. It is clearly essential for test users to understand the theoretical bases of the constructs measured by IQ tests and to be familiar with the volumes of research findings on various IQ tests. But test developers and test users alike need to integrate several aspects of psychology that extend beyond a particular theory. Test developers, in particular, need to be experienced in clinical settings and to understand the noncognitive aspects of intellectual assessment in such a way that the scales they develop will provide rich sources of clinical hypotheses and unveil important aspects of personality and temperament. They must be psychometrically sophisticated, feeling at ease with terms and concepts such as Rasch latent-trait models, item response theory, Mantel–Haenszel item-bias statistics, W-difficulty values, and the like. And they must have considerable knowledge of neuropsychology to understand brain–behavior relationships because, ultimately, the assessment of aspects of intelligence involves an insightful understanding of how test performance is related to brain function or dysfunction.

Tests that are powerful psychometric tools, that have a solid research history, and that are clinically and neuropsychologically relevant are quite valuable if used intelligently by highly trained examiners. Clinicians who employ the intelligent testing philosophy outlined earlier can make a meaningful difference in a client's life when interpreting the results of a test profile in the context of clinical observations during the test session, background information about the client, research findings, and theoretical models. The array of instruments described in this chapter, as well as others not included because of space constraints (such as the Detroit Tests of Learning Aptitude-3, by Hammill, 1991), can each serve quite well as the IQ test of choice for clinical evaluation. Perhaps when some of the highly respected theories of intelligence are translated into individual tests of intelligence it will be time to abandon existing instruments. But the test developers who attempt to translate the theories necessarily must be well versed in the clinical, neuropsychological, and psychometric aspects of assessment; otherwise, the perfect theory-based test will prove to be an imperfect clinical tool.

And what of the future? Though there has been considerable progress during the past two decades in providing options for clinicians apart from the Wechsler and Binet – and several of these options have impressive theoretical foundations – progress has not been as rapid as most would wish. By their very nature, test publishers have been a conservative lot, investing their money in proven ventures rather than speculating on new ideas for measuring intelligence. Unlike companies like Microsoft or Lucent with unfathomable budgets, research and development budgets are modest within the test publishing industry. The upshot is that progress will likely continue to be controlled as the 21st century unfolds. Nonetheless, there are certain predictions of where testing is heading. Managed care has had an impact on the tests psychologists use for clinical evaluations because reimbursement for assessments has become a thorny issue. The time spent on an evaluation often assumes more primacy than the quality of the evaluation. The result is likely to be new instruments that are shorter to administer but that retain strong psychometric properties despite their brevity. Once again, theory will take a back seat to pragmatics.

Meshing with the practical needs for saving the clinician's time is the emergence of computerized intelligence tests. The development of tests that can be administered by computer has already begun in earnest, such that Anastasi and Urbina (1997), when discussing group tests of multiple aptitudes, stated, "Like most major current tests, the DAT can be completely administered in a computerized version" (p. 288). The computerization has facilitated the growth of adaptive testing, a procedure that allows each examinee to be given a relatively small set of items; the person's response to each item determines the difficulty level of the next item administered. Computerization has already taken over group-administered tests in other domains of psychology, such as personality and vocational interests, and group-administered intelligence tests are clearly heading in the same direction. With the increasing computer skills of elementary school children and the increasing numbers of computers in the schools, it is feasible that conventional group testing of intelligence and achievement will soon give way to adaptive, computerized testing within the school systems. Indeed, testing on the Internet is now being explored in depth by test publishers, and a recent meeting was held in southern Florida to discuss that very issue (G. Jackson, personal communication, December 22, 1997).

It is only a matter of time before clinical tests of intelligence are computerized, especially as software continues to become more sophisticated in its ability to decipher words spoken by the human voice. When these tests become available, they will present clinicians with an answer to the practical issues raised by managed care and the need to conserve their professional time. At the same time, such tests will provide them with a professional dilemma regarding the importance of clinical observations in interpreting a test profile. Existing software (if a clip is attached to a person's earlobe or finger) can give continual readings of heart rate, galvanic skin response, and other psychophysical measures. Perhaps these data will substitute for direct observations in the future. The possibilities are limitless, and so are the ethical issues and controversies that will undoubtedly accompany the application of computer technology to clinical assessment.

Ultimately, during the next century, new and improved high-tech instruments will be available that will meet the rigors of psychometric quality and the demands of practical necessity. One hopes those tests will not abandon theory but will embrace it more fully, continuing the trend in the development of clinical tests of intelligence that began in the early 1980s and has continued to the present. But none of the excellent instruments that are now available for clinical assessment of intelligence – Wechsler or otherwise – should be left for dead until there is something of value to replace them.

ACKNOWLEDGMENT

The author is grateful to the following people for their contributions to this chapter: Drs. Nadeen L. Kaufman, Elizabeth O. Lichtenberger, and Jack A. Naglieri. Nadeen contributed primarily to the section on the KAIT, Liz to the section on the WAIS–III, and Jack to the section on the Das–Naglieri CAS. Nadeen and I are coauthors of the K–ABC and KAIT, and Jack is author of the Naglieri Nonverbal Ability Test and coauthor of the Das–Naglieri CAS, all of which are discussed in this chapter. We have made conscientious efforts to present and critique all intelligence tests fairly and objectively, including the four that we have developed.

REFERENCES

Anastasi, A. (1988). *Psychological testing* (6th ed.). New York: Macmillan.

Anastasi, A., & Urbina, S. (1997). *Psychological testing* (7th ed.). Upper Saddle River, NJ: Prentice Hall.

Baddeley, A. D. (1986). *Working memory*. Oxford, UK: Oxford University Press.

Bennett, G. K., Seashore, H. G., & Wesman, A. G. (1990). *Differential Ability Tests (DAT), 5th ed., technical manual*. San Antonio, TX: Harcourt Brace Educational Measurement.

Binet, A. (1903). *L'etude experimental de l'intelligence (Experimental study of intelligence)*. Paris: Schleicher.

Binet, A., & Henri, V. (1895). La psychologie individuelle (Psychology of the individual). *L'Année Psychologique, 2*, 411–465.

Bogen, J. E. (1975). Some educational aspects of hemispheric specialization. *UCLA Educator, 17*, 24–32.

Braden, J. P. (1992). Test Reviews: The Differential Ability Scales and special education. *Journal of Psychoeducational Assessment, 10*, 92–98.

Brown, D. T. (1994). Review of the Kaufman Adolescent and Adult Intelligence Test (KAIT). *Journal of School Psychology, 32*, 85–99.

Buckhalt, J. A. (1991). A critical review of the Wechsler Preschool and Primary Scale of Intelligence – Revised (WPPSI–R). *Journal of Psychoeducational Assessment, 9*, 271–279.

Carroll, J. B. (1995). Review of the book *Assessment of cognitive processes: The PASS theory of intelligence*. *Journal of Psychoeducational Assessment, 13*, 397–409.

Cattell, R. B. (1963). Theory of fluid and crystallized intelligence: A critical experiment. *Journal of Educational Psychology, 54*, 1–22.

Cohen, R. J., Montague, P., Nathanson, L. S., & Swerdlik, M. E. (1988). *Psychological testing*. Mountain View, CA: Mayfield.

Cronbach, L. J. (1975). Five decades of public controversy over mental testing. *American Psychologist, 30*, 1–14.

Das, J. P. (1984). Simultaneous and successive processes and K-ABC. *Journal of Special Education, 18*, 229–238.

Das, J. P., Kirby, J. R., & Jarman, R. F. (1975). Simultaneous and successive synthesis: An alternative model for cognitive abilities. *Psychological Bulletin, 82*, 87–103.

Das, J. P., Naglieri, J. A., & Kirby, J. R. (1994). *Assessment of cognitive processes: The PASS theory of intelligence*. Boston, MA: Allyn & Bacon.

Delugach, R. (1991). Test Review: Wechsler Preschool and Primary Scale of Intelligence – Revised. *Journal of Psychoeducational Assessment, 9*, 280–290.

Dennerll, R. D. (1964). Prediction of unilateral brain dysfunction using Wechsler test scores. *Journal of Consulting Psychology, 28*, 278–284.

Dumont, R., & Hagberg, C. (1994). Test reviews: Kaufman Adolescent and Adult Intelligence Test (KAIT). *Journal of Psychoeducational Assessment, 12*, 190–196.

Elliott, C. D. (1990). *Differential Ability Scales (DAS) administration and scoring manual*. San Antonio, TX: Psychological Corporation.

Elliott, C. D. (1997). The Differential Ability Scales (DAS). In D. P. Flanagan, J. L. Gensaft, & P. L. Harrison (Eds.). *Beyond traditional intellectual assessments: Contemporary and emerging theories, tests, and issues* (pp. 183–208). New York: Guilford.

Esters, I. G., Ittenach, R. F., Han, K. (1997). Today's IQ tests: Are they really better than their historical predecessors? *School Psychology Review, 26*, 211–223.

Flanagan, D. P. (1995). Review of the Kaufman Adolescent and Adult Intelligence Test. In J. C. Conoley & J. C. Impara (Eds.), *The twelfth mental measurements yearbook* (pp. 527–530). Lincoln, NE: University of Nebraska, Buros Institute.

Flanagan, D. P., Alfonso, V. C., & Flanagan, R. (1994). A review of the Kaufman Adolescent and Adult Intelligence

Test: An advancement in cognitive assessment? *School Psychology Review, 23*, 512–525.

Flanagan, D. P., & McGrew, K. S. (1997). A cross-battery approach to assessing and interpreting cognitive abilities: Narrowing the gap between practice and cognitive science. In D. P. Flanagan, J. L. Genshaft, & P. L. Harrison (Eds.), *Beyond traditional intellectual assessment: Contemporary and emerging theories, tests, and issues* (pp. 314–325). New York: Guilford.

Galton, F. (1869). *Hereditary genius: An inquiry into its laws and consequences*. London: Macmillan.

Galton, F. (1883). *Inquiries into human faculty and its development*. London: Macmillan.

Gardner, H. (1983). *Frames of mind: The theory of multiple intelligences*. New York: Basic Books.

Goddard, H. H. (1908). The Binet and Simon tests of intellectual capacity, *Training School, 5*, 3–9.

Golden, C. J. (1981). The Luria–Nebraska Children's Battery: Theory and formulation. In: Hynd, G. W. and Obrzut, J. E. (Eds.), *Neuropsychological assessment of the school-age child*. New York: Grune and Stratton.

Gresham, F. M., & Witt, J. C. (1997). Utility of intelligence tests for treatment planning, classification, and placement decisions: Recent empirical findings and future directions. *School Psychology Quarterly, 12*, 249–267.

Guilford, J. P. (1967). *The nature of human intelligence*. New York: McGraw-Hill.

Hammill, D. D. (1991). *Interpretive Manual for Detroit Tests of Learning Aptitude: Third Edition*. Austin, TX: PRO–ED.

Herrnstein, R. J., & Murray, C. (1994). *The bell curve: Intelligence and class structure in American life*. New York: The Free Press.

Horn, J. L. (1985). Remodeling old models in intelligence. In B. B. Wolman (Ed.), *Handbook of intelligence: Theories, measurements, and applications* (pp. 267–300). New York: Wiley.

Horn, J. L. (1989). Cognitive diversity: A framework of learning. In P. L. Ackerman, R. J. Sternberg, & R. Glaser (Eds.), *Learning and individual differences* (pp. 61–116). New York: Freeman.

Horn, J. L. (1991). Measurement of intellectual capabilities: A review of theory. In K. S. McGrew, J. K. Werder, & R. W. Woodcock (Eds.), *Woodcock–Johnson technical manual: A reference on theory and current research* (pp. 197–246). Allen, TX: DLM/Teaching Resources.

Horn, J. L., & Cattell, R. B. (1966). Refinement and test of the theory of fluid and crystallized intelligence. *Journal of Educational Psychology, 57*, 253–270.

Horn, J. L., & Cattell, R. B. (1967). Age differences in fluid and crystallized intelligence. *Acta Psychologica, 26*, 107–129.

Horn, J. L., & Hofer, S. M. (1992). Major abilities and development in the adult period. In R. J. Sternberg & C. A. Berg (Eds.), *Intellectual development* (pp. 44–99). Boston, MA: Cambridge University Press.

Inhelder, B., & Piaget, J. (1958). *The growth of logical thinking from childhood to adolescence*. New York: Basic Books.

Jackson, D. N. (1994). *Multidimensional Aptitude Battery (MAB) manual*. Port Huron, MI: Sigma Assessment Systems.

Jensen, A. R. (1984). The black-white difference on the K–ABC: Implications for future tests. *Journal of Special Education, 18*, 377–408.

Jensen, A. R. (1985). Methodological and statistical techniques for the chronometric study of mental abilities. In C. R. Reynolds & V. L. Willson (Eds.), *Methodological and statistical advances in the study of individual differences* (pp. 51–116). New York: Plenum.

Kamphaus, R. W. (1993). *Clinical assessment of children's intelligence*. Boston, MA: Allyn & Bacon.

Kamphaus, R. W., Beres, K. A., Kaufman, A. S., & Kaufman, N. L. (1995). The Kaufman Assessment Battery for Children (K–ABC). In C. S. Newmark (Ed.), *Major psychological assessment instruments* (2nd ed.) (pp. 348–399). Boston: Allyn & Bacon.

Kaufman, A. S. (1979). *Intelligent testing with the WISC–R*. New York: Wiley.

Kaufman, A. S. (1990a). *Assessing adolescent and adult intelligence*. Boston, MA: Allyn & Bacon.

Kaufman, A. S. (1990b). The WPPSI–R: You can't judge a test by its colors. *Journal of School Psychology, 28*, 387–394.

Kaufman, A. S. (1993a). Joint exploratory factor analysis of the Kaufman Assessment Battery for Children and the Kaufman Adolescent and Adult Intelligence Test for 11- and 12-year olds. *Journal of Clinical Child Psychology, 22*, 355–364.

Kaufman, A. S. (1993b). King WISC the Third assumes the throne. *Journal of School Psychology, 31*, 345–354.

Kaufman, A. S. (1994). *Intelligent testing with the WISC–III*. New York: Wiley.

Kaufman, A. S. (1998, August). What happens to our WAIS–R scores as we age from 16 to 89 years, and what do these changes mean for theory and clinical practice? Invited Division 16 Award Address presented at the meeting of the American Psychological Association, San Francisco.

Kaufman, A. S. (in press). David Wechsler. In A. E. Kazdin (Ed.). *Encyclopedia of psychology*. Washington, DC: American Psychological Association & Oxford University Press.

Kaufman, A. S., & Horn, J. L. (1996). Age changes on tests of fluid and crystallized intelligence for females and males on the Kaufman Adolescent and Adult Intelligence Test (KAIT) at ages 17 to 94 years. *Archives of Clinical Neuropsychology, 11*, 97–121.

Kaufman, A. S., Ishikuma, T., & Kaufman, N. L. (1994). A Horn analysis of the factors measured by the WAIS–R, Kaufman Adolescent and Adult Intelligence Test (KAIT), and two new brief cognitive measures for normal adolescents and adults. *Assessment, 1*, 353–366.

Kaufman, A. S., & Kaufman, N. L. (1983a). *Administration and scoring manual for Kaufman Assessment Battery for Children (K–ABC)*. Circle Pines, MN: American Guidance Service.

Kaufman, A. S., & Kaufman, N. L. (1983b). *K–ABC interpretive manual*. Circle Pines, MN: American Guidance Service.

Kaufman, A. S., & Kaufman, N. L. (1993). *Manual for Kaufman Adolescent & Adult Intelligence Test (KAIT)*. Circle Pines, MN: American Guidance Service.

Kaufman, A. S., & Kaufman, N. L. (1997). The Kaufman Adolescent and Adult Intelligence Test (KAIT). In D. P. Flanagan, J. L. Genshaft, & P. L. Harrison (Eds.), *Beyond traditional intellectual assessment: Contemporary and emerging theories, tests, and issues* (pp. 209–229). New York: Guilford.

Kaufman, A. S., Kaufman, J. C., Chen, T., & Kaufman, N. L. (1996). Differences on six Horn abilities for four teenage groups between 15–16 and 75–94 years. *Psychological Assessment, 8*, 161–171.

Kaufman, A. S., & Lichtenberger, E. O. (1998). Intellectual assessment. In C. R. Reynolds (Ed.), *Comprehensive clinical psychology, Volume 4: Assessment* (pp. 203–238). Tarrytown, NY: Elsevier Science.

Kaufman, A. S., & Lichtenberger, E. O. (1999). *Essentials of WAIS–III assessment*. New York: Wiley.

Keith, T. Z. (1991) Questioning the K–ABC: What does it measure? *Journal of Psychoeducational Assessment, 8*, 391–405.

Keith, T. Z. (1995). Review of the Kaufman Adolescent and Adult Intelligence Test. In J. C. Conoley & J. C. Impara (Eds.), *The twelfth mental measurements yearbook* (pp. 530–532). Lincoln, NE: University of Nebraska, Buros Institute.

Kinsbourne, M. (Ed.). (1978). *Asymmetrical function of the brain*. Cambridge, UK: Cambridge University Press.

Klove, H. (1959). Relationship of differential electroencephalographic patterns to distribution of Wechsler-Bellevue scores. *Neurology, 9*, 871–876.

Logie, R. H. (1995). *Visuo-spatial working memory*. Hove, East Sussex, UK: Erlbaum.

Levy, J., & Trevarthen, C. (1976). Metacontrol of hemispheric function in human split-brain patients. *Journal of Experimental Psychology: Human Perception and Performance, 2*, 299–312.

Luria, A. R. (1966). *Higher cortical functions in man*. New York: Basic Books.

Luria, A. R. (1973). *The working brain: An introduction to neuropsychology*. London: Penguin Books.

Luria, A. R. (1980). *Higher cortical functions in man* (2nd ed.). New York: Basic Books.

Luria, A. R., & Tsvetkova, L. S. (A. Mikheyev & S. Mikheyev, Trans.) (1990). *The neuropsychological analysis of problem solving*. Orlando, FL: Paul M. Deutsch Press.

Macmann, G. M., & Barnett, D. W. (1994). Structural analysis of correlated factors: Lessons from the Verbal–Performance dichotomy of the Wechsler scales. *School Psychology Quarterly, 9*, 161–197.

Matarazzo, J. D. (1972). *Wechsler's measurement and appraisal of adult intelligence* (5th and enlarged ed.). New York: Oxford University Press.

McGrew, K. S., Flanagan, D. P., Keith, T. Z., & Vanderwood, M. (1997). Beyond *g*: The impact of *Gf–Gc* specific cognitive abilities research on the future use and interpretation of intelligence test batteries in the schools. *School Psychology Review, 26*, 189–210.

Meeker, M. N., Mestyanek, L., Shadduck, R., & Meeker, R. (1975). *S.O.I. Learning Abilities Test*. El Segundo, CA: SOI Institute.

Mill, J. S. (1875). *A system of logic, ratiocinative and inductive, being a connected view of the principles of evidence and the methods of scientific investigation*. 2 vols., 9th ed. London: Longmans, Green, Reader and Dyer.

Miller, T. L., & Reynolds, C. R. (1984). Special issue . . . The K-ABC. *Journal of Special Education, 8*, 207–448.

Naglieri, J. A. (1997). *Naglieri Nonverbal Ability Test (NNAT) multilevel technical manual*. San Antonio, TX: Harcourt Brace Educational Measurement.

Naglieri, J. A., & Gottling, S. H. (1995). A cognitive education approach to math instruction for the learning disabled: An individual study. *Psychological Reports, 76*, 1343–1354.

Naglieri, J. A., & Gottling, S. H. (1997). Mathematics instruction and PASS cognitive processes: An intervention study. *Journal of Learning Disabilities, 30*, 513–520.

Naglieri, J. A., & Das, J. P. (1997a). *Das-Naglieri Cognitive Assessment System*. Chicago: Riverside.

Naglieri, J. A., & Das, J. P. (1997b). *Cognitive Assessment System interpretive handbook*. Chicago: Riverside.

Otis, A. S., & Lennon, R. T. (1997). *Otis–Lennon School Ability Test (OLSAT), 7th ed., technical manual, spring data*. San Antonio, TX: Harcourt Brace Educational Measurement.

Piaget, J. (1972). Intellectual evolution from adolescence to adulthood. *Human Development, 15*, 1–12.

Psychological Corporation. (1997). *WAIS–III and WMS–III technical Manual*. San Antonio, TX: The Psychological Corportion.

Reitan, R. M. (1955). Certain differential effects of left and right cerebral lesions in human adults. *Journal of Comparative and Physiological Psychology, 48*, 474–477.

Reynolds, C. R. (1987). Playing IQ roulette with the Stanford–Binet, 4th edition. *Measurement and Evaluation in Counseling and Development, 20*, 139–141.

Reynolds, C. R., Kamphaus, R. W., & Rosenthal, B. L. (1988). Factor analysis of the Stanford–Binet Fourth Edition for ages 2 years through 23 years. *Measurement and Evaluation in Counseling and Development, 21*, 52–63.

Richardson, J. T. E. (1996). Evolving concepts of working memory. In J. T. E. Richardson, R. W. Engle, L. Hasher, R. H. Logie, E. R. Stoltzfus, & R. T. Zacks (Eds.), *Working *memory and human cognition* (pp. 3–30). New York: Oxford University Press.

Roback, A. A. (1961). *History of psychology and psychiatry*. New York: Philosophical Library.

Roid, G. H., Prifitera, A., & Weiss, L. G. (1993). Replication of the WISC–III factor structure in an independent sample. In B. A. Bracken, & R. S. McCallum (Eds.), *Journal of Psychoeducational Assessment monograph series, advances in psychoeducational assessment: Wechsler Intelligence Scale for Children – Third Edition* (pp. 6–21). Germantown, TN: Psychoeducational Corporation.

Sandoval, J. (1992). Test Reviews: Using the DAS with multicultural populations: Issues of test bias. *Journal of Psychoeducational Assessment, 10,* 88–91.

Sattler, J. M. (1988). *Assessment of children* (3rd ed.). San Diego, CA: Jerome M. Sattler.

Shaw, S. R., Swerdlik, M. E., & Laurent, J. (1993). Review of the WISC–III. In B. A. Bracken, & R. S. McCallum (Eds.), *Journal of Psychoeducational Assessment monograph series, advances in psychoeducational assessment: Wechsler Intelligence Scale for Children – Third Edition* (pp. 151–160). Germantown, TN: Psychoeducational Corporation.

Smith, A. (1966). Verbal and nonverbal test performances of patients with "acute" lateralized brain lesions (tumors). *The Journal of Nervous and Mental disease, 141,* 517–523.

Sperry, R. W. (1968). Hemisphere deconnection and unity in conscious awareness. *American Psychologist, 23,* 723–733.

Sperry, R. W. (1974). Lateral specialization in the surgically separated hemispheres. In F. O Schmitt & F. G. Worden (Eds.), *The neurosciences: Third study program*. Cambridge, MA: MIT Press.

Sternberg, R. J. (1984). The Kaufman Assessment Battery for Children: An information-processing analysis and critique. *Journal of Special Education, 18,* 269–279.

Sternberg, R. J. (1985). *Beyond IQ: A triarchic theory of human intelligence*. New York: Cambridge University Press.

Sternberg, R. J. (1993). Rocky's back again: A review of the WISC–III. In B. A. Bracken & R. S. McCallum (Eds.), *Journal of Psychoeducational Assessment monograph series, advances in psychoeducational assessment: Wechsler Intelligence Scale for Children – Third Edition* (pp. 161–164). Germantown, TN: Psychoeducational Corporation.

Stone, B. J. (1992). Joint confirmatory factor analysis of the DAS and WISC–R. *Journal of School Psychology, 30,* 185–195.

TCS/2 *technical report*. (1993). *Test of Cognitive Skills*. Monterey, CA: CTB Macmillan/McGraw-Hill.

Terman, L. M. (1916). *The measurement of intelligence*. Boston, MA: Houghton Mifflin.

Terman, L. M., & Merrill, M. A. (1960). *Stanford–Binet Intelligence Scale*. Boston, MA: Houghton Mifflin.

Terman, L. M., & Merrill, M. A. (1973). *Stanford–Binet Intelligence Scale: 1972 norms edition*. Boston, MA: Houghton Mifflin.

Thorndike, R. L., & Hagen, E. P. (1993). *Cognitive Abilities Test (CogAT), Form 5, technical manual*. Chicago: Riverside.

Thorndike, R. L., Hagen, E. P., & Sattler, J. M. (1986). *Technical manual for the Stanford–Binet Intelligence Scale – Fourth Edition*. Chicago: Riverside.

Thurstone, L. L. (1938). Primary mental abilities. *Psychometric Monographs, 1.*

Vincent, K. R. (1991). Black/White IQ differences: Does age make the difference? *Journal of Clinical Psychology, 47,* 266–270.

Wada, J., Clarke, R., & Hamm, A. (1975). Cerebral hemisphere asymmetry in humans. *Archives of Neurology, 37,* 234–246.

Webster, R. E. (1994). Review of Woodcock–Johnson Psycho-Educational Battery – Revised. In D. J. Keyser, & R. C. Sweetland (Eds.), *Test Critiques* (pp. 804–815). Test Corporation of America.

Wechsler, D. (1939). *Measurement of adult intelligence*. Baltimore, MD: Williams & Wilkins.

Wechsler, D. (1946). *Manual for the Wechsler–Bellevue Intelligence Scale, Form II*. San Antonio, TX: The Psychological Corporation.

Wechsler, D. (1949). *Manual for the Wechsler Intelligence Scale for Children (WISC)*. San Antonio, TX: The Psychological Corporation.

Wechsler, D. (1950). Cognitive, conative, and non-intellective intelligence. *American Psychologist, 5,* 78–83.

Wechsler, D. (1955). *Manual for the Wechsler Adult Intelligence Scale (WAIS)*. San Antonio, TX: The Psychological Corporation.

Wechsler, D. (1974). *Manual for the Wechsler Intelligence Scale for Children – Revised (WISC–R)*. San Antonio, TX: The Psychological Corporation.

Wechsler, D. (1975). Intelligence defined and undefined: A relativistic appraisal. *American Psychologist, 30,* 135–139.

Wechsler, D. (1981). *Manual for the Wechsler Adult Intelligence Scale – Revised (WAIS–R)*. San Antonio, TX: The Psychological Corporation.

Wechsler, D. (1989). *Manual for the Wechsler Preschool and Primary Scale of Intelligence – Revised (WPPSI–R)*. San Antonio, TX: The Psychological Corporation.

Wechsler, D. (1991). *Manual for the Wechsler Intelligence Scale for Children – Third Edition (WISC–III)*. San Antonio, TX: The Psychological Corporation.

Wechsler, D. (1997). *Manual for the Wechsler Adult Intelligence Scale – Third Edition (WAIS–III)*. San Antonio, TX: The Psychological Corporation.

Wesman, A. G. (1968). Intelligent testing. *American Psychologist, 23,* 267–274.

Whitworth, R. H., & Chrisman, S. M. (1987). Validation of the Kaufman Assessment Battery for Children comparing Anglo and Mexican-American preschoolers. *Educational and Psychological Measurement, 47,* 695–702.

Williams, R. L. (1974). From dehumanization to black intellectual genocide: A rejoinder. In G. J. Williams and S. Gordon (Eds.), *Clinical child psychology* (pp. 320–323). New York: Behavioral Publications.

Woltz, D. J. (1988). An investigation of the role of working memory in procedural skill acquisition. *Journal of Experimental Psychology: General, 117,* 319–331.

Woodcock, R. W. (1990). Theoretical foundations of the WJ–R measures of cognitive ability. *Journal of Psychoeducational Assessment, 8,* 231–258.

Woodcock, R. W., & Johnson, M. B. (1977). *Woodcock–Johnson Psycho-Educational Battery.* Allen, TX: DLM/Teaching Resources.

Woodcock, R. W., & Johnson, M. B. (1989). *Woodcock–Johnson — Revised, Tests of Cognitive Ability: Standard and supplemental batteries.* Chicago: Riverside.

Woodcock, R. W., & Mather, N. (1989). *WJ–R Tests of Cognitive Ability–Standard and supplemental batteries: Examiner's manual.* In R. W. Woodcock & M. B. Johnson, Woodcock–Johnson Psycho-Educational Battery — Revised. Chicago: Riverside.

Yoakum, C. S., & Yerkes, R. M. (1920). *Army mental tests.* New York: Henry Holt.

CHAPTER TWENTY-ONE

Interpretation of Intelligence Test Scores

MARK H. DANIEL

Three fundamental questions in interpretating intelligence test batteries are the following:

1. What abilities underlie performance on the various scales?
2. How well do the scales measure those underlying abilities?
3. How can reliable information about those abilities be extracted from the test results?

This chapter considers how these questions may be addressed, without attempting to answer them for particular instruments.

One broad purpose of interpretation is to gain an understanding of the examinee's cognitive strengths and weaknesses; this requires focusing on the intelligence tests themselves and their theoretical underpinnings. For the purpose of understanding, a test score is interpretable only if it has a clear relationship to a meaningful construct. A second purpose of interpretation is prediction, such as of occupational or educational success, or of the likelihood that particular interventions will be effective ("treatment validity").

This chapter will focus on the first purpose, interpreting for understanding. Many psychologists consider such understanding to be helpful, if not essential, to their ability to serve a client effectively (Keith, 1994), although empirical demonstrations of the value of this understanding are rare (Reschly, 1997). Diagnosis is a particular form of understanding.

WHAT DO INTELLIGENCE TESTS MEASURE?

The question of what an intelligence battery measures can be addressed only with reference to a model of intelligence. The two dominant models underlying currently available intelligence tests are the hierarchical psychometric abilities model and the Das–Luria neuropsychological model. It is not the purpose of this discussion to advocate these or any other particular models, and all references to models are meant only to be illustrative of general issues in interpretation.

The two versions of the psychometric abilities model (*Gf–Gc* Theory, Horn & Noll, 1997) and the three-stratum theory (Carroll, 1993) are nearly identical in that they identify the same eight "broad abilities" (ability factors at Stratum Two, above the Stratum One narrow abilities and below the general ability factor at Stratum Three). In addition to fluid and crystallized intelligence, these broad abilities include visual and auditory processing, short-term memory, long-term retrieval, and two speed abilities (general cognitive speediness and correct-decision speed). One difference between the *Gf–Gc* and three-stratum models is that the former treats quantitative reasoning as a ninth broad ability, whereas the latter considers this ability dimension to be a part of fluid intelligence. A more important distinction, however, is that *Gf–Gc* theory does not include a third-order general ability factor above the broad abilities. In the three-stratum model, the general ability factor has differential degrees of influence on the broad abilities, ranging from strong influence on fluid and crystallized intelligence to fairly weak saturation of the broad abilities related to speed.

The Das–Luria model of intelligence (Das, Naglieri, & Kirby, 1994) identifies three main processing levels or units, each associated with a region of the brain. Arousal and attention make up the first unit; the second unit corresponds to the coding of information in either successive or simultaneous fashion; and the third unit consists of executive control functions such as planning and monitoring. The distinctive feature of this model is that it focuses on processes (i.e., *how* information is handled) rather than abilities (which are viewed as more dependent on task content and knowledge). The process measures are not intended to reflect integrity of the neurological system (Das et al., 1994, p. 22), and there is no analog in this model to the construct of general ability.

Both the *Gf–Gc*/three-stratum model and the Das–Luria model emphasize multiple dimensions of ability. Thus, the test batteries built on these models each offer a number of scores: multiple scores at the level of broad abilities or functional units, an overall composite score, and scores for individual subtests.

Methods of Investigation

The question of what the subtests and composite scales of an intelligence battery measure has been investigated in several major ways. At the subtest level, content and task analysis are a starting point and, in the case of tasks that are clearly defined and have been clearly located in the theoretical model, may go far. One of the more useful aspects of Carroll's (1993) factor analyses of over 400 multiability datasets is the summary information on the relative strength of relationship of cognitive tasks (i.e., narrow abilities often corresponding to subtests) to the broad ability factor to which they belong. The General Memory factor (short-term memory in the *Gf–Gc* model) offers an interesting example. On the basis of 20 datasets, the narrow ability of free-recall memory has an average loading of .79 on General Memory; the narrow ability of associative memory has a .66 average loading; meaningful memory, .46; and memory span, .36. Therefore, intelligence batteries whose measures of short-term memory consist largely or exclusively of memory-span tasks are not providing effective measurement of the broad short-term memory factor but instead are focusing on a narrow factor. Although on most of the broad abilities the range of narrow-ability loadings reported by Carroll is not as wide as

it is for General Memory, the lists of narrow abilities associated with each broad ability are a valuable reference for content and task analysis of instruments based on the psychometric abilities model.

For the tests built on the Das–Luria neuropsychological model – the Kaufman Assessment Battery for Children (K–ABC; Kaufman & Kaufman, 1983) and the Cognitive Assessment System (CAS; Naglieri & Das, 1997) – content and task analysis are relied on heavily for the construct validation of subtests because the model provides clear descriptions of the processes associated with each functional unit. As the first operationalizations of this theoretical perspective, these instruments did not have the opportunity enjoyed by psychometric ability batteries of relying on correlations with preexisting marker variables.

Another technique for exploring what a battery measures is correlational analysis of two or more batteries and the related procedure of joint exploratory factor analysis. Especially when there are marker subtests or scales believed to be strong and relatively pure measures of specified abilities, correlational analysis can be a powerful tool, although its results are not very informative when (as often happens) the cross-battery correlations are substantially lower than the subtests' or scales' reliabilities. Exploratory factor analysis is weakened as an explanatory tool by indeterminacy in the number of factors to extract; when a research study presents several sets of results for different numbers of factors (as is often found in test manuals), it can be difficult to form a clear understanding of what the battery measures. Indeterminacy in how the factors are rotated can also hamper the drawing of clear conclusions.

Confirmatory factor analysis (CFA), a subset of structural equation modeling, has become probably the most powerful tool for exploring the ability dimensions underlying cognitive batteries. It has several important advantages over exploratory factor analysis. First, whether one battery or a set of batteries is being analyzed, the pattern of subtest intercorrelations can be compared with the pattern that would be expected if the variables corresponded in a hypothesized way to components of a theoretical model, and the degree of misfit between observed and expected correlations can be quantified. The nature of the misfit may point to alternative hypotheses about what particular subtests or scales are measuring. When the data fit a model, the loadings have implications for interpretation.

Another valuable application of CFA is possible when two or more batteries are being analyzed jointly. One can test whether the latent trait underlying a scale on one battery is the same as that underlying a corresponding scale in another. This technique has been employed to show, for example, that the WISC–R Performance scale, the DAS Spatial Ability scale, and the K–ABC Simultaneous Processing scale all reflect the same ability factor. The chapter by Keith (1997) presented this finding as well others to illustrate a variety of ways in which CFA can contribute to construct validation and interpretation.

Understanding Factors versus Understanding Scales

A substantial research literature, based largely on CFA, is developing on how the factors underlying scales on different batteries relate to one another and, by implication, to a theoretical model (most often the psychometric abilities model). In combination, the development of CFA and the emergence of the consensual psychometric abilities model are giving impetus to fruitful research on the construct validation of intelligence tests. Although information of this type is useful for illuminating what these instruments measure, it does not address the equally important question of *how well* a particular scale measures its underlying factor. The demonstration that two scales, on different instruments, are explained by the identical ability dimension does not mean that scores on those scales will agree closely with each other or that either will be a highly valid measure of that dimension.

The validity of a scale in this sense – that is, the strength of correspondence between scale scores and the factor – depends on several characteristics. One is the validity of the individual subtests making up the scale as measures of the ability factor. How much of each subtest's variance is attributable to that factor? As the proportion of factor-determined variance in the subtests increases, the common variance among subtests will have an increasingly large influence on the composite scale score. Carroll's (1993) summary data on the loadings of narrow-ability tasks on broad-ability factors are relevant to this analysis.

A second characteristic is the adequacy with which the subtests sample the domain of narrow abilities subsumed in the broad ability factor. To the extent that a scale can be built from a set of subtests whose only common variance is broad-ability variance, the effect of subtest-specific variance (reflecting narrow abilities or task idiosyncrasies) on the composite is minimized. Selecting subtests that are dissimilar in their superficial features and in the narrow abilities they measure is a strategy for achieving a highly valid composite. It is not known how many different narrow abilities need to be included in a composite to produce a valid measure of the broad ability. Woodcock (1990) set the minimum at two, but it is possible that for some broad abilities a larger number must be included.

Finally, the reliabilities of the subtests affect the validity of the composite scale as a measure of its underlying factor. Error variance, being by definition uncorrelated between subtests, has a diminishing effect on the composite as the number of subtests increases; thus, when subtest reliabilities are low, more subtests are needed to form a valid scale.

In the light of the importance of the How well? question, an additional methodology for investigating what scales measure should be added to the list that already includes content and task analysis, correlational analysis, and exploratory and confirmatory factor analysis. This is the rarely used but potentially very informative procedure of computing the correlation of the scale with its underlying factor (defined through either exploratory or confirmatory methods). Procedures for computing scale-factor correlations are described by Gorsuch (1983, pp. 272–275). In the analysis of a single battery, it would be useful to know how strongly the scale score as actually computed (typically the sum of subtest scores) correlates with the latent trait. Parker and Atkinson (1994, 1995) have reported this information for the WISC–III and WAIS–R standardization samples, finding scale-factor correlations ranging from the mid-.80s, for the Verbal Comprehension Index, to the mid-.60s, for Freedom from Distractibility. (The surprisingly low level of these correlations is due in part to the orthogonal rotation of the factors.) Gustafsson and Undheim (1996) estimated a correlation of .84 between the WISC–III Full-Scale IQ and the general ability factor. Of even greater value to the practitioner would be joint factor analyses of two or more batteries to permit a comparison of the correlations of factorially similar scales with their common underlying ability dimension. By having that common factor be defined by several batteries instead of just one, the factor is likely to correspond more closely to the ability dimension in the theoretical model being used as the frame of reference. Information of this type would not only guide test selection but would also help practitioners interpret score discrepancies between purportedly similar scales.

For a variety of reasons, scales on different batteries that are measures of the same ability – even ones that have been shown through CFA to share the same underlying factor – often correlate at a level well below what might be expected given their reliabilities. This sometimes is true even for what should be the most robust of scores, those for the overall composites. The next sections are concerned with this phenomenon.

Overall Composites

Every intelligence battery, even those built on a theoretical model that does not include a general ability factor, yields an overall score. This testifies to the practical importance that professionals attach to the overall ability composite. The overall score is generally thought to be a powerful predictor and, at the least, a useful starting point for interpreting a cognitive assessment. From this point of view, there is no more important question about the meaning of intelligence-test scores than What do the overall composites measure?

It is an observable fact that not all overall composite scores measure the same construct. The way in which a test author conceptualized general ability will affect how the overall composite is designed and will significantly influence how it may be interpreted. Therefore, they should not all be interpreted or applied in the same way.

Table 21.1 shows the percentage of reliable variance shared by the overall composites of seven widely used intelligence batteries, using data on normal samples provided in the tests' manuals. The DAS, Wechsler scales, KAIT, and SB–4 have much in common; their overall composites correlate in the low .80s to low .90s. In contrast, the overall composites of the WJ–R, K–ABC, and CAS correlate with the four just-named instruments (and with one another) at substantially lower levels. The WJ–R composite correlates approximately .75 with the Wechsler scales, the SB–4, and the K–ABC Mental Processing Composite (MPC); and the K–ABC MPC and CAS Full Scale correlate in the .70s with overall composites on the Wechsler scales and the DAS. The correlation of the K–ABC MPC with the CAS Full Scale has not yet been reported but may be expected to be raised by both instruments' inclusion of scales for sequential and simultaneous processing and their exclusion of verbal ability.

Why do the composites of some instruments diverge so substantially from the others, and what do these results imply about what the different composites are measuring? The dissimilarities among composites mainly reflect different theoretical positions on whether a general ability dimension exists as a real psychological construct, and if it does, what its characteristics are.

A higher order general ability factor typically emerges in hierarchical factor analyses of batteries

TABLE 21.1. Percentage of Reliable Variance Shared by the Overall Composite Scores of Intelligence Batteries

	Wechsler[a] FSIQ	SB–FE Comp.	WJ–R BCA	DAS GCA	KAIT Comp.	K–ABC MPC	CAS FS
Wechsler		77%	59%	86%	79%	65%	50%
SB–FE	372		64%	83%	76%	66%	—
WJ–R	216	121		—	—	65%	—
DAS	153	55	—		—	63%	—
KAIT	461	79	—	—		—	—
K–ABC	252	245	70	27	—		—
CAS	87	—	—	—	—	—	

Note: All data taken from the tests' technical manuals for cases aged 5 and older. Total sample sizes are shown below the diagonal. Correlations were adjusted for restriction of range, averaged using Fisher's *z* transformation, disattenuated, and squared. Dashes indicate that no correlations were reported in the manuals.
[a] WPPSI–R, WISC–R, WISC–III, or WAIS–R.

of diverse cognitive tasks. The notion that this factor represents a unitary characteristic of individuals has had many adherents. For example, based largely on the apparent indivisibility of *g* in factor analysis, Carroll (1991) concluded: "It seems parsimonious to assume that *g* is unitary, that is, that it represents a single entity or constellation in the constitution of the individual that influences a great variety of behaviors and performances" (p. 434). And Gustafsson's hierarchical analyses of cognitive ability batteries led him to conclude that the higher order general factor is identical to the broad ability of fluid intelligence (Undheim & Gustafsson, 1987).

Horn, the primary author of the current *Gf–Gc* model, is perhaps the leading proponent of the contrary view that there is no unitary ability dimension that can be identified as *g*. Horn & Noll (1997) offer three arguments for this position. One is that the selection of tasks to make up a diverse cognitive battery has a large effect on the nature of the general factor extracted from that battery. "The problem for theory of general intelligences [sic] is that the factors are not the same from one study to another.... The general factors represent different mixture measures, not one general intelligence" (Horn & Noll, 1997, p. 68). Thus, Horn disagrees with Thorndike (1994) on the empirical question of whether general factors extracted from reasonably large and varied sets of tests will converge.

The second argument against *g* is that if, as Gustafsson argues, *g* and *Gf* are identical, then in the structural equation model the *g* factor is statistically underidentified, and it cannot account for the correlations among the other broad ability factors. It follows that the "general" factor does not reflect all of the abilities thought to characterize intelligence. A third argument against *g* is based on studies of sets of tasks that are diverse in their features and levels of complexity but are theoretically linked to a single broad ability such as *Gf*. The correlations among these tasks may meet criteria for a unifactorial set, but when a few subtests measuring a different broad ability (such as *Gc*) are added to the set, the criteria are no longer met. "The evidence thus indicates that a *g* factor of fluid intelligence is not a *g* factor of general intelligence" (Horn & Noll, 1997, p. 71).

The four batteries whose overall composites agree relatively closely – the DAS, SB–4, Wechsler scales, and KAIT – do so because the composites all are made up of several broad abilities that have high loadings on the general-ability factor in the three-stratum model. In the case of the SB–4 and DAS, the overall composites were intentionally structured in this way to optimize their validity as measures of *g*. The authors of both instruments viewed general ability as a meaningful and describable characteristic of individuals. For example, the SB–4 authors stated, "it is our strong belief that the best measure of *g*... will stem from a diverse set of cognitive tasks that call for relational thinking in a diversity of contexts" (Thorndike, Hagen, & Sattler, 1986, p. 6). Thorndike viewed *g* as having "a basic organismic reality" (Thorndike, 1994, p. 153). That instrument's overall composite consists of measures of verbal reasoning (crystallized intelligence), quantitative reasoning (crystallized or fluid intelligence), abstract–visual reasoning (fluid intelligence and visual processing), and short-term memory.

The overall composite of the DAS arrived at a similar composition (combining scales for verbal ability or *Gc*, nonverbal reasoning or *Gf*, and spatial ability or *Gv*) through a slightly different route. Following standardization, the scales having the highest loadings on the first unrotated common factor of the battery were selected for inclusion in the overall composite, whereas subtests with relatively low *g* loadings were excluded, although they were kept in the battery for the qualitatively different information they provided (Elliott, 1990). Like the SB–4 authors, the DAS author believed that the general factor is a psychological reality; he characterized it as "the general ability of an individual to perform complex mental processing that involves conceptualization and the transformation of information" (Elliott, 1990, p. 20).

Wechsler also believed in the meaningfulness of general ability, although he did not have the benefit of a well-defined taxonomy such as the *Gf–Gc* model to help guide his selection of content. Wechsler conceptualized intelligence as "the aggregate or global capacity of the individual to act purposefully, to think rationally, and to deal effectively with his environment" (1939, p. 3). He realized the value of sampling from varied types of tasks, but because he viewed these tasks as offering different means for the individual to demonstrate intelligence, he was not systematically selective in forming the overall composite. Current analyses of the Wechsler instruments find that the Full-Scale IQ is biased toward the measurement of verbal ability at the expense of visual processing and quantitative reasoning (Carroll, 1997; Parker & Atkinson, 1994, 1995).

The overall composite of the KAIT is made up of scales measuring the two most highly g-loaded of the broad abilities in the Gf–Gc model, fluid and crystallized intelligence. Consistent with that model, the KAIT authors view the composite "more as a summative score than as a theoretical construct" (Kaufman & Kaufman, 1993, p. 8). Yet because of the particular Gf–Gc broad abilities included in the composite, it provides a strong measure of the general factor in the three-stratum theory.

It is an interesting, and as yet unanswered, question which of these four instruments has a composite scale that most validly measures the general ability factor in the three-stratum model. One way to address that question would be to conduct a joint confirmatory factor analysis of the four batteries to determine whether they all reflect the same general ability dimension, and if they do, to compute scale-factor correlations to see how well each of them measures that dimension. The data in Table 21.1 indicate that the differences among these instruments will not be great.

An entirely different interpretive question arises when considering the construct meaning of the overall composites of the other three instruments included in Table 21.1, the WJ–R, K–ABC, and CAS. These composites cannot be said to approximate the general ability factor of three-stratum theory because the authors of these three batteries do not conceptualize general ability as a meaningful construct. Logically, therefore, there are no criteria against which to validate these general composite scales, and from the theoretical perspectives of these instruments it is meaningless to ask whether their composites are more or less construct-valid than those of other instruments. Also, if the overall composite is not intended to measure a describable construct, the selection of abilities to include in the composite becomes arbitrary or, at least, driven by considerations other than construct validity.

Woodcock, whose WJ–R adheres closely to the Gf–Gc model, agrees with Horn that a general factor is meaningless. "There is no question, technically, that broad scores of intelligence can be calculated, but what do such broad scores mean in practice? At best, they predict the average outcome in a variety of life situations that require a variety of cognitive abilities. They do not allow us to predict anything specific" (Woodcock, 1990, p. 257). The overall composite of the WJ–R is composed of scales measuring seven of the broad abilities of the Gf–Gc model, including some such as speed and auditory processing that in the three-stratum theory have relatively low g saturation. This may be the explanation for the low level of overlap with the composite scores on other batteries. The lack of a construct definition may introduce problems in application as well as interpretation. For example, the inclusion of weak g measures runs the risk of depressing the composite scores of examinees who have specific cognitive deficits, which such subtests often are designed to identify (Elliott, 1997).

The neuropsychological model on which the K–ABC and CAS are based also does not include the construct of general ability. In both instruments, the overall composite is offered as a summary of the individual's status in various process areas and as a score that may be useful for prediction but not as a measure of an underlying dimension. The CAS Full Scale "provides an index of the overall level of an individual's cognitive functioning" (Naglieri & Das, 1997, p. 7). The value of the Mental Processing Composite of the K–ABC is based on the belief that "intelligence is complex and that probably the most intelligent behavior results from an integration of sequential and simultaneous processing" (Kaufman & Kaufman, 1983, p. 31). As with the WJ–R, the relative lack of agreement of these instruments' overall composites with those of other instruments is probably explained by the fact that they are not designed to measure a general ability construct.

Overall composite scales that are not built to reflect an ability dimension may have practical advantages, such as the reduced influence of cultural background on instruments whose composites do not include measures of crystallized intelligence. However, they leave the test user with an interpretive problem, which may best be dealt with by downplaying the composite and focusing attention on lower order scales in the battery.

In summary, the way in which overall composite scales are constructed has a large effect on what they measure and how they should be interpreted (Jensen, 1992; Woodcock, 1990). With respect to the nature of the common factor underlying a test battery, it has been claimed that with any reasonably large and diverse set of cognitive tasks that factor will be very close to g (e.g., Thorndike, 1994). Yet, with respect to individually administered intelligence batteries, convergence does not always occur – or, it is more accurate to say, scores on the composite scales do not agree (even though the underlying common factors might). This might be the result of violating Thorndike's injunction that "the gamut of cognitive tasks [must] be sampled sufficiently broadly and uniformly that no relatively homogeneous subcluster of tests will introduce significant amounts of variance from factors other than a general cognitive ability" (1994, p. 153).

Practitioners should not assume that the overall composite scales of intelligence batteries can be interpreted interchangeably. Overall composites that intercorrelate highly may be interpreted in a similar way, perhaps using the construct descriptions presented by Carroll, Thorndike, or Elliott. When the correlational data indicate that composites diverge significantly, however, their interpretation should be based on a careful evaluation of their content and their theoretical underpinnings.

Lower Order Composites

All modern intelligence batteries include scales at a level below that of general ability representing in the psychometric abilities model what Carroll (1993) labels "broad abilities," and in the Das–Luria model, processing styles. Valid interpretation of these scales depends on a clear understanding of what they measure. Regarding the psychometric model, there is less disagreement about the construct interpretation of broad abilities than general ability; arguments about the nature of crystallized intelligence or visual processing abilities, for example, do not engage the wide attention that follows debates over g. Because lower order abilities are seen as having less serious implications for individual examinees, less thought may have been devoted to them. Whatever the reason, the low level of debate is *not* the result of a large amount of correlational data showing the convergence of scales on different batteries that purport to measure the same broad ability. To the contrary, the amount of such data is small for all broad abilities except crystallized intelligence.

Crystallized ability is well represented in the modern psychometrically based instruments. The median of 22 cross-battery intercorrelations reported in their manuals[*] is .78 (for normal samples; range, .51 to .85), and adjusting for range restriction would probably raise this average into the low .80s. Thus, there is good agreement among batteries on the measurement of crystallized intelligence. Nevertheless, given that these scales typically have reliabilities in the .90s and that confirmatory factor analyses have shown that the latent traits underlying at least some of these scales are identical (Keith, 1997), it must be concluded that there are differences among the scales in how, and how well, they reflect that broad ability.

For other broad abilities, there are little if any data. Only two instruments (the SB–4 and WJ–R) contain memory scales, for which two correlations have been reported (.65 and .71). The only batteries that have attempted to create scales focused on fluid intelligence, visual processing, or both, are the DAS, KAIT, and WJ–R, and their manuals contain no correlation studies between pairs of these instruments. (A similar condition exists for instruments built on the Das–Luria model; correlations between CAS and K–ABC process scales have not yet been published.) Overall, then, interpretation of scale scores with reference to the psychometric or neuropsychological models is not empirically grounded; the strength of relationship between scales and model constructs generally is not known.

The measurement of visual processing provides a clear example of the difference between understanding the ability factor(s) underlying a scale, and understanding scores on the scale itself. Confirmatory factor analysis has shown that the same factor underlies the WISC–R Performance scale and the DAS Spatial Ability scale (Keith, 1997). Nevertheless, the two scales correlate only in the low .70s (Elliott, 1990). The factor loadings in this analysis suggest that the Picture Completion and Picture Arrangement subtests add construct-irrelevant variance which weakens the validity of the Performance scale as a measure of the common underlying factor.

---

[*] Correlations among the following scales: DAS Verbal Ability; K–ABC Achievement; KAIT Crystallized; SB–4 Verbal Reasoning; WPPSI–R, WISC–R, WISC–III, and WAIS–R Verbal IQ; and WJ–R Comprehension-Knowledge.

Scale-factor correlations, described in the earlier section on methodology, would shed light on the construct validity of both the DAS and WISC–R scales.

Factor analyses performed on single batteries have been a primary source of scale construct validation. One positive feature of factor analysis for scale development is that it ensures cohesiveness among the subtests, which will share a common source of variance whose influence will be magnified when the subtest scores are summed. Also, especially if confirmatory factor analysis is used, correspondence of the battery's factor structure to a theoretical model can be evidence for the construct meaning of scales. Correlations among the factors, or, in the case of a hierarchical analysis, correlations of lower order factors with a higher order general factor, can be suggestive regarding scale validity. For example, if the third factor of the WISC–III has the highest loading (.90) on general ability of any of the four factors, as Keith and Witta's (1997) analysis of the standardization data found, then that factor should be interpreted as representing high-level intellectual processing rather than "freedom from distractibility." (Note, however, that in Gustafsson and Undheim's (1996) hierarchical analysis of the same data, the third factor's general ability loading was .80, which is lower than those for the first two factors.)

Single-battery factor analysis is nevertheless a limited tool for construct validation in comparison with multibattery analysis. For one thing, the factor structure of any battery is limited by the nature and variety of subtests it contains. Factor analysis of single batteries usually results in underfactoring because some broad abilities are represented by only one subtest and so cannot emerge as a factor (Woodcock, 1990). A good illustration is the effect of adding the Symbol Search subtest in the change from the WISC–R to the WISC–III. Introducing a second measure of speed created a fourth (Processing Speed) factor and altered the nature of the third factor. Thus, scales that have been formed on the basis of factor analysis may nevertheless be factorially complex and may never lend themselves to clear interpretation. And, as we have seen, single-battery factor analysis does little to achieve measurement consistency across instruments. Overall, this technique is not a sufficient foundation for scale interpretation.

Another important type of support for the interpretation of scales is analysis of the content,

task requirements, and empirical validity of the component subtests. Carroll (1993) and Woodcock (1990) offered empirically based analyses of the subtests and scales of many instruments. McGrew and Flanagan (1998; McGrew, 1997; Flanagan & McGrew, 1997) have furthered this type of analysis as part of a program to bring the scales and subtests of all intelligence batteries into a common interpretive system. Using this approach, the construct meaning of a scale on an intelligence battery is evaluated by tallying the narrow abilities measured by its component subtests, seeing how they fit into the *Gf–Gc* model, and judging where the scale belongs in the hierarchical structure. If the subtests were found to predominantly measure a single narrow ability, with relatively little construct-irrelevant variance, then the scale would be interpreted as reflecting that narrow ability. For example, the two WJ–R subtests in the Long-Term Retrieval cluster, Memory for Names and Visual–Auditory Learning, are both measures of the specific ability of associative memory, and thus that cluster is best interpreted at the narrow-ability level (Flanagan & McGrew, 1997). A similar conclusion would be drawn about a scale composed of a single, homogeneous subtest, such as the Speed of Information Processing subtest of the DAS.

On the other hand, if the subtests in a composite are good measures of two or more of the narrow abilities nested within a broad ability, and there is little extraneous variance, then, according to the guidelines suggested by Flanagan and McGrew (1997), the scale can be considered a valid measure of that broad ability. The dimension that the subtests have in common (i.e., the broad ability) will have a strong influence on the composite because the covariances between subtests will contribute to the composite's variance. For the same reason, extraneous variance present in only one of the component subtests will have little effect on the composite.

The construct validity of the scale will of course depend as well on the strength of relationship of each of the component subtests with the ability factor that the scale is intended to measure. Carroll (1993), Woodcock (1990), and McGrew (1997) all provide information relevant to this question, although, as McGrew (1997) observes, empirical groundwork for this kind of analysis is far from complete.

In evaluating results of this type, it is essential to keep in mind the distinction between factors and scales. The scale is a sum of subtest scores that may therefore contain a substantial amount of variance unrelated to the underlying factor, which accounts for the far from perfect correlations observed between scales whose underlying factors may correspond closely to the same broad ability (Jensen, 1992). The sizes of subtest loadings in a factor analysis indicate how tightly the scale composed of those subtests reflects the factor. For example, although the factor underlying the WJ–R subtests designed to measure Broad Visual Perception has a high g loading (Bickley, Keith, & Wolfle, 1995), as it should according to the three-stratum model, the subtest loadings on that factor are modest, and the scale score may therefore not be a strong indicator of this broad ability (McGrew, 1997).

HOW CAN USEFUL INFORMATION BE EXTRACTED FROM AN INTELLIGENCE TEST BATTERY?

Up to this point the discussion has concerned the construct validity of scales: What abilities do they measure, and how well do they measure them? Even after these questions have been answered satisfactorily for a battery, the practitioner faces the problem of how to extract information in a way that will be useful for understanding the examinee.

If only a single scale were being administered and interpreted, the procedure would be straightforward. The fundamental problem in interpreting a set of scores arises from the large amount of common variance among scales (reflecting general ability) and among subtests (reflecting in addition lower order factors such as broad abilities or processes; Gustafsson & Snow, 1997). The large amount of common factor variance tends to swamp and obscure information about abilities lower in the hierarchy. This is true whether or not the model underlying the battery incorporates a general ability factor, and it is true for neuropsychologically based instruments as well as psychometric ability tests (Kranzler & Weng, 1995). Much of the criticism of intelligence batteries can be traced to this phenomenon of shared variance across scores. Critics of profile analysis (e.g., Macmann & Barnett, 1992; McDermott & Glutting, 1997) probably overstate

the case when they suggest that the Wechsler scales and other batteries measure nothing other than general ability. Some of the techniques on which they base this conclusion, such as profile instability, exploratory factor analysis, and the amount of predictive validity added by lower order scores, are less direct ways of assessing dimensionality and construct validity than, for example, confirmatory factor analysis. But these critics are correct in pointing to the difficulties of deriving information on differential abilities from batteries containing large amounts of common variance.

Models for Representing Relationships between Abilities

A useful basis for conceptualizing the interpretive problem posed by multiple correlated ability scores is the distinction made by Gustafsson and Undheim (1996) between two types of hierarchical models. One type, which they label "weak," is built from the bottom up: factors are first extracted from observed variables (e.g., subtests); then, from the correlations among these factors, one or more second-order factors are extracted; and so on. Each factor at each level of the hierarchy is thought of as representing an ability. However, abilities at different levels are not distinct but instead share variance. It is as if each level were designed to be a complete, free-standing description of abilities, although different levels provide different degrees of detail.

The other type of hierarchical model, termed "strong," is built from the top down. First the general factor is identified and its variance is removed from all of the variables. Next, lower order factors are extracted from the correlations among the *residual* variances; these factors represent residualized abilities (i.e., abilities independent of general ability). The process could be repeated to create lower levels of residual factors. In this approach, the variance in a lower order scale can be decomposed into a part due to general ability and a part due to the residualized broad ability factor. That is, there are relations from higher order to lower order factors. Interpretation would consider all levels, not just a single level as in the weak model.

For the test interpreter, the strong type of model offers certain advantages, at least in principle. Practitioners often are interested in interpreting more than a single level of the hierarchy, especially if the test they are interpreting is based on a model that treats general ability as a meaningful construct. It is conceptually difficult to understand a set of ability scores that represent different levels of the hierarchy if those scores have overlapping variance; one continually faces the question of the extent to which a particular score reflects a lower order as opposed to a higher order ability. This problem is eliminated if ability scores are residualized.

In practice, however, interpreting a test battery according to the strong hierarchical model poses problems. At the conceptual level, although residualized ability scores are measures of real abilities, they are, in a sense, artificial (Carroll, 1993). They do not directly correspond to real-world demonstrations of ability, which are influenced by factors from several levels of the hierarchy. For example, an individual who is no better than average on the residualized broad ability of visual processing might nevertheless perform very well on real-world visualization tasks because of a high level of general ability.

Residualized ability scores also pose serious measurement problems, which existing tests probably are not prepared to handle (Gustafsson & Snow, 1997). Residualized scores are essentially difference scores and so tend to have lower reliability than raw scale scores. Assuming that accurately rank-ordering individuals on residualized abilities is a worthwhile goal, there would need to be a number of reliable and valid variables for each ability (Gustafsson & Undheim, 1996). Thus, the residualized-abilities approach to interpretation may be better suited to scales than to subtests. Also, because the reliability of difference scores is inversely related to the correlation between the higher order and lower order ability factors, the measurement demands would be particularly great for broad abilities that have high general-factor loadings.

The advantages and disadvantages of the commonly used methods of interpreting intelligence batteries can be more easily understood by reference to the distinction between strong and weak hierarchical models. One method, the "top–down" system of the type developed by Kaufman (1979) and widely recommended in textbooks (e.g., Sattler, 1988) and in the interpretive manuals of published tests (e.g., Elliott, 1990; Naglieri & Das, 1997), is closely related to the strong hierarchical model. Other methods are more compatible with the weak

hierarchical model because they start by evaluating a set of lower order scores simultaneously.

Top-Down Approach

Interpretive strategies of this type start by drawing inferences about general ability from the overall composite score. Then, scores at the next lower level of generality (scale scores, typically at the level of broad abilities or processes) are tested for variability. This may be done by making pairwise comparisons of scale scores (as suggested in the Wechsler, K–ABC, and CAS manuals) or by comparing scale scores with the score on the overall composite (as recommended in the manuals for the DAS and SB–4). If there is a statistically significant or rare degree of variation among scale scores, the variation may be interpreted to reflect clinically important strengths or weaknesses in lower order (e.g., broad) abilities. Modern tests typically provide numerical guidelines for this type of profile analysis in their manuals and, often, on their record forms.

The similarity of these approaches to the strong hierarchical model is clear. Scale scores are a function partly of general ability and partly of broad abilities. Either method of analyzing scale-score variability is an approximate way of determining whether, for this examinee, the non-g component of the broad ability (in other words, the residualized ability) is significantly high or low; otherwise, the scale scores are not interpreted individually. (To make this inference somewhat more accurate, each scale score could be compared with the scale score predicted from the general-ability score). An analogous procedure may be applied to subtests within a scale to test for significant strengths or weaknesses in narrow abilities.

To the extent that scales assess general ability, they must tend to be the same as one another and the same as the overall composite. It is only those portions of the broad ability scales independent of general ability that can produce interscale variation.

A standard feature of the top-down approach is the recommendation against interpreting the overall composite score if scale scores vary significantly. For example, Sattler comments that when the Verbal and Performance IQs on a Wechsler battery differ, the Full-Scale IQ is "merely" a "forced average of rather disparate primary skills" (1988, p. 182). In principle, the way in which variability is handled should depend on one's position regarding the nature and meaning of the composite. It is certainly the case that a composite score derived from highly varied component scores does not give a useful or accurate *summary* of the individual's cognitive abilities. For those who view the overall composite primarily as an average, whatever interpretive value it possesses is valid only when the components are relatively equal in level – which is to say, the overall composite then serves as a shorthand summary of the set of scores. For those who adopt this interpretive position, the recommendation against interpreting a composite derived from variable components is sensible. However, this approach diminishes the utility of the overall composite.

If, on the other hand, the overall composite is considered to measure a dimension of ability, then it may be argued that the degree of consistency of an individual's scores on the component broad abilities is irrelevant to the validity of that person's composite score. Except when there is independent reason to discount the accuracy of one or more of the component scores, variation in the subscores that make up the composite can be assumed to reflect strengths and weaknesses in broad abilities. Such patterns of strengths and weaknesses are normal, and there is no statistical reason why an overall composite score based on a "spiky" profile of broad abilities should be a less accurate measure of the general ability factor than a composite score based on a level profile. Furthermore, even if one suspected the composite to be less valid because of the variation among component scores, there is no statistical procedure that would be expected to yield a more valid estimate from such data. (This conclusion does not, of course, apply in situations where the validity of one or more of the component scores is questionable for reasons other than score variability itself, such as the effect on a crystallized ability scale of limited exposure to the dominant culture or the effect on a visual-processing scale of a motor impairment.)

IPSATIVE SCORES. Testing for significantly high or low scale or subtest scores in the top-down approach is a crude form of measuring residual ability dimensions in the strong hierarchical model. A closer approximation to residualized ability scores would be ipsative scores, that is, difference scores between the scale or subtest and a measure of

the higher order ability. The proper way to compute these scores would be to compare the obtained scale or subtest score with the score predicted from the higher order ability. This prediction would vary as a function of the higher-factor loading of the scale or subtest. For a scale or subtest where little variance is due to general ability, the score predicted from the battery's overall composite would be near the population average for all examinees, regardless of their general-ability level. For such a scale or subtest there would be little difference between the ipsative score and the unadjusted score. In contrast, the predicted score for a scale or subtest with a high general-ability loading would be nearly as far above or below the population mean as is the overall composite score.

Studies of ipsative scoring have generally reported disappointing results (Glutting, McDermott, & Konold, 1997; McDermott & Glutting, 1997). There are several reasons why this should be so. First, analyses usually have focused on subtests, which typically lack the reliability and specificity required to make difference scores reliable. Second, a simplified method has been used in which all subtests are compared with the same standard (the average subtest score) rather than with expected scores that take the subtests' general-ability loadings into account. Third, some studies have evaluated the validity of the ipsative subtest or scale scores without also considering scores on higher order ability factors (McDermott, Fantuzzo, & Glutting, 1990). Because ipsative scores have been stripped of a major source of ability variance, they need to be analyzed in concert with scores representing those other sources (Gustafsson & Snow, 1997). As discussed in a later section of this chapter, when well-constructed residualized ability scores are analyzed simultaneously with scores representing higher levels of the ability hierarchy, they can have substantial and informative relationships with external criteria.

Configural Analysis

An alternative to top-down profile analysis is evaluating the profile pattern and elevation – perhaps comparing it with prototypical profiles. This approach is well suited conceptually to weak hierarchical models such as the *Gf–Gc* model because it focuses on comparing broad abilities with one another rather than with a general factor. Inferences about broad abilities are based in a straightforward way on the normative scores associated with scales, bypassing the step of determining whether a scale score differs significantly from an overall composite. Inferences about relative strengths and weakness can be based on pairwise comparisons.

Configural analysis of intelligence batteries currently is out of favor because of disappointing results of attempts to establish diagnostically useful profiles for clinical groups and because this approach lacks the statistical significance and population frequency indexes yielded by the top-down method. Recently, McDermott and Glutting and their colleagues have presented "core" subtest profiles for several intelligence batteries identified by means of cluster analysis of cases in the standardization samples (Glutting, McDermott, Prifitera, & McGrath, 1994; Konold, Glutting, & McDermott, 1997). These are profiles that occur (with slight variation) relatively frequently in the normal population. The rationale for providing these core profiles is as follows. Before Kaufman (1976) and others publicized the fact that normal individuals frequently have considerable variability ("scatter") in their subtest or scale scores on an intelligence battery, such variation tended to be viewed as clinically significant, perhaps signifying psychopathology or neuropathology. In order to prevent this misinterpretation, test materials have in recent years made information available on the relative frequency of various amounts of scatter in the population so that intraindividual score differences are not presumed to be rare simply because they are statistically significant. Providing core profiles is another way of helping practitioners judge whether a particular profile is common or unusual. McDermott and his colleagues have provided algorithms that can be used for this purpose (e.g., Konold, Glutting, & McDermott, 1997). They recommend that any profile that meets their criteria of similarity to one of the core profiles should not be considered clinically significant, and only profiles that are among the 5% most dissimilar to the core profiles should be considered meaningful.

The most noticeable feature of the core profiles from any of the batteries is that most of them are nearly level, that is, the core profiles for an instrument primarily represent different levels of general ability. This is a consequence of the methodology employed by the authors (i.e., the use of normative rather than ipsative subtest scores and the choice of the statistical index of similarity between two profiles). Thus, the core profiles are unlikely to represent many cases in the population given that scatter is a typical rather than atypical feature of intelligence-test profiles. As Reschly (1997) put it, "what is abnormal in terms of occurring infrequently is a flat profile of subtest scores" (p. 443).

The rationale for core profiles confounds meaningfulness with rarity. Certainly, the once-common assumption that highly variable profiles are unusual and therefore likely to reflect pathology can now be seen to be invalid. But it goes too far in the other direction to say that because a profile is common it does not have clinical significance. The frequency of occurrence of a particular profile in the general population is not especially relevant to its usefulness for understanding the individual's cognitive strengths and weaknesses or making predictions about his or her success in various endeavors. Particularly for intelligence batteries that measure a number of broad abilities, it is not true that only unusual profiles can be clinically meaningful.

Specificity

Both the top-down and the configural approaches to profile analysis rest ultimately on difference scores: in the top-down analysis, differences between scores at lower and higher levels of the hierarchy; and in configural analysis, differences between scores at the same level. The measurement problems of using difference scores are reduced to the extent that scale or subtest scores have high reliabilities and low intercorrelations (Gustafsson & Snow, 1997). This combination of characteristics is referred to as *specificity* and is operationally defined as the proportion of score variance that is reliable and is unique to that scale or subtest. From the foregoing discussion, it is clear that extracting more valid and reliable ability information from intelligence batteries will require that efforts be made to raise their levels of specificity by ensuring that there are enough variables to measure ability dimensions reliably and by reducing sources of unwanted correlation between dimensions. In the interpretive process, the amount of specificity will manifest itself in the frequency with which statistically significant strengths and weaknesses are observed. Batteries having low specificity simply are less capable of revealing cognitive strengths and weaknesses.

Existing batteries vary in the average specificity of their scales and subtests (Elliott, 1997), and thus there is reason for optimism that careful test design can produce greater specificity. It is an interesting question whether there is an optimal level of specificity such that scales are not so thoroughly purged of the influence of general ability (assuming that were possible) that measurement of the general factor would be weakened.

Because correlations among cognitive variables are higher at low ability levels (Detterman & Daniel, 1989), the specificity of any particular cognitive battery will tend to be greater for high-ability examinees. This suggests that there is a firmer basis for profile analysis when intelligence tests are used with such individuals. Research on developing a residualized abilities method of interpretation might do well to utilize high-ability samples to maximize the reliability of residual scores.

Interpretive Models and Predictive Validity

Although the topic of this chapter has been ways of understanding and extracting the information captured by intelligence batteries, this topic has an implication for criterion-related validation that deserves mention. The same characteristic of cognitive batteries that makes it difficult to obtain reliable and distinctive information about lower order abilities – that is, the large proportion of variance that is due to the general factor – also appears to have hampered investigation of how lower order abilities are related to external criteria such as occupational and educational performance. This has led to the conclusion that general ability provides almost all of the predictive or explanatory power in a battery (Jensen, 1992; McNemar, 1964; McDermott & Glutting, 1997; Ree & Earles, 1993).

However, Gustafsson and Snow (1997) contended that the usual way of measuring broad and narrow abilities (i.e., as scale or subtest scores) has obscured what is in reality a substantial amount of validity for profiles of nonredundant scores. They observed that "the correlated factors approach cannot properly estimate the relative importance of predictors when broad factors influence two or more of the predictors..." (Gustafsson & Snow, 1997, p. 116). To demonstrate this point, they showed that when broad abilities are made orthogonal through the Schmidt–Leiman technique (thus removing variance due to higher order abilities), they can contribute large amounts of incremental validity to the prediction of occupational and educational criteria and that the patterns of prediction are informative about the differential roles of broad abilities in different real-world activities. For example, their studies show that academic success in English is predicted about equally well by crystallized and fluid abilities, whereas success in mathematics is much more strongly related to fluid ability than to crystallized ability. In these same datasets, analyses based on unadjusted scale scores fail to reveal such differential effects.

An alternative but conceptually similar way of validating broad or narrow abilities is through structural equation modeling, as illustrated by McGrew, Keith, Flanagan, & Vanderwood (1997). This technique allows the relationship of broad abilities to external criteria to be evaluated while the relationship of general ability to those criteria is taken into account. Like the residualized abilities approach, this method had shown substantial, differential and meaningful prediction of academic achievement by broad abilities. However, these investigators, like Gustafsson and Snow, are cautious in their expectations for practically useful applications of these more sophisticated approaches to validating profiles because the research is in an early stage and because translating the research findings to individual cases will require advances in assessment technology.

CONCLUSION

Interpreting intelligence batteries has never been easy, and the survey presented in this chapter does not suggest that new techniques or developments will dramatically change that situation in the near future. Steady work on identifying the abilities underlying test scales, referenced to widely accepted ability taxonomies, should tend to make interpretation more "instrument-free." But significant advances in interpretation are likely to result mainly from the development of new instruments that are built with interpretation in mind. To support interpretation of abilities at several levels of the hierarchy, such instruments will have to include enough carefully designed subtests to permit accurate measurement of abilities at lower levels while controlling the influence of higher-level abilities.

REFERENCES

Bickley, P. G., Keith, T. Z., & Wolfle, L. M. (1995). The three-stratum theory of cognitive abilities: Test of the structure of intelligence across the life span. *Intelligence, 20,* 309–328.

Carroll, J. B. (1991). No demonstration that *g* is not unitary, but there's more to the story: Comment on Kranzler and Jensen. *Intelligence, 15,* 423–436.

Carroll, J. B. (1993). *Human cognitive abilities: A survey of factor-analytic studies.* New York: Cambridge University Press.

Carroll, J. B. (1997). Commentary on Keith and Witta's hierarchical and cross-age confirmatory factor analysis of the WISC-III. *School Psychology Quarterly, 12,* 108–109.

Das, J. P., Naglieri, J. A., & Kirby, J. R. (1994). *Assessment of cognitive processes: The PASS theory of intelligence.* Needham Heights, MA: Allyn & Bacon.

Detterman, D. K., & Daniel, M. H. (1989). Correlations of mental tests with each other and with cognitive variables are highest for low IQ groups. *Intelligence, 13,* 349–359.

Elliott, C. D. (1990). *Differential Ability Scales introductory and technical handbook.* San Antonio, TX: The Psychological Corporation.

Elliott, C. D. (1997). The Differential Ability Scales. In D. P. Flanagan, J. L. Genshaft, & P. L. Harrison (Eds.), *Contemporary intellectual assessment: Theories, tests, and issues* (pp. 183–208). New York: Guilford.

Flanagan, D. P., & McGrew, K. S. (1997). A cross-battery approach to assessing and interpreting cognitive abilities: Narrowing the gap between practice and cognitive science. In D. P. Flanagan, J. L. Genshaft, & P. L. Harrison (Eds.), *Contemporary intellectual assessment: Theories, tests, and issues* (pp. 314–325). New York: Guilford.

Glutting, J. J., McDermott, P. A., & Konold, T. R. (1997). Ontology, structure, and diagnostic benefits of a normative subtest taxonomy from the WISC–III standardization sample. In D. P. Flanagan, J. L. Genshaft, & P. L. Harrison (Eds.), *Contemporary intellectual assessment: Theories, tests, and issues* (pp. 349–372). New York: Guilford.

Glutting, J. J., McDermott, P. A., Prifitera, A., & McGrath, E. A. (1994). Core profile types for the WISC–III and WIAT: Development and their application in identifying multivariate IQ-achievement discrepancies. *School Psychology Review, 23,* 619–639.

Gorsuch, R. L. (1983). *Factor analysis* (2nd ed.). Hillsdale, NJ: Erlbaum.

Gustafsson, J.-E., & Snow, R. E. (1997). Ability profiles. In R. F. Dillon (Ed.), *Handbook on testing* (pp. 107–135). Westport, CT: Greenwood.

Gustafsson, J.-E., & Undheim, J. O. (1996). Individual differences in cognitive functions. In D. C. Berliner & R. C. Calfee (Eds.), *Handbook of educational psychology* (pp. 186–242). New York: Macmillan.

Horn, J. L., & Noll, J. (1997). Human cognitive capabilities: Gf–Gc theory. In D. P. Flanagan, J. L. Genshaft, & P. L. Harrison (Eds.), *Contemporary intellectual assessment: Theories, tests, and issues* (pp. 53–91). New York: Guilford.

Jensen, A. R. (1992). Commentary: Vehicles of *g*. *Psychological Science, 3,* 275–278.

Kaufman, A. S. (1976). A new approach to the interpretation of test scatter on the WISC–R. *Journal of Learning Disabilities, 9,* 160–168.

Kaufman, A. S. (1979). *Intelligent testing with the WISC–R.* New York: Wiley.

Kaufman, A. S., & Kaufman, N. L. (1983). *Kaufman Assessment Battery for Children interpretive manual.* Circle Pines, MN: American Guidance Service.

Kaufman, A. S., & Kaufman, N. L. (1993). *Kaufman Adolescent and Adult Intelligence Test manual.* Circle Pines, MN: American Guidance Service.

Keith, T. Z. (1994). Intelligence *is* important, intelligence *is* complex. *School Psychology Quarterly, 9,* 209–221.

Keith, T. Z. (1997). Using confirmatory factor analysis to aid in understanding the constructs measured by intelligence tests. In D. P. Flanagan, J. L. Genshaft, & P. L. Harrison (Eds.), *Contemporary intellectual assessment: Theories, tests, and issues* (pp. 373–402). New York: Guilford.

Keith, T. Z., & Witta, E. L. (1997). Hierarchical and cross-age confirmatory factor analysis of the WISC–III: What does it measure? *School Psychology Quarterly, 12,* 89–107.

Konold, T. R., Glutting, J. J., & McDermott, P. A. (1997). The development and applied utility of a normative aptitude-achievement taxonomy for the Woodcock–Johnson Psycho-Educational Battery – Revised. *Journal of Special Education, 31,* 212–232.

Kranzler, J. H., & Weng, L. (1995). Factor structure of the PASS cognitive tasks: A reexamination of Naglieri *et al.* (1991). *Journal of School Psychology, 33,* 143–157.

Macmann, G. M., & Barnett, D. W. (1992). Redefining the WISC–R: Implications for professional practice and public policy. *Journal of Special Education, 26,* 139–161.

McDermott, P. A., Fantuzzo, J. W., & Glutting, J. J. (1990). Just say no to subtest analysis: A critique on Wechsler theory and practice. *Journal of Psychoeducational Assessment, 8,* 290–302.

McDermott, P. A., & Glutting, J. J. (1997). Informing stylistic learning behavior, disposition, and achievement through ability subtests – or, more illusions of meaning? *School Psychology Review, 26,* 163–175.

McGrew, K. S. (1997). Analysis of the major intelligence batteries according to a proposed comprehensive Gf–Gc framework. In D. P. Flanagan, J. L. Genshaft, & P. L. Harrison (Eds.), *Contemporary intellectual assessment: Theories, tests, and issues* (pp. 151–179). New York: Guilford.

McGrew, K. S., & Flanagan, D. P. (1998). *The intelligence test desk reference (ITDR): Gf–Gc cross-battery assessment.* Needham Heights, MA: Allyn & Bacon.

McGrew, K. S., Keith, T. Z., Flanagan, D. P., & Vanderwood, M. (1997). Beyond *g*: The impact of *Gf–Gc* specific cognitive abilities research on the future use and interpretation of intelligence tests in the schools. *School Psychology Review, 26,* 189–210.

McNemar (1964). Lost: Our intelligence. Why? *American Psychologist, 19,* 871–882.

Naglieri, J. A., & Das, J. P. (1997). *Cognitive Assessment System interpretive handbook.* Itasca, IL: Riverside.

Parker, K. C. H., & Atkinson, L. (1994). Factor space of the Wechsler Intelligence Scale for Children – Third Edition: Critical thoughts and recommendations. *Psychological Assessment, 6,* 201–208.

Parker, K. C. H., & Atkinson, L. (1995). Computation of Wechsler Adult Intelligence Scale – Revised factor scores: Equal and differential weights. *Psychological Assessment, 7,* 456–462.

Ree, M. J., & Earles, J. A. (1993). *g* is to psychology what carbon is to chemistry: A reply to Sternberg and Wagner, McClelland, and Calfee. *Current Directions in Psychological Science, 2,* 11–12.

Reschly, D. J. (1997). Diagnostic and treatment validity of intelligence tests. In D. P. Flanagan, J. L. Genshaft, & P. L. Harrison (Eds.), *Contemporary intellectual assessment: Theories, tests, and issues* (pp. 437–456). New York: Guilford.

Sattler, J. M. (1988). *Assessment of children* (3rd ed.). San Diego: Author.

Thorndike, R. L. (1994). *g. Intelligence, 19,* 145–155.

Thorndike, R. L., Hagen, E. P., & Sattler, J. M. (1986). *The Stanford–Binet Intelligence Scale: Fourth Edition technical manual.* Chicago: Riverside.

Undheim, J. O., & Gustafsson, J.-E. (1987). The hierarchical organization of cognitive abilities: Restoring general intelligence through the use of linear structural relations (LISREL). *Multivariate Behavioral Research, 22,* 149–171.

Wechsler, D. (1939). *The measurement of adult intelligence.* Baltimore: Williams & Wilkins.

Woodcock, R. W. (1990). Theoretical foundations of the WJ–R measures of cognitive ability. *Journal of Psychoeducational Assessment, 8,* 231–258.

CHAPTER TWENTY-TWO

Teaching Intelligence: A Performance Conception

TINA A. GROTZER AND DAVID N. PERKINS

INTRODUCTION

For years, scientists studying fish movement were puzzled. Their accumulated knowledge of the flow characteristics of a fish moving through water accounted for only a third of the speed at which scientists knew fish could actually swim. Recently, in broadening their investigation of possible causal factors by creating a robotic fish that swam for long time periods, they learned that a fish creates vortices as it moves and can push off from those vortices. Suddenly the performance of the fish made sense; they understood how the fish and the medium interact to explain how fish swim as fast as they do.

What has fish movement got to do with teaching intelligence? A lot actually. The perspective shift that scientists underwent to create a more powerful explanatory model is similar to the shift in current educational efforts to teach for intelligence. Historically, theorists and educators sought models to explain and teach for intelligence that focused on individual capability. Although such efforts met with limited success on some measures, a great deal of the variance in actual intelligent performance remained unexplained and unchanged. Current efforts are beginning to reflect (1) a performance conception of intelligence as a standard for explanation, and (2) a broadened vision of what it takes to teach for intelligent performance. These efforts adopt a more systemic approach and consider how the propensities, current understandings, and actions of individuals and the supporting structures of environments interact to result in intelligent performances.

In this chapter, we offer a brief review of the history of efforts to teach for intelligent behavior, focusing primarily on what was learned through these efforts. We then go on to outline three guiding principles of current efforts to teach for intelligence, provide examples of these efforts, and, where available, offer evidence to help evaluate the promise of current endeavors. First, we step back to provide context for why performance conceptions are increasingly common in teaching efforts and why we hold them as a standard for impacting intelligence.

A Performance Conception of Intelligence

How one defines intelligence has important implications for learning objectives and teaching pedagogy. It sets standards against which to measure whether one's objectives have been achieved. It guides how one builds and assesses understanding. Those who study intelligence agree on a number of common elements that define intelligence and give shape to what teaching efforts aim to impact. These include high-level abilities such as problem solving, abstract reasoning, mental representation, and decision making; executive processes; and learning ability. The ability to adapt in an evolutionary sense and to succeed at culturally valued endeavors further qualifies how researchers have defined intelligence (Neisser, 1979; Sternberg, 1997; Sternberg & Detterman, 1986). Although this general consensus around particular defining elements partially frames what it means to teach for intelligence, it leaves open the question of what criteria we use to show that individuals have gained these elements.

Increasingly, educators are adopting performance as a standard for learning. A wealth of research shows that education focused on what students "have in their heads" as opposed to what students can do with their understandings often leads to knowledge that is inert (e.g., Bransford, Goldman, & Vye, 1991; Perkins, 1992; Wiske, 1997). Students fail to recognize instances when the knowledge can be applied and, even when they do, they often have not yet discovered how actionable the knowledge is; they do not realize where their understanding has gaps, embedded misconceptions, a ritualistic character that does not map well to particular situations, or all of these limitations. In recognition of the perils of teaching to "what is in students' heads," there has been a movement towards performance conceptions in education more generally.

A performance conception of intelligence encompasses the common elements of intelligence outlined above. However, it refers specifically to the *enacting* of intelligence across and within different contexts. In addition to cognitive repertoire in the form of skill, knowledge, and understanding, it requires sensitivity to opportunities to behave intelligently and the inclination to engage in culturally valued forms of knowing and thinking that support intelligent behavior within and across particular contexts. A performance conception focuses on "authentic instances," culturally valued tasks that matter in people's lives, in contrast to tasks formulated for the purpose of testing and that are sometimes imported from a different cultural context (Greenfield, 1997). In addition to abilities, authentic instances require the detection of occasions calling for more thoughtfulness and an investment in following through on those occasions (Perkins & Tishman, in press; Perkins, Jay, & Tishman, 1993). A performance conception is consistent with a number of contemporary views of intelligence, among them those put forth by Sternberg (1985), Ceci (1990), Hunt (1961), and Baron (1985).

A performance conception can be broadly contrasted to a *capability* conception of intelligence. In attributing intelligence to a person, we often simply think of the person as capable of intelligent behavior. This leaves open the question of how the person actually behaves. Capability views can take many forms, from neural efficiency to learned metacognitive repertoire. Capability *is* im-

portant, of course. Although cautioning on the need to draw clear distinctions between intelligence, intelligent behavior, and intelligence as tested, Sternberg (1997) argued that intelligence has "a common core of mental processes that manifests itself behaviorally in different ways in different contexts" (p. 1031). Intelligent behavior *is* typically supported by a repertoire of intelligent thinking processes. However, from an educational standpoint, cognitive repertoire is not enough. Education in a deep sense must be concerned with how learners end up behaving in the world. A performance conception leads to a stringent test of learning and the need for a broader supporting repertoire. It requires sensitivity to opportunity, the skills to enact the behavior, and the inclination to engage in it (Perkins, Jay, & Tishman, 1993).

Whether or not one claims that intelligence can be taught to any meaningful degree often hinges upon what one's expectations are (Sternberg, 1996). In evaluating whether an effort is successful in teaching for a performance conception of intelligence, one might ask the following three questions related to the preceding discussion:

1. To what extent does the learner demonstrate the ability to enact more intelligent performance on authentic tasks?
2. Does the ability persist?
3. Does the learner demonstrate sensitivity and inclination to detect and follow through on occasions to behave intelligently such that it transfers to other authentic, culturally valued, and thought-demanding tasks?

These three questions provide criteria for determining the success of an intervention and offer insights into why efforts to teach intelligence have evolved as they have. The next section considers the lessons learned in previous attempts through the lens of a performance conception.

Lessons Learned From Previous Efforts to Teach Intelligence

How can one sort and examine the many efforts to teach for intelligent behavior? One useful strategy is to recognize three broad classes of causes for intelligent behavior: reflective, experiential, and neural. As the following paragraphs elaborate, reflective causes include cognitive skill and mental management; experiential causes include experience and expertise; and neurological causes include reaction and processing times, capacity, and efficiency. Although there may be other types of efforts, these three classes of causes are suggested by the sizeable literature on intelligence and also capture the spirit of the majority of efforts to enhance intelligence (Perkins, 1995).

Many efforts to teach for intelligence have attempted to impact reflective causes of intelligence at one level or another. *Reflective causes* refer to the active self-monitoring, assessing, and revising of behavior towards the goal of more intelligent behavior. These processes depend upon a repertoire of cognitive *strategies* and *dispositions* that enable one to monitor, assess, and enact more intelligent behaviors. For an informal example, while putting wiring in place for Internet access in schools, an installer reflected upon and repositioned the problem. Instead of tearing down walls, he trained a rat to pull wiring through the walls at considerable savings of time and money to local communities. Cognitive strategies call for thinking flexibly about the nature of the problem and defining it broadly so as to encourage a greater variety of solutions. The reflective tendency of asking what he could be doing differently and the strategy of repositioning problems led the installer to depart from typical practice.

Another kind of effort to teach intelligence focuses on the contribution of knowledge and acquired expertise to intelligent behavior. *Experiential causes* refer both to the development of a knowledge base and to the expertise that allows people to process patterns within a domain with deep understanding of the most relevant patterns, interactions, and nuances of how things work in that domain. They refer to accumulated knowledge and "knowing your way around" the domain (Perkins, 1995). The following example illustrates the unique contribution of experiential knowledge and acquired expertise to intelligent behavior. When a guest at a social event began experiencing heart failure and needed immediate attention, intelligent behavior eluded the many individuals present. Fortunately, a highly respected cardiologist was arriving who became aware of the guest's plight, quickly recognized the pattern of symptoms, and intervened. His expertise was the variable that enabled

intelligent behavior when others were incapable of it.

Some efforts to teach intelligence look to the contribution of the neurological system to intelligent behavior. As discussed in other chapters, some theorists (e.g., Anderson, 1992; Jensen, 1980) have suggested that characteristics of neural architecture and functioning can contribute to the speed, efficiency, access, and capacity of information processing at the level of synapses and cellular and networked memory. For instance, one might attribute the performance of a computer game whiz who demonstrates very quick reactions and is able to demonstrate these reactions across different types of games to *neural causes*. A dilemma concerning this category is whether processing speed and like indices can indeed be attributed to neural factors (e.g., Jensen, 1980), which is a matter of much debate (Ceci, 1990). Despite this disagreement, we review attempts to teach intelligence in this spirit and discuss some of the puzzles they present below.

Efforts in these three categories have led to an extensive literature pertaining to the teaching of intelligence. In the sections that follow, we survey attempts in each category broadly to cull what has been learned. We review one or two attempts in greater depth to provide evidence, where available, of the malleability of the aspect of intelligence in question. The chosen exemplars are not necessarily the most well-known cases but provide some of the clearest examples or most convincing evidence of impact in the particular category. The analysis refers to the most salient characteristics of the interventions reviewed and is not intended to imply that the intervention relies purely on the cause under discussion. (A greater range of examples can be found in such books as Baron and Sternberg, 1986; Chipman, Segal, & Glaser, 1985; Nickerson, Perkins, & Smith, 1985; Perkins, 1995; & Segal, Chipman, & Glaser, 1985). We then consider what has been learned about the intervention in terms of a performance conception of intelligence by revisiting the following three criteria: (1) whether and to what magnitude it enables learners to *enact* more intelligent performance, (2) whether the ability persists, and (3) whether it engenders sensitivity, ability, and inclination that transfer to other culturally valued thought-demanding tasks.

EFFORTS TO TEACH FOR REFLECTIVE CAUSES: COGNITIVE SKILL, REFLECTION, AND MENTAL MANAGEMENT. Interest in whether teaching cognitive skills resulted in more intelligent behavior evolved from research in information processing and cognitive science. Hunt (1961), reviewing research on conceptual development and animals learning how to learn, called for a new conception of intelligence as learnable through strategies. Whimbey (1975) argued that patterns of information-processing skills contributed to the differences among adults in intelligence. Cattell (1941, 1963) distinguished between fluid and crystallized intelligence, arguing that fluid intelligence is flexible in manner, not bound to any particular domain and can be directed to almost any problem. According to Cronbach and others (1977; Cronbach & Snow, 1977; Horn, 1985), fluid intelligence is learned and extractable from varied experience. Many researchers (e.g., Baron & Sternberg, 1986; Nickerson, 1989; Nickerson et al., 1985; Sternberg, 1985) have since studied the contributions of cognitive processes such as reasoning, decision making, problem solving and so on, to intelligent behavior.

In general, this research shows that high IQ and good thinking patterns are not the same thing. Regardless of IQ, people do not tend to reason very well in some respects. For instance, they often reason only about one side of a case, ignoring counter-arguments that might better inform a decision and getting trapped in goal-oriented biases, or they reason from a set of premises, failing to consider the validity of the premises (Baron, Granato, Spranca, & Teubal, 1993; Klaczynski, Gordon, & Fauth, 1997; Perkins, 1985; 1989; Perkins, Allen, & Hafner, 1983; Perkins, Farady, & Bushey, 1991; Stanovich, & West, 1997).

Several programs were developed throughout the 1960s, 1970s, and 1980s that sought to teach cognitive skill and strategy (see Costa, 1985, 1991, for explanations of programs). These programs varied in emphasis, grain of skills taught, directness of approach, and level of investment required. Programs such as the Structure of Intellect (SOI) (Meeker, 1969) and Instrumental Enrichment (Feuerstein, Rand, Hoffman, & Miller, 1980) focus on fine-grain mental operations. For instance, the SOI focuses first on foundational abilities such as visual closure, judgment of similarities, and comprehension of verbal relations and later on developing higher-level skills such as analytic, inferential, inductive and deductive reasoning and decision making. Others such as Philosophy for Children (Lipman, 1976) and the Creative Problem-Solving Program (Osborne, 1963; Parnes, 1981) focus more broadly. For instance, Philosophy for Children engages students in philosophical discussions to cultivate their ability to draw inferences, make analogies, form hypotheses, and so forth.

Instructing students in cognitive strategies has been shown to improve performance (see, e.g., Jones & Idol, 1990; Nickerson et al., 1985; Segal et al., 1985; Whimbey, 1975, for program reviews.) For instance, the Instrumental Enrichment Program (Feuerstein et al., 1980) has been shown to benefit certain types of learners in terms of magnitude of effects, persistence, and transfer to IQ-type tasks and general conduct (Feuerstein, Miller, Hoffman, Rand, Mintzker, & Jensen, 1981; Rand, Tannenbaum, & Feuerstein, 1979). Originally designed to improve the functioning of environmentally impoverished, seemingly retarded Israeli immigrants, the 2-year program includes over 400 abstract problems such as visual puzzles, numerical sequences, and syllogisms involving approximately 200–300 hours of intervention. A mediator scaffolds the learner's processing through questioning, facilitating learner focus, giving attention to relevant features, and task approach. Matched samples of low functioning, low socioeconomic status (SES) 12–15 year olds participated in instrumental (IE) or general enrichment (GE) programs (programs providing direct help, such as math or science tutoring). Instrumental Enrichment subjects made greater pre- to posttest gains on tests of interpersonal conduct, self-sufficiency, and adaptation to work demands. These subjects scored slightly above normal – far better than would have been expected without any special intervention and significantly better than GE subjects by about a third of a standard deviation on incidental follow-up testing on an Army Intelligence test (DAPAR) 2 years later (Feuerstein et al., 1981; Rand et al., 1979).

Examining ordinary students rather than those with special difficulties, Blagg (1991) found improvements in behavior but no advance in academic performance. It is not clear whether Instrumental Enrichment implemented for average learners in normal school settings generally has strong impact, but the results suggest that low-functioning students in intensive programs can benefit in terms of magnitude of effects, persistence, and transfer to similar-type tasks. Other studies (i.e., Haywood & Arbitman-Smith, 1981; Arbitman-Smith, Haywood, & Bransford, 1984) of Instructional Enrichment lend further support for its effectiveness.

Other interventions have demonstrated increased intelligent behavior on more authentic tasks and with a greater range of learners (e.g., Lipman, Sharp, & Oscanyon, 1980; Palinscar & Brown, 1984). For instance, Project Intelligence (Herrnstein, Nickerson, Sanchez, & Swets, 1986; Nickerson et al., 1985) enhanced the magnitude of students' intelligent behavior and transferability to new and authentic tasks, at least in the short term. The project was designed to improve cognitive development by teaching thinking strategies to Venezuelan seventh graders. The resulting program teaches foundations of reasoning, analysis of language, problem solving, decision making, and inventive thinking through about four 30-minute lessons per week (Wright, 1991). A formal evaluation with 24 classes of students from families of low SES and low parental education (Herrnstein et al., 1986) showed that intervention students gained significantly more than controls in general aptitude (effect sizes of $d = .43\delta$, $p < .001$ on the Otis–Lennon School Ability Test; $d = .11\delta$, $p < .02$ on the Cattell Culture Fair Test; and $d = .35\delta$, $p < .001$ on the General Abilities Test); on tests of targeted abilities (problem solving ($d = .46\delta$); decision making ($d = .77\delta$); reasoning ($d = .64\delta$); language ($d = .62\delta$); and inventive thinking ($d = .50\delta$), all significant at $p < .001$); on an open-ended design problem ($d = .70\delta$, $p < .001$); and on an everyday reasoning task that assessed students' ability to transfer what they had learned to new and authentic contexts ($d = .50\delta$, $p < .01$). The persistence of effects was not tested.

Periodic reinforcement following interventions may support the persistence of effects (e.g., Edwards, 1994). For instance, research on the CoRT (Cognitive Research Trust) Program (de Bono, 1973, 1987) suggests that low-investment follow-up may have a great deal of leverage. The CoRT Program teaches cognitive skills through a series of lessons that teach targeted thinking skills for dealing with various problem types. For instance, students are directly taught to explicitly consider the pluses, minuses, and interesting but otherwise neutral points about a matter at hand (PMI) through a developed set of practice problems. Another lesson would focus on a different aspect of a topic, such as the short-, medium-, and long-term consequences of an action (C&S). Evaluations of the CoRT Program were encouraging. Edwards (1994) reported that 12-year-olds taught all 60 lessons of the program showed improved scores on quantitative as well as qualitative measures. Compared with other seventh-grade students, scores of CoRT students ranged from 48 to 62% above the national mean on standardized tests, whereas other seventh graders' scores ranged from 25 to 43% (with a national norm of 31%). Teachers reported improvements in student thinking and confidence. Although students reported using the skills in other areas of their lives, there was no formal measure of transfer on this evaluation. Other evaluations revealed mixed results on transfer (Edwards & Bauldauf, 1983, 1987). Reviews of research on CoRT suggest that the effects were short-term (Edwards, 1991a, 1991b). However, a small amount of follow-up reinforcement given in the 2 years following the intervention resulted in increased persistence of effects with scores that were 1/3 better than controls 3 years after the intervention (Edwards, 1994).

Although the teaching of thinking skills met with some success, a number of criticisms were levied at the claims made. Reviewers cautioned that some findings can be difficult to interpret. (See Nickerson et al., 1985, and Sternberg & Bhana, 1986, for reviews). Some research was conducted by the creator of the thinking skills program; some had inadequate control groups, and others failed to examine long-term benefits of training and the application of the training to other areas. The success of the programs appeared to depend on many implementation-specific variables such as the quality of the teaching, administrative support, appropriateness of the program for the population taught, and the extent of implementation. Beyond this, although the preceding programs provide evidence of the teachability of more intelligent thinking, some interventions were less successful, meeting with mixed results (Covington, Crutchfield, Davies, & Olton, 1974; Mansfield, Busse, & Krepelka, 1978) or not including measures that would objectively measure improvements in thinking (Steiner, 1979; Wheeler, 1979). However, the sum of the results suggested a qualified yes to whether or not it was possible to teach more intelligent thinking and fueled interest in the best ways to ensure magnitude, persistence, and transfer of effects, for these concerns are at the heart of whether efforts to teach reflective intelligence in fact enable more intelligent behavior.

Early efforts also revealed that teaching mental management skills appeared to affect the magnitude, persistence, and generality of effects (e.g., Belmont, Butterfield, & Borkowski, 1978; Bornstein & Quevillon, 1976; Brown & Barclay, 1976; Brown, Campione, & Barclay, 1979). Comparisons of low- and high-achieving students showed that low achievers often have inadequate reflective management processes (Campione, 1984). Paris (1982) compared traditional instruction in memory strategies to instruction that informed students about when and why the strategies are useful. Controls were taught strategies to memorize a set of pictures and given an opportunity to practice them. Experimental students were given explanations about when to use the strategies and immediate feedback on their use of them. The average number of pictures recalled was 16 for controls and 19 for experimental students, and, after 5 days, controls no longer used the strategies, recalling 12 to 13 items as they had before instruction, whereas experimental students recalled 16 items. Reviews of research suggested that when instruction in mental management was included in instruction, the instruction was more likely to generalize and persist (Belmont Butterfield, & Ferretti, 1982), whereas when mental management instruction was lacking (Belmont & Butterfield, 1977) few generalized results were reported. A wealth of research (e.g., Baron, 1985; Baron & Sternberg, 1986; Campione, Brown, & Ferrara, 1982; Nickerson, 1989; Nickerson et al., 1985; Perkins, 1995; Sternberg, 1985) suggested the importance of encouraging a metacognitive stance in addition to teaching a repertoire of cognitive skills.

More recent, well-controlled efforts to teach for mental management in addition to cognitive skill have demonstrated a clear impact of mental management on magnitude of effects. White and Frederiksen (1998) demonstrated that adding a reflective self-assessment component to their inquiry-based physics program, ThinkerTools, has a clear impact on students' performance. After matching classes for average CTBS scores, one half of each teacher's classes took part in the physics program only, whereas the other half also participated in the reflective component. Intervention students learned a reflective-assessment framework and continually engaged in monitoring and evaluating their own and other's research. Controls also engaged in a discussion community but without the explicit reflective–assessment component. Intervention students significantly outperformed controls ($F(1, 106) = 6.82$, $p = .005$, one-tailed) with particular benefits for low achievers. Project scores for high and low CTBS students differed little in the intervention group (.39, an effect size of .4δ) and greatly in the control group (1.43, an effect size of 1.44δ). Pairing low and high achievers on research projects helped low achievers in the intervention but not the control group. The controlled nature of the study allows us to see the significant impact of reflection on magnitude of performance as an added component.

Empirical research on sensitivity and on mindfulness suggests that failure to detect occasions that call for thoughtful engagement is a major bottleneck limiting the deployment of strategic and metacognitive knowledge (Langer, 1989; Perkins & Tishman, in press; Perkins et al., 1993). Perkins and Tishman (in press) report a series of studies involving short stories with embedded opportunities to notice occasions in which certain types of thinking would improve the situation – reasons on the other side of a case, alternative options to the two obvious options in a decision-making situation, and so on. Various versions of the methodology were designed to separate sensitivity to occasion, from inclination to follow through and think deeply, from the ability to do so. The versions were used with groups ranging from fifth- to eighth-grade students. The findings persistently revealed that students' performance was sharply limited by sensitivity and inclination. That is, they tended not to notice situations where they might think on the other side of the case, think of more options, and so on. When alerted to such occasions, sometimes they saw no need to pursue them in order to reach a good decision or judgment. However, in general they proved quite capable of generating the called-for reasons or options. Thus, their intelligent behavior was not limited by ability but rather by sensitivity to the occasion in particular, as well as by inclination to follow through.

In the context of the three criteria for teaching a performance conception of intelligence (1) whether and to what magnitude intervention efforts enable learners to *enact* more intelligent performance; (2) whether the learned ability persists; and (3) whether the intervention engenders sensitivity, ability, and inclination such that it transfers to authentic, culturally valued and thought-demanding tasks, research on reflective causes of intelligent behavior suggests the following. Reflective causes of intelligent behavior can be impacted. The magnitude, persistence, and transfer of the impact require attention to mental management in addition to cognitive skill and strategy. Learners need to realize the importance of the skill and the mental management, and learners whose current ability is low appear to gain the most. Periodic follow-up reinforcement may facilitate persisting effects. Training on authentic, culturally valued, and thought-demanding tasks shows that intelligent performance on these tasks can be impacted. Some transfer has been demonstrated to other authentic, culturally valued tasks. However, transfer is not automatic but rather requires purposeful attention. Engendering sensitivity to occasions that call for high-level thinking may provide particularly high leverage in teaching for intelligent performance.

EFFORTS TO TEACH FOR EXPERIENTIAL CAUSES: EXPERTISE AND EXPERT NOVICES. A second category of efforts to teach for intelligent behavior concerns the role of experience. Historically and more recently, experiential causes have been recognized in different forms. Cattell (1963) argued that in contrast to "fluid" intelligence, "crystallized" intelligence represents knowledge that often takes the shape of the specific domain as new knowledge is integrated with other knowledge structures already present. Experiential causes have been characterized as practice (e.g., Fitts & Posner, 1967; Welford, 1968), as expertise (e.g., Chase & Simon, 1973; de Groot, 1965; Larkin, 1983), as orienting to and automatizing novelty (Sternberg, 1985), and as "knowing your way around" and being able to adapt to particular contexts (Perkins, 1995). More recently and in contrast to the parsing in this review, Sternberg (1998) argued that developing expertise

includes the kinds of thinking and metacognitive skills reviewed in the previous section.

Given the variety of views, what kinds of interventions should be examined as examples of teaching for experiential causes of intelligent behavior? Taken straightforwardly, experience refers to exposure and opportunities for practice. However, although practice can improve performance to a certain extent, the gains tend to drop off at a certain level (e.g., Fitts 1964; Fitts & Posner, 1967; Newell & Rosenbloom, 1981; Welford, 1968), and experience as mere exposure and practice tends to have disappointing results by the measure of more intelligent behavior (Bereiter & Scardamalia, 1993). Certainly, there are tasks or subroutines to tasks that are furthered through exposure and practice. For instance, in reading, children who do not achieve automaticity in terms of speed and word recognition end up with fewer cognitive resources to deploy for comprehension and sustain a disadvantage (Lesgold, Resnick, & Hammond, 1985). However, in general, experience as exposure and practice holds little promise for developing the elements of intelligence outlined above. More promising avenues include teaching for expertise and developing expert novices. We explain each avenue and an intervention intended to impact it in the following paragraphs.

The development of expertise entails effortfully acquired abilities involving intentionality (Bereiter & Scardamalia, 1993). If you have ever been driven somewhere repeatedly and then had to navigate the course on your own, you know the difference between experience and the mindful processing that contributes to expertise. A wealth of relevant information may be missed, such as traffic patterns or the larger mental map of the roadway dictating the best choices for alternate routes. Although expertise certainly provides the content knowledge to think with, the key distinction is in *how* experts think. Experts structure and construe meaning from information differently than novices. They notice and attach importance to deeper, more meaningful patterns (e.g., Chase & Simon, 1973; Chi, Feltovich, & Glaser, 1981; Larkin, McDermott, Simon, & Simon, 1980; Simon & Chase, 1973), allowing them to process patterns more efficiently and effectively. They reflectively monitor their activity, regulating their attention (Glaser, 1992), and are faster overall at solving problems because they routinize the process somewhat. Expert forms of pattern recognition come with the development of deep understanding of a domain – its rules, exceptions, and nuances. Experts tend to depend upon a great deal of informal background knowledge and to use self-regulatory knowledge that builds upon their self-knowledge relevant to the domain. They tend to work at the edge of their competence and to engage in a process of "progressive problem solving" by finding and pursuing problems that challenge them (Bereiter & Scardamalia, 1993).

Researchers have studied the patterns that experts employ in a variety of disciplines. For instance, researcher have developed models to illustrate how expert readers process information by studying details such as how their eyes move, how long they take to process certain kinds of words, and how often they regress in the test (Just & Carpenter, 1987). Scardamalia and Bereiter (1982) have studied the differences in how expert and novice writers plan out their work. Anderson and colleagues (see Bruer, 1993) have developed models of how experts think about geometry proofs. Similarly, a wealth of research offers insights into the differences between how scientists process information as compared with students (e.g., Chi, Glaser, & Rees, 1982; Clement, 1985).

Whether expertise can be taught has strong implications for a performance conception of intelligence given that expertise is typically grounded in authentic, culturally valued tasks. The acquisition of expertise tends to require a sustained, intense effort of deliberate and mindful practice over as many years as a decade (e.g., Bereiter & Scardamalia, 1993; Chase & Simon, 1973; de Groot, 1965). However, targeted attempts to teach patterns of disciplinary knowledge suggest that students can learn expert modes of thinking. Schoenfeld and colleagues (1982, Schoenfeld & Herrmann, 1982) helped college students become more expertlike in their mathematical behavior by introducing the relevant thinking processes for mathematical problem solving and making them explicit so students would learn and notice them in new instances. First, they asked 19 math students and a group of experts to sort a set of 32 math problems. Then they taught heuristics for solving mathematical problems to 11 of the students in the context of a mathematics

problem-solving course. The control group took a course that did not focus on the math problem-solving heuristics. Cluster analyses revealed that novices' initial sortings were based on surface similarity of the problems. After instruction, the experimental group sorted more like the experts and improved in their problem-solving performance. There was little change in the control groups' sorting patterns or performance. Correlations between the sort matrices for each of the groups before and after instruction were compared to the expert sorts: Pretest: Control = .551; Experimental = .540; Posttest: Control = .423; Experimental = .723 ($df = 496$, $p < .01$). At least for targeted interventions, it appears that expertlike patterns can be taught. Although persistence and generality were not assessed, the magnitude of the effects is well established.

A challenge for attempting to teach expertise is that high expertise involves acutely developed sensitivities in the domain in question, as evidenced, for example, by the classic studies of chess expertise conducted by de Groot (1965) and later by Chase and Simon (1973). Likewise, the time-on-task required for the development of expertise underscores the role of sustained commitment fueled by curiosity, passion, persistence, and like factors, which are features well-documented in the lives of individuals of high expertise (e.g., Barron, 1969; Gardner, 1993c; Roe, 1952). A problem characteristic of much of school instruction in particular domains is that it foregrounds problem solving in one or another sense with little attention to the shape of the domain, its more and less settled areas, its prominent puzzles, and the excitement and commitment of those who find in it a calling. A performance conception of intelligence foregrounds the importance of developing sensitivies and inclination in addition to expert-thinking patterns.

Whether expertise transfers in any sense raises important questions for the generality of developed intelligence. A number of researchers have claimed that intelligence is necessarily situated (e.g., Ceci, 1990; Ericsson & Smith, 1991; Detterman, 1992; Lave, 1988) and that expertise is rarely developed in more than one or two fields. However, an interesting twist in the study of expertise is that some novices in a domain behave like expert *learners* (e.g., Bereiter & Scardamalia, 1993; Bransford, Sherwood, Vye, & Reiser, 1986; Bransford & Stein, 1984). These "expert novices" know how to go about developing expertise, typically having learned how in one domain and subsequently applying this knowledge to new domains (Brown, Bransford, Ferrera, & Campione, 1983; Bruer, 1993). This led to another category of efforts to impact the experiential causes of intelligent behavior – developing expert novices. They appear to have processes for dealing with and automatizing novelty (Sternberg, 1985), such as structures for gaining knowledge efficiently. Such knowledge-building structures provide for efficient learning.

Bransford, Markman, and others have studied what it is that expert novices do (e.g., Bransford et al., 1982; Markman, 1985). They found that expert novices hold information about the nature of learning that helps them structure the learning enterprise. For instance, expert novices may know that it is hard to tell what is important when you first start out, that you should let your explanation evolve as you meet with increasing complexity; and so on. They also employ strategies based upon such knowledge of the nature of learning that help them learn well. For instance, they notice whether texts are easy or difficult and adjust their study strategies and the time they take to process the information (Bransford et al., 1982). They monitor their understanding and thus detect inconsistencies when reading text material (Markman, 1985). They ask themselves questions and use self-tests to assess their own understanding (Brown et al., 1983; Stein et al., 1982).

One might ask whether there is any difference between developing the expert novice and reflective intelligence. Although the skills of each certainly overlap and each is strongly about management and executive processes, they have a somewhat different center of gravity. Becoming an expert novice involves becoming an expert learner and developing knowledge acquisition skills rather than general thinking skills. Knowledge acquisition skills include both the explicit and implicit ways in which we set about learning and includes such things as how we encode information, differentiate relevant from irrelevant details, and relate new information to already stored information (Sternberg, 1998).

The behavior of expert novices stimulated researchers to ask, "To what extent can expertise in learning be learned?" (e.g., Bereiter & Scardamalia, 1993) and "Is it possible to teach knowledge-building schemas?" Although it is not a perfect example, for reasons explored below, the Practical Intelligences for Schools (PIFS) Program (Williams, Blythe, White, Li, Sternberg, & Gardner, 1996) can provide some insights into what such an endeavor might be like. Though PIFS did not attempt to teach knowledge-building structures directly, it was designed to help students learn to learn in more expertlike ways. Built around the concept of practical intelligence, it sought to teach coping strategies relevant to the learning process (Sternberg & Wagner, 1986). Stand-alone components taught skills for managing oneself (such as thinking about different types of intelligence, making pictures in your mind to help with memory tasks, and taking in new information) and for managing tasks (such as planning a way to prevent problems, noticing the way things are written, and seeing likenesses and differences in subjects). Infused components taught embedded PIFS skills in subject matter and cross-disciplinary units (such as discovering your learning profile). The performances of 100 seventh graders in three mixed-ability reading classes participating in PIFS stand-alone components 3 days per week for a semester and two control classes working with basal readers were compared. Intervention students made significantly larger gains in practical intellectual skills on the Survey of Study Habits (SSHA) ($F(4, 95) = 5.85$, $p < .001$); Learning and Study Skills Inventory (LASSI) ($F(10, 78) = 2.92$, $p < .01$); on the Sternberg Triarchic Abilities Test (STAT) ($F(3, 86) = 6.48$, $p < .001$); and on 14 out of 17 subscales. An evaluation of infused components with nine classes revealed significant intervention group gains in subject matter units as measured on assessments designed to include definitional, task-oriented, and metatask measures of understanding (Domain-specific units combined: $z = 6.57$, $p < .001$) with significant differences on five of six units (Gardner, Krechevsky, Sternberg & Okagaki, 1994). Although the persistence of effects is not known, the magnitude of effects and transfer of PIFS learning to subject matters suggest that the PIFS intervention helped students develop expertise in learning how to learn. A potential criticism levied against using the PIFS program as an example of developing expert novices in learning is that one might argue that the program is really about reflective intelligence.

Indeed, in a broad sense it is. However, the focus of PIFS is largely on learning rather than thinking in the typical "thinking skills" sense of problem solving, decision making, and so forth.

Revisiting our three criteria for teaching a performance conception of intelligence; the magnitude of ability to enact intelligent behavior and the persistence and transferability of intelligent behavior to culturally valued, thought-demanding tasks, research on experiential causes suggests the following. It is certainly possible to facilitate the development of expertlike patterns of processing and understanding, helping novices to behave in noticeably more expert ways within particular domains. The persistence of processing patterns is not clear. Although expertise is typically grounded in authentic and culturally valued tasks, transfer to other authentic and culturally valued tasks is perhaps best accomplished by encouraging the development of knowledge-building structures. A caveat for developing expert novices is that due attention must be given to acquiring sensitivities and inclination in addition to processing patterns.

EFFORTS TO TEACH FOR NEURAL CAUSES: NEURAL EFFICIENCY AND ACCESS. A third category of efforts represented in the literature concerns impacting neurology. This approach is somewhat vexed for a number of reasons set forth here. A significant puzzle concerns how to measure neural impact. Although reflective and experiential causes are fairly easily controlled and operationalized, it is difficult to isolate and demonstrate neurological impact.

Some neural researchers have focused on choice reaction times (the time a subject takes to respond to a choice between two buttons, for example), inspection times (how long it takes a subject to report a stimulus correctly from the time of exposure) (Deary & Stough, 1996; Jensen, 1980), or on both. Although some authentic, culturally valued tasks may depend upon quick reaction times, this represents only a small subset of valued tasks. The use of reaction times has been criticized because primates are characteristically faster than humans for simple reaction times (585 versus 597 ms) and dramatically so for tasks involving a decision-making component (12 versus 130 ms) (Washburn & Rumbaugh, 1997). This suggests that reaction times are not purely dependent upon neurological factors and that higher order executive processing may result in slower times.

IQ has commonly been taken as a measure of neural intelligence (e.g., Goddard, 1920; Jensen, 1980), and early enrichment has been shown to enhance IQ performance. For instance, the Abecedarian Project followed 111 children identified at birth as likely to be at high risk of retarded development owing to economic and social circumstances and randomly assigned them to an intervention or control group (Ramey & Smith, 1977). Both groups received medical, nutritional, and family supports where needed. Intervention infants began an early enrichment program with low student–teacher ratios and good nutrition at 6 weeks of age continuing until the beginning of kindergarten. By 6 months old, they tested 6 IQ points higher ($p = .0563$), and by 18 months old, 18 points higher than controls (Ramey & Campbell, 1987). In a crossed design, portions of the original intervention and control groups received intervention during the primary grades (K to second grade). Preschool-only enrichment had the greatest impact, and by ages 8 and 12, these children performed 5.1 points higher on the WISC–R than controls. Primary grade-only enrichment was no longer detectable by age 12 (Ramey, 1994). The intervention generalized to measures of IQ, and the greatest magnitude and persistence of effects were achieved with very early intervention.

However, impacting IQ does not necessarily mean that neural causes of intelligent behavior have been impacted (Ceci, 1990). The elements measured by IQ tests such as speed and efficiency of processing, reconstruction of memories from available cues, and handling increased cognitive load may be affected by other causes. Indeed factors such as prior experience and calling upon certain strategies can provide more memory cues, capacity, speed, and efficiency. Ceci (1990) argued, as have many others, that statistical derivations of a general intelligence factor do not imply that we know the mechanisms that give rise to it, that it "explains" neural contributions to intelligent behavior, or that it addresses more than certain domains (Gardner, 1983). According to Ceci (1990), it could result from any of the following: environmental variables, biological variables, metacognitive or executive processes, motivational and temperamental variables, and a "highly interlocked system of independent cognitive abilities

that are not easily separated through factor analysis''
(p. 107).

Although traditional neural approaches do not offer much guidance or hope for the enterprise of
teaching for intelligence, are there mechanisms and
evidence that might make some form of neural
approach to teaching for intelligence appropriate?
Some researchers find promise in recent neurological research that suggests early experience affects
the development of the neural pathways. It appears
that the human brain continues to undergo significant maturational development into the early
years of life (Chugani, 1994). Through positron
emission tomography (PET) scans, researchers are
able to study dendritic and synaptic proliferation, the myelinization of neurons, and glucose
metabolic utilization changes. Changes in local cerebral metabolic rates for glucose from birth to age 3
appear to relate to the greater reorganizational capacity and plasticity of developing brains as compared with those of adults (Chugani, 1994; Finger &
Wolf, 1988). Huttenlocher (1994) found a proliferation of neurons during the prenatal months and
a period of pruning and eliminating excessive neurons into the second postnatal year.

However, the link between this ''ontogenetic
sculpting'' and behavior is a highly tenuous one.
Edelman (1989) argued that the selective stimulus
and amplification of certain neuronal groups help to
define the cortical map, favoring certain circuits and
neuronal groups over time. Yet, there is currently little empirical support for his theory, nor is there any
mapping of how such groupings translate into behaviors. Dawson's work (1994) suggests that frontal
brain activity in infants is related to their emotional
interactions with parents; yet, it is unclear whether
the changes are temporary or persistent.

The style and timing of early intervention programs such as the Abecedarian Program are consonant with the possibility of neural impact. Even so,
without neurological evidence clearly linked to behavioral outcomes, there is no way to distinguish
whether the results are due to an impact on the
neurological structure or a strong experiential program and whether those are indeed separate factors.
Bruer (1997) has convincingly argued that it is far
too soon for the neurological research to provide a
direct bridge to educational advice. Before one could
even begin to consider our three criteria for a per-

formance conception of intelligence – magnitude,
persistence, and generality of effects – clear links
between neurology and behavior would be needed.
This is a long way off, according to Bruer, and perhaps an impossibility. The mapping between neurology and behavior may be complex in such a way
that we could never directly link them.

Bearing our three criteria for teaching a performance conception of intelligence in mind, the
commentary above suggests that little can be concluded here for lack of effective ways to isolate a
distinctively neurological impact. Although positive
results with older children and adults suggest reflective and experiential impact (because neural development has largely run its course), positive results with young populations do not distinctively
implicate neural impact because reflective or experiential impact may well account for any gains
there as well. Moreover, the neurological perspective
does not seem to offer much distinctive design advice other than ''start young'' – good advice in any
case.

In summary, we are perhaps better off focusing
our efforts on reflective and experiential causes until
a great deal more is understood about neurological
development. One avenue might be to apply our reflective and experiential skills to understanding better how to use our neurology well. People typically
do not understand their neurology well enough to
use it most intelligently. For example, many people view memory as storagelike. Yet, research shows
that our memories are reconstructed (e.g., Schacter,
1996), calling for different memorization strategies.
Indeed, knowing how our neurology works may provide some of the best advice for having an impact
on it.

A SUMMARY OF A HISTORY OF EFFORTS. Efforts to teach for intelligence are promising. There
is ample evidence for the malleability of cognitive
processes, and earlier interventions have informed
later efforts such that they met with greater success
in impacting the magnitude, persistence, and transferability of effects.

What would a critical perspective on this stance
look like? A common critique has been dissen-
sion on what counts as intelligence. Indeed, intelligence is multiply construable. An ''essentialist'' view argues that IQ is an index of general

neurological processing efficiency, which is the essence of intelligence. From a paradigm-building perspective, such arguments have a place. However, from an educators' stance, as long as "taught intelligence" improves people's abilities to think and act better on culturally valued and thought-demanding tasks, then whether "taught intelligence" is "real intelligence" is inconsequential.

The other common critique of the stance set forth here concerns whether the empirical findings around various efforts produce robust results. Do they yield improvements in performance that show magnitude, persistence, and transfer? Challenges have been raised on all three fronts. Often these have been theoretically motivated, but regardless of motivation, the issues are addressed in this chapter by the empirical story. Early efforts to teach intelligence revealed promise and indicated that interventions could be developed that met the challenges of a performance conception of intelligence: magnitude; persistence; and transfer ability. Current efforts are building upon what has been learned to provide new successes and insights into what is possible when increasingly systematic approaches are adopted. Next, we consider some current directions in teaching for intelligent performance and what is being learned from these.

Current and Promising Directions for Teaching Intelligence

As with the scientists studying fish movement, current efforts to explain and teach for intelligence reflect an increasingly broadened vision of the enterprise. In the past decade or so, efforts have woven the lessons learned from earlier reflective and experientially based interventions into more sophisticated approaches to teaching intelligent performance. Although the systemic nature of the interventions makes it difficult to characterize them as one type or another, these new directions attend to at least three aspects of how individuals and environments interact to result in intelligent performances. These approaches build powerfully on what we know about reflection and expertise while adopting (1) a cultural approach, (2) an encompassing view of the learner, and (3) a reorganizational stance towards learning. Many current interventions represent an amalgamation of these three aspects while attending to lessons learned from traditional approaches. Each

is described in turn below, and available research is summarized.

ADOPTING A CULTURAL APPROACH TO TEACHING INTELLIGENT BEHAVIOR. Although theories on intelligence have recognized the importance of context as a component of intelligent behavior (e.g., Gardne, 1983; Sternberg, 1985), it was not until the past decade or so that educators embarked on teaching interventions that attempt to enculturate the learning of intelligent behavior. Increasingly, educators have recognized that in order to sustain cognitive advances and to actualize intelligent behavior as opposed to capacity, the supporting structures of culture are needed (e.g., Brown & Campione, 1994; Scardamalia et al., 1994; Tishman, Perkins, & Jay, 1995). There has been a shift from strategy instruction aimed at students as individuals to an emphasis on building a classroom culture supportive of a social construction of knowledge (e.g., Scardamalia, Bereiter, & Lamon, 1994) and the development of patterns of good thinking (e.g., Tishman et al., 1993). Sfard (1998) has argued for the need to balance acquisition metaphors of learning: that knowledge is gained or made meaning of with participation metaphors: that learning is taking part in a dialogue and involves a constant flux of doing as opposed to a permanent sense of having.

Culture, construed broadly, refers to aspects of context including the physical, social, and symbolic surround (Pea, 1993; Perkins, 1993; 1995). The physical surround includes supports: computers, books, charts, and so on. (Salomon, 1993). The sociocultural surround encompasses the social dynamics of classrooms: schools, subcultures (e.g., inner-city youth), and cultures in a broad sense (e.g., North American). The symbolic context includes the symbols systems and notational structures – human inventions that range from spoken and written language to maps, codes, and dance notations – that have evolved to support abstract thought (Gardner, 1983). The sociohistorical dimension includes valued ways of knowing and thinking such as the epistemic forms of the disciplines that are part of our heritage in a Vygotskyian sense. Each of these aspects of culture provide supports for distributed intelligence, that is, scaffolding intelligent behavior beyond that which can be displayed by an individual mind (Perkins, 1995; Salomon, 1993).

Culture has been shown to play a powerful role in skill development, attitudes and beliefs, and values. It shapes what we attend to, care about and focus our energies on developing (e.g., Bruner, Olver, & Greenfield, 1966; Dasen, 1977; Super, 1980), and what we believe we can do. For instance, belief in the value of effort pervades Asian cultures. Japanese mothers emphasize effort and self-discipline, whereas American mothers emphasize ability (e.g., Stevenson & Lee, 1990). More American than Chinese mothers believe that early performance predicts later performance. These beliefs influence children's perception of their competence more than their own actual achievements and correlate with achievement differences (Americans performing consistently lower in computation and mathematical applications) as early as kindergarten (e.g., Stevenson, Lee, & Stigler, 1986).

Classroom cultures have been shown to play a similarly powerful role. For instance, Bezruczko, Kurland, and Eckert (1996) found that classroom practices can mediate, transmit, and extend the benefits of early childhood educational interventions. Following 379 African Americans in the Chicago Public Schools who received intervention from preschool through grade 3, they found that particular interaction variables and teacher behaviors affect student achievement. Kindergarten classrooms that valued children working together correlated positively with child performance measures (.14, .12, and .13, respectively, in Writing Content, ITBS (Iowa Test of Basic Skills) Reading, and ITBS Math, $p < .01$) as did those with interest centers (.14 and .19, respectively in ITBS Reading, and ITBS Math, $p < .01$) and classrooms that were orderly (.19, .25, and .23, respectively Knowledge of Print, ITBS Reading, and ITBS Math, $p < .01$). Students in classrooms with five or less positive cultural indicators declined nearly a half a grade from Kindergarten to Grade 1 in ITBS grade equivalents. Those in classrooms with a medium number of indicators (6 to 9) stayed about the same, whereas those in classrooms with a high number of indicators (10 or more) gained 1.5 grade equivalents.

Similarly, Deci and colleagues (Deci, Schwartz, Sheinman, & Ryan, 1981) found that the cultural values of the classroom as set by the teacher impact students' beliefs about the value of effort versus aptitude in determining success by the seventh week of school. Students of autonomy-oriented teachers grow more intrinsically motivated and feel better about themselves. Students of control-oriented teachers become less intrinsically motivated and feel worse about themselves – all this by the second month of school (motivational: prefers challenge .41, $p < .01$; curiosity .56, $p < .01$; mastery attempts .37, $p < .05$ and perceived competence: general self-worth .36, $p < .05$; cognitive .29, $p < .05$; social .27, $p < .05$).

Current efforts to teach for intelligence recognize that learning environments must transmit, in the sense of ongoing repertoire, culturally valued ways of knowing, cognitive and metacognitive skills, and forms of expertise that sustain intelligent behavior. Learners need to be immersed in cultures where these are valued and practiced regularly and where they will be able to build understandings through their performances. Sensitivity and inclination are difficult to teach in a direct sense (Perkins, Jay, & Tishman, 1993; Tishman et al., 1993). Although one can teach investigation techniques, it is hard to teach curiosity. It needs to be provoked and kindled. Not just teaching but *enculturation* is a richer way of conceptualizing the needed pedagogy (Tishman, Jay, & Perkins, 1993).

Educators are developing and assessing interventions that teach for intelligent behavior by using a cultural approach. For instance, Brown and Campione's *Guided Discovery in a Community of Learners* (1994) had an impact on student performance by changing the cultural norms in the classroom. A premium was placed on research, knowledge-building, and critical thinking. Individual responsibility was coupled with the communal sharing of expertise. Discourse (constructive discussion, questioning, and criticism) was the norm. "Ritual, familiar, participant structures" were introduced as navigation structures to help students understand the new culture. Approximately 90 fifth and sixth graders in the Community of Learners (CL) group outperformed a group using only a reciprocal teaching (RT) technique in which students led the learning in reading discussions (and this even though the group was given twice as much practice as the CL group) on criterion-referenced tests of reading comprehension. There was no improvement in a reading-only control group. Scores on questions dealing with inference, gist, and analogy improved dramatically. The results show magnitude of effects but require further study to assess the generality and persistence of effects. Further research is needed to determine whether the effects are sustaining in the sense of ongoing repertoire or whether their impact is limited to behaviors in the immediate culture.

Through CSILE (Computer Supported Intentional Learning Environments), Scardamalia and colleagues (Scardamalia et al., 1994) have encouraged the development of communities aimed at the social construction of knowledge. CSILE students are involved in the construction of a communal database. They pursue questions of interest, devise methodology for answering questions, and engage in dialogue about the questions. Because students sometimes find themselves investigating questions that others have investigated throughout history, they participate in a sociohistorical culture in addition to a classroom culture. CSILE students performed the same or better on standardized tests as non-CSILE students. (A significant effect of CSILE experience was found on the Canadian Test of Basic Skills using pretest as a covariate $(F(3,393) = 7.04, p < .001)$ with the three CSILE groups higher than the control group $(F(1,377) = 5.36, p < .05)$. They scored significantly higher on measures of depth of explanation $(M = 2.89$ versus $M = 1.20; t(35) = 7.09; p < .001)$ and knowledge representation involving description of causal–dynamic structures $(F(2,77) = 10.20, p < .001)$, were more accurate in solving problems from difficult text $(F(1,108) = 4.14, p < .05)$, and recalled more text information $(F(1,108) = 13.95, p < .001)$. CSILE students also held deeper conceptions of the nature of learning. They were more likely to make mastery-oriented choices (71 versus 50%), reported using understanding as a measure of whether they had learned something (80 versus 56%), were less likely to use test marks as a measure of learning (15 versus 40%), and reported that thinking deeply about what a book said was important for learning from text (64% (Year 1 CSILE students) and 78% (Year 2 CSILE students) versus 40%).

A cultural approach supports developing reflective tendencies and expertise, models sensitivity to opportunities for patterns of thinking, provides an authentic context for students' learning of powerful forms of thinking and knowing, and invites students to experience the cultural values, passion, and excitement that are part of contributing to a social-community-sustaining inquiry.

ADOPTING AN ENCOMPASSING VIEW OF THE LEARNER. Current attempts to teach for intelligent behavior take a more encompassing view of learners and attend more to the current aptitudes and propensities of individual learners. This includes having pluralistic notions of what it means to behave intelligently, teaching through multiple modalities, and matching modalities to learner strengths. The rise of pluralistic notions of intelligence in the 1980s (Gardner, 1983; Sternberg, 1985) engendered a broader vision of what it means to be intelligent as well as ways to encourage intelligence. Two of the most popular pluralistic notions are Sternberg's triarchic theory (1985) and Gardner's multiple intelligences theory (1983, 1993a).

Sternberg's triarchic theory (1985) describes three aspects of intelligence: contextual or practical intelligence, experiential, and componential. Contextual intelligence refers to how persons adapt to everyday environments and social settings; experiential intelligence to how persons deal with novelty, their insights and ability automatizing so as to deal efficiently with similar situations in the future; and componential or analytic intelligence to how persons process information cognitively and metacognitively.

Gardner's theory of multiple intelligences (MI) (1983) introduced seven forms of intelligence: linguistic and logical mathematical, the two most salient in school and on standardized tests; musical; spatial; bodily-kinesthetic; interpersonal; and intrapersonal. He recently added an eighth, naturalist, and has reviewed evidence pertinent to a possible ninth, existential (1999). MI theory defines intelligence as a biopsychological potential, which may or may not be realized, depending upon opportunities, motivations, and cultural norms. From an MI perspective, by virtue of their membership in the human species, all humans possess a range of discrete intelligences. Thus, the theory depicts what it means to be a human being, cognitively speaking. Yet because of genetic and experiential factors, no two individuals end up having exactly the same profile and blend of intelligences. In that sense, MI is a theory of the nature of individual differences in cognition, respecting a broad range of culturally valued, intelligent behaviors.

According to Gardner (1995), how these intelligences map onto various domains can be complex. A domain is a socially organized activity, that can be delineated in terms of relative levels of expertise. An intelligence such as spatial intelligence can be used in support of intelligent behavior in a range of domains, from geometry to sculpture to sailing to surgery. Correlatively, skill in a domain can reflect a variety of intelligences, and individuals may achieve comparable levels of skill using different intelligences. Skill in the domain of chess draws on logical, spatial, and interpersonal intelligences; but individual players may differ in the extent to which they use these and other intelligences to play chess at high level. Snow (1997) has argued that adaptive teaching involves attending to many types of symbols systems, such as those stemming from culture, native language, previous achievements and knowledge, and more general cases such as pictorial versus numerical forms of representation. He calls for using facility in one symbol system for building facility in another.

As outlined by Gardner (1999) a pedagogical approach based on MI can aid learning in at least three distinct ways: (1) through "entry points" for approaching a topic, for instance, evolution or civil war, through stories, works of art, role-playing, logical syllogism, and other kinds of symbol systems; (2) as suppliers of suggestive metaphors and analogies to elucidate unfamiliar topics through comparisons with familiar ones and; (3) through expression in different model languages. Expert understanding is demonstrated when an individual is able to represent the key features of a topic or concept in a number of complementary modes of representations, such as expressing the key features of the theory of natural selection in logical symbols, natural language, and through graphic or taxonomic representations. Kornhaber and colleagues are currently investigating efficacious uses of MI theory in schools (Kornhaber, 1998).

Some researchers (Sternberg, Ferrari, Clinkenbeard, & Grigorenko, 1996) are beginning to explore anew whether intervention programs are more effective in producing more intelligent behavior when they are matched to students' current aptitudes. It is assumed that the treatment used for teaching more intelligent behavior should be matched to learner needs in order for intelligence to be most learnable. Traditionally, this work has been referred to as Aptitude-Treatment Interactions (ATI).

A wealth of earlier research on ATI led to mixed results. Some of the problems, as summarized by Cronbach and Snow (1977), were as follows: The results of successful studies were difficult to replicate and generalize because of the many classroom variables that were difficult to control, which impacted outcome. Positive results were discounted or counted depending upon different criteria, making it difficult to determine if ATI exists. Although initially it was hoped that instruction adapted to aptitude would reduce individual differences, given the measures used, this was not the case. Though initial research on interactions between intelligent performance and specialized abilities was disappointing, Cronbach and Snow argued that the methods were not clearly specified and that the hypothesis was unclear.

Recently, Sternberg and colleagues (Sternberg et al., 1996) found more promising results by matching instruction and assessment in a highly focused manner to student aptitudes. Using Sternberg's triarchic theory (1985), they defined analytical, creative and practical aspects of abilities in verbal, quantitative, figural, and performance domains and measured the strengths of high school students who had been identified as gifted by their schools and were participating in the Yale Summer Psychology Program. Students took part in a 4-week intensive college course (about 140 hours of instruction) with two components (a college-level psychology text and lectures) in common and one (sections focused on one of four types of skills: memory [traditional], analytical, creative, and practical) either matched to students' aptitudes or not. Student performance was assessed via homework assignments, a midterm, independent project, and final exam. These were rated 1 to 9 (low to high) by four raters. A contrast analysis showed that matched students did better than nonmatched ones ($p < .01$). A log–linear analysis showed an interaction ($p < .05$) between ability and type of instruction (mixed versus mismatched). Those who performed the best on each task were those whose task assignment matched their abilities. They argued that the targeted nature of the intervention using specific factors with low correlations between them (no general *g* factor) contributed to the results.

These results suggest that attending to an encompassing view of the learner and mapping instruction to individuals accordingly hold promise for magnitude of effects. Persistence and transfer were not measured here. However, research on other aspects of learner individuality, such as that which addresses student's naive theories, as discussed in the next section, suggests greater persistence and transfer when individual students' current understandings are addressed.

Recognizing the difficulty of mapping educational interventions directly to students' individual aptitudes, Snow and others (e.g., Snow, 1997) have called for including "affordances" in classrooms. They call for classroom features that provide students with opportunities to use their personal strengths to further learning, to avoid weaknesses, and to remediate weaknesses through strengths.

An encompassing view of the learner promises to offer more avenues for more learners towards increasingly intelligent performances. Although there is more to be learned about magnitude, persistence, and generality of effects, this aspect of current endeavors holds promise and has captured the interest of many teachers (e.g., Armstrong, 1994; Gardner, 1993b).

ADOPTING A REORGANIZATIONAL STANCE TOWARDS TEACHING INTELLIGENT BEHAVIOR. Another new direction involves taking a reorganizational stance towards teaching for intelligent performance. Many programs have attempted to "exercise up" students' ability in order to affect the causes of intelligent behavior. However, as outlined below, an extensive literature shows that learners tend to hold maladaptive patterns of intellectual engagement that need to be reorganized into more adaptive patterns. Substantial gains come not just through improvements in fluency but through helping learners recognize and revise these patterns (Perkins, 1995; Perkins & Grotzer, 1997). They must realize the problems of their current beliefs, understandings, and thinking patterns (e.g., di Sessa, 1983; Driver, Guesne, & Tiberghien, 1985; Osborne & Freyberg, 1985). Evidence that a default pattern is problematic can introduce dissonance in learners' minds so that they become ready to accommodate

by reorganizing their thinking (e.g., Berlyne, 1965; Posner, Strike, Hewson & Gertzog, 1982). Models, experiences, and guidance within learners' zone of proximal development (Vygotsky, 1978) can help them reorganize their thinking around more powerful patterns. Research suggests that reorganization should take place in at least three dimensions: conceptual; procedural; and environmental.

Conceptual reorganization refers to discovering patterns in conceptual knowledge, beliefs, values and feelings that can hinder intelligent behavior and proactively seeking to replace those with more adaptive ones. This includes discovering naive theories and misconceptions in one's knowledge base (Gardner, 1991) such as the notion of a flat earth (Nussbaum, 1985) or heat as an entity (Erickson & Tiberghien, 1985) and evolving a more expert knowledge base. It includes identifying and reorganizing maladaptive beliefs, for instance, that our memory is storagelike as opposed to reconstructive (Schacter, 1996), that understanding is expressed by "knowing" as opposed to doing, and that the nature of intelligence is entitylike (Dweck, 1975). The belief that intelligence is limited (Dweck & Bempechat, 1983) can work against intelligent performance because, in the face of challenges, learners tend to assume that if they do not have and cannot gain what it takes to meet the challenge, there is no use persisting, and thus their strategy use diminishes and performance deteriorates (Diener & Dweck, 1978). Conceptual reorganization entails identifying feelings that hinder intelligent behavior such as "an illusion of knowing" (Druckman & Bjork, 1994) that often emerges in environments where learners are not asked to perform their understanding. Such feelings can prevent learners from pushing instances of inquiry as far as they might and from behaving intelligently in instances that call for the understandings in question.

Procedural reorganization refers to discovering and replacing maladaptive patterns in generic and discipline-specific processes for thinking, knowing and finding out, and reflecting upon and managing these. Perkins (1995) referred to four defaults that can be attributed to the pattern-driven character of cognition: Thinking tends to be *hasty* (impulsive, insufficient investment in deep processing, and examining alternatives), *narrow* (failure to challenge assumptions, examine other points of view), *fuzzy* (careless, imprecise, full of conflations), and *sprawling* (general disorganization, failure to advance or conclude). Beyond this, people often misconceive the nature of thinking in ways that translate into poor thinking; for instance, the notion that if problems cannot be solved quickly, they cannot be solved at all (Schoenfeld, 1989). This leads to premature closure on problems and the likelihood that the most creative options will be missed (Nickerson et al., 1985). Elementary students tend to think that effort means just working harder (Tishman, 1991), leading to more dogged but not necessarily more intelligent thinking. Students often have little understanding of the powerful forms of thinking in the disciplines. They think of science as a collection of facts, mathematics as a series of rituals, and history as an objective accounting of "what happened." School "rituals" can perpetuate these beliefs.

Students need to learn what good thinkers do and to learn to self-monitor, self-assess, and revise for more intelligent behavior. Valued forms of thinking need to be handed down as part of students' cultural heritage; for instance, proactive connection-making, breaking a learning problem down into progressive steps, and self-assessing to determine the next learning steps. Schools need to introduce culturally valued ways of knowing that have led to important insights, as in the disciplinary lenses – for instance, the process of gaining scientific knowledge by generating theories and then purposefully discarding those as more powerful theories are created (Pomeroy, 1992).

Environmental reorganization refers to discovering and replacing maladaptive patterns in how one views and uses the contexts of learning and behaving. Learners typically see the physical and cultural environment as a given, something that must be adapted to or coped with. Although some learners reshape their physical environments, most do not (Marcus, 1988 as cited in Zimmerman, 1989). Learners often behave as receptacles of information, assuming that responsibility for understanding rests with them, and thus they treat the social surround as static. They hesitate to ask questions, believing that they should already know the answers (Newman & Goldin, 1990; van der Meij, 1988). They pass up opportunities to reshape social learning opportunities in their favor; for instance, if it is easier for them to process information in a visual mode, asking someone to draw a diagram to illustrate an idea or simply asking someone to speak more slowly or repeat an idea. Commonly, people believe that "smart" people are able to do all thinking and learning in their heads. Thus, they pass up opportunities for distributing cognition that extend intelligent behavior (Salomon, 1993) such as "downloading" information onto a piece of chart paper to increase their cognitive capacity to deal with the complexity of a problem.

Students need opportunities to gain proactive patterns for shaping the social context so that others better support their learning and for adjusting and changing the physical environment proactively to support intelligent behavior. This could lead to seeking out new environments or changing the present one (e.g., Sternberg, 1997). Using distributed forms of cognition should be encouraged as advantageous ways to reduce cognitive load and increase "working space" rather than a display of inability to calculate the problem in one's head.

There is a great deal of interest in developing interventions to reorganize students' conceptual knowledge. Although these efforts have revealed the challenge of how robust students' conception are, successful examples exist as a testament to the possibility of the enterprise (e.g., Gabel, 1991; Lochhead & Clement, 1982; White & Horwitz, 1987). Fewer examples of efforts at procedural and environmental reorganization currently exist. Adey and Shayer (1993) explicitly tried to reorganize students' conceptual and procedural understandings in a program called Cognitive Acceleration through Science Education (CASE). It taught disciplinary patterns of thinking in science; for instance, the isolation and control of variables while paying particular attention to introducing cognitive dissonance so that students would examine their assumptions and rethink their prior conceptions. It explicitly fostered metacognition and transferring of knowledge and strategies between contexts. Significant improvements were found for 12-year-old boys ($d = .72$, $p < .05$) and 11-year-old girls ($d = .60$, $p < .025$) in the CASE group as compared with controls on school science achievement tests 1 year after the intervention following a 2-year program including 194 intervention and 230 control students. Significant differences persisted 2 years later for 12-year-old boys and 11-year-old girls (science: $d = .96$ and $d = .67$; math:

$d = .50$ and $d = .72$; and English: $d = .32$ and $d = .69$, respectively) between CASE students and controls on the General Certificate of Secondary Education Exam (GCSE) (Adey & Shayer, 1994, p. 92). These results are promising for the magnitude, persistence, and generalizability of effect. Further research is needed to assess the impact of reorganizational efforts on other aspects of conceptual organization, such as attitudes and beliefs, and on procedural and environmental organization more broadly.

A reorganizational stance holds promise for teaching for intelligent behavior, particularly for enabling effects that persist and are generalizable. This is not to imply that reorganization is easy to affect. However, the success of a number of studies speaks to the possibility of the enterprise.

A SUMMARY OF CURRENT EFFORTS. Current efforts to teach for intelligence draw together the three aspects described above to encourage more intelligent performances. The best of these efforts offers a strong cultural context in support of intelligent behavior – one that values reflection and growth in expertise and engages students in mentorship-like opportunities to gain from patterns of thinking, learning, and knowing that are part of their cultural inheritance. These efforts attend to individual and group learning, creating affordances for different learning approaches and propensities, and opportunities for students to build individual theories that are consonant with the current scientific theories. They provide opportunities for students to discover maladaptive conceptual, procedural, and environmental patterns and cultural supports for gaining adaptive ones. Such integrated and encompassing approaches currently hold the best promise for teaching intelligence using performance as a standard.

TWO CARICATURES AND A CONCLUSION

The history of efforts to teach intelligence is a vexed one. As long ago as the era of the Greek rhetoricians, some have taken it for granted that intelligence in some sense can be taught, and they set about designing ways to do so. However, others have vehemently argued the impossibility of the enterprise. The polarization is illuminating and can be caricatured as follows:

1. *Intelligence is a skill like skating or handwriting. Practice assiduously your problem solving, decision making, or learning and you will get much better at it!*
2. *Intelligence is a matter of neural speed, largely genetically determined. Do what you will, you will not get more intelligent in any fundamental sense.*

Although these caricatures represent extremes, both are present in the literature on teaching intelligence. The extremes illustrate a fundamental problem that has plagued the discourse around both positive and negative positions on the learnability and teachability of intelligence and imperil the enterprise – a persistent narrowness of conception. In reviewing efforts and evidence on the teachability of intelligence, our principal goal in this chapter has been to work against this hazard.

The hazard appears first in the meaning of intelligence. Both caricatures reveal a reductionist impulse. The first reduces intelligence to an acquired skill like any other skill. The second reduces intelligence to a matter of hardware and original equipment. They both aim to strip away complexity in favor of simple fundamental categorizations. They both treat intelligence as a capability, although one conceived very differently in the two cases. In pressing for a "performance conception" of intelligence, we urge that such reductionism is out of place, at least in educational contexts. Rather, it is important to look to intelligent behavior in realistic circumstances, which involves not only capabilities of various sorts but also sensitivities to occasion and values and commitments that spur the investment of mental effort.

The hazard of a narrow conception also surfaces around the causes of intelligent behavior. Here again, the caricatures betray a common impulse differently played out. Skill and neural speed are both efficiency conceptions, albeit very different in the sources of the presumed efficiency. Certainly efficiencies of various kinds have a lot to do with intelligent behavior – indeed with effective behavior of almost any sort. However, we have argued that a much broader range of causes plays important roles in shaping intelligent behavior. Although the interventions reviewed almost inevitably mix causes, they are interpretable as foregrounding one or another and suggesting that this cause of intelligence can be harnessed for purposes of teaching and learning.

The hazard of a narrow conception also troubles the pedagogy of intelligence. Our second caricature offers no hope at all here. The first does almost as much harm by proposing a glib recipe for success – practice, practice! Although practice undoubtedly is an important element in any trajectory of learning, effective efforts to teach intelligence must be broader. Initiatives that focus on the teaching of strategies with dogged attention to the procedural side of behavior are also narrow. The results of efforts to teach intelligent behavior signal that we must attend to the cultures of learning, to individuals' current abilities, propensities, and current conceptions, and to fundamental reorganizations of behavior, not just acceleration and fine-tuning.

It is natural to feel uneasy with this rich mix of considerations and to long for a simple, clean essentialist version like the two caricatures. But even supposing that both contain a grain of truth, they would be the wrong kinds of theory for educational ends. The challenge of education is not an essentialist one, but a complex, qualified, and situated one. To return to the analogy in our opening paragraph, as with the scientists who are studying fish movement, effective education requires a rich understanding of the learner, the medium, and the nature of their interaction. Analogously, it is rich conceptions of intelligence, its causes, and its pedagogy that inform and illuminate the enterprise of teaching intelligence.

ACKNOWLEDGMENTS

The authors would like to express their appreciation to Howard Gardner and Robert Sternberg for their substantive and helpful comments on earlier drafts of this chapter.

REFERENCES

Adey, P., & Shayer, M. (1993). An exploration of long-term far-transfer effects following an extended intervention program in the high school science curriculum. *Cognition and Instruction, 11*(1), 1–29.

Adey, P., & Shayer, M. (1994). *Really raising standards: Cognitive intervention and academic achievement*. London: Routledge.

Anderson, M. (1992). *Intelligence and development: A cognitive theory*. Oxford: Blackwell.

Arbitman-Smith, R., Haywood, W. C., & Bransford, J. D. (1984). Assessing cognitive change. In P. Brooks, R.

Sperber, & C. M. McCauley (Eds.), *Learning and cognition in the mentally retarded*. Hillsdale, NJ: LEA.

Armstrong, T. (1994). *Multiple intelligences in the classroom*. Alexandria, VA: ASCD.

Baron, J. (1985). *Rationality and intelligence*. New York: Cambridge University Press.

Baron, J., Granato, L., Spranca, M., & Teubal, E. (1993). Decision-making biases in children and early adolescents: exploratory studies. *Merrill–Palmer Quarterly, 39*(1), 22–46.

Baron, J., & Sternberg, R. S. (Eds.). (1986). *Teaching thinking skills: Theory and practice*. New York: W. H. Freeman.

Barron, F. (1969). *Creative person and creative process*. New York: Holt, Rinehart, & Winston.

Belmont, J. M., & Butterfield, E. C. (1977). The instructional approach to developmental cognitive research. In R. Kail & J. Hagen (Eds.), *Perspectives on the development of memory and cognition*. Hillsdale, NJ: LEA.

Belmont, J. M., Butterfield, E.C., & Borkowski, J. G. (1978). Training retarded people to generalize memorization methods across memory tasks. In M. M. Gruneberg, P. E. Morris, & R. N. Sykes (Eds.), *Practical aspects of memory*. London, Academic Press.

Belmont, J. M., Butterfield, E. C., & Ferretti, R. P. (1982). To secure transfer of training instruct self-management skills. In D. K. Detterman & R. J. Sternberg (Eds.), *How and how much can intelligence be increased* (pp. 147–154). Norwood, NJ: Ablex.

Bereiter, C., & Scardamalia, M. (1993). *Surpassing ourselves: An inquiry into the nature and implications of expertise*. Chicago: Open Court.

Berlyne, D. E. (1965). Curiosity and education. In J. D. Krumboltz (Ed.), *Learning and the educational process*. Chicago: Rand McNally.

Bezrucko, N., Kurland, M., & Eckert, K. (1996). *Elementary classroom practices show empirical relations to long-term benefits of early intervention: Sustaining the effects of early intervention*. A Symposium at the Head Start Third National Research Conference, Washington, DC, June 20–23.

Blagg, N. (1991). *Can we teach intelligence? A comprehensive evaluation of Feuerstein's Instructional Enrichment program*. Hillsdale, NJ: LEA.

Bornstein, P. H., & Quevillon, R. P. (1976). The effects of a self-instructional package on overactive preschool boys. *Journal of Applied Behavior Analysis, 9*, 179–188.

Bransford, J. D., Goldman, S. R., & Vye, N. J. (1991). Making a difference in people's abilities to think: Reflections on a decade of work and some hopes for the future. In L. Okagaki & R. Sternberg (Eds.), *Directors of development: Influences on the development of children's thinking* (pp. 147–180). Hillsdale, NJ: LEA.

Bransford, J. D., Sherwood, R., Vye, N., & Reiser, J. (1986). Teaching thinking and problem-solving. *American Psychologist, 41*(10), 1078–1089.

Bransford, J. D., & Stein, B. S. (1984). *The IDEAL problem solver*. New York: Freeman.

Bransford, J. D., Stein, B. S., Vye, N. J., Franks, J. J., Auble, P. M., Mezynski, K. J., & Perfetto, G. A. (1982). Differences in approaches to learning: An overview. *Journal of Experimental Psychology: General 111*, 390–398.

Brown, A. L., & Barclay, C. R. (1976). The effects of training specific mnemonics on the metamnemonic efficiency of retarded children. *Child Development, 47*, 70–80.

Brown, A. L., Bransford, J. D., Ferrara, R. A., & Campione, J. C. (1983). Learning, remembering, and understanding. In P. H. Mussen (Ed.), *Handbook of child psychology, Vol. 3: Cognitive development*. New York: Wiley.

Brown, A. L., & Campione, J. C. (1994). Guided discovery in a community of learners. In K. McGilly (Ed.), *Classroom lessons: Integrating cognitive theory and classroom practice*. Cambridge, MA: MIT Press/Bradford Books.

Brown, A. L., Campione, J. C., & Barclay, C. R. (1979). Training self-checking routines for estimating test readiness: Generalization from list learning to prose recall. *Child Development, 50*, 501–512.

Bruer, J. T. (1993). *Schools for thought: A science of learning in the classroom*. Cambridge, MA: MIT Press.

Bruer, J. T. (1997). Education and the brain: A bridge too far. *Educational Researcher, 26*(8), 4–16.

Bruner, J. S., Olver, R., & Greenfield, P. (1966). *Studies in cognitive growth*. New York: Wiley.

Campione, J. (1984). Metacognitive components of instructional research with problem learners. In F. Weinert & R. Kluew (Eds.), *Metacognition, motivation, and learning* (pp. 109–132). Stuttgart: Kohlhammer.

Campione, J., Brown, A., & Ferrara, R. (1982). Mental retardation and intelligence. In R. J. Sternberg (Ed.), *Handbook of human intelligence* (pp. 392–492). Cambridge, UK: Cambridge University Press.

Cattell, R. B. (1941). Some theoretical issues in intelligence testing. *Psychological Bulletin, 38*, 592.

Cattell, R. B. (1963). Theory of fluid and crystallized intelligence: A critical experiment. *Journal of Educational Psychology, 18*, 165–244.

Ceci, S. J. (1990). *On intelligence ... more or less: A bioecological treatise on intellectual development*. Englewood Cliffs, NJ: Prentice Hall.

Chase, W. C., & Simon, H. A. (1973). Perception in chess. *Cognitive Psychology, 4*, 55–81.

Chi, M., Feltovich, P., & Glaser, R. (1981). Categorization and representation of physics problems by experts and novices. *Cognitive Science, 5*, 121–152.

Chi, M., Glaser, R., & Rees, E. (1982). Expertise in problem-solving. In R. J. Sternberg (Ed.), *Advances in the psychology of human intelligence: Vol. 1*. Hillsdale, NJ: LEA.

Chipman, S. F., Segal, J. W., & Glaser, R. (Eds.). (1985). *Thinking and learning skills, Volume 2: Research and open questions*. Hillsdale, NJ: LEA.

Chugani, H. T. (1994). Development of regional brain glucose metabolism in relation to behavior and plasticity. In G. Dawson & K. W. Fischer (Eds.), *Human behavior and the developing brain* (pp. 153–175). New York: The Guilford Press.

Clement, J. (1985, April). *A method experts use to evaluate the validity of models used as problem representations in science and mathematics*. Paper presented at the annual meeting of the American Educational Research Association, Chicago.

Costa, A. (Ed.). (1985). *Developing minds: A resource book for teaching thinking*. Alexandria, VA: ASCD.

Costa, A. (Ed.). (1991). *Developing minds: Programs for teaching thinking: Rev. Ed.: Vol. 2*. Alexandria, VA: ASCD.

Covington, M. V., Crutchfield, R. S., Davies, L., & Olton, R. S. (1974). *The productive thinking program: A course in learning to think*. Columbus, OH: Merrill.

Cronbach, L. J. (1977). *Educational psychology*. (3rd ed.). New York: Harcourt Brace Janovich.

Cronbach, L. J., & Snow, R. E. (1977). *Aptitudes and instructional methods: A handbook for research on interactions*. New York: Irvington Publishers, Inc.

Dasen, P. R. (Ed.). (1977). *Piagetian psychology: Cross-cultural contributions*. New York: Gardner Press.

Dawson, G. (1994). Development of emotional expression and emotion regulation in infancy: Contributions of the frontal lobe. In G. Dawson & K. W. Fischer (Eds.), *Human behavior and the developing brain* (pp. 346–379). New York: The Guilford Press.

Deary, I. J., & Stough, C. (1996). Intelligence and inspection time: Achievements, prospects, and problems. *American Psychologist, 51*(6), 599–608.

de Bono, E. (1973). *CoRT Thinking Program: Workcards and teacher notes*. Sydney: Direct Educational Services.

de Bono, E. (1987). *CoRT Thinking Program: Workcards and teacher notes*. Chicago: Science Research Associates.

Deci, E. L., Schwartz, A. J., Sheinman, L., & Ryan, R. R. (1981). An instrument to assess adults' orientations toward control and autonomy with children: Reflections on intrinsic motivation and perceived competence. *Journal of Educational Psychology, 73*(5), 642–650.

de Groot, A. D. (1965). *Thought and choice in chess*. The Hague: Mouton.

Detterman, D. K. (1992). The case for the prosecution: Transfer as an epiphenomenon. In D. K. Detterman & R. J. Sternberg (Eds.), *Transfer on trial* (pp. 1–24). Norwood, NJ: Ablex.

Diener, C. I., & Dweck, C. S. (1978). An analysis of learned helplessness: Continuous changes in performance, strategy, and achievement cognitions following failure. *Journal of Personality and Social Psychology, 36*(5), 451–462.

di Sessa, A. (1983). Phenomenology and the evolution of intuition. In D. Gentner & A. L. Stevens (Eds.), *Mental models* (pp. 267–298). Hillsdale, NJ: LEA.

Driver, R., Guesne, E., & Tiberghien, A. (Eds.). (1985). *Children's ideas in science.* Philadelphia, PA: Open University Press.

Druckman, D., & Bjork, R. A. (Eds.). (1994). *Learning, remembering, believing: Enhancing human performance.* Washington, DC: National Academy Press.

Dweck, C. S. (1975). The role of expectations and attributions in the alleviation of learned helplessness. *Journal of Personality and Social Psychology, 31,* 674–685.

Dweck, C. S., & Bempechat, J. (1983). Children's theories of intelligence: Consequences for learning. In S. G. Paris, G. M. Olson, & H. W. Stevenson (Eds.), *Learning and motivation in the classroom* (pp. 239–255). Hillsdale, NJ: LEA.

Edelman, G. M. (1989). *The remembered present: A biological theory of consciousness.* New York: Basic Books.

Edwards, J. (1991a). Research work on the CoRT method. In S. Maclure & P. Davies (Eds.), *Learning to think: Thinking to learn* (pp. 19–30), Oxford: Pergamon.

Edwards, J. (1991b). The direct teaching of thinking skills. In G. Evans (Ed.), *Learning and teaching cognitive skills* (pp. 87–106). Melbourne: Australian Council for Educational Research.

Edwards, J. (1994). Thinking, education, and human potential. In J. Edwards (Ed.), *Thinking: International interdisciplinary perspectives* (pp. 6–15). Melbourne: Hawker Brownlow Education.

Edwards, J., & Baldauf, R. B. (1983). Teaching thinking in secondary science. In W. Maxwell (Ed.), *Thinking: The expanding frontier.* Philadelphia: The Franklin Institute Press.

Edwards, J., & Baldauf, R. B. (1987). The effects of the CoRT-1 thinking skills program on students. In D. N. Perkins, J. Lochhead, & J. C. Bishop (Eds.), *Thinking: The second international conference* (pp. 453–474), Hillsdale, NJ: LEA.

Erickson, G., & Tiberghien, A. (1985). Heat and temperature. In R. Driver, E. Guesne, & A. Tiberghien (Eds.), *Children's ideas in science* (pp. 52–84). Philadelphia: Open University Press.

Ericsson, K. A., & Smith, J. (Eds.). (1991). *Toward a general theory of expertise: Prospects and limits.* Cambridge, UK: Cambridge University Press.

Feuerstein, R., Miller, R., Hoffman, M. B., Rand, Y., Mintzker, Y., & Jensen, M. R. (1981). Cognitive modifiability in adolescence: Cognitive structure and the effects of intervention. *The Journal of Special Education, 15,* 269–286.

Feuerstein, R., Rand, Y., Hoffman, M. B., & Miller, R. (1980). *Instrumental enrichment.* Baltimore, MD: University Park Press.

Finger, S., & Wolf, C. (1988). The "Kennard Effect" before Kennard: The early history of age and brain lesions. *Archives of Neurology, 45,* 1136–1142.

Fitts, P. M. (1964). Perceptual–motor skill learning. In A. W. Melton (Ed.), *Categories of human learning* (pp. 243–285). New York: Academic Press.

Fitts, P. M., & Posner, M. I. (1967). *Human performance.* Belmont, CA: Brooks/Cole.

Gabel, D. (1991, April). *Improving chemistry achievement through emphasis on the particle nature of matter.* Paper presented at the annual meeting of the National Association for Research in Science Teaching, Lake Geneva, WI.

Gardner, H. (1983). *Frames of mind.* New York: Basic Books.

Gardner, H. (1991). *The unschooled mind: How children think and how schools should teach.* New York: Basic Books.

Gardner, H. (1993a). *Frames of mind: The theory of multiple intelligences.* Tenth Anniversary edition. New York: Basic Books.

Gardner, H. (1993b). *Multiple intelligences: The theory in practice.* New York: Basic Books.

Gardner, H. (1993c). *Creating minds: An anatomy of creativity seen through the lives of Freud, Einstein, Picasso, Stravinsky, Eliot, Graham, and Gandhi.* New York: Basic Books.

Gardner, H. (1995). Reflections on multiple intelligences: Myths and messages. *Phi Delta Kappan, 77*(3), 200–209.

Gardner, H. (1999). Are there additional intelligences? The case for naturalist, spiritual, and existential intelligences. In J. Kane (Ed.), *Education, Information and Transformation* (pp. 111–131). Upper Saddle River, NJ: Prentice Hall. Reprinted: *Gifted Education Press Quarterly, 11,* (2), Spring 1997, pp. 2–5.

Gardner, H. (1999). Multiple Approaches to Understanding. In C. M. Reigeluth (Ed.), *Instructional-Design Theories and Models: A New Paradigm of Instructional Theory, Vol. 2* (pp. 69–89). Mahwah, NJ: LEA.

Gardner, H., Krechevsky, M., Sternberg, R. J., & Okagaki, L. (1994). Intelligence in context: Enhancing students' practical intelligence for school. In K. McGilly (Ed.), *Classroom lessons: Integrating cognitive theory and classroom practice* (pp. 105–127). Cambridge, MA: MIT Press.

Glaser, R. (1992). Expert knowledge and the processes of thinking. In D. F. Halpern (Ed.), *Enhancing thinking skills in the sciences and mathematics* (pp. 63–75). Hillsdale, NJ: LEA.

Goddard, H. H. (1920). *Human efficiency and levels of intelligence.* Princeton, NJ: Princeton University Press.

Greenfield, P. M. (1997). You can't take it with you: Why ability assessments don't cross cultures. *American Psychologist, 52*(10), 1115–1124.

Haywood, H. C., & Arbitman-Smith, R. (1981). Modifications of cognitive functions in slow-learning adolescents. In P. Mittler (Ed.), *Frontiers of knowledge in mental retardation: Vol. 1: Proceedings of the fifth congress of IASSMD I-Social, educational, and behavioral aspects.* Baltimore, MD: University Park Press.

Hernstein, R. J., Nickerson, R. S., Sanchez, M., & Swets, J. A. (1986). Teaching thinking skills. *American Psychologist, 41,* 1279–1289.

Horn, J. L. (1985). Remodelling old models of intelligence. In B. B. Wolman (Ed.), *Handbook of intelligence* (pp. 167–300). New York: John B. Wiley & Sons.

Hunt, J. M. (1961). *Intelligence and experience*. New York: Ronald Press Co.

Huttenlocher, P. R. (1994). Synaptogenesis in human cerebral cortex. In G. Dawson & K. W. Fischer (Eds.), *Human behavior and the developing brain* (pp. 137–152). New York: Guilford Press.

Jensen, A. (1980). *Bias in mental testing*. New York: The Free Press.

Jones, B. F., & Idol, L. (Eds.). (1990). *Dimensions of thinking and cognitive instruction*. Hillsdale, NJ: LEA.

Just, M. A., & Carpenter, P. A. (1987). *The psychology of reading and language comprehension*. Boston: Allyn & Bacon.

Klaczynski, P. A., Gordon, D. H., & Fauth, J. (1997). Goal-oriented critical reasoning and individual differences in critical reasoning biases. *Journal of Educational Psychology, 89*(3), 470–485.

Kornhaber, M. (1998). *SUMIT: Schools using Multiple Intelligences theory* [On-line]. Available: http://pzweb.harvard.edu/Research/SUMIT.htm

Langer, E. J. (1989). *Mindfulness*. Menlo Park, CA: Addison–Wesley.

Larkin, J. (1983). The role of problem representation in physics. In D. Gentner & A. L. Stevens (Eds.), *Mental models* (pp. 75–100). Hillsdale, NJ: LEA.

Larkin, J. H., McDermott, J., Simon, D. P., & Simon, H. A. (1980). Models of competence in solving physics problems. *Cognitive Science, 4*, 317–345.

Lave, J. (1988). *Cognition in practice: Mind, mathematics, and culture in everyday life*. Cambridge, UK: Cambridge University Press.

Lesgold, A., Resnick, L., & Hammond, K. (1985). Learning to read: A longitudinal study of work skill development in two curricula. In G. E. MacKinnon & T. G. Waller (Eds.), *Reading research: Advances in theory and practice: Vol. 4*, New York: Academic Press.

Lipman, M. (1976). Philosophy for children. *Metaphilosophy, 7*(1).

Lipman, M., Sharp, A. M., & Oscanyon, F. (1980). *Philosophy in the classroom*. Philadelphia: Temple University Press.

Lochhead, J., & Clement, J. (1982). Does computer-programming enhance problem-solving ability? Some positive evidence on algebra word problems, In R. J. Seidel, R. Anderson, & B. Hunter (Eds.), *Computer literacy: Issues and directions for 1985*. New York: Academic Press.

Mansfield, R. S., Busse, T. V., & Krepelka, E. J. (1978). The effectiveness of creativity training. *Review of Educational Research, 48*(4), 517–536.

Markman, E. (1985). Comprehension monitoring: Developmental and educational issues. In S. F. Chipman, J. W. Segal, & R. Glaser (Eds.), *Thinking and learning skills: Vol. 2: Research and open questions*. Hillsdale, NJ: LEA.

Meeker, M. N. (1969). *The Structure of Intellect: Its interpretations and uses*. Columbus, OH: Charles Merrill.

Neisser, U. (1979). The concept of intelligence. In R. J. Sternberg & D. K. Detterman (Eds.), *Human intelligence: Perspectives on its theory and measurement* (pp. 179–189). Norwood: NJ: Ablex.

Newell, A., & Rosenbloom, P. S. (1981). Mechanisms of skill acquisition and the law of practice. In J. R. Anderson (Ed.), *Cognitive skills and their acquisition* (pp. 1–55). Hillsdale, NJ: LEA.

Newman, R. S., & Goldin, L. (1990). Children's reluctance to seek help with schoolwork. *Journal of Educational Psychology, 82*, 92–100.

Nickerson, R. S. (1989). On improving thinking through instruction. *Review of Research in Education, 15*, 3–57.

Nickerson, R., Perkins, D. N., & Smith, E. (1985). *The teaching of thinking*. Hillsdale, NJ: LEA.

Nussbaum, J. (1985). The earth as a cosmic body. In R. Driver, E. Guesne, & A. Tiberghien (Eds.), *Children's ideas in science* (pp. 170–192). Philadelphia: Open University Press.

Osborne, A. F. (1963). *Applied imagination*. New York: Scribner's.

Osborne, R., & Freyberg, P. (1985). *Learning in science: The implications of children's science*. Auckland: Heinemann.

Palinscar, A. S., & Brown, A. L. (1984). Reciprocal teaching of comprehension-fostering and comprehension-monitoring activities. *Cognition and Instruction, 1*, 117–175.

Paris, S. (1982). Learning the functional significance of mnemonic actions: A microgenetic study of strategy acquisition. *Journal of Experimental Child Psychology, 34*(3), 490–509.

Parnes, S. J. (1981). *The magic of your mind*. Buffalo: Brearly Limited Publishers.

Pea, R. D. (1993). Practices of distributed intelligence and designs for education. In G. Salomon (Ed.), *Distributed cognitions* (pp. 47–87). New York: Cambridge University Press.

Perkins, D. N. (1985). Postprimary education has little impact on informal reasoning. *Journal of Educational Psychology, 77*(5), 562–571.

Perkins, D. N. (1989). Reasoning as it is and could be. In D. Topping, D. Crowell, & V. Kobayashi (Eds.), *Thinking: The third international conference* (pp. 175–194). Hillsdale, NJ: LEA.

Perkins, D. N. (1992). *Smart schools: From training memories to educating minds*. New York: The Free Press.

Perkins, D. N. (1993). Person plus: A distributed view of thinking and learning. In G. Salomon (Ed.), *Distributed cognitions* (pp. 88–110). New York: Cambridge University Press.

Perkins, D. N. (1995). *Outsmarting I.Q.: The emerging science of learnable intelligence*. New York: The Free Press.

Perkins, D. N., Allen, R., & Hafner, J. (1983). Difficulties in everyday reasoning. In W. Maxwell (Ed.), *Thinking: The frontier expands* (pp. 177–189). Hillsdale, NJ: LEA.

Perkins, D. N., Farady, M., & Bushey, B. (1991). Everyday reasoning and the roots of intelligence. In J. Voss, D. N. Perkins, and J. Segal (Eds.), *Informal reasoning* (pp. 83–105). Hillsdale, NJ: LEA.

Perkins, D. N., & Grotzer, T. A. (1997). Teaching intelligence. *American Psychologist, 52*(10), 1125–1133.

Perkins, D. N., Jay, E., & Tishman, S. (1993). Beyond abilities: A dispositional theory of thinking. *The Merrill–Palmer Quarterly, 39*(1), 1–21.

Perkins, D. N., & Tishman, S. (in press). Intelligence in the wild: A dispositional view of intellectual traits. Educational Psychology Review.

Pomeroy, D. (1992, April). *Comparison of philosophies of scientists and science educators*. Paper presented at the National Science Teachers Association, Boston, MA.

Posner, G. J., Strike, K. A., Hewson, P. W., & Gertzog, W. A. (1982). Accommodation of a scientific conception: Toward a theory of conceptual change. *Science Education, 1982, 66*(2), 211–227.

Ramey, C. T. (1994). Abcedarian Project. In R. J. Sternberg (Ed.), *Encyclopedia of human intelligence: Vol. 1* (pp. 1–3) New York: Macmillan.

Ramey, C. T., & Campbell, F. A. (1987). The Carolina Abecedarian Project: An educational experiment concerning human malleability. In J. A. Gallagher & C. T. Ramey (Eds.), *The malleability of children* (pp. 127–139). Baltimore: Brookes.

Ramey, C. T., & Smith, B. J. (1977). Assessing the intellectual consequences of early intervention with high-risk infants. *American Journal of Mental Deficiency, 8*(4), 318–324.

Rand, Y., Tannenbaum, A. J., & Feuerstein, R. (1979). Effects of instrumental enrichment on the psychoeducational development of low-functioning adolescents. *Journal of Educational Psychology, 71*, 751–763.

Roe, A. (1952). *The making of a scientist*. New York: Dodd, Mead & Co.

Salomon, G. S. (Ed.). (1993). *Distributed cognitions*. New York: Cambridge University Press.

Scardamalia, M., Bereiter, C., & Lamon, M. (1994). The CSILE Project: Trying to bring the classroom into world 3. In K. McGilly (Ed.), *Classroom lessons: Integrating cognitive theory and classroom practice* (pp. 201–228). Cambridge, MA: MIT Press.

Schacter, D. (1996). *Searching for memory*. New York: Basic Books.

Schoenfeld, A. H. (1982). Measures of problem-solving performance and of problem-solving instruction. *Journal for Research in Mathematics Education, 13*(1), 31–49.

Schoenfeld, A. (1989). Teaching mathematical thinking and problem-solving. In L. Resnick & L. E. Klopfer (Eds.), *Toward the thinking curriculum: Current cognitive research* (pp. 83–103). Alexandria, VA: ASCD.

Schoenfeld, A. H., & Herrmann, D. J. (1982). Problem perception and knowledge structure in expert and novice mathematical problem-solvers. *Journal of Experimental Psychology: Learning Memory and Cognition, 8*(5), 484–494.

Segal, J. W., Chipman, S. F., & Glaser, R. (Eds.). (1985). *Thinking and learning skills, Volume 1: Relating instruction to research*. Hillsdale, NJ: LEA.

Sfard, A. (1998). On two metaphors for learning and the dangers of choosing just one. *Educational Researcher, 27*(2), 4–13.

Simon, H. A., & Chase, W. (1973). Skill in chess. *American Scientist, 61*, 394–403.

Snow, R. E. (1997). Aptitudes and symbol systems in adaptive classroom teaching. *Phi Delta Kappan 78*(5), 354–360.

Stanovich, K. E., & West, R. F. (1997). Reasoning independently of prior belief and individual differences in actively open-minded thinking. *Journal of Educational Psychology, 89*(2), 342–357.

Stein, B. S., Bransford, J. D., Franks, J. J., Vye, N. J., & Perfetto, G. A. (1982). Differences in judgments of learning difficulty. *Journal of Experimental Psychology: General 111*, 406–413.

Steiner, A. (1979). Why a practicum in thinking? In D. D. Wheeler & W. N. Dember (Eds.), *A practicum in thinking.* University of Cinicinnati, Department of Psychology.

Sternberg, R. J. (1985). *Beyond I.Q.: A triarchic theory of human intelligence*. New York: Cambridge University Press.

Sternberg, R. J. (1996). Myths, countermyths, and truths about intelligence. *Educational Researcher, 25*(2), 11–16.

Sternberg, R. J. (1997). The concept of intelligence and its role in lifelong learning and success. *American Psychologist, 52*(10), 1030–1037.

Sternberg, R. J. (1998). Abilities are forms of developing expertise. *Educational Researcher, 27*(3), 11–20.

Sternberg, R., & Bhana, K. (1986). Synthesis of research on the effectiveness of intellectual skills programs: Snake-oil remedies or miracle cures? *Educational Leadership, 44*, 60–67.

Sternberg, R. J., & Detterman, D. K. (Eds.). (1986). *What is intelligence?: Contemporary viewpoints on its nature and definition*. Norwood, NJ: Ablex.

Sternberg, R. J., Ferrari, M., Clinkenbeard, P., Grigorenko, E. L. (1996). Identification, instruction, and assessment of gifted children: A construct validation of a triarchic model. *Gifted Child Quarterly, 40*(3), 129–137.

Sternberg, R. J., & Wagner, R. K. (Eds.). (1986). *Practical intelligence: Nature and origins of competence in the everyday world*. New York: Cambridge University Press.

Stevenson, H. W., & Lee, S. (1990). Contexts of achievement. *Monographs of the Society for Research in Child Development, 55*(1–2, Serial No. 221).

Stevenson, H. W., Lee, S., & Stigler, J. (1986). Mathematics achievement of Chinese, Japanese, and American children. *Science, 231*, 693–699.

Super, C. (1980). Cognitive development: Looking across at growing up. In C. Super & S. Harkness (Eds.), *New directions for child development: Anthropological perspectives on child development* (pp. 59–69). San Francisco, CA: Jossey-Bass.

Tishman, S. (1991). *Metacognition and children's concepts of cognition*. Unpublished doctoral dissertation. Harvard University, Cambridge, MA.

Tishman, S., Jay, E., & Perkins, D. N. (1993). Thinking dispositions: From transmission to enculturation. *Theory Into Practice, 32*(3), 147–153.

van der Meij, H. (1988). Constraints on question-asking in classrooms. *Journal of Educational Psychology, 81*, 384–391.

Vygotsky, L. S. (1978). *Mind in society*. Cambridge, MA: Harvard University Press.

Washburn, D. A., & Rumbaugh, D. M. (1997). Faster is smarter so why are we slower?: A comparative perspective on intelligence and processing speed. *American Psychologist, 52*(10), 1147–1148.

Welford, A. T. (1968). *Fundamentals of skill*. London: Methuen.

Wheeler, D. D. (1979). A practicum in thinking. In D. D. Wheeler & W. N. Dember (Eds.), *A practicum in thinking*. University of Cinicinnati, Department of Psychology.

Whimbey, A. (1975). *Intelligence can be taught*. New York: E. P. Dutton.

White, B., & Frederiksen, J. (1998). Inquiry, modeling, and metacognition: Making science accessible to all students. *Cognition and Instruction, 16*(1), pp. 3–118.

White, B., & Horwitz, P. (1987). *Thinker Tools: Enabling children to understand physical laws*. Report 6470, Bolt, Beranek, & Newman Laboratories, Cambridge, MA.

Williams, W., Blythe, T., White, N., Li, J., Sternberg, R., & Gardner, H. (1996). *Practical intelligence for school handbook*. New York: Harper Collins.

Wiske, S. (Ed.). (1997). *Teaching for understanding*. San Francisco: Jossey-Bass.

Wright, E. D. (1991). Odyssey: A curriculum for thinking. In A. Costa (Ed.), *Developing minds: Programs for teaching thinking: Rev. Ed.: Vol. 2* (pp. 48–50), Alexandria, VA: ASCD.

Zimmerman, B. J. (1989). Models of self-regulated learning. In B. J. Zimmerman & D. H. Schunk (Eds.), *Self-regulated learning and academic achievement: Theory, research, and practice* (pp. 1–25), New York: Springer-Verlag.

PART VIII

INTELLIGENCE, SOCIETY, AND CULTURE

CHAPTER TWENTY-THREE

Intelligence and Education

RICHARD E. MAYER

INTELLIGENCE AND EDUCATION

The fields of intelligence and education are so intimately bound together that it would be impossible to understand intelligence without knowing about its relation to education. Quite literally, intelligence is the child of education, because the field of intelligence testing was born from the need to develop a test that would predict children's school success (Wolf, 1973). The thesis of this chapter is that the field of education has been instrumental in challenging psychologists to develop more authentic theories of individual differences in intellectual ability and that the emerging cognitive theories of intelligence can be instrumental in reforming educational practice. In short, the study of intelligence and education provides an example of the fruitful interaction between the practical demands of educators and the basic research focus of cognitive scientists. The first section of this chapter reviews education's contributions to the study of intelligence, and the second section reviews the study of intelligence's contributions to education.

EDUCATION'S CONTRIBUTIONS TO THE STUDY OF INTELLIGENCE

The historical connection between intelligence and education is no accident. As mandatory public education became commonplace by the late 1800s, educators were confronted with an overwhelming observation: Students of the same chronological age displayed a range of individual differences in intellectual ability. Like other advances in psychological theory, the study of intelligence has been motivated by the practical problems of education (Mayer, 1992). In this case, the practical pedagogic problem of how to address the needs of individual students touched off a worldwide search for an "instrument to differentiate children and adolescents on the basis on their ability to learn" (Wolf, 1973, p. 139).

By 1905 Binet and his colleagues achieved a solution that was innovative, straightforward, and most important, successful – the development of the Binet–Simon intelligence scale. Students of a given age were asked a battery of questions; if a child failed to answer correctly questions that most other children of the same age could answer, the child was considered below average in the ability to learn. Binet's logic was that if all children of the same age have the same exposure to learning experiences but some know less than others, they apparently have more difficulty in learning than their peers. Conversely, if a child was able to answer questions that most of the other same-aged children could not answer, the child could be considered above average in the ability to learn (if it is assumed all children at the same age level had the same opportunities to learn). What is important is that Binet's intelligence test was successful to some extent in predicting children's ability to learn in school.

The development of the first useful intelligence test is widely recognized as a "fundamental breakthrough that has had important influence on the subsequent development of both psychology and pedagogy" (Wolf, 1973, p. 139). Binet's test has been revised many times since the early 1900s and has served as the basis for subsequent intelligence tests.

In fact, the development of a test to predict school success has been heralded as one of psychology's major contributions to the world: "Probably no psychological innovation has had more impact on the societies of the Western world than the development of the Binet–Simon scales" (Jenkins & Paterson, 1961, p. 81).

The story of Binet's triumph parallels a larger pattern in which educational venues have freed cognitive scientists from narrow and contrived research methods that failed to account for real phenomena. For example, Binet (cited in Wolf, 1973, p. 91) criticized the methodology of experimental psychology of the early 1900s as follows:

Subjects go into a little room, respond by electrical signals, and leave without so much as a word to the experimenter... The latter want simple and precise results, even to carrying them out to three decimal places and measuring them to thousandths of a second. Simplicity is in fact obtained and in some ways imposed by this method.... Their aim is simplicity, but it is only a factitious one, artificial, produced by suppression of all troublesome complications. This simplicity comes about only when we efface all individual differences, thus coming to conclusions that are not true.

Instead, Binet (quoted in Wolf, 1973, p. 293) argued for applying the methods of science to issues raised in practical settings: "To observe and experiment, to experiment and observe, this is the only method that can obtain for us a particle of truth."

The birth of intelligence testing represents a case study in the intimate relation between advances in psychology and the practical demands of education (Mayer, 1992). Earlier attempts by Galton (1883) to develop a test of intelligence based on high-sounding psychological theory failed, leaving the scientific study of intellectual ability in disarray (Sternberg, 1990). Yet, when prompted by the practical demands of schools to create a way of identifying slow learners, Binet and his colleagues were able to build a new experimental psychology of individual differences that became the basis for a century of intelligence testing. Interestingly, the creation of the field of intelligence testing developed not from the hard-core scientific studies of Galton but rather from Binet's attempts to address an important pedagogic problem.

Today, as in Binet's time, the continuing search for an adequate understanding of individual differences in intellectual ability is enriched and challenged by the practical needs of education. In the remainder of this section, I review some commonsense views of intelligence and show how education-inspired research drives psychologists' changing views of intelligence. Far from being solely a place where psychological theories are applied, education can be a shaper of psychological theories of intelligence by challenging psychologists to develop viable theories.

Commonsense Views of Intelligence

Can education continue to drive psychology's search for a theory of intelligence? To answer this question, let us begin with some commonsense statements about intelligence based on observations of students in educational settings.

1. *Intelligence is a single cognitive skill: Some people have more intellectual ability than others.* Anyone who observes a classroom cannot help noticing that the students differ in their ability to learn and perform academic tasks.

2. *Intelligence is a general cognitive skill: People who have high intellectual ability learn more easily than people who do not.* Similarly, anyone who visits a classroom cannot help noticing that students considered to be "smart" seem to be able to apply their intelligence to a wide variety of academic tasks by learning faster and better than other students.

3. *Intelligence is an innate cognitive skill: People are born with their level of intellectual ability, and thus a person's level of intellectual ability is unlikely to show great changes during their life.* Again, anyone who observes schools could note that students who were "smart" last year tend to be "smart" this year, and so on.

4. *Intelligence is a static cognitive skill: A person's level of intellectual ability is reflected in his or her ability to produce solutions to problems.* Again, classroom observers can base their assessments of intellectual ability on tests in which students produce answers to questions. Students who are able to answer difficult questions and solve challenging problems are "smarter" than those who do not.

Each of these statements seems consistent with common knowledge about intelligence and education. They reflect a classic view of intelligence as a single skill, a general skill, an innate skill, and a static skill, respectively. However, in spite of the seeming correctness of the commonsense approach, there is growing consensus among intelligence researchers for changing views of intelligence. The theme of this section is that the impetus for changing views of intelligence comes from the need to understand intellectual ability in real academic settings.

Is Intelligence a Single Cognitive Skill?

The first commonsense statement presents the idea that intelligence is a single, monolithic ability; that is, intelligence is viewed as a single commodity of which students may possess varying amounts. Although the single-skill view of intelligence was supported by some early psychometric research (Galton, 1883; Spearman, 1927), it failed to stand the test of scrutiny in educational settings. A contrasting view – motivated by education-inspired research – is that intellectual ability depends on a collection of smaller component skills.

Is intelligence a single skill or a collection of smaller component skills? Psychometric psychologists attempted to answer this question during the first half of this century by using highly controlled experimental studies involving large numbers of subjects and based on ever more sophisticated statistical analyses (Spearman, 1927; Sternberg, 1990; Thurstone, 1938; Guilford, 1959). The resulting answers concerning the number of kinds of intelligence ranged from 1 (Spearman, 1927) to 7 (Thurstone, 1938) to 120 (Guilford, 1959). Eventually, the psychometric approach to intelligence faded from the scene partly because it failed to achieve a coherent answer to basic questions about the nature of intelligence.

In contrast, educationally relevant research has helped to usher in a new conception of intelligence as a collection of smaller component skills (Hunt, 1985; Sternberg, 1985). In the case of designating special education students – the same issue that motivated Binet's landmark research – the single-skill view of intelligence failed to square with the observations of educators. Students who scored low on intelligence tests – presumably because they did not possess enough of the stuff called intelligence – seemed to display a wide variety of different kinds of what can be called "learning disabilities" (Swanson & Keogh, 1990). For exam-

ple, Cermak (1983) has shown that children classified as learning disabled can exhibit a variety of information-processing deficits on simple academic learning tasks, including differences in rehearsal, encoding, and retrieval processes. Intensive research on learning disabilities such as dyslexia has led to the conclusion that a single-ability view of intelligence is no longer a useful construct (Stanovich, 1986).

For example, Belmont and Butterfield (1971) found that some students who scored low on intelligence tests did not engage in rehearsal processing on a simple list learning task in the same way as students who scored in the normal range. Instruction in how to rehearse greatly improved the learning of the low-scoring students, bringing them close to the level of higher-scoring students. These kinds of results suggest that failure to perform well on academic learning tasks can best be attributed to difficulties with small-component information-processing skills (such as rehearsal processes) rather than because of a lack of a single all-encompassing cognitive ability.

New theories of intelligence that emerged during the 1980s reflect the multiple-abilities view. For example, using a cognitive correlates approach, Hunt and his colleagues (Hunt, 1985; Hunt, Lunneborg, & Lewis, 1975) compared the information processing of students who scored high with those who scored low on a test of verbal ability. Interestingly, high- and low-verbal students differed in a variety of component processes such as retrieving a letter from long-term memory, mentally comparing two letters, and holding a list of letters in working memory. Using a cognitive components approach, Sternberg (1985) analyzed intelligence test problems into component processes and identified the specific processes responsible for differences better between high- and low-scoring students. Importantly, performance differences on intelligence tests could be described in terms of differences in how material is encoded, retrieved, and manipulated in people's information-processing systems.

In summary, the challenges of educators played an important role in the overthrow of the single-ability view of intelligence and the emergence of the multiple-abilities view. In special education, the changing view of intelligence is reflected in a shift from assessment based on a gross score on an intelligence test to diagnostic measures aimed at specific information-processing deficits. Similarly, modern theories of intellectual ability have shifted from a focus on general intelligence to an analysis of the cognitive processes required for performing intellectual tasks.

Is Intelligence a General Cognitive Skill?

The second commonsense statement is based on the idea that intelligence is a general cognitive skill that can be applied to a wide variety of tasks and situations. Even if one views intelligence as a collection of component skills – such as comprehension skills, generating skills, or planning skills – the general-skill view holds that each skill can be applied across a wide variety of domains from writing essays, to reading expository text, to solving arithmetic word problems. Although the general-skill view of intelligence is appealing, it was discredited long ago by educational psychologists interested in the issue of transfer across school subjects (Singley & Anderson, 1989; Thorndike, 1906; Thorndike & Woodworth, 1901). An alternative view – consistent with education-relevant research – is that intellectual skills are domain specific.

Is intellectual ability a general skill that can be applied across a wide variety of domains or a specific skill that applies only to a narrow domain? The general-skill view was at the heart of one of the earliest pedagogic principles, which was called the doctrine of formal discipline. The doctrine of formal disciple held that some school subjects such as Latin and geometry encourage students to develop cognitive skills such as mental discipline that help them learn other nonrelated school subjects. According to this view, certain cognitive skills are general and can be used across many school subjects.

When Thorndike and his colleagues (Thorndike, 1906; Thorndike & Woodworth, 1901) tested this doctrine in a series of research studies they found that students who had studied Latin (and presumably acquired useful cognitive skills) were no better at learning a new school subject such as bookkeeping than were students who had not studied Latin. The repeated failure to find evidence for general transfer of academic skills led to the conclusion that cognitive skills are domain specific; that is, they only apply to tasks that are identical or highly similar. Although Thorndike (1906) argued that only

specific behaviors could transfer from one situation to a similar one, Judd (1908) and Wertheimer (1959) later demonstrated that principles can also transfer within the same domain.

A current example of education's contribution to changing views of intelligence comes from one of educational psychology's most promising research areas: psychologies of school subjects (Bruer, 1993; Mayer, 1999; Shulman & Quinlan, 1996). Psychologies of school subjects focus on how students learn, think, and develop in content areas such as reading, writing, mathematics, and science. Instead of emulating experimental psychologists' traditional focus on a general theory of learning, psychologists of school subjects might seek to understand how students learn to read or write or compute. Instead of seeking a general theory of thinking, psychologists of school subjects may examine how students think mathematically, scientifically, or historically. Instead of building a general theory of cognitive development, psychologists of school subjects may pinpoint the development of literary, mathematical, or scientific competence. Whereas experimental psychologists have had to abandon their search for a general theory of learning or cognition or development, psychologists of school subjects have been far more successful (Mayer, 1992). Once again, educational issues have saved psychology from a scientific dead end by refocusing research on educationally relevant domains.

Research in the psychology of school subjects often is based on cognitive analyses of authentic tasks. For example, writing can be analyzed into processes such as planning – in which a student determines what to write and how to organize it; translating, in which a student produces written text; and reviewing, in which a student detects and corrects problems in what has been written (Hayes & Flower, 1980; Hayes, 1996). Similarly, mathematical problem solving can be analyzed into processes such as representing – in which a student constructs a mental representation of a word problem; planning, in which a student devises a plan for carrying out the solution; executing, in which the student carries out the plan; and monitoring, in which a student evaluates what has been done (Mayer, 1985; 1999). An important contribution of research on school subjects is that seemingly general skills, such as planning, are domain specific in that planning an essay is quite different from planning a solution to a word problem.

Research on expertise in school subjects provides complementary evidence for the domain specificity of cognitive skills (Chi, Glaser, & Farr, 1988; Smith, 1991). For example, researchers have examined the issue of what an expert in physics knows that a novice does not know (Chi, Feltovich, & Glaser, 1981; Larkin, McDermott, Simon, & Simon, 1980; Larkin, 1983). Specifically, physics experts (such as physics professors with at least 10 years of experience) differ from physics novices (students taking their first college physics course) in terms of factual knowledge – the amount and organization of their basic information; semantic knowledge – their underlying concepts used to understand problems; schematic knowledge – the way they categorize problems; and strategic knowledge – the methods for solving problems. A persistent finding is that skills that make one an expert in one domain do not necessarily help one become an expert in another domain, and thus possessing expert skills in physics does not necessarily transfer to expert problem solving in other areas.

Overall, research embedded in school subjects has helped intelligence theorists move from a general-skill view to a specific-skill view of intellectual skills. Cognitive task analyses of school subjects have demonstrated that seemingly general skills such as planning or monitoring or comprehending are specific to the subjects in which they are used. Similarly, expertise research has emphasized the domain-specificity of cognitive skills; that is, possessing expert problem-solving skills in one domain does not translate into expert problem solving in other areas. Rather than simply being a place for applying the scientific principles established in psychologists' laboratories, realistic educational settings have played an important role in shaping those principles.

Is Intelligence an Innate Cognitive Skill?

The third commonsense statement proposes that intelligence is an innate skill; that is, the range of people's intellectual ability is established in their genes just like other traits such as their height. Galton (1883) was the first to show that many cognitive skills are normally distributed in the population in a way similar to the distribution of physical characteristics. For example, people differ in the perfor-

mance of basic cognitive tasks such as response time (e.g., grasping a handle as soon as light comes on) or perceptual discrimination (e.g., detecting which of two objects weighs more). The fact that intelligence test scores are often normally distributed in the same way as physical characteristics has been offered as evidence that intelligence is genetically determined (Jensen, 1980). An alternative suggested by educationally relevant research is that students can learn to improve the way they process material; that is, cognitive processing can be taught.

Is intelligence innate or learned? When research moves from the laboratory to the classroom, intelligence theories are challenged to move from an innate-skill to a learnable-skill view. One of the most prominent contributions of educational psychology in the 1980s and 1990s has been a focus on cognitive process instruction (Pressley, 1990; Weinstein & Mayer, 1986) in which students learn component cognitive processes to be used in a specific domain. For example, Schoenfeld (1985) taught strategies for representing problems to mathematics students, Bradley and Bryant (1991) taught phonemic-awareness skills to prereaders, Cook and Mayer (1988) taught strategies for recognizing text structure to science students, and Kellogg (1994) taught planning strategies for writing essays. In each case, performance on academic tasks improved, suggesting that innate intelligence is not the sole determinant of academic success.

More recently, researchers have focused on cognitive apprenticeship to help students develop cognitive processes for academic tasks (Collins, Brown, & Newman, 1989). In cognitive apprenticeship, teachers and students work on authentic academic tasks such as interpreting a text; in this situation, teachers serve as mentors who model appropriate strategies and provide scaffolding and coaching as students work on the tasks. For example, Palinscar and Brown (1984) helped students learn basic reading comprehension processes such as how to summarize a passage, predict what will come next, clarify any potential comprehension difficulties, or produce a question that is answered by the text. Students and teachers took turns leading a group in the learning of these skills as they read a text. The results indicated that basic processes in reading comprehension are learnable, and thus in a sense, verbal ability appears to be a learnable ability.

Research on teaching of learning strategies contributes to changing views of intelligence by demonstrating that many aspects of intellectual performance are learnable. Although biology may place upper and lower limits on a person's intellectual potential, research on teaching of learning strategies shows that the potential range may be quite broad. The extent to which intelligence can be taught has been a hot topic in the field of intelligence (Detterman & Sternberg, 1982; Gustafsson & Undheim, 1996), but educationally relevant research suggests that the most success in improving performance on academic tasks occurs when students learn specific component skills that are directly relevant to academic tasks (Mayer, 1999). Once again, in looking towards the classroom, intelligence theorists are challenged to see intellectual ability as dependent on learnable skills.

Is Intelligence a Static Cognitive Skill?

The final commonsense statement assumes that intelligence is best measured by posing problems and examining the answers that people produce. This focus on product has a long history in the psychometric approach to intelligence testing and still permeates thinking about intelligence today (Carroll, 1993). However, educationally relevant research suggests that more can be learned about a person's intellectual ability through dynamic testing, which provides an opportunity to evaluate how the student learns over the course of a session. Rather than the static-skill view of intelligence, which assesses the product of intellectual activity, the dynamic-skill view of intelligence assesses the process of intellectual activity, including a student's ability to learn how to give better answers to test problems.

Is intellectual ability a static or a dynamic skill? Consider the situation in which a new student comes to a school, is given an intelligence test, and scores at the level of "mentally retarded." Although the assessment procedure may seem scientific and accurate, an educator may feel unsettled by the result. For example, Feuerstein (1980) examined newly arrived immigrant children who had been diagnosed as mentally retarded by their new school. Indeed, they performed poorly on intelligence tests, but interestingly, some were able to show substantial improvements over the course of a session in

which they learned how to solve testlike problems. In short, these students showed a discrepancy between their performance on a static test measuring what they had learned and their potential to learn on a dynamic test that gave a chance to learn. Feuerstein concluded that static testing fails to provide an accurate picture of a child's potential to learn, whereas dynamic testing, in which students are placed in a learning situation, allows them to demonstrate their ability to learn.

Similarly, Ginsberg (1997) argued that the best way to understand how a child thinks – such as how a child solves a math problem – is through a clinical interview that allows the child and adult to engage in an extended and flexible dialogue about how to solve a concrete problem. Ginsberg (1997, p. 10) points out that traditional intelligence tests – based on the static-skill view of intellectual ability – are "not suitable for studying dynamic change." Thus, the drive for a dynamic-skill view comes from the need to provide realistic assessments of students' intellectual skills. Consistent with Vygotsky's (1978) classic distinction between what a student does and what a student is capable of doing on a given task, dynamic assessments using authentic tasks can provide a much richer picture of student ability than can traditional measures.

Research on dynamic assessment provides an important incentive for revising the view of intelligence as a static skill and again demonstrates how education-based research can reshape theories of intelligence.

Changing Views of Intelligence

The foregoing review shows how educationally relevant research has contradicted each of the four commonsense statements about the nature of intelligence. In contrast to the commonsense statements, changing views of intelligence suggest the following four alternative statements, each warranting further scientific study:

1. *Intelligence is a collection of component skills.* Performance on a challenging academic task, such as writing an essay, critiquing a text passage, or solving a mathematics problem depends on many small component processes rather than a single all-encompassing ability. The shift from the single-skill view to the multiple-skills view was prompted by challenges

from education such as how to characterize learning disabilities or how to analyze school-relevant abilities.

2. *Intellectual skills are domain-specific.* Competence in a cognitive process for one domain, such as planning an essay, is different from corresponding competence in another domain such as planning a solution to a word problem. The shift from a general-skill to a specific-skill view of intellectual ability was prompted by challenges from education such as how to teach for transfer or how to characterize expert–novice differences in a given school subject area.

3. *Intellectual skills can be learned.* Instruction in specific, component skills can improve student performance on tests of intellectual ability, suggesting that such abilities are learnable to some extent. The shift from the innate-skill view to the learned-skill view was prompted by educationally relevant issues such as the degree to which learning skills can be taught.

4. *Intellectual skills are dynamic.* Intellectual skills emerge through extended realistic situations in which people have a chance to show how they learn and how they think. The shift from a static-skill to a dynamic-skill view of intelligence was motivated by educationally relevant issues such as dynamic assessment of students' potential to learn.

For more than a century the study of intelligence has been challenged, enriched, and ultimately guided by the field of education. As the study of individual differences in intellectual ability moves from the laboratory to the classroom, commonsense views of intelligence as a single, general, innate, and static skill give way to changing views of intelligence as a collection of multiple, specific, learnable, and dynamic skills. In short, scientific progress in understanding intelligence represents a case study in the rich reciprocal relationship between psychology and education.

THE STUDY OF INTELLIGENCE'S CONTRIBUTION TO EDUCATION

Consider a situation in which students who score high on a test of intellectual ability learn best under one instructional method, and students who score low learn best under a different method. For example, suppose that elementary school children

who score low in mathematical ability learn arithmetic best under a drill-and-practice method that emphasizes rote application of procedures whereas high-mathematical-ability students learn best under a guided discovery method that emphasizes conceptual understanding. One of the most important examples of how individual differences in intellectual ability are related to education is the aptitude x treatment interaction (ATI), such as in the example just described (Cronbach & Snow, 1977; Gustafsson & Undheim, 1996). An ATI occurs when one instructional method results in more learning for students who are high in one kind of intellectual ability and a different instructional method results in more learning for low-ability students.

There are several possible instructional implications of an ATI, including individualizing instruction or grouping students on the basis of ability, employing the same multiple instructional methods for all students, and providing ability training for low-ability students (Mayer, 1987). First, a straightforward instructional interpretation of an ATI is to provide different kinds of instructional methods for different kinds of learners. For example, in the mathematics example, high-ability students would be taught by meaningful guided discovery methods, whereas low-ability students would be taught by rote drill-and-practice methods. A shortcoming of this interpretation of an ATI is that low-ability students receive an instructional method believed to be inferior to that received by high-ability students.

A second way to address ATIs is to use multiple methods of instruction for all students so that students can learn from the method that is best for them. In the mathematics example, this means that an instructor would use both guided discovery and drill-and-practice methods in a class containing both high- and low-mathematics-ability students. A shortcoming of this approach is that instructional time is wasted because, at any given time, the teacher will be using methods that are not optimal for some students; furthermore, low-ability learners are still likely to focus on an instructional method believed to be inferior to that favored by high-ability students.

In contrast, a third approach is to provide pretraining for low-ability students. By bringing their ability level up to that of high-ability students, they can then benefit from the same high-quality methods of instruction used for high-ability students. In the mathematics example, this would mean helping low-performing students to improve their mathematical ability so they could then be taught using guided discovery methods of instruction. Until recently a shortcoming of this approach was a lack of understanding of how to teach intellectual ability, that is, how to teach students how to be better learners. In this section, we explore four criteria for developing lessons aimed at improving intellectual ability, and examine exemplary programs.

Criteria for Teaching Intellectual Ability

Can cognitive theories of intelligence inform educational practice? In particular, can theories of intelligence help determine how intelligence can be improved through instruction? In reviewing recent advances in addressing this classic issue, Sternberg (1997, p. 1137) noted that "there are now enough programs with positive results so that it seems reasonable to conclude that interventions can work." If you were going to develop an instructional program to make students smarter, what would you do? To answer these questions, let us examine some criteria for teaching students to be more intelligent based on an earlier analysis by Mayer (1992, 1997).

1. *What to teach: relevant component skills rather than global ability.* Although classic views of intelligence would suggest teaching of intelligence as a single, global ability, current views of intelligence suggest it makes more sense to teach well-specified component skills that have been shown to be prerequisites for academic learning. Concerning the issue of what to teach, the first criterion is to teach a small set of well-documented cognitive skills.

2. *How to teach: the process rather than the product of problem solving.* A classic view of intelligence suggests that instruction for intellectual ability should focus on practice in producing correct answers. The most popular instructional method for teaching motor skills is drill-and-practice with feedback, and thus it seems to make sense to use the same kind of method for teaching cognitive skills. In this case, "how to teach intellectual ability" is drill-and-practice on getting the right answer. However, current views of intelligence suggest that instruction should focus on underlying cognitive processes, that is, on developing appropriate methods of learning. Thus, the

second criterion is to emphasize the processes involved in learning.

3. *Where to teach: specific rather than general contexts.* According to classic views, instruction for intelligence should emphasize intellectual abilities that can be used across a wide variety of domains. Viewing intellectual ability as a general skill applicable across disciplines seems most efficient and consistent with sound pedagogy. In this case, "where to teach intellectual ability" is in general context-free courses. In contrast, according to recent views of intelligence, attempts to teach intellectual ability need to be tied to the specific contexts in which the skills will be used. Thus, the third criterion is that teaching of learning skills should be embedded within specific subject domains.

4. *When to teach: before rather than after mastering of low-level basic skills.* Classic views of intelligence suggest that instruction in high-level intellectual ability should not take place until the student has mastered relevant low-level basic skills. It seems to make pedagogic sense to teach in a systematic way by sequencing high-order cognitive skills after low-level skills. In this case, "when to teach intellectual ability" is after low-level skills are automatized. In contrast, recent views of intelligence promote the idea that knowing how to learn – that is, intellectual ability in a domain – may be a prerequisite to learning basic skills. Thus, the fourth criterion is to teach students how to learn before they try to master basic skills.

As can be seen, advances in the cognitive psychology of intelligence inform decisions concerning what, how, where, and when to teach intellectual ability. A theme of this review is that the impetus for improving educational practice comes from an understanding of the nature of human intellectual ability. In the following section we compare these criteria with several exemplary instructional programs.

Exemplary Programs for Teaching of Thinking

Although a review of intelligence-training programs is beyond the scope of this chapter, in this section I examine several exemplary programs categorized into three groups. Some early programs – those that I call the first phase – were not consistent with the criteria and seem to have been less than successful. Other programs, which I call the second phase, were loosely consistent with the criteria and met with limited success. Finally, more recent programs, which I call the third phase, are based on a sharpened version of the criteria and have been highly successful.

PHASE 1: PROGRAMS NOT TIED TO THE CRITERIA. Early attempts to improve the general intellectual functioning of students are exemplified in the Latin school movement. The premise underlying Latin schools was that training in subjects such as Latin and geometry would improve the mind in general. As noted earlier in this chapter, research studies failed to confirm that students who studied Latin were able to learn new school subjects any better than students who had not studied Latin (Thorndike, 1906; Thorndike & Woodworth, 1901). The failure of the Latin school movement as a means for improving intelligence parallels its failure to meet the criteria for successful intelligence-training programs: concerning what to teach, the focus was on intelligence as a single, global skill; concerning how to teach, the focus was on producing correct responses; concerning where to teach, intelligence was viewed as a general ability that could be applied across all domains; and concerning when to teach, mental ability was viewed as a high-level skill that required previous mastery of lower-level skills.

More recently, one of the most comprehensive national attempts to improve the cognitive functioning of young children is Project Head Start (Caruso, Taylor & Detterman, 1982; Zigler & Muenchow, 1992). Initiated in 1965 in the United States, Project Head Start established a national network of preschool programs aimed at increasing the cognitive ability of underprivileged children as measured by increases in IQ scores. Zigler and Muenchow (1992) note that no single instructional program was mandated, there was a shortage of trained teachers, a lack of quality control, and most important, Head Start was not designed primarily to improve cognitive ability. Zigler and Muenchow (1992, p. 53) noted that "Head Start had been designed to deemphasize cognitive development, yet it was being evaluated primarily on the most cognitive measure of all – IQ."

Evaluations of IQ changes attributable to Head Start and related programs have not been overly positive. In general, children in the program show immediate gains in IQ score over matched controls, but the differences disappear shortly after students leave the program (Carter, 1984; Caruso, Taylor & Detterman, 1982; Nurss & Hodges, 1982; Zigler & Muenchow, 1992). The fade-out effects for improvements in cognitive ability led many policy makers to question the effectiveness of the program, although defenders have argued that at-risk students may need instructional services that continue beyond preschool (Zigler & Muenchow, 1992).

Why has Head Start failed to show large and sustainable increases in cognitive ability? An explanation may be found in examining each of the criteria for successful training in cognitive ability. First, concerning what to teach, the program did not target individual cognitive processes but rather was aimed mainly at reducing school failure through improved motivation and health. When measured against standards such as reductions in special education placements or grade level retentions, Head Start has been effective. However, Head Start has not been very successful in improving intellectual ability, perhaps because its curriculum did not focus on improving individual cognitive processes. Second, concerning how to teach, the program lacked an agreed-upon instructional approach as well as a procedure for quality control, and thus it is unclear whether the program focused on process rather than product. Third, concerning where to teach, Head Start's global approach seems to violate the criterion of domain specificity. By attempting to improve general traits such as self-esteem and motivation, Head Start did not target individual cognitive processes in specific school subject areas. Finally, Head Start is consistent with the criterion of teaching students how to learn before they are required to master basic academic skills. Overall, Head Start failed to meet three of the four criteria for an effective teaching of cognitive ability, and thus its failure to demonstrate sustainable changes in cognitive ability may not be surprising.

The Latin School movement and the Head Start program are both examples of programs that fail to meet the criteria for teaching intellectual ability. In particular, the programs do not target specific cognitive processes that are taught within the context of specific school subject content areas. Interestingly, rigorous evaluations have revealed that both programs cannot be counted as highly successful in promoting gains in students' intelligence.

PHASE 2: PROGRAMS LOOSELY TIED TO THE CRITERIA. One of the earliest cognitive training programs to receive intensive research attention is the productive thinking program (Covington, Crutchfield, & Davies, 1966; Covington, Crutchfield, Davies, & Olton, 1974). The productive thinking program involves a self-paced set of 16 cartoonlike booklets aimed at improving high-level cognition in elementary school children. Each booklet – about 30 pages in length – presents a detective story that includes two children (Jim and Lila) and two adults (Jim's Uncle John and Mr. Search) who serve as cognitive models for describing various problem-solving methods. The story contains clues and often asks the student to answer questions aimed at "restating the problem in his own words," "formulating his own questions," and "generating ideas to explain the mystery" (Covington & Crutchfield, 1965, p. 3).

For example, in "The Riverboat Robbery," the student attempts to discover who committed a local robbery. After reading a portion of the booklet, students are asked to generate answers to questions (such as listing who the major suspects are) and then to compare their performance with cognitive models in the booklet who describe their methods for answering the same question. When the booklets are used in a classroom context, the authors suggest that teachers lead discussions for each booklet (Chance, 1986).

A review of over a dozen evaluation studies found that the productive thinking program is effective in promoting improvement on cognitive tasks like those emphasized in the training (Mansfield, Busse, & Krepelka, 1978). For example, Olton and Crutchfield (1969) found that fifth-graders who received intensive training in the productive thinking program exhibited a much greater pretest-to-posttest gain in solving detectivelike problems than a matched control group that did not receive training. However, Mansfield et al. (1978) note that students trained with the productive thinking program do not consistently show strong improvements in solving problems that are dissimilar to those presented during instruction.

The saga of the productive thinking program meshes well with the four criteria for successful teaching of intellectual ability. In considering what to teach, the authors focused on a collection of small component skills – such as generating ideas and evaluating ideas – rather than on trying to make the students smarter overall. In considering how to teach, the authors emphasized the process of problem solving by asking students to describe their thought processes at various points in the lesson and by providing descriptions of the thinking processes of various characters in the story. The issue of where to teach seems to violate the criterion of domain-specific teaching because the productive thinking program is taught as a general, stand-alone course. However, the evaluation results demonstrate that the positive effects of the program are largely limited to the domain of solving mystery and detective-like problems similar to those emphasized during instruction. Thus, the program turns out to fit the criterion of domain-specific learning. Finally, consistent with the fourth criterion, the authors do not require that their students have mastered all relevant basic skills before they receive training on improving higher-level cognitive skills. This is accomplished by using material that is familiar to elementary school students.

Another excellent representative of the second phase of cognitive training programs is instrumental enrichment, which was developed by Feuerstein (1980; Feuerstein, Jensen, Hoffman, & Rand, 1985) to improve the intellectual ability of immigrant children in Israel who were classified as retarded. The materials include 15 units of paper-and-pencil exercises, with each unit focusing on an instrument resembling a type of intelligence test item. For example, the first instrument is an organization of dots in which a student must connect a collection of dots to form some given geometric figures. Although the created figures must be the same size as the given figures, they can overlap and be in different orientations than the given figures. Other units include numerical progressions, transitive relations, and spatial relations.

In a typical session, the teacher presents a sample problem from the unit, asks students to work on the problem, and then leads a class discussion of how to solve the problem. The focus of the classroom discussion is on methods for solving the target problem. According to Chance (1986), students are expected to participate in three to five 1-hour sessions per week for 2 to 3 years. Over the course of the program, students gain experience in giving and receiving descriptions of the cognitive processes involved in solving a wide variety of problems like those on intelligence tests.

There is evidence that instrumental enrichment can be successful in improving students' performance on tests of intellectual ability. Feuerstein (1980) found that adolescent special education students who received instrumental enrichment training over a 2-year period showed more improvement in nonverbal tests of intelligence than did matched controls who received conventional instruction. There is also evidence that instrumental enrichment training helps low-IQ students perform like average-IQ students on test items similar to those used during the training (Arbitman-Smith, Haywood, & Bransford, 1978).

Instrumental enrichment meets each of the four criteria for successful intelligence training programs. First, concerning what to teach, instrumental enrichment focuses on a collection of small component processes – such as how to break a problem into parts – rather than on trying to improve mental functioning as a single ability. Second, concerning how to teach, instrumental enrichment emphasizes the process of problem solving, including giving and receiving descriptions of the problem-solving methods for each target problem, rather than the product of problem solving. However, a major criticism of the program is that the focus on cognitive modeling "requires a considerable investment of student time" (Chance, 1986, p. 85). Third, concerning where to teach, instrumental enrichment appears to opt for teaching intelligence as a general, stand-alone course; however, a closer examination reveals that "there is an emphasis on training students to solve certain types of problems so they will be able to solve similar problems on their own" (Bransford et al., 1985, p. 201). Thus, instrumental enrichment tends to focus on teaching within the specific domain of intelligence-test items. Finally, instrumental enrichment seeks to teach high-level skills before students have completely mastered all low-level basic skills. In particular, the program avoids the need for automated basic skills by using target problems that do not depend on a great deal of prior knowledge or experience. Overall, the success of the program – albeit costly and limited – is consis-

tent with the four criteria for teaching intellectual ability.

PHASE 3: PROGRAMS TIGHTLY TIED TO THE CRITERIA. The third major shift in programs aimed at teaching of cognitive ability involves a sharpening of each of the four criteria. It is reflected in teaching very focused skills that are embedded in specific school subject areas such as number-line instruction for improving mathematical ability (Griffin & Case, 1996; Griffin, Case, & Capodilupo, 1995; Griffin, Case, & Siegler, 1994) and phonological awareness instruction for improving verbal ability (Bradley & Bryant, 1978, 1985; Goswami & Bryant, 1992; Juel, Griffith, & Gough, 1986).

The rightstart program focuses on improving the mathematical ability of primary school students by ensuring they learn how to use a mental number line. Skill in using a mental number line is considered to be a critical step in the development of mathematical competence and a prerequisite for meaningful understanding of arithmetic procedures (Case & Okamoto, 1996). Many students entering school lack skill in using a mental line such as being able to compare two numbers, to visualize a number line, to determine the magnitude specified by number words, and to count objects systematically. Bruer (1993, p. 90) points out that "without this understanding [of the mental number line] . . . their only alternative is to try to understand school math as a set of arbitrary procedures."

The rightstart program consists of 40 half-hour sessions, each involving a different kind of number-line game (Griffin & Case, 1996). For example, in one game, two students each roll a die, and the student who rolled the highest number moves his or her token along a number-line path on a playing board. The first student to reach the end of the path wins. This game helps students learn how to evaluate number magnitudes, count forward and backwards along a number line, and make one-to-one mappings of numbers onto objects when counting.

Focused experience in using a number line was successful in helping students learn to think with number lines: Low-performing first-graders who participated in the rightstart program showed a large pretest-to-posttest increase in their number-line thinking skills, whereas similar children who received regular mathematics instruction did not.

More important, practice in using a number line had a strong effect on measures of mathematical ability: Low-performing first-graders who received right-start training showed a large pretest-to-posttest gain on arithmetic tests, whereas comparison students did not. Even more exciting, focused learning activities aimed at helping students acquire skill in thinking with number lines resulted in improved learning of mathematics in school. Twice as many of the rightstart-trained first-graders mastered their arithmetic lessons as did equivalent first-graders who received regular instruction.

These results demonstrate that intellectual ability can be taught. In this example, mathematical ability was taught by helping students acquire mathematical thinking skills considered to be prerequisites for early mathematics learning. Griffin and Case (1996, p. 102) noted that "a surprising proportion of children from low-income North American families – at least 50% in our samples – do not arrive in school with the central cognitive structure in place that is necessary for success in first grade mathematics." These students could easily be judged as low in mathematical ability and placed in learning tracks for slower learners. However, focused instruction on specific thinking skills needed for success in learning early mathematics allowed these students to perform like high-ability students in subsequent learning of mathematics. By improving their capacity to learn mathematics, teaching of number-line thinking skills served to increase the mathematical ability of students who entered school lacking these skills.

Number-line training as a means of improving mathematical ability exemplifies a sharpening of each of the four criteria for teaching of intellectual ability. The specification of what to teach for mathematical ability is sharp – a collection of skills related to using number lines rather than global mathematical ability. The issue of how to teach is resolved by emphasizing processes involved in using mental number lines in several gamelike settings rather than solely emphasizing getting the right answer. The sharpening of where to teach is reflected in rightstart's focus on mathematical ability as highly domain-specific (i.e., tied to the number-line context) rather than a more general ability. Finally, concerning when to teach cognitive ability, rightstart is based on teaching mathematical ability as a prerequisite to mastering basic skills (such as simple arith-

metic) rather than waiting to teach thinking skills until after basic skills have been mastered. In short, number-line training exemplifies how highly sharpened versions of the four criteria can be applied successfully to the teaching of mathematical ability.

Paralleling the role of number-line thinking skills as prerequisites for learning early arithmetic, phonological awareness skills have been implicated as possible prerequisites for learning to read (Adams, 1990; Bradley & Bryant, 1985; Juel, Griffin, & Gough, 1986; Wagner & Torgesen, 1987). Phonological awareness is knowing the sound units used in a language (called phonemes), including skill in hearing and producing separate phonemes; it can be measured by asking students to delete a phoneme from a spoken word (say "top" without the /t/), substitute a phoneme in a spoken word (for "park" instead of /k/ end the word with /t/), or identify which of four words lacks a sound contained in the others ("rag" for the set, "sun, sea, sock, rag"). For example, students who have difficulty in learning to read in elementary school – and therefore would be classified as low in verbal ability – often lack skill in phonological awareness, whereas students who are successful in learning to read tend have good phonological awareness skills (Bradley & Bryant, 1978; Stanovich, 1991). Similarly, longitudinal studies reveal a strong relation between children's phonological awareness skills upon entering school and reading achievement scores later in school, even when general cognitive ability is taken into account (Bradley & Bryant, 1985; Juel, Griffin, & Gough, 1986; Wagner & Torgesen, 1987).

Now that a collection of specific cognitive skills that appear to be crucial for early verbal learning has been pinpointed, the next step is to determine whether phonological awareness training helps students learn how to read. For example, Bradley and Bryant (1983, 1985, 1991) developed forty 10-minute sessions for teaching phonological awareness. In one session a child was shown a picture of a bus and asked to select the picture of a word starting with the same sound from a set a pictures, and in another, a child was given a set of pictures and asked to select the one that started with a different sound than the others. Five- and 6-year olds who received the 40 phonological awareness lessons produced larger improvements in phonological awareness and in reading achievement over the next 5 years than students given other kinds of pre-reading instruction.

In a review of phonological awareness training studies, Goswami and Bryant (1992, p. 49) concluded that "successful training in phonological awareness helps students learn to read." Furthermore, "without special training, children with poor phonemic awareness appear disadvantaged in learning to read" (Juel, et al., 1986, p. 249). In short, pretraining in phonological awareness improved students' ability to learn to read, and therefore phonological awareness training appears to have improved students' verbal ability.

As with number-line training, phonological awareness training is consistent with each of the four criteria for teaching of intellectual ability and, in fact, represents a sharpening of them. The delineation of what to teach is particularly clear – a collection of skills related to phonological processing rather than global verbal ability. Concerning how to teach, the instructional method does not focus solely on producing the correct answer (i.e., saying the correct sound for each phoneme) but rather emphasizes techniques for segmenting and blending words in a variety of gamelike settings. The issue of where to teach is razor sharp, for improvement in verbal ability is highly domain specific rather than general. Finally, the issue of when to teach cognitive ability appears to be turned on its head; rather than waiting for basic skills (such as reading and writing) to become automatic, basic verbal ability (in the form of phonological awareness) is seen as a prerequisite to learning of basic skills. In short, phonological awareness training exemplifies how highly sharpened versions of the four criteria can be applied successfully to the teaching of verbal ability.

Overall, the third phase in teaching of intellectual ability focuses on helping students acquire specific thinking skills that have been shown to be prerequisites for learning in specific subject areas such as mathematics and reading. According to this approach, the teaching of cognitive abilities such as mathematical or verbal ability no longer means exercising some sort of mental muscle. Rather, teaching of cognitive abilities involves pinpointing prerequisite cognitive skills and helping students to develop them. The teaching of domain-specific learning and thinking skills represents an emerging new component in school curricula (Bruer, 1993; Mayer, 1999; Pressley, 1990; Weinstein & Mayer, 1986).

GENERAL CONCLUSION

The thesis of this chapter is that the relation between intelligence and education is reciprocal. The first section of this chapter showed how the practical context of education influences fundamental changes in cognitive theories of intelligence. When intelligence researchers move from a laboratory to a school setting, intellectual ability can no longer be viewed as a single, general, innate, and static skill. Instead, education-driven research encourages intelligence researchers to view intellectual ability as consisting of multiple, specific, learnable, and dynamic skills.

The second section showed how the cognitive study of intelligence influences fundamental changes in educational practice. The view of intellectual ability as a collection of domain-specific cognitive skills suggests that the criteria for teaching of intellectual ability should focus on what to teach, how to teach, where to teach, and when to teach. In particular, changing views of intelligence suggest that school curricula should be expanded to include teaching of fundamental cognitive processing for students who lack them. The value of teaching cognitive processing that has been pinpointed as a prerequisite for basic academic achievement is exemplified in teaching number-line processing as a means of promoting mathematical ability and teaching phonological processing as a means of promoting verbal ability. Changing views of intelligence can be a driving force in curricular reform and, in particular, in the teaching of prerequisite cognitive process skills to students who lack them.

Overall, educational demands have influenced the development of more authentic views of intelligence, and modern views of intelligence have stimulated the development of more focused methods for teaching students to be better learners.

REFERENCES

Adams, M. J. (1990). *Beginning to read*. Cambridge, MA: MIT Press.

Arbitman-Smith, R., Haywood, H. C., & Bransford, J. D.

(1978). Assessing cognitive change. In C. M. McCauley, R. Sperber, & P. Brooks (Eds.), *Learning and cognition in the mentally retarded*. Baltimore, MD: University Park Press.

Belmont, J. M., & Butterfield, E. C. (1971). Learning strategies as determinants of memory deficits. *Cognitive Psychology, 2*, 411–420.

Bradley, L., & Bryant, P. (1978). Difficulties in auditory organization as a possible cause of reading backwardness. *Nature, 271*, 746–747.

Bradley, L., & Bryant, P. (1983). Categorizing sounds and learning to read – a causal connection. *Nature, 301*, 419–421.

Bradley, L., & Bryant, P. (1985). *Rhyme and reason in reading and spelling*. Ann Arbor, MI: University of Michigan Press.

Bradley, L., & Bryant, P. (1991). Phonological skills before and after learning to read. In S. A. Brady & D. P. Shankweiler (Eds.), *Phonological processes in literacy* (pp. 37–45). Hillsdale, NJ: Erlbaum.

Bransford, J. D., Arbitman-Smith, R., Stein, B. S., & Vye, N. J. (1985). Improving thinking and learning skills: An analysis of three approaches. In J. W. Segal, S. F. Chipman, & R. Glaser (Eds.), *Thinking and learning skills: Volume 1, Relating instruction to research* (pp. 133–206). Hillsdale, NJ: Erlbaum.

Bruer, J. T. (1993). *Schools for thought: A science of learning in the classroom*. Cambridge, MA: MIT Press.

Carroll, J. B. (1993). *Human cognitive abilities*. Cambridge, UK: Cambridge University Press.

Carter, L. F. (1984). The sustaining effects study of compensatory and elementary education. *Educational Researcher, 13*, 4–13.

Caruso, D. R., Taylor, J. J., & Detterman, D. K. (1982). Intelligence research and intelligent policy. In D. K. Detterman & R. J. Sternberg (Eds.), *How and how much can intelligence be increased?* (pp. 45–66). Norwood, NJ: Ablex.

Case, R., & Okamoto, Y. (1996). The role of central conceptual structures in the development of children's thought. *Monographs of the Society for Research in Child Development, 61*, Serial No. 246, Nos. 1–2.

Cermak, L. S. (1983). Information processing deficits in children with learning disabilities. *Journal of Learning Disabilities, 16*, 599–605.

Chance, P. (1986). *Thinking in the classroom*. New York: Teachers College Press.

Chi, M. T. H., Feltovich, P. J., & Glaser, R. (1981). Categorization and representation of physics problems by experts and novices. *Cognitive Science, 5*, 121–152.

Chi, M. T. H., Glaser, R., & Farr, M. J. (Eds.). (1988). *The nature of expertise*. Hillsdale, NJ: Erlbaum.

Collins, A., Brown, J. S., & Newman, S. E. (1989). Cognitive apprenticeship: Teaching the crafts of reading, writing, and mathematics. In L. B. Resnick (Ed.), *Knowing, learning, and instruction: Essays in honor of Robert Glaser* (pp. 453–494). Hillsdale, NJ: Erlbaum.

Cook, L. K., & Mayer, R. E. (1988). Teaching readers about the structure of scientific text. *Journal of Educational Psychology, 80*, 448–456.

Covington, M. V., & Crutchfield, R. S. (1965). Facilitation of productive problem solving. *Programmed Instruction, 4*, 3–5, 10.

Covington, M. V., Crutchfield, R. S., & Davies, L. B. (1966). *The productive thinking program*. Berkeley, CA: Brazelton.

Covington, M. V., Crutchfield, R. S., Davies, L. B., & Olton, R. M. (1974). *The productive thinking program*. Columbus, OH: Merrill.

Cronbach, L. J., & Snow, R. E. (1977). *Aptitudes and instructional methods*. New York: Irvington.

Detterman, D. K., & Sternberg, R. J. (Eds.). (1982). *How and how much can intelligence be increased?* Norwood, NJ: Ablex.

Feuerstein, R. (1980). *Instrumental enrichment: An intervention program for cognitive modifiability*. Baltimore: University Park Press.

Feuerstein, R., Jensen, M., Hoffman, M. B., & Rand, Y. (1985). Instrumental enrichment: An intervention program for structural cognitive modifiability. Theory and practice. In J. W. Segal, S. F. Chipman, & R. Glaser (Eds.), *Thinking and learning skills: Volume 1, Relating instruction to research* (pp. 43–82). Hillsdale, NJ: Erlbaum.

Galton, F. (1883). *Inquiry into human faculty and its development*. London: Macmillan.

Ginsberg, H. P. (1997). *Entering the child's mind*. Cambridge, UK: Cambridge University Press.

Goswami, U., & Bryant, P. (1992). Rhyme, analogy, and children's reading. In P. B. Gough, L. C. Ehri, & R. Treiman (Eds.), *Reading acquisition* (pp. 49–63). Hillsdale, NJ: Erlbaum.

Griffin, S., & Case, R. (1996). Evaluating the breadth and depth of training effects when central conceptual structures are taught. In R. Case & Y. Okamoto (Eds.), The role of central structures in the development of children's thought (pp. 83–102). *Monographs of the Society for Research in Child Development, 61*, Serial No. 246, Nos. 1–2.

Griffin, S., Case, R., & Capodilupo, A. (1995). Teaching for understanding: The importance of the central conceptual structures in the elementary mathematics curriculum. In A. McKeough, J. Lupart, & A. Marini (Eds.), *Teaching for transfer: Fostering generalization in learning* (pp. 123–152). Mahwah, NJ: Erlbaum.

Griffin, S. A., Case, R., & Siegler, R. S. (1994). Rightstart: Providing the central conceptual prerequisites for first formal learning of arithmetic to students at risk for school failure. In K. McGilly (Ed.), *Classroom lessons: Integrating cognitive theory and classroom practice*. Cambridge, MA: MIT Press.

Guilford, J. P. (1959). The three faces of intellect. *American Psychologist, 14*, 469–479.

Gustafsson, J., & Undheim, J. O. (1996). Individual differences in cognitive functions. In D. Berliner & R. Calfee (Eds.), *Handbook of educational psychology* (pp. 186–242). New York: Macmillan.

Hayes, J. R. (1996). A new framework for understanding cognition and affect in writing. In C. M. Levy & S. Ransdell (Eds.), *The science of writing* (pp. 1–28). Mahwah, NJ: Erlbaum.

Hayes, J. R., & Flower, L. (1980). Identifying the organization of the writing process. In L. W. Gregg & E. R. Steinberg (Eds.), *Cognitive processes in writing* (pp. 3–30). Hillsdale, NJ: Erlbaum.

Hunt, E. (1985). Verbal ability. In R. J. Sternberg (Ed.), *Human abilities: An information-processing approach* (pp. 31–58). New York: W. H. Freeman.

Hunt, E., Lunneborg, C., & Lewis, J. (1975). What does it mean to be high verbal? *Cognitive Psychology, 7*, 194–227.

Jenkins, J. J., & Paterson, D. G. (1961). *Studies in individual differences*. New York: Appleton-Century-Crofts.

Jensen, A. R. (1980). *Bias in mental testing*. New York: Free Press.

Judd, C. H. (1908). The relation of special training and general intelligence. *Educational Review, 36*, 28–42.

Juel, C., Griffith, P. L., & Gough, P. B. (1986). Acquisition of literacy: A longitudinal study of children in first and second grade. *Journal of Educational Psychology, 78*, 243–255.

Kellogg, R. T. (1994). *The psychology of writing*. New York: Oxford University Press.

Larkin, J. (1983). The role of representation in physics. In D. Gentner & A. L. Stevens (Eds.), *Mental models* (pp. 75–98). Hillsdale, NJ: Erlbaum.

Larkin, J., McDermott, J., Simon, D. P., & Simon, H. A. (1980). Expert and novice performance in solving physics problems. *Science, 208*, 1335–1342.

Mansfield, R. S., Busse, T. V., & Krepelka, E. J. (1978). The effectiveness of creativity training. *Review of Educational Research, 48*, 517–536.

Mayer, R. E. (1985). Mathematical ability. In R. J. Sternberg (Ed.), *Human abilities: An information-processing approach* (pp. 127–150). New York: W. H. Freeman.

Mayer, R. E. (1987). *Educational psychology: A cognitive approach*. New York: Harper Collins.

Mayer, R. E. (1992). Cognition and instruction: On their historic meeting within educational psychology. *Journal of Educational Psychology, 84*, 405–412.

Mayer, R. E. (1997). Incorporating problem solving into secondary school curricula. In G. D. Phye (Ed.), *Handbook of academic learning* (pp. 473–492). San Diego: Academic Press.

Mayer, R. E. (1999). *The promise of educational psychology: Learning in the content areas*. Columbus, OH: Merrill/Prentice Hall.

Nurss, J. R., & Hodges, W. L. (1982). Early childhood development. In H. E. Mitzel (Ed.), *Encyclopedia of educational research*. New York: Macmillan.

Olton, R. M., & Crutchfield, R. S. (1969). Developing the skills of productive thinking. In P. Mussen, J. Langer, & M. V. Covington (Eds.), *New directions in developmental psychology*. New York: Holt, Rinehart and Winston.

Palinscar, A. S., & Brown, A. L. (1984). Reciprocal teaching of comprehension-fostering and monitoring strategies. *Cognition and Instruction, 1*, 117–175.

Pressley, M. (1990). *Cognitive process instruction that really improves children's academic performance*. Cambridge, MA: Brookline.

Schoenfeld, A. H. (1985). *Mathematical problem solving*. New York: Academic Press.

Shulman, L. S., & Quinlan, K. M. (1996). The comparative psychology of school subjects. In D. Berliner & R. Calfee (Eds.), *Handbook of educational psychology* (pp. 399–422). New York: Macmillan.

Singley, M. K., & Anderson, J. R. (1989). *The transfer of cognitive skill*. Cambridge, MA: Harvard University Press.

Smith, M. U. (Ed.). (1991). *Toward a unified theory of problem solving: Views from the content domains*. Hillsdale, NJ: Erlbaum.

Spearman, C. (1927). *The abilities of man*. New York: Macmillan.

Stanovich, K. E. (1986). Mathew effects in reading: Some consequences of individual differences in the acquisition of literacy. *Reading Research Quarterly, 21*, 360–407.

Stanovich, K. E. (1991). Discrepancy definitions of reading disability: Has intelligence led us astray? *Reading Research Quarterly, 26*, 7–29.

Sternberg, R. J. (1985). *Beyond IQ: A triarchic theory of human intelligence*. Cambridge, UK: Cambridge University Press.

Sternberg, R. J. (1990). *Metaphors of mind*. Cambridge, UK: Cambridge University Press.

Sternberg, R. J. (1997). Intelligence and lifelong learning. What's new and how can we use it? *American Psychologist, 52*, 1134–1139.

Swanson, H. L., & Keogh, B. (Ed.). (1990). *Learning disabilities*. Hillsdale, NJ: Erlbaum.

Thorndike, E. L. (1906). *Principles of teaching*. New York: Seiler.

Thorndike, E. L., & Woodworth, R. S. (1901). The influence of improvement in one mental function upon the efficiency of other functions. *Psychological Review, 8*, 247–261.

Thurstone, L. L. (1938). *Primary mental abilities*. Chicago: University of Chicago Press.

Vygotsky, L. S. (1978). *Mind in society*. Cambridge, MA: Harvard University Press.

Wagner, R. K., & Torgesen, J. K. The nature of phonological processing and its causal role in the acquisition of reading skills. *Psychological Bulletin, 101*, 192–212.

Weinstein, C. E., & Mayer, R. E. (1986). The teaching of learning strategies. *Handbook of research on teaching (3rd ed.)* (pp. 315–327). New York: Macmillan.

Wertheimer, M. (1959). *Productive thinking*. New York: Harper & Row.

Wolf, T. H. (1973). *Alfred Binet*. Chicago: University of Chicago Press.

Zigler, E., & Muenchow, S. (1992). *Head start: The inside story of America's most successful educational experiment*. New York: Basic Books.

CHAPTER TWENTY-FOUR

Intelligence and Public Policy

CRAIG T. RAMEY AND SHARON LANDESMAN RAMEY

Make no mistake about it, intelligence matters. And numerous public policies affirm its importance. The legislation and regulations that relate to intelligence reflect assumptions about the nature and influence of intelligence on individual behavior in society as well as the value of intelligence to our society's well-being. The practical implications of these policies have been far-reaching and have affected virtually all areas of life, including citizenship rights, property rights, education and vocational training, marriage and reproduction, military service to our country, employment, and health care.

What are the origins of these policies? How did intelligence come to be so pervasive a concern in legislation and public policy? These questions and their answers are the subject of this article.

WHAT IS PUBLIC POLICY?

Public policy is a complex, multifaceted, and always-changing process in the United States. Individuals and groups vie for advantage and special consideration as well as for their views on the well-being of society as it is more generally construed. In the main it is a messy process.

Dr. Julius Richmond, former Surgeon General of the United States and a pediatrician concerned with policy formulation and enforcement, frequently defines public policy as an equation with three principal elements. This equation is as follows:

$$\text{Public Policy} = \text{Knowledge Base} + \text{Social Strategies} + \text{Political Will}$$

The *knowledge base* guiding public policy includes many different forms of knowing, from formalistic and scientific empirical forms to personal experience, perceived common sense, and logical inference. Strongly held beliefs by influential individuals and the general knowledge of the common man appear to be particularly important in shaping and reforming public policy related to intelligence.

The term *social strategies* refers to potential actions taken by a society in a collective and planned fashion to achieve specific goals. In essence, social strategies related to intelligence concern ways to improve the well-being of individuals and to ensure the betterment of society as a whole. Social strategies related to intelligence have been remarkably dual in nature: either designed to enhance the personal development of individuals or to exclude individuals with exceptionalities in intelligence from participation in mainstream activities. Sometimes this exclusionary focus has been guided by paternalistic concern, sometimes by anxiety and fear, and frequently by both operating in not well articulated ways.

Political will is a vital element in public policy reflecting the fact that laws and regulations, court decisions, and the allocation of resources are fundamentally linked to political processes. Politics, in an Aristotelian sense, deals with the structure, organization, and administration of the state. Elected officials, judges and juries, and government employees all seek to understand and influence "political will" as do pollsters, lobbyists, businesses, and social action and advocacy groups. Just as important, many individuals and organizations seek to create or change political will.

Political will is the engine that drives the decision-making process and the degree to which the knowledge base and social strategies are implemented.

In our definition of public policy, we include public laws, regulations, and professional practices as well as public expenditures. In the United States, public policies concerning intelligence exist in every municipality, county, and state as well as at the federal level. No centralized accounting has been conducted, to our knowledge, of the total expenditures associated with intelligence-related policies, but conservatively it is at least in the 300–500 billions of dollars annually given that, in 1997, the United States spent at least $300 billion on education which, we will argue, is directly related to intellectual concerns. In addition to public expenditures, there are large private and philanthropic expenditures ranging from test development and marketing to prevention programs and the provision of social supports and services, and health care. In short, intelligence is big business.

Americans are deeply concerned about intelligence, and they act upon their concerns frequently through public policy. These concerns reflect basic assumptions about humankind present when our nation was formed. Key among these are the following:

1. The vitality of a democracy requires an intelligent and informed citizenry, and
2. A successful open-market economy depends upon intelligent choices and a competent workforce.

Soon after the founding of the United States, the necessity of universal education as a means to raise the overall intelligence and social competence of citizens became apparent. The movement for universal, free public education became the first major public policy that related to intelligence. Unlike the numerous public policies that developed over the last century, this first public policy occurred in the context of a highly ambitious, optimistic, and generative worldview about how society can better itself. The initial details of public education and its future economic realities were far from clear, and the early enactment of public education was far from ideal by today's standards. Nonetheless, the conviction that for children to have more, rather than less, intelligence was a good thing, worthy of soci-

etal investment, was strongly endorsed in the public school movement. Intelligence was then understood in its commonsense definition of knowledge and good judgment. Only later did intelligence acquire the technical definition that is associated with the discipline of psychology.

Today, our country invests in science, via policy and programs, to enhance the knowledge base about intelligence, with a special emphasis on preventing mental retardation and treating learning disabilities. Practical knowledge about intelligence also derives from experience with evaluations of social strategies to improve the intellectual functioning of individuals. Sweeping legislation, most notably the Americans with Disabilities Act of 1990, has further raised awareness of how society has discriminated against and selectively excluded people because of their lack of measured intelligence (along with many other disabilities). In the remainder of this article we highlight key historical issues and briefly describe major current practices and controversies concerning intelligence and public policy.

WHAT IS INTELLIGENCE?

Intelligence represents a concept about individuals that is widely held and has had deep historical roots. It is especially the everyday definitions of intelligence, along with beliefs about its origins and expression, that have had such a pervasive and profound influence on public policy. Dictionary and encyclopedia definitions are illustrative of this point:

Intelligence, the capacity for learning, reasoning, understanding and similar forms of mental activity; aptitude in grasping truths, relationships, facts, meanings, etc. (*Random House Unabridged Dictionary*, 1993).

In its popular usage, the concept [of intelligence] refers to variations in the ability to learn, to function in society, and to behave according to contemporary social expectations. (*The Encyclopedia Britannica*, 1986).

The common understanding about intelligence is unquestionably that it represents a dimension of human competency that is far-reaching in its implications for functioning as a citizen, particularly in a democratic society dependent upon active engagement of individuals. Intelligence in this sense is not only an academic or scientific concept but rather reflects a fundamental human quality that influences almost every activity in life. In general, more intelligence is generally considered highly desirable, although there exists some ambivalence about the merits of genius level or extremely high amounts of intelligence within the general population. Historically, no such ambivalence existed about having very low levels of intelligence: This was clearly undesirable. Crude, pejorative terms were treated as synonyms for individuals with less intelligence, and many restrictive policies sought to deny them full citizenship rights and opportunities.

There is a vast and complex scientific literature that has accumulated about intelligence over the past century or so, as well documented in this and the earlier edition of Robert Sternberg's (1982) *Handbook of Human Intelligence*. Here, we highlight several broad issues and assumptions that have been the driving forces in shaping public policy. Specifically, we provide an overview of salient views about the following:

1. What intelligence is and how it is measured,
2. How intelligence is distributed in the population,
3. The ways that intelligence changes with age and historical time (i.e., it is developmental in nature),
4. The multiple forces that regulate the expression of intelligence,
5. The extent to which public policy influences the expression of intelligence.

What Intelligence Is and How it Is Measured

Vis-à-vis public policy, intelligence has had many different definitions. To our knowledge, many of the extremely oppressive laws enacted earlier in this century denying full citizenship rights to those with mental retardation (then often described as idiots and imbeciles) never provided a precise definition of intelligence or its lack. This likely reflected the belief that such a condition would be so apparent and well known in the community that professional diagnosis or determination was scarcely an issue. In this sense, early definitions of intelligence were essentially dichotomous and simply discriminated between those with adequate or normal intelligence and those with inadequate or abnormal intelligence. This principle derived from English

common law (under the so-called McNaughton rule) that excluded individuals from responsibility for illegal acts if the individual could not tell right from wrong when the act was committed owing to mental incompetence or insanity.

The dichotomous definition of intelligence was first operationalized in a large-scale way by Robert Yerkes in 1917 via development of the Army Alpha and Army Beta intelligence tests as part of mobilization and conscription into the U.S. Armed Forces for World War I. The prevailing assumption was that a certain *minimal* level of intelligence was required to function acceptably within the military and that a nontrivial proportion of adult American males possibly did not possess that minimal level. This assumption and the practice of universal intelligence screening are still in place, virtually unchallenged, in the military. In fact, as modern warfare becomes more complex and technological, the emphasis on intelligence may intensify.

On the basis of a similar belief system, children with mental retardation used to be regularly excluded from access to free public education on the assumption that they could not benefit from what teachers routinely provided to other children. Furthermore, the exclusion of children with low levels of intelligence from public education reflected the belief that they could not become contributing members of society and therefore did not need to be educated. Parents as education reform advocates in the early 1970s challenged this system and the de facto devaluation of children with low levels of intelligence. They argued that lack of educational opportunity was creating a self-fulfilling prophecy. They demanded truly *universal* free public education, and their demands resulted in "special education" for children whose learning needs differed from typically developing children. Indeed, the original Education for All Handicapped Children Act of 1974 (now replaced by the Individuals with Disabilities Education Act [IDEA] of 1997) reflects how the knowledge base, social strategies, and political will combine to shape public policy.

In the 1960s, basic research led to new knowledge that children with even severe forms of mental retardation were capable of substantial learning. The development of successful teaching strategies (mostly derived from basic principles of learning and reinforcement applicable to almost all living organisms) and the political will of influential upper middle-class parents who sought greater social and educational opportunities for their children with mental retardation resonated well in a political climate concerned with equal opportunities for *all* citizens. This concern led not only to an available public education for children with mental retardation but also to the creation of the National Institute of Child Health and Human Development, which had research on mental retardation and learning as two of its major focal points.

Definition of Mental Retardation

One of the most surprising facts to many people is that the definition of mental retardation is arbitrary, relativistic, and strongly influenced by social, political, and economic forces. In fact, the functional definition of mental retardation endorsed by the leading professional organization, the American Association on Mental Retardation, has changed four times in the past four decades. Before the mid-1960s, mental retardation was defined by performing below a prescribed level on a standardized test of intelligence, namely, a level that was two or more standard deviations below average for the population at any given age. On the basis of epidemiological and educational studies strongly suggesting that children from ethnic minorities and from economically impoverished families were likely to be incorrectly categorized as mentally retarded, *when in fact they functioned quite well in their everyday settings*, the definition was changed dramatically. The new definition had two quite distinctive features: first, the diagnosis of mental retardation could occur only after individuals who knew a child well suspected that there was a problem with the child's intellectual competency; and second, the diagnosis depended on significantly substandard performance on both a standardized test of general intelligence (which was individually administered) *and* comparable low performance on a standardized test of *adaptive behavior*. Adaptive behavior tests address areas of everyday competency such as social skills, self-help skills, communication, and learning. The implementation of this new definition had the anticipated consequences of identifying fewer individuals with the condition called mental retardation. Since then, the

diverse organizations that create professional standards for defining and diagnosing mental retardation have introduced further revisions, which, by the way, are not always compatible across the professions of psychology, psychiatry, and education and rarely are implemented to consistent and specific professional standards. It is interesting to note that, although there has been a lowering of the rate of mental retardation owing, in large part, to more restrictive diagnostic criteria and procedures, there has been a corresponding increase in *learning disabilities*, which is a field that itself continues to struggle with definitional and diagnostic issues.

From a public-policy perspective, some *quantitative system* for the measurement of intelligence is desirable. There are many practical and philosophical issues in which this becomes apparent. One area of concern deals with the issue of rights and responsibilities. When is a person competent to give legal consent, to stand trial, to be held responsible for his or her actions? Does a citizen need to show some minimal intellectual competency to drive a motor vehicle, to vote, to marry, to have children, to own property or to reside in the community, to serve his or her country, or to receive higher education? Another area of concern deals with potential benefits. The presence of an intellectual disability may qualify an individual for an entitlement to free health care, special educational and social service benefits, and, in some cases, to a lifetime cash income via Social Security. A quantitative system for determining the number of such individuals in a given society is a helpful tool in planning social strategies to meet individual needs and to benefit society in general.

Intelligence Testing

There are two important realities of intelligence testing as currently practiced that warrant emphasis. The first is that virtually all measurements to date of intelligence have been relativistic rather than absolute in nature. That is, they rely on statistical norming procedures that are analogous to grading on a curve. These procedures virtually ensure that there will always be a constant percentage of individuals who score below a given cut point. In theory, even if all people became much more intelligent – as determined by objective and constant standards – our current methods of norming and renorming tests would not capture this change and, indeed, would likely treat it as an artifact. This is because standardized tests are intermittently normed and renormed on representative samples of individuals (usually based on gender, and ethnic and social class variation within a nation at a given point in history). The resulting variation in performance of individuals is then transformed to fit a "normal curve." Within this framework, some people will always be judged inadequate simply because others score higher than they do, regardless of the absolute level of performance of the group or the individual.

A second issue is that almost all of the standardized tests in use have been developed to detect differences among individuals rather than primarily to measure the presence of particular competencies known to be important for domains of intellectual performance. Public policy generally is based on the implicit assumption that performance on a test of "general intelligence" or g is an adequate measure of intellectual skills. We think this remarkable, given the vast amount of scientific evidence that demonstrates the limits of this assumption, particularly when applied to predicting an individual's life course (rather than trends for very large samples or populations) and the many examples almost anyone can give of someone who did much better (or worse) in life than others would have thought based on his or her school performance or assessed general intelligence. Incidently, school performance and intelligence have been strongly linked since Alfred Binet began the intelligence testing movement in the Paris school system. His work was designed to divide children into two groups, the haves and have nots, so that children who could not benefit from formal education would not be admitted to that system.

We think it noteworthy that considerable innovative thinking about the nature of intelligence has occurred in recent decades, especially appreciation for multiple types or dimensions of intelligence by individuals such as Howard Gardner who, for example, distinguishes the following kinds of intelligence: interpersonal, linguistic, logical–mathematical, bodily–kinesthetic, spatial, musical, and intrapersonal. Yet these theoretical advances have had little detectable influence on public policies to date, and the concept of generalized intelligence is undeniably dominant in public life.

HOW INTELLIGENCE IS DISTRIBUTED IN THE POPULATION

The Normal Curve as an Assumption

The dominant assumption in the study of intelligence has always been that there is a Gaussian or normal curve for intelligence in the population such that approximately equal numbers of individuals have very high and very low scores and the vast majority score somewhere in the middle.* Figure 24.1 from Fontana and Sivan (1996) displays the percentage of cases under portions of the normal curve and various equivalents expressed in different metrics including percentiles, IQs, 2-scores, T scores, and SAT scores.

Numbers were selected as the means for measuring individual differences on the implicit assumption that these numbers reflect quantitative differences that have real-world meaning beyond the test score itself. These assumptions are broad and difficult, if not impossible, either to refute or support unequivocally. Nonetheless, it is fairly certain that, within the present system of scoring intelligence tests for individuals and comparing those tests to population norms, there is an excess of individuals with extremely high and low scores despite the efforts of test developers to minimize these bulges at the ends of the distribution (cf. Moser, Ramey, & Leonard, 1990, for a fuller discussion with respect to mental retardation).

A well-known fact is that there are regional and social class differences in the distribution of test scores from administration of standardized tests of intelligence and educational achievement dating back

---

* It should be noted that the normal curve distribution of intelligence is basically an uncheckable assumption because IQ scores do not have an absolute 0 and are therefore normed to a Gaussian distribution though a mathematical conversion using Z scores. Such norming transforms the raw score distribution as best it can to a Gaussian distribution. Historically, items have been added and deleted to the tests, based in part, on their ability to help the overall raw scores to approximate a normal distribution. One way this has been done is to eliminate items that were too easy or too difficult. Items were retained that improved the discrimination among individuals rather than on the basis of which ones measured some critical aspect of intellectual functioning, per se. Thus, we really do not know the natural distribution of raw intelligence in any given population. Psychometricians have assumed a normal distribution and have then adopted a number system and set of procedures that virtually ensure that distribution.

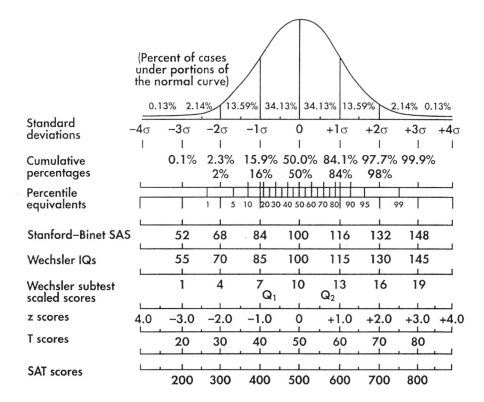

(Percent of cases under portions of the normal curve)

0.13%	2.14%	13.59%	34.13%	34.13%	13.59%	2.14%	0.13%	

Standard deviations
-4σ -3σ -2σ -1σ 0 $+1\sigma$ $+2\sigma$ $+3\sigma$ $+4\sigma$

Cumulative percentages
0.1% 2.3% 15.9% 50.0% 84.1% 97.7% 99.9%
2% 16% 50% 84% 98%

Percentile equivalents
1 5 10 20 30 40 50 60 70 80 90 95 99

Stanford–Binet SAS
52 68 84 100 116 132 148

Wechsler IQs
55 70 85 100 115 130 145

Wechsler subtest scaled scores
1 4 7 10 13 16 19
Q_1 Q_2

z scores
4.0 −3.0 −2.0 −1.0 0 +1.0 +2.0 +3.0 +4.0

T scores
20 30 40 50 60 70 80

SAT scores
200 300 400 500 600 700 800

FIGURE 24.1. Test results using curve equivalents.

to World War I and the work of Robert Yerkes discussed below. Regions with higher concentrations of poverty show lower average scores on general tests of intelligence as well as non-Gaussian or bell curve distributions of scores. Some of the presumed and documented correlates of these differences are discussed in the section below on the multiple forces that regulate the expression of intelligence.

Political Will as a Factor in Learning Disabilities

One of the most recent examples of how political will can alter presumed distribution of "intelligence" is the learning disabilities movement in which parents of children who are not performing well in traditional school settings have sought to create a classification system to distinguish their children from those with "mental retardation." Numerous studies have documented that the classification of children into the categories of "learning disabled" versus "mentally retarded" is strongly influenced by social class, ethnicity, and parental involvement in the testing and educational process of

the child. This means that there are many children whose functional behavior is virtually indistinguishable but whose administrative classification within the educational system entitles them to different treatment. Not surprisingly, those labeled *learning disabled* tend to be Caucasian and middle class and typically receive higher resources and more specialized interventions than those classified as mildly mentally retarded.

POLITICAL WILL AS A FACTOR IN EDUCATION FOR HIGHLY CAPABLE YOUTH. In contrast, many educators and human development researchers believe that children with exceptionally high intelligence, (typically defined as >+2 standard deviations above the population mean) could benefit substantially from "special education" to meet their unique needs. The political will, however, does not yet exist for this belief to translate into widely supported public policy and investments on behalf of highly capable youth. Many people in our society apparently believe that it is unfair to provide extra services to children who are already doing well or who are considered to be gifted. The public schools that serve this segment of the intellectual population tend to be populated by affluent and well-educated parents. There is an increasing knowledge base about highly intelligent children and the strategies that effectively promote their learning, their social–emotional well-being, and their potential to contribute to society (Robinson, 1998). In the meantime some of those children are receiving appropriate educational services in private schools or through idiosyncratic arrangements, depending on family circumstances and local resources. It remains to be seen if new social strategies to capitalize on the special talents and gifts of such individuals will achieve a high priority in the public sector in the United States, particularly as the so-called information age and its associated technologies mature.

THE WAYS THAT INTELLIGENCE CHANGES WITH AGE AND HISTORICAL TIME

There is a fundamental truth about intelligence that is often ignored: young children are much less intelligent than are adults according to any common-sense definition of intelligence. This fact is largely ignored because as a society we have implicitly accepted the notion that IQ is a constant feature of an individual. Granted that there are highly intelligent very young children who continue to seem remarkably intelligent at later ages and as adults; conversely, those with limited intelligence often *remain* at the lower end of the distribution. The agreement to use the same numerical scoring system ($M = 100$) to characterize individual intelligence from infancy through old age further reinforces the idea that intelligence is not fundamentally developmental in its nature. This scoring convention obscures the large, dramatic differences in intellectual abilities at different ages. To illustrate this by analogy, imagine a system for measuring physical growth (e.g., height and weight) only in terms that yielded 100 for "average" at all ages and never reported changes in an absolute metric. (Also, if the system for physical measurement followed the rules of intelligence testing and assumed a bell-shaped curve for all cohorts and ages, we could never detect any shifts in height and weight within populations.)

A landmark study in developmental science documented that individual children over the course of their childhood typically had IQ scores that varied as much as a dramatic 28 points *on average* between 3 and 17 years of age (McCall, Appelbaum, and Hogarty, 1973). This finding is based on careful longitudinal study of the same children, which is the only design that can adequately detect fluctuations in individual performance. Despite these impressive findings on intellectual variability during development, public policy continues to reflect the assumption that intelligence is a constant personal trait that can be assessed with reasonable certainty at any age beyond infancy. For example, the definition of mental retardation includes an assumption that the condition will be permanent.

What many people do not realize about intelligence test construction is that items have been selected for inclusion into tests in part because they correlate positively with one another over time. Thus, psychometricians have optimized the consistency and predictability of intelligence tests by eliminating items that do not show predictability over time. Therefore, it should come as no great surprise when they do what they were designed to do; however, this psychometric stability begs the question of whether and to what extend and under what conditions intellectual stability exists in nature. These are empirical issues that require careful and repeated inquiry – particularly for any society that is undergoing change likely to affect intellectual performance for individuals or for subgroups. Some major recent social changes in the United States that are particularly noteworthy with respect to population trends in intellectual performance include the civil rights movement, education and welfare reforms, and widespread adoption of mass media and telecommunication technologies to mention but a few.

THE MULTIPLE FORCES THAT REGULATE THE EXPRESSION OF INTELLIGENCE

Virtually all contemporary theories of intelligence recognize that its expression in brain and behavior is regulated by numerous factors, including genetics, health, nutrition, educational opportunities, social structure, social interactions, stress, culture, and chance events. Recently we have summarized this multifactorial model of intellectual development into a theoretical perspective that we call Biosocial Developmental Contextualism (Ramey and Ramey, 1998). This perspective highlights the potential of using public policies to prevent intellectual disabilities and of using treatment strategies to minimize secondary conditions that are the result of an existing intellectual disability. Examples of effective and promising strategies include the provision and access to the following service: genetic screening and counseling; nutritional supplements for women and children; public health services, including immunizations and medical treatment; special education; and early educational intervention. In addition, public laws concerning seatbelts and protective helmets seek, in part, to prevent intellectual disabilities secondary to traumatic brain injury. There is increasing public awareness of the value of such preventive strategies, both in terms of benefits to vulnerable individuals and in terms of significant cost savings to society.

THE EXTENT TO WHICH PUBLIC POLICY INFLUENCES THE EXPRESSION OF INTELLIGENCE

Because public policies can affect the expression of intelligence for individuals and populations, should they? This issue has ethical as well as feasibility and cost dimensions. For us, public policy is the most general embodiment of contextualism in our biosocial developmental perspective on intelligence. The laws and regulations of a society specify the hopes and fears of its dominant members. Dominance does not, of course, necessarily imply compassion or tolerance. Thus, we have historically witnessed severe actions by society in the intelligence domain, including involuntary sterilization, denial of civil rights, and involuntary commitment to institutions of persons with low intelligence. During the past 25 years, however, new trends have emerged that have favorably changed many of the laws, regulations, and supports for individuals and families affected by intellectual disabilities. Three themes strongly associated with the Developmental Disabilities Rehabilitation Act, The Americans with Disabilities Act

(ADA, 1990), and the Individuals with Disabilities Education Act (1997) are *inclusion, independence*, and *productivity*. These social concepts affirm the value of all citizens and their potential to be active, contributing members of a society when the right supportive contexts exist. Given a positive stance toward these broad goals, we believe that it is in the best interests of society to maximize its intellectual capital through thoughtful support programs implemented under explicitly stated policies derived from the political process.

The Pervasiveness of Public Policies Related to Intelligence

Collectively, the numerous public policies concerning intelligence may be characterized as vigorous, complex, compartmentalized, and largely uncoordinated. The policies derive from a combination of sources ranging from documented means to prevent disabilities to strongly held beliefs and hopes about how to create a more competitive, more humanitarian, or more integrated and cohesive society. An important fact to underscore is that many of the policies that influence intelligence and are guided by beliefs about intelligence do not necessarily mention intelligence per se. In part, this is due to the recognition that the topic of intelligence is an extremely sensitive and politically charged one. The social sensitivity of this topic is also due to ignorance, misinformation, and unresolved controversies about the nature of intelligence.

Some Current Public Policies

Public policies have see-sawed over the years, indicating the public's changing views concerning individuals with intellectual disabilities.

Historically, concern for individuals with mental retardation has been the primary focus of intelligence policy since Binet began his measurement of intelligence in France at the dawn of the 20th century. Within the last 25 years there has been an increasing emphasis on intelligence policy for individuals who are categorized as *learning disabled* but not mentally retarded. Years ago most states had laws permitting involuntary sterilization of persons categorized as mentally retarded even though genetic transmission of mental retardation accounts for only a small percentage of all cases (Moser, Ramey, &

Leonard, 1990). Owing to the vigorous and effective actions of advocates on behalf of persons with mental retardation, it is currently difficult to imagine even voluntary sterilization of mentally retarded individuals because of the threat of expensive lawsuits even though voluntary sterilization through vasectomies and laparscopies are widely used for birth control by the general population.

One way to think about current public policies is to summarize them according to executive level departments in government that have responsibilities for implementing relevant laws and regulations. At the federal level there are 13 cabinet level departments as follows:

- Agriculture,
- Commerce,
* Defense,
* Education,
- Energy,
* Health and Human Services,
* Housing and Urban Development,
- Interior,
* Justice,
- Labor,
- State,
- Transportation, and
- Treasury.

In concert with the judicial branch of government and the Congress these 13 departments have the responsibility of faithfully executing the federal laws (i.e., formally implementing federal policy).*

Policies about the intelligence of individuals can generally be divided into three broad strategies:

I. Exclusion from participation
II. General enhancement of intelligence via education
III. Prevention, treatment, and supports of intellectual disabilities

Examination of recent public laws reveals virtually every federal department has some responsibility in the area of intelligence policy. Under current disability law these are special provisions for employment, housing, health care, income, transportation, and justice to name but a few of the major ones. The five departments that we have starred, however, have the greatest direct involvement and control the vast bulk of public expenditures. We give example of public policies by strategy type below.

---

* Variations on this arrangement also exist at the state, county, and municipality levels, but this article, for the sake of brevity and illustrative purposes, will be concerned only with federal policy.

I. Exclusion

Beginning in 1917 the military establishment that is now called the Department of Defense used the Army Alpha and the Army Beta tests of intelligence to reject unqualified conscripts for military service. Conscription into the Armed Forces no longer exists in this country owing to the development of an all-volunteer personnel policy. Minimal competency requirements, however, still exist, but it is unclear to the authors if the stance is consistent with the Americans with Disability Act, which bars such discrimination in employment. To our knowledge no legal test case has addressed this issue.

In our opinion, minor variations on tests of intelligence commonly called achievement tests are widely used by public colleges and universities as a competitive selection device. There is substantial overlap in what is measured by these two kinds of tests, and one is a reasonably good predictor of the other, as they were designed to be. This begs the question of whether a proxy for intelligence is being used to limit educational opportunity unfairly and whether such procedures are in violation of the Americans with Disabilities Act of 1990 (ADA) that prohibits such discrimination. To our knowledge, no test case of this principle has occurred in federal courts although a somewhat comparable test case for K–12 occurred in California in 1972. Resolved as the *Larry P v. Wilson Riles* (1979) case it prohibited the use of intelligence tests to determine eligibility for special education at a time when placement in special education classes functionally meant being excluded from participation in regular education.

II. General Enhancement of Intelligence

The Department of Education is the main force in U.S. education policy even though the vast majority of educational expenditures, responsibility, and authority exists at the state and local levels. Total expenditures for all education in 1997 was approximately $300 billion according to the U.S. Department of Education. State and local laws regulate mandatory school attendance, usually until age 16, and increasingly there is pressure to improve the quality of education as we write in late 1998. Recent widely publicized polls indicate that the state of public education is a very high priority in the United States Businesses clamor for a better prepared work force, and parents, in the main, understand education to be an essential ingredient in good employment prospects and upward social mobility. In short, there is a clear, commonsense equation that developed intelligence equals social and economic competence. Although the mandate for better public education is clear, the social strategies by which to achieve it are currently receiving intense and complex debate. The next few years promise to be a watershed for American public education and its role in intellectual development.

III. Prevention, Treatment, and Support

Schools can no longer exclude children with intellectual disabilities from attendance and, in fact, are mandated by the IDEA legislation to provide a free public education for children from ages 3 to 21 years – a wider age range than for children without intellectual disabilities. Generally, states provide regular educational programs from 5 or 6 years to 18 or 19 years of age. The Department of Health and Human Services and the Department of Education together fund the bulk of services to intellectually disabled individuals. In the Department of Human Services, some main organizational entities include the following:

Administration on Children and Families
Administration on Developmental Disabilities
Centers for Disease Control
Head Start
Maternal and Child Health Division of the Public Health Service
Medicaid
National Institute of Child Health and Human Development
National Institute on Disability Research
Social Security Administration

Each of these branches of government has numerous programs and policies related to prevention, treatment, or supports for families affected by intellectual disabilities. The Department of Education, for example, uses two main social strategies with respect to intellectual disabilities: Early Intervention and Special Education.

EARLY INTERVENTION. Early intervention in human development is, historically, a relatively new concept, emerging in the 1960s and 1970s. Early intervention, in aggregate, represents a broad array of programs, treatments, and strategies designed to enhance the development of children who have risk conditions or identified developmental disabilities. Early intervention refers to a systematic and comprehensive process that begins with developmental concerns and extends through the delivery of appropriate supports and services to eligible children and their families. Active monitoring of the effectiveness of the early intervention is generally construed as an integral part of early intervention.

In early intervention, "early" typically refers to the first 5 years of life – the period when brain growth and development are most rapid and when young children acquire language, a sense of self, and the social skills essential for their everyday self-care and interactions with adults and peers. What is new about early intervention is that professional and societal attitudes have shifted from a predominantly care-providing mode to a more active teaching and stimulating orientation. Advocates for early intervention generally agree that the earlier intervention begins and the more intensive it is, the more likely it is to produce desired results for children and their families.

The term *early intervention* is used to refer to the process of planning and the actual provision of services designed to meet each child's individual developmental needs. A central component of many early intervention programs is a child development center or a structured home visiting program, or both, designed to facilitate the intellectual, motoric, communicative, and social development of the infant and young child. Specialized services and therapies (e.g., physical therapy and speech and language therapy) related to a child's individualized needs and to a family's unique knowledge and resources, are frequently delivered. Specialized health and nutritional services are frequently provided. In federally funded early intervention programs today, each family is required to have an Individualized Family Service Plan (IFSP). These individualized plans have grown out of an awareness and appreciation of the need to time, pace, and locate resources and services that are tailored to the idiosyncratic nature of the circumstances of particular children and their families.

Early intervention is designed (1) to prevent developmental disabilities and the secondary conditions arising from a disability, (2) to provide early treatment for specific conditions associated with a child's disability to maximize a child's likelihood of development gain, and (3) to provide systematic and high-quality support to families that are more knowledgeable in how to meet the developmental needs of their child, have more positive attitudes toward disability and the child's future opportunities, and become more informed advocates via awareness of the service delivery system and newly emerging treatments as well as their children's legal rights. Eligibility for early intervention services is determined by whether an individual child has a developmental disability or is at high risk for such a disability.

The U.S. government defines *developmental disability* as a severe, chronic disability of a person that

- is attributable to a mental or physical impairment or a combination of the two;
- is manifested before the person attains the age of 22;
- is likely to continue indefinitely;
- results in substantial limits in the following areas:
  - cognitive development
  - physical development
  - language and speech development
  - psychosocial development
  - self-help skills;
- or is a diagnosed physical or mental condition that has a high probability of resulting in developmental delay;
- reflects the person's need for a combination and sequence of special interdisciplinary or generic care, treatment, or other services that are of life-long or of extended duration and are individually planned and coordinated.

This complex defintion is operationalized by each state as it deems proper subject to federal oversight. A review of state definitions of developmental delay by Shackelford (1995) reveals states are expressing criteria for delay in various ways such as (a) the difference between chronological age and actual performance level on a developmentally normed examination expressed as a percentage of chronological age, (b) delay expressed as performance at a certain number of months below chronological age, (c) delay as indicated by standard deviations below the mean on a norm referenced instrument, or (d) delay indicated by atypical development or observed atypical behaviors. The first three of these are quantitative criteria, and the fourth allows for clinical judgment. Not only is there wide variability in the type of quantitative criteria used by states to describe developmental delay, but there also is a wide range in the level of delay required for eligibility. Common measurements of level of delay are 25% delay, 2 standard deviations' (SD) delay in one or more areas, or both of these criteria.

States may also, at their discretion, include individuals from birth to age 2 years who are at risk of having substantial developmental delays if early intervention services are not provided. In reality, there appears to be wide variation in operationalization and considerable inconsistency in the application of the definition in individual instances.

Before this definition was developed, the following specific conditions or syndromes were considered to define developmental disabilities:

- Mental retardation
- Autism
- Cerebral palsy
- Epilepsy
- Severe learning disorders

Now these conditions are frequently included by either clinical judgment or their past association with poor prognosis.

Beginning at birth early intervention programs can provide 17 services for children up to age 3. Table 24.1 specifies the services that may be provided under legislation known as the Individuals with Disabilities Education Act (IDEA).

From ages 3–5 years, public schools are mandated under Part B of IDEA to provide the services that are listed in Table 24.2.

SPECIAL EDUCATION. Beginning at age 5 years, children become eligible for special education when they have a diagnosed intellectual disability. Eligibility for educational services requires an Individualized Education Plan that mandates parental participation as well as special adaptations and services by teachers and other school personnel.

The two main categories of disability associated with intelligence are *mental retardation* and *specific learning disabilities*.

Mental Retardation

The definition of mental retardation according to the American Association on Mental Retardation is as follows:

Mental retardation refers to substantial limitations in present functioning. It is characterized by

- Significantly subaverage intellectual functioning existing concurrently with related limitations in two or more of the following applicable adaptive skill areas:

communication	self-care	self-direction
home living	social skills	community use
functional	health and	academics
work	safety	
	leisure.	

- Mental retardation is manifested before age 18.

The following four assumptions must be considered when applying the definition:

- Valid assessment considers cultural and linguistic diversity as well as differences in communication and behavioral factors.
- The existence of limitations in adaptive skills occurs within the context of community environments typical of the individual's age peers and is indexed to the person's individualized needs for supports.
- Specific adaptive limitations often coexist with strengths in other adaptive skills or other personal capabilities.
- With appropriate supports over a sustained period, the life functioning of the person with mental retardation will generally improve.

Learning Disabilities

The definition of learning disabilities adopted by the National Joint Committee on Learning Disabilities is as follows:

TABLE 24.1. Services Specified Under Part C (Birth to 3 Years) of the Individuals with Disabilities Education ACT (IDEA)

Services May Include but Are Not Limited to Following:

Assistive Technology Devices and Services	Occupational Therapy
Audiology	Physical Therapy
Family Training, Counseling, and Home Visits	Psychological Services
Health Services	Service Coordination Services
Medical Services for Diagnosis or Evaluation	Social Work Services
Nursing Services	Special Instruction
Nutrition Services	Speech–Language Pathology
	Transportation and Related Costs
	Vision Services

Note: From 34 Code of Federal Register (CFR) §303.12(d).

Learning disabilities is a generic term that refers to a heterogeneous group of disorders manifested by significant difficulties in the acquisition and use of listening, speaking, reading, writing, reasoning, or mathematical abilities. These disorders are intrinsic to the individual and presumed to be due to central nervous system dysfunction. Even though a learning disability may occur concomitantly with other handicapping conditions (e.g., sensory impairment, mental retardation, social emotional disturbance), or environmental influences (e.g., cultural differences, insufficient–inappropriate instruction, psychogenic factors), it is not the direct result of those conditions or influences.

TABLE 24.2. Special Education and Related Services Specified Under Part B of the Individuals with Disabilities Act (IDEA)

Services May Include but Are Not Limited to the Following:

Assistive Technology Devices and Services	Psychological Services
Audiology	Recreation
Counseling Services	Rehabilitation Counseling Services
Early Identification and Assessment	School Health Services
Medical Services for Diagnosis or Evaluation	Social Work Services in Schools
Occupational Therapy	Special Education
Parent Counseling and Training	Speech Pathology
Physical Therapy	Transportation

Note: See 34 CFR §§300.5, 300.6, 300.16, and 300.17.

Special Education Practices

Special education is a collection of social strategies that developed primarily as a result of effective advocacy by parents of children with mental retardation and severe learning disabilities. Before the enactment in 1975 of Public Law 94–142 (the Education for All Handicapped Children Act), children with significant cognitive and behavioral difficulties were frequently denied education in the public schools. The Education for All Handicapped Children Act guaranteed the right of every child to receive an individualized and appropriate free public education in the least restrictive educational environment. This law was updated in 1990 and renamed the Individuals with Disabilities Education Act (IDEA). Each state must set specific criteria for eligibility and provide a set of services consistent with federal guidelines or run the risk of losing federal funding, which augments state funding for special education programs.

The additional expenditures of special education are generally used to provide specially trained teachers, typically with a master's degree in education, who provide individualized instruction based on an *Individualized Education Plan* that is developed as the result of psychometric diagnostic testing and conferences concerning educational strategy and objectives involving teachers, other school personnel, and parents. This instruction must take place in the least restrictive educational environment and may occur in the child's regular classroom or in classes that contain only children with special needs. When so-called self-contained special classrooms are used there is almost always a significant reduction in teacher–child ratios in recognition of the additional instructional efforts needed.

Currently, the concepts of *mainstreaming* and *least restrictive environments* are central in special education owing to concerns about the educational and social effectiveness of segregated classrooms.

The federal government has influenced the growth and development of special education in two general ways: (1) by funding demonstration and research programs to explore the consequences of innovative educational approaches, and (2) by monitoring compliance of state education agencies with federal guidelines.

In general students with learning disabilities or mental retardation are instructed directly by an itinerant teacher on a regular basis or by a special education teacher in a resource room for part or all of each school day. Generally, the more severe the disability, the greater the time spent in a resource room, although mainstreaming remains a frequently stated goal.

Historically, the concept of special learning disabilities has been operationalized as a severe discrepancy between academic achievement in spelling, reading, mathematics, or other basic academic skills and the individual's IQ score. Each state adopts its own criteria contingent on federal guidelines. Two methods of calculating discrepancies have predominated: (1) a discrepancy defined by grade or age levels, or (2) discrepancies based on expected normal curve distribution of IQ and academic achievement within any given age level. Estimates of incidence range from 3 to 5% of the school age population to as high as 10% (Tucker, Stevens, & Ysseldyke, 1983). Both the issue of definition and the issue of treatment efficacy are undergoing careful examination from a scientific perspective under the leadership of the National Institute of Child Health and Human Development. Clearly, the knowledge base on these complex conditions needs substantial advancement.

VOCATIONAL EDUCATION. Vocational education is available to students with intellectual disabilities who qualify for special education services. The goal of vocational educational programs is to prepare special education students to enter the world of productive employment. Components of vocational education include remedial basic skills, job training, career information, social and personal skills, and on-the-job training. Students are eligible for these services at age 16 years.

SUMMARY AND CONCLUSIONS

Figure 24.2 presents an overview of prominent social strategies designed to provide services for persons affected by intellectual disabilities. As can be seen in Figure 24.2, these services are meant to aid families as well as the person with an intellectual disability. In principle at least some services are available from conception to old age.

During the past few decades several social and political trends that have been developing are noteworthy.

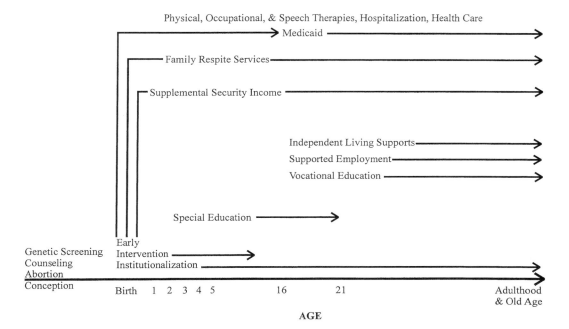

FIGURE 24.2. Services available to persons with intellectual disabilities.

First, as the importance of the early years has achieved scientific recognition, the pressure to start programs earlier in the life span has increased. As a result, there have been dramatic increases in the enrollment in early intervention programs.

Second, philosophical emphasis on the principles of *normalization* and *community integration* has led to a decrease in involuntary institutionalization and segregated special education classrooms. These forms of treatment are rapidly being phased out, and programs that emphasize community-based living and participation in nonsegregated settings, including regular education classrooms and competitive employment settings, are being scaled up.

Third, to expand the usable knowledge base, vigorous research programs are under way at the National Institutes of Health and the Department of Education to better understand, treat, and possibly prevent intellectual disabilities.

Fourth, an emphasis on the evaluation of differential outcomes associated with various treatments is emerging in the light of the significant public expenditures to improve the quality of life for persons affected by intellectual disabilities. This cost-effectiveness emphasis appears to be gaining social momentum.

Fifth, there is unquestionably a strong trend toward emphasizing the strengths and competencies of persons with intellectual disabilities and guiding their overall development under the principles of *inclusion, independence, and productivity*. As has been the case recently in other civil rights legislation, we see this emphasis as potentially beneficial to this segment of our society as well as individuals and families directly affected by intellectual disabilities.

Yes, intelligence does matter, and our society does act to enhance its expression. But, other important values help to put it into a broader context of social values that emphasize equity as well as excellence.

REFERENCES

McCall, R. B., Appelbaum, M. I., & Hogarty, P. S. (1973). Developmental changes in mental performance. *Monographs of the Society for Research in Child Development, 38* (Serial No. 150).

Moser, H. W., Ramey, C. T., & Leonard, C. O. (1990). Mental retardation. In A. E. H. Emery & D. L. Rimoin (Eds.), *The principles and practices of medical genetics* (Vol. II) (pp. 495–511). New York: Churchill Livingstone Inc.

Ramey, C. T., & Ramey, S. L. (1998). Early intervention and early experience. *American Psychologist, 53,* 109–120.

Robinson, N. M. (1998). Synergies in families of gifted children. In M. Lewis & C. Feiring (Eds.), *Families, risk, and competence* (pp. 309–324). Rahway, NJ: Erlbaum.

The Americans With Disabilities Act. (1990). U.S. Equal Employment Opportunity Commission. Washington, DC: U.S. Department of Justice.

Tucker, J., Stevens, L., & Ysseldyke, J. (1983). Learning disabilities: The experts speak out. *Journal of Learning Disabilities, 16,* 6–13.

CHAPTER TWENTY-FIVE

Intelligence and Culture

ROBERT SERPELL

A distinctive characteristic of the human species is that we live in societies that create their own niche within the larger ecosystem, imposing structure on the natural environment by means of a technology that is accumulated over many generations through the process known as culture. Culture consists of a set of practices (constituted by a particular pattern of recurrent activities with associated artifacts) that are informed by a system of meanings (encoded in language and other symbols) and maintained by a set of institutions over time. The history of the gradual change of these practices is part of the system of meanings shared by the members and owners of the culture as a function of their transformative participation in the culture's practices.*

The relations between intelligence and culture have been considered from three somewhat different perspectives that can be summarized under the metaphors of culture as a language, culture as a womb, and culture as a forum (Serpell, 1994). According to the language metaphor, each human culture constitutes a distinctive system of meanings for representing the mind, within which the concept of intelligence is defined. I shall illustrate this approach in the section on the cultural conceptualization of intelligence. According to the womb metaphor, different human cultures generate different kinds of nurturant environment for the growth of a person

that stimulate or mold the development of the individual's intelligence in different ways. I shall review some of the research evidence that supports this view in the section on theories of cognitive development. According to the forum metaphor, the culture shared by a community gives rise to, and feeds off, debates among its members about such matters as how to organize education, and the preoccupations of various participants in those debates assign particular significance to intelligence. I shall explain this perspective with several examples in the remaining sections of this chapter.

THE CULTURAL CONCEPTUALIZATION OF INTELLIGENCE

Intelligence is an ambitious word. Its range of connotations includes not only a particular set of mental functions but also the value-laden concepts of appropriateness, competence, and potential. As the moral philosopher Hare (1963) has noted, such terms tend to masquerade as purely descriptive but actually function in discourse to promote or endorse certain types of action; that is, they have "secondarily prescriptive" meaning (Serpell, 1974). Thus, when someone tells a parent that his or her child is "very intelligent," he or she is implicitly conveying some advice – advocating a certain attitude toward the child that might translate in practice, for instance, into setting high goals for the child's future achievement, investing in the child's education, or even tolerating a certain amount of deviance. A wide range of mental attributes are clustered under the descriptive meaning of the term

---

* The definition of culture has been a subject of extended debate summarized by Kroeber and Kluckhohn in 1952. For recent discussions of its meaning in cultural psychology, see Cole (1996), Miller (1997), & Shweder (1990), and in cross-cultural psychology see Berry, Poortinga, Segall, & Dasen (1992).

intelligent in contemporary English usage, including "clever, sensible, careful, methodical, inventive, prudent, acute, logical, witty, observant, critical, experimental, quick-witted, cunning, wise, judicious, and scrupulous" (Ryle, 1949, p. 45). In the United States and other English-speaking industrialized societies, a person with these characteristics is thought of as especially well placed to thrive within the academic domain and, more generally, to succeed in life.

The contemporary American understanding of these connotations draws on a web of meanings (Geertz, 1983) that informs people's lives as members of a particular society or community. In a society without schools, by contrast, the range of concepts available for describing the mind or behavior of an individual and expressing admiration for that person is liable to be connected with a different web of meanings. For instance, in the subsistence, agrarian societies of Africa, social cohesion is traditionally nurtured through a strong emphasis on cooperation and responsibility. Child-rearing practices in these societies aim to guide the developing minds of children toward those cultural values by requiring them to share with peers, to show respect for elders, and to care for younger children (Erny, 1972; Nsamenang, 1992; Rabain, 1969). The salience of these indigenous, traditional cultural values has been documented for several African cultures in the pattern of discourse about young people's behavior and intelligence (e.g., Bissiliat, Laya, Pierre, & Pidoux, 1967; Fortes, 1938).

A few studies have explored in detail the indigenous terminology of intellectual assessment in rural African communities (Dasen et al., 1985; Kingsley, 1985; Serpell, 1977; Super, 1983). In the central African language Chi-Chewa,* my Zambian informants convinced me that the key concept of *nzelu* (which means both wisdom and skill) includes the notions of cleverness (-*chenjela*) and ability to take responsibility (-*tumikila*). To qualify for the designation *wo-tumikila* (literally, a person worthy of being sent on errands), one must be both *wo-mvela* (attentive, understanding, and obedient) and *wo-khulupilika* (trustworthy). At the heart of this web

of meanings lies the principle that cleverness can be deployed either selfishly or in a socially productive way and that only when it is deployed responsibly is it worthy of our admiration (Serpell, 1993). A similar theme appears to inform the concept of *ng'louele* in the West African language Baoule according to the inquiries of Dasen and his Ivorian colleagues (Dasen, 1984; Dasen, Barthelemy, Kan, Kouame, Daouda, Adjei, & Assande, 1985).

Readers who received their primary socialization in an urban industrialized society may be inclined at first to view such interpretations as remote from the realities of their "modern" world. Yet a sample of the general public in an American city polled by Sternberg, Conway, Ketron, and Bernstein (1981) included in their concept of "an ideally intelligent person" such characteristics as "accepts others for what they are" and "has a social conscience." Indeed, when their ratings of various characteristics were factor analyzed, a whole cluster of characteristics emerged in these American "laypersons" collective representation of intelligence that the authors labeled "social competence." This factor, however, was conspicuously absent from the ratings of the same set of characteristics by a panel of American psychologists doing research on intelligence. According to the "experts," there are two main factors that define what we mean by intelligence: problem-solving ability and verbal skills. Because these aptitudes can occur with or without social competence, teachers and other professionals in the United States readily acknowledge the possibility that a child who behaves antisocially at school might even be intellectually gifted. Yet, a sample of teachers and parents in Japan (another highly industrialized society) reacted to such a suggestion with puzzlement. As one of them put it, "If he's so smart, how come he doesn't understand how to behave better?" (Tobin, Wu, & Davidson, 1989).*

In recent years, some American researchers have taken up the notion of a social dimension of intelligence (Gardner, 1983; Goleman, 1995), arguing that an individual's capacity to adapt to the full range of

---

* Also known as Chi-Nyanja, the language of the lake, referring to Lake Malawi, in whose general region it is spoken by some 10 million people.

* The wording cited here is that used on the videotape accompanying this book (also available from Yale University Press) but does not feature verbatim in the text, which however includes a detailed discussion of this and other Japanese interpretations of the same child's behavior and intelligence on pages 23–28.

demands of everyday life in American society calls for more than the analytical skills emphasized in standard IQ tests, which are mainly relevant to the performance of academic tasks. The wide readership these books have attracted suggests that they resonate with important preoccupations of contemporary American culture, which is one of the preconditions for a new idea to catch on in social science (Serpell, 1990). On the other hand, they have also encountered substantial resistance in academic circles – often considered the arbiters, if not the authorities, on what constitutes the mainstream of a society's culture. Several researchers have objected that to include social and emotional attributes under the heading of intelligence merely serves to obscure important technical distinctions between cognition and motivation, between ability and disposition, and between general competence and special talents. Sternberg (1997) observed that rather little empirical research has been conducted to date to validate Gardner's theory of multiple intelligences but also includes a social dimension in his own theoretical conception of practical intelligence for which he has accumulated substantial empirical support (e.g., Sternberg et al., 1996).

On the "lay" side, one might argue that a theoretical system that runs counter to received wisdom in the wider society runs the risk of being ignored by the public as irrelevant or even rejected as alien (cf. Joynson, 1974). The risk of academic theories becoming alienated from the mainstream of the culture appears to be particularly great in Third World countries where the "ivory tower" stereotype gains credence from its small numerical size, and from the tendency for much of its publication to be oriented toward the criteria of Western academia (Kashoki, 1979; Moghaddam & Taylor, 1986; Serpell, 1990; Sinha, 1986).

I shall argue in this chapter that as scientists and professional practitioners have sought to operationalize the construct of intelligence for purposes of research and policy formulation, they have drawn *unself-consciously* on the topical preoccupations of their particular historical epoch. Doing so may have enabled them to address some of the pressing needs of their particular social circumstances, but it has also narrowed the field in ways that need to be unpackaged and reformulated in much broader, less definitive terms if they are to have even faintly plausible applicability to the concerns and needs of other social groups in other places and in other times. At the end of the chapter I shall return to this theme and suggest, in the light of various examples discussed below, that three key themes running through the dominant Western cultural conception of intelligence have established a spurious orthodoxy in the context of a worldwide hegemony in the field of assessment: decontextualization, quantification, and biologization.

THEORIES OF COGNITIVE DEVELOPMENT IN CULTURAL CONTEXT

Within the human species,[*] the notion of intelligence as a capacity for understanding presupposes the significance of a subjective domain of thought that reflects and informs observable behavior. People not only act on the world and interact with other people, they also think about the world, represent it, and communicate with one another about their ideas (Bruner, 1990; Serpell & Boykin, 1994; Shweder 1990). Understanding the world involves inferences from the observable about what caused it and what it means. Some aspects of cognition manifestly change over the course of the life span: Infants, for instance, do not use language to represent the world, and toddlers often ask questions that reveal an incomplete understanding of the physical and social world.

The study of how these changes take place is known in the contemporary mainstream of psychology as the field of cognitive development. At least three broad strands of theory can be discerned within the field's vast literature: the genetic–epistemological perspective defined by Piaget (1983) and his colleagues and subsequently elaborated with important modifications by several neo-Piagetian scholars; the sociocultural–historical perspective originating from Vygotsky (1962, 1978) and elaborated by neo-Vygotskian scholars such as Cole (1975, 1996), Rogoff et al. (1990, 1995), and Wertsch (1975, 1991); and the information-processing

---

[*] Although a thriving field of research has focused on the "intelligence" of animal species other than humans (see Chapters 10 and 11 of this volume), I take the view that such terminology represents a metaphorical extension of the fundamental meaning of intelligence.

perspective (Siegler, 1991) that flows from the so-called cognitive revolution in American experimental psychology inspired on the one hand by transformational linguistics (Chomsky, 1957) and on the other by the metaphor of the digital computer (Bruner, Goodnow, & Austin, 1956). The extrapolation and testing of Piaget's theory and methods of inquiry across a range of different cultures have been one of the most carefully documented cases of a quite general phenomenon: the export of concepts originating in the West to other societies (cf. LCHC, 1982; Serpell, 1976, 1984). Other examples are the experimental psychology theories of mediated learning, memory clustering, depth perception, and so on (e.g., Cole & Bruner, 1971; Deregowski, 1989; Wagner, 1981), and the social psychology of cognitive styles developed by Witkin (1967) and his colleagues (e.g., Berry, 1981; Okonji, 1980). I shall focus on Piaget's theory because it centers more directly on the concept of intelligence than the other cases.

According to Piaget (1972), intelligence constitutes a state of equilibrium in which understanding approximates closely to the world as it really is. Piaget's principal interest is in how this understanding is constructed over time through processes of active exploration and experimentation.* The mind of the infant acts directly on the world through sensory–motor reflexes that later give rise to the cognitive processes of representation and reasoning. These processes are progressively refined and elaborated in the light of practical experience, enabling a gradual emancipation of thought from the domination of perceptual appearances and culminating in a system of formal operations that corresponds to the hypothetico–deductive methods of the experimental scientist.

This account of cognitive development as a process of gradual discovery rests on several cultural premises of mainstream Western philosophy that purchase a certain kind of clarity at the expense of other types of understanding. Bordo (1987) has dis-

cussed the epistemological limitations of Descartes' (1637) *Discourse on Method* with its dualistic separation of mind from body and prioritization of detached contemplation over emotional and moral engagement, which inspired many aspects of Enlightenment scholarship in Europe in the 18th and 19th centuries (Berlin, 1956). Merchant (1980) argued that during this period the mechanistic orientation of the new science pervaded the whole of Western culture, fostering technological development and the Industrial Revolution and legitimating professional practices in medicine that alienated people from their intuitive sense of being connected with nature.

Furthermore, as Buck-Morss (1975) has pointed out, the teleological theme of progress toward an ideal end state of intellectual development fits well with the preoccupations of the dominant bourgeoisie of 19th-century Europe. Drawing on the philosophy of Kant, Piaget's theory construes the hallmark of intellectual development as the ability to separate form from content. Following Marx and Lukacs, Buck-Morss argues that such formalism serves to legitimate the exploitative social relations of Western industrial capitalism by focusing on the abstract exchange value of commodities in the marketplace rather than their social-use value and alienating workers from the object of their production. Although Buck-Morss goes out of her way to distinguish this "socio-economic bias in Piaget's theory" from a position of cultural relativism, her analysis clearly highlights the socially and historically situated character of Piaget's theory (cf. Serpell, 1995).

Reducing her argument to its central critique, Buck-Morss asks, "Do Piaget's cognitive stages mark progressive assimilation of the structural principles of bourgeois industrialism? Do his tests capture a prototypical comprehension of alienation, reification and exchange value?" (pp. 38–39). If so, to claim cross-cultural universality for the theory and its instruments implies claiming also that a universal pattern of socioeconomic transformation is the goal for all societies. In other words, the Industrial Revolution and its sequelae represent a kind of modernization or social progress to which all peoples everywhere would do well to adapt. Some intelligence theorists have explicitly made such a claim

---

* Piaget's theory draws on three of the Western academic traditions: epistemology, mathematics, and biology. At the most fundamental level, the adaptation of an organism to its environment is characterized by the complementary processes of assimilation and accommodation.

(e.g., Vernon, 1967), whereas others have contended that it represents an unwarranted form of cultural hegemony (e.g., Serpell, 1972).

A second line of cultural critique of Piaget's theory came from within the community of Piagetian researchers. Accepting the view of the child as an explorer of the environment, a large number of researchers in the 1960s and 1970s noted that the physical and social characteristics of that environment are very different in many parts of the world from the settings in which Piaget and his colleagues situated their pioneering studies. They therefore posed as an empirical question whether the sequence of understandings documented by Piaget would have any generality across a wider range of cultural settings. The verdict, as summarized by Dasen (1972, 1977), was that most of the concepts hold up rather well across a wide range of cultures and that the basic sequence does not change, but that the rate at which children progress from one stage to the next is highly variable across cultures, and that in many communities there is no evidence of adults achieving what Piaget defined as the logical end state of cognitive development, namely, the stage of "formal operational" thinking. Indeed, in several studies conducted in less-industrialized countries, even the stage of "concrete operations" that Piaget found characteristic of Genevan 8-year-olds was not achieved by a majority of adults.

Adopting a more restricted focus, and drawing on Berry's (1971) ecological model (cf. also Berry, Poortings, Segall, & Dasen, 1992), Dasen (1977) set out to test specific hypotheses about the rate at which children would achieve the stage of "concrete operations," depending on the demands of their ecological setting. As predicted, he found that children of nomadic, hunting, and gathering communities in the Australian desert or in the ice-clad regions of northern Canada began to give concrete operational responses to Piagetian tasks in the domain of spatial reasoning (about orders, rotation, and horizontality) at a younger age than children of a sedentary agricultural community in West Africa, whereas children of the agricultural community began to give concrete–operational responses to questions about "conservation" (of quantity, weight and volume) at a younger age than children of the hunting and gathering communities. Thus, the ecological press

for children to develop an understanding of different domains varies across cultures with predictable consequences for their rates of cognitive development in each particular domain.

The phenomenon of domain specificity has been cited by many neo-Piagetian scholars (e.g., Biddell & Fischer, 1992; Fischer, 1980; Gardner, 1991) as one of the weaknesses of Piaget's original theory, which emphasized *structures d'ensemble* as integrative principles that serve to maintain coherence of intellectual perspective across many domains. Feldman (1980, 1994) argued that much of the structure that Piaget imputes to the intellect is really inherent in the ways in which information is coded in the practices and artifacts of a given domain of cultural activity such as geography. A classic study by Price-Williams, Gordon, & Ramirez (1974) showed that even within a single community the economic activities of different households can have significant consequences for the rate at which children acquire particular cognitive competencies. Children in Mexican villages who participated in the family craft of pottery making were more advanced on Piaget's scale of conservation of quantity than children of non-pottery-making families in the same villages. Intriguingly, in one experiment the precociousness of the pottery-apprenticed children was confined to tasks involving judgments of conservation with continuous quantities such as clay and water, whereas in the other replication they showed advanced performance across a wide range of conservation tasks, including content quite remote from the materials of their craft.*

The degree to which intellectual competencies are general or specific forms the basis of a third line of cross-cultural critique that focuses on Piaget's methods of inquiry. If we attribute intellectual competence to an individual on the basis of his or her

---

* Gardner (1991) argued that constraints not only canalize development but also potentiate it. Sternberg (1984a,b) added to the list of contextualist considerations for understanding intelligence the need to recognize that human adaptation often takes the form of selecting or transforming the environment in which we live. Thus, a culturally relativistic analysis needs to include the potential of such creative strategies of adaptation to transcend existing cultural tradition. Indeed, according to most theorists, it is the adaptability of an individual, rather than his or her adaptation to the status quo that merits attention as a criterion of intelligence.

performance on a given task, to some degree we extrapolate from the behavior we observe in that context to a wider range of behaviors that we infer would be likely to be manifested by that person in response to other challenges in other contexts. Like many other cross-cultural researchers, however, I have been struck by a marked discrepancy between the range of scores obtained by children on Western tests designed to measure cognitive competence and the conspicuous signs of intelligence displayed by children at work in their domestic settings and at play with peers in their local neighborhoods. In Zambia, for instance, the widespread play activity of making toy cars from scraps of wire seems to demand perceptual skills that formally resemble those required by tests on which most Zambian children perform poorly.

An experimental study to elaborate this idea (Serpell, 1979) followed the same "cross-over" design as Dasen's (1977) research described above. Children living in two ecoculturally contrasting groups were compared on several tasks with the prediction that their different ranges of prior experience would enable each group to outperform the other on selected tasks. However, in my study, the cognitive processes demanded by the different tasks were closely equated. All the tasks involved pattern reproduction, but the patterns were presented for reproduction in four different media. A relatively familiar medium for the sample of urban Zambian children was wire, whereas a relatively familiar medium for the urban English children was pencil and paper. The other two media were chosen to be equally familiar to both groups: modeling clay, and the child's own fingers. As predicted, each group significantly outperformed the other on the task in a relatively familiar medium, whereas there were no differences between the groups in the two equally familiar media.

In Brazil, Nunnes, Schliemann, and Carraher (1993) and Saxe (1989) have made similar observations of a marked discrepancy between the mathematical competence displayed by children in the context of street vending and their performance of the same mathematical operations in the form of paper-and-pencil sums as these are taught at school. Schliemann, Carraher, & Ceci (1997) have reviewed a substantial literature on such manifestations of

"everyday cognition," and have drawn the conclusion that decontextualized tests of intellectual performance generally afford an invalid estimate of competence as it is usually deployed in real life. Some researchers have taken this argument a step further and suggested that cognition itself is socially distributed (Salomon, 1993), and thus that attribution of intellectual power to an individual is somewhat arbitrary.

By comparison with several other lines of investigation of cognitive development, Piaget's classic studies are remarkably rich both in the variety of stimulus materials employed and in attention to "ecological validity" – at least for the particular cultural setting of his children. Nevertheless, his theory, like most if not all the Western theory in this field before 1950, was weakly articulated with respect to the characteristics of the environment to which children's development must adapt. It is now widely agreed in developmental psychology that different human communities organize the physical and social environment so differently for their children that behavioral adaptation can only be understood and evaluated with reference to the constraints of a particular ecocultural niche (Gallimore, Weisner, Kaufman, & Bernheimer, 1989; Super & Harkness, 1986). But the implications of this rather evident conclusion have yet to be fully incorporated within the technology of intelligence test development. The niche has been characterized by Super and Harkness (1986, 1997) as comprising three distinct but dynamically interacting cultural systems. In addition to a particular range of physical and social settings, the niche to which a child's development must adapt is constrained by culturally regulated customs or practices of child care and childrearing and by the implicit models or "ethnotheories" of psychology shared among the adult caregivers. The content of these indigenous psychologies includes ideas about the nature of child development, socialization goals, and optimal intervention methods for promoting them (Serpell et al., 1997).

Among the various contemporary accounts of interaction between cognitive development and context (Serpell, 1993b, in press), Piagetian theory, like the behavior–analytic tradition of Skinner (1953), Gibson's (1982) ecological theory of perceptual development, and the information-processing theories

(Siegler, 1991), tends to treat context as a source of external stimulation. However, researchers inspired by Vygotsky (1978) prefer to construe context as an incorporating system of social activity (Bronfenbrenner, 1979) informed by a cultural system of meanings (D'Andrade, 1984). Language functions not only as an amplifying tool for individual cognition (Bruner, 1966; Cole & Griffin, 1980) but also as a means of social intercourse and of cultural continuity over the course of history. The developing child appropriates the system of meanings encoded in language and other shared cultural resources by participating in structured activities (Gallimore & Goldenberg, 1993). Individual differences in intelligence are less conspicuous as a source of explanation in these accounts, which tend to focus more on interdependent, interactive processes such as intersubjectivity (Trevarthen, 1980) and co-construction (Valsiner, 1991; Zukow, 1989) and on their potential to support the growth of competence within the child's zone of proximal development (Cole, 1975).

The study of developmental change in cognition is relevant to an understanding of intelligence in several ways: as an account of its ontogenetic origins, as a source of ideas about its character, and as a frame of reference for evaluating individual differences. Yet, paradoxically, very little of the elaborate theoretical conceptualization of cognitive development reviewed in this section is explicitly reflected in the design of intelligence tests even though these are subjected to frequent revision (cf. Gardner & Clark, 1992). Instead the rationale of the most widely used intelligence tests is generally phrased in broad speculative terms combined with statistical evidence of psychometric reliability and empirical correlations with external criteria such as academic achievement, which are advanced as evidence of "validity."

THE CULTURAL PRACTICE OF TESTING APTITUDE AND INTELLIGENCE

Intelligence testing is an historically situated cultural practice whose formal procedures and instruments reflect not only their manifest psychological functions but also the institutional arrangements within which those functions were conceptualized and the political and economic concerns that motivated the creation of those arrangements.

The cultural practice account of literacy advanced by Scribner and Cole (1981) defines a practice as "a recurrent, goal-directed sequence of activities using a particular technology and particular systems of knowledge" (p. 236). The term *practice* can refer either to a very broad domain of activity such as law or to a more specific endeavor such as cross-examination, but in each case the term refers to "socially developed and patterned ways of using technology and knowledge to accomplish tasks" (p. 236). Viewing literacy in this broader perspective enabled Scribner and Cole to "understand ... the social factors that operated in the past and that operate now to shape the contexts and nature of ... the literacy practices" of a particular society, the Vai of Liberia. Heath (1983) has used a similar type of analysis to delineate different literacies within the English-speaking population of the United States, focusing on the "literacy events" of everyday life as defining for different communities what it means to be literate. (cf. Goodnow, Miller, & Kessel, 1995, for other applications of the concept of practice in cultural psychology). One of the important consequences of situating literacy within the context of a particular set of sociocultural circumstances is to explode the myth of its "autonomous" capacity to empower the mind of the individual to see the world in a different way (Street, 1984). The technology of script is only as useful as the practice in which it is embedded.

Assessment of intelligence as a distinct, formally structured activity, is a product of very particular cultural arrangements. Parents and other agents of primary socialization routinely make such evaluative judgments in the course of everyday social interaction with children. For them to call on an expert to assist them implies a lack of confidence in those judgments. Two types of contexts in which the need for technical assistance is often felt are discussed in the sections on mental retardation and on educational selection, guidance, and placement below: when a child appears to be unable to function within the normal range expected for her or his age, and when competing for admission to a selective educational program. Just as the scope of verbal communication is transformed, in both empowering and limiting ways, by the shift from spoken to written language (Olson, 1977, 1994), so the use of formal standardized procedures imposes an ambiguous set of constraints on the process of intellectual assessment. So long as we remain aware of the nature of those constraints and their costs and benefits, the technology of psychometrics can be a valuable resource for informing responsible decision making. Many teachers, physicians, and administrators, however, find it convenient to delegate the process of assessment to psychologists as technical experts. Both within and beyond the confines of American society, this professionalization of intellectual assessment carries some significant dangers.

Foremost among these dangers is what may be termed the synecdochic error of confusing the measure with the construct. Overwhelmed by the seemingly endless debates about how to define intelligence, some analysts have resorted to the sterile and evasive formulation that intelligence *is* what IQ tests measure. A close analysis of the instruments that purport to measure intelligence, however, reveals that the rationale for many of their particular features is not genuinely technical in the sense of enhancing the efficiency with which it performs its intrinsic functions of reliable assessment. Some of these *extrinsic* features reflect latent political and economic biases in the methodology of test development, and some of them clearly violate the premises of indigenous cultural practices in social groups to which they are applied. The "packaged" format of commercially marketed tests masks such distinctions with the result that software is effectively "buried in the hardware" – a phenomenon that may easily degenerate into "uncovenanted cultural transmission" (Cherns, 1984).

The technology of mental testing emerged from a change in the social arrangements in industrialized countries determining access to public basic schooling at the turn of the 19th to 20th centuries and was applied soon thereafter to the process of sorting adult recruits to the army into categories suited to training for different occupational roles within the mobilization of American troops for the First World War in 1917. The efficiency criteria of military mobilization bear a disturbing similarity to those governing tracking and progression in large public school systems: In both contexts, rapid, low-cost administration is perceived as a valuable feature of assessment procedures, as is their output of a re-

liable, easily interpretable index for decision-making. Considerations of impartiality became significant at a later stage in the history of mental testing and will be discussed in the section on cultural load and cultural bias below. Arguably, these were a secondary by-product of the primary efficiency criteria of speed, cost, simplicity and reliability.

The first impetus for systematic testing of intelligence originated in the context of a pattern of social reform that took place all over Europe and in the United States around the beginning of this century. Public policy in this period for the first time addressed in earnest a political program that had been advocated by social reformers for more than two centuries: the universalization of schooling. Literacy, schooling, and intelligence have become intimately linked within the orthodoxy of institutionalized public basic schooling (Serpell & Hatano, 1997) primarily as a result of sociocultural commitment to a particular set of institutional arrangements for imparting certain skills to children in a specific period of their development. Although it has been replaced in modern times by standardization with reference to the statistical concept of "normal distribution," the early emphasis of intelligence test construction on the developmental concept of growth is instructive. There is no logically necessary connection between the age of a child and his or her acquisition of the skills of reading, writing, and arithmetic, or the information encoded in the literate practices of a given community. But to grow up normally in Western society has become equated with progressing through an age-graded school curriculum at a standard rate. Thus, it made sense for Binet to include in his test of "normal" cognitive competence among French 8-year-olds in 1906 items that depended on a familiarity with numerals, writing, and line drawings, and it still makes sense in the 1990s to use such items for the assessment of intelligence in American 8-year-olds. In most parts of Africa, however, in 1906, such items would have been totally inappropriate for assessing the intelligence of 8-year-olds because literacy was still the province of a tiny elite, as it had been in earlier centuries in Europe. Even in the 1990s, it would be hazardous to use such items in many rural areas of Africa because only a small minority of local children are enrolled in school by that age, and scarcely any pictorial materials are available in their homes (cf. Serpell & Deregowski, 1980).

The curriculum of Western basic education only acquired its current paradigm of age-by-grade matching over a period of several centuries (Serpell, 1993a, 1995; Serpell & Hatano, 1997). Even to this day, literacy is acquired in some societies in a much more informal way (Scribner & Cole, 1981). According to Aries (1960), the institutionalization of schools in medieval Europe for instruction in the basic skills of reading, writing, and arithmetic initially grouped together students ranging widely in age, and the convention of separating students into classes of students with different levels of competence was established over several centuries with little or no reference to chronological age. Yet, by the time the social reformers began to push for mandatory universal basic education in the late 19th century, the range of ages enrolled in first grade had shrunk dramatically, and a corollary assumption had become part of educational orthodoxy, namely, that there is a *correct* age at which a child should first be enrolled in school.

Against this background, the ability of a child of a given age to perform those tasks normally assigned to his or her age group at school seemed to Binet an appropriate index of intellectual normality. Moreover, because the purpose of testing was to establish whether the child was intellectually fit for school enrollment, any narrowness of this field was easily excused on grounds of functional relevance.* However, Andersson-Levitt's (1996) comparative ethnography shows how the unilinearity and arbitrariness of the age-graded curriculum tends in both France and the United States to legitimize a social process of sorting and stigmatization under the disguise of maturational theory. Her analysis shows how the particulars of instructional practices mesh with each society's institutional policies and are framed by teachers in terms of an ideological construction of learning to read as if negotiating a racetrack (or obstacle course). She argues that the same conceptualization informed Binet's approach to the measurement of intelligence, and thus, "for all educators' talk about immaturity, schools operate over the long run to ensure that most failing children look 'stupid', not 'immature'" (pp. 73–74).

The consequences of its unique social history for the organization of the cultural practice of intelligence testing are momentous. We need to consider not only how tests are designed and administered but also how their results are communicated to outside audiences and how that information is interpreted by the recipients, many of whom will have much longer-lasting responsibility for the programming of the child's future developmental opportunities than the tester.* Parents, as noted earlier, have been shown to hold definite views about what constitute appropriate indices of their child's cognitive status and about appropriate ways of enhancing it in the course of home socialization. Many parents also hold definite views about the responsibilities of schooling in their child's intellectual development, and these are quite variable across cultural and subcultural groups (Okagaki & Sternberg, 1991; Stevenson, Chen, & Uttal, 1990).[†] But these ideas do not necessarily closely match those of school teachers or psychologists responsible for authoritative formulations on these matters, and a mismatch can have dire consequences for the child, as will be discussed in detail in the sections on mental retardation and on education selection, guidance, and placement below.

In the early 1970s a great debate erupted in American society about the degree to which an individual's intelligence is influenced by educational experience. The primary stimulus for the debate was an article published in the *Harvard Educational Review* provocatively entitled "How much can we boost IQ and scholastic achievement?" In it the author (Jensen, 1969) claimed that compensatory

---

* The arbitrariness of these criteria, however, becomes clear once the schooling practices are varied with respect to age. In Sweden, for instance, children are expected to enroll in the first grade at age 7, whereas in France and the United States the normal age of enrollment is 5.

* At one distinguished American center known to the author, an average of many hours of work is invested by each member of a team of five or six professionals in assessing the level of functioning of an individual child and co-constructing a diagnosis and referral plan, but scarcely any of the clients are followed up to assess whether the IPP has been implemented or has been found to be beneficial to the recipients.

† Super (1983) found that the Kipsigis people of Western Kenya had a different name for school intelligence to distinguish it from the regular intelligence that contributes to adaptive behavior in everyday life. In Zambia I have discussed a similar compartmentalization of thinking about the intellectual demands of home and school among primary school teachers (Serpell, 1993).

educational interventions such as Operation Head-start had failed to make any lasting impact on the school performance of children born into economically disadvantaged sectors of American society, that this was demonstrably due to enduring limitations in the intellectual capacity of such children to benefit from education, and that genetic factors, some of which can reliably be indexed by "race," were responsible for the association between social class and capacity to benefit from education. In short, intelligence was held to be highly "heritable." This thesis drew heavily on a long tradition of research with identical twins (whose genetic makeup is identical), some of whom were separated early in life and thus received their primary socialization in different families. Many criticisms were advanced against both the research and the conclusions drawn from it about the potential of educational intervention to raise children's level of functioning. But other scholars leaped to Jensen's defense, arguing that his thesis, although politically sensitive, was scientifically valid (see Chapter 4 in this volume for a review of these issues).

In the 1980s the debate flared up again following allegations that Burt had fraudulently concocted a substantial portion of the famous twin study data (Kamin, 1974; Mackintosh, 1995), to which Jensen and his colleagues replied that many other data collected by different researchers supported the same conclusions.

In 1994, many of the same issues were revisited in a book coauthored by a psychologist and a political economist (Hernnstein & Murray, 1994). The book is entitled *The Bell Curve*, an allusion to the line graph of the normal statistical distribution on which many of the techniques of psychometric standardization are based. In addition to the data on average differences in IQ test scores by different racial groups, these authors focused on trends in scores over time, arguing that the higher fertility of lower-class social groups poses a dysgenic threat to the pool of talent in the nation. This line of reasoning is reminiscent of that advanced in the 19th and early 20th centuries by the "Eugenic movement," which advocated "racially" selective immigration control and even compulsory sterilization as public policies designed to afford a reproductive advantage to the bearers of genes thought to underlie higher intelligence (Cravens, 1978; Thomas, 1982).

As Gould (1981) has noted in an influential critique, the data advanced to support those arguments were often fictitious, and their proponents were ostensibly motivated by an oppressive political agenda. On the other hand, many defenders of the thesis of IQ heritability have complained that an authoritarian adherence to egalitarian dogma, protected by considerations of "political correctness," has driven opponents of the thesis to suppress its public presentation, thus reducing the prospects for open and democratic debate.*

Both sides in the debate have accused the other of being motivated by ideological rather than "purely scientific" concerns (Mackintosh, 1995), a charge that is probably valid but also somewhat naive. The origins of psychological testing were so heavily tied into political conflict that as early as 1916 Terman wrote of "racial differences, which cannot be wiped out by any scheme of mental culture," and Dubois of "the new technique of psychological tests, which were quickly adjusted so as to put Black folk absolutely beyond the possibility of civilization" (cited by Dent, 1996). As I shall seek to explain below, the very essence of what is meant by intelligence and the methodology of assessing it are problematic issues central to an intense and enduring public debate in the forum of contemporary American society.

Two responses to the latest phase of the debate have recently been published, each of them designed in a different way to articulate an authoritative professional position on the strengths and limitations of psychometric technology. The first, a multiauthored statement of "mainstream science on intelligence," was originally published as a paid advertisement in a daily newspaper that specializes in coverage of the stock market, *The Wall Street Journal*, and subsequently reprinted with some contextual background in the academic journal *Intelligence* (Gottfredson et al., 1994 and 1997). The second, entitled "Intelligence: Knowns and Unknowns," was the report of a task force commissioned by the principal professional organization for psychologists in the United States, the American

---

* For instance, Jensen in the 1970s and Murray in the 1990s, as well as a number of other researchers in this tradition over the intervening years, were often the target of student demonstrations designed to prevent them from addressing audiences on university campuses.

Psychological Association, and published in their broad readership academic journal *The American Psychologist* (Neisser et al., 1996). It is interesting to note that even though the multiple authorship of these two documents includes some overlap (Professors Bouchard, Loehlin, and Perloff), the perspectives they offer on intelligence contain several substantial points of contradiction. For instance, the "mainstream science" manifesto states categorically that

Intelligence is a very general capability...It is not merely book learning, a narrow academic skill, or test-taking smarts. Rather it reflects a broader and deeper capability for comprehending our surroundings ...

and goes on to claim that

intelligence, so defined, can be measured, and intelligence tests measure it well (p. 13).

In contrast, the "knowns and unknowns" report summarizes its introductory survey as revealing

a wide range of contemporary conceptions of intelligence and how it should be measured,

concludes that

The psychometric approach is the oldest and best established, but others also have much to contribute,

and cautions that

We should be open to the possibility that our understanding of intelligence in the future will be rather different from what it is today (p. 80).

How may these two authoritatively phrased pronouncements be reconciled? One possibility* would be to construe intelligence tests as valid measures of a narrow range of cognitive skills that are unevenly represented across different cultural groups in U.S. society and hold different significance for different cultural groups. Although this may be a tenable position, however, it does not appear to be the view of

the authors of the "mainstream" statement, who explicitly underline the breadth and generality of the construct they claim to be validly measurable.

A related, and especially significant, difference between these two contrasting summaries of the field is their approach to the topic of cultural bias, which will be discussed in the section on cultural load and cultural bias in testing of intelligence below.

Psychologists around the world may be regarded as members of a geographically distributed community of practice (Lave & Wenger, 1991), especially with respect to their shared technology of mental testing. In the following two sections, two major applications of standardized intelligence testing will be discussed with reference to the particular needs for cultural adaptation that they demand. I shall argue that we need to foreground the fact that assessment of intelligence is fundamentally an evaluative judgment made by one human about the behavior of another based on social interaction and the projection of that judgment onto a future scenario over which the assessor has limited control. Using psychological tests as "instruments" in arriving at this judgment does not relieve the tester of the responsibility for that judgment and its consequences.

MENTAL RETARDATION AND LEARNING DISABILITIES

One of the most potent applications of the technology of psychological testing takes place in the context of medical diagnosis of mental retardation (cf. Chapter 12 in this volume). According to the World Health Organization (WHO, 1975) and the American Association for Mental Retardation (AAMR, 1992), the condition of mental retardation is defined by a combination of three criteria: (1) significantly subaverage intellectual functioning, (2) impaired adaptation relative to social expectations, and (3) manifestation during the period of child development. Assessment of an individual child's status on the first of these criteria is typically referred by modern physicians to a psychologist, who submits a report based on the application of a standardized test of intelligence, whereas the second is based primarily on informal inquiries from the child's family, a report of academic performance at school, or both.

Interpretation of the significance of this condition in Western cultures has given rise to considerable

---

* I am grateful to Dewi Smith, Steven Gorny, Brenda Haynes, and Yolanda Vauss-Berry, for helping me to clarify this issue in the context of our graduate seminar at UMBC on Cultural Aspects of Human Development, and to Dewi Smith for her subsequent assistance with compilation of the bibliography for this paper.

debate over classification and terminology (Clarke & Clarke, 1985). The classical medical terms "idiot" and "imbecile" are now widely regarded in Britain and the United States as offensively derogatory and unacceptably stigmatizing. The generic expression *mental deficiency*, widely used early in the century, has given way for similar reasons to *mental retardation* and *mental handicap*. Mittler and Serpell (1985) have summarized various social and technical considerations favoring the expression *intellectual disability*, whereas Fryers (1984) argued the case for *intellectual impairment*. Neither designation, however, has achieved wide currency. In the remainder of this discussion the abbreviation MR–ID will be used to refer to the condition with a minimum of surplus connotations.

In the case of severe degrees of MR–ID, research tends to suggest the presence of organic causes (Kushlick, 1966; Roberts, 1952; WHO, 1985), whereas the milder degrees have sometimes been designated as "sociocultural" in origin. Whatever its origins, mild MR–ID appears primarily to represent impaired adaptation to the demands of formal schooling because most of the individuals so designated in childhood cease to feature as a significant burden on the social services during adulthood (Richardson & Koller, 1985). Even in cases of relatively severe MR–ID, it is clear that "impaired adaptation relative to social expectations" represents an interactive relation between the individual and the environment, recognition of which has led the AAMR (1992) to propose a more dynamic definition that "assumes that the functioning of an individual can improve with the right supports." Warrant for this optimistic assumption can be derived from the growing visibility in Western cities of persons with Down's syndrome utilizing public transport and supermarkets without supervision. Many researchers and policymakers now prefer to represent physical and mental disabilities as a three-stage process: impairment – disability – handicap. Organic impairment (arising from genetic causes, disease, or injury) gives rise (unless secondary preventive measures are taken) to functional disability, which in turn places the individual at risk for handicap. The degree to which a functional disability is handicapping depends on social factors, including cultural beliefs and practices. Thus, individuals with MR–ID may be stigmatized as incompetent in the cultural context of IPBS but may be effortlessly included in the everyday social life of some subsistence agricultural communities (Serpell, 1989) and may even be accorded special privileges within the religious institutions of some societies (Miles, 1995, 1996).

A peculiar problem arises in this field from the quantitative operationalization of intelligence on a single dimension. Classification of an individual child as falling into one of the categories of normal intelligence, or of mild, moderate, or severe MR–ID tends to place his or her test scores on one or another side of quite arbitrary borderlines. Indeed, the zone between low normal intelligence and mild MR–ID has sometimes been labeled "borderline mental retardation." Moreover, in different epochs the dividing line between mild and moderate MR–ID has been shifted from IQ = 51–52 to 49–50 (Clarke & Clarke, 1985). When this degree of arbitrariness became known alongside striking differences in the diagnostic rates of MR–ID across ethnic groups, the general public understandably became suspicious that some type of measurement bias might be distorting the pattern of diagnosis and referral. More specifically, for instance, Tomlinson (1974) in the United Kingdom and Harry and Anderson (1994) in the United States, argued that children of disadvantaged minority ethnic groups were systematically overrepresented in school classes reserved for children with special needs, and that this represented a latent abuse of psychometric technology to promote socially discriminatory educational practices.

Opponents of this view contend that, on the contrary, psychometric approaches to assessment serve to minimize the scope for prejudice and that the higher proportions of children of particular ethnic groups in certain categories of low intelligence is merely evidence of the sociocultural and genetic disadvantage of those groups relative to others with respect to intellectual development. Assigning these minority group children to special educational classes, according to this position, is an act of remedial affirmative action calculated to redress historical injustices rather than to perpetuate them. The legitimacy of this counterargument depends on the degree to which special education is indeed attuned to the distinctive learning needs of children designated as MR–ID. Thus, although remedialism can theoretically be construed as a form of compensatory affirmative action, it may sometimes serve in practice to marginalize children of disadvantaged sociocultural groups still further.

Under the provisions of modern legislation, an enlightened policy prevails in many U.S. districts of requiring the consensual formulation of an Individualized Educational Plan for every child at an Admissions, Review, and Dismissal (ARD) meeting among several professionals from different disciplines and the child's parents. Harry, Allen, & McLanghlin (1995) reported on a longitudinal, 3-year study of the participation of 24 low-income African-American parents in special-education programs in a large urban school district. A recurrent experience of these parents was a process of disillusionment with what they initially perceived as "a benign and supportive intervention for their preschoolers," but eventually came to regard as "a potentially stigmatizing and limiting experience" (p. 373).

Particularly troubling in this compellingly documented account of the "preoccupation with compliance" displayed by apparently well-meaning professionals (many of whom were themselves African American) is the way in which the language of science, embedded in hyperliterate, bureaucratic procedures, was used to manipulate parents into formal acceptance of service arrangements they neither understood nor desired. Under current Federal U.S. law, case conferences are mandated in which parents are required to participate in the design of an individualized educational plan (IEP) for their child. Conceptually, such conferences are designed to focus the joint attention of several benevolent adults on the strengths and needs of an individual child and to generate cooperative, constructive discussion leading to an agreed plan of individually tailored education that will support the child's optimal development. Yet, "when parents were asked how they perceived their role in these conferences, the majority consistently replied that their main role was to receive information about their child's progress and to sign the documents" (p. 371).

The experience of these predominantly low-income African-American families stands in marked contrast to that of socioeconomically privileged American families that have successfully mobilized the diagnostic category of "learning disability" in recent years to protect their children's interests by affording them access to small classes in public schools, special tuition, and positive discrimination in admission to colleges (Sleeter, 1986; Sternberg & Grigorenko, in press). Thus, a privileged social class appears to have used their command of the language of power (Delpit, 1989) to appropriate the professional practices of diagnosis for purposes of class reproduction.

In Third World societies, the concepts of mild and borderline MR–ID appear even more vulnerable to misuse for exclusion of children of disadvantaged minority groups from educational opportunity than in the industrialized countries because the provision of special education of any kind is so limited that in practice many children identified as "slow learners" are excluded from school by silent consensus between teachers and parents (Serpell, Mariga, & Harvey, 1993). On the other hand, paradoxically, the condition of severe MR–ID may be quite amenable to a transculturally valid definition for a number of reasons. First, organic causes are demonstrable in many of these cases. Second, cross-cultural studies of cognitive development using theories such as Piaget's tend to reveal fewer differences in the earlier stages of ontogenesis. Third, data for the criterion of impaired adaptation relative to social expectations tend to be sought from the child's own family with the result that the criterion is adjusted to local cultural conditions. An international consultation among psychologists and psychiatrists in nine Third World countries revealed a high degree of consensus on assessment criteria for severe MR–ID across very diverse cultural settings (Serpell et al., 1989). The data, however, do not permit a definitive decision between the alternative hypotheses that the condition is clearly the same in all societies or that a particular nosology of Western science has pervaded the professional orientation of clinicians around the world.[*]

EDUCATIONAL SELECTION, GUIDANCE, AND PLACEMENT

A rationale for including estimates of general cognitive ability in the process of educational selection can be articulated in two different ways. The first rests on the elitist premise that instructional

---

[*] Similar considerations have been debated with respect to the concept of schizophrenia (WHO, 1975; Draguns, 1980).

resources should be invested in those persons with the greatest potential payoff. The other rationale centers on the principle of matching instruction to the learning characteristics of individual minds.

I have suggested in the preceding section on mental retardation that specifying the psychological construct of individual differences in intelligence is problematic in the field of mild MR–ID and specific learning disabilities. It becomes even more so in the field of superior intelligence and giftedness. Much of the research in this field has been driven by considerations of economic scarcity. Yet educational selection claims to draw on intelligence testing as a way of refining the match between students' aptitudes and the curriculum. A particularly troubling aspect of the rationale for this practice is the circularity with which tests are first validated with reference to educational outcomes and then used to predict the same outcomes as though they had some independent source of validity (Serpell, 1974, 1977; Sternberg, 1997). To the extent that the tests generated and used in this way are construed as measures of scholastic aptitude, the logic of the exercise is coherent, but educational selection is driven by a closed process of reproduction, allowing no room for student initiative to demand innovations in the curriculum. On the other hand, if the tests are to be construed more broadly as assessing intelligence, it seems clear that some independent criterion of validation is required other than the very activity for which they are to be used as a selection tool.

An interesting case study of the validity by academic and workplace performance norms of standardized test scores as admission criteria to a prestigious program of professional education was recently reported by Davidson and Lewis (1997). These authors analyzed examination scores and ratings of efficacy for a large sample of physicians trained over a 20-year period. During this time, the University of California at Davis School of Medicine operated an affirmative action program that admitted applicants from minority cultural backgrounds with lower test scores than those used to select from the general pool on grounds of "special considerations" designed to increase the representation of ethnic and cultural minorities in the medical profession. The school found that, although the trainees admitted with lower MCAT admission test scores consistently scored slightly lower than a control group on academic exams during their training, there was no significant difference between the groups in completion of residency training, evaluation of performance by residency directors, or completion of the requirements for certification. Moreover, after graduation the two groups moved into a very similar range of practices and expressed similar levels of satisfaction with their choice of career. The special consideration group expressed significantly higher overall satisfaction with their lives. Thus, it seems to have mattered much less how high a student scored on the MCAT once he or she was practicing medicine than during study and training.

As Harry and Anderson (1994) pointed out, admission to a program is only the first step in educational opportunity. What ultimately matters most is whether the education provided matches the abilities and aspirations of students (Allen & Boykin, 1992; Ciborowski, 1979; Cole & Bruner, 1971; Howard & Scott, 1981). Achieving such a match, especially when catering to the demands of a changing clientele, calls for adaptability on both sides – not only on the part of students, but also by curriculum developers and instructors. An ideological background that is shared by many of these African-American professionals is the principle of universal educability, encapsulated in the slogan "every child can learn." A recent study found that the same principle carries great weight with African-American teachers and tends to militate to some degree against the theme of "child-centered" individualization of instruction that dominates contemporary American educational orthodoxy (Akkari, Serpell, Baker, & Sonnenschein, in press; cf. also Delpit, 1989; Henry, 1996).

In Third World countries, the issue of bias in mental testing is less conspicuous than in the United States. Partly this may reflect the fact that inequities of educational opportunity across social groups tend to make psychological tests appear less biased against disadvantaged minorities than the most widely available alternative criteria for admission to higher levels of education, such as content-based tests of academic achievement. Another reason is the generally lower level of public information about the technology of psychometrics, which serves to protect the administrators of tests against informed criticism. But perhaps the most problematic reason for the low salience of the issue is a general, albeit largely latent and unquestioned, consensus in these societies on the desirability of achieving academic success within the boundaries of the existing academic curricula. These programs of "higher education" are widely viewed as definitive of a more advanced civilization than is enjoyed or understood by the general public and as holding the key to the nation's economic and social progress by generating an accumulation of "qualified manpower" equipped with technical knowledge essential for modernity. The underpinnings of this ideological package of technocracy and progressivist modernization are complex and sustained by international linkages (cf. Dore, 1976).

CULTURAL LOAD AND CULTURAL BIAS IN TESTING OF INTELLIGENCE

Drawing on the analyses of the two preceding sections, I return in this section to the perspective of intelligence testing as a situated cultural practice and argue that the topic of "test bias" has been formulated in various ways that reflect divergent sociocultural preoccupations arising from the agent's role in society. As I noted in the section on the cultural practice of testing aptitude and intelligence, American society has been gripped over a period of several decades by an intense and often acrimonious debate on how to use cognitive ability tests* to inform decisions about access to educational opportunity. The debate in this forum often tends to by-pass both the issue of how intelligence is to be conceptualized (with culture understood as a language) and how it is nurtured over the course of development (with culture regarded as a womb), and to focus instead on issues of social justice. Although there are undoubtedly grounds for attributing oppressive motivation to deliberate actions by particular agents in this scenario, I believe that the prevalence of biased uses of intelligence testing is best

understood as an indirect consequence of a basic inadequacy of the science that underpins the technology of intelligence testing, namely, its failure to acknowledge the cultural diversity of healthful, adaptive childrearing practices within the fundamental conceptualization of intelligence. The origins of this foundational flaw will be discussed in the next section.

According to the "mainstream science" manifesto (Gottfredson et al., 1997, p. 14),

intelligence tests are not culturally biased against American Blacks or other native-born, English-speaking peoples in the U.S. Rather IQ scores predict equally accurately for all such Americans, regardless of race and social class.

On the other hand, the APA task force report (Neisser et al., 1996, p. 93) draws a distinction between two senses of the term, bias: "outcome bias," and "predictive bias." According to the "outcome" sense, "the lower mean scores of African Americans reflect a bias in the intelligence tests themselves," which can be regarded as "just another example of a pervasive outcome bias that characterizes [U.S.] society as a whole," reflected in "average income, representation in high-level occupations, health and health care, death rate, confrontations with the legal system, and so on." The concept of "predictive bias" focuses more specifically on the function of intelligence tests as "predictors" of future performance in educational settings, and the report concludes that in this sense, "the tests do not seem to be biased against African Americans."*

A third sense in which tests can be construed as biased involves what I will term "sampling bias." The sample of knowledge and aptitudes contained in the major standardized tests of intelligence may be biased in favor of the range of skills, styles, and attitudes valued in the majority culture (and promoted within the developmental niche that it informs), according them priority over the range that is valued and promoted in minority cultural groups.

---

* In using this expression, I acknowledge the lead of Helms (1992), who makes the helpful point that the fine-grain distinctions drawn by many scientists among intelligence, aptitude, and attainment tests are in practice largely ignored by professionals and the lay public alike, who treat any formalized measure of cognitive functioning as a "test" along with all the trappings of legitimacy that term carries in modern societies.

* Indeed, detailed analyses by Jensen (1980) and others suggests that several IQ tests, such as Ravens Matrices, WISC, and even PPVT, as well as several more conspicuously culturally loaded academic aptitude tests such as the SAT and GRE predict academic performance as well for individuals from minority cultural groups as they do for individuals from the majority, or better.

Strikingly different conceptualizations of what constitutes intelligence were reviewed in the opening section when rural African communities were compared with those of urban Western societies. Within American society, Boykin (1984, 1986) has argued that certain aspects of an Afrocultural tradition shared among several indigenous African societies have continued to play a part in the socialization practices of certain segments of the contemporary African-American population, giving rise to the selective promotion of specifiable dimensions of human experience and behavior, such as communalism, affect, movement expressiveness, and verve. Moreover, he and his colleagues have conducted experimental studies confirming the hypothesis that educational methods designed to mesh with these cultural themes are particularly effective in achieving instructional goals with African-American students in inner-city schools (Allen & Boykin, 1992).*

Jensen (1980) has advanced yet another conception of bias focused on the inherent characteristics of the test. If a test is less adequate as a measure of intelligence for one population than another, he argues, then the rank order of difficulty of items may be expected to be different for the two populations. The finding that rank order of item difficulty in the Peabody Picture Vocabulary Test (PPVT) and Raven's Progressive Matrices remains quite stable across populations is interpreted by Jensen as evidence that the construct validity of the test is equivalent across cultures. This argument is somewhat similar to that of Piagetian theorists who argue that the constancy of the sequence of stages across cultures is evidence of the universality of the cognitive developmental processes. But the argument is much weaker in the case of tests such as the PPVT and Ravens Matrices because their items are not arranged according to a theoretical progression of cognitive structure as is the case for Piaget's stages. Whether or not readers are satisfied with such an approach to defining construct validity, it should be clear that it is irrelevant to the notion of "sampling bias." That the internal structure of the test remains constant in difficulty across different cultural groups tells us nothing about the equivalence of those groups' opportunities for acquiring the relevant abilities in their respective antecedent cultural contexts.

Concerns over outcome bias have generated a number of attempts to systematize "fairness," by making adjustments to enable members of underrepresented groups to gain access to educational opportunities they would otherwise be denied. Flaugher (1974) discussed four alternative versions of this approach, all of which disregard test content. As he notes, however, methods that involve merely "adding points" or "lowering the bar" amount to "avoidance of the issue for the psychometrician, in that it removes him from the focus of attention and turns the problem over to others for solution" (p. 7). Mercer's (1979) systematization of a method of adjusting raw scores to make allowance for various indices of social disadvantage such as socioeconomic status, home language, and ethnicity (SOMPAR) is open to the criticism that it violates technical assumptions of the standardization process on which it indirectly relies to claim validity for the test content (Messick, 1983).

Given that tests are used in educational selection to predict performance in a particular type of future cultural context on the basis of cognitive traits acquired in a quite different, antecedent cultural context, it seems clear that the content of the test needs to be sensitive both to the task demands of the future context and to the learning opportunities of the antecedent context. In response to the latter consideration, some researchers have attempted to incorporate indigenous cultural criteria into the design of assessment procedures. In Zambia, for instance, on the basis of experimental research described in the opening section of this chapter, a clay modeling version of the Draw-a-Person Test (Harris, 1962) has been developed and partly standardized (Kathuria & Serpell, 1996).

Church and Katigbak (1985, 1988) have reported, for a rural Philippines community, one of the most thorough attempts to develop an indigenous cultural mode of intelligence assessment (which they term "emic") and have compared it with a translated and content-adapted version of a standard Western test of intelligence (which they term "imposed etic," following Berry, [1969]; cf. Berry et al. [1992]. The indigenous mode involves application by a family member of an Adaptive Competencies Rating Form (ACRF), the content of which was derived from a survey of indigenous criteria similar to that carried out

---

* Serpell & Hatano (1997) have discussed how such cross-culturally variable values inform the educational practices of the different Sino–Japanese, Islamic, and Western educational traditions.

by Dasen and his colleagues in Cote d'Ivoire (1985), described in the first section. The ACRF comprises seven rating scales on which an adult family member rates the child. The scales measure skills that fall into two groups of competencies: barrio skills and responsibilities (including reports on the child's ability to perform everyday personal care functions, domestic chores, and outdoor livelihood activities, as well as initiative and perseverance in chores, and mannerly behavior) and verbal–intellective skills (covering the domains of literacy, numeracy, school performance, and verbal extroversion). Their "imposed etic" measure comprised a set of seven Western behavioral tests adapted to use local materials and language.* In one study they compared these various measures with respect to their predictive power for children's academic grades in the first three grades of the local school. As in the studies in rural African communities (Dasen, 1984, Dasen et al., 1985; Serpell, 1977, 1993), the indigenous assessments by rural Philippine parents generally bore no predictive relationship to children's success in first grade, with one exception. Indigenous ratings of first-grade children's verbal–intellective skills were reliably predictive of their concurrent school grades. The adapted Western behavioral tests, on the other hand, were predictive not only of concurrent academic scores by first-grade children but also of first-grade performance by children tested 2 years before they entered school.

Some readers might interpret these results as a validation of the "imposed etic" measure and as a vindication of their use for educational selection and guidance in non-Western societies. As the authors point out, however, the picture is complex because many analysts contend that the school curriculum itself is exogenous and thus serves as an "imposed etic" criterion of test validity. Moreover, the approach to assigning grades adopted by elementary school teachers is influenced by multiple considerations, some of which are quite particular to the dynamics of classroom interaction, to the school's relations with the community, or both. On this reading, indigenous informants may be sensitive and knowledgeable about the skills required for

their children's success in the local school and yet not perceive those skills as central to their indigenous conception of intelligence. Liddell, Lycett, & Rose (1997) have explored some of these issues in crowded, rural schools in South Africa. They found that the academic ranks assigned by teachers to their students in second grade were strongly predicted by mastery of simple curriculum skills such as counting, letter recognition, and handwriting, and by teacher ratings of attentiveness and helpfulness. By contrast, neither psychometric tests of broader competencies nor parent ratings of behavior were predictive of these academic achievement ranks.

According to some theorists (such as Vernon, 1967), the lack of correlation between indigenous home-based assessments of intelligence and children's academic achievement reflects the technological "backwardness" of indigenous culture and its irrelevance to success in the modern world. An alternative perspective on this mismatch construes the school culture as alien to that of the indigenous population. The latter view, which I have developed in my book *The Significance of Schooling* (Serpell, 1993a), has troubling implications for educational policy in societies that have adopted school curricula exported to them by their former colonial oppressors. First, by focusing on the demands of tasks that emanate from an exogenous culture (that currently dominates the design of the academy), assessment by Western standardized tests may tend to guide the selection process toward those individuals who, by accident or design, have made the fullest adjustment (acculturation) to the culture of the West (including both its characteristics that are positively valued in the host society and those that are viewed with skepticism or even outright rejected), rather than to identify the individuals with the broadest range of adaptability to the diverse demands of a rapidly changing society. Second, by ensuring that Western-acculturated students are admitted in large numbers and fare well in the imported curriculum, such educational selection may tend to inhibit enthusiasm for curricular innovation designed to serve the distinctive and emerging needs of a non-Western society better.

Similar concerns appear to me to be relevant to the process of educational selection in the 1990s in integrated American universities that aspire to serve a diverse cross section of the population. Although most ethnic and cultural groups in the United States

* This test battery included picture naming, detection of picture anomalies, object classification, picture assembly, oral definition of vocabulary, general knowledge and verbal comprehension, and block design.

aspire for some common resources, such as admission to prestigious universities or graduate programs, what they bring to those academic arenas and what they seek to derive from them may be quite different. Moreover, cultural diversity is valuable in such arenas for many reasons. A straightforward example is that people who speak Spanish will have certain advantages as teachers in Hispanic elementary schools, which will feed into the quality of a teacher training program (cf. Tharp, 1989). Many educational planners acknowledge that the college curricula developed in the 1960s are unlikely to be appropriate or adequate for students in the year 2000 as preparations for professional work in the United States of the next millennium. If we continue to select students from minority cultural backgrounds solely on their aptitude in cognitive domains emphasized by high schools geared to preparation for college entry in the 1970s, we are unlikely to diversify the cultural capital that college entrants bring to their further education.

Sternberg and Williams (1997) found in a recent study at Yale University that one of the tests widely used for selection among applicants to American graduate study programs in psychology was significantly predictive of several indices of outcome quality among men but not among women. As an explanation for this moderating effect of gender on predictive validity, these authors speculated that "certain complicating, non-ability variables might affect women's performance in graduate school more than men's performance, for example, concerns about role expectations or feelings of illusory incompetence" (p. 640). On the other hand, it is also quite possible that the most important intellectual strengths that women bring to a research degree program are just not sampled by the "Analytical" test of the Graduate Record Examination (GRE), just as the Verbal and Quantitative tests of the same exam failed to predict any of the outcome-quality indices for either women or men.

We may confidently predict, however, that at most universities around the United States, the GRE will continue for many years to be used as a major selection criterion for admission to doctoral programs in psychology. The practice is not only supported by long tradition but also permits considerable savings in time and effort by faculty. Yet, it may well serve to exclude significant numbers of potential scholars from the academic community by screening them out on largely irrelevant grounds. Moreover, because students from minority cultural backgrounds, in particular, are known to score significantly lower on average on these tests than students of European–American heritage with comparable college grades (ETS, 1996), they will continue to face considerable impediments to gaining access to programs of advanced education.

One way of situating the challenge for educational selection in a rapidly changing, culturally diverse society is to construe entry into higher education for underrepresented minority groups as analogous to cross-cultural immigration. In the United States, where testing for cognitive abilities has been most conspicuously institutionalized, the topic of test bias has attracted a great deal of attention because of the possibility that its prima facie impartiality may mask social injustices in the allocation of such benefits as educational opportunity and entry into professional occupations. Various language minority groups have lobbied with some success for the use of their indigenous languages for the assessment of their youth's verbal abilities (Laosa, 1984). But political advocates of the most conspicuously disadvantaged ethnic minority group have been less successful in identifying a tangible way of correcting for what they perceive as bias in standardized testing against African Americans.

Motivated by concerns over outcome inequities at both ends of the continuum of cognitive ability, a movement has begun to gather momentum in recent decades in the United States to design tests and measurements more appropriate to the distinctive situation and characteristics of the historically disadvantaged minority cultural groups. Helms (1992) poses the question, "Why is there no study of cultural equivalence in standardized cognitive ability testing?" Jones (1996, p. 9), on the other hand, argued that rather than searching for "etic," cross-culturally valid tests, "a more fruitful alternative activity – at least to understand and predict the behavior of African Americans – would be culture-specific tests and measures . . . not developed for use in comparative studies." He continues,

I believe it is now time for students of the Black experience to look inward in order to identify constructs, behaviors, and ideas that explain African American culture and African American behavior on their own terms. In order to accomplish this goal, culture specific constructs and assessment instruments will be necessary.

The *Handbook of Tests and Measurements for Black Populations* Jones (1996) that Jones' chapter introduces contains a total of 78 chapters in 2 volumes. This ambitious undertaking is not confined to the field of intelligence. Apart from six chapters on "cognitive approaches and measures," other sections are devoted to such topics as self-esteem, attitudes, coping strategies, values, world-view, acculturation, identity, stress, and organizational variables. In addition to the sheer volume and scope of these endeavors, a striking feature of the handbook's treatment of intellectual functioning is the emphasis on identifying positive rather than negative characteristics. As Patton (1996) puts it, assessment should assume that the learner "brings something to the table," that is, should focus on identifying strengths, and should be empowering, that is, should identify and mobilize supportive resources in the home and community. Chapters by Hilliard & Cummings (1996), Hamilton (1996), and Jackson (1996) are all concerned with the identification of giftedness.

Those authors in the handbook who acknowledge the social demands placed on practicing school psychologists to identify children with impaired intelligence and special needs (Dent, 1996; Taylor, 1996) stress the responsibility of the assessment process to generate promising suggestions for remedial intervention, and, whenever possible to locate such intervention within the mainstream of educational provision, rather than risk the stigmatizing consequences of segregation. Dent (1996) argued that an acceptable, nonbiased assessment model must serve to identify a specific problem and relate the results to specific instructional interventions.* This is consistent with the general principle that assessment of

---

* Dent links this concern to a critique of the disease model for diagnostic classification as "in the opinion of this writer, totally inappropriate in education." I have made a similar case for the inappropriateness of construing the various forms of intervention currently advocated for the promotion of literacy development as analogous to medical prescriptions (Serpell, 1997b). Dent favors dynamic assessment (an approach to assessment that examines the progress of the individual within his or her zone of proximal development) and also advocates a focus on evaluating the referral process by examining statistics and making on-site observations in class and at home.

childhood disabilities should always serve as a guide to action (Serpell, 1988).

Given the wide range of contrasting perspectives considered in this section on whether and, if so how, standardized tests of intelligence are biased, what guidelines can be offered for contemporary practice pending the outcome of future research? Tests, in my view, need to be treated as minor elements of a broad repertoire of assessment resources. As packaged formalizations of an inherently labile construct, they should be viewed as dangerously tempting, labor-saving devices. Their standardization needs to be acknowledged as both a strength and a limitation, grounding them firmly in a systematic database, but by the same token restricting their relevance to the population for which they were designed. Before invoking any test procedures, a responsible professional charged with assessment must examine closely the cultural background of the individual client and ascertain whether any suitably standardized instrument is available. If, as will often be the case, an instrument is used that has been standardized on a culturally different population, great caution should be used in interpreting the scores, and the report should estimate the direction and degree of error likely to arise from taking them at face value. Above all, when advising others without training in psychology, the assessor should strenuously resist any pressure to summarize the assessment in the form of a single score such as an IQ, which misleadingly implies the availability of a technically valid and reliable frame of reference for ranking the individual relative to others. Rather, each test score, with a suitably moderated interpretation should be presented as part of a multidimensional profile of strengths and needs, together with suggestions for how each of these strengths and needs can best be responded to by the resources available in the particular context for which assessment is being conducted.

ENDURING CULTURAL THEMES ABOUT INTELLIGENCE AND THEIR PAROCHIAL HISTORY

In this concluding section, I discuss the culturally particular conception of intelligence that informs most of the standardized tests of intelligence in current use in the United States, which in turn have emerged from a tradition that has dominated the design of intelligence tests elsewhere around the world. The summary statement of "mainstream science" (Gottfredson, 1997) provides a succinct account of how this tradition conceptualizes intelligence and reflects three significant cultural themes in contemporary Western, industrialized societies: decontextualization, quantification, and biologization.

Decontextualization

The theoretical concept of decontextualization derives its strong survival value in the literature of Western cognitive and educational psychology from its ideological loading. In Western thought, there is a very pervasive notion that what is important about academic intellectual functioning is to detach oneself from context, to rise above it and generalize. Generality and abstraction are construed as generating a "view from nowhere" (Nagel, 1954, 1961) that serves as a legitimating frame of reference for the taxonomic, linear, time-budgeted conceptions of cognition prioritized in what Berger, Berger & Kellner (1973) have termed "the homeless mind," a product of industrialization and bureaucracy. These themes have probably attained priority in the dominant culture of Western industrialized societies partly for functional reasons of efficiency, but also in some cases because of irrational tradition. Moreover, the efficiency they afford has been purchased at a price that has been the target of criticism from many different angles.

Gilligan (1982), for instance, argued from a feminine perspective that Kohlberg's (1971) hierarchy of stages of moral development exaggerates the value of impartial justice at the expense of interpersonal sensitivity and loyalty – values that command higher priority in a morality of care better suited to the needs of women in contemporary American society. Nsamenang (1992) suggested, from a West African perspective, that attachment to place, rather than representing a myopic concreteness or a restrictively parochial insularity, can be a source of social and cultural belonging that affords the developing individual a powerful base for personal identity. And Ignatieff (1984), from a social historical perspective, contended that moral and social responsibility in the abstract tend to be sterile unless they are grounded in lived experience with, and commitments to, particular persons – a grounding that has

become hard to achieve in the fragmented and alienating neighborhoods of modern cities.

All of these philosophical themes imply a relativity of intelligence to particular cultural circumstances. Yet Sternberg (1997), in the tradition of Western theorizing, insisted that a candidate for the designation of a type of intelligence should be both necessary and universal. What can justify such a proposal from a self-styled "contextualist" (Sternberg, 1984)? According to his theory, "the mental processes are universal but their instantiations in context are not.... For example, everyone needs to set up strategies to solve problems, but the problems and what the best solutions are, differ" (Sternberg, 1998). Note that what is claimed to be universal is highly abstract and stands above and beyond any particular context. The interest in such decontextualized, explanatory constructs seems to reflect a domineering tendency that is deeply entrenched in Western thought: an ambitious desire for one's explanations not merely to illuminate a particular problem, to enhance the quality of communication among an identifiable set of communicating participants, but to lay down a general law applicable across all societies and for all time.

A recurrent puzzle when talking about culture concerns the degree to which it makes sense to talk about culture in the abstract. When we make statements of the form "all human societies organize the assessment of intelligence with reference to the prevailing culture," we speak as if it were possible to stand outside culture (outside any and all cultures) and to survey the range of the world's societies and their various cultures. Yet to a large degree this presumption is fictional. The very act of committing an idea to words (let alone publishing it in print) is constrained by a multitude of cultural factors. Languages evolve over long periods to serve sociocultural functions; communication about abstract concepts such as intelligence is a socioculturally situated activity, and so forth. Thus, although it might appear reasonable at first blush to characterize a review of research from a wide range of societies on intelligence as a supracultural intellectual endeavor, the very notion that it represents the field from no particular cultural vantage point is evidently untenable. Rather than a "view from nowhere," such a survey is more akin to the fantasy of the ancient Greeks that their gods look down on human affairs from the summit of Mount Olympus (Berrien, 1967). Although the choice of metaphor may seem at first to be technically peripheral to the question of validity of the undertaking, it may be morally informative. If I think of myself by analogy with a Greek god, the hubris of supposing that I can be objective in my evaluations is immediately apparent, whereas the ontology of modern science claims such objectivity as an axiomatic principle.

Quantification

It appears that there are several ways in which the particular culture can modulate the conceptualization of intelligence. At one level, the very structure of the grammar and lexicon may serve to prioritize certain foci. As Miles (1957) has noted, the primary focus of the concept is on how an individual acts (an aspect of the world most readily captured in English by an adverb, e.g., *intelligently*). The manner in which a person answers a question, tackles a problem, or approaches another person is judged to be intelligent if it displays understanding. By extension, an individual who often behaves in ways that merit that description may be regarded as *intelligent* in disposition – an enduring character trait. A further step of reasoning generates the abstract noun *intelligence* to designate the characteristic shared by individuals who often act intelligently. The grammar of the English language is such that we speak of people as "having" such characteristics as kindness, beauty, or intelligence. However these are not concrete entities or substances. Indeed in other languages there is no word that carries this polysemic potential of the English verb *to have*. In the Central African language Chi-Nyanja we say that someone "is with" *nzelu*, but other attributes do not have an abstract noun form, and thus the link between the individual and the attribute has to be expressed with a verb or an adjective: *a-chenjela; ndi wo-tumikila.*

The grammar of nominalization, however, is less significant as a source of culturally particular definition of the concept of intelligence than two additional features that arguably are facilitated by nominalization. The first crucial step is reification. As Gould (1981) has cogently argued, this is a conceptual error that has played an important part in the thinking of many theorists of intelligence. Things have a location (e.g., in the brain) and a magnitude that can be measured. But to talk of intelligence in

this way is to commit what Ryle (1939) called a category mistake. We can no more locate or measure intelligence, as the concept operates in ordinary language, than we can beauty or sophistication – not because science has not yet made sufficient progress, but because the logic of discourse about such phenomena does not allow doing with them what we do with objects. In the language of modern science, however, we do indeed measure intelligence, and the proposition has acquired meaning by analogy with other types of measurement. As Lakoff and Johnson (1980) have pointed out, a great deal of human thought (both everyday and scientific) invokes and deploys metaphors, many of which involve projection into our image of the mind reflections of our body image (cf. Johnson, 1987). Following Freud, we *push* unwelcome thoughts away, *are driven* by emotion to contemplate actions, *take refuge* in fantasies, and so forth. Thus, for intelligence to be conceptualized as a concrete entity of which some people have more than others, or that parents might pass on to their children as an inheritance, is not an exceptionally fanciful way of talking about a quality of mind. However, the distinction between metaphorical analogy and objective description became blurred, to say the least, when researchers at the turn of the century began measuring the cranial capacity of distinguished men's skulls in search of evidence that they had room in their heads for more intelligence than ordinary folks (Gould, 1981).

Despite the patent absurdity of that particular episode of the scientific study of intelligence, the predilection of Western science for quantification has persisted, and thus it sounds rather radical today to maintain that intelligence, just like "personal growth," (Illich, 1973, p. 45) "is not a measurable entity." The whole elaborate edifice of psychometrics can quite reasonably be construed as an exercise in pseudoquantification that gives rise to escalating levels of confusion and mystification. For example, the educational psychologist Bloom (1964) put forward the aphoristic proposition that "the 'half development' of intelligence occurs at age 4," meaning that, within the American population studied longitudinally, half of the variance among individuals' IQ test scores at the age of 18 is accounted for by their IQ scores at 4 years of age. However, a team of economists (Lewin, Little, & Colclough, 1983) mistook this to mean that half of the entity called intelligence has finished growing by the time a child reaches the age of 4 and went on to build on this idea to advance an argument about the best age at which to intervene with education programs to enrich and promote intellectual growth (Serpell, 1993a). Similar confusion often surrounds quantitative estimates of "heritability" of intelligence based on twin studies, and members of the lay public often misinterpret the percentages to refer to the proportion of the stuff called intelligence that is passed on genetically from parents to their children. Indeed, so much of the debate discussed in the three preceding sections has been shadowed in the popular press that the implicit cultural models held by much of the general American public about intelligence have by now probably incorporated potted versions of this simplistic metaphor, much as contemporary French common sense has incorporated some of the tenets of Freudian theory (Moscovici, 1985).

Biologization

The cultural theme of biological determinism in late 20th-century Western society reflects not only the dramatic recent advances in genetic engineering (and fertility control) but also the continuation of a trend set in motion in the 19th century: evolutionary determinism (cf. Dixon & Lerner, 1992).

The key theoretical point about the ontogenesis of human cognition to emerge from comparative psychology is surely that, relative to other species of organisms, humans have a uniquely elaborate and open-ended mode of structuring their own environment. The ecological niches to which humans are adaptively tuned are staggeringly varied, and (as Sternberg, 1984a,b, wisely insists) we cannot capture the nature of human adaptation to the environment by focusing on what is out there today, let alone what was there when we (the adults) were growing up. Yet this widely acknowledged variability across time in the demands of the environment to which adaptive functioning is required to be attuned is not matched in salience for American theorists with the variability across cultural settings at a given point in time. Whereas it seems obvious that a world with television, personal computers, and the Internet places different types of demand on the intelligence than did the worlds portrayed by Western novelists of the 19th century, it has not appeared so

obvious that the world of a child growing up in an inner-city neighborhood and that of a child growing up in a wealthy suburb in the 1990s also place radically different demands on the intelligence. Yet, as Flynn (1987) has argued, the resources at the disposal of different segments of America's population in the present era may well differ as greatly as those of the middle class across a period of 40 years (cf. Williams, 1998).

Why then has it become so fashionable among intelligence theorists to speculate about the possible biological bases of intellectual differences between ethnic groups? One reason seems to be the confusion between intragroup genetic variation and between-group variation. A good deal of knowledge has accumulated over the past few decades about specific biological causes of mental retardation, a number of which have become amenable to preventive or ameliorative intervention (Berg, 1985; Magnusson, 1996), and these options have been widely publicized. However, to make the leap from these data to a biological explanation of group differences, it is necessary not only to impute differences in academic achievement to differences in intelligence but also to conceptualize ethnic groups in biological terms. In the United States, where a long history of miscegenation is so conspicuous, the notion of separate gene pools hardly seems very plausible based on observation alone. The biological emphasis in so much lay and scientific reasoning about group differences in intelligence appears to be primarily driven by ideologically motivated myths. The mythology of race that achieved prominence in 19th-century European and American thought has been well documented (James & Rattansi, 1992). Interestingly, its targets have shifted during the 20th century without many of the concepts changing in character. Thus, much of the mischievously derogatory writing published in the popular press about the intelligence of Irish and Italian immigrants to the United States in the late 19th and 20th centuries bears an uncanny resemblance to the pronouncements of racist groups about the intelligence of people of African-American heritage in the second half of the 20th century (Chase, 1977).

It seems that the misuses of intelligence testing to rationalize and accord unwarranted legitimacy to hostile stereotypes of oppressed and stigmatized social groups is a feature not only of American society but of other societies too (Ogbu, 1978).

Paradoxically, the biologization of explanations in this domain may afford one of the clearest lines of evidence that intelligence is a culturally constructed idea. The particular manifestation of its cultural construction in contemporary "mainstream science" reflects a fusion of ideas derived from systematic research with a complex of irrational myths that resonates with popular preconceptions and thus makes this so-called "mainstream science" peculiarly susceptible to widespread public acceptance (Serpell, 1990).

CONCLUSION

In sum, the contemporary "mainstream science" conception of intelligence represents a highly selective account of an extremely broad range of human behavioral phenomena. The cultural constraints guiding that selectivity arise from a long epistemological tradition, from a pattern of social organization that has developed during the 20th century for industrialized economies and from a technology designed for a particular set of professional practices in education, medicine, and psychology. Outside that unique constellation of epistemological, social, and professional factors, the mainstream science view of intelligence is virtually unintelligible. And yet, it is deployed by professionals to accord a spurious legitimacy to patently inappropriate practices and even sometimes to justify irrational decisions that have the potential to cause significant harm to individuals and their families. This pseudolegitimation constitutes an abuse of science. Yet it is not necessarily malicious in explicit purpose. Assessment of another person's intelligence is often an important part of decision making, and it is difficult. To be able to fall back on a simple, standard procedure to arrive at a definitive conclusion is an appealing option. But it is very seldom adequate to the full range of criteria for making a wise and humane decision.

REFERENCES

AAMR (American Association on Mental Retardation) (1992). *Mental retardation: The new definition*. Washington, DC.

Akkari, A., Serpell, R., Baker, L., & Sonnenschein, S. (in press). A comparative analysis of teacher ethnotheories. *The Professional Educator*.

Allen, B. A., & Boykin, A. W. (1992). African-American children and the educational process: alleviating cultural discontinuity through prescriptive pedagogy. *School Psychology Review, 21*(4), 586–596.

Anderson-Levitt, K. M. (1996). Behind schedule: Batch-produced children in French and US classrooms. In B. A. Levinson, D. E. Foley, & D. C. Holland (Eds.), *The cultural production of the educated person: Critical ethnographies of schooling and local practice* (pp. 57–78). Albany, NY: SUNY Press.

Aries, P. (1962). *Centuries of childhood*. London: Cape (trans. from the French by R. Baldick).

Berg, J. (1985). Biomedical amelioration and prevention. In A. M. Clarke, A. D. B. Clarke, & J. M. Berg (eds.), *Mental deficiency: the changing outlook. Fourth Edition* (pp. 403–439). London: Methuen.

Berger, P. L., Berger, B., & Kellner, H. (1973). *The homeless mind: Modernization and consciousness*. New York: Random House.

Berlin, I. (1956). Introduction. In I. Berlin (Ed.), *The age of enlightenment*. New York: Mentor.

Berrien, F. K. (1967). Methodological and related problems in cross-cultural research. *International Journal of Psychology, 2*, 33–44.

Berry, J. W. (1969). On cross-cultural comparability. *International Journal of Psychology, 4*, 119–128.

Berry, J. W. (1971). Ecological and cultural factors in spatial perceptual development. *Canadian Journal of Behavioural Science, 3*, 324–336.

Berry, J. W. (1981). Developmental issues in the comparative study of psychological differentiation. In R. L. Munroe, R. H. Munroe, & B. B. Whiting (Eds.), *Handbook of cross-cultural human development* (pp. 475–499). New York: Garland.

Berry, J. W., Poortinga, Y. H., Segall, M. H., & Dasen, P. R. (1992). *Cross-cultural psychology: Research and applications*. Cambridge, UK: Cambridge University Press.

Biddell, T. R., & Fischer, K. W. (1992). Beyond the stage debate: Action, structure, and variability in Piagetian theory and research. In R. J. Sternberg & C. A. Berg (Eds.), *Intellectual development* (pp. 100–140). Cambridge, UK: Cambridge University Press.

Bissiliat, J., Laya, D., Pierre, E., & Pidoux, C. (1967). La notion de lakkal dans la culture Djerma-Songhai (The concept of lakkal in the Djerma-Songhai culture). *Psychopathologie Africaine, 3*, 207–264.

Bloom, B. (1964). *Stability and change in human characteristics*. New York: Wiley.

Bordo, S. (1987). *The flight of objectivity: Essays on Cartesianism and culture*. Albany, NY: SUNY Press.

Boykin, A. W. (1986). The triple quandary and the schooling of Afro-American children. In U. Neisser (Ed.), *The school achievement of minority children*. (pp. 57–92). Hillsdale, NJ: Erlbaum.

Bronfenbrenner, J. (1979). *The ecology of human development*. Cambridge, MA: Harvard University Press.

Bruner, J. S. (1966). An overview. In J. S. Bruner, R. R. Olver, & P. M. Greenfield et al. (Eds.), *Studies in cognitive growth* (Ch. 14). New York: Wiley.

Bruner, J. S. (1990). *Acts of meaning.* Cambridge, MA: Harvard University Press.

Bruner, J. S., Goodnow, J. J., & Austin, G. A. (1956). *A study of thinking.* New York: Wiley.

Buck-Morss, J. (1975). Socioeconomic bias in Piaget's theory and its implications for cross-cultural studies. *Human Development, 18,* 35–49.

Chase, A. (1975). *The legacy of Malthus.* New York: Alfred A. Knopf.

Cherns, A. (1984). Contribution of social psychology to the nature and function of work and its relevance to societies of the Third World. *International Journal of Psychology, 19,* 97–111.

Chomsky, N. (1957). *Syntactic structures.* The Hague: Mouton.

Church, A. T., Katigbak, M. S., & Almario-Velazco, G. (1985). Psychometric intelligence and adaptive competence in rural Phillipine children. *Intelligence, 9,* 317–340.

Church, A. T., & Katigbak, M. S. (1988). Imposed-etic and emic measures of intelligence as predictors of early school performance of rural Philippine children. *Journal of Cross-Cultural Psychology, 19,* 164–177.

Ciborowski, T. (1979). Cross-cultural aspects of cognitive functioning. In A. J. Marsella, R. G. Tharp, & T. Ciborowski (Eds.), *Perspectives on cross-cultural psychology* (pp. 101–116). New York: Academic Press.

Clarke, A. M., & Clarke, A. D. B. (1985). Criteria and classification. In A. M. Clarke, A. D. B. Clarke, & J. M. Berg (Eds.), *Mental deficiency: The changing outlook. Fourth Edition* (pp. 27–52). London: Methuen.

Cole, M. (1975). The zone of proximal development: Where culture and cognition create each other. In J. V. Wertsch (Ed.), *Culture, communication and cognition: Vygotskian perspectives.* Cambridge, UK: Cambridge University Press.

Cole, M. (1996). *Cultural psychology: A once and future discipline.* Cambridge, UK: Cambridge University Press.

Cole, M., & Bruner, J. S. (1971). Cultural differences and inferences about psychological processes. *American Psychologist, 26,* 867–876.

Cole, M., & Griffin, P. (1980). Cultural amplifiers reconsidered. In D. R. Olson (Ed.), *The social foundations of language and thought.* New York: Norton.

Cravens, H. (1978). *The triumph of evolution: American scientists and the heredity–environment controversy, 1900–1941.* Philadelphia: University of Pennsylvania Press.

D'Andrade, R. G. (1984). Cultural meaning systems. In R. A. Shweder & R. A. Levine (Eds.), *Culture theory: Essays on mind, self and emotion* (pp. 88–119). Cambridge, UK: Cambridge University Press.

Dasen, P. R. (1972). Cross-cultural Piagetian research: a summary. *Journal of Cross-cultural Psychology, 3,* 23–40.

Dasen, P. R. (1977). Are cognitive processes universal? A contribution to cross-cultural Piagetian psychology. In N. Warren (Ed.), *Studies in cross-cultural psychology, Vol. 1.* London: Academic Press.

Dasen, P. R. (1984). The cross-cultural study of intelligence: Piaget and the Baoule. *International Journal of Psychology, 19,* 407–434.

Dasen, P. R., Barthelemy, D., Kan, E., Kouame, K., Daouda, K., Adjei, K. K., & Assande, N. (1985). N'glouele, l'intelligence chez les Baoule. *Archives de Psychologie, 53,* 295–324.

Davidson, R. C., & Lewis, E. L. (1997). Affirmative action and other special consideration admissions at the University of California, Davis, School of Medicine. *JAMA, 278*(14), 1153–1158.

Delpit, L. (1988). The silenced dialogue: The power and pedagogy of educating other people's children. *The Harvard Educational Review, 58,* 280–298.

Dent, H. E. (1996). Non-biased assessment or realistic assessment? In R. L. Jones (Ed.), *Handbook of tests and measurements for Black populations, Vol. 1* (pp. 103–122). Hampton, VA: Cobb & Henry.

Deregowski, J. B. (1989). Real space and depicted space: Cross-cultural perspectives. *Behavioral and Brain Sciences, 12,* 51–119.

Descartes, R. (1637). *Essais Philosophiques.*

Dixon, R. A., & Lerner, R. M. (1992). A history of systems in developmental psychology. In M. H. Bornstein & M. E. Lamb (Eds.), *Developmental psychology: An Advanced Textbook* (pp. 3–58). Hillside, NJ: Erlbaum.

Dore, R. P. (1976). *The diploma disease: Education, qualification, and development.* Berkeley, CA: University of California Press.

Erny, P. (1972). *L'enfant et son milieu en afrique noire* (The Child and this Environment in Black Africa). Paris: Payot.

ETS. (1996). *Sex, race, ethnicity, and performance on the GRE General Test.* Princeton, NJ: Educational Testing Service.

Feldman, D. H. (1980/1994). *Beyond universals in cognitive development.* Norwood, NJ: Ablex.

Fischer, K. W. (1980). A theory of cognitive development: The control and construction of hierarchies of skills. *Psychological Review, 87,* 477–531.

Flaugher, R. L. (1974). *The new definitions of test fairness in selection: Developments and interpretations.* Research Memorandum RM 73-17. Princeton, NJ: Educational Testing Service.

Flynn, J. R. (1987). Massive IQ gains in 14 nations: What IQ tests really measure. *Psychological Bulletin, 101,* 171–191.

Fortes, M. (1938). Social and psychological aspects of education in Taleland. *Africa, 11*(4). 1–64 (Supplement).

Fryers, T. (1984). *The epidemiology of severe intellectual impairment: The dynamics of prevalence.* London: Academic Press.

Gallimore, R., & Goldenberg, C. (1993). Activity settings of early literacy: Home and school factors in children's emergent literacy. In E. Foreman, E. Minnick, & A. Stone (Eds.), *Education and mind: The integration of institutional, social and developmental processes*. Oxford: Oxford University Press.

Gallimore, R., Weisner, T. S., Kaufman, S. Z., & Bernheimer, L. P. (1989). The social construction of ecocultural niches: Family accommodation of developmentally delayed children. *American Journal on Mental Retardation, 94*, 216–230.

Gardner, H. (1983, 1993). *Frames of mind: The theory of multiple intelligences*. New York: Basic Books.

Gardner, H. (1991). *The unschooled mind: How children think and how schools should teach*. New York: Basic Books.

Gardner, M. K., & Clarke, E. (1992). The psychometric perspective on intellectual development in childhood and adolescence. In R. J. Sternberg & C. Berg (Eds.), *Intellectual development*. Cambridge, UK: Cambridge University Press.

Geertz, C. (1983). *Local knowledge*. New York: Basic Books.

Gibson, E. J. (1982). The concept of affordances: The renascence of functionalism. In A. Collins (Ed.), *The concept of development: The Minnesota symposia on child development* (Vol. 15, pp. 55–81). Hillsdale, NJ: Erlbaum.

Gilligan, C. (1982). *In a different voice: Psychological theory and women's development*. Cambridge, MA: Harvard University Press.

Goleman, D. (1995) *Emotional intelligence: Why it can matter more than IQ*. New York: Bantam.

Goodnow, J. J., Miller, P. J., & Kessel, F. (1995). *Cultural practices as contexts for human development*. San Francisco: Jossey-Bass.

Gottfredson, L. S., et al. (1994). Mainstream science on intelligence. *The Wall Street Journal*, December 13, 1994.

Gottfredson, L. S. (1997). Mainstream science on intelligence: An editorial with 52 signatories, history and bibliography. *Intelligence, 24*(1), 13–23.

Gould, S. J. (1981). *The mismeasurement of man*. New York: Norton.

Hamilton, S. E. (1996). Optimal performer locator for parents and teachers. In R. L. Jones (Ed.), *Handbook of tests and measurements for Black populations* (Vol. 1, pp. 141–154).

Hare, R. M. (1963). *Freedom and reason*. Oxford: Clarendon Press.

Harris, D. B. (1963). *Children's drawing as measures of intellectual maturity: A revision and extension of the Goodenough draw-a-man test*. New York: Harcourt, Brace & World.

Harry, B., Allen, N., & McLaughlin, M. (1995). Communication versus compliance: African-American parents' involvement in special education. *Exceptional Children, 61*, 364–377.

Harry, B., & Anderson, M. G. (1994). The disproportionate placement of African-American males in special education programs: A critique of the process. *Journal of Negro Education, 63*(4), 602–620.

Heath, S. B. (1983). *Way with words*. New York: Cambridge University Press.

Helms, J. E. (1992). Why is there no study of cultural equivalence in standardized cognitive ability testing? *American Psychologist, 47*, 1083–1101.

Henry, A. (1996). Five Black women teachers critique child-centered pedagogy: Possibilities and limitations of oppositional standpoints. *Curriculum Inquiry, 26*(4), 363–384.

Herrnstein, R. J., & Murray, C. (1994). *The bell curve: Intelligence and class structure in American life*. New York: Free Press.

Hilliard, A., & Cummings, W. (1996). The "Who" and "O": Contextually-situated vehicles for the assessment of pupil potential. In R. L. Jones (Ed.), *Handbooks of tests and measurements for Black populations* (Vol. 1, pp. 155–168). Hampton, VA: Cobb & Henry Publishers.

Howard, A., & Scott, R. A. (1981). The study of minority groups in complex societies. In R. H. Munroe, R. L. Munroe, & B. Whiting (Eds.), *Handbook of cross-cultural human development*.

Ignatieff, M. (1984). *The needs of strangers*. London: Chatto & Winders.

Illich, I. (1973). *Deschooling society*. Hammondsworth, UK: Penguin Books.

Jackson, A. M. (1996). The Jackson competency scales. In R. L. Jones (Ed.), *Handbook of tests and measurements for Black populations* (Vol. 1, pp. 297–300). Hampton, VA: Cobb & Henry Publishers.

James, D., & Rattansi, A. (Eds.). (1992). *'Race', culture, and difference*. London: Sage.

Jensen, A. R. (1969). How much can we boost IQ and scholastic achievement? *Harvard Educational Review, 39*, 1–123.

Jensen, A. R. (1980). *Bias in mental testing*. New York: Free Press.

Johnson, M. (1987). *The body in the mind*. Chicago: University of Chicago Press.

Jones, R. L. (1996). Introduction and overview. In R. L. Jones (Ed.), *Handbook of tests and measurements for Black populations* (Vol. 1, pp. 3–15). Hampton, VA: Cobb & Henry.

Joynson, R. B. (1974). *Psychology and common sense*. London: Routledge & Kegan Paul.

Kamin, L. J. (1974). *The science and politics of IQ*. Potomac, MD: Erlbaum.

Kashoki, M. E. (1979). Indigenous scholarship in African universities. In B. Turok (Ed.), *Development in Zambia: A reader* (pp. 170–185). London: Zed Press.

Kathuria, R., & Serpell, R. (1996, April). *Standardization of Panga Munthu test: A non-verbal cognitive test developed in Zambia*. Paper for International Society for the study of Behavioral Development (ISSBD) African Regional Workshop, Lusaka, Zambia.

Kingsley, P. R. (1985). Rural Zambian values and attitudes concerning cognitive competence. In I. R. Lagunes & Y. H. Poortinga (Eds.), *From a different perspective: Studies of behavior across cultures* (pp. 281–303). Lisse: Swets and Zietlinger.

Kohlberg, L. (1971). From is to ought: How to commit the naturalistic fallacy and get away with it in the study of moral development. In T. Mischel (Ed.), *Cognitive development and epistemology*. New York: Academic Press.

Kushlick, A. (1966). Assessing the size of the problem of subnormality. In J. E. Meade, & A. S. Parkes (Eds.), *Genetic and environmental factors in human ability* (pp. 121–147). New York: Plenum.

Laosa, L. (1984). Social policies toward children of diverse ethnic, racial, and language groups in the United States. In H. W. Stevenson & A. E. Siegel (Eds.), *Child development research and social policy (Vol. 1*, pp. 1–109). Chicago: Chicago University Press.

Lakoff, G., & Johnson, M. (1980). *Metaphors we live by*. Chicago: University of Chicago Press.

Lave, J., & Wenger, E. (1991). *Situated learning: Legitimate peripheral participation*. Cambridge, UK: Cambridge University.

LCHC. (1983). Culture and cognitive development. In P. H. Mussen & W. Kessen (Eds.), *Handbook of child psychology, Vol. 1: History, theory and methods*. New York: Wiley.

LCHC. (1982). Culture and intelligence. In R. J. Sternberg (Ed.), *Handbook of human intelligence* (pp. 642–719). New York: Cambridge University Press.

Lewin, K., Little, A., & Colclough, C. (1983). Effects of education on development objectives. *Prospects, 13*(3), 299–311; (4), 413–25.

Liddell, C., Lycett, J., & Rose, G. (1997). Getting through Grade 2: Predicting children's early school achievement in rural South African schools. *International Journal of Behavioural Development, 21*, 331–348.

Mackintosh, N. J. (Ed.). (1995). *Cyril Burt: Fraud or framed?* Oxford: Oxford University Press.

Magnusson, D. (Ed.). (1996). *The lifespan development of individuals: Behavioral, neurobiological, and psychosocial perspectives: A synthesis*. New York: Cambridge University Press.

Mercer, J. R. (1979). *System of Multicultural pluralistic assessment (SOMPA) technical manual*. New York: Psychological Corporation.

Merchant, C. (1980). *The death of nature: Women, ecology, and the scientific revolution*. San Francisco, CA: Harper & Row.

Messick, S. (1983). Assessment of children. In W. Kessen (Ed.), *History, theory and methods, Volume 1 of P. H. Mussen (Ed.), Handbook of Child Psychology* (4th ed.) (pp. 477–526). New York: Wiley.

Miles, T. (1957). On defining intelligence. *British Journal of Educational Psychology, 27*, 153–165.

Miles, M. (1995). Disability in an Eastern religious context: Historical perspectives. *Disability and Society, 10*, 49–69.

Miles, M. (1996). Pakistan's microcephalic *chuas* of Shah Daulah: Cursed, clamped or cherished? *History of Psychiatry, 7*, 571–589.

Miller-Jones, D. (1991). Informal reasoning in inner-city children. In J. F. Voss, D. N. Perkins, & J. W. Segal (Eds.), *Informal reasoning and education*.

Mittler, P., & Serpell, R. (1985). Services: An international perspective. In A. M. Clarke, A. D. B. Clarke, & J. M. Berg (eds.), *Mental deficiency: The changing outlook. Fourth Edition* (pp. 715–787). London: Methuen.

Moghaddam, F. M., & Taylor, D. M. (1986). What constitutes an appropriate psychology for the developing world? *International Journal of Psychology, 21*, 253–267.

Montagu, A. (1974). *Man's most dangerous myth: The fallacy of race* (5th ed.). New York: Oxford University Press.

Moscovici, S. (1982). On social representations. In J. P. Forgas (Ed.), *Social cognition: Perspectives on everyday understanding* (pp. 181–209). London: Academic Press.

Nagel, E. (1954). *Sovereign reason, and other studies in the philosophy of science*. Glencoe, IL: Free Press.

Nagel, E. (1961). *The structure of science: Problems in the logic of scientific explanation*. New York: Harcourt Brace in World.

Neisser, U., Boodoo, G., Bouchard, T. J., Boykin, A. W., Brody, N., Ceci, S. J., Halpern, D. F., Loehlin, J. C., Perloff, R., Sternberg, R. J., & Urbina, S. (1996). Intelligence: Knowns and unknowns. *American Psychologist, 51*(2), 77–101.

Nsamenang, A. B. (1992). *Human development in cultural context*. Newbury Park, CA: Sage.

Nunes, T., Schliemann, A. D., & Carraher, D. W. (1993). *Street mathematics and school mathematics*. New York: Cambridge University Press.

Ogbu, J. U. (1978). *Minority education and caste: The American system in cross-cultural perspective*. New York: Academic Press.

Okagaki, L., & Sternberg, R. J. (1991). *Parental beliefs and children's school performance: A multi-ethnic perspective*. Unpublished MS.

Okonji, M. O. (1980). Cognitive styles across cultures. In N. Warren (Ed.), *Studies in cross-cultural psychology* (Vol. 2, pp. 1–50). London: Academic Press.

Olson, D. R. (1977). The language of instruction: The literate bias of schooling. In R. C. Anderson, R. J. Spiro, & W. E. Montague (Eds.), *Schooling and the acquisition of knowledge*. Hillsdale, NJ: Erlbaum.

Olson, D. R. (1994). *The world on paper*. Cambridge, UK: Cambridge University Press.

Patton, J. M. (1996). Identifying and assessing the gifts and talents of young African American learners: Promising paradigms and practices. In R. L. Jones (Ed.), *Handbook of tests and measurements for Black populations* (Vol. 1, pp. 123–140). Hampton, VA: Cobb & Henry Publishers.

Piaget, J. (1983). Piaget's theory. In W. Kessen (Ed.), *History, theory and methods, Volume 1 of P. H. Mussen (Ed.), Handbook of Child Psychology*, 4th ed. (pp. 103–128). New York: Wiley.

Price-Williams, D. R., Gordon, W., and Ramirez, M., III

(1974). Skill and conservation: A study of pottery-making children. *Developmental Psychology, 1,* 769.

Rabain, J. (1969). *L'Enfant du Lignage* (The child and its origin). Paris: Payot.

Richardson, S. A., & Koller, H. (1985). Epidemiology. In A. M. Clarke, A. D. B. Clarke, & J. M. Berg (Eds.), *Mental deficiency: The changing outlook* (4th ed.) (pp. 356–400). London: Methuen.

Roberts, J. A. F. (1952). The genetics of mental deficiency. *Eugenics Review, 44,* 71–83.

Rogoff, B., Baker-Sennett, J., Lacasa, P., & Goldsmith, D. (1995). Development through participation in sociocultural activity. In J. J. Goodnow, P. J. Miller, & F. Kessel (Eds.), *Cultural practices as contexts for development. New directions for child development* (Vol. 67, pp. 45–66). San Francisco: Jossey-Bass.

Ryle, G. (1949). *The concept of mind.* London: Hutchinson.

Salomon, G. (1993). *Distributed cognitions: Psychological and educational considerations.* Cambridge, UK: Cambridge University Press.

Saxe, G. B. (1991). *Culture and cognitive development: Studies in mathematical understanding.* Hillsdale, NJ: Erlbaum.

Schliemann, A. L., Carraher, D., & Ceci, S. (1997). Everyday cognition. In J. W. Berry, P. R. Dasen, & T. S. Saraswathi (Eds.), *Handbook of Cross-cultural psychology* (2nd ed.) (Vol. 2).

Scribner, S., & Cole, M. (1981). *The psychology of literacy.* Cambridge, MA: Harvard University Press.

Serpell, R. (1974). Aspects of intelligence in a developing country. *African Social Research, 17,* 578–596.

Serpell, R. (1976). *Culture's influence on behaviour.* London: Methuen.

Serpell, R. (1977). Estimates of intelligence in a rural community of Eastern Zambia. In F. M. Okatcha (Ed.), *Modern psychology and cultural adaptation* (pp. 179–216). Nairobi: Swahili Language Consultants and Publishers.

Serpell, R. (1979). How specific are perceptual skills? A cross-cultural study of pattern reproduction. *British Journal of Psychology, 70,* 365–380.

Serpell, R. (1984). Commentary: The impact of psychology on Third World development. *International Journal of Psychology, 9,* 179–192.

Serpell, R. (1988). Childhood disability in socio-cultural context: Assessment and information needs for effective services. In P. R. Dasen, J. W. Berry, & N. Sartorius (Eds.), *Health and cross-cultural psychology: Towards applications* (pp. 256–280). Newbury Park, California: Sage.

Serpell, R. (1989). Intellectual disability (mental retardation). In K. Peltzer & P. O. Ebigbo (Eds.), *Clinical Psychology in Africa* (pp. 365–382). Enugu, Nigeria: Working group for African Psychology.

Serpell, R. (1990). Audience, culture, and psychological explanation: A reformulation of the emic-etic problem in cultural psychology. *Quarterly Newsletter of the Laboratory Comparative Human Cognition, 12*(3), 99–132.

Serpell, R. (1993a). *The significance of schooling: Life-journeys in an African society.* Cambridge, UK: Cambridge University Press.

Serpell, R. (1993b). Interface between socio-cultural and psychological aspects of cognition. In E. Forman, N. Minick, & A. Stone (Eds.), *Contexts for learning: Socio-cultural dynamics in children's development.* New York: Oxford University Press.

Serpell, R. (1993c). Interaction of context with development: Theoretical constructs for the design of early childhood intervention programs. In L. Eldering & P. Leseman (Eds.), *Early intervention and culture.* Paris: UNESCO.

Serpell, R. (1994). The cultural construction of intelligence. In W. J. Lonner & R. M. Malpass (Eds.), *Psychology and culture.* Boston: Allyn & Bacon.

Serpell, R. (1995). Situated theory as a bridge between experimental research and political analysis. In L. Martin, K. Nelson, & E. Tobach (Eds.), *Cultural psychology and activity theory: Essays in honor of Sylvia Scribner.* New York: Cambridge University Press.

Serpell, R. (1997a, June). *Cultural dimensions of literacy development.* Paper presented at the international conference on reading promotion. Noordwijkerhout, Netherlands.

Serpell, R. (1997b). Literacy connections between school and home: how should we evaluate them? *Journal of Literacy Research, 29*(4), 587–616.

Serpell, R. (1997c). The struggle to make sense of school: Essay review of B. A. Levinson, D. E. Foley, & D. C. Holland (Eds.). (1996). The cultural production of the educated person: Critical ethnographies of schooling and local practice. *Human Development, 40,* 364–373.

Serpell, R. (in press, a). Local accountability: To rural communities: A challenge for educational planning in Africa. In F. Leach and A. Little (Eds.), *Schools, culture and economics in the developing world: Tension and Conflict.* New York: Garland.

Serpell, R. (in press, b). Theoretical conceptions of human development in context and their implications for the design of early education programs. In L. Eldering, & P. Leseman (Eds.), *Early education and culture: Culture-sensitive strategies for empowering parents and children.* New York: Garland.

Serpell, R., & Boykin, A. W. (1994). Cultural dimensions of cognition: A multiplex, dynamic system of constraints and possibilities. In R. J. Sternberg (Ed.), *Handbook of Perception and Cognition, Vol. 12: Thinking and Problem-solving* (pp. 369–408). San Diego, CA: Academic Press.

Serpell, R., & Deregowski, J. B. (1980). The skill of pictorial perception: An interpretation of cross-cultural evidence. *International Journal of Psychology, 15,* 145–180.

Serpell, R., & Hatano, G. (1997). Education, schooling, and literacy. In J. W. Berry, P. R. Dasen, & T. S. Saraswathi (Eds.), *Handbook of cross-cultural psychology, second edition* (Vol. 2, pp. 345–382). Boston: Allyn & Bacon.

Serpell, R., Mariga, L., & Harvey, K. (1993). Mental retardation in African countries: Conceptualization, services, and research. *International Review of Research in Mental Retardation, 19,* 1–39.

Serpell, R., Sonnenschein, S., Baker, L., Hill, S., Goddard-Truitt, V., & Danseco, E. (1997). *Parental ideas about development and socialization of children on the threshold of schooling* (Reading Research Report No. 78). Athens, GA: NRRC, Universities of Georgia and Maryland, College Park.

Shweder, R. A. (1990). Cultural psychology: What is it? In J. W. Stigler, R. A. Shweder, & G. Herdt (Eds.), *Cultural psychology*. Cambridge, UK: Cambridge University Press.

Siegler, R. (1991). *Children's thinking*. Englewood Cliffs, NJ: Prentice Hall.

Sinha, D. (1986). *Psychology in a Third World country: The Indian experience*. New Delhi: Sage.

Sinha, D. (1997). Indigenizing psychology. In J. W. Berry, Y. H. Poortinga, & J. Pandey (Eds.), *Handbook of cross-cultural psychology, second edition* (Vol. 1, pp. 129–169). Boston: Allyn & Bacon.

Skinner, B. F. (1953). *Science and human behavior*. New York: Macmillan.

Sleeter, C. (1986). Learning disabilities: The social construction of a special education category. *Exceptional Children, 53,* 46–54.

Sternberg, R. J. (1984a). Towards a triarchic theory of human intelligence. *Behavioral and Brain Sciences, 7,* 269–315.

Sternberg, R. J. (1984b). A contextualist view of the nature of intelligence. *International Journal of Psychology, 19,* 307–334.

Sternberg, R. J. (1997). The concept of intelligence and its role in lifelong learning and success. *American Psychologist, 52*(10), 1030–1037.

Sternberg, R. J., Conway, B. E., Ketron, J. L., & Bernstein, M. (1981). People's conceptions of intelligence. *Journal of Personality and Social Psychology, 41,* 37–55.

Sternberg, R., Ferrari, M., Clinkenbeard, P., & Grigorenko, E. L. (1996). Identification, instruction, and assessment of gifted children: A construct validation of a triarchic model. *Gifted Child Quarterly, 40*(3), 129–137.

Sternberg, R., & Grigorenko, E. L. (1999). *Our labeled children*. Needham Heights, MA: Perseus.

Sternberg, R., & Williams, W. M. (1997). Does the Graduate Record Examination predict meaningful success in the graduate training of psychologists? *American Psychologist, 52,* 630–641.

Stevenson, H. W., Chen, C., & Uttal, D. H. (1990). Beliefs and achievement: A study of Black, White and Hispanic children. *Child Development, 61,* 508–523.

Street, B. (1984). *Literacy in theory and practice*. Cambridge, UK: Cambridge University Press.

Super, C. M. (1983). Cultural variation in the meaning and uses of children's "intelligence." In J. B. Deregowski, S. Dziurawiec, & R. C. Annis (Eds.), *Explorations in cross-cultural psychology*. Lisse, The Netherlands: Swets & Zeitlinger.

Super, C., & Harkness, S. (1986). The developmental niche: A conceptualization at the interface between child and culture. *International Journal of Behavioural Development, 9,* 545–569.

Super, C., & Harkness, S. (1997). The cultural structuring of child development. In J. W. Berry, P. R. Dasen, & T. S. Saraswathi (Eds.), *Handbook of cross-cultural psychology, second edition* (Vol. 2, pp. 1–39). Boston: Allyn & Bacon.

Taylor, L. S. (1996). Informal assessment of intellectual ability using Piagetian tasks. In R. L. Jones (Ed.), *Handbook of tests and measurements for Black populations* (Vol. 1, pp. 169–184). Hampton, VA: Cobb & Henry Publishers.

Tharp, R. G. (1989). Psychocultural variables and constraints: Effects on teaching and learning in schools. *American Psychologist, 44,* 349–359.

Thomas, W. B. (1982). Black intellectuals' critique of Early mental testing: A little-known saga of the 1920s. *American Journal of Education, 90,* 258–292.

Tobin, J. J., Wu, D. Y. H., & Davidson, D. H. (1989). *Preschool in three cultures: Japan, China and the United States*. New Haven, CT: Yale University Press.

Tomlinson, S. (1981). *Educational subnormality: A study in decision-making*. London: Routledge & Kegan Paul.

Tomlinson, S. (1982). *The sociology of special education*. London: Routledge & Kegan Paul.

Trevarthen, C. (1980). The foundations of intersubjectivity: Development of interpersonal and cooperative understanding of infants. In D. R. Olson (Ed.), *The social foundations of language and thought: Essays in honor of Jerome S. Bruner* (pp. 316–342). New York: Norton.

Valsiner, J. (1991). Social co-construction of psychological development from a comparative-cultural perspective. In J. Valsiner (Ed.), *Child development within culturally structured environments, Vol. 3*. Norwood, NJ: Ablex.

Vernon, P. E. (1967). Abilities and educational attainments in an East African environment. *Journal of Special Education, 1,* 335–345.

Vygotsky, L. S. (1962). *Thought and language*. Cambridge, MA: Harvard University Press.

Vygotsky, L. (1978). *Mind in society: The development of higher psychological processes*. Cambridge, MA: Harvard University Press.

Wagner, D. A. (1981). Culture and memory development. In H. C. Triandis & A. Heron (Eds.), *Handbook of Cross-cultural psychology* (Vol. 4, pp. 187–232). Boston, MA: Allyn & Bacon.

Wertsch, J. V. (1985). *Vygotsky and the social formation of mind*. Cambridge, MA: Harvard University Press.

Wertsch, J. V. (1991). *Voices of the mind*. Cambridge, MA: Harvard University Press.

WHO (1975). *Schizophrenia: A multinational study*. Geneva, Switzerland: World Health Organization.

Williams, W. (1998). Are we raising smarter children today? School and home-related influences on IQ. In U. Neisser (Ed.), *The rising curve: Long-term changes in IQ and related measures*. Washington, DC: American Psychological Association.

Witkin, H. A. (1967). A cognitive style approach to cross-cultural research. *International Journal of Psychology, 2,* 233–250.

Zukow, P. G. (1989). Siblings as effective socializing agents: Evidence from central Mexico. In P. G. Zukow (Ed.), *Sibling interaction across cultures: Theoretical and methodological issues* (pp. 79–105). London: Springer.

PART IX

INTELLIGENCE IN RELATION TO ALLIED CONSTRUCTS

CHAPTER TWENTY-SIX

Intelligence and Personality

MOSHE ZEIDNER AND GERALD MATTHEWS

OVERVIEW

For more than half a century now psychologists have been exploring the avenues linking human intelligence to a wide array of personality traits in the hope of unravelling the mutual impact of intelligence and personality in the course of development and day-to-day behavior. Although these constructs are frequently kept apart, the artificiality of the distinction has been recognized by many of the key figures of differential psychology, including Binet, Terman, Thorndike, and Thurstone. Most notably, David Wechsler (1950) viewed intelligence as a manifestation of personality as a whole and argued that certain affective and motivational factors (interest, volition, etc.) are integral components of the construct of intelligence. According to Wechsler, because conative and affective factors function in concert with intelligence in determining intellectual performance, what is needed are not tests from which personality factors have been eliminated but tests in which these nonintellective factors are clearly present and objectively appraisable. Today, it is commonly agreed that some of the most interesting work in individual differences is being done at the interface of personality and intelligence (Snow, 1995). Because intelligence is often construed as the cognitive part of the construct of personality, the two constructs are in effect mutually intertwined (Brody, 1972).

This chapter sets out to survey some of the past and present attempts at shedding light on the nexus of relationships between intelligence and personality, two grand constructs of modern psychology.

We begin by comparing two approaches to understanding the personality–intelligence interface. The first is the traditional *psychometric* approach based on intercorrelating dimensions of individual differences as identified largely by factor analysis. We then survey empirical research on the direction and magnitude of the relationship between intelligence and personality constructs. The second approach is the *cognitive science* one that emphasizes process rather than structure. We review the biological, cognitive, and adaptive processes that may contribute to both personality and intelligence. We conclude by pointing out some potential directions for future research on the intelligence–personality interface.

The material included in this chapter is, perforce, exemplary rather than exhaustive; a full coverage of all relevant topics and studies would have required a chapter of monograph length. For further information, the reader is referred to two recently published edited books examining the interface between the constructs of personality and intelligence: *Personality and intelligence* (Sternberg & Ruzgis, 1994) and the *International Handbook of Personality and Intelligence* (Saklofske & Zeidner, 1995).

APPROACHES TO INTEGRATING PERSONALITY AND INTELLIGENCE

Following Eysenck (1994), we need to distinguish between psychometric and experimental approaches in examining the personality–intelligence interface. The psychometric approach is concerned with the alignments of ability and personality dimensions within a common measurement framework. For example, Cattell (1971) described the relationships between various cognitive (ability) and noncognitive (personality and motivation) dimensions. Cattell's model of individual differences accommodates the conjoint effects of intelligence, personality, and motivation on behavior. For example, test situations may evoke arousal and negative emotions that impact on test performance, affecting the inferences that may be drawn about intelligent behavior (Zeidner, 1998). Cattell (1971) also described developmental relationships between different constructs: there may be causal and reciprocal relationships between personality and intelligence. Hence, the main tasks for research are the operationalization and assessment of constructs and the modeling of correlational relationships between constructs, including longitudinal data to test causal models.

Experimental approaches require a theoretical framework. In recent years, the psychobiological theories promoted by Eysenck (1994) have been challenged by cognitive psychological analyses of intelligence (e.g., Sternberg, 1977). Analyses of cognitive processes may reveal interrelationships of intelligence and personality overlooked by purely psychometric analyses; for example, working memory is associated with both types of construct (Matthews & Dorn, 1995). However, cognition cannot be understand solely through development of the information-processing models now commonly used in individual differences research. According to the "classical theory" of cognitive science (Pylyshyn, 1984), three complementary levels of explanation are required. The first level is the biological or "hardware" level, which describes the behavioral consequences of neural functions. This approach is familiar in differential psychology through psychophysiological analyses, and, indirectly, through behavior genetics also (e.g., Eysenck & Eysenck, 1985). Secondly, cognitive phenomena may be described in terms of the formal properties of the cognitive architecture or "software" comprising (1) the rules governing the computational operations performed on symbols (algorithms) and (2) the processing structures supporting computation in real time, such as memory stores. Accounts of intelligence in terms of individual differences in processing limitations (e.g., Anderson, 1992) are ex-

pressed at this level. Thirdly, explanations in terms of the person's goals, intentions, and efforts at adaptation to the external environment are required (the semantic or knowledge level). Much traditional personality theory, such as psychoanalysis, is expressed at this level, but its neglect of other levels of explanation, especially the cognitive architecture, makes it difficult or impossible to test such theories empirically. Adaptive facets of intelligence have been explored through work on ability and motivation (Kanfer & Ackerman, 1989), and through Sternberg's (1985) concept of practical intelligence, the application of intelligence to real-life adaptive challenges.

Matthews (1997a) discusses how Pylyshyn's (1984) levels of explanations apply to differential psychology (see Figure 26.1). The three-rung ladder of explanation is reconceptualized as a loop to accommodate the partially genetic basis for ability and personality traits. Natural selection hard-wires successful adaptive choices into the brain, and thus knowledge and biological levels are linked as shown. Psychologists are perhaps more concerned with the other two bridging of levels. Studies of strategy use bridge the knowledge and architecture levels by specifying how the person's goals are translated into sequences of computation. Also, connectionism is a first attempt to represent computation in terms of biologically plausible models. Individual difference factors may require understanding at all three levels. For example, depending on the research context, it may be useful to conceptualize anxiety in terms of brain systems for handling punishment

FIGURE 26.1. Levels of explanation for the cognitive science of individual differences (Matthews, 1997a).

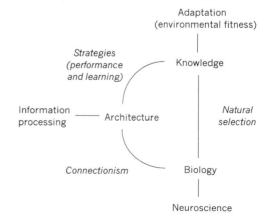

and fear cues (Gray, 1982) of flow diagrams for information processing (Williams et al., 1988), or in terms of the anxious individual's self-knowledge and motivations (Matthews & Wells, in press).

THE PSYCHOMETRIC FRAMEWORK

Operationalization and Assessment

Factor analytic research shows that when personality and intelligence measures are analyzed together the two constructs can generally be differentiated (McCrae, 1987). The question arises: On the basis of which criteria can we differentiate the two concepts? Table 26.1 provides a structure for this differentiation.

NATURE OF THE TRAIT. Intelligence is typically considered to be unidirectional, whereas personality can be considered bidirectional. Accordingly, intelligence is typically thought of as extending in a single direction, from "little of" to "much of" (Thorndike, 1982), and it is clear how to set optimal parameters for intelligent behavior. By contrast, personality is conceived of as being bipolar. A personality trait need not take on an extreme value for it to be set optimally, and midpoint values are often considered as optimal. Hence, a veridical criterion is generally employed in evaluating a response in the intelligence domain (cf. Nunnally, 1978), but behaviors falling under the domain of personality often have no veridical criteria for judging responses.

GOALS AND OPTIMAL ASSESSMENT SITUATION. An intelligence test aims at eliciting maximal performance from examinees, and they are expected to give their best shot in solving the problem or engaging the task at hand. Consequently, intelligence is generally measured in evaluative and maximal performance test conditions. By contrast, a personality measure is designed to gauge a person's typical performance in a real-life situation (Ackerman & Heggestad, 1997) to provide the best estimate of what a person is most likely to do. Conse-

quently, the examinee is expected to give as truthful a response as possible. The differentiation is not entirely straightforward: some researchers (Ackerman & Heggestad, 1997; Hofstee, 1997) have reflected on whether it may sometimes make sense to talk about personality as maximal performance (e.g., under intense stress) or "IQ typicality" (e.g., typical intellectual engagement).

MOTIVATION AND CONTROL IN MODIFYING BEHAVIOR. The individual has some degree of voluntary control in expressing personality. For example, the test-anxious person can cope with his or her anxiety through stress management techniques. By contrast, intelligence is under less personal control and is less amenable to instructions to change or modify behavior.

INSTRUCTIONS UNDER ASSESSMENT CONDITIONS. Intelligence is generally assessed using test conditions involving a set of standard tasks that examinees respond to at a designated time and place

---

TABLE 26.1. Some Relationships Differentiating Personality and Intelligence

Dimension	Intelligence	Personality
Trait	Unidirectional ("little of" to "much of")	Bidirectional (polar extremes)
Goals and optimal assessment situation	Test situation requiring maximal performance	Real-life situation
Motivation in taking the instrument	High motivation	Tends to vary
Instructions	To do one's best	To provide a candid response
Criteria for evaluating responses	Veridical criterion	Direction and intensity (no correct response)
Stability of the instrument	Relatively stable	Tends to fluctuate
Reliability of the instrument	Generally high	Varies from high to low
Interpreting results	Relatively straightforward	More open and controversial
Practical utility	Moderate	Low to moderate

Source: Adapted from B. Most & M. Zeidner, 1995. Constructing personality and intelligence test instruments: Methods and issues. In D. Saklofske & M. Zeidner (Eds.). *International handbook of personality and intelligence* (pp. 475–503). New York: Plenum.

(cf. Zeidner & Most, 1992). Intelligence has not been profitably assessed by observer ratings or self-reports. By contrast, personality researchers have worked most frequently with subjective media (e.g., projective devices), behavioral ratings, and self-inquiry modes of gathering evidence (e.g., inventories). In fact, most measures of personality rely on someone's impression, be it the individual's personal impressions or those of someone observing the individual.

STABILITY. Whereas theorists generally accept the fact that cognitive traits display considerable stability across situation and over time (Willerman, 1979), the cross-situational consistency of personality traits has been more controversial (Mischel, 1968). Some recent studies of personality (cf. Costa & McCrae, 1986) show promising findings of stability during the adulthood years, at least for basic traits (see Maciel, Heckhausen, & Baltes, 1994, for a recent review of the literature).

RELIABILITY OF THE INSTRUMENT. It follows from the modifiability of personality expression that the units of observation in personality assessment (moods, dispositions, emotional states) are quite troublesome for measurement purposes because they are "probabilistic" rather than "all or none" phenomena. Personality measures are also generally more susceptible to a wide variety of sources of measurement error (faking, response sets, social desirability). A considerable body of research attests to the lower reliability and validity of personality compared with intelligence measures (cf. Anastasi, 1986).

INTERPRETING RESULTS. Subjects' interpretations of personality tests may vary considerably from subject to subject, causing considerable ambiguity and further increasing measurement error. Furthermore, in contrast to ability measures, we may not get a typical response on personality measures because the subject chooses not to give it or because the subject does not have enough self-insight to give it (Thorndike, 1982). Interpretation of ability test scores is more straightforward, though it may be difficult to assess the roles of affective and conative factors.

PRACTICAL UTILITY. Both personality and intelligence measures have been used for practical de-cision-making purposes in a wide array of sectors and settings. Among the various practical uses of personality and intelligence measures are clinical diagnosis, vocational guidance and counseling, school prediction and placement college selection, and personnel selection and placement. The main difference between the two are that intelligence tests appear more valid and have been more widely used in school prediction and college placement and selection, whereas personality measures have been more used in clinical diagnosis and counseling (Jensen, 1980).

Despite the distinctions among the two constructs, it is commonly agreed that intelligence and motivational–personality processes are never utilized in isolation from each other; once activated there is basically no way to separate the processes or isolate the relative contribution of one from the other. Thus, in attempting to adapt to any practical situation, an individual needs to apply both mental and motivational–affective processes which, respectively, draw upon factual knowledge and knowledge related to values, beliefs, and standards. In most practical contexts, intelligence and personality contexts are bound to form a coalition of synergistic forces (Maciel, Heckhausen, & Baltes, 1994).

Empirical Links between Psychometric Measures of Intelligence and Personality

In the sections that follow we survey the results of empirical research exploring the links between personality and psychometric measure of intelligence. There now seems to be a more solid and coherent theoretical basis for examining the personality–intelligence interface than ever before. Although there are several competing theories of intellect, most theories converge on a hierarchical model of intelligence, specifying both general and group factor(s) (e.g., Cattell, 1971; Gustafsson, 1997; Snow, Kyllonen, & Marshalek, 1984). Although there is considerably less consensus about structure of individual differences in personality than intelligence, theoretical and empirical research over the past 30 years prompted several investigators to converge on a set of five factors (the Big Five: Costa & McCrae, 1992) that appear across numerous personality inventories (Extraversion, Agreeableness, Conscientousness, Neuroticism, Intellect).

Methodological Considerations

First, it may be useful to make a number of distinctions and methodological comments that may help the reader appraise the evidence relating intelligence to personality. To begin with, one should keep in mind the distinction between personality traits and states. Traits are broad determining tendencies or propensities to behave, whereas states are temporary states of mind and mood determined by the interaction between a person's trait and present state or situation (Spielberger, Gonzales, Taylor, Algaze, & Anton, 1978). States and traits are typically correlated because a trait is actually defined as a disposition that behavior is likely to be manifested in particular situations. For example, "trait anxiety" refers to an individual's disposition to respond with worry, tension, and physiological arousal across a variety of conditions (physical danger, evaluative situations, social encounters, sports events), whereas "state anxiety" refers to a specific level of anxiety experienced in a particular situation, such as an important athletic competition. Two people may have the same level of trait anxiety but differ in their anxiety elevations in a particular situation or "state."

Zeidner (1995) delineated several different models employed in studying the direction of the causal relationship between intelligence and personality. In Model A intelligence is depicted as the independent variable and personality as the dependent variable. In Model B the causal direction is reversed, and intelligence now serves as the dependent variable and personality as the independent variable. In Model C there is a bidirectional relationship and reciprocal determinism between the two constructs. In Model D the relationship is artifactual with a third extraneous variable responsible for the relationship. In Model E, personality is conceived as an intervening or "nuisance" variable intervening between the intelligence construct (as input) and manifest level of intelligence (as output, evidenced in intelligence test scores). Each of these models has been espoused as a possible model for the intelligence–personality relationship, although it is often difficult to discriminate among them.

Meta-Analytic Results for the Personality–Intelligence Interface

A recent meta-analysis (Ackerman & Heggestad, 1997), based on 135 separate studies, helps shed light on the magnitude and pattern of relationships between ability and the "Big Five" factors of personality. The largest effect observed in this analysis is the meaningful positive correlation between intelligence (g) and the Openness–Intellect factor ($r = .33$) – a factor associated with a broad class of intellectually oriented traits. In addition, a small but significant positive correlation was reported between g and Extraversion ($r = .08$), and a small but significant negative correlation with ability was reported for Neuroticism ($r = -.15$). Correlations between g and both Conscientiousness ($r = .02$) and Agreeableness ($r = .01$) were negligible. The authors suggest that the personality tests that have ubiquitous positive correlations with ability fall under the broad category of Positive Affect, whereas negative correlations with ability tend to be from broad categories of Negative Affect, such as Neuroticism (stress reaction) and Psychoticism. Kyllonen (1997) recently reported correlations between the Big Five factors and measures of General, Verbal, and Quantitative Ability in a U.S. sample of Air Force recruits. Just as in the reported meta-analysis, Openness and Neuroticism were the factors most strongly related to ability measures. Thus, Openness was meaningfully correlated with both g ($r = .45$), Verbal ability ($r = .58$), and Quantitative ability ($r = .29$), whereas Neuroticism was reported to be inversely correlated with both g ($r = -.23$) and Verbal ability ($r = -.20$). The correlations between Conscientiousness, Agreeableness, and Extraversion were very low, ranging from $-.11$ to $.11$. It is interesting to note, in passing, that only cognitive factors (working memory, knowledge, etc.), but not personality factors predicted short-term performance on learning tasks (e.g., computer programming, flight engineering, economics) and psychomotor performance (e.g., flying, control). However, personality did account for larger, long-term performance (e.g., productivity on the job).

The inference to be drawn from these data is that at the level of latent constructs, IQ and personality are orthogonal constructs (see Eysenck's, 1994, recent review). Furthermore, neither subtest patterns nor profiles of IQ have been systematically found to be related to personality variables (Eysenck, 1994). Although actual performance on IQ tests may be influenced by an array of noncognitive states (fatigue, anxiety, arousal), personality and intelligence are essentially unrelated. However, such conclusions may understate the personality–intelligence associations to be found through more fine-grained examination of the evidence. Three especially productive areas of research have focused on negative affectivity, extraversion–introversion, and openness. Another approach is to assess the IQs of people showing various abnormalities of behavior: the mentally ill, the deviant, and children with unusually high or low IQs.

Intelligence and Negative Affectivity

We now examine the relationship between intelligence and various personality traits subsumed under the higher order category of negative affectivity, including neuroticism, anxiety, depression and anger. Most studies have addressed negative affect through *anxiety*, which, as a state, is characterized by apprehension, worry, and emotional and somatic tension. Anxiety has received particular attention because it may impair intellectual functioning and performance in variety of contexts, ranging from intelligence test scores and school achievement (Sarason, 1980) to dating (Hope & Heimberg, 1990). In fact, the literature suggests that the relationship between trait anxiety and psychometric tests of intelligence is negligible (Matarazzo, 1972). Thus, neither pattern nor scatter-analysis approaches to the Wechsler scales have shown any relation to a trait measure of anxiety. However, studies utilizing situationally induced anxiety (i.e., state anxiety) do reveal decrements in performance on the same measures of intellectual functioning. Only when we separate the currently anxious (state anxious) from the chronically anxious (trait anxious) can we show a decrement in intellectual performance due to anxiety (Siegman, 1956). Discriminating different components of anxiety shows that worry, but not emotionality, is related to impaired intelligence test performance under time pressure (Matthews, 1986; Morris & Liebert, 1969).

Both test and trait anxiety may interact with situational variables (e.g., task complexity, test atmosphere, etc.) and personal variables (e.g., optimism, personal resources, social support) in impacting upon cognitive test performance (see Zeidner, 1998, for a review). For example, there is considerable evidence that the performance of highly test anxious individuals on complex tasks is detrimentally affected by evaluative stressors: the less com-

plex the task, the weaker the effect. Sarason (1975) reported that the differences between anxious and nonanxious students in performance are realized mainly in the competitive atmosphere; under neutral conditions the differences between anxious and nonanxious students are minimal.

Anxiety may have somewhat more general effects on intellectual performance in real-world contexts. It has been estimated that there is a correlation of about −.2 between anxiety and both measures of performance and achievement at school and college (Hembree, 1988; Siepp, 1991) and sports performance (Zeidner, 1997). The relationship between neurotic personality and occupational performance has also been estimated at about −.2 in studies in which there was an a priori rationale for performance being sensitive to neuroticism (Tett, Rothstein, & Jackson, 1991). Metanalytic data (Ackerman & Heggestad, 1997) show a mean correlation of −.33 between g and self-reports of test anxiety. Test anxiety measures may be a stronger predictor of situational anxiety than general anxiety in such contexts. However, meta-analysis also shows that there is little difference between state and trait anxiety measures as predictors of educational performance criteria. Hence, detrimental effects of anxiety in the real world may represent more than just distraction from performance by the person's immediate worries about the test situation, which relates to state rather than to trait anxiety.

Depression is characterized by strong negative emotions, impairment of everyday social functioning, and negative beliefs such as hopelessness and lack of self-worth. There is little evidence to suggest that subclinical levels of depression reliably relate to impaired intelligence test performance in laboratory settings (e.g., Matthews, 1986). Deficits are found in clinical populations, however, especially on the performance subtests of the Wechsler Adult Intelligence Scale (Endler & Summerfeldt, 1995). Impairment of performance appears to generalize across a variety of high-level cognitive tasks such as problem solving and reading comprehension (Hartlage, Alloy, Vazquez, & Dykman, 1993). The effects of depression on intellectual functioning in the real world are presently unclear. There has been little work on the manic symptoms central to some mood disorders, although low levels of symptoms (hypomania) may be associated with enhanced creativity

(Endler & Summerfeldt, 1995). Anger is another potentially important influence on intelligence test performance that remains to be investigated (cf. Zeidner, 1995).

The causal status of anxiety and other negative affects is somewhat controversial. It is often supposed that the worry component of state anxiety uses up working memory or attentional resources, and thus performance is impaired if the task is sufficiently demanding (e.g., Eysenck, 1992; Sarason, 1975). Subjects low in intelligence, for whom the task is objectively more difficult, may thus be especially vulnerable to more general anxiety-related impairments – an hypothesis confirmed by meta-analysis (Hembree, 1988). We will return to cognitive mechanisms for anxiety impairment in a later section. Causal effects of clinical depression on cognitive performance are generally accepted, especially for tasks requiring concentration or memory (Endler & Summerfeldt, 1995). However, there are alternative explanations for negative correlations between anxiety and intelligence. First, anxiety in the cognitive test situation may be generated by more or less veridical appraisals that failure is likely owing to low ability or lack of preparation and study. In other words, anxiety may be a marker for poor intellectual skills rather than a factor that directly affects performance (Mueller, 1992). Second, to the extent that anxiety leads to beliefs of lack of self-efficacy in achievement-oriented situations, individuals high in anxiety may avoid activities that enhance intellectual growth, and thus apprehension about academic contexts and lack of intellectual skills become mutually reinforcing (Cattell, 1971). Third, the observed relationship of anxiety to intelligence may be due to the artifactual influences of extraneous variables (e.g., social class, childrearing patterns, test situation) affecting both variables (Weiner, 1973). Similar explanations are possible for depression findings. It is conceivable that depression will result if low intelligence leads to a succession of performance failures, for example.

Extraversion–Introversion

Extraversion–introversion (E) is a basic dimension of individual differences in human behavior and is often construed as a source trait with a strong biological basis (Eysenck & Eysenck, 1985). Extraverts tend to be outgoing, sociable, and impulsive,

whereas introverts are socially reserved and cautious. Extraversion–Introversion relates to a variety of aspects of human performance (Matthews, 1992). However, as we have seen, it shows only small positive associations with intelligence in meta-analytic data (Ackerman & Heggestad, 1997). As in the case of anxiety, though, there may be some more subtle relationships. Relationships between extraversion and intelligence may be moderated by the nature of the test. Robinson (1985) claimed that E is intimately associated with different intellectual styles and intelligence profiles but not to absolute levels of performance on intelligence tests. Accordingly, introverts and extraverts were found not to differ in overall IQ, only on profile: introverts were found to do relatively better on verbal tests and extraverts on performance tests. However, these effects may not be replicable (Saklofske & Kostura, 1990). Matthews (1992) observed that introverts tend to do better on problem-solving tasks requiring insight and reflection. Conversely, extraverts may benefit from speeded tasks (Rawlings & Carnie, 1989). Eysenck (1994) reviewed studies showing that E is related to speed of working and that extraverted subjects spend lower total time doing the test. Thus, Jensen (1966) found that E correlated .44 with speed of solution of Raven's matrices, although extraverts made significantly more errors. Eysenck (1994) surveyed evidence suggesting that extraverts tend to give up towards the end of tests and take longer to obtain correct solutions towards the end of the test, a process he attributes to greater reactive inhibition or lower cortical arousal.

Extraversion effects are often moderated by factors related to stress, arousal, and emotion. Some of this work shows interactions between extraversion and arousal (e.g., Revelle et al., 1980) and has been inspired by the arousal theory hypothesis that the tonic or resting level of arousal for introverts is higher than that of extraverts (Eysenck & Eysenck, 1985). This hypothesis is further discussed in the section on neural processes. Extraversion has also been linked to positive emotionality (Watson & Clark, 1992), but associations between E and positive affect in performance contexts are small in magnitude (Matthews, 1997b). However, if extraverts are more energetic and lively in some real-world contexts, these positive moods may feed into superior intellectual performance. Studies of patients with chronic fatigue syndrome show wide-ranging deficits, including considerable impairment of full-scale IQ (Daugherty et al., 1991). Less dramatic but reliable attentional deficits are found in individuals whose mood is characterized by low energy, although there is no straightforward relationship between subjective tiredness and intelligence test performance (Matthews, 1992).

Finally, there may be a developmental or maturational link between intelligence and personality (Eysenck & Cookson, 1969). These authors suggest that around the ages of 13 or 14, there is a tendency for the correlation between extraversion and IQ to change from positive to negative. There seems to be some uncertainty over the age of the crossover point. For example, Crookes, Pearson, Francis, and Carter (1981) found a positive correlation between extraversion and IQ in 15–16 year old boys and girls. If the effect is genuine, there are various explanations. According to Eysenck (1994) it may relate to the change from the free and easy atmosphere at primary school, which accords well with the extraverted temperament, and the more formal atmosphere at secondary school, which agrees better with the introverted temperament. A second possible explanation is that more able children become introverted, whereas the less able become extraverted (Anthony, 1983). A further possible explanation is that because introverts mature more slowly, introversion in primary school age children is not advantageous to mental achievement, but by secondary school it becomes an assistance (Anthony, 1983). Eysenck (1994) suggested that the correlation between introversion and increasing relative success in academic exams is plausible because such success is presumably facilitated by private study, an introverted type of behavior.

Openness: Intellect and Authoritarianism

Openness is characterized by vivid fantasy, artistic sensitivity, depth of feeling, behavioral flexibility, intellectual curiosity, and unconventional attitudes. McCrae (1994) has argued that there is substantial overlap between Openness to experience and Intellectual Ability. Ackerman and Heggestad's (1997) meta-analysis established that this factor correlates more strongly with general intelligence than any of the other Big Five factors, although it related more strongly to crystallized than to fluid intelligence. However, interpretation of the data is complicated by uncertainty over the nature of Openness, which has been much debated in the personality literature (e.g., McCrae, 1996). Trapnell (1994), for example, picks out intellectual competency and liberalism as two distinct aspects of Openness, although he prefers to relate them to Conscientiousness (see Saucier, 1994, for a rebuttal of this view). Intellectual competency may mediate associations between Openness and intelligence test performance. Goff and Ackerman (1992) showed that three constructs were mutually intercorrelated: openness, crystallized intelligence, and a measure of "Typical Intellectual Engagement" (TIE), which assesses intellectual motives and interests. In a further study, Rolfhus and Ackerman (1996) showed that Openness correlated at .67 with TIE and that both measures related to knowledge of the arts and humanities, although the TIE scale was more broadly related to self-report knowledge. Plausibly, more Open individuals show greater crystallized intelligence because they are more motivated to engage in intellectual activities, especially those of a verbal and cultural nature.

In addition, the relationship between Openness and intelligence may also relate to its "liberal" element, that is, willingness to examine social, political and religious values and rejection of traditional conservative views. This link is shown most clearly by research on authoritarianism, an attitudinal system consisting of a set of interrelated antidemocratic sentiments, including ethnic prejudice, political conservatism, and moralistic rejection of the unconventional (Adorno, Frenkel-Brunswick, Levinson, & Sanford, 1950). Trapnell (1994) reported a correlation of −.57 between a right-wing authoritarianism scale and openness. The studies of Adorno et al., and those of other researchers show that Authoritarianism scores are negatively associated with intelligence and have correlations ranging between −.20 and −.50.

One possibility is that only individuals of relatively low intelligence are able to accept the kind of ideology represented by an extreme fascist orientation (Thompson & Michel, 1972). Another line of reasoning points out that both intelligence and authoritarianism are confounded by social class. Also, it may be chiefly education or cultural sophistication rather than intelligence per se that reduces authoritarianism. Cristie (1954) estimated that with education partialled out the correlation between authoritarianism and intelligence drops considerably.

Thus, those in society who are low in personal and social resources (e.g., social status, intelligence, education), feel threatened and frustrated and turn to authoritarian beliefs as a solution to problems.

Other evidence also points to the importance of socially shaped belief systems. A survey (Argyle, 1961) of American studies of children and students found negative correlations between intelligence and religious beliefs, attitudes, and experiences. The correlations are generally higher for religious conservatism (−.15 to −.55) than for attitudes and experiences (−.19 to −.27). Similarly, several studies showed that beliefs in the paranormal predicted low intelligence (see Zeidner, 1995, for a review), perhaps because higher intelligence may render an individual less vulnerable to the circular and ephemeral arguments put forth in defense of paranormal ideas (Zusne & Jones, 1982). Intriguingly, though, recent studies suggest that due to the antirationalism typical of many intellectually superior students during the 1960s and the 1970s, the historical relationship may have changed, and beliefs in the paranormal are now associated with higher rather than lower intelligence (cf. Jones, Russel, & Nickel, 1977).

Abnormality and Deviance

Work on abnormality of personality and intelligence has tended to use clinical typologies, although dimensional models based on normal personality structure are becoming more widely used in other contexts (Matthews, Saklofske et al., in press). Eysenck (1994) believed that research exploring statistical relations between measures of IQ and psychopathology is doomed to failure in view of the following three factors: the mindless "blunderbuss" approach adapted by many researchers in correlating measures of personality and intelligence; the notorious unreliability of the criterion, that is, diagnosed psychopathology; and problems in statistical analysis of difference scores. The role of intelligence in some aspects of abnormality has been neglected, notably in the case of personality disorders. Endler and Summerfeldt's (1995) review of the literature concluded that characteristic ways of organizing and processing information and experience appear to play major roles in the genesis and perpetuation of personality disorders. The cognitive characteristics of these disorders are important, but there is little systematic evidence on the role of intelligence from studies using psychometric tests.

Delinquency

On average, delinquents score eight IQ points lower than nondelinquents on standard intelligent tests (Lynam, Moffitt, & Stouthamer-Loeber, 1993). This relation holds up regardless of social class or ethnic background. Crime and even aggression may act over a long period of time to depress intellectual functioning (Huesmann, Eron, & Yarmel, 1987). Furthermore, recent meta-analytic research (Ackerman & Heggestad, 1997) reports a modest inverse correlation between aggression and g ($r = -.19$). Wechsler (1958) pointed out that the most outstanding single feature of the sociopath's test profile is his systematic high score on the Performance as compared with the Verbal part of the scale. Matarrazo (1972) listed about 30 studies that generally support this view, although he urges caution in individual diagnoses.

Researchers have argued over the meaning and interpretation of this negative relationship (Lynam, Moffitt, & Stouthamer-Loeber, 1993). For one, a delinquent life style may result in lower intellectual functioning. This lowering may be the result of one of a variety of factors, including poor school motivation, negative attitudes towards IQ testing, head injuries incurred in numerous street or gang fights, or the deleterious effects of drug abuse on the central nervous system. According to Block (1995), high impulsivity accounts for the lower Verbal IQ frequently characterizing serious delinquents. Because effective test performance requires constrained, slowed, and reflective behavior, impulsive and uncontrolled individuals are less able to modulate their actions and reactions, resulting in depressed test performance. Moreover, during their education, impulsive and undercontrolled children may cumulatively register less of the information, reasoning, and logic upon which verbal tests depend, and their IQ suffers because they are unprepared. It is the unresilient, undercontrolled child who will be disposed to conduct disorder, will more frequently miss days in school, and who will lose the opportunity to develop cognitive processes that underpin performance on intelligence tests. These behavioral deficits may be linked to deficiencies in self-regulation, including lack of self-control, preferences for coping through aggression, and distorted appraisals of others' attitudes towards oneself (Schwean & Saklofske, 1995; Matthews, Schwean et al., in press). Second, a low IQ may lead to delinquency as mediated by low scholastic performance and eventual school dropout. A third explanation is that the observed relationship is spurious, and a third variable (e.g., social class, race, etc.) may cause both low IQ and delinquency.

Schizophrenia

Schizophrenic thought and judgment is seriously impaired as mental health deteriorates with a growing tendency to confuse wish and reality (Coleman, Butcher, & Carson, 1984). The schizophrenic mind, although unselectively registering everything in its field of vision, is unable to distinguish between relevant and irrelevant cues (Williams & Beech, 1997). Decrements in intelligence test performance are common but may in part be attributed to the subject's low motivation to perform, minimal cooperation, and impaired contact with the examiner, leading to fluctuation of test scores across occasions.

It is somewhat unclear whether impairment of the intellect is a vulnerability factor for schizophrenia or whether it represents a consequence of psychosis: the direct empirical evidence is conflicting and often confusing. Although the intelligence of severely schizophrenic individuals may be below average, one is struck by the preservation of average or even remarkable intellectual superiority in many schizophrenics, especially those diagnosed as paranoid. Some studies report (Watson, Herder, Kucala, & Hoodecheck-Schow, 1987) substantial decline between premorbid assessment and hospitalization, whereas other studies show that intellectual decline among schizophrenics may be attributable to preexisting conditions and is not an inherent factor associated with the onset of schizophrenia. In one recent study, no significant decay in intelligence scores was observed for schizophrenics whose initial aptitude test scores were above average, and the observed decline in test scores was largely attributable to a drop in a specific skill – arithmetic performance (Watson et al., 1987). Because deterioration is limited to certain skills, it is best interpreted as a loss in particular intellectual functions rather than as a more generalized intellectual decay.

Some research shows that intelligence deteriorates under schizophrenic attack, but, under remission, performance on intelligence tests improves (Scheartzman & Douglas, 1962). Chronic schizophrenic inpatients with long histories of hospitalization manifest greater intellectual deficit than do patients with recent onset or brief hospitalization. However, this may be due to changes in the composition of hospitalized cohorts over time rather than to the effects of hospitalization or processes intrinsic to psychosis. Longitudinal studies of hospitalized patients fail to find progressive decline (Hamlin, 1963). That is, chronics may be less bright than acutes because of an association between IQ and retention in hospitals and readmission to hospitals. There is some research to suggest that brighter patients are less often rehospitalized several years after discharge than patients of lower IQ (Heffner, Strauss, & Grisell, 1975). Thus, there appears to be a prognostic significance for IQ that contributes to the differences in intelligence between acute and chronic schizophrenics.

The effects of psychosis on intellectual functioning for children may be more pernicious than for adults and children suffering from certain personality dysfunctions and disturbances, who have been reported to suffer from a severe deterioration of abilities (Sattler, 1988). Children with disintegrative psychosis usually have a period of normal development for the first 3–4 years, after which profound regression and behavioral disintegration occur, intelligence declines, speech and language abilities deteriorate, and social skills diminish. In addition, children become restive, irritable, anxious, and overactive. Overall, the prognosis is poor, although more intelligent children may have better prospects.

Personality Characteristics of the Gifted and Intellectually Challenged

The previous section considered the intellectual capabilities of individuals with abnormal personalities. We may also look at the personalities of people with abnormal intellect. By virtue of their exceptionally high and low intellectual talents, both gifted and intellectually challenged individuals are often viewed as suffering from special adjustment problems, especially during childhood (cf., Anastasi, 1958).

Intellectually Gifted Children

Paradoxically, it is often supposed that highly intelligent children have special problems in adjustment. The famous Stanford Gifted Child Study, initiated by L. Terman in 1921, systematically investigated the physical, mental, and personality traits of 1,528 gifted children from California (Mean IQ = 151), following them into late adulthood (Terman, 1935; Terman & Oden, 1947; Terman & Oden, 1959). Not only were these children above norms in height and overall health, but they were also rated by their teachers as considerably more "self confident," "optimistic," and "emotionally stable" compared with controls. In adulthood the gifted sample proved to be equal or superior to controls on marital adjustment and showed normal or below normal incidence of serious personality maladjustment. Data on the personality and social characteristics of these 70+ year-old subjects are still being gathered and disseminated. Interestingly, two of Terman's subjects, Lee Cronbach and Robert Sears, grew up to become famous psychologists in their own right and assumed professorships in psychology at the very university that sponsored the study! Comparable findings can be gleaned from the John Hopkins study of mathematically gifted youth (Stanley, Keating, & Fox, 1974). The personality profiles of these mathematically gifted students suggest social maturity and psychological health and are a far cry from maladjusted by any standards. A study (Mayer, Caruso, Zigler, & Dreyden, 1989) of 46 gifted adolescent students attending the Duke University Talent Identification Program has also suggested that gifted children are characterized by optimal levels on several intellect-related personality traits such as high intellectual absorption, the tendency to experience pleasure when working on problems, and low degrees of apathy or boredom in doing intellectual work. Overall, research provides a highly positive personality profile of the gifted, which is in sharp contrast to the common stereotype of the highly intelligent child as shy, unhealthy, weak, and generally socially maladjusted.

Intellectually Challenged Children

There is often a tendency to view mentally challenged children as a homogeneous group with specific personality deficits and problems. For example, some research suggests that these children are sometimes characterized by more rigid patterns of behavior than are those who are at the same mental age but who are chronologically younger. It has

also been suggested that personality may develop at a slower rate in these than in normal children. Thus, whereas the mentally challenged and normal children of the same mental age are similar in personality characteristics, the mentally challenged and regular children of the same chronological age may differ in personality (Nevo, 1998). In fact, aside from those children with clear physiological deficits, there is much evidence against the existence of unique personality characteristics intrinsically associated with mental retardation (Nevo, 1998). It is plausible, however, that poor cognitive performance and repeated failure in school and social settings may indirectly lead to problems of social adjustment and rejection. This, in turn, may influence both the development and expression of certain personality traits.

The Psychometric Approach: Conclusions

Correlations between personality and ability constructs are often small, although there are substantial associations between Openness and crystallized intelligence measures. However, closer empirical links are found in some contexts. Anxiety measures related to specific contexts, such as test anxiety, are moderately predictive of impaired test performance. Both anxiety and extraversion may be shown to predict test performance when situational factors such as level of time pressure, stress, or arousal are manipulated. Subject groups whose personality is abnormal, such as psychotic patients and delinquents, may also show impairment of intellectual function. However, groups of abnormal IQ (high and low) show relatively little sign of dysfunctional personality, and high IQ appears to be beneficial. It is often difficult to discriminate the causal hypotheses proposed for these various relationships. On one hand, personality may impair or facilitate the intellectual competence associated with IQ, as manifested in actual test performance illustrated by some of the detrimental effects of anxiety, depression, schizophrenia, and delinquency. On the other hand, IQ may influence the person's adjustment to real-world demands, and consequently, personality. For example, the educational difficulties of low-IQ children may variously lead to anxiety and conduct problems. In addition, personality–IQ relationships may be confounded by third variables, such as social class.

THE COGNITIVE SCIENCE PERSPECTIVE

Cognitive science emphasizes processes rather than structural factors, whether these processes are neural, computational, or adaptive. From this perspective, individual differences dimensions refer to stable parameters governing the behavior of dynamic systems. The first question to be addressed is whether ability and personality are associated with common parameters. For example, is it possible that intelligence and personality factors relate to a "clock-speed" parameter influencing rate of information processing? In general, the psychometric distinctiveness of the two kinds of dimension suggests that such overlaps are limited. The second, more subtle question is whether intelligence and personality influence common intelligent behaviors via different parameters. For example, both intelligence and some personality traits may influence response speed on some performance task, but the effect may be mediated by different processes, say, basic processing speed and strategy choice. This form of overlap may be quite prevalent. Initially, we will briefly review the evidence for process-oriented relationships between personality and intelligence at the three levels of explanation previously described: the biological, the cognitive–architectural, and the adaptive–knowledge levels. We will then outline an integrated cognitive–adaptive framework for interrelating personality and intelligence. It should be recognized from the outset that it is difficult to describe the static constructs of differential psychology in process-oriented terms. An empirical association between, say, intelligence and information-processing speed, does not necessarily imply either that intelligence is a direct expression of processing speed or that there is some unitary cognitive entity called intelligence that controls processing speed (Matthews & Dorn, 1995).

Neural Processes

The treatment here of the biological level will be brief. There is much work on the biological bases of both intelligence and personality constructs. Both appear to be partially inherited (Bouchard, 1995; Loehlin, 1992), and both have extensive psychophysiological correlates (Deary & Stough, 1996; Matthews & Gilliland, in press), implying that their behavioral expressions are influenced by neural pro-

cesses. However, there is little work that attempts to determine whether the two construct types relate to common neural bases. On the whole, intelligence and personality seem to relate to rather different psychophysiological indices, as shown by evoked potential studies, for example (Stelmack & Houlihan, 1995). It is also unclear whether behavior reflects interactions between distinct sets of neural processes associated with the two constructs. For example, is it possible that the cortical circuits controlling performance on an intelligence test are influenced by subcortical circuits linked to personality? A crude example might be disruption of cortical processing caused by fear circuits centered on the amygdala (LeDoux, 1995), if we may assume that chronically fearful individuals show abnormality of function in these circuits.

One strategy for integrating the two constructs has been through arousal theory. The electroencephalogram (EEG) and other psychophysiological measures may provide an index of the functional status of the organism, which integrates outputs from a variety of distinct neural systems (e.g., Mesulam, 1985). There have been occasional attempts to link intelligence to arousal (e.g., Necka, 1997), but individual differences in arousal are more usually seen as the basis for the personality traits of extraversion–introversion and neuroticism (Eysenck & Eysenck, 1985). Eysenck and Eysenck (1985) suppose that (1) extraverts tend to be less aroused than introverts and (2) arousal is linked to performance by an inverted-U function (the so-called Yerkes–Dodson law).

It follows that personality and arousing agents should have interactive effects on performance of various tasks, including intelligence tests. Consistent with prediction, arousal induced by caffeine and time pressure tends to enhance the test performance of extraverts but impairs introverts' performance (Revelle, Amaral, & Turiff, 1976). However, other work presents a more complex picture. Work by Revelle, Humphreys, Simon, & Gilliland (1980) demonstrated that when subjects are tested in the evening, caffeine benefits introverts, not extraverts, implying that the relationship between extraversion and arousal varies with time of day. Revelle et al. also showed that impassivity was more predictive than sociability of test performance. Matthews (1985) obtained results similar to those of

Revelle et al. using a self-report measure of arousal. However, these data showed that arousal moderated rather than mediated the effect of extraversion: the arousal–performance relationship appeared to be qualitatively different in extraverts and introverts. Similarly, Matthews & Amelang (1993) found that associations between EEG alpha and verbal intelligence test performance varied with extraversion. Matthews (1992, 1997b) attributed such effects to arousal having qualitatively differing effects on attentional efficiency in extroverted and introverted subjects.

Studies of this kind implicate neural arousal processes in both extraversion–introversion and in test performance, but their exact theoretical implications are unclear. The neural processes concerned are not specified precisely, and so there is no basis for modeling their interaction. Part of the problem is that extraversion is most likely associated with a variety of neurologically distinct functions. For example, studies of brainstem-evoked potentials permit extraversion to be linked to some specific brain structures, such as the inferior colliculus (Bullock and Gilliland, 1993). It is unlikely, however, that these structures directly influence intelligent behavior. Matthews & Harley (1993) have proposed a speculative connectionist model that attributes extraversion x arousal interaction effects on cognitive performance to variation in levels of random noise within a neural net. But, such attempts are in their infancy. Although arousal theory may serve as a useful heuristic for linking personality and intelligence, its well-known shortcomings (e.g., Matthews & Amelang, 1993) may limit its utility in developing neurally based theories.

Cognitive Processes

We can be fairly confident that intelligence is associated with individual differences in the cognitive architecture (strictly, the functional architecture, in Pylyshyn's, 1984, terms). It is clear that high IQ is associated with greater processing efficiency on some tasks, whether this advantage is attributed to working memory, attentional resources, rate of computation, or some other processing qualities. Reduced constraints on processing imposed by architectural features may also translate in superior acquired cognitive skills (Anderson, 1992). Like intelligence, personality traits also correlate with performance on information-processing tasks, but it is less clear that such correlations reflect individual differences in architecture, as opposed to voluntary strategy. For example, anxious individuals often behave as though they have a functional deficit in attentional capacity. However, this deficit may reflect diversion of capacity onto internal worries rather than a fundamental lack of resources (Matthews & Wells, in press; Sarason, 1975). Conversely, subjective arousal does seem to correlate with total availability of resources, a parameter of the architecture (Matthews & Davies, in press).

INTELLIGENCE. The pioneering studies of Hunt (1978) and Sternberg (1977) provided a major impetus to studies of intelligence and information processing. It has been claimed that special importance attaches to diverse processing constructs, including elementary processing speed (Neubauer, 1997), working memory (Kyllonen & Chrystal, 1990), and strategy use (Ferrara, Brown, & Campione, 1986). None of these constructs, however, seem likely to replace g on psychometric grounds alone (Carroll, 1993). Instead, as Sternberg (1977) claimed, intelligence may be associated with a multiplicity of lower level components and higher level "metacomponents" or control processes, and thus there is no single critical process for intelligence. Intelligence is distributed across a variety of independent processing components at different levels of the architecture. The observed correlations between intelligence and a specific task depend on the g loadings of the components controlling individual differences in performance (Sternberg, 1977). We can then ask questions about the role of personality similar to those posed at the biological level of explanation. Are there components associated with both intelligence and personality factors? To what extent is intelligent behavior controlled by cognitive processes sensitive to personality as well by g-loaded processes?

EXTRAVERSION. In previous reviews (Matthews, 1992, 1997b; Matthews & Dorn, 1995), one of us has concluded that, as with intelligence, personality traits are associated with a diversity of cognitive correlates or cognitive patterning. However, in contrast to intelligence, traits tend to be associated with performance deficits as well as enhancements,

TABLE 26.2. Cognitive Patterning of Extraversion–Introversion: Performance Characteristics of the Extravert Compared with the Introvert

Characteristics of Extraversion

Superiority in...	Divided attention
	Resistance to distraction
	Retrieval from memory
	Short-term memory
Inferiority in...	Vigilance
	Reflective problem solving
	Long-term memory
Lower response criterion	
Little systematic effect on...	Attentional selectivity
	Reaction-time tasks
	General intelligence

which may account for the small magnitude of personality–intelligence correlations previously discussed. Table 26.2 summarizes the cognitive correlates of extraversion–introversion. At least some of these effects, especially the associations with attentional and memory functions, appear sufficiently robust to represent individual differences in architecture, although there is little direct evidence. Superficially, at least, there appears to be overlap between some of these cognitive correlates and correlates of intelligence. For example, introverts appear more intelligent in their superior reflective problem solving, whereas extraverts resemble intelligent individuals in their superior dual-task performance (e.g., Stankov, 1989). At the least, then, individual differences in some aspects of performance may be sensitive to both personality and intelligence. However, more fine-grained analyses tend to suggest that the specific processes sensitive to extraversion and intelligence are often different from one another. For example, extraverts' dual-task superiority may reflect greater availability of resources (Eysenck, 1981), especially for verbal tasks. For intelligence, though, the crucial processes appear to be the control processes handling the additional complexity associated with dual-task performance (Spilsbury, Stankov, & Roberts, 1990).

The cognitive correlates of extraversion are highly sensitive to contextual factors such as level of stimulation (Eysenck & Eysenck, 1985) and motivational signals (Derryberry & Reed, 1994). As previously discussed, one interpretation of these interactional effects rests on analyses of neural processes such as arousal theory. Such explanations are, at the least, incomplete because extraversion x arousal interactions vary with the information-processing demands of the task. Matthews and Harley (1993) suggested that the typical interaction effect operates on lower-level spreading activation processes. They speculated that the effects of extraversion and arousal factors on intelligence test performance found by Revelle et al. (1980) may be mediated by "automatic" verbal processes. In other words, properties of the architecture may vary to some degree across both individuals and contexts. Overall, the impression is that intelligence and extraversion are associated with distinctive sets of parameter settings for the cognitive architecture, although there may be some overlap with regard to specific parameters.

ANXIETY. Like extraversion, anxiety effects may be characterized in terms of a cognitive patterning (for reviews see Eysenck, 1992; Wells & Matthews, 1994; Zeidner, 1998). In theory, anxiety may affect cognitive performance at each of the stages involved in processing information (i.e., encoding of new information, short- and long-term storage, elaboration and processing of encoded material, retrieval of content from long-term memory, and problem solving). Thus, anxiety may produce a narrowing of attention and increased distractibility, affecting encoding of intelligence test information and tasks particularly sensitive to distractibility (e.g., digit–symbol coding). Anxiety may impair the efficiency of short-term storage and tasks such as digit span. The short-term memory tasks most sensitive to anxiety tend to be those that also require active processing of information (working-memory tasks) and may require attentional resources as well as short-term retention. Intelligence tests vary in their demands on attentional resources and working memory, and thus impairment in these information-processing functions does not necessarily result in impairment on any given intelligence test (Matthews & Dorn, 1995). We would expect emotional disturbance to be most detrimental to tests making high demands on controlled processing, attention, or working memory, such as complex arithmetic calculations performed without paper and pencil. Anxiety may also affect students' long term memory, such that highly anxious subjects would show a greater retention loss over time (Eysenck & Eysenck, 1985).

Anxiety effects are not limited to deficits. Anxiety is also associated with negative biases in judgment and with selective attention to threat (Wells & Matthews, 1994; Zeidner, 1998). It may facilitate performance of easy tasks (Zeidner, 1998). Again, there is some uncertainty over whether anxiety effects should be linked to the cognitive architecture (Matthews & Wells, in press). The cognitive interference hypothesis for anxiety effects (Zeidner, 1998) implies that anxious individuals are not generally lacking in attentional resources or working-memory capacity; they simply allocate it to off-task processing. On the other hand, there may be more fundamental differences in some specific attentional functions such as attentional focusing and disengagement (Derryberry & Reed, 1997). Similarly, the nature of attentional bias in anxiety is controversial. According to Williams et al. (1988), anxiety is associated with individual differences in preattentive processes controlling threat evaluation, which are apparently a property of the architecture. Matthews and Wells (in press) point to numerous demonstrations that attentional bias effects are sensitive to contextual and strategic factors. They argue that bias reflects a coping strategy of monitoring for threat.

LIMITATIONS OF INFORMATION-PROCESSING MODELS. There is little dispute that intelligence and personality traits may conjointly influence many aspects of performance. Even intelligence test performance is sensitive to personality when contextual factors such as level of stimulation and time pressure are taken into account (e.g., Revelle et al., 1980). Cognitive psychological studies have been invaluable in generating detailed information-processing models of these findings. However, such models are often rather superficial in their explanations (Matthews, 1997a). The simplest explanation is that individual difference factors influence multiple parameters of the cognitive architecture in such a way that intelligence and personality factors relate to differing cognitive patterning. Such explanations may be adequate for explaining the performance data, although, in the larger picture, they may require supplementation with neural explanations. Humphreys and Revelle (1984) and Necka (in press) have discussed how individual differences

in resource availability (an architectural construct) may be influenced by arousal (a neural construct), for example.

In some respects, though, architectural explanations may not be just limited but wrong because they neglect volitional strategy choice. Individual differences in strategy may reflect either the architectural components supporting strategy implementation or the person's choices for dealing with task demands. In the latter case, we must invoke the knowledge-level explanations discussed in the next section. It is often difficult to ascertain which type of explanation is appropriate. Extraverts' deficiencies in certain kinds of problem solving may be attributed to use of "impulsive exit" strategies (Weinman, 1987). One explanation is that the computations used in deciding whether a valid solution has obtained are deficient in extraverts (architectural explanation). Alternatively, extraverts value speed relative to accuracy and so are at risk for making errors on the tasks concerned (knowledge explanation). In the next section, we explore the role of strategy as a construct bridging architectural and adaptive levels of explanation.

Adaptive Processes

At Pylyshyn's (1984) knowledge level, we are concerned with the processes of intentional adaptation to the demands of the external environment (cf. Lazarus, 1991). "Adaptation" here refers to the person's volitional management of real-world opportunities and threats and should be distinguished from adaptation in the evolutionary sense. Do personality and intelligence relate to common adaptive goals or to common adaptive outcomes? The motivational aspect of personality is commonplace: Consider the social motivations of extraverts or the concerns with self-protection of the anxious individual, for example. Motivational components of intelligence are less obvious. Motivation involves investment of time and energy in the pursuit of personal goals. In general, intelligence consists of abilities or aptitudes that help people achieve their basic long- and short-term goals or reach certain performance standards. Hence, intelligence is drawn into the domain of goal satisfaction and thus becomes more linked with general motivational dispositions. For example, the studies of openness previously described show that intelligent individuals are more likely to have intellectual interests. In this section, we review the evidence relating to motivational processes, their control by larger self-regulative systems, and the implementation of control through strategy selection.

MOTIVATION AND ENVIRONMENTAL CONTROL. A fundamental requirement for adaptation is a degree of control over the external environment. To achieve environmental control, individuals spend considerable time and effort assessing environmental contingencies and contextual changes as well as analyzing their own powers to cope and excel in relevant contexts (cf. Zeidner & Endler, 1996). Attribution theory (Weiner, 1973) posits that an essential motivation is to gain a measure of predictability and control over events with emphasis on gaining an accurate appraisal of one's personal characteristics. Locus of causality is an attributional dimension. Individuals with an *internal* locus of causality assume that their own behaviors and actions are responsible for the consequences that happen to them. *Externally* controlled people, by contrast, believe that the locus of causality is out of their hands and subject to the whims of fate. Internal locus of causality, especially for positive events, has commonly been associated with positive mental health and more adaptive functioning. Conversely, those who feel at the mercy of their environment and have little control over what happens to them may have low adaptive capacity.

Intelligence may affect the process of appraising personal control by allowing more complex reasoning and consideration of alternatives and choice among options, thus affording greater control during both primary and secondary appraisal (Zeidner, 1995). Furthermore, people who believe they can control their own lives will put forth the effort to gain competencies and skills, thus enhancing their acquired or crystallized intelligence and abilities. Consistent with these hypotheses, intelligence has been reported to be moderately and inversely correlated with external locus of causality in junior and high school students (Samuel, 1980). Also, some studies (Seligman, 1975) have specifically related deficits in mean IQ shown by Black examinees to the phenomena of low controllability (learned helplessness). Their motivation to cope with environmental contingencies is drastically diminished by preliminary exposure to uncontrollable aversive stimuli. Thus, people who have been successful at using their abilities come to believe in their abilities to control their destiny, and thus the locus of causality may shape the development of intelligence. However, we do not really know for sure what the causal direction is. Do attributions affect cognitive test performance, or do less intelligent people tend to rely more on luck and accidental or external factors than their own abilities?

Achievement motivation designates a general striving to perform one's best when the following two conditions hold: (a) the quality of one's performance is judged in terms of success or failure, (b) a relevant standard of excellence applies (Weiner, 1973). It may relate to people's need to seek a sense of control over their environment, which is often referred to as a motivation for "effectance." According to achievement motivation theory (Atkinson, 1964), all individuals have a basic motive to approach an achievement-related goal and an antagonistic motive to avoid failure. The strengths of these motives vary from person to person and situation to situation. Atkinson (1964) described in detail how motives and expectancies influence approach–avoidance conflict between the two opposing tendencies, the stronger of the two tendencies being expressed in action.

Achievement strivings are a defining characteristic of the Conscientiousness (C) trait of the Five-Factor Model (Costa & McCrae, 1992). Some authors have found it useful to distinguish achievement striving from the orderliness component of C (Hough, 1992). Achievement motivation may influence intellectual development and performance in one of several ways. First, achievement motivation may determine the level of interest, striving, and effort that persons invest in the development of their intellectual skills throughout all their life experiences prior to the test. Second, achievement motivation may help shape the level of attention, effort, concentration, and persistence applied in the evaluative or test situations. Recent research, in fact, suggests that a student's motivation, as expressed by basic interest in different school subjects, is significantly related to cognitive abilities and achievement (Snow, 1989). Third, intelligence may shape the person's motives. Thus, a person high in quantitative ability is likely to develop a motive to achieve in math. Furthermore, highly intelligent students develop a strong motivation to acquire or develop various intellectual skills tapped by IQ tests and to perform well in a testing situation.

In fact, some reviews have reported modest positive relations between need for achievement and intelligence, but others conclude the correlation is not statistically reliable (see Zeidner, 1995 for review). Achievement motivation research may underestimate the context dependence of motivation. Successful entrepreneurs who left school with few qualifications may be highly motivated to succeed – but not at schoolwork. Achievement striving predicts a variety of indices of occupational performance, as does the C trait (Barrick & Mount, 1991; Matthews, 1997c). The possibility of nonlinear relationships has also been rather neglected. Basic motivation theory predicts that need for achievement will show a linear relation to performance outcomes when measured as cumulative academic performance but a curvilinear relationship when immediate learning performance is measured (Snow, 1989). Thus, the optimum immediate learning should come from those students with middle positions on need for achievement. Motivation theory further predicts that only persons of average intelligence should be strongly motivated to achieve or avoid failure, depending on the relative strengths of their motivations for success or motivation to avoid failure (Weiner, 1972). Hence, performance differences as a function of motivation may tend to be confined to groups intermediate in ability (Atkinson, 1974). Contrary to this hypothesis, Heckhausen (1967) found that motivation was predictive of IQ only in high-ability groups. Kanfer (1990) suggested that the critical moderating factor is self-perceived ability. Motivation is beneficial only when ability is high, focusing attention on attaining performance goals. Low-perceived ability tends to lead to goal abandonment and performance impairment.

SELF-REGULATION. A more process-oriented analysis of individual differences in motivation and adaptation is provided by work on self-regulation. Self-regulation refers to people's management of their transactions with the environment under the guidance of cybernetic control loops that seek to align actual and ideal self-states (Carver & Scheier, 1991). Loosely, we can distinguish two aspects of self-regulation. Its more passive, state-oriented aspect refers to the person's self-representations and subsumes both self-appraisals and the goals of self-regulation. Its more action-oriented aspect (self-agency) refers to beliefs about the coping strategies used to meet those goals. Both aspects have been linked to intelligence.

SELF-REPRESENTATIONS: SELF-CONCEPT AND SELF-ESTEEM. A need for a positive self-concept or self-regard develops universally. People's self-image (how people come to see themselves) and their self-esteem (to what degree they feel positive about themselves) are crucial in determining their personal goals, perceptions, and behaviors. The earliest and most general aspects of the self concept develop in the interaction between the child and parent figures. Continuing changes in the self-concept should take place as a consequence of later interactions as well. Both theory and past research support the view that a positive self-concept and high self-esteem are related to higher academic ability and attainment. Negative beliefs about the self are associated with lower ability, scholastic underachievement, and failure (Purkey, 1970). Children who think of themselves poorly are likely to underestimate their ability, anticipate failure, and may well stop trying when difficulties arise.

The causal dynamics in the assumed relationship between intelligence and self-concept are ambiguous. One commonly held view is that the causality flows from intelligence to self-esteem. Accordingly, positive self-concept and adjustment only reflect past achievement and a person's subjective appraisals of his or her own social or educational standing and scholastic aptitudes. In fact, a causal modeling study by Maroyama, Rubin, and Kingsbury, (1981) suggested that self-esteem at age 12 is significantly predicted by ability at age 7. This suggests that the causal direction flows from ability to self-esteem. If correct, then efforts to improve adjustment would have little effect on ability and achievement.

SELF-AGENCY. According to current social–cognitive theory, human action is governed not so much by the objective properties of the environment but by the perceived level of personal efficacy to effect changes by productive use of capabilities and enlistment of sustained effort (Bandura, 1977). The term self-efficacy is used to refer to the belief of being able to master challenging demands by means of adaptive action. Self-efficacy can be conceptualized as a "can-do" cognition that mirrors a sense of control over the environment or as an optimistic view of one's capability to deal with stress and anxiety. Recent research from a social–cognitive perspective points to a meaningful relationship between self-efficacy and academic ability and attainment (Bandura, 1986). Students who view ability as reflecting an acquirable skill foster a resilient sense of self-efficacy. Thus, students who regard intellectual ability as a skill that can be acquired by gaining knowledge and competencies tend to adopt functional learning goals. These students seek challenges that provide opportunities to expand their knowledge and competencies. They regard errors as a natural part of the acquisition process rather than a source of distress. Self-efficacy varies dynamically with the person's experience of performing the task, depending on the goals the person sets and their perceived success in attaining them (Kanfer, 1990).

Ego resiliency is a somewhat similar construct: the capacity of the individual to modulate and monitor an ever-changing complex of desires and reality constraints effectively (Block & Kremen, 1996). A basic premise undergirding this conceptualization is that the human goal is to be as undercontrolled as possible and as overcontrolled as necessary. Thus, ego resiliency refers to the dynamic capacity of an individual to modify a characteristic level of ego control in either direction (i.e., overcontrol or undercontrol). This dynamic capacity is viewed as a function of the demand characteristics of the environmental context so as to preserve or enhance system equilibration (Block & Kremen, 1996). The ego-resilient person is adaptively attuned to the surrounding psychosocial environment, and thus he or she experiences feelings of zest for life, self-esteem, and harmony with others. Ego resiliency has elements of self-efficacy but places less emphasis on direct environmental control as the route to successful adaptation. Ego resiliency, as an index of human adaptability, might be expected to relate to cognitive function. Indeed, Block and Kremen (1996) found a significant relationship between IQ and a measure of ego resiliency among male students.

Linking Adaptation to the Architecture: The Role of Strategies

The research reviewed so far makes some broad predictions about how motivational and self-regulative aspects of personality may influence intelligence test performance. However, predicting effects on specific intelligent behaviors requires integration of the adaptive and cognitive architectural levels of explanation via the concept of strategy. First, we may seek to link the executive functions used in controlling intelligent behavior to self-regulation. Perhaps the more intelligent person is better able to attain personal goals in consequence. Second, we may investigate how personality factors influence strategy choice and the consequences of these choices for intellectual functioning. This approach provides a fresh perspective on effects of anxiety and depression on performance.

EXECUTIVE FUNCTIONS IN SELF-REGULATION AND INTELLIGENCE. One aspect of intelligence relates to cognitive self-regulatory processes ("metacognitive" or "executive functions") that control a person's cognitive functioning. A wide range of activities are included under the rubric of cognitive self-regulation. These include reflecting on the nature of the problem at hand, planning activities, predicting consequences of one's actions, monitoring ongoing activities, checking results of one's actions, testing for plausibility, and reflecting on one' actions (Flavell, 1985). Self-regulatory strategies and "metacognitive knowledge" are believed to be purposely constructed from the knowledge and experience one has acquired with respect to one's own problem-solving behavior (Flavell, 1985).

Increased intelligence is often believed to be associated with benefits in strategy regulation (Borkowski & Peck, 1986). The working methods of highly intelligent subjects are often claimed to be dominated by well-developed metacognitive strategies that are highly integrated into their rich cognitive repertoires. The three metacognitive skills perhaps most closely aligned with intelligence are (a) formation of a clear mental representation of learning–performance goals, (b) the capacity to devise and revise a plan of action, and (c) the ability to monitor one's behavior to detect mismatches between goals and standards and present behaviors (Boekaerts, in press). Other theoretical accounts of the link between metacognitive strategies and intelligence have been provided by Sternberg (1985) and Snow and Lohman (1984).

The person's use of metacognitive strategies should contribute to his or her adaptation to real-world environments through self-regulation of the attainment of personally salient goals (Kanfer, 1989). Self-regulation efficiency, that is, the ability to pursue one's goals despite alternative action tendencies, has been hypothesized to be an important variable subsumed under g (Kuhl & Kraska, 1989). Thus, whereas more intelligent students are hypothesized to use self-regulatory skills (actively setting goals, planning, monitoring their performance during problem solving, etc.), less intelligent students rely more on the task and environmental cues than self-regulatory cues to provide them with these structures. These hypotheses have been supported, in part, by recent research evidencing that external regulation may enhance the learning and performance of low-ability students. By contrast, self-regulation may interfere with the self-regulatory activities of high-ability students (Veenman & Elshout, 1995). Unfortunately, researchers have experienced considerable difficulties distinguishing the constructs used in conceptualizing self-regulation (or self-regulated learning) from those employed in more traditional theories of intelligence (Zeidner, Boekaerts, & Pintrich, in preparation). Researchers are still unclear whether these constructs should be conceptualized as independent constructs, overlapping constructs, or hierarchically related constructs (with self-regulation subsumed under the ability domain). Second, a review of the empirical literature suggests that the actual role of intelligence (with populations in the normal to gifted range) in strategy regulation is either weak or inconsistent and is still a matter of debate (Alexander & Schwanenflugel, 1994).

STRESS, MOTIVATION, AND STRATEGY USE. Current transactional perspectives on emotion (Lazarus, 1991) see stress as maladaptation to the perceived demands of the environment. Stress arises when the perceived demands of the environment tax or exceed the individual's perceived capacity to cope with these demands (Lazarus & Folkman, 1984). Stress may also be seen as a consequence of ineffective or misguided self-regulation (Matthews,

Schwean et al., in press). Emotional expressions of stress are closely linked to appraisals and coping tendencies. There has been much speculation but rather little evidence on the relationship between intelligence and stress reactions. Intelligence may be seen as a resource that facilitates personal growth and adjustment and possibly buffers the effects of environmental stress on stress reactions (Lazarus & Folkman, 1984). Possibly, intelligence leads to more positive appraisals through more accurate and flexible assessments of demanding situations. Furthermore, more intelligent persons may have better problem-solving skills used in deciding how to change themselves or their environment (cf. Payne, 1991). Haan (1977) found that changes in intelligence from early adolescence to middle adulthood correlate positively with increased usage of coping mechanisms but correlate negatively with defense mechanisms. However, intelligence is not necessarily beneficial in stressful situations: The more intelligent person may be able to work out negative consequences of a difficult situation that would not occur to a less intelligent person. Cognitive resource theory (Fiedler & Garcia, 1987) has set forth several interesting hypotheses relating leadership behavior under stress to individual differences in leader intelligence. Accordingly, stress is assumed to have a distracting effect on performance and limits the leader's ability to make use of his or her cognitive resources. A major hypothesis of this theory states that when a leader is under stress, his or her intellectual abilities will be diverted from the task. As a result, measures of leader intelligence will not correlate (or even correlate inversely!) with group performance under stressful conditions. Intelligent leaders may be better able than less intelligent leaders to foresee the consequences of failure, which makes them less able to function (Fiedler & Garcia, 1987).

Studies of personality factors related to stress vulnerability, such as anxiety, demonstrate the strategy choices that may influence intelligent behavior under stress (Matthews & Wells, 1996). Wells & Matthews' (1994) model of attention and emotion, the Self-Regulative Executive Function (S-REF) model, describes how choice of coping strategy is influenced by self-knowledge in states of distress. Matthews and Wells (in press) discuss how the model interrelates knowledge level and architectural concerns. At the knowledge level, the S-REF model states that coping is influenced by self-regulatory goals, such as self-protection from threats (generalized anxiety), reevaluation of personal failure (depression), maintenance of mental or physical health (panic disorder), and avoidance of contamination (obsessive-compulsive disorder). As the transactional theory of stress specifies (Lazarus & Folkman, 1984), coping also derives from individual evaluations of the demands of the situation and of personal ability to implement accessible coping strategies. The model also describes the cognitive architecture that supports self-regulation and coping: An executive system integrates intrusions from "automatic" processing with plans for coping retrieved from a stable store of self-knowledge.

In states of distress, the coping strategy selected is often "emotion-focused": The person may choose to replace task-focused goals by self-regulatory goals that generate worry and self-scrutiny (Matthews, Schwean et al., in press). In other words, cognitive interference reflects maladaptive self-regulation. In the case of depression, there is considerable evidence that lack of task motivation contributes to performance deficit (Johnson & Magaro, 1987). The intellectual performance of depressives is impaired by self-focus of attention (Strack, Blaney, Ganellen, & Coyne, 1985) and improved by a distracting secondary task. Foulds (1952) showed that depressives' deficit on the Porteus Maze intelligence test was eliminated when they also had to repeat digits back to the experimenter. This result is inconsistent with a simple resource-deficit explanation, which would suppose that the extra task would increase the requirement for resources and disadvantage the depressives further. Similarly, studies of driver stress have shown that negative emotions are most damaging to single-task driving; stress-vulnerable drivers appear to be able to mobilize sufficient effort to deal with dual-task situations (Matthews, Sparkes, & Bygrave, 1996).

The role of coping in anxiety is more controversial because there is no clear overall motivational deficit. Indeed, Eysenck & Calvo (1992) argued that anxious individuals may be motivated to compensate for their perceived deficit in performance through increased compensatory effort. Anxious subjects may counter cognitive interference resulting from emotion focus with increased task focus. Hence, anxiety may relate more strongly to processing efficiency than to observed performance effectiveness. The anxious individual may be compared with a car having a trailer hooked up to it. Additional acceleration is needed to reach a given level of speed compared with a car without a trailer. However, deficits in active strategy use have been observed in trait-anxious subjects and neurotic subjects (Mueller, 1992), implying that anxious individuals may sometimes have difficulty applying compensatory effort adaptively. In addition, the task-focused coping of anxious individuals may be applied to the "wrong" task. Selective attention to threat in anxiety may be a consequence of using the task-focused coping strategy of monitoring for threat (see Matthews & Harley, 1996, for a computational model). This "hypervigilance" for threat (Eysenck, 1992) may distract from the overt task at hand.

STRATEGIES AND ADAPTATION. In summary, the knowledge or adaptive level brings together several interrelated constructs: motivation, self-regulation, and stress processes such as appraisal and coping. Intelligence and personality may overlap in terms of adaptive goals and outcomes. Adaptive goals are perhaps primarily an attribute of personality, but achievement-related goals appear to relate to intelligence also. Personality and intelligence may interact also as influences on adaptive success. Both may be linked to constructs such as self-esteem, self-efficacy, and coping, though there is a shortage of evidence. Understanding the adaptive processes involved requires an understanding of how self-regulation is implemented by the cognitive architecture through selecting and executing strategies. Research should aim to specify the executive and coping routines involved in both adaptive and information-processing terms. Such research is in its initial stages, but some progress has been made in relating the performance consequences of anxiety and depression to choice and implementation of coping strategies.

The Longer View: A Cognitive–Adaptive Framework

The previous section showed how explaining the effects of anxiety on intellectual function within experimental settings requires analysis of both the information-processing routines involved and their adaptive significance. Matthews (1997d, in press) has developed a more general cognitive–adaptive framework that integrates the different levels of explanation over longer time periods. In part, individual differences reflect the relatively stable influences of genes and early learning, feeding forward into neural systems controlling nonspecific arousal (biological level of explanation) and into information-processing functions (cognitive architecture level). This tool kit of elementary functions provides the basis for subsequent skill acquisition: real-world adaptation depends on somewhat context-bound skills (remembering conversations) rather than on basic functions (short-term memory).

The right-hand side of Figure 26.2 illustrates the dynamic interplay at the adaptive level of explanation. "Knowledge" refers to the package of psychological functions involved in self-regulation, which are, of course, discriminated in more fine-grained models (e.g., Wells & Matthews, 1994). On the one hand, successful adaptation reflects the application of the skills the individual is predisposed to acquire. Ensuing real-world success then feeds into congruent self-knowledge – motivation and confidence in application of skill – which in turn is likely to enhance actual skill. On the other hand, adaptation is partially driven by knowledge itself, given that people may have unrealistic beliefs about the personal competencies. Self-beliefs and motivations influence the environments to which people choose to expose themselves, and, hence, the skills they have the opportunity to learn. Normally, there will be some positive feedback between the triangle of components to the extent that people gravitate towards environmental niches that suit their skills and interests.

Table 26.3 shows how the three individual difference constructs, g, E, and N, may relate to the cognitive–adaptive framework. Ability and personality traits are conceptualized as bundles of computationally independent processing functions that jointly support adaptation of the individual to specific informational environments. Intelligent individuals are adapted to novelty and complexity (cf. Sternberg, 1985), extraverts to social and informationally demanding environments, and more neurotic individuals to environments in which threats are subtle or disguised, and thus hypervigilance for threat (Eysenck, 1992) is required. These adaptations

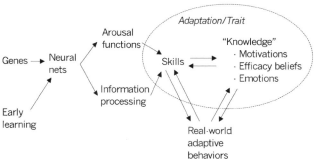

FIGURE 26.2. A cognitive–adaptive framework for personality and ability (Matthews, in press).

are supported both by acquired skills built on the platform provided by the cognitive architecture and by knowledge. For example, extraverts' processing functions equip them to learn how to converse effectively, to deal with challenging social encounters, and to act rapidly. At the knowledge level, extraverts have confidence in their own abilities, which feeds into more effective coping in demanding environments (Matthews, 1997b, in press). Conversely, introverts are adapted to environments characterized by infrequent stimuli, such as working as a writer or artist, within which they may capitalize on skills for sustained attention, reflective problem solving, and tolerance of monotony. Intelligence is perhaps more strongly influenced by feed-forward from basic neural and cognitive processing functions than is personality and could be identified with the acquired reasoning skills used for solving intelligence test problems, influenced by processing-level constructs such as speed of information processing.

The cognitive–adaptive approach provides a fresh perspective on relationships between personality and intelligence. The two kinds of individual difference factors are most sharply discriminated at the adaptive level, at which each dimension represents cognitive fitness for a different type of environment. However, the skills supporting different adaptations use some common processing building blocks. For example, a good short-term memory may be used to cultivate skills in fluent but nonintellectual conversation, an extraverted skill, or for more intellectual problem-solving skills related to g. In addition, specific real-world environments may sometimes relate to multiple adaptations. For example, training environments tend to possess both novelty and

TABLE 26.3. Relationship between Three Individual Difference Factors and Components of the Cognitive–Adaptive Framework

	Intelligence	Extraversion	Anxiety/ Neuroticism
Arousal functions	?	Cortico–recticular arousability Sensitivity to reward signals?	Autonomic arousal ? (1) Sensitivity to punishment signals?
Information processing	Processing speed (+) Working memory (+) Executive functions (+)	Dual task (+) Short-term memory (+) Response criterion (−) Vigilance (+) Problem solving (−) Arousal-dependent effects	Working memory (−) Attentional resources (−) Judgment (negative bias) Selective attention (negative bias)

Skills	Intellectual skills
	  – handling complexity
	  – handling novelty
	  – transfer across context
		Conversation
		Rapidity of action
		Social encounters
			Awareness of danger
			Safety behaviors
			More "substantive" decision making (1)

Knowledge	Achievement motivation Self-efficacy? Intellectual interest	Social motivation Self-efficacy Positive affect Task-focused coping	Self-protective motivations Low Self-efficacy Negative affect Emotion-focused coping Domain-specific knowledge (2)
Real-world adaptation	Academic and educational environments	High-pressure occupations (3) Dating and mating	Covert threats (4)

1. Relates to state anxiety only.
2. Knowledge referring to specific sources of threat: e.g., social or physical threat.
3. Introverts adapted to activities offering little external stimulation: e.g., literary and scientific work.
4. Emotionally stable individuals adapted to overtly threatening environments.

cognitive complexity (congruent with *g*) and potential information overload (congruent with *E*). Hence, job performance during training relates not just to *g* but also to *E*, although *E* does not relate to job performance in general (Barrick & Mount, 1991). In other words, personality may sometimes relate to the context-bound skills or practical intelligence (Sternberg, 1985) required for specific environments. Extraverts function more intelligently than introverts in the environments congruent with the trait. However, the underlying cognitive basis for this practical intelligence is not reasoning ability but the acquired information-management skills required for handling overload and social encounters.

It is readily apparent that an individual who is high in both intelligence and some personality factor such as Neuroticism or Extraversion will think, feel, and act differently from another person who has high intelligence but is very low in *N* or *E*, respectively. The different information processing characteristics of extraverts and introverts may not only underlie behavioral differences but also suggest the kinds of environments (e.g., vocational, social, interpersonal) they are most likely to seek out and function best in. More traditional views of intelligence may be somewhat limited in describing the interface between personality and intelligence and in describing how these two broad domains contribute to a description of human behavior and individual differences.

DIRECTIONS FOR FUTURE RESEARCH

The integration of research and assessment in the ability, personality, and motivational domains would appear to be an important goal for individual differences research in the 21st century. To achieve this goal, we conclude this chapter by highlighting several potentially useful directions for future research on the personality–intelligence interface recently suggested by Zeidner (1997).

More Refined Conceptualization and Taxonomies of Constructs

More thought needs to be given to the conceptualization of the personality–intelligence constructs and domains of discourse. Even quite loose provisional classification structures may help guide exploration and provide a useful framework to which to pin individual data as they accumulate. The growing consensus about the multidimensional nature of the ability domain (Carroll, 1993), together with more recent advances in the taxonomy of personality (McCrae & Costa, 1997) and conative aptitudes (cf. Corno, 1997), provides some solid ground for establishing personality–intelligence relations.

To that end, it may be useful to employ a facet–analytic approach to the investigation of the personality–intelligence interface by constructing a matrix with ability constructs (j) represented by rows and personality constructs (k) represented by columns and the entire two-dimensional matrix ($j \times k$), or Cartesian space, representing the domain of discourse for any future integrative attempt. A third facet, area of application (school, occupation, military) may be added to form a three-faceted cubic model. Furthermore, we need more theory-driven research to allow us to make focused predictions of the relationship between intelligence and personality. Thus, the optimal approach is to look at well-established theories concerning performance data and articulate focused hypotheses to test, arrange experimental conditions to test deductions from these theories, use appropriate measures to test hypotheses, and interpret results cautiously in the light of the theories in question (Eysenck, 1994).

Improving Research Design, Measurement, and Analysis

Further work is needed on the interrelations between different individual difference constructs and the underlying processes to which they relate (Snow, 1995). Various advances in design and analysis are ripe for application to the personality–intelligence interface such as modern confirmatory factor analysis, structural equation modeling, and multilevel modeling techniques (Boyle et al., 1995). Research would also benefit from using modern scaling techniques such as univariate or multivariate Item Response Theory (IRT) models in constructing affective assessment instruments. IRT technology has been available for some time now, but few individual difference researchers have taken advantage of modern test theory in constructing unidimensional scales (Most & Zeidner, 1995).

Within the psychometric approach, there is scope for testing for nonlinear relations as well as for multiplicative functions introducing both linear and quadratic functions of intelligence and motivational predictors of performance.

Clearer Specification of the Meaning and Nature of the Interaction between Intelligence and Personality

Much work needs to be done on modeling the complexity of personality–ability interactions while maintaining clarity and testability of hypotheses (Snow, 1995). Personality–intelligence interactions may take many forms and may reflect different hypotheses about particular causal mechanisms and types of interactive effects and mechanisms presumed to be operative. We need more longitudinal research modeling the dynamic transactions between personality and intellectual variables over time via such procedures as structural equation modeling.

Identifying Key Bridging Concepts

The psychometric approach tends to provide personality traits that are sharply discriminated from intelligence. Perhaps a more productive search would be to examine a gray area between intelligence and general personality, the domain of "cognitive" or "intellectual" styles (Messick, 1996). A variety of stylistic concepts may provide a useful bridge between affect and cognition and a means by which to conceptualize the intersection and crossroads between personality, conation, and intelligence domains. One of the difficulties in past research has been the application of inappropriate measurement models. Most measures of style have inappropriately followed the ability factor model and have yielded scores that are unipolar and value-directed rather than bipolar and value-differentiated. In fact, styles should be concerned with not "how much," but "how." One of the important contributions psychometricians can make to our field is through improved measurement of stylistic variables as a potential bridge between personality and intelligence variables. Recent research suggests that intelligence would be most closely and organically related to personality variables that reflect typical ways of dealing with information, and it might be useful to have another careful and methodologically sounder look at both old and new stylistic variables. Several stylistic variables, such as "mental self-government" (Sternberg & Grigorenko, 1995), "prudence" (Haslam & Baron, 1994), "wisdom" (Maciel, Heckhausen, & Baltes, 1994), "mindfulness" (Brown & Langer, 1990), and "intellectual absorption" (Mayer, Caruso, Agiler, & Dreyden, 1989) provide contemporary and dynamic examples of bridging concepts linking personality and intelligence.

In-Depth Research in Practical and Clinical Settings

Personality and intelligence variables are often used jointly for decision-making purposes in various practical domains. By necessity, the greatest amount of integration of cognitive and personality variables takes place in professional and applied settings. Research models such as Cronbach and Snow's (1977) Aptitude × Treatment Interaction attempted to demonstrate empirically how characteristics of the individual such as intelligence and personality (e.g., extraversion, anxiety) interacted with different possible treatments (e.g., therapies, instructional strategies, teacher characteristics) to produce particular outcomes. The clinical, vocational, counseling and school psychologist performs formal and informal ATIs each time a client is seen for assessment and diagnosis. However, we know very little about how practitioners and clinicians conduct the integration between personality, conative, and in-

telligence variables in the process of psychodiagnosis and decision making. More research is needed on the considerations practitioners bring to bear in making decisions based on the integration between affective and ability constructs.

As previously discussed, intelligence may relate to one's current level of organization and integrative functioning. Hence, intelligence may play an important role in the prognosis of maladjusted individuals. In fact, there is some research to support the claim that intelligence is a significant predictor of success in psychological treatment and therapy, although not all studies substantiate the link (Zeidner, Matthews, & Saklofske, 1998).

CONCLUSIONS

This review suggests a rather complex reciprocal relationship between intelligence and a variety of personality factors in which cognitive and affective–motivational variables dynamically impact upon each other in the course of development and day-to-day behavior. On one hand, personality dispositions and motivational factors may influence intellectual functioning. It is important to distinguish the effects personality may have on performance, in the short term, from effects on competence in the longer term. There is solid empirical evidence for various negative emotional and motivational states tending to impair intellectual performance to a moderate degree, especially when the task demands attention or working memory. It is likely that both loss of functional resources and motivational processes contribute to intellectual impairment in both emotional disorders and in subclinical stress states. Conversely, strategies driven by motivational factors such as self-efficacy and need to achieve may serve to maintain or enhance performance. Some of these effects may be context-dependent in that they are contingent upon stress or arousal. It is less clear whether personality factors affect basic competence in addition to the person's performance on specific occasions. Certain personality traits, such as poor self-concept and aggression, may act over extended periods of time to depress intellectual functioning by reducing a person's motivation to acquire and develop specific intellectual skills. Psychotic conditions and personality disorders too may affect both temporary performance and underlying competence. We have used a cognitive science framework to suggest that cognitive, adaptive, and (possibly) neural explanations may all be necessary in understanding the processes controlling these effects.

On the other hand, intelligence may impact upon personality and affective states through encouraging more positive cognitions of personal competence. Thus, individuals high in intellectual functioning are frequently shown to be better adjusted, both socially and emotionally, than their less intelligent counterparts. High intelligence can aid a student in learning the realities of general and school culture and the physical world as part of an integrated learning process and help the person acquire more socially desirable traits. Overall, intelligence may serve as a personal resource that can facilitate personal growth and adjustment and also serve as a buffer against the crippling effects of psychological stress and disease (cf. Lazarus & Folkman, 1984; Lazarus, 1991). Conversely, more or less veridical appraisals of negative outcomes on intellectual tasks may contribute to the development of negative affectivity.

From a practical point of view, personality variables seldom bear such a sizable impact on intellectual performance as to invalidate intelligence assessments or test scores as a whole. The impact of various personality and conative factors affecting performance (e.g., anxiety, motivation) may in fact be viewed as key aspects of the individual's global intellectual capacity (Matarazzo, 1972; Wechsler, 1944). Arguably, individuals who do poorly on intelligence tests because of the debilitating effects of certain personality factors (e.g., high test anxiety, low motivation) may also do poorly on the criterion measure of performance – and for much the same reasons. The cognitive–adaptive framework presented in this chapter emphasizes both information processing and the expression of individual differences in real-world skills. It leaves open causal questions concerning the origin of individual differences in feed-forward from genes and feedback from person–situation interactions. Plausibly, it may be the dynamic interplay between biologically based predispositions and the varying opportunities provided by the environment that determine personality and intelligence and relationships between them. Specifically, personality may relate to context-bound practical intelligence supported by

the skills acquired to handle the context concerned. Personality assessment tells us something about the situations in which the individual will behave more or less "intelligently".

Current trends in individual differences research allow for the hope of an integrated understanding of the ways that "each person is like all other people, some other people, and no other people" (Revelle, 1995). A truly integrative science of personality would help clear from our path some of the debris of disciplinary provincialism. However, there is a difference between simple eclecticism and an integrated model that forms the basis for a unified approach to, and rapprochement with, the domains of conation intelligence. Such an approach would not simply look at a person from intellectual and motivational or affective perspectives but instead integrate data from these perspectives. A true integration would certainly move us a step forward in understanding both normal as well as pathological states, and this appears to be a major challenge for individual differences research in the 21st century.

REFERENCES

Ackerman, P. L., & Heggestad, E. D. (1997). Intelligence, personality, and interests: Evidence for overlapping traits. *Psychological Bulletin, 121*, 219–245.

Adorno, T. W., Frenkel-Brunswick, E., Levinson, D. J., & Sanford, R. N. (1950). *The authoritarian personality*. New York: Harper & Row.

Alexander, J. M., & Schwanenflugel, P. J. (1994). Strategy regulation: The role of intelligence, metacognitive attributions, and knowledge base. *Developmental Psychology, 30*, 709–723.

Anastasi, A. (1958). *Differential psychology*. New York: Macmillan.

Anastasi, A. (1988). *Psychological testing* (4th ed.). New York: Macmillan.

Anderson, M. (1992). *Intelligence and development: A cognitive theory*. Oxford: Blackwell.

Anthony, W. S. (1973). The development of extroversion, of ability, and of the relation between them. *British Journal of Educational Psychology, 43*, 223–227.

Argyle, M. (1961). *Religious behavior*. Chicago: Free Press.

Atkinson, J. W. (1974). *An introduction to motivation*. Princeton, NJ: Van Nostrand.

Bandura, A. (1986). *Social foundations of thought and action: A social cognitive theory*. Englewood Cliff, NJ: Prentice Hall.

Bandura, A. (1977). Self-efficacy: Toward a unifying theory of behavioral change. *Psychological Review, 84*, 191–215.

Barrick, M. R., & Mount, M. K. (1991). The Big Five personality dimensions and job performance: a meta-analysis. *Personnel Psychology, 44*, 1–26.

Beech, A., & Williams, L. (1997). Investigating cognitive processes in schizotypal personality and schizophrenia. In G. Matthews (Ed.), *Cognitive science perspectives on personality and emotion.* Amsterdam: Elsevier Science.

Block, J. (1995). On the relation between IQ, impulsivity, and delinquency: Remarks on the Lynam, Moffitt, and Stouthamer-Loeber (1993) interpretation. *Journal of Abnormal Psychology, 104*, 395–398.

Block, J., & Kremen, A. M. (1996). IQ and ego-resiliency: Conceptual and empirical connections and separateness. *Journal of Personality and Social Psychology, 70*, 349–361.

Boekaerts, M. (in press). Self-regulated learning at the junction of cognition and motivation. *European Psychologist.*

Borkowski, J. G., & Peck, V. A. (1986). Causes and consequences of metamemory in gifted children. In R. Sternberg & J. Davidson (Eds.), *Conceptions of giftedness* (pp. 182–200). Cambridge, UK: Cambridge University Press.

Bown, J., & Langer, E. (1990). Mindfulness and intelligence: A comparison. *Educational Psychologist, 25*, 305–335.

Boyle, G. J., Stankov, L., & Cattell, R. B. (1995). Measurement and statistical models in the study of personality and intelligence. In D. H. Saklofske & M. Zeidner (Eds.), *International handbook of personality and intelligence* (pp. 417–446). New York: Plenum.

Brody, N. (1992). *Intelligence* (2nd ed.). New York: Academic Press.

Bullock, W. A., & Gilliland, K. (1993). Eysenck's arousal theory of introversion–extraversion: A converging measures investigation. *Journal of Personality and Social Psychology, 64*, 113–123.

Carroll, J. B. (1993). *Human cognitive abilities.* New York: Cambridge University Press.

Carver, C. S., & Scheier, M. F. (1981). *Attention and self-regulation: A control-theory approach to human behavior.* Berlin: Springer-Verlag.

Carver, C. S., & Scheier, M. F. (1991). A control-process perspective on anxiety. In R. Schwarzer & R. A. Wickland (Eds.), *Anxiety and self focused attention* (pp. 3–8). London: Harwood Publishers.

Cattell, R. B. (1971). *Abilities: Their structure, growth and action.* New York: Houghton Mifflin.

Christie, R. (1954). Authoritarianism re-examined. In R. Christie and M. Jahoda (Eds.), *Studies in the scope and method of ''The Authoritarian Personality.''* New York: Free Press.

Coleman, J. C., Butcher, J. N., & Carson, R. C. (1984). *Abnormal psychology* (7th ed.). Scott, Foresman, & Co.: NY.

Corno, L. (1997, July). *Conative individual differences in learning.* Paper presented at the Second Spearman Seminar on Intelligence and Personality, Plymouth, England.

Costa, P. T., Jr., & McCrae, R. R. (1986). Personality stability and its implications for clinical psychology. *Clinical Psychology Review, 1*, 144–149.

Costa, P. T., & McCrae, R. R. (1992). *Revised NEO personality inventory and NEO five factor inventory. Professional manual.* Odessa, FL: Psychological Assessment Resources, Inc.

Crookes, T. G., Pearson, P. R., Francis, L. J., & Carter, M. (1981). Extraversion and performance on Raven's Progressive Matrices in 15–16 year old children. *British Journal of Educational Psychology, 51*, 109–111.

Cronbach, L. J., & Snow, R. E. (1977). *Aptitudes and instructional methods.* New York: Irvington.

Daugherty, S. A., Henry, B. E., Peterson, D. L., Swarts, R. L., Bastien, S., & Thomas, R. S. (1991). Chronic fatigue syndrome in Northern Nevada. *Reviews of Infectious Diseases, 13*, pp. 539–44 (supplement).

Deary, I. J., & Stough, C. (1996). Intelligence and inspection time: Achievements, prospects and problems. *American Psychologist, 51*, 599–608.

Derryberry, D., & Reed, M. A. (1994). Temperament and attention: Orienting toward and away from positive and negative signals. *Journal of Personality and Social Psychology, 66*, 1128–1139.

Derryberry, D., & Reed, M. A. (1997). Motivational and attentional components of personality. In G. Matthews (Ed.), *Cognitive science perspectives on personality and emotion.* Amsterdam: Elsevier Science.

Endler, N. S., & Summerfeldt, L. J. (1995). Intelligence, personality, psychopathology, and adjustment. In D. H. Saklofske & M. Zeidner (Eds.), *International handbook of personality and intelligence* (pp. 249–284). New York: Plenum.

Eysenck, H. J. (1994). Personality and intelligence: Psychometric and experimental approaches. In R. J. Sternberg & P. Ruzgis (Eds.), *Personality and intelligence* (pp. 3–31). New York: Cambridge University Press.

Eysenck, H. J., & Eysenck, M. W. (1985). *Personality and individual differences: A natural science approach.* New York: Plenum.

Eysenck, H. J., & Cookson, D. (1969). Personality in primary school children – Ability and achievement. *British Journal of Educational Psychology, 39*, 109–130.

Eysenck, M. W. (1981). Learning, memory and personality. In H. J. Eysenck (Ed.), *A model for personality.* Berlin: Springer-Verlag.

Eysenck, M. W. (1982). *Attention and arousal: Cognition and performance.* New York: Springer-Verlag.

Eysenck, M. W. (1992). *Anxiety: The cognitive perspective.* Hillsdale, NJ: Erlbaum.

Eysenck, M. W., & Calvo, M. G. (1992). Anxiety and performance: The processing efficiency theory. *Cognition and Emotion, 6*, 409–434.

Ferrara, R. P., Brown, A. L., & Campione, J. C. (1986). Children's learning and transfer of inductive reasoning rules: Studies of proximal development. *Child Development, 57*, 1087–1099.

Fiedler, F. E., & Garcia, J. E. (1987). *New approaches to effective leadership: Cognitive researches and organizational performance.* New York: Wiley.

Flavell, J. H. (1985). *Cognitive development.* Englewood Cliffs, NJ: Prentice Hall.

Foulds, G. A. (1952). Temperamental differences in maze performance II: The effect of distraction and of electroconvulsive therapy on psychomotor retardation. *British Journal of Psychiatry, 43*, 33–41.

Goff, M., & Ackerman, P. L. (1992). Personality–intelligence relations: Assessment of typical intellectual engagement. *Journal of Educational Psychology, 84*, 537–552.

Gray, J. A. (1982). *The neuropsychology of anxiety: An inquiry into the functions of the septo–hippocampal system.* Oxford: Oxford University Press.

Grigorenko, E. L., & Sternberg, R. J. (1995). In D. Saklofske, & M. Zeidner (Eds.). (1995). Thinking styles. *International handbook of personality and intelligence* (pp. 205–229). New York: Plenum.

Gustafsson, J. (1997, July). *On the hierarchical structure of personality and ability.* Paper presented at the 2nd Spearman Seminar, Plymouth, England.

Haan, N. (1977). *Coping and defending: Processes of self-environmental organization.* New York: Academic Press.

Hamlin, R. M. (1963). The stability of intellectual functioning in chronic schizophrenia. *Journal of Nervous and Mental Disease, 136*, 360–364.

Hartlage, S., Alloy, L. B., Vazquez, C., & Dykman, B. (1993). Automatic and effortful processing in depression. *Psychological Bulletin, 113*, 247–278.

Haslam, N., & Baron, J. (1994). Intelligence, personality, and prudence. In R. J. Sternberg & P. Ruzgis (Eds.), *Personality and intelligence* (pp. 32–60). New York: Cambridge University Press.

Heckhausen (1967). *The anatomy of achievement motivation.* New York: Academic Press.

Heffner, P. A., Strauss, M. E., & Grisell, J. (1975). Rehospitalization of schizophrenics as a function of intelligence. *Journal of Abnormal Psychology, 84*, 735–736.

Hembree, R. (1988). Correlates, causes, effects and treatment of test anxiety. Review of *Educational Research, 58*, 47–77.

Hofstee, W. (1997, July). *Conceptual issues in the relation between personality and intelligence.* Paper presented at the Second Spearman Seminar, Plymouth, UK.

Hope, D. A., & Heimberg, R. G. (1990). Dating anxiety. In H. Leitenberg (Ed.), *Handbook of social and evaluative anxiety* (pp. 217–246). New York: Plenum Press.

Hough, L. M. (1992). The "Big Five" personality variables construct confusion: Description versus prediction. *Human Performance, 5*, 139–155.

Huesman, L. R., Eron, L. D., & Yarmel, P. W. (1987). Intellectual functioning and aggression. *Journal of Personality and Social Psychology, 52*, 218–231.

Humphreys, M. S., & Revelle, W. (1984). Personality, motivation and performance: A theory of the relationship between individual differences and information processing. *Psychological Review, 91*, 153–184.

Hunt, E. B. (1978). Mechanics of verbal ability. *Psychological Review, 85*, 109–130.

Jensen, A. (1980). *Bias in Mental Testing.* New York: Free Press.

Johnson, M. H., & Magaro, P. A. (1987). Effects of mood and severity on memory processes in depression and mania. *Psychological Bulletin, 101*, 28–40.

Jones, W. H., Rusell, D. W., & Nickel, T. (1977). Belief in the paranormal scale: An objective instrument to measure belief in magical phenomena and causes. *JSAS Catalog of selected documents in psychology, 7*, 100.

Kanfer, R. (1989). Conative processes, dispositions, and behavior: Connecting the dots within and across paradigms. In R. Kanfer, P. L. Ackerman, & R. Cudeck (Eds.), *Abilities, motivation, and methodology* (pp. 375–388). Hillsdale, NJ: Erlbaum.

Kanfer, R. (1990). Motivation and individual differences in learning: An integration of developmental, differential and cognitive perspectives. *Learning and Individual Differences, 2*, 221–239.

Kuhl, J., & Kraska, K. (1989). Self-regulation and meta-motivation: Computational mechanisms, development, and assessment. In R. Kanfer, P. L. Ackerman, & R. Cudeck (Eds.), *Abilities, motivation, and methodology* (pp. 343–374). Hillsdale, NJ: Erlbaum.

Kyllonen, P. (1997, July). *Learning, cognition, personality, and emotion.* Paper presented at the 2nd Spearman Seminar, Plymouth, England.

Kyllonen, P. C., & Christal, R. E. (1990). Reasoning ability is (little more than) working-memory capacity?! *Intelligence, 14*, 389–433.

Lazarus, R. S. (1991). *Emotion and adaptation.* New York: Oxford University Press.

Lazarus, R. S., & Folkman, S. (1984). Coping and adaptation. In W. D. Gentry (Ed.), *The handbook of behavioral medicine* (pp. 282–325). New York: Guilford.

LeDoux, J. E. (1995). In search of an emotional system in the brain: Leaping from fear to emotion and consciousness. In M. S. Gazzaniga (Ed.), *The cognitive neurosciences* (pp. 1049–1062). Cambridge, MA: MIT Press.

Loehlin, J. C. (1992). *Genes and environment in personality development.* Newbury Park, CA: Sage.

Lynam, D., Moffitt, T., & Stouthame-Loeber, L. M. (1993). Explaining the relation between IQ and delinquency: Class, race, test motivation, school failure, or self control? *Journal of Abnormal Psychology, 102*, 187–196.

Maciel, A. G., Heckhausen, J., & Baltes, P. B. (1994). A life-span perspective on the interface between personality and intelligence. In R. J. Sternberg & P. Ruzgis (Eds.), *Personality and intelligence* (pp. 61–103). New York: Cambridge University Press.

Maroyama, G., Rubin, R. A., & Kingsbury, G. G. (1981). Self-esteem and educational achievement: Independent constructs with a common cause. *Journal of Personality and Social Psychology, 40,* 962–975.

Matarazzo, J. D. (1972). *Wechsler's measurement and appraisal of adult intelligence* (5th ed.). Baltimore: Williams & Wilkins.

Matthews, G. (1986). The effects of anxiety on intellectual performance: When and why are they found? *Journal of Research in Personality, 20,* 385–401.

Matthews, G. (1992). Extraversion. In A. P. Smith & D. M. Jones (Eds.), *Handbook of human performance.* Vol. 3: State and trait, pp. 95–126. London: Academic.

Matthews, G. (1997a). An introduction to the cognitive science of personality and emotion. In G. Matthews (Ed.), *Cognitive science perspectives on personality and emotion.* Amsterdam: Elsevier Science.

Matthews, G. (1997b). Extraversion, emotion and performance: A cognitive-adaptive model. In G. Matthews (Ed.), *Cognitive science perspectives on personality and emotion* (pp. 339–342) Amsterdam: Elsevier Science.

Matthews, G. (1997c). The Big Five as a framework for personality assessment. In N. Anderson & P. Herriot (Eds.), *International handbook of selection and appraisal* (2nd ed.), pp. 175–200. London: Wiley.

Matthews, G. (1997d). Intelligence, personality and information processing: An adaptive perspective. In W. Tomic & J. Kingsma (Eds.), *Advances in cognition and educational practice. Volume 4: Reflections on the concept of intelligence,* pp. 475–492. Greenwich, CT: JAI Press.

Matthews, G. (1999). Personality and skill: A cognitive-adaptive framework. In P. L. Ackerman, P. C. Kyllonen, & R. D. Roberts (Eds.), *The future of learning and individual differences research: Processes, traits, and content* (pp. 251–273) Washington, DC: American Psychological Association.

Matthews, G., & Amelang, M. (1993). Extraversion, arousal theory and performance: A study of individual differences in the EEG. *Personality and Individual Differences, 14,* 347–364.

Matthews, G., & Davies, D. R. (in press). Arousal and vigilance: The role of task factors. In R. B. Hoffman, M. F. Sherrick, & J. S. Warm (Eds.), *Integrating perception across psychology. Perspectives on motivation, choice, and individual differences* (pp. 113–144), Washington, DC: American Psychological Association.

Matthews, G., & Dorn, L. (1995). Personality and intelligence: Cognitive and attentional processes. In D. Saklofske & M. Zeidner (Eds.), *International handbook of personality and intelligence* (pp. 367–396). New York: Plenum.

Matthews, G., & Gilliland, K. (1999). The personality theories of H. J. Eysenck and J. A. Gray: A comparative review. *Personality and Individual Differences, 26,* 583–626.

Matthews, G., & Harley, T. A. (1993). Effects of extraversion and self-report arousal on semantic priming: A connectionist approach. *Journal of Personality and Social Psychology, 65,* 735–756.

Matthews, G., & Harley, T. A. (1996). Connectionist models of emotional distress and attentional bias. *Cognition and Emotion, 10,* 561–600.

Matthews, G., Saklofske, D. H., Costa, P. T., Jr., Deary, I. J., & Zeidner, M. (1998). Dimensional models of personality: A framework for systematic clinical assessment. *European Journal of Psychological Assessment, 14,* 36–49.

Matthews, G., Schwean, V. L., Campbell, S. E., Saklofske, D. H., & Mohamed, A. A. R. (1999). Personality, self-regulation and adaptation: A cognitive-social framework. In M. Boekaerts, P. R. Pintrich, & M. Zeidner (Eds.), *Handbook of self-regulation.* New York: Academic.

Matthews, G., & Wells, A. (1999). The cognitive science of attention and emotion. In T. Dalgleish & M. Power (Eds.), *Handbook of cognition and emotion* (pp. 171–191), New York: Wiley.

Matthews, G., Sparkes, T. J., & Bygrave, H. M. (1996). Stress, attentional overload and simulated driving performance. *Human Performance, 9,* 77–101.

Mayer, J. D., Caruso, D. R., Zigler, E. & Dreyden, J. I. (1989). Intelligence and intelligence-related traits. *Intelligence, 13,* 119–133.

McCrae, R. R. (1987). Creativity, divergent thinking, and openness to experience. *Journal of Personality and Social Psychology, 52,* 1258–1265.

McCrae, R. R. (1994). Openness to experience: Expanding the boundaries of Factor V. *European Journal of Personality. 13,* 39–55.

McCrae, R. R., & Costa, P. T., Jr. (1997). Personality trait structure as a human universal. *American Psychologist, 53,* 509–516.

Messick, S. (1996). *Bridging cognition and personality in education: The role of style in performance and development.* Research Report, Educational Testing Service.

Mesulam, M. M. (1985). Principles of behavioral neurology. Philadelphia: F. A. Davis.

Mischel, W. (1968). *Personality and assessment.* New York: John Wiley.

Morris, L. W., & Liebert, R. M. (1969). Effects of anxiety on timed and untimed intelligence tests: Another look. *Journal of Consulting and Clinical Psychology, 33,* 240–244.

Most, B., & Zeidner, M. (1995). Constructing personality and intelligence test instruments: Methods and issues. In D. Saklofske & M. Zeidner (Eds.). *International handbook of personality and intelligence* (pp. 475–503). New York: Plenum.

Mueller, J. H. (1992). Anxiety and performance. In A. P. Smith & D. M. Jones (Eds.), *Handbook of human performance* (3rd ed.) (pp. 127–160). London: Academic Press.

Necka, E. (1997). Attention, working memory and arousal: Concepts apt to account for the process of intelligence. In G. Matthews (Ed.), *Cognitive science perspectives on personality and emotion.* Amsterdam: Elsevier Science.

Neubauer, A. C. (1997). The mental speed approach to the assessment of intelligence. In W. Tomic & J. Kingsma

(Eds.), *Advances in cognition and educational practice. Volume 4: Reflections on the concept of intelligence.* Greenwich, CT: JAI Press.

Nevo, B. (1998). *Human intelligence.* Tel-Aviv: Open University Press (in Hebrew).

Nunnally, J. C. (1978). *Psychometric theory.* New York: McGraw-Hill.

Payne, R. (1991). Individual differences in cognition and the stress process. In C. L. Cooper & R. Payne (Ed.), *Personality and stress: Individual differences in the stress process.* New York: John Wiley.

Purkey, W. W. (1970). *Self-concept and school achievement.* Englewood Cliffs, NJ: Prentice Hall.

Pylyshyn, Z. W. (1984). *Computation and cognition: Toward a foundation for cognitive science.* Cambridge, MA: MIT Press.

Rawlings, D., & Carnie, D. (1989). The interaction of EPQ extraversion with WAIS subtest performance under timed and untimed conditions. *Personality and Individual Differences, 10,* 453–458.

Revelle, W. (1995). Personality processes, *Annual Review of Psychology, 46,* 295–328.

Revelle, W., Amaral, P. & Turriff, S. (1976). Introversion/extraversion, time stress, and caffeine: Effects on verbal test performance. *Science, 192,* 149–150.

Rolfhus, E. L., & Ackerman, P. L. (1996). Self-report knowledge: At the crossroads of ability, interest and personality. *Journal of Educational Psychology, 88,* 174–188.

Revelle, W., Humpheys, M. S., Simon, L., & Gilliland, K. (1980). The interactive effects of personality, time of day, and caffeine: A test of the arousal model. *Journal of Experimental Psychology: General, 109,* 1–31.

Robinson, D. L. (1985). How personality relates to intelligence test performance: Implications for a theory of intelligence, aging research, and personality assessment. *Personality and Individual Differences, 6,* 203–216.

Saklofske, D. H., & Kostura, D. D. (1990). Extraversion-intraversion and intelligence. *Personality and Individual Differences, 11,* 547–551.

Saklofske, D. H., & Zeidner, M. (Eds.). (1995). *International handbook of personality and intelligence.* New York: Plenum.

Samuel, W. (1980). Mood and personality correlates of IQ by race and sex of subject. *Journal of Personality and Social Psychology, 38,* 993–1004.

Sarason, I. G. (1975). Test anxiety, attention, and the general problem of anxiety. In C. D. Spielberger & I. G. Sarason (Eds.), *Stress and anxiety* (Vol. 1, pp. 165–210). New York: Hemisphere/Halstead.

Sarason, I. G. (1980). (Ed.). *Test anxiety: Theory, research and applications.* Hillsdale, NJ: Lawrence Erlbaum.

Saucier, G. (1994). Trapnell versus the lexical factor: Much ado about nothing? *European Journal of Personality, 8,* 291–298.

Sattler, J. M. (1988). *Assessment of children.* (3rd ed.). San Diego: Author.

Schwartzman, A. E., & Douglas, V. I. (1962). Intellectual loss in schizophrenics. Part I. *Canadian Journal of Psychology, 16,* 1–10.

Schwean, V. L., & Saklofske, D. H. (1995). A cognitive–social description of exceptional children. In D. H. Saklofske & M. Zeidner (Eds.), *International handbook of personality and intelligence* (pp. 185–204). New York: Plenum.

Siegman, A. W. (1956). The effect of manifest anxiety on a concept formation task, a nondirected learning task, and on timed and untimed intelligence tests. *Journal of Consulting Psychology, 20,* 176–178.

Seligman, M. E. P. (1975). *Helplessness.* San Francisco: Freeman.

Seipp, B. (1991). Anxiety and academic performance: A meta-analysis of findings. *Anxiety Research, 4,* 27–41.

Snow, R. (1989). Cognitive-conative aptitude interactions in learning. In R. Kanfer, P. L. Ackerman, & R. Cudeck (Eds.), *Abilities, motivation, and methodology* (pp. 435–474). Hillsdale, NJ: Erlbaum.

Snow, R. (1995). Foreword. In D. H. Saklofske & M. Zeidner (Eds.), *International handbook of personality and intelligence* (pp. 11–15). New York: Plenum.

Snow, R., & Lohman, D. F. (1984). Toward a theory of cognitive aptitude for learning from instruction. *Journal of Educational Psychology, 76,* 347–376.

Snow, R. E., Killonen, P. C., & Marshalek, B. (1984). The topography of ability and learning correlations. In R. J. Sternberg (Ed.), *Advances in the psychology of human intelligence* (Vol. 2). Hillsdale, NJ: Erlbaum.

Spielberger, C. D., Gonzales, H. P., Taylor, C. J., Algaze, B., & Anton, W. D. (1978). Examination stress and test anxiety. In C. D. Spielberger & I. G. Sarason (Eds.), *Stress and anxiety* (Vol. 5, pp. 167–191). New York: Wiley.

Stankov, L. (1989). Attentional resources and intelligence: A disappearing link. *Personality and Individual Differences, 10,* 957–968.

Spilsbury, G., Stankov, L., & Roberts, R. (1990). The effect of a test's difficulty on its correlation with intelligence. *Personality and Individual Differences, 11,* 1069–1077.

Tett, R. P., Jackson, D. N., & Rothstein, M. (1991). Personality measures as predictors of job performance: A meta-analytic review. *Personnel Psychology, 44,* 703–742.

Trapnell, P. D. (1994). Openness versus intellect: A lexical left turn. *European Journal of Personality, 8,* 273–290.

Stanley, J. C., Keating, D. P., & Fox, L. H. (1974). *Mathematical talent: Discovery, description, development.* Baltimore: John Hopkins University Press.

Stelmack, R. M., & Houlihan, M. (1995). Event-related potentials, personality, and intelligence. In D. H. Saklofske & M. Zeidner (Eds.), *International handbook of personality and intelligence* (pp. 349–366). New York: Plenum.

Strack, S., Blaney, P. H., Ganellen, R. J., & Coyne, J. C. (1985). Pessimistic self-preoccupation, performance deficits and depression. *Journal of Personality and Social Psychology, 49,* 1076–1085.

Sternberg, R. J. (1977). Intelligence, information processing, and analogical reasoning. *The componential analysis of human ability*. Hillsdale, NJ: Erlbaum.

Sternberg, R. J. (1985). Beyond IQ: *A triarchic theory of human intelligence*. New York: Cambridge University Press.

Sternberg, R. J., & Ruzgis, P. (Eds.). (1994). *Personality and intelligence*. New York: Cambridge University Press.

Terman, L. M. (Ed.). (1935). *Mental and physical traits of a thousand gifted children*. Volume I. Stanford: Stanford University Press.

Terman, L. M., & Oden, M. H. (1947). The gifted child grows up. In L. M. Terman (Ed.). *Genetic studies of genius* (Vol 4). Stanford: Stanford University Press.

Thompson, R. C., & Michel, J. B. (1972). Measuring authoritarianism: A comparison of the F and D scales. *Journal of Personality, 40*, 180–190.

Thorndike, R. L. (1982). *Applied psychometrics*. Boston: Houghton Mifflin.

Veenman, M. V. J., & Elshout, J. J. (1995). Differential effects of instructional support on learning in simulation environments. *Instructional Science, 22*, 363–383.

Watson, C. G., Herder, J., Kucala, T., & Hoodecheck-Schow, E. (1987). Intellectual deterioration and personality decompensation in schizophrenia. *Journal of Clinical Psychology, 43*, 447–455.

Watson, D., & Clark, L. A. (1992). On traits and temperament: General and specific factors of emotional experience and their relation to the five-factor model. *Journal of Personality, 60*, 441–476.

Wechsler, D. (1944). *The measurement of adult intelligence* (3rd ed.). Baltimore, MD: Williams & Wilkins.

Wechsler, D. (1950). Cognitive, conative, and nonintellective intelligence. *American Psychologist, 5*, 78–83.

Wechsler, D. (1958). *The measurement and appraisal of adult intelligence* (4th ed.). Baltimore: Williams & Wilkins.

Weiner, B. (1972). *Theories of motivation: From mechanisms to cognition*. London: Markham.

Weiner, B. (1973). *Theories of motivation*. Chicago: Rand McNally.

Wells, A., & Matthews, G. (1994). *Attention and emotion: A clinical perspective.*: Hillsdale, NJ: LEA.

Willerman, L. (1979). *The psychology of individual and group differences*. San Francisco: W. H. Freeman & Co.

Weinman, J. (1987). Non-cognitive determinants of perceptual problem-solving strategies. *Personality and Individual Differences, 8*, 53–58.

Williams, J. M. G., Watts, F. N., MacLeod, C., & Mathews, A. (1988). *Cognitive psychology and emotional disorders*. Chichester, UK: Wiley.

Zeidner, M. (1995). Personality trait correlates of intelligence. In D. Saklofske & M. Zeidner (Eds.), *International handbook of personality and intelligence* (pp. 299–319). New York: Plenum.

Zeidner, M. (1997, July). Personality, conation, and intelligence: Directions for future research. Paper presented at the 2nd Spearman Seminar, Plymouth, England.

Zeidner, M. (1998). *Test anxiety: The state of the art*. New York: Plenum.

Zeidner, M., Boekaerts, M., & Pintrich, P. (in press). Self-regulation: Current perspectives and directions for future research. In M. Boekaerts, P. Pintrich, & M. Zeidner (Eds.), *Handbook of self-regulation*. New York: Academic Press.

Zeidner, M., & Endler, N. (Eds.), *Handbook of coping: Theory, research, applications*. New York: Wiley.

Zeidner, M., Matthews, M., & Saklofske, D. H. (1998). Intelligence and mental health. *Encyclopedia of Mental Health*. New York: Academic Press.

Zusne, L., & Jones, W. H. (1982). *Anomalistic psychology: A study of extraordinary phenomena, of behavior, and experience*. Hillsdale, NJ: LEA.

CHAPTER TWENTY-SEVEN

Intelligence and Creativity

ROBERT J. STERNBERG AND LINDA A. O'HARA

INTELLIGENCE AND CREATIVITY

Intelligence has long been conceived of as critical in adaptation to existing environments, whereas creativity, which involves the production of an idea or product that is both novel and useful, has been viewed as critical to the modification or shaping of those environments ("Intelligence and its Measurement," 1921; Sternberg, 1985a,b). Although there are many other definitions of both intelligence (see "Intelligence and its measurement," 1921; Sternberg & Detterman, 1986) and creativity (see Glover, Ronning & Reynolds, 1989; Rothenberg & Hausman, 1976; Sternberg, 1988), these definitions tend to share at least some elements with these simple consensual definitions.

Definitions leave it unclear exactly what the relationship between intelligence and creativity is. A broad definition of intelligence can include shaping of the environment (Sternberg, 1985a), and a broad definition of creativity recognizes that creative ideas need to be not only novel but adaptive in some sense (Sternberg & Lubart, 1995). Just what is the relationship between intelligence and creativity?

Ochse (1990) suggested that to the extent intelligence involves selecting and shaping environments, it is creativity. To select or shape the environment to suit oneself, the imagination is required to create a vision of what the environment should be and of how this idealized environment can become a reality. On the other hand, the ability to adapt to the environment – to change oneself to suit the environment – typically involves little or possibly no creativity and may even require one to suppress creativity. For example, adaptation to a school or job environment can in some instances mean keeping one's creative ideas to oneself or else risking a low grade or job evaluation. According to Getzels and Csikszentmihalyi (1972), creativity and intelligence may represent different processes. Intelligence is required in different degrees across fields of creative endeavor. For example, great amounts of intelligence may not be needed to be a creative artist but certainly would be expected in a Nobel-prize-winning physicist. One could also say that creativity is required in widely different degrees in different fields of intelligent behavior.

Are intelligence and creativity the same or not? If not, how are they related, if at all? In this chapter, we will review work that covers the five possible answers to that question: (1) intelligence is a superset of creativity, (2) intelligence is a subset of creativity, (3) intelligence and creativity are overlapping sets, (4) intelligence and creativity are essentially the same thing (coincident sets), and (5) intelligence and creativity bear no relation at all to each other (disjoint sets). All of these relations have been proposed. The most conventional view is probably that of overlapping sets: Intelligence and creativity overlap in some respects, but not in others. But the other views deserve serious attention as well.

We shall consider each of the relations in turn, realizing that these set relations are idealizations that cannot possibly do justice to the complexity and richness of extant theories of either intelligence or creativity. We shall limit our consideration primarily to theories and research on human intelligence, although, of course, artificial intelligence also can provide key insights into the nature of creativity (see, e.g., Boden, 1991, 1994; Johnson-Laird, 1988; Langley, Simon, Bradshaw, & Zytkow, 1987).

INTELLIGENCE AS A SUPERSET OF CREATIVITY

One view of the relation between intelligence and creativity is that of intelligence as a superset of creativity, or equivalently, of creativity as a subset of intelligence. In his original test of intelligence, Binet (1896, as cited in Brown, 1989) included an inkblot for children to describe as a measure of imagination, but Binet later dropped it because he could not develop a reliable scoring system for it. Later, in the 1905 scale, Binet and Simon included open-ended items such as giving rhyming words, completing sentences, and constructing sentences that contain three given words in order to tap creativity; but again, Binet dropped the items measuring creativity in a later version of the test (Brown, 1989). It appears that Binet's troubles with creativity tests foreshadowed the frustrations future researchers would have for a over a century. J. P. Guilford is one researcher who persisted with creativity tests despite the frustrations.

Guilford's Structure-of-Intellect Model

Guilford (1950, 1967, 1970, 1975) had an enormous impact on the field of creativity when he pointed out (Guilford, 1950) that creativity was a relatively neglected field of study, a claim that has been made recently as well (Sternberg & Lubart, 1996). Guilford almost single-handedly created psychometric interest in the study of creativity. He was also a major theorist in the field of intelligence.

In his structure of intellect (SI) model, Guilford (1967) suggested three basic dimensions of intelligence, which form a cube: (1) operations – cognition, memory, divergent production, convergent production, evaluation; (2) content – figural, symbolic, semantic, behavioral; and (3) products – units, classes, relations, systems, transformations, implications. By crossing the 5 operations, 4 contents, and 6 products, one gets 120 factors (a number Guilford increased to 150 in his later life). Most relevant for creativity is divergent production, which involves a broad search for information and the generation of numerous novel answers to problems as opposed

to one single correct answer, which represents convergent production. Because divergent production is just one of the five operations of the intellect, intelligence can be seen as a superset of creativity. Guilford also pointed out that the facets of his model of intelligence that involved creativity were typically not measured by conventional tests of intelligence (and, half a century later, they still are not). Conventional tests of intelligence most often require convergent operations to produce a single correct answer to multiple choice questions.

Guilford (1975) identified several factors involved in creative problem solving (see also Ochse, 1990, for a review), including (a) sensitivity to problems – the ability to recognize problems, (b) fluency – number of ideas, (c) flexibility – shifts in approaches, and (d) originality – unusualness. These abilities could be further broken down. For example, Guilford distinguished among ideational fluency (the ability to produce various ideas rapidly in response to certain preset requirements), associational fluency (the ability to list words associated with a given word), and expressional fluency (the ability to organize words into phrases or sentences). Similarly, flexibility could be broken down into spontaneous flexibility (the ability to be flexible, even when it is not necessary to be so) and adaptive flexibility (the ability to be flexible when it is necessary, as in certain types of problem solving).

Guilford devised several tests of creativity, which were then adapted and expanded upon in the battery of Torrance (1974). For example, a test of divergent production of semantic units is, "Name all the things you can think of that are white and edible." A test of production of alternative relations is, "In what different ways are a father and daughter related?" A test of production of systems is, "Write as many sentences as you can using the words *desert*, *food*, and *army*." Other tests include producing clever titles for short stories, listing unusual uses for common objects such as bricks or coat hangers, and listing the consequences of a given event such as "What if people didn't need to sleep?"

Guilford and Hoepfner (1966) gave 204 ninth-graders 45 different divergent production tests and found a mean correlation of .37 between the California Test of Mental Maturity (CCTM, an IQ measure) and the semantic divergent production tests and a mean correlation of .22 between the

CCTM and the visual–figural divergent production tests. They also noted that the scatter plots of the IQ and divergent production data points were triangular as opposed to the customary elliptical distribution seen in correlations. The triangular plots indicated that students low in IQ were also low in divergent production tests, but students high in IQ were scattered over much of the whole range in divergent production tests (Guilford & Christensen, 1973). This finding was replicated by Schubert (1973) with an Army sample.

Guilford's approach to intelligence has lost much of its appeal. There are several reasons why the approach has been on the wane. The major one is that Guilford's method of rotating axes, called Procrustean rotation, has been found to produce spuriously good fits between data and theory (Horn & Knapp, 1973). A second one is that 120 factors departs so far from any kind of parsimonious interpretation of the nature of intelligence that it has proved too cumbersome for most researchers. It is also very difficult to construct tests that are relatively pure measures of such a large and diverse number of constructs. But as is usual, people are most likely to lose interest in a theory when another more attractive one comes along, and other theories have grabbed the attention of those whose attention might once have been grabbed by Guilford's theory.

Guilford's approach to testing has been enormously influential in the field of creativity but today has lost some of its appeal in part because the tests seem to relate only weakly to other kinds of ratings of creativity and to measure somewhat trivial aspects of the phenomenon (Amabile, 1996; Beittel, 1964; Merrifield, Gardner, & Cox, 1964; Piers, Daniels, & Quackenbush, 1960; Skager, Schultz, & Klein, 1967; Wallach & Kogan, 1965; Yamamoto, 1964).

Cattell's Model

Raymond Cattell (1971) is most well known for his theory of crystallized and fluid intelligences. He suggested that intelligence be viewed hierarchically with general ability at the top and two broad factors right below it. Crystallized ability, measured by tests of verbal comprehension and general knowledge, refers to one's accumulated store of information. Fluid ability, measured by tests of abstract inductive reasoning, refers to one's abil-

ity to acquire and utilize information, especially in novel contexts. Cattell expanded further upon these factors, however. He also posited a list of primary abilities that are similar to, but less complex than, Guilford's model of 120 factors. Cattell's list of primary abilities includes Verbal, Numerical, Spatial, Perceptual Speed (Figural Identification), Speed of Closure (Visual Cognition, Gestalt Perception), Inductive Reasoning, Deductive Reasoning, Rote Memory, Mechanical Knowledge and Skill, Word Fluency, Ideational Fluency, Restructuring Closure (Flexibility of Closure), Flexibility-versus-Firmness (Originality), General Motor Coordination, Manual Dexterity, Musical Pitch and Tonal Sensitivity, Representational Drawing Skill, Expressional Fluency, Motor Speed, Musical Rhythm and Timing, and Judgment. Cattell, then, saw the primary abilities as a superset of the creativity-relevant abilities of originality and ideational fluency.

Cattell (1971) was a critic of Guilford's. Some of his criticisms overlapped with those discussed above. For example, Cattell criticized Guilford for his factor-analytic rotational procedures which, according to Cattell, led to Guilford's overrating the role of divergent thinking in creativity. And, like the other critics of Guilford's tests, Cattell argued that

the verdict that a test measures creativity is only a projection of the test constructor's personal view about what creativity is. Thus, in the intellectual tests designed by Guilford's students and many others who have worked on creativity in this decade, creativity has finished up by being evaluated simply as oddity or bizarreness of response relative to the population mean or as output of words per minute, etc. This indeed comes close to mistaking the shadow for the substance (Cattell, 1971, p. 409).

Cattell believed real-life creative performance is determined by one's general intelligence first, particularly fluid intelligence as opposed to crystallized intelligence, and then by personality factors.

Gardner's Theory of Multiple Intelligences

Similar to but less extensive than Cattell's set of abilities is the proposed set of intelligences in Howard Gardner's (1983, 1993, 1995) theory of multiple intelligences (MI). According to Gardner, intelligence is not a unitary entity but rather a collection of eight distinct intelligences. These intelligences each occupy a separate module of the brain. According to this view, people can be intelligent in a variety of ways. For example, a poet is intelligent in a way that is different from the way that an architect is, who is intelligent in a way that is different from the way a dancer is. Moreover, these intelligences can be used in a variety of ways including, but not limited to, creative ways. Thus, creative functioning is one aspect (a subset) of the multiple intelligences. The eight intelligences are (a) linguistic (as in writing a poem or a short story), (b) logical–mathematical (as in solving a logical or mathematical proof), (c) spatial (as in getting the "lay of the land" in a new city), (d) bodily–kinesthetic (as in athletics or dancing), (e) musical (as in composing a sonata or playing the cello), (f) interpersonal (as in finding an effective way to understand or interrelate to others), (g) intrapersonal (as in achieving a high level of self-understanding), and (h) naturalist (as in seeing complex patterns in the natural environment).

Gardner (1993) has analyzed the lives of seven individuals who made highly creative contributions in the 20th century, each of whom specialized in one of the multiple intelligences: Sigmund Freud (intrapersonal), Albert Einstein (logical–mathematical), Pablo Picasso (spatial), Igor Stravinsky (musical), T. S. Eliot (linguistic), Martha Graham (bodily–kinesthetic), and Mohandas Gandhi (interpersonal). Charles Darwin would be an example of someone with extremely high naturalist intelligence. Gardner points out, however, that most of these individuals actually had strengths in more than one intelligence and that they had notable weaknesses as well in others (e.g., Freud's weaknesses may have been in spatial and musical intelligences).

Although creativity can be understood in terms of uses of the multiple intelligences to generate new and even revolutionary ideas, Gardner's (1993) analysis goes well beyond the intellectual. For example, Gardner points out two major themes in the behavior of these creative giants: They tended to have a matrix of support at the time of their creative breakthroughs, and they tended to drive a "Faustian bargain" whereby they gave up many of the pleasures people typically enjoy in life in order to attain extraordinary success in their careers. It is not clear that these attributes are intrinsic to creativity, per se, however; rather, they seem to be associated with those who have been driven to exploit their creative gifts in a way that leads them to attain eminence.

Gardner further follows Csikszentmihalyi (1988, 1996) in distinguishing between the importance of the domain (the body of knowledge about a particular subject area) and the field (the context in which this body of knowledge is studied and elaborated, including the persons working with the domain, such as critics, publishers, and other "gate-keepers"). Both are important to the development, and ultimately, the recognition of creativity.

INTELLIGENCE AS A SUBSET OF CREATIVITY

According to a second model, intelligence can be viewed as a subset of creativity. Creativity comprises intelligence plus other things, whatever these other things may be.

Sternberg and Lubart's Investment Theory

A representative theory of this kind is Sternberg and Lubart's (1991, 1995, 1996) investment theory of creativity (see also Rubenson & Runco, 1992, for a related approach wherein the theorists postulate the existence of creative potential for each individual as the product of initial endowments and active investments in creative ability). According to Sternberg and Lubart's theory, creative people, like good investors, buy low and sell high. But their buying and selling is in the world of ideas. In particular, they generate ideas that – like stocks with low price-to-earnings ratios – are relatively unpopular or even openly disrespected. They attempt to convince other people of the worth of these ideas. Then they sell high, meaning that they let other people pursue their extant ideas while they move on to their next unpopular idea.

Sternberg and Lubart (1995) argue that there are six main elements that converge to form creativity: intelligence, knowledge, thinking styles, personality, motivation, and the environment. Intelligence is thus just one of six forces that, in confluence, generate creative thought and behavior.

According to the theory, three aspects of intelligence are key for creativity: synthetic, analytical, and practical abilities. These three aspects are drawn from Sternberg's (1985a, 1988, 1996) triarchic theory of human intelligence. They are viewed as interactive and as working together in creative functioning.

Synthetic ability is the ability to generate ideas that are novel, high in quality, and task appropriate. Because creativity is viewed as an interaction between a person, a task, and an environment, what is novel, high in quality, or task appropriate may vary from one person, task, or environment to another.

The first key element of synthetic ability is what Sternberg (1985a) refers to as a metacomponent, which is a higher order executive process used in planning, monitoring, and evaluating task performance. This metacomponent is one of redefining problems. In other words, creative people may take problems that other people see, or they themselves have previously seen, in one way, and redefine them in a totally different way. In this sense, they "defy the crowd." For example, they may decide that because many of their friends are buying houses in a certain community indicates not good value, but bad value, for houses in that community have already been bid up in price by high demand. Or they may take a problem they have seen in one way and redefine it. For example, they may decide that, rather than trying to make more money to meet expenses, they should instead lower their expenses. Sternberg and Lubart point out that redefining problems involves both an ability and an attitude – the ability to do it effectively but also the attitude whereby one decides to do it in the first place.

Creative giants effect major changes in the way we define problems. For example, Einstein redefined the way physicists and others understand physical laws and how they function in the universe. Darwin redefined the way we view the development of organisms over the aeons. Picasso redefined the way we perceive possibilities for artistic expression. People also redefine problems in their everyday lives, however, although in less momentous ways.

Sternberg devised several convergent tests of the ability to see problems in new ways. In one kind of problem (Sternberg, 1982; Tetewsky & Sternberg, 1986), based on Nelson Goodman's so-called new riddle of induction (see Goodman, 1955), participants were taught about novel concepts, such as *grue* (green until the year 2000 and blue thereafter) and *bleen* (blue until the year 2000 and green thereafter). The participants were then tested in their ability to solve induction problems using conventional concepts as well as novel concepts. Scores on these tests were moderately related to scores on conventional tests of fluid intelligence (i.e., tests of the ability to think flexibly and in novel ways, such as geometric matrix problems). Most important, the information-processing component that seemed best to identify the creative thinkers was one that involved flexibly switching back and forth between conceptual systems (*green–blue*, on the one hand, and *grue–bleen*, on the other).

Another type of item (Sternberg & Gastel, 1989a, 1989b) required participants to solve analogies and other kinds of induction problems but with either factual premises (e.g., "Birds can fly") or counterfactual premises (e.g., "Sparrows can play hopscotch"). Scores on the counterfactual items were moderately related to scores on conventional fluid-intelligence tests, and the counterfactual items seemed to be the better measure of the ability to redefine conventional ways of thinking.

Yet another kind of problem (Sternberg & Kalmar, 1997) required participants to make predictions or postdictions about relations between events. For example, participants might be told about a carton of milk with a certain date on it, and they might be asked to predict whether by a certain future date the milk would have spoiled. Or they might be asked whether leaves that now are brown would have been green on a certain prior date. Some of the problems involved relatively straightforward predictions and postdictions; others, fairly complex ones.

The synthetic part of intelligence as applied to creativity also involves three knowledge-acquisition components or processes used in learning. These three processes, in the context of creativity, are bases of insightful thinking. They are called selective encoding, which involves distinguishing relevant from irrelevant information; selective combination, which involves combining bits of relevant information in novel ways; and selective comparison, which involves relating new information to old information in novel ways. For example, Bohr's model of the atom as a miniature "solar system" was based on a selective-comparison insight relating the atom to the solar system. Freud's hydraulic model of the mind was also based on a selective-comparison insight.

Sternberg and Davidson (1982; see also Davidson, 1986, 1995; Davidson & Sternberg, 1984) tested this theory of insight in a variety of studies, including one using mathematical insight problems (e.g., "If you have blue socks and brown socks in a drawer mixed in a ratio of 4 to 5, how many socks do you have to take out of the drawer in order to be assured of having a pair of the same color?"). They found that the three kinds of insights could be separated via different kinds of problems and that correlations between the insight problems and conventional tests of fluid intelligence were moderate. They also found that it was possible to teach elementary-school students to improve their insightful thinking.

According to this theory, the analytical part of intelligence – that which is measured in part by conventional tests of intelligence – is also involved in creativity. This ability is required to judge the value of one's own ideas and to decide which of one's ideas are worth pursuing. Then, if a given idea is worth pursuing, analytical ability can further be used to evaluate the strengths and weaknesses of the idea and thereby to suggest ways in which the idea can be improved. People with high synthetic but low analytical abilities will probably need others to fulfill this judgmental role lest they pursue their less rather than more valuable ideas.

The third intellectual ability involved in creativity is practical ability – the ability to apply one's intellectual skills in everyday contexts. Because creative ideas often tend to be rejected, it is very important for people who wish to have a creative impact to learn how to communicate their ideas effectively and how to persuade others of the value of their ideas. In essence, practical ability is involved in the "selling" of the idea, whether the idea is in the domain of art (where selling may be to a gallery or to potential purchasers or to critics), literature (where selling may be to a publisher or a public), science (where selling may be to relatively conservative scientific peers), or entrepreneurship (where selling may be to venture capitalists who are willing to fund only the most promising business innovations). Because creativity is in the interaction of the person, task, and environment, the failure to sell the idea properly may result in its never being dubbed creative or in its being recognized as creative only after the creator's death.

Sternberg, Ferrari, Clinkenbeard, and Grigorenko (1996; see also Sternberg, 1997; Sternberg & Clinkenbeard, 1995; Sternberg, Grigorenko, Ferrari, & Clinkenbeard, 1999) suggested that because the analytical, synthetic, and practical aspects of abilities are only very weakly related, students who are adept in one of these abilities may not benefit particularly from instruction aimed at another of the abilities. In particular, students who are intelligent in a traditional sense – high in memory and analytical abilities – will tend to profit from conventional instruction, which emphasizes these abilities. At the same time, creative students may not benefit particularly well from instruction as it is given in the schools because it typically emphasizes memory and analytical rather than creative abilities. In an experiment, Sternberg, Ferrari, Clinkenbeard, and Grigorenko found that high school students who were taught in a way that better matched their own pattern of abilities (e.g., analytic or synthetic) tended to achieve at higher levels than students who were taught in a way that more poorly matched their pattern of abilities. In a follow-up study, Sternberg, Torff, and Grigorenko (1998) showed that third-grade students (about 8 years old) and eighth-grade students (about 14 years old) taught analytically, creatively, and practically achieved at higher levels than did students whose instruction emphasized only memory abilities or primarily analytical as well as memory abilities.

It is important to say something about the role of knowledge in the investment theory because knowledge is itself the basis of an important aspect of intelligence, sometimes called crystallized intelligence (e.g., Cattell, 1971; Horn & Cattell, 1966). According to the investment theory, knowledge is a double-edged sword with respect to creativity. On the one hand, in order to advance a field beyond where it is, one needs the knowledge to know where the field is. Even reactions in opposition to existing ideas require knowledge of what those existing ideas are. On the other hand, knowledge can impede creativity by leading an individual to become entrenched or fixated. The individual can become so used to seeing things in a certain way that he or she starts to have trouble seeing them, or even imagining them, in any other way. The expert therefore may sacrifice flexibility for knowledge. There is actually evidence that experts in a field may have more difficulty than novices in adjusting to changes in the fundamental structure of the domain in which they are working (Frensch & Sternberg, 1989).

According to Sternberg and Lubart's (1995) investment theory, creativity also demands the investment of thinking style, personality, motivation, and the environment. Thinking style refers to a preference for thinking in novel ways of one's own choosing rather than following the crowd. To prefer this thinking style, one needs a certain personality capable of defying the crowd and the motivation to be persistant and determined to overcome the many obstacles encountered in any creative endeavor. The environment most conducive to creativity is one that reduces some of these obstacles, that reduces the risks inherent in any new idea or activity, and that rewards the people who take those risks.

Sternberg and Lubart (1995) tested the investment theory by asking people to generate creative products in four domains, choosing two from among a variety of topics they were given: writing (e.g., "The Keyhole," "2983"), art (e.g., "Earth from an Insect's Point of View," "Beginning of Time"), advertising (e.g., "Brussels sprouts," "Cuff links"), and science (e.g., "How could we know if there were extraterrestrial aliens hidden among us?"). They found only moderate correlations across the four domains, as well as moderate correlations of averaged ratings of creativity of products with tests of fluid intelligence, although the generality of creative intelligence may depend in part upon the population being tested (see Runco, 1987).

In a recent study (Grigorenko & Sternberg, in press), analytical, creative, and practical intelligence were all investigated as bases of coping in, and adaptation to, a rapidly changing socioeconomic and political landscape, that of contemporary Russia. Variables indicative of physical and mental health were used as criterion measures. It was found that the best predictor of coping and adaptation was practical intelligence. The second best was analytical intelligence. Creative intelligence showed some mixed results, with some trivial correlations, but also with correlations that were significant either in the positive or the negative direction. These results suggest that conventional analytical intelligence and creative intelligence show quite distinct patterns in their prediction of adaptation to everyday life – at least in a society such as contemporary Russia's.

In sum, although analytical skills tend to be strongly interrelated (Jensen, 1998), creative abilities show weaker interrelations (as do practical abilities – Sternberg, Wagner, Williams, & Horvath, 1995). What appears to be a general factor in human cognitive abilities, therefore, really seems to apply primarily or perhaps even exclusively to analytical abilities. Once one looks at abilities more broadly, the general factor largely disappears.

Smith's Hierarchy

Another interesting view of intelligence as a subset of creativity is one based on Bloom's *Taxonomy of Educational Objectives* and tested by Smith (1970, 1971). The basic assumption of the taxonomy is that cognitive processes can be placed along a cumulative and hierarchical continuum beginning with the major class of Knowledge and proceeding through the classes of Comprehension, Application, Analysis, Synthesis, and Evaluation. Intellectual ability is required in the first four processes, and creative ability is required for the last two: Synthesis and Evaluation. Because the categories are cumulative and hierarchical, Synthesis and Evaluation demand the skills underlying the preceding levels (i.e., intelligence) in addition to the new behavior – creativity. Hence, in Smith's view, intelligence is a subset of creativity.

Smith (1970) gave 141 eleventh graders an intelligence test, two creativity tests, and taxonomic tests. He used the intelligence and creativity tests to predict performance in the taxonomic tests via a multiple regression analysis. He found that the percentage of variance that intelligence accounted for was significant for each of the first four classes (Knowledge – 34%, Comprehension – 53%, Application – 50%, and Analysis – 28%). Creativity did not significantly explain any further variance for these four classes, consistent with the theory. Again, in accordance with the theory, both intelligence (contributing 49 and 31%, respectively) and creativity (contributing 20 and 14%, respectively) made significant, independent, and overall contributions to individual-differences variation on the Synthesis and Evaluation subtests.

INTELLIGENCE AND CREATIVITY AS OVERLAPPING SETS

The view of intelligence and creativity as overlapping sets implies that in some ways intelligence and creativity are similar, but in other ways they are different. Discussing the similarities, Barron (1963) proposed:

> If one defines originality as the ability to respond to stimulus situations both adaptively and unusually, and if one defines intelligence simply as the ability to solve problems, then at the upper levels of problem-solving ability the manifestation of intelligence will be also a manifestation of originality. That is to say, the very difficult and rarely solved problem requires by definition a solution that is original. (p. 219)

Highlighting the differences between intelligence and creativity, Roe (1963/1976) suggested that

> the creative process is probably closest to problem solving, but it differs from it in a number of ways. In problem solving, the immediate goal is a specific one, and logical and orderly modes of approach are appropriate – if not always used. In the creative process there is no such clear goal as a rule, and illogical and orderly modes of thought are common. Newell, Shaw, and Simon (1958) consider that "creative activity appears simply to be a special class of problem-solving activity characterized by novelty, unconventionality, persistence, and difficulty in problem formulation." A major differentiation is the extent of the involvement of the whole person; in the creative process this is very great, and noncognitive and emotional elements loom large, but they are a barrier to effective problem solving. (p. 172)

Another way of distinguishing creativity from intelligence has been proposed by Shouksmith (1973), who said that judging the correctness or "rightness" of a response is an attempt to measure logical reasoning or intelligence, whereas judging the "goodness" of a response, that is, the extent to which an answer or problem solution is fitting or appropriate to the problem or situation, is a creativity measure. The overlap would represent responses that are both right and good.

One reason the view of creativity and intelligence as overlapping sets may be the most conventional view is that it is the most well-known owing to the impressive amount of work done by its proponents. Examples are Catherine Cox and Lewis Terman's investigations of historical geniuses (Cox, 1926) and all of the studies done with the various professional occupations conducted by researchers connected with the Institute of Personality Assessment and Research (IPAR) at the University of California at Berkeley, such as MacKinnon (1962, 1967, 1975), Barron (1963, 1969), Helson (1971/1976), and Gough (1957).

Cox's 301 Geniuses

Cox (1926), working with Lewis Terman, published IQ estimates for 301 of the most eminent persons who lived between 1450 and 1850. They selected their list from a list of 1,000 prepared by James McKeen Cattell, who determined eminence by the amount of space allotted in biographical dictionaries. From Cattell's list, they deleted hereditary aristocracy and nobility unless those individuals distinguished themselves beyond status due to their birth, those born before 1450, those with a rank over number 510 on the original list, and 11 names for whom no records were available. These deletions left 282 persons whose IQs were summarized as Group A. In addition, they discussed a Group B, which consisted of 19 miscellaneous cases from those over number 510 on the original list, bringing the grand total to 301.

To estimate IQ, Cox, Terman, and Maud Merrill (Cox, 1926) examined biographies, letters, and other writings and records for evidence of the earliest period of instruction; the nature of the earliest learning; the earliest productions; age of first reading and of first mathematical performance; typical precocious activities; unusually intelligent applications of knowledge; the recognition of similarities or differences; the amount and character of the reading; the range of interests; school standing and progress; early maturity of attitude or judgment; the tendency to discriminate, to generalize, or to theorize; and family standing. Their IQ estimates are, of course, necessarily subjective. In a sense, though, the estimates have an ecological validity with regard to real-life intelligence that is not seen in standard IQ tests. The reported IQs were the average of the three expert raters mentioned above, namely, Cox, Terman, and Merrill. Interrater reliability was .90 for the childhood estimate and .89 for the young adulthood estimate (calculated from intercorrelations in Cox, 1926, pp. 67–68).

An example of some of the factors that contributed to their estimates can be seen in a description of Francis Galton (not in the list; he was born in 1822 and published *Hereditary Genius* in 1869), whose IQ Terman estimated to be 200. "Francis knew his capital letters by twelve months and both his alphabets by eighteen months; ... he could read a little book, *Cobwebs to Catch Flies*, when $2^1/_2$ years old, and could sign his name before 3 years" (Cox, 1926, pp. 41–42). By 4 years of age, he could say all the Latin substantives and adjectives and active verbs, could add and multiply, read a little French, and knew the clock. At 5, he was quoting from Walter Scott. By 6, he was familiar with the *Iliad* and the *Odyssey*. At 7, he was reading Shakespeare for fun and could memorize a page by reading it twice. Clearly, Galton's record is one of an exceptional child.

Cox concluded that the average IQs of the group, 135 for childhood and 145 for young adulthood, were probably too low because of instructions to regress toward the mean of 100 for unselected populations (whereas this group's means were 135 and 145) whenever data were unavailable. Also, unreliability of the data may have caused regression to the mean. One of the problems Cox noted in the data was a strong correlation, .77, between IQ and the reliability of the available data: the more reliable the data, the higher the IQ, and the higher the IQ, the more reliable the data upon which it was based. She concluded that if more reliable data had been available, all of the IQs would have been estimated to be higher. She therefore corrected the original estimates, bringing the group average up to 155 for childhood and 165 for young adulthood.

As Cox was careful to point out, the IQs are not estimates of the actual person's IQ, but rather, estimates of the record of that person. "The IQ of Newton or of Lincoln recorded in these pages is the IQ of the Newton or of the Lincoln of whom we have record. But the records are admittedly incomplete" (Cox, 1926, p. 8).

Cox found the correlation between IQ and rank order of eminence to be .16, plus or minus .039 (Cox, 1926, p. 55), after correcting for unreliability of the data. Dean Simonton (1976) reexamined the Cox data using multiple regression techniques and showed that the correlation between intelligence and ranked eminence that Cox found was an artifact of unreliability of data and, especially, of a timewise sampling bias – those more recently born had both lower estimated IQs and lower ranks of estimated eminence. In Simonton's analysis, the relationship between intelligence and ranked eminence

was zero controlling for birth year (Simonton, 1976, p. 223–224). In any case, Cox recognized the role of factors other than IQ in eminence and concluded that "high but not the highest intelligence, combined with the greatest degree of persistence will achieve greater eminence than the highest degree of intelligence with somewhat less persistence" (Cox, 1926, p. 187).

IPAR

The Institute of Personality Assessment and Research (IPAR) was established at the University of California at Berkeley in 1949. Its objective was the development and use of psychological assessment techniques in the study of effectively functioning persons as opposed to persons with some pathology. The stimulus for this center had been the experiences of several psychologists in the assessment program during World War II of the Office of Strategic Services, whose mission it had been to select men to be spies, counterespionage agents, leaders of resistance groups behind enemy lines, creators of propaganda designed to destroy the enemy's morale, and leaders of other irregular warfare assignments (Barron, 1963; MacKinnon, 1967, 1975). The group's first study, as could be predicted, was with graduate students at Berkeley. But over the years, MacKinnon studied architects and the members of the American Mount Everest expedition; Barron studied Air Force officers, business administrators, artists, and writers; Helson studied male and female mathematicians; and Gough studied research scientists and validated the Adjective Check List and the California Psychological Inventory in the course of many studies.

A typical study would involve a nomination and ranking of the most creative people in a field by some experts in that field (such as professors, superiors, journal editors, and critics) and the administration of a battery of tests, including many of Guilford's divergent thinking tests, some intelligence measure, and various personality self-descriptions and projective tests, such as the Thematic Apperception Test or the Rorschach Inkblot Test, to those who agreed to attend a 3-day weekend assessment workshop in Berkeley. The weekend provided numerous occasions for several staff members to interview and observe the participants in informal social interaction, situational tests, group discussions, charades, and other exercises. Typically, 10 participants would be assessed in a weekend by 6 or 7 staff members. Ratings from the weekend assessments would be compared with ratings of the less creative professionals in a field of participants matched for age and geographic location of their practice and assessed through a battery of procedures sent to them through the mail.

Describing the relationship between creativity and intelligence ratings was just one part of the IPAR studies. Much more emphasis was placed on the personality variables identified in creative persons, which are not covered at length in this chapter. One study of 343 military officers sheds light on some personality variables that distinguish creative persons from intelligent persons. Barron (1963) found that those who scored high in originality but low in intelligence (measured by the Concept Mastery Test, which includes synonyms–antonyms and verbal analogies) described themselves as "affected, aggressive, demanding, dependent, dominant, forceful, impatient, initiative, outspoken, sarcastic, strong, suggestible. [Those who scored high in intelligence but low in originality described themselves as] mild, optimistic, pleasant, quiet, unselfish" (Barron, 1963, p. 222). Barron said:

When one compares these self-descriptions with the staff descriptions of subjects who are both original and intelligent, it appears that intelligence represents the operation of the reality principle in behavior, and is responsible for such characteristics as the appropriate delay of impulse-expression and the effective organization of instinctual energy for the attainment of goals in the world as it is. (p. 223)

Barron (1963) summarized the many IPAR studies as follows:

Over the total range of intelligence and creativity a low positive correlation, probably in the neighborhood of .40, obtains; beyond an I.Q. of about 120, however, measured intelligence is a negligible factor in creativity, and the motivational and stylistic variables upon which our own research has laid such stress are the major determiners of creativity. (p. 242)

The relative importance of intelligence and personality or motivation variables can be demonstrated in this anecdote about Edison. Once Cyrus Eaton, who was hard of hearing, asked Thomas Edison, who

also was hard of hearing, to perfect the hearing aid. Edison refused, saying, "I don't want to hear that much" (Crovitz, 1970, p. 56).

Three basic findings concerning conventional conceptions of intelligence as measured by IQ and creativity are generally agreed upon (see, e.g., Barron & Harrington, 1981; Lubart, 1994).

First, creative people tend to show above-average IQs, often above 120 (see Renzulli, 1986). This figure is not a cutoff but rather an expression of the fact that people with low or even average IQs do not seem to be well represented among the ranks of highly creative individuals. Cox's (1926) geniuses had an estimated average IQ of 165. Barron estimated the mean IQ of his creative writers to be 140 or higher based on their scores on the Terman Concept Mastery Test (Barron, 1963, p. 242). The other groups in the IPAR studies, that is, mathematicians and research scientists, were also above average in intelligence. Roe (1952, 1972), who did similarly thorough assessments of eminent scientists before the IPAR group was set up, estimated IQs for her participants that ranged between 121 and 194, with medians between 137 and 166, depending on whether the IQ test was verbal, spatial, or mathematical.

Second, above an IQ of 120, IQ does not seem to matter as much to creativity as it does below 120. In other words, creativity may be more highly correlated with IQ below an IQ of 120, but only weakly or not at all correlated with it above an IQ of 120. (This relationship is often called the threshold theory. See the contrast with Hayes's, 1989, certification theory discussed below). In the architects study, in which the average IQ was 130 (significantly above-average), the correlation between intelligence and creativity was −.08, not significantly different from zero (Barron, 1969, p. 42). But in the military officer study, in which participants were of average intelligence, the correlation was .33 (Barron, 1963, p. 219). These results suggest that extremely highly creative people often have high IQs but not necessarily that people with high IQs tend to be extremely creative.

Some investigators (e.g., Simonton, 1994; Sternberg, 1996, 1999) have suggested that very high IQ may actually interfere with creativity. Those who have very high IQs may be so highly rewarded for their IQ-like (analytical) skills that they fail to develop the creative potential within them, which may then remain latent. In a reexamination of the

Cox (1926) data, Simonton (1976) found that the eminent leaders showed a significant negative correlation, −.29, between their IQs and eminence. Simonton explained that

leaders must be understood by a large mass of people before they can achieve eminence, unlike the creators, who need only appeal to an intellectual elite.... Scientific, philosophical, literary, artistic, and musical creators do not have to achieve eminence in their own lifetime to earn posterity's recognition, whereas military, political, or religious leaders must have contemporary followers to attain eminence (Simonton, 1976, pp. 220, 222).

Third, the correlation between IQ and creativity is variable, usually ranging from weak to moderate (Flescher, 1963; Getzels & Jackson, 1962; Guilford, 1967; Herr, Moore, & Hasen, 1965; Torrance, 1962; Wallach & Kogan, 1965; Yamamoto, 1964). The correlation depends in part upon what aspects of creativity and intelligence are being measured and how they are being measured as well as in what field the creativity is manifested. The role of intelligence is different in art and music, for instance, than it is in mathematics and science (McNemar, 1964).

The Three-Ring Model

These facts suggest another conceptualization of the relation between creativity and intelligence whereby the two overlap (e.g., creative people need a certain IQ level) but are nonidentical. Renzulli (1986), for example, has proposed a three-ring model whereby giftedness is at the intersection among above-average ability (as measured in the conventional ways), creativity, and task commitment. The circles for ability and creativity thus overlap.

Renzulli distinguishes between "schoolhouse" and "creative–productive" giftedness, noting that to be gifted in the one way does not necessarily imply giftedness in the other. Schoolhouse giftedness is conventional giftedness in taking tests and learning lessons, whereas creative–productive giftedness is giftedness in the generation of creative ideas. The people gifted in the two ways are often different. We therefore need to be very careful in using conventional IQ tests to identify the gifted, because we are likely to miss the creatively productive gifted. This point is further elaborated below in the section on creativity and intelligence as disjoint sets.

Mednick and the RAT

An obvious drawback to the tests used and assessments done by the researchers at IPAR, as well as by Anne Roe and Guilford, is the time and expense involved in administering them as well as the subjective scoring of them. In contrast, Mednick (1962) produced a 30-item, objectively scored, 40-minute test of creative ability called the Remote Associates Test (RAT). The test is based on his theory that the creative thinking process is the "forming of associative elements into new combinations which either meet specified requirements or are in some way useful. The more mutually remote the elements of the new combination, the more creative the process or solution" (Mednick, 1962). Because the ability to make these combinations and arrive at a creative solution necessarily depends on the existence of the stuff of the combinations, that is, the associative elements, in a person's knowledge base and because the probability and speed of attainment of a creative solution are influenced by the organization of the person's associations, Mednick's theory suggests that creativity and intelligence are very related; they are overlapping sets.

The RAT consists of the test-taker's supplying a fourth word that is remotely associated with three given words. Samples (not actual test items) of given words are

1) rat	blue	cottage
2) railroad	girl	class
3) surprise	line	birthday
4) wheel	electric	high
5) out	dog	cat

We will give the answers later in the chapter so readers can have the fun of trying the examples first.

Correlations of .55, .43, and .41 have been shown between the RAT and the WISC (Wechsler Intelligence Scale for Children), the SAT verbal, and the Lorge–Thorndike Verbal intelligence measures, respectively (Mednick & Andrews, 1967). Correlations with quantitative intelligence measures were lower ($r = .20$–$.34$). Correlations with other measures of creative performance were more variable (Andrews, 1975).

Implicit Theories

Another approach that has suggested an overlapping-circles model for creativity and intelligence makes use of people's implicit theories, or folk conceptions, of intelligence and creativity. Sternberg (1985b) asked laypeople as well as specialists in four fields (physics, philosophy, art, and business) to give information that, through a data-analytic technique called nonmetric multidimensional scaling, could yield their implicit theories of intelligence and creativity (as well as of wisdom).

Sternberg found that people's implicit theories of intelligence involved six components: (a) practical problem-solving ability, (b) verbal ability, (c) intellectual balance and integration, (d) goal orientation and attainment, (e) contextual intelligence (i.e., intelligence in their everyday environments), and (f) fluid thought. People's implicit theories of creativity seemed to involve eight main components: (a) nonentrenchment (seeing things in novel ways), (b) integration and intellectuality, (c) aesthetic taste and imagination, (d) decisional skill and flexibility, (e) perspicacity (intuition, acuteness of perception, discernment, or understanding), (f) drive for accomplishment and recognition, (g) inquisitiveness, and (h) intuition. The two constructs are thus seen to have some overlap, for example, in the importance of setting and reaching goals and of thinking in flexible (fluid) and nonentrenched ways. When people were asked to rate hypothetically described individuals in terms of their creativity and intelligence, Sternberg (1985b) found a correlation of .69 between their ratings of creativity and intelligence.

The degree of overlap between intelligence and creativity may depend somewhat on the particular population whose implicit theories are being queried. For example, an earlier study by Sternberg, Conway, Ketron, and Bernstein (1981) identified three factors of intelligence in the implicit theories of laypersons: practical problem solving, verbal ability, and social competence. None of these seem to involve much overt creativity, although practical problem solving might in some instances. A more recent study of Taiwanese Chinese conceptions of intelligence – yielding factors of general cognitive competence, interpersonal competence, intrapersonal competence, intellectual self-assertion, and intellectual self-effacement – revealed little overlap with creativity (Yang & Sternberg, 1997).

CREATIVITY AND INTELLIGENCE AS COINCIDENT SETS

Haensly and Reynolds (1989) argued that creativity and intelligence should be viewed as a "unitary phenomenon," that is, as a conjoint set. They proposed that creativity is not just another kind of mental processing, but rather, is the ultimate expression of intelligence.

Some researchers, such as Weisberg (1986, 1988, 1993) and Langley et al. (1987), have argued that the mechanisms underlying creativity are no different from those underlying normal problem solving of the kind involved in problems that do not seem, on their surface, to involve any need for creative thinking. According to these investigators, work is adjudged as creative when ordinary processes yield extraordinary results. Perkins (1981) refers to this view as the "nothing special" view. According to this view, if we want to understand creativity, we need look no further than to studies of ordinary problem solving.

For example, Weisberg and Alba (1981) had people solve the notorious nine-dot problem in which people are asked to connect all of the dots, which are arranged in the shape of a square with three rows of three dots each, using no more than four straight lines, never arriving at a given dot twice, and never lifting their pencil from the page. The problem can be solved only if people allow their line segments to go outside the periphery of the dots. Typically, solution of this task had been viewed as hinging upon the insight that one had to go "outside the box." Weisberg and Alba showed that even when people were given the insight, they still had difficulty in solving the problem. In other words, whatever is required to solve the nine-dot problem, it is not just some kind of extraordinary insight.

INTELLIGENCE AND CREATIVITY AS DISJOINT SETS

Several investigators have taken great pains to show that intelligence is different from creativity, that is, that they are disjoint sets (e.g., Getzels & Jackson, 1962; Torrance, 1975; Wallach & Kogan, 1965). Although none of these investigators suggested and many explicitly denied that creativity and intelligence are completely unrelated, their emphasis is clearly in that direction. Their goal seems to have been to focus attention on a problem with relying on traditional IQ tests to identify gifted children. A story told by Donald MacKinnon (which he believed was first told by Mark Twain) illustrates the issue and the importance of recognizing potential talent in order to provide the kind of environment that will facilitate its development and expression. The story

is about a man who sought the greatest general who had ever lived. Upon inquiring as to where this individual might be found, he was told that the person he sought had died and gone to Heaven. At the Pearly Gates he informed St. Peter of the purpose of his quest, whereupon St. Peter pointed to a soul nearby. "But that, protested the inquirer, "isn't the greatest of all generals. I knew that person when he lived on earth, and he was only a cobbler." "I know that," replied St. Peter, "but if he had been a general he would have been the greatest of them all." (MacKinnon, 1962, p. 484)

The risks of failing to identify talent are also evident in Hayes's (1989) proposed alternative to the 120 IQ threshold theory discussed in the overlapping sets section. According to Hayes's certification theory, creativity and IQ are not intrinsically related. However, in order to display creativity in one's work, one must have attained a position with a certain degree of freedom of expression. For instance, a college professor has more freedom to display creativity in his or her work than does an assembly line worker. Positions with this kind of freedom typically require a college degree, sometimes also a graduate degree. Academic performance is correlated with IQ. Therefore, it may be that one's opportunity to be creative depends on an IQ high enough to get the degree that is a certification for the types of jobs in which one can display creativity.

Getzels and Jackson

Getzels and Jackson (1962) gave five creativity measures to 245 boys and 204 girls in 6th through 12th grade and compared the results with scores from IQ tests (either a Binet, a Henmon–Nelson, or a WISC) the school had already administered. The focus of their work was to identify two groups of students (one high in intelligence but not in creativity and one high in creativity but not in intelligence) and study the nature of their behavior in school, their value orientations, fantasies and imaginative productions, and their family environment.

Their five creativity measures were word association, uses for things, hidden shapes, fables, and make-up problems. These tests are typical examples of creativity tests used by other researchers.

In word association, children were asked to give as many definitions as possible to fairly common objects (e.g., bolt, bark, sack). The score depended on absolute number of definitions and number of different categories into which these definitions could be placed. For example, a high score for *bolt* would be given to "to fasten down, to run away quickly, to eat food rapidly, a bolt of cloth, a horse bolts, a bolt of lightning."

In uses for things, children were asked to give as many uses as they could for objects that customarily have a stereotyped function attached to them. This test is similar to Guilford's test items, such as uses for a brick, paper clip, or toothpick. The score depended on the number of uses and their originality. A high score for *brick* would be given to "bricks can be used for building. You can also use a brick as a paperweight. Use it as a doorstop. You can heat a brick and use it as a bed warmer. You can throw a brick as a weapon. You can hollow out the center of a brick and make an ashtray."

In hidden shapes, which is part of Cattell's objective–analytical test battery, children were presented with 18 simple geometric figures, each of which was followed by 4 complex figures. The children were asked to find the geometric figures hidden in the more complex form.

In fables, children were presented with four fables in which the last lines were missing. The children were then asked to compose three different endings for each fable: a moralistic, a humorous, and a sad ending. The Mischievous Dog is an example:

A rascally dog used to run quietly to the heels of every passerby and bite them without warning. So his master was obliged to tie a bell around the cur's neck that he might give notice wherever he went. This the dog thought was very fine indeed, and he went about tinkling it in pride all over town. But an old hound said . . . (p. 18)

The score again depended on the number, appropriateness, and originality of the endings. Here are sample moralistic, humorous, and sad endings that received credit. "Pride cometh before a fall." "This is your plight, you dogs that bite." "That the dog would go insane from the constant tinkling."

In make-up problems, children were presented with four complex paragraphs, each containing many numerical statements, and were required to make up as many mathematical problems as they could with the information given. One example describes a man who buys a house for so much money, puts so much down, and makes monthly payments for the mortgage and other expenses. The question, "How long will it be before Mr. Smith had saved enough on heating costs to make up for what he had paid for insulating the house?" received more credit than did the question, "How much did Mr. Smith still owe after his down payment?"

Intercorrelations among the creativity measures ranged from .153 between fables and hidden shapes to .488 between make-up problems and word association. The average of the correlations between IQ and the creativity measures was .26. The lowest correlation was between IQ and fables, .12 for girls and .13 for boys; the highest was .39 between IQ and make-up problems for girls and .38 with word association for boys. It should be noted that the average IQ in the school was 132, beyond the point at which there is much expected relationship between creativity and IQ. The correlations, then, may support Burt's (1962/1970) criticism that "the new tests for creativity would form very satisfactory additions to any ordinary battery for testing the general factor of intelligence." McNemar (1964) estimated the correlation of the combined creativity scores and IQ for the total sample, which Getzels and Jackson failed to provide, to be .40. This correlation of .40, McNemar said, was greatly attenuated because of the usual measurement errors, the restricted range of IQ (mean of 132), and the fact that the IQs were a mixture from the Stanford–Binet, Henmon–Nelson, and Wechsler. A correlation corrected for these attenuating factors would lend even more support to Burt's and McNemar's points that the creativity tests used here are very much like intelligence tests.

The high-creativity group in Getzels and Jackson's (1962) study (15 boys and 11 girls) consisted of those students who scored in the top 20% of the summed creativity measures but below the top 20% in IQ. The high-intelligence group (17 boys and 11 girls) scored in the top 20% in IQ but below the top 20% in creativity. Wallach and Kogan (1965) criticized Getzels

and Jackson for summing the creativity measures when the tests were no more correlated with each other than they were with IQ.

Getzels and Jackson (1962) made a major point of the fact that despite a 23 point difference in mean IQ between the high-creativity group (127) and the high-IQ group (150), surprisingly, the school achievement scores of the two groups were equally superior to the achievement scores of the school population as a whole. McNemar (1964), in a scathing criticism, said that if the authors had bothered to give the correlations among IQ, creativity, and total school achievement for the entire group, one could have deduced "that creative ability is not as important as IQ for school achievement – just the opposite of their position" (p. 879).

Getzels and Jackson (1962) found that the students in the high-IQ group were more desirable to their teachers than were the students in the high-creative group. The high-IQ students desired the same qualities for themselves that they believed were important for success and that they believed teachers approved of more so than did students in the high-creative group. For high-IQ students, the relationship between the qualities they valued for themselves and those they believed would lead to success as adults was quite close, $r = .81$. That is, these students appeared to be highly success oriented. For the high-creativity students, there was practically no relationship ($r = .10$) between the qualities *they* valued and those they believed would lead to success as adults. These students appeared not to buy into the conventional standards of adult success, and, indeed, reported much more unusual career aspirations, such as adventurer, inventor, and writer, than did the high-IQ students, who more often aspired to be doctors, lawyers, and professors.

Sense of humor stood out as a high-ranking ideal quality for the high-creative group over the high-IQ group. The high-creative students ranked sense of humor third out of 13 qualities, after getting along with others and emotional stability, as a quality they aspired to have in their ideal selves, whereas the high-IQ students ranked it ninth. High marks, high IQ, and goal directedness were all higher in the ideal selves of the high-IQ students.

In the various open-ended tests and drawings, high-creative students were significantly higher than the high-IQ students in stimulus-free themes, unexpected endings, humor, incongruities, and playfulness, as well as violence. The high-creative students seemed to use the stimulus largely as a point of departure for self-expression, versus the high-IQ students, who focused on the stimulus as the point to be communicated or the task to be accomplished. Some noteworthy examples are presented below.

In response to the picture stimulus perceived most often as a man sitting in an airplane reclining his seat on his return from a business trip or professional conference, one high-IQ student gave this response:

Mr. Smith is on his way home from a successful business trip. He is very happy and he is thinking about his wonderful family and how glad he will be to see them again. He can picture it, about an hour from now, his plane landing at the airport and Mrs. Smith and their three children all there welcoming him home again.

One high-creative student gave this response to the same picture:

This man is flying back from Reno where he has just won a divorce from his wife. He couldn't stand to live with her anymore, he told the judge, because she wore so much cold cream on her face at night that her head would skid across the pillow and hit him in the head. He is now contemplating skid-proof face cream.

When asked to draw a picture of "Playing Tag in the School Yard," high-IQ students were much more likely than high-creative students to draw details and label parts of their drawing, such as drawing a building and labeling it a school, concentrating on communicating and being understood, whereas high-creative students were much less bound by the specific details of the instructions and less worried about being misunderstood. For instance, for the playing tag drawing, one high-creative student returned the blank sheet of paper with the title changed to "Playing Tag in the School Yard – During a Blizzard."

Wallach and Kogan

Wallach and Kogan (1965) argued that a serious flaw in the work of Getzels and Jackson (1962) was that creativity is not measured well in the test-like situations they used. To correct this flaw, Wallach and Kogan devised a series of gamelike, untimed tests for 151 fifth graders. Their five creativity mea-

sures were rated as to uniqueness and number and included the following:

1. Instances – Name all the round things, things that make a noise, square things, things that move on wheels that you can think of. For round things, life savers, mouse hole, and drops of water were unique responses; buttons, plate, and door knob were not.
2. Alternate Uses – Name all the different ways you could use a newspaper, automobile tire, shoe, button, knife, cork, key, chair. For newspaper, "rip it up if angry" was a unique response; "make paper hats" was not.
3. Similarities – Tell all the ways in which a ____ and a ____ are alike: cat and mouse, milk and meat, curtain and rug, potato and carrot, train and tractor, grocery store and restaurant, violin and piano, radio and telephone, watch and typewriter, desk and table. For milk and meat, "they are government inspected" was a unique response; "they come from animals" was not.
4. Pattern Meanings – Tell me all the things you think this could be? Students were presented with eight drawings of various combinations of geometric shapes. For a picture of a triangle surrounded by three circles, "three mice eating a piece of cheese" was a unique response; "three people sitting around a table" was not.
5. Line Meanings – similar to pattern meanings, except with drawings of lines. For a simple straight horizontal line, "stream of ants" was a unique response; "stick" was not.

Wallach and Kogan (1965) also had 10 general intelligence measures, which included subtests from the WISC, School and College Ability Tests (SCAT), and Sequential Tests of Educational Progress (STEP). They noted correlations of .41 among the creativity measures, .51 among the intelligence measures, and .09 between the creativity and intelligence measures.

Wallach and Kogan (1965, 1972) divided their students into four groups based on their scores on the various tests: High Creativity and High Intelligence (HC–HI), Low Creativity and High Intelligence (LC–HI), High Creativity and Low Intelligence (HC–LI), and Low Creativity and Low Intelligence (LC–LI).

In the HC–HI group, students had the highest level of self confidence and self-control as well as freedom of expression, were outgoing and popular with their peers, had the highest levels of attention span and concentration and interest in academic work, and were the most sensitive to physiognomic stimuli, that is, they were able to discuss affective and expressive connotations of stimuli beyond just physical or geometric descriptions. They also demonstrated high-disruptive, attention-seeking behavior, which suggested enthusiasm and overeagerness. They had a tendency to admit to some feelings of anxiety, which seemed to serve as an energizing factor for them.

In the LC–HI group, students were more reserved and addicted to school achievement to the extent that they believed academic failure would be a catastrophe. They were also less likely to seek attention in disruptive ways and less likely to express unconventional ideas but were still popular with peers. They were the least anxious of all the groups. They performed best in the presence of evaluation pressures. They appeared to have an excessive fear of making a mistake. Having a clear understanding of the expectations of others allowed them to know the "right" way of behaving.

In the HC–LI group, students were at the greatest disadvantage in the classroom. They were the most cautious and hesitant, the least self-confident, the least sought after by peers, the most deprecatory of their own work, and the least able to concentrate. They displayed high-disruptive, attention-seeking behavior, which suggested an incoherent protest against their plight. They were more likely to cope with academic failure by social withdrawal and performed best when evaluation pressures were absent. They seemed to have an excessive fear of being evaluated in contrast to the LC–HI group. Like the HC–HI group, they were more willing to postulate relationships between somewhat dissimilar events.

In the LC–LI group, students appeared to compensate for poor academic performance by social activity. They were more extroverted, less hesitant, and more self-confident than the HC–LI group.

Torrance

Torrance (1963) replicated the Getzels and Jackson (1962) study and found similar results to theirs. He also followed up on their sample and noted that 55% of the high-creative group ended up in un-

conventional occupations compared with only 9% of the high-intelligence group, lending some support to the ecological validity of the creativity tests (Torrance, 1975). In a separate long-range predictive validity study of 236 high school students tested with the Torrance Tests of Creative Thinking (TTCT) in 1959 and followed up in 1971, Torrance (1975) found a canonical correlation of .51 for the combined scores on the creativity test battery and later creative achievement.

In developing the TTCT, Torrance (1975) experimented with variations in time limits as well as with unlimited time and various instructions and found that in thousands of administrations of the TTCT, none of the stress due to a testing environment that Wallach and Kogan (1965) tried to eliminate by using their gamelike exercises was evident.

In a summary of a total of 388 correlations from a variety of dissertation studies and published studies, Torrance observed that "all along the data have seemed to support the conclusion that these two variables [intelligence and creativity] are related only moderately" (Torrance, 1975, p. 287). "The median of 114 coefficients of correlation involving figural measures was .06; for the 88 correlations involving verbal measures, the median was .21; and for the 178 correlations involving both verbal and figural measures combined, the median was .20" (Torrance, 1975, p. 287). He emphasized the finding that "no matter what measure of IQ is chosen, we would exclude about 70% of our most creative children if IQ alone were used in identifying giftedness" (Torrance, 1963, p. 182).

Practice Effects

Recently, some investigators have suggested that intelligence and creativity may be disjoint because of practice effects (Ericsson, 1996; Ericsson & Faivre, 1988; Ericsson, Krampe, & Tesch-Römer, 1993). According to this view, expertise of any kind, including creative expertise, develops as a result of deliberate practice, whereby an individual practices with a mind to improve him or herself in his or her performance. Creative expertise thus is not really an ability at all but rather a result of deliberate practice in a domain, and particularly, in doing creative work in a domain. Indeed, many researchers have spoken of the 10-year rule (e.g., Gardner, 1993; Simonton, 1994), whereby significant creative production seems to require 10 years of active work in a field.

Ericsson and his colleagues have done several studies showing that expertise of various kinds does indeed seem to correlate with deliberate practice. In a variety of fields, deliberate practice is correlated with eminence. Roe (1952) concluded, after her investigation of eminent scientists, that more than your capacity for a particular field, how well you do is "a function of how hard you work at it" (p. 170). At the present, however, the evidence is largely correlational, meaning that it is difficult to assess the causal chain. It may be, for example, that people with creative or other talent are more motivated to engage in deliberate practice than are those without such talent. Nevertheless, the deliberate-practice view of creativity cannot be ruled out, and clearly, deliberate practice facilitates creative work and may even be necessary for it, whether or not it is also sufficient.

CONCLUSION

At the very least, creativity seems to involve synthetic, analytical, and practical aspects of intelligence: synthetic to come up with ideas, analytical to evaluate the quality of those ideas, and practical to formulate a way of effectively communicating those ideas and of persuading people of their value. But beyond the basics, it is difficult to find substantial agreement among those working in the field.

Despite a substantial body of research, psychologists still have not reached a consensus on the nature of the relation between intelligence and creativity, nor even of exactly what these constructs are. All possible set relations between intelligence and creativity have been proposed, and there is at least some evidence to support each of them. The negative side of this state of affairs is that we can say little with certainty about the relation between intelligence and creativity and creativity's fate as a legitimate area of research is still debated between "hard" and "soft" scientists. The debate is old, dating back to Francis Galton, who in 1879 argued that scientific phenomena must be quantified (cited in Crovitz, 1970, p. 24). The positive side is that for those seeking an important, open research question, that of the relation between creativity and intelligence is worth considering. The question is theoret-

ically important, and its answer probably affects the lives of countless children and adults. We therefore need elucidation of good answers as soon as possible.

AUTHOR NOTES

This chapter draws on "Creativity and Intelligence," a chapter in the *Handbook of Creativity* (1999) edited by Robert J. Sternberg and published by Cambridge University Press.

1. The work reported herein was supported under the Javits Act program (Grant No. R206R950001) as administered by the Office of Educational Research and Improvement, U.S. Department of Education. The findings and opinions expressed in this report do not reflect the positions or policies of the Office of Educational Research and Improvement or the U.S. Department of Education.
2. Answers to the sample RAT items: (1) cheese, (2) working, (3) party, (4) chair or wire, (5) house.

REFERENCES

Amabile, T. M. (1996). *Creativity in context.* Boulder, CO: Westview.

Andrews, F. M. (1975). Social and psychological factors which influence the creative process. In I. A. Taylor & J. W. Getzels (Eds.), *Perspectives in creativity* (pp. 117–145). Chicago: Aldine.

Barron, F. (1963). *Creativity and psychological health.* Princeton: D. Van Nostrand.

Barron, F. (1969). *Creative person and creative process.* New York: Holt, Rinehart & Winston.

Barron, F., & Harrington, D. M. (1981). Creativity, intelligence, and personality. *Annual Review of Psychology, 32,* 439–476.

Beittel, K. R. (1964). Creativity in the visual arts in higher education: Criteria, predictors, experimentation and their interactions. In C. W. Taylor (Ed.), *Widening horizons in creativity.* New York: Wiley.

Boden, M. (1991). *The creative mind: Myths and mechanisms.* New York: Basic Books.

Boden, M. (Ed.). (1994). *Dimensions of creativity.* Cambridge, MA: MIT Press.

Brown, R. T. (1989). Creativity: What are we to measure. In J. A. Glover, R. R. Ronning, & C. R. Reynolds (Eds.), *Handbook of creativity* (pp. 3–32). New York: Plenum Press.

Burt, C. L. (1970). Critical notice. In P. E. Vernon (Ed.), *Creativity: Selected readings* (pp. 203–216). Baltimore: Penguin Books. (Reprinted from *British Journal of Educational Psychology, 32,* 1962, 292–298).

Cattell, R. B. (1971). *Abilities: Their structure, growth and action*. Boston: Houghton Mifflin.

Cox, C. M. (1926). *The early mental traits of three hundred geniuses*. Stanford, CA: Stanford University Press.

Crovitz, H. F. (1970). *Galton's walk: Methods for the analysis of thinking, intelligence, and creativity*. New York: Harper & Row.

Csikszentmihalyi, M. (1988). Society, culture, and person: A systems view of creativity. In R. J. Sternberg (Ed.), *The nature of creativity* (pp. 325–339). New York: Cambridge University Press.

Csikszentmihalyi, M. (1996). *Creativity*. New York: Harper-Collins.

Davidson, J. E. (1986). The role of insight in giftedness. In R. J. Sternberg & J. E. Davidson (Eds.), *Conceptions of giftedness* (pp. 201–222). New York: Cambridge University Press.

Davidson, J. E. (1995). The suddenness of insight. In R. J. Sternberg & J. E. Davidson (Eds.), *The nature of insight*. Cambridge, MA: MIT Press.

Davidson, J. E., & Sternberg, R. J. (1984). The role of insight in intellectual giftedness. *Gifted Child Quarterly, 28*, 58–64.

Ericsson, K. A. (Ed.). (1996). *The road to excellence*. Mahwah, NJ: Lawrence Erlbaum Associates.

Ericsson, K. A., & Faivre, I. A. (1988). What's exceptional about exceptional abilities? In I. K. Obler & D. Fein (Eds.), *The exceptional brain: Neuropsychology of talent and special abilities* (pp. 436–473). New York: Guilford Press.

Ericsson, K. A., Krampe, R. T., & Tesch-Römer, C. (1993). The role of deliberate practice in the acquisition of expert performance. *Psychological Review, 100*, 363–406.

Flescher, I. (1963). Anxiety and achievement of intellectually gifted and creatively gifted children. *Journal of Psychology, 56*, 251–268.

Frensch, P. A., & Sternberg, R. J. (1989). Expertise and intelligent thinking: When is it worse to know better? In R. J. Sternberg (Ed.), *Advances in the psychology of human intelligence* (Vol. 5, pp. 157–158). Hillsdale, NJ: Erlbaum.

Gardner, H. (1983). *Frames of mind: The theory of multiple intelligences*. New York: Basic.

Gardner, H. (1993). *Creating minds*. New York: Basic Books.

Gardner, H. (1995). *Leading minds*. New York: Basic Books.

Getzels, J. W., & Csikszentmihalyi, M. (1972). The creative artist as an explorer. In J. McVicker Hunt (Ed.), *Human intelligence* (pp. 182–192). New Brunswick, NJ: Transaction Books.

Getzels, J. W., & Jackson, P. W. (1962). *Creativity and intelligence: Explorations with gifted students*. New York: John Wiley & Sons.

Glover, J. A., Ronning, R. R., & Reynolds, C. R. (Eds.). (1989). *Handbook of creativity*. New York: Plenum Press.

Goodman, N. (1955). *Fact, fiction, and forecast*. Cambridge, MA: Harvard University Press.

Gough, H. G. (1957). *California psychological inventory manual*. Palo Alto, CA: Consulting Psychologists Press.

Grigorenko, E. L., & Sternberg, R. J. (in press). Analytical, creative, and practical intelligences as predictors of adaptive functioning: A case study in Russia. *Intelligence*.

Guilford, J. P. (1950). Creativity. *American Psychologist, 5*, 444–454.

Guilford, J. P. (1967). *The nature of human intelligence*. New York: McGraw-Hill.

Guilford, J. P. (1970). Creativity: Retrospect and prospect. *Journal of Creative Behavior, 4*, 149–168.

Guilford, J. P. (1975). Creativity: A quarter century of progress. In I. A. Taylor & J. W. Getzels (Eds.), *Perspectives in creativity*. Chicago: Aldine.

Guilford, J. P., & Christensen, P. W. (1973). The one-way relation between creative potential and IQ. *Journal of Creative Behavior, 7*, 247–252.

Guilford, J. P., & Hoepfner, R. (1966). Creative potential as related to measures of IQ and verbal comprehension. *Indian Journal of Psychology, 41*, 7–16.

Haensly, P. A., & Reynolds, C. R. (1989). Creativity and intelligence. In J. A. Glover, R. R. Ronning, & C. R. Reynolds (Eds.), *Handbook of creativity* (pp. 111–132). New York: Plenum.

Hayes, J. R. (1989). Cognitive processes in creativity. In J. A. Glover, R. R. Ronning, & C. R. Reynolds (Eds.), *Handbook of creativity* (pp. 135–145). New York: Plenum.

Helson, R. (1976). Women and creativity. In A. Rothenberg & C. R. Hausman (Eds.), *The creativity question* (pp. 242–250). Durham, NC: Duke University Press. (Reprinted from Women mathematicians and the creative personality, *Journal of Consulting and Clinical Psychology, 36*, 1971, pp. 210–211, 217–220).

Herr, E. L., Moore, G. D., & Hasen, J. S. (1965). Creativity, intelligence, and values: A study of relationships. *Exceptional Children, 32*, 114–115.

Horn, J. L., & Cattell, R. B. (1966). Refinement and test of the theory of fluid and crystallized intelligence. *Journal of Educational Psychology, 57*, 253–270.

Horn, J. L., & Knapp, J. R. (1973). On the subjective character of the empirical base of Guilford's structure-of-intellect model. *Psychological Bulletin, 80*, 33–43.

"Intelligence and its measurement": A symposium (1921). *Journal of Educational Psychology, 12*, 123–147, 195–216, 271–275.

Jensen, A. R. (1998). *The g factor*. Greenwich, CT: Greenwood.

Johnson-Laird, P. N. (1988). Freedom and constraint in creativity. In R. J. Sternberg (Ed.), *The nature of creativity* (pp. 202–219). New York: Cambridge University Press.

Langley, P., Simon, H. A., Bradshaw, G. L., & Zytkow, J. M. (1987). *Scientific discovery: Computational explorations of the creative processes*. Cambridge, MA: MIT Press.

Lubart, T. I. (1994). Creativity. In R. J. Sternberg (Ed.), *Thinking and problem solving* (pp. 290–332). San Diego: Academic Press.

MacKinnon, D. (1962). The nature and nurture of creative talent. *American Psychologist, 17*, 484–495.

MacKinnon, D. (1967). The highly effective individual. In R. L. Mooney & T. A. Razik (Eds.), *Explorations in creativity* (pp. 55–68). New York: Harper & Row.

MacKinnon, D. (1975). IPAR's contribution to the conceptualization and study of creativity. In I. A. Taylor & J. W. Getzels (Eds.), *Perspectives in creativity* (pp. 60–89). Chicago: Aldine.

McNemar, Q. (1964). Lost: Our intelligence? Why? *American Psychologist, 19*, 871–882.

Mednick, S. A. (1962). The associative basis of the creative process. *Psychological Review, 69*, 220–232.

Mednick, M. T., & Andrews, F. M. (1967). Creative thinking and level of intelligence. *Journal of Creative Behavior, 1*, 428–431.

Merrifield, P. R., Gardner, S. F., & Cox, A. B. (1964). *Aptitudes and personality measures related to creativity in seventh-grade children.* Reports of the Psychological Laboratories of the University of Southern California, No. 28.

Newell, A., Shaw, J. C., & Simon, H. A. (1958). Elements of a theory of human problem solving. *Psychological Review, 65*, 151–166.

Ochse, R. (1990). *Before the gates of excellence.* New York: Cambridge University Press.

Perkins, D. N. (1981). *The mind's best work.* Cambridge, MA: Harvard University Press.

Piers, E. V., Daniels, J. M., & Quackenbush, J. F. (1960). The identification of creativity in adolescents. *Journal of Educational Psychology, 51*, 346–351.

Renzulli, J. S. (1986). The three-ring conception of giftedness: A development model for creative productivity. In R. J. Sternberg & J. E. Davidson (Eds.), *Conceptions of giftedness* (pp. 53–92). New York: Cambridge University Press.

Roe, A. (1952). *The making of a scientist.* New York: Dodd, Mead.

Roe, A. (1972). Patterns of productivity of scientists. *Science, 176*, 940–941.

Roe, A. (1976). Psychological approaches to creativity in science. In A. Rothenberg & C. R. Hausman (Eds.), *The creativity question* (pp. 165–175). Durham, NC: Duke University Press. (Reprinted from *Essays on creativity in the sciences*, pp. 153–154, 166–172, 177–182, by M. A. Coler & H. K. Hughes, Eds., 1963, New York: New York University Press).

Rothenberg, A., & Hausman, C. R. (Eds.). (1976). *The creativity question.* Durham, NC: Duke University Press.

Rubenson, D. L., & Runco, M. A. (1992). The psychoeconomic approach to creativity. *New Ideas in Psychology, 10*, 131–147.

Runco, M. A. (1987). The generality of creative performance in gifted and nongifted children. *Gifted Child Quarterly, 31*(3), 121–125.

Schubert, D. S. (1973). Intelligence as necessary but not sufficient for creativity. *The Journal of Genetic Psychology, 122*, 45–47.

Shouksmith, G. (1973). *Intelligence, creativity and cognitive style.* London: Angus & Robertson.

Skager, R. W., Schultz, C. B., & Klein, S. P. (1967). Quality and quantity of accomplishments as measures of creativity. *Journal of Educational Psychology, 56*, 31–39.

Simonton, D. K. (1976). Biographical determinants of achieved eminence: A multivariate approach to the Cox data. *Journal of Personality and Social Psychology, 33*, 218–226.

Simonton, D. K. (1994). *Greatness: Who makes history and why?* New York: Guilford.

Smith, I. L. (1970). IQ, creativity, and the taxonomy of educational objectives: Cognitive domain. *The Journal of Experimental Education, 38*(4), 58–60.

Smith, I. L. (1971). IQ, creativity, and achievement: Interaction and threshold. *Multivariate Behavioral Research, 6*(1), 51–62.

Sternberg, R. J. (1982). Natural, unnatural, and supernatural concepts. *Cognitive Psychology, 14*, 451–488.

Sternberg, R. J. (1985a). *Beyond IQ: A triarchic theory of human intelligence.* New York: Cambridge University Press.

Sternberg, R. J. (1985b). Implicit theories of intelligence, creativity, and wisdom. *Journal of Personality and Social Psychology, 49*, 607–627.

Sternberg, R. J. (1988). *The triarchic mind: A theory of human intelligence.* New York: Viking.

Sternberg, R. J. (1996). *Successful intelligence.* New York: Simon & Schuster.

Sternberg, R. J. (1997). What does it mean to be smart? *Educational Leadership, 54*, 20–24.

Sternberg, R. J. (1999). A propulsion model of creative contributions. *Review of General Psychology, 3*, 83–100.

Sternberg, R. J., & Clinkenbeard, P. (1995). A triarchic view of identifying, teaching, and assessing gifted children. *Roeper Review, 17*(4), 255–260.

Sternberg, R. J., Conway, B. E., Ketron, J. L., & Bernstein, M. (1981). People's conceptions of intelligence. *Journal of Personality and Social Psychology, 41*, 37–55.

Sternberg, R. J., & Davidson, J. E. (1982). The mind of the puzzler. *Psychology Today, 16*, 37–44.

Sternberg, R. J., & Detterman, D. K. (Eds.). (1986). *What is intelligence? Contemporary viewpoints on its nature and definition.* Norwood, NJ: Ablex.

Sternberg, R. J., Ferrari, M., Clinkenbeard, P., & Grigorenko, E. L. (1996). Identification, instruction, and assessment of gifted children: A construct validation of a triarchic model. *Gifted Child Quarterly, 40*, 129–137.

Sternberg, R. J., & Gastel, J. (1989a). Coping with novelty in human intelligence: An empirical investigation. *Intelligence, 13*, 187–197.

Sternberg, R. J., & Gastel, J. (1989b). If dancers ate their shoes: Inductive reasoning with factual and counterfactual premises. *Memory and Cognition, 17*, 1–10.

Sternberg, R. J., Grigorenko, E. L., Ferrari, M., & Clinkenbeard, P. (1999). Triarchic analysis of an aptitude-treatment interaction. *European Journal of Psychological Assessment, 15*, 1–11.

Sternberg, R. J., & Kalmar, D. A. (1997). When will the milk spoil? Everyday induction in human intelligence. *Intelligence, 25*(3), 185–203.

Sternberg, R. J., & Lubart, T. I. (1991). An investment theory of creativity and its development. *Human Development, 34*(1), 1–32.

Sternberg, R. J., & Lubart, T. I. (1995). *Defying the crowd: Cultivating creativity in a culture of conformity.* New York: Free Press.

Sternberg, R. J., & Lubart, T. I. (1996). Investing in creativity. *American Psychologist, 51*(7), 677–688.

Sternberg, R. J., Torff, B., & Grigorenko, E. L. (1998). Teaching triarchically improves school achievement. *Journal of Educational Psychology, 90*(3), 1–11.

Sternberg, R. J., Wagner, R. K., Williams, W. M., & Horvath, J. (1995). Testing common sense. *American Psychologist, 50*, 912-927.

Tetewsky, S. J., & Sternberg, R. J. (1986). Conceptual and lexical determinants of nonentrenched thinking. *Journal of Memory and Language, 25*, 202–225.

Torrance, E. P. (1962). *Guiding creative talent.* Englewood Cliffs, NJ: Prentice–Hall.

Torrance, E. P. (1963). Explorations in creative thinking in the early school years: A progress report. In C. W. Taylor & F. Barron (Eds.), *Scientific creativity: Its recognition and development* (pp. 173–183). New York: John Wiley & Sons.

Torrance, E. P. (1974). *The Torrance Tests of Creative Thinking: Technical-norms manual.* Bensenville, IL: Scholastic Testing Service.

Torrance, E. P. (1975). Creativity reasearch in education: Still alive. In I. A. Taylor & J. W. Getzels (Eds.), *Perspectives in creativity* (pp. 278–296). Chicago: Aldine.

Wallach, M., & Kogan, N. (1965). *Modes of thinking in young children.* New York: Holt, Rinehart, & Winston.

Wallach, M., & Kogan, N. (1972). Creativity and intelligence in children. In J. McVicker Hunt (Ed.), *Human Intelligence* (pp. 165–181). New Brunswick, NJ: Transaction Books.

Weisberg, R. (1986). *Creativity, genius and other myths.* New York: Freeman.

Weisberg, R. (1988). Problem solving and creativity. In R. J. Sternberg (Ed.), *The nature of creativity* (pp. 148–176). New York: Cambridge University Press.

Weisberg, R. W. (1993). *Creativity: Beyond the myth of genius.* New York: Freeman.

Weisberg, R. W., & Alba, J. W. (1981). An examination of the alleged role of "fixation" in the solution of several "insight" problems. *Journal of Experimental Psychology: General, 110*, 169–192.

Yamamoto, K. (1964). Creativity and sociometric choice among adolescents. *Journal of Social Psychology, 64*, 249–261.

Yang, S.-Y., & Sternberg, R. J. (1997). Taiwanese Chinese people's conceptions of intelligence. *Intelligence, 25*, 21–36.

CHAPTER TWENTY-EIGHT

Intelligence and Wisdom

ROBERT J. STERNBERG

INTELLIGENCE AND WISDOM

Some people, like Mohandas Gandhi or Nelson Mandela, radiate both intelligence and wisdom. Other people, like Joseph Stalin or Adolph Hitler, seem to have been intelligent in a narrow sense, but certainly were not wise. Still others seem to be wise but perhaps not conventionally intelligent: Many of us have known older people, perhaps relatives, who have shown their wisdom but who have not shown the kinds of achievements or talents typically associated with conventional intelligence. And of course, there are many people who are neither wise nor intelligent. Given all the possible relations we see in people between wisdom and intelligence, just what is the nature of their interrelation?

Theories of intelligence seem to have little to say about wisdom. Regardless of the metaphor of mind underlying the theory of intelligence (Sternberg, 1990a), wisdom seems to be viewed as outside the purview of the large majority of theories of intelligence. But intelligence plays an important role in many theories of wisdom (see Sternberg, 1990b). In this chapter, I will consider the interrelation between the two, suggesting that the asymmetry in reference across the two literatures results from wisdom being a special case of a special kind of intelligence, practical intelligence. One possibly can discuss intelligence without dealing with wisdom, but one cannot adequately discuss wisdom without dealing with intelligence.

Wisdom can be defined as the "power of judging rightly and following the soundest course of action, based on knowledge, experience, understand-

ing, etc." (*Webster's New World College Dictionary*, p. 1533). But dictionary definitions usually do not suffice for psychological understanding. Several scholars have attempted to understand wisdom in different ways. Some of these approaches are philosophical (see Robinson, 1990), but I will limit the discussion here to psychological approaches. The approaches underlying some of these attempts are summarized in Sternberg (1990b) and in Baltes (in preparation). The approaches may be classified as implicit–theoretical approaches and explicit–theoretical approaches.

APPROACHES TO WISDOM AND THEIR INTERRELATION TO INTELLIGENCE

There are two major approaches that have been taken to understanding the relation of intelligence to wisdom: implicit–theoretical and explicit–theoretical.

Implicit–Theoretical Approaches

Implicit–theoretical approaches to wisdom have in common the search for an understanding of people's folk conceptions of what wisdom is. Thus, the goal is not to provide a "psychologically true" account of wisdom but rather an account that is true with respect to people's beliefs, whether these beliefs are right or wrong.

Some of the earliest work of this kind was done by Clayton (1975, 1976; 1982; Clayton & Birren, 1980), who multidimensionally scaled ratings of pairs of words potentially related to wisdom for three samples of adults differing in age (younger, middle-aged, older). In her earliest study (Clayton, 1975), the terms that were scaled were ones such as *experienced, pragmatic, understanding*, and *knowledgeable*. In each study, participants were asked to rate similarities between all possible pairs of words. The main similarity in the results for the age cohorts for which the scalings were done was the elicitation of two consistent dimensions of wisdom, which Clayton referred to as an affective dimension and a reflective dimension. The reflective dimension seems to be the one of these two that more overlaps with intelligence. There was also a suggestion of a dimension relating to age. The greatest difference among the age cohorts was that mental representations of wisdom seemed to become more differentiated (i.e., to increase in dimensionality) with increases in the ages of the participants, which is reminiscent of work by Yussen (1977) suggesting that children's conceptions of intelligence also become more differentiated with age. Some theorists also have suggested that intelligence itself differentiates with age (see review in Sternberg & Powell, 1983).

Holliday and Chandler (1986) also used an implicit-theories approach to understanding wisdom. Approximately 500 participants were studied across a series of experiments. The investigators were interested in determining whether the concept of wisdom could be understood as a prototype (Rosch, 1975) or central concept. This same approach of applying the Roschian prototype model previously has been applied to intelligence by Neisser (1979). Principal-components analysis of one of Holliday and Chandler's studies revealed five underlying factors: exceptional understanding, judgment and communication skills, general competence, interpersonal skills, and social unobtrusiveness. All of these factors except the last could also apply to Western notions of intelligence. Moreover, Yang and Sternberg (1997a) found a factor similar to the last one in Taiwanese Chinese conceptions of intelligence. In these conceptions, the last extracted factor seemed to measure the individual's understanding of when *not* to show his or her intelligence. Indeed, the Chinese conception of intelligence seems to bear a close relation to conceptions of wisdom, perhaps because, in Chinese, there is no clear linguistic differentiation between the two constructs (Yang & Sternberg, 1997a,b).

Sternberg (1985b, 1990c) has reported a series of studies investigating implicit theories of wisdom. In one study, 200 professors, each of art, business, philosophy, and physics, were asked to rate the characteristicness of each of the behaviors obtained in a prestudy from the corresponding population with respect to the professors' ideal conception of each of an ideally wise, intelligent, or creative individual in their occupation. Laypersons were also asked to provide these ratings but for a hypothetical ideal individual without regard to occupation. Correlations were computed across the three ratings. In each group except philosophy, the highest correlation was between wisdom and intelligence; in philosophy, the highest correlation was between intelligence and creativity. The correlations between wisdom and intelligence ratings ranged from .42 to .78 with a median of .68. For all groups, the lowest correlation was between wisdom and creativity (which ranged from −.24 to .48 with a median of .27). In a second study, 40 college students were asked to sort three sets of 40 behaviors each into as many or as few piles as they wished. The 40 behaviors in each set were the top-rated wisdom, intelligence, and creativity behaviors from the previous study. The sortings then each were subjected to nonmetric multidimensional scaling. For wisdom, six components emerged: *reasoning ability, sagacity, learning from ideas and environment, judgment, expeditious use of information*, and *perspicacity*. These components can be compared with those that emerged from a similar scaling of people's implicit theories of intelligence, which were *practical problem-solving ability, verbal ability, intellectual balance and integration, goal orientation and attainment, contextual intelligence*, and *fluid thought*. In both cases, cognitive abilities and their use are important. In wisdom, however, some kind of balance appears to emerge as important that does not emerge as important in intelligence, in general.

In a third study, 50 adults were asked to rate descriptions of hypothetical individuals for intelligence, creativity, and wisdom. Correlations were computed between pairs of ratings of the hypothetical individuals' levels of the three traits. Correlations between the ratings were .94 for wisdom and intelligence, .62 for wisdom and creativity, and .69 for intelligence and creativity, again suggesting that wisdom and intelligence are highly correlated in people's implicit theories, at least in the United States.

Explicit–Theoretical Approaches

Explicit theories are constructions of (supposedly) expert theorists and researchers rather than of laypeople (Sternberg, Conway, Ketron, & Bernstein, 1981). In the study of wisdom, most explicit-theoretical approaches are based on constructs from the psychology of human development.

The most extensive program of research has been that conducted by Baltes and his colleagues. This program of research is related to Baltes's longstanding program of research on intellectual abilities and aging. For example, Baltes and Smith (1987, 1990) gave adult participants life-management problems, such as "A fourteen-year-old girl is pregnant. What should she, what should one, consider and do?" and "A fifteen-year-old girl wants to marry soon. What should she, what should one, consider and do?" This same problem might be used to measure the pragmatics of intelligence, about which Baltes has written at length. Baltes and Smith tested a five-component model of wisdom on participants' protocols in answering these and other questions, based on a notion of wisdom as expert knowledge about fundamental life matters (Smith & Baltes, 1990) or of wisdom as good judgment and advice in important but uncertain matters of life (Baltes & Staudinger, 1993).

Three kinds of factors – general person factors, expertise-specific factors, and facilitative experiential contexts – were proposed to facilitate wise judgments. These factors are used in life planning, life management, and life review. Wisdom is in turn then reflected in five components: (a) rich factual knowledge (general and specific knowledge about the conditions of life and its variations), (b) rich procedural knowledge (general and specific knowledge about strategies of judgment and advice concerning matters of life), (c) life-span contextualism (knowledge about the contexts of life and their temporal [developmental] relationships), (d) relativism (knowledge about differences in values, goals, and priorities), and (e) uncertainty (knowledge about the relative indeterminacy and unpredictability of life and ways to manage). An expert answer should reflect more of these components, whereas a novice answer should reflect fewer of them. The data collected to date generally have been supportive of the model. These factors seem to reflect the pragmatic aspect of intelligence but to go beyond it, for example, in the inclusion of factors of relativism and uncertainty.

Over time, Baltes and his colleagues (e.g., Baltes, Smith, & Staudinger, 1992; Baltes & Staudinger, 1993) have collected a wide range of data showing the empirical utility of the proposed theoretical and measurement approaches to wisdom. For example, Staudinger, Lopez, and Baltes (1997) found that measures of intelligence (as well as personality) overlap with, but are nonidentical to, measures of wisdom in terms of constructs measured and Staudinger, Smith, and Baltes (1992) showed that human–services professionals outperformed a control group on wisdom-related tasks. They also showed that older adults performed as well on such tasks as did younger adults and that older adults did better on such tasks if there was a match between their age and the age of the fictitious characters about whom they made judgments. Baltes, Staudinger, Maercker, and Smith (1995) found that older individuals nominated for their wisdom performed as well as did clinical psychologists on wisdom-related tasks. They also showed that up to the age of 80, older adults performed as well on such tasks as did younger adults. In a further set of studies, Staudinger and Baltes (1996) found that performance settings that were ecologically relevant to the lives of their participants and that provided for actual or "virtual" interaction of minds increased wisdom-related performance substantially.

Thus, wisdom seems to behave more like crystallized than like fluid intelligence in its development over the life course (see Horn, 1994; Horn & Cattell, 1966). In particular, crystallized intelligence, like wisdom, appears to increase during most of the life span and then perhaps to level off (cf. Meacham, 1990). Fluid intelligence, in contrast, appears to decline after some point in adulthood.

Sternberg (1990c) also proposed an explicit theory, suggesting that the development of wisdom can be traced to six antecedent components: (a) knowledge, including an understanding of its presuppositions and meaning as well as its limitations; (b) processes, including an understanding of what problems should be solved automatically and what problems should not be so solved; (c) a judicial thinking style, characterized by the desire to judge and evaluate things in an in-depth way; (d) personality, including tolerance of ambiguity and of the role of obstacles in life; (e) motivation, especially the motivation to understand what is known and what it means; and (f) environmental context, involving an appreciation of the contextual factors in the environment that lead to various kinds of thoughts and actions. The first two of these components correspond very roughly to crystallized and fluid aspects of intelligence, whereas the other components go beyond intelligence as it is usually understood.

Whereas the Sternberg (1990c) theory specified a set of *antecedents* of wisdom, the balance theory proposed here (see also Sternberg, in press-a, for a more nearly complete presentation) specifies the *processes* (balancing of interests and of responses to environmental contexts) in relation to the *goal* of wisdom (achievement of a common good). The Sternberg (1990c) theory is incorporated into the balance theory as specifying antecedent sources of developmental and individual differences, as discussed later.

Some theorists have viewed wisdom in terms of postformal–operational thinking, thereby viewing wisdom as a form of intellectual functioning that extends the development of thinking beyond the Piagetian stages of intelligence (Piaget, 1972). These theorists seem to view wisdom in a way that is similar or even identical to the way they perceive the development of intelligence past the Piagetian (1972) stage of formal operations. For example, some authors have argued that wise individuals are those who can think reflectively or dialectically, in the latter case with the individuals' realizing that truth is not always absolute but rather evolves in an historical context of theses, antitheses, and syntheses (e.g., Basseches, 1984; Kitchener, 1983, 1986; Kitchener & Brenner, 1990; Kitchener & Kitchener, 1981; Labouvie-Vief, 1980, 1982, 1990; Pascual-Leone, 1990; Riegel, 1973). Consider a very brief review of some specific dialectical approaches.

Kitchener and Brenner (1990) suggested that wisdom requires a synthesis of knowledge from opposing points of view. Similarly, Labouvie-Vief (1990) has emphasized the importance of a smooth and balanced dialogue between logical forms of processing and more subjective forms of processing. Pascual-Leone (1990) has argued for the importance of the dialectical integration of all aspects of a person's affect, cognition, conation (motivation), and life experience. Similarly, Orwoll and Perlmutter (1990) have emphasized the importance to wisdom of an integration of cognition with affect. Kramer (1990) has suggested the importance of the integration of relativistic and dialectical modes of thinking, affect, and reflection. And Birren and Fisher (1990), putting together a number of views of wisdom, have suggested as well the importance of the integration of cognitive, conative, and affective aspects of human abilities. A common feature of these models is the balancing of different aspects of the mind – what Baltes (in preparation) refers to as the orchestration of the mind. In contrast, the balance theory described in this chapter (Sternberg, 1998a) views balance as referring to competing interests and reactions to the environment in response to these competing interests.

Other theorists have suggested the importance of knowing the limits of one's own extant knowledge and of then trying to go beyond it. For example, Meacham (1990) has suggested that an important aspect of wisdom is a kind of metacognition – an awareness of one's own fallibility and a knowledge of what one does and does not know. Kitchener and Brenner (1990) similarly have also emphasized the importance of knowing the limitations of one's own knowledge. Arlin (1990) has linked wisdom to problem finding, the first step of which is the recognition that how one currently defines a problem may be inadequate. This view perhaps links wisdom not just with intelligence but with creativity in that problem finding is often viewed as important to creative thinking (see Getzels & Csikszentmihalyi, 1976; Sternberg & Lubart, 1995). Arlin views problem finding as a possible stage of postformal operational thinking. Such a view is not necessarily inconsistent with the view of dialectical thinking as such a postformal–operational stage. Dialectical thinking and problem finding could represent distinct postformal–operational stages or two manifestations of the same postformal–operational stage.

Although most developmental approaches to wisdom are ontogenetic, Csikszentmihalyi and Rathunde (1990) have taken a philogenetic or evolutionary approach, arguing that constructs such as wisdom must have been selected for over time, at least in a cultural sense. Intelligence, too, has been understood by some in a cultural–evolutionary sense (see essays in Sternberg & Kaufman, in press). In other words, wise ideas should survive better over time than unwise ideas in a culture. The theorists define wisdom as having three basic dimensions of meaning: (a) that of a cognitive process, or a particular way of obtaining and processing information; (b) that of a virtue, or socially valued pattern of behavior; and (c) that of a good, or a personally desirable state or condition. The first of these dimensions seems to be primarily intellectual, whereas the latter two are not.

A BALANCE VIEW: TACIT KNOWLEDGE AS THE CORE OF WISDOM

A different approach to the relation between intelligence and wisdom is taken by Sternberg (1998a). Sternberg (1985a) proposed that intelligence has three main aspects: analytical, creative, and practical. Although all three aspects enter into wisdom, at least indirectly, wisdom is understood primarily as an outgrowth of practical intelligence in much the same way creativity would be understood as an outgrowth of creative intelligence. A somewhat restricted definition of intelligence used by many theorists (e.g., Brand, 1996; Carroll, 1993; Jensen, 1998) would understand intelligence primarily as an outgrowth of analytical intelligence. But in Sternberg's (1985a) triarchic theory, intelligence is understood in a broader sense as encompassing as well the creative and practical aspects of intelligence. Thus, arguments about what intelligence *really* is are fruitless. What it really is depends on whether one is defining it narrowly or broadly. Similarly, arguments about the general factor of intelligence (see Schmidt, & Hunter 1993; Jensen, 1993; Ree & Earles, 1993; Sternberg & Wagner, 1993) are fruitless because the general factor applies to the narrow conception of intelligence but not to the broad one. Thus, whether there is a general factor depends on how broadly one chooses to define intelligence.

The Nature of Tacit Knowledge

The view of wisdom proposed here has at its core the notion of tacit knowledge (Polanyi, 1976) about oneself, others, and situational contexts. Tacit knowledge is action-oriented, typically acquired without direct help from others, and allows individuals to achieve goals they personally value

(Sternberg, Wagner, Williams, & Horvath, 1995). Tacit knowledge thus has three main features: (a) it is procedural, (b) it is relevant to the attainment of goals people value, and (c) it typically is acquired with little help from others. Tacit knowledge forms an important part of practical intelligence, and indeed, the particular notion of tacit knowledge used here derives from the triarchic theory of intelligence (Sternberg, 1985a, 1997a). An advantage of the proposed theory is that it draws upon a theory of intelligence (the triarchic one) at the same time that it makes explicit how wisdom is different from the various aspects of intelligence as they are typically encountered.

When we refer to tacit knowledge as being procedural, and as intimately related to action, we are viewing it as a form of "knowing how" rather than of "knowing that" (Ryle, 1949). In our work, we view condition–action sequences (production systems) as a useful formalism for understanding the mental representation of tacit knowledge. For example, if one needs to deliver bad news to one's boss, and if it is Monday morning, and if the boss's golf game was rained out the day before, and if the boss's staff seems to be "walking on eggshells," then it is better to wait until later to deliver the news. Note that tacit knowledge is always wedded to particular uses in particular situations or classes of situations.

Tacit knowledge also is practically useful. It is instrumental to the attainment of goals people value. Thus, people use this knowledge in order to achieve success in life, however they may define success. Abstract academic knowledge about procedures for solving problems with no relevance to life would not be viewed, in this perspective, as constituting tacit knowledge.

Finally, tacit knowledge typically is acquired without direct help from others. At best, others can guide one to acquire this knowledge. Often, environmental support for the acquisition of this knowledge is minimal, and sometimes organizations actually suppress the acquisition of tacit knowledge. For example, an organization might not want its employees to know how personnel decisions are really made, as opposed to how they are supposed to be made. From a developmental standpoint, this view suggests that wisdom is not taught so much as indirectly acquired. One can provide the circumstances for the development of wisdom and case studies to help students develop wisdom, but one cannot teach particular courses of action that would be considered wise, regardless of circumstances. Indeed, tacit knowledge is wedded to contexts, and thus the tacit knowledge that would apply in one context would not necessarily apply in another context. To help someone develop tacit knowledge, one would provide mediated learning experiences rather than direct instruction as to what to do at what time.

Measurement of Tacit Knowledge

In a series of studies on practical intelligence (summarized in Sternberg, Wagner, & Okagaki, 1993; Sternberg et al., 1995), we have sought to develop assessments of tacit knowledge in real-world pursuits. The methodology for constructing assessments is rather complex (Horvath et al., 1996) but involves interviewing individuals for how they have handled critical situations on their jobs. We then extract the tacit knowledge implicit in these interviews. Assessments then are constructed that ask people to solve the kinds of problems they find in managing themselves, others, and tasks on the job. Examples of two tacit-knowledge problems, one for an academic psychologist and one for a business manager, are shown in the appendix of Sternberg et al. (1995). Each of these problems typically presents a scenario about a job-related problem along with possible options for dealing with that problem. For example, an academic psychologist might be asked to solve a problem in which a psychology professor has too much to do in the time available to do it. The participant (academic psychologist) would be given statements suggesting how the hypothetical professor might allocate his or her time and would be asked to rate the goodness of each of the options on a 1–9 Likert scale. The response profile for all items, then, is typically scored against the averaged profile of a nominated expert group.

Tacit Knowledge as an Aspect of Practical Intelligence

We have argued that tacit knowledge is a key aspect of practical intelligence (Sternberg, 1985b, 1997b; Sternberg & Wagner, 1993; Sternberg, Wagner, & Okagaki, 1993; Sternberg et al., 1995) or the ability to apply various kinds of information-processing components of intelligence to experience for the purposes of adaptation to, shaping

of, and selection of environments. Practical intelligence requires adaptation, shaping, and selection, in that different kinds of environments and environmental situations require different kinds of responses. It has been distinguished conceptually and statistically in research from analytical and creative aspects of intelligence (Sternberg, 1985a; Sternberg, Ferrari, Clinkenbeard, & Grigorenko, 1996; Sternberg, Grigorenko, Ferrari, & Clinkenbeard, 1999).

In a series of studies (see review in Sternberg et al., 1995), we have shown that tacit knowledge tends to increase with experience on a job but that it is what one learns from the experience rather than the experience itself that seems to matter. Measures of tacit knowledge tend to be correlated with each other, both within and across measures for different occupations. For example, Wagner (1987) found a correlation at the .6 level between scores on tacit-knowledge measures for academic psychology and management with undergraduates as participants. Our measures of tacit knowledge also predict actual performance in jobs such as sales, management, and college teaching. Not only is this prediction statistically significant and fairly substantial in magnitude (with correlations typically at about the .3 level), but this prediction is largely independent of the prediction provided by conventional tests of academic intelligence. In a study at the Center for Creative Leadership (described in Sternberg, Wagner, & Okagaki, 1993), we found that tacit knowledge for management was the best single predictor of performance on two managerial simulations. This relation held even after entering (conventional) cognitive abilities, personality-scale measures, styles, and interpersonal orientation into a hierarchical regression equation predicting performance on the simulations. Tacit knowledge still contributed significantly and substantially to prediction of performance on the simulations. This is true within a fairly broad range of academic abilities (Eddy, 1988). But the prediction is not always independent and may even be negative in other cultures (see Sternberg & Grigorenko, 1997a).

Why should tacit knowledge be relatively independent of academic intellectual abilities, or even, in some cases, inversely related to them? Along with Neisser (1979), we believe it is in part because the characteristics of academic and practical problems differ. In particular, academic problems tend (a) to be formulated by others, (b) often to be of little or no intrinsic interest, (c) to have all needed information available from the beginning, (d) to be disembedded from an individual's ordinary experience, (e) to be well defined, (f) to be characterized by a "correct" answer, and (g) to be characterized by a single method of obtaining the correct answer. In contrast, practical problems tend to be (a) unformulated or in need of reformulation; (b) of personal interest; (c) lacking in information necessary for solution; (d) related to everyday experience; (e) poorly defined; (f) characterized by multiple "correct" or at least "acceptable" solutions, each with liabilities as well as assets; and (g) characterized by multiple methods for picking a problem solution (Sternberg et al., 1995).

Practical intelligence and the role of tacit knowledge in it provide an entrée for understanding wisdom, but they do not provide a complete basis for its understanding. Practical intelligence does not always involve the same particular kinds of balances involved in wisdom. In particular, although it always involves a balancing of different possible responses to the environment, it does not always involve a balance among different competing interests. Consider the balance theory of wisdom in more detail.

THE BALANCE THEORY OF WISDOM

Balance is a crucial construct in the theory proposed here (see Sternberg, 1998a). Several of the theories described above also emphasize the importance of various kinds of integrations or balances in wisdom. At least three major kinds of balances have been proposed: among various kinds of thinking (e.g., Labouvie-Vief, 1990); among various self systems, such as the cognitive, conative, and affective (e.g., Kramer, 1990); and among various points of view (e.g., Kitchener & Brenner, 1990). The view presented here expands on but also differs from these kinds of notions in providing for particular kinds of balance in wisdom.

The balance theory views wisdom as inherent in the interaction between an individual and a situational context, much as intelligence (Sternberg, 1997a, Valsiner & Leung, 1994) involves a person-context interaction, as does creativity (Csikszentmihalyi, 1996; Sternberg & Lubart, 1995). For this reason, the balances proposed by the theory are in the interaction between a person and his or her context, rather than, say, in internal systems of functioning (such as cognitive, conative and affective). In the current view, someone could be balanced in terms of the internal systems by which they *process* information but not in the *products* that result from these processes. Because wisdom is in the interaction of person and situation, information processing in and of itself is not wise or unwise. Its degree of wisdom depends on the fit of a wise solution to its context.

In this view, the same balance of cognitive, conative, and affective processes that in one situational context may result in a wise solution in another context may not. This result may derive, for example, from a lack of tacit knowledge or incorrect tacit knowledge about one situation but not another. Judgments in any domain require a substantial tacit-knowledge base in order consistently to be wise.

Wisdom as Tacit Knowledge Used for Balancing Interests

The definition of wisdom proposed here (see Figure 28.1) draws both upon the notion of tacit knowledge, as described above, and on the notion of balance. In particular, wisdom is defined as the application of tacit knowledge as mediated by values toward the goal of achieving a common good through a balance among multiple:

1. *interests*: (a) intrapersonal, (b) interpersonal, and (c) extrapersonal in order to achieve a balance among
2. *responses to environmental contexts*: (a) adaptation to existing environmental contexts, (b) shaping of existing environmental contexts, and (c) selection of new environmental contexts.

Thus, wisdom is like all practical intelligence (Sternberg, 1985a) in requiring a balancing of responses to environmental contexts but only constitutes that subset of practical intelligence that involves balancing of interests, something that is not a necessary aspect of all practical intelligence.

In its application to wisdom, the features of tacit knowledge take on a special cast. Wisdom is procedural knowledge – it is about what to do in usually difficult and complex circumstances. Wisdom is also relevant to the attainment of particular goals people value, not just any goals, but rather, a balance of responses to the environment – adapting, shaping,

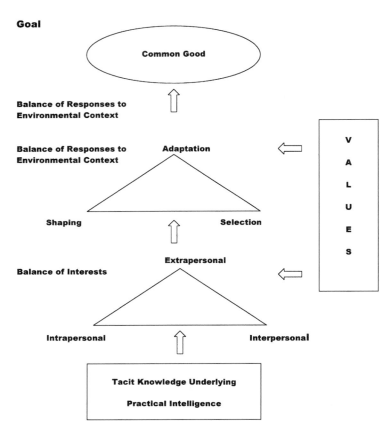

FIGURE 28.1. A balance theory of wisdom. Tacit knowledge underlying practical intelligence is applied to balance intrapersonal, interpersonal, and extrapersonal interests to achieve a balance of the responses to the environmental context of adaptation to, shaping of, and selection of environments in order to achieve a common good. Values mediate how people use their tacit knowledge in balancing interests and responses. (Another related construct is creativity. The relation between intelligence and creativity is discussed at some length in Sternberg and O'Hara [this volume].)

and selecting – so as to achieve a common good for all relevant stakeholders. Finally, wisdom typically is acquired with little direct help from others. One typically learns it from experience, not from formal instruction. Formal instruction may give one contexts in which to develop wisdom, but it cannot impart wisdom the way, say, multiplication facts can be imparted.

Wisdom is probably best developed through role modeling and through the incorporation of dialectical thinking into one's processing of problems – the same kind of thinking that is the hallmark of levels of intelligence that develop quite late, according to the neo-Piagetian theories (Basseches, 1984; Labouvie-Vief, 1990; Pascual-Leone, 1990; Riegel, 1973; Sternberg, 1998-b, 1999). Dialectical thinking can be either with respect to time or with respect to place. When it is with respect to time, it involves the recognition that ideas evolve over time through an ongoing, unending process of thesis followed by antithesis followed by synthesis, with the synthesis in turn becoming the next thesis (Hegel, 1807/1931). When dialectical thinking occurs with respect to place (or space), it involves the recognition that at a given point in time, people may have diverging viewpoints on problems that seem uniquely valid or at least reasonable to them.

Thus, wisdom is related to practical intelligence in that it draws upon tacit knowledge about oneself, others, and situational contexts, but it is only a refined subset of the tacit knowledge involved in practical intelligence. Practical intelligence has been defined in terms of maximizing practical outcomes. The practical outcomes may be for anyone or any ones, but usually these outcomes are the outcomes of an individual and most typically of oneself. For example, when one manages oneself, others, or tasks (Wagner, 1987; Wagner & Sternberg, 1985), one's ultimate goal often is to maximize one's self-interest. Wisdom is involved when practical intelligence is applied to maximizing not just one's own or someone else's self-interest, but rather a balance of various self-interests (intrapersonal) with the interests of others (interpersonal) and of other aspects of the context in which one lives (extrapersonal), such as one's city or country or environment or even God.

Thus, whereas practical intelligence can be applied toward the maximization of any set of interests – whether of an individual or a collective – wisdom is practical intelligence applied in particular to a *balance of intrapersonal, interpersonal, and extrapersonal interests*. It is a very special case of practical intelligence – one that requires balancing of multiple and often competing interests. Practical intelligence may or may not involve a balancing of interests, but wisdom must. Its output is typically in the form of advice, usually to another person, but sometimes for oneself.

An implication of this view is that when one applies practical intelligence, one deliberately may seek outcomes that are good for oneself or one's family and friends but bad for the common good. For example, despots typically are practically intelligent, managing to control an entire country largely for their own benefit. Despots such as Hitler or Stalin even may have balanced factors in their judgments, but *not* for the common good. Or one may apply practical intelligence to maximize someone else's benefit, as does a lawyer. In the subset of practical intelligence that is wisdom, one certainly may seek good ends for oneself (intrapersonal interests), but one also seeks to balance them with good outcomes for others (interpersonal interests) and with the contextual factors (extrapersonal interests) involved. The balance is then used to adapt to, shape, and select environments. For example, after hearing about as many relevant factors as possible, one might advise a college student to stay with his or her major but to work harder (adapt), to stay with the major but try to obtain a waiver of a certain requirement or set of requirements (shape), or to find another major (select).

If one's motivations are to maximize certain people's interests and minimize other people's, wisdom is not involved, although other aspects of practical intelligence well may be. In wisdom, one seeks a common good, realizing that this common good may be better for some than for others. A person who uses his or her mental powers to become an evil genius may be academically or practically intelligent, but the person cannot be wise. I will not attempt here a disquisition on what constitutes "good" and "evil," believing such questions to be better dealt with by moral philosophy and religion.

I refer here to "interests," which, together with the perceived facts of a situation, are the content to which wisdom is applied. Interests are related to the multiple points of view that are a common feature of many theories of wisdom (as reviewed in Sternberg, 1990b). Diverse interests encompass multiple points of view, and thus the use of the term "interests" is intended to include "points of view."

Interests go beyond points of view, however, in that they include not only cognitive aspects of divergences but affective and motivational divergences as well. Sometimes differences in points of view derive not so much from differences in cognitions as from differences in motivations. For example, executives in the tobacco industry for many years have defended their products. Their point of view may be divergent from those of many others, but the motivation of maintaining a multimillion dollar business may have more to do with the divergences in points of view than do any kinds of cognitive analysis. Economic interests no doubt motivate these executives to adopt a point of view favorable to the continued use in society of tobacco products. In order to be wise, therefore, one must understand not only people's cognitions but also their motivations and even their affects. Such understanding may involve applying one's own cognitions, motivations, and affects to the understanding of other people's. Wisdom involves, then, understanding people's cognitions, motivations, and affects. But in the balance theory, unlike in many other theories of wisdom, wisdom itself does not necessarily draw on any kind of balance of these three kinds of functions.

Problems requiring wisdom always involve at least some element of each of intrapersonal, interpersonal, and extrapersonal interests, although the weights may be different in different instances, just as they may be different for adaptation, shaping, and selection. For example, one may decide that it is wise to go to college, a problem that seemingly involves only one person. But many people are typically affected by an individual's decision to go to college – parents, friends, significant others, children, and the like. And the decision always has to be made in the context of what the whole range of available options is. In making the decision, one selects a future environment, and in doing so adapts to and shapes one's current environment, as well as the environments of others. Similarly, a decision about whether to have an abortion requires wisdom because it involves not only oneself, but the baby who would be born, others to whom one is close such as the father, and the rules and customs of the society. One also simultaneously is profoundly adapting to, shaping, and selecting the environment, both for oneself and for a potential infant. In each case, one might make a practically intelligent decision for oneself without balancing interests. But for the decision to be wise, it must take into account other interests and seek a common good.

The Role of Values

It is impossible to speak of wisdom outside the context of a set of values, which in combination may lead one to a moral stance, or, in Kohlberg's (1969, 1983) view, stage. The same can be said of all practical intelligence: Behavior is viewed as practically intelligent as a function of what is valued in a societal–cultural context. Values mediate how one balances interests and responses and collectively contribute even to how one defines a common good. I do not believe it is the mission of psychology, as a discipline, to specify what the common good is or what values should be brought to bear in what proportion toward its attainment. Such specifications are perhaps more the job of religion or moral philosophy. I, at least, would be skeptical of any psychologist who claims to specify *what* people should think rather than *how* or *why* they think or should think. But I believe the intersection of wisdom with the moral domain can be seen by there being some overlap in the notion of wisdom presented here and the notion of moral reasoning as it applies in the two highest stages (4 and 5) of Kohlberg's (1969) theory. At the same time, wisdom is broader than moral reasoning. It applies to any human problem involving a balance of intrapersonal, interpersonal, and extrapersonal interests, whether or not moral issues are at stake.

Mental Processes Underlying Wisdom

As is true with all aspects of practical intelligence (Sternberg, 1985a, 1997a), wisdom involves a balancing not only of the three kinds of interests, but also of three possible courses of action in response to the balancing of interests: adaptation of oneself or others to existing environments, shaping of environments to render them more compatible with oneself or others, and selection of new environments. In adaptation, the individual tries to find ways to conform to the existing environment that forms his or her context. Sometimes adaptation is the best course of action under a given set of circumstances. But typically one seeks a balance between adapting and shaping, realizing that fit to an environment requires not only changing oneself, but

changing the environment as well. When an individual finds it impossible or at least implausible to attain such a fit, he or she may decide to select a new environment altogether, leaving, for example, a job, a community, a marriage, or whatever.

Underlying wisdom in action is a series of processes executed in a manner that is typically cyclical and variable with respect to order of process execution. Among these processes are what I have referred to as "metacomponents" of intelligence (Sternberg, 1985a), including (a) recognizing the existence of a problem, (b) defining the nature of the problem, (c) representing information about the problem, (d) formulating a strategy for solving the problem, (e) allocating resources to the solution of a problem, (f) monitoring one's solution of the problem, and (g) evaluating feedback regarding that solution. In deciding about college, for example, one first has to see both going to college and not going as viable options (problem recognition); then figure out exactly what going or not going to college would mean for oneself (defining the problem); then consider the costs and benefits to oneself and others of going or not going to college (representing information about the problem); and so forth.

The use of these metacomponents is a hallmark of intelligent thinking, in general (Sternberg, 1985a), and they are used in all of analytical, creative, and practical thinking. What distinguishes their use in wisdom is that these processes are applied to balancing off the various interests of parties about which one needs to make a judgment or series of judgments.

The balance theory suggests that wisdom is at least partially domain specific in that tacit knowledge is acquired within a given context or set of contexts. It typically is acquired by selectively encoding new information that is relevant for one's purposes in learning about that context, selectively comparing this information with old information to see how the new fits with the old, and selectively combining pieces of information to make them fit together into an orderly whole (Sternberg, Wagner, & Okagaki, 1993). These processes are referred to as knowledge-acquisition components in the triarchic theory of intelligence (Sternberg, 1985a). Again, the processes are used in all aspects of intelligence (analytical, creative, and practical). Acquisition of knowledge can be in the service of wisdom, but it is not in itself wise. Thus, there is nothing peculiar to wisdom in the uses of these components other than that the knowledge may later be used for wise purposes.

The use of metacomponents and knowledge-acquisition components in wisdom or any other kind of practical intelligence points out a key relationship between wisdom and intelligence (as conceptualized by the triarchic theory). All aspects of intelligence – analytical, creative, and practical – involve utilization of metacomponents for executive processing and of knowledge-acquisition components for learning. What differs is the kind of context in which they are applied. Analytic intelligence is called upon for relatively familiar decontextualized, abstract, and often academic kinds of situations. Creative intelligence is called upon for relatively unfamiliar, novel kinds of situations. Practical intelligence is called upon for highly contextualized situations encountered in the normal course of one's daily life. Wisdom only applies to highly contextualized situations. It does not apply to the kinds of abstract situations to which one might apply one's intelligence (e.g., in the context of ability-test or achievement-test problems) or one's creativity (e.g., in formulating original, high-quality, but abstract ideas).

People who acquire wisdom in one context may be those who would be well able to develop it in another context, but the tacit knowledge needed to be wise in different contexts may itself differ. For example, the wise individual in one society may be able to give useful advice in the context of that society. But the same advice may be suicidal in another society (e.g., to criticize a governmental policy as it applies to a particular individual). Thus, the ability to be wise may transfer, but the actual content of wise advice may vary. A wise person will therefore know not only when to give advice but when not to (see Meacham, 1990) because the individual will know the limitations of his or her own tacit knowledge.

As noted above, however, our research has found significant correlations on scores of tacit knowledge across domains. For example, we have found that scores on tests of tacit knowledge for academic psychology and management correlate significantly (Wagner & Sternberg, 1985), as do scores on tests of tacit knowledge for management and military leadership (Forsythe et al., 1998). Thus, although one's development of wisdom may be domain-specific,

the tacit knowledge one learns in one domain can extend to other domains.

Although tacit knowledge is acquired within a domain, it more typically applies to a field, following a distinction made by Csikszentmihalyi (1988, 1996). Csikszentmihalyi refers to the domain as the formal knowledge of a socially defined field. So, for example, knowing how to construct, conduct, or analyze the results of experiments would be knowledge important to the *domain* of experimental psychology. But knowing how to speak about the results persuasively, how to get the results published, or knowing how to turn the results into the next grant proposal would constitute knowledge of the *field*. Thus, academic intelligence would seem to apply primarily in the domain, whereas practical intelligence in general and wisdom in particular would seem to apply primarily in the field. Because the field represents the social organization of the domain, it is primarily in the field that intrapersonal, interpersonal, and extrapersonal interactions take place.

The much greater importance for wisdom of the field than of the domain helps to clarify why, in the balance theory, tacit, informal knowledge rather than explicit formal knowledge is the basis of wisdom. Formal knowledge about the subject matter of a discipline is certainly essential to expertise in that discipline (Chi, Glaser, & Farr, 1988; Hoffman, 1992) but domain-based expertise is neither necessary nor sufficient for wisdom. All of us most likely know domain-based experts who seem pretty near the bottom of any scale when it comes to wisdom. At least some of us also know very wise individuals who have little formal education. Their education is in the "school of life," which is in the acquisition of tacit (informal) knowledge.

Sources of Developmental and Individual Differences in Wisdom

The balance theory suggests several sources of developmental and individual differences in wisdom. In particular, there are two kinds of sources, those directly affecting the balance processes and those that are antecedent.

INDIVIDUAL AND DEVELOPMENTAL DIFFERENCES DIRECTLY AFFECTING THE BALANCE PROCESSES. There are five such sources:

1. *Goals.* People may differ in terms of the extent to which they seek a common good and thus in the extent to which they aim for the essential goal of wisdom. The seeking of a common good does not apply to intelligence in general, however. One could be analytically, creatively, or even practically intelligent without looking out for the interests of others.

2. *Balancing of Responses to Environmental Contexts.* People may differ in their balance of responses to environmental contexts. Responses always reflect an interaction of the individual making the judgment and the environmental context, and people can interact with contexts in myriad ways. Such balancing is a hallmark of all uses of practical intelligence.

3. *Balancing of Interests.* People may balance interests in different ways. This balancing is unique to wisdom and does not necessarily apply to analytical, creative, or other kinds of practical intelligence.

4. *Practical Intelligence Manifested as Tacit Knowledge.* People bring different kinds and levels of tacit knowledge to judgmental situations, which are likely to affect their responses. This aspect of wisdom applies to all of practical intelligence but typically does not apply to analytical or creative intelligence.

5. *Values.* People have different values mediating their utilization of tacit knowledge in the balancing of interests and responses. Values covertly enter into all aspects of intelligence just as soon as intelligence is measured because any test of intelligence reflects someone's (usually the author's) values as to what is worth measuring on a test of intelligence.

These sources of differences produce variation in how wise people are and in how well they can apply their wisdom in different kinds of situations. To the extent that wisdom typically is associated with greater intellectual and even physical maturity, it presumably is because the development of tacit knowledge and of values is something that unfolds over the course of the life span and not just in childhood or even in early years of adulthood.

The preceding sources of individual differences pertain to the balancing processes. Other sources are antecedent to these processes.

DEVELOPMENTAL AND INDIVIDUAL DIFFERENCES IN ANTECEDENT VARIABLES. Antecedent variables leading to developmental and individual differences are those specified by my earlier the-

ory (Sternberg, 1990c). They include (a) knowledge, (b) analytical and creative as well as practical thinking (Sternberg, 1997a), (c) a judicial thinking style (Sternberg, 1997b), (d) personality variables, (e) motivation to think wisely, and (f) environmental variables.

Relation of the Proposed Balance Theory to Balance Theories of Intelligence

In the cognitive and developmental literatures, balance has been suggested as important in some theories of intelligence. For example, Piaget (1972) proposed that the development of intelligence involves an equilibration or balance between assimilation (modification of the way one understands an object or concept in order to fit it into existing cognitive schemas) and accommodation (modification of one's existing cognitive schemas in order to fit the way one understands a concept or object). As another example, Sternberg and Frensch (1989) proposed a balance-level theory of intelligent thinking involving a balance between coping with novelty and proceduralization. These kinds of balance, too, are not directly relevant to the theory proposed in this article.

The notion of balance also has played an important role in theories of wisdom. Philosophical conceptions of wisdom (reviewed in Baltes, in preparation; see especially Hartshorne, 1987) and especially Chinese conceptions (reviewed in Yang, in preparation) note the importance of balance, as do psychological theories such as the ontogenetic theory of wisdom proposed by Baltes and his colleagues (see Baltes, 1993, Staudinger & Baltes, 1994; Staudinger, Lopez, & Baltes, 1997). However, as mentioned earlier, these theories emphasize balance in the orchestration of the workings of the mind (Baltes, in preparation) rather than in interests and responses to the environment.

Staudinger and Baltes (1996) specify a family of five criteria, mentioned above, that characterize wisdom and wisdom-related performance. In contrast, the theory proposed here views wisdom as inhering in the extent to which a task requires a person to balance the interests of him or herself, others, and the context, for a common good, such that the decision making leads to adaptation to, shaping of, and selection of environments. Although the basic claim is simple, the actual balancing is extremely complex, and it is unlikely that any theory of wisdom can provide a normative "formula" to be used to achieve this balance.

What is new in the balance theory is not the concept of balance, per se, but the proposed specification of the particular *conjunction of elements* that are balanced (intrapersonal, interpersonal, and extrapersonal interests balanced to achieve a common good through a balance among adaptation to, shaping of, and selection of environments). Also new is the proposed specification of the relation between wisdom and practical intelligence, in particular, and intelligence, more generally. The balance theory is further related to other theories of wisdom in a variety of ways. For example, the nature of balance in the theory proposed here is somewhat different from the nature of balance in some of the other models (e.g., Kramer, 1990), which are intrapersonal balances of cognitive, conative, and affective systems. In the present model, the individual can use whatever internal systems he or she wants in making judgments. But the individual must understand how these systems work in him or herself and in others. Intrapersonal balance refers not to a balance of such systems but of the various kinds of interests one has oneself. For example, wisdom from an intrapersonal standpoint might balance one's own short- and long-term interests, or one's desire to engage in an activity that one enjoys with the recognition that the activity one enjoys poses substantial risks (for further discussion, see Sternberg, 1998a).

Relation of Wisdom to Various Constructs in the Study of Intelligence

According to the balance view, wisdom is related to practical intelligence, a point made as well in the extensive work of Baltes and his colleagues (e.g., Baltes & Smith, 1990), but the two constructs are not the same. In practical intelligence in general, tacit knowledge may be used in a way that does not balance interests to achieve a common good. The subset of practical intelligence that is wisdom applies when the tacit knowledge is used maximally to advance the balanced joint interests of oneself, others, and the context for a common good to adapt to, shape, and select environments. One may actually take a loss for oneself in advancing the joint benefit. In this view, wisdom and egocentricity are incompatible. People who are practically intelligent but not wise, however, can be quite egocentric. Some of the most successful individuals, at least by the conventional standards of society, seem to be people who have gotten where they are by not taking other people's interests into account, or even by actively thwarting the interests of others. They might be viewed as practically intelligent, but in the view proposed here, they would not be viewed as wise.

Consider a concrete example in which practical intelligence and wisdom are not the same. In a negotiation between management and a union, negotiators are often chosen for their practical intelligence – their ability maximally to advance the interests of their respective parties. But negotiations in which the two sides seek only to advance their own interests typically go nowhere. If the two parties do not have the wisdom to reach an agreement, sometimes a third party is brought in whom it is hoped will have the wisdom to help the negotiating parties reach a settlement. Such an individual must take into account his or her own (intrapersonal) role as well as the interpersonal and extrapersonal factors involved in the negotiation. Similarly, in international relations, if the parties to a dispute cannot reach an agreement, a mediating party (such as the UN) is hoped to have the wisdom to help the disputants reach some kind of settlement.

Wisdom seems to bear at least some relation to constructs such as social intelligence (Cantor & Kihlstrom, 1987; Sternberg & Smith, 1985), emotional intelligence (Goleman, 1995; Mayer & Salovey, 1993; Salovey & Mayer, 1990), and interpersonal and intrapersonal intelligences (Gardner, 1983). There are also differences, however. Social intelligence can be applied to understanding and getting along with others, to any ends, for any purposes. Wisdom seeks out a good through a balancing of interests. Thus, a salesperson who figures out how to sell a worthless product to a customer may do so through using social intelligence to understand the customer's wants but has not applied wisdom in the process. Emotional intelligence involves understanding, judging, and regulating emotions. These skills are an important part of wisdom. But making wise judgments requires going beyond the understanding, regulating, or judging emotions. It requires processing the information to achieve a balance of interests and formulating a judgment that makes effective use of the information to achieve a common good. Moreover, wisdom may require a balance of interpersonal and intrapersonal intelligences, but it also requires an understanding of extrapersonal factors and a balance of these three factors to attain a common good. Thus wisdom seems to go somewhat beyond these two theoretically distinct kinds of intelligences as well. Perhaps the most salient difference among constructs is that wisdom is applied toward the achievement of ends that are perceived as yielding a common good, whereas the various kinds of intelligences may be applied deliberately toward achieving either good ends or bad ones, at least for some of the parties involved. Interestingly, the conception of wisdom proposed here is substantially closer to Chinese conceptions of intelligence than to American conceptions of intelligence (Yang & Sternberg, 1997a,b). Indeed, one of the words used in Chinese to characterize intelligence is the same as the word used to characterize wisdom.

Problems Measuring (and Not Measuring) Wisdom

If one looks at the kinds of problems that have been used to measure wisdom in empirical work, notably of Baltes and his colleagues, one can evaluate the degree to which they measure wisdom, at least according to this balance theory. A life-planning task (Baltes et al., 1995) would be an excellent task for measuring wisdom because it involves one's own interests but may and usually will take into account the interests of others about whom one cares deeply as well as the context in which one lives and may live in the future. A task in which one must decide what to do when a good friend calls and says he or she wants to commit suicide (Staudinger & Baltes, 1996) would also involve the interests of the other, one's own interest in getting involved and possibly failing to convince the person not to commit suicide, and also the difficulty of acting in the context of an unexpected telephone call. Similarly, counseling a 14-year-old girl who is pregnant or a 16-year-old boy who wants to marry soon (Baltes & Smith, 1990) both involve balancing of the interests of the individuals to be counseled, the other people in their lives, and the costs of giving the wrong advice.

Perhaps the ideal problems for measuring wisdom in the light of the balance theory proposed here are complex conflict-resolution problems involving the formation of judgments given multiple competing interests and no clear resolution of how these interests can be reconciled (see, e.g., Sternberg & Dobson, 1987; Sternberg & Soriano, 1984). For example, one

might be asked to resolve a conflict between a couple over whether the husband's mother should be allowed to come to live with the couple. Such problems measure an aspect of practical intelligence, and Sternberg and Dobson (1987) found that a strategy of mitigating conflicts is related to higher levels even of academic intelligence. Given the relevance of such problems, it makes sense that Baltes and his colleagues (Smith, Staudinger, & Baltes, 1994) would have found that clinical psychologists would do particularly well on wisdom-related tasks. Another group who might be expected to do well would be experienced foreign-service officers and other negotiators who have helped nations in conflict reach resolutions of their disagreements.

Part of wisdom is deciding not only what course of action best balances off various interests but whose interests are at stake and what the contextual factors are under which one is operating. A high-level display of wisdom requires identification of all relevant stakeholders. Thus some wisdom may be involved in resolving a conflict between management and a union in a way that provides equitable benefits to both. But a higher level of wisdom may be needed to take into account as well that other stakeholders' interests are involved, including shareholders, customers, people who live near to the organization, and perhaps others as well.

The tacit-knowledge approach to measurement described above may present a useful way of measuring wisdom. The exact problems would differ, however, from those we have used to measure practical intelligence. In particular, the problems would involve solutions that maximize not just one's own self-interest but a variety of intrapersonal, interpersonal, and extrapersonal interests. The stakes, therefore, would be higher and more complex because so many different interests would be involved. In our current work, we are using tacit-knowledge problems of these kinds to assess wisdom and its relation to other constructs.

In contrast to problems such as the ones we have suggested above or the ones Baltes and his colleagues have used, typical problems found on conventional tests of intelligence, such as the Stanford–Binet (Thorndike, Hagen, & Sattler, 1986) or the Wechsler (Wechsler, 1991), measure wisdom minimally or not at all, according to the balance theory. There is no obvious similarity between these problems and the kinds of problems described above that would measure wisdom. Even when they measure thinking in a variety of domains, they typically do not involve balancing judgments about intrapersonal, interpersonal, and extrapersonal interests for purposes of adapting to, shaping, and selecting environments. Similarly, there is little apparent similarity between problems measuring wisdom and those measuring creativity, whether from a psychometric point of view (e.g., Torrance, 1974) or from a systems point of view (e.g., Sternberg & Lubart, 1995). For example, wisdom-related problems seem remote either from finding unusual uses of a paper clip or from writing creative short stories, drawing creative pictures, or devising creative scientific experiments or explanations.

Although wisdom problems seem remote from problems found on conventional intelligence tests, people's implicit theories of wisdom are rather close to their implicit theories of intelligence, and people expect, to a large degree, that people high in wisdom will be high in intelligence. The same relation holds true, but to a lesser extent, for creativity (see Sternberg, 1985b). Scores on wisdom-related tasks also overlap with scores on tasks measuring intelligence and other abilities as well as tasks measuring personality and thinking styles (Staudinger, Lopez, & Baltes, 1997). For example, the groups of participants that Baltes and his colleagues have tested and identified as high in wisdom, such as expert clinical psychologists, could be expected to be high in IQ. But we do not know that other groups as high or higher in IQ (e.g., expert physicists or mathematicians) necessarily would be as wise (and of course they might be wiser – we just do not know at this point). The evidence that old adults perform about as well as young adults on wisdom-related tasks (e.g., Staudinger, Smith, & Baltes, 1992) suggests that, to the extent that wisdom covaries with intelligence, it covaries more with crystallized than with fluid abilities (Cattell, 1971).

CONCLUSION

Much is still to be learned about how wisdom functions in the world and as an individual-differences variable in psychology. It is plausible to speculate that the potential for wisdom may be in part genetic, given that other kinds of potentials seem to be at least in part genetic (see Sternberg & Grigorenko, 1997b). But the tacit knowledge necessary for wisdom must be environmentally acquired, and thus genetic factors could only be necessary but never sufficient for the development of wisdom. (Indeed, the same argument could be made for any ability, for abilities always manifest themselves in covariance or interaction with an environmental context.) Far more important, it would seem, would be the kinds of experiences one has and what one learns from them. The development and display of wisdom also would seem to be partly attitudinal, involving a decision that one wishes to use one's tacit knowledge for the balanced benefit of others and the environment, not just for the benefit of oneself.

There is one source of evidence that suggests that, as individual-difference variables, wisdom and academic intelligence may be rather different "kettles of fish." We know that IQs have been rising substantially over the past several generations (Flynn, 1987; Neisser, 1998). The gains have been experienced both for fluid and for crystallized abilities, although the gains are substantially greater for fluid than for crystallized abilities. Yet it is difficult for some to discern any increase in the wisdom of the peoples of the world. Of course tests administered over time might have revealed otherwise. But the levels of conflict in the world show no sign of deescalating, and conflicts recently have intensified in many parts of the world where formerly they lay dormant (as in ex-Yugoslavia). So maybe it is time that psychologists, as a profession, take much more seriously the measurement of wisdom and the formulation of theories and theory-based measures of wisdom. Although there has been work in the area, the amount of work is dwarfed by work on intelligence. And perhaps we even need to be concerned about how we might create experiences that would guide people to develop wisdom, much as we have been concerned in some quarters about guiding people to develop their intelligence (see, e.g., Perkins & Grotzer, 1997).

From a theoretical standpoint, wisdom is quite distinct both from intelligence as traditionally defined and from creativity. In terms of the triarchic theory (Sternberg, 1985a), wisdom derives primarily from practical intelligence, traditional intelligence primarily from analytical intelligence, and creativity primarily from creative intelligence. The three aspects of intelligence are statistically quite distinct (Sternberg, 1997a). In terms of the theory of mental self-government (Sternberg, 1997b), wisdom draws primarily upon a judicial (judgmental, evaluative) style, traditional intelligence primarily on an executive (implementing, executing) style, and creativity primarily on a legislative (inventive, rebellious) style. The wise person uses knowledge primarily to make balanced judgments about problems in the context of a field, whereas the creative person typically uses knowledge primarily in extending a domain, often in a decidedly unbalanced and extreme way. The traditionally intelligent person is someone who has shown an ability to use knowledge that is as abstracted as possible from traditional context-rich domains (as can be seen by the inclusion of abstract-reasoning items on conventional intelligence tests). In terms of personality, the wise individual seeks to resolve ambiguities whereas the traditionally intelligent person excels in problems that have few or no ambiguities (and thus can be "objectively" scored as right or wrong). The creative person often creates ambiguity or at least must be tolerant of it (according to the investment theory of creativity – Sternberg & Lubart, 1995).

Intelligence and wisdom, then, are closely related, with wisdom a special part of intelligence. With a world in turmoil, perhaps we need to turn our attention in schools not only to the development of knowledge base or even of intelligence, narrowly or broadly defined. Perhaps we need to turn our attention to the development of wisdom. We ignore wisdom at our peril.

ACKNOWLEDGMENT

Portions of this chapter draw on Sternberg (1998a). Preparation of this chapter was supported by a government grant under the Javits Act Program (Grant No. R206R950001) as administered by the Office of Educational Research and Improvement, U.S. Department of Education. Grantees undertaking such projects are encouraged to express freely their professional judgment. This chapter, therefore, does not necessarily represent the positions or the policies of the U.S. government, and no official endorsement should be inferred.

REFERENCES

Arlin, P. K. (1990). Wisdom: the art of problem finding. In R. J. Sternberg (Ed.), *Wisdom: Its nature, origins, and development* (pp. 230–243). New York: Cambridge University Press.

Baltes, P. B. (1993). The aging mind: Potential and limits. *The Gerontologist, 33,* 580–594.

Baltes, P. B. (in preparation). *Wisdom: The orchestration of mind and virtue.* Boston: Blackwell.

Baltes, P. B., & Smith, J. (1987, August). *Toward a psychology of wisdom and its ontogenesis.* Paper presented at the Ninety-Fifth Annual Convention of the American Psychological Association, New York.

Baltes, P. B., & Smith, J. (1990). Toward a psychology of wisdom and its ontogenesis. In R. J. Sternberg (Ed.), *Wisdom: Its nature, origins, and development* (pp. 87–120). New York: Cambridge University Press.

Baltes, P. B., Smith, J., & Staudinger, U. M. (1992). Wisdom and successful aging. In T. Sonderegger (Ed.), *Nebraska Symposium on Motivation* (Vol. 39, pp. 123–167). Lincoln, NE: University of Nebraska Press.

Baltes, P. B., & Staudinger, U. M. (1993). The search for a psychology of wisdom. *Current Directions in Psychological Science, 2,* 75–80.

Baltes, P. B., Staudinger, U. M., Maercker, A., & Smith, J. (1995). People nominated as wise: A comparative study of wisdom-related knowledge. *Psychology and Aging, 10,* 155–166.

Basseches, J. (1984). *Dialectical thinking and adult development.* Norwood, NJ: Ablex.

Birren, J. E., & Fisher, L. M. (1990). The elements of wisdom: overview and integration. In R. J. Sternberg (Ed.), *Wisdom: Its nature, origins, and development* (pp. 317–332). New York: Cambridge University Press.

Brand, C. (1996). *The g factor: General intelligence and its implications.* Chichester, UK: Wiley.

Cantor, N., & Kihlstrom, J. F. (1987). *Personality and social intelligence.* Englewood Cliffs, NJ: Prentice–Hall.

Carroll, J. B. (1993). *Human cognitive abilities: A survey of factor-analytic studies.* New York: Cambridge University Press.

Cattell, R. B. (1971). *Abilities: Their structure, growth, and action.* Boston: Houghton Mifflin.

Chi, M. T. H., Glaser, R., & Farr, M. J. (Eds.). (1988). *The nature of expertise.* Hillsdale, NJ: Erlbaum.

Clayton, V. (1975). Erickson's theory of human development as it applies to the aged: Wisdom as contradictory cognition. *Human Development, 18,* 119–128.

Clayton, V. (1976). *A multidimensional scaling analysis of the concept of wisdom.* Unpublished doctoral dissertation, University of Southern California.

Clayton, V. (1982). Wisdom and intelligence: The nature and function of knowledge in the later years. *International Journal of Aging and Development, 15,* 315–321.

Clayton, V., & Birren, J. E. (1980). The development of wisdom across the life-span: A reexamination of an ancient topic. In P. B. Baltes & O. G. Brim (Eds.), *Life-span development and behavior* (Vol. 3, pp. 103–135). New York: Academic Press.

Csikszentmihalyi, M. (1988). Society, culture, and person: A systems view of creativity. In R. J. Sternberg (Ed.), *The nature of creativity* (pp. 325–339). New York: Cambridge University Press.

Csikszentmihalyi, M. (1996). *Creativity.* New York: Harper-Collins.

Csikszentmihalyi, M., & Rathunde, K. (1990). The psychology of wisdom: an evolutionary interpretation. In R. J. Sternberg (Ed.), *Wisdom: Its nature, origins, and development* (pp. 25–51). New York: Cambridge University Press.

Eddy, A. S. (1988). *The relationship between the Tacit Knowledge Inventory for Managers and the Armed Services Vocational Aptitude Battery.* Unpublished master's thesis, St. Mary's University, San Antonio, TX.

Flynn, J. R. (1987). Massive IQ gains in 14 nations. *Psychological Bulletin, 101,* 171–191.

Forsythe, G. B., Hedlund, H., Snook, S., Horvath, J. A., Williams, W. M., Bullis, R. C., Dennis, M., & Sternberg, R. J. (1998, April). *Construct validation of tacit knowledge for military leadership.* Paper presented at the Annual Meeting of the American Educational Research Association, San Diego, California.

Gardner, H. (1983). *Frames of mind: The theory of multiple intelligences.* New York: Basic Books.

Getzels, J., & Csikszentmihalyi, M. (1976). *The creative vision: A longitudinal study of problem finding in art.* New York: Wiley–Interscience.

Goleman, D. (1995). *Emotional intelligence.* New York: Bantam Books.

Hartshorne, C. (1987). *Wisdom as moderation: A philosophy of the middle way.* Albany: State University of New York Press.

Hegel, G. W. F. (1931). *The phenomology of the mind* (2nd ed.; J. D. Baillie, Trans). London: Allen & Unwin. (Original work published 1807).

Heider, F. (1958). *The psychology of interpersonal relations.* New York: Wiley.

Hoffman, R. R. (Ed.). (1992). *The psychology of expertise: Cognitive research and empirical AI.* New York: Springer–Verlag.

Holliday, S. G., & Chandler, M. J. (1986). *Wisdom: Explorations in adult competence.* Basel, Switzerland: Karger.

Horn, J. L. (1994). Theory of fluid and crystallized intelligence. In R. J. Sternberg (Ed.), *The encyclopedia of human intelligence* (Vol. 1, pp. 443–451). New York: Macmillan.

Horn, J. L., & Cattell, R. B. (1966). Refinement and test of the theory of fluid and crystallized intelligence. *Journal of Educational Psychology, 57,* 253–270.

Horvath, J. A., Sternberg, R. J., Forsythe, G. B., Sweeney, P. J., Bullis, R. C., Williams, W. M., & Dennis, M. (1996). *Tacit knowledge in military leadership: Supporting instrument development* (Technical Report 1042). Alexandria, VA: U.S. Army Research Institute for the Behavioral and Social Sciences.

Jensen, A. R. (1993). Test validity: *g* versus "tacit knowledge," *Current Directions in Psychological Science, 1,* 9–10.

Jensen, A. R. (1998). *The g factor: The science of mental ability.* Westport, CT: Praeger/Greenwoood.

Kitchener, K. S. (1983). Cognition, metacognition, and epistemic cognition: A three-level model of cognitive processing. *Human Development, 4,* 222–232.

Kitchener, K. S. (1986). Formal reasoning in adults: A review and critique. In R. A. Mines & K. S. Kitchener (Eds.), *Adult cognitive development.* New York: Praeger.

Kitchener, K. S., & Brenner, H. G. (1990). Wisdom and reflective judgment: Knowing in the face of uncertainty. In R. J. Sternberg (Ed.), *Wisdom: Its nature, origins, and development* (pp. 212–229). New York: Cambridge University Press.

Kitchener, K. S., & Kitchener, R. F. (1981). The development of natural rationality: Can formal operations account for it? In J. Meacham & N. R. Santilli (Eds.), *Social development in youth: Structure and content.* Basel, Switzerland: Karger.

Kohlberg, L. (1969). Stage and sequence: The cognitive-developmental approach to socialization. In G. A. Goslin (Ed.), *Handbook of socialization theory and research* (pp. 347–380). Chicago: Rand McNally.

Kohlberg, L. (1983). *The psychology of moral development.* New York: Harper & Row.

Kramer, D. A. (1990). Conceptualizing wisdom: The primacy of affect-cognition relations. In R. J. Sternberg (Ed.), *Wisdom: Its nature, origins, and development* (pp. 279–313). New York: Cambridge University Press.

Labouvie-Vief, G. (1980). Beyond formal operations: Uses and limits of pure logic in life span development. *Human Development, 23,* 141–161.

Labouvie-Vief, G. (1982). Dynamic development and mature autonomy. *Human Development, 25,* 161–191.

Labouvie-Vief, G. (1990). Wisdom as integrated thought: Historical and developmental perspectives. In R. J. Sternberg (Ed.), *Wisdom: Its nature, origins, and development* (pp. 52–83). New York: Cambridge University Press.

Mayer, J. D., & Salovey, P. (1993). The intelligence of emotional intelligence. *Intelligence, 17,* 433–442.

Meacham, J. (1990). The loss of wisdom. In R. J. Sternberg (Ed.), *Wisdom: Its nature, origins, and development* (pp. 181–211). New York: Cambridge University Press.

Neisser, U. (1979). The concept of intelligence. In R. J. Sternberg & D. K. Detterman (Eds.), *Human intelligence: Perspectives on its theory and measurement* (pp. 179–189). Norwood, NJ: Ablex.

Neisser, U. (Ed.). (1998). *The rising curve.* Washington, DC: American Psychological Association.

Orwoll, L., & Perlmutter, M. (1990). The study of wise persons: Integrating a personality perspective. In R. J. Sternberg (Ed.), *Wisdom: Its nature, origins, and development* (pp. 160–177). New York: Cambridge University Press.

Pascual-Leone, J. (1990). An essay on wisdom: Toward organismic processes that make it possible. In R. J. Sternberg (Ed.), *Wisdom: Its nature, origins, and development* (pp. 244–278). New York: Cambridge University Press.

Perkins, D. N., & Grotzer, T. A. (1997). Teaching intelligence. *American Psychologist, 52,* 1125–1133.

Piaget, J. (1972). *The psychology of intelligence.* Totowa, NJ: Littlefield–Adams.

Polanyi, M. (1976). Tacit knowledge. In M. Marx & F. Goodson (Eds.), *Theories in contemporary psychology* (pp. 330–344). New York: Macmillan.

Ree, M. J., & Earles, J. A. (1993). g is to psychology what carbon is to chemistry: A reply to Sternberg and Wagner, McClelland, and Calfee, *Current Directions in Psychological Science, 1,* 11–12.

Riegel, K. F. (1973). Dialectical operations: The final period of cognitive development. *Human Development, 16,* 346–370.

Robinson, D. N. (1990). Wisdom through the ages. In R. J. Sternberg (Ed.), *Wisdom: Its nature, origins, and development* (pp. 13–24). New York: Cambridge University Press.

Rosch, E. (1975). Cognitive representations of semantic categories. *Journal of Experimental Psychology: General, 104,* 192–233.

Ryle, G. (1949). *The concept of mind.* London: Hutchinson.

Salovey, P., & Mayer, J. D. (1990). Emotional intelligence. *Imagination, Cognition, and Personality, 9,* 185–211.

Schmidt, F. L., & Hunter, J. E. (1993). Tacit knowledge, practical intelligence, general mental ability, and job knowledge. *Current Directions in Psychological Science, 1,* 8–9.

Smith, J., & Baltes, P. B. (1990). Wisdom-related knowledge: Age/cohort differences in response to life-planning problems. *Developmental Psychology, 26,* 494–505.

Smith, J., Staudinger, U. M., & Baltes, P. B. (1994). Occupational settings facilitating wisdom-related knowledge: The sample case of clinical psychologists. *Journal of Consulting and Clinical Psychology, 66,* 989–999.

Staudinger, U. M., & Baltes, P. B. (1994). Psychology of wisdom. In R. J. Sternberg (Ed.), *Encyclopedia of human intelligence* (Vol. 2, pp. 1143–1152). New York: Macmillan.

Staudinger, U. M., & Baltes, P. M. (1996). Interactive minds: A facilitative setting for wisdom-related performance? *Journal of Personality and Social Psychology, 71,* 746–762.

Staudinger, U. M., Lopez, D. F., & Baltes, P. B. (1997). The psychometric location of wisdom-related performance: Intelligence, personality, and more? *Personality & Social Psychology Bulletin, 23,* 1200–1214.

Staudinger, U. M., Smith, J., & Baltes, P. B. (1992). Wisdom-related knowledge in life review task: Age differences and the role of professional specialization. *Psychology and Aging, 7,* 271–281.

Sternberg, R. J. (1985a). *Beyond IQ: A triarchic theory of human intelligence.* New York: Cambridge University Press.

Sternberg, R. J. (1985b). Implicit theories of intelligence, creativity, and wisdom. *Journal of Personality and Social Psychology, 49,* 607–627.

Sternberg, R. J. (1990a). *Metaphors of mind.* New York: Cambridge University Press.

Sternberg, R. J. (Ed.). (1990b). *Wisdom: Its nature, origins, and development.* New York: Cambridge University Press.

Sternberg, R. J. (1990c). Wisdom and its relations to intelligence and creativity. In R. J. Sternberg (Ed.), *Wisdom: Its nature, origins, and development* (pp. 142–159). New York: Cambridge University Press.

Sternberg, R. J. (1997a). *Successful intelligence.* New York: Plume.

Sternberg, R. J. (1997b). *Thinking styles.* New York: Cambridge University Press.

Sternberg, R. J. (1998a). A balance theory of wisdom. *Review of General Psychology, 2,* 347–365.

Sternberg, R. J. (1998b). The dialectic as a tool for teaching psychology. *Teaching of Psychology, 25*(3), 177–180.

Sternberg, R. J. (Ed.). (1999). *The nature of cognition.* Cambridge, MA: MIT Press.

Sternberg, R. J., Conway, B. E., Ketron, J. L., & Bernstein, M. (1981). People's conceptions of intelligence. *Journal of Personality and Social Psychology, 41,* 37–55.

Sternberg, R. J., & Dobson, D. M. (1987). Resolving interpersonal conflicts: An analysis of stylistic consistency. *Journal of Personality and Social Psychology, 52,* 794–812.

Sternberg, R. J., Ferrari, M., Clinkenbeard, P. R., & Grigorenko, E. L. (1996). Identification, instruction, and assessment of gifted children: A construct validation of a triarchic model. *Gifted Child Quarterly, 40,* 129–137.

Sternberg, R. J., & Frensch, P. A. (1989). A balance-level theory of intelligent thinking. *Zeitschrift für Pädagogische Psychologie, 3,* 79–96.

Sternberg, R. J., & Grigorenko, E. L. (1997a). The cognitive costs of physical and mental ill-health: Applying the psychology of the developed world to the problems of the developing world. *Eye on Psi Chi, 2,* 20–27.

Sternberg, R. J., & Grigorenko, E. L. (Eds.). (1997b). *Intelligence, heredity, and environment.* New York: Cambridge University Press.

Sternberg, R. J., Grigorenko, E. L., Ferrari, M., & Clinkenbeard, P. R. (1999). A triarchic analysis of an aptitude-treatment interaction. *European Journal of Psychological Assessment, 15,* 1–11.

Sternberg, R. J., & Kaufman, J. C. (Eds.). (in press). *The evolution of intelligence.* Mahwah, NJ: Lawrence Erlbaum Associates.

Sternberg, R. J., & Lubart, T. I. (1995). *Defying the crowd: Cultivating creativity in a culture of conformity.* New York: Free Press.

Sternberg, R. J., & Powell, J. S. (1983). The development of intelligence. In P. H. Mussen (Series Ed.), J. Flavell & E. Markman (Volume Eds.), *Handbook of child psychology* (Vol. 3, 3rd ed., pp. 341–419). New York: Wiley.

Sternberg, R. J., & Smith, C. (1985). Social intelligence and decoding skills in nonverbal communication. *Social Cognition, 2,* 168–192.

Sternberg, R. J., & Soriano, L. J. (1984). Styles of conflict resolution. *Journal of Personality and Social Psychology, 47,* 115–126.

Sternberg, R. J., & Wagner, R. K. (1993). The g-ocentric view of intelligence and job performance is wrong. *Current Directions in Psychological Science, 2,* 1–5.

Sternberg, R. J., Wagner, R. K., & Okagaki, L. (1993). Practical intelligence: The nature and role of tacit knowledge in work and at school. In H. Reese & J. Puckett (Eds.), *Advances in lifespan development* (pp. 205–227). Hillsdale, NJ: Erlbaum.

Sternberg, R. J., Wagner, R. K., Williams, W. M., & Horvath, J. A. (1995). Testing common sense. *American Psychologist, 50,* 912–927.

Thorndike, R. L., Hagen, E. P., & Sattler, J. M. (1986). *Stanford–Binet Intelligence Scale* (4th ed.). Itasca, IL: Riverside.

Torrance, E. P. (1974). *Torrance tests of creative thinking: Technical-norms manual.* Bensenville, IL: Scholastic Testing Services.

Valsiner, J., & Leung, M.-C. (1994). From intelligence to knowledge construction: A sociogenetic process approach. In R. J. Sternberg & R. K. Wagner (Eds.), *Mind in context* (pp. 202–217). New York: Cambridge University Press.

Wagner, R. K. (1987). Tacit knowledge in everyday intelligent behavior. *Journal of Personality and Social Psychology, 52,* 1236–1247.

Wagner, R. K., & Sternberg, R. J. (1985). Practical intelligence in real-world pursuits: The role of tacit knowledge. *Journal of Personality and Social Psychology, 49,* 436–458.

Webster's New World College Dictionary (3rd ed.). (1997). New York: Simon & Schuster.

Wechsler, D. (1991). *Wechsler Intelligence Scale for Children* (3rd ed.). San Antonio, TX: The Psychological Corporation.

Yang, S. (in preparation). Implicit theories of wisdom and intelligence in Chinese people in Taiwan.

Yang, S., & Sternberg, R. J. (1997a). Conceptions of intelligence in ancient Chinese philosophy. *Journal of Theoretical and Philosophical Psychology, 17,* 101–119.

Yang, S., & Sternberg, R. J. (1997b). Taiwanese Chinese people's conceptions of intelligence. *Intelligence, 25,* 21–36.

Yussen, S. R. (1977). Characteristics of moral dilemmas written by adolescents. *Developmental Psychology, 13,* 162–163.

Author Index

Subject Index